HALLIDAY'S INTRODUCTION TO FUNCTIONAL GRAMMAR

Fully updated and revised, this fourth edition of *Halliday's Introduction to Functional Grammar* explains the principles of systemic functional grammar, enabling the reader to understand and apply them in any context. Halliday's innovative approach of engaging with grammar through discourse has become a worldwide phenomenon in linguistics.

Updates to the new edition include:

- Recent uses of systemic functional linguistics to provide further guidance for students, scholars and researchers
- More on the ecology of grammar, illustrating how each major system serves to realise a semantic system
- A systematic indexing and classification of examples
- More from corpora, thus allowing for easy access to data
- Extended textual and audio examples and an image bank available online at www. routledge.com/cw/halliday

Halliday's Introduction to Functional Grammar, fourth edition is the standard reference text for systemic functional linguistics and an ideal introduction for students and scholars interested in the relation between grammar, meaning and discourse.

M.A.K. Halliday is Emeritus Professor of Linguistics at the University of Sydney, Australia.

Christian M.I.M. Matthiessen is Chair Professor of the Department of English in the Faculty of Humanities at Hong Kong Polytechnic University.

Related titles include:

The Functional Analysis of English, third edition
Thomas Bloor and Meriel Bloor
ISBN 978 0 415 825 931 (hbk)
ISBN 978 1 444 156 652 (pbk)

Introducing Functional Grammar, third edition
Geoff Thompson
ISBN 978 0 415 826 303 (hbk)
ISBN 978 1 444 152 678 (pbk)

HALLIDAY'S INTRODUCTION TO FUNCTIONAL GRAMMAR

FOURTH EDITION

M.A.K. Halliday

Revised by Christian M.I.M. Matthiessen

Routledge
Taylor & Francis Group

LONDON AND NEW YORK

Third edition published 2004 by Hodder Education, an Hachette UK company

This fourth edition published in 2014
by Routledge
2 Park Square, Milton Park, Abingdon, Oxon OX14 4RN

Simultaneously published in the USA and Canada
by Routledge
711 Third Avenue, New York, NY 10017

Routledge is an imprint of the Taylor & Francis Group, an informa business

British Library Cataloguing in Publication Data
A catalogue record for this book is available from the British Library

Library of Congress Cataloging-in-Publication Data
Halliday, M. A. K. (Michael Alexander Kirkwood), 1925–
[Introduction to functional grammar]
Halliday's introduction to functional grammar / M.A.K. Halliday and Christian Matthiessen. – Fourth Edition
pages cm
Previous ed. published as: Introduction to functional grammar, 2004.
Includes bibliographical references and index.
1. Functionalism (Linguistics) 2. Grammar, Comparative and general. I. Matthiessen, Christian M. I. M., author. II. Title.
P147.H35 2013
410.1'8–dc23
2013006799

ISBN: 9780415826280 (hbk)
ISBN: 9781444146608 (pbk)
ISBN: 9780203431269 (ebk)

Typeset in 10 on 12.5pt Berling
by Phoenix Photosetting, Chatham, Kent

MIX
Paper from
responsible sources
FSC® C013056
www.fsc.org

Printed and bound in Great Britain by
TJ International Ltd, Padstow, Cornwall

CONTENTS

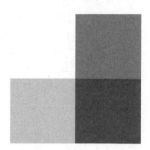

CONTENTS

CONVENTIONS

Systemic description

Capitalization labels used in systems and realization statements

Capitalization	Convention	Example
lower case, or lower case with single quotes	name of term in system (feature, option)	'indicative'/'imperative'
small capitals	name of name of system	MOOD, MOOD TYPE, SUBJECT PERSON
initial capital	name of structural function (element)	Mood, Subject; Theme, Rheme

Operators in system specifications

Operator	Symbol	Example
entry condition leading to terms in system	:	indicative : declarative/ interrogative
systemic contrast (disjunction)	/	declarative/interrogative; declarative/imperative: tagged/ untagged
systemic combination (conjunction)	&	intensive & identifying: assigned/ non-assigned

Operators in realization statements

Operator	Symbol	Example
insert	+	indicative ↘ + Finite
order	^	declarative ↘ Subject ^ Finite
expand	( )	indicative ↘ Mood (Finite, Subject)
preselect	:	mental ↘ Senser: conscious

Graphic conventions in system networks

$a \rightarrow \begin{bmatrix} x \\ y \end{bmatrix}$ there is a system x/y with entry condition a [if a, then either x or y]

$a \begin{cases} \rightarrow \begin{bmatrix} x \\ y \end{bmatrix} \\ \rightarrow \begin{bmatrix} m \\ n \end{bmatrix} \end{cases}$ there are two simultaneous systems x/y and m/n, both having entry condition a [if a, then both either x or y and, independently, either m or n]

$a \rightarrow \begin{bmatrix} x \rightarrow \begin{bmatrix} m \\ n \end{bmatrix} \\ y \end{bmatrix}$ there are two systems x/y and m/n, ordered in dependence such that m/n has entry condition x and x/y has entry condition a [if a then either x or y, and if x, then either m or n]

$\begin{matrix} a \\ \quad \rbrace \rightarrow \begin{bmatrix} x \\ y \end{bmatrix} \\ b \end{matrix}$ there is a system x/y with compound entry condition, conjunction of a and b [if both a and b, then either x or y]

$\begin{matrix} a \\ \quad \rbrack \rightarrow \begin{bmatrix} m \\ n \end{bmatrix} \\ c \end{matrix}$ there is a system m/n with two possible entry conditions, disjunction of a and c [if either a or c, or both, then either m or n]

Annotation of text

Boundary markers

Stratum	Symbol	Unit (complex)	Example
lexicogrammar	|||	clause complex	
	||	clause	
			phrase, group	
	[[[ ]]]	rankshifted (embedded) clause complex	
	[[ ]]	rankshifted (embedded) clause	
	[ ]	rankshifted (embedded) phrase, group	
phonology	///	tone group complex	
	//	tone group	
	/	foot	
	^	silent beat	

Other forms of annotation

Symbol	Gloss	Example
†	Constructed example	† John's father wanted him to give up the violin. His teacher persuaded him to continue.
*	Overlapping turns, starting at the location of the asterisk	Jane: We were all exactly * the same. Kate: * **But** I don't know that we were friends.
[ø: 'x']	element of structure ellipsed, reinstatable as 'x'	You've lost credibility and also you've probably spent more than you wanted to, so [ø: **'you'**] do be willing to back away from it, because there's always something else next week or the month after.

Example sources

Sources of examples are given in square brackets after examples. The main types are listed in the table below.

Type of reference		Comment	Example
[number]		Example taken from our archive of examples held in a database; these will be listed on the IFG companion website	[Text 370]
[corpus name]	[ICE]	Example take from one of the corpora in the collection known as International Corpus of English (ICE)	[ICE-India]
	[ACE]	Example take from the Australian Corpus of English (ACE)	
	[LOB]	Example take from the Lancaster-Oslo-Bergen Corpus of British English	
	[BROWN]	Example take from the BROWN Corpus of American English	
	[COCA]	Example take from the Corpus of Contemporary American English (COCA)	
	[BE]	Bank of English corpus	

Other conventions

Bold font is used to indicate (first mention of) technical terms, as in:

Each foot, in turn, is made up of a number of **syllables**

Italic font is used to indicate grammatical and lexical items and examples cited in the body of the text, as in:

Here, the Theme *this responsibility* is strongly foregrounded

INTRODUCTION

The first edition of *Halliday's introduction to functional grammar* (IFG) appeared in 1985. It was, among other things, an introduction to the systemic functional **theory** of grammar that M.A.K. Halliday initiated through the publication of his 1961 article 'Categories of the theory of grammar' (although his publications on the grammar of Chinese go back to 1956). It was at the same time an introduction to the **description** of the grammar of English that he had started in the early 1960s (see e.g. Halliday, 1964). Thus, the first edition of IFG was an introduction both to a functional theory of the grammar of human language in general and to a description of the grammar of a particular language, English, based on this theory. The relationship between theory and description was a dialogic one: the theory was illustrated through the description of English, and the description of English was empowered by the theory. Halliday could have used any other language for this purpose rather than English – for example, Chinese, since he had worked on Chinese since the late 1940s. The theory had been developed as a theory of grammar in general, and by the mid-1980s it had already been deployed and tested in the description of a number of languages.

Around half a century has passed since Halliday's first work on the general theory of grammar and his first work on the description of English, and around a quarter of a century has passed since IFG1 appeared: that edition represents the mid-point between the early work and today's continued theoretical and descriptive research activities, activities that were enabled by IFG1 and are reflected in IFG4. When IFG1 appeared, it was the only introduction of its kind, a summary of the work by Halliday and others undertaken since the early 1960s. It was a 'thumbnail sketch'. He had already published accounts of various areas, accounts that were in many respects more detailed than the sketches in IFG – e.g. his account of transitivity and theme (Halliday, 1967/8), his interpretation of modality (Halliday, 1970) and his description of grammar and intonation (Halliday, 1967a). He had also worked on a manuscript presenting a comprehensive account of the grammar of English, *The meaning of modern English*; many aspects of this account such as his interpretation of tense in English were only sketched in IFG1. In addition, researchers had contributed significant text-based studies of grammar and of intonation based on his framework. These informed the description of English, but have not been published since text-based accounts were not welcomed by publishers in the period dominated by formal generative linguistics.

Since IFG1 appeared a quarter of a century ago, and IFG2 followed nine years later in 1994, systemic functional linguists have published other complementary volumes drawing on IFG in different ways, designed to serve different communities of users; these include Geoff Thompson's *Introducing functional grammar* (first edition in 1996; second in 2004, with the third about to appear), Meriel and Thomas Bloor's *Functional analysis of English: a Hallidayan approach* (first edition in 1995; second in 2004), my own *Lexicogrammatical cartography: English systems* (1995), Graham Lock's *Functional English grammar: An introduction for second language teachers* (1996), and the IFG workbook by Clare Painter, J.R. Martin and myself (first edition: *Working with functional grammar*, 1998; second edition: *Deploying functional grammar*, 2010). In addition, researchers have contributed many journal articles and book chapters to thematic volumes dealing with particular aspects of IFG or reporting on research based on the IFG framework. For a summary of the rich work in the IFG framework, see Matthiessen (2007b). However, researchers have also complemented IFG stratally, moving from the account of lexicogrammar presented in IFG to the stratum of semantics; book-length accounts include Martin's *English text* (1992) and Halliday's and my *Construing experience* (1999, republished in 2006).

By the time Halliday generously invited me to take part in the project of producing IFG3, the ecological niche in which IFG operates had thus changed considerably – certainly for the better. It had, in a sense, become more crowded; but this meant that IFG3 could develop in new ways. Thanks to Geoff Thompson's more introductory *Introducing functional grammar* and to other contributions of this kind, we were able to extend IFG in significant ways, perhaps making the third edition more of a reference work and less of a beginner's book than the previous two editions had been. We certainly included features of the grammar of English that had not been covered before, and we provided a more comprehensive sketch of the overall theoretical framework in Chapters 1 and 2. In preparing the third edition, we worked extensively with corpora of different kinds – resources that had become more accessible since IFG1, supported by computational tools that had been developed since that edition; and we included many examples drawn from corpora, and from our own archives of text. In addition, we included system networks for all the major areas of the grammar.

In my own *Lexicogrammatical cartography: English system* (1995), LexCart, I had used system networks as a cartographic tool, organizing the presentation of the description of the grammar in terms of the system networks – ranging across metafunctions and down ranks and taking a number of steps in delicacy. These system networks were derived from a system network of the clause that Halliday had put together for a computational project initiated by Nick Colby at UC Irvine and then taken over as the seed of the Nigel grammar as part of the Penman project directed by Bill Mann at the Information Sciences Institute, USC, in 1980 (this system network has now been published as part of Halliday's collected works). As a research linguist working on Mann's project since the beginning, I expanded this clause network, and added networks for other parts of the grammar – with

the help of Halliday and other systemic functional linguists (see Matthiessen, 1995a, and cf. Matthiessen, 2007b). When we added system networks to IFG3, we did not try to organize the overall presentation in terms of them as I had done in LexCart, since IFG already had its own logic of presentation, which included more reasoning about the development of the account than I had included in LexCart.

In preparing IFG4, I have followed the trajectory from IFG1 to IFG3, while at the same time keeping in mind changes in the environment in which this fourth edition will appear. I have continued working with corpora, benefiting from new resources generously made available to the research community such as COCA (see Chapter 2). A great deal of this work is, quite naturally, 'under the hood': as with IFG3, many fishing expeditions are reflected by only one or two examples, or by just a brief note in passing, and many other expeditions are only reflected indirectly. Along the way, there have been various interesting findings that there is no space to report on in IFG4, like changes in the use of 'gush' as a verb in *Time Magazine* since the 1920s, or more generally in the use of verbs of saying over that period. In working with corpora, I was at various points tempted to replace all examples from older corpora dating back to the 1960s with examples from more recent ones; but I decided against it for various reasons – an important one being that, like any other language, English is an assemblage of varieties of different kinds (cf. Chapter 2, Section 2.4), including temporal dialects: the collective system of a language typically spans a few generations – never in a state of being, always in a process of becoming. And even more than a few generations: while Chaucer is almost out of range, Shakespeare is not.

One new feature in IFG4 is the introduction of a scheme for classifying texts according to contextual variables, presented in Chapter 1. In Chapter 2 through to Chapter 10, I have classified all the short texts and text extracts according to this scheme. This is a step in the direction of illuminating the grammar at work in different text types – of supporting the understanding of a language as an assemblage of registers. We hope that the website companion to IFG4 (see below) will make it possible to provide many more text examples.

Another feature of IFG4 is the continued expansion of references to theoretical frameworks and to descriptive work on English in systemic functional linguistics but also in other frameworks. Here it is, of course, impossible to be comprehensive, or even to achieve a balanced representation of references to relevant contributions. In his preface to Volume 1 of his *Basic linguistic theory*, Dixon refers to 'quotationitis', introducing it as 'a fashion in linguistics', and characterizing it as 'attempting to cite every single thing published on or around a topic, irrespective of its quality or direct relevance', and then pointing to problems with this 'fashion'. At the same time, it is very important that readers of IFG should be able to follow up on particular points mentioned in the book and go beyond the material presented here; and these days scholars are increasingly subjected by governments to ill-conceived and destructive frameworks designed to measure their output and impact in terms of publications, so citations make a difference. At one point, I thought that the solution in the area of description might be to cite central passages in the major reference grammars of English. However, on the one hand, this would actually be a significant project in its own right, and on the other hand, these reference grammars are not, on the whole, designed as gateways to the literature. I hope that the website companion to IFG4 will be able to provide more bibliographic information. And various online search facilities are helping students and researchers find relevant references.

IFG4 can be used as a reference work supporting more introductory accounts, or as a textbook in its own right. In either case, there are a number of books that are an important part of the environment in which IFG operates – theoretical and descriptive accounts of grammar (e.g. Halliday, 2002b, 2005; Butt *et al.*, 2000; Thompson, 2004; Bloor & Bloor, 2004; Eggins, 2004; Matthiessen, 1995a; Martin, Matthiessen & Painter, 2010; Matthiessen & Halliday, 2009; Caffarel, Martin & Matthiessen, 2004), of (prosodic) phonology (e.g. Halliday & Greaves, 2008) and of semantics (e.g. Martin, 1992; Eggins & Slade, 2005; Martin & Rose, 2007; Halliday & Matthiessen, 2006). Accounts of language development both in the home and the neighbourhood before school (e.g. Halliday, 1975, 2004; Painter, 1984, 1999) and in school (see Christie & Derewianka, 2008, for a recent summary of research and report on their own research from early primary school to late secondary school in Australia) give a unique insight into the ontogenetic beginnings and continual expansion of lexicogrammar, and also a very rich understanding of the grammar at work in everyday and educational contexts. Recent overviews of systemic functional linguistics include Hasan, Matthiessen & Webster (2005, 2007), Halliday & Webster (2009); and, through the window of terminology, Matthiessen, Teruya & Lam (2010). Here it is very important to note that Systemic Functional Grammar (SFG) is only one part of Systemic Functional Linguistics (SFL). If one is working on English, it is, of course, always helpful to have the standard reference grammars of English within easy reach – Quirk *et al.* (1985), Biber *et al.* (1999) and Huddleston & Pullum (2002), as well as overviews of descriptions of English such as Aarts & McMahon (2006).

In addition, IFG4 will be supported by a dedicated website. At the time of writing, I am still working on material for the website, but it is clear that the site will offer additional examples, extended text illustrations, sources of examples cited, additional pointers to the literature, colour versions of a number of figures in IFG4 and probably additional displays, the appendices from the first two editions of IFG and the foreword, and, I hope, in-depth discussions of certain topics. I also hope that it will, at least to some extent, be possible to take account of alternative descriptions, both systemic functional ones based on the framework of the 'Cardiff grammar', developed by Robin Fawcett, Gordon Tucker and their team of colleagues, researchers and students, and functional ones from other traditions, as well as formal ones where there are interesting convergences or illuminating differences. I hope the website will make it possible to treat IFG4 as a 'live document'.

Let me round off this introduction on a personal note. When I saw the first drafts of parts of IFG1 around 1980 or 1981, I was working as a research linguist on a computational linguistic text-generation project directed by Bill Mann (cf. Matthiessen & Bateman, 1991; Matthiessen, 2005). Halliday was a consultant on the project and had (as mentioned above) already contributed an 'algebraic' representation of the core systems of the clause as a foundation of the computational grammar part of the text generation system, the 'Nigel grammar', and with the help of the first drafts and earlier published system networks, I expanded the description for the computational grammar. Halliday and I had both started on the project in mid-1980. In the course of this project and its successors, I was very fortunate to learn from him how to develop grammatical descriptions – holistically, as global outlines rather than as local grammar fragments; and I learned how to model grammar and how to produce descriptions that are explicit enough for computational modelling.

However, my interest in Halliday's work and in systemic functional linguistics more generally had started during my undergraduate days in general linguistics and English linguistics at Lund

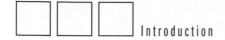

University in the 1970s. As an undergraduate student in linguistics, I was taught to develop descriptions of fragments of grammar using the version of Chomsky's generative grammar that was current at the time (a version of the 'Extended Standard Theory'); I remember working on mood tags – without any of the insights that Halliday's account brings to this area of the grammar of English. But we were also encouraged to explore different theoretical frameworks, by the two professors of Linguistics during my time there as a student, Bertil Malmberg and then Bengt Sigurd. And in the Department of English, where I was also a student, there was a great deal of interest in Halliday & Hasan's (1976) account of cohesion – a contribution that stimulated a number of PhD theses in that department, as part of the reorientation to corpus-based research brought about by the new Professor of English linguistics, Jan Svartvik. (In those days, it was still possible for students to construct their own study paths; I had added Arabic and Philosophy to my particular mix.)

When I first came across Systemic Functional Linguistics back at Lund University, something clicked – or rather a number of things clicked. I realized that Halliday had solved a problem that had puzzled and bothered me for quite a long time – since secondary school, where I had come across Alvar Ellegård's highly original introduction to generative semantics and also Bertil Malmberg's introduction to European structuralism. Both approaches seemed full of insight and promising – one providing a deeper understanding of structure and the other showing the power of the paradigmatic axis. However, they appeared to be completely incompatible. It was only when I read Halliday's work that I understood how systemic (paradigmatic) organization could be related to structural (syntagmatic) organization through realization statements. His theory of paradigmatic organization and the relationship between the paradigmatic axis and the syntagmatic one is one of the major breakthroughs in twentieth-century theoretical linguistics. Later I became aware of other breakthroughs he had quietly made, including his theory of metafunctions, his theory of instantiation and his theory of grammatical metaphor.

In working on the description of English in a computational linguistics context, and on the description of Akan in a typological linguistic context, I also came to appreciate the descriptive power of systemic functional theory, including the heuristic value of developing a description with the help of a function-rank matrix (see Chapter 2). I still remember very clearly the quite extraordinary sensation I had when I began auditing the first seminars I had ever attended by Halliday – a course he gave at UC Irvine starting around March 1980: this was the first time anyone had ever given me a clear sense of the overall organization of language as a complex semiotic system. I thought to myself that he was the first linguist to teach me about language; previously other linguists had taught me about linguistics. There is a very significant fundamental difference between the two; and language is much harder to understand (and so to teach about) than linguistics!

I was very fortunate to start working on the systemic functional description of English in 1980 under Halliday's guidance. His descriptions were often quite 'unorthodox' in the sense that they differed significantly from 'mainstream' accounts — for example, his account of the clause as a metafunctional grammatical construct, his account of grammar and lexis as zones within a lexicogrammatical continuum (rather than as separate 'modules'), his account of transitivity in English based on the complementarity of the transitive and ergative models, his account of theme and information as complementary textual systems, his account of modality as a cline for propositions and proposal between positive and negative polarity extended through interpersonal grammatical metaphor, his account of tense as a logical system for construing serial time (as opposed to a combination of tense and aspect), his account of hypotactic verbal group complexes and of clause complexes (contrasting with accounts based on the notion of complementation).

Naturally, in working on the computational grammar in the 1980s, I tried out more fashionable accounts that were part of the received tradition; but every time I experimented I came to realize how much more insightful Halliday's accounts were – being part of (and thus revealing patterns within) the overall system of the grammar. He never tried to convince me – never tried to pull rank (although in his position, I would've been very tempted to tell me: 'just take my word for it'), but, instead, he taught me how to work things out for myself.

One of the early areas I worked on was tense; when I finally understood his account, and was able to appreciate the advance it represented over both tense-aspect accounts that were popular at the time and Hans Reichenbach's sketch of a temporal logic from the 1940s that had been adopted in a number of more recent linguistic and computational linguistic accounts, I experienced the sense of an *Aha-Erlebnis* for the first time in my life – the term had been introduced to us in high school (I probably learned the term 'epiphany' much later), but I think I had only understood it theoretically before: I suddenly understood the deep insight embodied in Halliday's description of the English grammar of serial time.

On another occasion I was trying to come to grips with 'serial verb constructions' in Akan in the mid-1980s and I suddenly realized that Halliday's account of hypotactic verbal group complexes was a much better model than the assumption (still common at the time) that some form of complementation was involved. But I've already gone on too long … I just wanted to convey both my sense of the extraordinary intellectual excitement of being involved in the long-term research programme of which IFG has turned out to be an important part and my enormous sense of gratitude to Halliday for his mentorship, and also for his fortitude – for daring to be so dramatically different from the mainstream even at the cost of being ignored and effaced by its practitioners and for daring to develop appliable linguistics at a time when application was a sign of theoretical impurity.

As I tinker with Michael Halliday's *Introduction to functional grammar*, I am yet again reminded of my enormous debt to him — a debt that I am very happy to see increase over the decades; it will continue to accumulate interest for as long as I live. At the same time, I'm also happily aware of all the colleagues and students who have engaged with IFG, asking questions and giving comments that have informed my work on the fourth edition. I am deeply grateful to all of them. It's impossible to mention everyone; but I have benefited in particular from the researchers who have done PhDs with me developing comprehensive descriptions of the clause grammars of a rich range of languages: Alice Caffarel on French, Kazuhiro Teruya on Japanese, Minh Duc Thai on Vietnamese, Eden Li on Chinese, Pattama Patpong on Thai, Ernest Akerejola on Òkó, Abhishek Kumar on Bajjika and Mohamed Ali Bardi on Arabic.

Christian M.I.M. Matthiessen
The Hong Kong Polytechnic University
Hong Kong

PART I
THE CLAUSE

CHAPTER
ONE

THE ARCHITECTURE OF LANGUAGE

1.1 Text and grammar

When people speak or write, they produce **text**; and text is what listeners and readers engage with and interpret. The term 'text' refers to any instance of language, in any medium, that makes sense to someone who knows the language; we can characterize text as language functioning in context (cf. Halliday & Hasan, 1976: Ch. 1; Halliday, 2010). Language is, in the first instance, a resource for making meaning; so text is a process of making meaning in context.

To a grammarian, text is a rich, many-faceted phenomenon that 'means' in many different ways. It can be explored from many different points of view. But we can distinguish two main angles of vision: one, focus on the text as an object in its own right; two, focus on the text as an instrument for finding out about something else. Focusing on text as an object, a grammarian will be asking questions such as: Why does the text mean what it does (to me, or to anyone else)? Why is it valued as it is? Focusing on text as instrument, the grammarian will be asking what the text reveals about the system of the language in which it is spoken or written. These two perspectives are clearly complementary: we cannot explain why a text means what it does, with all the various readings and values that may be given to it, except by relating it to the linguistic system as a whole; and, equally, we cannot use it as a window on the system unless we understand what it means and why. But the text has a different status in each case: either viewed as **artefact**, or else viewed as **specimen**.

The text itself may be lasting or ephemeral, momentous or trivial, memorable or soon forgotten. Here are three examples of text in English:

> ### Text 1-1: Exploring text (spoken, monologic)
> Today all of us do, by our presence here, and by our celebrations in other parts of our country and the world, confer glory and hope to newborn liberty.

THE ARCHITECTURE OF LANGUAGE

Out of the experience of an extraordinary human disaster that lasted too long, must be born a society of which all humanity will be proud. Our daily deeds as ordinary South Africans must produce an actual South African reality that will reinforce humanity's belief in justice, strengthen its confidence in the nobility of the human soul and sustain all our hopes for a glorious life for all.

All this we owe both to ourselves and to the peoples of the world who are so well represented here today.

Text 1-2: Recommending text (written, monologic)

Cold power is the **ideal brand for any family**.

We understand that there is more than one thing you want to achieve out of every wash load.

As such, we have developed a formula capable of achieving **a wide range of benefits** for all types of wash loads.

Text 1-3: Sharing text (spoken, dialogic)

'And we've been trying different places around the island that – em, a couple of years ago we got on to this place called the Surai in East Bali and we just go back there now every time. It is –'

'Oh I've heard about this.'

'Have you heard about it? Oh.'

'Friends have been there.'

'It is the most wonderful wonderful place. Fabulous.'

Text (1-3) was a spontaneous spoken text that we are able to transpose into writing because it was recorded on audiotape. Text (1-2) is a written text, which we could (if we wanted to) read aloud. Text (1-1) is more complex: it was probably composed in writing, perhaps with some spoken rehearsal; but it was written in order to be spoken, and to be spoken on an all-important public occasion (Nelson Mandela's inaugural speech as President, 10 May 1994).

When grammarians say that from their point of view all texts are equal, they are thinking of them as specimens. If we are interested in explaining the grammar of English, all these three texts illustrate numerous grammatical features of the language, in meaningful functional contexts, all equally needing to be taken into account. Seen as artefacts, on the other hand, these texts are far from equal. Text (1-1) constituted an important moment in modern human history, and may have left its imprint on the language in a way that only a very few highly valued texts are destined to do. But here too there is a complementarity. Text (1-1) has value because we also understand texts like (1-2) and (1-3); not that we compare them, of course, but that each text gets its meaning by selecting from the same meaning-making resources. What distinguishes any one text is the way these resources are deployed.

Our aim in this book has been to describe and explain the meaning-making resources of modern English, going as far in detail as is possible within one medium-size volume. In deciding what parts of the grammar to cover, and how far to go in discussion of theory, we have had in mind those who want to use their understanding of grammar in analysing and interpreting texts. This in turn means recognizing that the contexts for analysis of discourse are numerous and varied – educational, social, literary, political, legal, clinical and so on; and in all these the text may be being analysed as specimen or as artefact, or both (specimen here might mean specimen of a particular functional variety, or **register**, such as 'legal English'). What is common to all these pursuits is that they should be grounded in an

account of the grammar that is coherent, comprehensive, and richly dimensioned. To say this is no more than to suggest that the **grammatics** – the model of grammar – should be as rich as the grammar itself (Halliday, 1984b, 1996; for educational considerations, cf. also Williams, 2005). If the account seems complex, this is because the grammar is complex – it has to be, to do all the things we make it do for us. It does no service to anyone in the long run if we pretend that **semiosis** – the making and understanding of meaning – is a simpler matter than it really is.[1]

1.1.1 Constituency: (1) phonological

Perhaps the most noticeable dimension of language is its **compositional** structure, known as 'constituency': larger units of language consist of smaller ones. The patterns of any sub-system of language such as the sub-system of sounding, or **phonology**, are distributed across units of varying size, ranging from the largest units of that sub-system to the smallest. Units of different sizes carry different kinds of pattern; for example, in phonology, the largest units carry melodic patterns, and the smallest units carry articulatory patterns.

If we listen to any of these texts – to any text, in fact – in its spoken form we will hear continuous melody with rising and falling pitch, and with certain moments of prominence marked by either relatively rapid pitch changes or extended pitch intervals (cf. Halliday & Greaves, 2008). These moments of prominence define a snatch of melody – a melodic unit, or **line**; and within this melodic progression we will be able to pick up a more or less regular beat, defining some rhythmic unit, or **foot**. We can perhaps recognize that the 'line' and the 'foot' of our traditional verse metres are simply regularized versions of these properties of ordinary speech.

Each foot, in turn, is made up of a number of units of articulatory movement, or **syllables**; and each syllable is composed of two parts, one of which enables it to rhyme. We refer to this rhyming segment, simply, as the **rhyme**; the preceding segment to which it is attached is called the **onset**. Both onset and rhyme can be further analysed as articulatory sequences of consonants and vowels: consonant and vowel **phonemes**, in technical parlance.

The stretch of speech is continuous; we stop and pause for breath from time to time, or hesitate before an uncertain choice of word, but such pauses play no part in the overall construction. None of these units – melodic line (or 'tone group'), foot (or 'rhythm group'), syllable or phoneme – has clearly identifiable boundaries, some definite point in time where it begins and ends. Nevertheless, we can hear the patterns that are being created by the spoken voice. There is a form of order here that we can call **constituency**, whereby larger units are made up out of smaller ones: a line out of feet, a foot out of syllables, a syllable out of sequences of phonemes (perhaps with 'sub-syllable' intermediate between the two). We refer to such a hierarchy of units, related by constituency, as a **rank scale**, and to each step in the hierarchy as one **rank** (cf. Halliday, 1961, 1966c; Huddleston, 1965).

---

[1] Throughout this book we will show the first mention of technical terms such as 'register', 'grammatics' and "semiosis" in bold. Most scientific disciplines use technical terms quite extensively as part of the linguistic resources for construing their field of study. Technical terms are *not* unnecessary 'jargon'; they are an essential part of construction of scientific knowledge. Many of the terms used here can be found in Matthiessen, Teruya & Lam (2010). If this introduction to functional grammar seems to have many technical terms, we recommend a comparison with a university textbook introducing, e.g., anatomy or geology!

What we have been setting up here is the rank scale for the sound system of English: the **phonological rank scale** (see Halliday, 1967a: 12ff.; Halliday & Greaves, 2008). Every language has some rank scale of phonological constituents, but with considerable variation in how the constituency is organized (cf. Halliday, 1992c, on Mandarin): in patterns of articulation (syllables, phonemes), of rhythm (feet), and of melody (tone groups), and in the way the different variables are integrated into a functioning whole. We get a good sense of the way the sounds of English are organized when we analyse children's verses, or 'nursery rhymes'; these have evolved in such a way as to display the patterns in their most regularized form. *Little Miss Muffet* can serve as an example (Figure 1-1).[2]

	foot			foot			foot			foot		
	syll.	syll.	syll.	syll.	syll.	syll.	syll.	syll.	syll.	syll.	syll.	syll.
line	Lit	tle	Miss	Muf	fet		sat	on	a	tuf	fet	
line	Eat	ing	her	curds	and		whey					There
line	came	a	big	spi	der	which	sat	down	be	side	her	And
line	frigh	tened	Miss	Muf	fet	a	way					

Fig. 1-1 Example of phonological constituency

We will say more about phonology in Section 1.2 below. Meanwhile we turn to the notion of constituency in writing.

1.1.2 Constituency: (2) graphological

As writing systems evolved, they gradually came to model the constituent hierarchy of spoken language, by developing a rank scale of their own. Thus, in modern English writing, we have a graphological rank scale of four ranks: the **sentence** (beginning with a capital letter and ending with a major punctuation mark: a full stop, question mark or exclamation mark), **sub-sentence** (bounded by some intermediate punctuation mark: colon, semicolon or comma; or a dash), **word** (bounded by spaces) and **letter**. Here is the same text written in orthographic conventional form (see Figure 1-2).

		word	word	word	word	word	word	word
sentence	sub-sentence	Little	Miss	Muffet	sat	on	a	tuffet,
	sub-sentence	eating	her	curds	and	whey.		
sentence	sub-sentence	There	came	a	big	spider,		
	sub-sentence	which	sat	down	beside	her,		
	sub-sentence	and	frightened	Miss	Muffet	away.		

Fig. 1-2 Examples of graphological constituency: sentence, sub-sentence and word

---

2 Versions of nursery rhymes are those given in Iona & Peter Opie, *The Oxford dictionary of nursery rhymes*.

The constituent structure is represented by a combination of **spelling** (combining letters to form words) and **punctuation** (using special signs, and also the case of the letter, to signal boundaries; cf. Halliday, 1985a). The system is more complex than we have illustrated here, in three respects: (1) word boundaries are somewhat fuzzy, and there is a special punctuation mark, the hyphen, brought in to allow for the uncertainty, e.g. *frying pan, fryingpan, frying-pan*; (2) there is a further rank in the hierarchy of sub-sentences, with colon and semicolon representing a unit higher than that marked off by a comma; (3) there is at least one rank above the sentence, namely the paragraph. These do not affect the principle of graphological constituency; but they raise the question of why these further orders of complexity evolved.

The simple answer is: because writing is not the representation of speech sound. While every writing system is related to the sound system of its language in systematic and non-random ways (exactly how the two are related varies from one language to another), the relationship is not a direct one. There is another level of organization in language to which both the sound system and the writing system are related, namely the level of **wording**, or 'lexicogrammar'. (We shall usually refer to this simply as 'grammar', as in the title of the book; but it is important to clarify from the start that grammar and vocabulary are not two separate components of a language – they are just the two ends of a single continuum (see Halliday, 1961; Hasan, 1987; Matthiessen, 1991b; Tucker, 1998, 2007).) The sound system and the writing system are the two modes of **expression** by which the lexicogrammar of a language is represented, or **realized** (to use the technical term).

Since language evolved as speech, in the life of the human species, all writing systems are in origin parasitic on spoken language (cf. Halliday, 1985a; Matthiessen, 2006b); and since language develops as speech, in the life of every hearing individual, this dependency is constantly being re-enacted. Even with the deaf, whose first language uses the visual channel, this is not writing; Sign is more closely analogous to spoken than to written language, signs being in a sense visible forms of articulation and facial expressions visible prosodies. But as writing systems evolve, and as they are mastered and put into practice by the growing child, they take on a life of their own, reaching directly into the wording of the language rather than accessing the wording via the sound; and this effect is reinforced by the functional complementarity between speech and writing. Writing evolved in its own distinct functional contexts of book keeping and administration as 'civilizations' first evolved – it never was just 'speech written down'; and (at least until very recent advances in technology) the two have continued to occupy complementary domains.

So, still keeping for the moment to the notion of constituency, as a way in to exploring how language is organized, let us look at the phenomenon of constituency in lexicogrammar. This will help to explain the principles that lie behind this kind of hierarchic construction, and to understand what is common to different manifestations (such as melodic unit of speech, the line of metric verse, and the sub-sentence of the written text).

1.1.3 Constituency: (3) lexicogrammatical

We will visit Little Miss Muffet just one more time. The punctuation of the text, in the previous section, clearly indicated its graphological composition, in terms of sentences, sub-sentences and words. When we now break down the same text into its grammatical constituents, we find a high degree of correspondence across the higher units: each written sentence in the graphology is one **clause complex** in the grammar, and each sub-sentence is one **clause**. This is obviously not a coincidence: the two sets of units are related (see Figure 1-3).

		word group	word group	word group	word group
clause	clause	*little miss muffet*	*sat*	*on*	*a tuffet*
complex	clause	*eating*	*her curds and whey*		
clause	clause	*there*	*came*	*a big spider*	
complex	clause	*which*	*sat down*	*beside*	*her*
	clause	*and*	*frightened*	*miss muffet*	*away*

Fig. 1-3 Example of grammatical constituency

But they are not identical; the correspondence will not always hold. Little Miss Muffet evolved as a spoken text, so when someone decided to write it down they chose to punctuate it according to the grammar. In Nelson Mandela's text, on the other hand, the first (written) sentence is grammatically a single clause – but it is written as five sub-sentences. Here the punctuation is telling us more about the phonological structure (the division into tone groups) than about the grammar. There is nothing unusual about this: many writers punctuate phonologically rather than grammatically, or in some mixture of the two. And there are many kinds of written text that are carefully punctuated into sentences and sub-sentences (i.e. with full stops, colons and commas) but containing no clauses or clause complexes at all, like the following:

Text 1-4: Recommending – 'Classified rates'
CLASSIFIED RATES

£5.10 per line (average six words per line); display £12 per single column centimetre; box numbers £5.

Discounts: 20 per cent for four insertions, 30 per cent for eight insertions, 50 per cent for twelve insertions.

Prices do not include VAT.

London Review of Books, 28 Little Russell Street, London WC1A 2HN.

It is often uncertain whether someone writing about grammar is talking about graphological units or grammatical units. To avoid this confusion we shall call them by different names (as has become the usual practice in systemic functional grammar). We will use **sentence** and **sub-sentence** to refer only to units of orthography. In referring to grammar we will use the term **clause**. When a number of clauses are linked together grammatically we talk of a **clause complex** (each single linkage within a clause complex can be referred to as one **clause nexus**).

Below the clause, the situation is rather different. Graphologically, sub-sentences consist of words – there is no written unit in between. The word is also a grammatical unit; and

here we shall continue to use the same term for both, because the correspondence is close enough (both categories, orthographic word and grammatical word, are equally fuzzy!). Grammatically, however, the constituent of a clause is not, in fact, a word; it is either a phrase or a word group (which we shall call simply **group** from now on). (We have not shown phrases in Little Miss Muffet; there are two examples, *on a tuffet* and *beside her*. For the important difference between a group and a phrase, see Section 6.1 'Groups and phrases' in, Chapter 6.) Grammatically, a word functions as constituent of a group.

Words have constituents of their own, **morphemes**. These are not marked off in the writing system; sometimes they can be identified as the parts of a written word, e.g. *eat + ing, curd + s, frighten + ed,* or else recognized as traces of its history (*beside, away* were both originally dimorphemic). We shall not be dealing systematically with word morphology in this book (see Matthiessen & Halliday, in prep.); but it illustrates the limits of compositional structure in language (and hence the problems of trying to explain all of grammar in constituency terms). Grammarians used to worry a lot about whether to analyse *sat, came* as consisting of two morphemes (*sit/come* plus an abstract morpheme 'past' realized as a vowel change); but this is a problem created by the theory. Composition is an important semogenic (meaning-creating) resource; but it should not be allowed to dominate our thinking about grammar.

Let us summarize here the five principles of constituency in lexicogrammar.

(1) There is a **scale of rank** in the grammar of every language. That of English (which is typical of many[3]) can be represented as:
   clause
   phrase/group
   word
   morpheme.

(2) Each consists of ***one or more*** units of the rank next below. For example, *Come!* is a clause consisting of one group consisting of one word consisting of one morpheme.[4]

(3) Units of every rank may form **complexes**: not only clause complexes but also phrase complexes, group complexes, word complexes and even morpheme complexes may be generated by the same grammatical resources.

(4) There is the potential for **rank shift**, whereby a unit of one rank may be down-ranked (downgraded) to function in the structure of a unit of its own rank or of a

---

[3] Languages vary, however, with respect to the 'division of grammatical labour' among the ranks. In particular, certain languages do relatively more grammatical work at group (and clause) rank, while other languages do relatively more work at word rank. Thus, for example, Japanese, Turkish, and Inuit do relatively more work at word rank, whereas, for example, Thai, Chinese, and Vietnamese do relatively more work at group rank. For instance, verbal affixes operating at word rank in one language may correspond to verbal auxiliaries operating at group rank in another, or even to modal particles operating at clause rank in yet another. This distribution of grammatical work across the rank scale is likely to change over time as a language evolves: there is a strong tendency for higher-ranking items to drift down the rank scale, as when pronouns and auxiliaries lose their status as free words and gradually become bound verbal affixes.

[4] This is not an arbitrary 'rule'. It is what explains the fact that such an instance is selecting simultaneously in systems of every rank: *Come!* is an 'imperative' (as opposed to 'indicative') clause, a 'positive' (as opposed to 'negative') verbal group, a base (as opposed to derived) form of the verb (word).

rank below. Most commonly, though not uniquely, a clause may be down-ranked to function in the structure of a group.

(5) Under certain circumstances it is possible for one unit to be **enclosed** within another; not as a constituent of it, but simply in such a way as to split the other one into two discrete parts.

To represent the lexicogrammatical constituents in a passage of written text we adopt the notational conventions set out in Table 1-1 Notational conventions for representing lexicogrammatical constituency (see Table 1-1).

Table 1-1 Notational conventions for representing lexicogrammatical constituency

|||	clause complex	⟦⟦ ⟧⟧	downranked clause complex	<<< >>>	enclosed clause complex
||	clause	⟦ ⟧	downranked clause	<< >>	enclosed clause
		phrase or group	[ ]	downranked phrase/group	< >	enclosed phrase/group
# [space]	word				

Examples:

|| out of [the experience [of [an extraordinary human disaster ⟦that | lasted | too long ⟧]]] | must be born | a society ⟦of which | all humanity | will be | proud ⟧||

|| did <you> read | that article [the other day] [about [this woman ⟦who | was driving | along | somewhere | on [this country road] || when | hail | just suddenly | started pouring down ⟧]] ||

||| we | understand || that | there | is | more [than [one thing]] ⟦you | want to achieve | out of [every wash load] ⟧|||

|| today | all of us | do < by [our presence here] and | by [our celebrations [in [other parts [of [our country and the world [ ]]]] > confer | glory and hope | to [newborn liberty] ||

The clause is the central processing unit in the lexicogrammar – in the specific sense that it is in the clause that meanings of different kinds are mapped into an integrated grammatical structure. For this reason the first half of this book is organized around the principal systems of the clause: theme, mood and transitivity. In Part II we move outward from the clause, to take account of what happens above and below it – systems of the clause complex, of groups and phrases, and of group and phrase complexes; and also beyond the clause, along other dimensions so to speak.

The perspective moves away from structure to consideration of grammar as system, enabling us to show the grammar as a meaning-making resource and to describe grammatical categories by reference to what they mean. This perspective is essential if the analysis of grammar is to be an insightful mode of entry to the study of discourse. But first, in the remainder of the present chapter, we will say a little more about compositional structure, including a more detailed sketch of phonology, so that we can take the relevant aspects of it for granted throughout the rest of the book.

1.2 Phonology and grammar

If we want to take a comprehensive view of English grammar, we must first make an excursion into phonology. This is because there are some grammatical systems that are realized by prosodic means: for example, by the contrast between falling and rising tone.

As we have seen in Section 1.1.1, the units of phonology are organized from largest to smallest according to the phonological rank scale – tone group (melodic line), foot (rhythm group), syllable and phoneme. Each unit is the domain of certain phonological systems, and it can be characterized in terms of a characteristic structure (the exception being the smallest unit, the phoneme): see the summary in Table 1-2. These units can be divided into two regions of articulation and prosody. Articulatory features are associated with smaller units, typically phonemes (vowels and consonants). Prosodic features are associated with larger units; they are features of intonation and rhythm (for an overview of the phonetics of prosody, see Nooteboom, 1997). The gateway between the two regions is the syllable; it realizes prosodic features of intonation and rhythm (and may carry its own, e.g. syllabic tone in 'tone languages' such as Chinese) and it 'choreographs' articulatory gestures (sequences of phonemes).

Table 1-2 The phonological rank scale

Rank	Nature of unit	Major systems	Structure
tone group	prosody: melody (intonation)	TONE, TONICITY, TONALITY	(Pretonic ^) Tonic
foot	prosody: rhythm	FOOT COMPOSITION, ICTUS STATE	Ictus (^ Remiss)
syllable	prosody: salience articulation: articulatory gesture	SYLLABIC COMPOSITION	(Onset ^) Rhyme
phoneme	articulation: articulatory sub-gesture	[ARTICULATORY SYSTEMS:] MANNER, PLACE, NASALITY ETC.	–

As a general principle, articulation is **arbitrary** (conventional), in the sense that there is no systematic relation between sound and meaning (as emphasized by Saussure and further developed by other European structuralist linguists, in particular Hjelmslev and Martinet; see e.g. Halliday, 1985b/2003: 196). Prosody, on the other hand, is **natural** (just as grammar is in relation to semantics; see Halliday & Matthiessen, 1999: 18–22): it is related systematically to meaning, as one of the resources for carrying contrasts in grammar. In this section we give a sketch of the prosodic region of the phonology from the standpoint of its importance to the grammatical description. For a more comprehensive account, see Matthiessen & Halliday (in prep.), Halliday (1967a) and Halliday & Greaves (2008).

1.2.1 Rhythm: the foot

Consider another well-known piece of traditional children's literature:

Text 1-5: Expounding – nursery rhyme
If all the world was apple pie,

And all the sea was ink,

And all the trees were bread and cheese,

What should we have to drink?

Say it aloud; or, better still, get a pre-literate child to say it aloud for you, so as to avoid imposing any artificial conventions in the reading of written verse. You will hear the lines of melody, and you will hear the rhythm.

The rhythm is carried by a succession of beats, occurring at more or less regular intervals (Abercrombie, 1967: 96–98; Catford, 1977: 85–91, 1985).[5] In this verse, the beats occur in alternate syllables, which happen to be the even-numbered syllables in the line: *all*, *world*, *ap-*, *pie*, *sea*, *ink*; *all*, *trees*, *bread*, *cheese*; *should*, *have*, *drink*. For contrast, here is a verse with the beat on the odd-numbered syllables in the line:

Text 1-6: Recreating – nursery rhyme
Better Botter bought some butter.

But, she said, the butter's bitter;

If I put it in my batter,

It will make the batter bitter ...

Accompanying the beat syllable are other, off-beat syllables that are rhythmically dependent on it. In these examples there was only one off-beat syllable attached to each one that carried a beat. There may be two, as in Little Miss Muffet (cf. Figure 1-1 above). We will refer to the syllable that carries the beat as a **strong** syllable (but noting at the same time that there is also a technical term, **salient**, for it) and to the off-beat syllables as **weak**. The structural unit formed by one strong, or salient, syllable together with any weak syllable(s) following on from it is called a **foot**. The foot is one of the constituents of the English sound system; it is the unit of rhythm.

The foot is easily recognized in children's nursery rhymes, (1) because the strong syllables are very regular in tempo and (2) because a pattern is set up with a fixed number of syllables in the foot. This second point does not mean that every foot contains exactly that number; there may be a moment of silence, like a rest in music, or one syllable may be lengthened to stretch over the time allowed for two, like *curds* in *eating her curds and whey*. But each verse establishes is own basic pattern, either of two or of three syllables in the foot, or sometimes of four; and every foot adapts to that pattern.

---

[5] Note that the account of rhythm presented here is based on the study of natural, connected speech. This contrasts sharply with accounts of rhythm that are based on isolated words and expressions (as in metrical phonology) or constructed examples that are read aloud. There is, however, a trace of the connection between the word (as a unit of grammar) and the foot (as unit of phonology) in the form of **accent**: a grammatical word is realized phonologically by a sequence of syllables, and one of them will be the default location of the beat. But this may be overridden in connected speech; and there are words where the beat may fall on either syllable (as with *Chinese*) to accommodate the rhythmic pattern of connected speech.

The question then is: how does this relate to the natural rhythm of English speech? All poetry ultimately derives from natural spoken language; over time it evolves a rich array of patterns of its own, at all levels of language, but all of them have their origin in speech. Every language has its own natural rhythm, some patterned way of modulating the pulse of the air-stream that comes from the diaphragm (cf. Catford, 1977: 85–91). In English, the rhythm of speech derives from the marked contrast between strong and weak syllables (cf. Grabe & Low, 2002). When you speak, naturally and spontaneously, without paying attention to the process of speaking, the strong syllables tend to occur at roughly even intervals: nothing like so exact, of course, as in children's verses, or in recitations like counting or listing the days of the week, but enough to provide a clear measure, a rhythmic progression with which the listener keeps in phase.

This rhythmic progression represents a form of constituency: the foot is a constituent of the sound system of English. The foot in poetry has its origin in the foot of the spoken language. But there are three factors that need to be taken into account when we compare the two.

(1) In natural speech, the number of syllables in the foot continually varies; there may be just one (the salient syllable), or there may be two, three, four, or even five or six in speech with rapid tempo. This was, in fact, the pattern followed in Old English and Early Middle English verse; the line had a definite number of feet (typically four), but the number of syllables in the foot could vary freely. The metric foot – that is, a foot with a fixed number of syllables – became established in Chaucer's time, largely through the influence of Chaucer himself, and it remained the norm of mainstream English verse for the next five centuries. In the twentieth century it ceased to dominate, and there has been a new wave of input into poetry from spoken language – including, in the past few decades, from speakers of new varieties of English whose rhythms are very different from those of the original native speakers of the language.

(2) Part of the tradition of metric verse was the analysis of verse forms in terms of **metrics**: this was an analysis based on the number of feet per line, and the number and distribution of syllables in the foot. A line might have two, three, four, five or six (occasionally seven or eight) feet; the favourite line, that of Chaucer, Shakespeare, Milton, Pope and Keats, was the pentameter (five feet). A foot might have two, three or four syllables, but, in addition, it might be either 'descending' or 'ascending' – that is, the salient syllable might occur either at the beginning or at the end. For example, a two-syllable foot might be **trochaic** (strong + weak) or **iambic** (weak + strong). Of the verses cited above, *Betty Botter* is trochaic, while *the world of apple pie and ink* is iambic.

This last distinction, between descending and ascending rhythm, is a property of metric verse form, accounting for how the line is organized into metric feet; it has no significance for the sound system of English. In spoken English the salient syllable always occurs at the beginning of the foot; a foot is thus like a bar in music, defined as beginning with a beat. The phonological foot, therefore, as distinct from the metric foot, consists of one strong syllable optionally followed by one or more weak syllables. The functional interpretation of this structure is

Ictus (^ Remiss)

where ^ means 'followed by' and the parentheses indicate that the Remiss element is optional. The Ictus and the Remiss are **elements** of the functional structure of the foot, and

they are realized by units of the rank below that of the foot, i.e. by syllables. The Ictus is realized by a strong syllable (or a silent beat; see immediately below), and the Remiss (if present) by one or more weak syllables.

(3) The tradition of metric analysis was faulty in certain respects, particularly in confusing the opposition of 'strong/weak' with the quite different phenomenon of 'long/short'. But its main defect in relation to our present discussion is that it failed to recognize silence. Silence is a systematic feature of the rhythm of spoken English; there are many instances of what is usually called a **silent beat**, where the Ictus is clearly present in the sound pattern (i.e. there *is* a beat), but it is realized in the form of silence – just as a bar might begin with a silent beat in music. So we may have an entirely silent foot, and many of the standard metres of English verse depend on this; there is in fact a silent foot at the end of the second and fourth lines of *If all the world was apple pie*, as you can tell by beating out the time while saying it. In spontaneous dialogue, speakers and listeners can maintain the tempo across at least two feet of total silence; and the silent beat also plays a part in grammar, in making a contrast in meanings (see Chapter 7, Section 7.4.1.2).

Below the foot on the phonological rank scale (see Section 1.1.1) is the **syllable**; a foot consists of one or more syllables (unless the foot consists of only an Ictus realized by a silent beat). The syllable is the fundamental unit of an articulatory gesture (see, e.g., Catford, 1977: 88–91; Fujimura & Erickson, 1997: 98–99; and in auditory terms it can be characterized as being organized around a peak of high sonority). Like the foot, the syllable is also a structured unit; it consists of Onset + Rhyme. These are, in turn, realized by consonant and vowel phonemes. The Onset is realized as initial consonant or consonant cluster, or zero. The Rhyme is, naturally, the part of the syllable that is involved in rhyme: vowel plus following consonant or consonant cluster if any. We shall say a little more about the organization of syllables later, in Section 1.2.3; but here it is important to note that the realization of the phonemes serving as Onset + Rhyme will depend on the rhythmic nature of connected speech. The syllable is 'elastic' so that it can accommodate itself to the rhythmic requirements of the foot. This is the property of the syllable that enables the foot to function as a rhythmic unit: given a constant tempo, the more syllables there are in a foot, the shorter those syllables have to be.

1.2.2 Intonation: the tone group

The foot, then, is a 'rhythm group': it is the unit that manages the rhythm of spoken English. It is a constituent in the phonological structure. But it is not the highest constituent; there is a more extended sound pattern constructed out of a succession of feet. If you listen again to the apple pie quatrain you will hear a clear melodic pattern emerging, probably corresponding fairly closely to the line: one line of verse, one 'snatch' or line of melody. The name for this systematic melodic variation in language is **intonation**, the melodic line is an **intonation contour**, or more shortly a **tone contour**; and the snatch is called a **tone group** (Halliday, 1967a; Halliday & Greaves, 2008; Elmenoufy, 1988; Tench, 1990, 1996; Wells, 2006; other names used are 'tone unit' and 'intonation unit').

If we are given a text in writing, there will always be various possible ways of intoning it, each with a somewhat different meaning (cf. Davies, 1986); but generally one or a small number of these possible intonation patterns will stand out as more natural and more likely. If we say the apple-pie verse, we probably start the first three lines with a fairly high-pitched note on *all*, descend step by step, and then end with a slight but noticeable rising

pitch on the last syllable in the line: *pie, ink, cheese.* (Note that the melody is constructed by the strong syllables; the weak ones fit in with them in the place of least effort – here the *if* and the *and* at the beginning of the line would be on a neutral, medium pitch.) The third line might also have a little rise on *trees* to go with the internal rhyme. The last line, on the other hand, would probably have a highish level pitch on *should*, a similar but marginally lower one on *have*, and a clearly marked falling pitch on the final word *drink*, with a total effect of an overall movement from high to low.

The tone group is the phonological constituent that ranks above the foot: each tone group consists of a whole number of feet – one or more. This relationship whereby syllables are grouped into rhythm groups, or feet, and feet into tone groups, is the way the sounds of English are organized into larger patterns. But unlike writing, which is captured (even if very briefly) in time, so that written units can be clearly marked off one from another, speech is fluid and kinetic: there are no clear boundaries between its constituents. So in a given passage of speech we can tell how many syllables there are, how many feet, and how many tone groups; and we can tell within limits where each one is located; but we cannot pinpoint exactly where each one begins and ends. So we determine the boundaries on theoretical grounds, making generalizations that have the greatest explanatory force. One example of such a generalization is the principle just stated, whereby each unit consists of a whole number of units of the rank next below; this means that a tone group boundary will always also be a foot boundary, and a foot boundary always also a syllable boundary, and this in turn makes it easier – makes it possible, in fact – to explain how these phonological patterns function in the making of meaning (cf. Figure 1-1 above).

While the rhythm group, or foot, is largely a timing unit (it has one or two specific functions in the grammar, but its domain of operation is principally phonological), the tone group does a great deal of work in the construal of meaning: it organizes continuous speech as a sequence of units of information (see further Chapter 3, Section 3.5). In other words, it manages the flow of the discourse. It is thanks to the tone group, as defined here, that listeners get the message: not only how it is framed into items of news but also what value the speaker attaches to each. Hence it is on the basis of the tone group that, as grammarians, we are able to analyse spoken language and 'chunk it up' into grammatical units of a particular and important kind.

The tone group is the point of entry into the system of TONE: the systematic use of melody as a grammatical resource. While the potential (and actual) variation in the pitch movement in speech is immense, each snatch in the melody represents one of a small number of systemically distinct tones. At the phonological level there are just five of these: falling, rising, 'level', falling-rising, and rising-falling. These are realized in the form of a characteristic pitch movement located on one particular foot within the tone group, the **tonic** foot. (The 'level' tone is actually realized as a low with a slight rise.) Whereas the organization of speech into a sequence of tone groups carries **textual** meaning, the choice among the different tone carries **interpersonal** meaning, via the grammatical systems of KEY (see further Section 4.4.4). For the metafunctional categories of interpersonal and textual, see below Section 1.3.5.

The tone group itself has an internal structure of the form (P ^) T: an obligatory Tonic segment, optionally preceded by a Pretonic segment. Each of these consists of at least one complete foot; the tonic foot is the first foot within the Tonic segment.

Let us return briefly to the relationship among spoken language, written prose, and written verse. The 'line', in verse, evolved as the metric analogue of the tone group: one line of verse corresponded to one tone group of natural speech. In children's nursery rhymes this correspondence is often preserved intact (this is why they are valuable in helping children learn the patterns of the language); but in adult verse of course it is not – on the contrary, it becomes an idealized motif on which endless meaningful variations can be played. And this illustrates a principal strategy whereby the meaning potential of a language comes to be extended.

We can postulate an 'initial' state where the two **variables** are fully **associated**: at this point, the 'line' is just the poetic incarnation of the tone group. Then the two become **dissociated**: the poetic line takes on a life of its own, and new meanings are construed by mapping a line into more than one tone group, or having the intonation patterns cut right across those set up by the poetic form. This 'dissociation of associated variables' is one of the main semogenic resources of a language; for a theoretical discussion, see Halliday (1991).

As it happens, the verse form helps us recognize that there is a still higher unit of organization above the tone group. Listening to the four lines of the apple-pie rhyme we can hear that they make up a sequence of interrelated tone groups: beginning with a series that are alike, all ending on a rise, and ending with one that is distinct, with its final falling movement on *drink*. The rising tones suggest non-finality, whereas the fall sounds (and in fact is) culminative: it brings the sequence to an end. Together these tone groups make up a **tone group complex** (see further Chapter 7, Section 7.6); and this, in turn, is the origin of the metric **stanza**, as a higher pattern of organization in poetry.

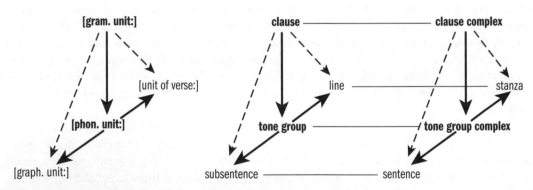

Fig. 1-4   Analogic patterning of units across content (lexicogrammar) and expression (phonology, graphology)

The explanation for all this analogic patterning lies in the grammar. When children start to speak English as their mother tongue, they soon learn to construct a unit that is a conflation of clause and tone group (later, again, they will learn to dissociate these two). This is also manifested as a unit in the rhymes they hear. When they start learning to read and write they find this unit reappearing as a (simple) sentence, with a capital letter at the beginning and a full stop or other major punctuation mark at the end; and this also turns

up as a line in written verse. Behind all these diverse entities – tone group, spoken line, sentence in writing and written line – lies the one fundamental grammatical unit, the clause.

By the same token, an analogous relationship is set up among a series of higher units: tone group complex, spoken stanza, 'compound/complex' sentence, and stanza of written verse, all of which originate as different incarnations of the grammatical **clause complex** (see Chapter 7, *passim*). And when the rhymes have been set to music, and are sung, the same patterns are reinforced over again, with the line of melody representing the clause, and the melody as a whole representing the clause complex. We could diagram these two sets of analogies as in Figure 1-4.

Then, in the very act of developing these fundamental unities, the child is also learning to pull them apart: to deconstrue the pattern, so that each of its modes of being becomes a carrier of meaning in its own right. Once a clause, for example, may be mapped either into one tone group or into two, this enhances its meaning potential in the flow of discourse; moreover, there are likely to be various places where the transition can take place. The phonological patterns (and, for a literate person, the graphological ones also) are the semogenic resources of a language; any systemic variation that they embody has the potential for making systematic distinctions in meaning – and most of these are likely to be taken up.

Here are the notational conventions for the higher units of phonology – the tone group complex, the tone group and the foot (rhythm group): see Table 1-3. Examples:

(a)   /// ∧ if / all the / world was / apple / pie and // all the / sea was / ink and // all the / trees were / bread and / cheese what // would we / have to / drink ///

(b)   /// ∧ and we've been / trying / different / places a/round the / island that / ∧ em // ∧ a / couple of / years a/go we // got on to this / place / called the / Surai in // east / Bali and we // just go / back there / now / every / time // ∧ it / is ... ///

// oh I've / heard about / this //

/// have you / heard about it // oh ///

// friends have / been there //

/// ∧ it / is the most / wonderful / wonderful / place // fabulous ///

Table 1-3 Notational conventions for higher phonological units

///	tone group complex		
//	tone group		
/	foot	∧	silent ictus

Figure 1-5 shows the system network for prosodic systems in English phonology. Note that the network represents the phonological resources; it does not show how these resources are exploited in the lexicogrammar. Some illustrations of this will be found in Chapters 3, 4 and 7.

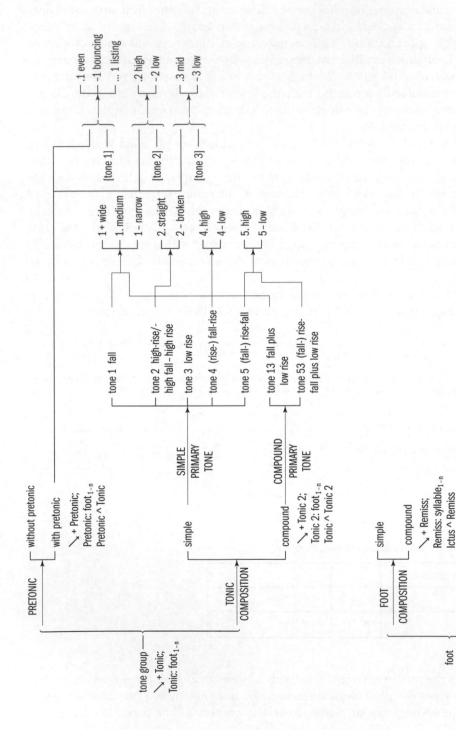

Fig. 1-5   System network for prosodic systems in English phonology

1.2.3 Syllables and phonemes

Next below the foot is the **syllable**; as already remarked, a foot consists of a whole number of syllables, one or more. From an articulatory point of view, the syllable is an articulatory gesture; Catford (1977: 89) characterizes is as a '"ripple" on the surface of the initiator-power curve' – that is, the articulatory correlate of a foot. From an auditory point of view, this gesture is typically organized around a peak of sonority. All languages have something that can be called a syllable; but these somethings are far from being the same – if we compare just Russian, Japanese, Arabic and English we find great variation in how syllables are structured and how they function (for a systemic account of syllables in Mandarin, see Halliday, 1992c). In some languages, it is clear where a syllable begins and ends; but in others it may not be quite so clear – in English it is not at all obvious how to divide up a word such as *colour* or *basket* into syllables, and people dispute whether words like *chasm*, *rhythm*, *fathom* consist of one syllable or two (I once watched a game of charades dissolve into chaos as the players argued whether *comfortable* had three syllables in it or four). But the fact that English verse came to depend on counting syllables means that syllables must have been perceived as things that were able to be counted, even if there is indeterminacy in certain places. Musical settings of verse also impose a syllable pattern – which is not always the same as that required by the metre.

What is there below the syllable? English verse makes extensive use of rhyme; from that point of view, a syllable consists of two parts, the non-rhyming part, or **Onset** (which may be empty), and the **Rhyme**. This analysis is helpful in explaining the relative duration of different syllables in English, since this depends entirely on the structure of the rhyme. On the other hand, the English writing system is made up of letters, and the letters stand for smaller units of sound called **phonemes** – the individual consonants and vowels out of which both parts of the syllable are built.

The English script is not 'phonemic' if by that we understand a strict one-to-one correspondence between phonemes and letters. It never could be phonemic in this sense, because the criteria for identifying phonemes in English are internally contradictory: what are one and the same phoneme from one point of view may be two separate phonemes from another. But it clearly is phonemic in its general principle: the symbols represent consonants and vowels that contrast systemically with one each other and combine to form regular structures. Many of its symbols have more than one phonemic value; some pairs of letters ('digraphs') have to be treated as single symbols, like *th* in *thin*, *sh* in *shin*; and there are various other departures from an imaginary phonemic ideal – some of them systematic, some random. Nevertheless, speakers of English readily become aware of the phoneme as a minimal phonological unit; the fact that there is no one right answer to the question 'How many phonemes are there in English?', and there is indeterminacy where some of them begin and end (is the sound *ch* in *chin* one phoneme or two?), merely brings them into line with all the other constituents in the phonological system – syllables, feet and tone groups – and, it might be added, with most other phenomena pertaining to natural languages.

In this book we shall not need to be concerned with the detailed analysis of syllables and phonemes. For discussion of the grammar, the important part of phonology is prosody – features of intonation and rhythm. The transcription that will be needed is one that shows the intonational and rhythmic features of speech but which uses ordinary orthography for the spelling – an elaboration of the conventions introduced in the previous section.

1.3 Basic concepts for the study of language

The discussion so far has raised a number of theoretical issues, as can be seen from the variety of technical terms that have had to be used. We have referred to language (i) as text and as system, (ii) as sound, as writing and as wording, (iii) as structure – configurations of parts, and (iv) as resource – choices among alternatives. These are some of the different guises in which a language presents itself when we start to explore its grammar in functional terms: that is, from the standpoint of how it creates and expresses meaning.

At this point, we begin to need a map: some overview of language that will enable us to locate exactly where we are at any point along the route. A characteristic of the approach we are adopting here, that of systemic theory, is that it is *comprehensive*: it is concerned with language in its entirety, so that whatever is said about one aspect is to be understood always with reference to the total picture. At the same time, of course, what is being said about any one aspect also *contributes to* the total picture; but in that respect as well it is important to recognize where everything fits in. There are many reasons for adopting this systemic perspective; one is that languages evolve – they are not designed, and evolved systems cannot be explained simply as the sum of their parts. Our traditional compositional thinking about language needs to be, if not replaced by, at least complemented by a 'systems' thinking whereby we seek to understand the nature and the dynamic of a semiotic system as a whole (cf. Matthiessen & Halliday, in prep., Chapter 1, and references therein to Capra, 1996, and other proponents of systems thinking; Matthiessen, 2007a).

In the remainder of this chapter we shall present in a very summary way the critical dimensions of the kind of semiotic that language is. By 'language' we mean natural, human, adult, verbal language – natural as opposed to designed semiotics like mathematics and computer languages (cf. Halliday & Matthiessen, 1999: 29–46; O'Halloran, 2005); adult (i.e. post-infancy) as opposed to infant protolanguages (see Halliday, 1975, 2003); verbal as opposed to music, dance and other languages of art (cf. Kress & van Leeuwen, 1996; O'Toole, 1994; van Leeuwen, 1999). Of course, all these other systems share certain features with language in this specified sense; but none of them incorporates all. The dimensions, or forms of order, in a language, and the ordering principles, are set out in Table 1-4 and represented diagrammatically in Figure 1-6.

Table 1-4 The dimensions (forms of order) in language and their ordering principles

	Dimension	Principle	Orders
1.	structure (syntagmatic order)	rank	clause ~ group/phrase ~ word ~ morpheme [lexicogrammar]; tone group ~ foot ~ syllable ~ phoneme [phonology]
2.	system (paradigmatic order)	delicacy	grammar ~ lexis [lexicogrammar]
3.	stratification	realization	semantics ~ lexicogrammar ~ phonology ~ phonetics
4.	instantiation	instantiation	potential ~ subpotential/ instance type ~ instance
5.	metafunction	metafunction	ideational [logical ~ experiential] ~ interpersonal ~ textual

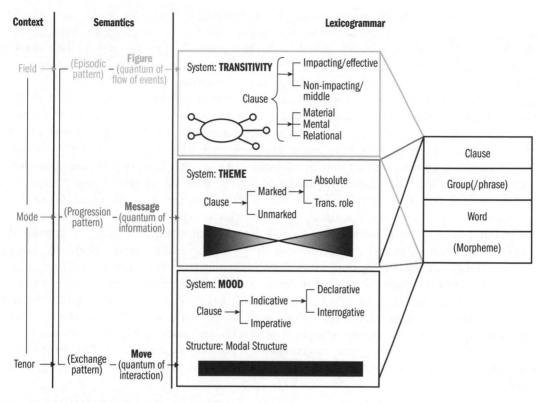

Fig. 1-6   The dimensions in language

1.3.1 Structure (syntagmatic order)

This is the compositional aspect of language, referred to in linguistic terminology as 'constituency'. The ordering principle, as defined in systemic theory, is that of **rank**: compositional layers, rather few in number, organized by the relationship of 'is a part of'. We have identified four such compositional hierarchies in English, as shown in Table 1-5.

Table 1-5 Compositional hierarchies in English

Domain	Compositional hierarchy
(a) in sound:	tone group ~ foot (rhythm group) ~ syllable (~ hemisyllable) ~ phoneme
(b) in writing:	sentence ~ sub-sentence ~ word (written) ~ letter
(c) in verse (spoken):	stanza ~ line ~ foot (metric) ~ syllable
(d) in grammar:	clause ~ phrase/ group ~ word ~ morpheme

The guiding principle is that of **exhaustiveness**: thus, in the writing system, a word consists of a whole number of letters, a sub-sentence of a whole number of words, a sentence of

a whole number of sub-sentences; the number may be more than one, or just one. At the same time, as always in language, there is much indeterminacy, or room for manoeuvre: should we recognize just one layer of sub-sentences, marked off by any punctuation mark, or two – a higher layer marked off by (semi)colons, a lower one marked off by commas? This may well depend on the practice of the particular writer.

As we have seen, all these compositional hierarchies are ultimately variants of a single motif: the organization of meaning in the grammar. As the language has evolved, they have drifted apart (as will tend to happen in the history of every language); but traces of their equivalence remain (e.g. tone group : sub-sentence : line : clause). When we come to analyse the grammar, we find that the structure of each unit is an **organic configuration** such that each part has a distinctive function with respect to the whole; and that some units may form **complexes**, iterative sequences working together as a single part. Grammar is the central processing unit of language, the powerhouse where meanings are created; it is natural that the systems of sound and of writing through which these meanings are expressed should reflect the structural arrangement of the grammar. They cannot, obviously, copy the functional configurations; but they do maintain the grammatical principle that units of different rank construe patterns of different kinds. In English phonology, for example, the foot is the unit of rhythm; it is the constituent that regulates the pulse of continuous speech. In this it is distinct from other units both above it and below it: from the syllable, which organizes the articulatory sequences of vowels and consonants, and from the tone group, which organizes the pitch movement into patterns of intonation. This functional specialization among units of different rank is a feature of the structure of language as a whole.

1.3.2 System (paradigmatic order)

Structure is the syntagmatic ordering in language: patterns, or regularities, in what *goes together with* what. System, by contrast, is ordering on the other axis: patterns in what *could go instead of* what. This is the paradigmatic ordering in language (cf. Halliday, 1966a; Fawcett, 1988; Butt & Matthiessen, forthcoming).

Any set of alternatives, together with its condition of entry, constitutes a **system** in this technical sense. An example would be 'all clauses are either positive or negative', or more fully 'all clauses select in the system of POLARITY whose terms are positive and negative'; diagrammatically as in Figure 1-7. To get a more rounded picture, we attach probabilities to the two terms: 'positive, 0.9; negative, 0.1' (cf. Halliday & James, 1993).

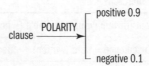

Fig. 1-7   The system of POLARITY

It will be clear that this is a more abstract representation than that of structure, since it does not depend on how the categories are expressed. Positive and negative are contrasting features of the clause, which could be made manifest in many different ways. They represent

an aspect of the **meaning potential** of the language, and they are mutually defining: 'not positive' means the same thing as 'negative', and 'not negative' means the same thing as 'positive'.

The relationship on which the system is based is 'is a kind of': a clause having the feature 'positive' is a kind of clause. Suppose we now take a further step, and say that negative clauses may be either generalized negative, like *they didn't know*, or some specific kind of negative like *they never knew* or *nobody knew*. Here we have recognized two paradigmatic contrasts, one being more refined than the other: see Figure 1-8. The relationship between these two systems is one of **delicacy**: the second one is 'more delicate than' the first. Delicacy in the system ('is a kind of a kind of ...') is the analogue of rank in the structure ('is a part of a part of ...').

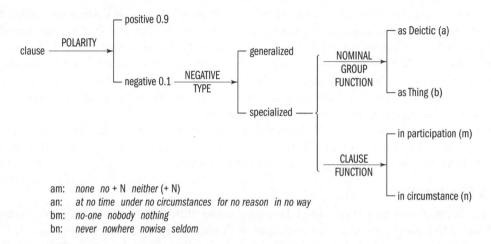

Fig. 1-8   The system of POLARITY, next step in delicacy

A text is the product of ongoing selection in a very large network of systems – a **system network**. Systemic theory gets its name from the fact that the grammar of a language is represented in the form of system networks, not as an inventory of structures. Of course, structure is an essential part of the description; but it is interpreted as the outward form taken by systemic choices, not as the defining characteristic of language. A language is a resource for making meaning, and meaning resides in systemic patterns of choice.

The way system and structure go together can be illustrated by showing a simplified version of the system network for MOOD (this will be explained in detail in Chapter 4): see Figure 1-9. This can be read as follows. A clause is either major or minor in STATUS; if major, it has a Predicator in its structure. A major clause is either indicative or imperative in MOOD; if indicative, it has a Finite (operator) and a Subject. An indicative clause is either declarative or interrogative (still in MOOD); if declarative, the Subject comes before the Finite. An interrogative clause is either yes/no type or WH-type; if yes/no type, the Finite comes before the Subject; if WH-type, it has a Wh element.

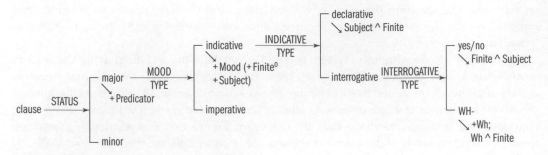

Fig. 1-9   The MOOD system network

What this means is that each system – each moment of choice – contributes to the formation of the structure. Of course, there is no suggestion here of **conscious** choice; the 'moments' are analytic steps in the grammar's construal of meaning (for the relationship between semantic choice and what goes on in the brain see Lamb, 1999). Structural operations – inserting elements, ordering elements and so on – are explained as **realizing** systemic choices. So, when we analyse a text, we show the functional organization of its structure; and we show what meaningful choices have been made, each one seen in the context of what might have been meant but was not.

When we speak of structural features as 'realizing' systemic choices, this is one manifestation of a general relationship that pervades every quarter of language. Realization derives from the fact that a language is a stratified system.

1.3.3 Stratification

We are accustomed to talking about language under different headings. School grammar books used to have chapters on pronunciation, orthography, morphology (earlier 'accidence') and syntax, with a vocabulary added at the end. This acknowledged the fact that a language is a complex semiotic system, having various levels, or **strata**. We have made the same assumption here, referring to the sound system, the writing system and the wording system, i.e. **phonology**, **orthography** (or **graphology**) and **grammar**. (We also noted, on the other hand, that grammar and vocabulary are not different strata; they are the two poles of a single continuum, properly called **lexicogrammar** (cf. Hasan, 1987). Likewise, syntax and morphology are not different strata; they are both part of grammar – the distinction evolved because in Indo-European languages the structure of words (**morphology**) tends to be strikingly different from the structure of clauses (**syntax**); but this is not a feature of languages in general.)

What does it mean to say that these are different 'strata'? In infants' protolanguage, which has as yet no grammar in it, the elements are simple signs; for example, a meaning 'give me that!' is expressed directly by a sound, like *nananana*, or maybe by a gesture of some kind. Here we have just two strata, a stratum of content and a stratum of expression (cf. Halliday, 1975, 2004).

Adult languages are more complex. For one thing, they may have two alternative modes of expression, one of sounding (i.e. speech) and one of writing. More significantly, however, they have more strata in them.

The 'content' expands into two, a **lexicogrammar** and a **semantics** (cf. Halliday, 1984a; Halliday & Matthiessen, 1999). This is what allows the meaning potential of a language to expand, more or less indefinitely. The reason for this can best be explained in terms of the functions that language serves in human lives.

We use language to make sense of our experience, and to carry out our interactions with other people. This means that the grammar has to interface with what goes on outside language: with the happenings and conditions of the world, and with the social processes we engage in. But at the same time it has to organize the construal of experience, and the enactment of social processes, so that they can be transformed into wording. The way it does this is by splitting the task into two. In step one, the interfacing part, experience and interpersonal relationships are transformed into meaning; this is the stratum of semantics. In step two, the meaning is further transformed into wording; this is the stratum of lexicogrammar. This is, of course, expressing it from the point of view of a speaker, or writer; for a listener, or reader, the steps are the other way round.

This stratification of the content plane had immense significance in the evolution of the human species – it is not an exaggeration to say that it turned *homo ...* into *homo sapiens* (cf. Halliday, 1995b; Matthiessen, 2004a). It opened up the power of language and in so doing created the modern human brain. Some sense of its consequences for the construction of knowledge will be given in Chapter 10, where we raise the question of whether learned forms of discourse, in education, science, technology and the humanities, could ever have evolved without the 'decoupling' of these two aspects of the semogenic process.

It might be asked whether an analogous stratification took place within the expression plane; and the answer would appear to be 'yes, it did', and for analogous reasons, namely separating the organizing function from the function of interfacing with the environment. Here, however, the environment is the human body, the biological resource with which sounding (or signing) is carried out. Taking sound (spoken language) as the base, the stratification is into **phonetics**, the interfacing with the body's resources for speech and for hearing, and **phonology**, the organization of speech sound into formal structures and systems (see Figure 1-10).

When we say that language is stratified in this way, we mean that this is how we have to model language if we want to explain it. A language is a series of redundancies by which we link our eco-social environment to non-random disturbances in the air (soundwaves). Each step is, of course, masterminded by the brain. The relationship among the strata – the process of linking one level of organization with another – is called **realization**.[6] Table 1-6 presents this model from the point of view of the speaker – it is hard to present it in a way that is neutral between speaking and listening. Figure 1-10 represents the stratal organization of language, and shows how the stratified linguistic system is 'embedded' in context (cf. Halliday, 1978; Halliday & Hasan, 1985; Hasan, 1999, and other contributions to Ghadessy, 1999; Martin, 1992).

---

[6]   With a primary semiotic system, like the infant protolanguage (see immediately below), consisting only of content and expression, we could still use the word 'express'. But with a higher order (multi-stratal) semiotic this is no longer appropriate; we could not really say that wording 'expresses' meaning. Hence the use of a distinct technical term.

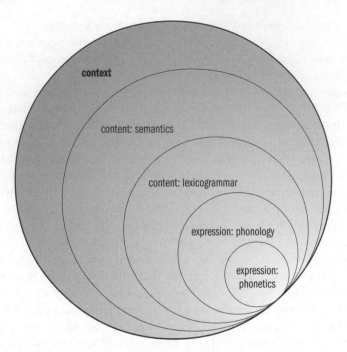

Fig. 1-10 Stratification

Table 1-6 From eco-social environment to soundwaves: speaker perspective

[from environment to] meaning:	interfacing, via receptors	**semantics**
[from meaning to] wording:	internal organization	**lexicogrammar**
[from wording to] composing:	internal organization	**phonology**
[from composing to] sounding:	interfacing, via motors	**phonetics**

Language is thus organized into four strata – semantics, lexicogrammar, phonology, and phonetics. But these four strata are grouped into two stratal planes, the content plane and the expression plane. When children learn how to mean, they start with a very simple semiotic system, a **protolanguage**, usually sometime in the second half of their first year of life (see Halliday, 1973, 2003); and we hypothesize that language evolved in the same way (see Matthiessen, 2004a). This system is organized into two stratal planes, content and expression; but neither is internally stratified: content is mapped directly onto expression (vocal or gestural). This protolanguage is a child tongue rather than a mother tongue; it is not yet like the adult language spoken around young children. Children develop their protolanguages in interaction with their immediate caregivers, gradually expanding their protolinguistic meaning potentials. In doing so, they learn the principles of meaning. At some point, typically in the second year of life, they are ready to build on this experience and to begin to make the transition into the mother tongue spoken around them. This transition involves a number of fundamental changes in the linguistic system. A key

change – one that makes possible other changes – is the splitting up of each of the two stratal planes into two content strata and two expression strata. Content gradually splits into semantics and lexicogrammar, and expression gradually splits into phonology and phonetics. The realizational relationship between content and expression, more specifically between lexicogrammar and phonology is largely **conventional**, or 'arbitrary' (with certain interesting exceptions relating to prosody and to two areas of articulation, phonaesthesia and onomatopoeia). However, the realizational relationship between the two sets of content strata (semantics and lexicogrammar) and the two sets of expression strata (phonology and phonetics) is **natural** rather than conventional. Patterns of wording reflect patterns of meaning. Part of the task of a functional theory of grammar is to bring out this natural relationship between wording and meaning. The natural relationship between semantics and lexicogrammar becomes more complex and less transparent with the development of lexicogrammatical metaphor, as we shall see in Chapter 10; but the relationship is still fundamentally natural rather than arbitrary.

1.3.4 Instantiation

When we want to explain how language is organized, and how its organization relates to the function it fulfils in human life, we often find it difficult to make things clear; and this is because we are trying to maintain two perspectives at once. One perspective is that of language as system; the other perspective is that of language as text.

The concept we need here is that of **instantiation**. The **system** of a language is 'instantiated' in the form of **text**. A text may be a trivial service encounter, like ordering coffee, or it may be a momentous event in human history, like Nelson Mandela's inaugural speech; in either case, and whatever its intrinsic value, it is an instance of an underlying system, and has no meaningful existence except as such. A text in English has no semiotic standing other than by reference to the system of English (which is why it has no meaning for you if you do not know the language).

The **system** is the underlying potential of a language: its potential as a meaning-making resource.[7] This does not mean that it exists as an independent phenomenon: there are not two separate objects, language as system and language as a set of texts. The relationship between the two is analogous to that between the weather and the climate (cf. Halliday, 1992a). Climate and weather are not two different phenomena; rather, they are the same phenomenon seen from different standpoints of the observer. What we call 'climate' is weather seen from a greater depth of time – it is what is instantiated in the form of weather. The weather is the text: it is what goes on around us all the time, impacting on, and sometimes disturbing, our daily lives. The climate is the system, the potential that underlies these variable effects.

Why then do we refer to them as different things? We can see why, if we consider some recent arguments about global warming, the question is asked: 'Is this a long-term weather pattern, or is it a blip in the climate?' What this means is, can we explain global warming

---

[7] This use of 'system' is thus different from – although related to – its meaning as a technical term in the grammar (see Section 1.3.2 above). The system in this general sense is equivalent to the totality of all the specific systems that would figure in a comprehensive network covering every stratum.

in terms of some general theory (in this case, of climatic change), or is it just a set of similar events? An analogous question about language would be if we took a corpus of, say, writings by political scientists and asked, are these just a set of similar texts, or do they represent a sub-system of the language? The climate is the *theory* of the weather. As such, it does have its own separate existence – but (like all theoretical entities) it exists on the semiotic plane. It is a virtual thing. Likewise with the system of language: this is language as a virtual thing; it is not the sum of all possible texts but a theoretical entity to which we can assign certain properties and which we can invest with considerable explanatory power.

System and text are thus related through instantiation. Like the relationship between climate and weather, the relationship between system and text is a cline – the **cline of instantiation** (Figure 1-11). System and text define the two poles of the cline – that of the overall potential and that of a particular instance. Between these two poles there are intermediate patterns. These patterns can be viewed either from the system pole as

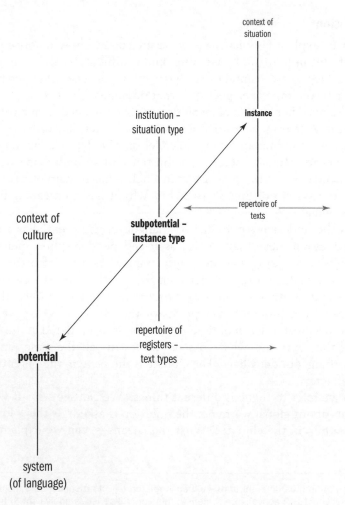

Fig. 1-11   The cline of instantiation

sub-systems or from the instance pole as instance types. If we start at the instance pole, we can study a single text, and then look for other texts that are like it according to certain criteria. When we study this sample of texts, we can identify patterns that they all share, and describe these in terms of a **text type**. By identifying a text type, we are moving along the cline of instantiation away from the text pole towards the system pole. The criteria we use when we compare the texts in our sample could, in principle, come from any of the strata of language – as long as they are systematic and explicit. However, research has shown that texts vary systematically according to contextual values: texts vary according the nature of the contexts they are used in. Thus recipes, weather forecasts, stockmarket reports, rental agreements, e-mail messages, inaugural speeches, service encounters in the local deli, news bulletins, media interviews, tutorial sessions, walking tours in a guide book, gossip during a tea-break, advertisements, bedtime stories, and all the other innumerable text types we meet in life are all ways of using language in different contexts. Looked at from the system pole of the cline of instantiation, they can be interpreted as **registers**. A register is a functional variety of language (Halliday, McIntosh & Strevens, 1964; Halliday, 1978) – the patterns of instantiation of the overall system associated with a given type of context (a **situation type**).[8] These patterns of instantiation show up quantitatively as adjustments in the systemic probabilities of language; a register can be represented as a particular setting of systemic probabilities. For example, the future tense is very much more likely to occur in weather forecasts than it is in stories (for examples of quantitative profiles of registers, see Matthiessen, 2002a, 2006a).

If we now come back to the question of stratification, we can perhaps see more clearly what it means to say that the semantic stratum is language interfacing with the non-linguistic (prototypically material) world. Most texts in adult life do not relate directly to the objects and events in their environment. Mandela's text was highly abstract, and even when he talked about *the soil of this beautiful country* and *the jacaranda trees of Pretoria* it is very unlikely that he could actually see them at the time. They were not a part of the setting in that instance. Nevertheless the meanings that are realized by these wordings, and the meanings realized by *an extraordinary human disaster* and *humanity's belief in justice* are, ultimately, construals of human experience; and when we now read or listen to that text we are understanding it as just that. Interfacing with the eco-social environment is a property of language as system; it is also, crucially, a feature of those instances through which small children come to master the system; but it is not something that is re-enacted in every text. Experience is remembered, imagined, abstracted, metaphorized and mythologized – the text has the power to create its own environment; but it has this power because of the way the system has evolved, by making meaning out of the environment as it was given.

As grammarians we have to be able to shift our perspective, observing now from the system standpoint and now from that of the text; and we have to be aware at which point we are standing at any time. This issue has been strongly foregrounded by the appearance of the computerized corpus. A corpus is a large collection of instances – of spoken and written

---

8 Here the term 'register' thus refers to a functional variety of language (see e.g. Halliday, 1978; Hasan, 1973; Matthiessen, 1993b; Ghadessy, 1993; Lukin *et al.*, 2008). It has also been used in a related, but different way, to refer to the contextual values associated with such a functional variety (see Martin, 1992, and other contributions to the 'genre model' within systemic functional linguistics; cf. Matthiessen, 1993b).

texts; the corpuses now available contain enough data to give significantly new insights into the grammar of English, provided the data can be processed and interpreted. But the corpus does not write the grammar for you, any more than the data from experiments in the behaviour of light wrote Newton's *Opticks* for him; it has to be theorized. Writing a description of a grammar entails constant shunting between the perspective of the system and the perspective of the instance. We have tried in this edition to take account of the new balance that has arisen as a result of data becoming accessible to grammarians in sufficient quantity for the first time in the two and a half millennia history of the subject.

1.3.5 Metafunction

This brings us back to the question asked in Section 1.3.3: what are the basic functions of language, in relation to our ecological and social environment? We suggested two: making sense of our experience, and acting out our social relationships.

It is clear that language does – as we put it – **construe** human experience. It names things, thus construing them into categories; and then, typically, goes further and construes the categories into taxonomies, often using more names for doing so. So we have *houses* and *cottages* and *garages* and *sheds*, which are all kinds of *building*; *strolling* and *stepping* and *marching* and *pacing*, which are all kinds of *walking*; *in, on, under, around* as relative locations, and so on – and the fact that these differ from one language to another is a reminder that the categories are in fact construed in language (cf. Halliday & Matthiessen, 1999: Chapter 7; Caffarel, Martin & Matthiessen, 2004). More powerfully still, these elements are configured into complex grammatical patterns like *marched out of the house*; the figures can be built up into sequences related by time, cause and the like – there is no facet of human experience that cannot be transformed into meaning. In other words, language provides a **theory** of human experience, and certain of the resources of the lexicogrammar of every language are dedicated to that function. We call it the **ideational** metafunction, and distinguish it into two components, the **experiential** and the **logical** (see Chapter 5 and Chapter 7).

At the same time, whenever we use language there is always something else going on. While construing, language is always also **enacting**: enacting our personal and social relationships with the other people around us. The **clause** of the grammar is not only a figure, representing some process – some doing or happening, saying or sensing, being or having – together with its various participants and circumstances; it is also a proposition, or a proposal, whereby we inform or question, give an order or make an offer, and express our appraisal of and attitude towards whoever we are addressing and what we are talking about. This kind of meaning is more active: if the ideational function of the grammar is 'language as reflection', this is 'language as action'. We call it the **interpersonal** metafunction, to suggest that it is both interactive and personal (see Chapter 4).

This distinction between two modes of meaning is not just made from outside; when the grammar is represented systemically, it shows up as two distinct networks of systems (Halliday, 1969; cf. Martin, 1991, on intrinsic functionality). What it signifies is that (1) every message is both about something and addressing someone, and (2) these two motifs can be freely combined – by and large, they do not constrain each other. But the grammar also shows up a third component, another mode of meaning that relates to the construction of text. In a sense this can be regarded as an enabling or facilitating function, since both the others – construing experience and enacting interpersonal relations – depend on being able

to build up sequences of discourse, organizing the discursive flow, and creating cohesion and continuity as it moves along. This, too, appears as a clearly delineated motif within the grammar. We call it the **textual** metafunction (see Chapters 3 and 9).

Why this rather unwieldy term 'metafunction?' We could have called them simply 'functions'; however, there is a long tradition of talking about the functions of language in contexts where 'function' simply means purpose or way of using language, and has no significance for the analysis of language itself (cf. Halliday & Hasan, 1985: Ch. 1; Martin, 1991). But the systemic analysis shows that functionality is *intrinsic* to language: that is to say, the entire architecture of language is arranged along functional lines. Language is as it is because of the functions in which it has evolved in the human species. The term 'metafunction' was adopted to suggest that function was an integral component within the overall theory (Figure 1-12).

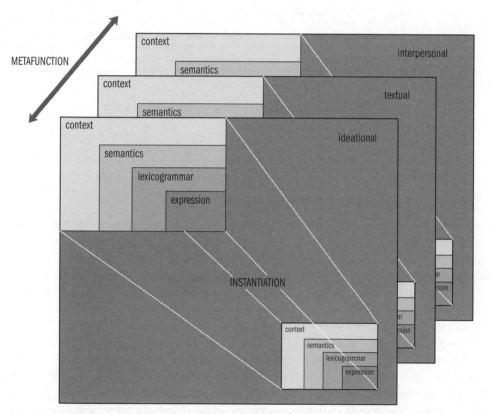

Fig. 1-12   Metafunction

1.4 Context, language and other semiotic systems

We have now introduced the major semiotic dimensions that define the 'architecture' of language in context (cf. Halliday, 2003: 1–29; Matthiessen, 2007a). Some of these dimensions enable us to locate lexicogrammar in relation to the other sub-systems that make up the total system of language; these are known as **global dimensions** because they determine the overall organization of language in context: the hierarchy of stratification, the cline of instantiation, and the spectrum of metafunctions. The other dimensions enable us to characterize the internal organization of lexicogrammar and also of the other sub-systems of language, and of context; these are known as **local dimensions** because they operate locally within linguistic sub-systems. Let us summarize the semiotic dimensions of language in context under these two headings: see Table 1-7.

Table 1-7 The global and local semiotic dimensions of language in context

Scope of dimension	Dimension	Orders	Section in this book
global	stratification	context – language [content [semantics – lexicogrammar] – expression [phonology – phonetics]]	1.3.3
	instantiation	potential – sub-potential/instance type – instance	1.3.4
	metafunction	ideational [logical – experiential] – interpersonal – textual	1.3.5
local	axis	paradigmatic – syntagmatic	1.3.1–1.3.2
	rank	(for lexicogrammar:) clause – group/phrase – word – morpheme	1.1.1–1.1.3; 1.2.1–1.2.3
	delicacy	(for lexicogrammar:) the continuum from grammar to lexis	(1.3.3); 2.2

1.4.1 Context; language in relation to context

As we have noted above (in particular in Section 1.3.4), language operates in context. In terms of linguistic theory, we recognize this important principle by developing an 'ecological' theory of language – one in which language is always theorized, described and analysed within an environment of meanings; a given language is thus interpreted by reference to its semiotic habitat. This way of approaching language was given a considerable theoretical and empirical boost by the anthropologist Bronislaw Malinowski in the 1920s and 1930s, based initially on his extensive fieldwork in the Trobriand Islands in the 1910s; and his insights were taken up and developed within linguistic theory by J.R. Firth, and then built into a general theory of language in context by systemic functional linguists (e.g. Halliday, McIntosh & Strevens, 1964; Halliday, 1978, 1992a; Halliday & Hasan, 1985; Ghadessy, 1999; Butt & Wegener, 2007). This is the conceptualization of context that we use here.

Like language, context is extended along the cline of instantiation (Section 1.3.4) from instance to potential; and like language, it is functionally diversified (Section 1.3.5). Let us discuss these two different aspects of the organization of context, and then introduce a context-based typology of texts that we will be using throughout this book when we give examples of grammar operating in text.

As shown in Figure 1-11, context extends along the cline of instantiation (Section 1.3.4) from the overall contextual potential of a community to the contextual instances involving particular people interacting and exchanging meanings on particular occasions. The contextual potential of a community is its culture – what we call the **context of culture**,

following Malinowski. The context of culture is what the members of a community can mean in cultural terms; that is, we interpret culture as a system of higher-level meanings (see Halliday, 1978) – as an environment of meanings in which various semiotic systems operate, including language, paralanguage (gesture, facial expression, voice quality, timbre, tempo, and other systems of meaning accompanying language and expressed through the human body; cf. Thibault, 2004) and other human systems of meaning such as dance, drawing, painting and architecture (e.g. Kress & van Leeuwen, 1996; O'Toole, 1994; Martinec, 2005). Describing the cultural potential of a community is obviously a huge undertaking – one requiring the kind of commitment, support, recognition and funding given to the Human Genome Project, started in 1990. Perhaps we can imagine a vast number of Human Sememe Projects given the task of mapping out the cultural potentials of all human societies (or Human Meme Projects, to relate to Richard Dawkins' notion of meme as a cultural replicator). While no project on this scale has yet been undertaken, it is certainly possible to see the theoretical significance of such a project.

From a practical point of view, one research strategy is to move along the cline of instantiation from the potential pole towards the instance pole: for researchers, it is considerably easier to take on the task of describing a particular **cultural domain**, or **institution**, based on evidence gathered from the various **contexts of situation** operating within that institution (cf. Matthiessen, 2009c: Section 3.6). Malinowski (e.g. 1944) called institutions the 'real isolates of culture', advocating the study of institutions; and we can investigate an institution linguistically through the register that operates within it (cf. Section 1.1 above). While describing the overall potential of a culture is a daunting task, mapping out an institution by identifying and describing the different types of situation that collectively constitute the institution is a more manageable undertaking, and systemic functional contributions along these lines have been made in a number of areas including the family, education, administration, the media, and healthcare.

While there are still no comprehensive descriptions of the context of culture, the general categories of context have been known for a long time – see Halliday, McIntosh & Strevens (1964: 90–94); and they have been explored under the headings of **field**, **tenor** and **mode** (e.g. Hasan, 1973; Halliday, 1978; Halliday & Hasan, 1985; Martin, 1992). Thus any situation type can be characterized in terms of field, tenor and mode:

- **field** – what's going on in the situation: (i) the nature of the social and semiotic activity; and (ii) the domain of experience this activity relates to (the 'subject matter' or 'topic')
- **tenor** – who is taking part in the situation: (i) the roles played by those taking part in the socio-semiotic activity – (1) institutional roles, (2) status roles (power, either equal or unequal), (3) contact roles (familiarity, ranging from strangers to intimates) and (4) sociometric roles (affect, either neutral or charged, positively or negatively); and (ii) the values that the interactants imbue the domain with (either neutral or loaded, positively or negatively)
- **mode** – what role is being played by language and other semiotic systems in the situation: (i) the division of labour between semiotic activities and social ones (ranging from semiotic activities as constitutive of the situation to semiotic activities as facilitating); (ii) the division of labour between linguistic activities and other

semiotic activities; (iii) rhetorical mode: the orientation of the text towards field (e.g. informative, didactic, explanatory, explicatory) or tenor (e.g. persuasive, exhortatory, hortatory, polemic); (iv) turn: dialogic or monologic; (v) medium: written or spoken; (vi) channel: phonic or graphic.

Field, tenor and mode are thus sets of related variables, with ranges of contrasting values. Together they define a multi-dimensional semiotic space – the environment of meanings in which language, other semiotic systems and social systems operate. The combinations of field, tenor and mode values determine different uses of language – the different meanings that are at risk in a given type of situation. There are systematic correspondences between the contextual values and the meanings that are at risk in the contexts defined by these values. As Halliday (1978) suggested, field values **resonate** with ideational meanings, tenor values resonate with interpersonal meanings, and mode values resonate with textual meanings (see also Halliday & Hasan, 1985: 26)[9]. In other words, the correspondences between context and language are based on the functional organization of both orders of meaning.

The ideational, interpersonal and textual *meanings at risk* can be stated in terms of systems at the semantic stratum in the first instance. However, since semantics stands in a natural relation to lexicogrammar, the two being the content plane systems of language, meanings at risk can also be stated, by another stratal step, in terms of systems at the lexicogrammatical stratum as *wordings at risk*. For example, when we consider the correlations between tenor values and terms in interpersonal systems, we should really focus on interpersonal semantic systems such as SPEECH FUNCTION in the first instance rather than on lexicogrammatical ones such as MOOD (to take an area of content from Chapter 4). Thus combinations of tenor values relating to (a) status and (b) contact correlate with different semantic strategies open to speakers for demanding goods-&-services of their listeners – for commanding their listeners. If (a) the status is unequal, with the speaker being subordinate to the listener and (b) the contact is minimal, the speaker's semantic options are very limited: it is very hard to command a stranger who is of superior status to do something; but there will be certain semantic strategies. Lexicogrammatically, these strategies will be far removed from the congruent realization of a command, a clause of the imperative mood – perhaps something like *I wonder if you would be so kind as to* ... and they will be 'dispersed' in the grammar of mood, involving not only 'imperative' clauses but also 'declarative' and 'interrogative' ones and in fact not only clauses but also combinations of clauses (see Chapter 10, Section 10.4); but semantically, they are still within range of options associated with commands. Thus accounts of 'politeness' have tended to be cast in semantic terms rather than in lexicogrammatical ones (e.g. Brown & Levinson, 1987 – an influential contribution: see Watts, 2003, for a critical review of their framework and the literature since their work; and systemic functional accounts, e.g. Bateman, 1988; Butler, 1988). Tenor is, as it were, refracted through semantics so that the lexicogrammatical resonances with tenor values are more indirect than the semantic ones.

---

[9]   We use the term 'resonate with' because the relationship is not a one-way causal relationship, but rather a two-way realizational relationship (cf. Jay Lemke's, 1984, notion of **metaredundancy**, discussed in Halliday, 1992d). Contextual values influence linguistic choices but are also influenced by them.

Still, while field, tenor and mode resonate with semantic systems in the first instance, they do penetrate into lexicogrammar: field values put ideational wordings at risk, tenor values put interpersonal wordings at risk, and mode values put textual wordings at risk. This was in fact shown by Brown & Gilman's (1960) classic study of 'the pronouns of power and solidarity': the tenor variables of power (or 'status') and solidarity (related to 'contact', in our characterization of tenor above) resonate with different uses of the system of pronouns in various languages[10]. Indeed, the tenor variables of power and contact may be grammaticalized as part of the core interpersonal system of mood in a language, as in Japanese and Korean (see Matthiessen, Teruya & Wu, 2008, and references therein).

Field, tenor and mode variables are the basis for any attempt to develop a taxonomy of situations. At the same time, since text is language functioning in context, the field, tenor and mode variables are also the basis of any attempt to develop a taxonomy of texts operating in situations. It is certainly true that in developing a taxonomy of texts, we can adopt – we need to adopt – a trinocular perspective (see Section 1.5.1 below), matching up contextual, semantic and lexicogrammatical considerations to support the taxonomy. However, to be meaningful, a taxonomy of texts must be grounded in contextual considerations. If the taxonomy is 'on the right track', semantic and lexicogrammatical considerations will align themselves with the contextual ones.

In principle, such a taxonomy would be based on all three contextual variables – on field, tenor and mode. However, here we will present a contextual taxonomy of text that is based on field in the first instance, more specifically on the variable of socio-semiotic activity (see Matthiessen, 2006c; Matthiessen, Teruya & Lam, 2010; Teruya, 2007). We will use this taxonomy throughout the book, classifying the illustrative texts we introduce according to this taxonomy (as we have already done – e.g. Texts 1-1 through to 1-3).

So let's consider the nature of the socio-semiotic activity that constitutes a situation. In a sense, the activity that constitutes a situation is either one of behaviour or one of meaning; this is the traditional distinction between action and reflection. So we will make a basic distinction between activities of 'doing' and of 'meaning', and then further distinctions within 'meaning':

- 'doing': the situation is constituted in some form of social behaviour, involving one or more persons. Language or other semiotic systems such as gesture, gaze and facial expression may be engaged to facilitate the performance of the activity, as when language is used to coordinate a team
- 'meaning': the situation is constituted in some process of meaning. There are seven primary types:
  - 'expounding': expounding knowledge about the world – about general classes of phenomena, categorizing them or explaining them
  - 'reporting': reporting particular phenomena, chronicling the flow of events, surveying places or inventorying entities

---

[10] Another classic study that illuminates the relationship between tenor and lexicogrammar is Ervin-Tripp's (1972) account of terms of address in American English in relation to tenor values. The general point is that a given interpersonal system can mean in more than one way depending on the tenor values of the context in which it operates.

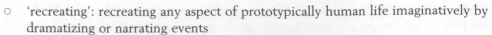

- ○ 'recreating': recreating any aspect of prototypically human life imaginatively by dramatizing or narrating events
- ○ 'sharing': sharing personal experiences and values, prototypically in private
- ○ 'enabling': enabling some course of activity, either enabling the activity by instructing people in how to undertake it or regulating the activity by controlling people's actions
- ○ 'recommending': recommending some course of activity, either for the sake of the speaker through promotion of some commodity or for the sake of addressee through advice
- ○ 'exploring': exploring societal values and positions, prototypically in the public arena.

These primary types of socio-semiotic activity can be represented typologically as a system network, of course; but we can also represent them topologically, as shown in Figure 1.13. This 'pie' diagram suggests that different types shade into one another, which is indeed the case. For example, 'reporting' and 'recreating' shade into one another to provide a context for fictionalized biographies ('fake histories': see Halliday, 2010: Section 5.3), and 'recommending' and 'reporting' shade into one another to provide a context for infomercials.

Figure 1-13 represents two steps in delicacy – the eight primary types, and secondary distinctions within each type. When we reach secondary delicacy, we can begin to discern the structuring of situations belonging to the different types. And if we take one step further, we can relate tertiary types to generic structures in the literature on 'genres'. For example, situations characterized by processes of explaining can be structured in a number of different ways, but once we differentiate these explanation strategies at tertiary delicacy, for example distinguishing factorial explanations from sequential ones, we can assign the distinct structures described by Veel (1997) for explanations in school science. Similarly, there are different ways of staging narrative situations, but once we take another step and differentiate folk tales, exempla, anecdotes and other narrative strategies, we can refer to the different narrative structures that have been described in the literature (e.g. Hasan, 1984; Eggins & Slade, 1997; Martin & Rose, 1994: Chapter 2). (Clearly, the specification of the structure of situation is staged in terms of delicacy. For example, narrative situations in general share structures that embody temporal sequence, but they differ in terms of other structural elements and even with respect to what factors 'drive' the temporal sequence.)

The question of how many steps in delicacy we have to take before we can begin to discern the distinct structures of different types of situation is obviously important from the point of view of contextual description. This question is also significant from the point of view of the description of lexicogrammar. Here the issue is at what point we can begin to discern interestingly distinct uses of the resources of lexicogrammar. As a rule of thumb, we can say that this happens at the point at which the contextual structure of a situation can be fully specified. This will mean, among other things, that the elements of the structure of a situation can be investigated in terms of their distinct patterns of lexicogrammatical realization, as illustrated by e.g. Halliday (1982) and Fries (1985).

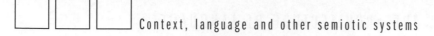
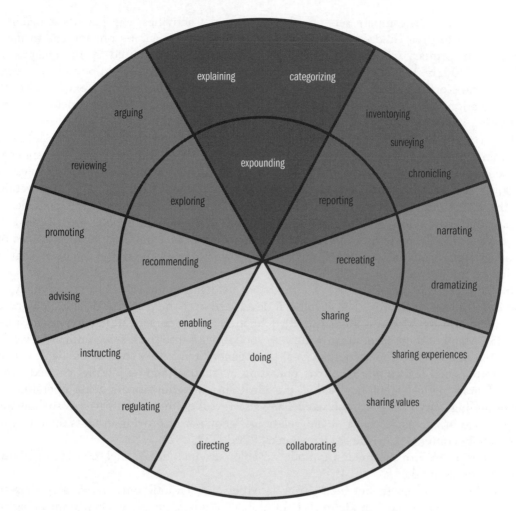

Fig. 1-13   Field – socio-semiotic process (activity) represented as a topology

The socio-semiotic activity types in Figure 1-1 combine with values from the other field variable, i.e. with values from experiential domains (areas of subject matter); and these combinations are likely to yield somewhat different patterns. For example, explanations in school science (e.g. Veel, 1997) and in school history (e.g. Coffin, 2006) are similar in various ways, but they are also different in certain respects. For example, the repertoire of explanations deployed in school history appears to be narrower; and they differ lexicogrammatically: scientific terms are construed and used very frequently in school science but hardly at all in school history (cf. Eggins, Wignell & Martin, 1993).

The socio-semiotic activity types in Figure 1-1 also combine with variables within the tenor and mode parameters of context. In terms of **tenor**, we can consider the different socio-semiotic activities in relation to different role combinations of those taking part in the activity. For example, we can imagine a series of concentric circles for different institutional role combinations as children would meet them in the course of their development as they grow up, and then compare sets of roles for different activities, e.g. parents explaining phenomena to their children in the home versus teachers explaining phenomena to their students in primary school – or the other way around, as illustrated by the analysis in Halliday (2002b: 313–322) on an explanation offered by a five-year-old boy to his father of why the North Star stays still but the other stars don't (see Chapter 3, Text 3-7). Tenor considerations thus include the range of 'voices' taking part in the different socio-semiotic activities, including degrees of expertise and of professionalism.

In terms of **mode**, we can intersect the socio-semiotic activity types with different combinations of (a) turn: dialogic vs. monologic, and (b) medium: written vs. spoken; these combinations are represented as four different concentric circles in e.g. Matthiessen (2006c: 46), Teruya (2007), and Matthiessen, Teruya & Lam (2010: 221). The intersection of the socio-semiotic activity types with (a) turn and (b) medium makes it possible to locate the short numbered text examples we give throughout this book: see Table 1-8. Quite a few cells are empty, but most of them could in fact be filled with examples of lexicogrammatically analysed texts, and we hope that systematic overviews can be presented in future publications.

In the same way, we could use this matrix of field and mode values to locate many of the descriptions of 'genres' that have been developed over the past few decades: compare the summaries in Martin & Rose (2008), Christie & Derewianka (2008), Eggins & Slade (2005). Many of these accounts provide very good insights into the lexicogrammar 'at work' in different contexts. The accounts reveal fairly general tendencies such as the deployment of interpersonal lexis in various texts operating in 'sharing' and 'exploring' contexts, the use of grammatical metaphor within the ideational metafunction in texts operating in 'expounding' and 'exploring' contexts. They also reveal quite specific patterns such as the emergence in late adolescence of the 'relational' grammar of proving in texts operating in 'exploring' contexts (Christie & Derewianka, 2008: 222, 232).

In addition to turn and medium, mode variables also include channel, division of labour and rhetorical mode.

The division of labour between social activities and semiotic ones varies according to the activities represented in Figure 1-1. In 'doing' contexts, people exchange meanings to facilitate the social tasks they are concerned with, as when medical teams collaborate to perform surgery or when removalists talk and gesture (if their hands are free!) to coordinate difficult tasks (as in Text 4-3 in Chapter 4). In all other contexts, most of the socio-semiotic labour is semiotic in the first instance: the exchange of meanings in language and other semiotic systems is constitutive of the contexts in which it operates.

The division of labour between language and other semiotic systems covers the whole range, from contexts where language does all the semiotic work to contexts where all the semiotic work is done by some semiotic system or systems other than language. The possible combinations naturally depend on the nature of the channel, but they also vary according to field. For example, recounts in history using a graphic channel might be accompanied by timeline diagrams, but instructions in software manuals might be accompanied by flowcharts (cf. Matthiessen, 2009a).

Rhetorical mode encompasses a number of rhetorical categories concerned with the contribution of the text to the situation it operates in: informative, didactic, persuasive, exhortatory, pragmatic, and so on. However, we can relate these particular categories to

Table 1-8 Matrix of socio-semiotic activity types intersected with turn and medium, with classification of text samples used in this book (examples of 'genres' in italics)

		Spoken & monologic	Spoken & dialogic	Written & dialogic	Written & monologic
expounding	**explaining** [explanations]		Text 3-7, Table 9-7		Text 1-5
	categorizing [reports: descriptive, taxonomic]				Text 3-2, Table 5-13, Text 5-16, Text 6-2, Text 9-12, Text 9-13
reporting	**inventorying** [inventory lists]				
	surveying [topographic reports]				Text 3-1
	chronicling [recounts: historical, procedural; news reports; forecasts]		Text 3-3, Text 4-5, Text 4-7, Text 4-8, Text 5-17, Text 9-6, Text 10-1		Text 5-6, Text 5-8, Text 5-13, Text 7-10, Text 8-1, Text 9-10, Text 10-2, Text 10-3, Text 10-4
recreating	[folk stories, short stories, novels, plays]			Text 4-2, Text 7-7	Text 1-6, Text 3-5, Text 5-2, Text 5-3, Text 5-5, Text 5-9, Text 5-11, Text 5-14, Text 5-15, Text 6-1, Text 7-1, Text 7-6, Text 7-9, Text 9-11, Text 9-14, Table 9-18
sharing	[anecdotes, exempla, reminiscences, opinion texts, gossip, banter]		Text 1-3, Text 3-4, Text 3-8, Text 3-9, Text 4-1, Text 5-1, Text 5-7, Text 5-12, Text 7-2, Text 9-1, Text 9-2, Text 9-3, Text 9-4, Text 9-5, Text 9-6, Text 9-7		

continued overleaf

Table 1-8 *continued*

		Spoken & monologic	Spoken & dialogic	Written & dialogic	Written & monologic
doing	**directing** [administrative directives]				
	collaborating [service encounters; kinds of team work]		Text 4-3, Text 7-8, Text 9-1		
enabling	**instructing** [procedures, demonstrations]		Text 3-6, Text 9-1		Text 5-11, Text 7-3, Text 7-5, Table 10-2
	regulating [constitutions, laws]				Text 4-4, Text 10-6, Text 10-7
recommending	**advising** [consultations, advice columns]		Text 4-6		
	promoting [advertisements, commercials, book blurbs]				Text 1-2, Text 1-4, Text 9-15, Text 10-8
exploring	**reviewing (valuing)** [reviews, speeches]	Text 1-1, Text 2-1			
	arguing [expositions, debates, discussions, speeches]		Text 6-3, Text 7-4		Text 9-4, Table 9-20, Text 10-5

the **orientation** of the text (i) towards the field of the situation, (ii) towards the tenor or (iii) towards some mixture of both.

(i)   Orientation towards field means that the goals of the situation, or intended outcomes, are concerned with field, more specifically with the development of field, as in an 'expounding' context where the speaker's goal might be to construe a taxonomy for the addressee, a classification of some classes of phenomena. When texts operate in such situations, they tend to be organized in terms of field – in terms of the structure of the field, as when a text is organized according to the classes of a taxonomy (e.g. Text 9-12, Text 9-13). Orientation towards field is characteristic of 'expounding', 'reporting' and 'doing' contexts, and also in principle of 'enabling' contexts of the 'instructing' subtype.

(ii) Orientation towards tenor means that the goals of the situation, or intended outcomes, are concerned with tenor, more specifically with the relationship between speaker and addressee – with maintaining or changing this relationship, as when speakers try to bring their addressees closer to their own positions (e.g. the text in Table 9-20). When texts operate in such situations, they tend to be organized in terms of tenor, with a central proposition or proposal supported by text segments that provide evidence for the proposition, increasing the likelihood that the addressee will agree, or motivation for the proposal, increasing the likelihood that the addressee will comply (if the proposal is some form of command) or accept (if the proposal is some form of offer). The orientation towards tenor is thus likely to be reflected in the semantic organization of texts operating in 'recommending' and 'exploring' contexts in the use of fairly global **internal relations** – called internal conjunctive relations (see Halliday & Hasan, 1976; Martin, 1992) or internal rhetorical relations (see Mann & Matthiessen, 1991). Both evidence and motivation can be interpreted as internal versions of cause – evidence: 'I claim/you should believe that ... because ... '; motivation: 'I want you/you are obliged to ... because ...'. In general, orientation towards tenor is characteristic of 'sharing', 'recommending' and 'exploring' contexts, and also in principle of 'enabling' contexts of the 'regulatory' subtype (but see immediately below). In contrast, texts operating in contexts with an orientation towards field are much less likely to involve internal relations; instead, they are organized both globally and locally in terms of **external relations**. For the contrast between internal and external relations, see further Chapter 9, Section 9.3.2; for the orientation in the organization of text towards interpersonal or ideational meanings, see Halliday (2001).

(iii) Orientation towards both field and tenor means that the goals of the situation, or intended outcomes, are concerned with field and/or tenor. Thus the goals of 'recreating' situations may be concerned with the construal of some imaginary world, ranging from a slight variant of our own world to a world of pure fantasy; but the goals may at the same time involve moral principles embodied in tenor. In this way, utopias and dystopias are concerned with both field and tenor. The orientation towards both field and tenor is reflected in the structure of traditional folk tales or nursery tales: field is reflected in the sequence of events (initiating, sequent and final), and tenor is reflected in evaluations, which may be strung out prosodically through the narrative and/or encapsulated in a separate 'moral' at the end of the tale (cf. Hasan, 1984). The goals of 'enabling' situations can also be said to relate to both field and tenor, but in a different way. They concern the addressee's activities in some field, but tenor comes into the picture as well because these activities are 'modulated': the addressee is either capacitated to undertake them (instruction) or required to do so (regulation). In terms of their organization, instructional texts tend to be more field-like, being organized as the sequence of steps that make up a procedure. In contrast, regulatory texts have a less clearly field-based organization; and like 'promoting' texts, they may include motivations – although typically threats of forms of punishment rather than the irresistible features of a product or service!

Channel determines the 'bandwidth' of the flow of meanings in a situation. For most of human history, the channel was only phonic, but typically with visual contact (thus also allowing for accompanying gestures, facial expressions and other forms of visual 'paralanguage'); but with the gradual emergence of writing, initially in certain city-based civilizations around five thousand years ago, graphic channels were added, and archival uses of language became possible. Technological advances have continued to enhance the potential of both phonic and graphic channels, and to enable mixed channels (cf. Halliday, 2008: 140–141). Importantly, mobile and web-based technologies (for hardware and software) have changed the possibilities of 'sharing' in rather dramatic ways, with a whole host of new options like e-mail messages, text messages, blogs, tweets and other formats associated with social media, as investigated and discussed by Macnamara (2010). As a result, the distinction between the private sphere of 'sharing' values and opinions and the 'public' sphere of exploring them has become blurred. This can be seen in places where users post reviews of commodities such as film and music, such as the Internet Movie Data Base. Reviews range from opinions that might be shared in casual conversation to analytical evaluations of the kind we would expect from expert reviewers contributing to quality newspapers. Since both 'sharing' and 'exploring' contexts are important sites for the instantiation, and (in the phylogenetic time-frame) for the evolution, of interpersonal meaning, there are likely to be interesting changes in patterns of interpersonal meaning-making – more profound than the addition of 'emoticons' to written conversation to make up for some of the loss of intonation and voice quality in spoken language. Of course, technological advances do not affect only 'sharing' and 'exploring' contexts, but also the other types of situation characterized in terms of socio-semiotic activities in Figure 1-1. However, the development of social media does indicate the extent to which companies are trying to leverage people's need for 'sharing' and orientation towards the interpersonal.

1.1.2 Semantics

Semantics is the highest stratum within language; it serves as an 'interface' between language and the environment outside language, as shown in Table 1-5. This means that semantics interfaces with context, but not only with context – it also interfaces with other systems that operate within context, viz. with the content systems of other semiotic systems and

with bio-semiotic systems such as our systems of perception and our system of bodily action (cf. Halliday & Matthiessen, 1999).

As the upper of the two content strata within language, semantics is the interface between context and lexicogrammar. Semantics transforms experience and interpersonal relationships into linguistic meaning, and lexicogrammar transforms this meaning into words, as we put it above (see Table 1-5), adopting the speaker's perspective.

The basic unit of semantics is the **text** – language functioning in context, an instance of the semantic system. A text is organized internally as patterns of logical, experiential, interpersonal and textual meaning. At the same time, it is organized externally as a unit operating in context: the structure of the context of situation that a text operates in is, as it were, projected onto the text. If the situation is one of 'meaning' in terms of the socio-semiotic activity in Figure 1-1 then the entire structure of the situation is projected onto the text. For example, in a situation of telling a traditional folk tale, the structure would be (from Hasan, 1984, but slightly simplified):

(Placement ^) Initiating Event ^ Sequent Event^{1-n} ^ Final Event (^ Finale) (° Moral)

This structure is projected onto the text operating in the situation, as illustrated in Text 5-2, Chapter 5 – and possibly also onto other accompanying semiotic processes such as a musical score. Each element, or stage, of the structure of the situation is realized by distinctive semantic patterns, as illustrated for Placement by Hasan (1984). These distinctive semantic patterns are, in turn, realized by distinctive lexicogrammatical patterns; but the patterns of wording in the lexicogrammar are always mediated by the patterns of meaning in the semantics. In Text 5-2, the beginning of the Placement is realized (via the semantics) by an 'existential' clause, followed by a 'material' clause (to characterize them in the experiential terms that we will introduce in Chapter 5):

Once, a very long time ago, there lived a man called Noah. He and his wife and his sons and their wives all worked very hard.

The 'existential' clause serves to introduce the protagonist of the tale, *a man called Noah*, as the Existent – the participant in the process of living; and the Existent is given the textual status of New information, the main point of the message (to use textual terms we will introduce in Chapter 3). The protagonist is presented in this way against the background of Time, *once, a very long time ago*; and this temporal circumstance is given the textual status of Theme, the orientation chosen for the message. The next clause still contributes to the development of the Placement: elaborating on Noah, it construes a habitual activity he and his family took part in.

The need for a placement in a traditional situation of narration thus 'trickles' down from context via the semantics to the lexicogrammar, and this need is met by the lexicogrammatical choices that we have just illustrated. However, unless texts are very short (like traffic signs), there are layers of semantic patterning between the whole text and the local units that are realized lexicogrammatically by clauses such as *Once, a very long time ago, there lived a man called Noah*. Texts have 'depth' – ordered layers of semantic patterns, ranging from the global semantic domain of the whole text to local semantic domain corresponding to domains of lexicogrammatical patterning. This depth is reflected in traditional accounts within composition and rhetoric in notions like rhetorical paragraph and topic sentence, and linguists and other scholars concerned with the analysis of texts and the description of the systems that lie behind them have proposed various frameworks for accounting for the 'depth' of texts, including pioneering contributions from the broad tradition of tagmemic linguistics (e.g. Grimes, 1975; Beekman, Callow & Kopesec, 1981; Longacre, 1996; Longacre & Hwang, 2012; Pike, 1992).

In general, two approaches to the account of the depth of texts have emerged in various traditions: the depth of layering may be modelled in terms of a **semantic rank scale** operating with some kind of constituency structure (analogous to the lexicogrammatical and phonological rank scales discussed above), as in Longacre's work since the 1970s; or it may be modelled in terms of **internal nesting of relational organization** – along the lines of Grimes (1975) and Beekman, Callow & Kopesec (1981). Within systemic functional linguistics, we also find these two models of the depth of text – the rank-scale model with rhetorical units proposed by Cloran (1994) and the internal-nesting model derived from Rhetorical Structure Theory (RST, e.g. Matthiessen & Thompson, 1988; Matthiessen, 1992, 2002a). The two are applied to the analysis of the same text by Cloran, Stuart-Smith & Young (2007). They are not, of course, mutually exclusive; they can be interpreted as capturing different aspects of the 'depth' of texts. And as grammarians we do not have to choose between the two as long as they provide us with motivated accounts of how to relate semantics to grammar. However, at various points in our account of grammar, we will make use of the internal nesting model derived from RST since this model will enable us to explore the nature of clause complexing (Chapter 7), of the use of cohesive conjunctions (Chapter 9), of grammatical metaphor (Chapter 10), and of the source of methods of development relating to the choice of Theme (Chapter 3).

Let us try to summarize the salient features of the relationship between situation (context), text (semantics) and clause (lexicogrammar) by means of a diagram: see Figure 1.14. Globally, a text is structured according to the situation it operates in; the contextual structure is projected onto the text, and the contextual elements are realized by patterns of meaning in the text. As a semantic unit, the text consists of semantic domains of different sizes. It is likely to consist of **rhetorical paragraphs** (or **parasemes** (see Halliday, 2002d), which may or may not correspond to orthographic paragraphs in writing). In turn, these consist of **sequences** – sequences of **figures**, i.e. configurations of processes, participants involved in these and attendant circumstances. These more local domains, sequences and figures, are typically realized grammatically: sequences are realized by clause complexes, and figures by clauses. Here the grammar provides a good deal of guidance through the grammatical structure of the clause complex (Chapter 7), the clause (Chapters 3 through to 5) and its constituent parts (Chapters 6 and 8). Thus the grammar makes the local structure of the text 'tighter', more highly integrated, by constructing it not only as meaning but also as wording. However, the grammar also provides some important guidance beyond the domain of the clause complex, i.e. beyond the most extensive domain of grammatical structure. It does this by means of the resources of cohesion (Chapter 9), e.g. by means of cohesive conjunctions such as *for example*, *in addition*, *in contrast*, *therefore*, *meanwhile*, which can mark relations between sequences realized by clause complexes and also between (groups of) rhetorical paragraphs.

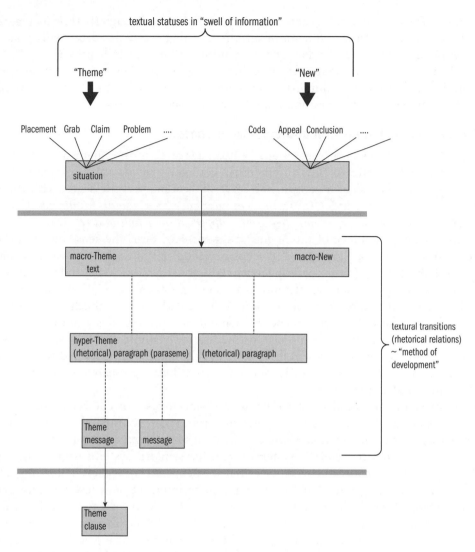

Fig. 1-14   Semantics as an 'interlevel' between context and lexicogrammar

In describing the structure of the text, we have foregrounded the perspective of the ideational metafunction. Sequences are construed through logical resources and figures through experiential ones; and rhetorical paragraphs and groups of paragraphs can be interpreted as being formed by logical resources – in terms of logico-semantic relations (cf. Halliday, 2001; Matthiessen, 2002a). At the same time, texts are also organized in terms of interpersonal and textual patterns of meaning. Interpersonally, a text is a series of **exchanges** between speaker and addressee – even if it is a one-sided monologue that is essentially a series of statements acknowledged silently by the addressee. These exchanges are propelled forward locally by **moves**, which are realized by clauses in their interpersonal guise (Chapter 4). Textually, a text is a flow of information, or, more accurately, waves of

45

information. These wave patterns extend from the whole text through rhetorical paragraphs to local waves, or **messages** – quanta of information that are realized by clauses in their textual guise, and (in spoken language) also by information units (Chapter 3).

We will discuss the complementary metafunctional perspectives on the text at various points in the book in order to illuminate the grammar, and we will return to the relationship between semantics and lexicogrammar in Chapter 10, Section 10.1.

1.4.3 Language and other semiotic systems in context

The term 'text' includes both spoken and written instances of the linguistic system. As a scientific term in linguistics, it thus differs from a common everyday sense of text as a piece of writing – and now also as a verb, in the sense of 'sending text messages' with the help of some mobile message service (as in *In what may have been a final, frantic act, Conaway texted relatives an hour later, saying they were trapped in the trunk of a car.*). In linguistics, 'text' thus means an instance of the linguistic system. However, the sense of text is being extended to other semiotic systems, and scholars refer to instances of e.g. 'visual semiotic' systems as '(visual) texts' (thus a painting would be a visual semiotic text) and they also refer to 'multimodal texts' – instances of more than one semiotic system. While this extended sense of 'text' is still hard to find in dictionaries, it has clearly been established; for example, ACARA, the Australian Curriculum and Assessment Authority glosses 'multimodal text' as 'combination of two or more communication modes (for example, print, image and spoken text, as in film or computer presentations)'[11]. And the same has happened to 'discourse' (see e.g. Kress & van Leeuwen's, 2001, pioneering contribution; researchers now talk about 'MDA': 'multimodal discourse analysis'.

Most accounts of 'multimodal text' so far have probably focused on combinations of written texts and instances of 'visual semiotic' systems. From a developmental and evolutionary point of view, it would make more sense to start with spoken texts unfolding together with instances of other **somatic semiotic systems** (i.e. other semiotic systems using some aspect of the body as their expression plane; see Matthiessen, 2009a, and cf. Thibault's, 2004, notion of the 'signifying body') before moving on to interpret and describe **exo-somatic semiotic systems**. Indeed, the protolanguages of early childhood tend to be both vocal and gestural in their expression (see Halliday, 1975, 1992d, 2004); and we can hypothesize that the same was true of protolanguages in human evolution (see Matthiessen, 2004a). Using this starting point, we could investigate the relationship (including relative timing) between choices in lexicogrammar and choices in semiotic systems other than language such as gesture, facial expression and vocal paralanguage in face-to-face conversation, building on contributions such as McNeill (2000). Here the research by James Lantolf and his team of researchers in the context of (advanced) second language learning is a source of insights and ideas. For example, he has shown that English and Spanish differ in how they construe motion through space in terms of the division of labour between lexicogrammar and gesture: certain features of motion are construed lexicogrammatically in English, but gesturally in Spanish; and the other way around. While Lantolf's framework is not derived from systemic functional linguistics, it is quite compatible (cf. contributions in Byrnes,

---

[11] See: http://www.australiancurriculum.edu.au/Glossary?a=E&t=multimodal+texts

2006), and it is a valuable demonstration of the importance of investigating lexicogrammar 'ecologically' instead of treating it as an 'autonomous' system: clearly, lexicogrammar and gesture evolved together as complementary systems in both English and Spanish[12]. An early systemic functional contribution to the study of language and gesture is Muntigl (2004), and the systemic functional work on language and gesture has been followed up by Hood (2011).

If we take 'text' to mean an instance of the system of a language operating in a context of situation, then we can ask: (1) how it relates to instances of other semiotic systems operating in the same context of situation, and (2) how semiotic labour is divided among these different semiotic systems – how they complement one another. Taking gesture as an example of a semiotic system operating alongside language, we can represent the basis for these two questions diagrammatically: see Figure 1-15. Both language and gesture operate in the same context of situation, and are thus coordinated within it: as spoken text unfolds, it is accompanied by gesturing. Studies like those referred to above show that speakers (and addressees) are very adept at synchronizing speech and gesture so that gesture may relate to any of the metafunctional strands of meaning that run through the spoken text, e.g. a beckoning gesture accompanying a command to the addressee such as *Come here!* (interpersonal), a pointing gesture accompanying a reference (exophoric) such as *That's huge* (textual), or a depictive gesture accompanying a description such as *It is shaped like a five-pointed star* (experiential). (2) The division of semiotic labour between language and gesture seems to vary from one language to another, as already noted; but with a given language, there will also be variation

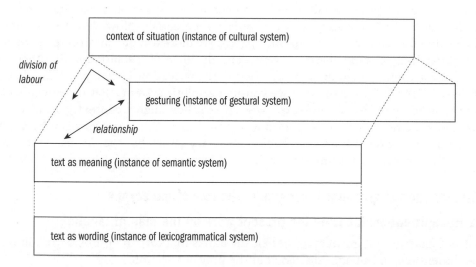

Fig. 1-15   Gesturing accompanying linguistic meaning and wording in context

---

[12] This is a fundamental insight into lexicogrammar – and it is very relevant in the context of the extensive body of research on the lexicogrammar of motion, going back to Talmy's (1985) pioneering typological study. (For a recent contribution to, and review of the extensive literature in, this area, see Beavers, Levin & Thao, 2010.)

according to the nature of the context, and thus of the register. In a game of charades, or in pantomime more generally, gesture and other visually realized semiotic systems must, of course, take over entirely from language; but in contexts where speakers need their hands and arms for other purposes, as often happens in 'doing' contexts, they have to rely more on language, and even though speakers tend to gesture when they engage in a telephone conversation, their listeners do not see these gestures (unless there is a video link).

One interesting issue that relates to both questions posed above is to what extent the different semiotic systems operating in context are integrated with one another and to what extent they operate independently of one another. To explore this issue, we can posit a **cline of integration**, extending from completely integrated systems to completely independent ones (cf. Matthiessen, 2009a). An example of complete integration is grammar and intonation. In English, and in many other languages, intonation is in fact not a separate semiotic system but rather a medium of expression deployed within the interpersonal and textual systems of the language (see e.g. Halliday, 1967a; Halliday & Greaves, 2008). An example of more or less complete independence would be the use of images in early printed books in Europe: illustrations were not produced or even chosen by the author as illustrations of points in the text but were instead added by the printer as decorations.

Another interesting issue is to what extent different semiotic systems extend all the way along the cline of instantiation from the instance pole to the potential pole (cf. Figure 1-11). We can ask of any one given semiotic system how systemic it is – which clearly relates to the question of how much individual variation there is across a speech fellowship (or speech community). Language has evolved as a fully systemic semiotic system: it is possible to posit and describe the overall meaning potential for a given language, interpreting this meaning potential as an aggregate of registerial subpotentials. However, it is theoretically quite possible that certain other semiotic systems are more usefully interpreted as operating with systems located somewhere midway along the cline of instantiation; in other words, they are most usefully described in register-specific terms (cf. Halliday, 1973: Chapter 4; Matthiessen, 1990). For example, if we consider semiotic systems that have been included under the heading of 'visual semiotics', we can note how highly contextually adapted and specialized systems such as technical drawing, mass transport route cartography and press photography are; it is not immediately clear that they can all be regarded as registerial sub-systems of a general visual semiotic system (cf. Bateman, 2008; Matthiessen, 2009a).

1.5 The location of grammar in language; the role of the corpus

1.5.1 Recapitulation: locating the present work on the map of language

This is not exactly a recapitulation; rather, the aim is to locate the present work in relation to the dimensions of language discussed in the previous section.

In terms of **stratification**, the book deals with lexicogrammar, the stratum of wording. If we use the familiar metaphor of vertical space, as implied in the word 'stratum', the stratum 'above' is the semantics, that 'below' is the phonology. We cannot expect to understand the grammar just by looking at it from its own level; we also look into it 'from above' and 'from below', taking a **trinocular perspective** (Halliday, 1978: 130–131; 1996). But since the view from these different angles is often conflicting, the description will inevitably be a form of compromise. All linguistic description involves such compromise; the difference between

a systemic description and one in terms of traditional school grammar is that in the school grammars the compromise was random and unprincipled whereas in a systemic grammar it is systematic and theoretically motivated. Being a 'functional grammar' means that priority is given to the view 'from above'; that is, grammar is seen as a resource for making meaning – it is a semanticky kind of grammar. But the focus of attention is still on the grammar itself.

Giving priority to the view 'from above' means that the organizing principle adopted is that of **system**: the grammar is seen as a network of interrelated meaningful choices. In other words, the dominant axis is the paradigmatic one: the fundamental components of the grammar are sets of mutually defining contrastive features (for an early statement, see Halliday, 1966a). Explaining something consists not in stating how it is structured but in showing how it is related to other things: its pattern of systemic relationships, or **agnateness** (**agnation**, a term introduced into linguistics by Gleason (1965: 199) based on Latin *agnatus* 'related on the father's side').[13]

Each system has its point of origin at a particular **rank**: clause, phrase, group and their associated complexes. Since the clause is the primary channel of grammatical energy, the first part of the book deals with systems of the clause. The second part deals with systems at other ranks; and also those of the information unit, which is the grammatical reflex of the phonological tone group. The final chapter will describe movement across the rank scale, one of the forms taken by grammatical metaphor.

Systems at every rank are located in their **metafunctional** context; this means, therefore, that every system has its address in some cell of a **metafunction-rank matrix** (see e.g. Halliday, 1970/2005: 169; 1973: 133; 1976a; 1978: 132), as shown schematically in Figure 1-16 and in more detail in Chapter 2, Table 2-8. For example, the system of MOOD, referred to above, is an interpersonal system of the clause; so it is located in the 'clause' row, 'interpersonal' column in the matrix.

Structure is analysed in functional terms, explaining the part played by each element in the organic configuration of the whole. We shall see later on that the configurational view of structure is oversimplified, if not distorted, because the way linguistic units are structured tends to vary according to metafunction (see Halliday, 1979; Martin, 1996; Matthiessen, 1988). But it is possible to reduce all types of structure to a configurational form, as a strategy for exploring the grammar.

Figure 1-16 provides a map of this general conceptual framework. It also shows the dimension of **instantiation**; and this is the route by which we return to the text. In preparing this new edition we have made considerable use of a corpus, to check the details and extend the scope of the description; and also as a source of authentic examples. Whenever we shift our perspective between text and system – between data and theory – we are moving along this instantiation cline. The **system**, as we have said, is the potential that lies behind the **text**.

---

[13] This was true of the earlier editions also. But there the grammar was *presented* in the form of structure, whereas in this edition we have introduced the category of system into the ongoing account.

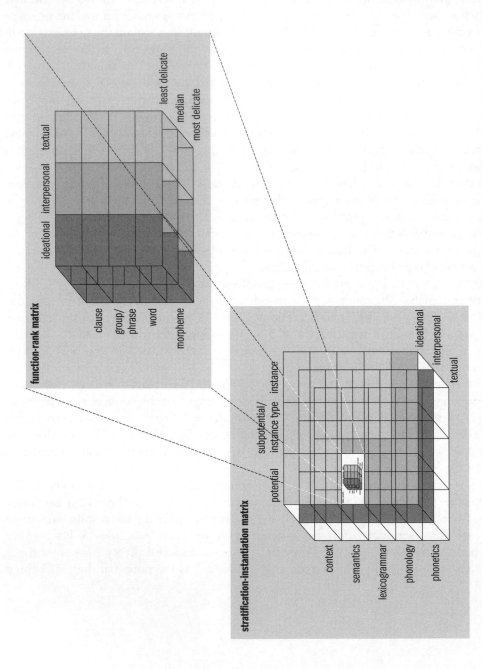

Fig. 1-16 Matrices defined by the semiotic dimensions: the lexicogrammatical function-rank matrix in relation to the stratification-instantiation matrix

But 'text' is a complex notion. In the form in which we typically receive it, as spoken and written discourse, a text is the product of two processes combined: instantiation, and realization. The defining criterion is instantiation: text as instance. But realization comes in because what becomes accessible to us is the text **as realized** in sound or writing. We cannot directly access instances of language at higher strata – as selections in meaning, or even in wording. But it is perhaps helpful to recognize that we can produce text in this way, for ourselves, if we compose some verse or other discourse inside our heads. If you 'say it to yourself', you can get the idea of text as instance without the additional property of realization.

1.5.2 Text and the corpus

Text is the form of data used for linguistic analysis; all description of grammar is based on text. Traditionally this has been mainly 'virtual' text of the kind just described: examples made up by grammarians inside their heads to illustrate the categories of the description. The only 'real' text that was available was written text, and some notable grammarians of English, such as Otto Jespersen, made considerable use of written texts as sources of data.

In the late 1940s two inventions appeared which were to change the work of a grammarian: tape recorders, and computers. The tape recorder made it possible to capture spontaneous speech; the computer made it possible to store and access data in increasing quantities. Ten years later, when Randolph Quirk at the University of London and W. Freeman Twaddell at Brown University in Providence designed and began to implement the first corpuses of written text, they foresaw that the operation would soon become computerized. At the same time grammarians such as Halliday were recording natural speech and analysing it for intonation and rhythm (Halliday, 1963a and b, 1967a). We now have indefinitely large computerized corpuses of both written and spoken text (for recent overviews of corpus linguistics, see e.g. Cheng, 2011; McEnery & Hardie, 2012; for the use of corpora in the investigation of English, see McEnery & Gabrielatos, 2006; for the relationship to systemic functional research, see also Hunston & Thompson, 2006; Wu, 2009).

The text is typically presented in written form, on the screen or else printed as hard copy. If the original was written, its format is – or at least can be – preserved. If the original was spoken, it is usually transcribed into regular orthography; this has two drawbacks, one of omission (there is no record of intonation and rhythm) and one of commission (it is 'normalized' according to conventions designed to make it look as though it had been composed in writing) – thus for a grammarian it has rather limited value. It is still not automatically made available as speech.

The corpus is fundamental to the enterprise of theorizing language. Until now, linguistics has been like physics before 1600: having little reliable data, and no clear sense of the relationship between observation and theory. But precisely because the corpus is so important it is better to be aware of what is good about it, and also what is potentially not so good. Let us enumerate four points – three plusses and one minus – which relate particularly to our use of the corpus.

First, its data are **authentic**. This one property underlies all its other advantages. What people actually say is very different from what they think they say; and even more different from what they think they ought to say (Halliday, McIntosh & Strevens, 1964). Likewise, what people say or understand under experimental conditions is very different from what they say or understand in real life (for example, children aged 4 to 5 were found, when they were probed, not to understand or be able to produce relative clauses and passives; whereas these appear regularly in the natural speech of children before the age of 2). The difference is less marked in writing, although it is still there. Would Jane Austen (or our own teachers in school) have acknowledged the double ' –ing' form she used in *Mansfield Park*: *'But it would rather do her good after being stooping among the roses;'* ? (New York: Hyperion, n.d., p. 64). But it is in speech that authenticity becomes critical; and this leads us to the second point.

Second, then, its data include **spoken** language, ranging from fairly formal or at least self-monitored speech (as in interviews) to casual, spontaneous chatter. The reason this is so important is not, as people sometimes think, a sort of inverted scale of values in reaction against earlier attitudes that dismissed everyday speech as formless and incoherent; it is a more positive factor – namely, that not only is natural spoken language every whit as highly organized as writing (it is simply organized along somewhat different lines; Halliday, 1985a, 1987a) but, more significantly, it is in the most un-selfmonitored spontaneous speech that people explore and expand their meaning potential. It is here that we reach the semantic frontiers of language and get a sense of the directions in which its grammar is moving (cf. Halliday, 2002a).

There is another point that should be brought in here. Now that spontaneous speech is becoming available for study,[14] some grammarians propose to write separate grammars for it. This approach has the merit that it can highlight special features of spoken language and show that it is systematic and highly organized; but it tends to exaggerate the difference between speech and writing and to obscure the fact that they are varieties within a unitary system. Spoken and written English are both forms of English – otherwise you could not have all the mixed and intermediate forms that are evolving in electronic text. In my own work, including earlier editions of this book, I have always taken account of both, with a slight bias towards spoken language for reasons given above; I have wanted to preserve the underlying unity of the two. Either way, what matters is that spoken language can now occupy the place in linguistic scholarship that it must do if the theory is to continue to advance.

Third, the corpus makes it possible to study grammar in **quantitative** terms. It is clear by this time that grammatical systems are probabilistic in nature: that, for example, the system of POLARITY in English has to be modelled not simply as 'positive/negative' but as 'positive/negative with a certain probability attached' (which has been found to be of the order of 0.9 : 0.1).[15] Computerized parsing and pattern-matching is now reaching the point where quantitative studies can be undertaken of a number of primary systems in the grammar, using samples large enough to permit comparison among different registers (where it seems likely that probabilities may be systematically reset). Not enough work has yet been undertaken along these lines for us to build it in to the total picture; but it is a high priority field for future research. (The exploration of the probabilistic nature

---

[14] Though now that technological obstacles have gone, legal ones have arisen. If you record surreptitiously, you lay yourself open to being sued.

[15] See Halliday & James (1993); also Halliday (1993a), Nesbitt & Plum (1988), Matthiessen (1999, 2006a).

of language has been part of systemic functional linguistics from the start – in fact, since before the start: see Halliday, 1959. After decades of resistance in formal linguistics, there is now more general acceptance of the probabilistic nature of language, thanks to advances in both 'corpus linguistics' and 'statistical natural language processing': see e.g. Bod, Hay & Jannedy, 2003.)

What then is the problematic aspect of the large-scale corpus? Linguists who specialize in corpus studies tend to refer to themselves, rather disingenuously, as 'mere data-gatherers'. We doubt whether they truly deceive themselves; they are well aware of the theoretical significance of what they are doing and what they are finding out. But they may perhaps deceive others, encouraging them to believe that there is some disjunction between data-gathering and theorizing. It is just such a dichotomy that has hassled the linguistics of the past few decades, isolating the system of language from the text as if they were two different orders of phenomena.[16] Of course, new data from the corpus will pose problems for any theory, systemic theory included – as Steve Jones has said, 'a science without difficulties is not a science at all' (Jones, 1999: 152). But such data will not contribute towards raising our understanding unless cultured by stock from within the pool of theoretical knowledge.

We emphasize this because there was a strong current of anti-theoretical ideology in late twentieth-century thinking, at least in certain intellectual domains. This was part of a self-conscious postmodern reaction against 'grand designs'; as often happens in such shifts of fashion, what starts out as a steadying correction to the course of knowledge becomes a lurch to a position more extreme than that which it was correcting. All modelling becomes micromodelling, all categories become collections of instances. We share the commitment to data and to the study of small-scale phenomena, in semiotic systems as in systems of any kind. But to banish the macro and the system from one's thinking is simply to indulge in another kind of grand design; being 'atheoretical' disguises a particular theoretical conviction which in our view is ill-judged and ill-informed (cf. Halliday & Martin, 1993: Ch. 11). We would argue for a dialectical complementarity between theory and data: complementarity because some phenomena show up best if illuminated by a general theory (i.e. from the 'system' end), others if treated as patterns within the data (i.e. from the 'instance' end) (cf. on global warming, above); dialectical because each perspective interpenetrates with and constantly redefines the other. This is the kind of thinking we have tried to adopt throughout the present work.

---

16 A 'corpus-based grammar' is fine; there is no excuse now for a grammar of a well-researched language such as English not to be corpus-based. A 'corpus grammar' would seem to be a contradiction in terms, if it means a grammar emerging by itself out of the corpus. Data do not spontaneously generate theory. Some corpus specialists now favour a 'corpus-driven' approach (cf. Tognini Bonelli, 2001). In the terms described, the present grammar would, we think, qualify as corpus-driven; the difference would lie in the relative weight given to a general linguistic theory (and to the place of theory scientific praxis). We make more use of the explanatory power of a comprehensive model of language. In this connection, it is also important to emphasize that the present grammar has been tested extensively against authentic text in a way most 'corpus-based grammars' never are: it has been applied in systematic and exhaustive analysis of large volumes of text.

1.6 Theory, description and analysis

In this chapter, we have outlined the contours of language in general – what we might call the 'architecture' of human language, using a common metaphor for the organization of a system, although a term such as 'anatomy' would arguably be more appropriate since language is an evolved system rather than a designed one. We have drawn our illustrations from English since one of the aims of this book is to present a description of the grammar of English that can be applied in the analysis of spoken and written English text, as illustrated in Halliday (1985c). However, it would be equally possible, and highly desirable, to do the same for any other language. Lexicogrammatical text analysis is an important tool to be used in addressing many problems in a community in different spheres such as education, healthcare, administration, and commerce. The number of systemic functional descriptions of languages spoken around the world has been growing steadily. In Caffarel, Martin & Matthiessen (2004), linguists present summary accounts of eight languages (German; French; Telugu; Vietnamese; Mandarin Chinese; Japanese; Tagalog; Pitjantjatjara), and these are part of the basis for cross-linguistic comparison and typology. Since then, linguists have added accounts of a number of other languages (including Danish; Spanish; Arabic; Òkó; Bajjika; Cantonese), and some of them have now been published as books.

In the next chapter, we will begin to sketch a description of the lexicogrammar of English based on the general theory of language we have sketched in this chapter. But let us first pause briefly to distinguish between **analysis** and **description**, and between description and **theory**. In empirical approaches to language, all three are grounded in data – in the first instance, in spoken and written text; but they differ in their relation to data – they differ in degree of abstraction from data.

When we observe a language, we observe it as text – as a flow of speech or as (typically) discrete pieces of writing. Texts lie at the instance pole of the cline of instantiation (Section 1.3.4), and once we have observed and collected them and made them accessible to study (e.g. by transcribing spoken text), we can proceed by **analysing** them, noting patterns in these instances. (i) If we have access to an existing account of the system of the language (at the potential pole of the cline of instantiation), then we will analyse texts by relating instantial patterns in the system. In other words, we undertake the analysis of texts by means of the **description** of the system that lies behind them, as in Figure 1-9 above, identifying terms in systems and fragments of structures that are instantiated in the text. In the course of undertaking the analysis, we are likely to find gaps in the description, or even mistaken generalizations. Text analysis is a very rigorous way of testing, and thus improving, existing descriptions because everything in a given text has to be accounted for in the description (cf. Matthiessen, 2007b: 791–792). (ii) If there is no description to draw on, this means that we will gradually have to develop one based on the analysis of a representative sample of texts (a corpus; see Section 1.3.4 above, and Chapter 2, Section 2.4). In other words, **describing** a language is a process of generalizing from the analysis of textual data. The outcome of this process is a **description** of the system of the language, and we keep testing such descriptions by deploying them in continued text analysis and by applying them to different tasks such as language education or natural language processing.

Analysis and description thus operate at the outer poles of the cline of instantiation within a given language. Regions intermediate between these two poles can be approached in terms of either analysis or description: the account of a text type can be interpreted as a

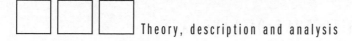
generalized analysis of a sample of texts, and the account of a register can be interpreted as specialized description of the general system; but, in either case, the account will ultimately be grounded in textual data.

While a description is an account of the system of a ***particular*** language, a **theory** is an account of language in ***general***. So we have descriptions of various languages such as English, Akan and Nahuatl; but we have a theory of human language in general (see e.g. Halliday, 1992e, 1996; Matthiessen & Nesbitt, 1996). This introduction to (systemic) functional grammar is both an introduction to the general theory of grammar and to the description of the grammar of a particular language, English. The theory includes the 'architecture' of grammar – the dimensions that define the overall semiotic space of lexicogrammar, the relationships that inhere in these dimensions – and its relationship to other sub-systems of language – to semantics and to phonology (or graphology). Thus, according to systemic functional theory, lexicogrammar is diversified into a metafunctional spectrum, extended in delicacy from grammar to lexis, and ordered into a series of ranked units: see Figure 1.17. This figure shows the general 'template' according to which the lexicogrammar of any particular language will be organized.

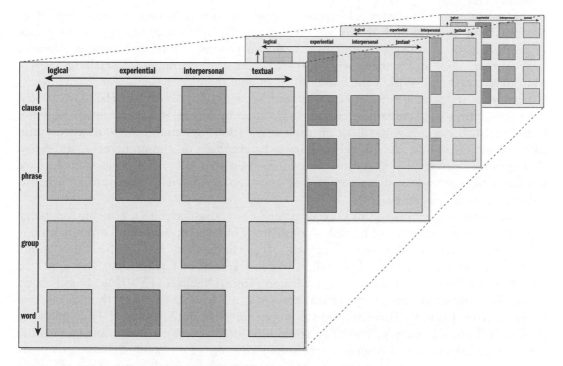

Fig. 1-17   Theoretical dimensions of lexicogrammar: hierarchy of rank, spectrum of metafunctions and cline of delicacy

However, this theoretical template does not include details that are specific to particular languages or even to large sets of languages. For instance, the description of the system of MOOD shown in Figure 1-9 is specific to English: according to this description, there is a system of INDICATIVE TYPE, with 'indicative' as its entry condition and 'declarative' and 'interrogative' as its two terms, and the term 'declarative' is realized by the sequence of Subject followed by Finite. This description is grounded in generalizations about English data, i.e. spoken and written texts; and all descriptions must be based on empirical evidence[17]. Naturally, when we develop descriptions for other languages, we may find similarities; for example, many languages can be described systemically in terms of a contrast between 'declarative' and 'indicative', although very few languages realize 'declarative' structurally by putting Subject before Finite, in contrast with Finite before Subject in 'yes/no' interrogative clauses (cf. Teruya *et al.*, 2007). Typological generalizations are both possible and desirable, serving many purposes (cf. Matthiessen, Teruya & Wu, 2008); but they are still grounded in empirical evidence, not based on theoretical hypotheses.

The template illustrated in Figure 1-17 will accommodate innumerable possible descriptions – a number of which correspond to languages actually spoken today. In Chapter 2, we will provide an overview map or matrix of the lexicogrammar of English in terms of metafunction and rank, and in the remainder of the book (Table 2-8), we will present a more detailed description, up to a certain point in delicacy – a point that is still a far distance from lexis, and even some distance from the region intermediate between grammar and lexis.

This introduction to (systemic) functional grammar differs in various ways from other accounts – in terms of both theory and description. (i) In terms of theory, we can locate systemic functional theory of grammar within a general family of functional theories of grammar, contrasting these with formal theories of grammar (cf. Halliday, 1977; Matthiessen, 2009b). Within the family of functional theories, systemic functional theory is unique in its paradigmatic orientation (see Section 1.3.2 above; cf. Halliday, 1966a) – its orientation to grammar as system, represented by means of system networks; other functional theories are syntagmatic in their orientation. Systemic functional theory also differs from many other functional theories in its emphasis on comprehensive, text-based descriptions – descriptions that can be used in text analysis; other functional theories have tended to foreground linguistic comparison and typology based on descriptive fragments from a wide range of languages.

(ii) In terms of description, this book is of course an introduction to a systemic functional description of the grammar of English – constituting one descriptive strand evolving among other ones in systemic functional linguistics (cf. Matthiessen, 2007b). This description may be compared with other descriptions of the grammar of English that have appeared over the past 500 years or so: see, e.g., Gleason (1965), Michael (1970) and Linn (2006). These descriptions naturally vary in many ways, e.g. relationship to theory (homogenous or heterogeneous ['eclectic']), relationship to corpus (cf. Chapter 2, Section 2.4), relationship to time (diachronic vs. synchronic, or some kind of synthesis), relationship to dialectal variation (what varieties of English are included), coverage of phenomena – from grammars of very selective coverage via grammars with a registerial focus (such as grammars of spoken English) to reference grammars, and relationship to intended users – ranging from language

---

[17] It is important to be clear whether technical terms are theoretical or descriptive in nature; theoretical and descriptive terms are distinguished systematically in Matthiessen, Teruya & Lam (2010).

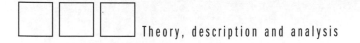

learners to professional grammarians. Reference grammars are, in principle, the most comprehensive descriptions.

In the first half of the twentieth century, there appeared a number of single-authored reference grammars largely by Danish or Dutch grammarians – the most comprehensive being Otto Jespersen's *Modern English grammar on historical principles*, in seven volumes, which were published from 1909 to 1949 – completed by Niels Haislund after Jespersen passed away in 1943 during the Nazi occupation of Denmark. In the second half of the twentieth century, English-speaking grammarians took over the task of producing reference grammars, with Jan Svartvik and Stig Johansson representing the Nordic tradition, both of them making substantial contributions to corpus-based research into English grammar: Quirk *et al.* (1972, 1985), Biber *et al.* (1999) and Huddleston & Pullum (2002). The description of English grammar presented here is not designed as a reference grammar. However, unlike the recent reference grammars – or all previous ones for that matter, this description has been designed as one that can be used in text analysis (cf. Halliday, 1985c) – a task that imposes quite stringent demands on the description. Since the first edition of IFG appeared in 1985, researchers have analysed quite a large volume of registerially varied texts using the description presented here (see e.g. Matthiessen, 2007b: 824–830).

CHAPTER
TWO

TOWARDS A FUNCTIONAL GRAMMAR

2.1 Towards a grammatical analysis

Let us take a passage of three sentences from the transcript of Nelson Mandela's speech and start exploring its lexicogrammar:

> **Text 2-1: Exploring – passage from Nelson Mandela's inaugural speech**
> To my compatriots I have no hesitation in saying that each of us is as intimately attached to the soil of this beautiful country as are the famous jacaranda trees of Pretoria and the mimosa trees of the bushveld.
>
> Each time one of us touches the soil of this land, we feel a sense of personal renewal. The national mood changes as the seasons change.
>
> We are moved by a sense of joy and exhilaration when the grass turns green and the flowers bloom.

Starting at the lexical end – with the 'content words' of the vocabulary – we find names of entities (persons and things), names of processes (actions, events, etc.) and names of qualities:

(1)	*names of entities*	
	(a) common names:	
	persons	compatriots
	things, concrete, general	soil, country, trees, bushveld, land, grass, flowers
	things, concrete, specific	jacaranda, mimosa
	things, abstract	hesitation, sense, renewal, mood, seasons, joy, exhilaration
	(b) proper names:	Pretoria
(2)	*names of processes*	
	(a) doing & happening	touches, change(s), bloom

(b)	sensing & saying	saying, feel, moved
(c)	being & having	have, is, are, turns

(3) *names of qualities*

evaluative	beautiful, famous
emotive	attached, intimately, personal, national

Here persons and things are named by nouns, qualities by adjectives (one in the form of an adverb: *intimately*) and processes by verbs. Verb, noun and adjective are grammatical **classes** – classes of word.

Word classes can be viewed 'from above' – that is, semantically: verbs typically refer to processes, nouns to entities and adjectives to qualities (of entities or of processes). They can also be viewed 'from round about', at their own level, in terms of the relations into which they enter (cf. Halliday, 1963c): paradigmatic relations (the options that are open to them) and syntagmatic relations (the company they keep). On either of these two axes we can establish relationships of a lexical kind (collocations and sets) and of a grammatical kind (structures and systems). Here are some we find construed in this text.

(i) syntagmatic/lexical [collocation]

change ... mood, season

grass ... flower, green

flower ... bloom

move ... sense ... joy, exhilaration

soil ... land, country

tree ... jacaranda, mimosa

say ... hesitation

country ... beautiful

The measure of collocation is the degree to which the probability of a word (lexical item) increases given the presence of a certain other word (the **node**) within a specified range (the **span**). This can be measured in the corpus. Thus, the word *season* occurs 1,000 times in the corpus of ten million words: this would give it a certain overall probability of occurrence. But it might be found that, given the node *change* and a span of ± 4 (that is, four words on either side), the probability of *season* occurring went up by a significant extent. This would mean that, if you hear or read the word *change* in a text, you have a heightened expectancy that the word *season* may be somewhere in the immediate neighbourhood. It is a significant feature of the meaning of the word *season* that it collocates with the word *change*. Such conditioning effects can, of course, be measured in both directions: both the increased probability of *season* in the environment of *change*, and the increased probability of *change* in the environment *season*.[1]

---

[1] The effects will be different if the words have notably different overall frequencies in the language: for example, a rare word *jacaranda* collocating with a common word *tree*.

Collocational patterns of this kind contribute significantly to the unfolding meaning of a text[2].

(ii) syntagmatic/grammatical [structure]

the	famous	jacaranda	trees	of Pretoria
the		mimosa	trees	of the bushveld
the			soil	of this beautiful country

The words in these (or any other) sequences can be assigned to grammatical classes. Given that *the* is a determiner and *of* a preposition, in the first example we have determiner + adjective + noun + noun + preposition + noun. Such a sequence of classes is called a **syntagm** (e.g. Halliday, 1966a). However, this tells us very little about how it is organized or what it means. The significance of such a syntagm is that here it is the realization of a **structure**: an organic configuration of elements, which we can analyse in functional terms. *trees* denotes the category of entity being referred to; we designate its function as Thing. *jacaranda* denotes the class within this general category; it functions here as Classifier. *the* has a pointing out function, known as Deictic: it signals that some particular member(s) of this class is or are being referred to. *famous* is one of a special set of adjectives that occur straight after the Deictic, still contributing to the pointing function; we call these simply Post-Deictic. We then have to wait until after the Thing to find out which jacaranda trees are meant: it is those 'of Pretoria', with *of Pretoria* functioning as Qualifier. (We will leave out the analysis of its own internal structure for the moment.) So we can analyse as:

the	famous	jacaranda	trees	of Pretoria
Deictic	Post-Deictic	Classifier	Thing	Qualifier

There is a similar structure in *the mimosa trees of the bushveld*, except that it has no Post-Deictic, and the Qualifier is 'common' not 'proper'; and *the soil of this beautiful country* is again comparable – here there is no Classifier, while, on the other hand, the Qualifier is rather longer (showing that it can in fact contain a fully expanded nominal group). Each of the three nominal groups has the same functional outline, *the* + Thing + Qualifier with *of*; each happens to contain six words, but, more relevantly, in Mandela's speech each one contains (from the first Ictus) three feet:

// ^ the	/ famous jaca	/randa trees of Pre	/ toria //
// ^ the mi	/ mosa	/ trees of the	/ bushveld //
// ^ the	/ soil of this	/ beautiful	/ country ///

---

2 The notion of collocation was first introduced by J.R. Firth (1957) (but note Hoey, 2005), and gained wide acceptance, particularly in work based on corpus analysis, as in the Birmingham tradition, e.g. Sinclair (1987, 1991), Coulthard (1993), Hoey (2005) and Cheng et al. (2009). For further systemic functional accounts of collocation, see e.g. Halliday (1966b), Halliday & Hasan (1976: Section 6.4), Benson & Greaves (1992), Gledhill (2000), Tucker (2007) and Matthiessen (2009b); Matthiessen (1995a) relates collocational patterns to structural configurations such as Process + Medium, Process + Range, Process + Degree; Thing + Epithet (for a corpus-based study of Process + Degree, see Matthiessen, 2009b).

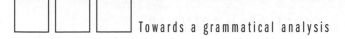
This combination of grammatical (functional) parallelism with phonological (rhythmic) parallelism foregrounds the grammatical pun in the word *attach* (*be attached to*, (1) mental process 'love', (2, 3) 'be rooted in' – which then sets one to rethinking (1) in terms of roots). The analysis points up how the interaction among patterns at different strata plays a significant part in the construction of meaning.

(iii) paradigmatic/lexical [the lexical set]

Paradigmatically, lexical items function in sets having shared semantic features and common patterns of collocation. Thus *tree*, *flower*, *grass* share the feature of being generic names of plants; the corpus might show that they have in common a tendency to collocate with names of colours, various forms of the item *grow*, and so on. Such sets are typically fuzzy, with doubtful or part-time members (for example, *bush*, *blossom*).

Word association tests carried out many years ago showed that people associated words along both axes: if asked what other words sprang to mind when they heard *tree* they would come up both with words that were related syntagmatically, like *green* and *grow*, and with words that were related paradigmatically like *grass* and *bush*. Of course, many pairs of words are related in both ways, like *tree* and *branch*; they enter into a systemic contrast (a *branch* is part of a *tree*), but they also collocate, as in *climbed up the branch of a tree*.

Typically, the semantic features that link the members of a lexical set are those of synonymy or antonymy, hyponymy and meronymy: that is, they are words that are alike or opposed in meaning, words that are subtypes of the same type (cohyponyms: *oak, palm, pine* ... as kinds of *tree*), or parts of the same whole (comeronyms: *branch, root, trunk* ... as parts of *tree*). Thus in the text by Nelson Mandela, in the environment of *trees, jacaranda* and *mimosa* suggest other flowering varieties of tree (and also resonate with *flower*); *personal* and *national* encompass other contexts of intermediate scope like *regional* and *familial*. *Pretoria* and *the bushveld* are parts of (*this beautiful*) *country* – its capital city and its open countryside; and they likewise suggest all the other parts. *joy* is related to *happiness, gladness* and *pleasure*, and also to its opposites *sadness* and *distress*. These 'absent' items do not need to be mentioned; they are part of the meaning of the items that are there in the text, virtually present once the relevant vectors have been established. Figure 2-1 illustrates the lexical relations set up within this passage.

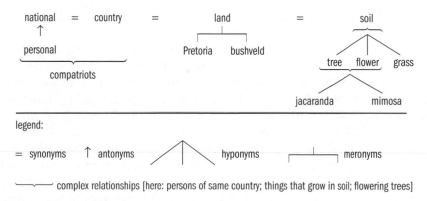

Fig. 2-1 Some lexical patterns in the Mandela extract (Note shift in sense of *land*: (1) = country, (2) = soil)

(iv) paradigmatic/grammatical [the grammatical system]

As discussed in Chapter 1, grammatical categories are organized in systems. For example, there is a system of PERSON, based (in English, as in most other languages) on the opposition of 'you-&-me' versus 'everyone (and perhaps everything) else', and then on that of 'you' as opposed to 'me' (see Figure 2-2):

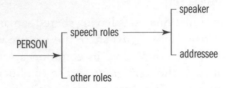

Fig. 2-2 The system of PERSON

This intersects with a system of NUMBER, opposing 'one' to 'more than one' (see Figure 2-3).

Fig. 2-3 The system of NUMBER

The way these two combine varies among different languages; for the version found in (modern standard) English, see Table 2-1 and, for further detail, Chapter 6.

Table 2-1 Systems of PERSON and NUMBER intersected

PERSON: NUMBER:	speaker (+) ('1st person')	addressee (+) ('2nd person')	other (+) ('3rd person')
singular	I/me	you	he/him, she/her; it
plural	we/us		they/them

'First person plural' can mean 'more than one speaker', like a congregation in a religious assembly; more usually it means 'speaker + other person(s)'. In this case, Mandela is the only speaker (hence *I*); but the 'other persons' are made explicit as *my compatriots*, a semantically complex expression in which the meaning of 'possessive' *my* is defined by (the *com-* in) the word *compatriots* 'those who belong to the same nation'. Thus *my compatriots* means 'those who belong to the same nation as I do'; these are 'others' making up *we*. Here another grammatical system intersects (see Figure 2-4), contrasting collective *we* with distributive *each (one) of us*. In the environment of *compatriots* this means 'each person who belongs to the same nation as I do', and so this system grammaticalizes the opposition that is lexicalized as *national/personal*. Thus, through the resources of his lexicogrammar, Mandela construes each South African as an individual while at the same time linking them all inclusively with himself and with each other.

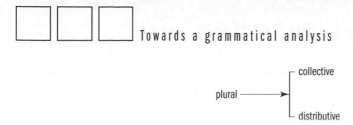

Fig. 2-4   The system of PLURALITY

Mandela is, of course, making a very large number of grammatical choices with every clause in his text. All of them contribute to the total meaning; certain ones among them may stand out as creating patterns that resonate strongly with the context of the occasion. As another example of this, we may note the way in which, in the course of these three paragraphs, Mandela combines selections in the system of process type in the clause (system of TRANSITIVITY; see Chapter 5) with the selections in the system of expansion in the clause complex (system of LOGICAL-SEMANTIC RELATIONS; see Chapter 7). These can be summarized in tabular form as shown in Table 2-2.

Table 2-2 Combinations of selections in process type and in expansion in Mandela's Inaugural

Process type: material	Process type: mental	Expansion
attach (grow in)	attach (love)	as ... as [comparative]
touch	feel	each time [temporal]
change (season)	change (mood)	as [comparative/temporal]
bloom	move	when [temporal]

In the material clauses, the central participant is some part of the environment: *trees*, *soil*, *flowers* and the abstract *seasons*. In the mental clauses, it is *we/us* and the abstract *national mood*. The two sets of processes are then linked by a relationship of time or comparison 'as the same time as/in the same way as', with the abstract ones combining these two motifs. The overall effect of these highly patterned selections from within the grammar is to create a powerful sense of identity among individual, nation and physical environment, through a network of semantic relationships that we might represent diagrammatically as in Figure 2-5.

This brief commentary on a few sentences from Nelson Mandela's speech may serve to illustrate the lexicogrammar 'at work' creating meaning in the form of text (for further discussion of texts by Mandela, see Martin, 1999). We gain an insight into this process by placing some features of the wording, both lexical items and grammatical categories, in their syntagmatic and paradigmatic contexts in the system of the language. As the text unfolds, patterns emerge, some of which acquire added value through resonating with other patterns in the text or in the context of situation. The text itself is an instance; the resonance is possible because behind it lies the potential that informs every choice made by the speaker or writer, and in terms of which these choices are interpreted by listeners and readers. We refer to this ongoing creation of meaning in the unfolding of text as **logogenesis** (Halliday & Matthiessen, 1999: 18; cf. also Matthiessen, 2002b); this concept will become salient especially when we come to consider the relationship between different varieties

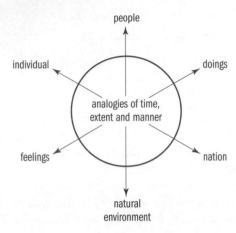

Fig. 2-5 Semantic relationships in Mandela text construed by grammatical systems

of text (for example, spoken and written) in later sections of the book (for a review, see Chapter 9, Section 9.1).

2.2 The lexicogrammar cline

We have stressed the **unity** of lexis and grammar, as the two poles of a single cline, or continuum; cf. Figure 2-6.

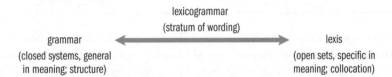

Fig. 2-6 The lexicogrammar cline

Because the two ends of the continuum are organized differently, when it came to describing them different techniques evolved: dictionary and thesaurus for lexis (Halliday *et al.*, 2004: Part one; Landau, 1989: Ch. 2; McArthur, 1986), and the 'grammar book' (typically, in the European tradition, syntactic constructions and morphological paradigms) for the grammar (e.g. Michael, 1970, and Linn, 2006). Either of these techniques may be extended all the way along the cline – but with diminishing returns: what the dictionary has to say about 'grammatical words' like *the* and *to* and *if*[3] is not very helpful; and while we can quite helpfully describe lexical items in terms of systems of features, the level of generality achieved is low. It is helpful because it shows how, when you choose a word, you are selecting among certain sets of contrasting features: for example, in Figure 2-7 the features that are 'lexicalized' (realized in words) are those of the degree of forcefulness of the order, the kind of authority behind it, and the positive or negative loading; lexical verbs

---

[3] i.e. words functioning as the direct realization of terms in grammatical systems.

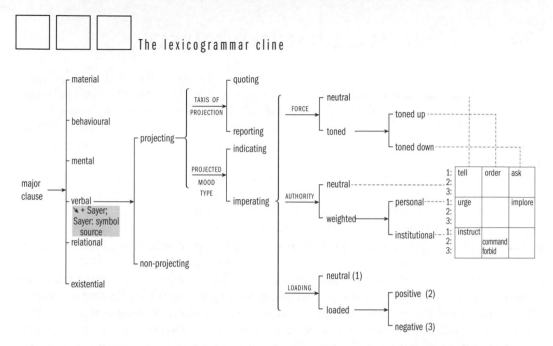

Fig. 2-7 Extension of the grammar of transitivity in delicacy towards lexis: a fragment of the lexicogrammar of the verbal process type (subtype 'imperating': see Table 5-25)

differentiated by these systems are given in Table 2-3[4]. Note that these are not definitive descriptions of these words; they are introduced here to show the principle of 'lexis as delicate grammar'. For other examples, see Hasan (1985a, 1987), Tucker (1998, 2007), and Halliday & Matthiessen (1999) and cf. Matthiessen (forthc.); and for the complementarity of grammar and lexis, see Halliday (2008: Chapter 2).

Table 2-3 Some verbs of saying differentiated by the delicate verbal process type systems in Figure 2-7

FORCE	AUTHORITY	LOADING	Process:
neutral (1)	neutral (1)	neutral (1)	*tell*
toned up (2)	neutral (1)	neutral (1)	*order*
toned down (3)	neutral (1)	neutral (1)	*ask*
neutral (1)	personal (2)	neutral (1)	*urge*
neutral (1)	institutional (3)	neutral (1)	*instruct*
toned up (2)	institutional (3)	positive (2)	*command*
toned up (2)	personal (2)/institutional (3)	negative (3)	*forbid*
toned down (3)	personal (2)	neutral (1)	*implore, beg*
toned up (2)	institutional (3)	positive (3)	*require*

---

[4] To be more precise: these systems differentiate *senses* of lexical verbs. Such senses are typically given separate subentries in dictionaries. For example, the relevant sense of *tell* is 'order, instruct, or advise' rather than any of the many other senses of this verb such as 'narrate or relate (a tale or story)'. High-frequency lexical items always have more than one sense, typically many. Verb senses are likely to correspond to different process types or subtypes within one process type (cf. Matthiessen, forthc.).

The example we have just given is taken from the lexicogrammar of the clause, more specifically from the experiential system of PROCESS TYPE (see Chapter 5), which is located at the grammatical pole of the lexicogrammatical cline: taking one of the terms in this system, that of 'verbal' processes, we have illustrated how to extend the account in delicacy to the point where we can begin to discern lexical contrasts of the type exemplified in Table 2-3.

But if grammar and lexis are interpreted as the endpoints of a continuum, what lies in between them, around the middle? It is here that we locate those items that, on the paradigmatic axis, enter into series which could be regarded from both angles of vision: either, in a grammatical perspective, as rather large and fuzzy closed systems or, in a lexical perspective, as somewhat determinate and limited open sets. This would include, in English, things like prepositions, temporal and other specialized adverbs, and conjunctions of various kinds. Since this is a grammar book, we shall be treating these semi-grammatical patterns grammatically, although there will be space to give them only limited coverage.

But what sort of syntagmatic patterns would we locate around the midpoint of the cline? These are patterns that lie somewhere in between structures and collocations, having some of the properties of both (cf. Tucker, 2007). Consider patterns of wording such as the following:

take + pride/pleasure/delight + in + ... -ing

to make + things/matters + (even +) worse/more ...

waste/squander/spend + time/energy/money + on/in + ...-ing

Patterns of this mixed or intermediate type were brought to attention in the context of teaching English as a foreign language, notably in the work of A.S. Hornby (e.g. Hornby, 1954); and they have been investigated in linguistics within the framework of **construction grammar** (e.g. Kay & Fillmore, 1999; Fillmore, 2002). But it is thanks to the corpus that they can now be accessed and studied in detail; see especially Hunston & Francis (2000), also Partington (1998) – note Hunston & Francis' subtitle '[Pattern Grammar:] a corpus-driven approach to the **lexical grammar** of English' (our emphasis).

Patterns of this kind raise two distinct questions (which, however, sometimes get mixed up): How do we find them? How do we describe them? The answer to the first is provided by the corpus; patterns of this kind are difficult to retrieve by introspection, which is in any case unreliable, and require more reading and listening than linguists have usually been able or willing to devote; but they can be brought into visibility fairly easily by the use of standard concordancing techniques.

The answer to the second will, of course, depend on the grammatical theory. In systemic terms they appear as moderately delicate choices in the grammar, typically in transitivity and its related systems, having complex realizations involving both grammatical and lexical selections: see Tucker (2007). They are, on the whole, at a greater degree of delicacy than we shall be dealing with in this book; but several such patterns are brought in to the discussion (see Chapters 5, 7, 10) in order to show where they are located – their place in the overall map – and how they are approached from the grammar – how they are theorized as part of the total system of a language. We shall also see some of the problems they

present, especially the complex manner in which they may be realized (e.g. a pattern that is selected as a system of the clause but realized disjointedly throughout an entire clause complex/nexus).

Hunston & Francis (2000) refer to their object of study as 'lexical grammar', suggesting (appropriately) that these are mixed patterns which they are viewing in a lexical perspective. Such patterns have also been explored under the heading of 'phraseology' (e.g. Greaves, 2009; Cheng *et al.*, 2009), and Tucker (2007) outlines a systemic functional account of this intermediate region of the lexicogrammatical continuum.

In our grammatical perspective they appear, as we have said, as medium delicacy grammar – the most delicate grammar being lexis itself. If we maintain the grammarian's viewpoint all the way across the cline, lexis will be defined as grammar extended to the point of maximum delicacy. It would take at least a hundred volumes of the present size to extend the description of the grammar up to that point for any substantial portion of the vocabulary of English; and, as we have noted, the returns diminish the farther one proceeds. Nevertheless, there are certain contexts in which such a systemic interpretation of lexis can be valuable (cf. Hasan, 1985a, 1987; Tucker, 1998); and even in a general account of the grammar it is important to maintain a comprehensive picture that will show the relation between choice of words (lexical items) and choice of grammatical categories – especially in view of the complementarity between these two (see next section).

2.3 Grammaticalization

Consider a series of expressions:

didn't succeed ... nowise (or in no way) succeeded ... failed

These all contain a semantic feature 'negative'; but it is construed in different ways – at different points along the lexicogrammatical cline. In *failed* the 'negative' is **lexicalized**; in *didn't succeed* it is grammaticalized; while in *nowise succeeded* it is semi-grammaticalized – it is construed somewhere around the mid-point, with *nowise* occurring in an extended system including *never, at no time/seldom, rarely/hardly ever/nowhere/...*

These expressions also contain a semantic feature 'past time'. But this is **grammaticalized** in all three, with the v^d form (the past tense form) of the verb (*failed, succeeded, did*; see Chapter 6).

Imagine a 'language' in which all meanings were construed lexically. There would be different words for every lexical item in every grammatical category; not just positive/negative, as in *succeed/fail, trust/distrust* (with words meaning 'not see', 'not go', 'not know', 'not ...') but also for every tense and person of every verb, singular and plural of every noun (like *person/people*), comparison of every adjective (like *good/better*), and so on. Such a 'language' would need billions of different words; in other words, it would be impossible – impossible to learn as a system and impossible to process as text, except on so limited a scale that functionally it would not be a language at all.

It is a necessary condition of language that some meanings should be grammaticalized. These need not be the same meanings in every language; and in fact they are not – categories of place, time, size, value, number, sex are quite variable in this respect. In any case there are, as we have seen, differing degrees of grammaticalization; it is not an all-or-nothing phenomenon. Nevertheless, some meanings (polarity is one of the most clear-cut) always seem to be grammaticalized, and many others are extremely likely to be so.

If a meaning is 'grammaticalized', this means that it is organized in the language (i) as a closed system of mutually exclusive terms, (ii) associated with some general category, and (iii) displaying proportionality throughout. For example: (i) positive/negative, singular/plural, past/present/future; (ii) a feature of all clauses, all count nouns, all verbs; (iii) [clause$_1$] positive : negative :: [clause$_2$] positive : negative :: [clause$_3$] positive : negative :: ... ; and likewise throughout. These are the three properties – **closure**, **generality** and **proportionality** – that characterize a grammatical system.

Grammaticalization is not dependent on how the categories are realized. They may be realized in a variety of ways: a change in the form, articulatory or prosodic, of some word or words; an addition of some element, to a word, a group or a clause; a change in the order of words, groups, or clauses. The realization may not be the same for all categories or in all environments; but it will be systematic in some way in the majority of cases, enough to establish and maintain the proportionality – with only a minority of 'exceptions' (which are likely to include some of the more frequent items). For example: past tense in English is usually realized as +(e)d, in so-called 'weak' verbs; second, there may be a change of vowel, in 'strong' verbs; some have change of vowel plus final -d/t (e.g. *think/thought, do/did, mean/meant*); and a tiny number are lexicalized (*am/was, are/were; go/went*). The varied nature of these realizations has no effect on the proportionality, which is exact: the relationship of 'past' to 'present' remains constant throughout.[5]

A systemic grammar is one that is organized around this concept of grammaticalization, whereby meaning is construed in networks of interrelated contrasts.[6] The term 'grammaticalization' itself, however, is problematic; it foregrounds the sense of 'process' – something being **turned into** a grammatical system, and this obscures the point that it is the inherent nature of language to be organized in grammatical systems. Nevertheless, we can recognize grammaticalization as a process taking place in time – in fact, in three distinct dimensions of time (Halliday & Matthiessen, 1999: 17–18). (i) We can see it in **ontogenetic time** when we observe children's early language development, which is built around the creation of proto-grammatical and then grammatical systems (Halliday, 1975, 2004). (ii) We cannot observe it directly in **phylogenetic time**, the evolution of human language; but we can track examples in the history of particular languages (for example, secondary tenses and the passive voice in English; see Chapter 6; Strang, 1970). (iii) We can see it in **logogenetic time**, the unfolding of discourse, when a passage of some extent – a clause or more – is recapitulated in a single word or group (see Chapter 10). So when we talk of the 'system' of language, as the underlying potential that is instantiated in the form

---

5   This does not mean that the meaning of each category remains constant across all **grammatical** environments. We shall see in Chapter 5, for example, that the meaning of present tense differs between material and mental processes. But this has nothing to do with how the tenses are realized.

6   We use 'contrast' rather than the Saussurean term 'opposition' simply because the latter suggests that all contrasts are binary. Reducing systems of more than two terms to sets of binary oppositions, which is always possible as a formal operation, can be arbitrary and misleading semantically. For example, the English tense system past/present/future patterns in some respects as past/non-past, in some as present/non-present and in some as future/non-future (but in most respects as a system of three terms). Any form of binary representation of such a three-term system is equally arbitrary.

of text, we are in effect theorizing a language as the outcome of ongoing grammaticalization in all these three dimensions of time.

The evidence that we use for theorizing in this way is, of course, obtained from what people say and write – in other words, from text. This is where the corpus (cf. Chapter 1, Section 1.4.2) comes in.

2.4 Grammar and the corpus

The **corpus** was originally conceived as a tool for the study of grammar: Quirk referred to his Survey as 'an NED of English usage', and it played a fundamental part in the preparation of *A comprehensive grammar of the English language* (Quirk, Greenbaum, Leech & Svartvik, 1985). But as it evolved into its present computerized form, the corpus was taken over by lexicologists (particularly lexicographers), and it is still thought of mainly in this connection today[7] although the recent *Longman grammar of spoken and written English*, developed by D. Biber *et al.* (1999), is a corpus-based grammar.

It is much easier, if one is using automated techniques, to retrieve lexical information than to retrieve grammatical information (cf. Halliday, 2002a). The data are stored in orthographic form, using standard spelling and punctuation: if the text originated in writing, it is stored exactly in the original form (at first keyed in on a word processor, subsequently either scanned or obtained already in electronic form); if the text was originally spoken, it is transcribed (and often normalized) according to the same orthographic conventions.

The most readily accessible element is the (orthographic) word: a string of letters bounded by spaces, or rather by some combination of space and punctuation mark (cf. Chapter 1, Section 1.1.2). Not only can words be immediately identified; they can also be organized into an existing conventional sequence, that of 'alphabetical order'. Tokens of the same type (that is, instances of the same sequence of letters) can then be counted, and the types (words) can be ranged in order of their frequency of occurrence. It is not difficult to pick out instances of text in which a given word occurs and to display these in the form of a concordance, showing their collocations on either side; the collocations can then be treated as single items and investigated quantitatively in their turn. All this information feeds in to the making of a dictionary.

It is much harder to retrieve information about the grammar. The orthography does not show any higher units than the word – or rather, it does, by virtue of punctuation; but these as we have seen are graphological units that do not reliably correspond with units in the grammar (cf. the methodology outlined in Halliday & James, 1993). Nor does it show word classes; still less does it give any indication of the structure of groups, phrases or clauses[8]. It has taken a long time to develop 'taggers' (systems for marking word classes) and 'parsers' (systems for analysing the structure of higher units) to a degree of accuracy enough to make them into viable tools for research. Even now we are still some way away from being able

---

[7]   And it has supported lexical approaches to, and conceptions of, grammar (cf. Hoey, 2005).

[8]   There are of course some corpora of English that have been tagged for word classes, and even parsed. For example, the excellent web-based interface of COCA, a corpus of contemporary American English (see Footnote 11 below), enables users to specify searches in terms of strings enhanced with word class specifications, lexical items (lemmas), and so on.

to input a text in orthographic form and come out with a description of its grammar – particularly, a rich systemic and functional description (cf. O'Donnell & Bateman, 2005).

How then do we use the corpus as a tool for grammatical research? If we want to draw on the full potential of the corpus, we have to deploy computational tools to explore the corpus (see Teich, 2009; Wu, 2009). These tools are both enabling and constraining. They are enabling because they make it possible to process much greater volumes of text than is possible by hand, allowing us to see features of language that were previously hidden from view. They are constraining because the kind of analysis they can perform automatically is still a long way away from being as informative and rich as manual analysis. We can characterize the current ability of automatic analysis in terms of the semiotic dimensions of organization introduced in Chapter 1 (see Table 1-3, Figure 1-6). Broadly speaking, automatic analysis gets harder the higher up we move along the hierarchy of stratification: it can handle any patterns that are stated in terms of orthographic words and it can handle certain low-ranking patterns within lexicogrammar, but is not able to handle full-fledged systemic functional analysis of clauses, and semantic analysis is also beyond its reach[9]. In lexicogrammatical analysis, it is thus possible to automate the identification of classes of words (handled by (word class) taggers) and grammatical structure stated in terms of classes of words and groups/phrases (syntagms, handled by (formal) parsers); but analysis involving function structures and systemic features is much harder to automate for a free flow of text (cf. O'Donnell, 1994; Teich, 2009). So we have a trade-off between volume of analysis and richness of analysis: low-level analysis can be automated to handle large volumes of text, but high-level analysis has to be carried out by hand for small samples of text.

To address the current situation, we have adopted a two-pronged approach where we use certain computational concordancing tools to look for low-level patterns in large corpora and a computational database system to record and interpret our manual analysis of higher-level patterns in small samples of text: see Table 2-4[10]. The kinds of tools we have used in preparing this book are shown in bold italics; they were developed by Wu Canzhong and Christian Matthiessen (see Wu, 2000, 2009).

The concordancing tools have been applied to various corpora and the database system, SysFan, has been used to analyse texts from an archive of texts that we have selected from a range of different sources: see Table 2-5.[11] The difference between a **corpus** and a **text archive** is not a sharp one; but the general principle is that a corpus represents a systematic sample of text according to clearly stated criteria whereas a text archive is assembled in a

---

[9] We are talking about computational systems designed to process a free flow of text. It is always possible to build systems capable of handling short, registerially constrained texts.

[10] There are now various initiatives to provide non-commercial tools and resources for the research community, e.g. http://www.clarin.eu/vlo/ and Mick O'Donnell's UAM tools (http://www.wagsoft.com/CorpusTool/) developed for and used by the community of systemic functional researchers.

[11] Information about corpora can be accessed through the Linguistic Data Consortium (LDC), the University of Pennsylvania: http://www.ldc.upenn.edu/. The Corpus of Contemporary American English (COCA), at Brigham Young University, comes with a very user-friendly and powerful interface for corpus-searchers: http://corpus.byu.edu/coca/ Corpora of professional texts in different areas are available for free, with a web-based search engine at the PolyU Language Bank: http://langbank.engl.polyu.edu.hk/indexl.html (cf. Greaves, 2009). For an overview of corpora of English, see McEnery & Gabrielatos (2006).

Table 2-4 Tools for automatic and manual analysis of texts and corpuses

Highest rank of analysis:	Highest axis of analysis:	Automatic analysis	Manual analysis
Clause	paradigmatic + syntagmatic		**SysFan** [Wu, 2000]; WAG Coder [O'Donnell, 1994]; UAM CorpusTool [O'Donnell, 2011]
	syntagmatic only: function structure		Functional Grammar Processor [Webster, 1993]; Systemics [Kay O'Halloran & Kevin Judd]
	syntagmatic: syntagm	Standard parsers, e.g. Helsinki functional dependency parser	
Word		Taggers; concordancing programs, e.g. MonoConc, WordSmith, ConcGram [Greaves, 2009], **SysConc** [Wu, 2000], **COBUILD tools**	

more opportunistic fashion; thus given such criteria, a corpus can be extracted from a text archive – see Matthiessen (2006a).

The corpora listed in Table 2-5 differ in **registerial composition**. Some are corpora of spoken English, some of written English. The traditional one-million word corpora of written English, starting with the Brown corpus, are composed of samples from fifteen very broad categories, each of which is further classified into two to six subcategories. These categories are close to folk categories of genres, categories such as 'press', 'learned' and 'fiction'. When we review

Table 2-5 Corpuses and text archive used for description and exemplification in IFG

Size: # words	Corpus (explicit criteria)	Text archive (opportunistic sample)
> 50 m.	COBUILD corpus of spoken and written British, American, Australian English (c. 60 m. out of 330 m. words); COCA (450 m. word corpus of contemporary spoken and written American English)	
c. 1 m.	ACE corpus of written Australian English (1 m. words) Brown corpus of written American English (1 m. words) LOB corpus of written British English (1 m. words) Kolhapur corpus of written Indian English (1 m. words)	Archive of written and spoken British, American, Australian English texts (c. 850 K words) [referred to as Text 1, Text 2, etc.] – manual analysis of various samples
c. 500 K	London-Lund corpus of spoken British English (c. 500 K words)	Archive of screenplays (c. 450 K words)
≤ 250 K	UTS/Macquarie corpus of spoken Australian English (subpart used: c. 250 K words)	Archive of Larry King interviews (c. 70 K words)

these categories in terms of field, tenor and mode (see Chapter 1, Section 1.4.1), we find that there are considerable gaps in the sampling of texts and also skews; for example, texts operating in 'recreating' contexts seem over-represented (categories K, L, M, N and P in the Brown corpus). In the first corpus-based reference grammar with quantitative information, Biber *et al.* (1999), the authors give counts for grammatical features investigated in texts from four 'primary registers', viz. conversation, fiction, news, and academic prose. These are very broad, and each covers a considerable degree of registerial variation – variation that is lexicogrammatically quite significant, but which only becomes visible when we increase the delicacy in our differentiation of registers, using the field, tenor and mode variables. In work on compiling corpora, there is now a tendency to work towards samples of what Gu (1999) calls 'situated discourse', making it possible to study language 'at work' in well-defined contexts. A good example of a corpus of situated discourse is the extensive sample of texts for sociolinguistic research collected by the Language in the Workplace Project led by Janet Holmes (e.g. Holmes, 2000); another is MICASE, the Michigan Corpus of Academic Spoken English. In our view, compiling a corpus of situated discourse means using field, tenor and mode to define 'ecological' criteria for sampling text in context. While there is as yet no large-scale general corpus of English, a considerable number of 'situated discourses' have been analysed lexicogrammatically based on the description presented in the successive editions of IFG, and this research informs the current version of the description. To give a sense of the grammar 'at work', we present short texts or text extracts in each chapter categorized according to field and mode: see Chapter 1, Table 1-8.

Corpora thus differ in registerial composition, but they also differ in terms of **dialectal composition**. As can be seen from the corpora listed in Table 2-5, we have drawn on corpora from different 'dialectal' varieties of English – British English, American English, Australian English and Indian English; and, in addition, we have included text examples from South African English and Nigerian English. Naturally, there are other varieties of English; and different varieties of the language play different roles, with different registerial ranges, and have different statuses in the communities that they are spoken in (see e.g. Kachru, Kachru & Nelson, 2006; Schneider, 2007; Kortmann *et al.*, 2004). In the account of English presented here, the focus is not on distinctive features characteristic of different varieties but rather on features that are common across many varieties. At the same time, there are certainly interesting features found in particular varieties that are not covered in the current description. For example:

Yorkshire English:

Nobbut t'fireless arth an tgeeable end/Mark t'spot weear t' Carter family could mend, /An mek onny ilk o' cart. [From Halliday, 2003/2006]

Singaporean English:

Because she wants to sing **mah.** So she want to use, she want to join to sing, so we just groom her **lor**. [From Leimgruber, 2011]

Indian English:

They'd come in a bus, **isn't it**? [ICE-India]

Thus varieties of English differ with respect to the realizational resources they deploy to realize features within the interpersonal grammar of MOOD. Where standard British, American

and Australian English use a particular construction of mood tagging ('tag questions') with variable copies of the Mood element of the clause (see Chapter 4), Indian English uses a generalized tag *isn't it*, and Singaporean English uses clause-final interpersonal particles, drawn from southern dialects of Chinese.

In general, like any other language, English needs to be interpreted and described as an **assemblage of varieties** – varieties that are differentiated along different dimensions, with fuzzy boundaries. Thus, English is subject to **dialectal**, **codal** and **registerial** variation, each type of variation having a different locus within the strata of the language and covering a different range along the cline of instantiation: see Halliday (1994) and Matthiessen (2007a: 538–540).

Using the framework originally proposed by Bateman *et al.* (1991), we can represent such variation as an inherent property of lexicogrammatical system networks (for a more detailed account, see Bateman, Matthiessen & Zeng, 1999; for the application to register variation, see Matthiessen, 1993b; for examples in comparative and typological descriptions, see Teruya *et al.*, 2007; Matthiessen, Teruya & Wu, 2008). In this framework, systemic and structural specifications that are common across the varieties covered by the description are represented as in system networks in general, but specifications that apply only to one or a subset of these varieties are represented as **partitions** within the system network. Such partitions are conditioned by the variety or varieties that they are valid for.

For example, 'tagged' clauses are realized in most standard varieties of English by a Mood tag consisting of Finite ^ Subject, where the Finite is a copy of the Finite of the Mood element and the Subject is a (pronominal) copy of the Subject of the Mood element (see e.g. Chapter 4, Figure 4-6). In a description covering different varieties of English, this realization statement would be represented in a partition specific to (say) British, American, Australian and New Zealand English. The generalized Mood tag, Finite = *isn't* ^ Subject = *it*, would be represented in a partition specific to Indian English (as would *innit?* in an account of certain varieties of English in London). Such partitions are concerned with structural variation in the realizations of the same systemic option of 'tagged'. In addition to such **structural partitions** representing differences in realizations of the same systemic option across varieties of English, **systemic partitions** are also possible. In a description covering Australian English, there would be a systemic partition representing the option of tagging 'yes/no interrogative' clauses in addition to 'declarative' and 'imperative' ones (e.g. *Were you in England, were you?*; *Did Jane used to be a really close friend of hers, did she?*). In an account covering (colloquial) Singaporean English, there would probably be a partition representing the mood potential for interactive stances realized by the different interpersonal particles of this variety of English.

Variation in lexicogrammar across varieties of English is, of course, not only qualitative but also quantitative; the system of lexicogrammar is **probabilistic** in nature (cf. Chapter 1, Section 1.3.2; see Halliday, 1991, in relation to the corpus), and probabilities vary across varieties of English – dialectal, codal and registerial varieties (see e.g. Tottie & Hoffmann, 2006, on the significantly higher frequency of tags in British English than in American English, and Hoffman, 2006, on the gradual increase in frequency from early to late Modern English based on a corpus of plays). If we include probabilistic information in the description of the lexicogrammar, we also pave the way for interpreting the system as one that is always in the process of becoming, not one that is in a frozen state of being: the evolution of language involves gradual changes in probabilities, over long periods of time

(see e.g. Ellegård, 1953) but also over much shorter periods. We have used samples of English typically taken from the mid-twentieth century onwards, but during this period, there have certainly been changes in the system that are reflected as changes in relative frequencies in text (see e.g. Mair & Leech, 2006).

2.5 Classes and functions

What grammarians do, as we have been suggesting in these first two chapters, is to construct an abstract model of the system of language, based on observation of language instantiated in use. The computerized corpus has made this evidence available in sufficient quantity for the first time. But the relation between what we observe on the screen (or take in in any other form, as written or spoken discourse) and the abstract categories that we construct in order to explain how the language works – how people exchange meanings discursively in real-life situations – is extremely complex and indirect. We have tried to set out the grammarian's resources for doing this, the list of abstract tools we use to think with, in the course of these two chapters.

At the end of this chapter we will enlarge one of the cells of our linguistic map in Table 2-9 to display a **metafunction-rank matrix** for English grammar (cf. also Figure 1-16 in Chapter 1). Let us now move on to that bit of the territory and zero in to the clause. The clause, as we said, is the mainspring of grammatical energy; it is the unit where meanings of different kinds, experiential, interpersonal and textual, are integrated into a single syntagm. Chapters 3 to 5 will be exploring these three facets of the clause in turn.

Two concepts that we need to invoke from the start are those of grammatical class and grammatical function.

A **class** is a set of items that are in some respect alike (cf. Halliday, 1963c). The most familiar, in our traditional grammar, are classes of words: verb, noun, adjective, adverb, pronoun, preposition, conjunction (and sometimes also interjection), in the usual list. But every unit can be classified: there are classes of group and phrase, classes of clause, and, at the other end of the rank scale, classes of morpheme.

Word classes were traditionally called 'parts of speech', through mistranslation of the Greek term *meroi logou*, which actually meant 'parts of a sentence'. These began, with the Sophists, as functional concepts, rather close to the Theme and Rheme of Chapter 3; but they were progressively elaborated into, and replaced by, a scheme of word classes, defined by the kinds of inflexion that different words underwent in Greek (and which were largely paralleled in Latin; see Robins, 1966, for an account of the development of the account of word classes in the European tradition): see Table 2-6.

Table 2-6 Classical definitions of word classes

Inflection for:	(defines)	Word classes:
number, case		noun
number, case, gender		adjective
tense, person		verb
(none)		(other words)

This could have been carried further, to take account of inflexion for voice and aspect in verbs, and for comparison in adjectives and adverbs. But the criterion of inflexion will not serve all relevant word classes, even in a highly inflected language such as Greek or Latin; and in languages with little or no inflexion, such as English or Chinese, other principles have to be invoked. These may be either grammatical or semantic, or some combination of the two.

There are many ways in which one word may be like another, and the resultant groupings do not always coincide; a word will typically be like one word in one respect and like a different word in another. For example, *upper* and *lower* (which may have the same function, as in *upper case* and *lower case*) both belong to the class of adjective; but *lower* is a comparative adjective, contrasting with *low*, whereas *upper* is not – we cannot say *this roof is upper than that one*. In this respect, *lower* is like *higher*; but *lower* is also a verb, whereas *higher* is not – we cannot say *that roof needs highering*. Sometimes rather clear and definite criteria do present themselves, like grammatical inflexions with fairly consistent meanings; but often they do not, and in such instances the criteria on which classes are defined tend to be rather mixed, and membership of the classes rather indeterminate, with some items clearly belonging and others whose status is doubtful.

Consider for example the class of 'noun' in English. A general definition would involve both grammatical and semantic considerations, with some of the grammatical features having an overt manifestation and others not:

(semantic:)	expresses a person, other being, inanimate object or abstraction, bounded or unbounded, etc.
(grammatical:)	is either count or mass; if count, may be either singular or plural, plural usually inflected with *-s*; can be made possessive, adding *-'s/-s'*; can take *the* in front; can be Subject in a clause, etc.

When we say that something is a noun, in English, we mean that it displays these characteristics, or most of them, in common with some (but not all) other words in the language.

The word classes that we shall need to recognize in English are shown in Figure 2-8.

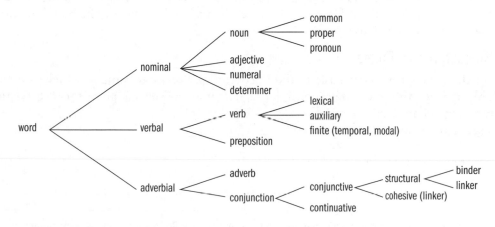

Fig. 2-8   Word classes recognized in a functional grammar of English

We shall also refer to three classes of group: verbal group, nominal group, adverbial group (also preposition group and conjunction group); and to one class of phrase: prepositional phrase. These will be clarified in the course of discussion (see Chapter 6); but we shall assume that the traditional word classes are reasonably familiar (cf. Coffin, Donohue & North, 2009). We shall not need to discuss clause classes explicitly, although they are in fact present as part of the overall description, as in the distinction between major and minor clauses and within major clauses between free and bound clauses.

The **class** of an item indicates in a general way its *potential range of grammatical functions*. Hence words can be assigned to classes in a dictionary, as part of their decontextualized definition. But the class label does not show what part the item is playing in any actual structure. For that we have to indicate its **function**. The functional categories provide an interpretation of grammatical structure in terms of the overall meaning potential of the language. For example, see Figure 2.9.

	our daily deeds as ordinary South Africans	must produce	an actual South African reality that … for a glorious life for all
[function]	Actor	Process	Goal
[class]	nominal group	verbal group	nominal group

Fig. 2-9   Function structure of clause with syntagm of classes realizing functions

The functional labels could be further elaborated to show what kind of Process, what kind of Goal, etc.; but this is not necessary to the description because these more delicate functions can be derived from the systemic analysis, which shows the features selected by any particular clause (in this case, see Chapter 5). An extended example of correspondences between classes and functions is given in Figure 2-10 below.

Note, however, that most elements of a clausal structure have more than one function in the clause.[12] This is where the concept of metafunction comes into play. We presented this in outline in Chapter 1; we will now explore its significance for the grammar by reference to one of the most familiar, and also most problematic, functional concepts in the Western grammatical tradition – that of Subject. This will then open the way into the metafunctional analysis of the English clause.

2.6 Subject, Actor, Theme

One of the concepts that are basic to the Western tradition of grammatical analysis is that of Subject. Since this is a familiar term, let us take it as the starting point for investigating the functions in an English clause.

Consider the clause:

the duke gave my aunt this teapot

---

12 The boundaries of the functional elements may not exactly coincide, for reasons that will emerge in Chapters 3 to 5.

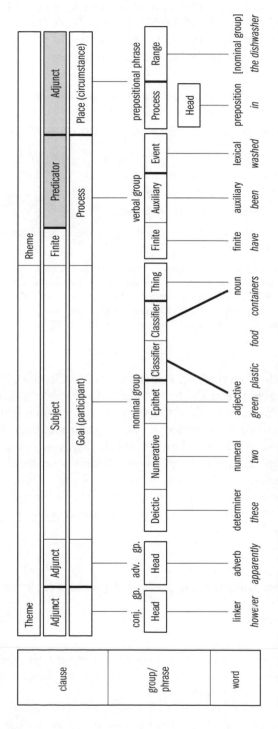

Fig. 2-10 Example illustrating class-function correspondences

In accordance with the syntactic principles established by medieval grammarians, which were themselves based on the grammarians of ancient Greece and Rome, each clause contains one element which can be identified as its Subject (see e.g. Covington, 1984; Seuren, 1998: 34–37); and in this instance, the Subject would be *the duke*.

Here are some other clauses with the Subject shown in italic:

Oh, *I*'m just starving and *all* [[*you'll feed me*]] is something rotten, or something [[*I* hate]] . *I* hate lasagne and *I* don't want rotten carrots – *I* only want salted carrots. [Text 76]

I wasn't making a cubby house; *that* wasn't a cubby house. – What were *you* making with it, then? [Text 76]

Adam, do *you* like red or white? – *I* would like red but only if *you*'re opening it. [UTS/Macquarie Corpus]

[S04:] *That*'s [[how *my nan* used to do them in Manchester]] – parboil them. – [S02:] What parboil them? – [S04:] Yeah. – [S01:] Did *she*? – [S04:] Yeah. [UTS/Macquarie Corpus]

They fit me. – Do *they*? – *They* will. [UTS/Macquarie Corpus]

The thought occurred to me on Air Force One a few weeks ago ‖ when *I* was escorted into President Clinton's cabin for a farewell interview. [Text 110]

Guinness's entertaining memoir, "Blessings in Disguise," <<published in 1985, >> told more about the talented and eccentric people [[*he* knew]] than about himself. *He* was seldom recognized in public. In one of the stories [[*he* told about himself]], *Guinness* checks his hat and coat at a restaurant ‖ and asks for a claim ticket. "*It* will not be necessary," ‖ *the attendant* smiles. Pleased at [[being recognized]], ‖ *Guinness* later retrieves his garments, ‖ puts his hand in the coat pocket ‖ and finds a slip of paper [[on which is written, "Bald with glasses."]] [Text 90]

It is possible to conclude from these examples that 'Subject' is the label for a grammatical function of some kind (*subject* being the Latin translation of a word in Greek, *hypokeimenon*, used as a grammatical term by Aristotle in the sense of 'that which is laid down, or posited'). There seems to be something in common, as regards their status in the clause, to all the elements we have labelled in this way. But it is not so easy to say exactly what this is; and it is difficult to find in the grammatical tradition a definitive account of what the role of Subject means (cf. Halliday, 1984b, on the ineffability of the category of Subject).

Instead, various interpretations have grown up around the Subject notion, ascribing to it a number of rather different functions . These resolve themselves into three broad definitions, which can be summarized as follows:

(i)   that which is the concern of the message
(ii) that of which something is being predicated (i.e. on which rests the truth of the argument)
(iii) the doer of the action.

These three definitions are obviously not synonymous; they are defining different concepts. So the question that arises is, is it possible for the category of 'Subject' to embrace all these different meanings at one and the same time?

In *the duke gave my aunt this teapot*, it is reasonable to claim that the nominal group *the duke* is, in fact, the Subject in all these three senses. It represents the person with whom

the message is concerned; the truth or falsehood of the statement is vested in him; and he is represented as having performed the action of giving.

If all clauses were like this one in having one element serving all three functions, there would be no problem in identifying and explaining the Subject. We could use the term to refer to the sum of these three definitions, and assign the label to whichever element fulfilled all the functions in question. But this assumes that in every clause there is just one element in which all three functions are combined; and this is not the case. Many clauses contain no such element that embodies all three. For example, suppose we say

this teapot my aunt was given by the duke

— which constituent is now to be identified as the Subject?

There is no longer any one obvious answer. What has happened in this instance is that the different functions making up the traditional concept of Subject have been split up among three different constituents of the clause. The duke is still represented as the doer of the deed; but the message is now a message concerning the teapot, and its claim for truth is represented as being vested in my aunt.

When these different functions came to be recognized by grammarians as distinct, they were first labelled as if they were three different **kinds** of Subject. It was still implied that there was some sort of a superordinate concept covering all three, a general notion of Subject of which they were specific varieties.

The terms that came to be used in the second half of the nineteenth century, when there was a renewal of interest in grammatical theory (see Seuren, 1998: 120–133, on the subject–predicate debate that lasted from the nineteenth century until the 1930s), were 'psychological Subject', 'grammatical Subject', and 'logical Subject'.

(i) Psychological Subject meant 'that which is the concern of the message'. It was called 'psychological' because it was what the speaker had in his mind to start with, when embarking on the production of the clause.

(ii) Grammatical Subject meant 'that of which something is predicated'. It was called 'grammatical' because at the time the construction of Subject and Predicate was thought of as a purely formal grammatical relationship; it was seen to determine various other grammatical features, such as the case of the noun or pronoun that was functioning as Subject, and its concord of person and number with the verb, but it was not thought to express any particular meaning.

(iii) Logical Subject meant 'doer of the action'. It was called 'logical' in the sense this term had had from the seventeenth century, that of 'having to do with relations between things', as opposed to 'grammatical' relations, which were relations between symbols.

In the first example, all these three functions are conflated, or 'mapped' on to one another, as shown in Figure 2-11.

79

the duke	gave my aunt this teapot
psychological Subject grammatical Subject logical Subject	

Fig. 2-11   Same item functioning as psychological, grammatical and logical Subject

In the second example, on the other hand, all three are separated (Figure 2-12). In *this teapot my aunt was given by the duke*, the psychological Subject is *this teapot*. That is to say, it is 'this teapot' that is the concern of the message – that the speaker has taken as the point of embarkation of the clause. But the grammatical Subject is *my aunt*: 'my aunt' is the one of whom the statement is predicated – in respect of whom the clause is claimed to be valid, and therefore can be argued about as true or false. Only the logical Subject is still *the duke*: 'the duke' is the doer of the deed – the one who is said to have carried out the process that the clause represents.

this teapot	my aunt	was given	by the duke
psychological Subject	grammatical Subject		logical Subject

Fig. 2-12   Psychological, grammatical and logical Subject realized by different items

As long as we concern ourselves only with idealized clause patterns like *John runs* or *the boy threw the ball*, we can operate with the label Subject as if it referred to a single undifferentiated concept. In clauses of this type, the functions of psychological, grammatical and logical Subject all coincide. In *the boy threw the ball*, *the boy* would still be Subject no matter which of the three definitions we were using, like *the duke* in the first of our examples above.

But as soon as we take account of natural living language, and of the kinds of variation that occur in it, in which the order of elements can vary, passives can occur as well as actives, and so on, it is no longer possible to base an analysis on the assumption that these three concepts are merely different aspects of one and the same general notion. They have to be interpreted as what they really are – three separate and distinct functions. There is no such thing as a general concept of 'Subject' of which these are different varieties. They are not three kinds of anything; they are three quite different things. In order to take account of this, we will replace the earlier labels by separate ones that relate more specifically to the functions concerned:

psychological Subject: Theme

grammatical Subject: Subject

logical Subject: Actor

We can now relabel Figure 2-12 as in Figure 2-13.

this teapot	my aunt	was given	by the duke
Theme	Subject		Actor

Fig. 2-13   Theme, Subject and Actor

In *the duke gave my aunt this teapot*, the roles of Theme, Subject and Actor are all combined in the one element *the duke*. In *this teapot my aunt was given by the duke*, all three are separated. All the additional combinations are also possible: any two roles may be conflated, with the third kept separate. For example, if we keep *the duke* as Actor, we can have Theme = Subject with Actor separate, as in Figure 2-14.

(a)

my aunt	was given	this teapot	by the duke
Theme Subject			Actor

(b)

this teapot	the duke	gave	to my aunt
Theme	Subject Actor		

(c)

by the duke	my aunt	was given	this teapot
Theme Actor	Subject		

Fig. 2-14   Different conflations of Subject, Actor and Theme

In any interpretation of the grammar of English we need to take note of all these possible forms, explaining how and why they differ. They are all, subtly but significantly, different in meaning; at the same time they are all related, and related in a systematic way. Any comparable set of clauses in English would make up a similar **paradigm**. Often, of course, there are not three distinct elements that could carry the functions of Theme, Subject and Actor, but only two, as in Figure 2-15.

(a)

I	caught	the first ball
Theme Subject Actor		

(b)

I	was beaten	by the second
Theme Subject		Actor

(c)

the third	I	stopped
Theme	Subject Actor	

(d)

by the fourth	I	was knocked out
Theme Actor	Subject	

Fig. 2-15   Narrative embodying different conflations of Subject, Actor and Theme

Note how the series of clauses in (a)–(d) forms an entirely natural sequence such as a speaker might use in a personal narrative of this kind.

And often no variation at all is possible, if there is only one element that can have these functions; for example *I ran away*, where *I* is inevitably Theme, Subject and Actor. (Even here there is a possibility of thematic variation, as in *run away I did* or *the one who ran away was me*; see Chapter 3 below.) On the other hand, while explaining all these variants, we also have to explain the fact that the typical, **unmarked** form, in an English declarative (statement-type) clause, is the one in which Theme, Subject and Actor are conflated into a single element. That is the form we tend to use if there is no prior context leading up to it, and no positive reason for choosing anything else.

2.7 Three lines of meaning in the clause

What is the significance of there being these three distinct functions in the clause, Subject, Actor and Theme?

Each of the three forms part of a different functional configuration, making up a separate strand in the overall meaning of the clause. As a working approximation, we can define these different strands of meaning as follows (based on the notion of metafunction, introduced in Chapter 1, Section 1.3.5):

(i) The Theme functions in the structure of the **clause as a message**. A clause has meaning as a message, a quantum of information; the Theme is the point of departure for the message. It is the element the speaker selects for 'grounding' what he is going on to say.

(ii) The Subject functions in the structure of the **clause as an exchange**. A clause has meaning as an exchange, a transaction between speaker and listener; the Subject is the warranty of the exchange. It is the element the speaker makes responsible for the validity of what he is saying.

(iii) The Actor functions in the structure of the **clause as representation**. A clause has meaning as a representation of some process in ongoing human experience; the Actor is the active participant in that process. It is the element the speaker portrays as the one that does the deed.

These three headings – clause as a message, clause as an exchange, and clause as a representation – refer to three distinct kinds of meaning that are embodied in the structure of a clause. Each of these three strands of meaning is construed by configurations of certain particular functions. Theme, Subject and Actor do not occur as isolates; each occurs in association with other functions from the same strand of meaning. We have not yet introduced these other functions; they will be presented in Chapters 3 to 5 and we have summarized the most important functions in each metafunctional configuration in Table 2-7. But one example was given in Figure 2-9 above: that of Actor + Process + Goal. A configuration of this kind is what is referred to in functional grammars as a **structure** (as opposed to a syntagm of classes: see Halliday, 1966a, Section 2.1 above, and Chapter 1, Section 1.3.1).

Table 2-7 Three lines of meaning in the clause

Metafunction	Clause as ...	System	Structure
textual	message	THEME	Theme ^ Rheme
interpersonal	exchange	MOOD	Mood [Subject + Finite] + Residue [Predicator (+ Complement) (+ Adjunct)]
experiential	representation	TRANSITIVITY	process + participant(s) (+ circumstances), e.g. Process + Actor + Goal

The significance of any functional label lies in its relationship to the other functions with which it is structurally associated. It is the structure as a whole, the total configuration of functions, that construes, or realizes, the meaning. The function Actor, for example, is interpretable only in its relation to other functions of the same kind – other representational functions such as Process and Goal. So, if we interpret the nominal group *I* as Actor in *I caught the first ball*, this is meaningful only because at the same time we interpret the verbal group *caught* as Process and the nominal group *the first ball* as Goal. It is the relation among all these that constitutes the structure. In similar fashion, the Subject enters into configurations with other functional elements as realization of the clause as exchange; and likewise the Theme, in realizing the clause as message.

By separating out the functions of Theme, Subject, and Actor, we have been able to show that the clause is a composite entity. It is constituted not of one dimension of structure but of three, and each of the three construes a distinctive meaning. We have labelled these 'clause as message', 'clause as exchange' and 'clause as representation'. In fact, the three-fold pattern of meaning is not simply characteristic of the clause; these three kinds of meaning run throughout the whole of language, and in a fundamental respect they determine the way that language has evolved. They are referred to in systemic accounts of grammar as **metafunctions** (see Chapter 1, Section 1.3.5), and the concept of 'metafunction' is one of the basic concepts around which the theory is constructed.

We shall not pursue the concept of metafunction in further detail at this stage; rather, it will be built up step by step throughout the book. But there is one thing to be said here about how the metafunctions relate to constituent structure, because this will arise as soon as we begin to consider the various specific dimensions of meaning in the clause. So far, we have referred to constituent structure as if it was something uniform and homogeneous (as in Chapter 1, Section 1.1.3); but as we embark on the detailed analysis of clause structures this picture will need to be modified. The model of constituent structure that we presented – the **rank scale** – is the prototype to which all three metafunctions can be referred. But the actual forms of structural organization depart from this prototype, each of them in different ways.

(1) The general principle of **exhaustiveness** means that everything in the wording has some function at every rank (cf. Halliday, 1961, 1966c). But not everything has a function in every dimension of structure; for example, some parts of the clause (e.g. interpersonal Adjuncts such as *perhaps* and textual Adjuncts such as *however*, as in Figure 2-10) play no role in the clause as representation.

(2) The general principle of **hierarchy** means that an element of any given rank is constructed out of elements of the rank next below (as in Figure 1-3). This is a feature of the constituent hierarchy made up of units and their classes: clause, verbal group, and so on. But the configurations of structural functions show further ramifications of this general pattern. Thus, in the clause as exchange there is slightly more layering in the structure, while in the clause as message there is rather less.

(3) The general principle of **discreteness** means that each structural unit has clearly defined boundaries. But while this kind of **segmental** organization is characteristic of the clause as representation, the clause in its other guises – as message, and as exchange – departs from this prototype. In its status as an exchange, the clause depends on **prosodic** features – continuous forms of expression, often with indeterminate boundaries; while in its status as message it tends to favour **culminative** patterns – peaks of prominence located at beginnings and endings.

It is not yet clear how far English is typical in these particular respects; but the evidence so far suggests that it is (see e.g. Caffarel, Martin & Matthiessen, 2004) and it is certainly true that, while the kinds of structure found in language are rather varied, the realizations of the different metafunctions tend to follow certain regular principles (see Halliday, 1979; Matthiessen, 1988; Martin, 1996). It may be helpful to try and summarize the picture as it is in English, so (with apologies for the terminological overload!) Table 2-8 introduces the technical names for the metafunctions, matches them up with the different statuses of the clause, and shows the kind of structure favoured by each. It will be seen that there is a fourth metafunctional heading that does not show up in the 'clause' column, because it is not embodied in the clause but in the clause complex – clauses linked together by logico-semantic relations to form sequences; this will figure as the topic of Chapter 7.

Table 2-8 Metafunctions and their reflexes in the grammar

Metafunction (technical name)	Definition (kind of meaning)	Corresponding status in clause	Favoured type of structure
experiential	construing a model of experience	clause as representation	segmental (based on constituency)
interpersonal	enacting social relationships	clause as exchange	prosodic
textual	creating relevance to context	clause as message	culminative
logical	constructing logical relations	–	iterative

It is the segmental kind of structure, with clearly separated constituent parts organized into a whole, that has traditionally been taken as the norm in descriptions of grammar; the very concept of 'structure', in language, has been defined in constituency terms. This is partly because of the kind of meaning that is expressed in this way: experiential meaning has been much more fully described than meaning of the other kinds (see e.g. Martin, 1990). But there is also another reason, which is that constituency is the simplest kind of structure, from which the other, more complex kinds can be derived; it is the natural one to take as prototypical – in the same way as digital systems are taken as the norm from which analogue systems can be derived, rather than the other way round.

For both these reasons, in the remaining chapters of Part One (Chapters 3 to 5) we shall use constituent-type descriptions of structure, merely pointing out now and again where meaning in the clause will be described independently in its own terms. This in itself will involve some sleight of hand, since although there are clearly these three motifs running side by side in every clause, a clause is still one clause – it is not three. It is a familiar problem for functional grammarians that everything has to be described before everything else; there is no natural progression from one feature in language to another (when children learn their mother tongue they do not learn it one feature at a time!).

We have chosen to start with the clause as message, because we find that the easiest aspect of the clause to discuss in its own terms and because it provides a window on the other two metafunctional strands within the clause; but even here it will be necessary to make some forward references to other parts of the book. These will be kept to a minimum; in general, we have tried to turn the exploration of grammar into a linear progression. Each chapter will presuppose the chapters that have gone before, and will only rarely have recourse to matters that are yet to come.

In conclusion, we present an overview of the lexicogrammatical resources of English in the form of a **function-rank** matrix: see Table 2-9. Each cell represents the **semiotic address** of one or more systems. This address is defined in terms of metafunction (columns) and ranks (rows); group/phrase rank systems are also differentiated according to primary class. For example, the matrix shows that the system of THEME is a textual system operating within the clause, while the system of TENSE is a logical system operating within the verbal group. We shall confine ourselves to systems at clause rank and group/phrase rank; systems at word rank and at morpheme rank are also part of the overall meaning-making resources of lexicogrammar, but their systems are, in a sense, subservient to the higher-ranking systems. We have also included the highest-ranking phonological systems – the systems of the tone group, since these systems realize patterns of wording directly, and will be discussed in this book (cf. Chapter 1, Section 1.2). Note, finally, that we have also included the information unit, placing it next to the clause (cf. Chapter 1, Section 1.3.1).

Table 2-9 Function-rank matrix: the systems of lexicogrammar

Stratum	Rank	Class	Logical		Experiential	Interpersonal	Textual
lexicogrammar	clause		TAXIS & LOGICO-SEMANTIC TYPE [Ch. 7]	–	TRANSITIVITY [Ch. 5]	MOOD [Ch. 4]	THEME [Ch. 3]
	info. unit				–	KEY [Ch. 4]	INFORMATION [Ch. 3]
	group/phrase [Ch. 6]	nominal [§ 6.2]	[Ch. 8]	MODIFICATION	THING TYPE, CLASSIFICATION, EPITHESIS, QUALIFICATION	nominal MOOD, PERSON, ASSESSMENT	DETERMINATION
		verbal [§ 6.3]		TENSE	EVENT TYPE, ASPECT	POLARITY, MODALITY	CONTRAST, VOICE
		adverbial [§ 6.4]		MODIFICATION	CIRCUMSTANCE TYPE	COMMENT TYPE	CONJUNCTION TYPE
		prepositional phrase [§ 6.5]		–	minor TRANSITIVITY	minor MOOD	
	word			DERIVATION	DENOTATION	CONNOTATION	
	morpheme						
phonology	tone group		TONE SEQUENCE; TONE CONCORD [Ch. 7]			TONE [Ch. 4]	TONICITY [Ch. 3]
			complexes	simplexes			

CHAPTER
THREE

CLAUSE AS MESSAGE

3.1 Theme and Rheme

In Section 2.6 we introduced the notion of a clause as a unit in which meanings of three different kinds are combined. Three distinct structures, each expressing one kind of semantic organization, are mapped on to one another to produce a single wording (cf. Table 2-7 (Three lines of meaning in the clause) in Chapter 2).

In the next three chapters we shall consider these three 'lines of meaning' in turn, beginning with the one that gives the clause its character as a message. The structure that carries this line of meaning is known as **thematic** structure.

We may assume that in all languages the clause has the character of a **message**, or quantum of information in the flow of discourse: it has some form of organization whereby it fits in with, and contributes to, the flow of discourse (cf. Matthiessen, 2004b: Section 10.5). But there are different ways in which this may be achieved. In English, as in many other languages, the clause is organized as a message by having a distinct **status** assigned to one part of it. One part of the clause is enunciated as the theme; this then combines with the remainder so that the two parts together constitute a message. For example, *From Raffles Place MRT* is given the status of the theme of the message in *From Raffles Place MRT, walk through the office blocks of Chulia Street*; it combines with *walk through the office blocks of Chulia Street* to form a message in a text that sets out a walking tour around a part of Singapore.

In some languages that have a pattern of a similar kind, the theme is announced by means of a particle: in Japanese, for example, there is a special postposition *-wa*, which signifies that whatever immediately precedes it is thematic (see Teruya, 2004, 2007). This element tends to come early in the clause, and may be preceded by other elements such as cohesive conjunctions that are also given thematic status. In other languages, of which English is one, the theme is indicated only by position in the clause. In speaking or writing English we signal that an item has thematic status by putting it first. No other

signal is necessary, although it is not unusual in spoken English for the theme to be marked off also by the intonation pattern (see Section 3.5).

Following the terminology of the Prague school of linguists (e.g. Garvin, 1964; Firbas, 1992), we shall use the term **Theme** as the label for this function. (Like all other functions it will be written with an initial capital.) The Theme is the element that serves as the point of departure of the message; it is that which locates and orients the clause within its context. The speaker chooses the Theme as his or her point of departure to guide the addressee in developing an interpretation of the message; by making part of the message prominent as Theme, the speaker enables the addressee to process the message. The remainder of the message, the part in which the Theme is developed, is called in Prague school terminology the **Rheme**. As a message structure, therefore, a clause consists of a Theme accompanied by a Rheme; and the structure is expressed by the order – whatever is chosen as the Theme is put first.[1] The message thus unfolds from thematic prominence – the part that the speaker has chosen to highlight as the starting point for the addressee – to thematic non-prominence. (As we shall see below, in Section 3.5, the Rheme typically contains another kind of prominence, prominence as news.)

In the following example, which is the first sentence of the Introduction to Roget's *Thesaurus*, the Theme is *the present Work*:

> The present Work is intended to supply, with respect to the English language, a desideratum hitherto unsupplied in any language; ...

Here is a short passage from a guidebook, illustrating how the choice of Theme functions to organize and carry forward the discourse (Text 3-1). The boundary between Theme and Rheme is shown by +.

Text 3-1: Reporting – passage from a guidebook (written, monologic)

Goa Gajah + is the 'elephant cave' on the road to Gianyar, a Hindu-Buddhist temple area with several open structures, bathing pools and flowing fountains. The atmosphere outside + is peaceful, one of holiness and worship, while inside the small cave + it is surprisingly humid and dry. *<sic>*

Beyond the main complex + is a lovely stream that bubbles under a wooden bridge, and further on + are steep stone steps leading to another complex and a large, lily-covered pond. For this popular tourist attraction, + dress properly; otherwise, *sarongs* (waist wrap-around skirt) + are available for rental at the door.

Yeh Pulu + is a beautiful hill area filled with rock carvings and relics just a kilometre or so from Goa Gajah. Continuing northwards, Bedulu village + marks the former site of the powerful Dalem Bedulu the last king of the Pejeng dynasty who were eventually defeated by Java's Gajah Mada in 1340s.

---

[1] Some grammarians have used the terms Topic and Comment instead of Theme and Rheme (e.g. Hockett, 1958: 201–203; cf. also Li & Thompson, 1976). But the Topic–Comment terminology carries rather different connotations. The label 'Topic' usually refers to only one particular kind of Theme, the 'topical Theme' (see Section 3.4); and it tends to be used as a cover term for two concepts that are functionally distinct, one being that of Theme and the other being that of Given (see Sections 3.5 and 3.6; and cf. Fries, 1981). It seems preferable to retain the earlier terminology of Theme-Rheme. In the generative linguistic literature, Gruber (1976: 38) introduced the term 'theme' in an experiential (rather than textual) sense for a kind of participant role, a 'theta role' in generative terms. In work drawing on Fillmore's (1968) 'case grammar', the term 'theme' has also been used as a label for deep case, or semantic case. In a different context, 'theme' is also used as the name of a stratum in verbal art: see Hasan (1985b: 96).

Still further along the road + is Pura Kebo Edan, otherwise known as the 'crazy buffalo' temple, where + a statue of Bima (one of the five Pandawa brothers of the Mahabharata epic) is particularly well-endowed.

(Holly Smith *et al.*, *Indonesia*. Singapore & London: Sun Tree Publishing Ltd (Travbugs Travel Guides). 1993. p.317.)

Contrast this with a geological text (Text 3-2):

Text 3-2: Expounding – categorizing (written, monologic): taxonomic report
Chert + is microscopically fine-grained silica (SiO$_2$).

It + is equivalent to chalcedony. ...

Chert + originates in several ways.

Some + may precipitate directly from sea water ...

Most + comes from the accumulation of silica shells of organisms.

These silica remains + come from diatoms, radiolaria, and sponge spicules, ...

[Robert J. Foster, *Physical geology*. Columbus, Ohio: Merrill. 1971. p.87.]

As can be seen from 3-1 and 3-2, the Theme always starts from the beginning of the clause (for the status of *while* and *and* in Text 3-1, see Section 3.4 below). It is what sets the scene for the clause itself and positions it in relation to the unfolding text. In the first text the reader is being led around and invited to notice and appreciate; in the second, the reader is held firmly to the topic that is being described.

This suggests that the speaker/writer is selecting the desired Theme – that there can be variation in what is chosen as the thematic element in the clause; and this is so. In the following paradigm of constructed examples the three agnate clauses differ just in respect of which nominal group is functioning as Theme (see Figure 3-1). Compare the following snatch of dialogue from an interview, where the second speaker switched from one Theme to another (Text 3-3).

Text 3-3: Reporting – admission interview (spoken, dialogic) [LLC, p.753]
A: (I'm hoping that) all financial and domestic considerations + have been gone into?

B: (Yes) we + 've taken them into account.

(Yes) they + have.

The interviewee, faced with this bureaucratic mouthful, obviously feels that the natural Theme for the response is *we*; it is after all she and her partner whose actions are the key to providing the information requested. But she then adapts to the thematic structure of the question, and switches over to *they* (= *all ... considerations*) as Theme.

the duke	has given my aunt that teapot
my aunt	has been given that teapot by the duke
that teapot	the duke has given to my aunt
Theme	Rheme

Fig. 3-1   Theme-Rheme structure

It will have been clear from the earlier examples that the Theme is not necessarily a nominal group; it may be some other class of group or phrase. John B. Carroll's 'Foreword' to Whorf's *Language, Thought and Reality* begins with the adverbial Theme, *once in a blue moon*:

Once in a blue moon a man comes along who grasps the relationship between events which have hitherto seemed quite separate, and gives mankind a new dimension of knowledge.

As a general guide to start off with, we shall say that the Theme of a clause is the first group or phrase that has some function in the experiential structure of the clause, i.e. that functions as a participant, a circumstance or the process. We shall return to this in a little more detail in Section 3.4 below (and more fully in Chapter 5); meanwhile this definition will be elaborated in the next few sections to take account of complex and multiple Themes, as well as special types of thematic patterning that create order in the discourse.

The most common type of Theme is a participant, realized by a nominal group. Such Themes are sometimes announced explicitly, by means of some expression like *as for …, with regard to …, about …* ; this has the effect of **focusing** the Theme. For example:

As for Pope John Paul himself, + he is known to be very keen on sport. [BE bbc/06 S1000900 531]

Compare:

As to that teapot, + my aunt was given it by the duke.

Typically, the Theme is then 'picked up' by the appropriate pronoun in its natural place in the clause. Such picking up may occur even if the Theme is not explicitly announced by a thematic marker (as usually the case in speech, where intonation can be used; see below), as in

That teapot – my aunt was given it by the duke.

Oh, my little toe, look at it. [Text 76]

A man who succeeds as a farmer, who succeeds as a householder – these things are highly regarded. [Text 16]

'The barge she sat in', do you remember that passage in The Waste Land? [Text 125]

Now about 'The Love Song of Alfred J. Prufrock', what is that poem about? [Text 125]

Sometimes the Theme is not picked up in this way and it is left to the listener to infer the relationship:

But corporations, you've got to make sure you know what you're doing, because otherwise you're out of business. [Text 101]

As for the other players, I've got no apprehensions. [ACE_A]

This device enables the speaker/writer to select a Theme without disturbing the overall arrangement of the clause (cf. below on marked Themes, Section 3.3).

The Theme of a clause is frequently marked off in speech by intonation, being spoken on a separate tone group; this is especially likely when the Theme is either (i) an adverbial group or prepositional phrase; or (ii) a nominal group not functioning as Subject – in other words, where the Theme is anything other than that which is most expected (see Section 3.3 below). But even ordinary Subject Themes are often given a tone group to themselves in everyday speech. One tone group expresses one unit of information (cf. Section 3.5); and if a clause is organized into two information units, the boundary between the two is overwhelmingly likely to coincide with the junction of Theme and Rheme. This is, in fact, an important piece of evidence for understanding the Theme + Rheme structure, for example (from Text 3-6 below):

// in this job + Anne we're // working with silver // [marked theme]

// the people that buy silver + // love it // [unmarked theme]

3.2 Group/phrase complexes as Theme; thematic equatives

As a first step we have made two assumptions: that the Theme of a clause consists of just one structural element, and that that element is represented by just one unit – one nominal group, adverbial group or prepositional phrase. These two assumptions hold for the examples given above; similarly, in the first sentence of the Preface to J.R. Firth's *Papers in linguistics 1934–1951* the Theme is *the first chair of General Linguistics in this country*, which is still one single nominal group:

The first chair of General Linguistics in this country was established in the University of London in 1944, at the School of Oriental and African Studies ...

In each of these examples the Theme is one element, which, in turn, is one nominal group or one prepositional phrase.

A common variant of this elementary pattern is that in which the Theme consists of two or more groups or phrases forming a single structural element. Any element of clause structure may be represented by a complex of two or more groups or phrases (see Chapter 8). Such a group or phrase complex functions as a Theme in the normal way. This is illustrated in Figure 3-2.

the Walrus and the Carpenter	were walking close at hand
Tom, Tom, the piper's son	stole a pig [and away did run]
from house to house	I wend my way
on the ground or in the air	small creatures live and breathe
Theme	Rheme

Fig. 3-2   Group complex or phrase complex as Theme

Such Themes still fall within the category of **simple** (as opposed to **multiple**) Themes. Any group complex or phrase complex constitutes a single element within the clause; for example, two nominal groups joined by *and*, like *the Walrus and the Carpenter*, make up a nominal group complex. This is just one element in the clause, and therefore constitutes a simple Theme. The two prepositional phrases *from house to house* likewise make up a prepositional phrase complex, and this is also therefore one simple Theme. The different kinds of relationship that may be expressed in these **complex** structures are discussed in Chapter 8.

The first sentence of Hjelmslev's *Prolegomena to a theory of language*, Whitfield's translation, has as its Theme the nominal group complex *language – human speech*, consisting of two nominal groups in apposition:

Language – human speech – is an inexhaustible abundance of manifold treasures.

Another example of apposition in the Theme is the following, from the blurb to Hunter Davies' biography of George Stephenson:

One hundred and fifty years ago, on 15 September 1830, the world's first passenger railway – the Liverpool to Manchester – was opened, an event which was to change the face of civilization.

Here the Theme consists of two phrases forming a phrase complex, ending at *1830*.

In the above examples, the group or phrase complex is a single constituent of the clause; it is not specially constructed by the thematic system. There is, in addition, a special thematic resource whereby two or more separate elements are grouped together so that they form a single constituent of the Theme + Rheme structure. An example of this would be:

What the duke gave to my aunt was that teapot.

Here the Theme is *what the duke gave to my aunt*. Technically, this is still a simple Theme, because it has now been organized as a single constituent of the clause – but it is a clause of a particular kind. The clause *what the duke gave to my aunt was that teapot* is a thematic variant of *the duke gave my aunt that teapot*. Here *what* can be interpreted as 'that which'.

This kind of clause is known as a **thematic equative** (cf. Halliday, 1967/8), because it sets up the Theme + Rheme structure in the form of an equation, where Theme = Rheme. The particular clause type that is being exploited to form a thematic equative is the **identifying** clause; this will be described in Chapter 5, Section 5.4.4; but since it plays such an important part in the construction of the clause as a message we need to introduce it here.

In a thematic equative, all the elements of the clause are organized into two constituents; these two are then linked by a relationship of identity, a kind of 'equals sign', expressed by some form of the verb *be*. There is an example of this in the first clause of the second paragraph of Lewis Carroll's *Through the looking-glass*:

The way Dinah washed her children's faces was this:

where the Theme is *the way Dinah washed her children's faces*. (Strictly speaking the *was*, or other form of *be*, serves to link the Rheme with the Theme; but for the sake of simpler analysis it can be shown as part of the Rheme.) We can construct a thematic paradigm around the gift of the teapot (see Figure 3-3).

what (the thing) the duke gave to my aunt	was	that teapot
the one who gave my aunt that teapot	was	the duke
the one the duke gave that teapot to	was	my aunt
what the duke did with that teapot	was	give it to my aunt
how my aunt came by that teapot	was	she was given it by the duke
Theme	Rheme	

Fig. 3-3   Thematic equatives

A form such as *what the duke gave to my aunt* is an instance of a structural feature known as nominalization, whereby any element or group of elements is made to function as a nominal group in the clause. This nominal group consists of a Head and a post-modifying relative clause, as in *the one who gave my aunt that teapot*; but the Head and the marker of the relative clause may be fused in one item: *what* 'that which', *how* 'the way in which', *when* 'the time at which' and *where* 'the place at which'.[2] In this case the nominalization serves a thematic purpose. The thematic equative pattern allows for all possible distributions of the parts of the clause into Theme and Rheme, as in Figure 3-3. It even includes one variant such as the following:

what happened was that the duke gave my aunt that teapot

where the Theme is simply *what happened*, meaning 'I want to tell you that something happened', and every component of the happening is put into the Rheme.

In the typical instance the nominalization functions as Theme, because in the Theme-Rheme structure it is the Theme that is the prominent element. All the examples above were of this type. But – as so often happens in language – in contrast with the typical pattern there is a standing-out or marked alternative, exemplified by *you're the one I blame for this*, with *you* as Theme, in which the usual relationship is reversed and the nominalization becomes the Rheme. Further examples of this can be seen in Figure 3-4. The following corpus examples include both unmarked and marked theme equatives:

The Sri Lanka Constitution's claim to distinction lies in the fact that it follows neither the Presidential system nor the Prime Ministerial one, a claim with which none need quarrel for Constitutional straitjackets are the invention of professors. **What needs to be noted**, however, is that even President Jayawardane admits, by implication, that the Constitution contains the possibility of a 'dictator-motivated individual' ruling for six years. [KOHL_A]

All these were attractive and vivacious young ladies, but **the one who stuck in the memory of the Minister** was Miss Sheila Patterson, an Anglo-Indian beauty who was introduced to him as 'Durga's English teacher'. [KOHL_K]

---

[2]   We might thus expect *who gave my aunt that teapot was the duke* (cf. *whoever gave my aunt that teapot was a generous person*) but this use of *who* is not possible, and *the one who* fills the hole in the paradigm.

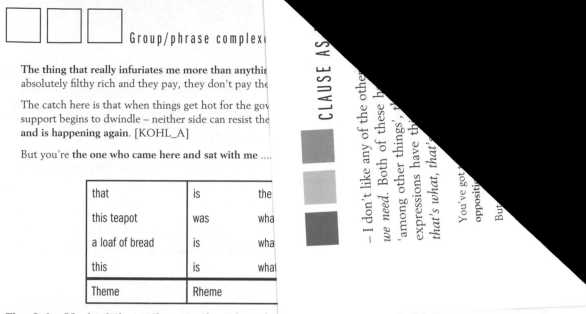

The thing that really infuriates me more than anythi
absolutely filthy rich and they pay, they don't pay th

The catch here is that when things get hot for the gov
support begins to dwindle – neither side can resist the
and is happening again. [KOHL_A]

But you're **the one who came here and sat with me** ....

that	is	the
this teapot	was	wha
a loaf of bread	is	wha
this	is	what
Theme	Rheme	

Fig. 3-4   Marked thematic equatives (nominalization as Rheme)

A thematic equative (which is usually called a 'pseudo-cleft sentence' in formal grammar) is an identifying clause which has a thematic nominalization in it. Its function is to express the Theme-Rheme structure in such a way as to allow for the Theme to consist of any subset of the elements of the clause. This is the explanation for the evolution of clauses of this type: they have evolved, in English, as a thematic resource, enabling the message to be structured in whatever way the speaker or writer wants.

Let us say more explicitly what this structure means. The thematic equative actually realizes two distinct semantic features, which happen to correspond to the two senses of the word *identify*. On the one hand, it identifies (specifies) what the Theme is; on the other hand, it identifies it (equates it) with the Rheme.

The second of these features adds a semantic component of exclusiveness: the meaning is 'this and this alone'. So, the meaning of *what the duke gave my aunt was that teapot* is something like 'I am going to tell you about the duke's gift to my aunt: it was that teapot— and nothing else'. Contrast this with *the duke gave my aunt that teapot*, where the meaning is 'I am going to tell you something about the duke: he gave my aunt that teapot' (with no implication that he did not give – or do – other things as well).

Hence even when the Theme is not being extended beyond one element, this identifying structure still contributes something to the meaning of the message: it serves to express this feature of exclusiveness. If I say *what the duke did was give my aunt that teapot*, the nominalization *what the duke did* carries the meaning 'and that's all he did, in the context of what we are talking about'. [3] This is also the explanation of the marked form, which has the nominalization in the Rheme, as in *that's the one I like*. Here the Theme is simply *that*, exactly the same as in the non-nominalized equivalent *that I like*; but the thematic equative still adds something to the meaning, by signalling that the relationship is an exclusive one

---

[3]   It further indicates, by the choice of the 'pro-verb' *did*, something about the role of the duke: that he did something – he was an active participant in the process. Contrast *what happened to that teapot* ... , where the role of the teapot is shown to have been a passive one. See Chapter 5, Section 5.2.

s. Compare *a loaf of bread we need* and *a loaf of bread is what*
ve *a loaf of bread* as Theme; but whereas the former implies
e latter implies 'and nothing else'. Note that some very common
s marked thematic equative structure, including all those beginning
why, etc.; e.g. *that's what I meant, that's why it's not allowed.*

o be confident in this game. And I reckon I'm one of the best. That's **why I never worry about the**
n; **never respect too many players**. I let them worry about me. [ACE_A]

you can't ride into the Ferry. That's **what they'll expect you to do**. [BROWN1_N]

We shall see in the next section that there is a further significant difference between equative and non-equative agnates in those cases where the non-equative has something other than Subject as Theme; for example:

[equative]	that	's what they don't tell us
	Subject	
[non-equative]	that	they don't tell us
	Subject	

Meanwhile, Figure 3-5 gives some further examples that help to bring out the difference between a thematic equative and a clause with ordinary Theme-Rheme structure.

(a) thematic equative

(i) nominalization as Theme

what no one seemed to notice	was	the writing on the wall
the thing that impresses me the most	is	their enthusiasm for the job
the ones you never see	are	the smugglers
Theme		Rheme

(ii) nominalization as Rheme

twopence a day	was	what my master allowed me
the Walrus	is	the one I like the best
Theme		Rheme

(b) non-equative equivalents (assuming Subject as Theme; see Section 3.3 below)

No one	seemed to notice the writing on the wall
their enthusiasm for the job	impresses me the most
you	never see the smugglers
I	like the Walrus best
Theme	Rheme

Fig. 3-5   **Further examples of thematic equatives**

96

3.3 Theme and mood

What is the element that is typically chosen as Theme in an English clause? The answer to that question depends on the choice of MOOD.

MOOD is the major interpersonal system of the clause; it provides interactants involved in dialogue with the resources for giving or demanding a commodity, either information or goods-&-services – in other words, with the resources for enacting speech functions (speech acts) through the grammar of the clause: statements (giving information), questions (demanding information), offers (giving goods-&-services), and commands (demanding goods-&-services). MOOD will be discussed in Chapter 4. Here we shall need to anticipate the first steps in that discussion, and introduce the primary categories of the mood system. We will restrict ourselves to **free** clauses, those that can stand by themselves as a complete sentence, in contrast with **bound** clauses (see Chapter 4, Section 4.4.5).

Every free clause selects for mood. Some, like *John!* and *good night!*, are **minor** clauses (Chapter 4, Section 4.6.2); they have no thematic structure, and so will be left out of account. The others are **major** clauses. A free major clause is either indicative (giving or demanding information) or imperative (demanding goods-&-services) in mood; if indicative, it is either declarative (giving information) or interrogative (demanding information); if interrogative, it is either 'yes/no' interrogative or 'WH-' interrogative. Examples:

indicative: declarative	Bears eat honey. Bears don't eat honey.
indicative: interrogative: yes/no	Do bears eat honey? Don't bears eat honey?
indicative: interrogative: WH-	What eats honey? What do bears eat?
imperative:	Eat! Let's eat!

We will consider each of these moods in turn, from the point of view of their thematic structure.

(1) Theme in declarative clauses. In a declarative clause, the typical pattern is one in which Theme is conflated with Subject; for example, *Little Bo-peep has lost her sheep*, where *Little Bo-peep* is both Subject and Theme. All the examples in Figure 3-1 were of this kind; likewise those in Figure 3-3 to Figure 3-5.

We shall refer to the mapping of Theme on to Subject as the **unmarked Theme** of a declarative clause. The Subject is the element that is chosen as Theme unless there is good reason for choosing something else. Note that this adds a further explanation for the use of a thematic equative in clauses such as *you're the one I blame for this, that's what they don't tell us*: here the Theme is Subject, and therefore unmarked, whereas in the non-equative variants *you I blame for this, that they don't tell us, you* and *that* – not being Subject – are now marked Themes. The effect of this is to add a feature of contrastiveness that the speaker may not require.

In everyday conversation, in sharing contexts, the item most often functioning as unmarked Theme (Subject/Theme) in a declarative clause is the first person pronoun *I*. Much of our talk consists of messages concerned with ourselves, and especially with what we think and feel. Next after that come the other personal pronouns *you, we, he, she, it, they*; and the impersonal pronouns *it* and *there*. For example:[4]

Text 3-4: Sharing – casual conversation

Son 1 (Joshua): <u>Do you</u> want to go?

Mother: <u>I</u> don't know; <u>I</u> haven't been. I don't **what** it's like, but **everyone** else said <u>it</u>'s not very good; <u>it</u>'s just boring.

Son 2: <u>It</u> isn't very exciting.

Mother: Joshua is – **what** do you think of it, Joshua?

Son 2: Bit of a disappointment.

Son 1 (Joshua): Oh well, you know... [snicker]

Mother: (what?

Son 1 (Joshua): I think **you** should go ... if **you** haven't been.

Mother: Yes but **why** do you think he should go?

Son 1 (Joshua): If <u>he</u> hasn't been before.

Son 2: <u>Yeah, why</u> would I go?

Son 1 (Joshua): <u>I</u> don't know. <u>There</u>'s all these, you know, old –

Then come other nominal groups – those with common noun or proper noun as Head – and nominalizations. Providing these are functioning as Subject, then having them as Theme is still the unmarked choice.

A Theme that is something other than the Subject, in a declarative clause, we shall refer to as a **marked theme**. The most usual form of marked Theme is an adverbial group, e.g. *today, suddenly, somewhat distractedly*, or prepositional phrase, e.g. *at night, in the corner, without any warning* functioning as **Adjunct** in the clause. Least likely to be thematic is a **Complement**, which is a nominal group that is not functioning as Subject – something that could have been a Subject but is not, as in the examples *you I blame for this, that they don't tell us*.[5] (For discussion of Complement and Adjunct see Chapter 4, Section 4.3.) Marked Adjunct and Complement Themes are followed by the Subject in Modern English

---

4   From UTS-Macquarie Corpus: family conversation involving Mother and her two sons about whether Son 2 should join a school excursion to Old Sydney Town.

5   As we have just noted, a marked Theme in a declarative clause is something other than the Subject: a (circumstantial) Adjunct or a Complement. But what about the Predicator? It only occurs as Theme in a fairly rare construction where the whole Residue element is Theme followed by the Mood element with a substitute as Finite carrying the Focus of New information (cf. Halliday, 1967/8/2005: 79), e.g. *Get better she did.* [ACE_E] In the limiting case, the Residue consists only of the Predicator, as in *This filly is another Adios that wants to trot, and <u>trot</u> she did until forced to do otherwise* [BROWN1_E] (cf. with an Adjunct as part of Residue: *and trot fast she did*). However, what is thematized is really the Residue rather than the Predicator, as is brought out by relational clauses with a finite form of *be* as Finite but without a Predicator, e.g. *The grammar, in its ideational function, is a theory of human experience. <u>And a very effective theory</u> it is* [Halliday, 2008: 147]. If, in a 'projection' nexus, the projecting 'verbal' or 'mental' clause follows the projected part, the sequence may be either Sayer (Senser) + Process or Process + Sayer (Senser): ... *Henry said*; ... *said Henry*. In the latter case, the combination of Finite and Predicator, i.e. Finite/Predicator, proceeds the Subject; and the whole projecting clause is as it were downgraded through tonal cliticization

– a historical departure from the general principle in Germanic languages that the Theme is followed by, and thus marked off by, the Finite in a declarative clause. The general exception to this departure in Modern English is a clausal negative item as Theme – an Adjunct or Complement with a negative feature that pertains to the clause.[6] Such negative Themes are followed by the Finite, as in:

> Nowhere **has** this decline been more painfully evident than in the New York City area. [BROWN1_H]

> No longer **does** the truism 'everyone has to eat' mean that producers and marketers can afford to ignore the valuable information consumers can provide. [ACE_E]

The main tendencies for the selection of Theme in declarative clauses are summarized in Table 3-1.

The 'most marked' type of Theme in a declarative clause is thus a Complement: for example *this responsibility* in *this responsibility we accept wholly* (see below). This is a nominal element that, being nominal, has the potentiality of being Subject; which has not been selected as Subject; and which nevertheless has been made thematic. Since it could have been Subject, and therefore unmarked Theme, there must be very good reason for making it a thematic Complement – it is being explicitly foregrounded as the Theme of the clause.[7] Let us look at one example, taken from the end of Bally and Sechehaye's Preface to Saussure's *Course in general linguistics* (English translation by Wade Baskin):

> We are aware of our responsibility to our critics. We are also aware of our responsibility to the author, who probably would not have authorized the publication of these pages. This responsibility we accept wholly, and we would willingly bear it alone.

Here the Theme *this responsibility* is strongly foregrounded; it summarizes the whole burden of the preface – the special responsibility faced by scholars reconstructing from others' lecture notes the work of an outstanding colleague for publication after his death – and enunciates this as their point of departure, as what the undertaking is all about. Similarly:

> In the worst scenario, if most of a teacher's lessons are 'poor', he or she will be asked to sign a sheet explaining any extenuating circumstances. This they should refuse until there is union advice, and then all the circumstances – the whole demoralising history of oversized classes, or teaching without books, inadequate training or lack of special needs support – should be recorded. [Text 97]

The general principle is that Complements are highly marked as Theme. However, certain types of Complement may be highly motivated as Theme in texts of a certain type because

---

(see Chapter 7, Table 7-29). In certain types of news reports, a projecting clause that proceeds the projected part may have Finite/Predicator as Theme, e.g. *Says Senator Pepper in support of his bill: 'I think it would do wonders'* [*Time Magazine*]. Here the journalist's choice of Theme serves to flag that s/he is attributing what follows to a particular source.

[6] This applies to circumstantial Adjuncts with a negative feature, e.g. *nowhere* as a locative Adjunct; and it also applies to modal Adjuncts with a negative (or quasi-negative) feature, e.g. *never, hardly*.

[7] It is also likely to be given the status of New information within its own unit of information. At the same time, some element other than the Complement will be a candidate for the status of New within the Rheme of the clause, as in the example from the next extract: *this* they should **refuse**.

Table 3-1 Examples of Theme in declarative clause. Theme-Rheme boundary is shown by #.

	Function[8]	Class	Clause example
unmarked Theme	Subject	nominal group: pronoun as Head	I # had a little nut-tree
			she # went to the baker's
			there # were three jovial Welshmen
		nominal group: common or proper noun as Head	a wise old owl # lived in an oak
			Mary # had a little lamb
			London Bridge # is fallen down
		nominal group: nominalization (nominalized clause) as Head	what I want # is a proper cup of coffee
marked Theme	Adjunct	adverbial group	merrily # we roll along
		prepositional phrase	on Saturday night # I lost my wife
	Complement	nominal group: common or proper noun as Head	a bag-pudding # the King did make
			Eliot # you're particularly fond of
		nominal group: pronoun as Head	all this # we owe both to ourselves and to the peoples of the world ⟦who are so well represented here today⟧
			this # they should refuse
		nominal group: nominalization (nominalized clause) as Head	what they could not eat that night # the Queen next morning fried

of the 'method of development' of such texts. For example, in topographic reports such as Text 3-1 above, locations in place play a major role in the organization of the texts as reference point in the construction of a verbal map of some territory, and locative Adjuncts and Complements are highly motivated as Themes since they enable speakers to guide their addressees in the development of the verbal map (cf. Matthiessen, 1992: 60–61; 1995c: 37–39). They occur frequently in 'existential' clauses such as *Beyond the main complex is a lovely stream that bubbles under a wooden bridge* and in 'circumstantial' relational clauses such as *Still further along the road is Pura Kebo Edan*; and also, of course, in clauses of other types. Such examples from topographic reports (and also from topographic procedures) illustrate a general principle of marking: while a given term may be marked globally in the language, it may be locally unmarked because it is motivated by register-specific considerations.

Sometimes even the Complement from within a prepositional phrase (see Chapter 6, Section 6.5) functions as Theme, particularly in idiomatic combinations of preposition and

---

8   Function in clause as exchange; see Chapter 4.

verb: for example, *that* in *that I could do without*, *two things* in *two things we need to comment on*. Perhaps the type of Complement/Theme that stands out, however, is a pronoun, such as *me* in *me they blame for it*. This is, as it were, the opposite end of the scale of thematic tendency from the unmarked Subject/Theme *I* with which we started.

There is one sub-category of declarative clause that has a special thematic structure, namely the exclamative. These typically have an exclamatory WH-element as Theme, as in Figure 3-6.

what a self-opinionated egomaniac	that guy is
how dreadful	she sounds
Theme	Rheme

Fig. 3-6 Theme in exclamative clauses

(2) Theme in interrogative clauses. The typical function of an interrogative clause is to ask a question; and from the speaker's point of view asking a question is an indication that he wants to be told something. The fact that, in real life, people ask questions for all kinds of reasons does not call into dispute the observation that the basic meaning of a question is a request for an answer. The natural theme of a question, therefore, is 'What I want to know'.

There are two main types of question: one where what the speaker wants to know is the POLARITY 'yes or no?', e.g. *Can you keep a secret? Is anyone at home?*; the other where what the speaker wants to know is the identity of some element in the content, e.g. *Who will you take as your partner? Where has my little dog gone?* In both types, the word indicating what the speaker wants to know comes first.

In a yes/no interrogative, which is a question about polarity, the element that functions as Theme is the element that embodies the expression of polarity, namely the **Finite verbal operator**. It is the Finite operator in English that expresses positive or negative: *is, isn't; do, don't; can, can't*; etc. So in a yes/no interrogative the Finite operator is put first, before the Subject. The meaning is 'I want you to tell me whether or not'.

In a WH- interrogative, which is a search for a missing piece of information, the element that functions as Theme is the element that requests this information, namely the WH-element. It is the WH- element that expresses the nature of the missing piece: *who, what, when, how*, etc. So in a WH- interrogative the WH- element is put first no matter what other function it has in the mood structure of the clause, whether Subject, Adjunct or Complement. The meaning is 'I want you to tell me the person, thing, time, manner, etc.'.

Interrogative clauses, therefore, embody the thematic principle in their structural make-up. It is characteristic of an interrogative clause in English that one particular element comes first; and the reason for this is that that element, owing to the very nature of a question, has the status of a Theme. The speaker is not making an instantial choice to put this element first; its occurrence in first position is the regular pattern by which the interrogative is expressed. It has become part of the system of the language, and the explanation for this lies in the thematic significance that is attached to first position in the English clause. Interrogatives express questions; the natural theme of a question is 'I want to be told something'; the answer required is either a piece of information about an element of the clause or an indication of polarity. So the realization of interrogative mood involves selecting an element that indicates the kind of answer required, and putting it at the beginning of the clause.

In a WH- interrogative, the Theme is constituted solely by the WH- element: that is, the group or phrase in which the WH- word occurs. See the examples in Figure 3-7.

who	wants a glass of white wine?
where	did you get that from?
how many hours	did you want?
and how long	's she there for?
why	was he opposed to coming in?
Theme	Rheme

Fig. 3-7 Theme in WH- interrogative

Here the WH- element is an element serving directly in the interrogative clause – a participant serving as Subject or Complement or a circumstance serving as Adjunct. However, under certain conditions it may be an element that is not directly part of the clause (see Matthiessen, 1995a: 416–417). If the WH- word is, or is part of, a nominal group functioning as Complement in a prepositional phrase, this nominal group may function as Theme on its own, e.g. *what* in *what shall I mend it with?*, *which house* in *which house do they live in?* If the WH- element serves in a projected clause (see Chapter 7), it may serve as the Theme of the projecting clause, as in *Who do you think pays the rent?*, which is the interrogative version of *you think somebody pays the rent*. Similarly: *And what do you think you could have done about it before?*, *What did you say your name was?*, *What does he think a remark like this 'lousy' one does to our prestige and morale?*

In a yes/no interrogative, the picture is slightly different, for reasons that will be explained more fully in Section 3.5 below. Here, the Theme includes the Finite operator; but, since that is not an element in the experiential structure of the clause, the Theme extends over the following Subject as well. For examples, see Figure 3-8.

could	you	eat a whole packet of tim tams?
has	he	got the car back by the way?
did	you	sleep okay?
didn't	it	smell terrible?
shall	I	make some toast?
are	they	still together?
Theme (1)	Theme (2)	Rheme

Fig. 3-8 Theme in yes/no interrogative

Thus in both kinds of interrogative clause the choice of a typical 'unmarked' thematic pattern is clearly motivated, since this pattern has evolved as the means of carrying the basic message of the clause. Hence there is a strong tendency for the speaker to choose the unmarked form, and not to override it by introducing a marked Theme out in front. But marked Themes do sometimes occur in interrogatives, as illustrated in Figure 3-9.

at lower latitudes [[where there are no stratospheric ice crystals]],	is the role of ice mimicked by other aerosols such as volcanic dust?
on the right	is it?
In such circumstances	is it any wonder that motorists, for their own safety as well as that of other road users, are reluctant to 'obey the signals of a police officer?' [ACE_B]
aesthetically, in terms of the vision in your head,	what is the relationship between the fiction and the non-fiction?
After all, except for music,	what did they have in common? [KOHL_R]
Theme	Rheme

Fig. 3-9   Marked Theme in interrogative clauses

(3) **Theme in imperative clauses.** The basic message of an imperative clause is either 'I want you to do something' or 'I want us (you and me) to do something'. The second type usually begins with *let's*, as in *let's go home now*; here *let's* is clearly the unmarked choice of Theme. But with the first type, although the 'you' can be made explicit as a Theme (e.g. *you keep quiet!*, meaning 'as for you, ... '), this is clearly a marked choice; the more typical form is simply *keep quiet*, with the verb in thematic position. The function of the verb, in the mood structure (clause as exchange), is that of **Predicator**; here, therefore, it is the Predicator that is the unmarked Theme.

In negative imperatives, such as *don't argue with me*, *don't let's quarrel about it*, the principle is the same as with yes/no interrogatives: the unmarked Theme is *don't* plus the following element, either Subject or Predicator. Again there is a marked form with *you*, e.g. *don't you argue with me*, where the Theme is *don't you*. There is also a marked contrastive form of the positive, such as *do take care*, where the Theme is *do* plus the Predicator *take*. See the examples in Figure 3-10.

The imperative is the only type of clause in which the Predicator (the verb) is regularly found as Theme. This is not impossible in other moods, where the verb may be put in first position precisely to give it thematic status, e.g. *forget* in *forget it I never shall*; but in such clauses it is the most highly marked choice of all.

Imperative clauses may have a marked Theme, as when a locative Adjunct in thematic in a clause giving directions:

From this crossroads town # follow the main road south through increasingly arid landscapes towards Rembitan, a pretty little village claiming a 17th-century mosque, then Sade. [Text 142]

turn	it down.
just place	a blank CD in the drive,
and click	the Burn CD icon.
try	to prevent any teacher being singled out as inadequate.
you	take the office
well Jane think	of smoked salmon.
don't do	that
no don't worry	
let's	do lunch at the Ivy.
let's	all think about that for a moment.
don't let's	quarrel about it
let me	send Lesley a photocopy.
Theme	Rheme

Fig. 3-10   Theme in imperative clauses

The Adjunct part of a phrasal verb (see Chapter 6, Section 6.3.5) may serve as marked Theme in an imperative clause with an explicit Subject, as in *Up you get!*, *Off you go – go and bond!*. Thus the question which element of the clause is typically chosen as Theme depends on the choice of mood.[9] The pattern can be summarized as shown in Table 3-2.

Table 3-2 MOOD TYPE and unmarked Theme selection

MOOD of clause	Typical ('unmarked') Theme
declarative	nominal group functioning as Subject
interrogative: yes/no	first word (finite operator) of verbal group plus nominal group functioning as Subject
interrogative: wh-	nominal group, adverbial group or prepositional phrase functioning as interrogative (Wh-) element
imperative: 'you'	verbal group functioning as Predicator, plus preceding *don't* if negative
imperative: 'you and me'	*let's* plus preceding *don't* if negative
exclamative	nominal group or adverbial group functioning as exclamative (Wh-) element

[9]   This orientation of theme towards mood is a principle of metafunctional unification in English, and in a number of other languages as well; but there is considerable variation across the languages of the world (see Matthiessen, 2004b: Section 10.5). For example, Japanese is very different (see Teruya, 2004, 2007): while the beginning of the clause is thematically significant, it is the end of the clause that indicates the nature of the clause as exchange. In many languages, Wh- elements are associated with the focus of New information rather than with Theme; and in yet other languages it is not given a special textual status at all.

When some other element comes first, it constitutes a 'marked' choice of Theme; such marked Themes usually either express some kind of setting for the clause or carry a feature of contrast. Note that in such instances the element that would have been the unmarked choice as Theme is now part of the Rheme.

The following passage from Dickens' *David Copperfield* shows a typical context for the choice of marked Themes in declarative clauses (see Figure 3-11):

Text 3-5: Recreating – narrative (written, monologic)

'We came,' repeated Mrs Micawber, 'and saw the Medway. My opinion of the coal trade on that river is, that it may require talent, but that it certainly requires capital. Talent, Mr Micawber has; capital, Mr Micawber has not... We are at present waiting for a remittance from London, to discharge our pecuniary obligations at this hotel. Until the arrival of that remittance, ... I am cut off from my home ..., from my boy and girl, and from my twins.'

talent	Mr Micawber has
capital	Mr Micawber has not
Theme/Complement: nominal group	Rheme

until the arrival of that remittance	I am cut off from my home
Theme/Adjunct: prepositional phrase	Rheme

Fig. 3-11 Examples of marked Theme in declarative clauses

At this point it may be useful if we introduce a system network showing the thematic potential of the English clause as far as we will be taking it in this book: see Figure 3-12.

3.4 Textual, interpersonal and topical Themes

In our brief sketch of the metafunctions, at the end of Chapter 2, we said that the clause, in its representational function, construes a quantum of human experience: some process – some change, or in the limiting case lack of change, in the external or our own internal environment. Processes are construed as a configuration of components of three types: (i) the process itself; (ii) the participants in that process; and (iii) any circumstantial factors such as time, manner or cause.

The guiding principle of thematic structure is this: the Theme contains one, and only one, of these experiential elements.[10] This means that the Theme of a clause ends with the first constituent that is either participant, circumstance or process. We refer to this constituent, in its textual function, as the **topical Theme**.

---

[10] Although they are rare, we may find more than one circumstantial Adjunct as marked topical Theme (see Halliday, 1967/8/2005: 80; Matthiessen, 1992: 51).

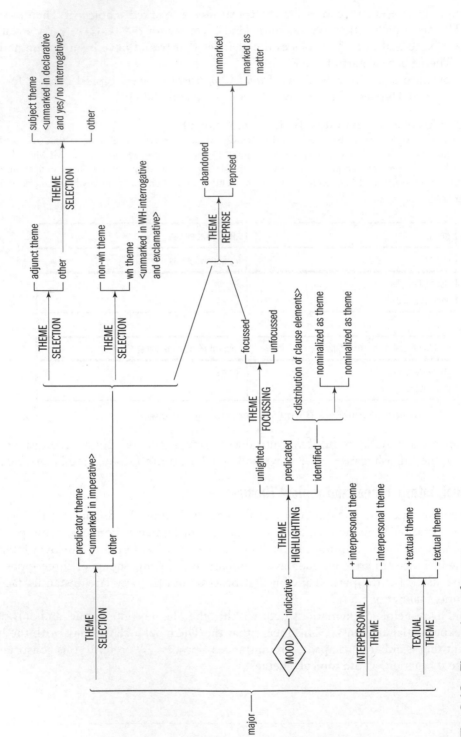

Fig. 3-12 The system of THEME

There may however be other elements in the clause preceding the topical Theme. These are elements that are either textual or interpersonal in function, playing no part in the experiential meaning of the clause. They can be summarized as shown in Table 3-3.

Table 3-3 Textual and interpersonal Themes

textual:	continuative
	conjunction ['structural Theme']
	conjunctive Adjunct
interpersonal:	modal/comment Adjunct ['modal Theme']
	vocative
	finite verbal operator [in yes/no interrogative]

They are listed in Table 3-3 in the order in which combinations typically occur. Most of the time we find only one or two such elements in any one clause, although we could construct an example to illustrate a **multiple Theme** containing each of these six types of non-topical element in thematic position:

well	but	then	surely	Jean	wouldn't	the best idea	be to join in
cont	stru	conj	modal	voc	finite	topical	
Theme							Rheme

Let us flesh out these categories, so that we can explain why such 'multiple Themes' occur.[11]

1 [textual] **continuative**. A continuative is one of a small set of words that signal a move in the discourse: a response, in dialogue, or a new move to the next point if the same speaker is continuing. The usual continuatives are *yes no well oh now*. See Halliday & Hasan (1976: Chapter 5).

2 [textual] **conjunction**. A conjunction is a word or group that either links (paratactic) or binds (hypotactic) the clause in which it occurs structurally to another clause. Semantically, it sets up a relationship of **expansion** or **projection**; see Chapter 7. Among the commonest are:

---

[11] This is an area of the grammar of theme where languages vary considerably. For example, Tagalog makes a sharp distinction between textual and interpersonal Themes on the one hand and experiential (topical) ones on the other: the former are indicated positionally, being placed at the beginning of the clause, whereas the latter are marked segmentally (by *ang*) and appear at the end of the clause in the unmarked case (see Martin, 2004). Japanese makes a similar distinction, although, like textual and interpersonal Themes, experiential ones tend to come early in the clause (Teruya, 2004, 2007). Germanic languages other than Modern English have much lower tolerance for multiple Theme (see Steiner & Teich, 2004, on German, and Andersen, Helm Petersen & Smedegaard, 2001, on Danish): apart from a structural conjunction, only one textual, interpersonal or experiential element appears as Theme and is followed by the Finite (thus overriding the principle of Subject before Finite in a declarative clause). In respect of its potential for multiple Themes, English is similar to Romance languages (see e.g. Caffarel, 2000, 2004, 2006, on French; Lavid, Arús & Zamorano-Mansilla, 2009, on Spanish).

(paratactic) *and or nor either neither but yet so then for*

(hypotactic) *when while before after until because if although unless since that whether to by with despite as even if in case supposing (that) assuming (that) given that provided (that) so that to as to in order to in the event that in spite of the fact that*

3   [textual] **conjunctive Adjunct** ('discourse Adjunct'). These are adverbial groups or prepositional phrases that relate the clause to the preceding text (see Table 3-4): they cover roughly the same semantic space as conjunctions. See Chapter 9, Section 9.3.

4   [interpersonal] **Vocative**. This is any item, typically (but not necessarily) a personal name, being used to address. See Chapter 4, Section 4.3.4.

5   [interpersonal] **Modal/comment Adjunct**. These express the speaker/writer's judgment on or attitude to the content of the message (see Table 3-5). See Chapter 4 (cf. also Chapter 10, Section 10.2.2).

6   [interpersonal] **Finite verbal operator**. These are the small set of finite auxiliary verbs construing primary tense or modality; they are the unmarked Theme of yes/no interrogatives. See Chapter 4, Table 4-4 and Chapter 6, Section 6.3.1.

(primary tense) *am is are was were do does did have has had shall will*

(modality) *can could may might shall should will would must ought*

need dare

— including their negatives *aren't, can't,* etc.

Table 3-4 Conjunctive adjuncts

	Type	Meaning	Examples
I	appositive	'i.e., e.g.'	that is, in other words, for instance
	corrective	'rather'	or rather, at least, to be precise
	dismissive	'in any case'	in any case, anyway, leaving that aside
	summative	'in short'	briefly, to sum up, in conclusion
	verificative	'actually'	actually, in fact, as a matter of fact
II	additive	'and'	also, moreover, in addition, besides
	adversative	'but'	on the other hand, however, conversely
	variative	'instead'	instead, alternatively
III	temporal	'then'	meanwhile, before that, later on, next, soon, finally
	comparative	'likewise'	likewise, in the same way
	causal	'so'	therefore, for this reason, as a result, with this in mind
	conditional	'(if ...) then'	in that case, under the circumstances, otherwise
	concessive	'yet'	nevertheless, despite that
	respective	'as to that'	in this respect, as far as that's concerned

Table 3-5 Modal Adjuncts

	Type	Meaning	Examples
I	probability	how likely?	probably, possibly, certainly, perhaps, maybe
	usuality	how often?	usually, sometimes, always, (n)ever, often, seldom
	typicality	how typical?	occasionally, generally, regularly, for the most part
	obviousness	how obvious?	of course, surely, obviously, clearly
II	opinion	I think	in my opinion, personally, to my mind
	admission	I admit	frankly, to be honest, to tell you the truth
	persuasion	I assure you	honestly, really, believe me, seriously
	entreaty	I request you	please, kindly
	presumption	I presume	evidently, apparently, no doubt, presumably
	desirability	how desirable?	(un)fortunately, to my delight/distress, regrettably, hopefully
	reservation	how reliable?	at first, tentatively, provisionally, looking back on it
	validation	how valid?	broadly speaking, in general, on the whole, strictly speaking, in principle
	evaluation	how sensible?	(un)wisely, understandably, mistakenly, foolishly
	prediction	how expected?	to my surprise, surprisingly, as expected, by chance

Of these six categories, the first two, continuatives and conjunctions, are **inherently thematic**: if they are present in the clause at all, they come at the beginning. The remainder are what we might call **characteristically thematic**: they are very frequently found in a thematic position (i.e. before the topical Theme), but they also occur in other locations in the clause.

Why do these items favour thematic position in the clause – or, to put the question more meaningfully, why are they associated with thematic function, either characteristically or, in some cases, inherently? In the most general sense, they are all natural Themes: if the speaker, or writer, is making explicit the way the clause relates to the surrounding discourse (textual), or projecting his/her own angle on the value of what the clause is saying (interpersonal), it is natural to set up such expressions as the point of departure. The message begins with 'let me tell you how this fits in', and/or 'let me tell you what I think about this'.

Those that are inherently thematic are the (textual) continuatives and conjunctions. As the language evolved, they have, as it were, migrated to the front of the clause and stayed there. Essentially they constitute a setting for the clause (continuative), or else they locate it in a specific logical-semantic relationship to another clause in the neighbourhood (conjunction). In either case, their thematic status comes as part of a package, along with their particular discursive force.

109

By the same token, however, since these items are thematic by default, when one of them is present it does not take up the full thematic potential of the clause in which it occurs. What follows it will also have thematic status, almost if not quite as prominently as when nothing else precedes. We can demonstrate this by reference to the concept of 'marked (topical) Theme', as described in Section 3.3. On the one hand, after a continuative or a conjunction it is still possible to introduce a marked type of topical Theme, either in contrast or as a setting; for example (from Charles Darwin, *The origin of species*):

> When in any country several domestic breeds have once been established ...

Note that the only reason for choosing this marked order of elements is to make *in any country* thematic. On the other hand, such marked Themes appear to be slightly less frequent when there is some inherently thematic item in the clause, suggesting that some of the 'quantum of thematicity' has already been taken up.

The items that are characteristically thematic are the (textual) conjunctive Adjuncts, and the (interpersonal) vocatives, modal and comment Adjuncts, and (in yes/no interrogative) finite verbal operators.

The conjunctive Adjuncts (often called 'discourse Adjuncts'), as noted above, cover roughly the same semantic space as the conjunctions; but whereas conjunctions set up a grammatical (systemic-structural) relationship with another clause, which may be either preceding or following, the relationship established by conjunctive Adjuncts, while semantically cohesive, is not a structural one (hence they can relate only to what has gone before). These Adjuncts often are thematic; but they do not have to be. We may have either *therefore the scheme was abandoned*, with *therefore* as textual Theme, or *the scheme was therefore abandoned*, with *therefore* falling within the Rheme. Note how the Theme + Rheme analysis enables us to explain the difference in meaning between pairs of agnate clauses such as these.

The same principle extends to the interpersonal elements. If there is a Vocative in the clause, or a modal or comment Adjunct, it is quite likely to be thematic: these items are characteristic of dialogue, in which the speaker may be calling the attention of the listener, or else expressing his or her own angle on the matter in hand, whether probable, desirable and so on, and hence they tend to be brought in as key signature to the particular move in the exchange – in other words, as Theme of the clause. For example (Theme indicated by underlining),

> <u>Maybe we</u> could develop our listening skills. [UTS/Macquarie Corpus]

> <u>Kate, I must say this fish</u> is cooked beautifully. [Text 82]

> <u>YOUR MAJESTIES, YOUR ROYAL HIGHNESSES, DISTINGUISHED GUESTS, COMRADES AND FRIENDS, today</u> all of us do, by our presence here, and by our celebrations in other parts of our country and the world, confer glory and hope to newborn liberty. [Mandela's Inaugural]

> King: <u>Senator Rudman,</u> what does it say to you?

> Rudman: <u>Well, Larry, unfortunately,</u> << as you know – we discussed it the other night – >> <u>the reason our commission came to the conclusion that terrorism was the No. 1 threat – we talked about chemical, biological and nuclear – and the reason we came to that conclusion</u> is we had information, intelligence and other, over the last 3 1/2 years that indicated to us that efforts were under way to manufacture a number of

instrumentalities that could be delivered to this country to cause mass destruction, which is what this is doing, as opposed to mass destruction, which is what would happen with certain types of chemical and certainly nuclear weapons. [KING_Interviews]

Well look, honestly, Mrs Finney, my suggestion to you would be that if you want to read English honours you should spend a year in solid preparation for it and then reapply. [Text 135]

Again, the difference in meaning stands out if one transfers either or both of these items to a location within the Rheme:

It's alright **Kate**. [Text 82]

Well you are proposing taking on quite something, **Mrs Finney**, aren't you? [Text 135]

Well, usually means mostly, doesn't it, **Mary**? [Text 76]

How about the test referred to earlier: when any of these characteristically thematic items is present in the Theme, may it still be followed by a marked topical Theme? The answer is clearly yes (as illustrated by the example above from Mandela's Inaugural, with Vocative followed by Time: *your majesties ... today*), but rather more seldom. It seems as if the presence of one of these elements, since it does involve a choice on the part of the speaker, uses up rather more of the thematic energy of the clause – but still not all of it. The fact that we do find clauses such as *unfortunately protein you can't store*, with marked topical Theme in such an environment, shows that the experiential element following the interpersonal Adjunct still carries thematic status – otherwise there would be no sense in fronting it. This, in turn, means that an ordinary unmarked Theme under the same conditions is just that – an unmarked topical Theme. We could set up a paradigm as follows, showing the effect of different initial selections in the clause: (1) no non-topical Theme, (2) with inherently thematic non-topical Theme, (3) with characteristically thematic non-topical theme; it will be seen that the marked topical Theme becomes, as it were, more and more marked at each step.

	topical Theme unmarked	topical Theme marked
(1)	you + can't store protein	protein + you can't store
(2)	but you + can't store protein	but protein + you can't store
(3)	however you + can't store protein	however protein + you can't store

What we learn from studying this kind of variation in the order of clause elements in spoken and written discourse could be summed up as follows. (i) Initial position in the English clause is meaningful in the construction of the clause as a message; specifically, it has a thematic function. (ii) Certain textual elements that orient the clause within the discourse, rhetorically and logically, are inherently thematic. (iii) Certain other elements, textual and interpersonal, that set up a semantic relation with what precedes, or express the speaker's angle or intended listener, are characteristically thematic; this includes finite operators, which signal one type of question. (iv) These inherently and characteristically thematic elements lie outside the experiential structure of the clause; they have no status as participant, circumstance or process. (v) Until one of these latter appears, the clause

111

lacks an anchorage in the realm of experience; and this is what completes the thematic grounding of the message. We can now approximate more closely to the identification of the Theme: the Theme of a clause extends from the beginning up to, and including, the first element that has an experiential function – that is either participant, circumstance or process. Everything after that constitutes the Rheme.

There is one further category that is 'characteristically thematic', namely the WH- items. We have already mentioned WH- interrogatives: these function as the unmarked Theme of a WH- interrogative clause. We can now see that these items have in fact a two-fold thematic value: they are at the same time both interpersonal and topical – interpersonal because they construe the mood, topical because they represent participant or circumstance. Note that it is the group or phrase in which the WH- interrogative word occurs that has this status, not the interrogative word by itself. For example, see Figure 3-13.

to what extent		is *The Snow Leopard* a shaped creation?
interpersonal	topical	
Theme		Rheme

Fig. 3-13   Wh- element (interrogative) as Theme

WH- items also function as **relatives**, marking a 'relative clause' – one that is structurally related to another by hypotaxis or embedding; see Chapter 7, Sections 7.4.1.2 and Section 7.4.5 on. Like WH- interrogatives, WH- relatives are also characteristically thematic – the group or phrase in which they occur is the unmarked Theme of a relative clause; and likewise they combine topical with a non-topical function, in this case textual.[12] For example, see Figure 3-14.

(the book is faithful to the time)	in which		it took place
	textual	topical	
	Theme		Rheme

Fig. 3-14   Wh- element (relative) as Theme (Text 7)

---

[12] The textual Theme of a relative element is inherently thematic; in this respect, it is like other structural Themes – binders and linkers. Consequently, the topical Theme part is also inherently thematic; but since it is inherent, it seems that it leaves some potential for other experiential elements to follow the Wh- element, preceding the Finite, as in: ||| *Palos Verdes Estates is a residential community of fine homes on large lots,* || *which until the 1950s was restricted to Spanish-style architecture of white stucco with red tile roofs* ||| [Text 140]. Here the Wh- element is followed by the circumstance of Time *until the 1950s*, preceding the Finite element *was*. There is clearly a variant with the temporal circumstance within the Rheme (showing that *until the 1950s* is not part of a nominal group complex with *which*): *which was restricted to Spanish-style architecture of white stucco with red tile roofs until the 1950s*. Similarly: *It is also the founding principle of the Freedom Charter [[we adopted as policy in 1955]], || which in its very first lines, places before South Africa an inclusive basis for citizenship* [Text 181]; *and yet, the outcome was [[[he'd committed himself to flying to Trinidad || to renew a friendship with a man [[[who in his youth had been his closest friend || but who now was no more than a stranger]]]]]]* [ACE_L].

WH- relatives are either definite or indefinite; see Table 3-6.

Table 3-6 Relatives

Type	Examples
definite	which, who, that, whose, when, where (why, how)
indefinite	whatever, whichever, whoever, whosoever, whenever, wherever, however

Thus all WH- groups and phrases have this dual function: on the one hand, as an element in the experiential structure; on the other hand, as marker of some special status of the clause, interrogative (mood) or relative (dependence). These two values, interrogative and relative, are themselves related at a deeper level, through the general sense of 'identity to be retrieved from elsewhere'; the 'indefinite' ones illustrate a kind of transition between the two:

Where are you going?	('I don't know; tell me')	[interrogative: definite]
Wherever are you going?	('I can't imagine!')	[interrogative: indefinite]
Wherever you're going, ...	('it doesn't matter')	[relative: indefinite]
The town where you're going ...	('it's a certain town')	[relative: definite]

The category of WH- element opens up this semantic space, of an identity that is being established by interrogation, perhaps with an element of challenge or disbelief; or put aside as irrelevant; or established relative to some other entity. The WH- element in turn is part of a wider set embracing both WH- and TH- forms, which taken together fulfil a deictic or 'pointing out' function, as set out in Table 3-7 TH-items and WH-items – see Table 3-7.

Table 3-7 TH-items and WH-items

	TH- items	WH- items
nominal	the this that	which what who whose
adverbial	there then thus	where when how/why
	[thence thither]	[whence whither]
	there- fore/b, etc.	where- fore/by, etc.

Examples (nominal) are shown in Table 3-8.

Table 3-8 Examples of nominal TH-items and WH-items

	Meaning	Deictic type	Example
(1)	I'm telling you which	TH-	I saw the one, this/that (one)
(2)	I'm not telling you which:	WH-	
(a)	I'm asking you (bounded)	int. def.	which/who/what did you see?
(b)	I'm asking you (unbounded)	int. indef.	Whichever, etc. did you see?
(c)	I'm not concerned	rel. indef.	Whichever, etc. you saw
(d)	I'm telling you about something else	rel. def.	the one which/who I saw

The 'defining relative clause' (d) is anomalous, in that, while it does not itself identify the thing or person seen, it uses the fact of my seeing for the purpose of identification. This is why there is an alternative form using a TH- item as relative: *the one that I saw* – and also a 'contact' type, which avoids choosing either, *the one I saw.*

The generalization we can make here is that all deictic elements are characteristically thematic; we shall see later that this same principle applies also at group rank, in the verbal and nominal group (Chapter 6). This in turn sheds light on the nature of the Theme as a grounding for the clause as message.

We suggested earlier that the Theme + Rheme structure is not so much a configuration of clearly bounded constituents as a movement running through the clause; this is one perspective which it is useful to keep in view (cf. Matthiessen, 1992). At the same time, there is one significant feature that does tend to create a clearly defined boundary between the two, given that the Theme is delineated as suggested here. This depends on another feature that we will explore in the next section, that of **information** as introduced in Chapter 1.

3.5 The information unit: Given + New

We referred in Chapter 1 to the concept of 'discourse flow', and introduced the textual component within the grammar as the resource for creating discourse – text that 'hangs together', with itself and with its context of situation.

These textual resources are of two kinds: (i) structural, (ii) cohesive. What this means is as follows. The grammar construes ***structural*** units up to the rank of the clause complex (which is what lies behind the sentence of written English); there it stops. But although the grammar stops here, the semantics does not: the basic semantic unit is the text (cf. Chapter 1, Section 1.4.2), which can be as long as a novel, an epic, or a treatise. So the grammar provides other, ***non-structural*** resources for managing the flow of discourse: for creating semantic links across sentences – or rather, semantic links that work equally well either within or across sentences. These latter are referred to collectively under the name of **cohesion** (see Halliday & Hasan, 1976, 1985) and will be dealt with in Chapter 9.

Below the clause complex, the grammar manages the discourse flow by structural means; and here there are two related systems at work. One is a system of the clause, viz. THEME; this we have been discussing throughout the present chapter so far. The THEME system construes

the clause in the guise of a message, made up of Theme + Rheme. The other is the system of INFORMATION. This is a system not of the clause, but of a separate grammatical unit, the **information unit** (cf. Halliday, 1967a, 1967/8; Halliday & Greaves, 2008: Section 5.1). The information unit is a unit that is parallel to the clause and the other units belonging to the same rank scale as the clause:

clause   information unit

group/ phrase

word

morpheme

Since it is parallel with the clause (and the units that the clause consists of), it is variable in extent in relation to the clause, and may extend over more than one clause or less than one clause; but in the unmarked case it is co-extensive with the clause (see further below).

In Chapter 1 we introduced the **tone group**, defining it as a unit of English phonology (Section 1.2.2); we then went on to say that the tone group functions grammatically as realization of a quantum of information in the discourse. It is this quantum of information that we have called the information unit. Spoken English unfolds as a sequence of information units, typically one following another in unbroken succession – there is no pause or other discontinuity between them.

Text 3-6 is a passage of transcribed speech showing some features of intonation: tone group boundary, marked by double slash //, foot boundary by single slash, silent beat by ^; beginning of tonic segment, shown by bold type.

Text 3-6: Enabling – instructing (spoken, dialogic): the 'Silver Text' showing tonality and tonicity
Manageress: // ^ in / **this** job / Anne we're // working with / **silver** // ^ now / silver / needs to have / **love** // {Anne: // yeah. //} you / **know** ^ the // people that / **buy** silver // **love** it //

Anne: // **yeah** // guess they / **would** //

Manageress: // **yeah** // mm / ^ well / **naturally** I / mean to / say that it's // got a / lovely / **gleam** a/bout it you / **know** // ^ and / if they come / **in** they're // usually / people who / love / beautiful / **things** // ^ so / you / have to be / beautiful / **with** it you / know // ^ and you / **sell** it with / beauty //

Anne: // **um** //

Manageress: // ^ you / ^ I'm / **sure** you know / how to do // **that** // ^ // oh but you / **must** // let's hear / ^ / let's hear / ^ / **look** / ^ you say // **madam** // isn't that / **beautiful** // ^ if / you sug/**gest** it's beautiful // they / **see** it as / beautiful //

An information unit does not correspond exactly to any other unit in the grammar. The nearest grammatical unit is in fact the clause; and we can regard this as the unmarked or default condition: other things being equal, one information unit will be co-extensive with one clause. But other things are often not equal, for reasons that will be brought out in the following sections. Thus a single clause may be mapped into two or more information units; or a single information unit into two or more clauses. Furthermore, the boundaries may overlap, with one information unit covering, say, one clause and half of the next.

So, the information unit has to be set up as a constituent in its own right. At the same time, its relationship to the clausal constituents is by no means random, and instances of overlapping boundaries are clearly 'marked'; so the two constituent structures, the clausal and the informational, are closely interconnected.

The information unit is what its name implies: a unit of information. Information, in this technical grammatical sense, is the tension between what is already known or predictable and what is new or unpredictable. This is different from the mathematical concept of information, which is the measure of unpredictability. It is the interplay of new and not new that generates information in the linguistic sense. Hence the information unit is a structure made up of two functions, the New and the Given.

In the idealized form each information unit consists of a Given element accompanied by a New element. But there are two conditions of departure from this principle. One is that discourse has to start somewhere, so there can be discourse-initiating units consisting of a New element only. The other is that by its nature the Given is likely to be **phoric** – referring to something already present in the verbal or non-verbal context; and one way of achieving phoricity is through ellipsis, a grammatical form in which certain features are not realized in the structure (see Chapter 9). Structurally, therefore, we shall say that an information unit consists of an obligatory New element plus an optional Given.

The way this structure is realized is essentially 'natural' (non-arbitrary), in two respects: (i) the New is marked by prominence; (ii) the Given typically precedes the New. We will look at these two features in turn.

(i) Each information unit is realized as a pitch contour, or **tone**, which may be falling, rising or mixed (falling-rising, rising-falling) (for the details of the tones see Chapter 4, Section 4.3). This pitch contour extends over the whole tone group. Within the tone group, one foot (and in particular its first syllable) carries the main pitch movement: the main fall, or rise, or the change of direction. This feature is known as **tonic prominence**, and the element having this prominence is the **tonic** element (tonic foot, tonic syllable). We indicate tonic prominence by a form of graphic prominence: bold type for print, wavy underlining for manuscript and typescript. The element having this prominence is said to be carrying **information focus**.

(ii) The tonic foot defines the culmination of what is New: it marks where the New element ends.[13] In the typical instance, this will be the last functional element of clause structure in the information unit. As this implies, the typical sequence of informational elements is thus Given followed by New. But whereas the end of the New element is marked by tonic prominence, there is nothing to mark where it begins; so there is indeterminacy in the structure. If we take an instance out of context, we can tell that it culminates with the New; but we cannot tell on phonological grounds whether there is a Given element first, or where the boundary between Given and New would be. (This is not always true; see below.)

---

[13] In some languages there may be special focus particles (as in Hindi), which may be derived from a theme predication construction (cf. Harris & Campbell, 1995).

For example, in Figure 3-15, we know that *on the burning deck* is New, because that is the element on which the prominence falls; but we cannot tell whether the New extends also to *stood* and *the boy*.

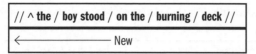

Fig. 3-15   Unit with New element only

In real life we do not usually meet with text out of context, so there is other evidence for interpreting the information structure. For example, the first two clauses of the silver text were: *In this job, Anne, we're working with silver. Now silver needs to have love.* The second clause was spoken as follows:

// ^ now / silver / needs to have / **love** //

Taken by itself, this also is undecidable: all we know is that at least *love* is New. But given the preceding clause, we know that *silver* was in fact Given; the New element starts at *needs* (see Fig. 3-16).

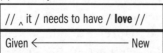

Fig. 3-16   Unit with Given and New elements

(It is not quite true to say that there are no phonological indices of the Given-New structure before the tonic prominence; this is one of the functions of variation in rhythm. Compare the two following versions in Figure 3-17:

(a) I'll tell you about silver. It needs to have love.

// ˄ it / needs to have / **love** //
Given ←——————— New

(b) I'll tell you what silver needs. It needs to have love.

// ˄ it needs to have /   **love** //
Given ——————→   New

Fig. 3-17   Rhythmic indications of information structure

In (a), *needs* is salient, which indicates that it is the beginning of the New; whereas in (b) it is part of the initial proclitic foot, reflecting the fact that in this instance it is Given, being mentioned in the preceding clause. But not all Given elements are characterized by this absence of salience.)

117

The unmarked position for the New is at the end of the information unit. But it is possible to have Given material following the New; and any accented matter that follows the tonic foot is thereby signalled as being Given. For example, see Figure 3-18:

You say 'Madam, isn't that beautiful?' If you suggest it's beautiful, they see it as beautiful.

//∧ if / you sug/**gest**	it's / beautiful		// they / **see**	it as / beautiful //
New	Given		New	Given

Fig. 3-18 Marked information structure

Here *suggest* and *see* are New; *you* and *they* are also New, not because they have not been mentioned before but because they are contrastive (in this case with each other). But 'it + be beautiful' is Given. The fact that the two occurrences of *beautiful* are both post-tonic makes explicit the fact that they refer back to the question *Isn't that beautiful?* in the preceding sentence. This is an instance of **marked information focus**.

We can now see more clearly what the terms Given and New actually mean. The significant variable is: information that is presented by the speaker as recoverable (Given) or not recoverable (New) to the listener. What is treated as recoverable may be so because it has been mentioned before; but that is not the only possibility. It may be something that is in the situation, like *I* and *you*; or in the air, so to speak; or something that is not around at all but that the speaker wants to present as Given for rhetorical purposes. The meaning is: this is not news. Likewise, what is treated as non-recoverable may be something that has not been mentioned; but it may be something unexpected, whether previously mentioned or not. The meaning is: attend to this; this is news. One form of 'newness' that is frequent in dialogue is contrastive emphasis such as that on *you* and *I* in the following:

// **you** can / go if you / like // **I'm** not / going //

There are a number of elements in language that are inherently 'given' in the sense that they are not interpretable except by reference to some previous mention or some feature of the situation: anaphoric elements (those that refer to things mentioned before) and deictic elements (those that are interpreted by reference to the 'here-&-now' of the discourse). Typically these items do not carry information focus; if they do, they are contrastive. So when we say that, for any information unit, the unmarked structure is that with the focus on the final element, this excludes any items that are inherently given. So, for example, in *How'd you go at that interview today?* the unmarked form, and the one actually used by the speaker, was

// how'd you / go at that / **interview** to/day /

with *today*, which is a deictic element, occurring as a post-tonic item.

Here is a little text (Text 3-7) from a five-year-old child showing clearly his mastery of the information structure:

Text 3-7: Sharing leading into expounding – explaining: the 'North Star' text

Child: Shall I tell you why the North Star stays still?

Parent: Yes, do.

Child: Because that's where the magnet is, and it gets attracted by the earth. But the other stars don't; so they move around.

// shall I / tell you / why the / North / Star / stays / **still** //

// **yes** // **do** //

// ^ because / **that's** // where the / **magnet** / is// ^ and it gets at/**tracted** by the // **earth** // ^ but the / **other** / stars // **don't** // ^ so / **they** // move a/**round** //

The child begins with an offer of information in which everything is fresh; the focus is in its unmarked place, at the end. The offer is accepted, and he continues with the explanation. The pattern is now as in Table 3-9:

Table 3-9 Given and New elements in the North Star text

	Given	New	
1	because	that's	contrastive
2	where	the magnet	fresh
3	and it	gets attracted	"
4		by the earth	"
5	but	the other	contrastive
6	stars	don't	"
7	so	they	"
8		move around	fresh

(Note in relation to the discussion in Chapter 9, that all the Given items, and also the New items that are contrastive, are also cohesive in the discourse.) In the explanation, each of the four clauses is structured into two information units; the focus is (i) on items containing new (fresh) information (*the magnet, gets attracted, by the earth*); and (ii) on contrastive items (*that* (= the North Star), *the other* (stars, i.e., not the North Star), *don't* (get attracted), *they* (again by contrast to the North Star) *move around* (move around also contrasts with stays still). Note in connection with Section 4.3 that all fresh items are tone 1 and all contrastive items tone 4. The Given items are the anaphoric reference item *it*; the word *stars* (post-tonic following *other*), and the conjunctives *because ... and ... but ... so* (harking back to *why* in the first turn.)

3.6 Given + New and Theme + Rheme

There is a close semantic relationship between the system of INFORMATION and the system of THEME – between information structure and thematic structure. This is reflected in the unmarked relationship between the two. Other things being equal, one information unit is co-extensive with one (ranking) clause ('unmarked tonality'); and, in that case, the ordering of Given ^ New ('unmarked tonicity') means that the Theme falls within the Given, while the New falls within the Rheme.

But although they are related, Given + New and Theme + Rheme are not the same thing. The Theme is what I, the speaker, choose to take as my point of departure. The Given is what you, the listener, already know about or have accessible to you. Theme + Rheme is speaker-oriented, while Given + New is listener-oriented.

But both are, of course, speaker-selected. It is the speaker who assigns both structures, mapping one on to the other to give a composite texture to the discourse and thereby relate it to its environment. At any point of the discourse process, there will have been built up a rich verbal and non-verbal environment for whatever is to follow; the speaker's choices are made against the background of what has been said and what has happened before. The environment will often create local conditions that override the globally unmarked pattern of Theme within Given, New within Rheme.

Within any given scenario, or set of contextual conditions, the speaker can exploit the potential that the situation defines, using thematic and information structure to produce an astonishing variety of rhetorical effects. He can play with the system, so to speak. A very frequent type of linguistic game-playing is the use of these two systems to achieve complex manoeuvres of putting the other down, making him feel guilty and the like. Since these strategies usually have a lengthy history of interaction behind them, it is hard to exemplify in a short space; but Text 3.8 is a little conversation overheard on a commuter train:

Text 3.8: Sharing – casual conversation (spoken, dialogic)
Are you coming back into circulation?

— I didn't know I was out.

— I haven't seen you for ages.

// ^ are / you coming / **back** into / circu/lation //

// ^ I / didn't / know I was / **out** //

// ^ I / haven't / **seen** you for / ages //

Figure 3-19 gives the analysis in thematic and informational terms.

are	you	coming	**back**	into circulation
interpersonal	topical			
Theme		Rheme		

←————————————————————————— New   Given

Fig. 3-19   Theme and information (1)

Speaker 1 initiates the dialogue: (i) Theme *are you* 'I want to know something about you; give an account of yourself – yes or no?'; (ii) *into circulation* treated as Given, 'that's the

norm', with the New made up of contrastive *back* 'but you've been away' plus fresh *are you coming* 'so I need an explanation' – see Figure 3-20.

I	didn't	know	I	was	**out**	
Theme	Rheme					'in my opinion +
Theme			Rheme			I wasn't out'
Given ←					New	

Fig. 3-20   Theme and information (2)

Speaker 2 recognizes the attack and defends himself with mild irony: (i) Theme 'from my angle', with *I didn't know* as interpersonal metaphor for 'in my estimation' plus negative (see Chapter 10 below); (ii) Information: New = contrastive *out* (contrasting with *back*) and extending back over everything except perhaps the initial *I*; 'as I see it, I was not away, so you are wrong' – see Figure 3-21.

I	haven't	**seen**	you	for ages
Theme	Rheme			
←		New	Given	

Fig. 3-21   Theme and information (3)

Speaker 1 returns to the attack in a vein which a fiction writer might label 'accusingly': (i) Theme *I*, i.e. 'I stick to my perspective (the only one that counts)'; (ii) Information: New = contrastive *seen* (and hence the clause element *haven't seen*) 'so you were out of circulation'; *for ages* treated as Given by reference back to *into circulation* with implication of regularity over a long period. The overall message is: 'you weren't where I was, to be kept tabs on; so it's your fault'. It is not hard to make a character sketch of the two speakers on the basis of this little bit of dialogue. Note that because something is not phonologically prominent this does not mean it is not important to the message!

The intonation and rhythm shown here are as they were on the occasion observed. One can think of many variants in the textual semantics. Speaker 1, for example, might have put another focus on *I* in the last line:

// I haven't // **seen** you for / ages //

thus making his own self-centredness a little more explicit. It is a useful exercise to take a passage of spontaneous dialogue and vary the texture of Theme + Rheme and Given + New, noting the effect. One sees very clearly how this interplay of thematic and information structure carries the rhetorical gist of the clause. For a more detailed treatment of these features, see Halliday & Greaves (2008).

3.7 Predicated Themes

There is one further resource that figures prominently in the organization of the clause as a message. This is the system of THEME PREDICATION (see Halliday, 1967/8/2005: 99–103[14]), which involves a particular combination of thematic and informational choices. Here are some examples from spoken discourse:

> it was **Jane** that started it
>
> it wasn't **the job** that was getting me down
>
> is it **Sweden** that they come from?
>
> it was **eight years ago** that you gave up smoking

Any element having a representational function in the clause can be marked off by predication in this way. Let us go back to the duke, the aunt and the teapot – but perhaps with a slight variation: corresponding to *the queen sent my uncle that hat-stand* we could have:

> it was the queen who sent my uncle that hat-stand
>
> it was my uncle the queen sent that hat-stand
>
> it was that hat-stand the queen sent my uncle

This system resembles that of THEME IDENTIFICATION (see Section 3.2), in that it does identify one element as being exclusive at that point in the clause. Both are in fact equative constructions. But there are also differences between the two. Let us take one of the above examples and derive a paradigm from it, controlling for information focus:

> it wasn't **the job** that was getting me down
>
> [exclusive: job as Theme/New]
>
> **the job** wasn't getting me down
>
> [non-exclusive: job as Theme/(marked) New]
>
> **the job** wasn't what was getting me down
>
> [exclusive: job as Theme/(marked) New]
>
> what was getting me down wasn't **the job**
>
> [exclusive: job as Rheme/New]

The neutral variant of the clause lacks the 'equative' feature: none of the elements is identified as the unique filler of the role. The identifying and predicated forms share the equative feature; but they differ in the choice of Theme, and in the mapping of Theme + Rheme onto

---

[14] Theme predication is often discussed under the heading of 'cleft sentence' – a term going back to Jespersen (e.g. 1928: 37, 88–92; 1937: Section 25.4), or 'it-clefts' to distinguish them from 'wh- clefts' or 'pseudo-clefts' (theme identification).

Given + New. In the identifying type, *the job* is either non-thematic or, if thematic, then marked for informational status. In other words, the cost of choosing *the job* as Theme is that it becomes strongly foregrounded information – just as it is in the neutral form of the clause; the meaning is something like 'take special note: this is improbable, or contrary to expectation' (for a corpus-based investigation of the uses of theme predication, see Collins, 1991).

In the predicating type, on the other hand, *the job* retains its thematic status; but it also carries the focus of information without such additional foregrounding: the conflation of Theme with New is a regular feature. The sense is, of course, contrastive, because of the exclusive equation:

it wasn't **the job** that was getting me down 'it was something else'

— but there is no implication that the proposition is difficult to accept.

It is this mapping of New and Theme, in fact, that gives the predicated theme construction its special flavour. The difference may be felt from some other pairs of agnate clauses (see Text 3-9).

Text 3-9: Sharing – casual conversation (spoken, dialogic)

A: Craig was saying, when we were driving over here, about in Sweden, you know, when Nokia – is it Sweden that they come from?

B: Finland.

A: Finland or ... anyway one of those Scandinavian countries, ... the mobile is used for everything, like —

B: Opening the garage door and letting the kids in the house and ...

Contrast *is Sweden where/the place they come from?*

A: I was only 29 back then. I had the whole of my life ahead of me.

B: 29? That means it was eight years ago that you gave up smoking.

Contrast *eight years ago was when/the time you gave up smoking.*

A: It was on fire and that was the first day after it came back from getting fixed.

B: The horn was on fire was it?

C: It was the wire going into the horn that burnt out.

A: Was it?

Contrast *the wire going into the horn was what burnt out.*

The predicated Theme structure is frequently associated with an explicit formulation of contrast: *it was not ... , it was ... , who/which ...* ; for example (from the report of the *Sydney Morning Herald*'s London correspondent on the publication of *The Holy Blood and the Holy Grail*, 21 January 1982):

And, say the authors, it was Mary Magdalen, not Mary the Mother of Jesus, who has been the real, if secret, object of Mariolatry cults down the ages.

123

Here the Theme is *And ... (it was) Mary Magdalen, not Mary the Mother of Jesus, (who)*. In such cases, the contrast between the two Mary's clearly indicates that both should be read as New. But even without the contrast being made explicit, the unmarked focus still falls on the Theme; hence this structure is often used by writers to signal that this is the reading that is intended.

Since tonic prominence is not marked in writing, the predication has the additional function in written English of directing the reader to interpret the information structure in the intended way. Suppose we have the sequence:

†John's father wanted him to give up the violin. His teacher persuaded him to continue.

In the second sentence, the natural place for the tonic accent is *continue*, which makes the effective contrast that between giving up and continuing. If we replace this with

John's father wanted him to give up the violin. It was his teacher who persuaded him to continue.

the tonic accent now falls on *teacher*; the fact that John continued is taken as given, and the contrast is between his teacher's attitude and that of his father.

It may be helpful here to give the full thematic analysis: see Figure 3-22. Version (a) shows the local thematic structure; here both Themes are unmarked (*it* and *who* are both Subjects). Version (b) shows the thematic structure of the whole clause as predicated Theme. Note that here the Subject is *it ... who persuaded him to continue* (see Chapter 4, Section 4.7, especially Figure 4-29).

	It	was	his teacher	who	persuaded him to continue
(a)	Theme	Rheme		Theme	Rheme
(b)	Theme			Rheme	

Fig. 3-22 Thematic structure of clause with predicated Theme

A structure that can look superficially like Theme predication, but is not, is that involving postposition, where one nominal element of the clause – typically the Subject, though not always – is delayed to the end and the appropriate pronoun is inserted as a substitute in its original slot. This may be a nominal group, as in:

they don't make sense, these instructions

shall I hang it above the door, your Chinese painting?

in some places they've become quite tame, the wombats

Here the Theme is, as usual, the item(s) in first position: *they, shall + I, in some places*; while the postposed nominal functions as **Afterthought**, realized prosodically by a second, minor tonic with tone 3:

// 1 ^ they / don't make / **sense** these in// 3 **struc**tions //

Now, one common type of these clauses is that where the postposed Subject is an embedded 'fact' clause (see Chapter 5, Section 5.3, and Chapter 7, Section 7.5.7). Here the pronoun substitute is always *it*:

it helps a lot to be able to speak the language

I don't like it that you always look so tired

So if the postposed fact clause is introduced by *that*, and the matrix clause has the verb *be* plus a nominal, the result may look like a predicated Theme; for example:

it was a mistake that the school was closed down

it's your good luck that nobody noticed

But these are not predicated Themes; the postposed Subject is not a relative clause, and there is no agnate form with the predication removed, proportional to *it was his teacher who persuaded him to continue*: *his teacher persuaded him to continue*. The last example is in fact ambiguous, and could be used to illustrate the difference: *it's your good luck (that) nobody noticed*

(i) predicated Theme: agnate to

nobody noticed your good luck

(ii) postposed Subject: agnate to

the fact that nobody noticed was your good luck

(Cf. Chapter 4, Section 4.7.)

3.8 Theme in bound, minor and elliptical clauses

We have not explicitly considered Theme in clauses other than free ones, although by referring to conjunctions and relatives as structural Themes we have suggested that such clauses do display thematic structure.

There is thematic structure, in fact, in all major clause types: that is, all clauses expressing mood and transitivity, whether independent or not. But, as we have seen, there is a kind of scale of thematic freedom: whereas in a free declarative clause the speaker has a free choice of Theme – other things being equal he will map it on to the Subject, but this is merely the unmarked option – the further one moves away from this most open-ended form of the clause, the more the thematic options are restricted by structural pressures from other parts of the grammar, pressures that are themselves thematic in origin. In interrogatives and imperatives, and even more strongly in clauses that are not independent, the thematic principle has determined what it is that will be the Theme of the clause, leaving only a highly marked alternative option (as in interrogative) or else no alternative at all.

However, we have also seen that there is a compensatory principle at work whereby, if what comes first is 'fixed' (in the sense that its being first is an essential or at least typical characteristic), then what comes next may retain some thematic flavour. If the initial element is there as the expression not of thematic choice but of some other option

125

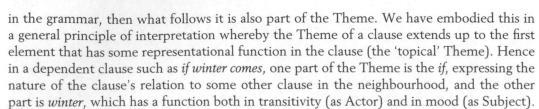

in the grammar, then what follows it is also part of the Theme. We have embodied this in a general principle of interpretation whereby the Theme of a clause extends up to the first element that has some representational function in the clause (the 'topical' Theme). Hence in a dependent clause such as *if winter comes*, one part of the Theme is the *if*, expressing the nature of the clause's relation to some other clause in the neighbourhood, and the other part is *winter*, which has a function both in transitivity (as Actor) and in mood (as Subject).

The significance of these patterns emerges when we come to consider the importance of clause theme in the overall development of a text. By itself the choice of Theme in each particular instance, clause by clause, may seem a fairly haphazard matter; but it is not. The choice of clause Themes plays a fundamental part in the way discourse is organized; it is this, in fact, that constitutes what has been called the 'method of development' of the text (see e.g. Fries, 1981, and contributions to Ghadessy, 1995; and to Hasan & Fries, 1995). In this process, the main contribution comes from the thematic structure of independent clauses. But other clauses also come into the picture, and need to be taken account of in Theme-Rheme analysis. This can be seen in the text that is analysed in Section 3.9.

We shall not treat other types of clause in very great detail, partly because their thematic structure is less variable and partly because in any case we could not do so without making frequent reference to later chapters, to the discussion that is still to come. Here, however, is a summary of the thematic organization of clauses other than those that are independent, major, and explicit.

(1) **Dependant Bound clauses** (Chapter 7). (i) If **finite**, these typically have a conjunction as structural Theme, e.g. *because*, *that*, *whether*, followed by a topical Theme; for example, see Figure 3-23.[15]

[I asked]	whether	pigs	have wings
[they knew]	that	in spring	the snow would melt
[he left]	because	his work	was done
	structural	topical	
	Theme		Rheme

Fig. 3-23 Theme in finite bound clauses (with conjunctions)

If the bound clause begins with a WH- element, on the other hand, that element constitutes the topical Theme, e.g. see Figure 3-24.

---

[15] With bound intensive relational clauses that are concessive, there is a special thematic option with the topical Theme coming before the binder *though*, e.g. *Achyut Abhyankar << talented though he is >>, should be more restrained in his vocal 'sangat'* [KOHL_C]; *Vicious though she looked || the Contessa was no exception* [LOB_N]. The clause culminates with the Process, which is thus likely to be the Focus of New information. Contrast: *though she looked **vicious*** and *vicious though she **looked**.*

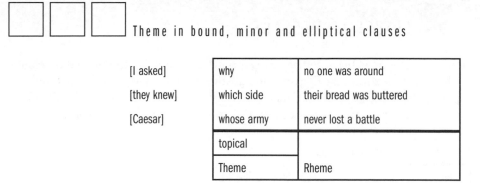

[I asked]	why	no one was around
[they knew]	which side	their bread was buttered
[Caesar]	whose army	never lost a battle
	topical	
	Theme	Rheme

Fig. 3-24 Theme in finite bound clauses (with WH- elements)

The reason for this, as we have seen, is that the WH- element also has a function in the transitivity structure of the clause.

(ii) If **non-finite**, there may be a conjunction or preposition as structural Theme, which may be followed by a Subject as topical Theme; but many non-finite clauses have neither, in which case they consist of Rheme only. See Figure 3-25.

with	all the doors	being locked	[we had no way in]
for	that printer	to work off your machine	[you need a cable]
while		not blaming them	[I'm still disappointed]
		to avoid delay	[have your money ready]
structural	topical		
Theme		Rheme	

Fig. 3-25 Theme in non-finite dependent clauses

(2) **Embedded clauses** (Chapters 6 and 7). These are clauses that function inside the structure of a nominal group, as **defining relative** clauses, e.g. *who came to dinner, the dam broke, requiring travel permits* in *the man who came to dinner, the day the dam broke, all personnel requiring travel permits*. The thematic structure of such clauses is the same as that of dependent clauses. However, because of their down-ranking, the fact that they do not function as constituents of a sentence, their thematic contribution to the discourse is minimal, and for practical purposes can be ignored.

(3) **Minor clauses** (Chapter 4, Section 4.6.2). These are clauses with no mood or transitivity structure, typically functioning as calls, greetings, exclamations and alarms, like *Mary!, Good night!, Well done!* They have no thematic structure either. (In this they resemble an important class of items such as titles and labels – not regarded as clauses because they have no independent speech function.)

(4) **Elliptical clauses** (Chapter 4, Section 4.6.1). (i) **Anaphoric ellipsis**. Here some part of the clause is presupposed from what has gone before – for example, in response to a question. The resulting forms are very varied. Some are indistinguishable from minor clauses, e.g. *Yes. No. All right. Of course.*; these have

127

no thematic structure, because they presuppose the whole of the preceding clause (see Chapter 9, Section 9.5: Ellipsis and substitution). Others, which presuppose only part of the preceding clause, have their own thematic structure; the details will depend on which part is presupposed. Figure 3-26 gives some examples.

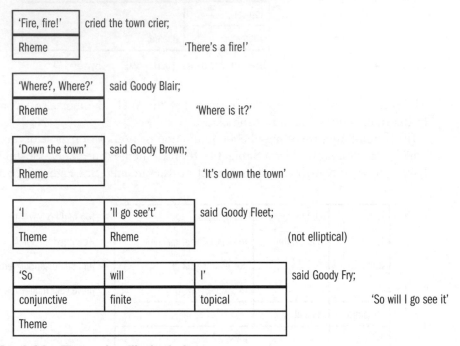

Fig. 3-26   Theme in elliptical clauses

(ii) **Exophoric ellipsis.** In this type of ellipsis the clause is not presupposing anything from what has gone before, but simply taking advantage of the rhetorical structure of the situation, specifically the roles of speaker and listener (Chapter 4, Section 4.6). Hence the Subject, and often also the finite verb, is 'understood' from the context; e.g. *Thirsty?* ('are you thirsty?'), *No idea.* ('I've no idea'), *A song!* ('let's have a song!'), *Feeling better?* ('are you feeling better?'). Such clauses have, in fact, a thematic structure; but it consists of Rheme only. The Theme is (part of) what is omitted in the ellipsis.

For the meaning of the terms 'anaphoric' and 'exophoric', see further in Chapter 9.

3.9 Thematic interpretation of a text

The following extract illustrates theme selections in biographical text. The analysis is presented in tabular form, to make it easy to scan it and detect patterns in the text. The structural analysis is marked by various typographic conventions in the running text; the systemic analysis is set out to the right of the text. The systemic value of 'unmarked' and 'marked' theme depends on the mood selection, as shown in the system network in Figure 3-12 above.

	TEXTUAL THEME	INTERPERSONAL THEME	THEME SELECTION
Apart from a need to create his own identity <<having been well and truly trained and educated and, indeed, used by his father for so long, emotionally and practically>> **Robert** felt	–	–	marked
that at twenty the last thing ⟦he wanted to do⟧ was ⟦to join a family firm up in Newcastle, in however important a position⟧.	+	–	marked
He must have felt	–	–	unmarked
that he was being forced into a corner.	+	–	unmarked
This was it, for ever, a lifetime's occupation.	–	–	unmarked
And he'd better be duly grateful for ⟦what his father and his father's friends were doing for him⟧.	+	–	unmarked
⟦*what* his father and his father's friends were doing for him⟧	+	–	unmarked
For all his integrity and high principles, **Robert** pulled a slightly fast one over his father and business partners.	–	–	**marked**
He did eventually get permission, <<however reluctantly it was given,>> from his father and partner to have leave of absence from the Newcastle locomotive works,	–	–	unmarked
<<however reluctantly it was given,>>	–	–	unmarked
telling them	–	–	unmarked
that he'd designed a contract for only one year.	+	–	unmarked
It was only after his departure that they discovered			**marked & predicated**
that in fact he'd signed on for three years.	+	–	unmarked
It was **no doubt** fear ⟦that he'd never get away, rather than deceit⟧, which made him mislead them.	–	+	unmarked & **predicated**
A slight feeling of fear of his father, mixed with awe, comes through many of his letters.	–	–	unmarked
George finally realized	–	–	unmarked
that his son wanted to go off	+	–	unmarked
and stretch his wings in a new country	+	–	unmarked
and there was nothing more ⟦he could do about it⟧, no further inducements ⟦he could offer⟧.	+	–	unmarked
As it was only for a year,	+	–	unmarked

	TEXTUAL THEME	INTERPERSONAL THEME	THEME SELECTION
so he thought,	+	–	unmarked
he might as well make the best of it,	–	–	unmarked
though it couldn't have come at a worse time,	+	–	unmarked
with the Darlington and Liverpool lines now both under way	+	–	unmarked
and though he had personally been very hurt and saddened by his son's decision.	+	–	unmarked
In a letter ⟦written to Longridge⟧ on 7 June, eleven days before Robert's departure, **George** sounds distinctly miserable, even bitter, <<though trying hard to hide it,>> at the prospect ⟦of travelling to Liverpool in time to see Robert off⟧	–	–	**marked**
'I am a little more cheerful to night	–	–	unmarked
as I have quite come to a conclusion	+	–	unmarked
that there is nothing for me but hard work in this world	+	–	unmarked
therefore I may as well be cheerful as not'	+	–	unmarked
After he arrived in Liverpool	+	–	unmarked
and met up with Robert	–	–	unmarked
to bid him farewell,	–	–	unmarked
George wrote to Longridge, this time on 15 June,	–	–	unmarked
saying	–	–	unmarked
what a pleasure it had been ⟦to see Robert again⟧.	–	+	unmarked
He describes the smart dinner parties ⟦that he and Robert have been to together⟧.	–	–	unmarked

From: Davies, 1980, pp.112–13

Notational conventions:

<u>Single underlining</u>	Theme
plain	topical Theme
bold	interpersonal Theme
italic	textual Theme

Bold without underlining	Displaced Theme[16]
<< >>	included clause boundary
〚 〛	downranked clause boundary

Summary of thematic analysis

Paragraph 1 (*he* = Robert)

paragraph Theme (from clause 1)	his need to create identity
Displaced Theme	Robert
clause Themes:	
bound clause	[feeling] that + at twenty
free clause	he
bound clause	[feeling] that + he
free clause	this [prospect]
free clause	and + he

Paragraph 2 (*he* = Robert)

paragraph Theme (from clause 1)	despite his integrity and high principles
Displaced Theme	Robert
clause Themes:	
free clause	he
bound clause	however reluctantly
free clause	after his departure
bound clause	[discovery] that in fact + he
free clause	no doubt + fear that he wouldn't get away

Paragraph 3 (*he* = George)

paragraph Theme (from clause 1)	George
clause Themes:	
bound clause	[realized] that + his son
bound clause	and + there [was nothing]
clause complex Theme	as it was to be only for a year
clause Themes:	

---

[16] A displaced Theme is a topical element which would be unmarked Theme (in the ensuing clause) if the existing marked topical Theme was reworded as a dependent clause. In the first example here, if we reworded more congruently as *Besides needing to create his own identity, Robert ...* , then in the ensuing clause *Robert* becomes unmarked Theme.

bound clause	as + it [the departure]
free clause	so + he
free clause	He
bound clause	though + it [the departure]
bound clause	and + though + he

Paragraph 4 (*I* = George)

paragraph Theme (from clause 1)	in a letter written [by George]
Displaced Theme	George
clause Themes:	
free clause	I
bound clause	as + I
bound clause	[realized] that + there [was nothing]
free clause	therefore + I

Paragraph 5 (*he* = George)

paragraph Theme (from clause complex)	after arriving in Liverpool and meeting Robert
clause Themes:	
bound clause	after + he
free clause	George
bound clause	what a pleasure [seeing Robert]
free clause	He

Commentary

The thematic organization of the clauses (and clause complexes, where relevant) is the most significant factor in the development of the text. In this little extract, there are five paragraphs, the first two having Robert as dominant Theme and the remaining three George. But whereas in the latter it is George himself, and his thoughts and actions, that form the paragraph Themes, in the first two it is the author's characterization of Robert – his needs and his principles; and these remain thematic throughout the paragraph. (Note that the only interpersonal Theme, apart from the interrogative *what a pleasure*, is the authorial *no doubt* qualifying Robert's fear of being restrained.) It is George who is the Theme of the book, not Robert. (George is also the Theme of the book's opening clause: *George Stephenson was born in the village of Wylam, about nine miles west of Newcastle-on-Tyne, on 9 June 1781.*)

Paragraph by paragraph, the development proceeds as follows:

(1) (apart from) Robert's need for self-identity ... [he felt] (that) at 20 ... this [his prospects]
(2) (despite) Robert's integrity and high principles ... (after) his departure ...

[discovered] (that) he ... (no doubt) his fear of restraint ... his fear of his father
(3) George ... [realized] (that) his son ... (as) it [his son's departure] ... (so) he ... (though) it ... (though) he
(4) George's letter ... I [George] ... (as) I .ll (so) I
(5) (after) George met Robert for leavetaking ... what a pleasure ... he [George]

First come Robert's needs and contrasting prospects; his principles and, behind his departure, his fears, including fear of his father George; then George, in relation to his son's departure; George's letter, and George himself; finally, George's meeting with Robert, and his pleasure at it. This is the thematic line, from which we know where the text is going.

   The Theme provides the environment for the remainder of the message, the Rheme. In the Rhemes of the various clauses are expressed, first, the explanation of Robert's malaise, followed in the second paragraph by the details of his actions; then George's sad resignation, his attempts at cheerful acceptance, and finally his activities in Robert's company.

   In the Theme-Rheme structure, it is the Theme that is the prominent element. This example shows how, by analysing the thematic structure of a text clause by clause, we can gain an insight into its texture and understand how the writer made clear to us the nature of his underlying concerns.

CHAPTER
FOUR

CLAUSE AS EXCHANGE

4.1 The nature of dialogue

In the last chapter we set out an interpretation of the clause in its textual function as a **message**, analysing it as a two-part structure with the elements Theme and Rheme. We shall now turn to another aspect of the meaning of the clause, its interpersonal meaning as an **exchange**. Here the principal grammatical system is that of MOOD (for a simple version of this system, see Chapter 1, Figure 1-9). We shall start with clauses that make a direct contribution to the development of exchange – 'free' clauses: these clauses select for different types of mood, and have various other interactive features. Having presented all the different mood types, and summarized them as a system in Section 4.5, we shall then add a note on 'bound' clauses, i.e. clauses that are either dependent on other clauses in clause complexes or embedded in groups (Section 4.4.5).

Simultaneously with its organization as a message, the clause is also organized as an interactive event involving speaker, or writer, and audience. Let us use the term 'speaker' as a cover term for both speaker and writer. In the act of speaking, the speaker adopts for himself a particular speech role, and in so doing assigns to the listener a complementary role that he wishes him to adopt in his turn (see Halliday, 1984a; Martin, 1992: Ch. 2; Eggins & Slade, 2005: Ch. 3). For example, in asking a question, a speaker is taking on the role of seeker of information and requiring the listener to take on the role of supplier of the information demanded. In Text 4-1 is a short extract from a conversation between a mother and her nine-year-old daughter:

Text 4-1: Sharing – casual conversation [Text 78]

Daughter:	Mummy, Boof keeps scaring me. Keeps getting into my bed, and kind of like he's going to bite me.
Mother:	He won't bite you, darling.
Daughter:	Well, I'm still afraid of him 'cause he's bitten me.
Mother:	Just push him off.

Daughter:	I'm trying really hard but he doesn't go off.
Mother:	Boof, you stay away from Jana.
Daughter:	I'm scared because I've had an experience where Boof has bit me.
Mother:	When?
Daughter:	When I was young at Bay's house, I was swimming and he jumped up and bit my bum.
Mother:	Oh, yeah. All right, we're gonna –

Like all interactants, mother and daughter 'co-author' the text: they take turns at this interactive process, each time adopting a speech role and assigning a complementary one to the other, as in ... *where Boof has bit me. – When? – When I was young ...* . Most of the clauses here are free clauses, clauses where Mother and Daughter adopt speech roles (see immediately below), thus contributing to the development of the dialogue; but there are some bound clauses supporting free clauses, e.g. *'cause he's bitten me, when I was young at Bay's house.* But as we noted above, we will start with free clauses.

The most fundamental types of speech role, which lie behind all the more specific types that we may eventually be able to recognize, are just two: (i) **giving**, and (ii) **demanding** (see Halliday, 1984a). Either the speaker is giving something to the listener (a piece of information, for example, as in *Boof keeps scaring me*) or he is demanding something from him (as in *just push him off; when [has Boof bit you]?*). Even these elementary categories already involve complex notions: giving means 'inviting to receive', and demanding means 'inviting to give'. The speaker is not only doing something himself; he is also requiring something of the listener. Typically, therefore, an 'act' of speaking is something that might more appropriately be called an **interact**: it is an exchange, in which giving implies receiving and demanding implies giving in response.

Cutting across this basic distinction between giving and demanding is another distinction, equally fundamental, that relates to the nature of the commodity being exchanged: see Figure 4-1. This may be either (a) **goods-&-services** or (b) **information**. Examples are given in Table 4-1. If you say something to me with the aim of getting me to do something for you, such as 'kiss me!' or 'get out of my daylight!', or to give you some object, as in 'pass the salt!', the exchange commodity is strictly nonverbal: what is being demanded is an object or an action, and language is brought in to help the process along. This is an exchange of goods-&-services. But if you say something to me with the aim of getting me to tell you something, as in 'is it Tuesday?' or 'when did you last see your father?', what is being demanded is information: language is the end as well as the means, and the only answer expected is a verbal one. This is an exchange of information. These two variables, when taken together, define the four primary speech functions of **offer**, **command**, **statement** and **question**.[1] These, in turn, are matched by a set of desired responses: accepting an offer, carrying out a command, acknowledging a statement and answering a question – see Table 4-2.

---

[1] These four primary speech functions are 'terminal' features in Figure 4-1 (with the exception of 'question'); but in extended descriptions of the system of speech function, each is the 'root' of a whole network of further speech-functional options: see Hasan *et al.* (2007) and references therein.

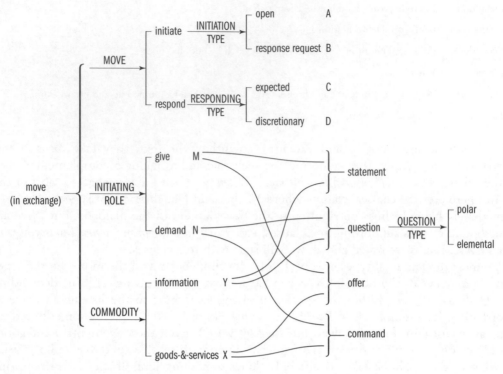

Fig. 4-1 The semantic system of SPEECH FUNCTION

Table 4-1 Giving or demanding, goods-&-services or information

	Commodity exchanged	
role in exchange	(a) goods-&-services	(b) information
(i) giving	'offer' would you like this teapot	'statement' he's giving her the teapot
(ii) demanding	'command' give me that teapot!	'question' what is he giving her?

Of these, only the last is essentially a verbal response; the others can all be nonverbal. But typically in real-life situations all four responses are verbalized, with or without some accompanying non-verbal action (Table 4-3). Examples:

Speaker:	Listener (becoming Speaker in his turn):
Would you like this teapot?	Yes, I would. No, I wouldn't.
Give me that teapot!	All right, I will. No, I won't.
He's giving her the teapot.	Oh, is he? Yes, he is. No, he isn't.
What is he giving her?	A teapot. I don't know; sha'n't tell you.

Table 4-2 Speech functions and responses

		Initiation [A/B]	Response	
			expected [C]	discretionary [D]
give [M]	goods-&-services [X]	offer shall I give you this teapot?	acceptance yes, please, do!	rejection no, thanks
demand [N]		command give me that teapot!	undertaking here you are	refusal I won't
give [M]	information [Y]	statement he's giving her the teapot	acknowledgement is he?	contradiction no, he isn't
demand [N]		question what is he giving her?	answer a teapot	disclaimer I don't know

Table 4-3 Typical realizations in grammar of speech functions

Initiate: full clause			Respond: elliptical clause	
AMX	(I'll ... / shall I ...?)		CMX	(yes; do)
BMX	(I'll ... , shall I?		DMX	(no; don't)
AMY	declarative		CMY	(oh; is it?)
BMY	declarative + moodtag		DMY	(no it isn't)
ANX	imperative		CNX	(yes; I will)
BNX	imperative + moodtag		DNX	(no I won't)
ANYP	interrogative: yes/no		CNYP	(yes/no)
			DNYP	(don't know/won't say)
ANYQ	interrogative: WH-		CNYQ	group/phrase
			DNYQ	(don't know/won't say)

In moving into the role of speaker, the listener has considerable discretion. Not only can he give any one of a wide range of different responses to a question, or carry out a command in different ways; he may refuse to answer the question altogether, or to provide the goods-&-services demanded. The speaker on his part has a way of forestalling this: he can add a (mood) **tag**, which is a reminder of what is expected, e.g. *will you?*, *isn't he?*, as in:

Give me that teapot, **will you**? He's giving her the teapot, **isn't he**?

Come and sit here, **will you**? [LLC_03]

Betty Nguyen: Good morning. Get that guy a coat, **will you**?

Rebecca Jarvis: He doesn't want one. [COCA]

Mr Mortlake: You could study literature in a foreign language, **couldn't you**?

Miss Detch: Yes, I could. [Text 125]

King: You will never retire-retire, **will you**?

Cronkite: No, I never intended to retire. [King Interviews]

This is the function of the tag at the end of the clause. It serves to signal explicitly that a response is required, and what kind of response it is expected to be.

As long as what is being exchanged is goods-&-services, the choices open to the listener are relatively limited; accept or reject the offer, obey or refuse the command. He may hedge, of course; but that is merely a way of temporarily avoiding the choice. Now, in the life history of an individual child, the exchange of goods-&-services, with language as the means, comes much earlier than the exchange of information: infants typically begin to use linguistic symbols to make commands and offers at about the age of nine months, whereas it may be as much as nine months to a year after that before they really learn to make statements and questions, going through various intermediate steps along the way (see Halliday, 1984a). It is quite likely that the same sequence of developments took place in the early evolution of language in the human race, although that is something we can never know for certain. It is not difficult to see why offering and requesting precede telling and asking when a child is first learning how to mean. Exchanging information is more complicated than exchanging goods-&-services, because in the former the listener is being asked not merely to listen and do something but also to act out a verbal role – to affirm or deny, or to supply a missing piece of information, as in

It's Tuesday.—Oh, is it?

Is it Tuesday?—Yes.

What day is it?—Tuesday.

What is more significant, however, is that the whole concept of exchanging information is difficult for a young child to grasp. Goods-&-services are obvious enough: I want you to take what I am holding out, or to go on carrying me, or to pick up what I have just dropped; and although I may use language as a means of getting what I want, the requirement itself is not a linguistic commodity – it is something that arises independently of language. Information, on the other hand, does not; it has no existence except in the form of language. In statements and questions, language itself is the commodity that is being exchanged; and it is by no means simple for a child to internalize the principle that language is used for the purpose of exchanging language. He has no experience of 'information' except its manifestation in words.

When language is used to exchange information, the clause takes on the form of a **proposition**. It becomes something that can be argued about – something that can be affirmed or denied, and also doubted, contradicted, insisted on, accepted with reservation, qualified, tempered, regretted, and so on. But we cannot use the term 'proposition' to refer to all the functions of the clause as an interactive event, because this would exclude the exchange of goods-&-services, the entire range of offers and commands. Unlike statements

and questions, these are not propositions; they cannot be affirmed or denied. Yet they are no less significant than statements and questions; and, as already noted, they take priority in the ontogenetic development of language.

Nevertheless there is an important reason why, when we are considering the clause as exchange, it is useful to look at propositions first. This is the fact that propositions have a clearly defined grammar (cf. Teruya *et al.*, 2007). As a general rule languages do not develop special resources for offers and commands, because in these contexts language is functioning simply as a means towards achieving what are essentially non-linguistic ends. But they do develop grammatical resources for statements and questions, which not only constitute ends in themselves but also serve as a point of entry to a great variety of different rhetorical functions. So, by interpreting the structure of statements and questions we can gain a general understanding of the clause in its exchange function.

We will continue to use the term 'proposition' in its usual sense to refer to a statement or question. But it will be useful to introduce a parallel term to refer to offers and commands. As it happens, these correspond more closely to the everyday sense of the word 'proposition', as in *I've got a proposition to put to you*; so we will refer to them by the related term **proposal**. The semantic function of a clause in the exchange of information is a proposition; the semantic function of a clause in the exchange of goods-&-services is a proposal.

4.2 The Mood element

4.2.1 Structure of the Mood

When we come to look closely at statements and questions, and at the various responses to which these naturally give rise, we find that in English they are typically expressed by means of a particular kind of grammatical variation: variation which extends over just one part of the clause, leaving the remainder unaffected.

Consider the traditional rhyme:

> He loves me. He don't. He'll have me. He won't. He would if he could. But he can't, so he don't.

Compare this with a typical piece of information-exchanging dialogue:

> The duke's given away that teapot, hasn't he? – Oh, has he? – Yes, he has. – No he hasn't! – I wish he had. – He hasn't; but he will. – Will he? – He might.

What is happening in these discourses is that one particular component of the clause is being, as it were, tossed back and forth in a series of rhetorical exchanges; this component carries the argument forward. Meanwhile the remainder, here *give(n) away that teapot*, is simply left out, being taken for granted as long as the discourse continues to require it.[2] Similarly in the rhyme: *love(s) me* and *have me* are 'understood' from one line to the next, only a small part of the clause being used to carry the sentiments forward.

---

[2] Where there is some change other than just a switch of mood or polarity, the verb substitute *do* may be used to stand in for the rest of the clause, as in *he might do*, *I wish he had done*. See Chapter 9.

What is the component that is being bandied about in this way? It is called the **Mood** element, and it consists of two parts: (1) the **Subject**, which is a nominal group, and (2) the **Finite** operator, which is part of a verbal group. (See Chapter 6 below for detailed discussion of these two types of group.) Thus in *he might*, *he* is Subject and *might* is Finite.

The Subject, when it first appears, may be any nominal group. If it is a personal pronoun, like *he* in the rhyme, it is simply repeated each time. If it is anything else, like *the duke*, then after the first occurrence it is replaced by the personal pronoun corresponding to it. So *the duke* becomes *he*, *my aunt* becomes *she*, *the teapot* becomes *it*. Nominal groups functioning as Subject include embedded, down-ranked clauses serving as Head (see Section 4.7), as in *It is clear* [[*that the current pace of peacetime operations has a major impact on service members and their families*]]. In 'circumstantial' relational clauses (see Chapter 5, Section 5.3), the Subject may be a prepositional phrase or an adverbial group:

By airline from Concord to Burlington is a distance of about 150 miles [BROWN1_F]

The Finite element is one of a small number of verbal operators expressing tense (e.g. *is*, *has*) or modality (e.g. *can*, *must*); these are listed in Table 4-5. Note, however, that in some instances the Finite element and the lexical verb are 'fused' into a single word, e.g. *loves*. This happens when the verb is in simple past or simple present (tense), active (voice), positive (polarity) and neutral (contrast): we say *gave*, not *did give*; *give(s)* not *do(es) give*. See Table 4-4.

Table 4-4 Finite elements in simple present and past tenses

Tense	Other categories	In body of clause	In tag
simple present	negative (polarity)	(he) doesn't have	does (he)?
	contrastive (contrast)	(he) does love	doesn't (he)?
	passive (voice)	(she) is loved	isn't (she)?
	none of above, i.e. positive, neutral, active	(he) loves ['present' + love]	doesn't (he)?
simple past	negative (polarity)	(he) didn't give	did (he)?
	contrastive (contrast)	(he) did give	didn't (he)?
	passive (voice)	(it) was given	wasn't (it)?
	none of above, i.e. positive, neutral, active	(he) gave ['past' + give]	didn't (he)?

These 'fused' tense forms are in fact the two most common forms of the English verb. When one of these occurs, the Finite *did*, *do(es)* will then make its appearance in the subsequent tags and responses, e.g. *He gave it away, didn't he? Yes, he did.* But it is already lurking in the verb as a systemic feature 'past' or 'present', and is explicit in the negative and contrastive forms (e.g. *He didn't give it away; He did give it away*).

Examples of Subject and Finite, in the body of the clause and in the tag, are given in Figure 4-2. Note the analysis of the simple tense form, in the final example.

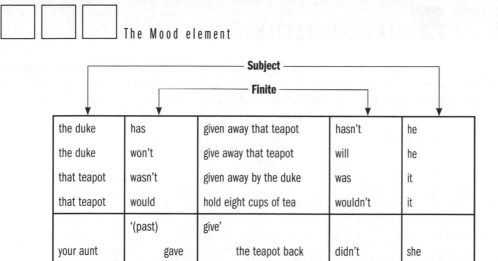

Fig. 4-2   Subject and Finite

As was pointed out in Chapter 2, the term 'Subject' as we are using it corresponds to the 'grammatical Subject' of earlier terminology; but it is being reinterpreted here in functional terms. The Subject is not a purely formal category; like all grammatical functions it is semantic in origin. What it means will be discussed in Section 4.2.2; here we will first describe how the Subject may be recognized.

The Subject, in a declarative clause, is that element which is picked up by the pronoun in the tag (cf. Figure 4-2). So in order to locate the Subject, add a tag (if one is not already present) and see which element is taken up. For example, *that teapot was given to your aunt*: here the tag would be *wasn't it?* – we cannot add *wasn't she?*. On the other hand with *that teapot your aunt got from the duke* the tag would be *didn't she?*; we cannot say *didn't he?* or *wasn't it?*. (At the same time, the Subject is also that element of the clause that precedes the Finite in a declarative clause but follows it in a yes/no interrogative one: *that teapot was : was that teapot?* Such observations can be derived from the system network in Figure 4-13 (cf. Figure 4-4).)

This is not the functional definition of the Subject; it is the way to *identify* it. Note that the category that is identified in this way will in fact accord with the classical conception of the Subject as 'that noun or pronoun that is in person and number concord with the verb': Subjects *he, she, it* go with *has*, and *I, you, we, they* go with *have*. This formulation however has a rather restricted application in Modern English, because apart from the verb *be*, the only manifestation of person and number in the verb is the *-s* on the third person singular present tense. The other part of the classical definition of the Subject, 'that noun or pronoun which is in the nominative case', is even more restricted, since the only words in English that display case are *I, we, he, she* and *they* (and in formal language also *who*). The criterion for recognizing the Subject that we are using here – 'that nominal group that is repeated in pronoun form in the tag' – can be followed up in every declarative clause.[3]

---

[3]   Checking the agnate 'yes/no interrogative' clause will also work (cf. Fawcett, 1999, 2000), since the relative sequence of Subject and Finite distinguishes 'declarative' clauses from 'yes/no interrogative' ones: *the duke has given away that teapot – has the duke given away that teapot*. The general point is the Subject can be identified by reference to any system in which it appears in a realization statement.

Note that it does bring in certain things that are not traditionally regarded as Subject: not only *it* in *it's raining* but also *there* in *there's trouble in the shed*, both of which function as Subject in Modern English. Some further examples are given in Figure 4-3.

	Subject	Finite		
what the duke gave my aunt	was	that teapot	wasn't	it
my aunt	has	been given a teapot	hasn't	she
it	's	not going to rain	is	it
there	won't	be a storm	will	there
the weather bureau	should	have warned us	shouldn't	they
nobody	'(present) takes	take' any notice	do	they

Fig. 4-3 Subject and Finite: further examples

   Subject and Finite are closely linked together, and combine to form one constituent which we call the **Mood**.[4] (For the other function that can occur within the Mood, see Section 4.3 below.) The Mood is the element that realizes the selection of mood in the clause; and it is also the domain of agreement between Subject and Finite.[5] It has sometimes been called the 'Modal' element; but the difficulty with this is that the term 'modal' is ambiguous, since it corresponds both to mood and to modality.

---

[4]   Note the distinction in capitalization between 'Mood' as the name of an element of the interpersonal structure of the clause (Mood + Residue; see below) and 'MOOD' as the name of the primary interpersonal system of the clause – the grammaticalization of the semantic system of SPEECH FUNCTION. This follows the general convention whereby names of structural functions are spelt with an initial capital and names of systems with all small caps or upper case.

[5]   Certain other languages operate with a similar Mood element consisting of Subject + Finite: the relative sequence of Subject and Finite serves to realize the selection of mood in the clause. However, around the languages of the world, this strategy is quite rare, being restricted mainly to certain languages (originally) from Europe (see Teruya *et al.*, 2007). It is far more common for languages to use tone (as English also does) and/or special interpersonal mood particles, as in languages in East and South-East Asia (as in Chinese [see Halliday & McDonald, 2004], Vietnamese [see Thai, 2004], Japanese [see Teruya, 2004, 2007a,b], and Thai [see Patpong, 2005]). Such mood particles serve the interpersonal function of Negotiator, and tend to come either at the beginning of the clause or at the end – that is, at either of the junctures of the clause as an exchange, where the speaker may take over from the previous speaker, or hand over to the next speaker. The element that is 'bandied about' in exchanged involving a change in polarity is often the Predicator ± polarity.

The remainder of the clause we shall call the **Residue**[6]. It has sometimes been labelled 'Proposition', but this term is also not very appropriate; partly because, as has been mentioned, the concept of proposition applies only to the exchange of information, not to the exchange of goods-&-services, and partly because, even in the exchange of information, if anything it is the Mood element that embodies the proposition rather than the remainder of the clause. We shall return to the structure of the Residue below.

The general principle behind the expression of MOOD in the clause is as follows.[7] The grammatical category that is characteristically used to exchange information is the **indicative**; within the category of indicative, the characteristic expression of a statement is the **declarative**, that of a question is the **interrogative**; and within the category of interrogative, there is a further distinction between **yes-no interrogative**, for polar questions, and **WH-interrogative**, for content questions. (These were outlined in Chapter 3, Section 3.3.) These features are typically expressed as follows:

(1) The ***presence*** of the Mood element, consisting of Subject plus Finite, realizes the feature 'indicative'.
(2) Within the indicative, what is significant is the ***order*** of Subject and Finite:
    (a) The order Subject before Finite realizes 'declarative'[8];
    (b) The order Finite before Subject realizes 'yes-no interrogative';
    (c) In a 'WH- interrogative' the order is: (i) Subject before Finite if the WH-element is the Subject; (ii) Finite before Subject otherwise.

The structure is as shown in Figure 4-4.

(a) declarative

the duke	has	given that teapot away
Subject	Finite	
Mood		Residue

(b) yes/no interrogative

has	the duke	given that teapot away
Finite	Subject	
Mood		Residue

Fig. 4-4 **Structure of declarative and yes/no interrogative**

---

[6] The combination of Mood plus Residue embody the proposition or proposal of the clause (with the Mood element as the key to the distinction between the two); but, as we shall see below, there are certain interpersonal elements of the clause that do not belong to either the Mood element or the Residue: the Vocative, and comment and conjunctive Adjuncts. These relate to, but are not part of the proposition/proposal enacted by the clause.

[7] Note that the system of MOOD is a system of the clause, not of the verbal group or of the verb. Many languages also have an interpersonal system of the verb(al group) that has been referred to as 'mood': it involves interpersonal contrasts such as indicative/subjunctive, indicative/subjunctive/optative. To distinguish these verbal contrasts from the clausal system of MOOD, we can refer to them as contrasts in **mode**. The subjunctive mode tends to be restricted to the environment of bound clauses – in particular, reported clauses and conditional clauses having the sense of irrealis. In Modern English, the subjunctive mode of the verb is marginal, although there is some dialectal variation.

[8] For exceptions, see Section 4.3.2 on Mood Adjuncts and Chapter 9, Section 9.5 on ellipsis. Note also that in verbal clauses (Chapter 5, Section 5.5.2), the Subject/Sayer may follow the Finite/Predicator/Process when the clause follows quoted material, as in *'Kukul is compassionate,' replied* **the priest**.

For the analysis of WH- interrogatives, which involve a consideration of the Residue, see Section 4.4, Figure 4-13, Figure 4-15 and Figure 4-16 below.

4.2.2 Meaning of Subject and Finite

Why have Subject and Finite this special significance in the English clause? We need to consider each of these elements in turn, since both are semantically motivated but the contribution they bring to the clause is not the same. We will take a look at the Finite element first.

4.2.2.1 The Finite element

The Finite element, as its name implies, has the function of making the proposition finite.[9] That is to say, it circumscribes it; it brings the proposition down to earth, so that it is something that can be argued about. A good way to make something **arguable** is to give it a point of reference in the here and now; and this is what the Finite does. It relates the proposition to its context in the speech event.

This can be done in one of two ways. One is by reference to the time of speaking; the other is by reference to the judgement of the speaker. An example of the first is *was* in *an old man was crossing the road*; of the second, *can't* in *it can't be true*. In grammatical terms, the first is **primary tense**, the second is **modality**.

(i) Primary tense means past, present or future at the moment of speaking; it is time relative to 'now'. A proposition may become arguable through being located in time by reference to the speech event. (There is no primary tense in proposals; *cross the road!* doesn't embody a choice of past, present or future relative to the now of speaking.) (ii) Modality means likely or unlikely (if a proposition), desirable or undesirable (if a proposal). A proposition or proposal may become arguable through being assessed in terms of the degree of probability or obligation that is associated with it.

What these have in common is **interpersonal deixis**: that is, they locate the exchange within the semantic space that is opened up between speaker and listener. With primary tense, the dimension is that of time: primary tense construes time interpersonally, as defined by what is 'present' to you and me at the time of saying. With modality the dimension is that of assessment: modality construes a region of uncertainty where I can express, or ask you to express, an assessment of the validity of what is being said.

Finiteness is thus expressed by means of a verbal operator that is either temporal or modal. But there is one further feature that is an essential concomitant of finiteness, and that is **polarity**. This is the choice between positive and negative. In order for something to be arguable, it has to be specified for polarity: either 'is' or 'isn't' (proposition), either 'do!' or 'don't!' (proposal). Thus the Finite element, as well as expressing primary tense or modality, also realizes either positive or negative polarity. Each of the operators appears in both positive and negative form: *did/didn't, can/can't*, and so on.

---

[9] In certain formal accounts, Finite has been discussed in terms of 'I', or 'Inflection', one difference being that this category also includes the infinitive marker *to*.

Table 4-5 lists the Finite verbal operators, positive and negative[10]. Note that some of the negative forms, such as *mayn't*, are rather infrequent; if they occur in a negative clause, the negative is usually separated (*may not, used not to*). In such cases, the *not* can be analysed as part of the Residue; but it is important to note that this is an oversimplification – sometimes it belongs functionally with the Finite, for example

> you may not leave before the end ('are not allowed to'): *not* is part of Finite
>
> you may not stay right to the end ('are allowed not to'): *not* is part of Residue

For further discussion of polarity and modality, and of the relation between the two, see Section 4.5.

Table 4-5 Finite verbal operators

Temporal operators:			
	Past	**Present**	**Future**
positive	did, was, had, used to	does, is, have	will, shall, would, should
negative	didn't, wasn't, hadn't, didn't + used to	doesn't, isn't, hasn't	won't, shan't, wouldn't, shouldn't
Modal operators:			
	Low	**Median**	**High**
positive	can, may, could, might, (dare)	will, would, should, is/was to	must, ought to, need, has/had to
negative	needn't, doesn't/didn't + need to, have to	won't, wouldn't, shouldn't, (isn't/ wasn't to)	mustn't, oughtn't to, can't, couldn't, (mayn't, mightn't, hasn't/hadn't to)

Finiteness combines the specification of polarity with the specification of either temporal or modal reference to the speech event. It constitutes the verbal component in the Mood. But there has to be also a nominal component; and this is the function of the Subject.

4.2.2.2 The Subject

The Subject supplies the rest of what it takes to form a proposition: namely, something by reference to which the proposition can be affirmed or denied (cf. Chapter 2, Section 2.6, and Halliday, 1984b, on the interpretation of the category of subject). For example, in *the duke has given away that teapot, hasn't he?*, the Finite *has* specifies reference to positive

---

[10] These operators obviously vary considerably in frequency. As modal operators, *shall* and *shan't* are very rare, although in regulatory texts operating in 'enabling' contexts, *shall* is quite common, as illustrated in Text 4-4 below. Like other grammatical systems, the system of MODALITY is in constant flux – in a process of becoming rather than in a state of being; for a corpus-based study of changes in the inventory of modal operators, see Mair & Leech (2006).

polarity and present time, while the Subject *the duke* specifies the entity in respect of which the assertion is claimed to have validity.

It is the duke, in other words, in whom is vested the success or failure of the proposition. He is the one that is, so to speak, being held responsible – **responsible** for the functioning of the clause as an interactive event. The speaker rests his case on *the duke + has*, and this is what the listener is called on to acknowledge.

It is perhaps easier to see this principle of responsibility in a proposal (a 'goods-&-services' clause), where the Subject specifies the one that is actually responsible for realizing (i.e., in this case, for carrying out) the offer or command. For example, in *I'll open the gate, shall I?* (offer) the opening depends on me; in *Stop shouting, you over there!* (command) it is for you to desist or otherwise. Hence the typical Subject of an offer is the speaker, and that of a command is the person being addressed. (Note that this is not the same thing as the Actor. The Subject in such clauses usually is the one that is also the Actor; but not necessarily so – both offers and commands can be passive with participants other than Actor as Subject, as in:

> I'll be guided by your wishes, shall I?
>
> [∅: 'you'] Get (yourself) invited to their meeting, will you?
>
> You've lost credibility and also you've probably spent more than you wanted to, so [∅: 'you'] do be willing to back away from it, because there's always something else next week or the month after. [COCA]
>
> [∅: 'you'] Stay warm, and please, [∅: 'you'] do be safe. [COCA]
>
> This might look like a sweet suburban cottage but [∅: 'you'] do not be deceived. Inside it is a construction zone, a destruction zone, a war zone. [COCA]
>
> If you do decide to write, you will soon become acquainted with rejection slips and dejection. Don't [∅: 'you'] be discouraged! This is just being a normal writer. [BROWN1_F]

Here the Subject is dissociated from the Actor[11]; but the Subject still specifies the one who is responsible for the success of the proposal.) This role is clearly recognizable in the case of offers and commands; but it is the same principle that is at work in statements and questions. Here, too, the Subject specifies the 'responsible' element; but in a proposition this means the one on which the **validity** of the information is made to rest. (It is important to express it in these terms rather than in terms of true or false. The relevant concept is that of exchangeability, setting something up so that it can be caught, returned, smashed, lobbed back, etc. Semantics has nothing to do with truth; it is concerned with consensus about validity, and consensus is negotiated in dialogue.)

Note the different Subjects in the examples in Figure 4-5.

The responses would be, respectively:

(a) . . . hasn't he?	Yes, he has.	No, he hasn't.
(b) . . . hasn't she?	Yes, she has.	No, she hasn't.
(c) . . . hasn't it?	Yes, it has.	No, it hasn't.

---

[11] This applies to 'material' clauses, but the same principle applies to clauses of other process types (see Chapter 5), as in *do be safe; don't be discouraged!*

the duke	has	given my aunt that teapot		hasn't	he	(a)
my aunt	has	been given that teapot by the duke		hasn't	she	(b)
that teapot	has	been given my aunt by the duke		hasn't	it	(c)
Subject	Finite			Finite	Subject	
Mood		Residue		Mood tag		

Fig. 4-5 Variation of Subject in declarative clauses

So, if we want to know why the speaker chooses this or that particular item as Subject of a proposition, there are two factors to be borne in mind. One is that, other things being equal, the same item will function both as Subject and as Theme. We saw in Chapter 3 that the unmarked Theme of a declarative clause is the Subject; so if the speaker wants to make the teapot his Theme, and to do so without the added implication of contrast that would be present if he made it a marked Theme (i.e. a Theme which is not also Subject, as in *that teapot the duke gave to my aunt*), he will choose an option with *that teapot* as Subject, namely *that teapot was given by the duke to my aunt*. Here there is an integrated choice of an item realizing two functions simultaneously: Subject in the proposition, and Theme in the message.

At the same time, however, the selection of this item as Subject has a meaning in its own right: the speaker is assigning to the teapot not only the function of starting point of the message but also that of 'resting point' of the argument. And this is brought out if we dissociate one from the other, selecting different items as Subject and as Theme. For example:

> That teapot the duke gave to your aunt, didn't he? – No he didn't. He put it up for auction.

Here the teapot is Theme ('now about that teapot:'), but the duke is Subject; it is the duke who is made to sustain the validity of the statement. Hence only *he*, not *she* or *it*, can figure in the tag and the response. In the next the teapot is still the Theme, but the Subject has now switched to the aunt:

> That teapot your aunt was given by the duke, wasn't she? – No she wasn't. She bought it at an auction.

Finally, let us reverse these two roles, having the aunt as Theme and the teapot as Subject:

> To your aunt that teapot came as a gift from the duke, didn't it?
>
> – No it didn't. It was the first prize in a Christmas raffle.

4.2.2.3 A further note on the Subject

The interpretation of the functional category of Subject in English has always been rather problematic. As we noted above (Chapter 2, Section 2.6), the definition of Subject inherited from classical times was a morphological one: it was that nominal element – 'noun or pronoun' – that is in the nominative case, and that displays person and number concord with the (finite) verb. But few traces remain, either of case in the noun or of person and number in the verb.[12] What made the situation more problematic was that, in the structuralist tradition, the Subject was said to be a purely grammatical element, operating at the syntactic level but without semantic significance. That something should be a grammatical function whose only function is to be a grammatical function is already somewhat anomalous; it becomes even more anomalous if it has no clear syntactic definition[13].

In fact the Subject in English has got a distinct identity, as we have pointed out; its identity can be established if we adopt a **trinocular perspective**, as suggested by the stratificational model of language (see Chapter 1, Section 1.3.3). (i) From below, it is that nominal element (nominal group or nominalized phrase or clause) that is picked up by the pronoun in the mood tag.[14] (ii) From round about, it is that which combines with the Finite (operator) to form the Mood element in the clause; it is also that which constitutes the unmarked Theme if the mood is declarative, and which switches place with the Finite if the mood is yes/no interrogative. (iii) From above, it is that which carries the **modal responsibility**: that is, responsibility for the validity of what is being predicated (stated, questioned, commanded or offered) in the clause. This last point is the basic insight that informed the original, pre-structuralist interpretation of the Subject function, that in terms of a configuration of Subject + Predicate. The problem only arises when predication is interpreted in terms of truth value, since proposals – commands and offers – have no truth value. This mistake arose because predication was assumed to be an experiential relation; but it is not – it is an interpersonal relation, enacting the form of exchange between speaker and listener. The notion of **validity** relates to the arguing of the case, if it is a proposition, or to the putting into effect if it is a proposal. The Subject is that element in which the particular kind of validity (according to the mood) is being invested. Examples below.

Since the Subject is interpersonal in nature, being vested with modal responsibility, it interacts with other interpersonal aspects of the clause; it is treated in a different way from Complements and Adjuncts. There are various interpersonal reactances showing the special

---

[12] And in those pronouns which retain a distinct form of nominative case, this is no longer restricted to functioning as Subject, since in current usage the nominative also occurs in expressions such as *you and I* following a preposition (cf. *'I think it's best for he and I to have our discussion first, and I look forward to it,'* Bush said. [AP news report]). This is of course 'bad grammar' – the result of hypercorrection; but it has become the norm, and so further muddies the small remaining pool of morphologically recognizable Subjecthood.

[13] In the context of seminal work on Philippine languages such as Tagalog in particular, Schachter (1976, 1977, 1994) has argued for distinguishing different sets of properties that have been associated with 'subject'. From a systemic-functional point of view, this makes perfect sense: properties that have been associated with 'subject' are metafunctionally diverse, being textual, interpersonal or experiential (as we noted in Chapter 2). Understandably, some scholars have abandoned the term 'subject' altogether, preferring to use other terms to avoid confusion. For example, drawing on the framework of Role and Reference Grammar, Van Valin & LaPolla (1997: 274 ff.) distinguish between 'controller' and 'pivot', instead of retaining the traditional term 'subject'. These may be either 'semantic' or 'syntactic'. In contrast, in our systemic-functional account of English, Subject is interpreted metafunctionally as an interpersonal grammatically category; but like other such categories, e.g. Theme and Actor (see Chapter 2, Section 2.6), Subject is both grammatical and semantic at the same time – the notion of 'modal responsibility'.

[14] We have noted that existential *there* (as in *there is, there isn't*), is not, in fact, an exception; this *there* is a pronoun. The proportionality is:
the : that : it :: a(n) : one : there
This is explained more fully in Chapter 6, Section 6.2.1.1.

status of Subject. For example, we have seen that modals serving as Finite orient to the Subject as the element being held modally responsible; and we find a class of comment Adjuncts that are similarly oriented towards the Subject (see Section 4.3.2.2 below):

> Gaunt was compelled to give up his search for an elusive foe, and, afraid to return home without something to show, <u>he</u> **foolishly** attempted to besiege the well-protected fortress of St Malo. [LOB_G]

> <u>They</u> **rightly** point out that the first the profession learnt of the proposed tribunal was by way of a press release on September 12. [ACE_B]

They occur with Subjects that are not 'active' participants, e.g. Sensers (Chapter 5), and also with Subjects in passive clauses:

> <u>They</u> **rightly** understood that nothing would be saved if we simply defend it on economic grounds. [COCA]

> on April 1, <u>she and husband Scott Pelletier</u> were **foolishly** surprised with the birth of our daughter, Caroline Vera [COCA]

> Well, <u>he</u> was **rightly** awarded a white hat for standing up to the president, but now he should be awarded a black hat again for caving in. [COCA]

These have agnates where the subject-orientation is explicit, as in *he was foolish to attempt to besiege* .... When reference items in Complements and Adjuncts have the referent of the Subject as their antecedent, they are usually represented by reflexive pronouns rather than by simple personal pronouns, e.g.:

> 'What a wonderful pet this funny creature would make,' <u>he</u> thought to **himself**. [ACE_D]

> Having migrated to Australia from Britain in 1960, <u>Alun Leach-Jones</u> has established **himself** as an important Australian artist over the past twenty-five years. [ACE-G]

> <u>Alex</u> was obliged to prepare **himself** in haste. [BROWN1_K]

> Publicly, he denied everything. Privately, <u>he</u> created and magnified an image of **himself** as a hired assassin. [BROWN1_N]

> 'The snake was beautiful, wasn't it?' asked Keith, <u>his voice</u> getting harsher in spite of **himself**, as he struggled to control his growing anger. [BROWN1_N]

> But the other thing I want to say to you is that you can't sober up for him. You've got to lead your life and <u>you</u> have to get help **for yourself**. [King Interviews]

So the Subject is a thick, well-rounded category along with all the other elements in the structure of the clause. The fact that it proves difficult to define does not distinguish it from Theme or Actor or Medium or many other equally pregnant categories. All are subject to the general principle of **ineffability** – they mean themselves (see Halliday, 1984b). The guiding axiom is the metafunctional one: just as the Theme is best understood by starting from the concept of the clause as a message, so the Subject is best understood by starting from the concept of the clause as an exchange, a move in dialogic interaction. Each of the two can be thought of as an anchor; and we shall see in Chapter 5 that the Medium plays an analogous role in the clause as representation. (Medium rather than Actor, for reasons that will appear in Section 5.7.) The notion of the Subject as a 'purely syntactic' element arose because it proved difficult to understand Subject + Predicate in an account of the grammar that recognized only the ideational kind of meaning; once we open up the other metafunctional spaces, just as Theme comes powerfully into the picture, so Subject becomes (equally powerful but) less mysterious. But to see the interpersonal significance of Subject, we have to take natural dialogic interaction seriously as a source of insight into the grammar; if we only focus on monologic discourse such as narrative, Subject will appear to be the same as Theme since Subject = Theme is the unmarked mapping (cf. Chapter 2, Section 2.6).

4.2.3 Function of the Mood element

Hence the Mood element has a clearly defined semantic function: it carries the burden of the clause as an interactive event. So it remains constant, as the nub of the proposition, unless some positive step is taken to change it, as in

> The duke has given your aunt a new teapot, hasn't he?
>
> – No, he hasn't. But
>
>> (a) the duchess has.
>>
>> (b) he's going to.

Here the proposition is first disposed of, by being rejected, in (i); this then allows for a new proposition, with change of Subject, as in (a), or change of Finite, as in (b). Each of these two constituents, the Subject and the Finite, plays its own specific and meaningful role in the propositional structure.

In the next section, we shall discuss the structure of the Residue. We shall then return to a consideration of the Mood element, with an analysis of mood in WH-interrogative, imperative, and exclamative clauses. Here meanwhile in Text 4-2 is a short text example from Alice's conversation with Humpty Dumpty:

Text 4-2: Recreating – dramatic dialogue in narrative

(1)	My name	is	Alice, but—		
	Subject	Finite			
(2)	It	's	a stupid name enough		
	Subject	Finite			
(3)	What	does	it	mean?	
		Finite	Subject		
(4)	Must	a name	mean	something?	
	Finite	Subject			
(5)	Of course	it	must		
		Subject	Finite		
(6)	My name	means	the shape I am		
	Subject	Finite [present]			
(7)	And a good handsome shape		it	is,	too
			Subject	Finite	

The flow of the dialogue is as follows:

Mood I	(1–3):	Subject – Alice's name; Finite – present tense
Mood II	(4–5):	Subject – name in general; Finite – 'high' modality
Mood III	(6):	Subject – Humpty Dumpty's name; Finite – present tense
Mood IV	(7):	Subject – Humpty Dumpty's shape; Finite – present tense

There are two non-thematic Subjects, in clauses (3) and (7), (7) having a marked Theme.

4.3 Other elements of Mood structure

4.3.1 Structure of the Residue

The Residue consists of functional elements of three kinds: Predicator, Complement and Adjunct. There can be only one Predicator, one or two Complements, and an indefinite number of Adjuncts up to, in principle, about seven. An example is given in Figure 4-6.

Sister Susie	's	sewing	shirts	for soldiers
Subject	Finite	Predicator	Complement	Adjunct
Mood		Residue		

Fig. 4-6   Structure of the Residue

4.3.1.1 Predicator

The Predicator is present in all major clauses, except those where it is displaced through ellipsis (see Chapter 9, Section 9.5).[15] It is realized by a verbal group minus the temporal or modal operator, which as we have seen functions as Finite in the Mood element; for example, in the verbal groups *was shining, have been working, may be going to be replaced* the parts functioning as Predicator are *shining, been working, be going to be replaced*. The Predicator itself is thus non-finite; and there are nonfinite clauses containing a Predicator but no Finite element, for example *eating her curds and whey* (following *Little Miss Muffet sat on a tuffet*). For the discussion of non-finite clauses, see Chapter 7, Section 7.4 below.

The function of the Predicator is fourfold. (i) It specifies time reference **other than** reference to the time of the speech event, i.e. 'secondary' tense: past, present or future relative to the primary tense (see Chapter 6, Sections 6.3.2–6.3.4). (ii) It specifies various other aspects and phases like seeming, trying, hoping (in verbal group complexes; see Chapter 8, Section 8.4-6). (iii) It specifies the voice: active or passive (see Chapter 6, Section 6.3.2). (iv)

---

[15] Note that the name of this function is 'Predicator', not 'Predicate'. The latter term has been used in traditional grammar, formal grammar (where it is roughly equivalent to VP, or Verb Phrase) and logic (for the origins of 'Subject' and 'Predicate' in traditional grammar and logic, see e.g. Law, 2003: 168; Seuren, 1998: 120–133). From a functional point of view, its use in accounts of grammar represents an attempt to characterize Rheme and/or Residue.

It specifies the process (action, event, mental process, relation) that is predicated of the Subject (see Chapter 5)[16]. These can be exemplified from the verbal group *has been trying to be heard*, where the Predicator, *been trying to be heard*, expresses (i) a complex secondary tense, *been + ing*; (ii) a conative phase, *try + to*; (iii) passive voice, *be + -d*; (iv) the mental process *hear*. See the examples below (verbal group underlined, Predicator part in bold):

All the people in the affected areas <u>are **panicking**</u> [Text 15]

One of the little trials that a man <u>must **learn to bear**</u> when he <u>**admits**</u> the telephone to his home <u>is</u> that, when he <u>**hurries**</u> to its side <u>**to answer**</u> a call, it <u>will</u> sometimes <u>**stop ringing**</u> before he <u>**gets**</u> there. [LOB_B]

We <u>are **going to release**</u> the document to the press [Text 12]

<u>Can</u> you <u>**tell**</u> us a little about your early life? [Text 7]

You'<u>ll **have to make**</u> it a lot clearer [Text 10]

You'd <u>**better look**</u> at it [Text 8]

Brazil <u>wasn't **discovered**</u> [Text 12]

The Indians <u>had</u> originally <u>**planned to present**</u> the document to President Fernando Henrique Cardoso [Text 12]

As the examples illustrate, a finite verbal group serves as both Finite and Predicator, the two being fused under the conditions shown in Table 4-4. When the Finite and the Predicator are not fused, the Predicator follows the Finite, but certain other elements may come between them, making the verbal group discontinuous: the Subject in 'interrogative' clauses where the Finite precedes the Subject (as in *can <you> tell*) and Adjuncts (as in *had <originally> planned to present*: see Figure 4-7).

The Indians	had	originally	planned to present	the document	to President Fernando Henrique Cardoso
Subject	Finite	Adjunct	Predicator	Complement	Adjunct
Mood		Residue			
nominal group	verbal group	adverbial group		nominal group	prepositional phrase

Fig. 4-7: Discontinuous verbal group

---

[16] Note that if the lexical verb is a phrasal one (Chapter 6, Section 6.3.6), the non-verbal part, the adverb and/or preposition, serves as Adjunct, thus falling outside the scope of the Predicator. The combination of Predicator + Adjunct corresponds to the Process. This analysis enables us to account for discontinuous Processes realized by phrasal verbs, as in *look that one up in the dictionary* with *look up* as Process, and *look* as Predictor and *up* as Adjunct: [Predicator:] *look* [Complement:] *that one* [Adjunct:] *up* [Adjunct:] *in the dictionary*.

There are two lexical verbs in English, *be* and *have*, where, strictly speaking, the simple past and simple present forms consist of Finite element only, rather than of a fusion of Finite with Predicator. This is shown by the negatives: the negative of *is, was* is *isn't, wasn't* – not *doesn't be, didn't be*. Similarly with *have* (in the sense of 'possess', not *have* in the sense of 'take'): the negative forms are *hasn't, hadn't*, as in Table 4-6. The pattern with *have* varies with the dialect: some speakers treat *have* 'possess' just like *have* 'take', with negative *doesn't have*; others expand it as *have + got* (cf. *I haven't a clue / I don't have a clue / I haven't got a clue*). But since in all other tenses *be* and *have* function as Predicators in the normal way, it seems simpler to analyse them regularly, as '(past/present) + *be/have*'.

Table 4-6 Simple past and present forms of be and have

	past positive	past negative	present positive	present negative
be	was. were	wasn't, weren't	am, is, are	isn't, aren't, (ain't)
have	had	hadn't	have, has	haven't, hasn't

4.3.1.2 Complement

A Complement is an element within the Residue that has the potential of being Subject but is not; in other words, it is an element that has the potential for being given the interpersonally elevated status of modal responsibility – something that can be the nub of the argument. It is typically realized by a nominal group. So, in *the duke gave my aunt that teapot* there are two Complements, *my aunt* and *that teapot*. Either of these could function as Subject in the clause: *my aunt was given that teapot by the duke* and *that teapot was given my aunt by the duke*. (These variants contrast in voice; see Chapter 5, Section 5.8.) Here are some corpus examples illustrating the assignment of subjecthood and complementhood to elements of the clause (Subject in bold; Complement underlined):

We also should ask um ... – And **Joan** has been invited. [UTS/Macquarie Corpus]

Son (crying): **It** hurts. Oh, my little toe, look at <u>it</u>.

Father (to son): Oh, **your little toe** has been scraped by the –

Mother (to Father): Did **you** scrape <u>it</u>, did **you**?

Father (to Mother): Must have, accidentally. ... [UTS/Macquarie Corpus]

I must tell <u>Betty</u> <u>that</u> when *I* go down at the end of the month. – Yeah! [laughing] **Most of it** has been said by Sandy now about the savoury muffins. [UTS/Macquarie Corpus]

Any nominal group not functioning as Subject will be a Complement (with the exception of certain circumstantial Adjuncts of Extent realized by nominal groups without the preposition *for*, e.g. *180 miles* in *he sailed 180 miles north on the Company's armed schooner* [ACE_G]: see Chapter 5, Section 5.6.2.1); and this includes nominal groups of one type which could not function as Subject as they stand, namely those with adjective as Head, e.g.

Inspection can be <u>frightening</u>, but staff morale has to be kept high. [Text 97]

The clergy's concern was, of course, still <u>spiritual</u>. [Text 122]

(Note that in a clause such as *a right nit proper barmy was uncle Algernon, wasn't he?*, *uncle Algernon* is the Subject.)

There is an explanation of this 'from above' in terms of function in transitivity: nominal groups with adjective as Head can function in the clause only as Attributes, and the Attribute cannot be mapped to the interpersonal role of Subject. This is because only participants in the clause can take modal responsibility, and the Attribute is only marginally, if at all, a participant. As illustrated above, the Attribute serves primarily in 'attributive' relational clauses (see Chapter 5, Section 5.4.3); but it serves in certain 'material' clauses (see Chapter 5, Section 5.2.4), as in *Her father slowly wiped himself dry* [ACE_W], where *dry* can be analysed as Complement/Attribute.

Nominal groups as Complement include those with an embedded, down-ranked clause as Head, e.g.:

Calculations by Anderson show ⦀that ozone depletion at the 410-and 420-K isentropic surfaces between August 23 and September 22 can be almost entirely explained by the amount of ClO present ‖ if one assumes that the ClO-ClO mechanism is effective⦀. [Text 33]

In 'circumstantial' relational clauses, the Complement may be a prepositional phrase or an adverbial group, as in:

He is Minister for Industry but his degree is <u>in agricultural science</u>. [ACE_B]

When I said she was not <u>here</u> I meant to say that she was not <u>in the house</u> [LOB_K]

<u>Where</u>'s our cake? [Text 10]

(We can also note metaphorical locative Attributes as Complement, e.g. *in love, in a rage, in denial, in luck, in clover*, as in *Nellie is in love with Clayton Roy* [BROWN1_N]. These are more like Attributes in intensive relational clauses, but may at the same time be variants of clauses of other process types, e.g. 'mental': *Nellie loves Clayton Roy*.) Such examples constitute the limiting case of complement-hood. Looked at 'from below', they would appear to be Adjuncts rather than Complements since they are prepositional phrases or adverbial groups rather than nominal groups; but viewed 'from above', they are similar to other Complements in that they are participants inherent in the process rather than attendant circumstances.

It will be noted that the Complement covers what are 'objects' as well as what are 'complements' in the traditional school grammar ('predicative complements', usually serving as Attribute or Value in a 'relational' clause). But that distinction has no place in the interpersonal structure; it is imported from the experiential analysis, that of transitivity. Since the term 'object' is strongly associated with the formal analysis of transitivity, we use Complement as the term for this single element within the Residue.

4.3.1.3 Adjunct

An Adjunct is an element that has not got the potential of being Subject; that is, it cannot be elevated to the interpersonal status of modal responsibility. This means that arguments

cannot be constructed around those elements that serve as Adjuncts; in experiential terms, they cannot be constructed around circumstances, but they can be constructed around participants, either actually, as Subject, or potentially, as Complement (we shall see in Chapter 5 that all participants are not construed as equal; some are more likely than others to be given the status of Subject – or as we noted in the previous subsection with respect to the Attribute, some may be marginal participants). We thus have three degrees of interpersonal ranking or elevation in the clause, as shown in Figure 4-8: Subject – Complement – Adjunct.

Fig. 4-8   Degree of interpersonal 'elevation' in the clause

An Adjunct is typically realized by an adverbial group or a prepositional phrase (i.e. preposition + nominal group rather than by a nominal group). In *my aunt was given that teapot yesterday by the duke* there are two Adjuncts: the adverbial group *yesterday* and the prepositional phrase *by the duke*. (As noted above, certain circumstantial Adjuncts of Extent may be realized by nominal groups without the preposition *for*; contrast *he had walked for miles* with *he had walked four miles*.)

A prepositional phrase, however, has its own internal structure, containing a nominal group serving as Complement within it (see Chapter 6, Section 6.5). In *by the duke*, *the duke* is a Complement with respect to the preposition *by* (which serves as a Predicator). So, although *by the duke* is itself an Adjunct, and could not become Subject, it has as one of its constituents *the duke*, which is a Complement at another rank, and could become Subject.

In the case of *by the duke*, if *the duke* comes to function as Subject then the preposition simply disappears: *the teapot was presented by the duke, the duke presented the teapot*. Similarly with the Adjunct *to my aunt*; if *my aunt* becomes Subject, then *to* disappears: *that teapot was given to my aunt, my aunt was given that teapot*. (The principle behind this is explained in Chapter 5, Section 5.7 'Transitivity and voice: another interpretation'.) But increasingly in modern English the Complement to any preposition has the potential of becoming Subject, even where the preposition has to be retained and hence to function as an Adjunct on its own. For example, in *that paper's already been written on*, *that paper* functions as Subject, leaving *on* behind as a truncated Adjunct (Figure 4-9).

The typical order of elements in the Residue is: Predicator ∧ Complement(s) ∧ Adjunct(s), as in *the duke gave my aunt that teapot last year for her birthday*. But, as we have noted, an Adjunct or Complement may occur thematically, either as a WH- element in an interrogative clause or as marked Theme in a declarative clause. This does not mean that it becomes part of the Mood element; it is still within the Residue. As a result, therefore, the Residue is split into two parts; it becomes discontinuous. In *that teapot the duke had given to my aunt last year*, where *that teapot* is a marked-thematic Complement, the Residue is *that teapot ... given to my aunt last year*. Discontinuous constituents can be represented in the box and tree diagrams as in Figure 4-10.

(a)

that paper	's	already	been written	on
Subject	Finite	Adjunct	Predicator	Adjunct
Mood			Residue	

(b)

someone	's	already	written	on that paper
Subject	Finite	Adjunct	Predicator	Adjunct
Mood			Residue	

Fig. 4-9   Related clauses with same item as (a) Subject, (b) Complement in prepositional phrase

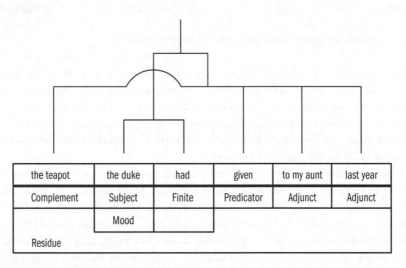

the teapot	the duke	had	given	to my aunt	last year
Complement	Subject	Finite	Predicator	Adjunct	Adjunct
	Mood				
Residue					

Fig. 4-10   Discontinuous Residue

4.3.2 Types of Adjunct; Adjuncts outside Residue

Within the general category of Adjunct, however, there are two special types that do not follow the same principles of ordering, and do not fall within the Residue at all. These are the modal Adjuncts and the conjunctive Adjuncts, which were already identified in Chapter 3 in the discussion of 'characteristic Themes' (Section 3.4, especially Tables 3-2 and 3-3).

The distinction among these different kinds of Adjunct is a metafunctional one. The type of Adjuncts discussed in the previous paragraphs (Section 4.3.1 (iii)) was what we refer to collectively as **circumstantial Adjuncts** (because they function as 'circumstance' in the transitivity structure of the clause; see Chapter 5, Section 5.7). These are experiential in metafunction. **Modal Adjuncts** and **conjunctive Adjuncts** are, respectively, interpersonal and textual in metafunction; hence they occur at different locations within the clause. The general picture is as shown in Table 4-7.

Table 4-7 Metafunction and type of Adjunct

Metafunction	Type of Adjunct		Location in mood structure
experiential	circumstantial Adjunct		in Residue
interpersonal	modal Adjunct	mood Adjunct	in Mood
		comment Adjunct	(not in mood structure)
textual	conjunctive Adjunct		(not in mood structure)

In Table 3-5, the modal Adjuncts were introduced under the two subheadings of **mood Adjunct** and **comment Adjunct**; but only those subcategories were included that typically function as Theme. Here we need to consider the full range of modal Adjuncts, having regard to their interpersonal role. The distinction into mood Adjunct and comment Adjunct is made on this interpersonal basis. They represent different types of assessment of the proposition or proposal, and will be discussed in more detail in Section 4.5.3.

4.3.3 Conjunctive Adjuncts

With conjunctive Adjuncts, we come to the limits of the concept of the clause as exchange. Strictly speaking, they do not belong in this chapter at all; unlike modal Adjuncts, which are interpersonal in function, conjunctive Adjuncts are textual – they set up a contextualizing relationship obtaining between the clause as a message and some other (typically preceding) portion of text. The semantic basis of this contextualizing function is that of the logical-semantic relationships of **expansion** described in Chapter 7. But the conjunctive Adjuncts construct these relationships by **cohesion** – that is, without creating a structural link in the grammar between the two parts (see Halliday & Hasan, 1976: Ch. 5; Halliday & Hasan 1985; Martin, 1992: Ch. 2). They are therefore described in greater detail in Chapter 9, Section 9.3.

The conjunctive Adjuncts were introduced in Chapter 3, because they typically operate in the clause as part of the Theme. But, as pointed out there, they are not necessarily thematic; they may occur elsewhere in the clause, and in fact their distribution – where they can go, and what difference it makes to the meaning – is quite similar to that of modal Adjuncts, especially those of Comment. For example (conjunctive Adjuncts underlined; Mood elements in bold):

At present all the three posts in the Engineering Department, one of the biggest and most important departments of the corporation, are being held by those who are not eligible according to the rules and regulations prescribed by the UPSC. However, **Mr Dayal has** made a representation to the commissioner that he should be considered as Superintending Engineer since April 1969, when he was given the charge on an *ad hoc* basis, though the Departmental Promotion Committee had regularised him in March, 1976. [KOHL_A]

Today, however, **the paths of denominational religion have often** become the hotbeds of intolerance and fanaticism, dogmatism and obscurantism, persecution and oppression, and training grounds of reaction and exploitation. [KOHL_D]

This device, however, **gives** the President the whip hand of Parliament and can, in the case of authoritarian Presidents, prove disastrous. [KOHL_A]

It was not, <u>however</u>, to be a precedent, he said. [KOHL_A]

I maintain, <u>however</u>, that if anybody has to go, it should be myself. [KOHL_A]

Fr R. Hambye rightly remarks: 'if he had succeeded in reaching Malabar and in governing his archdiocese for some time, it can hardly be doubted that he would have gathered all the Catholic Thomas Christians under his leadership'. **This did not** happen, <u>however</u>. [KOHL_D]

The two types of Adjunct are also similar both in their own composition (as adverbial groups and prepositional phrases) and in how they may be differentiated from circumstantial Adjuncts. Whereas circumstantial Adjuncts fall most naturally at the end of the clause, where they carry the unmarked tonic (intonational) prominence, modal and conjunctive Adjuncts occur finally only as Afterthought (see Chapter 3, Section 3.7) and can never carry the only tonic prominence in the clause. Contrast:

(circumstantial)	it rains more heavily on the hill
(modal: comment)	it rains more heavily, on the whole
(circumstantial)	it rains more heavily on the other side
(conjunctive)	it rains more heavily, on the other hand

And while they all can occur thematically, only the circumstantial Adjuncts can normally occur as predicated Theme (see Chapter 3, Section 3.7): we can say *it's on the hill that it rains more heavily*, but not *it's on the whole that it rains more heavily* or *it's on the other hand that it rains more heavily*. Similarly, only circumstantial Adjuncts can serve in thematic equatives: we can say *where it rains more heavily is on the other side* but not *where it rains more heavily is on the other hand* (in the intended conjunctive sense).

What is common to the modal and conjunctive Adjuncts, as distinct from the circumstantials, is that they are both constructing a context for the clause. Thus even though the same semantic feature may be involved – for example, time – it has a different significance in each case. A modal Adjunct of time, like *just*, *yet*, *already*, relates closely to the primary tense, which is the 'shared time' of speaker and listener; a conjunctive Adjunct of time such as *next*, *meanwhile*, locates the clause in time with respect to the preceding textual environment; and both are different from time as circumstance, such as *in the afternoon*. And the same item may function sometimes circumstantially and sometimes conjunctively; for example *then*, *at that moment*, *later on*, *again*, as in:

circumstantial Adjunct:

The fund did not have a cent in the local market **then**. [ACE_A] 'at that time'

conjunctive Adjunct:

Grahame courteously listened as Shepard spoke of his plans for the book. **Then**, leaning forward, he said to the artist: "I love these little people, be kind to them." [ACE_C] 'next'

So for purposes of analysis we can include conjunctive Adjuncts within the framework of this part of the description. But note that they form a constituent on their own; they are not part of the Mood or the Residue. See the example in Figure 4-11.

such men	however	seldom	make		good husbands
Subject	conjunctive Adjunct	mood Adjunct	'(present) Finite	make' Predicator	Complement
Mood				Residue	

Fig. 4-11 **Clause with conjunctive Adjunct**

4.3.4 Vocatives and Expletives

Another element that figures in the structure of the clause as exchange, but outside the scope of the Mood and Residue, is the Vocative. This also is fairly mobile, occurring (a) thematically (cf. Chapter 3, Section 3.5 above on interpersonal Themes); (b) at the boundary between Theme and Rheme (not usually between Mood and Residue), or (c) clause-finally; and with the same intonation patterns as the comment Adjuncts. The Vocative can accompany a clause of any mood, but it is relatively more frequent in 'demanding' clauses (interrogatives and imperatives) than in 'giving' ones (declaratives).

> It's lovely **darling**. – Thanks. Thank you **Craig** so much for saying so. [UTS/Macquarie Corpus]
>
> **Mum** you're not enjoying your dinner, are you? – I am. [UTS/Macquarie Corpus]
>
> You're not stupid, are you, **darling**? [UTS/Macquarie Corpus]
>
> **Mum**, do you know where the scissors are? [UTS/Macquarie Corpus]
>
> What do you want **darling**? – Nothing for me. [UTS/Macquarie Corpus]
>
> No, no, **darling**, that's – go the other way. [UTS/Macquarie Corpus]
>
> Oh **darling** don't you worry; that's quite easily arranged. [UTS/Macquarie Corpus]

In using a Vocative the speaker is enacting the participation of the addressee or addressees in the exchange. This may serve to identify the particular person being addressed, or to call for that person's attention; but in many dialogic contexts the function of the Vocative is more negotiatory: the speaker uses it to mark the interpersonal relationship, sometimes thereby claiming superior status or power (see Poynton, 1984). The Vocative is also brought in as a text signal – for example, when signing off in a telephone conversation.

Likewise outside the structure of Mood and Residue, and occurring in more or less the same places as Vocatives in the clause, are Expletives, whereby the speaker enacts his own current attitude or state of mind. These are perhaps on the fringe of grammatical structure; but since they participate fully in the intonation and rhythm of the clause they do figure in the analysis.

> **God**, mine's terrific. [Text 82]
>
> And then there was a child crying in the background, so I was thinking 'oh **God**, you know, this isn't the man'. [UTS/Macquarie Corpus]
>
> Now straight – straight – **Jesus**! Ok; open the door. [Text 4-3]

Both Vocatives and Expletives are features of dialogue, especially casual conversation where they often occur one after the other and together reinforce the 'you-&-me' dimension of the meaning.

We should distinguish from Expletives the individual lexical items ('swear words') that may be sprinkled prosodically anywhere throughout the discourse and have no grammatical function in the clause (as with *bloody* in *it's a bloody taxation bloody policy, God*). In fact, they have very little function of any kind, except to serve as the ongoing punctuation of speech when the speaker has nothing meaningful to say.

To round off this presentation of the elements of the interpersonal structure of the clause in English, let us represent the elements schematically in relation to the textual and experiential structures of the clause: see Figure 4-12.

This diagram shows which interpersonal elements can serve as Theme – textual Theme (conjunctive Adjunct), interpersonal Theme (comment Adjunct, mood Adjunct, Finite, Vocative), topical Theme (Subject, Complement, circumstantial Adjunct; Predicator in an 'imperative' clause, WH- element in a 'wh- interrogative clause) – or as Rheme. The diagram also shows the correlations between interpersonal elements and experiential ones. Subject and Complement are participants, Finite and Predicator correspond to the process, and circumstantial Adjuncts to circumstances.

4.4 Mood as system; further options

The network in Figure 4-13 shows the full range options in MOOD that we are discussing in the present chapter. The mood types that we have already discussed, declarative and yes-no interrogative are terms in the systems of INDICATIVE TYPE and INTERROGATIVE TYPE. In this section we will introduce further options: wh- interrogative – a subtype of interrogative contrasting with yes/no interrogative, exclamative – a subtype of declarative contrasting with affirmative, and imperative – the primary mood type contrasting with indicative (declarative and interrogative).

4.4.1 WH- interrogatives

The WH- element is a distinct element in the interpersonal structure of the clause. Its function is to specify the entity that the questioner wishes to have supplied. For reasons outlined in Chapter 3 above, it typically takes a thematic position in the clause.

The WH- element is always conflated with one or another of the three functions Subject, Complement or Adjunct. If it is conflated with the Subject, it is part of the Mood element, and the order within the Mood element must therefore be Subject ^ Finite, as shown in Figure 4-14.

If, on the other hand, the WH- element is conflated with a Complement or Adjunct, it is part of the Residue; and in that case the typical interrogative ordering within the Mood element reasserts itself, and we have Finite preceding Subject, as in Figure 4-15.

What about WH- / Predicator? There is always the possibility that the missing piece the speaker wishes to have supplied may be something that is expressed in the verb – an action, event, mental process or relation – and hence functioning as Predicator. But the WH- element cannot be conflated with the Predicator; there is no verb *to what* in

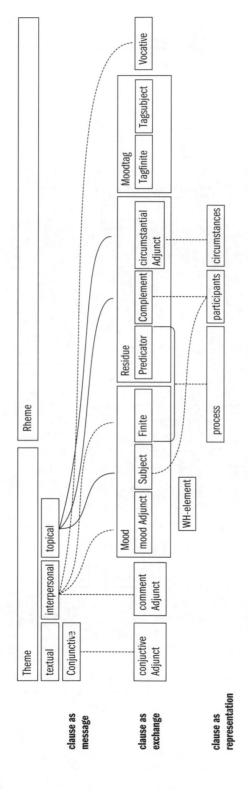

Fig. 4-12 The interpersonal structure of the clause in relation to the textual and experiential structures

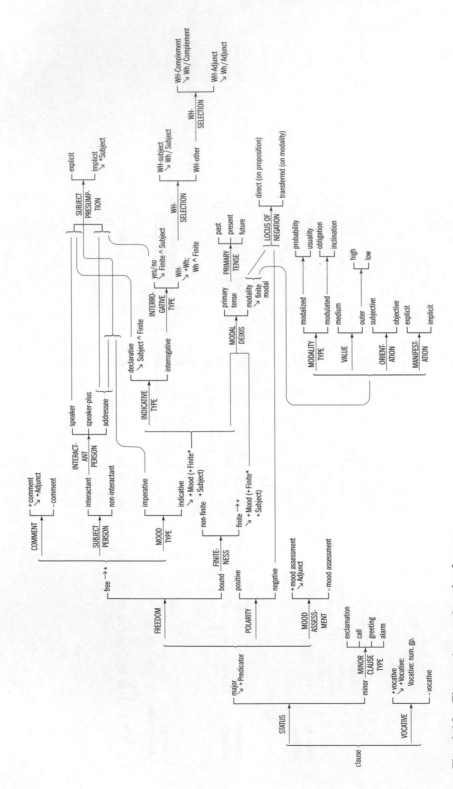

Fig. 4-13 The system network of MOOD

who	killed		Cock Robin
Subject/WH-	'past' Finite	'kill' Predicator	Complement
Mood		Residue	

Fig. 4-14   WH- element conflated with Subject

(a)

whose little boy	are	you
Complement/ WH-	Finite	Subject
Residue	Mood	

(b)

where	have	all the flowers	gone
Adjunct/ WH-	Finite	Subject	Predicator
	Mood		
Residue			

Fig. 4-15   WH- element conflated with (a) Complement, (b) Adjunct

English[17], so we cannot ask *whatted he?* Questions of this kind are realized as *do + what* (Complement), or *what* (Subject) + *happen*, and whatever had something done to it, or happen to it, comes in as an Adjunct, in the form of a prepositional phrase, usually with the preposition *to*. An example is given in Figure 4-16.

what	have	the elephants	done	to the pier
Complement/ WH-	Finite	Subject	Predicator	Adjunct
	Mood			
Residue				

Fig. 4-16   WH- clause having question related to the process

This is one kind of Adjunct that is almost never thematic, for obvious reasons – not only would it have to override a WH- element, but it is not functioning as a circumstantial element anyway.

In the selection of the WH- element, the category of Complement can extend to include the minor Complement of a prepositional phrase (cf. Chapter 5, Section 5.7 on, and Chapter 6, Section 6.5). Here the WH- element is conflated with the minor Complement of a prepositional phrase serving as a circumstantial Adjunct in the clause. Since the WH-

---

[17]   There are languages with interrogative verbs, as illustrated for Tagalog by Martin (2004: 287).

element is thematic, the minor Complement of the prepositional phrase is given the status of Theme, while the minor Predicator appears within the Rheme, in the position the Adjunct has when it is not thematic; for example:

Who were you talking to? – Speaking to Margaret. [UTS/Macquarie Corpus]

Whose room is it in? – Um, Lily's. [UTS/Macquarie Corpus]

How long do you cook the food for? – Errm, well it says an hour ... [UTS/Macquarie Corpus]

Who are you going with? – Oh it's um ... Oh we've got this civil law training thing at Legal Aid tomorrow. Some of the you know the groovier ones want to go out for dinner. [UTS/Macquarie Corpus]

In addition, the WH- element may be conflated with an element from a clause that is projected by the WH- interrogative clause (cf. Chapter 7, Section 7.5; cf. also Matthiessen, 1991a); for example:

How much chicken do you think → I had __ Kate? – I don't know darling. I know it's hard to believe but I wasn't watching. [UTS/Macquarie Corpus]

So how many quarters do you reckon → you could have __ ? – I've had heaps. [UTS/Macquarie Corpus]

4.4.2 Exclamatives

These clauses have the WH- element *what* or *how*, in nominal or adverbial group. Examples:

What a self-opinionated egomaniac that guy is! – Who is it? – Bob Hawke. [UTS/Macquarie Corpus]

Oh what a case Nata Nasimovah was! [UTS/Macquarie Corpus]

What a darling you are! [UTS/Macquarie Corpus]

What a wise man we have for an Emperor! [Amadeus]

What a disagreeable old man I've become. [Citizen Kane]

How secretive you are! [Of Human Bondage]

How beautifully you make love! [Of Human Bondage]

what conflates with a Complement, as in *what tremendously easy riddles you ask*; this is often an attributive Complement, as in *what a fool he is*. *how* conflates with an Adjunct, as in *how beautifully you make love*. In earlier English the Finite in these clauses preceded the Subject, as in *how are the mighty fallen*; but since the Finite ^ Subject sequence became specifically associated with the interrogative mood, the normal order in exclamatives has become Subject ^ Finite. An example is given in Figure 4-17.

Exclamative clauses of the kind just described have a distinctive grammar; but other mood types may also realize exclamations; this includes yes/no interrogative clauses that are negative in polarity:

And then every... come out with a bag full of sweets. – Isn't it amazing! [UTS/Macquarie Corpus]

Oh, you mean, you just happened to go to Darlington? Isn't it wonderful! [UTS/Macquarie Corpus]

However, unlike clauses that are exclamative in mood, such clauses do not have a distinctively exclamative grammar.

What a disagreeable old man	I	've	become
Complement/ WH-	Subject	Finite	Predicator
	Mood		
Residue			

Fig. 4-17 Exclamative clause

4.4.3 Imperatives

The imperative has a different system of PERSON from the indicative. Since the imperative is the mood for exchanging goods-&-services, its Subject is 'you' or 'me' or 'you and me'. If we take the 'second person', 'you', as the base form, an imperative clause displays the following paradigm:

	unmarked for person or polarity	marked for person	marked for polarity
positive	look	YOU look	DO look
negative	DON'T look	DON'T YOU look	DO NOT look

The capitalized forms indicate salience: these syllables must be rhythmically prominent (they may be, but are not necessarily, tonically prominent; see Chapter 1, Section 1.2.1). Thus there is a contrast between the imperative // you / look //, with *you* as Ictus, and the typical declarative // ∧ you / look //, with *you* as Remiss and usually phonetically reduced. (Where two are shown capitalized, at least one is salient.)

In the analysis, the unmarked positive has no Mood element, it consists of Residue (Predicator): the verb form (e.g. *look*) is Predicator only, with no Finite in it. The other forms have a Mood element; this consists of Subject only (*you*), Finite only (*do, don't*), or Finite followed by Subject (*don't you*). Any of these can be followed by a Mood tag: *won't you?, will you?* – showing that the clause is finite, even though the verb is non-finite (the imperative of *be* is *be*, as in *Be quiet!*, not the finite form *are*). Historically the forms *do, don't* derived from non-finite forms of the verb *do*, but they now function analogously to the Finite operator in an indicative clause; compare the dialogic sequence *Look! – Shall I? – Yes, do!* or *No, don't!*, with the response consisting of Mood element only.

Corresponding forms of the imperative with 'you and me' are:

	unmarked for person or polarity	marked for person	marked for polarity
positive	let's look	LET's look	DO let's look
negative	DON'T let's look	DON'T LET'S look	LET'S NOT look

The tag is *shall we?*, and the response form is *Yes, let's (do let's); No, don't let's (let's not)*. Note that the meaning of *let's* always includes 'you'; it is quite different from *we/us* in indicative, which may be either inclusive or exclusive of the listener. Hence a sequence

165

such as *let's go*; *you stay here* is self-contradictory, unless there is a change of addressee; an offer which is non-inclusive is realized either as declarative *we'll go*, or as *let us go*, with imperative on the verb *let*.

What is the analysis of *let's*? Given its place in the paradigm, it is best interpreted as a wayward form of the Subject 'you and I' (note that the marked person is realized by Ictus on *let's*, parallel to that on *you*). The only anomalous form then is the response *Yes, let's!*, *No, let's not!*, which on this analysis has Subject and no Finite; but in each case there is an alternative form with the Finite element in it, *Yes, do let's!*, *No, don't let's!*, which also suggests that *let's* is felt to be a Subject. (The order *do let's* corresponds to the earlier second person ordering as in *Do you look!*.)

The second person imperative ('you ...!') is the typical realization of a demand for goods-&-services, i.e. a command (Section 4.1 above). The 'you-&-me' type, with *let's*, realizes a **suggestion**, something that is at the same time both command and offer. Is there also a 'me' type, a first person imperative realizing a simple offer? The forms most commonly found are *let me* and *I'll*; the latter is clearly declarative, but *let me* may be interpreted as imperative on the analogy of *let's*. We can in fact set up a comparable paradigm, with forms such as

	unmarked for person or polarity	marked for person	marked for polarity
positive	let me help	LET me help	DO let me help
negative	DON'T let me object	DON'T LET ME object	LET ME NOT object

Note however that the meaning of 'offer' is dependent only on the particular goods-&-services referred to: if the meaning required is 'allow me to', the same form will be heard as a command with *let* as second person imperative. Hence an expression such as *let me go* is ambiguous: either offer, first person imperative (= 'I offer to go', with the tag *shall I?*), or command, second person imperative (= 'release me', with the tag *won't you?* or *will you?*). An expression such as *let me help you* is similarly interpretable either way; but here the effect is a blend, since even the second person imperative 'allow me to help you' will still be functioning as an offer.

We may also recognize a third person imperative form as in *Lord save us!*; these are rare except in exclamations and in young children's speech (e.g. *Daddy carry me!*). Here, too, there is a Subject but no Finite operator. These never occur with pronoun Subject; if the Subject required is a pronoun it will always be accompanied by *let* as in *let them beware!*. This is therefore comparable to *let me*, and also to *let us*, from which, of course, the modern *let's* originally derives. (The older variant *let you* ... no longer occurs.)

Examples of imperative clauses are given in Figure 4-18.

4.4.4 MOOD and TONE

We noted in Chapter 1, Section 1.2.2 that intonation makes a significant contribution to the interpersonal meaning of the clause. Here what is significant is the choice of **tone**, the melodic contour of the tone group: whether the pitch is falling or rising, or neither, or some combination of the two (see Halliday, 1967a; Halliday & Greaves, 2008). (Tone is a

(a)

come	into my parlour	will	you
Predicator	Adjunct	Finite	Subject
Residue		Mood tag	

(b)

do	take	care	won't	you
Finite	Predicator	Complement	Finite	Subject
Mood	Residue		Mood tag	

(c)

let's	go	home	shall	we
Subject	Predicator	Adjunct	Finite	Subject
Mood	Residue		Mood tag	

(d)

don't	you	believe	it
Finite	Subject	Predicator	Complement
Mood		Residue	

Fig. 4-18   Imperative clauses

prototypical example of the prosodic mode of expression characteristic of the interpersonal metafunction: see Chapter 2, Table 2-7.)

The fundamental opposition is that between falling and rising; the whole of the tone system can in fact be constructed out of that simple contrast. At the most general level, falling tone means certainty, rising tone means uncertainty. A neutral, more or less level tone, is one that opts out of the choice. There are then two possibilities for forming more complex tones: falling-rising, which means something like 'seems to be certain but isn't', and rising-falling, complementary to that, which means 'seems not to be certain but is'. This defines the five **simple** tones of spoken English. In addition, two **compound** tones are formed by adding the neutral tone to one that ends with a fall. The simple tones are numbered 1 to 5, the compound ones 13 and 53 ('one three', 'five three'). See Table 4-8.

The actual pitch contour traced by any one tone group may be extremely complex; but the distinctive movement takes place at the point of tonic prominence. Whatever direction is taken by the tonic foot (tonic segment) determines the tone of the tone group. We shall assume, for the purposes of this chapter (as we did in Chapter 3), that tonality is unmarked: that is, each tone group is mapped onto one clause (as shown in Chapter 1, Figure 1-4). This will help us to bring out the relationship of tone to mood: we can identify the typical patterns of association between the two.

Let us start with the indicative, which realizes the speech function of proposition. **Declarative** clauses most frequently combine with tone 1, the feature of certainty; but there is a secondary motif, also very common, whereby the declarative goes with tone 4, showing some kind of reservation.

Table 4-8 The primary tones of spoken English

Tone		Symbol	Pitch movement
simple	tone 1	\	falling
	tone 2	/	rising
	tone 3	⌐	level (actually showing a low rise in pitch)
	tone 4	V	falling-rising
	tone 5	⋀	rising-falling
compound	tone 13	∟	falling + level
	tone 53	⋁	rising-falling + level

Within the **interrogative**, the yes/no type is usually found with tone 2, the 'uncertain' rising tone. WH- interrogatives, on the other hand, favour tone 1, because although they are asking for a missing element, the proposition itself is taken as certain. Another way of putting this would be to say that 'certainty' means certainty about the polarity; there is no issue of 'yes or no?' with a WH- interrogative clause.

Proposals are typically combined with tones 1 and 3. **Imperative** clauses, functioning as commands, typically favour tone 1, as also do modulated declaratives (see Section 4.5); but a mild command, such as a request, and also a negative command, often comes with tone 3, which has the effect of leaving the decision to the listener. For the same reason offers are commonly associated with tone 3.

Tone 5 is the one most typical of **exclamative** clauses, where the meaning is 'wow!' – something that is (presented as) contrary to expectation.

Text 4-3 illustrates tone selections in combination with the declarative, yes/no-interrogative, wh- interrogative and imperative clauses. This is language in action, a 'doing' context: three removalists are struggling to get a large fridge through a fairly narrow kitchen entrance, past an oven that's near the entrance.

Text 4-3: Doing – collaborating: language in action, mood and tone combinations
[13] Got to bring it out **sideways** a little **bit** [1] yeah [1] **right** [1] like **that**. [3] In we **come** again. [13] **In a bit** [3] come in around **here** [3] now **straight** [3] **straight** [1] **Jesus!** [3] **OK** [3] open the **door** [1] so you can butterfly around the **oven**.

[1] Got to get it **back**.

[1] Which way d'you want to **go**? [2] Is it **jagging** or anything? [2] Can you get that **door** round? [1] You can't get that **door** round [1] is that the **trouble**? [4] No chance of moving that **oven** [1] **is** there?

The tones are not, however, simply additional markers attached to the realization of mood. They realize distinct grammatical systems of their own, which are associated with the mood categories. The general name for systems that are realized by tone is KEY. The term KEY covers a number of systems; here we will note just those that relate to the contrasts mentioned above (for a fuller treatment, see Halliday & Greaves, 2008).

(1) declarative clauses

>   unmarked statement: tone 1
>   reserved statement: tone 4
>   insistent statement: tone 5
>   tentative statement: tone 3
>   protesting statement: tone 2

(2) WH- interrogative clauses

>   unmarked WH- question: tone 1
>   tentative question: tone 2
>   echo question: tone 2 with tonic on WH- element

(3) yes/no interrogative clauses

>   unmarked yes/no question: tone 2[18]
>   peremptory question: tone 1

(4) imperative clauses

>   command: tone 1 (unmarked in positive)
>   invitation: tone 3 (unmarked in negative)
>   request (marked polarity): tone 13, with tonic on *do/don't*
>   plea: tone 4

Minor clauses – exclamations, calls, greetings and alarms (see Section 4.6.2) – have varied tones depending on their function. Greetings, and also alarms, tend to have tone 1 or tone 3; exclamations tone 5, calls (vocatives) have every possible tone in the language, with noticeable differences in meaning, as in (examples from Halliday & Greaves, 2008).

// 1 Eileen // ('come here!', 'stop that')

// 2 Eileen // ('is that you?', 'where are you?')

// 3 Ei/**leen** // ('listen!', 'I've got something to say to you')

// 4 Eileen // ('listen carefully!', 'don't tell anyone', 'be honest')

// 5 Eileen // ('now I've told you before!', 'take a look at that!')

Many set phrases have one particular tone associated with them, for example:

// 5 far / **from** it //   // 5 certainly //   // 4 **hardly** //   // 13 **never** / **mind** //

// 3 your / **turn** //   // 1 good / **evening** //   // 3 good / **night** //

---

[18] This tone 2 may also occur with a declarative or imperative clause, querying a preceding statement or command.

There are a number of further systems of this kind, some realized by more delicate distinctions within the primary tones (e.g. tone 1: high falling/mid falling/low falling; tone 2: high rising/sharp fall-rise), others by contrasts within the pretonic segment of the tone group.

In this section, we have sketched the extension in delicacy of the basic mood types that is available in spoken English thanks to the phonological resources of tone. Because a systemic account of grammar takes paradigmatic organization as fundamental (see Chapter 1, Section 1.3.2), there is no problem with incorporating considerations of tone (or intonation, in general) into the account since terms in systems may realized by different syntagmatic patterns such as fragments of constituency-like structure, e.g. 'declarative' ↘ Subject ^ Finite or prosodic patterns, e.g. 'reserved statement' ↘ tone 4. Such realizational patterns may change over time in a given language, as they have in English in terms of the function in the grammar of the relative sequence of Subject and Finite, gradually over a few centuries (cf. Ellegård, 1953). In the grammar of MOOD in English, the general principle is that less delicate distinctions in mood are realized through the Mood element – its presence and the nature and relative sequence of its element, Subject and Finite, plus the presence of the WH- element, whereas more delicate distinctions are realized by distinctions in tone. But such patterns vary across languages. For example, in Vietnamese and Cantonese, mood distinction of all degrees of delicacy are essentially realized by interpersonal (modal) particles (which may, of course, have special prosodic features), and in yet other languages the Predicator may be the main domain of realizations in terms of verbal morphology (see Matthiessen, 2004b: Section 10.4; Teruya *et al.*, 2007, and references therein).

In English, tones also play a role in some interpersonal systems other than MOOD, viz. in certain parts of the system of MODAL ASSESSMENT. For example, speech-functional comment Adjuncts of the type 'assurance' are associated with tone 1, whereas those of 'concession' are associated with tone 4. Similarly, certain modalities are associated either with tone 1 or tone 4.

4.4.5 FREEDOM: 'free' and 'bound' clauses

Let us now turn to the system of FREEDOM that was shown in Figure 4-16. So far we have been concerned with 'free' clauses; the term 'free' is the entry condition to the system of MOOD TYPE. Semantically, this means that 'free' clauses realize either propositions or proposals, serving to develop exchanges in dialogue either by initiating new exchanges or by responding to ones that have already been initiated.

In contrast, 'bound' clauses are not presented by the speaker as being open for negotiation. For instance, in Text 4-1, Jana presents her mother with a problem in the form of a proposition realized by a 'free' clause, and she backs this up with a reason realized by a 'bound' clause:

Statement: give & information	Supporting reason: presume & information
↘ free: declarative	↘ bound
Well, I'm still afraid of him	'cause he's bitten me.
I'm scared	because I've had an experience where Boof has bit me.

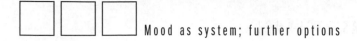

Jana thus presents the reason not as a challengeable statement but as supporting information to be taken for granted. Thus Jana's mother would be more likely to say *Are you?* rather than *Has he?* in response to *Well, I'm still afraid of him 'cause he's bitten me*; or at least, this is how Jana positions her mother – in response to her mother's immediately preceding, reassuring statement *He won't bite you darling*. Jana contests this indirectly, by propositionalizing her fear and downgrading the issue of biting to the states of presumed information about what happened in the past.

In this example, the bound clauses are hypotactically dependent on a dominant (main) clause in a hypotactic clause nexus (see Chapter 7): the dominant part of the nexus is realized by a 'free' clause and the dependent part by a 'bound' one. This is a very common pattern, although a dependent clause may of course be dependent on another dependent clause; e.g.

> ||| Two men were killed by lethal injection in Texas this year, || **even though** they were 17 || **when** they committed their offences ||| [Text 2]

> ||| Tours leave from Circular Quay at 10.15am, 12.15am and 2.00pm Tuesday to Sunday, || **although** you will certainly need to book in advance || **by** ringing Captain Cook Cruises on 2515007. ||| [Text 22]

By another step, 'bound' clauses may be further removed from the line of negotiation. They may be down-ranked, and embedded as elements in the structure of a group, either a nominal group or an adverbial one:

> ||| I know || this is in our reach || because we are guided by a power larger than ourselves [[who creates us equal in His image]]. ||| [Text 307: George W. Bush Inaugural in 2001]

> ||| The next step is [[to remove some impurities]]. ||| [Text 410]

> ||| But there was a kind of common moral ground [[in which a good bit of the debate took place]], || and as it resolved, || which it essentially did, || you see [[a consciousness emerging of [[what really is right]]]], || which must mean [[it reflects our built-in conception of [[what's right]]]]. ||| [Text 172]

Whether they are dependent or downranked, 'bound' clauses may be either 'finite' or 'non-finite'. 'Finite' clauses are typically introduced by a binder (or relative/interrogative item), and have the same modal structure as 'declarative' clauses, i.e. Mood: Subject ^ Finite – even when they are reports of questions (see Chapter 7, Section 7.5): (*they told me*) *that **he had** left*; (*they asked me*) *whether **he had** left*; (*they asked me*) *when **he had** left*. 'Non-finite' clauses may be introduced by a binder, a structural preposition or conjunctive preposition; but they may also appear without one (see Chapter 7, Section 7.4.4). Most of the examples we have given so far have been of 'finite' clauses, so let us add a few 'non-finite' ones.

> ||| The worsening concentration of global corporate power over our government has turned that government frequently against its own people, || denying its people their sovereignty [[to shape their future]]. ||| [Text 174]

> ||| Then he went in the Navy || and helped design various gunnery training devices [[used during World War II]]. ||| [Text 7]

> ||| My dear Ellen: Your kind letter of October 19th, 1917, has just been received || and it seems nice [[to hear something of the family]] || and I shall be thankful to you for further communications. ||| [Text 111]

Non-finite clauses are even further removed from the status of negotiability than finite ones.

When we consider the negotiability or challengeability of 'bound' clauses, we thus find two variables: (i) is the clause dependent on another clause (or combination of clauses) in a clause nexus or is it down-ranked, embedded in the structure of a group; (ii) is the clause finite or non-finite? See Table 4-9.

Table 4-9 'Bound' clauses – function and finiteness

	Finite	**Non-finite**
dependent	they left || after they had eaten dinner	they left || after eating dinner
down-ranked	their departure ⟦after they had eaten dinner⟧	their departure ⟦after eating dinner⟧

'Bound' clauses are, as we have suggested, presented as presumed rather than as negotiable. They lack a number of the interactive features of 'free' clauses. They are very unlikely to be tagged even if they are 'finite' and thus look structurally like 'declarative' clauses. For example, while *they left after they had eaten dinner, didn't they?* is perfectly fine since it is the 'free' clause *they left* that is tagged, *they left after they had eaten dinner, hadn't they* is decidedly odd; and *their departure after they had eaten dinner, hadn't they* seems impossible. And 'non-finite' clauses cannot be tagged. Similarly, Vocatives and speech-functional comment Adjuncts – both highly interactive features – are unlike to occur with 'bound' clauses. Thus, *frankly they left after they had eaten dinner* is straightforward, but *they left after frankly they had eaten dinner* is unlikely. As everywhere else, the grammar operates with clines rather than with dichotomies, and it is possible to find what look like tagged bound clauses, as in the following example from Matthiessen (1995a: 432):

||| That's the one ⟦⟦I should have || if I had any⟧⟧ || because it's jolly, isn't it? ||| [LLC: 210]

At the same time, if clauses have more interactive features such as tags, they are closer to being 'free' rather than 'bound'. Compare the actual example with the following constructed variant: *because it's jolly, isn't it, that's the one I should have if I had any.* This version seems much less likely because the reason clause precedes the consequence clause – it is thematic within the clause nexus (see Chapter 7), so it can no longer be interpreted paratactically as a 'free' clause on the model of *for it's jolly, isn't it?*

4.5 POLARITY and MODAL ASSESSMENT (including modality)

We referred above, in discussing the Finite verbal operator (Section 4.2.2), to the systems of POLARITY and MODALITY: POLARITY as the opposition between positive (*It is. Do that!*) and negative (*It isn't. Don't do that!*); MODALITY as the speaker's judgement, or request of the judgement of the listener, on the status of what is being said (*It could be. Couldn't it be? You mustn't do that. Must you do that?*). Both POLARITY and MODALITY are realized through the Mood element, either through the Finite element (*It is/It isn't; It is/It must be*) or through a separate mood Adjunct (*It is/It is not; It is/It certainly is*). But interpersonal judgements, or assessments, extend beyond the 'core' grammatical system of modality to include assessments of temporality and intensity realized like modality through mood

172

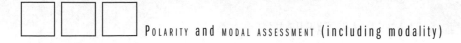

Adjuncts (e.g. *It is/It already is/It almost is*), and also other types of assessments beyond the mood itself that relate either to the proposition being exchanged (e.g. *Fortunately it is*: 'it is, which is fortunate') or to the act of exchanging it (e.g. *Frankly it is*: 'I'm telling you frankly it is'). We will discuss POLARITY first, then introduce MODALITY as cline between positive and negative polarity, and finally extend the description to other types of MODAL ASSESSMENT based on our account of modality.

4.5.1 POLARITY

The positive/negative opposition is one that is fairly certain to be grammaticalized in every language, in association with the clause as proposition or proposal. Typically the positive clause is formally unmarked, while the negative is realized by some additional element: in English, by the word *not* located in the neighbourhood of the verb (for other languages, see Matthiessen, 2004b: Section 10.4.2.7).[19]

If we take account of a wide range of discourse types, positive probably works out around ten times as frequent as negative (see Halliday & James, 1993). But it would be wrong to think of positive as simply the absence of a negative feature; choosing positive is just as substantive and meaningful as choosing negative, and this is suggested symbolically in English by the way the negative marker may get reduced to the point where positive and negative are more or less equivalent in weight and the negative marker can no longer be detached to leave a positive form intact, e.g. *can/can't, will/won't*, and, in rapid speech, *i'n't, doe'n't* (for *isn't, doesn't*).

This kind of fusion happens only in conjunction with the Finite element – *not* does not get reduced if the verb is non-finite; and this reflects the systemic association of polarity with mood. What carries the polarity feature, positive or negative, is the speech functional component of the proposition or proposal; hence when the speaker adds a **mood tag**, meaning 'please check!', the unmarked form of the tag is the one that reverses the polarity:

You know them don't you?	I didn't hurt you, did I?
Keep quiet can't you!	Don't tell him will you!

If the polarity in the tag remains constant, the meaning is assertive rather than seeking corroboration (cf. Section 4.1).

It's you is it? ('It would be!')	They won't pay won't they? ('I'll see about that.')

It is this reversal of polarity in the tag that enables us to identify the polarity of clauses containing other negative expressions, such as *no, never, no one, nowhere, seldom*:

---

[19] The term 'polarity' was introduced by Halliday (e.g. 1956) to fill a terminological gap. Linguists have also used the term 'negation'. The drawback with this term is that it foregrounds 'negative' over 'positive' and does not highlight the nature of the contrast. As an alternative to 'positive', linguists have also used 'affirmative', but this term has also been used as an alternative to 'declarative'.

There's no more paper in the box, is there?

They never came back again, did they?

It seldom works that way, does it?

No one with any sense would behave like that, would they?

These clauses all have negative polarity; so if a negative tag is added, it becomes assertive: *there is no more paper isn't there?*[20] By contrast, if the negative word is part of some element in the Residue, the clause itself may be positive:

It's a question that's never really been addressed, isn't it?

She could have not known about it, couldn't she?

Well you can not go, can't you?

What is the meaning of polarity in interrogative? In a yes/no interrogative clause, which is precisely a request for polarity and hence presumably cannot itself pre-empt the choice, both positive and negative can occur; and here the negative does appear as a marked option, in that while the positive contains no suggestion regarding the likely answer, the negative is, in the traditional formulation, a 'question expecting the answer "yes" ':

Haven't you seen the news?

Aren't those potatoes done yet?

Aren't you pleased with it?

(the mother's question to a child showing no great enthusiasm for a gift). In fact the typical meaning is slightly more complex than this formulation suggests; what the speaker is saying is something like 'I would have expected the answer yes, but now I have reason to doubt'.

How then is the negative question answered? The responses *yes, no* (see below) state the polarity of the answer, not the agreement or disagreement with that of the question:

Haven't you seen the news? – No (I haven't). Yes (I have).

– whereas some languages reverse the pattern, or (like French, German and Swedish) have a third form for the contradictory positive term (cf. Halliday & Hasan, 1976: 208–209).

In the WH- interrogative, the negative is more variable. It is common enough with *why*, especially in contexts of disapproval; e.g. *Why didn't you tell me before?* With the other WH- items the negative is more restricted. It does occur straightforwardly as a question, e.g. *Which ones don't contain yeast?*; and especially perhaps in questions of the echo type:

---

[20] The tendency in speech is to prefer the 'not ... any' combination: rather than *it goes nowhere*, which seems awkward to tag, we get *it doesn't go anywhere* (tag: *does it?*). Likewise *it doesn't often work that way, does it?* This form of realization shows whether the negative is located in the Mood or in the Residue. Thus in *there isn't any more paper in the box, is there?*, the negative is shown to be located in the Mood element, in contrast with: *there is no more paper in the box, is there?*; but in either case, the unmarked reversed polarity of the tag reveals the location of the negative item.

They didn't have any bananas. – What didn't they have? Otherwise it tends to function as the equivalent of a generalized positive:

I'd love to live in a house like that! – Who wouldn't? (= 'Everybody would.')

To return briefly to the words *yes* and *no*: these are direct expressions of polarity, but they have more than one functional status. If they are expressing a speech function, they are mood Adjuncts; if not, they are continuatives (Chapter 3, Section 3.4 on (1)) and have no place in the mood structure.

(1) *yes* and *no* may function as statements; either in answer to a question, in acknowledgement to a statement, in undertaking of a command or in acceptance of an offer (cf. Table 4-1). They are then mood Adjuncts. In this function they are phonologically salient and often carry tonic prominence. They may occur elliptically, as a clause on their own; or thematically within the responding clause. So, in answer to *It's Tuesday, isn't it?* we might have various forms of denial, as in Figure 4-19. Note that in (b) the response consists of two clauses; the *no* is tonic, as shown by the comma in writing, and could have stood alone as an answer. In (c) the *no* is salient but not tonic, and the response is a single clause.

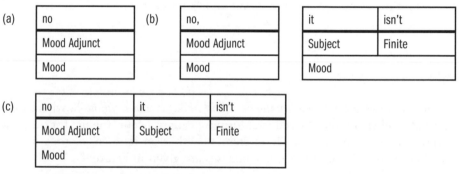

Fig. 4-19   Yes and no as mood Adjunct

(2) *yes* and *no* may function as part of a textual Theme (like *oh, well*). Here they are continuatives and serve to signal that a new move is beginning, often but not necessarily a new speaker's turn; they have no speech function of their own, and therefore merely reflect the current polarity – they are not selecting for positive/negative (and so cannot bring about a switch). In this case they are almost always phonologically weak. Examples are given in Figure 4-20.

(3) *yes* (but not *no*) may function as a minor clause, as response to a call; it carries tonic prominence, typically on a rising tone, for example *Paddy! – Yes?* It does not seem necessary to label this function grammatically (see Section 4.6.2, on minor clauses). Finally, we should note that the negative word *not* occurs in two functions: either it is simply a formal or written variant of the Finite negative element *n't*, in which case it is part of the Finite; or it is a distinct modal Adjunct in Mood or Residue. In the latter case it is phonologically salient and may also be tonic, e.g.

(a)   They're late. — [new speaker:]

yes	they	usually	are
	Subject	Mood Adjunct	Finite
	Mood		
textual: continuative	topical		
Theme		Rheme	

(b)   I don't like it. — [same speaker:]

no	I	don't	like	the idea
	Subject	Finite	Predicator	Complement
	Mood		Residue	
textual: continuative	topical			
Theme		Rheme		

Fig. 4-20   Continuatives yes and no: mood and theme structure

// I will / not al/**low** it //

// we were / **not** im/pressed //

In non-finite clauses such as *not having been told about it, not to allow it*, where there is, of course, no Finite element and the reduced form *n't* cannot occur, the *not* (or other negative modal Adjunct) may constitute a Mood element either on its own, or together with the Subject if there is one.[21] Some specimen analyses are given in Figure 4-21.

4.5.2 Modality

Polarity is thus a choice between yes and no. But these are not the only possibilities; there are intermediate degrees, various kinds of indeterminacy that fall in between like 'sometimes' or 'maybe'. These intermediate degrees, between the positive and negative poles, are known collectively as MODALITY. What the modality system does is to construe the region of uncertainty that lies between 'yes' and 'no'.

But there is more than one route between the two, (1) one for propositions, and (2) one for proposals. (1) In between the certainties of 'it is' and 'it isn't' lie the relative probabilities of 'it must be', 'it will be', 'it may be'. (2) Likewise, in between the definitive 'do!' and 'don't!' lie the discretionary options 'you must do', 'you should do', 'you may do'.

---

[21] The principle is rather complex, but it works as follows: if the agnate finite clause is negative (as shown by the tag; e.g. *she was never given a proper chance, was she?*) then the negative Adjunct functions as Mood element. If the agnate finite clause is positive (e.g. *she could **not** have known about it, couldn't she?*) then the negative Adjunct forms part of the Residue.

176

she	couldn't	possibly		not		have known	about it
Subject	Finite	Mood Adjunct		Mood Adjunct		Predicator	Adjunct
Mood						Residue	

never		having been given		a proper chance	
Mood Adjunct		Predicator		Complement	
Mood		Residue			

for	anyone	not		to take	such a warning	seriously
	Subject	Mood Adjunct		Predicator	Complement	Adjunct
	Mood			Residue		

Fig. 4-21 **Modal Adjunct of polarity in finite and non-finite clauses**

The space between 'yes' and 'no' thus has a different significance for propositions and for proposals.

(1) Propositions. In a proposition, the meaning of the positive and negative pole is asserting and denying; positive 'it is so', negative 'it isn't so'. There are two kinds of intermediate possibilities: (i) degrees of probability: 'possibly/probably/certainly'; (ii) degrees of usuality: 'sometimes/usually/always'. The former are equivalent to 'either yes or no', i.e. maybe yes, maybe no, with different degrees of likelihood attached. The latter are equivalent to 'both yes and no', i.e. sometimes yes, sometimes no, with different degrees of oftenness attached. It is these scales of probability and usuality to which the term 'modality' strictly belongs. We shall refer to these, to keep them distinct, as **modalization**.

Both probability and usuality can be expressed in the same three ways: (a) by a finite modal operator in the verbal group (see Table 4-5), e.g. *that will be John, he'll sit there all day*; (b) by a modal Adjunct of (i) probability or (ii) usuality (see Table 3-5), e.g. *that's probably John, he usually sits there all day*; (c) by both together, forming a prosody of modalization (cf. Halliday, 1970, 1979) e.g. *that'll probably be John, he'll usually sit there all day*.

Note that in a statement the modality is an expression of the speaker's opinion: *that will be John* 'that's John, I think'; whereas in a question it is a request for the listener's opinion: *will that be John?* 'is that John d'you think?'. Modality is thus grounded in the initiating role of an exchange (cf. Figure 4-1). Note also that even a high value modal ('certainly', 'always') is less determinate than a polar form: *that's certainly John* is less certain than *that's John*; *it always rains in summer* is less invariable than *it rains in summer*. In other words, you only say you are certain when you are not.

(2) Proposals. In a proposal, the meaning of the positive and negative poles is prescribing and proscribing: positive 'do it', negative 'don't do it'. Here also there are two kinds of intermediate possibility, in this case depending on the speech function, whether command or offer. (i) In a command, the intermediate points represent degrees of obligation: 'allowed

177

to/supposed to/required to'; (ii) in an offer, they represent degrees of inclination: 'willing to/anxious to/determined to'. We shall refer to the scales of obligation and inclination as **modulation**, to distinguish them from modality in the other sense, that which we are calling modalization.

Again, both obligation and inclination can be expressed in either of two ways, though not, in this case, by both together: (a) by a finite modal operator, e.g. *you should know that*, *I'll help them*; (b) by an expansion of the Predicator through verbal group complexing (see Chapter 8, Section 8.5), (i) typically by a passive verb, e.g. *you're supposed to know that*, (ii) typically by an adjective, e.g. *I'm anxious to help them*.

Proposals that are clearly positive or negative, as we have seen, are goods-&-services exchanges between speaker and hearer, in which the speaker is either (i) offering to do something, e.g. *shall I go home?*, (ii) requesting the listener to do something, e.g. *go home!*, or (iii) suggesting that they both do something, e.g. *let's go home!* They rarely have third person Subjects, except as prayers or oaths. Modulated clauses, on the other hand, while they also occur frequently as offers, commands and suggestions (*I'll be going, you should be going, we ought to be going*), regularly implicate a third person; they are statements of obligation and inclination made by the speaker in respect of others, e.g. *John's supposed to know that, Mary will help*; such statements of obligation are common in regulatory texts, as in

> Subject to the provisions of Article 6, <u>a Member</u> **shall not** provide support in favour of domestic producers in excess of the commitment levels specified in Section I of Part IV of its Schedule. [WTO: Uruguay Round Agreement]

– see Text 10-7, and in such texts, Subjects are often realized by nominal groups denoting inanimate entities and also abstractions (see Text 4-4 below):

> <u>Any casual vacancy on the Executive</u> **shall** be filled by a ballot of the members of the Association at any general meeting. [From continuation of Text 4-4]

Such statements of obligation function **as propositions**, since to the person addressed they convey information rather than goods-&-services. But they do not thereby lose their rhetorical force: if Mary is listening, she can now hardly refuse; and we know what happens if we don't obey the law!

Thus once a proposal becomes discretionary, it shifts into the indicative mood to accommodate the modal operator; this also means that it takes the full indicative person system, not the restricted person system of the imperative. Modal clauses are thus in principle ambiguous as between proposition and proposal (cf. Halliday & Matthiessen, 1999: 558– 560, on indeterminacy in the system of modality): this is shown up when the experiential meaning of the clause points strongly in one direction or the other, for example, *she must be very careless* is likely to be interpreted as proposition (modalization), because one does not usually enjoin people to be careless, whereas *she must be very careful* is more likely to be interpreted as a proposal (modulation).

Both modalization and modulation can of course occur in texts of all kinds; but texts operating in certain situation types are likely to favour either modalization or modulation. For example, modalization is favoured in 'expounding' contexts where the certainty of the

knowledge being expounded needs to be assessed. There is one example in the taxonomic report analysed experientially in Table 5-13 in Chapter 5: [10.1] *The creature **may** have been able to swing the club with great force*, where *may* indicates low probability. At the same time, there are also examples in such texts of the 'potentiality' type of modulation (rather than of the 'obligation' type), as in Predicator of the clause just quoted, *been able to*, and in clause [6] of the same text: *With its small teeth and weak jaws the dinosaur **could** take only plants which **could** be easily bitten off*. Potentialities associated with this dinosaur is part of the characterization of it.

In contrast, as we noted above, modulation of the 'obligation' subtype is highly favoured in texts operating in regulating texts, as illustrated by Text 4-4, an extract from the constitution of an association (for another illustration, see Chapter 10, Text 10-7). In such texts, modals of obligation are very common; in addition to *shall* and *may* and *be required to*, this text also includes *must*. While *shall* is quite uncommon in English in general as a modal of obligation, in regulatory texts, it is highly favoured. The regulatory nature of the text also comes through in the lexis: *rule, contravene, constitution, act*.

Text 4-4: Enabling – regulating (written, monologic): extract from the constitution of an association[22]
RULE MAKING POWER

The Association **shall** make such rules as **are required** to carry out its functions. The rules **shall not** contravene the terms of this constitution, the Education Reform Act, 1990, or the Parents and Citizens' Associations Incorporation Act, 1976. The rules **may** be adopted, altered or withdrawn according to a simple majority vote at any meeting of the Association for which a month's notice has been given. Such notice **shall** include details of the proposed changes. The rules **shall** provide for the procedure to be followed –

(a) at meetings of the Association

(b) to convene a substitute meeting when a quorum is not attained at a meeting

(c) in making an application for membership.

What is the nature of these modal systems? Since modality is an expression of indeterminacy, it might be expected that the systems themselves would be notably indeterminate; but they are no more so than grammatical systems in general. Let us take the system of probability as one with which to explore further. As we have seen, probability may be construed by Finite operators, by modal Adjuncts, and by a combination of the two. We can therefore set up the following paradigm.

certain	that must be true	that's certainly true	that must certainly be true
probable	that will be true	that's probably true	that will probably be true
possible	that may be true	that's possibly true	that may possibly be true

What justifies us in setting this up as a systemic paradigm? These examples are all positive; let us now make the proposition negative.

---

[22] 'Constitution for Epping Heights Public School Parents' and Citizens' Association'. Text due to Mira Kim.

certain	that must be not true	that's certainly not true
probable	that will be not true	that's probably not true
possible	that may be not true	that's possibly not true

Suppose now we transfer the negative feature from the proposition itself to the modality:

certain	that can't be true	that's not possibly true
probable	that won't be true	that's not probably true
possible	that needn't be true	that's not certainly true

Notice what happens. The middle row is unaffected: it makes no difference whether we say *that's probably not true* or *that's not probably true* (or more commonly *that's not likely to be true*). But the top and bottom rows reverse the modality: 'certain + not' = 'not + possible'; 'possible + not' = 'not + certain'. If the domain of the negation is switched from the proposition to the modality, the value of the modality in the outer rows also has to be switched. There is some variation in the items that most typically occur: *can't*, rather than *mayn't*; *needn't*, rather than *mustn't*; *not necessarily*, rather than *not certainly*; but these do not affect the principle at work.

This paradigm shows that probability is organized as a system of three values: a median value 'probable' where the form of the negative is the same whether it is attached to the modality or the proposition, and two outer values, high 'certain' and low 'possible', where there is a switch from high to low, or from low to high, if the negative is shifted between the two domains. We can represent this in a network as shown in Figure 4-22.

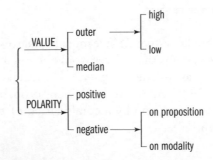

Fig. 4-22 **The systems of** VALUE **and** POLARITY

All nine feature combinations may be realized by Finite operator, modal Adjunct, or both.

Exactly the same set of possibilities arises in respect of the three other dimensions of modality. With usuality, for example, whereas 'not usually' is the same as 'usually not', 'sometimes not' is equivalent to 'not always' and vice versa. Similarly with obligation: 'not supposed to' is the same as 'supposed not to', whereas 'allowed not to' is equivalent to 'not required to', and vice versa. And finally with inclination, 'anxious not to' is the same as 'not anxious to', whereas 'not willing to' is equivalent to 'determined not to', and vice versa. It is

this parallelism in their construction of semantic space, all lying within the region between the two poles of positive and negative, that gives the essential unity to this particular region of the grammar.

Up to now we have treated the different ways of expressing modality simply as if they were free variants: as if *that must be true* and *that's certainly true* are just different ways of saying the same thing. But they are not. In order to explore the difference between them, we should introduce two further variants that cover the same range of meanings. Keeping to the same category of high probability, we will also find expressions such as *it is certain (that) that is true* and *I'm certain (that) that is true*. Notice what is happening here. With these last examples, the speaker is explicitly stating the source of the conviction: it is either being said to be **objective**, as in *it is certain ...*, or presented as a **subjective** judgement on the speaker's part, as in *I'm certain that ...*. By contrast with these, the versions presented earlier leave implicit the source of the conviction. But they also differ along the subjective/objective dimension: whereas the adverbial form *certainly* is a way of objectifying the speaker's evaluation, the verbal form *must* carries a subjective loading – it is the speaker's own judgement on which the validity of the proposition is made to rest[23]. We thus arrive at a matrix of four feature combinations as follows:

	subjective	objective
	subjective	objective
implicit	must	certainly
explicit	I'm certain that ...	it is certain that ...

These options are present throughout the system; we can therefore rewrite the network for modality as shown in Figure 4-23.

We have taken the description of modality up to this degree of detail because in the analysis of discourse, especially the more conversational, dialogic forms, all these variants are likely to be met with, and their differences in meaning may have a marked effect on the unfolding and impact of the discourse[24]. Text 4-5 gives an example of Robert Morley deploying the resources of modality in response to a question during a talk show.

---

[23] We see the difference in orientation between mood Adjuncts such as *certainly* and modal Finites such as *must* in the tag. With the subjective type, the speaker gives his or her subjective assessment, and then asks for the addressee's subjective assessment: *they must've left, mustn't they?* In contrast, with the objective type, the speaker does not ask for the addressee's subjective assessment; the modality is not part of the tag: *they certainly left, didn't they?* Similarly, *can they have left?* means 'in your opinion, have they left?', but *have they perhaps left?* means 'have they left? – it is possible' (cf. *haven't they left?*: 'have they left? – I thought it was so'). In other words, with the subjective orientation, the modality is queried, but not with the objective orientation. Yes/no interrogatives with mood Adjuncts are more restricted than yes/no interrogatives with modal Finites. For example, *has he perhaps left?* is fine, but *has he probably left?* and *has he surely left?* seem less likely; and interrogatives with thematic Adjuncts seem unlikely (e.g. *perhaps has he left?*).

[24] There is an extensive literature on modality in English, and in other languages; and many studies are now corpus-based, providing us with empirical evidence for extending the description of modality. Such studies include Tucker's (2001) systemic functional investigation of *possibly* as a modal adverb.

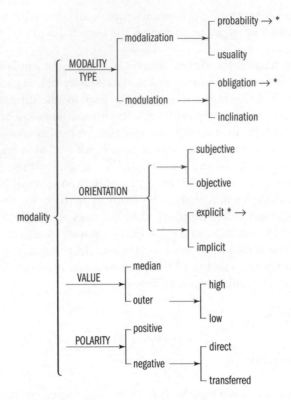

Fig. 4-23 System network of MODALITY

Text 4-5: Reporting – chronicling (spoken, dialogic): extract from media interview with Robert Morley[25]

Simon Dee: Actually, Robert, we **should** have your son on here tonight because <u>I believe</u> Sheridan once said you **would**'ve made an excellent pope. What is your reply to that?

Robert Morley: I don't know why he said I **would** have made – <u>I think</u> if he had taken a more positive attitude and said I **may** make a very excellent pope. I'm very young to be pope still; I'm only 61 and popes are *usually* about 70 when they start – the slight trouble is that I'm not a Roman Catholic but – indeed I don't believe any religion – but if I was – if they insisted that I **should** become pope {Simon Dee: Yes.} I **would** submit. Yes, I **would** like a go at pope; I'**d** like a go at most things. <u>I think</u> it **would** be very nice – very pretty town, Rome, and I **could** do a good deal. I **would probably** be the last pope. I **would** close the Café de Paris, and I **might** close down the Roman Catholic religion, and that **would** be a pity because <u>I think</u> I've met the next pope, actually – without dropping names – and then I have a grandson, you know, who is being brought up in the faith and we all say he is going to be pope one day.

Let us conclude with one more text illustration, an extract from a medical consultation in the emergency department of a hospital (Text 4-6). This is part of the 'interview' phase

---

25 Simon Dee interviews Robert Morley, January 1969. Available through YouTube http://www.youtube.com/watch?v=nJzcLaVHJmc.

of the consultation. Prompted by the doctor, the patient gives an account of how he was injured. Since he is uncertain about what exactly happened, he modalizes his account, ranging over the three values – low (*may*; *maybe*), median (*I think*) and high, but negative (*I don't really know*; *I'm not sure*). All his modalizations except for one (*maybe*) are 'subjective', one of the 'implicit' (*may*) and the rest 'explicit' (*I think*; *I think*; *I don't really know*; *I'm not sure*). In addition, there is one 'subjective' modulation – typical of the way symptoms and signs are described by patients and probed by doctors and nurses: *I couldn't put any pressure on it at all*. If we consider the system of modality in Figure 4-23, we can see that it is easy to profile the patient's selections against this potential, pinpointing which parts he uses and which remain unactivated.

Text 4-6: Recommending – advising (spoken, dialogic): extract from medical[26] consultation

Doctor: So what's been happening? What happened two weeks ago?

Patient: Okay. It's a long story. I was out surf boat rowing. = = Surf board -

Doctor: = = Surfing.

Patient: You know, with the surf boats and we were in the waves {Doctor: Oh, right.}, okay, and waves hit me from behind. I can't really remember how it happened, but **I think** it **may** have foot straps {Doctor: Ah-hm.} so **I think** I've been pushed forward; **I don't really know**, like I thought '**maybe** something hit it', so **I'm not sure**. But being cold water, I didn't really – and then when I got out of the boat and go oh, that doesn't feel very good and I **couldn't** put any pressure on it and swell – like it swelled up and I thought, 'mm'. And I have a fairly high tolerance of pain and I kind of iced it and put it up and everyday I'd go to work and I'd ice it. Went to the physio …

Doctor: But you've been walking like this?

Patient: Yeah, like, kind of like a = = [].

We will return to modality in Chapter 10, Section 10.3, where we shall explain the workings of the system in more detail and show how it depends on the underlying potential for metaphor that is present as an essential property of human language.

4.5.3 Modal assessment

As noted above, there are types of modal assessments that extend beyond the 'core' systems of POLARITY and MODALITY. Polarity is a highly grammaticalized system, in the sense discussed in Chapter 2, Section 2.2; and it defines the outer limits within which modality operates (as shown in Figure 10-6 in Chapter 10). The system of polarity is most likely one of the most highly grammaticalized system in all languages, although the forms of realization vary considerably (see e.g. Matthiessen, 2004b: Section 10.4.2.7).

The system of modality is highly grammaticalized in English, but when we move around the languages of the world, we find a great deal of variation in the grammaticalization of modality and other types of interpersonal judgement (cf. Matthiessen, Teruya & Wu, 2008). For example, some languages foreground evidentiality rather than modality, and some languages do not bring modalization and modulation together into a unified system

---

[26] From the EDCOM corpus (Text 070925P017P).

the way English does. Among Germanic languages, English is unusual in its treatment of 'modal verbs': while such modal verbs have retained a fuller verbal paradigm in other Germanic languages (and also in other Indo-European languages in the 'neighbourhood': see e.g. Caffarel, 2006, on French), English has evolved a closed set of finite modal auxiliary verbs, creating a kind of distance in the grammar between modal auxiliaries and lexical verbs, and of quasi-modals, supplemented by 'periphrastic' forms (e.g. *can – to be able*).

One aspect of the highly grammaticalized nature of modality in English is – not surprisingly – that it has expanded its domain of realization: within the clause, this domain includes not only Finite verbal operators (e.g. *will*) but also Adjuncts within the Mood element (e.g. *probably*); and beyond the clause, it includes 'bi-clausal' realizations such as *I think that ...*; and *it is probable that* serving as 'explicit' manifestations of 'subjective' and 'objective' orientation, as illustrated in 4-5 and Text 4-6 above for explicitly subject orientation, e.g. *I think I've met the next pope, actually*, where *I think* is an explicitly 'subjective' modalization, contrasting with the explicitly 'objective' version *it's probable* in *it's probably that I've met the next pope*. Such manifestations are, in fact, metaphorical extensions of the system of modality, and we shall return to them in Chapter 10, as part of our general account of grammatical metaphor. Since they are metaphorical realizations, they are also analysed as if they were expressions serving as mood Adjuncts, as in Chapter 10, Figure 10-3.

Modality embodies a number of simultaneous systems, as shown in Figure 4-23. Other kinds of modal assessment are characterized by a narrower range of simultaneous systems. One key reason for this is simply that modal operators serving as Finite have evolved in the grammar of English as one type of realization of modality (see Table 4-5), other kinds of modal assessment cannot be realized by finite operators. This is one indication that they are less highly grammaticalized than modality. The one type of realization that is shared by all kinds of modal assessment is the modal Adjunct.

We can recognize two types of modal Adjuncts, (i) mood Adjuncts and (ii) comment Adjuncts. (i) Mood Adjuncts serve within the Mood element, and are closely associated with the meaning of the Finite element – the limiting case being modality, which (as we have seen) can also be realized by the operator serving as Finite. (ii) Comment Adjuncts serve outside the Mood + Residue structure of the clause. They are not part of the proposition realized by Mood + Residue, but are instead comments on it (propositional) or on the act of exchanging it (speech-functional). These different types of modal Adjuncts are characterized by different grammatical properties, including different agnation patterns in terms of possible alternative forms of realization: see Table 4-10 and Figure 4-24. In Table 4-10, we have also included incongruent realizations that serve to make the orientation of the assessment explicit; we will return to these in Chapter 10. We have also noted realizations within the Predicator by verbal group complexes (see Chapter 8, Sections 8.7 and 8.8). Here we will discuss mood Adjuncts first and then turn to comment Adjuncts.

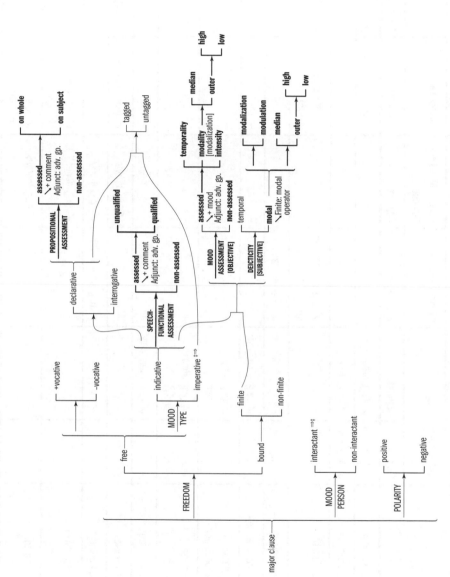

Fig. 4-24 Systems of MODAL ASSESSMENT (PROPOSITIONAL ASSESSMENT, SPEECH-FUNCTIONAL ASSESSMENT, MOOD ASSESSMENT & DEICTICITY: modal) in relation to MOOD and other interpersonal systems of the clause

Table 4-10 Types of modal assessment and forms of realization

Type			Implicit [congruent]				Explicit [incongruent]	
			within Mood		within Residue	outside Mood + Residue	subjective	Objective
			Finite	Adjunct	Predicator	Adjunct	[Adjunct]	[Adjunct]
mood	modality	probability	✓ (e.g. *will*)	✓ (e.g. *probably*)	–	–	✓ (e.g. *I think*)	✓ (e.g. *it's probable*)
		usuality	✓ (e.g. *will*)	✓ (e.g. *usually*)	–	–	–	(✓)
		obligation	✓ (e.g. *will*)	–	✓ (e.g. *be expected to*)	–	√ (e.g. *I expect you to*)	✓ (e.g. *it is expected*)
		inclination	✓ (e.g. *will*)	–	✓ (e.g. *be keen to*)	–	–	–
	temporality	relative to now	–	✓ (e.g. *soon, just*)	–	–	–	–
		relative to expectation	–	✓ (e.g. *still, already*)	–	–	–	–
	intensity	degree	–	✓ (e.g. *almost, hardly*)	–	–	–	–
		counterexpectancy	–	✓ (e.g. *even, only*)	–	–	–	–
comment	propositional	on whole	–	–	–	✓ (e.g. *fortunately*)	✓ (e.g. *I'm happy*)	✓ (e.g. *it's fortunate*)
		on Subject	–	–	✓ (e.g. *be wise to*)	✓ (e.g. *wisely*)	–	–
	speech-functional	unqualified	–	–	–	✓ (e.g. *honestly*)	✓ (e.g. *I tell you honestly*)	–
		qualified	–	–	–	✓ (e.g. *tentatively*)	✓ (e.g. *I tell you tentatively*)	–

186

4.5.3.1 Mood Adjuncts

These are so called because they are closely associated with the meanings enacted by the mood system: modality and temporality, and also intensity. This means that their neutral position in the clause is next to the Finite verbal operator, either just before it or just after it. But there are two other possible locations: before the Subject (i.e. in thematic position – those of temporality and modality have a strong tendency to function as Theme; cf. Chapter 3, Section 3.4), and at the end of the clause as Afterthought. This gives the following paradigm:

(a) but usually they don't open before ten   (thematic)

(b) but they usually don't open before ten   (neutral)

(c) but they don't usually open before ten   (neutral)

(d) but they don't open before ten usually   (afterthought)

The difference between (b) and (c) is also in fact systematic, as becomes clear with some of these Adjuncts when the polarity is negative: contrast *they always don't open* 'they never open' with *they don't always open* 'they open (only) sometimes'. Where this happens the meaning of options (a) and (d) corresponds to that of (b), not (c): e.g. *possibly he couldn't decide* corresponds to *he possibly couldn't decide*, not to *he couldn't possibly decide*. Technically, in (c) the mood Adjunct is actually functioning in the Residue (as can also happen with Adjuncts of negative polarity, e.g. *not* in *One cannot not communicate: every behaviour is a kind of communication.*). But where the polarity is positive, and even (with some categories) where it is negative, the difference between (b) and (c) is effectively neutralized; cf. the example with *usually* above (and on modality in Section 4.5).

The Adjuncts of modality have already been discussed. Adjuncts of temporality relate to interpersonal (deictic) time, as introduced earlier in Section 4.2.2. They relate either (i) to the time itself, which may be near or remote, past or future, relative to the speaker-now; or (ii) to an expectation, positive or negative, with regard to the time at issue (sooner or later than expected, as in *Many have already achieved a degree of financial security.* [ACE_A]: they have achieved it sooner than could be expected). (The latter may also relate to selections in secondary tense; see Chapter 6, Section 6.3.) For example:

I suspect that they **still** think that this is a very different way of learning, and not the way that they would prefer to do things. [UTS/Macquarie Corpus]

They've been typed up and they were the responses to the various things which you had **already** raised in relation to the questions that we were asking in that short survey, so I thought you'd **probably** want to keep a record of that; and **already** when I look back over this, I was absolutely astounded. [UTS/Macquarie Corpus]

Oh, I can't do it **yet**. [UTS/Macquarie Corpus]

And we **still** don't know. [UTS/Macquarie Corpus]

Adjuncts of modality and temporality containing the feature 'negative' have the special property that, when they occur in thematic position, the order of Subject and Finite is typically reversed; e.g.

Never before have fans been promised such a feast of speed with reigning World Champion Ove Fundin sparking the flame that could set the meeting alight. [LOB_A]

This is a relic of an older pattern whereby the Finite operator always followed immediately after the first element in the mood structure (a pattern still found in other Germanic languages). It is not very widespread in current usage, being restricted largely to certain styles of narrative, and to public speaking.

Adjuncts of intensity fall into two classes, of which again one relates to expectation. (i) Those of degree may be total, high degree or low degree; the total display the same shift in value where the clause carries negative polarity (contrast *I entirely disagree, I don't entirely agree*). These Adjuncts (especially the 'total' ones) are typically associated with interpersonally loaded Processes or Attributes; the same adverbs also function regularly as Submodifiers within a nominal group (see Chapter 6, Section 6.2.5). (ii) Those of counterexpectancy are either 'limiting' or 'exceeding' what is to be expected: the meaning is either 'nothing else than, went no further than' or 'including also, went as far as'. Adjuncts of intensity occur medially or finally in the clause, but seldom initially – they cannot be thematic (hence there is no occasion for those containing the feature 'negative' to cause inversion of Subject and Finite). Examples:

This time, however, it **almost** came unstuck, or rather stuck in the mud. [LOB_A]

'These two men **almost** ended up in the West Auckland Cemetery – in more senses than one,' said Mr. H. Hewitt, prosecuting. [LOB_A]

Have they **actually** calculated all the consequences of what they are doing with their tanks and planes in Berlin? [LOB_B]

It suggested, **in fact**, that Miss Kind is a very much better harpsichordist than this recital as a whole revealed. [LOB_C]

A more detailed network for the mood Adjuncts is given in Figure 4-25. Examples of adverbs serving as mood Adjuncts are given in Table 4-11, Table 4-12 and Table 4-13.

Table 4-11 Adverbs serving as mood Adjuncts of temporality

	remote	near
future	eventually	soon
non-future (past/present)	once	just

	since	by
positive	still	already
negative	no longer	not yet

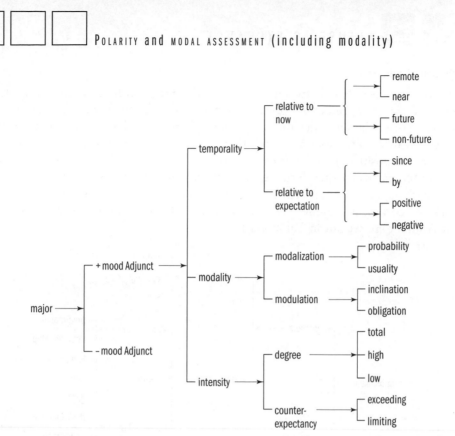

Fig. 4-25   System of mood Adjuncts

Table 4-12 Adverbs serving as mood Adjuncts of modality

	median	outer: high	outer: low
probability	probably	certainly, definitely; no way (no how)	possibly, perhaps, maybe; hardly
usuality	usually	always; never	sometimes, occasionally; seldom, rarely

Table 4-13 Adverbs serving as mood Adjuncts of intensity

degree	total	totally, utterly, entirely, completely
	high	quite, almost, nearly
	low	scarcely, hardly
counterexpectancy	exceeding	even, actually, really, in fact, indeed
	limiting	just, simply, merely, only

4.5.3.2 Comment Adjuncts

There is no very clear line between these and the mood Adjuncts; for example, the 'comment' categories of prediction, presumption and desirability overlap semantically with the mood categories shown under modality. The difference is that comment Adjuncts are less closely tied to the grammar of mood; they are restricted to 'indicative' clauses (those functioning as propositions), and express the speaker's attitude either to the proposition as a whole or to the particular speech function. In other words, the target of the comment may be either ideational (the content of the proposition) or interpersonal (the speech function). A network for comment Adjuncts is given in Figure 4-26; examples of items serving as comment Adjunct are set out in Table 4-14.

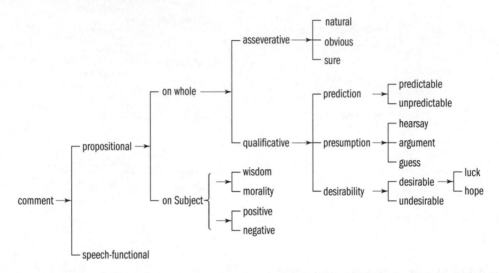

Fig.4-26 System of comment Adjuncts

(1) **The propositional (ideational) type** occur only with declarative clauses. They appear at the same locations in the clause as the mood Adjuncts – though for different reasons: they are less integrated into the mood structure, being located rather according to their significance for the textual organization of the clause. In particular, they are strongly associated with the boundary between information units – realized as a boundary between tone groups: hence the commas that typically accompany them in writing. So they often occur medially, following the item that is prominent; otherwise, they may occur as Theme, frequently as a separate information unit, or in final position as Afterthought. For example:

(a) // **Unfortunately**, // the doctor hasn't left an **address**. //

(b) // The **doctor**, unfortunately, // hasn't left an **address**. //

(c) // The doctor **hasn't**, unfortunately, // left an **address**. //

(d) // The doctor hasn't left an **address**, unfortunately. //

With this type, the speaker is commenting either on the proposition as a whole or on the part played by the Subject. In the first case, the comment may be either asseverative ('it is

Table 4-14 Examples of realizations of comment Adjunct

type					examples of realizations
propositional	on whole	asseverative	natural		naturally, inevitably, of course
			obvious		obviously, clearly, plainly, of course
			sure		doubtless, indubitably, no doubt
		qualificative	prediction	predictable	unsurprisingly, predictably, to no one's surprise
				surprising	surprisingly, unexpectedly
			presumption	hearsay	evidently, allegedly, supposedly
				argument	arguably
				guess	presumably
			desirability	desirable: luck	luckily, fortunately
				desirable: hope	hopefully
				undesirable	sadly, unfortunately
			amusement		amusingly, funnily
			significance		importantly, significantly
	on Subject	wisdom	& positive		wisely, cleverly
			& negative		foolishly, stupidly
		morality	& positive		rightly, correctly, justifiably
			& negative		wrongly, unjustifiably
		typicality			characteristically, typically
speech-functional	unqualified	persuasive	assurance		truly, honestly, seriously (+ tone 1)
			concession		admittedly, certainly, to be sure (+ tone 4)
		factual			actually, really, in fact, as a matter of fact
	qualified	validity	general		generally, broadly, roughly, ordinarily, by and large, on the whole
			specific		academically, legally, politically, ethically, linguistically
		personal engagement	honesty		frankly, candidly, honestly, to be honest
			secrecy		confidentially, between you and me
			individuality		personally, for my part
			accuracy		truly, strictly
			hesitancy		tentatively

so'; typically tone 1) or qualificative ('this is what I think about it'; typically tone 4). These items cannot function as circumstantial Adjuncts: it makes no sense to say *it happened evidently*. Examples:

> Jazz Legend: Billy Higgins was **reportedly** the most recorded jazz drummer in history. He played with such greats as Dexter Gordon, Thelonious Monk, John Coltrane and Herbie Hancock. Higgins died Thursday at the age of 64. Check out the NPR Jazz tribute to Higgins. [www.npr.org, 5v01]

> **Unfortunately** he did not know that his wife had been polishing the furniture that day and she had made too much furniture polish. [ACE_G]

> Referring to spending cuts, Brown said '**unfortunately** our work is not finished.' [Reuters]

In the second case the Subject's role is being evaluated for its wisdom or morality, or typicality; such expressions can occur circumstantially (contrast *wisely*, *he didn't act*, comment Adjunct, with *he didn't act wisely*, circumstance of Manner); for example:

> I think <u>Dr Chatterji</u> is **wisely** implying that reverence is open, faith is blind; reverence permits freedom, faith demands obedience. [KOHL_G]

> <u>They</u> **rightly** thought that juries could not be relied on to convict in certain sorts of cases. [ACE_G]

Such subject-oriented comments may also be expressed as predications, through verbal group complexes serving as Predicator, e.g.

> <u>Jim</u> was **too wise** to push me. [ACE_K] 'Jim wisely didn't push me'

> <u>Harold Clurman</u> is **right** to say that 'Waiting for Godot' is a reflection (he calls it a distorted reflection) 'of the impasse and disarray of Europe's present politics, ethic, and common way of life'. [BROWN1_G] 'Harold Clurman rightly says ... '

> <u>He</u> is **wrong** to inject Eisenhower into this campaign [BROWN1_A] 'he wrongly injects ...'

> during the whole Napoleonic era, <u>the major dramatic critics</u> were **wont** to look upon opera as their exclusive prerogative. [LOB_G]

(2) The speech functional (interpersonal) type may occur with either declarative or interrogative clauses, but with a change of orientation: in a declarative, they express the speaker's angle (as in Text 4-7), while in an interrogative they seek the angle of the listener. Their locations in the clause are more restricted; they strongly favour initial or final position. For example:

> (a) Frankly, were you surprised at the outcome?

> (b) Were you surprised at the outcome, frankly?

The speech functional type also falls into two subtypes, qualified and unqualified. The qualified types are closely related to projection (Chapter 7, Section 7.5 below); they can be expanded by ~ *speaking* as in *generally speaking*, and if construed as a separate intonation unit they will typically take tone 4.

Text 4-7: Reporting – media interview (spoken, dialogic) [Text 184]

REPORTER: Can I ask you first, as a very prominent Liberal MP how you think the row over Shane Stone's memo has affected the party?

ANDREW: Oh Laurie, I'm on your show as the Speaker and **frankly** as the Speaker, as long as I've had this office, I've not made a political comment other than the comments I make to constituents in my electorate. I'm not about to make one this morning.

The unqualified, which cannot be followed by ~ *speaking*, are either claims of veracity ('factual'; if separate, then tone 4) or signals of assurance or admission (if separate, then tone 1; the clause is then typically tone 1 if assurance, tone 4 if admission); for example:

Admittedly, merely denying the right to strike or imposing heavy penalties for such strikes without providing for acceptable procedures to resolve them was too one-sided an approach. Let us, therefore, look for a clue in the Conventions of the ILO that deal with the Freedom of Association. [KOHL_H]

The networks of mood and comment Adjuncts are drawn up in the perspective 'from the same level': they encompass just those items that function as interpersonal Adjunct. Thus they do not include expressions from the same semantic domain which do not function as Adjuncts: typically 'mental'/'verbal' clauses (e.g. *I regret, I admit*) or 'relational' clauses (e.g. *it is regrettable*), non-finite clauses e.g. *to be honest, to tell you the truth, come to think of it*. Such expressions would be included in a network drawn up in the perspective 'from above' (cf. Table 4-10 above). Networks of this kind are beyond the present scope; but the principle is illustrated in the discussion of modality above (followed up in Chapter 10).

4.6 Absence of elements of the modal structure

4.6.1 Ellipsis

We noted in Section 4.2 that a typical pattern of dialogue in English is one where the dialogue is carried forward by the Mood element in the clause. An exchange centring on the validity of an assertion – the identity of the Subject, the choice and degree of polarity – may be realized by clauses consisting of the Mood only, the Residue being established at the start and then presupposed by ellipsis, or by substitution with *do*.

Exchanges involving not the yes/no variable but the WH- variable, where just one element is under discussion, lead to a different form of ellipsis in which everything is omitted except that element. Its function in the clause is presupposed from the preceding discourse.

Examples of both kinds of ellipsis are given in Figure 4-27. The question of ellipsis is taken up again in Chapter 9.

There is also a form of ellipsis of the Subject. In general, every free clause in English requires a Subject, because without a Subject it is impossible to express the mood of the clause, at least in the usual fashion. We have already noted that the difference between declarative and yes/no interrogative is realized by the order of the elements Subject and Finite; and it is impossible to arrange two elements in order if one of them is not there. So while the *it* in *it's raining*, and the *there* in *there was a crash*, do not represent any entity participating in the process of raining or of crashing, they are needed in order to distinguish these from *is it raining, was there a crash*.

I	might	do
Subject	Finite	Predicator
Mood		Residue

I	won't
Subject	Finite
Mood	

(a) (Will you join the dance?)

I	(said the sparrow)	with my bow and arrow
Subject		Adjunct
Mood		Residue

(b) (Who killed Cock Robin?)

Fig. 4-27   (a) Substitution and ellipsis of the Residue (yes/no response); (b) Ellipsis of other presupposed elements (WH- response)

However, there is another feature associated with the realization of these two structures, and that is the intonation: declaratives usually go down in pitch at the end, while yes/no interrogatives typically go up (see Section 4.3). So it is possible to signal mood by intonation, which does not depend on the presence of a Subject; and this makes it possible for a clause to occur without one. There is, in fact, one condition in which clauses in English systematically occur without Subjects, one that depends on the notions of giving and demanding that were discussed as the very beginning of this chapter.

For any clause, there is one choice of Subject that is 'unmarked' – that is assumed, in the absence of evidence to the contrary. In a giving clause (offer or statement), the unmarked Subject is 'I'; while in a demanding clause (question or command), the unmarked Subject is 'you'. This means that, if a clause that on other grounds can be interpreted as offer or statements without a Subject, the listener will understand the Subject 'I' – that is, Subject equals speaker, for example:

(a)   Carry your bag? ('Shall I ...?')

– Would you? Thanks.

(b)   Met Fred on the way here. ('I ...')

– Did you? Where?

Whereas if it is a question or command the listener will understand the Subject 'you' – that is, Subject equals listener, for example:

(c)   Seen Fred? ('have you ...?')

– No, I haven't.

(d)   Play us a tune. ('Will you ...?')

– Shall I? Alright.

Notice that (d) is an ordinary imperative clause. In most accounts of English grammar the imperative is presented as if it was a special case, without any explanation. But it is not; it is simply an instance of this general principle by which a Subject is 'understood'. Being a demanding clause, its unmarked Subject is 'you'.

As these examples show, typically it is the whole of the Mood element that is left implicit in such instances: (*shall I*) *carry your bag?*, (*will you*) *play us a tune!* In an information clause, however, the Finite element may be present either because it is needed to express tense or modality, as in *might see you this evening* ('I ...'), or because it is fused with the Predicator as in (b) above. In such instances only the Subject is 'ellipsed'.

The principle that the Subject to be supplied in a case of ellipsis is always the modally unmarked one, *I* or *you* according to mood, can also be overridden by the context; for example in

(d)   Seen Fred? ('Have you ...?')

        – No; must be away. ('He ...')

the Subject in the response is understood as 'he (Fred)' by presupposition from the preceding question ('anaphoric ellipsis'; see Chapter 9, Section 9.5).

We remarked in Section 4.2 above on the relation between the semantic categories of statement, question, offer and command on the one hand and the grammatical categories of the mood system on the other. The relationship is a rather complex one. For statements and questions there is a clear pattern of congruence: typically, a statement is realized as declarative and a question as interrogative – but at the same time in both instances there are alternative realizations. For offers and commands the picture is even less determinate. A command is usually cited, in grammatical examples, as imperative, but it is just as likely to be a modulated interrogative or declarative, as in *Will you be quiet?*, *You must keep quiet!*; while for offers there is no distinct mood category at all, just a special interrogative form *shall I ...?*, *shall we ...?*, which again is simply one possible realization among many. This would seem to complicate the question just raised, namely which Subject is to be understood if none is present. But in general this follows the grammar; for example, in *Have an orange!* (imperative 'will you'), *Like an orange?* (interrogative 'would you?'), the listener will supply 'you' as Subject and at the same time interpret the clause as an offer. There is rarely any misunderstanding, since the listener operates on the basic principle of all linguistic interaction – the principle that what the speaker says makes sense in the context in which he is saying it.

4.6.2 Minor clauses

The other circumstance in which a clause does not display a Mood + Residue structure is if it is realizing a minor speech function. Minor speech functions are exclamations, calls, greetings and alarms.

These speech functions may be realized by a major clause; for example, exclamations by a particular kind of declarative (the exclamative, discussed in Section 4.4.2), greetings by an interrogative or imperative. But there are other forms used in these speech functions which are not constructed as propositions or proposals. Many of these do not need to be assigned any internal structure of their own.

Exclamations are the limiting case of an exchange; they are verbal gestures of the speaker addressed to no one in particular, although they may, of course, call for empathy on the part of the addressee. Some of them are in fact not language but protolanguage, such as *Wow!*, *Yuck!*, *Aha!* and *Ouch!*. Others are made of language, with recognizable words and sometimes even traces of structure; for example *Terrific!*, *You sod!*, *God's boots!*, *Bugger you!*, *Bullshit!*. They can be analysed as nominal groups (Chapter 6, Section 6.2), or as clauses in terms of transitivity (Chapter 5), if desired.

Calls are the speaker calling to attention another person, or other entity treated as capable of being addressed: deity, spirit, animal or inanimate object. These do relate to the clause as exchange; the structural function is that of Vocative, as in *Charlie!*, *You there!*, *Madam President*, *Oh Lord our Heavenly Father*. Under this heading we could also include the response to a call, where relevant; typically the word *yes* on a rising tone (Section 4.5).

Greetings include salutations, e.g. *Hullo!*, *Good morning!*, *Welcome!*, *Hi!*, and valedictions, such as *Goodbye!*, *See you!*; together with their responses, largely the same set of forms. Under this heading we could include **well-wishings**, like *Your very good health!*, *Cheers!*, *Good shot!*, *Congratulations!*. Both calls and greetings include some that are structured as clauses or nominal groups.

Alarms bear some resemblance to exclamatives, if only in voice quality; but they are addressed to another party, and they are in general derivable from the grammar of the clause – they are intermediate between major and minor clauses. Alarms include (a) warnings, such as *Look out!*, *Quick!*, *Careful!*, *Keep off!*; (b) appeals, like *Help!*, *Fire!*, *Mercy!*, *A drink!*. Many of these are clearly imperative and can be analysed as such: Residue only, consisting of Predicator (*help*), Predicator plus Adjunct (*keep off*), optional Predicator plus Complement (*[be] careful*), and so on. Other are nominal groups; these could in principle be functioning either as Subject or as Complement, but it is usually impossible to decide between these two: would *Fire!*, for example, be 'filled out' as *there's a fire*, or as *fire's broken out*, or even *the house is on fire*? This is one place where it is useful to recognize a distinct structural function; a nominal group which could be either Subject or Complement in an agnate major clause is said to have the function **Absolute**. This is not assigned either to Mood or to Residue. The concept of 'Absolute' function is also relevant to headlines, labels, lists and suchlike.

We've seen that Vocatives can function on their own as minor clauses. At the same time, they can also function as an element of a major clause. When the Vocative functions within a major clause, it is fairly 'loosely' integrated: it falls outside the Mood + Residue structure. There is one other element that occurs in major clauses but which can also function on its own in dialogue. This is a textual element – the Continuative (see Chapter 3, Section 3.4), which is used to indicate how the clause relates to the preceding move in a dialogue: *well*, *oh*, *yes*, *no*, and so on. Such items can also function on their own in dialogue, indicating that the listener is tracking the current speaker's contribution. This tracking has been called 'backchannelling' and items serving this function have been called 'backchannel-continuers' or 'backchannels'; we can extend the category of minor clauses to included instances of this. For example, see Text 4-8:

Text 4-8: Reporting – admission interview [Text 135]

Professor Hart: ||| Yes, || it's not as though you have already tried for two or three months to see how this works out. |||

Mrs Finney: ||| Working. ||| No, no; || what I did do a certain amount – || I've done – || I did a certain amount of reading during the last few months || and I have been and I went away || to did it || to do it. ||| I went a way from home {{Professor Hart: **Yes.**}} || so that I wouldn't be there {{Professor Hart: **Yes.**}} || and it worked very well. |||

Such minor clauses include *yes, mmh, aha, sure*. They do not constitute turns in their own right; rather they serve to ensure the continuity of the interaction by supporting the current speaker's turn (e.g. Stenström, 1994), as when Professor Hart says *yes* to indicate that he's following what Mrs Finney is saying. In face-to-face conversation, they may of course be accompanied – or even replaced – by other, 'paralinguistic', indicators such as nodding.

4.7 Clause as Subject

Up to this point, in our discussion of the clause as exchange, we have been illustrating the Subject with fairly simple, straightforward nominal groups: *I, Mary, this teapot, the man in the moon* and so on. This has been done to avoid complicating the issue with longer and structurally more complex examples.

In real discourse, obviously, there is vastly greater scope and variation in the choice of Subject in a clause. Depending on the register, we will regularly find examples such as the following (the Subject is shown by underlining):

(a) The scientific treatment of music had been popular ever since the days of Pythagoras, but most theorists, like the famous Greek, let their passion for numerical order override practical considerations. Thus even so outstanding a scientist as Kepler held fast, in his *De harmonice mundi* (1619), to the old astrological belief in the association between interval ratios and the structure of the universe, even of human society. The same delight in a neatly arranged system can be seen in the *Gradus ad Parnassum* (1725) of the Austrian composer Fux, …

(*Pelican History of Music*, Vol. II p. 246)

(b) Only about four out of every 10 residents 'affected' even know their new number, || said Kevin Read, spokesman for The Big Number, the phone industry umbrella organization. [Text 15]

(c) A system that just keeps you warm in winter isn't a very good idea.

(d) Somehow this sort of traditional Hamlet aspect in the untraditional character he was playing didn't seem to fit together.

(e) The people who want to play with the cards that have goods trains on have to sit here.

Apart from that in (b), which is a **nominal group complex** (consisting of two nominal groups in paratactic relation; see Chapter 8, Section 8.1), each of these Subjects is a single nominal group. All of them, however, except *most theorists* in (a), contain some embedded material: either a prepositional phrase, or a clause, or both. Thus in (a) *of music, as Kepler, in a neatly arranged system* are prepositional phrases functioning as Qualifier/Postmodifier in the nominal group, and therefore form part of the Subject of the clause; likewise the phrase *for business or personal use* in the first nominal group in (b).

The Postmodifier in the nominal group functioning as Subject in (c) is an embedded clause: *that just keeps you warm in winter*. It is a **defining relative clause**, as described in Chapter 6, Section 6.2.2. This, too, falls within the Subject.

In (d) and (e), which are taken from spontaneous speech, the Subject nominal groups are more complex, since they contain both clauses and phrases in the Postmodifier. That in (d) has the clause *he was playing* embedded in the phrase *in the untraditional character he was playing* which in turn is embedded in the nominal group having *aspect* as its Head noun. In

197

(e), which was spoken by a child of four, the clause *that have goods trains on* is embedded in the phrase *with the cards that have goods trains on* which is embedded in the clause *who want to play with the cards that have goods trains on*; the whole thing is a single Subject, with the noun *people* as Head.

Such items are not difficult to recognize and identify as Subjects. There is another type of embedded clause which does not figure among the examples above, and this is a clause functioning not as Postmodifier in the nominal group but as Head: in other words, functioning as if it constituted a nominal group on its own. Examples are:

(f) <u>To argue with the captain</u> was asking for trouble.

(g) <u>Ignoring the problem</u> won't make it go away.

(h) <u>That all this wealth might some day be hers</u> had simply never occurred to her.

The analysis is shown in Figure 4-28.

to argue with the captain	was	asking for trouble
Subject	Finite	Complement
Mood		Residue
nominal group: clause as Head	verbal group	nominal group: clause as Head

Fig 4-28 Embedded clause as Subject

Note that in this example the Complement is also an embedded clause. (This is a characteristic pattern of one type of identifying relational clause; see Chapter 5, Section 5.4.4.)

In many instances an embedded clause functioning as Subject appears at the end of the clause in which it is embedded, with an **anticipatory *it*** occurring in the normal Subject position, as in *it's no use crying over spilt milk*. In such cases there will be a marked variant with the clause Subject at the beginning: *crying over spilt milk is no use*. Here are some further examples (for analysis of (l), see Figure 4-29):

(j) <u>It</u> was fortunate for me <u>that the captain was no naturalist</u>.

(k) <u>It</u> is impossible <u>to protect individuals against the ills of poverty, sickness and decrepitude</u> without some recourse to the machinery of the state.

(l) Doesn't <u>it</u> worry you <u>that you might get stung</u>?

doesn't	it	worry	you	that you might get stung
Finite	Sub-	Predicator	Complement	-ject
		Residue		
Mood				
	1 [nominal group]			=2 [nominal group]

Fig. 4-29 Embedded clause Subject with anticipatory *it*

(As we shall see in Chapter 5, clauses such as (j) and (k) are attributive relational ones, while clauses such as (l) are emotive mental ones of the 'please' type.) With an example such as (l), the more likely agnate form would be one in which the clause is Postmodifier to a fact noun as Head:

Doesn't the fact that you might get stung worry you?

It is important to distinguish clausal Subjects of this kind from those occurring in Theme predication (cf. Chapter 3, Section 3.7). Let us give three further examples of predicated Theme:

(m) It was not until fairly recently that this problem was solved.

(n) Pensioner Cecil Burns thought he had broken the slot machine; but it was not the machine he had broken – it was the bank.

(o) It was last year that he fell ill.

In both these examples and the (j) to (l) type above the Subject will be discontinuous, consisting of *it* plus the clause in final position; but the relation between the two parts of the Subject is different in the two cases. In Theme predication, the final clause is a relative clause functioning as Postmodifier to the *it* (where *it* means 'the thing that', 'the time that/ when', and so on). The clause as postposed Subject, on the other hand, is a fact clause (see Chapter 5, Section 5.3, and Chapter 7, Section 7.5.7); and it is related to the *it* by apposition (paratactic elaboration: see Chapter 7, Section 7.4.1).

As pointed out in Section 3.7, a clause with predicated Theme always has the verb *be*, and has a non-predicated agnate:

it was last year that he fell ill : he fell ill last year

it was the bank he had broken : he had broken the bank

A clause with postposed Subject has no such agnate form; moreover, such clauses are not restricted to the verb *be* (cf. example (l) above). Being facts they typically occur in clauses where the proposition has an interpersonal loading; e.g. a Complement expressing modality or comment (*it is possible unfortunate that* ...), or a Predicator expressing affection or cognition (*it worries/puzzles me that* ...). See Chapter 5, Sections 5.3 and 5.4 for the status of these in the transitivity system.

It may be helpful to show both the thematic and the modal analysis here; see Figure 4-30.

it	was not	the machine		(that)	he had broken
Theme	Rheme			(Theme)	Rheme
Theme				Rheme	
	Finite	Complement			
Subject					
		Residue			
Mood					
nominal				group	
Head				Postmodifier	

it	was	the bank
Theme	Rheme	
Subject	Finite	Complement
Mood		Residue

Fig. 4-30   Subject in Theme predication

4.8 Texts

Text 1: conversation between Nigel (age 4;2) and his father

			MOOD	POL.	DEICTICITY	SUBJECT PERSON
1	N	Drown a mermaid!	exclamative	pos	–	–
1	F	What?	wh-inter.	pos		–
2	N	(laughing) You can't drown a mermaid,	decl.	neg	mod	*non-inter.*
		the mermaid goes under the water, very deep.	decl.	pos	temp	non-inter.
2	F	No, you can't drown a mermaid,	decl.	neg	mod	*non-inter.*
		a mermaid lives in the water.	decl.	pos	temp	non-inter.
		You can't drown a fish, either, can you?	decl.: tag.	neg	mod	*non-inter.*
3	N	But you can drown a deadly stonefish.	decl.	pos	mod	*non-inter.*
3	F	You can't –	decl.	neg	mod	*non-inter.*
		that's a fish too.	decl.	pos	temp	non-inter.

			MOOD	POL.	DEICTICITY	SUBJECT PERSON
4	N	But it only goes in very shallow water,	decl.	pos	temp	non-inter.
		so it will drown	decl.	pos	mod	non-inter.
		if you make it go deep.	*bound*	pos	temp	*non-inter.*
4	F	I don't think it will!	decl.	neg	mod	non-inter.
		It might get rather uncomfortable,	decl.	pos	mod	non-inter.
		that's all.	decl.	pos	temp	non-inter.
		We must go to the Shedd Aquarium	decl.	pos	mod	speaker+
		and [we must] have a look at one.	decl.	pos	mod	speaker+
5	N	No: it wasn't in the Shedd Aquarium;	decl.	neg	temp	non-inter.
		it was in the Steinhart Aquarium,	decl.	pos	temp	non-inter.
		They haven't got one at the Shedd	decl.	neg	temp	non-inter.
5	F	They may have.	decl.	pos	mod	non-inter.
6	N	No they haven't.	decl.	neg	temp	non-inter.
6	F	Well you don't know.	decl.	neg	temp	addressee
		We only saw a little bit of it.	decl.	pos	temp	speaker+
		There's lots more [[that we didn't see]].	decl.	pos	temp	non-inter.
		[[	*bound*	neg	temp	speaker+
7	N	I liked that fish [[that we saw at the Steinhart]], the one [[that its tail wasn't like a fish]].	decl.	pos	temp	speaker
		[[	*bound*	pos	temp	speaker+
		[[	*bound*	neg	temp	non-inter.
		It was eating lettuce.	decl.	pos	temp	non-inter.
7	F	Oh yes I remember.	decl.	pos	temp	speaker
		What was it called?	wh- inter.	pos	temp	non-inter.
		I can't remember its name.	decl.	neg	mod	speaker
		Wasn't it funny,	y/n-inter.	neg	temp	non-inter.
		eating lettuce?	*bound*	pos	–	non-inter.
		Actually I think it was a cabbage, wasn't it?	decl.	pos	temp	non-inter.

			MOOD	POL.	DEICTICITY	SUBJECT PERSON
8	N	No – yes I think it was a cabbage.	decl.	pos	temp	non-inter.
		And it ate it (laughing).	decl.	pos	temp	non-inter.
8	F	It's funny [[that it liked cabbage]].	decl.	pos	temp	non-inter.
		[[	*bound*	pos	temp	non-inter.
		There isn't any cabbage in the sea.	decl.	neg	temp	non-inter.
9	N	I expect the people at the museum ... the zoo ... I mean the aquarium (laughing) gave it the cabbage.	decl.	pos	temp	non-inter.
9	F	Yes, but, I mean, why did it like cabbage?	wh- inter.	pos	temp	non-inter.
		There aren't any cabbages	decl.	neg	temp	non-inter.
		where it actually lives, in the sea.	*bound*	pos	temp	non-inter.
10	N	Yes there are cabbages –	decl.	pos	temp	non-inter.
		no not in the sea,	decl.	neg	temp	non-inter.
		but in its water.	decl.	pos	temp	non-inter.
10	F	But that is sea water, in its tank.	decl.	pos	temp	non-inter.
		The cabbage doesn't grow there;	decl.	neg	temp	non-inter.
		the aquarium people put it in.	decl.	pos	temp	non-inter.
11	N	No that's not sea ...	decl.	neg	temp	non-inter.
		I mean it isn't the sea [[that's deep]], the sea [[that ...	decl.	neg	temp	non-inter.
		[[	*bound*	pos	temp	non-inter.
		(hesitating) that's [[where the ships can go, far far away]].	decl.	pos	temp	non-inter.
		[[	*bound*	pos	mod	non-inter.
11	F	No but it's water from the sea –	decl.	pos	temp	non-inter.
		it's the same kind of water.	decl.	pos	temp	non-inter.

Analysis of selected clauses from the text (in terms of mood)

drown	a mermaid
Predicator	Complement
Residue	

What
Absolute/WH-

you	can't	drown	a mermaid
Subject	Finite	Predicator	Complement
Mood		Residue	

a mermaid	lives		in the water
Subject	'present' Finite	live Predicator	Adjunct
Mood		Residue	

because	the mermaid	goes		under the water, very deep
	Subject	'present' Finite	go Predicator	Adjunct
	Mood		Residue	

you	can't	drown	a fish	either	can	you
Subject	Finite	Predicator	Complement		Finite	Subject
Mood		Residue			Mood tag	

you	can't	that	's	a fish	too
Subject	Finite	Subject	Finite	Complement	
Mood		Mood		Residue	

but	it	only	goes		in very shallow water
	Subject	Modal Adjunct	'present' Finite	go Predicator	Adjunct
	Mood			Residue	

so	it	will	drown
	Subject	Finite	Predicator
	Mood		Residue

if	you	make		it	go	deep
		'present'	make	Complement		
	Subject	Finite	Predi-		-cator	Adjunct
	Mood		Residue			

oh yes	I	remember	
	Subject	'present' Finite	remember Predicator
	Mood		Residue

what	was	it	called
Complement/ WH-	Finite	Subject	Predicator
	Mood		
Resi-		-due	

wasn't	it	funny
Finite	Subject	Complement
Mood		Residue

eating	a lettuce
Predicator	Complement
Residue	

(1)

actually	I	think	
Adjunct	Su	'present' Finite	think Pred
Mood			Residue

it	was	a cabbage	wasn't	it
Su	Finite	Compl	Finite	Su
Mood		Residue	Mood tag	

(2)

actually	I think	it	was	a cabbage	wasn't	it
	Adjunct	Subject	Finite	Complement	Finite	Subject
	Mood			Residue	Mood tag	

(2)

no – yes –	I think	it	was	a cabbage
	Adjunct	Subject	Finite	Complement
	Mood			Residue

it	's	funny	that	it	liked		cabbage
Sub-	Finite	Complement	Finite	-ject			
				Subject	Finite	Predicator	Complement
				Mood		Residue	
		Residue					
Mood							

there	isn't	any cabbage	in the sea
Subject	Finite	Complement	Adjunct
Mood		Residue	

Table 4-15 Summary of Subjects and Finites in the text

No. of occurrences		Subject	Finite	Turn no.: clause no.
	(5)	you (= 'one')	can/can't	2N: 1; 2F: 1, 3; 3N:1, 3F: 1
	(2)	mermaid	Does	2N:2; 2F:2
(5)	(1)	that ('stonefish')	Is	3F: 2
	(1)	it (")	Does	4N: 1
	(3)	it (")	will/might	4N: 2; 4F: 1,2
	(1)	we	Must	4F: 3
	(2)	it ('the stonefish')	was/ wasn't	5N: 1,2
	(3)	they ('Shedd')	have/haven't	5N: 3; 5F:1; 6N: 1
	(1)	you	don't	6F: 1
	(1)	we	Did	6F: 2
	(1)	there	Is	6F: 3
(3)	(1)	I ('Nigel')	Did	7N: 1
	(2)	I ('father')	do/can't	7F: 1
(6)	(3)	it ('that fish')	Was	7N: 2; 7F: 2,4
	(3)	it (")	Did	8N: 2; 8F: 1; 9F: 1
	(2)	it ('lettuce')	Was	7F: 5; 8N: 1
	(3)	there	is/isn't/aren't	8F: 2; 9F: 2; 10N: 1
	(2)	aquarium people	Did	9N: 1; 10F: 3
	(5)	that/it (the fish's water)	is/isn't	10F: 1; 11N: 1,2; 11F: 1,2
	(1)	the cabbage	doesn't	10F: 2

By looking at the mood structure, clause by clause, we can see the way the dialogue proceeds as a series of exchanges. It begins with a discussion of a proposition, initiated by Nigel, that something is not possible (*you can't*), interspersed with general assertions about mermaids; these are followed by general assertions about stonefishes, which move from unmodalized (*does*) to modalized (*will, might*), and then by assertions about a particular stonefish (*was*), and about the current holdings of the Shedd Aquarium.

This sequence is terminated by his father, who shifts the orientation away from the third person (non-interactant) to themselves, with *we* (speaker+) and *you* (addressee) as Subjects (*we must, you don't*). Nigel reopens the exchange, beginning with a proposition about himself and a past experience (*I [like]d*); he then reorients the past event to the third person, investing the validity in a particular fish (*it* 'that fish'). This leads on to a series of exchanges in which the dialogue centres on the fish, on its food, on presence or absence (*there is/isn't*), on the activities of the aquarium people, and on the nature of the water in which the fish was kept and fed.

We have ignored 'embedded' clauses (see Chapters 6 and 7) and also clauses functioning as modalities (*I think, I expect, I mean*); cf. Section 3.6), since these do not function as propositions or proposals – they play no part in the structure of the interaction. These aside, there are 43 clauses that are functioning as propositions, of which 41 are taken account of in the movement of the dialogue as described above.

Unlike the Theme, which – while it is itself a property of the clause – carries forward the development of the text as a whole, the Mood element has little significance beyond the immediate sequence of clauses in which it occurs. It tends to be the overall organization of the text that determines the choice of Theme in any particular clause, or that determines at least the general pattern of thematic choices; whereas there may be no general pattern in the choice of Subject, but only a specific propositional basis for each exchange. In this particular text, all the Themes are unmarked, which means that in every declarative clause the Theme is also the Subject. Naturally when this happens the overall sequence of Subjects will also be patterned; but the pattern displayed is first and foremost a thematic one – it depends on the status of each of the items as a Theme.

Nevertheless the ongoing selection of Subjects by a speaker or writer does give a characteristic flavour to a piece of discourse. In this particular example it is clear that initially Nigel is determining the direction of the dialogue, and that his argument has a strong orientation towards the outside world; that he starts from general propositions in the present (which being general are therefore interpreted as valid for any time) and proceeds to propositions about specific past events. This is the pattern throughout roughly the first half of the text; so much we can tell simply from looking at the Mood elements, the configurations of Subject plus Finite. In the second half, by contrast, the argumentation is much more fluid. Nigel's father raises a problem that Nigel is unable to grasp; and in the course of his attempts to elucidate it the argument switches from one Subject to another from among the various entities that figured as participants in the event in question. Here the rapid changes of orientation from one proposition to another give a rather fragmentary character to the dialogue as a whole.

Text 2: from Peter Calvocoressi: The British Experience 1945–75, pp. 106–7

In this text, both Mood and Theme are marked: Mood by bold, Subject by italics, Theme by underlining. No commentary is given.

	MOOD	POL.	DEICTICITY	SUBJECT PERSON
What then **were** *governments* trying to do?	**wh-inter.**	pos	temp: past	non-inter.
There **was not** so very much difference between them, extremists on either side excepted –	decl.	**neg**	temp: past	non-inter.
and *these* **were** ineffective.	decl.	pos	temp: past	non-inter.
All governments **accepted** an obligation to contribute positively to the prosperity of both sectors.	decl.	pos	temp: past	non-inter.
This contribution **was** in the nature of things essentially financial;	decl.	pos	temp: past	non-inter.
governments **provided** money	decl.	pos	temp: past	non-inter.
or **facilitated** credit,	decl.	pos	temp: past	non-inter.
and with this money *private and nationalized businesses* **would** invest, modernize and grow.	decl.	pos	**mod**	non-inter.
At the same time, and from the very earliest postwar years, *governments of both colours* also **saw** it as part of their job ⟦to intervene in economic affairs to keep wages in check, whether by bargaining of by subsidizing the cost of living or by law⟧.	decl.	pos	temp: past	non-inter.
Broadly speaking therefore *governments* **were** actively involved ⟦in priming industry and restraining wages⟧.	decl.	pos	temp: past	non-inter.
This **was** their economic strategy.	decl.	pos	temp: past	non-inter.
It **did not** distinguish fundamentally between the private and the public sector,	decl.	**neg**	temp: past	non-inter.
which **were** treated as parts of a single whole.	bound	pos	temp: past	non-inter.
There **was** no fixed dividing line between them.	decl.	**neg**	temp: past	non-inter.
Government intervention of this nature **was** inflationary.	decl.	pos	temp: past	non-inter.
The inflation **was** modified	decl.	pos	temp: past	non-inter.
so far as *wage rises* **were** restrained	bound	pos	temp: past	non-inter.
(or matched by higher output)	bound	pos	temp: past	non-inter.
but *some inflation* **was** inseparable from a policy ⟦which set out to make things happen by supplying money and credit to make them happen⟧	decl.	pos	temp: past	non-inter.

	MOOD	POL.	DEICTICITY	SUBJECT PERSON
– the more so of course if *governments* were simultaneously supplying money for social services and social security benefits,	bound	pos	temp: past	non-inter.
the former as of right	bound	pos	–	non-inter.
and *the latter* in return for contributions [[which did not cover the whole cost]].	bound	pos	–	non-inter.
For about twenty years *inflation* proceeded at around 3% a year.	decl.	pos	temp: past	non-inter.
Then, in the early seventies, *it* averaged nearly 10%	decl.	pos	temp: past	non-inter.
and was soon to shoot up much higher.	decl.	pos	temp: past	non-inter.
A modern democratic capitalist economy is based on inflation,	decl.	pos	temp: pres	non-inter.
and in these years *the wherewithal for recovery and expansion* was provided to a significant degree by government, either through fiscal policy or by direct central or local government expenditure.	decl.	pos	temp: past	non-inter.
(*Complaints* [[*that governments were impeding industry and commerce, e.g. by excessive taxation,*]] were at bottom pleas for further inflation.)	decl.	pos	temp: past	non-inter.
At the same time *governments* hoped	decl.	pos	temp: past	non-inter.
that *the private sector in particular* would quickly get on its own feet,	bound	pos	**mod**	non-inter.
attaining a degree of profitability [[which would make it sturdily independent of governments]];	bound	pos	–	non-inter.
wages policies were designed to this end	decl.	pos	temp: past	non-inter.
and when *the end* was not attained	bound	**neg**	temp: past	non-inter.
government, in later years of our period, remitted taxes on business,	decl.	pos	temp: past	non-inter.
thereby shifting the fiscal burden from companies to individuals.	bound	pos	–	non-inter.
These policies did not work.	decl.	**neg**	temp: past	non-inter.
Unions were powerful enough to insist, if sometimes tardily, on wage rises [[to match more or more than match the rise in the cost of living]].	decl.	pos	temp: past	non-inter.
Wage claims were increasingly geared not to price rises but to these plus anticipated further rises.	decl.	pos	temp: past	non-inter.

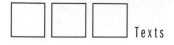

	MOOD	POL.	DEICTICITY	SUBJECT PERSON
Profitability **remained** therefore elusive,	decl.	pos	temp: past	non-inter.
or **was** achieved only on paper	decl.	pos	temp: past	non-inter.
by presenting accounts in new ways:	bound	pos	–	non-inter.
on the hard test of how much cash there was in the bank *profits* **were** meagre.	decl.	pos	temp: past	non-inter.
Real wage increases **were** also elusive.	decl.	pos	temp: past	non-inter.
By the late sixties not only *rates of profit* **were** falling	decl.	pos	temp: past	non-inter.
but so too **was** *the share of wages as a proportion of the national product*.	decl.	pos	temp: past	non-inter.
Governments **were** committed to inflation	decl.	pos	temp: past	non-inter.
because *they* **were** themselves part of the system ⟦which required it⟧.	bound	pos	temp: past	non-inter.
Modern capitalism **thrives** on expansion and credit,	decl.	pos	temp: <u>pres</u>	non-inter.
and without them *it* **shrivels**.	decl.	pos	temp: <u>pres</u>	non-inter.
Equally however *it* **requires** the right context,	decl.	pos	temp: <u>pres</u>	non-inter.
which **is** an expanding world economy:	bound	pos	temp: <u>pres</u>	non-inter.
a national economy **is** distinct and severable from other national economies in some senses but not all.	decl.	pos	temp: <u>pres</u>	non-inter.
If *the total economy* ⟦*of which it is part*⟧ **does not** expand,	bound	**neg**	temp: <u>pres</u>	non-inter.
then *the inflation in the particular economy* **ceases** to be fruitful	decl.	pos	temp: <u>pres</u>	non-inter.
and **becomes** malignant.	decl.	pos	temp: <u>pres</u>	non-inter.
Furthermore, the more *the particular economy* **flourishes**,	bound	pos	temp: <u>pres</u>	non-inter.
the more dependent *it* **is** upon the total economy ⟦to which it is directing a part of its product⟧,	decl.	pos	temp: <u>pres</u>	non-inter.
and the more dangerous **is** *any pause in its alimentation* –	decl.	pos	temp: <u>pres</u>	non-inter.
the easier *it* **is** to turn from boom to bust.	decl.	pos	temp: <u>pres</u>	non-inter.
Finally, *any government* ⟦*operating within such a system*⟧ **becomes** overwhelmingly committed to maintaining it,	decl.	pos	temp: <u>pres</u>	non-inter.
more especially when *symptoms of collapse* **appear** –	bound	pos	temp: <u>pres</u>	non-inter.
as *they* **did** in the last decade of our period	bound	pos	temp: past	non-inter.

	MOOD	POL.	DEICTICITY	SUBJECT PERSON
when *governments* **felt** compelled to help not only lame ducks but lame eagles too.	bound	pos	temp: past	non-inter.
All this **was** inflationary.	decl.	pos	temp: past	non-inter.
No government **could simply** deflate:	decl.	**neg**	**mod**	non-inter.
every government **did** both,	decl.	pos	temp: past	non-inter.
aiming to deflate on balance	bound	pos	–	non-inter.
but constantly inflating to such an extent ⟦that the compensating deflation became increasingly harsh and politically dangerous⟧.	bound	pos	–	non-inter.
Simply to turn off the tap **would** have been a double disaster,	decl.	pos	**mod**	non-inter.
not only putting millions out of work	bound	**neg**	–	non-inter.
but also ringing down the curtain once and for all on Britain's career as an industrial and trading nation.	bound	pos	–	non-inter.
If *industries* **were** allowed to shrivel and fail	bound	pos	temp: past	non-inter.
they **would** cease producing the goods ⟦which the country exchanged for food || (which it had ceased to produce for itself || when it took the industrial option)⟧ and for the industrial raw materials ⟦which it did not possess within its own borders || (now much reduced by loss of empire)⟧.	decl.	pos	**mod**	non-inter.

CHAPTER
FIVE

CLAUSE AS REPRESENTATION

5.1 Modelling experience of change

5.1.1 Construing experience as a third line of meaning in the clause

As we showed in Chapter 2, Section 2.7, the clause – like any other grammatical unit – is a multifunctional construct consisting of three metafunctional lines of meaning: see the examples in Figure 2-15. In the last two chapters we have introduced two out of these three metafunctional lines – the textual line of Theme ^ Rheme (the clause as message) and the interpersonal line of Mood + Residue (the clause as exchange). We now come to the third mode of meaning in the organization of the clause – the experiential line of organization. The three metafunctional lines are unified within the structure of the clause; textual, interpersonal and experiential functions are conflated with one another, so that e.g. Theme = Subject = Actor as in Figure 2-15 (a). Let's consider an authentic example, *Well, 'usually' means mostly, doesn't it, Mary?*, taken from the following passage of dialogue:

> **Text 5-1: Sharing – casual conversation (spoken & dialogic) [Text 76]**
> Dano: I don't want a shower; I had one yesterday.
>
> Father: Oh, I have one every day, Dano, every single day.
>
> Dano: Every single day?
>
> Father: Yeah. So does Mum. Don't you?
>
> Mother: Usually.
>
> Dano: Usually? See, Dad?
>
> Father: Well, usually means mostly, doesn't it, Mary?
>
> Mother: It means more often than not.

	Well,	*usually*	means		mostly,	doesn't	it,	Mary?
textual	Theme		Rheme					
	textual	topical						
interpersonal		Mood		Residue		Mood tag		Vocative
		Subject	Finite	Predicator	Complement	Finite	Subject	
experiential		Token	Process		Value			
syntagm:	conjunction group	adverbial group	verbal group		adverbial group	verbal group	nominal group	nominal group

Fig. 5-1 Clause with three metafunctional lines of meaning

The example is analysed in Figure 5-1 in terms of the textual, interpersonal and experiential lines of structure.

(i) Textually, the clause *Well, usually means mostly, doesn't it, Mary?* presents a **message** as a new turn in response to a query (the continuative *well*) concerned with an English word (*usually*) that has just been queried; this is the Theme of the message. The topical Theme established in this clause is maintained as the Theme of the next clause and is elaborated further within the Rheme: [Theme:] *It* [Rheme:] *means more often than not.*

(ii) Interpersonally, the clause enacts a **proposition**, in this case a consultative statement (realized by a tagged declarative: *usually means ... doesn't it*) that is explicitly addressed to a particular person, Mary (Vocative: *Mary*). This statement has been prompted by Dano's query of *usually* and it elicits a response from Mary, adjusting the proposition. The 'nub of the argument' is realized by the Subject of clause and the Finite fixes it as 'present' in relation to the now of speaking: *usually means ... doesn't it? – it means ...*

(iii) And experientially, the clause construes a quantum of change in the flow of events as a **figure**, or configuration of a process, participants involved in it and any attendant circumstances. In the example, the clause construes a relationship of signification between a word and its meaning: 'usually' signifies (represents, expresses) 'mostly'. There are three elements in this relationship, one process (*means*) and two participants involved in this process (*usually* and *mostly*).

- One of these elements is the Process – the process of 'meaning'. This process is represented as being located in, and unfolding through, time: the process is realized by a verb marked for 'present' tense, contrasting with 'past' *meant* and 'future' *will mean.*

- The other two elements are participants involved in the process of meaning: one of them represents the expression (*usually*) and the other its meaning (*mostly*). These participants are the Token and Value in the relationship of signification.

In the unified structure of the clause shown in Figure 5-1, the (topical) Theme is the Subject, and the Subject is the Token in the experiential structure of the clause; the alignment of these three functions in the box diagram shows that (topical) Theme = Subject = Token (*usually*). Similarly, two of the other interpersonal functions that fall within the Rheme of the clause have distinct roles in the experiential structure: the combination of Finite and Predicator = Process (*means*), Complement = Value (*mostly*). However, in this example, certain textual and interpersonal functions do not play roles in the experiential structure. The textual Theme (*well*) serves no experiential function, nor an interpersonal one; it serves simply to mark the continuity of the message of the clause to what's come before. The Moodtag (consisting of the tag Finite and Subject) and the Vocative are interpersonal functions that make an important contribution to the clause as a move in the exchange of meanings in the dialogue, eliciting an indication of agreement with the proposition (*doesn't it*) from the addressee (*Mary*).

In the example in Figure 5-1, the process is one of signification. These processes constitute one of a small number of different process types in the experiential grammar of the clause, just as the declarative mood constitutes one of a small number of different mood types in the interpersonal grammar of the clause. There is one further example of a clause of signification – *It means more often than not*; but the other clauses represent other types of process – wanting a shower ([Senser:] *I* + [Process:] *don't want* + [Phenomenon:] *a shower*), and having a shower ([Actor:] *I* + [Process:] *had* + [Scope:] *one* + [Time:] *yesterday*). Let us now turn to a general account of types of process in the grammar of the English clause.

5.1.2 Types of process

Our most powerful impression of experience is that it consists of a flow of events, or 'goings-on'. This flow of events is chunked into quanta of change by the grammar of the clause: each quantum of change is modelled as a **figure** – a figure of happening, doing, sensing, saying, being or having (see Halliday & Matthiessen, 1999). All figures consist of a process unfolding through time and of participants being directly involved in this process in some way; and in addition there may be circumstances of time, space, cause, manner or one of a few other types. These circumstances are not directly involved in the process; rather they are attendant on it. All such figures are sorted out in the grammar of the clause. Thus as well as being a mode of action – or rather of interaction: of giving and demanding goods-&-services and information, the clause is also a mode of reflection, of imposing linguistic order on our experience of the endless variation and flow of events. The grammatical system by which this is achieved is that of TRANSITIVITY (cf. Halliday, 1967/8). The system of TRANSITIVITY provides the lexicogrammatical resources for construing a quantum of change in the flow of events as a figure – as a configuration of elements centred on a process. Processes are construed into a manageable set of PROCESS TYPES. Each process type constitutes a distinct model or schema for construing a particular domain of experience as a figure of a particular kind – a model such as the one illustrated above for construing signification: Token (*usually*) + Process (*means*) + Value (*mostly*); and for construing wanting to shower: [Senser:] *I* + [Process:] *don't want* + [Phenomenon:] *a shower*, and showering: [Actor:] *I* + [Process:] *had* + [Scope:] *one* + [Time:] *yesterday*.

What are the different types of process, as construed by the transitivity system in the grammar? The picture we derive from English is something like this (for other languages, cf. Matthiessen, 2004b: 581–602, and references therein). There is a basic difference, that we become aware of at a very early age (three to four months), between inner and outer experience: between what we experience as going on 'out there', in the world around us, and what we experience as going on inside ourselves, in the world of consciousness (including perception, emotion and imagination). The prototypical form of the 'outer' experience is that of actions and events: things happen, and people or other actors do things, or make them happen. The 'inner' experience is harder to sort out; but it is partly a kind of replay of the outer, recording it, reacting to it, reflecting on it, and partly a separate awareness of our states of being. The grammar sets up a discontinuity between these two: it distinguishes rather clearly between outer experience, the processes of the external world, and inner experience, the processes of consciousness. The grammatical categories are those of **material** process clauses (see Section 5.2) and **mental** process clauses (see Section 5.3), as illustrated by *I'm having a shower* (material) and *I don't want a shower* (mental). Text examples of these, and of other process types, are given in Table 5-1. For instance, *you produce so much money* is a 'material' clause, construing the outer experience of the creation of a commodity, but *I was fascinated by it* is a 'mental' one, construing the inner experience of an emotion. Or, to construct a contrastive pair, *the machine is producing (sorting, destroying) money* is 'material', whereas *people love (hate, want) money* is 'mental'.

Table 5-1 Examples of different process types from 'Interview of Chinua Achebe' (process in bold; process + participants underlined; circumstances in italics)

PROCESS TYPE	Example [Process + participants underlined; Process in bold; circumstances in italics]
material	*During the European scramble for Africa,* Nigeria **fell** *to the British.*
	and the British **ruled** it *until 1960*
behavioural	people **are laughing**.
mental	The Ibos **did not approve of** kings.
verbal	so we **say** → that every fourth African is a Nigerian
	Can you **tell** us *about the political and cultural make-up of Nigeria?*
relational	that every fourth African **is** a Nigerian.
existential	so *today* there**'s** Christianity *in the south*

In addition to material and mental processes – the outer and inner aspects of our experience, a third component has to be supplied, before this can become a coherent theory of experience. We learn to generalize – to relate one fragment of experience to another in some kind of taxonomic relationship: this is the same as that, this is a kind of the other. Here the grammar recognizes processes of a third type, those of identifying and classifying; we call these **relational** process clauses (see Section 5.4), as in *usually means mostly*. For instance, *every fourth African is a Nigerian* is a classifying 'relational' clause and *The three major groups in the nation are the Yoruba in the southwest, the Ibo in the southeast, and the Hausa, finally, in the north* is an identifying one, as is the example in Figure 5-1 above.

214

Material, mental and relational are the main types of process in the English transitivity system (they are, among other things, the most frequent types, with 'material' and 'relational' being significantly more frequent than 'mental', as shown in Figure 5-2: see e.g. Matthiessen, 1999, 2006a). But we also find further categories located at the three boundaries (see Section 5.5); not so clearly set apart, but nevertheless recognizable in the grammar as intermediate between the different pairs – sharing some features of each, and thus acquiring a character of their own. On the borderline between 'material' and 'mental' are the **behavioural** processes: those that represent the outer manifestations of inner workings, the acting out of processes of consciousness (e.g. *people are laughing*) and physiological states (e.g. *they were sleeping*). On the borderline of 'mental' and 'relational' is the category of **verbal** processes: symbolic relationships constructed in human consciousness and enacted in the form of language, like saying and meaning (e.g. the 'verbal' clause *we say*, introducing a report of what was said: *that every fourth African is a Nigerian*). And on the borderline between the 'relational' and the 'material' are the processes concerned with existence, the **existential**, by which phenomena of all kinds are simply recognized to 'be' – to exist, or to happen (e.g. *today there's Christianity in the south*). This closes the circle.[1]

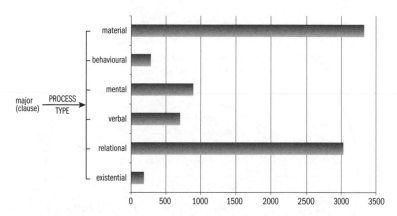

Fig. 5-2   Relative frequency of selection of terms in the system of PROCESS TYPE in a registerially mixed sample of texts (n = 8425 clauses)

---

[1]   The minor process types appear to vary more across languages than the major ones. For example, in certain languages (English being one of them), existential clauses appear as a distinct type, but in other languages they may be very close to possessive and/or locative relational clauses (see e.g. Matthiessen, 2004a: 600). The description of process type in English presented here was developed over a number of years by Halliday (e.g. 1967/8, 1969, 1976a). In the earlier accounts, there was a primary distinction between 'intensive' clauses and 'extensive' ones. This was developed further into 'action'/'mental'/'relational', where 'action' was an earlier term for 'material' and 'mental' covered both 'mental' in the current narrower sense of a process of sensing and 'verbal' in the sense of a process of saying (e.g. Halliday, 1967/8: Section 8.4). In the description of process type that was included in the computational 'Nigel grammar' (e.g. Matthiessen & Bateman, 1991), 'behavioural' clauses were treated as a subtype of 'material' ones and 'existential' clauses as a subtype of 'relational' ones (see Matthiessen, 1995a: 211). Other variants of the account have also been explored and proposed. For example, the boundary between 'material' and 'relational' clauses is drawn in a different place from where we draw it in the description of English within the Cardiff Grammar (see Fawcett, 1987, and Halliday & Matthiessen, 1999: 504, for some comments).

It does not matter, of course, where we move in: we started with the material, partly because they are the most accessible to our conscious reflection, but also because (for that very reason) throughout most of the history of linguistics they have been at the centre of attention. They have, for example, been the source of the traditional distinction between 'transitive' and 'intransitive' verbs. There is no priority of one kind of process over another. But they are ordered; and what is important is that, in our concrete visual metaphor, they form a circle and not a line. (More accurately still, they could be shown to form a sphere; but that becomes too complex a metaphor to handle graphically in a printed book.) That is to say, our model of experience, as interpreted through the grammatical system of transitivity, is one of regions within a continuous space (cf. our reference to a topology of process types in Footnote 3); but the continuity is not between two poles, it is round in a loop. To use the analogy of colour: the grammar construes experience like a colour chart, with red, blue and yellow as primary colours and purple, green and orange along the borders; not like a physical spectrum, with red at one end and violet at the other. A diagrammatic summary is given in Figure 5-3.

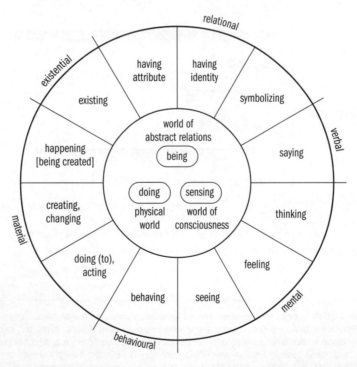

Fig. 5-3   The grammar of experience: types of process in English

Figure 5-3 represents process type as a semiotic space, with different regions representing different types. The regions have core areas and these represent prototypical members of the process types; but the regions are continuous, shading into one another and these border areas represent the fact that the process types are fuzzy categories (for discussions of the implications of the visual metaphor, see Martin & Matthiessen, 1991; Matthiessen,

1995b). Thus we can contrast prototypical examples of 'verbal' and 'relational' clauses. (1) *David told us that the moon was a balloon* is a prototypical example of a 'verbal' clause; this 'verbal' clause includes a Sayer (*David*) and a Receiver (*us*) – thus construing the interaction between speaker and addressee in a speech event, and it projects a 'locution', a reported clause representing the content of saying (*that the moon was a balloon*); this content could alternatively be quoted (*David told us: 'the moon is a balloon'*). (2) In contrast, *red indicates danger* is a prototypical example of a 'relational' clause; this relational clause construes a relationship between an expression and its content, not between the interactants in a speech event; the the Process is realized by a 'be' type of verb (cf. *red is danger*). Intermediate between such prototypical examples are instances such as *the data indicate that the moon is a balloon*; but this is on the 'relational' side of the borderline between 'verbal' and 'relational'. There are reasons for interpreting *the data indicate that the moon is a balloon* as 'relational' (since, for example, there is no quoted version; we cannot say, retaining the intended meaning: *the data indicate 'the moon is a balloon'*. But wherever we draw the line between 'verbal' and 'relational', *the data indicate that the moon is a balloon* will be closer to the border area than any of the prototypical examples are. This is not an artefact of the way we describe the system; it is a fundamental principle on which the system is based – the principle of **systemic indeterminacy**. The world of our experience is highly indeterminate; and this is precisely how the grammar construes it in the system of process type (see Halliday & Matthiessen, 1999: 547–562). Thus one and the same text may offer alternative models of what would appear to be the same domain of experience, construing, for example, the domain of emotion both as a process in a 'mental' clause (e.g. *she liked it; it pleased her*) and as a quality serving as a participant in a 'relational' one (e.g. *she was happy [about it]; it made her happy*), as in Text 4:1 in Chapter 4 ('mental': *Boof keeps scaring me*; 'relational': *I'm still afraid of him, I'm scared*) and as in the following extract from a retelling for children of a story from Genesis:

> **Text 5-2: Recreating – narrating (written, monologic): beginning and ending of a traditional narrative**
> [Placement:] Once, a very long time ago, there lived a man called Noah. He and his wife and his sons and their wives all worked very hard. Now Noah was a good man and this **pleased** God. But all around him, Noah's neighbors were lying and fighting and cheating and stealing. This **made** God <u>sad</u>. [Main body of the narrative: sequence of events.] One day God spoke to Noah. [...] Noah and his wife and his sons and their wives built new homes and planted fields. [Finale:] In time the earth was filled with people once again. And God **was** <u>happy</u>.

Generic stages such as Placement and Finale are realized by meanings at the semantic stratum in the first instance, and these meanings are then realized by wordings at the lexicogrammatical stratum (see Hasan, 1984/1996: Ch. 3, and Chapter 1, Section 1.4.2). In this story, the fate of the world hinges on God's emotions, more particularly the contrast between happiness and sadness in the Placement and Finale. His sadness in the Placement precipitates his destruction of the world; and the story ends with his happiness in the Finale. Divine emotions and their causes and consequences are thus one key to the story, perhaps helping young children accept that their fates depend on parental emotions. In the lexicogrammar, this semantic motif of divine emotion in the Placement and the Finale is realized by 'mental' and 'relational' clauses, bringing out the nature of emotion

217

as both process and quality: ['mental':] *this pleased God* – ['relational':] *this made God sad* – ['relational':] *and* ['so'] *God was happy*. (There is a switch in AGENCY (see Section 5.7 below) from 'effective' in the Placement to 'middle' in the Finale.)

Emotion is one of a number of experiential domains that are construed in more than one way within the system of transitivity. Such domains are experientially difficult to come to terms with, and the grammar solves the problem by offering complementary models for construing them. Halliday (1998) shows how the grammar has solved the problem of dealing with our experience of pain by offering an impressively rich range of complementary interpretations[2], with pain construed as process, quality or thing in clauses of different process types (cf. *my head is painful, my head hurts, my head hurts me, my head is hurting, I have a headache, I feel a pain in my head*); and his investigation of English has been followed up by Hori (2006) for Japanese and Lascaratou (2007) for Greek.

The semiotic space shown in Figure 5-2 can be interpreted systemically as a system network; see Figure 5-4. Like all system networks, this network construes a continuous semiotic space. There are a number of simultaneous systems, the systems of AGENCY and PROCESS TYPE and a set of circumstantial systems. We will deal with AGENCY and the circumstantial systems in Section 5.1.3 below and discuss PROCESS TYPE briefly here.

The system of PROCESS TYPE represents the overall space in Figure 5-2 above; and the terms represent the regions within this space that shade into one another.[3] The system has six terms (exemplified in Table 5-1) – 'material', 'behavioural', 'mental', 'verbal', 'relational' and 'existential'; and each term is the entry condition to a more delicate part of the network that represents the grammar of that particular process type. The account is taken only a few steps in delicacy; but it could be taken much further, towards systems that are realized lexically (as is shown for certain 'material' clauses by Hasan, 1987). The grammar of each process type will be presented below in Sections 5.2 through to 5.5. Meanwhile, we shall discuss the different process types at work in the construction of discourse.

The examples given in Table 5-1 have not been constructed to illustrate the full range of each type of process. Rather, they are natural examples from a particular text, selected to illustrate the contribution made by different process types in the construction of experience in discourse. The text is an interview with the Nigerian writer Chinua Achebe, an extract of which is analysed below in Table 5-4. In this extract, the interviewer starts with a 'verbal' clause, demanding information from Achebe. His response consists mainly of 'material'

---

[2]   When we say that 'the grammar has solved the problem', we are, of course, referring to very complex processes taking place over long periods of time involving innumerable unconscious acts of meaning by generations of speakers collectively construing commonsense folk models of experience (cf. Halliday & Matthiessen, 1999: Chapter 14). The patterns in the lexicogrammar – the systems, structures and items (both grammatical and lexical) – are **emergent**, in the sense of the term that has been used in the study of complex adaptive systems of different kinds (for a recent summary, see Beckner *et al.*, 2009, and other contributions to the special issue of *Language Learning* that their article appears in).

[3]   Systemic terms are not Aristotelian categories. Rather they are fuzzy categories; they can be thought of as representing fuzzy sets rather than 'crisp' ones (cf. Matthiessen, 1995b). Right from the start, systems in system networks were used to represent clines in the description of intonation (Halliday, 1967a). Martin & Matthiessen (1991) discuss how the 'topological' view exemplified by Figure 5-3, 'The grammar of experience: types of process in English,' and the 'typological' one exemplified by Figure 5-4 complement one another. For a general discussion of the problem with Aristotelian categories in accounts of language, see Ellis (1993); for discussion of this book, see Halliday (1995a).

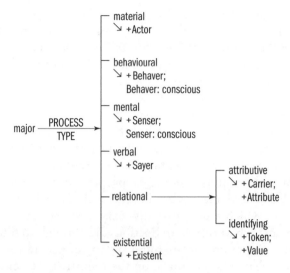

Fig. 5-4 TRANSITIVITY: PROCESS TYPE **represented as system network**

and 'relational' clauses: the 'material' clauses construe events and actions in Nigeria's history, with Nigeria or the British as the Actors (e.g. *during the European scramble for Africa, Nigeria fell to the British*), while the 'relational' ones serve to characterize Nigeria and its population (e.g. *it was a large number of independent political entities*). There are two 'existential' clauses with *there* as Subject (ellipsed in the second clause), representing the existence of Christianity and Islam in different parts of the country (e.g. *so today there's Christianity in the south*); and these is one 'verbal' clause, *we say*, serving to introduce a report of what is said, the 'relational' clause *that every fourth African is a Nigerian*. This first response contains no 'mental' or 'behavioural' clauses, but in Achebe's second response there are four 'mental' clauses, with either the speaker (*I*) or the Ibos as the Senser (e.g. *the Ibos did not approve of kings*). One of these 'mental' clauses, *I suspect*, is like the 'verbal' clause *we say*: it sets up or introduces what is suspected as a report – *they did*.

Clauses of different process types thus make distinctive contributions to the construal of experience in text. We can see this in sequences of clauses of different process types, as in Text 1 in Chapter 4:

['mental':] Mummy, Boof keeps scaring me. ['material':] Keeps getting into my bed, and ['material':] kind of like he is going to bite me.

['relational':] Well, I'm still afraid of him ['material':] 'cause he's bitten me.

Part of the 'flavour' of a particular text, and also of the register that it belongs to, lies in its mixture of process types. For example, in enabling contexts, recipes and other procedural texts are almost entirely 'material', whereas, in reporting contexts, 'verbal' clauses play an important role in news reports and, in sharing contexts, 'mental' clauses are a typical motif in casual conversation. The mixture of process types characteristic of a text belonging to a particular register typically changes in the course of unfolding of the text[4]. For example, recreating contexts, the Placement of a story is often dominated by 'existential' and 'relational' clauses, but the main event line is construed predominantly by 'material' clauses. In making these varied contributions to discourse, the different process types have evolved distinctive grammatical properties. Even in the short extract from the interview, we can begin to see the properties characteristic of each process type. Thus 'relational' clauses are characterized by a few favourite verbs – in particular, *be* and *have*. 'Mental' clauses must be construed with one conscious participant (*I*, *the Ibos*), while 'material' clauses have a more varied central participant that may or may not be a conscious being (*Nigeria*, *the British*, *this*, *you*). Both 'verbal' and 'mental' clauses are characterized by their ability to introduce what is said or thought as a report – a property distinguishing them from all the other process types. 'Existential' clauses are unique in that the Subject is not a participant but rather the item *there*, which represents only 'existence', not the participant that exists; this participant comes after the Process. In Sections 5.2 through to 5.5, we shall introduce the process types and their grammatically more systematically. In the meantime, we shall explore the experiential elements that make up the transitivity structure of a clause.

5.1.3 Process, participants and circumstances

What is the status of a figure, as set up in the transitivity grammar of a clause? The framework is very simple; it makes sense to very young children, who are learning their mother tongue (cf. Halliday, 1975, 2003; Painter, 1984, 1999). A figure consists, in principle, of three components (see Halliday & Matthiessen, 1999):

    (i)   a process unfolding through time
    (ii) the participants involved in the process
    (iii) circumstances associated with the process.

These are organized in **configurations** that provide the models or schemata for construing our experience of what goes on.

    Imagine that we are out in the open air and that there is movement overhead. Perceptually the phenomenon is all of a piece; but when we talk about it we analyse it as a semantic configuration – something that we express as, say, *birds are flying in the sky*. This is not the only possible way of organizing such a fragment of experience; we might have turned it into a meaning structure – 'semanticized' it, so to speak – quite differently. We might have said something like *it's winging*; after all, we say *it's raining*, without analysing that process into components, although it would be quite possible to do so – many languages represent the phenomenon of rain as 'water is falling' and there is, in fact, one dialect of Chinese

---

[4]   This is reflected in the realizations of the elements of the generic structure of the context in which a text unfolds (cf. Chapter 1, Section 1.4.3): different elements are likely to favour different experiential meanings, and thus also different selections in PROCESS TYPE: see e.g. Halliday (1982); Hasan (1984/1996: Ch. 3); Fries (1985). Thus while 'existential' clauses constitute a minor type of process, and are not very common in text in general (cf. Matthiessen, 1999, 2006a), they are very likely to occur in the text segment realizing the Placement element of a folk tale, as illustrated in Text 2 (*Once, a very long time ago, there lived a man called Noah.*).

that represents it as 'the sky is dropping water'. In English, there are a few processes, like raining, which are left unanalysed; but more typically the English language structures each experience as a semantic configuration on the principle illustrated above, consisting of process, participants and (optionally) circumstantial elements. So in this instance we have a process *are flying*, a participant *birds*, and a circumstantial element *in the sky*. In this interpretation of what is going on, there is doing, a doer, and a location where the doing takes place.

Circumstantial elements are almost always optional **augmentations** of the clause rather than obligatory components. In contrast, participants are **inherent** in the process: every experiential type of clause has at least one participant and certain types have up to three participants – the only exception being, as just noted above, clauses of certain meteorological processes without any participants such as *it's raining, it's snowing, it's hailing* (but not all; for example, we say *the wind's blowing* rather than *it's winding*). The difference in status between participants and circumstances can be seen very clearly from Text 17, analysed in Table 5(46). While every clause has at least one participant, only certain clauses are augmented circumstantially. In text in general, the average number of circumstances per clause is roughly 0.45, but there is considerable difference among clauses belonging to the different process types (see Matthiessen, 1999, 2006a).

How can we explain the difference in status between participants and circumstances in the configuration of process + participants + circumstances? One way of looking at the situation is this. The process is the most central element in the configuration. Participants are close to the centre; they are directly involved in the process, bring about its occurrence or being affected by it in some way. The nature of participants will thus vary according to the type of process set out in Figure 5-3 and we can say that the configuration of process + participants constitutes the **experiential centre** of the clause. Circumstantial elements **augment** this centre in some way – temporally, spatially, causally, and so on; but their status in the configuration is more peripheral and, unlike participants, they are not directly involved in the process. This model of the clause is represented diagrammatically in Figure 5-5[5]. (We shall make certain adjustments to this model in Section 5.7 below.)

This tripartite interpretation of figures, shown in Figure 5-5, is what lies behind the grammatical distinction of word classes into verbs, nouns, and the rest, a pattern that in some form is probably universal among human languages. We can express this as in Table 5-2, and an example is given in Figure 5-6. Here the process is realized by a discontinuous verbal group, *can ... tell*. The source of the discontinuity is interpersonal, not experiential. Interpersonally, the clause is 'yes/no interrogative' in mood, and as we have seen in Chapter 4, such clauses are realized by the sequence Finite ^ Subject, with the Predicator coming after the Subject. Thus in the example, we get Finite: *can* ^ Subject: *you* ^ Predicator:

---

5   This is the model developed in SFL since the 1960s. It is discussed in semantic terms in more detail in Halliday & Matthiessen (1999: Chapter 4). Comparable accounts have been proposed within other theoretical frameworks under headings such as case frame or grid and argument structure, an early account being Tesnière's (1959) characterization of the clause as a little drama, couched in terms of a dependency model; like Tesnière, many linguists have recognized some kind of syntagmatic cline from the process nucleus of a clause via different kinds of participant to a circumstantial periphery or margin (cf. Halliday, 1979): see e.g. Van Valin & LaPolla (1997).

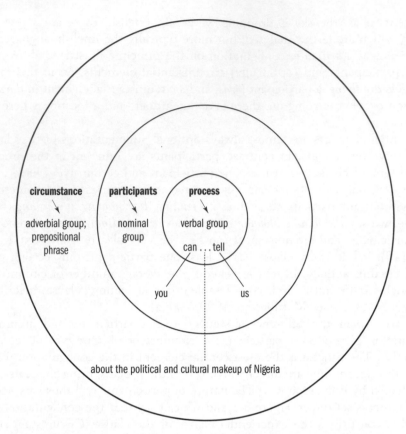

Fig. 5-5   Central and peripheral elements in the experiential structure of the clause

tell. In the agnate 'declarative' clause, the verbal group is not discontinuous: *you can tell us about the political and cultural makeup of Nigeria.* As far as the experiential structure of the clause is concerned, it makes no difference whether the verbal group is continuous or discontinuous.

Table 5-2 Typical experiential functions of group and phrase classes

Type of element	Typically realized by
(i) process	verbal group
(ii) participant	nominal group
(iii) circumstance	adverbial group or prepositional phrase

The units that realize the process, participant, and circumstance elements of the clause make distinct contributions to the modelling of a quantum of change. The elements that make up the 'centre' of the clause – the process and the participants involved in it – construe complementary facets of the change. These two facets are **transience** and

Can	you	tell	us	about the political and cultural makeup of Nigeria
pro- verbal ...	participant nominal group	-cess ... group	participant nominal group	circumstance prepositional phrase

Fig. 5-6   Clause as process, participants and circumstances

permanence. Transience means that a phenomenon is construed as unfolding through time by a verbal group serving as the process. Permanence means that a phenomenon is construed as continuous through time, being located in (concrete or abstract) space, by nominal groups serving as participants. Thus participants are construed as being relatively stable through time, and an instance of a participant can take part in many processes, as happens for example in narrative (see Text 5-3):

> **Text 5-3: Recreating – narrating (written, monologic): the Placement stage of a Mexican folk tale**
> During the first part of the nineteenth century, there **was** a lighthouse keeper who was in charge of the lighthouse. His name **was** Felipe. He **was** a brave young man, very dedicated to his work. He **lived** very happily in the lighthouse with his wife, Catalina, and his little daughter Teresa. He **loved** them both very much.

Here we have one instance of a participant that is first introduced into the narrative in one process of existence (*there was ...*) and then maintained as a participant in other processes: *a lighthouse keeper ...* – *(his name)* – *he* – *he* – *he*. In contrast, processes are ephemeral; every instance is a unique occurrence – every *was* in the passage above refers to a unique occurrence of a process of being. This contrast between participants and processes explains why there are names of individual participants – 'proper names', as well as names of classes of participants – 'common nouns', but only names of classes of processes: all lexical verbs are 'common' verbs. The contrast is also reflected in the organization of nominal groups and verbal groups in two ways (see Table 5-3): while nominal groups have evolved the system of DETERMINATION for locating referents in a referential space, verbal groups have evolved the system of TENSE for locating a unique occurrence of a process in time (see Chapter 6).

Table 5-3 Deictic systems of verbal group and nominal group

Type of element	Location in	System	Terms
process ➘ verbal group	referential time	TENSE	past (*did do*) present (*does do*) future (*will do*)
participant ➘ nominal group	referential space	DETERMINATION	specific (*the/this/that thing*; *it*) non-specific (*a/some/any/every thing*)

Change is thus construed as involving both transience and permanence, and the phenomena of experience are construed either as transient processes or as permanent participants. The borderline between these two is indeterminate; the lexicogrammar of every language will allow considerable discretion in how phenomena are treated in discourse, and lexicogrammars of different languages draw the borderline in different places. For example, in English, *rain* and other forms of precipitation may be construed either as process, as in *it's started to rain again*, or as participant, as in *the rain's started again*. This is an area of considerable fluidity; but most phenomena are treated either as process or as participant, and have to be reconstrued metaphorically to change their status in the grammar: e.g. *purchases of durables depend on prior stock*, where the process of purchasing is objectified as a participant and is represented in the grammar as a nominal group with traces of clausal structure (see Chapter 10, Section 10.5).

The concepts of process, participant and circumstance are semantic categories that explain in the most general way how phenomena of our experience of the world are construed as linguistic structures. When we come to interpret the grammar of the clause, however, we do not use these concepts as they stand because they are too general to explain very much. We shall need to recognize participant and circumstance functions that are more specific than these and which, in the case of participant functions, differ according to the type of process being represented. Nevertheless they all derive from, and can be related to, these three general categories. In the following sections we shall explore the different types of process that are built into the grammar of English, and the particular kinds of participant role that are systematically associated with each. In Section 5.6, we shall present the different types of circumstance that enter into the clause.

5.2 Material clauses: processes of doing-&-happening

5.2.1 Introductory examples

As the examples given in Table 5-1 illustrate, 'material' clauses are clauses of doing-&-happening: a 'material' clause construes a quantum of change in the flow of events as taking place through some input of energy. We have already seen what kind of contribution such clauses make to the interview illustrated in Table 5-1 (taken from the text represented by the extract in Text 5-17 at the end of this chapter); but let us now consider an extract from a text that is predominantly 'material' – a text instructing readers in gardening procedures. Here is short example of concrete 'material' clauses serving to construct the procedure:

> **Text 5-4: Enabling – instructing (written, monologic): extract from a gardening procedure**
> Each year, **replace** the fruiting rod by **tying down** a lateral in its place. Either **tie down** 1 shoot and **cut** it **off** where it meets the next vine, or **tie down** 2, one each way, and **cut** them where they meet the neighbouring lateral. This is called the Double Guyot. (Mary Spiller, *Growing fruit*, 1982, Penguin Books.)

The 'material' clauses construe the procedure as a sequence of concrete changes in the trees brought about by the person being instructed – the implicit 'you' (which could be made explicit, as in *you replace the fruiting rod*). In the examples above, and in 'material' clauses in general, the source of the energy bringing about the change is typically construed as a participant – the **Actor**. This participant role was introduced in Chapter 2 as the 'logical Subject' of older terminology. The Actor is the one that does the deed – that is, the one

that brings about the change.[6] In instructional texts such as the one exemplified above, the Actor is typically also the Subject – the element held modally responsible for the proposal or proposition, as in *replace the fruiting rod, won't you?* However, as we saw in Chapter 2, Figure 2-14, Actor and Subject are distinct in a 'passive' – or, 'receptive' – clause, as in *the fruiting rod was replaced by the gardener (wasn't it?)*. Here the Actor is not interpersonally 'charged' with the role of Subject, but is rather given the lower status of Adjunct and can thus be left out: *the fruiting rod was replaced*. We therefore have to be careful to distinguish the experiential notion of 'the one doing the deed' (or 'the one bringing about the change') from the interpersonal notion of 'the one held modally responsible' (or 'the one given the status of the nub of the argument').

Processes of all types unfold through time; but the way the process unfolds may vary from one process type to another. In particular, processes of the 'material' type tend to differ from all the other types (with the partial exception of 'behavioural' processes, as we shall see below), and this is seen in how present time is reported. The unmarked tense selection is the present-in-present (e.g. *is doing*) rather than the simple present (e.g. *does*; cf. Chapter 6, Section 6.3.4):

> We're all **eating** now. [UTS/Macquarie Corpus: Bandon Grove]
>
> Who's **acting** for him, Jane? – Well we **are**. [UTS/Macquarie Corpus: Bandon Grove]
>
> He's always here; he's **living** up there now. [UTS/Macquarie Corpus: All men 3]
>
> We need to take more initiative in showing how the halting progress we **are making** across the broad front of understanding really **is improving** our ability to deal with specific problems. [Global Change and the Changing Atmosphere]

The present-in-present serves to **narrow down** the present from the extended now of habits and 'general truths' that is characteristic of the simple present with 'material' clauses; contrast *we're all eating now* : *we all eat out on Saturdays* [habitual occurrence]; *the progress is improving our ability* : *the progress improves our ability* [generalized occurrence].[7]

5.2.2 Transitive and intransitive material clauses

Let us recapitulate. In a 'material' clause, there is always one participant – the Actor. This participant brings about the unfolding of the process through time, leading to an outcome that is different from the initial phase of the unfolding. This outcome may be confined to the Actor itself, in which case there is only one participant inherent in the process. Such a 'material' clause represents a **happening** and, using traditional terminology (see below), we can call it **intransitive**. Alternatively, the unfolding of the process may extend to another

---

6 The 'Actor' of a 'material' clause (Halliday, 1967/8) is distinct from the 'Agent' of an 'effective' clause; as we shall see in Section 5.8, the two represent different generalizations about the experiential organization of the clause. There is considerable variation in the use of the terms 'agent' and 'actor' in linguistics. For example, Dik (1978: 37) uses 'agent' (paired with 'goal') in a sense that is close to our 'actor', whereas Foley & van Valin (1984: 29ff) use 'actor' (paired with 'undergoer') in a sense that is closer to our 'agent'.

7 This narrowing-down effect of the present-in-present is not brought out by the names most commonly used for this tense – the 'present progressive', or the 'present continuous'.

participant, the Goal, impacting it in some way: the outcome is registered on the Goal in the first instance, rather than on the Actor. Such a 'material' clause represents a **doing** and we can call it **transitive**. The constructed examples in Figure 5-7 illustrate the contrast.

(a)

the lion	sprang
Actor	Process
nominal group	verbal group

(b)

the lion	caught	the tourist
Actor	Process	Goal
nominal group	verbal group	nominal group

Fig. 5-7 Happening represented by an 'intransitive' material clause (a) and doing represented by a 'transitive' material clause (b)

In both clauses, the Actor (realized by the nominal group *the lion*) is an inherent participant. The implication is that in both cases the lion did something; but in (a) the doing was confined to the lion, whereas in (b) it was directed at, or extended to, the tourist. This is the **Goal**. The term implies 'directed at'; another term that has been used for this kind of function is 'Patient', meaning one that 'suffers' or 'undergoes' the process.[8] We will keep the familiar term Goal in the present analysis (taken from Bloomfield, 1933: e.g. 135, and introduced in systemic work in Halliday, 1967/8), although neither of the two really hits the mark; the relevant concept is more like that of 'one to which the process is extended'. The concept of extension is in fact the one that is embodied in the classical terminology of 'transitive' and 'intransitive', from which the term 'transitivity' is derived. According to this theory the verb *spring* is said to be intransitive ('not going through') and the verb *catch* is said to be transitive ('going through' – that is, extending to some other entity). This is an

---

[8] Note that 'Goal' refers to the goal of impact – the participant construed as being impacted by the Actor's performance of the process (this term is also used by Dik, 1978: 37, in his framework of 'Functional Grammar': 'the entity to which the Action is applied by the Agent'). This sense of the goal of impact is distinct from (though obviously ultimately related to) the sense of destination – the destination of a process of motion, as in the goal of a journey. Thus the prepositional phrase *to a thicket* in *he came to a thicket* is not a Goal: it is not a participant at all; rather it is a circumstance of Location: place, more specifically the place of destination. In addition to the terms 'goal' and 'patient', other terms have also been used, corresponding to different descriptive generalizations; these include 'object', 'objective', 'theme', 'target' and 'undergoer'. In his highly influential article that gave rise to 'Case grammar' and stimulated other approaches, Fillmore (1968: 25) did not use the term 'patient', the closest being the 'objective' case for 'the semantically most neutral case'. Also in the 1960s, Gruber (1976: 38) introduced the term 'theme' for 'the entity that is conceived as moving or undergoing transitions' (taken up by Jackendoff, 1972), and 'theme' has been used widely in this experiential sense in the generative linguistic literature (contrasting with the textual sense that derives from the Prague School much earlier in the twentieth century: see Chapter 3). Needless to say, these different terms are not synonymous. They have to be interpreted together with other terms in different accounts of the grammar of transitivity of a language; and such accounts differ theoretically from one another in terms of their location in the overall model of language: they may be grammatical, lexical or semantic in nature.

accurate interpretation of the difference between them; with the proviso that, in English and in many other languages – perhaps all, these concepts relate more appropriately to the clause than to the verb. Transitivity is a system of the clause, affecting not only the verb serving as Process but also participants and circumstances.[9]

It will be noticed that the term Actor is used in the interpretation of both the intransitive clause and the transitive one; and this embodies a further assumption, namely that *the lion* has the same function in both. In both cases, the lion is construed as 'doing' something – as bringing about the unfolding of the process. This assumption is related to the fact that, in those Indo-European languages in which nouns are marked for case, like Greek and Latin, and modern German and Russian, *the lion* would be in the nominative case in both (a) and (b), whereas *the tourist* would be in an oblique case, typically the accusative; which suggests that the function of *the lion* is constant across both types. The same point can be made in relation to English; although nouns have no case, personal pronouns have, so if we replace the nouns *lion* and *tourist* by personal pronouns we would have *he sprang, he caught him*. This is highly suggestive; there is undoubtedly some reason for the cases to be distributed as they are. But it may not tell the whole story. For one thing, not all processes necessarily have the same grammar; and for another, even where they have there may be more than one principle at work. We shall explore the first point in Sections 5.2–5.4, and the second in Section 5.7.

The assumptions that lie behind the notions of Actor and Goal are valid for 'material' clauses, but not, as we shall see, for clauses of other process types. Material clauses construe figures of 'doing-&-happening'. They express the notion that some entity 'does' something – which may be 'to' some other entity. So we can ask about such processes, or 'probe' them, in this way (cf. Chapter 4, Figure 4-18): *What did the lion do? What did the lion do to the tourist?* Looked at from the tourist's point of view, on the other hand, the process is not one of doing but one of 'happening'; so we can also say *What happened to the tourist?* Consequently if there is a Goal of the process, as well as an Actor, the representation may come in either of two forms: either **operative** (active), *the lion caught the tourist* (Figure 5-8), or **receptive** (passive), *the tourist was caught by the lion*.[10] Note the analysis in Figure 5-9 (for the significance of *by* see Section 5.7 below). The contrast between 'operative' and 'receptive' is a contrast in **voice** open to 'transitive' clauses, as shown in the lower half of the system network in Figure 5-10. The clauses are the same experientially; they both represent a configuration of Actor + Process + Goal. But they differ in how these roles are mapped onto the interpersonal functions in the modal structure of the clause. In the 'operative' variant, the Actor is mapped on to the Subject, so it is given modal responsibility and in the 'unmarked' case (in a 'declarative' clause) it is also the Theme; and the Goal is mapped on to the Complement, so in the 'unmarked' case it falls within the Rheme. However, in the

---

[9] The interpretation would be different in a dependency model (due in modern times to Tesnière, 1959), where the verb is treated as the 'head' of the clause. But the model we use is one of ranked constituency, where the clause and the verb constitute different ranking domains (see Chapter 2). One of the reasons for preferring the ranked constituency model is precisely the need to differentiate the clause as the domain of transitivity and the verb, or rather the verbal group, as the domain of tense and other purely verbal systems.

[10] It is helpful to make a terminological distinction between the voice contrast of the clause – operative/ receptive, and the voice contrast of the verbal group – passive/active (see Chapter 6, Section 6.1): cf. Halliday (1967/8).

the lion	caught		the tourist
Actor	Process: active		Goal
Subject	Finite	Predicator	Complement
Mood		Residue	
Theme	Rheme		

Fig 5-8 Operative transitive material clause

the tourist	was	caught	by the lion
Goal	Process: passive		Actor
Subject	Finite	Predicator	Adjunct
Mood		Residue	
Theme	Rheme		

Fig 5-9 Receptive transitive material clause, with Process realized by passive verbal group

'receptive' variant, it is the Goal that is mapped on to the Subject, so it is assigned modal responsibility and it is also the Theme in the 'unmarked' case; and the Actor has the status of an Adjunct within the Rheme of the clause and, as an Adjunct, it may in fact be left out: *the tourist was caught by the lion : the tourist was caught.*

5.2.3 Types of doing-&-happening

So far we have mentioned the properties of 'material' clauses in general. There are other properties that are specific to particular subtypes of 'material' clauses. The material realm is, as noted in Section 5.1, quite vast, covering events, activities, and actions involving both animate Actors and inanimate ones. But we can discern some features in the material landscape, taking the description a few steps further in delicacy. To do so, we need to discuss the nature of the unfolding of a material process through time.

The quantum of change represented by a material clause is construed as unfolding through distinct phases, typically over a fairly short interval of time – with at least an initial phase of unfolding and a separate final phase, as with *tying down, replacing, cutting off,* and *cutting.* The final phase of unfolding is the **outcome** of the process: it represents a change of some feature of one of the participants in the material clause. In the procedural gardening text above, the outcome is that a shoot has been tied down, cut or cut off, and so on: texts instructing people in procedures are typically concerned with achieving such material outcomes.

The nature of the outcome affecting the Actor of an 'intransitive' clause and the Goal of a 'transitive' one turns out to be the general criterion for recognizing more delicate subtypes

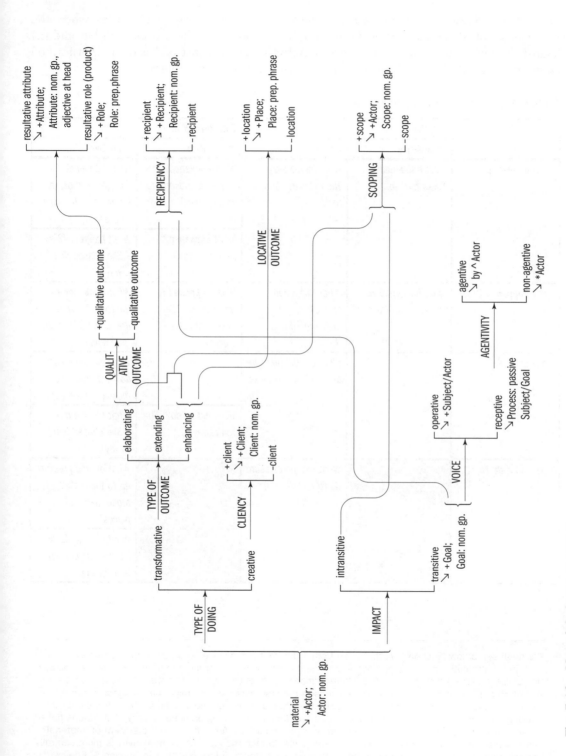

Fig. 5-10 Material clause systems

of 'material' clauses.[11] The most general contrast is between (i) 'creative' clauses, where the Actor or Goal is construed as being brought into existence as the process unfolds, and (ii) 'transformative' ones, where a pre-existing Actor or Goal is construed as being transformed as the process unfolds: see Figure 5-10. Examples are given in Table 5-4.

Table 5-4 type of doing: 'creative'/'transformative'

	Creative		Transformative	
	intransitive	transitive	intransitive	transitive
what **happened**?	What **happened**? - Rocks formed.	What **happened**? - The pressure formed rocks.	What **happened**? - The rocks broke (into small pieces).	What **happened**? - The pressure broke the rocks (into small pieces).
			What **happened**? - He ran (away).	What **happened**? - She chased him (away).
what **happened to** X?	What **happened to** rocks? - They formed.	What **happened to** rocks? - *The pressure formed them.	What **happened to** the rocks? - They broke (into small pieces).	What **happened to** the rocks? - The pressure broke them (into small pieces).
what did X **do**?		What did the pressure **do**? - It formed rocks.		What did the pressure **do**? - It broke the rocks (into pieces).
			What did he do? - He ran (away).	What did she do? - She chased him (away).
what did X **do to** Y?		What did the pressure **do to** rocks? - *It formed them.		What did the pressure **do to** the rocks? - It broke them (into pieces).
				What did she **do to** him? - She chased him (away).

---

[11] We shall see below (Section 5.7) that seen from a different perspective from that of the traditional transitive/intransitive model, these two functions, the intransitive Actor and the transitive Goal, are actually one and the same – the Medium. The differentiation of different subtypes of 'material' clauses is thus based on the combination of Medium + Process in the first instance. One might have expected that it would be based on Actor + Process instead, as the traditional model would suggest; but it turns out that although they have been favoured by philosophers of language drawing on action theory, distinctions based on Actor + Process such as animacy, potency and volitionality are less central to the system of 'material' clauses than distinctions based on Medium + Process. In fact, the grammar of transitivity is more centrally concerned with consciousness rather than with animacy, potency or volitionality: see Section 5.3 below.

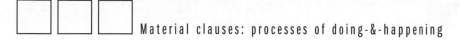

(i) In **a 'creative' clause**, the outcome is the coming into existence of the Actor ('intransitive') or the Goal ('transitive'). The outcome is thus this participant itself, and there is no separate element in the clause representing the outcome. The Process is realized by a verb such as *form, emerge, make, create, produce, construct, build, design, write, compose, draw, paint, bake*. For example:

(a) intransitive

> '*An icicle* **formed** in the cold air of the dining vault.' [ACE_P]

> In addition, *the iodoamino acid* **formed** in largest quantity in the intact thyroid is di-iodotyrosine. [BROWN1_J]

> *Limestone* **can form** in many ways ‖ as shown in Table 4-4. [Text 68]

> He is of the view that the writer's use of one language or the other is determined by the objective conditions under which *the spiritual life of the given people* **is developing**. [KOLH_A]

(b) transitive

> Well, *he* **was making** a cubby house a minute ago. [Text 76]

> *I* **started writing** short stories while I was at Yale.[Text 7]

> These **are formed** *by chemical precipitation, by biological precipitation, and by accumulation of organic material*. [Text 68]

> Given plenty of advance notice, ... *businesses* **have printed** new stationery and supplies. [News/ Britain Readies to Change Numbers]

Even the verb *do* can be used in a creative sense, typically with a semiotic product such as a play, film or book: *I **did** a book called Sand Rivers, just before the Indian books*. In the category of 'creative' clauses, we can perhaps also include phases of creation, as in *Then I started my first novel*, where *started* can be interpreted as 'began to write', and *I'd better try some more non-fiction*, where *try* can be interpreted as 'try to write'.[12] (However, processes of destruction seem to be treated by the grammar as 'transformative' rather than as 'creative': *but the wild places were being destroyed in many parts of the world; the bar and all the marble fittings of the interior were painstakingly dismantled*.) 'Intransitive' 'creative' clauses have the sense of 'come into existence' and shade into clauses of the 'existential'

---

[12] Compare the discussion in Section 8.5 on of phased processes in hypotactic verbal group complexes. In hypotactic verbal group complexes, the phase (starting, continuing; trying, succeeding; and so on) is an expansion of the process itself; but in the examples discussed here, the phase is construed as a process in its own right. Such examples may involve a participant that is 'eventive' in character, as in *music has started in the ballroom; the war had started; the 'excellent' relationship would continue; (he) had started the voyage as an ordinary seaman; you continue your journey*; and there are certain verbs that are collocationally restricted to certain nouns, e.g. *dawn* + period of time, e.g. *day: Marathon day dawned a little foggy and cool*. Examples of this kind shade into metaphorical variants of clauses with phased verbal group complexes; the participant involved in the phased process is a reified process realized by a nominal group with a nominalization as Head: *the next dance started; preparation started; the current decline in population continues; (he) immediately started constructions again; his widow started the circulation of petitions*.

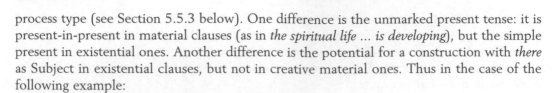

process type (see Section 5.5.3 below). One difference is the unmarked present tense: it is present-in-present in material clauses (as in *the spiritual life ... is developing*), but the simple present in existential ones. Another difference is the potential for a construction with *there* as Subject in existential clauses, but not in creative material ones. Thus in the case of the following example:

> *A similar pattern* **emerges** for the country's 1.7 million prisoners. [Text 1]

there is an agnate variant with *there*: *there emerges a similar pattern*.

(ii) In **a 'transformative' clause**, the outcome is the change of some aspect of an already existing Actor ('intransitive') or Goal ('transitive'). Thus while *she painted a portrait of the artist* is 'creative' since the outcome is the creation of the portrait, *she painted the house red* is 'transformative' since the outcome is the transformation of the colour of the house. In the limiting case, the outcome of the final phase is to maintain the conditions of the initial phase, as in *hold it vertically in your hand* – that is, so that it does not fall or change position (cf. a 4-year-old's definition of balance, discussed in Painter, 1999: 108: *balance means you hold it on your fingers and it doesn't go*).

Unlike 'creative' clauses, 'transformative' ones can often have a separate element representing the outcome (see further below), as in *she painted the house red*, where *red* serves as an Attribute specifying the resultant state of the Goal (cf. Halliday, 1967b: 62-66/2005: 32-37). Even where the sense of outcome is inherent in the process, the outcome may be indicated by the 'particle' of a phrasal verb (cf. Chapter 6, Section 6.3.6), as in *shut down, turn on, start up, tie up, cut off, rub out, throw away, use up, fill up*. The Goal of a 'transitive' 'transformative' clause exists before the process begins to unfold and is transformed in the course of the unfolding. It can thus be probed by means of *do to, do with* in a special 'manipulative' construction, as in the following narrative passage.

Text 5-5: Recreating - narrating (written, monologic)

Father McCarthy told him that he should not have more than one wife. 'What then should *he* **do with** the second wife?' he asked. **Should** *he* just **turn** her **out** to starve? If *he* **sent** her **back** to her parents, they would certainly not return the bride-price with which he had bought her. Oh, no, said Father McCarthy, *he* **should keep** her, but *he* **should not use** her as a wife. [LOB_G]

Turning out, sending back, keeping and using are all examples of processes of transformation. The Actor of an intransitive transformative clause can be probed by *happen to*, as in *You know what could have happened to them? – They could have fallen through the hole on the deck.* Neither *happen to* nor *do to/with* can be used with creative clauses: see Table 5-4. Thus we cannot say *what he did to a cubby house was make it* because the *do to* 'manipulative' construction presupposes the prior existence of the 'done-to'.

The 'transformative' type of 'material' clause covers a much wider range than the 'creative' type. As always, it is difficult to find an appropriate term for the grammatical category. We have to understand it in the context of the relevant systemic contrast. Thus 'transformative' means that the Actor ('intransitive') or Goal ('transitive') exists prior to the onset of the unfolding of the process, and is changed in some way or other through the unfolding of the process. The outcome of the transformation is an (1) **elaboration**, (2) **extension** or (3)

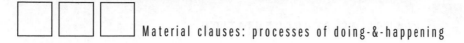

enhancement of the Actor ('intransitive') or Goal ('transitive'), as represented in the system network in Figure 5-10[13]; for example:

(1) elaboration

> Beat <u>the butter and sugar</u> *to a cream* [LOB_E]
>
> Be careful ‖ that *they* **do not boil *dry*** ‖ and catch. [LOB_E]
>
> <u>The breeding flock</u> **was reduced** *to 30 ewes* [LOB_E]

(2) extension

> when he first sees <u>light machine-guns</u> **being assembled**, ‖ his stomach goes cold. [LOB_K]
>
> <u>Too many books and articles</u> **are** just **assembled** ‖ by putting one word after another. [BROWN1_C]
>
> I've got some cake here; ‖ look, *she* **gave** *me* <u>that</u>. [Text 10]
>
> when you leave ‖ *you* **will give** *her* <u>your little present</u> ‖ as you thank her ‖ for looking after you [LOB_E]
>
> *He* **was awarded** in 1980 <u>the A.C. Benson Medal</u> by the Royal Society of Literature [Text 152]

(3) enhancement

> *He* **threw** <u>green stuff</u> *on it*, ‖ and *a thin blue column of smoke* **rose**. [BROWN1_F]
>
> *I'll* **put** <u>him</u> *in the shower* [Text 76]
>
> *I* **limped** back *to the door* [LOB_N]

Ferris's face turned a deep red ‖ as *his blood pressure* **rose**. [ACE_N]

Examples of verbs serving as Process in these different material clause types are given in Table 5-5. There are two columns of examples, 'intransitive' and 'transitive'; but many verbs cut across this distinction – an interesting feature of the lexicogrammar of current English that we will explain in Section 5.7 below. Any of the rows of examples could be explored further to reveal patterns intermediate between grammar and lexis (cf. Chapter 2, Figure 2-6); many of them have been discussed in the linguistic literature (see e.g. Levin, 1993, and Matthiessen's, forthc., classification of her verb classes according the system of PROCESS TYPE). Certain processes of 'extension' are described systemically by Hasan (1985a, 1987); her account provides a model for the extension of the grammatical description in delicacy towards lexical distinctions. In such investigations, the corpus is an invaluable source of evidence (cf. Neale, 2006).

In 'transformative' clauses, the participant being affected is typically construed as having changed in some fundamental way. Here the process unfolds through distinct phases, with a clear difference between the initial state and the final state, the outcome[14]; but the process may also be more uniform through time, as in the following examples:

---

13 As we shall see in Section 5.4, these three types of outcome correspond to the three types of relation in relational clauses: elaboration – intensive relational clauses, extension – possessive ones, and enhancement – circumstantial ones.

14 Cf. Chapter 6, Section 6.3.6, on phrasal verbs with a completive or directional sense.

I **served** in World War II. [Text 7]

Below, in the Champs Elysees, *the cars* **glittered** in the sun and *the pedestrians* **were dappled** by leaf shadows. [LOB_P]

While I was in Paris I had written a non-fiction piece for The New Yorker ... together with Ben Bradlee, *who* now **runs** <u>The Washington Post</u> and was also in Paris at that time. [Text 7]

Here the outcome is the continuous unfolding of the process; the Actor keeps this process going. This type of 'outcome' can be interpreted as 'elaborating'; the performance of the process ensures that intransitive Actor or transitive Goal has a certain quality like being operational.

Table 5-5 Examples of verbs serving as Process in different material clause types

			Intransitive	**Transitive**
creative	general		appear, emerge; occur, happen, take place	
			develop, form, grow, produce	
				create, make, prepare
	specific			assemble, build, construct; compose, design, draft, draw, forge, paint, sketch, write; bake, brew, cook; knit, sow, weave; dig, drill; found, establish; open, set up
transformative	elaborating	state	burn, singe, boil, fry, bake, dissolve, cool, freeze, warm, heat, melt, liquefy, pulverize, vaporize, harden, soften	
		make-up	blow up, break, burst, chip, collapse, crack, crash, explode, shatter, tear; mend, heal	
			erupt	crush, demolish, destroy, damage, mash, smash, squash, wreck
			chop, cut, mow, prune, slice, trim [intransitive: 'easily']	
				axe, hack, harpoon, knife, pierce, prick, spear, skewer, stab, sting
		surface	polish, rub, dust, scratch, wipe [intransitive: 'easily']	
				brush, lick, rake, scrape, shave, sweep
		size	compress, decompress, enlarge, extend, expand, grow, stretch, reduce, shrink, shrivel	
		shape	form, shape; arch, bend, coil, contort, curl, uncurl, curve, deform, distort, fashion, flatten, fold, unfold, stretch, squash, twist	

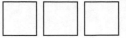

			Intransitive	Transitive
		age	age, ripen, mature, modernize	
		amount	increase, reduce; strengthen, weaken	
		colour	colour; blacken, whiten; darken, brighten, fade; solarize	
			blush, redden, yellow, pale	
		light	twinkle; glimmer, glisten, glitter, gleam, glow, flash, flicker, sparkle, shimmer	
			Shine	
				light, illuminate
		sound	boom, rumble, rustle, roar, thunder, peal	
			chime, toll, sound, ring	
		exterior (cover)	peel, skin, peel [intransitive: 'easily']	
				bark, husk, pare, scalp, shuck
				cover, strip, uncover, remove, drape, paper, plate, roof, unroof, wall-paper, shroud, wrap, unwrap
				clothe, attire, dress, strip, undress, robe, disrobe
				coat; butter, enamel, gild, grease, lacquer, paint, pave, plaster, stucco, tar, varnish, veneer, whitewash
		interior		gut, disembowel, dress, pit
		contact		hit, strike; bump; knock, tap; punch, slap, spank; elbow; kick; belt, cane, shoot, stone, whip
		aperture	open, close, shut	
		operation	run, operate, work; ride, drive, fly, sail [but also as motion]	
				captain, command, rule, govern; bring up, nurse, mother
	extending	possession		give; offer; tip; advance; bequeath, will, leave, donate, grant, award; cable, fax, post, mail, e-mail, hand; deliver, send; lend, lease, loan; deny (sb sth; sth to sb)

Table 5-5 Examples of verbs serving as Process in different material clause types (*contd*)

			Intransitive	Transitive
			hire, rent, sell	
				feed, serve, supply, provide, present, furnish (sb with sth; sth to sb)
				deprive, dispossess, divest, rob, strip, cheat (sb of sth); acquire, get, take, grab, steal, pilfer, buy, borrow, hire, rent (sth from sb)
		accompaniment	join, meet; assemble, accumulate, collect, cluster, crowd, flock, herd; separate; disassemble, disband, disperse, scatter, spread	
	enhancing	motion: manner	bounce, gyrate, rock, shake, tremble, spin, swing, wave; walk, amble, limp, trot, run, jog, gallop, jump, march, stroll; roll, slide; drive, fly, sail	
		motion: place	come, go	bring, take
			approach, arrive, reach, return; depart, leave; circle, encircle, surround, cross, traverse; enter, exit, escape; follow, tail, precede; pass, overtake; land, take off	
			down, drop, fall/fell, rise/raise; capsize, overturn, tilt, tip, topple, upset	

5.2.4 Different types of material clauses and additional participants

We have met two participant roles in material clauses – the Actor and the Goal. The Actor is an inherent participant in both intransitive and transitive material clauses; the Goal is inherent only in transitive clauses. In addition to these two roles, there are a number of other participant roles that may be involved in the process of a 'material' clause; these are: **Scope**, **Recipient**, **Client** and (more marginally) **Attribute**. For example:

Scope:
Then cross **Hyde Park and the Domain** to the Art Gallery of N.S.W. [Text 22]

the administration was not optimistic of reaching **a final deal** before George W. Bush becomes president on Jan. 20. [Text 108]

The British brought this rather complex association into being as one nation and ruled it until 1960 when Nigeria achieved **independence**. [Text 16]

Recipient:
Did Kerry give **you** those files there? [Text 72]

236

One of the most important posts was given **to Tsai Ying-wen, an expert on international trade who will head the Mainland Affairs Council** [Text 13]

She had been given medicine which kept her husband sedated for short periods. [Text 24]

Client:
The last phrase he told me was that our fate is to build **for our children** an assuring future. [Text 66]

Do you want us to make up the full pallet **for you**? [UTS/Macquarie Corpus]

She's poured **herself** a mineral water. – Just a plain water but I think maybe I should have something fizzy. [UTS/Macquarie Corpus]

Attribute:
Mr Bannister described how an unarmed black American, Mr William Whitfield, was shot **dead** in a New York supermarket on Christmas Day last year when an officer mistook the keys he was carrying for a gun. [Text 2]

They stripped her **clean** of every bit of jewellery [[she ever had]]. [Text 24]

Of these four participant roles, **Scope** is the most general across different types of 'material' clause introduced in the previous subsection; but they are all more restricted than Actor and Goal. Figure 5-10 shows how these different participant roles are distributed across the subtypes of 'material' clause; examples are given in Table 5-6.

The two functions of **Recipient** and **Client** resemble one another in that both construe a benefactive role (cf. Halliday, 1967/8: 51–58/2005: 19–27; and see Section 5.7.3.1 below); they represent a participant that is benefitting from the performance of the process, in terms of either goods or services. The Recipient is one that goods are given to; the Client is one that services are done for. Either may appear with or without a preposition, depending on its position in the clause (*gave John the parcel, gave the parcel to John*); the preposition is *to* with Recipient, *for* with Client. To find out if a prepositional phrase with *to* or *for* is Recipient/Client or not, see if it could occur naturally without the preposition. Thus in *she sent her best wishes to John, to John* is Recipient (*she sent John her best wishes*); in *she sent her luggage to Los Angeles, to Los Angeles* is not Recipient but rather a circumstance of Location (we do not say *she sent Los Angeles her luggage*).[15] Clients tend to be more restricted than Recipients; in *I'm doing all this for Mary, for Mary* is not a Client but a type of circumstance of Cause (Behalf; see Section 5.7 below). An example of a Client would be *(for) his wife* in *Fred bought a present for his wife/bought his wife a present*.

---

[15] And there are clauses with *give* which, though superficially like transfer of possession, differ from these in that they do not exhibit the contrast between + preposition and – preposition. These are clauses with a nominalized verb as one participant, as in *give somebody a kick/punch/kiss/hug*. Thus while we can say, *he gave the dog a kick*, we are much less likely say *he gave a kick to the dog*. Such clauses are in fact mildly metaphorical variants of clauses where *kick, punch, kiss, hug*, etc. is a verb serving as the Process: *he gave the dog a kick: he kicked the dog*. This suggests that the nominalized verb is in fact a Scope (see below) rather than a Goal and that what might at first appear to be a Recipient is in fact construed as a Goal (and can thus be probed with *do to/with*): [Actor:] *he* [Process:] *gave* [Goal:] *the dog* [Scope: *a kick*] (cf. *what he did to the dog was give it a kick* but not *what he did with the kick was give the dog it*) but not *he gave a kick to the dog*, which we would have predicated if the structure had been [Actor:] *he* [Process:] *gave* [Goal:] *a kick* [Recipient:] *to the dog*.

Table 5-6 Type of doing and additional participants in 'material' clauses

		Intransitive	Transitive + Goal
creative		*Icicles formed.*	*They built a house.* **+Client:** *They built me a house.*
transformative	elaboration	*They washed.* *They played.* **+Scope (process):** *They played **a game of tennis**.* **+Scope (entity):** *They played **the piano**.*	*They washed the plates.* **+Attribute (resultative):** *They washed the plates **clean**.* **+Role (product):** *They cut it **into cubes**.*
	extension		*They donated a house.* **+Recipient:** *They gave **him** a house.* **+Accompaniment:** *provide sb with something*
	enhancement	*She crossed.* **+Scope (entity):** *She crossed **the room**.* **+Place:** *She crossed (the room) **into the opposite corner**.*	*She threw it.* **+Place:** *She threw it **across the room**.*

Recipients and Clients occur in systemically different environments, as indicated in Table 5-6. Recipients occur only in 'transitive transformative' clauses of the 'extending' type; and within that category, they occur with those clauses that denote a transfer of the Actor's possession of goods – transfer to the Recipient.[16] Here the Goal represents the 'goods' being transferred, as in Figure 5-11 below. (Note that the transfer of possession can alternatively be modelled in the grammar as depriving somebody of something rather than as giving something to somebody; in this model, the original owner is construed

---

[16] They are thus the material version of possessive relational clauses (see Section 5.4.5.2). Fawcett (e.g. 1988) treats them as relational rather than as material. But in our interpretation, they are simply part of a general pattern of agnation between material clauses on the one hand and relational and existential ones on the other: creative material clauses are related to existential clauses and transformative material clauses to relational clauses (more specifically, elaborating transformation – intensive relation, extending transformation – possessive relation, and enhancing transformation – circumstantial relation).

either circumstantially as a locative source, as in *take/steal/borrow money from a friend*, or participantally as the Goal, with the goods being transferred construed circumstantially as Matter, as in *rob/deprive him of* ['in respect of'] *his money*.[17])

With a Client, the 'service' may likewise be construed as the Goal, especially a Goal of the 'created' as distinct from the 'transformed' type, one that is brought into being by the process – the 'creative' type of 'transitive material' clause; e.g. *a picture, this house* in *he painted John a picture, built Mary a house*. But it is really the process that constitutes the service; hence a Client may also appear in an 'intransitive' clause – one that has no Goal, but has either Process + Scope, as described below, e.g. *played Mary a tune*, or else Process only, as in *play for me*. These last cannot appear without *for* (*play me*); in order to show that they are Client it is necessary to add a Scope element in final position (*play for me – play a tune for me – play me a tune*).

I	gave	my love	a ring that has no end
Actor	Process	Recipient	Goal

Fig 5-11 Material clause with Recipient

Most typically the Recipient/Client is realized by a nominal group denoting a human being; especially a personal pronoun, and most commonly of all a speech role (*me, you, us*), e.g. *me* in Mae West's famous line *Peel me a grape!* But this is not necessarily so; the Recipient is a plant in *did you give the philodendron some water?*, and an abstract entity *privilege* in *we... have today been given the rare privilege to be host to the nations of the world on our own soil*. Nor, of course, is the 'benefit' necessarily beneficial: *Claudius* is Recipient in *Locusta gave Claudius a dose of poison*.

Like the Goal, both Recipient and Client are affected by the process; but while the Goal is the participant that is impacted by the process, the Recipient/Client is the one that benefits from it. In contrast, the **Scope** of a 'material' clause is not in any way affected by the performance of the process.[18] Rather it either (i) construes the domain over which the process takes place (as with *the path* and *some steps which soon divide* in *Follow the path and climb some steps which soon divide*) or (ii) construes the process itself, either in general or specific terms

---

17 These two models for construing the experience of transfer of possession are thus grammatically distinct in English. The 'giving' model constitutes a distinct type in the grammar of transitivity – the configuration of Actor + Process + Goal + Recipient. In contrast, the 'depriving' model is not a distinct one; it is based on a more general pattern of participant + circumstance: (i) [possession as participant] Actor + Process + Goal + Place (e.g. *they took his most cherished belongings from him*) or (ii) [original owner as participant] Actor + Process + Goal + Matter (e.g. *they robbed him of his most cherished belongings*). To account for the relationship between these two lexicogrammatical models in English, we have to move up to the level of semantics.

18 As we shall see later (Section 5.7.3), the Scope of a 'material' clause is the **Range** element in the ergative model of a clause. In the first two editions of this book, there was no special term for the Range of a 'material' clause, so the Scope was simply called Range, as it was in Halliday (1967/8: 58–62/2005: 27–32). Certain types of Scope were recognized in traditional accounts under the heading of 'cognate object'.

(as with *a shower* in *In the morning you'd just wake up in a sweat and have a shower*). There is not, in fact, a sharp line between these two; they really lie along a single continuum. In either case, the Scope is restricted to 'intransitive' clauses (with the minor exception of clauses with *give*; cf. under (ii) below): see above Table 5-6. This means that a material clause consisting of the syntagm 'nominal group + verbal group + nominal group can be either Actor + Process + Goal or Actor + Process + Scope. We shall discuss the difference between them once we have characterized and exemplified the two types of Scope.

(i) The Scope may construe an entity which exists independently of the process but which indicates the domain over which the process takes place. An example is *You will be crossing some lonely mountains, so make sure you have enough petrol*. In our experience, mountains exist whether anyone crosses them or not and this is how the grammar construes them – as participants that can enter into different kinds of process; and *some lonely mountains* specifies the range of the tourist's crossing. Note that this is not a 'doing' relationship; you cannot say *what you will do to some lonely mountains is cross them* (compare with a 'doing' process such as levelling, where *do to* is fine: *what the mining company did to the mountain was level it*). Similarly in *Does Hogey Carmichael play the piano in that?*, where *the piano* is Scope; in our experience pianos also exist, independently of the act of playing them and this is how their grammar construes them – as participants that can enter into different kinds of process (compare *play the piano* with *polish/tune/move the piano*). There is a difference between playing pianos and climbing mountains – pianos exist for the purpose of being played, and would not exist otherwise. But in both cases the Scope is the domain of the process rather than another name for the process itself. When we come to *the boys were playing football*, however, although there exists an object called a football, *football* is really the name of the game in this example; it is doubtful whether this is referring to the ball as a material entity. And this leads us to those of the second type.

(ii) The Scope may be not an entity at all but rather another name for the process; for example:

Has anyone you have known or heard of died '**a good death**'? [Text 24]

So they decide to play **this rather elaborate game of murder** to pep things up. [Text 119]

Consider *I play tennis*, where *tennis* is Scope. The game of tennis is clearly not an entity; there is no such thing as tennis other than the act of playing it. Likewise with *sing a song*; if we look up *song* in the dictionary we are likely to find it defined as 'act of singing', just as *game* is 'act of playing'.

Why are these processes expressed as if they were a kind of participant in the clause? In other words, why do we say *play games*, rather than simply *play*, or *sing songs*, rather than simply *sing*? The answer is that this structure enables us to specify further the number or kind of processes that take place. The main types of 'process Scope' are as follows:

general:	they played games
specific: quantity	they played five games
specific: class	they played tennis
specific: quality	they played a good game

240

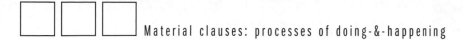

All these can of course be combined, as in *they played five good games of tennis*.

This pattern has given rise to a form of expression that is very common in modern English, exemplified by *have a bath, do some work, make a mistake, take a rest*. Here the verb is lexically very general; the process of the clause is expressed only by the noun functioning as Scope.[19]

There are various reasons in English grammar why this has become a favoured construction. The main reason for its prevalence is the greater potential that is open to nouns, in contrast to verbs, for being modified in different ways: it would be hard to replace the nouns by verbs in examples such as *have a hot bath, do a little dance, made three serious mistakes, take another quick look, gave her usual welcoming smile, made minor revision*. Compare the example *the jewellers hadn't done the evaluation yet*, where if the Scope is replaced by a process *hadn't valued*, on the one hand this would require an explicit Goal, and on the other hand it could not be made specific with *the*. The resulting nominal groups can then function as Themes and also as participants in other clause types; for example *three serious mistakes is three too many*.

It is useful to label the Scope in a 'material' clause more specifically as either 'Scope: entity' or 'Scope: process'. Examples of Scope are given in Figure 5-12.

the doormouse	crossed	the court
Actor	Process: material	Scope: entity

the whole country	is paying	a heavy price
Actor	Process: material	Scope: process

Fig. 5-12   Examples of Scope: entity and Scope: process

As noted above, the Scope typically occurs in 'intransitive' clauses, those in which there is only one direct participant – hence where there is Actor only, no Goal. As a result it is not always easy to distinguish a Scope from a Goal: both are possible interpretations of a nominal group following the verbal group serving as Process. Semantically the Scope element is not in any very obvious sense a participant in the process – it is not directly involved in the process by bringing it about, being affected by it or benefitting from it; but grammatically the Scope is treated as if it was a participant. So it can become Subject of the clause, as in *five games were played before tea*.

---

[19] Jespersen (1942: 117) called verbs in such constructions 'light verbs', and this term is often used in the contemporary literature on English and also on other languages (e.g. Butt, 2003) – another term being 'vector verb'. The Scope element in examples such as *the candidate dances three dances, Waltz, Foxtrot and Quickstep, with an Amateur or Professional partner* [LOB_E] was traditionally recognized as a 'cognate object'. Poutsma (1926) had noticed constructions with (in our terms) Process + Scope, characterizing the verb realizing the Process as having 'vague meaning' and calling the Scope an 'effective object'; he analysed such configurations as 'intransitive'.

The exception was the finale of the symphony, <u>which</u> **was played** just a shade too fast ... [LOB_C]

Enthusiasm grew, and in a few more months we gave a concert at which the accompanist was the village schoolmaster, and <u>the tenor solo 'Onaway awake'</u> **was sung** by the Rector. [LOB_G]

<u>Minor revisions</u> **were made** to the text.

However, there are some grammatical distinctions between a Scope and a Goal.

As we have already noted, the Scope cannot be probed by *do to* or *do with*, whereas the Goal can. Since nothing is being 'done to' it, a Scope element can never have a resultative Attribute (for resultative Attribute, see immediately below) added within the clause, as a (transformative) Goal can: we can say *they trampled the field flat* meaning 'with the result that it became flat', where *the field* is Goal, but not *they crossed the field flat*, where *the field* is Scope, even though the flattening may have resulted from their continued crossing of it. Similarly, a Scope element can never be configured with a circumstance of Role of the 'product' type (for Role, see Section 5.6.2.3). The Scope is less commonly a personal pronoun, and it cannot normally be modified by a possessive. Moreover, although generalized Scope-receptive clauses such as *this mountain has never been climbed* are quite common, Scope-receptive clauses with specific Actors are rare. Thus while a Goal readily becomes Subject in clauses such as *This teapot wasn't left here by your aunt, was it?*, it is unusual to make a Scope element 'modally responsible' in this way: *This mountain wasn't climbed by your aunt, was it?*, where the validity of the proposition is being asserted with respect to the mountain, sounds decidedly odd.

There is one more role noted in Table 5-6, that of **Attribute**. The Attribute really belongs to the realm of 'relational' clauses and will be introduced in that context below. However, it enters into 'material' clauses in a restricted way. In certain clauses with an 'elaborating' outcome, the Attribute may be used to construe the resultant qualitative state of the Actor or Goal after the process has been completed, as in

They stripped her **clean** of every bit of jewellery she ever had [Text 24]

where *clean* serves as an Attribute specifying the resultant state of the Goal, *her*. Such Attributes are called **resultative Attributes**. They are only marginal participants. While they are unlike circumstances in that they are not marked by prepositions, they are also unlike true participants in that they cannot serve as Subject. There is in fact a closely related circumstance – the resultative Role or 'product' (see Section 5.6.2).

if everything you touch crumbles **into dust and ashes,** [Text 16]

but she was reduced, by reason of spinal cancer, **into a howling virago** [Text 24]

There is also a non-resultative variant of the Attribute. This is the **depictive Attribute** serving to specify the state which the Actor or Goal is in when it takes part in the process; for example:

What – so it's not fresh here? You don't get it **fresh**. [UTS/Macquarie Corpus]

As soon as I could, I left the flat and drove home in my utility, sober for once and half-hoping as I always did on the few occasions when I was driving **sober** late at night that I would be picked up by the cops. [ACE_K]

In a 'material' clause, the Attribute is always an optional added specification. In contrast, it is an inherent part of the configuration of a 'relational' clause and cannot be left out. The following example is thus 'relational' rather than 'material':

the more one sets the record **straight**. [Text 24]

We cannot say *the more one sets the record* without the Attribute *straight*. Similarly, a prepositional phrase with *into* serves as an Attribute in a 'relational' clause if it is an inherent part of the clause, as in the following example:

I could turn that **into a novel** in a few months. [Text 7]

This clause is not agnate with *I could turn that* (without *into a novel*).

Certain types of 'material' clause may thus be configured with an additional participant – a Scope, a Recipient, a Client or an Attribute. Scope, Recipient and Client are clearly treated by the grammar as participants; for example, they are all candidates for subjecthood in a 'receptive' clause. However, at the same time, they are clearly located some distance towards circumstances on the cline between participants and circumstances, which is reflected in the fact that, under certain conditions, they may be marked by a preposition. There are also, in fact, certain circumstances that are construed as inherent in a process. This happens with 'enhancing' clauses construing movement through space of a participant: here a circumstance of Place represents the destination of that movement and may be inherent in the process. For example:

Did these books and articles **put** groceries <u>on the table</u>? [Text 7]

They carved its image into stone ‖ and **placed** it <u>on their temples and palaces</u>. [Text 65]

5.2.5 Concrete and abstract material clauses

Material clauses do not necessarily represent concrete, physical events; they may represent abstract doings and happenings, as in the passage of financial news shown in Text 5-6:

Text 5-6: Reporting – chronicling: financial news report (written & monologic) [Text 26]
AT&T's stock **slid** 14 percent Tuesday as the company **issued** its first profit warning under chief executive C. Michael Armstrong, **fueling** worries about whether his radical remake of the nation's largest long-distance company **will succeed**. The disappointing forecast, which **came** as AT&T **posted** first-quarter results that met most expectations, **dampened** the enthusiasm **created** by last week's initial public offering of $10.6 billion worth of stock in the company's wireless business. In fact, shares of the new AT&T Wireless Group also **fell** Tuesday even as three major brokerages **initiated** coverage of the stock with a 'buy' recommendation.

These are treated grammatically in the language as types of action; the appropriate probes would be for example *What did AT&T's stock do?*, *What did AT&T do to the first-quarter results?*, thus showing that *AT&T's stock* is interpretable as Actor and *the first-quarter results* as Goal. Thus *A&T's stock slid* is modelled on the concrete *the car* (or other concrete entity) *slid*, *fueling worries* on the concrete *fueling fires*, *dampened the enthusiasm* on the concrete *dampened the fire*, and so on.

But as the process becomes more abstract, so the distinction between Actor and Goal becomes harder to draw. With a concrete process it is usually clear which role a given participant is playing: there is a sharp distinction between *the boy kicked*, where *the boy* is Actor, and *the boy was kicked*, where *the boy* is Goal. Even with concrete processes, however, we have to recognize that there are some where the Actor is involuntary, and thus in some respects like a Goal; for example *the tourist collapsed*. Despite the fact the verb is active, this is a happening rather than a doing: the probe is not *what did the tourist do?* but *what happened to the tourist?* With more abstract processes, we often find 'operative' and 'receptive' forms side by side with little difference between them: for example (transformative: extending) *the girls' school and the boys' school combined/were combined*; (creative) *a new approach is evolving/is being evolved*. There is still some difference: if the 'receptive' form is used, we can probe for an explicit Actor – we can ask *who by?*, whereas with the 'operative' form we cannot. And this is what justifies us in still giving a different functional status to the participant in the two cases, as in Figure 5-13, where *the two schools* is Actor in one case and Goal in the other:

the two schools	combined
Actor	Process

the two schools	were combined
Goal	Process

Fig. 5-13   Operative and receptive in abstract material clauses

But this clearly exaggerates the difference, and we shall return to this point with an alternative interpretation below (Section 5.7).

Meanwhile we need to take cognizance of the fact that much of the time people are not talking about concrete processes like springing and catching, or even abstract ones like evolving and combining. We are talking about such momentous phenomena as what we think and feel, what Mary said to John, what is good or bad, here or there, mine or yours; these are the flesh and blood of everyday encounters. In sayings of this kind, however, the concepts of Actor and Goal do not make much sense. If we say

I hate lasagna. [Text 76]

it can hardly be said that *I* is an Actor and is 'doing something to' *lasagna*. And this is not because it is casual or colloquial; the same would be true of a majority of expressions in more highly valued modes of discourse. It would be difficult, for example, to identify an Actor in any of the following:

To be or not to be: that is the question.

We hold these truths to be self-evident.

The square on the hypotenuse of a right-angled triangle equals the sum of the squares on the other two sides.

To understand expressions such as these we need to broaden our view of what constitutes 'goings-on' – a quantum of change in the flow of events. It is important to recognize that there may be more than one kind of process in the grammar of a language; and that the

functions assumed by the participants in any clause are determined by the type of process that is involved.

5.3 Mental clauses: processes of sensing

5.3.1 Introductory examples of 'mental' clauses

While 'material' clauses are concerned with our experience of the material world, 'mental' clauses are concerned with our experience of the world of our own consciousness. They are clauses of sensing: a 'mental' clause construes a quantum of change in the flow of events taking place in our own consciousness. This process of sensing may be construed either as flowing from a person's consciousness or as impinging on it; but it is not construed as a material act.

Here is a short example of 'mental' clauses in casual chat leading up to an anecdote about cockroaches (which is given in full, together with generic analysis, in Eggins & Slade, 1997: 228):

> **Text 5-7: Sharing – casual conversation: anecdote about personal experience (spoken & dialogic) [Eggins & Slade, 1997: 228]**
> Pat: I **hate** cockroaches more than rats.
>
> Pauline: I **don't like** cockroaches either. [...]
>
> Pat: I **remember** we were sitting for our analytical chemistry exam, and it was the final exams and they have sort of like bench desks where there's three to a bench normally and they had the middle seat empty and two sat either side and I was sitting there, and **thought** geez I **can feel** something on my foot and I **thought** no, no **don't worry** about it.

The Processes of the 'mental' clauses are shown in bold. When the clause refers to present time, the tense of the verbal group serving as Process is the simple present rather than the present-in-present that is characteristic of 'material' clauses. For example, Pat says *I hate cockroaches* rather than *I'm hating cockroaches*; the latter is highly marked and requires some special interpretation such as inception (e.g. *I'm hating cockroaches more and more every day*).

The 'mental' clauses are all the same in that the Subject is the speaker, *I* – with the exception of *don't worry about it*, where the subject is the addressee, 'you' – which is, however, the speaker addressing herself; that is, they serve to construe the speaker's own processes of consciousness. This is very typical of casual conversation. As we shall see, this turns out to be a special case of a general property of one class of 'mental' clause: the Subject is a nominal group denoting a conscious being (as in *where many experts believe ...*, *investigators found evidence ...*, *he had heard ...*, *and police presume ...*, *Indians now think ...*). In contrast to the Subject, the Complement is realized by a nominal group that can denote entities of any kind – animals such as cockroaches, objects such as guns, substances such as cough medicine, abstractions such as greed. Thus, while *I hate greed* is perfectly fine, *greed hates me* is odd; and *guns hate me* would have to be interpreted figuratively as some kind of personification.

The first two clauses construe emotions – *I hate cockroaches more than rats* and *I don't like cockroaches either*. The verbs serving as Process are lexically gradable; they form points on a scale (*detest, loathe – hate – dislike – like – love*), expressing degrees of affection. The

245

first clause is also graded grammatically, by a circumstance of degree – *more than rats*. This property of lexical and grammatical gradability is typical of 'mental' clauses construing emotions.

These two turns are followed by Pat's anecdote, illustrating the negative evaluation of cockroaches. The anecdote is in fact launched by a 'mental' clause – *I remember*. This is a 'mental' clause, not of **emotion** but of **cognition**, of a type characteristically used to introduce an anecdote or other narrative passage, for example:

> When I was younger when I went to my first disco I **remember** how it was and the boys didn't behave like you saw on Happy Days or anything like that.

> I **remember** once I went to a film, and ah, I'd just bought this new outfit and it was long silky, black pants that came up all in one.

Interestingly, there is a variant of this strategy where the thing remembered is a nominal group serving as Subject and the person remembering is a nominal group serving as Complement:

> But this **reminds** me of Tamara. She comes back from two months away, organises an extra month the following year – and how she accumulates so many holidays is beyond me. [UTS-Macquarie Corpus]

In such clauses, the phenomenon remembered is construed as impinging on the person's consciousness. We thus have a pair of related processes, *remember : remind*, where the sensing is construed from two different angles.

In Pat's introduction to her anecdote, the 'mental' clause is followed by a representation of the content of thinking – *we were sitting for our analytical chemistry exam ...* . Compare: *I remember [that] once I went to a film ...* These representations of the content of thinking are clauses in their own right. They are related to the 'mental' clause; but they are not part of it. They do not serve as Complements in the 'mental' clause since we do not find 'receptive' variants with them as Subject: we would not expect to find *once I went to a film is remembered by me*, and so on. Two of the 'mental' clauses that follow in Pat's anecdote are similar: *and [I] thought geez I can feel something on my foot; and I thought no, no don't worry about it.* These are also 'mental' clauses of cognition; and all these examples illustrate a general feature of such clauses: they are able to set up another clause or set of clauses as the content of thinking – as the ideas created by cognition. As we shall see later, the relationship between the 'mental' clause and the 'idea' clause is one of projection: the 'mental' clause projects another clause or set of clauses, giving them the status of ideas or of the content of consciousness. Such examples are very common in casual conversation.

The cockroach passage thus illustrates 'mental' clauses of emotion and cognition. There is one further type of 'mental' clause: *I can feel something on my foot*. This is a clause of **perception**, the *can feel* as the Process, *I* as the Senser and *something on my foot* as the Phenomenon being perceived. Such clauses are similar to emotive and cognitive 'mental' clauses in that the Senser is construed as a conscious being. But they also have properties that set them apart from the other subtypes of 'mental' clause. For example, while Pat could have said *I feel something on my foot* with the Process in the simple present, she has

used a modulation of readiness instead – *can feel* (for modulation, see Chapter 4, Section 4.5.2). This is quite common with 'mental' clauses of perception, as with *Can you see those pelicans flying across the lagoon* alongside *Do you see ....* This example also illustrates another feature specific to clauses of perception: what is construed as the phenomenon being perceived can be a thing (such as cockroach); but it can also be an **act**, realized by a non-finite clause (cf. Chapter 7, Table 7-14), as in *I can feel* [[*something crawling up my foot*]].

5.3.2 Interpreting 'mental' clauses

We have identified some of the properties of 'mental' clauses that are either shared by them as a class or characteristic of a significant subclass. These properties differentiate them from 'material' clauses, so it is reasonable to ask if the Actor + Process + Goal model used in the analysis of 'material' clauses is or is not applicable to 'mental' ones. It might be argued that the terms Actor and Goal are just conventional labels; and that since grammatical and semantic categories are not in one-to-one correspondence, then if we use grammatical terms that are semantic in import (as nearly all grammatical terms are) we cannot expect them to be appropriate for all instances. The reasoning is quite valid; grammatical labels are very rarely appropriate for all instances of a category (cf. Halliday, 1984b) – they are chosen to reflect its central or 'core' signification (what has been called 'prototype' in the work by Eleanor Rosch, e.g. Rosch, 1978). These core areas are the central regions for each process type in Figure 5-3; and the non-core areas lie on the borders between different process types, shading into one another as the colours on a colour spectrum. In the case of Actor and Goal, the range of different clause types to which they are readily applicable would be suspiciously few. But there is a more serious reason for questioning their relevance to the analysis of examples such as *I hate cockroaches*.

Consider the pair of clauses (i) *Mary liked the gift* (cf. *I hate cockroaches*), (ii) *the gift pleased Mary*. These are not synonymous; they differ in their choice of both Theme and Subject, both these roles being assigned to *Mary* in (i) and to *the gift* in (ii). But they are obviously closely related; considered from the standpoint of the present chapter, they could be representations of the same state of affairs. Yet if we apply an Actor-Process-Goal analysis we shall be saying that in (i) *Mary* is Actor and *the gift* is Goal, while in (ii) it is the other way round. This seems somewhat artificial.

Could we perhaps interpret one of these as being the receptive variant of the other? Assuming we could find some criterion for deciding which was which, this could yield a proportion as in Figure 5-14. This says that *Mary liked the gift* is the realization of a semantic configuration that would be realized as *Mary was pleased by the gift* if such a clause existed. The drawback is, of course, that *Mary was pleased by the gift* does exist; it is a normal, and indeed very frequent, clause type in English. We can hardly explain some other clause by saying that it is doing duty as a replacement for this one. Furthermore the other clause has its own 'receptive' variant: *the gift was liked by Mary*, although a much less common type, undoubtedly exists also. So we cannot explain either of the 'operative' forms by saying that it is a special kind of 'receptive' of the other; each one has a 'receptive' variant of its own. This is not an isolated instance; pairs of this kind are typical of clauses of feeling, thinking and perceiving, for example:

No one believed his story   his story convinced no one

I hadn't noticed that   that hadn't struck me

children fear ghosts   ghosts frighten children

I freaked out   it freaked me out

(For a fuller list see Table 5-10 later on.) The contemporary language goes on creating such pairs: the slang expressions *I dig it* and *it sends me* both evolved at about the same time. Nonetheless speakers of English do not seem to feel that doublets like *believe* and *convince*, or *notice* and *strike*, semantically related though they may be, are so close that they ought to be interpreted as different forms of the same word (in the way that, for example, *go* and *went* are different forms of the same verb *go*).

Mary	liked	the gift
Goal	Process	Actor
the tourist	was caught	by the lion

the gift	pleased	Mary
Actor	Process	Goal
the lion	caught	the tourist

Fig. 5-14   Verbs *like* and *please* interpreted as operative/receptive pair

It seems therefore that we should abandon the Actor-Goal trail at this point and recognize that 'mental' clauses are unlike 'material' process clauses and require a different functional interpretation. Obviously clauses construing doing and clauses construing sensing are different in meaning, but that is not enough to make them constitute distinct grammatical categories. There are indefinitely many ways of drawing lines on purely semantic grounds, for example, by invoking contextual considerations 'from above', as we do when we describe the semantic strategies specific to a particular situation type (cf. Halliday, 1973: Ch. 4; Matthiessen, 1990); but the question we are concerned with here is which of these have systematic repercussions in the grammar.

We shall treat Actor and Goal as participant roles that are confined to the grammar of 'material' clauses and instead of these two we now introduce two distinct participant roles for 'mental' clauses. These are Senser and Phenomenon: see Figure 5-15. We shall present these in more detail in Sections 5.3.3.1 and 5.3.3.2.

Mary	liked	the gift
Senser	Process	Phenomenon
nom. group	verbal group	nom. group

the gift	pleased	Mary
Phenomenon	Process	Senser
nom. group	verbal group	nom. group

Fig. 5-15   Verbs *like* and *please* interpreted as 'mental' clauses

5.3.3 Properties of 'mental' clauses

The category of 'mental process clauses' turns out to be grammatically distinct from that of material process clauses on the basis of a number of properties; these are set out in Table 5-7 and discussed in the following subsections (and cf. Table 5-45 below).

Table 5-7 Properties differentiating 'material' and 'mental' clauses

	Material	Mental
participant: central	Actor: ± conscious; prototypically a potent thing	Senser: +conscious
participant: second	Goal: things Scope: things – typically either places or events	Phenomenon: things, macro-things (acts) or meta-things (facts)
ability to project	–	can project ideas
Process, tense: reporting present time	present-in-present unmarked	simple present unmarked
Process: substitute	substitute verb *do*	–

5.3.3.1 The nature of the Senser

In a clause of 'mental' process, there is always one participant who is human; this is the **Senser**, introduced above: the one that 'senses' – feels, thinks, wants or perceives, for example, *Mary* in *Mary liked the gift*. More accurately, we should say human-like; the significant feature of the Senser is that of being 'endowed with consciousness'. Expressed in grammatical terms, the participant that is engaged in the mental process is one that is referred to pronominally as *he* or *she*, not as *it*.[20]

Which particular creatures we choose to endow with consciousness when we talk about them may vary according to who we are, what we are doing or how we are feeling at the time; different registers show different preferences. Pets, domestic animals and other higher animals are often treated as conscious; the owner says of the cat *she doesn't like milk*, whereas someone who is not a cat lover, or who has been annoyed by that particular specimen, is more likely to refer to the animal as *it*. But any entity, animate or not, can be treated as conscious; and since mental process clauses have this property, that only something that is being credited with consciousness can function in them as the one who feels, thinks, wants or perceives, one only has to put something into that role in order to turn it into a conscious being. Thus in *The Rabbit sighed. He thought it would be a long time before this magic called Real happened to him*, the Senser is the nominal group *he*, which refers to a velveteen toy rabbit; but the example comes from a story for children about this velveteen rabbit and in the imaginary world construed by the story, toys are endowed with

---

[20] In languages with nominal case marking, the Senser – or certain types of Senser – may be in the dative case, as in Hindi and Telagu (cf. Prakasam, 2004), setting it formally apart from the Actor. In some languages, the Senser is realized by a nominal group denoting a certain body part (see Matthiessen, 2004b: 591), as in Akan (cf. English *it breaks my heart, it blows my mind*).

consciousness. Similarly, in *the empty house was longing for the children to return*, the nominal group *the empty house* is Senser. Simply by putting *the empty house* in this grammatical environment, as something that felt longing, we cause it to be understood as endowed with consciousness. This explains the anomalous character of clauses such as *it really likes me*, *it knows what it thinks*, where there is a tension between the *it* and the meaning of the verb. Not that such clauses are ungrammatical; far from it. But the ambiguous status of the 'sensing' participant, who on the one hand is capable of liking, knowing and thinking, and therefore is 'plus consciousness', but on the other hand is referred to as *it*, and therefore is 'minus consciousness', gives them a flavour that is somewhat humorous or quaint.[21]

'Conscious being' typically means a person or persons; but as the following examples illustrate, a human collective (*the British public*, *the whole house*, *the world*) can also be construed as conscious:

> I think the British public **doesn't dislike** force provided that it's short, sharp and rewarding. [LOB K]

> Surely you don't want the whole house **to know** of this occurrence? [Agatha Christie, 'Styles']

> The judging must come from one's own experience, one's own conscience, and understanding. What the world **thought** didn't matter. [LOB_K]

It can even be a product of human consciousness:

> The film **imagines** that the FBI imported a free-lance black operative to terrorize the town's mayor into revealing the murderers' names. [Time 89 9i]

The Senser may also be represented by part of a person (*the brain*), as in:

> On the theory that the brain '**thinks** by virtue of its organization,' it is susceptible of explanation. [LOB_D]

This strategy also includes figurative expressions that are construed on a material model – *it breaks my heart that ...*, *it blew my mind that ...* .

While the Senser is construed as being endowed with consciousness in 'mental' clauses, there is no trace of this pattern in 'material' clauses. In 'material' clauses, no participant is required to be human, and the distinction between conscious and non-conscious beings simply plays no part. The Actor of a 'material' clause is thus much less constrained than the Senser of a 'mental' clause. Prototypically, it is realized by a nominal group that denotes some kind of 'potent' entity; but even this is, in Modern English, a very relaxed constraint, particularly when we move into the realm of abstract examples such as *Politically committed art took over one wing of the modernist movement* and the realm of non-volitional happenings, as in *Limestone can form in many ways* (cf. Section 5.2.5, and Halliday & Matthiessen, 1999: 482–483).

---

[21] There is one type of 'mental' clause of perception where the Senser is a period of time and the Process is either see or find, as in *Summer finds campers and hikers descending on the mountains in throngs*; *Ten minutes later saw us speeding through London*. These are metaphorical constructions where a circumstance of Time has been construed as if it were a Senser: see Chapter 10, Section 10.5.

5.3.3.2 Phenomenon

The Senser of a 'mental' clause is thus highly constrained. With regard to the other main element in a clause of mental process, namely the **Phenomenon** – that which is felt, thought, wanted or perceived, the position is in a sense reversed. That is to say, the set of things that can take on this role in the clause is not only not restricted to any particular semantic or grammatical category, it is actually wider than the set of possible participants in a 'material' clause. It may be not only a **thing** but also an **act** or a **fact**.

In a 'material' clause, every participant is a **thing**; that is, it is a phenomenon of our experience, including of course our inner experience or imagination – some entity (person, creature, institution, object, substance or abstraction). Any of these 'things' may also, of course, be the object of consciousness in a 'mental' clause; for example:

> *You* **recognize** <u>her</u>? [Text 8]

> *I* **don't understand** <u>you</u> Inspector. [Text 8]

> **Do** *you* **want** <u>lasagna</u>? – Oh, *I* **hate** <u>lasagna</u>. [Text 76]

> *Only about four out of every 10 residents affected* even **know** <u>their new number</u>. [News/Britain Readies to Change Numbers]

> *I* **learned** <u>that lesson</u> a long time ago. [UTS/Macquarie Corpus/Men]

> <u>Ashtray</u> **upsets** *him*. [UTS/Macquarie Corpus/Men]

> After that war <u>nothing</u> **could frighten** *me* anymore. [Text 24]

The thing construed as Phenomenon may even be a metaphorical one – a nominal group with a nominalization as Head denoting a process or quality reified as a thing (see Chapter 10, Section 10.5):

> where *Amnesty* **found** <u>persistent abuses</u> [Text 2]

> As the new year of 1855 dawned, Johan Heinrich pondered that he would turn 26 in February, and *he* **saw** <u>a bleak future</u> ahead of him. [ACE_G]

> Westbrook further **bemoans** <u>the Southern writers' creation of an unreal image of their homeland</u> [BROWN1_G]

These 'things' could all appear in a 'material' clause as well. However, the concept of 'thing' is extended in 'mental' clauses to include **macrophenomenal** clauses where the Phenomenon is an act and **metaphenomenal** clauses where the Phenomenon is a fact.

In a 'macrophenomenal mental' clause, the Phenomenon is realized by a non-finite clause denoting an act; for example:

> *He* **saw** [[<u>the sand dredger heading for the cruiser</u>]] [Text 30]

> *Neighbours* **noticed** [[<u>him return home later that day</u>]], but it was the last time the old man was seen alive. [COBUILD/OzNews]

An act is a configuration of a process, participants involved in that process and possibly attendant circumstances, as in *the sand dredger heading for the cruiser*. Macrophenomenal

Phenomena are typically restricted to one subtype of 'mental' clause – clauses of perception (see further below under TYPE OF SENSING): the act is seen, heard, tasted or perceived in some other way; but it is not normally thought, felt emotionally or desired. The non-finite clause realizing an act is either a present participial one ([*he saw*] *the sand dredger heading for the cruiser*) or an infinitival one without the 'infinitive marker' *to* ([*he saw*] *the sand dredger head for the cruiser*). The difference between them is a temporal one: the participial clause represents the process as unbounded in time, while the infinitival one represents it as bounded in time (cf. Kirsner & Thompson, 1976). One of the interesting features of 'macrophenomenal' clauses is the form of what would seem to be the 'receptive' variant: instead of the expected *the sand dredger heading for the cruiser was seen by him*, where the whole Phenomenon is the Subject, we are much more likely to get *the sand dredger was seen (by him) heading for the cruiser*, where only the Subject of the non-finite clause serving as Phenomenon is 'picked out' to serve as the Subject of the 'mental' clause. For example:

Smoke **was seen** billowing from the police headquarters after an explosion.

This might suggest a different analysis of macrophenomenal clauses: what appears to be the 'receptive' variant could be interpreted not as a 'receptive' variant of a 'macrophenomenal' clause but rather as a clause with a verbal group complex serving as Process, *was seen billowing*, on the model of *the sand dredger was rumoured (said) to be heading for the cruiser*. Such constructions could be interpreted as markers of evidentiality – of the nature of the evidence for the information being negotiated. (We shall discuss such verbal group complexes in Chapter 8, Section '8.8 Hypotaxis: verbal group, projection'.)[22]

In a 'metaphenomenal mental' clause, the Phenomenon is realized by a (typically finite) clause denoting a fact; for example:

[[That this was not the ideal solution]] **was recognised** *by the Chairman* in his letter to the President, while submitting the Commission's report. [KOHL_A]

Police divers late last night **discovered** [[[the Marchioness had broken in two || and sunk in 10 m of water]]]. [Text 30]

'*I* **can see** [[this town is going to hell fast]],' says Mike Day, a lobster fisherman. [Time 89 9i]

I **regret** very much [[that I was away from home]]. [Dumb Witness]

I'm **not surprised** [[[he died thinking || the novel was a failure]]] [Text 17]

What really **irritates** *me* is [[[that a lot of people go || to socialise in pubs]]] [UTS/Macquarie Corpus/A's dinner]

It **beats** *me* [[[how people think up such things, || let alone say them]]]. [A. Christie, 4.50 from Paddington]

A fact is on a higher level of abstraction than an ordinary thing or an act. Ordinary things and acts are both material phenomena; they can be seen, heard and perceived in other ways.

---

[22] A receptive variant such as *the sand dredger heading for the cruiser wasn't spotted by the navy* would in fact be ambiguous: it could be a macrophenomenon, but alternatively *heading for the cruiser* might be an embedded relative clause. These two are significantly different in meaning. The interpretation as embedded relative clause would not be plausible where the non-finite clause occurs after the process of perception.

Thus while an act is more complex than an ordinary thing, it still exists in the same material realm. In contrast, a fact is not a material phenomenon but rather a semiotic one: it is a proposition (or sometimes a proposal) construed as existing in its own right in the semiotic realm, without being brought into existence by somebody saying it.[23] The most common environment for a metaphenomenal Phenomenon is that of a clause of emotion (see further below) where the Phenomenon is construed as impinging on the Senser's consciousness (as with *irritate, trouble* in the examples above). The status of the 'fact' clause is often signalled by the noun *fact* itself, as in *I regret the fact that you should have left him out in the cold*, or by another 'fact' noun such as *notion, idea, possibility* (see further Chapter 7, Section 7.5.7).

Given the semiotic nature of facts, it stands to reason that they cannot serve as participants in 'material' clauses. When they do occur in what might appear to be 'material' clauses, these clauses are abstract; and they have to be interpreted either mentally or relationally, as in the following examples:

> The problem with Huck Finn is not [[that Twain is trapped by the voice of the narrator]]. He's **trapped** by the fact [[that the river flows south]]. [Text 17]

> The fundamental nature and importance of these advances **are not diminished** by the fact [[that many of them came about in response to specific problems of environmental change [[thought to offer threats to society]]]]. [Text 32]

> But it is an urban legend, he said, largely **fueled** by the fact [[that suicides there are often shockingly public]]. [COCA]

Thus the first example means 'the fact that the river flows south confines him mentally'; and the second example means 'the fact that many of them came about in response to specific problems of environmental change thought to offer threats to society does not make the fundamental nature and importance of these advances smaller'. As we shall see below, facts occur regularly in 'relational' clauses.

5.3.3.3 Projection

As we have seen, 'metaphenomenal mental' clauses are configured with a fact as Phenomenon. But there is one further option open to such clauses – an option that sets them apart not only from 'material' clauses but also from 'relational' ones. This option is the ability to set up another clause 'outside' the 'mental' clause as the representation of the 'content' of consciousness. This kind of meaning is recognized very explicitly in the conventions of comic strips: sensers are shown with 'clouds' emanating from them and the content of consciousness is represented linguistically within these clouds (cf. Chapter 7, Figure 7-5). For example:

> ||| An unknown number of passengers are still missing || and police presume || they are dead. ||| [Text 5]

> ||| I don't believe || that endorsing the Nuclear Freeze initiative is the right step for California CC. ||| [Text 6]

---

[23] We could say that a fact is an act that has been propositionalized – that has been given existence as a semiotic phenomenon.

Here the 'mental' clause **projects** another clause (or combination of clauses) as a representation of the content of thinking, believing, presuming, and so on; the projected clause is called an **idea** clause. Thus while 'fact' clauses serve as the Phenomenon of a 'mental' clause and can therefore be made Subject and be theme-predicated, 'idea' clauses are not part of the 'mental' clause but are rather combined with the 'mental' clause in a clause nexus of projection. We shall explain and illustrate the difference in some detail in Chapter 7, Section 7.5.

5.3.3.4 Process: the system of TENSE

'Material' and 'mental' processes also differ with respect to the way that they unfold in time and this is reflected in the grammatical system of TENSE. What is the basic form of the present tense in modern English? In the teaching of English as a foreign language there has been much controversy about which to teach first, the simple present *takes* or the so-called 'present continuous' or 'present progressive' *is taking* (which we shall characterize as 'present in present' in Section 6.3.4, Chapter 6); and claims have been made on behalf of both. There is a reason for the controversy; in fact, either one of these tenses may be the basic, unmarked form depending on the type of process expressed by the clause. In a 'mental' clause, the unmarked present tense is the **simple present**; we say

She likes the gift	(not *she is liking the gift*)
Do you know the city?	(not *are you knowing the city?*)
I see the stars	(not *I am seeing the stars*)

But in a 'material' clause the unmarked present tense is the **present in present**; we say

They're building a house	(not *they build a house*)
Are you making the tea?	(not *do you make the tea?*)
I'm going home	(not *I go home*)

We are not saying that the other tense cannot occur; both tenses are used with both types of process. But the other one is the marked option in each case; and this means that it is less frequent and that it carries a special interpretation. Thus the following examples of 'mental' clauses with the present-in-present are all marked:

I think that you you're **wanting** your little captive breeding program here. [UTS/Macquarie Corpus]

Good morning, CSR. [7 seconds] Who **are** you **wanting**, sorry? [UTS/Macquarie Corpus]

And people were diagnosing all these things, and so she was very concerned at what was really happening, and nobody **was believing** it – particularly my brother-in-law. He thought she was, you know, a drama queen. [UTS/Macquarie Corpus]

I think we're all **forgetting** one little thing here, and that is that Bill is Hillary. [COCA]

The simple present with a material process is general or habitual – that is, the **occurrence** of the process is construed as generalized or as habitual, e.g. *they build a house for every*

employee.[24] The present in present with a mental process is a rather highly conditioned kind of inceptive aspect, as in *I feel I'm knowing the city for the first time* ('I'm getting to know'); this is somewhat difficult to contextualize, with the result that, taken out of context, it is quite likely to be understood as something else (e.g. *I'm seeing the stars* as a 'material' clause 'I'm interviewing the leading performers'). These tense patterns are set out in Table 5-8.

Table 5-8 Unmarked present tense with material and mental processes

	Present	**Present in present**
material	[marked] they build a house (for every employee) [habitual; generalized]	[unmarked] they're building a house
mental	[unmarked] I know the city	[marked] I'm knowing the city (for the first time) [inceptive]

The present-in-present is thus highly marked with 'mental' clauses. We can note the success of McDonald's attention-grabbing advertising slogan *I'm lovin' it*, which has surely been more effective that *I love it* would have been. In Justin Timberlake's promotional song, *I'm loving it* is followed (after two repetitions interspersed with *ba da ba ba ba*) by *Don't you love it too?* rather than by *Aren't you loving it too?*

5.3.3.5 Substitute verb

Mental clauses also differ from material ones with respect to the use of *do* as a substitute verb. We referred above to the fact that material processes are 'doing' processes, which can be probed, and substituted, by the verb *do*; for example:

> What did John do? – He ran away. What John did was run away.
>
> What did Mary do with the gift? – She sold it.

Mental processes, on the other hand, are processes of feeling, wanting, thinking and seeing. They are not kinds of doing, and cannot be probed or substituted by *do*. We cannot say *What John did was know the answer*, or *What did Mary do with the gift? – She liked it*. This lack of a substitute verb can render some things unsayable, as in the following text example from casual conversation:

> That's because I prefer small boats, which other people don't necessarily ...

If the process had been a material one such as *build small boats*, there would have been no problem in ending *which other people don't necessarily do*.

---

[24] In addition, there is a registerially restricted use of the simple present tense. In commentary accompanying demonstrations and the like, the simple present is used.

5.3.4 TYPE OF SENSING

Within the general class of 'mental' clauses (Figure 5-16), there are four different subtypes of sensing: 'perceptive', 'cognitive', 'desiderative' and 'emotive'[25]. These are treated by the grammar as distinct types. They differ with respect to phenomenality, directionality, gradability, potentiality and ability to serve as metaphors of modality; the typical patterns are set out in Table 5-9. (For additional differences and discussion, see Halliday & Matthiessen, 1999: 137–144; Matthiessen, 1995a: 263–270; Davidse, 1991/1999.) Examples of verbs serving in the different types of mental clause are given in Table 5-10.

Table 5-9 type of sensing

		Perceptive	Cognitive	Desiderative	Emotive
phenomenality	phenomenal	✓ [he saw the car]	✓ [he knows the car]	✓ [he wants the car]	✓ [he likes the car/ the car pleases him]
	macro-phenomenal	✓ [he saw the car speeding]	–	–	✓ [he likes the car speeding]
	meta-phenomenal	✓ [typically fact: he saw that they had left]	✓ [typically idea: proposition: he thought that they had left]	✓ [typically idea: proposal: he wanted them to leave]	✓ [fact: he regretted (the fact) that they had left]
directionality	'like' type	✓	✓	✓	✓
	'please' type	[restricted: strike, assail]	[restricted: strike, occur to, convince, remind, escape]	[marginal: tempt]	✓
gradability		–	[restricted: imagine – think – know]	[restricted: would like – want – desire]	✓ [pervasive] [like – love – adore]
potentiality		I can see them/I see them	≠	≠	≠
metaphorical modality		– (evidentiality [I hear/see that ...])	modalization: probability [I think that's the courier : that'll be the courier]	modulation [I'd like to be there at 8 : you should be there at 8]	– (appraisal [I fear/ regret that ...])

---

[25] In Figure 5-3, 'feeling' covers both desideration and emotion.

Table 5-10 Examples of verbs serving as Process in mental clauses

	'Like' type	'Please' type
perceptive	perceive, sense; see, notice, glimpse; hear, overhear; feel; taste; smell	(assail)
cognitive	think, believe, suppose, expect, consider, know; understand, realize, appreciate; imagine, dream, pretend; guess, reckon, conjecture, hypothesize; wonder, doubt; remember, recall, forget; fear (think fearfully)	strike, occur to, convince; remind [26], escape; puzzle, intrigue, surprise
desiderative	want, wish, would like, desire; hope (for), long for, yearn for; intend, plan; decide, resolve, determine; agree, comply, refuse	(tempt)
emotive	like, fancy, love, adore, dislike, hate, detest, despise, loathe, abhor; rejoice, exult, grieve, mourn, bemoan, bewail, regret, deplore; fear, dread; enjoy, relish, marvel	allure, attract, please, displease, disgust, offend, repel, revolt; gladden, delight, gratify, sadden, depress, pain; alarm, startle, frighten, scare, horrify, shock, comfort, reassure, encourage; amuse, entertain, divert, interest, fascinate, bore, weary, worry

Like all other experiential systems, the system of TYPE OF SENSING construes experience as indeterminate: the four different types of sensing shade into one another. For example, perception shades into cognition, with *I see* coming to mean not only 'I perceive visually' but also 'I understand'. And cognition shades into perception with clauses where *remember* or *imagine* serves as the Process; unlike 'cognitive' clauses in general such clauses can be construed with a macrophenomenal Phenomenon:

I **remember** ⟦ a coffee cup falling off the table and being broken ⟧ – Elsa did that. And I **remember** ⟦ her running – suddenly running for all she was worth down the path ⟧ – and the awful look there on her face. [p. 192] I **remember** ⟦her saying once: ... ⟧ [p. 206] [A. Christie, Five Little Pigs]

I **can't** even **imagine** ⟦ her buying a gun⟧. I **can't imagine** ⟦ her knowing how to shoot a gun⟧.

well it surprises me that Eileen should be surprised I **can imagine** ⟦ Leslie being surprised ⟧ but ... [LLC_01]

---

[26] As is often the case of with verbs, *remind* has different senses corresponding to uses in different transitivity environments. (i) In a 'mental' clause, *remind* may have different senses. (1) *Remind* may serve as a causative equivalent of *remember*, 'cause somebody to remember' with the causer in the role of Inducer (cf. Section 5.7.4 if the clause is 'phenomenal', the Phenomenon represented on the model of a circumstance of Matter (e.g. [Inducer:] *This reminds* [Senser:] *me* [Phenomenon:] *of an interesting encounter I had a few years ago with the late Col M.S. Rao, the celebrated physician.* [KOHL_E]) and if the clause is 'hyperphenomenal' with a project 'idea' clause, *remind* is configured with only Inducer + Senser (e.g. [Inducer:] *The church clock striking the hour reminds* [Senser:] *me* → *that I must hurry if this is to be ready on time for the printer.* [LOB_F]; for the participant role of Inducer, see Section 5.7.4). (2) Alternatively, *remind* may have the sense of 'cause somebody to see a relationship of similarity' (e.g. *They* ['the children'] reminded *old Amai of a flock of bright birds gathering together to peck corn.* [KOHL_K]). (ii) In a 'verbal' clause, *remind* has the sense of 'tell somebody something so that s/he will remember it', the 'verbal' clause projects a report or quote (e.g. *'Don't forget, there was the hope it would pass for a natural death', Pauling reminded him.* [BROWN1_L]). (iii) In a hypotactic verbal group complex, *remind* serves as a causative variant of *remember* (e.g. *Mary reminded John to do it*; see Chapter 8, Section 8.7.3).

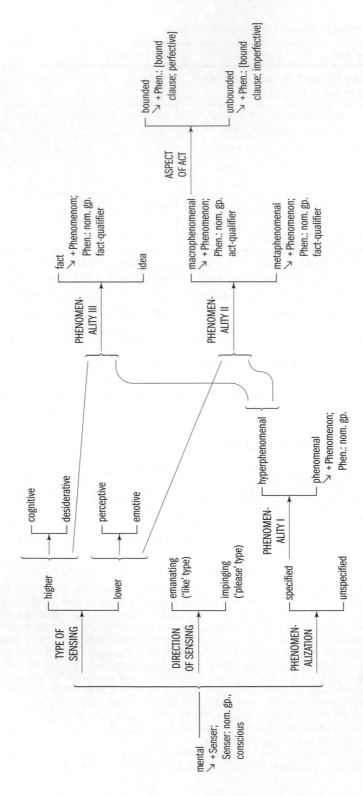

Fig. 5-16 Mental clause systems

5.4 Relational clauses: processes of being & having

5.4.1 Nature of 'relational' clauses

We now come to the third major type of process – 'relational' clauses. 'Relational' clauses serve to characterize and to identify. Thus, when Chinua Achebe is asked, in an interview, to say something about Nigeria, he draws on the resources of 'relational' clauses, as shown in the extract in Table 5-46 on pp. 356–8:

(i)　characterization

> One quarter of the entire population of Africa **is** in Nigeria, so we say that every fourth African **is** a Nigerian.

> It **wasn't** one nation at that point; it **was** a large number of independent political entities.

(ii)　identification

> The three major groups in the nation **are** the Yoruba in the southwest, the Ibo in the southeast, and the Hausa, finally, in the north.

> ... because its final requirement **was** [[that the man [[who aspires to be king]] would first pay all the debt [[owed by every single man and every single woman in the community]]]]!

When we look at these clauses 'from below', we can immediately see that they have something in common: the Process is realized by the verb *be* in the simple present or past (i.e., *every fourth African is a Nigerian* rather than *every fourth African is being a Nigerian*) and they appear to have two inherent participants, e.g. *it* and *a large number of independent political entities* in *it was a large number of political entities*. The view 'from below' also reveals that there are differences among the clauses. Thus the second participant may be a 'non-specific' ('indefinite') nominal group – *a Nigerian, one nation, a large number of independent political entities* – or a 'specific' ('definite') one – *the Yoruba in the southwest, the Ibo in the east and the Hausa, finally, in the north*; or it may be a prepositional phrase – *in Nigeria*. And if we probe the clauses 'from around' for a voice-like contrast, we find a further distinction. While the clauses with a 'non-specific' second participant have no agnate reversed variant – *a large nation was it* is either impossible or marginal, the clause with a 'specific' second participant does have an agnate reversed variant – *the Yoruba in the southwest, the Ibo in the east and the Hausa, finally, in the north are the three major groups in the nation* seems like a very normal systemic variant of the clause that actually occurs in the text.

Looking at 'relational' clauses 'from below' (how are they realized?) and 'from around' (what other systemic variants are possible?), we begin to see that such clauses have a distinct grammar of their own – one that has no doubt evolved to serve distinct uses in discourse, as in the example above. But before we explore this relational grammar further, we shall view 'relational' clauses 'from above', asking what kind of experience they construe. As we have seen, 'material' clauses are concerned with our experience of the material world and 'mental' clauses are concerned with our experience of the world of our own consciousness. Both this outer experience and this inner experience may be construed by 'relational' clauses; but they model this experience as 'being' rather than as 'doing' or 'sensing': see the examples in Table 5-11. What does it mean to say that experience is modelled as 'being'?

259

We can answer this in two related steps by considering (i) how 'being' is construed as unfolding through time and (ii) how 'being' is construed as being configured with process plus participants.

Table 5-11 Inner and outer experience construed by different process types

	Inner experience	Outer experience
material [doing]	–	she's walking (into the dining room); she's getting a mahogany table; she's emptying the bottle
mental [sensing]	she rejoices, she fears stupidity; his behaviour amuses her, stupidity frightens her	–
relational [being]	she's happy, she's afraid (of stupidity); his behaviour is amusing (to her), stupidity is frightening (to her)	she's in the dining room; she has a mahogany table; the bottle's empty

(i) **Nature of unfolding**. Unlike 'material' clauses, but like 'mental' ones, 'relational' clauses prototypically construe change as unfolding 'inertly', without an input of energy – typically as a uniform flow without distinct phases of unfolding (unlike the contrast in material processes between the initial phase and the final phase of the unfolding of a process, the outcome). Thus, static location in space is construed relationally – *she's in the dining room*, but dynamic motion through space is construed materially – *she's walking into the dining room*. Similarly, static possession is construed relationally – *she has a mahogany dining table*, but dynamic transfer of possession is construed materially – *she's getting a mahogany dining table; she's being given a mahogany dining table*; and static quality is construed relationally – *the bottle's empty*, but dynamic change in quality is construed materially – *the bottle's emptying; she's emptying the bottle*. In the nature of the unfolding of the process, 'relational' clauses thus pattern like 'mental' ones rather than like 'material' ones; and this is reflected in the unmarked present tense. We can add one row for 'relational' clauses to Table 5-8 above: (simple) present: [unmarked] *she's in the dining room, she has a mahogany table, the bottle's empty*; present in present [marked] *she's being in the dining room, she's having a mahogany table, the bottle's being empty*. The present in present is in fact highly marked and is largely restricted to 'relational' clauses of behavioural propensity such as:

> Si: I walked in, right, and the first thing that happens is Maryanne's got the shits with Ian, right, for some reason. – Di: Well, he's **being** macro-neurotic again. [UTS/Macquarie Corpus]

> and I was really ... I don't know how much of a chameleon I **was being** in this common-room conversation [LLC 01]

Here 'being' is no longer construed as inert and is nudged closer to 'behaving' (we also need to take note of clauses of 'becoming', which we shall discuss below in Section 5.4.3.2 under point (ii)).

(ii) **Nature of configuration**. If the way in which a process is construed as unfolding through time was the only consideration, 'relational' and 'mental' clauses might appear to

be two variants of the same type of process; and this is in fact how they have been classified in some (typically philosophical) approaches – as 'states' (cf. Halliday & Matthiessen, 1999). But the nature of unfolding is only one out of many considerations and most of these considerations show that 'relational' and 'mental' clauses are quite distinct. For example, while one participant in a 'mental' clause, the Senser, is always endowed with consciousness, this is not the case with 'relational' clauses. If anything, the participants in 'relational' clauses are more like the Phenomenon of a 'mental' clause – not only things, but also acts and facts can be construed as participants in a 'relational' clause; for example: *it ... to depend solely on the US constitution* in *it was not enough to depend solely on the US constitution*; and *that she never left* in *that she never left is clear*; and *that the quantity of the literature is not overwhelming yet* in *another reason is that the quantity of the literature is not overwhelming yet*.

In being able to be construed not only with things as participants, but also with acts and facts, 'relational' clauses clearly differ from 'material' ones; but they resemble 'mental' ones in this respect. However, in a relational clause, these things, acts and facts are not construed as a phenomenon of consciousness; rather, they are construed as one element in a relationship of being. Thus while a thing, act or fact construed as a Phenomenon in a 'mental' clause is configured with a Senser (as in *that she never left pleased them*), in a 'relational' clause, a thing, act or fact construed as a participant is configured with another relational participant that has to come from the same domain of being; for example, *clear* in *that she never left is clear* is a semiotic property that can be attributed to a fact,[27] which is itself a semiotic entity. There is a further difference between 'mental' and 'relational' clauses relating to the construal of semiotic phenomena. With a 'mental' clause, the phenomenon of consciousness can be construed as an idea brought into existence through the process of consciousness and represented grammatically as a separate clause (as in *the witness thought that she never left*); but this is not possible with 'relational' clauses.

The fundamental properties of 'relational' clauses derive from the nature of a configuration of 'being'. As the term 'relational' suggests, this is not 'being' in the sense of existence. There is a related, but distinct, category of 'existential' clauses, such as *there was a storm*; these are discussed in Section 5.5.3 below. In 'relational' clauses, there are two parts to the 'being': something is said to 'be' something else. In other words, a relationship of being is set up between two separate entities. This means that in a 'relational' clause in English, there are always two inherent participants – two 'be-ers'. In contrast, the general classes of 'material' and 'mental' clause have only one inherent participant (the Actor and the Senser, respectively). Thus, while we can have a 'material' clause with one participant such as *she was walking* or *she was walking into the room*, we cannot have a 'relational' clause such as *she was*, with only one participant; we have to have two: *she was in the*

---

[27] *Clear* in this sense is a member of a lexical set (cf. Chapter 2, Section 2.1) that includes *obvious, evident, self-evident, doubtful* and other names of semiotic properties. It is, of course, related to the material sense of *clear* 'transparent', as in *the water was very clear*; but *clear* in this sense is a member of a different lexical set, with members such as *muddy, transparent, cloudy, milky*. The difference between the two is indicated by the oddity of examples such as *the water and that she never left are very clear*; *that she never left is very cloudy*; *the water is obvious*.

room. Similarly, a 'mental' clause with one participant such as *she rejoiced* is possible; but the nearest 'relational' equivalent must have two participants – *she was happy*, not *she was*.

This tells us something significant about a prototypical configuration of 'being': the experiential 'weight' is construed in the two participants, and the process is merely a highly generalized link between these two participants (and this is pushed the furthest in registers of science, administration, business and the law, as in the following example involving both a thematic equative (see Section 3.3.2 above) and grammatical metaphor (*conviction that ...*: see Section 10.10.3 below): *What is really new in the last 10 years is the pervasive conviction that the connections among the relatively well researched problem areas are not side effects but are central to our basic understanding of environmental change.*). Thus the verbs that occur most frequently as the Process of a 'relational' clause are *be* and *have*; and they are typically both unaccented and phonologically reduced (e.g. /z/ in *she's happy*) – the 'copula' or 'copular verb' of traditional grammar. Verbs in general in 'relational' clauses are typically non-salient, whereas verbs in 'material' and 'mental' clauses are salient at the accented syllable; compare 'material' // Herbert/Smith/stood for/parliament // (in the sense of 'contested'; unmarked present tense: *is standing for*) with 'relational' // Mary/Jones stood for/women's/rights // (in the sense of 'represented'; unmarked present tense: *stands for*). This weak phonological presence of the Process represents iconically its highly generalized, grammatical nature. The limiting case of weak presence is absence; and the Process is in fact structurally absent in certain 'non-finite' 'relational' clauses in English (e.g. 'non-finite' clauses introduced by *with* as in *the animals might have moved about in family groups, with the younger ones in the middle for protection*, where *with the younger ones in the middle for protection* means '... being in the middle ...') and in many languages there is no structurally present Process in the 'unmarked' type of 'relational' clause (as in e.g. Arabic and Russian). Here the 'relational' clause is simply a configuration of 'Be-er1' + 'Be-er2'.[28]

The configuration of Process + 'Be-er1' + 'Be-er2' opens up the potential for construing the abstract relationships of **class-membership** and **identity** in all domains of experience. Class-membership is construed by **attributive** clauses and identity by **identifying** ones. These two 'relational' clause types cut across the inner and outer experience of 'mental' and 'material' clauses illustrated in Table 5-11 above. Thus being in the dining room, having a table and being happy are just special cases of classification; and being happy and being empty are construed on the same relational model – *she was happy, the bottle was empty* – although one relates to the inner experience of 'mental' clauses and the other to the outer experience of 'material' ones – *she rejoiced, the bottle emptied*.

Class-membership and identity are, as we have said, abstract relationships. If we say *every fourth African is a Nigerian*, we are construing *every fourth African* and *a Nigerian* as

---

[28] Such clauses have often been called 'nominal clauses', in contrast to 'verbal clauses', where there is a Process present in the structure of the clause. But this reflects only the view 'from below' and hides the fact that in languages such as Arabic 'relational' clauses that are marked for aspect and/or polarity, typically have a structurally present Process (see Matthiessen, 2004b: 595–600). (There is, however, a deeper sense in which 'relational' clauses are nominal: they construe the same range of relations as those of modification within the nominal group: *the house was old : the old house :: the house was in Wessex : the house in Wessex :: the house was Thomas's : Thomas's house.*)

being related not materially, but semiotically as member to class: 'every fourth African is a member of the class of Nigerians'. Similarly, if we say *the three major groups in the nation are the Yoruba in the southwest, the Ibo in the southwest and the Hausa, finally in the north* or *the Yoruba in the southwest, the Ibo in the southwest and the Hausa, finally in the north are the three major groups in the nation*, we are construing *the three major groups in the nation* and *the Yoruba in the southwest, the Ibo in the southwest and the Hausa, finally in the north* as being related not materially, but semiotically as two identical descriptions: one is, as it were, a restatement of the other.

In her account of 'relational' clauses, Davidse (1992, 1996) adopts a semiotic approach, interpreting class-membership by reference to the semiotic relation of instantiation and identity by reference to the semiotic relation of realization (see Chapter 1, Section 1.3 for these concepts). This can be exemplified from Painter's (1999) case study in the development of language as a resource for learning. At an early stage, the young child she studied produced 'relational' clauses such as *that's a circle*. Here he construed a phenomenon in the perceptual field he shared with his listener as an instance of a class; and we can say that the conceptualization of class-membership was grounded for him in his experience of instantiation. He theorized the perception of a concrete, material object as an instance of a semiotic abstraction – a class of things. Somewhat later came examples such as *a platypus is a mammal*. Here one class is construed as a subclass of another class. This is no longer instantiation in its true sense; it is a relationship of delicacy construed between two classes that are equally abstract but differ in generality in a taxonomy of things. However, we can see how this more abstract kind of class-membership is developmentally related to instantiation. Later still he produced clauses such as *balance means you hold it on your fingers and it doesn't go* ('fall'). Here the relationship between *balance* and *you hold it on your fingers and it doesn't go* is not one of class-membership but one of identity and, as Davidse points out, this can be interpreted as based on realization: the word *balance* realizes the meaning 'you hold it on your fingers and it doesn't go'. This is the same kind of example as we analysed in Figure 5-1 above, and we can see how the grammar models the realizational relationship between two strata in the form of 'relational' clauses of identity. Identifying clauses are also used to construe 'exhaustive' class membership where a class is identified with its members, as in Text 9-12: *The fuels of the body are carbohydrates, fats and proteins*. In this way, the grammar of 'relational' clauses is based on the dimensions of a semiotic system (cf. Matthiessen, 1991a, on the grammar of semiosis).

5.4.2 Principal types of 'relational' clause

After our introductory exploration of 'relational' clauses, we are now ready to sketch a picture of this part of the grammar of transitivity. Every language accommodates, in its grammar, some systematic construction of relational processes. The English system operates with three main types of relation – 'intensive', 'possessive' and 'circumstantial'; and each of these comes in two distinct modes of being – 'attributive' and 'identifying'. These are set out as two simultaneous systems in the system network of TRANSITIVITY in Figure 5-4. These two systems intersect to define six categories of 'relational' clause, as set out in Table 5-12. These different categories are further elaborated in the grammar of 'relational' clauses; the first few steps in delicacy are shown in Figure 5-17. We shall explore these more delicate options in 'relational' transitivity below.

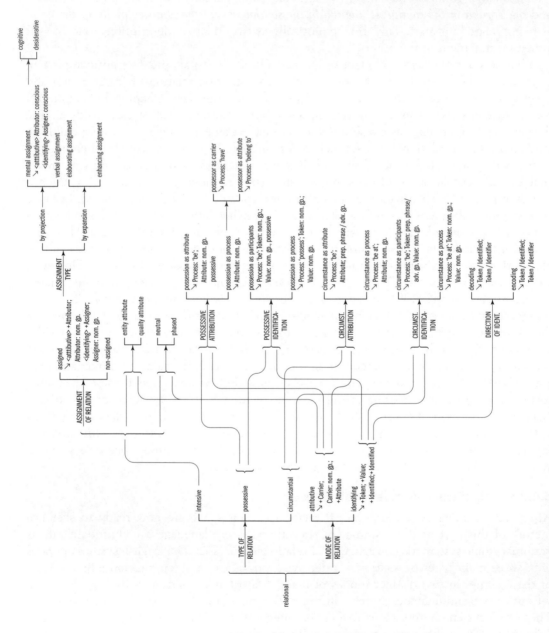

Fig. 5-17 Relational clause systems

Table 5-12 The principal categories of 'relational' clause

	(i) Attributive '*a* is an attribute of *x*'	(ii) Identifying '*a* is the identity of *x*'
(1) intensive '*x* is *a*'	Sarah is wise	Sarah is the leader; the leader is Sarah
(2) possessive '*x* has *a*'	Peter has a piano	the piano is Peter's; Peter's is the piano
(3) circumstantial '*x* is at *a*'	the fair is on a Tuesday	tomorrow is the 10th; the 10th is tomorrow

The examples given in this Table bring out one important difference between the 'attributive' and 'identifying' mode. The 'identifying' ones are reversible, so that the *x* and the *a* can be switched around: *Sarah is the leader/the leader is Sarah*. The 'attributive' ones are not reversible: there is no form *wise is Sarah* which is agnate (systemically related) to *Sarah is wise*. This is one of a number of significant distinctions between the two modes, which will be brought out in the discussion which follows.

It is difficult to illustrate all the different categories of 'relational' clause in a short text; but the text presented and analysed in Table 5-13 has a fair sprinkling of them. This is a report on one group of dinosaurs and like such texts in general it is predominantly relational in character (cf. Text 9-12, Chapter 9). It characterizes and identifies various aspects of a general class of entity, Ankylosaurus – construing a language-based model or picture of the creature. This model is illustrated in a small drawing that accompanies the text. The creature is assigned to a class, described in terms of physical qualities such as length, outlined in terms of body parts, and identified as unique in terms of the property of size. Here the different categories of 'relational' clause make distinctive contributions; thus while 'intensive' clauses dominate, the other two types of being are also significant: the 'possessive' clauses relate body parts to the whole (... *had a club* ...; ... *did not have any teeth*) and the 'circumstantial' ones construe the extension in space of certain smaller body parts in relation to larger ones (as in *These plates **went** from the head to the tail*, with *go* used not as a material process of motion but as a circumstantial process of static location in space). There is one 'existential' clause (# 7.1), which also contributes to the linguistic picture of the creature. In addition to these relational and existential clauses of 'being', there are four 'material' clauses, all construing events of generalized past occurrence and three with the modal feature of ability (*could take, may have been able to swing, [may have been able to] aim*). These 'material' clauses thus complement the 'relational' and 'existential' ones by adding limited animation to the 'relational' and 'existential' composition; but even with this 'material' animation, the text is located in the realm of being rather than that of doing. The text is similar to descriptive passages in other registers such as narratives; but such descriptions tend to be concerned with particularized entities rather than generalized ones and are usually woven into sequences of 'material' clauses denoting habitual time if the description is part of the placement of the narrative (e.g. *My grandmother Ammani was a busy person. She performed a variety of tasks all through the day* ...) or particular time if the description is part of the

event sequence of the narrative (e.g. *One summer evening, the Rabbit saw two strange beings creep out of the bracken. They were rabbits like himself, but quite furry.*).

Table 5-13 Expounding – categorizing: entry on dinosaur[29]

	Ankylosaurus	Relational		Other
		Attributive	Identifying	process type
1	The Ankylosaurs **were** armored lizards [[which varied greatly in size]]	intensive		
1 [[ ]]	[[... **varied** ...]]	intensive		
2.1	The largest **was** as long as a bus,	intensive		
2.2	while the smallest **was not** much bigger than a man.	intensive		
3	Ankylosaurs **were** extremely sturdily built, with armor plates, knobs, and spikes [[which were embedded in the leathery skin]].	intensive		
3 [[ ]]	[[... were ...]]	intensive		
4.1	These plates **went** from the head to the tail	circumstantial		
4.2	but **did not cover** the body.		circumstantial	
5.1	Ankylosaurus – the 'fused lizard' – **was** the largest of the ankylosaurs,		intensive	
5.2	but in spite of its size and frightening appearance it **fed** only on plants.			material
6	With its small teeth and weak jaws the dinosaur **could take** only plants [[which could be easily bitten off]].			material
7.1	At the end of the head, << which was covered with armor plates>>, **was** a horny beak [[which did not have any teeth]].			existential
7.2	<< ... **was covered** ...>>		circumstantial	
7.1 [[	[[... **did not have** ...]]	possessive		
8	Flesh-eating carnosaurs **were** potentially dangerous to the ankylosaurs.	intensive		
9	As an added means of self-defense the ankylosaur **had** a club on its tail.	possessive		
10.1	The creature **may have been able to swing** the club with great force			material
10.2	and **aim** a savage blow at an enemy.			material

---

[29] From Wilson, 1986, p.10.

In order to explain the concepts of 'attributive' and 'identifying', we shall concentrate first on the 'intensive' type, '*x* is *a*', as in the contrast in the text in Expounding – categorizing: entry on dinosaur between the 'attributive' *the Ankylosaurs **were** armored lizards which varied greatly in size* and the 'identifying' *Ankylosaurus – the 'fused lizard' – **was** the largest of the ankylosaurs*. In this type of 'relational' clause, the most typical verb is *be*, and *x* and *a* are nominal groups. At the same time, many verbs other than *be* also occur, and this is another distinguishing feature: the verbs used in 'identifying' and 'attributive' clauses belong to two different classes. There are also differences in the kinds of nominal element that occur as attribute and as identity. Let us introduce one more short text example to illustrate the similarity and difference between attribution and identity:

> 'Why should I want to murder a perfectly strange woman?' said Dr Quimper.

> 'She wasn't a strange woman', said Inspector Craddock. 'She was your wife.' [A. Christie, 4.50 From Paddington]

In both *she wasn't a strange woman* and *she was your wife*, the meaning is '*x* was *a*'; but Inspector Craddock's rhetorical punch is the shift from 'attributive' to 'identifying' – from common class-membership to unique identity.

5.4.3 'Intensive' clauses: 'attributive'

5.4.3.1 Characteristics of 'attributive intensive' clauses

In the 'attributive' mode, an entity has some class ascribed or attributed to it. Structurally, we label this class the **Attribute**, and the entity to which it is ascribed is the **Carrier** – the 'carrier' of the 'attribute'. Examples are given in Figure 5-18 and in the entry on dinosaurs in Table 5-13. This type of clause is a resource for characterizing entities serving as the Carrier; and it is also a central grammatical strategy for assessing by assigning an evaluative Attribute to the Carrier.

today's weather	is going to be	warm and sunny
she	's	atrocious
the minister	didn't seem	sure of himself
your story	sounds	complete nonsense
the baby	turned into	a pig
mice	are	timid creatures
Carrier	**Process: intensive**	**Attribute**
nominal group	verbal group	nominal group

Fig. 5-18   Some examples of 'intensive attributive' clauses

There are four characteristics of 'attributive' clauses that distinguish them from 'identifying' ones.

(i) The nominal group functioning as Attribute construes a class of thing and is typically indefinite: it has either an adjective or a common noun as Head and, if appropriate, an indefinite article (e.g. *is/are warm*, *is a creature*, *are creatures*). It cannot be a proper noun or a pronoun since these do not construe classes. (Thus *he is Charles Darwin* would be interpreted as 'identifying'; but if we say *he is another Charles Darwin*, the clause is 'attributive' and the proper name *Charles Darwin* has been re-construed as the common noun – the name of a class of people that are like Charles Darwin.)

(ii) The lexical verb in the verbal group realizing the Process is one of the 'ascriptive' classes: see Table 5-14. If the Attribute is realized by a nominal group with a common noun as Head without a pre-modifying adjective, it is usually expressed as if it was a circumstance (with a preposition following the verb, as indicated in the table; for example: *he grew old* but *he grew into a man*); Attributes with noun Head are rare with the verbs *keep*, *go* and *get*, where they would be highly ambiguous.

(iii) The interrogative probe for such clauses is *what?*, *how?* or *what ... like?*, e.g. *what is Paula?*, *how did the minister seem?*, *what will today's weather be like?*

(iv) The clauses are not reversible: there are no 'receptive' forms, such as *complete nonsense is sounded by your story*; while clauses such as *a poet is Paula*, *wise is Sarah*, are archaic or literary variants, not systemically agnate forms.

5.4.3.2 Kinds of intensive attribution

Within clauses of intensive attribution, we can distinguish three simultaneous contrasts: (i) the class denoted by the Attribute may be defined by reference to an entity or to a quality; (ii) the process of attribution may be neutral or phased; and (iii) the domain of attribution may be either material or semiotic.

(i) MEMBERSHIP SPECIFICATION: **entity/quality.** The class is specified either by naming the class itself by reference to the entity that constitutes the class, as in *What did your father do? – He was an architect*, or by naming a criterion for class-membership by reference to a quality or qualities of the entity that constitutes the class, as in *The New Yorker is very generous*.

The two kinds of Attribute differ in how they are realized: entity Attributes are realized by nominal groups with Thing as Head, e.g. *architect* in *an architect*; quality Attributes are realized by nominal groups with Epithet as Head, e.g. *very generous*.[30] With the latter, the Thing is thus implicit; the general sense is 'one' – that is, the class of the Thing is presumed from the context. This means that the norm of the quality denoted by the Epithet depends on the context; and this is made explicit when the substitute *one* serves as Head. Thus in an example such as *It's a big one I think*, the norm of the size depends on what *one* substitutes for – *reef* in this case:

> [S01:] What reef? – [S02:] There's reefs around bloody Australia, isn't there? – [S01:] Yeah. A Great Barrier one I believe. – [S02:] It's a <u>big</u> *one* I think. [UTS/Macquarie Corpus]

---

[30] There is a metaphorical variant (cf. Chapter 10), where the Attribute is realized by *of* + a nominal group with a nominalization as Thing/Head; for example, *of crucial importance* in: *In India now, the question of the minorities and how to satisfy their aspirations is of crucial importance.* [KOHL_A] The congruent version is ... *is crucially important.*

Table 5-14 Examples of verbs serving as Process in intensive clauses

		Attributive	Identifying
neutral		be, feel	be
phase: time	inceptive	become; turn (into), grow (into)	become; turn into, grow into
		get, go, fall, run;	
	durative	remain, stay (as), keep	remain, stay as
phase: reality	apparent	seem, appear, qualify as,	seem (+ superlative)
	perceptive	look, sound, smell, feel, taste (like)	
	realized	prove, turn out, end up (as)	prove
measure		weigh, cost, measure	
quality		[Process/Attribute:] seem, appear ['be apparent']; matter, count ['be important'], apply ['be relevant'], figure ['be sensible'], suffice ['be enough'], abound ['be plentiful'], differ, vary ['be different'], dominate ['be dominant'], do ['be acceptable, enough']; hurt, ache ['be painful']; stink, smell ['be smelly']; reek, drip, ooze ['be overfull']; suck, stink ['be awful']	
role		play, act as, function as, serve as	
sign			mean, indicate, suggest, imply, show, betoken, mark, reflect,
equation			equal, add up to, make
kind/part			comprise, feature, include
significance			represent, constitute, form
example			exemplify, illustrate
symbol			express, signify, realize, spell, stand for, mean
assignment: neutral		make; [Process/Attribute:] ensure, guarantee ('make it certain that …'), prove, confirm ('make it a fact that …')	make
assignment: elaborating			elect, choose (as); dub; name, christen, term; spell, pronounce
assignment: projection		think, consider; wish, want; prove	think, consider; prove; call, declare

Attribution of the 'entity' kind approaches qualitative attribution when the Thing in the nominal group is a very general one such as *thing, person* or *fellow*. Thus in *I started it in Paris in late '51 with a guy called Harold Humes, who was an absolutely brilliant fellow but rather erratic*, the attributive nominal groups *an absolutely brilliant fellow* (Thing/Head) and *rather erratic* (Epithet/Head) are both qualitative characterizations; from an experiential point of view, *an absolutely brilliant fellow* is very close to *absolutely brilliant* and *rather erratic* to *a rather erratic fellow*, and the two could be switched (*who was absolutely brilliant but a rather erratic fellow*) without a great difference in meaning – because *fellow* does not add any new classificatory information beyond what we have already learnt from *a guy* – *Harold* (a male proper name) – *who* (a person).

Qualitative Attributes are, as noted, realized by nominal groups with Epithet as Head. The Epithet is realized by an adjective (or participial verb form), which is frequently submodified by adverbs of degree such as *very, extremely, greatly*, including the comparative adverbs *as; more, most; less, least; too*. The comparatives may be expanded by a standard of comparison introduced by *as, than; for*. These are either phrases or clauses and are placed after the Head/Thing, in the same position as post-modifying Qualifiers; for example:

> I think mum's <u>more</u> **upset** <u>than he is</u>. [UTS/Macquarie Corpus]

> Nothing gets past those kids. They're <u>as</u> **sharp** <u>as old razor blades</u>. [UTS/Macquarie Corpus]

> [S 03:] And, well, this baby possum was **so cute**, it was about this tiny. – [S 02:] Aha. – [S 04:] That tiny? – [S 02:] That's just tiny, <u>too</u> **tiny** <u>for words</u>. [UTS/Macquarie Corpus]

Structurally such expressions are Submodifiers within the Epithet rather than Qualifiers (see Chapter 6, Section 6.2.5); but nominal groups with Epithet as Head may also be constructed with Qualifiers[31]:

> She's not very **interested** <u>in the food</u>. [UTS/Macquarie Corpus]

These may be difficult to differentiate from circumstantial elements in the transitivity structure of the clause. To differentiate them in analysis, we can apply textual probes: in principle, being an element of the clause, a circumstance is subject to all the different textual statuses brought about by theme, theme predication and theme identification. Thus *with it* in *so you have to be beautiful with it* is a circumstance (of Accompaniment), if we interpret the clause to mean 'so you and it [silver] have to be beautiful together', since it can be Theme (*so with it you have to be beautiful* rather than *so it you have to be beautiful with*) and predicated Theme (*so it is with it that you have to be beautiful* rather than *so it is it that you have to be beautiful with*). In contrast, a Qualifier cannot on its own be given a textual status in the clause since it is a constituent of a nominal group, not of the clause;

---

[31] Note that sequences of 'verb: be + adjective + verb' such as *be eager to do, be keen to do, be willing to do* are interpreted as verbal group complexes, as in *she was terribly keen to get out of London*: see Chapter 8, Section 8.8. Note that unlike adjectives serving as Epithet/Head in nominal groups functioning as Attribute, these adjectives cannot be expanded with nouns serving as Thing/Head; contrast *he is keen : he is a keen fellow*, which is fine, with *he is keen to keen to finish the job : he is a keen fellow to finish the job*, which does not seem possible. Note also the pattern of ellipsis: *he is keen to do it, but he isn't able to [∅: do it]*.

so it can only be thematic together with the rest of the nominal group that it is part of. Thus *of a quid* in *and Mal's not short of a quid* would be grouped with *short* by the textual metafunction as Theme (*short of a quid he may be, but ...* rather than *of a quid he may be short, but ...* or *short he may be of a quid, but ...*), as predicated Theme (*it is short of a quid that he is* rather than *it is of a quid that he is short* or *it is short that he is of a quid*), and as identified Theme (*short of a quid is what he is* rather than *short is what he is of a quid* or *of a quid is what he is short*). And this resonates with the fact that *short* would not occur without *of* + nominal group in this sense: *he is short* is not a possible variant of *he is short of a quid*; but *he is afraid* is a variant of *he is afraid of snakes*, indicating that *of snakes* is a circumstantial element whereas *of a quid* is a Qualifier relating to *short*. However, there is a considerable degree of indeterminacy in this area (cf. the possibility of *a quid is what he is short of/what he is short of is a quid; it is a quid that he is short of*).

Certain circumstances are common with particular types of attribution. For example, circumstances of Cause, Matter and Angle are common with 'mental' qualities as Attribute ([Cause:] *I did get angry <u>with him</u>*; [Matter:] *no, I am fussed <u>about the speakers</u> and the speaker cabling; so I think we have to be a bit sensible <u>about what we are doing</u>*; [Angle:] *it's all Greek <u>to me</u>; next one sounds even sexier <u>to me</u>; that's been really important <u>to me</u>*).

Within 'quality' attribution, there is a further option: a small number of qualities may be construed as a qualitative Process rather than as a qualitative Attribute. Thus, alongside *will it be enough?* we have *will it suffice?* (Alternatively, we can interpret such clauses as having a conflation of Process and Attribute.) We have in fact already met such an example with the qualitative verb *vary* in the text in Table 5-13: *The Ankylosaurs were armored lizards which **varied** greatly in size*. Verbs of this kind include *matter, count* 'be important' (as in [*the cities*] *that now counted* [*were North Atlantic in location or access*]), *suffice* 'be enough', *abound* 'be plentiful'; *figure* 'make sense'; *differ, vary* 'be different, varied'; *hurt, ache* 'be painful' (see Halliday, 1998); *dominate* 'be dominant', *apply* 'be relevant' (as in *and Styron's remark **applies***), *do* 'be acceptable, enough' (as in *that **won't do***), *remain* 'be + still', *stink, smell, reek* (+ *of* + source of smell) 'be smelly' e.g. (*a place called Desire that **stinks** of rotting rubbish; the air **reeks** of bee venom as they furiously attack our white suits and screened head veils*) and a number of verbs of negative appraisal, some of them abstract versions of 'be + smelly', e.g. *stink, suck* (as in *her best friend, Mike, is 14 and thinks science **sucks**, preferring a life of horses and guitars; and the system **stinks** – I'll never forgive them*).[32]

(ii) PHASE OF ATTRIBUTION: **neutral/phased**. Like other processes, processes of attribution unfold through time. In the unmarked case, the phase of the unfolding is left unspecified ('neutral'); alternatively, the phase is marked as either (1) 'time phase' – 'inceptive' (e.g. *become, go, grow, turn*) or 'durative' (e.g. *keep, remain*) or (2) 'reality phase' – 'apparent'

---

[32] The verbs *reek, drip* and *ooze* are used in the sense of 'be [over-]ful' or 'have [too] much of' (shading into the 'possessive' area); but they always seem to be configured with a nominal group, introduced by a preposition in the case of *drip* and *reek*, and this element can be interpreted as Attribute: *it certainly **reeks** to me of sexual exploitation; I don't care that the English choose to maintain their royalty, but I object to the tone of the stateside reportage. It **drips** with press agentry; Greenoak's book **drips** with bird lore like no other; she **oozes** self-confidence; but although it's a platform game that has been crafted to include the vital ingredients of the genre, it lacks substance and **oozes** mediocrity.*

(e.g. *seem*, *appear*), 'perceptive' (e.g. *look*, *sound*, *taste*) or realized (e.g. *prove*, *turn out*): see above, Table 5-14; for example:

(1)   time phase

When a child loves you for a long, long time, you **become** Real. Generally, by the time you are Real, most of your hair has been loved off, and you **get** very shabby. [Text 28]

This **remains** national policy all over the world. [LLC_05]

(2)   reality phase

At least we remember them as young before they decayed and **grew** old. [LLC_05]

She said 'well that **seems** pretty expensive but if they're all right I don't mind'. [LLC_01]

You **don't look** bad yourself either, Betty. [King Interviews]

He doesn't know he **looks** very funny, does he? [LLC_02]

that you **might have proved** too strong and independently minded a figure to be in exactly that role [LLC_06]

In the case of 'time phase', in particular 'inceptive', the tense may be like that of 'material' clauses rather than like that of 'relational' ones; for example:

Text 5-8: Reporting – chronicling: historical recount (written & monologic)
But one sharp line can be traced: the economy moved from a Mediterranean base to an Atlantic one. The scope of European trade **was becoming** oceanic and worldwide; the cities that now counted were North Atlantic in location or access: London and Bristol in England; Bordeaux and Nantes in France; Amsterdam in Holland. [Europe in Retrospect]

That is, coming into being is construed on the same model as activities as far as time is concerned; but it is still construed as a configuration of being, with Carrier (*the scope of European trade*) + Process (*was becoming*) + Attribute (*oceanic and worldwide*). If the Attribute is an 'entity' rather than a 'quality', the nominal group realizing it may be marked by the preposition *into*; alongside 'become' + nominal group, we thus have 'turn', 'grow' + *into* + nominal group, as in:

Those who have quality will outgrow the experience; the rest will **turn** beat, or into dentists, or into beat dentists. [BROWN1_G]

Clauses of 'inceptive' attribution are subject to collocational patterns between Process: verb and Attribute: adjective; for example *go* + *mad*, *run* + *dry*, *turn* + *sour*, *fall* + *ill*. And the collocational pattern may also involve the Head noun of the nominal group serving as Carrier, as with Process: *run* + Attribute: *dry*, where the Carrier includes a noun such as *well*, *lake*, *river*, *sea*, *water supply*, *tap*; *blood bank*; *mouth* (in the COBUILD corpus).

   (iii) DOMAIN OF ATTRIBUTION: **material/semiotic.** As we noted above, 'relational' clauses may construe both 'outer experience' and 'inner experience' (cf. Table 5-11). So both these modes of experience are included within the domains of attribution of an 'attributive' clause; but these domains transcend the two modes. In particular, 'inner experience' is generalized to include not only subjective sensations but also attributes that are construed

as objective properties of macrothings and metathings – properties such as the one denoted by the adjective *true* in *it's true the food down there it's really fresh*. The general contrast in domains of attribution is thus not that of material vs. mental but rather 'material' vs. 'semiotic'. The attributes assigned to the carrier in an 'attributive' clause are either material ones or semiotic ones, and the 'thing' serving as carrier has to be of the same order as the attribute. Thus with *true* as Attribute, the Carrier has to be a metathing – represented by a fact clause such as *the food down there it's really really fresh* or by *it, that, this* referring to a fact, the clause *that's (not) true* being a popular form of comment in conversation: *Well not all states have executions. – Yes that's true, but some states do.* Examples of Attributes in the 'semiotic' domain are given in Table 5-15.

Table 5-15 Examples of Attributes within the 'semiotic' domain

Type	Attribute
emotion/attitude	sad, tragic/a tragedy; delightful/a delight, a joy, a relief, extraordinary
	good/a good thing, bad/a bad thing
cognition/probability	doubtful, certain, likely, unlikely, probable, possible, a question
desideration/obligation	desirable, acceptable, appropriate, important, justified

Within the 'semiotic' domain of attribution, there is one variety of 'attributive' clause in which the Attribute denotes a quality of sensing equivalent to the Process of a 'mental' clause (cf. Table 5-11), and may be formed as a participle from a mental process verb; for example, *I'm sorry, it is amazing how effective this system is*. 'Mental' and 'relational' variants may occur within the same passage of text, as in the example in Text 5-9.

Text 5-9: Recreating – narrating (written, monologic): extract from retelling of traditional narrative [Noah's Ark]

[1] Once, a very long time ago, there lived a man called Noah. [2] He and his wife and his sons and their wives all worked very hard. [3] Now Noah was a good man and this **pleased** God. [4] But all around him, Noah's neighbours were lying and fighting and cheating and stealing. [5] This **made** God **sad**.

'Relational' clauses with a quality of sensing fall into two types: those that match the *like* type of 'mental' clause, with Carrier equivalent to Senser; and those that match the *please* type, with Carrier equivalent to Phenomenon. In the former, a typical Carrier is *I* in 'declarative', *you* in 'interrogative'; e.g. *I am not all that pleased anymore with what I got from it, I'm very worried, aren't you glad that's over?* Here the equivalent of the Phenomenon of a 'mental' clause can be construed as a circumstance of Cause marked by *at, of, with* or as a circumstance of Matter typically marked by *about*: *she was upset at the news, she was very anxious about the delay*. In the latter, the Carrier is commonly *that* or *this*, or else *it* plus postposed clause, and the Attribute may have adjective/participle or noun as Head; e.g. *that's encouraging, isn't it a pity that photograph got spoilt?, (I've always thought that my real writing was the fiction,) which seems odd*. Here the equivalent of the Senser of the 'mental' clause may be construed as a circumstance of Angle marked by *to*: *it sounds funny <u>to me</u> that*

he was afraid. Examples of common adjectives, participles and nouns serving as Attribute are given in Table 5-16 together with agnate verbs serving as Process in 'mental' clauses. As can be seen from the table, many of the Attributes are evaluative in nature; this type of clause is an important grammatical strategy in the enactment of appraisal.

Table 5-16 Sensing as Attribute and as Process

| | 'Like' type | | 'Please' type | |
	Mental – Process:	Relational – Attribute:	Mental – Process:	Relational – Attribute:
emotive	rejoice	glad, happy, pleased	gladden, please	gladdening, pleasing; a good thing
	mourn, grieve	sorry, sad	sadden	sad, saddening
	fear	afraid, scared	frighten, scare	frightening, scary
	worry	worried	worry	worrying
		upset	upset	upsetting
	like	pleased; fond	please	pleasing, lovely
		disgusted	disgust	dreadful, awful, disgusting
			encourage	encouraging
		ashamed, embarrassed	shame, embarrass	shameful, pitiful, embarrassing; a shame, a pity
		irritated, annoyed	irritate, annoy	irritating, annoying; a nuisance
		relieved	relieve	a relief
		surprised	surprise	surprising, strange
		puzzled	puzzle	odd, funny, puzzling
desiderative	want	keen (on)	tempt	tempting
	desire			desirable
cognitive	know	aware; certain		known
	guess, suppose			likely
	doubt	doubtful		doubtful
	suspect	suspicious		suspect
	believe			believable
	wonder	curious		curious

There is overlap here between 'mental' and 'relational' clauses, and some clauses such as *I was scared*, could be interpreted either way. There are four main indicators: (1) submodification; (2) marked phase; (3) tense; and (4) clause structure.

(1) Submodifiers like *so, very, too* (see Chapter 6, Section 6.2.5) go with nominal groups but not with verbal groups[33]: we can say *I was very afraid of it* but not *I very feared it*; *you're not too keen on it* but not *you don't too want it*. All the words listed in Sensing as Attribute and as Process as 'adjective/participle', *glad, sorry, worrying, frightening*, etc., readily accept these submodifying items; hence a clause featuring *be + worrying, frightening* etc. is likely to be 'relational' rather than 'mental'.

(2) As noted above, attributive verbs other than *be*, namely those of marked phase, occur in 'attributive' clauses; e.g. *it seems encouraging, you look pleased*. These would not occur in this way in a 'mental' clause; we could not say *you look enjoying (it), it seems delighting (you)*.

(3) As far as tense is concerned, since a quality is typically the outcome of a preceding event, the same phenomenon will appear in present tense if represented as an Attribute but in past tense if represented as a Process in a 'mental' clause: for example, *he's frightened* (present) is likely to be 'relational attributive', with the agnate 'mental' clause being (past in present) *he's been frightened*.

(4) In clause structure, a 'mental' clause typically has (and always can have) both Senser and Phenomenon; whereas in the 'attributive', such other entities can appear only circumstantially as Cause or Matter (agnate to Phenomenon) or Angle (agnate to Senser). Examples are given in Table 5-17.

Table 5-17 Examples of circumstantial agnates in 'relational' clauses of Senser and Phenomenon

Mental	Relational
he's been frightened by a snake	he's frightened/afraid of snakes [not *'s been afraid by …*]
that report is puzzling me	that report is puzzling/odd to me [not *is odd me*]
were you pleased by what happened?	are you pleased/happy about what happened? [not *were you happy by …*]

But these four criteria do not always coincide, and not every instance can be clearly assigned to one category or the other.[34]

No doubt because of this overlap, the situation regarding the status of what were referred to above (Section 5.3) as 'facts' is also blurred. In principle, if a second figure comes into the picture representing the source or origin of the mental condition, it appears as 'fact' with a 'mental' clause but as 'cause' with a 'relational' one; for example:

(mental) it distresses me/I regret + that you failed

It **distresses** him <u>that</u> women ask him, to this day, to remove his dark glasses so that they can witness the marvel of his magical peepers. [COBUILD/Today]

(relational) I'm very distressed + because you failed

Well, I'm still **afraid** of him <u>'cause</u> he's bitten me. [UTS/Macquarie Corpus]

---

[33] Except colloquially nowadays with *so*, as in *you're gonna just so want one* [Text 176].

[34] Thus we find clauses where the participial form of the mental process verb is submodified but where the Phenomenon is also present in the form it takes in a 'receptive' clause; for example: *she was very intrigued by alternative ideas*; *I was very depressed by some feedback I was getting*.

But 'relational attributive' clauses with Attributes of this kind, agnate to the Process of a 'mental' clause, are regularly construed with 'fact' clauses:

(relational) I'm very distressed/it's a great pity + that you failed

I **am extremely distressed** <u>that</u> these unfounded allegations should then have been leaked to newspapers. [COBUILD/Times]

The Attribute has become, in effect, a metaphorical expression of the Process of a 'mental' clause, and can be accompanied by a clause that is projected (see Chapter 7, Section 7.5).[35]

The 'relational' clauses we have just discussed fall within the 'semiotic' domain of attribution and they shade into 'mental' clauses. Within the other major domain of attribution, the 'material' domain, we find an analogous situation where Attribute denotes a material quality equivalent to the Process of a 'material' clause, and may be formed as a participle from a material process verb; for example, *they said that our disk was **corrupted** when it arrived; Kate, I must say this fish is **cooked** beautifully; So the door needs to have the lock taken off – alright and the alarm is not **connected** any more and the exit sign's gone; I've just hitched recently from Byron to Sydney because my money was **locked** in a car and I did not have any; it was **bolted** with a deadlock; this room was **absolutely flooded**.* Indicators (1), (2) and (3) listed above also apply here. Thus we have for example (1) *our disk was very corrupted* (since *corrupted* denotes a quality that is gradable – but not all participial forms of material process verbs do), (2) *our disk seemed corrupted*, and (3) *our disk was corrupted (when it arrived)* rather than *our disk had been corrupted (when it arrived)*. In addition, while 'material' clauses are typically construed with the present-in-present, 'relational' ones are construed with the simple present. Thus has to be interpreted as 'material' – *market research **is being conducted** this week*; and *our disk was being corrupted (when it arrived)* would be 'material' rather than 'relational'.

5.4.4 'Intensive' clauses: 'identifying'

5.4.4.1 General characteristics

In the 'identifying' mode, some thing has an identity assigned to it. What this means is that one entity is being used to identify another: '*x* is identified by *a*', or '*a* serves to define the identity of *x*'. Structurally we label the *x*-element, that which is to be identified, as the **Identified**, and the *a*-element, that which serves as identity, as the **Identifier**. Examples are analysed in Figure 5-19 and we can draw additional examples from entries on dinosaurs. There is only one 'identifying' clause of the 'identifying' kind in the entry in Table 5-13; but other such entries in the same book include: *these dinosaurs **were** the longest ever to live on the Earth; Antarctosaurus **was** one of the group of sauropods, or 'lizard feet'; one feature of the skeleton **was** that the rear thighbones were longer than the front ones; Antarctosaurus **means***

---

[35] As in many other areas of the grammar, English has moved away from the common Germanic construction. In Germanic languages in general, it is possible to construct the equivalent of 'fact' clauses marked by *that* with prepositions. Thus the Swedish translation equivalent of *I'm extremely distressed that ...* is something along the lines of *Jag är oerhört bedrövad över att ...*, where *över att* corresponds to *that* in English and can be glossed as 'because of that'.

'not northern lizard'; research **suggests** *that Brachiosaurus's relative was Cetiosauriscus; close examination of the finds* **showed** *that this group had some puzzling features.* These illustrate some of the uses of 'identifying' clauses in the construction of knowledge – establishing uniqueness, glossing (technical) names, and interpreting evidence. There are others as well; here we can add the use of 'identifying' clauses in definitions such as the one we already cited from Painter (1993, 1999) – *balance* **means** *you hold it on your fingers and it doesn't go: Tagmemics* **is** *a slot-and-filler approach which is primarily designed to allow fieldworkers to reduce corpora of data to coherent descriptions efficiently* [Trask, 1993]; *repression* **is** *an extreme form of denial in which children completely erase a frightening event or circumstance from their awareness* [Craig, *Human Development*] (for a systemic functional account of definitions in technical discourse, see Harvey, 1999). Such clauses are important because they represent a strategy for expanding the naming resources of language, in both everyday discourse and technical or scientific discourse. They underpin dictionary definitions, where the Process is often absent from the structure: *gauge: a measurement according to some standard or system.*

The deadliest spiders in Australia	are	the funnelwebs
the one in the backrow	must be	you
usually	means	mostly
today's meeting	represents	the last chance for a compromise
Mr Garrick	played	Hamlet
c-a-t	spells	'cat'
Identified	Process: intensive	Identifier
nominal group	verbal group	nominal group

Fig. 5-19   Some examples of 'intensive identifying' clauses

In the examples cited above we are evidently not talking about membership of a class. Class membership does not serve to identify; if I say *Sarah is wise*, this allows that there are other wise ones besides Sarah – it does not provide her with an identity. One way of looking at the 'identifying' clause would be to say that here we are narrowing down the class in question to a class of one. If we say *Alice is the clever one*, or *Alice is the cleverest*, this does serve to identify Alice, because we have specified that there is only one member in the class, a single instance. It does not say, of course, that there are no other clever people in the world; only that there are no others within a previously specified population, e.g. *There are three children in the family; ...* . This will now function as a possible answer to a question about Alice's identity: 'which is Alice?' – *Alice is the clever one*.

Before exploring this further, let us first enumerate the characteristics of 'identifying' clauses that contrast with those of 'attributive' clauses listed above. We will take them in the same order.

(i)   The nominal group realizing the function of Identifier is typically definite: it has a common noun as Head, with *the* or another specific determiner as Deictic (see

Chapter 6, Table 6-1), or else a proper noun or pronoun. The only form with adjective as Head is the superlative; for example:

> S01: You know ... interestingly enough I think the tastiest part of this dinner has been the vegetables. – S02: Yeah I agree. – S03: I disagree. – S01: Disagree. – S03: The chicken skin was definitely **the best**. [UTS/Macquarie Corpus]

(ii) The lexical verb of the verbal group realizing the Process is one from the 'equative' classes: see Table 5-14.

(iii) The interrogative probe for such clauses is *which?*, *who?*, *which/who ... as?* (or *what?* if the choice is open-ended); for example, *who is the one in the back row?*, *which are the deadliest spiders?*, *who/what did Mr Garrick play?*

(iv) These clauses are reversible. All verbs except the neutral *be* and the phased *become*, *remain* (and those with following prepositions like *as* in *act as*) have passive forms, e.g. *Hamlet was played by Mr Garrick*, *cat is spelt c-a-t*. Clauses with *be* reverse without change in the form of the verb and without *by* marking the non-Subject participant; e.g. *the deadliest spiders in Australia are funnelwebs* : *funnelwebs are the deadliest spiders in Australia*.

Let us now come back to *Alice is the clever one*. Note that this also serves as a possible answer to a different question, namely 'which is the clever one?'. Since each of the two entities *Alice* and *the clever one* is unique in the context, either can be used to identify the other. But this means that instead of one possible analysis, we have two (see Figure 5-20).

(which is Alice?)

Alice	is	the clever one
Identified		Identifier

(which is the clever one?)

Alice	is	the clever one
Identifier		Identified

Fig. 5-20   Two analyses of *Alice is the clever one*

The two are, of course, likely to have different intonation patterns, with the Identifier as the focus of the New marked by tonic prominence:

Which is Alice? – Alice is **the clever one**.

Which is the clever one? – **Alice** is the clever one.

In other words, Identified and Identifier can come in either order. But since they can come in either order, and either element can take either of the two functions, this means that there are four possibilities here, not two:

(which is the clever one?)

the clever one is **Alice** / **Alice** is the clever one

(which is Alice?)

Alice is **the clever one** / **the clever one** is Alice

For the present discussion, we shall take it that the Identifier always carries the tonic prominence. This is not, in fact, true; it is the typical pattern, since it is the identity that is likely to be new information, but there is a marked option whereby the Identified is construed as the New. (Note therefore that Identified-Identifier cannot simply be explained as Given-New in an 'identifying' clause; not surprisingly, since the former are experiential functions whereas the latter are textual.)

But how exactly are these identities being established? What is the nature of the relationship between the two parts? Let us construct a sketchy but reasonably plausible context. Suppose you are taking part in a play; but I don't know whether you are hero or villain. Here is our conversation:

Which are you? – Which am I? Oh, I'm the villain.

Next you show me a photograph of the cast all made up; the dialogue now goes:

Which is you? – Which is me? Oh, the ugly one is me.

Note how Subject and Complement have been switched around; we can verify this by substituting another verb, say *represent* (see Figure 5-21).

(which are you?)

which	am	I
Complement		Subject

I		represent	**the villain**
Subject/Identified			Complement/Identifier

(which is you?)

which	is	me
Subject		Complement

the ugly one		represents	me
Subject/Identifier			Complement/Identified

Fig. 5-21   Subject-Complement and Identified-Identifier

5.4.4.2 Token and Value

What is happening here is this. In any 'identifying' clause, the two halves refer to the same thing; but the clause is not a tautology, so there must be some difference between them. This difference can be characterized as a stratal one of 'expression' and 'content' (cf. the reference to Davidse, 1992, 1996; Matthiessen, 1991a, above); or, in terms of their generalized labels in the grammar, of **Token** and **Value** – and either can be used to identify the other. If we say *Tom is the treasurer*, we are identifying 'Tom' by assigning him to a Value; if we say *Tom is the tall one*, we are identifying 'Tom' by assigning a Token to him. Every 'identifying' clause faces either one way or the other: the structure of the clause is either Identified/Token ^ Identifier/Value (as in *Tom is the treasurer*) or Identified/Value ^ Identifier/Token (as in *Tom is the tall one*). These two directions are represented in Figure 5-22. The figure represents Token and Value as stratally distinct, with Token being the lower 'expression' and Value the higher 'content'. The figure also shows that either the

Token is 'decoded' or else the Value is 'encoded'. If the Token is construed as Identified and the Value as Identifier, the clause is a **decoding** one (as in *Tom is the treasurer*); if the Value is construed as Identified and the Token as Identifier, the clause is an **encoding** one (as in *Tom is the tall one*). In other words, the identity either decodes the Token by reference to the Value or it encodes the Value by reference to the Token. The two types, 'decoding' and 'encoding', are structurally distinct, which is why examples such as *Tom is the tall one and the treasurer* and *The tall one and the treasurer is (are) Tom* are odd. That is, since *the tall one* is heard as Token and *the treasurer* as Value, they cannot be coordinated.

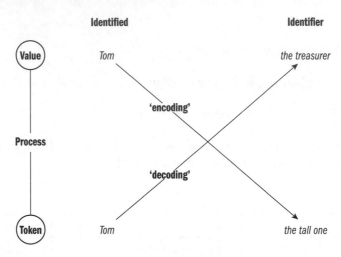

Fig. 5-22 'Identifying' clauses: direction of coding

It is this directionality that determines the voice of the clause – whether it is 'operative' or 'receptive'; and in order to explain this we need to operate with Token and Value as structural functions. Let us fill out the possible answers to the questions in the previous examples set out in Figure 5-21 above: see Figure 5-23.

In other words, 'identifying' clauses select for voice; they have an 'operative' and a 'receptive' variant. The difference is entirely systematic, once we recognize the structure of Token and Value: the **'operative' voice** is the one in which the Subject is also the Token (just as, in a 'material' clause, the 'operative' is the variant in which the Subject is also the Actor: cf. Figure 5-8 above). The most important difference is that the typical verb of the 'identifying' clauses, namely *be*, has no 'passive' form; so clauses like *the villain is me* and *I am the ugly one* do not look like 'receptive' clauses. But they are. This appears clearly when we substitute a different verb, one which has a 'passive' form, as in *the villain is played by me*. There is a strict proportionality, such as is displayed in Figure 5-24. This proportion is clear enough for children to construct such 'passive' forms of the verb *be* (We have heard both *been* and *be'd* in this context, e.g. while playing hospitals, *well then the doctor won't be been by anyone!*).

There is therefore a systemic distinction between *which am I?*, with *I* as Subject ('which do I represent?'), and *which is me?*, with *which* as Subject ('which represents me?'). In the second of these, the form of the personal pronoun is the oblique *me* – naturally, since here *me* is Complement, not Subject, and Complements in English are in the oblique case.

(which are you? — which part do you play?)

Which	am	I
Identified/ Value		Identifier/ Token
Complement/ Wh-		Subject

I	am (= play)	**the villain**
Identified/ Token		Identifier/ Value
Subject		Complement

the villain	is (= is played by)	me
Identifier/ Value		Identified/ Token
Subject		Complement

(which is you? — which picture shows you?)

Which	is	me
Identified/ Token		Identifier/ Value
Subject/Wh-		Complement

the ugly one	is (= shows)	me
Identifier/ Token		Identified/ Value
Subject		Complement

I	am (= am shown by)	**the ugly one**
Identified/ Value		Identifier/ Token
Subject		Complement

Fig. 5-23   Subject-Complement, Identified-Identifier, and Token-Value

Henry	is	the villain	**is to**	the villain	is	Henry
Token/ Subject	Process	Value/ Complement	**as**	Value/ Subject	Process	Token/ Complement
Henry	plays [active]	the villain	**is to**	the villain	is played [passive]	by Henry

Fig. 5-24   'Operative' and 'receptive' in 'identifying' clauses

The form that would be impossible is *which is I?*, with its clash between nominative case and Complement function (cf. the impossible *which represents I?*). Equally anomalous, for exactly the same reason, is *it is I*, which was constructed on a false analogy with Latin (and used to be insisted on by English teachers, though they seldom used it themselves). The clause *it is I* is simply 'bad grammar', in the sense that it conflicts with the general principles that apply to such a clause. The corresponding 'correct' forms – that is, those that are

consistent with the rest of the grammar – are either (1) *I'm it*, with *I* as Subject, or (2) the form that is commonly used, namely *it's me*.[36]

We can now see an explanation for the preferences people show for certain combinations rather than others. Let us add one more component to the paradigm. If we are looking for Fred in the photograph, identifying him by means of a Token, the two clauses *the tall one is Fred* and *Fred is the tall one* are both equally likely. But if we are seeking his role in the organization, identifying him by means of a Value, the preferred form is *Fred is the treasurer*; here *the treasurer is Fred* is rather rare. The analysis shows why (see Figure 5-25).

(1)

the tall one	is	Fred
Identifier/ Token	Process: active	Identified/ Value
Subject		Complement

('which is [represents] Fred?')

(2)

Fred	is	**the tall one**
Identified/ Value	Process: passive	Identifier/ Token
Subject		Complement

(3)

Fred	is	**the treasurer**
Identified/ Token	Process: active	Identifier/ Value
Subject		Complement

('which is Fred? [which does Fred represent?]')

(4)

the treasurer	is	Fred
Identifier/ Value	Process: passive	Identified/ Token
Subject		Complement

Fig. 5-25   Unmarked, singly marked and doubly marked variants

The relevant variable is the extent of marking (markedness) involved in respect of the two systemic parameters of (i) voice and (ii) information (see Chapter 3, Section 3.5): see Table 5-18. Here (1) is unmarked for voice ('operative'), but marked for information (with New preceding Given). (2) on the other hand is marked for voice ('receptive') but unmarked for information (with Given preceding New). In other words, each is marked in respect of one variable. But (3) is unmarked both for voice and information, whereas (4) is marked for both. What this means, furthermore, is that the choice of 'receptive' in (4) is unmotivated. The reason for choosing the 'receptive' in English is to get the desired texture, in terms of Theme-Rheme and Given-New; in particular, it avoids marked information focus (which carries an additional semantic feature of contrast). Here, however, the 'receptive' has the opposite effect; it actually **leads to** a marked focus of information (New before Given); hence the resulting form is doubly marked, both for information and for voice. Such a form is by no means impossible; but the meaning is such that it assumes a highly specific context.

With a verb other than *be* it is clear which is Token and which is Value, since as pointed out above this can be determined by the voice: if the clause is 'operative', the Subject is Token,

---

[36] Since tonic prominence sits uneasily on *it*, a usual variant of (1) is *I'm the one*, although children use *I'm it* when *it* is the name of a role, as in the game of tig. The Late Middle English form was *it am I*; but this disappeared under the modern word order principle whereby all non-Wh Subjects come first.

Table 5-18 Markedness in voice and information

	Unmarked voice: operative	Marked voice: receptive
unmarked information	(3) Fred is **the treasurer**	(2) Fred is **the tall one**
marked information	(1) **the tall one** is Fred	(4) **the treasurer** is Fred

whereas if the clause is 'receptive', the Subject is Value. (For verbs such as *consist of, comprise,* see under 'possessive' in Section 5.4.5.2.) With the verb *be* one cannot tell whether the clause is 'operative' or 'receptive'; the best strategy for analysing these is to substitute some other verb, such as *represent*, and see which voice is chosen. For example, *this offer is/represents your best chance to win a prize; one criterion is/is represented by genetic diversity.*

Any 'identifying' clause with *be*, like *Tom is the leader*, if constructed out of context and presented in written form, is obviously highly ambiguous. In real life, there is usually some relevant context, and misunderstanding seldom occurs – at least, misunderstanding that is subsequently brought to light: how much occurs that is not brought to light is something that a teacher begins to wonder about when it turns out that students have misconstrued a key sentence in the textbook. In dialogue the context usually suffices; and when an instance does show up it often provides good insight into the meaning of Token and Value. Here is an example from a conversation between one teacher and another:

A: So the best students are the greatest worriers, is that it?

B: Oh, I don't think there's any virtue in worrying, is there?

A: No, I didn't mean is it because they worry that they get to be the best. I meant it is because they're the best students that they worry.

Speaker A meant 'the best students worry most', i.e. because they're good they worry. Here *the best students* is Token and *the greatest worriers* is Value. Speaker B misinterpreted as 'the greatest worriers study best', i.e. because they worry they're good; in other words, she took *the best students* as Value and *the greatest worriers* as Token.

Another way of becoming sensitized to the Token-Value relation is to notice when one's expectations turn out to be wrong. For example, in an article on winter sports there was a clause beginning *but the most important piece of equipment is* ... I read this as Value (unconsciously, of course!) and so predicted that it would be followed by a Token, something like ... *a safety helmet*. What actually followed was ... *the one you can least afford.* I had to go back and reinterpret the first part as Token, so as to construe the whole as Token-Value. As we have noted, the two cannot be coordinated; so, in this example you could not have *the most important pieces of equipment are the one you can least afford and a safety helmet* – except as conscious play on the grammar.

Identifying clauses of different coding orientations make distinct and complementary contributions in the development of text. Thus 'encoding' clauses serve as a resource for presenting the steps in the organization of a text, as in the following extract from a consequential explanation in history taken from Coffin (2006: 69–70):

World War II affected Australian society both during and after the war. [Identified/Value:] The focus of this essay [Process:] is [Identifier/Token:] its impact on Australia after it ended in 1945, and an explanation

283

of how six years of involvement in warfare led to major economic, political and social changes. [Identified/ Value:] One major effect of World War II [Process:] was [Identifier: Token:] a restructuring of the Australian economy: the unavailability of goods meant that Australia had to begin to produce its own.

Similarly:

There are three kinds of reasons that justify the protests and these should carry weight with the US Government, Earl Russell suggested. '[Identified/Value:] The first of these reasons [Process:] is [Identifier: Token:] the importance of preserving the hitherto cordial relations between the US and Great Britain, not only in Government circles, but in public opinion.' [LOB_A]

In contrast, 'decoding' clauses can be used as a strategy for interpreting phenomena that have been observed, as in (from the same consequential explanation as above):

In fact between 1937 and 1945 the value of industrial production almost doubled. This increase was faster than would otherwise have occurred and the momentum was maintained in the post-war years. [Identified/ Token:] This [Process:] was partly [Identifier/Value:] the result of the post-war influx of immigrants which led to an increase in the demand for goods and services and therefore a growth in industry.

5.4.4.3 Subtypes of 'identifying' clause

The Token-Value structure is probably the most difficult to come to terms with in the entire transitivity system. It is also, arguably, the most important, in that it tends to dominate in certain highly valued registers (such as scientific, commercial, political and bureaucratic discourse) where the meanings that are being construed are inherently symbolic ones. Let us draw attention to, and exemplify, some of the subtypes of 'identifying' clauses (for a discussion of the system of 'identifying' clauses seen from the point of view of the field of semiotics, see Martin, 1992: 280–285).

equation:

For example, if [Token/Identified:] A [Process:] = [Value/Identifier:] {a, b, c, d} and [Token/Identified:] B [Process:] = [Value/Identifier:] {x, y, z}, then the coordinate diagram of A × B is as shown in Fig. 5-2 above. [Set Theory and related topics, p. 67]

equivalence:

[Token/Identified:] Such energies **correspond** to [Value/Identifier:] nearly 95% of the speed of light.

role-play:

[Token/Identified:] You [Process:] **will be** [Value/Identifier:] our primary interface with clients.

Naming[37]:

[Token/Identified:] I [Process:] **am** [Value/Identifier:] Mrs Fitzfassenden. I am not a pronoun.

---

[37] Languages are full of mysteries. Like contemporary Germanic languages such as German and Swedish, Old English had a very useful verb meaning 'be:called', viz. *hight* (cf. German *heißen* and Swedish *heta*, and also e.g. French *s'appeler*), but this verb was lost. English lexicogrammar has accommodated for this loss by evolving a new paradigm for naming; in Modern English, one would say *My name is Fitzfassenden* (cf. *What's your name?*), with the feature of 'naming' construed as part of the Value – or simply *I'm Fitzfassenden*; 'naming' can only be construed as part of the Process with verbs like *call, term*, in the receptive (unless the assigner of the name is made explicit; see Section 5.7): *I'm called Mrs. Fitzfassenden.* Contrast Swedish *Jag heter Fitzfassenden* 'I am:called Fitzfassenden' (cf. *Vad heter du?* 'What are:called you?'). Why was Old English *hight* lost? Of course, it was part of a general change: a great number of Old English lexical items disappeared as part of the 'transformation' of Old English into Middle English. No doubt somebody has written a Ph.D. thesis about the history of the lexicogrammar of naming in English – or else there is one waiting to be written!

definition:

> It'd have to 'cause [Token/Identified:] politics is [Value/Identifier:] the art of negotiation, you have to decide a compromise. [UTS/Macquarie Corpus]

symbolization (including glossing and translation):

> [Value/Identified:] The entire floor of the fourth ventricle [Process:] **is indicated** [Token/Identifier:] by the strippled area in the figure to the right.

> [Token/Identified:] Heinz [Process:] **means** [Value/Identifier:] beans.

exemplification:

> [Token/Identified:] Frogs, toads, and salamanders [Process:] **are** [Value/Identifier:] some amphibians we know today.

> [Value/Identified:] One criterion [Process:] **is** [Token/Identifier:] that of genetic diversity.

demonstration:

> [Token/Identified:] A study of more than one syllable [Process:] **shows** [Value/Identifier:] ⟦ that in connected speech, or what may be called 'combinative style', the syllable structure proper to the isolative style is modified in some degree⟧ .

> [Token/Identified:] The fluorocarbon-halon theory [Process:] **suggests** [Value/Identifier:] ⟦ that there should be a change in the partitioning of chlorine from the inactive forms of chlorine, namely hydrochloric acid and chlorine nitrate, into the active forms of chlorine, namely chlorine atoms and chlorine oxide radicals⟧ . [Text 65]

> [Token/Identified:] The evidence ⟦ that I have seen from laboratory studies⟧ [Process:] **indicates** [Value/Identifier:] ⟦⟦ that liquid sulfuric acid particles will not provide such an efficient surface for heterogeneous chemistry, ‖ partly because the rate of reaction proceeds more slowly compared to that with ice crystals, ‖ and partly because the typical density of the sulfuric acid aerosols is less than that for ice crystals over Antarctica⟧⟧ . [Text 33]

> [Token/Identified:] the boom in new buildings and road construction [Process:] **indicates** [Value/Identifier:] 'full steam ahead' for a long time to come. [LOB_A]

These subtypes contrast with the general sense of the Token-Value relation which we find in clauses such as:

> [Value:] The converse of that [Process:] **is** [Token:] that the same is true in war. [LLC 454]

> [Token:] These people [Process:] **constitute** [Value:] a reservoir for the transmission of the virus.

It is this general sense of identifying that we have seen in the thematic equatives described in Chapter 3, Section 3.2, e.g.

> [Token:] This [Process:] is [Value:] what happened to me the last few weeks. [UTS/Macquarie Corpus]

> [Value:] what you could – what you should do [Process:] is [Value:] get the different components [UTS/Macquarie Corpus]

Note that in a thematic equative, the nominalization is always the Value.

5.4.4.4 Summary of attributive and identifying (intensive) clauses

Let us now look back over the distinction between the 'attributive' and the 'identifying' and try to see it as something rather more continuous – as a continuum within the overall continuum of process types represented in Figure 5-3 above.

In attribution, some entity is being said to have an attribute. This means that it is being assigned to a class; and the two elements that enter into this relation, the attribute and the entity that 'carries' it, thus differ in generality (the one includes the other) but are at the same level of abstraction. So for example

my brother	is	**tall**
Carrier = member		Attribute = class

means 'my brother belongs to the class of people who are tall'. This specifies one of his attributes; but it does not serve to identify him – there are other tall people besides. The only means of identifying something by assigning it to a class is to make that a class of one member. But if the one-member class is at the same level of abstraction as its member, we have a tautology: *my brother is my brother*. The relation is not a tautology; on the other hand, if the two differ in abstraction then the one-member class becomes a value to which the member is assigned as a token:

my brother	is	the tallest in the **picture**
Identified/Value		Identifier/Token

The element that is of the lower order of abstraction now becomes the Identifier; and as a result of the switch, the verb becomes passive. Instead of *my brother represents the tallest one in the family*, we have *my brother is represented by the tallest one in the picture*. Of course, in a context like this we should be likely to use *be* in both, and the verb *be* does not show the passive in its own form; but the contrast can be brought out with a pair of clauses such as:

his best work	is (represents)	the high point of the tradition
Identified/Token		Identifier/Value
his best work	is (is represented)	by the last novel he wrote
Identified/Value		Identifier/Token

We have seen how these roles are mapped onto that of Subject: the Subject is always Token in the 'operative', Value in the 'receptive'.

What this means is that the type of 'identifying' clause where the Identifier is the Value (that is, the identity is given by function) is intermediate between the attributive and the other type of identifying, the one where the Identifier is the Token (the identity is given by form):

Pat is rich	Attribute	attributive
Pat is the richest	Identifier/Value	decoding
the richest is Pat	Identifier/Token	encoding

The former is the 'decoding' type introduced above (cf. Figure 5-22) and the latter is the 'encoding' type. The 'decoding' type of 'identifying' clause is intermediate between the 'attributive' and the 'encoding' type: see Figure 5-26.

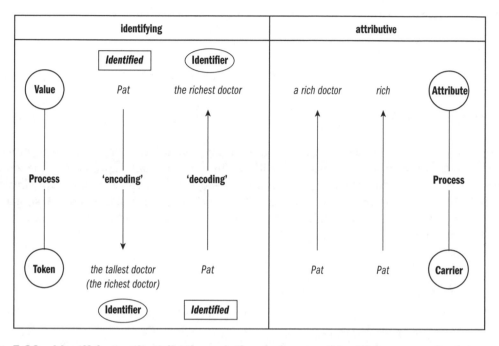

Fig. 5-26   Identifying and attributive relational clauses: 'identifying: encoding' – 'identifying: decoding' – 'attributive: entity' – 'attributive: quality'

The continuity becomes clearer when we set up as Value/Identifier something that is explicitly worded as membership of a class, using the expression 'one of ...'

Pat	is	one of the richest people I know
Identified/Token		Identifier/Value

And on the other hand we often interpret an Attribute not just as an instance of a class but in some sense the value of the entity it carries, e.g. *Pat is a millionaire*. Nominal Attributes are closer to Values than adjectival ones; and these, in turn, are very close to the 'is an example of' type of 'identifying' clause, like *those missiles constitute a threat to our security*. Most problematic of all are clauses of naming and defining, which lie exactly at the crossover point between the two types of 'identifying' clause:

my name	is	'Alice'	
Value		Token	
I	am	Alice	['am called']
Value		Token	

Naming and defining are linguistic exercises, in which the word is Token and its meaning is the Value. In 'calling', on the other hand, it is the name that is the Value. Contrast the following pair:

a 'gazebo'	is	a pavilion on an eminence	(= 'the word *gazebo* means [names, is defined as] a pavilion on an eminence')
Token		Value	
a poet	is	an artist in words	(= 'one who makes verbal art has the standing of [is called] a poet')
Value		Token	

Both 'identifying' and 'attributive' clauses of the 'intensive' kind have the option of ASSIGNMENT: they may be configured with a third participant representing the entity assigning the relationship of identity of attribution – for example, *they* in *they made Mary the leader* and *they made Mary happy*. In the case of 'identifying' clauses, this is the **Assigner**; in the case of 'attributing' clauses, this is the **Attributor**. In a 'receptive' clause, this participant may be left implicit. For example:

[i]   Assigner in 'identifying' clause:

We might call it the authorial voice. [Text 16]

DPP Secretary-general Yu Shyi-kun was named vice premier. [Text 13]

[ii]   Attributor in 'attributive' clause:

In the Spirit of Crazy Horse would make a marvelous novel – **I** could turn that into a novel in a few months. [Text 7]

People like bloody Kerry Packer and Rupert Murdoch and Bill Gates they, they employ their smart lawyers and taxation experts and they pay very little tax and I think that's –, **it** makes me absolutely furious. My blood boils when I think about that. [UTS/Macquarie Corpus]

Schools can be declared 'failing' for a number of reasons, including high levels of racial harassment or expulsions. [Text 97]

Just make sure you're not. [UTS/Macquarie Corpus]

[S 02:] Okay, Jana ... – [S 03:] I'm the best. – [S 02:] Yeah, but I don't want to compare your jokes ... 'cause if **you** make someone a winner, then the other people become losers. And they're all good. Just different. Okay, Jana. What's yours? [Text 57]

We may note that there is a type of clause that is agnate to those with verbs of appearance (see Table 5-14)) in which the Carrier is construed on the model of a circumstance of Means (of the subtype 'material'; see Table 5-28) marked by *of* or *out of*; for example:

'**It** makes a mockery of the slogan which many of them use, "To Protect and Serve",' he said. [Text 2]

I mean, I think **she**'s made an absolute fool of herself. [UTS/Macquarie Corpus]

No one's gonna make a fool out of me [COCA]

These relational clauses resemble creative material ones with a circumstance of Means such as *you could make fortune out of any one of your loves*. However, in such material clauses the circumstance of Means can be left out: *you could make a fortune*, whereas the Carrier/Means cannot be left out of an assigned relational clause: we cannot say *she's made an absolute fool* without *of herself*. Creative verbs other than *make* can serve as the Process, e.g. *create, produce, develop*. Further, there is a receptive option with such material clauses, e.g. *a fortune could be made (by you) out of any of your loves*, but there is no receptive version of assigned relational clauses of this type: *an absolute fool has been made (by her) of herself* is odd.

5.4.5 Circumstantial and possessive clauses

We now turn to the other two types of being, 'circumstantial' and 'possessive' clauses. These two types also come in two modes of being, 'attributive' and 'identifying'. We can thus recognize the following series of proportions:

intensive	Emily is a poet :	attributive
	Emily is the poet ::	identifying
possessive	Emily has a piano :	attributive
	the piano is Emily's ::	identifying
circumstantial	the meeting is on Friday :	attributive
	the time of the meeting is Friday	identifying

The verb *be* can be used in all categories set out in Section 5.4.2 although *have* is the unmarked verb in 'attributive' clauses of possession (in standard English we say *Emily has a piano* rather than *with Emily is a piano*). The variants of 'possessive' and 'circumstantial' clauses with *be* (and *have*) are analogous to 'intensive' clauses. Thus *Emily has a piano* can be interpreted as 'Emily is a member of the class of piano-owners' and *the meeting is on Friday* as 'the meeting is a member of the class of events on Friday'. Similarly *the piano is Emily's* can be interpreted as 'the piano is identified as the one belonging to Emily' and *Friday is the best time* as 'Friday is identified as the best time'.

If all 'possessive' and 'circumstantial' clauses had the intensive verb *be* as the Process, we could perhaps interpret them as subtypes of 'intensive' clauses – subtypes where possessor and possessed are related to one another and where circumstances are related to one another. Here *the piano is Emily's* would be like our earlier example *her name is Alice*, where naming is construed as an aspect of one of the participants (cf. also *the owner of the Piano is Emily*). Under this interpretation a clause such as *Emily has a piano* would be the odd one out because here the sense of possession is construed in the process in the first instance (the verb *have*), not in (one of) the participants. However, *Emily has a piano* is not the odd one out; it exemplifies a regular option throughout for all 'possessive' and 'circumstantial' clauses. This is the option of construing possession or circumstantiation as process. Thus alongside *the piano is Emily's*, we have *the piano is owned by Emily*; and alongside *Emily is like her mother*, we have *Emily resembles her mother*. Here *own* means 'be + possession' and *resemble* means 'be + like'.

With 'possessive' and 'circumstantial' clauses, there is thus a systemic contrast between 'possession/circumstantiation as participant' and 'possession/circumstantiation as process'.

The contrast is a general one, construed in the grammatical zone of lexicogrammar rather than the lexical one; and just as with the 'like'/'please' contrast in the grammar of 'mental' clauses, we often find lexical pairs manifesting the contrast such as *be x's/be owned, be like/ resemble, be with/accompany, be in/inhabit, be around/surround, be opposite of/face, be about/ concern* – but just as in the mental case there may be gaps in the lexical paradigm. The contrast between 'as participant' and 'as process' is, as we have just noted, a grammatical one and in a sense it applies also to 'intensive' clauses. Thus we have for example:

the <u>meaning</u> of 'kita:bun' **is** 'book'/	'kita:bun' **means** 'book',
the <u>name</u> of his mother is Anna/	his mother **is** <u>called</u> Anna,
<u>examples</u> of amphibians **are** frogs, toads and salamanders/	amphibians **are** <u>exemplified</u> by frogs, toads and salamanders

But a special feature of the 'intensive' type is that the sense of 'meaning', 'name', 'example' and the like may be left implicit in the participant (for the reason, see Matthiessen, 1991a): *'kita:bun' is 'book', his mother is Anna*.

We shall now discuss 'circumstantial' and 'possessive' clauses in turn, using the systemic description set out in the system network in Figure 5-17.

5.4.5.1 Circumstantial clauses

In the 'circumstantial' type, the relationship between the two terms is one of time, place, manner, cause, accompaniment, role, matter or angle. These are also manifested as circumstantial elements in the English clause, and they are discussed in more detail in Section 5.6.

(i) Attributive. In the 'attributive' mode, the circumstantial element is an attribute that is being ascribed to some entity; for example *my story is about a poor shepherd boy*. These take two forms: (a) one in which the circumstance is construed in the form of the Attribute, as here (*about a poor shepherd boy*); (b) the other in which the circumstantial relation is construed in the form of the Process, e.g. *my story concerns a poor shepherd boy, the rain lasted forty days and forty nights*. In the first case, the circumstantial relation is construed as a minor process realized by a preposition; in the second it is construed as a process realized by a verb: *about/concern + a poor shepherd boy*.

(a) Circumstance as attribute. Here the Attribute is realized (1) by a prepositional phrase, in which case the circumstantial relation is expressed by the preposition,[38] e.g. *in, from, among, without* in *after 1954, the editorial office was mostly in New York; the victims are mostly from ethnic minority backgrounds; he is among more than 3,000 Indians from 186 Brazilian tribes who have assembled to draft a list of grievances against government policies that affect Indians; so I was without a teacher* and/or (2) by an adverbial group, e.g. *she was there with three Zen masters; I'd been back about a year and a half, two years; where's our cake?*.

---

[38] Clauses with ascriptive verbs of marked phase such as *turn* and *look*, were treated as 'intensive' even when they had a prepositional phrase after them: e.g. *caterpillars turn into butterflies, Penelope looked like an angel*. This reflects their constituent structure; cf. *what they turn into are butterflies* (not *what they turn is into butterflies*), *Penelope looked angelic*. But there is overlap at this point, and these could also be interpreted as circumstantial.

Unlike the Attribute of an 'intensive' clause, the Attribute of a 'circumstantial' one is frequently Theme in registers where the thematic status is rhetorically motivated, as in touring texts in guide books, topographic procedure (operating in 'enabling' contexts):

> Turn left after the Entertainment Centre. <u>On your right</u> is the historic Pump House which formerly provided hydraulic pressure to operate lifts in the city. The building now accommodates the refurbished Tavern and Boutique Brewery.

And unlike intensive Attributes, such circumstantial Attributes frequently have a 'definite' nominal group such as *on your right* in the example above and *at the centre* in *at the centre is Alice Springs*; here the combination of definiteness with denoting something that provides an orientation constitutes a strong motivation for thematic status in the clause. However, note that clauses such as *on the north wall inside the Cathedral hangs a Union Jack which was carried by Mr R Fair of the Australian 8th Division, through all this work runs a strong vein of cynicism*, are not 'attributive' but 'existential' (see Section 5.5). The thematically unmarked form of these clauses is that beginning with existential *there: there is (hangs) a Union Jack on the north wall*. The prepositional phrase then appears initially as a marked Theme; in that case the existential feature may be left implicit, although the *there* may still be present and will appear in any case in the mood tag: *on the north wall (there) is a Union Jack, isn't there?* In contrast, in a 'circumstantial attributive' clause, the Subject/Carrier is picked up in the mood tag: *the sounds and smell of the ocean hang in the air – don't they?; on your right is the historic Pump House, isn't it?*

(b) Circumstance as process. Here the Attribute is realized by a nominal group and the circumstantial relation is expressed by the lexical verb in the verbal group serving as Process: see the 'attributive' column in Table 5-20. For example: *the voyage from Oban to Castlebay (Barra)* **takes** *about five hours; but the 'Thousand Year Reich' that* **had lasted** *but thirteen years was now only publicly displayed through its regalia offered for sale at flea markets.* The verb expresses a circumstantial relation such as 'be + extent in time' (e.g. *last, take*), 'be + condition' (e.g. *depend on*), 'be + matter' (e.g. *concern*). Being attributive, these are non-reversible; there are no 'receptive' equivalents such as *about five hours are taken by the voyage; but thirteen years had been lasted by that.*

In (b), therefore, the Process is circumstantial; whereas in (a) it is the Attribute that is circumstantial, the Process being the same as in the 'intensive' type. Examples are shown in Figure 5-27.

(a)

my story	is	about a poor shepherd boy
Carrier	Process: intensive	Attribute: circumstantial
nominal group	verbal group	prepositional phrase

(b)

my story	concerns	a poor shepherd boy
Carrier	Process: circumstantial	Attribute
nominal group	verbal group	nominal group

Fig. 5-27 'Circumstantial attributive' clauses

Verbs serving in clauses with a circumstantial process are often derived from a basic use in 'material' clauses of motion – for example, see Text 5-10:

Text 5-10: Enabling – instruction (written, monologic): extract from a topographic procedure [Text 22]

From the high point of the craggy Castle Rock, the Royal Mile, backbone of the Old Town, **runs** down to the royal Palace of Holyroodhouse.

Built by TNT Harbourlink in 1988, the Monorail **runs** in a 3.6 kilometre loop and has six stations: ...

The unmarked present tense is the simple present (*the Royal Mile runs down to the royal Palace*), rather than the present in present of 'material' clauses (we would not say *the Royal Mile is running down to the royal Palace*; but with a 'material' clause: *look, she's running down to the royal Palace*). The Carrier is typically some immobile physical feature, whereas the Actor of a 'material' clause of motion is typically an animate being or a mobile entity. Because of the overlap of a large set of verbs, there will, of course, be cases that are indeterminate (cf. Halliday, 1973/2002c: 109, commenting on examples such as [*the bushes*] *waded out*).

(ii) Identifying. In the 'identifying' mode, the circumstance takes the form of a relationship between two entities; one entity is being related to another by a feature of time or place or manner, etc. As with the circumstantial attributive, this pattern may be organized semantically in either of two ways. The relationship is expressed either (a) as a feature of the participants, as in *tomorrow is the tenth*, or (b) as a feature of the process, as in *the fair takes up the whole day*.

(a) Circumstance as participants. In this type it is the participants – Identified and Identifier – that are circumstantial elements of time, place and so on. For example, in *tomorrow is the tenth*, *tomorrow* and *the tenth* are both time elements. Similarly in *the best way to get there is by train*, both *the best way* and *by train* express manner; in *the real reason is that you're scared*, Identified and Identifier are both expressions of cause. The Token can be quite varied in grammatical class – a nominal group, an adverbial group, a prepositional phrase or an embedded clause, whereas the Value is often a nominal group with the name of a class of circumstance as Thing: see Table 5-19.

Table 5-19 Token and Value in circumstantial identifying clauses with circumstance as participants

Token	Value	Example
clause	nominal group: Thing: name of circumstance (*reason*)	one reason is [[[that foxes, << being small, >> often fail to kill their prey]]]
prep. phrase	nominal group: Thing: name of circumstance (*way*)	perhaps the best way [[to measure it]] is by the number of different kinds of cells an organism has
adverbial group	nominal group: Thing: name of circumstance (*birthday*)	(you told me) today was your birthday
nominal group	nominal group: Thing: name of circumstance (*time*)	the time is 19 minutes past the hour

(b) Circumstance as process. In this type it is not the participants that are the expression of time, place or other circumstantial features, but the Process. In examples such as the following the verbs *take up, span, cross, cause* are so to speak 'circumstantial' verbs: *US bases **take up** almost one-fifth of the land of the cramped island; more than 50 years **span** her age and mine; Turtle Ridge **would span** maybe three blocks; this situation **is** apparently **caused** by anomalous low temperatures; about half way the track turns inland amid a lot of prickly hakea then **crosses** Wattamolla Creek at waterfalls; A bikeway also **circles** The Village.* Circumstantial verbs encode the circumstance of time, place, accompaniment, manner, etc. as a relationship between the participants (verbs are listed in the identifying column of Table 5-20). Thus *take up* means 'be + for (extent in time)'; *follow* means 'be + after (location in time)'; *cross, span* mean 'be + across (extent in place)'; *accompany* means 'be + with'; *resemble* means 'be + like'.[39] This means that in terms of the concept of grammatical metaphor discussed in Chapter 10 all clauses of this type are metaphorical.

Like those in the previous paragraph, these clauses are reversible in voice. In this case, however, not only are the participants reversed but also the verb appears in the passive: *the whole day **is taken up** by the fair; apart from economic issues it's likely that some of his time **will be taken up** by a proposal Mr Ben Ali made yesterday; It replaces the 0 plus ClO rate-limiting step with a pressure-dependent dimerization step that **is followed** by photodissociation of that dimer; in France, nationalization **was accompanied** by state planning.* There is no difficulty in recognizing these as 'receptive' clauses.

The line between the 'attributive' and 'identifying' modes is less clear in the 'circumstantial' than in the 'intensive' type of 'relational' clause. This is natural, since it is less obvious whether an expression such as *on the mat* designates a class (that has members – the class of things on the mat) or an identity (the thing that is identified by being on the mat). Nevertheless, there is a distinction, which we can recognize if we set up typical examples side by side:

	attributive	identifying
(a)	the cat is on the mat	the best place is on the mat
		on the mat is the best place
(b)	the fair lasts all day	the fair takes up the whole day
		the whole day is taken up by the fair

In the 'identifying' mode, we can also recognize Token and Value, with exactly the same application as in the 'intensive' – see Figure 5-28.

---

[39] We can also see the sense of 'be' in variants where the circumstantial type is named within the nominal group serving as Value: *US bases take up almost one-fifth of the land ...* : *The extent of US bases is (is represented by) almost one-fifth of the land; the situation is apparently caused by anomalous low temperatures* : *the cause of the situation is (is represented by) apparently anomalous low temperatures.*

operative

(a)

tomorrow on the mat	is is	the tenth the best place
Identified/ Token	Process: intensive	Identifier/Value
Subject	Finite	Complement
Mood		Residue

receptive

the tenth the best place	is is	tomorrow on the mat
Identified/Value	Process: intensive	Identifier/ Token
Subject	Finite	Complement
Mood		Residue

(b)

the fair	occupies		the whole day
Identified/ Token	Process: circ.		Identifier/Value
Subject	Finite	Pred.	Complement
Mood		Residue	

the whole day	is	occupied	by the fair
Identified/ Value	Process: circ.		Identifier/Token
Subject	Finite	Pred.	Adjunct
Mood		Residue	

Fig.5-28 Circumstantial identifying clauses

Table 5-20 Circumstantial verbs

	Attributive	**Identifying**
temporal	last, take, date (from); range (from ... to);	greet, predate, anticipate, co-occur with; take up, follow, precede;
spatial	run, extend (from ... to), reach	cross, circle, surround, enclose, follow, cover, crown, span, overhang, extend over, permeate, dominate, support, face, parallel, overlook, inhabit,
comparative	differ from; become, suit	resemble, match, fit; exceed, outnumber
causal: reason		bring about, cause, lead to, produce, result in; arise from
causal: concession		conflict with, contradict, contravene, preclude, prevent
causal: condition	depend on, hinge on	condition, determine
accompaniment		accompany, complement
matter	concern, be concerned with, deal with, treat of, go into	cover, touch upon, take up, discuss, expound on

5.4.5.2 Possessive clauses

In the 'possessive' type, the relationship between the two terms is one of ownership; one entity possesses another; for example: *we **had** a wonderful piece of property in Connecticut, back up in the hills* [Text 7]; *most impressive of all was the staggering statistic that 80 percent of European electronics production **was owned** by American firms* [Europe in Retrospect]. In addition to possession in the narrow sense of 'owning', the category of 'possessive' clauses

also includes possession in a broader, more generalized sense – possession of body parts and other part-whole relations, containment, involvement and the like; for example: *in some places, the walks **have** simple guide leaflets; the vessel **lacked** life vests and other safety equipment; non-fiction usually **involves** research* [Text 7] – and also possession of abstractions; for example: *but I **have** this idea that American writers, by and large, do weak work in their later years; public men, Mr Birling, **have** responsibilities as well as privileges.* Possession thus has to be interpreted quite broadly, in the sense of 'extension': one entity is construed as being extended by another.

Just like 'circumstantial' clauses, 'possessive' ones are construed in both the 'attributive' and 'identifying' modes.

(i) Attributive. In the 'attributive' mode, the possessive relationship may again be construed either as attribute, e.g. *Peter's* in *the piano is Peter's*, or as process, e.g. *has, belongs to* in *Peter has a piano, the piano belongs to Peter.*

(a) Possession as Attribute. If the relationship is construed as the Attribute, then it takes the form of a possessive nominal group, e.g. *Peter's*; the thing possessed is the Carrier and the possessor is the Attribute. These are not, in fact, syntagmatically distinct from 'identifying' clauses; the clause *the piano is Peter's* could be either 'attributive'. 'the piano is a member of the class of Peter's possessions' or 'identifying', 'the piano is identified as belonging to Peter'. (Note that the reversed from *Peter's is the piano* can only be 'identifying'.)

(b) Possession as Process. If the relationship of possession is construed as the Process, then two further possibilities arise. Either (one) the possessor is the Carrier and the possessed is the Attribute (we will call the thing possessed the 'possessed' rather than the 'possession', to avoid ambiguity; 'possession' refers to the relationship), as in *Peter has a piano*. Here piano-ownership is an attribute being ascribed to Peter. Verbs other than *have* combine the sense of possession with other features, e.g. *lack* 'need to have', *boast* 'have as a positive feature'. Or (two) the possessed is the Carrier and the possessor is the Attribute, as in *the piano belongs to Peter*. Here Peter-ownership is an attribute being ascribed to the piano. Neither of the two, of course, is reversible; we do not say *a piano is had by Peter*, or *Peter is belonged to by the piano*. Examples are shown in Figure 5-29.

Additional examples are as follows:

The Sydney casino **will boast** 400 gaming tables and 1500 video slot machines with a capacity for 11,000 people at one time. [ACE_B]

The ceiling cornices in the main rooms **feature** patterns of WA wildflowers – geraldton wax, wattle, gumnuts and leaves – with a different flower in various rooms. [ACE_A]

Besides Evans and Thompson the mini-series **stars** Judy Morris, Jason Robards and Tony Bonner. [ACE_C]

(ii) Identifying. In the 'identifying' mode, the possession takes the form of a relationship between two entities; and again this may be organized in two ways, with the relationship being expressed either (a) as a feature of the participants, as in *the piano is Peter's*, or (b) as a feature of the process, as in *Peter owns the piano.*

(a) Possession as participants. Here the participants embody the notion of possession, one signifying property of the possessor, e.g. *Peter's*, the other signifying the thing possessed, e.g. *the piano*. Thus in *the piano is Peter's*, both *the piano* and *Peter's* express 'that which

295

(a)	the piano	is	Peter's
	Carrier	Process: intensive	Attribute: possession

(b)	(one)	Peter	has	a piano
		Carrier: possessor	Process: possession	Attribute: possessed
(b)	(two)	the piano	belongs to	Peter
		Carrier: possessed	Process: possession	Attribute: possessor

Fig. 5-29 Possessive attributive clauses

Peter possesses', the relationship between them being simply one of identity. Note that here *the piano* is Token and *Peter's* is Value.

(b) Possession as process. Here the possession is encoded as a process, typically realized by the verb *own* as in *Peter owns the piano*. (Notice we do not normally say *Peter has the piano*, in the sense of ownership; *have* is not used as an identifying verb of possession.) The participants are possessor *Peter* and possessed *the piano*; in this case *Peter* is Token and *the piano* is Value.

In addition to possession in the usual sense of 'owning', this category includes abstract relationships of containment, involvement and the like[40]. Among the verbs commonly occurring in this function are *include, involve, contain, comprise, consist of, provide*. Some verbs combine the feature of possession with other semantic features; for example *exclude* '[negative] + have', *owe* 'have on behalf of another possessor', *deserve* 'ought to have', *provide* 'have as a resource', *require* 'need to have', *lack* 'fail to have'. (Most verbs meaning 'come to have', on the other hand, function as Process in 'material' clauses; for example *get, receive, acquire* – compare the tense forms in *You deserve a medal. – I'm getting one.*) See Table 5-21. Examples of possessive identifying clauses:

General Motors, had $20 billion in world sales and **owned** production facilities in some twenty-four countries.

the vessel, << ..., >> **lacked** life vests and other safety equipment [News report/Thai ferry (SMH)]

Would you say that a lot of fiction **lacks** this compassion or empathy? [Text 21]

Our men and women **deserve** a retirement system [[that more appropriately rewards their service]]. [Text 115]

Yes, GFCI [ground fault circuit interrupter] outlets do have a reputation for tripping easily – especially when confronted by large motor loads. That rap was **deserved** by the first generation of GFCI receptacles. [COCA]

The report quoted a retired senior police officer as saying that in 47 years in law enforcement, he had never seen anything from the State Department or the FBI on the Vienna Convention, which **contains** the consular access provision. [Text 1]

---

[40] Examples in this area of the relational grammar illustrate the connection between possession and location (cf. Matthiessen, 2004b: 598), as in: *A portrait of Robert Jameson **is housed** by the National Portrait Gallery in London, and a bust of him **is in** the Old College of the University of Edinburgh*. [Wikipedia entry].

Many, if not most, of the products we use daily **contain** or **are contained** by plastic. [COCA]

Manufacturing paint **requires** high levels of both technical expertise and financial resources [[**lacked by** many would-be competitors]]. [COCA]

On the left the seven storey Convention Centre **provides** seating for 3,500 people [Text 22]

Interim financing of construction costs **is provided** by a short term loan from The Chase Manhattan Bank. [BROWN1_H]

As expected, types (a) and (b) are both reversible, the latter having the verb in the passive: (a) *Peter's is the piano*, (b) *the piano is owned by Peter*. Examples can be seen in Figure 5-30.

(a) operative

the piano	is	**Peter's**
Identified/Token: possessed	Process: intensive	Identifier/Value: possessor

receptive

Peter's	is	**the piano**
Identified/Value: possessor	Process: intensive	Identifier/Token: possessed

(b) operative

Peter	owns	**the piano**
Identified/Token	Process: possession	Identifier/Value

receptive

the piano	is owned by	**Peter**
Identified/Value	Process: possession	Identifier/Token

Fig. 5-30 Possessive identifying clauses

In principle, possession can be thought of as another kind of circumstantial relation, which could be embodied in some such expression as 'at Peter is a piano', 'the piano is with Peter'. Many languages typically indicate possession by circumstantials of this kind. The nearest English is the verb *belong*; compare the dialectal form *is along o'me*.

Table 5-21 Possessive verbs

	Attributive	**Identifying**
neutral	have; belong to	possess
feature	feature, boast, sport, star	
ownership		own, deserve, need, lack
containment		comprise, contain, consist of, house; include, exclude, involve
benefaction		provide (sb with sth), afford (sb sth: this affords us many possibilities); owe (sb sth)

5.4.6 Summary of relational clauses

Table 5-22 brings together in a single display all the categories of the 'relational' clauses that have been introduced in this section. These include (i) the type of relation: 'intensive/circumstantial/possessive' with their subcategories; (ii) the relation-mode: 'attributive/identifying': within 'identifying', (a) the voice: 'operative/receptive', and (b) the information focus: 'marked/unmarked'.

The picture seems complex partly because it is a less familiar area, one that was little explored in the grammatical tradition. But these processes are critical in many types of text; the 'circumstantial identifying' ones, for example, figure centrally in the kind of grammatical metaphor that is characteristic of scientific discourse (see Chapter 10). More than other process types, the relationals have a rich potential for ambiguity, which is exploited in many registers from technocratic and political rhetoric to the discourse of poetry and folk sayings. Here is an example from the United States Congress, quoted in *Time Magazine*:

The loopholes that should be jettisoned first are the ones least likely to go.

Apart from the lexical puzzle of how to jettison a loophole, is this Token ^ Value ('because they are least likely to go they should be jettisoned first'), or it is Value ^ Token ('although they ought to be jettisoned first they are likely to be around the longest')? Compare the lines from Tennyson's *Choric Song* from the *Lotos-Eaters: Death is the end of life. – Ah, why Should life all labour be?* Here *why should life all labour be?* is clearly an 'attributive' clause. On the other hand *death is the end of life* is 'identifying'; but which is Token and which is Value? Does it mean 'once we die, life ends (that is what death means)', as in (a), or 'we die when life ends (that is how death may be recognized)', as in (b)?

(a) death	is	**the end of life**	(b) death	is	**the end of life**
Id/Tk		Ir/Vl	Id/Vl		Ir/Tk

It seems likely that we build both these interpretations into our understanding of the text. If we then give it a marked information focus, as in (c) and (d), we get two further senses with the roles recombined:

(c) **death**	is	the end of life	(d) **death**	is	the end of life
Ir/Tk		Id/Vl	Ir/Vl		Id/Tk

– where (c) means 'life ends when we die (that is how we know that life is ended)', and (d) means 'once life ends, we die (that is what it means for life to end)'. Precisely the same multiple ambiguity is present in sayings such as *home is where your heart is* (Token ^ Value 'because you live in a place you love it', or Value ^ Token 'because you love a place you feel at home there'), *an Englishman's home is his castle*, and other such distillations of age-old wisdom.

We will return for another look at the main types of process in Section 5.7. Meanwhile there are other aspects of transitivity to cover. In the next section we shall briefly survey the other three types that lie along each of their borders (cf. Figure 5-3).

Table 5-22 Summary of 'relational' clauses

(I) attributive (Carrier/Subject)								
(1) intensive			Sarah	is/seems	wise			
			John	became	a plumber			
			Carrier	Process: intensive	Attribute			

(2) circumstantial	(a) circ. as attr.		Pussy	is	in the well			
			the daughter	is/looks	like the mother			
			Carrier	Process: intensive	Attribute			
	(b) circ. as proc.		the poem	concerns	a fish			
			the fair	lasts	all day			
			Carrier	Process: circumstantial	Attribute			

(3) possessive	(a) poss. as attr.		the piano	is	Peter's			
			Carrier/ Possessed	Process: intensive	Attribute: Possessor			
	(b) poss. as proc.	(i) possessor as Carrier	Peter	has	a piano			
			Carrier/ Possessed	Process: possession	Attribute/ Possessed			
		(ii) Possessed as Carrier	the piano	belongs to	Peter			
			Carrier/ Possessed	Process: possession	Attribute/ Possessor			

(II) identifying			A: operative (Token/Subject)			B: receptive (Value/Subject)		
(1) intensive	(i) unmarked focus		Sarah	is	**the wise one**	the wise one	is	**Sarah**
			Mr Garrick	plays	**Hamlet**	Hamlet	is played	**by Mr Garrick**
			Id/Tk	Process: intensive	Ir/Vl	Id/Vl	Process: intensive	Ir/Tk
	(ii) marked focus		**Sarah**	is	the wise one	**the wise one**	is	Sarah
			Mr Garrick	plays	Hamlet	**Hamlet**	is played	by Mr Garrick
			Ir/Tk	Process: intensive	Id/Vl	Ir/Vl	Process: intensive	Id/Tk

(2) circumstantial	(a) circ. as part.	(i) unmarked focus	tomorrow	is	**the tenth**	the tenth	is	**tomorrow**
			by train	is	**the best way**	the best way	is	**by train**
			Id/Tk/Circ	Process: intensive	Ir/Vl/Circ	Id/Vl/Circ	Process: intensive	Ir/Tk/Circ

Table 5-22 Summary of 'relational' clauses (*contd*)

		(ii) marked focus	**tomorrow**	is	the tenth	**the tenth**	is	tomorrow
			by train	is	the best way	**the best way**	is	by train
			Ir/Tk/Circ	Process: intensive	Id/Vl/Circ	Ir/Vl/Circ	Process: intensive	Id/Tk/Circ
	(b) circ. as proc.	(i) unmarked focus	the daughter	resembles	**the mother**	the mother	is resembled	**by the daughter**
			applause	followed	**her act**	her act	was followed	**by applause**
			Id/Tk	Process: circ.	Ir/Vl	Id/Vl	Process: circ.	Ir/Tk
		(ii) marked focus	**the daughter**	resembles	the mother	**the mother**	is resembled	by the daughter
			applause	followed	her act	**her act**	was followed	by applause
			Ir/Tk	Process: circ.	Id/Vl	Ir/Vl	Process: circ.	Id/Tk

(3) possessive	(a) poss. as part.	(i) unmarked focus	the piano	is	**Peter's**	Peter's	is	**the piano**
			Id/Tk/Poss.	Process: intensive	Ir/Vl/Poss.	Id/Vl/Poss.	Process: intensive	Ir/Tk/Poss.
		(ii) marked focus	**the piano**	is	Peter's	**Peter's**	is	the piano
			Ir/Tk/Poss.	Process: intensive	Id/Vl/Poss.	Ir/Vl/Poss.	Process: intensive	Id/Tk/Poss.
	(b) poss. as proc.	(i) unmarked focus	Peter	owns	**the piano**	the piano	is owned	**by Peter**
			Id/Tk	Process: poss.	Ir/Vl	Id/Vl	Process: poss.	Ir/Tk
		(ii) marked focus	**Peter**	owns	the piano	**the piano**	is owned	by Peter
			Ir/Tk	Process: poss.	Id/Vl	Ir/Vl	Process: poss.	Id/Tk
			Subject			Subject		

5.5 Other process types; summary of process types

In the last three sections (5.2 to 5.4) we have been discussing the three principal types of process in the English clause: 'material', 'mental', 'relational'. They are the principal types in that they are the cornerstones of the grammar in its guise as a theory of experience, they present three distinct kinds of structural configuration, and they account for the majority of all clauses in a text ('material' and 'relational' seem to be roughly balanced in frequency over the language as a whole, followed by 'mental', although the pattern varies considerably among different registers). We can then go on to recognize three subsidiary process types, located at each of the boundaries: behavioural at the boundary between material and mental, verbal at the boundary between mental and relational, and existential at the boundary between relational and material (see Figure 5-3).

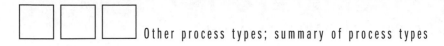

5.5.1 Behavioural clauses

These are processes of (typically human) physiological and psychological behaviour, like breathing, coughing, smiling, dreaming and staring (Table 5-23). They are the least distinct of all the six process types because they have no clearly defined characteristics of their own; rather, they are partly like the material and partly like the mental. The participant who is 'behaving', labelled **Behaver**, is typically a conscious being, like the Senser; the Process is grammatically more like one of 'doing'. The usual unmarked present tense for behavioural processes is present in present, like the material (e.g. *you're dreaming!*); however, we also find a simple present *in its unmarked* sense (i.e. not meaning habitual), e.g. *why do you laugh?*, alongside *why are you laughing?* (with scarcely any difference between them), which suggests an affiliation with a mental. For example:

> Sub Inspector Guha too **had fainted** and the others were looking at APV as at a unique building or beauty – as at a miracle. In that atmosphere of tension APV **laughed**, unconsciously sinister cynicism, causing the two nurses to jump on to the constable's inert body. [KOHL_L]

> He was foolish not to realize that this was happening to him, that he **could** possibly **have dreamt** about it. [Text 125]

> The amusing thing is, I woke of my own accord, a little bit before. I thought I **was dreaming**. But it was really happening. [KOHL_L]

Table 5-23 Inner and outer experience construed by different process types

	Inner	Inner => outer	Outer
material [doing]	–		she's walking (into the dining room)
behavioural [behaving]		she's laughing	
mental [sensing]	she rejoices		–
relational [being]	she's happy		she's in the dining room

The boundaries of behavioural processes are indeterminate; but we can recognize the kinds set out in Table 5-24 as typical.

Many of these verbs also occur behaviourally; contrast *think* as behavioural process, in *Be quiet! I'm thinking*, with *think* as mental process, in *they think we're stupid*.

Behavioural processes are almost always middle; the most typical pattern is a clause consisting of Behaver and Process only, like *Don't breathe!*, *No one's listening*, *He's always grumbling*. A common variant of these is that where the behaviour is dressed up as if it was a participant, like *she sang a song, he gave a great yawn*; this structure is typical in the everyday spoken language. The participant is analogous to the Scope of a 'material' clause (both being manifestations of the general function of Range; Section 5.7.3 on Range); we shall call it **Behaviour**.

301

Table 5-24 Examples of verbs serving as Process in behavioural clauses

(i)	[near mental]	processes of consciousness represented as forms of behaviour	look, watch, stare, listen, think, worry, dream
(ii)	[near verbal]	verbal processes as forms of behaviour	chatter, grumble, talk, gossip, argue, murmur, mouth
(iii)		physiological processes manifesting states of consciousness	cry, laugh, smile, frown, sigh, sob, snarl, hiss, whine, nod
(iv)		other physiological processes	breathe, sneeze, cough, hiccup, burp, vomit, faint, shit, yawn, sleep
(v)	[near material]	bodily postures and pastimes	sing, dance, lie (down), sit (up, down)

Certain types of circumstance are associated with behaviour processes: those of Matter with groups (i) and (ii), e.g. *dreaming of you, grumbled about the food*; Manner with the remainder, e.g. *breathe deeply, sit up straight*. Some of those in groups (i)–(iii) also regularly feature a prepositional phrase in it with *to*, *at* or *on*: *I'm talking to you, don't look at me, fortune is smiling on us*. These are, in origin, circumstances of Place; in the behavioural context they express orientation but we may continue to use that label. (The verb *watch* is anomalous: in *I'm watching you*, the tense suggests a behavioural process but the *you* appears as a participant, like the Phenomenon of a 'mental' clause. Since this is restricted to *watch*, we can label this participant as Phenomenon, indicating the mental analogue.) Note, finally, that while 'behavioural' clauses do not 'project' indirect speech or thought, they often appear in fictional narrative introducing direct speech, as a means of attaching a behavioural feature to the verbal process of 'saying' (see Chapter 7, Section 7.5.1):

'I was under the impression you just had, Miss Radcliffe – taken in a few details, if not actually down. Come, come,' he **chided** with a sardonic ***smile*** as Julia **frowned** her incomprehension. [Edwina Shore, 1991, *Not his property*, Mills & Boon, p. 10]

5.5.2 Verbal clauses

These are clauses of saying, as in *What did you say? – I said it's noisy in here*. Such clauses are an important resource in various kinds of discourse. They contribute to the creation of narrative by making it possible to set up dialogic passages, as in the following written narrative (Processes in 'verbal' clauses in bold; Processes in 'mental' ones in italics):

Text 5-11: Recreating – narrating (written, monologic): extract from a traditional folk tale [Text 65]

Chirumá would find any opportunity **to talk** to that priest about Kukul. Another day, he **told** him, 'Kukul is reckless. He stops to take care of the wounded and puts his men in danger.'

'Kukul is compassionate,' **replied** the priest.

'He is inexperienced,' **countered** Chirumá, as he sowed the seeds of doubt.

Here the 'verbal' clauses are all except for one accompanied by quotes. Similarly, when narrative passages are constructed in conversation, 'verbal' clauses are often used to develop

accounts of dialogue on the model of 'x said, then y said', together with quotes of what was said; for example:

Text 5-12: Sharing – casual conversation (spoken, dialogic): gossip [Text 72]

And Joanne came up and she **said**, 'Oh, can you do this?' and I **said**, 'Look you're at the end of a very long line; be prepared to wait' and she **said**, 'Well, she's at the Oncology clinic right now.' and I **said**, 'But these have to be done as well; I can't help.' and sort of smiled all the way through it and she **went**, ... I **said**, 'Look, it's three minutes to three; these should be done in a minute, if you want to wait till then.' and she **went** '(sigh) ahhh'.

The second example illustrates the fact that *say* is the unmarked member of the set of verbs serving as Process in 'verbal' clauses. The first example illustrates that as well, but it also includes two other common verbs, *told* and *talk*, and examples of verbs representing features of dialogic exchange, *reply* and *counter*. There is always one participant, representing the speaker; there may also be an additional one representing the addressee (e.g. *to that priest* in *to talk to that priest*, *him* in *he told him*). In news reporting, 'verbal' clauses allow the reporter to attribute information to sources, including officials, experts and eye witnesses, as in the following extract from a report of a ferry disaster:

Text 5-13: Reporting – chronicling: extract from a news report (written & monologic) [Text 4]

Several of the 18 survivors **said** the vessel, which appeared to be overloaded, lacked life vests and other safety equipment.

'In less than one minute, everything was gone,' survivor Somsak Thongtraipop **told** Thailand's The Nation newspaper.

He had heard the captain on the radio **being warned** by a crew member from another boat that there were big waves ahead and he should turn back.

There are, of course, innumerable other discourse uses of 'verbal' clauses. For example, they play an important role in academic discourse, making it possible to quote and report from various scholars while at the same time indicating the writer's stance with verbs like *point out*, *suggest*, *claim*, *assert*. But even from the examples above, we can already begin to see the main features of clauses of 'saying'.

'Saying' has to be interpreted in a rather broad sense; it covers any kind of symbolic exchange of meaning, like *the notice tells you to keep quiet*, or *my watch says it's half past ten*. The grammatical function of *you, I, the notice, my watch* is that of **Sayer**.

What about the function of *it's noisy in here, to keep quiet, it's half past ten?* In formal grammar what is said is treated as a 'noun clause object of the verb *say*', meaning a clause that is rankshifted by nominalization (see Chapter 6). But functionally this clause is not rankshifted; it functions as the secondary clause in a 'clause complex' (see Chapter 7), being either (a) directly quoted, as in (*he said*) *'I'm hungry'*, or (b) indirectly reported, as in (*he said*) *he was hungry*. This means that such sequences consist of two clauses, as in Figure 5-31. (Only the primary clause is a 'verbal' one, of course; the other may be a process type of any kind.) The status of the reported and quoted clause is analogous to that of an 'idea' clause introduced by a 'mental' clause: it is, as we have just noted, not rankshifted and in this respect such clauses differ from rankshifted 'fact' clauses serving as the Phenomenon of a 'mental' clause. This makes sense historically. In Old English, the structure was *he said/thought that: he was not hungry*, with *that* as a demonstrative in the 'verbal' or 'mental' clause 'pointing' to the clause representing the reported content of saying or sensing (see e.g. Hopper & Traugott, 1993). This demonstrative came to be reanalysed as a structural conjunction introducing the reported clause; but the reported clause itself remained outside the structure of the reporting clause – it has not been incorporated through downranking (in contrast with 'fact' clauses). Thus we would not expect to find such reported clauses serving as the Subject of a 'receptive' 'verbal' or 'mental' clause; for example, *that he was not hungry was said/thought by him* is highly unlikely.

The projected clause may be either (a) a proposition, realized by a finite clause, as in *Mr Deshmukh **said** that some dissidents had met him and **asked** him whether they should vote according to their conscience or discretion;* or (b) a proposal, realized by a perfective non-finite clause, as in *Bush **urges** China to release crew; The States **are asked** to mobilize additional resources for development as their contribution.* The proposal may be expressed alternatively by a modulated finite clause (see Chapter 4, Section 4.5): *Yet somebody **told** me that I mustn't repudiate my non-fiction, because it's saying very much what the fiction is saying.* For further discussion of these see Chapter 7, Section 7.5.

	John	said	'I'm hungry'
(a)	Sayer	Process	
	1: Quoting		2: Quoted

	John	said	he was hungry.
(b)	Sayer	Process	
	α: Reporting		β: Reported

Fig. 5-31 Verbal clauses projecting quotes and reports

It follows from what was said above about saying that, unlike 'mental' clauses, 'verbal' ones do not require a conscious participant. The Sayer can be anything that puts out a signal; for example:

And they've got *a great big sign* out the front **saying** pokies

The study **says** that such a diversified village structure produces a dualistic pattern of migration, ... [KOHL_A]

The letter **says**: 'It is observed that neither Mr J. D. Goyal nor Mr B. Dayal is eligible for appointment as Dy. ME as their regular service as Superintending Engineer commences from 24. 3. 76.' [KOHL_A]

In view of the nature of the 'Sayer', verbal processes might more appropriately be called 'symbolic' processes (cf. below on relationship to 'relational' processes). (It is worth noting, however, that there are other languages where the nature of the Sayer is more constrained than in English, essentially being confined to speakers and writers; see e.g. Steiner & Teich, 2004, on German, and Teruya, 2004, 2007, on Japanese.)

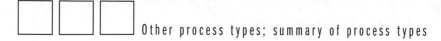

The Process of a 'verbal' clause is realized by a verbal group where the lexical verb is one of saying: see Table 5-25. The verb may be unaccented as in a 'relational' clause or accented as in a 'material' one. The tense is also in a sense intermediate between that of 'material' clauses and that of 'relational' ones. When the Sayer is realized by a nominal group denoting a conscious speaker, the tense selection may be like that of a 'material' clause, with the simple present indicating habit or generalization (i.e., an extended 'now') and the present in present indicating a narrower period of time; and the present in past often indicates simultaneity, just as it does with 'material' clauses:[41]

> But I **say** that sort of thing all the time. Didn't make a hoot of a difference to my situation. I **say**, I'm not applying for the job and, you know, you whinge on side. [UTS/Macquarie Corpus]

> [Di S:] **Were** you **saying** that you're engaged, when I walked in; I thought you **said** that you were engaged. – [Di:] Sort of, sort of … – [Di S:] That's wonderful; you **didn't tell** me that last time. [UTS/Macquarie Corpus]

However, the simple present also occurs in a more 'relational' sense of 'expresses the opinion that', as in *She **says** she prefers cigarettes to fish* [UTS/Macquarie Corpus]. And when the Sayer is realized by a nominal group denoting a symbol source other than a human speaker, the tense selection is likely to be more like that of a 'relational' clause, as in *the study **says** that such a diversified village structure produces a dualistic pattern of migration.* Here the 'present in' is unlikely: *the study is saying that* … would not occur. While such clauses are still clearly 'verbal', they are closer to 'relational' clauses than are 'verbal' ones with a human speaker as Subject (cf. below).

Table 5-25 Examples of verbs serving as Process in verbal clauses

TYPE		Examples of verbs
activity	targeting	praise, flatter, commend, compliment, congratulate; insult, abuse, slander, blame, criticize, chide, censure, pillory, rebuke
	talking	speak, talk
semiosis	(neutral quoting)	say, tell; go, be like
	indicating	tell (sb that), report, announce, notify, explain, argue, convince (that), persuade (sb that), promise (that)
		ask (sb whether), question, enquire (whether)
	imperating	tell (sb to do), ask (sb to do), order, command, require, promise, threaten, persuade (sb to do), convince (sb to do), entreat, implore, beg

---

[41] The present can alternate with the past in conversational narratives just as it can with 'material' clauses: *The guy **says** sorry she hasn't got her ticket, you have to speak to my supervisor blah blah blah and finally after about another two minutes he **said** oh alright two dollars. So we **go** okay so Brenda gets her money out gives him two bucks and he **says** as she sort of driving away by the way what's your rego? And Brenda **calls** out I don't know I've stolen it and drives off.* [UTS/Macquarie Corpus]

In certain respects, 'verbal' clauses are thus like 'behavioural' ones, exhibiting certain characteristics of other process types – tense like 'material' or 'relational', ability to project like 'mental'. But while 'behavioural' process clauses are not so much a distinct type of process, but rather a cluster of small subtypes blending the material and the mental into a continuum, 'verbal' process clauses do display distinctive patterns of their own. Besides being able to project, in the unique manner described above, they accommodate three further participant functions in addition to the Sayer: (1) Receiver, (2) Verbiage, (3) Target. The first two of these are 'oblique' participants, as described in Sections 5.6.1 and 5.6.2 below.

(1) The **Receiver** is the one to whom the saying is directed; e.g. *me, your parents, the court* in *tell me the whole truth, did you repeat that to your parents?, describe to the court the scene of the accident*. The Receiver may be Subject in a clause which is 'receptive'; e.g. *I* in *I wasn't told the whole truth*. The Receiver is realized by a nominal group typically denoting a conscious being (a potential speaker), a collective or an institution; the nominal group either occurs on its own or is marked by a preposition – almost always *to* but sometimes *of*. The range of realizational possibilities depends on the lexical verb of the verbal group realizing the Process; for example, *tell sb, say to sb, demand of sb* (see Matthiessen, 1995a: 292).

(2) The **Verbiage** is the function that corresponds to what is said, representing it as a class of thing rather than as a report or quote; e.g. *what* in *What did you say?* above. This may mean one of the two things.

(a) It may be the ***content of what is said***; e.g. *your family* in *But when people describe your family, they don't talk about your nephews and nieces; the latest decision of Bihar to ban English in schools* in *How else would you explain the latest decision of Bihar to ban English in schools?* The Verbiage may construe the topic of what is said, as with *describe your family* above; as the following clause illustrates, this type of Verbiage is close in meaning to a circumstance of Matter (*talk about your nephews and nieces*). If the verbal process is one that projects goods-&-services rather than information, like *order* or *promise*, the Verbiage refers to these: e.g. *a steak* in *I ordered a steak, those earrings* in *those earrings were promised to another customer*.[42]

(b) It may be the ***name of the saying***; for example *a question* in *let me ask you a question, another word* in *now don't you say another word!* This type also occurs with very general verbs like *give* and *make* (as in 'material' clauses with Process + Scope), e.g. *give the order, make a statement*. The name of the saying includes speech functional categories such as *question, statement, order, command* – often with collocational constraints in relation to the lexical verb in the Process (*ask + question, make + statement, give + order, issue + command, tell + lie*) and generic categories such as *story, fable, joke, report, summary*. The name of a language can be construed as Verbiage, e.g. *they were speaking Arabic*; alternatively, this is construed circumstantially as Manner, e.g. *they were speaking a few words in Arabic*.

The two types of Verbiage are not sharply distinct; in between (a) *tell me your experience* and (b) *tell me a story* is something such as *tell me the truth*, where *the truth* could be interpreted either as (a) 'the events as they happened' or as (b) 'a narrative that is factual'.

---

[42] *Order, promise* and other such processes can be construed with a Beneficiary (see Section 5.7.3). With *promise* this Beneficiary is the Receiver of a 'verbal' clause, but with *order* this Beneficiary is more like the Client of a 'material' clause denoting the creation of goods or the performance of a service; for example: *You felt alright on Friday 'cause you ordered yourself a nice big pizza* (cf. *you ordered a nice big pizza for yourself*). Here the 'Receiver' would be represented like a circumstance: *you ordered yourself a nice big pizza from the waiter*.

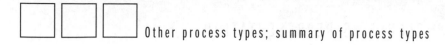

(3) The **Target** occurs only in a subtype of 'verbal' clauses; this function construes the entity that is targeted by the process of saying, which may be a person, an object or an abstraction; e.g.

He also **accused** <u>Krishan Kant</u> of conspiring with Bansi Lal in destabilising the set-up in Haryana who, in turn, issued a press statement saying that Devi Lal was suffering from 'hallucinations'. [KOHL_A]

I think there are serious problems in her work traceable to the writer's distance, or lack of it, from all this; but <u>she</u> **is** rightly **praised** at least for showing it. [ACE_G]

Rather than **criticize** <u>my teaching ability</u>, he actually **praised** <u>it</u>. [COCA]

Here the Sayer is, as it were, acting verbally on another party, judging them positively or negatively (cf. Martin & White, 2005, on appraisal of the judgement type). Verbs that accept a Target (see Table 5-25) do not easily project reported speech[43]; but some aspect of the Sayer's words may be quoted in the representation of the Target, of a circumstance of Cause or Role, or of an enhancing clause of reason for the judgement:

In June, Gates **praised** 'the unprecedented cooperation between the nations of the gulf.' [COCA]

Charles C Jones's 1883 The History of Georgia **praised** Zubly as 'learned and eloquent, public spirited, and of marked ability' and described his early career as 'consistent and patriotic.' [COCA]

Targeted verbal clauses are closer to the Actor + Goal structure of a 'material' clause (cf. *what he did to Krishan Kant was accuse him*). The source of praise, blame, etc. is construed either as a circumstance or as an enhancing hypotactic clause (e.g. *of conspiring with Bansi Lal ...; for showing it*) – but not as a projection (Japanese is interestingly different in that 'targeted verbal' clauses may project; see Teruya, 2007).

As the different types in Table 5-25 illustrate, different aspects of our experience of speech events may be lexicalized in verbs of saying, including the speech function (e.g. *ask, urge*), the turn (e.g. *reply, add*), the medium (e.g. *write*), manner (e.g. *enthuse, gush, rave*) and the channel (e.g. *email, phone*). As technology is opening up new channels, new verbs are added to the resources of the 'verbal' lexicogrammar and are pressed into reporting or quoting service, e.g.:

'Ruiz's passing at 70 represents a tremendous loss for contemporary filmmaking,' **blogs** Dave Kehr.

He **texted** me back that Somer didn't come home from school. [COCA]

5.5.3 Existential clauses

These represent that something exists or happens, as in *In the caves around the base of Ayers Rock, there are aboriginal paintings that tell the legends of this ancient people; In Bihar, there was no comparable political campaign; There was confusion, shouting and breaking of chairs.* While 'existential' clauses are not, overall, very common in discourse – on the

---

[43] When verbs that serve in targeted verbal clauses occur in verbal clauses together with quotations, the participant construed as being addressed by the Sayer functions as Receiver rather than as Target: *'Those are fine letters,' I **praised** her* [COCA].

order of 3 to 4 per cent of all clauses are 'existential', they make an important, specialized contribution to various kinds of text. For example, in narrative, they serve to introduce central participants in the Placement (Setting, Orientation) stage at the beginning of a story (cf. Hasan, 1984/1996: Ch. 3); limericks illustrate this in compressed form:

Text 5-14: Recreating – narrating (written, monologic): limerick [Edward Lear]
There was <u>an old person of Dover</u>,

Who rushed through a field of blue Clover;

But some very large bees, stung his nose and his knees,

So he very soon went back to Dover.

Textually, the Theme is just the feature of existence (*there*), allowing the addressee to prepare for something that is about to be introduced; and this something is presented as New information. (For this reason, 'existential' clauses have been interpreted as 'presentative' or 'presentational' constructions; see e.g. Hetzron, 1975; Van Valin & LaPolla, 1997: 208; Downing, 1990.) After the Placement stage, existential clauses are also used to introduce phenomena into the (predominantly) material stream of narration; and in guidebook texts, they serve to introduce places or features of interest that may be encountered on walking and driving tours; for example:

I had just put the baby down on the beach, and was going in the water to see if it was okay, for the kids to go in the water, and the crocodile came waaaah out at me and at the baby that I'd sat on the beach. I had seconds, to rab, to grab that baby and run up the beach, with that crocodile coming out at me, coming out towards me. And do you know what? **There was** <u>a big</u>, **there was** <u>a big, sort of platform, rock platform</u>, near the beach and the kids all raced up onto the platform, it's about as this roof up there. And I grabbed the baby, who was crying its head off [yawn], by this stage terrified. Can you imagine if you saw a crocodile coming towards you with an open mouth, how you'd feel? [Text 57]

Llantwit Major. An attractive small town that was one of the first major centres of learning in Europe. Saints like David, Teilo and Samson of Dol studied here in what were the Dark Ages for the rest of Europe but the Golden Age of the Welsh saints. In the church **there is** <u>a fine collection of Celtic crosses</u>.

The word *there* in such clauses is neither a participant nor a circumstance – it has no representational function in the transitivity structure of the clause; but it serves to indicate the feature of existence, and it is needed interpersonally as a Subject (Chapter 4, Section 4.6).[44] Unlike participants and circumstances this existential *there* cannot be queried, theme-predicated or theme-identified; we cannot say *Where is?* in response to *there is a fine collection of Celtic crosses*, we cannot say *it is there that is a fine collection of Celtic crosses* (cf.

---

[44] Contrast English with languages where there is no interpersonal requirement for the presence of Subject in a clause (cf. Matthiessen, 2004b: 600). In such languages, 'existential' clauses typically have only Process + Existent without a Subject (unless the Existent is the Subject); and the Process is an existential/possessive/locative verb such as *hay* in Spanish, *you* in Mandarin or *var/yok* in Turkish. The English *there* is locative in origin; but in some other Germanic languages the Subject is the equivalent of *it*, as in the German construction *es gibt*. Such existential clauses are, not surprisingly, concerned more with ontological existence than with locative existence (cf. Matthiessen, 2001). For a discussion of English *there* as a locative setting, see Davidse (1992b).

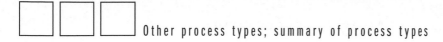

it is there that they keep a fine collection of Celtic crosses) and we cannot say *there is where (what) is a fine collection of Celtic crosses/where (what) is a fine collection of Celtic crosses is there*. Phonologically *there* is non-salient, and the vowel is often reduced to schwa (hence identical with *the*); it is thus distinct from the Adjunct *there* which is a circumstantial element. Contrast (i) existential *there's your father on the line*, with reduced *there* [ðə] as Subject, and response *Oh, is there?*, and (ii) circumstantial relational *there's your father*, with salient *there* [ðɛə] as Adjunct, and response *Oh, is he?* In (ii), but not in (i), *there's* is in contrast with *here's*.

'Existential' clauses typically have the verb *be*; in this respect also they resemble 'relational' clauses. But the other verbs that commonly occur are mainly different from either the 'attributive' or the 'identifying': see Table 5-26.

Frequently an 'existential' clause contains a distinct circumstantial element of time or place, as in *there was a picture on the wall*; if the circumstantial element is thematic, the Subject *there* may be omitted – but it will turn up if there is a tag: *on the wall (there) was a Picasso painting, wasn't there?*, *all around (there) grew a thick hedge*. Another common way of 'locating' the process in space-time is to follow it with a non-finite clause, e.g. *there was an old woman tossed up in a basket, there's someone waiting at the door, there's a patient to see you*; the two together form a clause complex (cf. Chapter 7, Section 7.4.2.2(ii)).

The entity or event that is being said to exist is labelled, simply, **Existent**. In principle, there can 'exist' any kind of phenomenon that can be construed as a 'thing': person, object, institution, abstraction; but also any action or event, as in *is there going to be a storm?, there was another robbery in the street*. And here the 'existential' merges into the 'material' type of clause: there is little difference in meaning between 'existential' *there was a robbery* and 'material: creative' *a robbery took place* (note the present tense *a robbery is taking place*). Existentials are illustrated in Figure 5-32.

there	was	a storm
	Process	Existent: event

on the wall	there	hangs	a picture
circumstance		Process	Existent: entity

there	is	a man	at the door
	Process	Existent: entity	Circumstance

there	was	an old woman	tossed up	in a basket
	Process	Existent: event	Process	circumstance
α: Extended			β: Extending	

Fig. 5-32 Existential clauses

On this borderline between the 'existential' and the 'material' there is a special category of processes to do with the weather: **meteorological** processes like *it's raining, the wind's blowing, there's going to be a storm*. Some are construed existentially, e.g. *there was a storm/ hurricane/breeze/gale/shower/blizzard*. Some are construed as material events, e.g. *the wind's* *blowing, the sun's shining, the clouds are coming down.* Some are construed as relational attributives: *it's foggy/cloudy/misty/hot/humid/sunny/frosty*; here the *it* can be interpreted as a Carrier, since it is possible to substitute the weather, the sky or the (time of) day. Finally, some are construed as *it* + a verb in the 'present in present' tense: *it's raining/hailing/snowing/freezing/pouring/drizzling/lightning/thundering.*

This last type is unique in English, in that it has no participant in it. The *it* serves the interpersonal function of Subject, like the *there* in an 'existential' clause, but has no function in transitivity – if you are told that it's raining, you cannot ask *What is?* and the *it* cannot be theme-predicated (we cannot say *it's it that's raining*) or serve as an identified Theme or Rheme (we cannot say *it is what's raining/what's raining is it*). On the other hand the tense is clearly that of a 'material' process. These clauses can be analysed as consisting of a single element, the Process; they are the limiting case of a 'material' process clause. With meteorological events the grammar completes the circle of experience, tying these in with the concrete happenings with which we started.

Table 5-26 Examples of verbs serving as Process in existential clauses

Type		Verbs
neutral	exist	exist, remain
	happen	arise; occur, come about, happen, take place
+ circumstantial feature	time	follow, ensue
	place	sit, stand, lie; hang, rise, stretch, emerge, grow
abstract		erupt, flourish, prevail

5.5.4 Summary of process types

Table 5-27 gives a summary of the types of process that we have identified in the grammar of English, together with their general category meaning and the participants that are associated with each.

Section 5.6 describes the circumstantial functions. The total set of functions used in interpreting the clause as representation, with criteria for recognizing the various types of process, is set out at the end of the chapter, in Table 5-41 and Table 5-45.

5.6 Circumstantial elements

5.6.1 General characteristics

We began this chapter with the concept of process types, taking in the Process function, together with those participant functions which were critical to the distinction between one process type and another (Sections 5.1–5.5). We now come to the circumstantial elements, which lie at the other end of the continuum (cf. Figure 5-5): typically, they occur freely in all types of process, and with essentially the same significance wherever they occur. There are, of course, some combinations that are less likely, and some special interpretations. For example, circumstances of Matter are fairly common with 'mental' and 'verbal' clauses but quite rare with the other process types, except for certain 'behavioural' clauses. And in an

Table 5-27 Process types, their meanings, and characteristic participants

PROCESS TYPE	Category meaning	Participants, directly involved	Participants, obliquely involved

material:
   action
   event
	'doing'
	   'doing'
	   'happening'
		Actor, Goal	Recipient, Client; Scope; Initiator;
			Attribute

behavioural	'behaving'	Behaver	Behaviour

mental:
   perception
   cognition
   desideration
   emotion
	'sensing'
	   'seeing'
	   'thinking'
	   'wanting'
	   'feeling'
		Senser, Phenomenon	Inducer

verbal	'saying'	Sayer, Target	Receiver; Verbiage

relational:
   attribution
   identification
	'being'
	   'attributing'
	   'identifying'
		Carrier, Attribute
		Identified, Identifier; Token, Value
			Attributor; Beneficiary
			Assigner

existential	'existing'	Existent	

'attributive' clause, Manner circumstances are fairly unusual, and circumstances of Place often carry a feature of time as well, e.g. *I get hungry on the beach* 'when I am on the beach'. But these tend to be rather specific, and we shall not deal with them here.

There is thus a continuity between the categories of participant and circumstance; and the same continuity can be seen in the forms by which the two are realized. The distinction between participant and circumstance is probably relevant in all languages; but in some it is drawn relatively sharply, while in others it is shaded and blurred. We shall see in the next section (5.7) that it has become blurred in English, and for an interesting reason: it has been superseded by something else.

Let us look at the notion of 'circumstance' from our usual three perspectives. (i) As far as meaning is concerned, we used the expression 'circumstances associated with' or 'attendant on the process', referring to examples such as the location of an event in time or space, its manner, or its cause; and these notions of 'when, where, how and why' the thing happens provided the traditional explanation, by linking circumstances to the four WH-forms that were adverbs rather than nouns. (ii) This ties in with the second perspective, that from the clause itself: whereas participants function in the mood grammar as Subject or Complement, circumstances map onto Adjuncts; in other words, they have not got the potential of becoming Subjects, of taking over the modal responsibility for the clause as exchange. (iii) Thirdly, looked at from below, they are typically expressed not as nominal groups but as either adverbial groups or prepositional phrases – mostly the latter, since adverbial groups are largely confined to one type, those of Manner.

But a prepositional phrase is an odd sort of hybrid construction. It has a nominal group inside it, as a constituent, so it looks bigger than a group; and yet it is still not quite a clause. In English, this nominal group inside a prepositional phrase is no different from a nominal

group functioning directly as a participant in a clause, and in principle every nominal group can occur in either context; e.g. *the mighty ocean*, participant in *little drops of water make the mighty ocean*, circumstance in *I'll sail across the mighty ocean*. And if we focus attention on the nominal group in its relation to the overall process, it still seems to be some kind of participant: even in the sailing, the mighty ocean does play some part. But it is allowed in, as it were, only indirectly – through the intermediary of a preposition, as we expressed it above.

We can make a contrast, then, between **direct** and **indirect participants**, using 'indirect participant' to refer to the status of a nominal group that is inside a prepositional phrase. (For the structure of the prepositional phrase see Chapter 6, Section 6.5.) We have already seen that the participant roles of (1) Client, Recipient and Receiver and (2) Scope, Behaviour and Verbiage are sometimes expressed 'indirectly' in this sense, as in *gave money to the cashier, plays beautifully on the piano*. The elements we are treating as 'circumstantial' are those in which the participant typically – and in many cases obligatorily – is indirect, being linked into the process via some preposition or other.

What, then, is the set of functions that is construed as circumstantial in the grammar of the clause as representation? We can start from time, place, cause and manner; but we need to realign them somewhat, to add to them, and to interpret them in relation to the process types as a whole. The list of circumstantial elements will then be as in Table 5-28. Set out in this way they appear as a fairly arbitrary list. But if we think of 'circumstantiation' as a general concept, in the context of the overall interpretation of transitivity as the grammar of experience, we can get a sense of the semantic space that is being constructed by these circumstantial elements. One way of doing this is to relate them to the various types of process that have been described above.

We are able to do this because a circumstantial element is itself, from this point of view, a process that has become parasitic on another process. Instead of standing on its own, it serves as an expansion of something else. Most circumstantials can be derived from the three types of relational process; the largest group, not surprisingly, from that type of relational process for which we used the label 'circumstantial'. We could illustrate the principles as follows:

(a) relational: circumstantial	Jack was building a house ...	
1 when? ('it was during')	throughout the year	Extent: duration
2 where? ('it was at')	near the river	Location: place
3 how? ('it was by')	out of brick	Manner: means
4 why? ('it was for')	for his retirement	Cause: purpose
5 under what conditions?	despite his illness	Contingency: concession
(b) relational: possessive	Jack was building a house ...	
6 who with? ('he had')	with his daughters	Accompaniment: comitation
(c) relational: intensive	Jack was building a house ...	
7 what as? ('it was')	as a vacation home	Role: guise

Table 5-28 Types of circumstantial element

		TYPE		Wh- item	Examples of realization
enhancing	1	Extent	distance	*how far?*	*for; throughout* 'measured' nominal group
			duration	*how long?*	*for; throughout* 'measured' nominal group
			frequency	*how many times?*	'measured' nominal group
	2	Location	place	*where?* [*there, here*]	*at, in, on, by, near; to, towards, into, onto, (away) from, out of, off; behind, in front of, above, below, under, alongside ...* adverb of place: *abroad, overseas, home, upstairs, downstairs, inside, outside; out, up, down, behind; left, right, straight ...; there, here*
			time	*when?* [*then, now*]	*at, in, on; to, until, till, towards, into, from, since, during, before, after* adverb of time: *today, yesterday, tomorrow; now, then*
	3	Manner	means	*how?* [*thus*]	*by, through, with, by means of, out of* [+ material], *from*
			quality	*how?* [*thus*]	*in* + *a* + quality (e.g. *dignified*) + *manner/way, with* + abstraction (e.g. *dignity*); *according to* adverbs in *-ly, -wise; fast, well; together, jointly, separately, respectively*
			comparison	*how? what like?*	*like, unlike; in* + *the manner of ...* adverbs of comparison *differently*
			degree	*how much?*	*to* + *a high/low/... degree/extent;* adverbs of degree *much, greatly, considerably, deeply* [often collocationally linked to lexical verb, e.g. *love* + *deeply, understand* + *completely*]
	4	Cause	reason	*why?*	*because of, as a result of, thanks to, due to, for want of, for, of, out of, through*
			purpose	*why? what for?*	*for, for the purpose of, for the sake of, in the hope of*
			behalf	*who for?*	*for, for the sake of, in favour of, against* ['not in favour of'], *on behalf of*
	5	Contingency	condition	*why?*	*in case of, in the event of*
			default		*in default of, in the absence of, short of, without* ['if it had not been for']
			concession		*despite, in spite of*

Table 5-28 Types of circumstantial element (*contd*)

		TYPE		Wh- item	Examples of realization
extending	6	Accompaniment	comitative	*who/what with?*	*with; without*
			additive	*and who/what else?*	*as well as, besides; instead of*
elaborating	7	Role	guise	*what as?*	*as, by way of, in the role/shape/guise/form of*
			product	*what into?*	*into*
projection	8	Matter		*what about?*	*about, concerning, on, of, with reference to, in ['with respect to']*
	9	Angle	source		*according to, in the words of*
			viewpoint		*to, in the view/opinion of, from the standpoint of*

The other two, Matter and Angle, can be related to verbal processes:

(d) verbal: Verbiage	Jack told his friends	
8 what about? ('said ...')	about the sale	Matter
(e) verbal: Sayer	the price was good	
9 says who? ('... said')	according to Jack	Angle: source

We shall see later on that both these patterns – both types of process and types of circumstantial element – are in turn part of a more general picture which we shall be able to establish after we have explored the clause complex and conjunction (see Chapter 10, especially Table 10-3; see also Table 5-6 above). For the present discussion, what is important is the notion of 'circumstance' as a kind of additional minor process, subsidiary to the main one, but embodying some of the features of a relational or verbal process, and so introducing a further entity as an indirect participant in the clause.

5.6.2 Types of circumstance

5.6.2.1 Expansion: enhancing

Enhancing circumstances augment the configuration of process + participants through the specification of extent or location in time or space of the unfolding of the process, the manner of the unfolding of the process, the cause of the unfolding of the process, or the contingency of the unfolding of the process. These enhancing circumstances range on a cline (1) from circumstances that are like a feature of the process construed circumstantially, e.g. *unsteadily* (Manner: quality) in

> He swayed like a drunkard, his arms milling in slow circles. He paced forward **unsteadily**, leaning too far back, his head tilted oddly. [BROWN1_K]

(2) to circumstances that are like indirect participants, e.g. *because of his asthma* (Cause: reason) in

Cam could not sleep **because of his asthma**. [ACE_A]

The location of circumstances on this cline will determine patterns of agnation. For example, around (1), Process with lexically incorporated feature of manner: *sway* can be glossed as Process + Manner, 'move slowly or rhythmically', and *wobble* as 'move unsteadily from side to side'; but around (2), Cause: *because of his asthma* is agnate with either a participant, e.g. *asthma prevented Cam from sleeping* or to an enhancing clause of cause, e.g. *Cam could not sleep because he had asthma*.

(1) Extent and (2) Location. The circumstantials of Extent and Location construe the unfolding of the process in space and time. They form a four-term set as shown in Table 5-29.

Table 5-29 Circumstantials of extent and location

	Spatial	Temporal
extent (including interval)	**Distance** walk (for) seven miles stop every tend yards	**Duration** stay (for) two hours pause every ten minutes **Frequency** knock three times
location	**Place** work in the kitchen	**Time** get up at six o'clock

Extent construes the extent of the unfolding of the process in space-time: the distance in space over which the process unfolds or the duration in time during which the process unfolds. The interrogative forms for Extent are *how far?*, *how long?*, *how many* [measure units]?, *how many times?* The typical structure is a nominal group with quantifier, either definite, e.g. *five days*, or indefinite, e.g. *many miles, a long way*; this occurs either with or without preposition, the most usual preposition being *for*:

||| Clay particles are very small || and sink slowly; || they can be carried **thousands of miles** by gentle currents. ||| [Text 68]

||| He and seven others survived || by clinging to a floating fish container **for hours**.||| [Text 4]

||| Er, well now, **how far** are you going away? ||| [Text 34]

||| **How long** were you at camp **for**? ||| [Text 34]

(Note that this is *how far?* in the sense of 'over what distance?', not in the sense of 'at what distance' (*how far away?*), which is Location.) The category of Extent includes 'interval', which has a corresponding question form *how often?*, in the sense of 'at what intervals?'. In the temporals there is an additional category of 'frequency', *how many times?* This is related to the interpersonal category of usuality (see Chapter 4, Section 4.5), but it is not identical to it; usuality is a modal assessment referring to position on a scale between positive and negative (always/never), whereas frequency is the extent of repetition of the occurrence of the process. The categories of extent and usuality may, however, work together, as in a narrative where habitude is established: [Extent:] *Every day, all day long, Ka-ha-si slept on a warm caribou hide near the lamp in his igloo. 'Why do you not play with other children?' his mother* [Finite: usuality] *would ask. 'You should be learning how to hunt and fish so you will grow to be a good man.' But Ka-ha-si* [Adjunct: usuality] *never answered.*

There is no very sharp line separating (circumstantial) expressions of Extent from (participant) expressions of Scope of the enhancing type; but there is a distinction between them: Extent is expressed in terms of some unit of measurement, like yards, laps, rounds, years, whereas Scope in terms other than measure units (contrast *they walked five miles* with *they walked the streets*); and being a participant, the Scope has the potential of being able to serve as Subject.

Location construes the location of the unfolding of the process in space-time: the place where it unfolds or the time when it unfolds. The general interrogatives of Location are *where?*, *when?*. Place includes not only static location in space, but also the source, path and destination of movement. Similarly, time includes not only static location in time, but also the temporal analogues of source, path and destination. For example:

||| **Outside the station**, turn **right into Pitt Street then right again at Park** l **Street** || and **at George Street** turn **left** || and walk **to St. Andrews Cathedral**. ||| [Text 22]

||| The foundation stone of the cathedral was laid by Governor Macquarie **on August 31, 1819**, || but construction was axed on the recommendation of Colonial Commissioner Bigge || and the project wasn't restarted **until 1837**. ||| [Text 22]

The typical structure is an adverbial group or prepositional phrase; examples are *down*, *underneath*, *by the door*, *in Canberra*, *long ago*, *before sunset*, *on Wednesday evening*, *among friends*, *between you and me*. Note adverbial group/prepositional phrase complexes expressing spatial and temporal paths (see Chapter 8), as in:

||| It's different for a woman though as opposed to a man || because I've just hitched recently **from Byron to Sydney** || because my money was locked in a car || and I did not have any. ||| [UTS/Macquarie Corpus]

Under certain conditions a temporal preposition may be left out, as in *let's meet next Wednesday, they left last week.*

There are close parallels between temporal and spatial expressions, the most significant ones being the following. (i) As already indicated, both incorporate the notions of extent and location: we recognize not only extent and location in space but also extent and location in time. (ii) In both time and space, extent is measurable in standard units: we have hours and years, and we have inches and miles, and acres, or their metric equivalents (which have not yet become domesticated in the English language). (iii) In both time and space, both extent and location may be either definite or indefinite; see Table 5-30. (iv) In both spatial and temporal location, the location may be either absolute, or relative to the 'here-&-now'; and, if relative, may be either near or remote; see Table 5-31. (v) In both spatial and temporal location there is a distinction between rest and motion; and, within motion, between motion towards and motion away from, as shown in Table 5-32.

Table 5-30 Definite and indefinite extent and location

		Spatial	**Temporal**
extent	**definite**	five miles	five years
	indefinite	a long way	a long time
location	**definite**	at home	at noon
	indefinite	near	soon

Table 5-31 Absolute and relative location

			Spatial	**Temporal**
location	absolute		in Australia	in 1985
	relative	**near**	here, nearby	now, recently
		remote	there, a long way away	then, a long time ago

Table 5-32 Rest and motion

			Spatial	**Temporal**
location	rest		in Sydney, at the airport	on Tuesday, at noon
	motion	**towards**	to Sydney	till Tuesday
		away from	from Sydney	since Tuesday

However, this spatio-temporal parallelism is far from complete; and in recent centuries the language seems to have been moving away from it.

Space includes not only concrete space, but also abstract space. Abstract space covers a range of experiential domains that are construed on the model of space; for example:

||| Nearby he could see the raspberry canes, || in whose shadow he had played with the Boy || and a great sadness came **over him**. ||| [Text 28]

||| So, **where** is all this taking us? ||| Many places, but most obviously to the International Geosphere-Biosphere Program (IGBP). ||| [Text 32]

||| This brings us back **to the purpose of this symposium**. ||| [Text 32]

||| But the fact that I'd sort of gone **from that status position down to a mere housemaid**, you know? ||| [UTS/ Macquarie Corpus]

||| We pledge our-selves to liberate all our people **from the continuing bondage of poverty, deprivation, suffering, gender and other discrimination**. ||| [Text 104]

As the examples illustrate, the construal of abstract space often involves a 'material' process of motion through space like *come, go, bring, take*. The abstractness is a feature of the clause as a whole, not just of a single element; but the 'clue' to the abstract interpretation may be a single element or a combination of elements. The Location itself may be an abstract one, as with *the purpose of this symposium* in *this brings us back to the purpose of this symposium* (contrast *this bus brings us back to Sydney*); the participant placed in relation to the Location may be an abstraction, as with *sadness* in *a great sadness came over him* (contrast *a small bird came over him*); or a participant causing this participant to be placed in relation to the Location may be an abstraction, as in *where is all this taking us?* (contrast *where is the bus taking us?*).

Abstract space is the source of various expressions that serve as realizations of other types of circumstance such as Manner (e.g. *walk on one's legs*, *make wine out of grapes*), Role (e.g. *cut into cubes*, *translate from Spanish into English*). It can be difficult to determine whether such an expression serves as an abstract Location or as a circumstance of another type. But probes involving Wh- items usually help us drawn the line (cf. the Wh- item column in Table 5-28). For example, using spatial *where*, we can say *where the dollar rose was to its highest point in the past year*, which indicates that *to its highest point in the past year* is a Location in abstract space rather than a circumstance of some other kind. In contrast, we cannot say *where she talked was on the meaning of life*, which indicates that *on the meaning of life* is not a Location in abstract space but rather a circumstance of another kind.

(3) Manner. The circumstantial element of Manner construes the way in which the process is actualized. Manner comprises four subcategories: Means, Quality, Comparison, Degree. These cover a considerable range; Means is close to the participant role of Agent and Comparison is like a participant in a clause with the same kind of process, whereas Quality and Degree are like features of the Process itself. These differences in status are reflected in realizational tendencies: Means and Comparison tend to be realized by prepositional phrases, whereas Quality and Comparison tend to be realized by adverbial groups.

(a) Means refers to the means whereby a process takes place; it is typically expressed by a prepositional phrase with the preposition *by* or *with*. The interrogative forms are *how?* and *what with?*. Examples:

||| It seems to me [[that answers to most such questions have to be learned **by experiment**]]. ||| [Text 212]

||| What were you making **with that**? ||| [Text 76]

||| These men were the philosophes, the popularizers of the new thought, || who sought to convince the educated public **by means of the written word**. ||| [Text 122]

||| You don't learn about it **through hearsay** either. ||| [Text 17]

||| Can you hop **on your hind legs**? ||| [Text 28]

||| The Conservatives have not hesitated to make political capital **out of the defence chief's tactless observations**. ||| [KOHL_B]

In addition to generalized expressions of means such as *by train*, *by chance*, the category includes, in principle, the concepts of both agency and instrumentality. The instrument is not a distinct category in English grammar; it is simply a kind of means. So given *the pig was beaten with the stick*, the corresponding active form is *she beat the pig with the stick*; in both, *with the stick* is a circumstantial expression of Manner.

The agent, however, although it is expressed as a prepositional phrase, typically functions as a participant in the clause; given *the pig was beaten by the stick*, the corresponding active

is *the stick beat the pig* (not *she beat the pig by the stick*), where *the stick* has the function of Actor.

The line between agent and instrument is not always very sharp. In a mental process clause we may have either *she was pleased by the gift* or *she was pleased with the gift*, without any real difference in function, and either one could remain as a Manner element in the active: *he pleased her with his gift, he pleased her by his gift*. Nevertheless, there is a significant distinction in the grammar between manner and agency, such that a passive *by* phrase, if it could not remain unchanged in the corresponding active clause, is interpreted as a participant, not as a circumstance of Manner. This reflects the fact that semantically, whereas the instrument is not usually an inherent element in the process, the agent typically is – although less clearly so when the process is expressed in the passive. For more on the concept of agency, see Section 5.7 below.

(b) **Quality** is typically expressed by an adverbial group, with *-ly* adverb as Head; the interrogative is *how?* or *how ... ?* plus appropriate adverb. Less commonly, Quality is realized by a prepositional phrase. The general type is one where the preposition is *in* or *with* and the Head/Thing of the nominal group is the name of 'manner', either *manner* or *way*, or of a qualitative dimension such as *speed, tone, skill, ease, difficulty, term*; but phrasal expressions of Quality also include more specific types such as specifications of the manner of movement (e.g. *on your hind legs* below). Quality expressions characterize the process in respect of any variable that makes sense; for example:

||| Morgan **calmly** surveyed the scenery from the top of Rock Island ||| [Text 22]

||| I experienced the despair of [[watching [[my partner and manager die **wretchedly, slowly, bitterly**]]]] . ||| [Text 24]

||| We know it **well** || that none of us [[acting **alone**]] can achieve success. ||| [Text 104]

||| He learned to walk **in a certain way**, || to have a certain accent, || all based on the nose. ||| [Text 17]

||| I don't think **that way** at all anymore, || ... ||| [Text 17]

||| The model boat caught the tone || and referred to the rigging **in technical terms**. ||| [Text 28]

As the examples illustrate, circumstances of Quality may also embody positive or negative interpersonal evaluations (e.g. the positively evaluated *eloquently*), and they may include comparative reference, as with *that way, similarly, thus*, thus contributing to cohesion in the text (see Chapter 9, Section 9.4.4).

(c) **Comparison** is typically expressed by a prepositional phrase with *like* or *unlike*, or an adverbial group of similarity or difference; for example:

||| That stands **like a pillar in the course of their history**, a place [[from which they can take bearing]]. ||| [Text 16]

||| As you well know, || we sometimes work **like the devil** with them. ||| [Text 21]

||| **Like all Mayan boys**, Kukul learned the art of warfare from his elders. ||| [Text 65]

||| All at once, Kukul saw [[an arrow flying straight toward Chirumá]], || and Kukul positioned himself **like a shield** in front of his uncle. ||| [Text 65]

|| **unlike Proust**, this chap Robbe Grillet starts from nothing at all || [Text 135]

319

The interrogative is *what ... like?*

(d) Degree is typically expressed by an adverbial group with a general indication of degree such as *much, a good deal, a lot,* or with a collocationally more restricted adverb of degree such as *deeply, profoundly, completely, heavily, badly.* The collocationally restricted adverbs collocate with verbs serving as Process, as in 'mental' clauses: *love + deeply, understand + completely, believe + strongly, want + badly* (see Matthiessen, 1995a: 279–281, 1998a, 2009b). Less commonly Degree may be expressed by a prepositional phrase, usually with *to* plus a nominal group with *extent, degree* as Thing and an intensifying adjective such as *high, large, great* as Epithet. Degree expressions characterize the extent of the actualization of the process and they often occur immediately before or immediately after the Process; for example:

‖‖ As a writer of short-stories for adults, she has worked **a great deal** with these themes. ‖‖ [Text 100]

‖‖ Their seams didn't show **at all** ‖‖ [Text 28]

‖‖ I enjoyed it **so much** [[I didn't want to stop working on it]]. ‖‖ [Text 7]

‖‖ He built a giant campaign war chest, ‖ advertised **heavily** ‖ and quickly climbed in the polls. ‖‖ [Text 87]

‖‖ We **deeply** appreciate the role [[[that the masses of our people and their political mass democratic, religious, women, youth, business, traditional and other leaders have played ‖ to bring about this conclusion]]]. ‖‖ [Text 104]

‖‖ **To what extent** is The Snow Leopard a shaped creation? ‖‖ [Text 7]

Circumstances of Degree shade into Mood Adjuncts of intensity (see Chapter 4, Section 4.3.2.1). The difference between them can be seen in an example such as *it almost destroyed the house*: (Degree) 'it destroyed the house to a large extent', (mood Adjunct) 'it didn't destroy the house'[45]. Circumstances of Degree construe the extent to which the process is actualized, and are thus agnate with lexical grading, as is seen particularly clearly in the lexicogrammar of emotion (cf. *adore* 'love deeply'; *detest* 'dislike intensely'). In contrast, Adjuncts of intensity assess the proposition – how close it comes to being actualized, and are thus agnate with other types of assessment and related to polarity. Thus with *almost* as mood Adjunct, it makes sense to say *it almost destroyed the house but it didn't* but with *almost* as Degree, it is odd to say *it almost destroyed the house but it didn't.* The contrast is clear with 'negative' polarity; contrast *almost* as mood Adjunct in *it almost didn't destroy the house* with *almost* as Degree in *it didn't almost destroy the house.*

Some examples of Manner circumstantials are given in Table 5-33.

(4) Cause. The circumstantial element of Cause construes the reason why the process is actualized. It includes not only Reason in the narrow sense of existing conditions leading to the actualization of the process, but also Purpose in the sense of intended conditions for which the process is actualized (what has been called 'final cause'). Both Reason and Purpose tend to be eventive (and are therefore commonly construed as clauses in a clause nexus: see below); but there is another kind of Cause that tends to denote a person –

---

[45] Such contrasts have been described in terms of 'scope' in formal semantics.

Table 5-33 Examples of Manner circumstantials

Type	WH- form	Examples
means	how? what with?	(mend it) with a fusewire
quality	how?	(they sat there) in complete silence
comparison	what like?	(he signs his name) differently
degree	how much?	(they all love her) deeply

the circumstance of Behalf. Cause thus comprises three subcategories: Reason, Purpose, Behalf.

(a) A circumstantial expression of **Reason** represents the reason for which a process takes place – what causes it; they have the sense of 'because'. It is typically expressed by a prepositional phrase with *through, from, for* or a complex preposition such as *because of, as a result of, thanks to, due to*; also the negative *for want of*, as in

||| Assad died **of heart failure**. ||| [Text 66]

||| Some newspapers reported || that Guinness died **from liver cancer,** || but the hospital would not confirm the cause of death. ||| [Text 90]

||| Is it worse **because of your asthma**? ||| [UTS/Macquarie Corpus]

||| **Thanks to the plentiful gold and silver of New World mines**, the Spanish could lavishly purchase [[what they needed elsewhere]]. ||| [Text 122]

||| Sometimes the guards punish them **for minor violations of rules** [[which have never been explained to them]], ... ||| [Text 1]

for want of a nail the shoe was lost.

There is also one class of expressions with *of*, one of the few places where *of* functions as a full preposition (i.e. representing a minor process) as distinct from being merely a structure marker; for example, *die of starvation*. The corresponding WH- forms are *why?* or *how?*.

(b) Circumstantials of **Purpose** represent the purpose for which an action takes place – the intention behind it; they have the sense of 'in order that'. They are typically expressed by a prepositional phrase with *for* or with a complex preposition such as *in the hope of, for the purpose of, for the sake of*; for example:

||| He has thus always worked **for an interdisciplinary environment** [[in which computer scientists and engineers can talk to neuroscientists and cognitive scientists]]. ||| [Text 86]

||| 'This is the only way [[to show President Estrada || that he has to step down **for the good of the country and the love of the nation**]]' || said Teddy Casino, a protest leader. ||| [Text 114]

||| It is rather curious, isn't it, [[that the Guardian, so highly respected and regarded, sees fit to actually, just **for the sake of a headline**, if you like, a little nice quote – it's a good quote, isn't it: 'Milosevic is innocent, says Pinter.']] ||| [Text 381]

||| President Bush is rallying the nation **for a war against terrorism's attack on our way of life**. ||| [Text 337]

321

The interrogative corresponding is *what for?*. As the examples above illustrate, the Head/ Thing of the nominal group introduced by the purposive preposition tends to be either a noun denoting entity that is to be obtained through the actualization of the process or a nominalization representing a reified process. The latter is in fact a metaphorical variant of what would be congruently realized as a clause (see Chapter 10).

The semantic relations of reason and purpose tend to be realized as separate clauses rather than as phrases within the clause; for example *I did it to get my own back* (cf. *for (the sake of) revenge*), *because he's ardent* in *I love my love with an A because he's ardent*, *to watch them* in *she went nearer to watch them*. These 'clause complex' structures are discussed further in Chapter 7.

(c) Expressions of **Behalf** represent the entity, typically a person, on whose behalf or for whose sake the action is undertaken – who it is for. They are expressed by a prepositional phrase with *for* or with a complex preposition such as *for the sake of*, *in favour of* (negative: *against*), *on behalf of*; for example:

||| Do any of your characters ever speak **for you**? ||| [Text 17]

||| At USC, he is founder and first Director of the Center for Neural Engineering, || and has developed an active Industrial Affiliates Program **for the Center**. ||| [Text 86]

||| The clergy was responsible for the community's spiritual well-being || and therefore interceded by prayer and sacred ceremony with an inscrutable God **on behalf of His 'creatures here below'**. ||| [Text 122]

||| Is that [[why you've decided to speak out **in favour of voluntary euthanasia legislation**]]? ||| [Text 24]

||| ||| Therefore, I urge you || to vote **against a CCC endorsement of the nuclear freeze initiative**. ||| [Text 6]

The usual interrogative is *who for?*

This category includes in principle the concept of the Client, the person for whom something is performed (see Section 5.2.4). But the Client is treated in the grammar as a kind of participant: it occurs without preposition, except when in a position of prominence, and can become Subject in the passive. Hence we have to distinguish between *she gave up her job for her children* ('for the sake of': Behalf), where we could not say *she gave her children up her job*, and *she built a new house for her children* ('for the use of': Client), where we could say *she built her children a new house*. Semantically, the former is something that is not inherently a service, whereas the latter is; here the process itself has a benefactive implication, in this case because it creates a usable product. Compare the distinction introduced above between Agent and Means; and see also the immediately following Section, 5.7.

Some examples of Cause circumstantials are given in Table 5-34.

Table 5-34 Examples of Cause circumstantials

Type	WH- form	Examples
Reason	why? how?	(they left) because of the draught
Purpose	what for?	(it's all done) with a view to promotion
Behalf	who for?	(put in a word) on my behalf

(5) Contingency. Circumstances of Contingency specify an element on which the actualization of the process depends. Again, there are three subtypes: Condition, Concession, Default.

(a) Circumstantials of **Condition** construe circumstances that have to obtain in order for the process to be actualized; they have the sense of 'if'. They are expressed by prepositional phrases with complex prepositions *in case of, in the event of, on condition of*:

‖‖ The U.S. provides air verification platforms, ‖ and we have joined in NATO planning for possible military actions ‖ to stabilize the situation **in the event of a large-scale humanitarian crisis**. ‖‖ [Text 115]

‖‖ Get back to the bedroom and change clothes **in case of bloodstains**. ‖‖ [LOB_N]

‖‖ An accord ⟦that included all the tough issues⟧ would be 'a difficult undertaking,' ‖ said the official, ‖ who accompanied Clinton to New York ‖ and spoke **on condition of anonymity**. ‖‖ [Text 108]

As the examples illustrate, the Head/Thing of the nominal group introduced by the preposition tends to be a noun denoting an entity whose existence is conditional (e.g. *bloodstains*: 'if there are bloodstains'), a noun denoting an event that might eventuate (e.g. *crisis, emergency*: 'if a crisis/emergency breaks out'), or a nominalization denoting a reified process or quality (e.g. *invasion*: 'if we were invaded', *anonymity*: 'as long as the official could be anonymous'; see Chapter 10, Section 10.5). Eventive nouns include those naming meteorological processes like typhoons. There used to be this notice displayed on the old Hong Kong trams: *In the event of a typhoon, open all windows*. Note that *in case of* is ambiguous (in the same way that the conjunction *in case* is ambiguous): (1) *in case of fire proceed calmly down the stairs*, (2) *in case of fire refrain from smoking in bed*; the first means 'if fire breaks out' and could be replaced by *in the case of*, the second means 'because fire might break out'.

(b) **Concession** circumstantials construe frustrated cause, with the sense of 'although'; they are expressed by prepositional phrases with the prepositions *despite, notwithstanding* or the complex prepositions *in spite of* or *regardless of*: e.g.

‖‖ **In spite of its beacon**, many ships have been wrecked on this rocky coast during storms or in dense fog. ‖‖ [Text 140]

‖‖ The performance exists **regardless of the mental state of the individual**, ‖ as persona is often imputed to the individual **in spite of his or her lack of faith in – or even ignorance of – the performance**. ‖‖ [Text 188]

‖‖ To the extent ⟦that the system works at all⟧, it works **despite Ofsted**, ‖ not because of it. ‖‖ [Text 97]

Note concessive expressions with *for all*, e.g.

And you know, **for all his success**, he was a helluva nice guy as well. [ACE_A]

(c) **Default** circumstantials have the sense of negative condition – 'if not, unless'; they are expressed by prepositional phrases with the complex prepositions *in the absence of, in default of*, e.g.

‖‖ **In the absence of any prior agreement between the parties as to the rate of salvage payable**, the amount is assessed, as a rule, by the Admiralty Court. ‖‖ [LOB_F]

Since the semantic relations involved in contingency are typically relations between processes, they are often realized clausally (cf. reason and purpose above); the most usual conjunctions are *if, although, unless*. Therefore, as we noted above for circumstances of Condition, when they are construed as circumstances, with a prepositional phrase, the noun is typically the name of an event, like *typhoon*, or a nominalized process as in *in spite of popular objections* (cf. *although people objected*).

5.6.2.2 Expansion: extending

Extending circumstances augment the configuration of process + participants through the specification of an element that stands in an extending relation to one of the participants in relation to its participation in the process. This element ranges on a scale from a co-participant, as in

> Restaurateur and chef Basil Amanatidis will fly out of Adelaide **with his 18-year-old son** on Tuesday, heading for Athens. [ACE_A]

to an 'appendix' to one of the participants, as in:

> He used to go to bed here every night **with his boxing gloves**. [ACE_A]

Contrast the acceptability of *Basil and his 18-year-old son will fly out to Adelaide* with the oddity of *he and his boxing gloves used to go to bed here every night*. There is only one type of extending circumstance: Accompaniment.

(6) Accompaniment. Accompaniment is a form of joint participation in the process and represents the meanings 'and', 'or', 'not' as circumstantials; it corresponds to the interrogatives *and who/what else?, but not who/what?*. It is expressed by prepositional phrases with prepositions such as *with, without, besides, instead of*. We can distinguish two subcategories, comitative and additive; each has a positive and a negative aspect. They are set out in Table 5-35.

(a) The **comitative** represents the process as a single instance of a process, although one in which two entities are involved. It ranges from some cases where the two entities could

Table 5-35 Examples of Accompaniment circumstantials

	WH- form	**Examples**
comitative, positive: 'accompanied by'	who/what with? and who/what else?	Fred came with Tom Jane set out with her umbrella
comitative, negative: 'not accompanied by'	but not who/what?	Fred came without Tom I came without my key
additive, positive: 'in addition to'	and who/what else?	Fred came as well as Tom
additive, negative: 'as alternative to'	and not who/what?	Fred came instead of Tom

be conjoined as a single element, as in *Fred and Tom set out together*, to others where they could not, like *Jane and her umbrella set out together*:

||| I was traveling up the west coast of Florida **with my father** in a boat, ... ||| [Text 96]

||| Karaca said || one of the Pakistanis had told rescuers || he had been locked in the hold **with about 50 other people**. ||| [Text 105]

Sometimes the comitative element is actually an accompanying process, as in *the Dormouse woke up with a shriek* 'woke up and shrieked simultaneously'; see Chapter 10 for the general principle of grammatical metaphor involved.

A circumstance of Accompaniment may have an additional sense of cause or contingency – 'since/if x has/hasn't'. Here the closest clausal agnate is a 'possessive' one of reason or condition; for example:

||| **Together with a well thought-out, disciplined approach to potential uses of force**, the guidelines should help us manage OPTEMPO and PERSTEMPO ... ||| [Text 115] 'if we also have ...'

||| **Without skilled, committed people**, we will be unable to exploit the full potential of our advanced weapons systems on the battlefield. ||| [Text 115] 'if we haven't got ...'

(b) The **additive** represents the process as two instances; here both entities clearly share the same participant function, but one of them is represented circumstantially for the purpose of contrast. We could say *Fred and Tom both came*; but *Fred came as well as Tom* distinguishes the two as regards their news value ('not only Tom but also Fred came'). In the same way, when one participant is represented circumstantially it can be given the status of Theme:

||| **As well as five collections of short stories, A Horse and Two Goats, An Astrologer's Day and Other Stories, Lawley Road, Under the Banyan Tree and Malgudi Days**, he has published a travel book, The Emerald Route, three collections of essays, a Writer's Nightmare, Next Sunday and Reluctant Guru, three books on the Indian epics, and a volume of memoirs, My Days. ||| [Text 152]

Similarly we could say *Fred came and Tom did not*; but *Fred came instead of Tom* makes it clear which it was that was unexpected ('not Tom but Fred came'):

||| Well [[what – what those lot do]] is [[that they wear them **instead of hair nets**]]. ||| [UTS/Macquarie Corpus]

and the same principle again applies to thematic status:

||| **Instead of dingy velveteen** he had brown fur, soft and shiny. ||| [Text 28]

5.6.2.3 Expansion: elaborating

Elaborating circumstances augment the configuration of process + participants through the specification of the role in which one of the participants participates in the process: this participant is elaborated circumstantially. There is only one type of elaborating circumstance: Role.

325

(7) Role. This category construes the meanings 'be' and 'become' circumstantially; the Role corresponds to the Attribute or Value of an 'intensive relational' clause. Role includes the subcategories of Guise ('be') and Product ('become').

(a) **Guise** corresponds to the interrogative *what as?* and construes the meaning of 'be' (attribute or identity) in the form of a circumstance; e.g. example *she was installed as chancellor, I come here as a friend* (i.e. 'she is the chancellor', 'I am friendly'). The usual preposition is *as*; other, complex prepositions with this function are *by way of, in the role/shape/guise/form of*; e.g. *they leave the place untidy by way of protest* ('to signal their protest'). Thematic circumstances of Role may indicate a period of time in a person's life; for example:

||| Kukul grew into a handsome young man with jet black hair and skin the colour of cinnamon. ||| He was quick of mind || and excelled at any task [[he was given]]. ||| **As a young boy**, he spent long hours with his father. ||| Together, they would study the stars. ||| [Text 65]

This is distantly agnate with a temporally enhancing relational clause – *when he was a young boy* in the example above (cf. the causal-conditional sense of Accompaniment noted above).

A circumstance of Role usually relates to a participant in the clause – more specifically, to the Medium (see Section 5.7 below); but we also find circumstances of Role that do not. The following example illustrates both possibilities:

||| **As an operating system,** *Mac OS X* offers a glitzy new look with many 'cool' interface features – as well as significant 'under the hood' troubleshooting benefits || (perhaps the best one is protected memory; || it may put an end to system crashes [[that require restarting your Mac]]). ||| **But as a troubleshooter**, it also offers significant hurdles [[to overcome]]. ||| While I enthusiastically look forward to using Mac OS X, || I remain wary of these obstacles. ||| [From http://www.macfixit.com/reports/macosx.shtml]

||| **As socialists,** *we* understand all too well the impact of staffing cuts, insufficient books, decaying buildings, and inner city life in general on teachers and pupils ... ||| [Text 97]

||| **As a token of its commitment to the renewal of our country**, the new interim Government of National Unity will, as a matter of urgency, address the issue of amnesty for various categories of our people [[who are currently serving terms of imprisonment]]. ||| [Text 104]

Here *as a troubleshooter* means 'when you are a troubleshooter', not 'when it [= Mac OS X] is a troubleshooter'.

(b) **Product** corresponds to the interrogative *what into?*, with the meaning of 'become', likewise as attribute or identity; e.g. *aren't you growing into a big girl?* ('becoming a big girl'), *he moulded the army into a disciplined fighting force.*

||| Kukul grew **into a handsome young man with jet black hair and skin the colour of cinnamon** ||| [Text 65]

||| Proteins are first broken down **into amino acids**. ||| [Text 150]

||| His short stories, << which have received extraordinary acclaim, >> have been translated **into many languages** || and have been bestsellers all over the world. ||| [Text 160]

||| If they could gain power || they would then beat the people **into submission**. ||| [Text 234]

It was noted in Section 5.4 that in some instances, such as *act as, turn into*, the preposition *as, into* was so closely bonded with the verb that it should be analysed as part of the Process (cf. Chapter 6, Section 6.3.6 on phrasal verbs). Contrast the following pair:

you'll grow + into a big girl [material process + Role]

you'll turn into + a real terror [relational process + Attribute]

The boundary is indeterminate; but the second analysis is suggested where the verb could not easily occur without the prepositional phrase, or is separated from the preposition thematically – here *grow* could occur alone (*how you're growing!*), whereas *turn* could not (cf. *I don't know what you're turning into!*). As already pointed out, the difference is also realized phonologically: if *grow* is a material process it will be salient, whereas *turn* into is typically non-salient.

There is a related pattern in the clause which could be regarded as a circumstance of Role, except that it does not involve a prepositional phrase. This is the structure whereby an **Attribute** is added to a material process, either (i) as **depictive**, corresponding to the guise, or (ii) as **resultative**, corresponding to the product; e.g. (i) *he came back rich*, (ii) *bend that rod straight*. Typically such an Attribute appears as an adjective; the pattern can occur with a general noun (*he came back a rich man/a millionaire*), but the related nominal attribute is usually construed circumstantially, with *as*: *he came back as a millionaire*, *it's frozen into a solid mass* (cf. *it's frozen solid*). We shall analyse these as follows:

he	set out	poor
Actor	Process: material	Attribute: depictive

he	set out	as a pauper
Actor	Process: material	Role: guise

bend	that rod	straight
Process: material	Goal	Attribute: resultative

bend	that rod	into a straight line
Process: material	Goal	Role: product

We shall return to consider the relation between Role and Attribute in Section 5.7 below.

5.6.2.4 Projection

While circumstances of expansion relate to 'relational' clauses, circumstances of projection relate to projecting 'mental' and 'verbal' clauses – either to the Senser or Sayer of that clause (Angle) or to the Verbiage (Matter).

(8) Matter. Matter is related to verbal processes; it is the circumstantial equivalent of the Verbiage, 'that which is described, referred to, narrated, etc.'. The interrogative is *what about?*. Matter is expressed by prepositions such as *about, concerning, with reference to* and sometimes simply *of*:

||| Tell me **about the Paris Review**. ||| [Text 7]

||| We generally talk **of Africa** as one || because that's [[the way Europe looks at Africa]], ... ||| [Text 16]

||| ||| We must warn **of the consequences of this truth**. ||| [Text 327]

||| We were scared to death of all four-letter words || because in those days we had to worry **about the censors in the US** [[who could keep the issues from coming in]]. ||| [Text 119]

It is frequent with both 'verbal' clauses and 'mental' ones (especially of the 'cognitive' subtype). In mathematical expressions, there is a special form of Matter, typically with 'relational' clauses: *for all x such that x > 5, ...*

For $x \neq 0$, we can find $f'(x)$ by using the standard rules: it's $2x \, sin\left(\dfrac{1}{x}\right) - cos\left(\dfrac{1}{x}\right)$.

One way of giving prominence to a Theme is to construe it as if it was a circumstance of Matter; e.g. *as for the ghost, it hasn't been seen since*. By being first introduced circumstantially, *the ghost* becomes a focused Theme (cf. Chapter 3, Section 3.3).

(9) Angle. Angle is related either to (i) the Sayer of a 'verbal' clause, with the sense of 'as ... says' or (ii) to the Senser of a 'mental' clause, with the sense of 'as ... thinks'. We can call type (i) 'source' since it is used to represent the source information, as in:

||| Torture and sexual violence against prisoners is widespread in jails across the United States, **according to a report** [[**published yesterday**]]. ||| [Text 2]

||| **According to the phlogistic theory**, the part [[remaining after a substance was burned]] was simply the original substance [[deprived of phlogiston]]. ||| [Text 259]

It is expressed by complex prepositions such as *according to, in the words of.* (Note that *according to* can also mark a circumstance of Manner, as in *The 'Garden of Friendship' was designed according to southern Chinese tradition by Sydney's sister city, Guangzhou in China*.)

We can call type (ii) 'viewpoint' since it is used to represent the information given by the clause from somebody's viewpoint (as is illustrated by the following natural example *and I think that's important, that's been really important to me*). This type is expressed by the simple preposition *to* or by complex prepositions such as *in the view/opinion of, from the standpoint of*; for example, *to Mary it seemed unlikely, they're guilty in the eyes of the law*:

||| It seems **to me** [[that answers to most such questions have to be learned by experiment]]. ||| [Text 212]

||| Simple in the most beautiful ways: generous, soulful, giving, humorous, loving – all those things [[that are important **to me**]]. ||| [Text 206]

||| Philip's not tall. ||| – ||| Everybody's tall **to me**. ||| [UTS/Macquarie Corpus]

||| Secretary Cohen has noted in the past || that while we can never pay our men and women in uniform enough, || we can pay them too little || – and **in my view**, we are. ||| [Text 115]

This type of Angle occurs in 'relational' clauses that are agnate with Senser in 'mental' clauses (cf. Section 5.4.3.2 above): *that's very interesting **to me*** (cf. *that interests **me***).

5.6.3 The status of circumstances

Rounding off our discussion of circumstances, let us now review their status in the grammar, focusing on the prepositional phrases in the grammar since most circumstances are realized by prepositional phrases (see Chapter 6, Section 6.5). Issues arise because while

prepositional phrases serve as circumstances by default, they can also serve as participants in the clause, and even as elements of groups (nominal or adverbial). Issues also arrive because while prepositions serve in prepositional phrases by default, they can also come to serve as extensions of verbs, so-called phrasal verbs (and we can also note conjunctive prepositions, prepositions used as structural conjunctions in bound clauses, as in *who will authorise payment **on** ascertaining that the item was really received*: see Chapter 7).

5.6.3.1 Circumstances: preposition as minor process

Most circumstances are realized by prepositional phrases. A prepositional phrase can be interpreted as a shrunken clause, in which the preposition serves as a 'minor process', interpreted as a kind of mini-verb, and the nominal group as a participant in this minor process. This needs explaining.

The preposition, it was suggested, acts as a kind of intermediary whereby a nominal element can be introduced as an 'indirect' participant in the main process. We saw also that in circumstantial and possessive relational processes there are often close parallels between *be* + preposition and a verb, e.g.

> the delay was because of a strike ~ was caused by a strike
>
> a carpet was over the floor ~ covered the floor
>
> the bridge is across the river ~ crosses/spans the river
>
> a path is along(side) the wood ~ skirts the wood
>
> a halo is around the moon ~ surrounds the moon

This similarity between verb and preposition can also be seen in cases where there is a close relationship between a prepositional phrase and a non-finite dependent clause (Chapter 7, Section 7.4):

> he cleaned the floor with a mop ~ using a mop
>
> grass grows after the rain ~ following the rain

In this way certain prepositions are themselves derived from non-finite verbs; e.g. *concerning, according to, given, excepting*. These considerations suggest that the nominal group stands to the preposition in some kind of transitivity relation, as well as in a relationship like that of Complement to Predicator in mood structure (discussed further in Chapter 6, Section 6.5).

At the same time, there are many instances where a nominal group seems to have more or less the same function whether it is brought into the clause directly, or indirectly via a prepositional phrase: for example, *John* in *sent John a message/sent a message to John*. We have interpreted these as participant functions, rather than as circumstantial elements, for reasons that will be given in Section 5.7. But they also suggest that the line between participants and circumstances is not a very clear one, and that the preposition does function like some highly generalized kind of process, by reference to which the nominal group that is attached to it establishes a participant status. These instances are summarized in Table 5-36.

Table 5-36 Participant functions realized by prepositional phrases

Preposition	Examples	Process type	Process-type specific function	General function
by	the bridge was built by the army	material	Actor	Agent
	the children were frightened by a ghost	mental	Phenomenon	
	the calm was followed by a storm	relational	Token	
to	I sent a letter to my love	material	Recipient	Beneficiary
	don't tell these secrets to anybody	verbal	Receiver	
for	she baked a pie for the children	material	Client	
on, in, etc.	he plays well on all three instruments	material	Scope	Range
	I spoke to him in fluent Russian	verbal	Verbiage	
as	she acted magnificently as St. Joan	relational	Value	

5.6.3.2 Some difficulties in identifying circumstantial elements

Because of the status of prepositions and of prepositional phrases noted above, there are perhaps five main sources of difficulty in identifying circumstantial elements.

(i) Prepositional phrase as participant. As discussed in the last sub-section, some prepositional phrases realize participant functions, which can be grouped under a few general headings as shown. Wherever there is systematic alternation between a prepositional phrase and a nominal group, as in all the instances in Table 5-36, the element in question is interpreted as a participant.

(ii) Preposition attached to verb. This also involves prepositional phrases functioning as participants; but here there is no alternation between prepositional phrase and nominal group. Instead, the preposition is closely bonded with a verb, so that it is functioning as part of the Process (see Chapter 6, Section 6.3.6 on phrasal verbs), as with *turn into* in Section 5.6.2.3 (7)(b) above; similarly *look at the sky* consists of Process *look at* + Phenomenon *the sky*. There is no simple diagnostic criterion for deciding every instance; but a useful pointer is provided by the thematic structure, which gives an indication of how the clause is organized as a representation of the process. Consider the following sets of clauses:

(a) where were you waiting?—I was waiting on the shore

    (i) it was on the shore that I was waiting *not* it was the shore that I was waiting on

    (ii) on the shore I was waiting all day *not* the shore I was waiting on all day

    (iii) where I was waiting was on the shore *not* what I was waiting on was the shore

(b) what were you waiting for?—I was waiting for the boat

    (i) it was the boat that I was waiting for *not* it was for the boat that I was waiting

    (ii) the boat I was waiting for all day *not* for the boat I was waiting all day

    (iii) what I was waiting for was the boat *not* why I was waiting was for the boat

These suggest that (a) consists of process *wait* plus circumstance *on the shore*, while (b) consists of process *wait for* plus participant *the boat*. If the thematic variants of pattern (a) seem more natural, the prepositional phrase can be interpreted as a circumstance; if those of (b) seem more natural, the preposition can be taken as part of the verbal group serving as Process.

(iii) Prepositional phrase (as Qualifier) inside nominal group. Prepositional phrases also function in the structure of nominal groups, following the noun, like in *the wall* in *the hole in the wall*. In some varieties of English, especially the more elaborated registers of adult writing, this is the predominant function of prepositional phrases, and they may nest one inside the other up to a considerable length, as in:

a reduction [in the level [of support [among members] [for changes [to the regulations

[concerning assistance [to people [on fixed incomes]]]]]]]

In general it is clear whether any given prepositional phrase is circumstance in the clause or Qualifier in the nominal group; where it is uncertain, there will often be some thematic variation that can be used to question the text. For example,

The report favours the introduction of water spray systems in aircraft cabins.

Semantically, it seems clear that *in aircraft cabins* belongs with the nominal group *the introduction* ... , not with the clause *the report favours* ... ; this can be verified by the passive:

The introduction of water spray systems in aircraft cabins is favoured by the report.

– not *the introduction of water spray systems is favoured in aircraft cabins by the report*. (For the Qualifier, see Chapter 6, Section 6.2.2.)

(iv) Prepositional phrase as Modal or Conjunctive Adjunct. In Chapter 4 we introduced the distinction among Modal, Conjunctive and circumstantial Adjuncts, pointing out that while all three are similar in their own make-up (as adverbial group or prepositional phrase), they differ in their function. Modal and Conjunctive Adjuncts are outside the transitivity system, hence while typically thematic, they are not topical Theme and therefore cannot normally be given special thematic prominence; nor will they carry the only focus of information in the clause. Contrast Modal *in principle* with circumstantial (Cause) *on principle*:

I disagree **on principle**. (Why I disagree is **on principle**.)

I disagree, in principle. In principle I **disagree**.

but not *how I disagree is in principle*. Likewise, contrast Conjunctive in that case with circumstantial (Matter) *in your case*:

That might be true **in your case**. (Where that might be true is **in your case**.)

That might be **true**, in that case. In that case that might be **true**.

but not *where that might be true is in that case*.

But many items can occur both as circumstance and in one of the other functions. In particular, prepositional phrases having a nominal group consisting of, or starting with, the word *that* are potentially either Conjunctive or circumstantial; thus, *at that moment* might well be a circumstance of Time in a history textbook ('at that moment in history') but conjunctive in a vivid personal narrative ('and just at that very moment'). What the grammar offers here, so to speak, are three planes of reality so that for (say) time, it construes experiential time, interpersonal time and textual time. Experiential time is time as a feature of a process: its location, its duration or its repetition rate in some real or imaginary history. Interpersonal time is time as enacted between speaker and listener: temporality relative to the speaker-now, or usuality as a band of arguable space between positive and negative poles. Textual time is time relative to the current state of the discourse: 'then' in the text's construction of external reality, or in the internal ordering of the text itself. Very often only the overall context will suggest which of the three is being foregrounded in a particular prepositional construction.

(v) Abstract and metaphorical expressions of circumstance. In the modern elaborated registers of adult speech and (especially) writing, the circumstantial elements have evolved very far from their concrete origins – especially the spatial ones. It is beyond our scope here to treat these developments systematically; here are a few examples, with suggested interpretations:

they closed down with the loss of 100 jobs [Accompaniment: addition]

the directive was now with the Council of Ministers [Accompaniment: comitation]

we have now been introduced to a new topic [Location: place]

we learn from this experiment [Manner: means]

the committee decided against their use [Cause: behalf 'not + in favour of']

the problem lies in our own attitudes [Location: place]

the group will work through all these materials [Extent: distance]

the venture would have failed without the bank's support [Contingency: default]

my colleague works for the transport section [Cause: behalf]

these products are made to a very high standard [Manner: quality]

we have been asked to assist in a further project [Matter]

consult the chart for the full operational details [Cause: purpose]

Some less problematic examples are set out in Figure 5-33.

5.7 Transitivity and voice: another interpretation

In this chapter we have distinguished the types of process represented by the English clause, and the various participant functions that are associated with each. The circumstantial elements we were able to treat independently, without distinguishing them according to process type; this is because, although there are natural restrictions on the way particular circumstantials combine with other elements, these often go with rather small classes and in any case do not affect either the structure or the meaning. Each type of process, on the

the Dodo	pointed	to Alice	with one finger
Actor	Process: material	Location: spatial	Manner: means

the whole party	at once	crowded	round her
Actor	Location: temporal	Process: material	Location: spatial

in despair	Alice	put	her hand	in her pocket
Manner: quality	Actor	Process: material	Goal	Location: spatial

Alice	handed	the comfits	round	as prizes
Actor	Process: material	Goal	Extent: spatial	Role: guise

the two creatures	had been jumping about	like mad things	all this time
Actor	Process: material	Manner: comparison	Extent: temporal

we	can dance	without lobsters
Behaver	Process: behavioural	Accompaniment: comitative

Fig. 5-33 Clauses with circumstantial elements

other hand, is characterized by process-participant configurations where the functions are particular to that type.

For purposes of analysis we could leave it at that. But it is not the whole story; so we shall pursue the investigation one stage further, although only in a rather sketchy manner.

It is true that, from one point of view, all these types of process are different. Material, behavioural, mental, verbal, relational and existential processes each have a grammar of their own. At the same time, looked at from another point of view they are all alike. At another level of interpretation, they all have the same grammar: there is just one generalized representational structure common to every English clause.

These two perspectives complement one another, giving us a balance in the account of transitivity between similarity and difference among the process types. The two perspectives constitute two different modes of modelling transitivity. We shall call these the **transitive model** and the **ergative model** of transitivity (see Halliday, 1967/8).[46] These models are

---

[46] Note that 'transitivity' is the name for the whole system, including both the 'transitive' model and the 'ergative' one. 'Ergativity' is thus not the name of a system, but of a property of the system of transitivity: within this system of transitivity, we can recognize the 'transitive model' and the 'ergative model' – while of course leaving open the possibility of other transitivity models (cf. Martin, 2004).

summarized in Table 5-37. We have constructed the table to suggest that (i) generalization across process types and (ii) transitivity model are independently variable. In English and in many other languages, it is the transitive model that differentiates the different process types and it is the ergative model that generalizes across these different process types. But the alignments could be different (for examples, see the description of different languages in Caffarel, Martin & Matthiessen, 2004, in particular Martin's account of Tagalog transitivity and Rose's account of Pitjantjatjara transitivity).

We shall introduce the ergative model in two steps. We begin by examining two passages of text, one from the point of view of the transitive model and the other from the point of view of the ergative model. Then we explore the ergative model in more general terms.

Table 5-37 The complementarity of the transitive and ergative models of transitivity in English

	Transitive model	Ergative model
generalized (across process types)		Process + Medium (± Agent) [middle/effective]
particularized (for each process type)	**material:** Actor + Process ± Goal [intransitive/transitive], confined to 'material' clauses, so leading to a range of other configurations as well: **behavioural:** Behaver + Process **mental:** Senser + Process + Phenomenon **verbal:** Sayer + Process (± Receiver) **relational:** Carrier + Process + Attribute; Token + Process + Value **existential:** Existent + Process	

5.7.1 The transitive model

As we have seen in this chapter, the transitive model is based on the configuration of Actor + Process. The Actor is construed as bringing about the unfolding of the Process through time; and this unfolding is either confined in its outcome to the Actor or extended to another participant, the Goal. The Goal is construed as being impacted by the Actor's performance of the Process. This model is illustrated by Text 5-15, an extract from a traditional narrative – a retelling for children of the Noah's Ark biblical story.

The entities serving as Actor in a 'transitive' or 'intransitive' clause and as Goal are set out in Table 5-38. The transitive Actors are all 'beings' – God or humans (but not animals) – with the exception of 'flood'; but this natural force is construed as being under God's control (*I am going to send a great flood*). This means that they are all 'potent' and all except for 'flood' are also 'volitional'. These beings may also serve as intransitive Actors; but this role admits of a greater range of entities, including not only animals but also various kinds of natural phenomena, which can all be construed as 'volatile', and also one kind of artefact (the ark). The picture that emerges is thus one where a range of entities can serve as Actor; and the most 'potent' ones can serve not only as intransitive Actor but also as transitive Actor, bringing about a Process that impacts a Goal: see Figure 5-32. Turning to the Goal, we find that 'beings' can take on this role; but when they do, a more potent entity serves as Actor:

Actor: 'God' + Goal: 'Noah & family', Actor: 'Noah & family' + Goal: 'animal'. In addition, natural phenomena, artefacts, plants and food can serve as Goal, the last three being largely restricted to the role of Goal. The transitivity grammar of this text thus construes a particular 'world view': this is a world where God can act on humans and on natural phenomena, where natural forces can act destructively on the world under God's control, where humans in turn can act on animals, artefacts and plants but where plants do not act.

This world view is, of course, specific to this particular text; but at the same time it is representative of the world view embodied in the traditional commonsense theory of everyday grammar (cf. Halliday, 1993b).

Table 5-38 Distribution of entities in transitive participant roles

		Actor (transitive)	Actor (intransitive)	Goal
(i) beings	God	✓		
	Noah & family	✓	✓	✓
	animals		✓	✓
(ii) natural phenomena	*flood*, lake	✓		
	rain; rivers, lakes, water, *flood*; clouds, <u>rainbow</u>; breeze; sun		✓	
	flood, ocean, <u>rainbow</u>; world; fields			✓
(iii) artefacts	ark		✓	✓
	ship, ark, door, window, stalls, cages, cracks; homes			✓
(iv) plants & food:	trees, fruit, grain, vegetables; food			✓

Text 5-15: Recreating – narrating (written, monologic): Extract from Noah's Ark

[9] At first Noah was frightened. How **could** <u>God</u> save <u>him</u> from the waters of a great flood?

[10] Then God spoke to Noah again. [11] He told him **to build** <u>a ship called an ark</u>. [12] 'The ark must be 450 feet long, 75 feet wide, and 45 feet high,' he said, 'big enough for you and your wife, your three sons, and their wives. [13] **Take** with you also into the ark <u>two of every living thing that creeps on the earth or flies in the air</u>. [14] **Take** <u>a male and a female of every creature, large and small</u>. [15] **Do** as I say and <u>you</u> **will be saved**.'

[16] God told Noah many more things. [17] Then <u>Noah</u> **went** home to tell his family all that God had said.

[18] The very next morning <u>Noah and his sons</u> **went** to the cypress forest **to cut down** <u>the tallest trees</u> for timber. [19] For many days <u>they</u> **sawed and chopped**.

[20] <u>Noah's wife and his sons' wives</u> **went** to the fields **to gather** <u>fruit and grain and vegetables</u>. [21] They would need plenty of food for themselves and the animals on the dark.

These Actors occur in both 'happening' and 'doing' clauses; they remain constant across the two types, which is in keeping with the transitive model of 'material' clauses , see Figure 5-34:

335

happening	the very next morning	Noah and his sons	went		to the cypress forest
		we	must hurry		
doing		[they]	to cut down	the tallest trees	for timber
		[we]	collect	the animals	
	(circumstance)	**Actor**	Process	**Goal**	(circumstance)

Fig. 5-34   Actor and Goal in *Noah's Ark*

5.7.2 The ergative model

Noah's Ark is construed according to the transitive model; but there is a hint of ergative patterning. In the transitive model, the great flood and its various manifestations (rain, rivers, water) serve either as Actor in 'happening' clauses or as Goal in 'doing' clauses:

'I **am going to send** a great flood to **wash** the world away,'

The great flood spread and *the water* kept rising. *It* covered fields and hills and mountains.

Thus in *I am going to send a great flood* the nominal group *a great flood* serves as Goal, but other occurrences of nominal groups denoting forms of water all serve as Actor. This is the transitive generalization. However, in the ergative model, there is also a generalization to be made: the great flood serves the same ergative role in *I am going to send a great flood* and *the great flood spread*: see Figure 5-35. This is the role of **Medium** – the medium through which the process is actualized[47]; in this case, it is the medium through which the movement of sending or spreading is actualized. The difference between 'doing' and 'happening' derives from a different principle from the transitive one of extension-&-impact: 'happening' means that the actualization of the process is represented as being self-engendered, whereas 'doing' means that the actualization of the process is represented as being caused by a participant that is external to the combination of Process + Medium. This external cause is the **Agent**.

	Agent	Process	**Medium**	
doing	I'm	going to send	a great flood	
happening			the great flood	spread
			Medium	Process

Fig. 5-35   Ergative patterning in 'material' clauses of motion

---

[47] Halliday (1968: 185/2005: 117) originally suggested the term 'affected' for what is now called 'medium', although Fawcett and other linguists working with and developing descriptions within the 'Cardiff Grammar' continue to use the term 'affected' in their accounts. Within other linguistic frameworks, something like the role of Medium has been characterized by means of other labels. For example, in Starosta's (1988: 128) Lexicase theory, '"Patient" corresponds to Halliday's **medium**'.

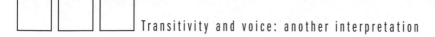

Even if there is a trace of it in a traditional narrative like *Noah's Ark*, the ergative model is not foregrounded in the text (cf. Halliday, 1971). However, there are many registers of current modern English where the ergative model is foregrounded, playing a role that is as important as, or more important than, that of the transitive model. These registers include those that are collectively known as Scientific English – registers that that evolved over the past 500 years or so (see Halliday, 1988); but they also include those that are collectively known as casual conversation – the frontier of change in English. The ergative model is now fully systemic in English; that is, it is not restricted to certain registers, but together with the transitive model it makes up the general system of transitivity, and it has been gaining ground over the last half a millennium. The two models complement one another, which is why they are variably foregrounded across registers: they embody different generalizations about the flux of experience, resonating with different situation types. Let us consider examples taken from samples of Scientific English:

Text 5-16: Expounding – categorizing: extract from geology text book

[72] Evaporite deposits **are formed** by the evaporation of sea water. [73] Gypsum and rock salt are the main rocks ⟦**formed** in this way⟧. [74] When sea water is evaporated at surface temperatures, such as in a restricted basin, the first mineral precipitated is calcite. [75] Dolomite is the next mineral precipitated, but only very small amounts of limestone and dolomite **can be formed** in this way. [76] Evaporation of a half-mile column of sea water would only produce an inch or two of limestone and dolomite. [77] After about two-thirds of the water is evaporated, gypsum is precipitated; and when nine-tenths of the water is removed, halite **forms**.

Here the verb *form* occurs in four clauses, all of which are 'material'. According to the transitive model, the first three are passive, transitive clauses, while the last one is intransitive: the intransitive clause *halite forms* would be analysed as Actor + Process, and the transitive clauses as agnate variants where the process extends to impact a Goal, that is, as Actor + Process + Goal. But this is not, in fact, how these clauses pattern. (1) The intransitive clause *halite* forms cannot be interpreted as an intransitive variant of a clause such as *evaporite deposits are formed by the evaporation of sea water*. This is why there is no intransitive clause in *the evaporation of sea water forms*. That is, the Actor of the intransitive clause and the Actor of the transitive one are not in fact agnate. (2) Instead, the Actor of the intransitive clause is agnate with the Goal of the transitive one: *evaporite deposits, the main rocks* and *limestone and dolomite* are all of the same type of thing as *halite*; but *the evaporation of sea water* is of an entirely different class of thing. (3) This is related to the fact that the intransitive clause is very close in meaning to the passive variant of the transitive clause with only one participant: alongside *halite forms* we could have *halite is formed*, and alongside *only very small amounts of limestone and dolomite can be formed* in this way, we could have *only very small amounts of limestone and dolomite can form in this way*.

These facts are not idiosyncratic properties of the use of the verb *form* in the paragraph quoted above. There are many other verbs in Modern English that pattern in this way; in a random sample of 100 verbs taken from a standard dictionary, 60 per cent were labelled 'vb, trans & intrans', among them being almost all those of high frequency. Some examples taken from recipes are given in Table 5-39. More generally, many of

337

the verbs serving in material clauses in Table 5-5 are listed under both 'intransitive' and 'transitive'; we can see that this is because they pattern ergatively (see Table 5-40 for examples in 'material' clauses). But ergativity is not restricted to the lexical zone of lexicogrammar.[48] Rather it is also a grammatical phenomenon, and the explanation can be stated in grammatical, rather than lexical, terms since it is the grammar that engenders the lexical patterns: this is the ergative model of transitivity referred to above and illustrated in Figure 5-35. Examples taken from the geological text are analysed in Figure 5-36.

Table 5-39 Recipe examples of the same verb in 'effective' and 'middle' clauses

doing – effective
    Agent + [Process + Medium]
	happening – middle
	    [Process + Medium]

Simmer for 1/2 an hour, **remove** the flavourings if desired, **adjust** the seasonings and **serve**.	until **simmering** well
cook slowly in the water with salt	as they **cook** in the sauce
by **boiling** rapidly	once the custard **has boiled** for several seconds
These **can be cooked** in 15–20 minutes	It **should cook** in 40–50 minutes Whilst they **are cooking**
Evaporate the cooking liquor	as the liquid **may evaporate** too much
Fry some wholemeal breadcrumbs in butter	[if you leave any more than a smear of grease] the pancakes **will fry**
Do not on any account **burn** it	otherwise they **would burn**
[If you are making the richest mixture you may find] that the last egg **curdles** the mixture	it **will curdle**
Melt the butter in a saucepan	until butter **melts**

[48] Some linguists have in fact thought that English is only lexically ergative. But this is not a tenable position once we realize that lexis and grammar are not separate modules or components, but merely zones within a continuum (Chapter 2, Section 2.2): 'lexical ergativity' in English is an extension in delicacy of 'grammatical ergativity' within the experiential clause grammar; and the explanation for the evolution of ergative patterning in English is grammatical in the first instance rather than lexical. The account of lexical ergativity has sometimes been supported by reference to pronominal case marking in English, with the claim that it is 'nominative-accusative' in nature rather than 'ergative'. But this is also a mistake; pronominal case marking is not a feature of the experiential system of transitivity but rather of the interpersonal system of mood: the non-oblique ('nominative') case is used for Subjects in finite clauses and the oblique ('accusative') case in all other environments (including Subjects in non-finite clauses). It is thus related to arguability status, not to the transitive model of transitivity.

middle	**Limestone**	can		form		in many ways
effective: receptive	**Limestone**	is	presently	being formed	by chemical precipitation	on the shallow Bahama banks
	Medium	Pro-		-cess	Agent	(circumstance)
	Theme	Rheme				

Fig. 5-36   Analysis of 'middle' and 'effective' clauses with Process = 'form'

Table 5-40 Ergative and transitive functions in 'material' clauses

		Initiator	**Actor**	**Goal**
effective	Agent + Medium	**Agent/Initiator** 'Ag/In makes ...'	**Medium/Actor** ... Me/Ac do sth'	
		The police exploded the bomb The sergeant marched the prisoners		
middle	Medium		**Medium/Actor**	
			The bomb exploded The prisoners marched	
middle	Medium		**Medium/Actor**	
			(The cake cut easily) The tourist ran	
effective	Agent + Medium		**Agent/Actor** 'Ag/Ac does sth ...	**Medium/Goal** ... to Me/Go'
			Alice cut the cake The lion chased the tourist	

The arguments for the ergative interpretation are long and technical. But while, as we have seen, there is clear evidence in the grammar for distinguishing one process type from another, there is also clear evidence for saying that, in a more abstract sense, every process is structured in the same way, on the basis of just one variable. This variable relates to the source of the process: what it is that brought it about. The question at issue is: is the process brought about from within, or from outside?

This is not the same thing as the intransitive/transitive distinction. There, as we saw, the variable is one of extension. The Actor is engaged in a process; does the process extend beyond the Actor, to some other entity, or not? So *the lion chased the tourist* relates to *the lion ran*: 'the lion did some running; either the running stopped there (intransitive, *the lion ran*), or else it extended to another participant (transitive, *the lion chased the tourist*).

In the second interpretation, the question is, again, how many participants there are, one or two; but the relationship between the two possible answers is quite different. To understand it we have to restructure our thinking, rather in the way that we have to

339

restructure our perception when looking at a figure that can be seen as either concave or convex.

Looked at from this point of view, the variable is not one of extension but one of causation. Some participant is engaged in a process; is the process brought about by that participant, or by some other entity? In this perspective, *the lion chased the tourist* relates not so much to *the lion ran* as to *the tourist ran*: 'the tourist did some running; either the running was instigated by the tourist himself (intransitive *the tourist ran*), or else by some external agency (transitive *the lion chased the tourist*)'. Note however that the terms 'transitive' and 'intransitive' are no longer appropriate here, since they imply the extension model. The pattern yielded by this second interpretation is known as the ergative pattern. The clauses *the lion chased the tourist/the tourist ran* form an **ergative/non-ergative** pair[49].

As we noted above, if we examine the lexis of modern English, and look up large samples of verbs in a good dictionary, we find that many of them, including the majority of those that are in common use, carry the label 'both transitive and intransitive' (just as in Table 5-5). If we investigate these further, we find that where the same verb occurs with each of these two values the pairs of clauses that are formed in this way, with the given verb as Process, are not usually intransitive/transitive pairs but non-ergative/ergative ones. There are intransitive/transitive pairs, like *the tourist hunted/the tourist hunted the lion*, where *the tourist* is Actor in both. But the majority of verbs of high frequency in the language yield pairs of the other kind, like *the tourist woke/the lion woke the tourist*, where the relationship is an ergative one. If we express this structure in transitive terms, *the tourist* is Actor in the one and Goal in the other; yet it is the tourist that stopped sleeping, in both cases. Compare *the boat sailed/Mary sailed the boat*, *the cloth tore/the nail tore the cloth*, *Tom's eyes closed/Tom closed his eyes*, *the rice cooked/Pat cooked the rice*, *my resolve weakened/the news weakened my resolve*.

The coming of this pattern to predominance in the system of modern English is one of a number of related developments that have been taking place in the language over the past five hundred years or more, together amounting to a far-reaching and complex process of semantic change. These changes have tended, as a whole, to emphasize the textual function, in the organization of English discourse, by comparison with the experiential function; and, within the experiential function, to emphasize the cause-&-effect aspect of processes by comparison with the 'deed-&-extension' one. There is no such thing, of course, as 'completed' change in language; waves of change are passing through the system all the time. But this aspect of English – its transitivity system – is particularly unstable in the contemporary language, having been put under great pressure by the need for the language continually to adapt itself to a rapidly changing environment, and by the increasing functional demands that have been made on it ever since Chaucer's time. Let us try and give a brief sketch of the clause in its experiential function as it now appears in the contemporary language, looking at it as a way of making generalizations about processes in the real world.

---

[49] In the typological literature on 'case marking' or 'alignment' systems, such pairs are often referred to as 'ergative/absolutive', contrasting with the 'nominative/accusative' pair of the transitive model.

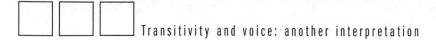

Every process has associated with it one participant that is the key figure in that process; this is the one through which the process is actualized, and without which there would be no process at all. Let us call this element the **Medium**, since it is the entity through the medium of which the process comes into existence. In the examples above, the Medium is *the boat, the cloth, his (Tom's) eyes, the rice, my resolve*. Hence in a material process the Medium is equivalent to Actor in an intransitive clause and Goal in a transitive clause. See Figure 5-37.

(a) transitive interpretation

the boat	sailed
the cloth	tore
Tom's eyes	closed
the rice	cooked
my resolve	weakened
Actor	Process

Mary	sailed	the boat
the nail	tore	the cloth
Tom	closed	his eyes
Pat	cooked	the rice
the news	weakened	my resolve
Actor	Process	Goal

(b) ergative interpretation

the boat	sailed
the cloth	tore
Tom's eyes	closed
the rice	cooked
my resolve	weakened
Medium	Process

Mary	sailed	the boat
the nail	tore	the cloth
Tom	closed	his eyes
Pat	cooked	the rice
the news	weakened	my resolve
Agent	Process	Medium

Fig. 5-37   Transitive and ergative interpretations

Except in the special case of the medio-receptive voice (see Figure 5-38), the Medium is obligatory in all processes; and it is the only element that is, other than the process itself. (For the sake of simplicity we represent meteorological processes such as *it's raining* as having no Medium; but it would be more accurate to say that here the Medium is conflated with the Process.) The Medium is also the only element that is never introduced into the clause by means of a preposition (again with the same exception of medio-receptives); it is treated as something that always participates directly in the process. (Note that the structure *the cooking of the rice*, where the Medium follows *of*, is not an exception; *of* is functioning here, as it typically does, not as preposition but as structure marker – cf. genitive *'s* in *the rice's cooking*.)

The Process and the Medium together form the **nucleus** of an English clause; and this nucleus then determines the range of options that are available to the rest of the clause. Thus the nucleus 'tear + cloth' represents a small semantic field that may be realized as a

(a) 'true' receptive: effective; Medium/Subject, Agent: *by ...*

| (material) | the glass | was | broken | by the cat | |
| (mental) | Mary | as | upset | by the news | |

Medium	Process		Agent	
Subject	Finite	Predicator	Adjunct	
Mood		Residue		
nominal group	verbal group		prepositional phrase	

(b) Beneficiary – receptive: effective; Beneficiary/Subject, Agent: *by ....*

| (material) | my aunt | was | given | this teapot | by the duke |

Beneficiary	Process		Medium	Agent
Subject	Finite	Predicator	Medium	Adjunct
Mood		Residue		
nominal group	verbal group		nominal group	prepositional phrase

(c) Range – receptive: middle (i.e. medio-receptive); Range/Subject, Medium: *by ...*

| (material) | songs | were | sung | by the choir | |
| (mental) | the music | was | enjoyed | by the audience | |

Range	Process		Medium	
Subject	Finite	Predicator	Adjunct	
Mood		Residue		
nominal group	verbal group		prepositional phrase	

Fig. 5-38 Types of receptive clause

clause either alone or in combination with other participant or circumstantial functions. (The lexical spread of such a semantic field is very roughly that of a paragraph in *Roget's Thesaurus*.)

The most general of these further options, 'most general' because it turns up in all process types, is the ergative one whereby, in addition to the Medium, there may be another participant functioning as an external cause. This participant we will refer to as the **Agent**. Either the process is represented as self-engendering, in which case there is no separate Agent; or it is represented as engendered from outside, in which case there is another participant functioning as Agent. Thus the clauses *the glass broke, the baby sat up, the boy ran* are all structured as Medium + Process. In the real world, there may well have been some external agency involved in the breaking of the glass; but in the semantics of English it is

represented as having been self-caused. For that matter there may have been some external agency also in the baby's sitting up, and even in the boy's running (such as the lion referred to earlier). We may choose to put the Agent in, as in *the heat broke the glass*, *Jane sat the baby up*, *the lion chased the boy*; notice that if the receptive is used, e.g. *the glass got broken*, it is always possible to ask who or what by. A large number of processes may be represented either way: either as involving Medium only, or as involving Medium plus Agent.

By using the ergative standpoint to complement the transitive one in our interpretation of English, we can match up the functions in the various process types. The table of equivalents is given as Table 5-41. In this table, the generalized ergative functions are listed first in a single column; then their equivalents in specific transitive terms are shown for each of the process types. For example, the ergative function Medium is equivalent:

in material process	to Actor (middle), Goal (effective)
in behavioural process	to Behaver
in mental process	to Senser
in verbal process	to Sayer (middle), Target (effective)
in attributive process	to Carrier
in identifying process	to Token
in existential process	to Existent

Thus the Medium is the nodal participant throughout the system. It is not the doer, nor the causer, but the one that is critically involved, in some way or other according to the particular nature of the process.

The **Agent** is the external agency where there is one. In a material process, it is the Actor – provided the process is one that has a Goal; otherwise, it may be present as the **Initiator** of the process. In a mental process, it is the Phenomenon – provided the process is encoded in one direction, from phenomenon to consciousness and not the other way round. The Agent can also be present in a relational process. In the attributive type, this is a distinct function analogous to the material Initiator: the one that brings about the attribution, e.g. *the heat* in *the heat turned the milk sour*. This is the Attributor. In the identifying type, it is normally possible to add a feature of agency (an Assigner) provided the clause is operative (Token as Subject): thus, to ('which is Tom?'—) *Tom is (serves as) the leader* corresponds an agentive such as *they elected Tom the leader* (cf. Figure 5-35); and, with second order Agent, *they got Tom elected the leader* (cf. Figure 5-37). We have seen that, with such **decoding** clauses (those where Token = Identified) the receptive is in any case rather rare (see Section 5.4.4 a). By contrast, in an **encoding** identifying clause, passive is more or less as frequent as active, e.g. ('which is the leader?'—) active *Tom is the leader*, passive *the leader is Tom*; but only the active will accommodate a further agency – we do not say *they elected the leader Tom*. Hence in an active/passive pair such as ('who are now the main suppliers?'—) active *our company are now the main suppliers*, passive *the main suppliers are now our company*, the agentive form is *this decision leaves our company the main suppliers*; the passive does not readily expand to *this decision leaves the main suppliers our company*. See also Table 5-42.

343

Table 5-41 Table of transitivity functions, showing transitive and ergative equivalents (participant functions only)

| | Typical preposition | Ergative function | Transitive function | | | | | | |
			material	behavioural	mental	verbal	relational: attributive	relational: identifying	Existential
process	–	1 Process							
participants		2 Medium	Actor [mid.]; Actor or Goal [eff.]	Behaver	Senser	Sayer [mid.]; Target [eff.]	Carrier	Token	Existent
	by	3 Agent	Initiator or Actor [eff.]	–	Inducer or Phenomenon ['please']	Sayer [eff.]	Attributor	Assigner	–
	to, for	4 Beneficiary	Recipient; Client	–	–	Receiver	(Beneficiary)	–	–
	at, on, etc.	5 Range	Scope	Behaviour	Phenomenon ['like']	Verbiage	Attribute	Value	–
circumstances	for, over, across, etc.	6 Extent	duration, frequency (temporal), distance (spatial)				how long? how far? how often?		
	at, in, on, from, etc.	7 Location	time (temporal), place (spatial)				when? where?		
	with, by, like	8 Manner	means, quality, comparison, degree				how? what with? in what way? like what? to what extent?		
	through, for, etc.	9 Cause	reason, purpose, behalf				why? what for? who for?		
	in case of, etc.	10 Contingency	condition, concession, default				under what conditions?		
	with, besides, etc.	11 Accompaniment	comitation, addition				who/what with? who/what else?		
	as, into, etc.	12 Role	guise, product				what as? what into?		
	about, etc.	13 Matter					what about?		
	according to; to, etc.	14 Angle	source, viewpoint				who says? who thinks?		

Table 5-42 Transitive and ergative in identifying relational clauses[50]

decoding (which is Tom?)	Tom	is/plays	**the leader**	**the leader**	is/is played	by Tom
transitive:	Id/Tk	Process	Ir/Vl	Ir/Vl	Process	Id/Tk
ergative	Medium		Range	Range		Medium

encoding (who's the leader)	**Tom**	is/plays	the leader	the leader	is/is played	by **Tom**
transitive:	Ir/Tk	Process	Id/Vl	Id/Vl	Process	Ir/Tk
ergative	Agent		Medium	Medium		Agent

We will now introduce the other participant functions, Beneficiary and Range.

5.7.3 Ergative and transitive participant roles

In addition to Medium and Agent, we can recognize two further ergative participant roles – the **Beneficiary** and the **Range**. Like Medium and Agent, they take on different transitivity values according to the nature of the process type. Thus, for all the participant roles we have one functional concept that is specific to the process type, and another that is general to all process types; and the general concept derives naturally from an ergative interpretation of the grammar of the clause.

5.7.3.1 Benefactive clauses: Beneficiary

The Beneficiary is the one to whom or for whom the process is said to take place. It appears in 'material' and 'verbal' clauses, and occasionally in 'relational' ones. (In other words, there are no Beneficiaries in 'mental', 'behavioural' or 'existential' clauses.)

(a) In a 'material' clause, the Beneficiary is either the Recipient or the Client. The Beneficiary is realized by (*to* +) nominal group (Recipient) or (*for* +) nominal group (Client); the presence of the preposition is determined by textual factors (see below Section 5.7.4).

(b) In a 'verbal' clause, the Beneficiary is the Receiver.

(c) There are also a few 'relational' clauses of the 'attributive' mode containing a Beneficiary, e.g. *him* in *she made him a good wife, it cost him a pretty penny*. We shall just refer to this as Beneficiary, without introducing a more specific term, since these hardly constitute a recognizably distinct role in the clause.

The Beneficiary regularly functions as Subject in the clause; in that case the verb is in the 'receptive' voice. An example of this is shown in Figure 5-39.

---

[50] Note: Those in the top row are **decoding** clauses; the receptive is a medio-receptive and hence rare. Those below are **encoding**; the receptive is a 'true' receptive.

were	you	asked	a lot of questions
	Receiver		
Process:		verbal	Verbiage
Finite	Subject	Predicator	Complement
Mood		Residue	
verbal ...	nominal group	... group	nominal group

Fig. 5-39 Beneficiary as Subject

5.7.3.2 Ranged clauses: Range

The Range is the element that specifies the range or domain of the process. A Range may occur in 'material', 'behavioural', 'mental', 'verbal' and 'relational' clauses – but not in 'existential' ones: see Table 5-43.

In a 'material', the Range is the Scope; in a 'behavioural' clause, the Range is the Behaviour.

In a 'mental' clause, the concept of Range helps to understand the structure we have already identified, that of Senser and Phenomenon. It is not an additional element, but an interpretation of the Phenomenon in one of its structural configurations.

Table 5-43 Range in different process types

PROCESS TYPE	Range:	Examples:
material	Scope	he rode his motorbike to work you haven't signed your name on this letter I'm following your example
behavioural	Behaviour	the child wept copious tears
mental	Phenomenon	you can feel the pressure on your skull do you prefer tea for breakfast? I would recognize that face anywhere
verbal	Verbiage	he made a defiant speech she speaks Russian with her children what question did you want to ask me?
relational	Attribute	she is a captain
	Value	she is the captain
existential	–	

We saw that mental processes are distinguished by being bi-directional: we say both *it pleases me* and *I like it*. The first of these shares certain features of an effective material process: it occurs freely in the 'receptive' (*I'm pleased with it*), and it can be generalized as a kind of 'doing to' (*What does it do to you? – It pleases me*). Here the Phenomenon shows

some resemblance to an Actor: from the ergative point of view, they are both Agent. The *like* type, on the other hand, displays none of these properties; in this type the Phenomenon bears no kind of resemblance to a Goal. But it does show certain affinities with the Scope. It figures as Subject, in the 'receptive', under similarly restricted conditions; and it appears in expressions like *enjoy the pleasure, saw a sight, have an understanding of*, which are analogous to material Scope expressions of the 'process' type like *play a game, have a game*. So we can interpret the role of Phenomenon in the *like* type of mental process as a counterpart of that of Scope in the material; it is the element which delimits the boundaries of the sensing.

Likewise, the concept of Range turns out to be applicable to a 'verbal' clause, in this case to the function we have referred to above as the Verbiage (not to be taken as a derogatory term!). The two kinds of Verbiage, that which refers to the content, as in *describe the apartment*, and that which specifies the nature of the verbal process, like *tell a story*, are analogous respectively to the material 'entity Scope' and 'process Scope'. The latter type includes configurations of Process: general verb + Range: lexical content analogous to those found with 'material' clauses (e.g. *take a bath, have a shower*): *make a statement, make an offer, issue a command, give an order*.

The ergative analysis of relational clauses is complex. In the attributive, the Attribute is clearly analogous to a Range; but in the identifying the criteria tend to conflict. For purposes of simplicity, we will interpret the Token as Medium and the Value as Range in all types, although this does ignore some aspects of the patterning of such clauses in text.

What is common to all these functions – Scope in material clauses, Behaviour in behavioural clauses, Phenomenon in the *like* type of mental clauses, Verbiage in verbal clauses, and Attribute or Value in 'relational' clauses – is something like the following. There may be in each type of clause one element that is not so much an entity participating in the process as a refinement of the process itself. This may be the name of a particular variety of the process, which being a noun can then be modified for quantity and for quality: (material) *play another round of golf*, (mental) *enjoy the pleasure of your company, see an amazing sight, think independent thoughts*, (verbal) *tell those tales of woe*. Since here the kind of action, event, behaviour, sensing or saying is specified by the noun, as a participant function, the verb may be entirely general in meaning, as in *have a game of, have an idea about, have a word with* (cf. Footnote 19 above). Or, second, this element may be an entity, but one that plays a part in the process not by acting, or being acted upon, but by marking its domain, e.g. *play the piano, enjoy the scenery, recount the events*. It is a characteristic of this second type that they are on the borderline of participants and circumstances; there is often a closely related form of prepositional phrase, e.g. *play on the piano, delight in the scenery, tell about the events*.

5.7.4 The complementarity of the transitive and ergative models

Probably all transitivity systems, in all languages, are some blend of these two semantic models of processes, the transitive and the ergative. The transitive is a linear interpretation; and since the only function that can be defined by extension in this way is that of the Goal (together with, perhaps, the analogous functions of Target in a verbal process and Phenomenon in a mental process of the *please* type), systems that are predominantly transitive in character tend to emphasize the distinction between participants (i.e. direct participants, Actor and Goal only) and circumstances (all other functions). But the ergative

347

is a nuclear rather than a linear interpretation; and if this component is to the fore, there may be a whole cluster of participant-like functions in the clause: not only Agent but also Beneficiary and Range. These, seen from a transitive point of view, are circumstantial: Agent is a kind of Manner, Beneficiary a kind of Cause and Range a kind of Extent; and they can all be expressed as minor processes. But from an ergative point of view they are additional participants in the major process: the nucleus of 'Process + Medium' has an inner ring of additional participants as well as an outer ring of circumstances surrounding it: see Figure 5-40.

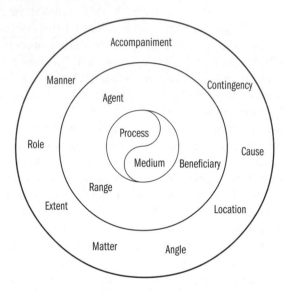

Fig. 5-40 Clause nucleus of Process + Medium, inner ring of Agent, Beneficiary and Range and outer ring of circumstances

Semantically, therefore, Agent, Beneficiary and Range have some features of participants and some of circumstances: they are mixed. And this is reflected in the fact that grammatically also they are mixed: they may enter in to the clause either directly as nominal groups (participant-like) or indirectly in prepositional phrases (circumstance-like).

But the choice of 'plus or minus preposition' with Agent, Beneficiary and Range is not just random variation; it serves a textual function. This is, in fact, another instance of the importance attached to the message structure in modern English. The principle is as follows. If a participant other than the Medium is in a place of prominence in the message, it tends to take a preposition (i.e. to be construed as 'indirect' participant); otherwise it does not. Prominence in the message means functioning either (i) as marked Theme (i.e. Theme but not Subject) or (ii) as 'late news' – that is, occurring after some other participant, or circumstance, that already follows the Process. In other words, prominence comes from occurring either earlier or later than expected in the clause; and it is this that is being reinforced by the presence of the preposition. The preposition has become a signal of special status in the message. Examples in Table 5-44.

Table 5-44 Association of prepositional phrase with textual prominence

	Non-prominent	Marked Theme	'Late news'
Agent (her nephew)	her nephew sent her flowers	by her nephew she was sent flowers	she was sent flowers by her nephew
Beneficiary (his aunt)	he sent his aunt flowers	to his aunt he sent flowers	he sent flowers to his aunt
Range (the high jump)	John wins the high jump every time	at the high jump John wins every time	John wins every time at the high jump

The other elements in the clause are represented clearly as circumstances; they are adverbial groups or prepositional phrases. But even here there is some indeterminacy; in other words, just as those elements that are treated essentially as participants can sometimes occur with a preposition, so at least some elements that are treated essentially as circumstances can sometimes occur without one. With expressions of Extent and Location there is often no preposition, as in *they stayed two days, they left last Wednesday*. Furthermore, as pointed out in Section 4.3, the Complement of the preposition can often emerge to function as a Subject, as in *the bed had not been slept in, she hasn't been heard from since, I always get talked to by strangers*, and an example overheard in a cinema queue *look at all these people we've been come in after by*. This pattern suggests that Complements of prepositions, despite being embedded in an element that has a circumstantial function, are still felt to be participating, even if at a distance, in the process expressed by the clause.

The same tendency away from a purely transitive type of semantic organization can be seen in the system of voice. In a transitive pattern the participants are obligatory Actor and optional Goal; if there is Actor only, the verb is intransitive and active in voice, while if both are present the verb is transitive and may be either active or passive. This is still the basis of the English system; but there is little trace of transitivity left in the verb, and voice is now more a feature of the clause.

The way the voice system works is as follows. A clause with no feature of 'agency' is neither active nor passive but **middle**. One with agency is non-middle, or **effective**, in agency. An effective clause is then either operative or receptive in voice. In an operative clause, the Subject is the Agent and the Process is realized by an active verbal group; in a receptive the Subject is the Medium and the Process is realized by a passive verbal group. The basic system is shown in Figure 5-41.

Strictly speaking an effective clause has the feature 'agency' rather than the structural function Agent, because this may be left implicit, as in *the glass was broken*. The presence of an 'agency' feature is, in fact, the difference between a pair of clauses such as *the glass broke* and *the glass was* (or *got*) *broken*: the latter embodies the feature of agency, so that one can ask the question 'who by?', while the former allows for one participant only.

If the clause is effective, since either participant can then become Subject there is a choice between operative and receptive. The reasons for choosing receptive are as follows: (1) to get the Medium as Subject, and therefore as unmarked Theme ('I'm telling you about the glass'); and (2) to make the Agent either (i) late news, by putting it last ('culprit: the cat'), or (ii) implicit, by leaving it out. In spoken English the great majority of receptive clauses

349

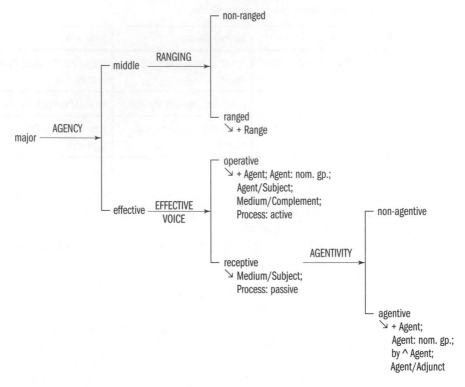

Fig. 5-41   The systems of AGENCY, RANGING and VOICE

are, in fact, Agent-less; *the glass was broken* is more common than *the glass was broken by the cat*. The speaker leaves the listener to locate the source.

But, as we have seen, there are other potential Subjects besides Agent and Medium. There are the other participants, the Beneficiary and the Range, either of which may be selected as Subject of the clause; the verb will then likewise be in the passive. Examples of these are given in Figure 5-38. Then there are the 'indirect' participants functioning as Complements to prepositions, some of which (as referred to above) are potential Subjects; these give various other kinds of passive such as 'location-receptive', e.g.

> The china had never been used. <u>The sheets</u> **had** never **been slept in**. Titanic was called the ship of dreams. [COCA]

'manner-receptive', e.g. *this pen's never been written with*, and so on. Normally these are also medio-receptives, i.e. they are middle not effective clauses. But receptives with idiomatic phrasal verbs, such as

> <u>Garbage collection</u>, always sporadic, **had been done away with** entirely the last few weeks. [COCA]

> And <u>both President Obama and Michelle Obama</u> **are** really **looked up to** there and, yes, on that rock star type status. [COCA]

> that prize has never been put in for

are often 'true' receptives in the sense that the prepositional phrase really represents a participant, as in the examples *look at the sky*, *wait for the boat* discussed above. Analysis in Figure 5-42.

(a) locative receptive: middle (medio-receptive); Location/Subject, Medium: *by ...*

the bed	hadn't	been slept	in		by anyone
Location	Process				Medium
Subject	Finite	Predicator	Adjunct		Adjunct
Mood		Residue			
nominal group	verbal group		prepositional phrase		prepositional phrase

(b) 'true' receptive: effective; Medium/Subject, Agent: *by ...*

it	's	been done	away	with	by the government
Medium	Process				Agent
Subject	Finite	Predicator	Adjunct	Adjunct	Adjunct
Mood		Residue			
nominal group	verbal group				prepositional phrase

Fig. 5-42 Circumstantial receptive clauses

By interpreting processes ergatively as well as transitively we are able to understand many features of English grammar that otherwise remain arbitrary or obscure. We will take up just one such example, that of clauses such as *the police exploded the bomb*, *the sergeant marched the prisoners*, where – as suggested by the agnate clauses *the bomb exploded*, *the prisoners marched* – the meaning is not so much 'do to' as 'make to do' (what the sergeant made the prisoners do was march). Ergatively, there is no difference between these and clauses like *the lion chases the tourist*. Transitively, these appear as different configurations; we have to introduce the function of **Initiator** to take account of the executive role. But in modern English they are very much alike; and the ergative analysis expresses their likeness – both consist of a Medium and an Agent. In ergative terms, '*a* does something to *x*' and '*a* makes *x* do something' are both cases of '*x* is involved in something, brought about by *a*'. The analyses are shown in Figure 5-44.

Putting the two analyses together, we would expect to find that these two types of clause are not identical, but that there is no clear line between them; and that is precisely the case. One difference is whether or not there can be an **analytic causative** with *make* (see Chapter 8, Section 8.7): we can say *the police made the bomb explode*, but not *the lion made the tourist chase*. But this leaves many uncertain: what about *Mary made the boat sail*, *the nail made the cloth tear*? – and, with a different verb, *the lion made the tourist run*? The distinction becomes somewhat clearer if we ask whether, if the second participant is removed, the role of the first participant changes. In *the sergeant marched the prisoners/the sergeant marched*, it clearly does; it is now the sergeant who is doing the marching (cf. *the police exploded*, which we now have to interpret in a transferred sense) – whereas in *the lion chased* no such interpretation is possible. Those where the role changes will have Initiator + Actor rather than Actor + Goal. There is a large class of material processes of this kind where the agnate causatives are, or may be, attributive: *the sun ripened the fruit/made the fruit ripen*, *her voice calmed the audience/made the audience calm*; these will belong to the 'initiating' type – if we say *the sun ripened, her voice calmed*, the meaning changes from 'make (ripe, calm)' to 'become (ripe, calm)'.

From the transitive point of view, in these initiating structures there is a feature of 'cause' added. This is also possible with (i) mental clauses and with (ii) relational ones. (i) Corresponding to the initiating structure in material clauses, we find an inducing structure in mental clauses; for example, *remind* can be interpreted as 'induce to remember' (cf. Footnote 25 above), as in:

> **The Saudis** also reminded Hariri that King Abdullah's July 2010 arrival in Beirut aboard the same plane as Syrian president Assad was intended to underscore Riyadh's acquiescence in Damascus's superior role in Lebanon. [COCA]

Here *the Saudis* is Inducer and *Hariri* is Senser. Such examples are, of course, close to 'verbal' clauses; compare [Sayer:] *the Saudis* [Process:] *told* [Receiver:] *Hariri that ...* . Just as *remind* can be analysed as 'cause to remember', so a small number of other verbs can analysed as operating in 'mental' clauses with an added feature of 'cause', e.g. *instruct, teach* – 'cause to learn' (see Halliday, 1976b/2005: 302), *convince* – 'cause to believe', *persuade* – 'cause to believe', or (desiderative) 'cause to want'.

(ii) Corresponding to the initiating structure in material clauses, we find attributed and assigned structures in relational clause. As we have seen, for the transitive analysis we have to recognize the additional functions of Attributor and Assigner, as in Figure 5-43; but from the ergative point of view, these clauses simply add a feature of agency. Examples:

> In the instant case, **Butterworth** considered it appropriate to commence both sets of proceedings in the Supreme Court. [ACE_J]

> He was considered bolshie **by the European establishment** [ACE_A]

> **They** elected her president of the Council of Superior Court Judges of Georgia. [COCA]

If the clause already has an Agent in the structure, the only way this can be done is by using an analytic causative; this makes it possible to bring in an Agent of the second order, as Figure 5-44. Figure 5-45 shows how these clauses appear in the receptive voice.

The ergative structure is open-ended, and a further round of agency can always be added on:

> the ball rolled: Fred rolled the ball: Mary made Fred roll the ball: John got Mary to make Fred roll the ball: ...

The transitive structure, on the other hand, is configurational; it cannot be extended in this way. Thus, from a transitive point of view, *Mary made Fred roll the ball* is not a single process; it is two processes forming one complex. But at this point, to take up the notion

(a) attributive

the news	made	Bill	happy
the result	proves	you	right
transitive Attributor	Process	Carrier	Attribute
ergative Agent		Medium	Range

(b) identifying

the mother	called	the baby	Amanda
the team	voted	Tom	captain
transitive Assigner	Process	Identified/Token	Identifier/Value
ergative Agent		Medium	Range

Fig. 5-43 Transitive and ergative analyses of relational clauses

the police	exploded	the bomb
Initiator	Process	Actor
Agent		Medium

They	got	the police	to explode	the bomb
	Pro-	Initiator	-cess	Actor
Agent$_2$		Agent$_1$		Medium

the story	frightened	you
Phenomenon	Process	Senser
Agent		Medium

What	made	the story	frighten	you?
	Pro-	Phenomenon	-cess	Senser
Agent$_2$		Agent$_1$		Medium

Fig. 5-44 Second-order Agent in material and mental clauses

they	got/had	the bomb	exploded	by the police
	Pro-	Actor	-cess	Initiator
Agent$_2$		Medium		Agent$_1$

what	made	you	be frightened	by the story?
	Pro-	Senser	-cess	Phenomenon
Agent$_2$		Medium		Agent$_1$

they	had/got	Tom	voted	captain	by the team
	Pro-	Id/Tk	-cess	Ir/Vl	Assigner
Agent$_2$		Medium		Range	Agent$_1$

Fig. 5-45 Second-order Agent in receptive (material, mental and relational) clauses

of a complex, we have to hand the discussion over to Part II. For the analysis of these particular structures, see Chapter 8, Section 8.5.

Table 5-45 sets out the principal criteria for distinguishing the types of process discussed in the present chapter, taking account of the number and kind of participants, the directionality and voice, the pro-verb, the form of the unmarked present tense, and the phonological properties of the verb. Figure 5-46 shows the systems of PROCESS TYPE and AGENCY interact in the system network of TRANSITIVITY. This system network adds a sub-network for 'verbal' clauses to the sub-networks given in Figure 5-10 (material clauses), Figure 5-16 (mental clauses), and Figure 5-17 (relational clauses). Note that the mental distinction between 'emanating' and 'impinging' is now interpreted as the distinction between 'middle' and 'effective' (but mental clauses with an Inducer are not covered by the system network).

Table 5-45 Criteria for distinguishing process types

| | Material | Behav. | Mental | | Verbal | Relational | | Existential |
						attributive	identifying	
Category meaning:	doing (doing, happening, doing to/ with)	behaving	sensing		saying	being (attribute)	being (identity)	being (existence)
Number of inherent participants:	1 or 2	1	2		1	2	2	1 or 0
Nature of first participant:	thing	conscious thing	conscious thing		symbol source	thing or fact	thing or fact	thing or fact
Nature of second participant:	thing		thing or fact				[same as 1st]	
Ability to project:	−	−	projection of ideas		projection of locutions	−	−	−
Directionality:	one way		one way	two way: please type	like type	one way	one way	one way	one way
Voice:	middle or effective		middle	effective	middle	middle or effective [target type]	middle or effective	middle or effective	middle
Type of receptive:		receptive		receptive	medio-receptive			receptive	
Pro-verb:	do	do to/ with	do	(do to)					
Unmarked present tense:	present in present	present in present	simple present		simple present	simple present	simple present	simple present
Accentuation of verb:	accented	accented	accented	(either)	(either)	unaccented	unaccented	unaccented

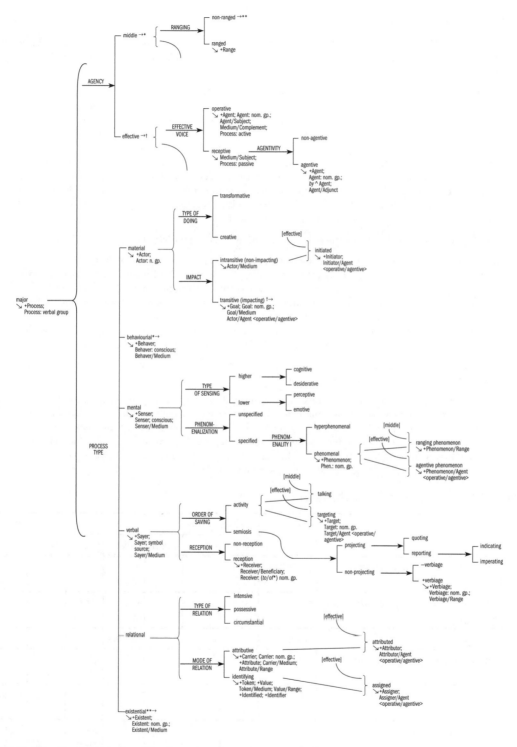

Fig. 5-46 System network of TRANSITIVITY (AGENCY and PROCESS TYPE)

5.8 Text illustrations

Text 5-17: Reporting – chronicling (spoken, dialogic): interview with Chinua Achebe

Interviewer: When people speak of African literature, they say African literature, as opposed to Nigerian literature, South African literature, Somalian literature. Is there a reason for that?

Achebe: We generally talk of Africa as one because that's the way Europe looks at Africa, and many people in Europe and America who have not travelled, or who are perhaps not well educated, probably think that Africa is one small state or something somewhere. Another reason is that the quantity of the literature is not overwhelming yet, so one can put them all together. But it is growing. Suddenly Nigerian literature is a substantial body of literature. Somalian literature is not enough yet to form a body by itself, but it can fit into the general name of African literature. We ourselves do not have any difficulty at all in recognizing regional differences, but there are distinctive qualities – even within Nigeria. The literature which is beginning, just beginning, to come out of the Moslem part of Nigeria is very different from the literature which is coming out of the south. Very few people know of this yet, outside of Nigeria. As time goes on, I think there will be greater and greater and greater emphasis on the differences.

Interviewer: Can you tell us about the political and cultural makeup of Nigeria?

Achebe: One quarter of the entire population of Africa is in Nigeria, so we say that every fourth African is a Nigerian. During the European scramble for Africa, Nigeria fell to the British. It wasn't one nation at that point; it was a large number of independent political entities. The British brought this rather complex association into being as one nation and ruled it until 1960 when Nigeria achieved independence. Christian missionaries from Europe were active in the southern part of Nigeria, so today there's Christianity in the south and Islam in the north. The three major groups in the nation are the Yoruba in the southwest, the Ibo in the southeast, and the Hausa, finally, in the north. This is simplifying it, but that's roughly the picture.

Interviewer: The differences, as I understand it, between the Yoruba and the lbo was that the Yoruba had a system of royalty, and the Ibo were more egalitarian.

Achebe: Yes, yes. The Ibos did not approve of kings. They may have had kings in the past, and I suspect they did because they seem to know a lot about kings. They had five titles and the fifth and the highest title was that of king. For every title there is something you do for the community, you feast the community, you entertain the community, you produce so much money, you produce so many yams. The title for king fell out of use because its final requirement was that the man who aspires to be king would first pay all the debt owed by every single man and every single woman in the community!

Table 5-46 Extract from interview with Chinua Achebe

		AGENCY	PROCESS TYPE						CIRC.
			mat.	behav.	mental	verbal	relat.	exist.	
I:	**Can** you **tell** us *about the political and cultural makeup of Nigeria?*	mid: non-ra				non-verb.			matter
A:	One quarter of the entire population of Africa **is** in Nigeria,	mid: ra					attr & circ		–
	so we **say**	mid: non-ra				reporting			–
	that every fourth African **is** a Nigerian.	mid: ra					attr & intens		–
	During the European scramble for Africa, Nigeria **fell** *to the British.*	mid: non-ra	transf: enh						locative
	It **wasn't** one nation *at that point;*	mid: ra					attr & intens		locative

Table 5-46 Extract from interview with Chinua Achebe (*contd*)

		AGENCY	PROCESS TYPE						CIRC.
			mat.	behav.	mental	verbal	relat.	exist.	
	it **was** a large number of independent political entities.	mid: ra					attr & intens		–
	The British **brought** this rather complex association *into being as one nation*	eff	creative [transf: elab]						role
	and **ruled** it *until 1960*	eff	transf: elab						locative
	when Nigeria **achieved** independence.	mid: ra	transf: enh						–
	Christian missionaries from Europe **were** active *in the southern part of Nigeria,*	mid: ra					attr & intens		locative
	so *today* there**'s** Christianity *in the south*	mid: non-ra						✓	locative
	and [there**'s**] Islam *in the north.*	mid: non-ra						✓	locative
	The three major groups in the nation **are** the Yoruba in the southwest, the Ibo in the southeast, and the Hausa, finally, in the north.	mid: ra					ident & intens		–
	This **is simplifying** it,	eff	transf: elab						–
	but that**'s** roughly the picture.	mid: ra					ident & intens		–
I:	The differences, <<as I understand it,>> between the Yoruba and the Ibo **was** ⟦that the Yoruba had a system of royalty, and the Ibo were more egalitarian⟧.	mid: ra					ident & intens		–
	<< as I **understand** it>>	mid: ra			cog & phen				–
	⟦that the Yoruba **had** a system of royalty,	mid: ra					attr & poss		–
	and the Ibo **were** more egalitarian⟧	mid: ra					attr & intens		–
A:	Yes, yes.								
	The Ibos **did not approve of** kings.	mid: ra			emot & phen				–
	They may **have had** kings *in the past,*	mid: ra					attr & poss		locative
	and I **suspect**	mid: non-ra			cog & idea				–

Table 5-46 Extract from interview with Chinua Achebe (*contd*)

	AGENCY	PROCESS TYPE						CIRC.
		mat.	behav.	mental	verbal	relat.	exist.	
they **did**	mid: ra					attr & poss		—
because they **seem to know** a lot about kings.	mid: ra			cog & phen				—
They **had** five titles	mid: ra					attr & poss		—
and the fifth and the highest title **was** that of king.	mid: ra					ident & intens		—
For every title there **is** something ⟦you do for the community⟧,	mid: non-ra						✓	matter
⟦you **do** for the community⟧	mid: non-ra	transf						behalf
you **feast** the community,	eff	transf: ext						—
you **entertain** the community,	eff	transf: elab						—
you **produce** so much money,	eff	creative						—
you **produce** so many yams.	eff	creative						—
The title for king **fell** out of use	mid: ra					attr & intens		—
because its final requirement **was** ⟦that the man ⟦who aspires to be king⟧ would first pay all the debt ⟦owed by every single man and every single woman in the community⟧ ⟧ !	mid: ra					ident & intens		—
⟦that the man ⟦who aspires to be king⟧ **would** first **pay** all the debt ⟦owed by every single man and every single woman in the community⟧ ⟧	eff	transf: ext						—
⟦who **aspires to be** king⟧	mid: ra					ident & intens		—
⟦**owed** by every single man and every single woman in the community⟧	eff					ident & poss		—

PART II

ABOVE, BELOW AND BEYOND THE CLAUSE

C H A P T E R
S I X

BELOW THE CLAUSE: GROUPS AND PHRASES

6.1 Groups and phrases

We have seen in Chapters 3–5 that the English clause is a composite affair, a combination of three different structures deriving from distinct functional components. These components (called 'metafunctions' in systemic theory) are the ideational (clause as representation), the interpersonal (clause as exchange) and the textual (clause as message). What this means is that the three structures serve to express three largely independent sets of lexicogrammatical choice. (1) Transitivity structures express representational meaning: what the clause is about, which is typically some process, with associated participants and circumstances; (2) modal structures express interactional meaning: what the clause is doing, as a verbal exchange between speaker-writer and audience; (3) thematic structures express the organization of the message: how the clause relates to the surrounding discourse, and to the context of situation in which it is being produced. These three sets of options together determine the structural shape of the clause.

The three functional components of meaning, ideational, interpersonal and textual, are realized throughout the grammar of a language (see e.g. Chapter 2, Table 2-8). But whereas in the grammar of the clause each component contributes a more or less complete structure, so that a clause is made up of three distinct structures combined into one (three lines of meaning, as we put it in Chapter 2, Section 2.7), when we look below the clause, and consider the grammar of the group, the pattern is somewhat different. Although we can still recognize the same three components, they are not represented in the form of separate whole structures, but rather as partial contributions to a single structural line. The difference between clause and group in this respect is only one of degree; but it is sufficient to enable us to analyse the structure of the group in one operation, rather than in three operations as we did with the clause.

At the same time, in interpreting group structure we have to split the ideational metafunction into two modes of construing experience: **experiential** and **logical**. So far what we have been describing under the ideational heading has been meaning as organization of experience; but there is also a logical aspect to it – language as the construal of certain very general logical relations – and it is this we have to introduce now. The logical component defines complex units, e.g. the **clause complex** discussed in the next chapter and **group and phrase complexes** discussed in Chapter 8. It comes in at this point because a group is in some respects equivalent to a **word complex** – that is, a combination of words built up on the basis of a particular logical relation. This is why it is called a **group** (= 'group of words'). It is also the reason why in the western grammatical tradition it was not recognized as a distinct structural unit: instead, simple sentences (that is, clauses, in our terms) were analysed directly into words. Such an analysis is still feasible provided we confine our attention to the sort of idealized isolated sentences that grammarians have usually dealt with, such as *Socrates runs* or *John threw the ball*[1]; even there, however, the 'words-in-sentences' model ignores several important aspects of the meanings involved, and in the analysis of real-life discourse it leads to impossible complexity. Describing a sentence as a construction of words is rather like describing a house as a construction of bricks, without recognizing the walls and the rooms as intermediate structural units.

In this chapter we shall examine the structure of the three main classes of group: **nominal group**, **verbal group** and **adverbial group**; along with a brief reference to **preposition** and **conjunction groups**. These classes of group are complexes of nominals, verbs, and adverbs (see Chapter 2, Figure 2-8); for example:

> [nominal group:] the police [verbal group:] will conduct [nominal group:] an investigation [adverbial group:] thoroughly and efficiently [ACE_A]

> [nominal group:] people [verbal group:] didn't take [nominal group:] the universities [adverbial group:] very seriously [LLC_06]

> [nominal group:] An aircraft [with a load of small nuclear weapons] [verbal group:] could < [adverbial group:] very conceivably > be given [nominal group:] a mission [[to suppress all trains [[operating within a specified geographic area of Russia]]]] [BROWN1_E]

They serve different functions in the clause (unless they are rankshifted and embedded in other units). In terms of the modal structure of the clause, nominal groups serve as Subject, Complement or Vocative, verbal groups as Finite + Predicator, and adverbial groups as Adjunct (either circumstantial or modal ones); and in terms of the experiential structure, nominal groups serve in participant roles, verbal groups as Process, and adverbial groups in circumstance roles. The correspondences between class and function were illustrated in Chapter 2, Figure 2-10, and will be discussed in more detail in this chapter. They are summarized in Table 6-1.

The final section will be concerned with the prepositional phrase. A **phrase** is different from a group in that, whereas a group is an expansion of a word, a phrase is a contraction

---

[1]   The model of words in clauses can be applied to simple structures during Phase II of language development, e.g. *squeeze orange* (pragmatic, spoken on rising tone) and *chuffa stuck* (mathetic, spoken on a falling tone) from the case study presented in Halliday (1975). Phase II is the transition from a child's protolanguage (Phase I) into the mother tongue spoken around him or her (Phase III). As children move further into the mother tongue, groups begin to emerge.

of a clause. Starting from opposite ends, the two achieve roughly the same status on the rank scale, as units that lie somewhere between the rank of a clause and that of a word.[2] In terms of the modal structure of the clause, prepositional phrases serve as Adjuncts, and in terms of the experiential structure, they serve as circumstances (e.g. *without cream* in *you didn't have it without cream, surely?* [Text 371]); see Table 6-1. Groups and phrases can form complexes, e.g. *violently and without reason* in *The Royal Australian Nursing Federation state secretary, Ms Irene Bolger, said yesterday police had acted violently and without reason* [ACE_A].

Table 6-1 Group and phrase classes in relation to clause function

		Modal structure	Experiential structure
groups	nominal	Vocative	–
		Subject, Complement	participant role (Medium, Agent, Range, Beneficiary)
	verbal	Finite + Predicator	Process
	adverbial	Adjunct (circumstantial)	circumstance role (primarily Manner: quality, Manner: degree)
		Adjunct (modal)	–
	conjunction	Adjunct (textual)	–
phrases	prepositional	Adjunct (circumstantial)	circumstance role (Location, Extent, Manner, Cause ...); participant role with special textual status
		Adjunct (modal)	–
		Adjunct (textual)	–

As can be seen from Table 6-1, there is functional overlap between adverbial group (and conjunction group) and prepositional phrase. They have the same general functional potential (cf. Chapter 2, Section 2.5); but they differ in two related respects. (1) Since prepositional phrases include a nominal group, they have greater expressive potential than adverbial groups. (2) Consequently they can construe more experientially complex circumstances. While adverbial groups tend to realize circumstances of Manner: quality (as with *beautifully* in *you've coped beautifully tonight*) and Manner: degree (as with *completely* in

---

[2] As we noted in Chapter 1, there is considerable variation across languages in the division of grammatical labour between groups and words: some languages have more elaborated group grammars, some have more elaborated word grammars; and some are intermediate. Phrases also appear to be quite variable. For example, some languages (like Finnish and Hungarian) realize many circumstantial relations by means of nominal cases rather than by prepositions (or postpositions), whereas other languages construe such relations verbally in verbal group complexes (so-called 'serial verb constructions', as in Akan and other languages in West Africa and Thai and other languages in South-East Asia). Over time, items tend to drift down the rank scale, so prepositions/postpositions (adpositions) and case markers often derive from verbs in verbal group complexes. Phrases may also develop via another, nominal, route: the adposition may derive from a noun in a possessive construction, which is why adpositions may take the genitive, as with certain prepositions in German and many in Arabic (cf. English: *sake* in *for somebody's sake*).

Big Pond had completely stuffed their computer up) – as well as modal and textual Adjuncts, other, experientially more complex circumstances that are more like indirect participants (e.g. Location, Cause, Accompaniment) tend to be realized by prepositional phrases. But prepositional phrases encroach on the functional ground of adverbial groups, partly by means of phrasal templates such as *in a … way (manner)*, as in *yeah it's not done in an antagonistic way* (instead of *…. not done antagonistically*); and adverbial groups may serve as Location in time or space. These latter often have as Head an adverb that derives from preposition + noun (e.g. *upstairs, outside, overseas; today, tomorrow*). (Here we can note that certain 'adverbs' such as *up, out, over* can be analysed alternatively as prepositions in prepositional phrases without a Range: see the end of Section 6.5.)

There is also some overlap between nominal groups and prepositional phrases. As noted in Chapter 5, Section 5.7, the distinction between participants and circumstances is less clear in the ergative organization of the clause, and this means that certain participants (Agent, Range and Beneficiary) are realized by prepositional phrases to indicate a special status in the clause as message (when they are presented as early or late news; cf. Table 5-44). At the same time, circumstances of location and extent may be realized by nominal groups without a preposition marking the circumstantial relation (cf. Chapter 5, Section 5.6).

6.2 Nominal group

Consider the following clause, spoken by a three-year-old child:

Look at those two splendid old electric trains with pantographs!

Most of this clause consists of one long nominal group, *those two splendid old electric trains with pantographs*. This group contains the noun *trains* preceded and followed by various other items all of them in some way characterizing the trains in question. These occur in a certain sequence; and the sequence is largely fixed, although some variation is possible.

We can interpret the first part of this nominal group structurally as in Figure 6-1.

those	two	splendid	old	electric	trains
Deictic	Numerative	Epithet$_1$	Epithet$_2$	Classifier	Thing
determiner	numeral	adjective	adjective	adjective	noun

Fig. 6-1 Experiential structure of part of a nominal group

This is an experiential structure which, taken as a whole, has the function of specifying (i) a class of things, namely *trains*, and (ii) some category of membership within this class. We shall refer to the element expressing the class by the functional label **Thing**.

6.2.1 Experiential structure of the nominal group: from Deictic to Classifier

Categorization within the class is typically expressed by one or more of the functional elements **Deictic**, **Numerative**, **Epithet** and **Classifier**. They serve to realize terms within different systems of the system network of the nominal group. We will consider each of these systems and elements in turn.

6.2.1.1 Deictic

The Deictic element indicates whether or not some specific subset of the Thing is intended; and if so, which. The nature of the Deictic is determined by the system of DETERMINATION: see Figure 6-2. The primary distinction is between (i) specific or (ii) non-specific. Here is an example of the use of Deictics from the beginning of a narrative; as we shall note below, the absence of the Deictic element is also systemically meaningful within the system of non-specific determination: see Text 6-1.

> **Text 6-1: Recreating – narrating (written, monologic): extract from the beginning of a folk tale (Placement followed by beginning of Initiating Event) [Text 65]**
> Pyramids, palaces, and temples of stone stand silent and abandoned, hidden by dense rain forests. But that was not always so. Long, long ago, great cities built by **the** Mayan people were centers of activity. In one of **those** cities – one **whose** name has long been forgotten – there lived **an** old halac uinic, or chief. Since he had **no** son to succeed him, he knew that **his** younger brother, Chirumá, would **one** day take **his** place. But **the** chief's wife wanted **a** child. **Each** day, she prayed with all **her** heart. And, **one** day, **her** prayers were answered. She gave birth to **a** son. **The** child was born on **the** 13th day of **the** month, **a** lucky day.

Here *a(n)*, *one*, *no* and *each* are non-specific determiners, and the absence of a determiner (∅) similarly marks a nominal group as non-specific when it is plural (e.g. *pyramids*) or mass (e.g. *stone*); and *the, those, his, her, whose*, and *the chief's* function as specific ones. Note the characteristic move from non-specific to specific: *great cities – those cities; an old halac uinic, or chief – the chief; a son – the child*; that is, non-specific determiners are used to introduce the discourse referent of the Thing, and specific determiners are used to track this referent in the text (see further, Chapter 9, Section 9.4).

(i) The specific Deictics are given in Table 6-2; they are **demonstrative** or **possessive** determiners, or embedded possessive nominal groups. The subset in question is specified by one of two possible deictic features: either (1) demonstratively, i.e. by reference to some

Table 6-2 Items (determiners, or [embedded] nominal groups) functioning as specific Deictic

	Determinative			Interrogative
Demonstrative	this	that		which(ever)
	these	those		
			the	what(ever)
Possessive	my	your	our	
	his	her	its	
	their			whose(ever)
	one's			
	[John's]			[which person's], etc.
	[my father's], etc.			

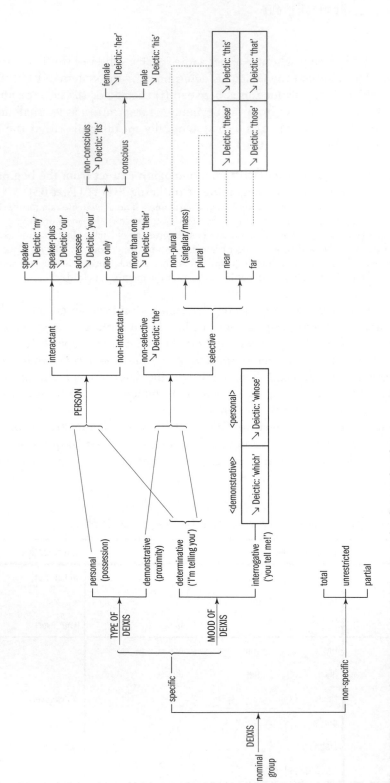

Fig.6-2 The nominal group system network: determination

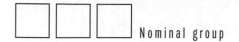

kind of **proximity** to the speaker (*this, these* = 'near me'; *that, those* = 'not near me'), or (2) by possession, i.e. by reference to **person** as defined from the standpoint of the speaker (*my, your, our, his, her, its, their* (see Figure 6-4 below); also *Mary's, my father's* etc.) together with the possibility of an interrogative in both these categories (demonstrative *which?*, possessive *whose?*). All these have the function of identifying a particular subset of the 'thing' that is being referred to.

Many languages embody these two forms of deixis in the structure of the nominal group. The two are closely related, both being (as indicated by the term 'deixis') a form of *orientation* by reference to the speaker – or more accurately, to the 'speaker-now'; the temporal-modal complex that constitutes the point of reference of the speech event. In some languages they are more systematically related to each other, the demonstrative having three terms instead of two: 'near me', 'near you' and 'not near either of us'. (Note that 'near' is not restricted to a local interpretation; the meaning is 'associated with' in some sense.) Some dialects of English have a system of this kind, the three terms being *this, that* and *yon*, with corresponding locative adverbs *here, there* and *yonder*.

There is one more item in this class, namely *the*. The word *the* is a specific, determinative Deictic of a peculiar kind: it means 'the subset in question is identifiable; but this will not tell you how to identify it – the information is somewhere around, where you can recover it'. So whereas *this train* means 'you know which train: – the one near me', and *my train* means 'you know which train: – the one I own', *the train* means simply 'you know which train'. Hence *the* is usually accompanied by some other element that supplies the information required: for example, *the long train* means 'you know which train: you can tell it by its length'. Compare *the night train, the train with a pantograph, the next train to arrive*. If there is no such information supplied, the subset in question will either be obvious from the situation, or else will have been referred to already in the discourse: for example, if you are on the platform you can say *get on the train!*, while *the train was coming nearer and nearer* might occur as part of a narrative.

In an incongruent nominal group that corresponds to a congruent clause, a possessive Deictic may correspond to one of the participants in the transitivity structure of the clause, e.g.:

The Minister's <u>decision</u> follows **his** <u>efforts</u> to mediate since the board decided to sack the matron several weeks ago. [ACE_A]

For 26 years journalists have followed John Paul II's every move. **His** world <u>travels</u>, **his** Sunday <u>blessings</u>, **his** <u>creation</u> of cardinals and saints, and now **his** every <u>sneeze</u>. [COCA]

or even (more restrictedly) to one of the circumstances, e.g.:

Yesterday's <u>decision</u> by the Arbitration Commission effectively said 'no' to ordering employers to pay into superannuation schemes. [ACE_A]

At **today's** official <u>fixing</u> by the five leading dealers, it was cut by 2s. 4d. per fine ounce – the lowest point for six weeks. [LOB_A]

(cf. further Chapter 10, Section 10.5).

(ii) Non-specific Deictics are given in Table 6-3; they are **total** or **partial** determiners[3]. The total ones convey the sense of 'all' (positive) or 'none' (negative), and the partial ones convey the sense of some unspecified subset; for example, *both trains have left, is there a train leaving soon?, there are some trains on the track, some trains are very comfortable, I haven't noticed any trains go by*. Note that there are two different types of *some*, one selective and one non-selective. The selective *some* contrasts with *any*, and is pronounced some [s^m]. The non-selective *some* is reduced in spoken form, being pronounced [sṃ], with a syllabic ṃ; the limiting case of phonological reduction is absence, and [sṃ] does indeed alternate with the absence of a determiner (∅). Thus in George Orwell's *All animals are equal but some animals are more equal than others*, the determiner *all* is a positive total Deictic, whereas the determiner *some* [s^m] is a selective partial Deictic.

Table 6-3 Determiners functioning as non-specific Deictic

		singular		non-singular		unmarked
				dual	mass/plural	
total	positive	each every		both	all	
	negative		neither (not either)			no (not any)
partial	selective	one	either			some [s^m] any
	non-selective	a(n)			some [sṃ] ∅	
		'one'	**'two'**		**'not one'**	**(unrestricted)**

Thus the so-called 'articles' of English, 'definite article' *the* and 'indefinite article' *a(n)*, are determiners realizing terms in, respectively, the specific and non-specific systems of nominal deixis. They enter into a proportional pattern as follows (for Head, see Sections 6.2.5 and 6.2.6 below): see Table 6-4.

Table 6-4 Parallel between specific and non-specific determiners

	'Weak' determiner [cannot be Head]	'Full' determiner [may be Head]	Non-personal pronoun [Head]
specific	the	that	it
non-specific	a(n)	one	there

---

[3] In predicate logic, some of these determiners have been interpreted as quantifiers – the 'universal quantifier' (∀ 'for all') and the 'existential quantifier' (∃ 'there exists'). These are part of one form of designed formal symbolic logic, but although they have been used in formal semantic interpretations of natural languages, they do not match the categories that have evolved in natural languages like English.

Historically *the* and *a(n)* are reduced forms of (respectively) *that* and *one*; *it* is also a reduced form of *that* (but preserving the final part, since it functions as Head, where *the* preserves the initial part). *there* is a reduced form of locative *there*.

It should be pointed out here that there are two different systems of NUMBER in the English nominal group, one associated with each of the two kinds of Deictics.

(i) With specific Deictics, the number system is 'non-plural/plural'; mass nouns are grouped together with singular, in a category of 'non-plural'. So *this*, *that* go with non-plural (singular or mass), *these*, *those* with plural, as in Table 6-5.

Table 6-5 Number in specific nominal groups

Non-plural		Plural
singular	mass	
this train	this electricity	these trains

(ii) With non-specific Deictics, the system is 'singular/non-singular'; mass nouns are grouped together with plural, in a category of 'non-singular'. So *a, an* goes with singular, weak *some* with non-singular (mass or plural), as in Table 6-6.

Table 6-6 Number in non-specific nominal groups

Singular	Non-singular	
	mass	plural
a train	(some) electricity	(some) trains

As noted above, if there is no Deictic element, the nominal group is non-specific and, within that, non-singular.[4] In other words, a nominal group may have no Deictic element in its **structure**, but this does not mean it has no value in the Deictic **system** – simply that the value selected is realized by a form having no Deictic in the expression.

The two different number systems operating with specific and non-specific determination apply to all nominal groups, but the typical range of determiners and the semantic patterns of agnation depend on whether a given nominal group refers to (i) a member or members of a class (particular reference) or to (ii) to a class to which members belong (general, or 'generic', reference): see Table 6-7. We will discuss these briefly in turn.

(i) When a given nominal group refers to a member or members of a class – i.e. to a particular thing or set of things, the full ranges of specific and non-specific determiners can serve as Deictic and the values within the specific and non-specific number systems are

---

[4]   The forms *trains* and *some trains*, as in *there are (some) trains on the track*, are not in fact identical. But the distinction is a more delicate one, and for the purpose of this analysis they will be treated as variant expressions of the same category.

BELOW THE CLAUSE: GROUPS AND PHRASES

Table 6-7 Nominal groups referring to members of a class ('particular') or to the class itself ('general')

			Singular	Mass	Plural
non-specific [Table 6-6]			singular [a(n)]	non-singular [(some)]	
specific [Table 6-5]			non-plural [this]		plural [these]
(i) particular (members)		non-specific	there was **an elephant** in the glade	there were **(some) elephants** in the glade / there was **(some)** water in the river	
		specific	**the/this elephant** charged / **the/this water** was brownish		**the/these** elephants charged
(ii) general (class)	as Attribute	non-specific	this is **an elephant**	these are **elephants/** this is **water**	
		specific	––	––	––
	as other than Attribute	non-specific	[1] **an elephant** lives long	[2] **elephants** live long/ **water** consists of hydrogen and oxygen	
		specific	[3] **the elephant** lives long	––	––

quite distinct. Thus, when they refer to members of the class of elephant, *an elephant, the elephants* and *elephants* are not interchangeable; for example:

After four months, on New Year's Eve, Russell reportedly proposed while on **an elephant** in India. [COCA]

Do you suppose I'm going to find **an elephant** walking about the streets of London? [COCA]

An African elephant lay dying alongside a well-traveled trail. Researchers noted that **38 elephants** made a total of 56 visits to **the dying elephant** – including six visits by her mother and sister. After **the elephant** died, 54 individuals made 73 visits to her corpse – none by her mother and sister. [COCA]

Here we could not replace *an elephant* in *Russell reportedly proposed while on an elephant in India* with *the elephant* or *elephants*. These alternatives would have quite different meanings. Typically, the member of a class is introduced by a non-specific reference, e.g. *an African elephant*, and once it has been introduced into the discourse, it is referred to again anaphorically (see Chapter 9) by specific nominal groups, as with *the dying elephant, the elephant* (or, pronominally, *it*).

(ii) In contrast, when a nominal group refers to a class, the use of determiners as Deictic is more constrained. For example, while *this dying elephant* and *this elephant* are both possible as anaphoric references to a particular member of the class of elephant, only *the elephant* would normally be possible as a reference to the general class of elephants. In addition,

370

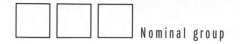

Nominal group

certain options that are quite distinct as references to members of a class are much closer in meaning as references to the class itself; these are marked [1], [2] and [3] in Table 6-7 above[5]. Consider the following examples of references to the class of elephants:

An elephant can pound mightily on the ground, but the pressure its foot exerts is less than that exerted by a mole rat's teeth. *Smaller and thinner animals* can even push their way through the soil with their heads. [COCA]

Elephants communicate in a complicated, sophisticated language that scientists are trying to decipher and compile into the world's first elephant dictionary. [COCA]

The elephant, that noble creature known for **its** long memory, is no longer an appropriate symbol for a political party which has so quickly forgotten the eight rudderless years of unfettered corporate greed the nation experienced when one of its own occupied the Oval Office. [COCA]

[Voiceover:] For **the elephant, the herd** is home. It is family. Elephant researcher, Gay Bradshaw. [Gay Bradshaw:] **The herd** is the most important component of elephant culture. **They**'re very affectionate with **their** children, with each other. Always touching and talking to each other. **They** have a culture that they pass on through generations. **They** even have grieving rituals. When someone in the family dies, **people** gather around. **They** touch the body. [COCA]

You might think that **the elephant**'s peculiar way of 'running' arose solely because of **its** huge size. But consider **the white rhinoceros, the second-largest land animal**, which can weigh more than 5,000 pounds. That's half as much as **an adult African elephant**. Yet **the rhinoceros** runs exactly like **a horse – a really big, nearly blind, very grumpy horse**. All four of **its** feet leave the ground, springing **the behemoth** forward from step to step. Compare that with the gait of **a baby elephant**. [COCA]

An elephant's heart beats much slower than **a hummingbird**'s, but **elephants** live longer than **hummingbirds** so **they** have about the same number of heartbeats over their lives. [COCA]

In the first example, *the elephant* illustrates type [1] in Table 6-7 above; it refers to the general class of elephants. The reference item *the* is homophoric, rather than anaphoric, as it would have been in reference to a particular member of the class of elephants: when we meet *the elephant pounded mightily on the ground*, we can assume that the elephant has already been introduced into the discourse. While not identical in meaning, types [2] and [3] are close in meaning, and could be used instead: (type [2]:) *elephants can pound mightily on the ground*, and (type [2]:) *the elephant can pound mightily on the ground*. All three constitute ways of generalizing about elephants as a class of animal; but as references to members of a class, they would be quite distinct; compare: *when I approached the river, an elephant pounded mightily on the ground*; *I saw an elephant some 30 yards way, but when I approached it, the elephant pounded mightily on the ground*; and *when I approached the river, elephants pounded mightily on the ground*. Similarly, instead of *for the elephant, the herd is home*, we could have *for an elephant, the herd is home* or *for elephants, the herd is home*. In the last example, we can note the switch from *an elephant* (in *an elephant's heart beats ...*)

---

[5] References to general classes of countable things do usually not take the form of specific plural nominal groups; we do not expect to find *the elephants* alongside *elephants*, *an elephant* and *the elephant*. But there are principled exceptions to this generalization, including references to classes of people (e.g. nationalities: *the French*; certain references with Epithet as Head: *the rich*). Compare also with biological taxonomies: *the Ankylosaurs* in the text analysed in Table 5-13, Chapter 5.

371

to *elephants* (in *elephants live longer* ...); but both nominal groups constitute generalizations about the class of elephants.

Generalizations about masses, whether they are concrete substances such as 'water' or abstractions such as 'justice', are restricted to type [2], i.e. non-specific nominal groups, as in the following example of a general reference to 'ozone':

> **Ozone** is one of the gases in Earth's atmosphere. It is a cousin of the oxygen molecule on which we depend for life. The oxygen molecule is two oxygen atoms bound together. The ozone molecule is three. That extra atom makes a big difference. [COCA]
>
> **Wine** has an archeological record dating back more than 7.5 thousand years.

The nominal group *ozone* is non-specific; but subsequent nominal groups referring to classes of countable things are represented according to type [1]: *the oxygen molecule*, *the ozone molecule*. Generalizations about abstractions take the same form, e.g.:

> **Morality**, **democracy**, and **intellectual honesty** are dying. [COCA]
>
> **Rationality** is therefore an essential aspect of integrating the miraculous into a theology of nature. [COCA]

In certain other languages, such nominal groups would be specific, as in French *la liberté*, in contrast with English *freedom*; but there are exceptions even in English, with nominal groups where Epithet = Head (e.g. *from the sublime to the ridiculous*), as with *the miraculous* above.

The contrast between references to (i) (particular) members of a class and to (ii) the class itself affects the deployment of the resources of the nominal group; but it actually relates to the whole clause in which the nominal group serves as an element. For example, in *An African elephant lay dying alongside a well-traveled trail*, the verbal group is 'temporal' rather than 'modal', and it is 'past' rather than 'present'; but in *An elephant can pound mightily on the ground*, the verbal group is 'modal', more specifically: 'modulation: readiness: potentiality' – potentiality being a way of generalizing about classes, and in *An elephant's heart beats much slower than a hummingbird's*, the verbal group is 'temporal', but 'present' rather than 'past', and 'simple present' rather than 'present-in-present' – 'simple present' being the tense of the extended now with 'material' clauses (see Chapter 5, Section 5.2.1). In the following example, the choice of a modality of 'modalization: usuality' reinforces the general reading, as would other forms of modal assessment such as *generally*, *typically* (although it is of course perfectly possible to generalize about particular members of classes, as when we talk about somebody's habits):

> Esoteric culture **always** exists in some sort of relationship to the general, or exoteric, culture, sharing a common tradition even while interpreting its basic realities quite differently, so that tense and unstable juxtapositions are the norm. [ACE_D]

The contrast between general and particular is thus based on selections within the clause as a whole.

Nominal groups referring to classes of things have been studied extensively in philosophy, logic and linguistics under the heading of 'generics'; for an overview, see Lyons (1999:

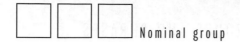

179–198). Studies based on constructed examples need to be supplemented by corpus-based investigations. Here we can recognize that texts of different types will be more likely to involve references to particular members of classes or to the classes themselves. For example, in 'recreating' and 'reporting' texts, we are more likely to find references to particular members, but in 'expounding' texts, we are more likely to find references to classes of things, as in the entry on Ankylosaurs analysed experientially in Table 5-13, Chapter 5.

In addition to the Deictic element we have just discussed, there may be a second Deictic element in the nominal group, one which adds further to the identification of the subset in question. We will refer to these as **post-Deictic** or **Deictic₂**.

The post-Deictic identifies a subset of the class of 'thing' by referring to its fame or familiarity, its status in the text, or its similarity/dissimilarity to some other designated subset. For example:

> Virgil has enumerated abstractions and the **customary** grisly inhabitants of Tartarus [LOB_J]

> A **typical** elution curve is shown in Figure 3. [LOB_J]

> Of these, at the time of the search, there were three, in a sealed container; and there is irrefutable evidence to prove that this **same** container was still there, still sealed and intact, when Wynter's body was discovered. [LOB_L]

> The plane has a built-in stereo tape-recorder which can play for the **whole** four hours it will take to fly to Majorca. [LOB_A]

> There are many **self-styled** anarchists who insist, often with great passion, that theirs is the only right way, and that others do not merit the term (and maybe are criminals of one or another sort). [Text 212]

> This is the **necessary** first step. [LOB-B]

> Further information is required to elucidate fully the **possible** role of these contaminants. [LOB_J]

These can be interpreted in terms of (1) the categories of expansion and (2) the categories of projection. The words occurring as post-Deictic are adjectives, and may also occur in the function of Epithet but with a different sense; those that frequently occur as post-Deictic are shown in Table 6-8. Also found in the post-Deictic position in the nominal group are words expressing the speaker's attitude (to the thing, or else to the world in general), such as *wretched, miserable, lousy, lovely, splendid, magnificent* as in *those lovely two evenings in Bali*:

> The Sphinx and the **splendid** three <u>Pyramids</u> are one of the remaining Seven Wonders of the World.

> A larger group of unfortunate organizations spend all their time east of the merge point, on those **miserable** two <u>miles of asphalt and concrete</u>.

The attitude may be focused on the number represented by the Numerative (with a singular determiner *a(n)* as Deictic and a plural noun as Thing):

> For a **lousy** <u>two</u> weeks in New Jersey, you'll make a shitload of dough [COCA]

> Flashback digital recorder weighs just three ounces – but its Intel memory cartridges hold an **impressive** <u>30 or 60</u> minutes of high-quality recordings. [COCA]

It sold a **disappointing** 9,000 copies, but by the second half of 1924, weekly circulation had increased to 70,000, and Time Inc. had its first profit.

Table 6-8 Adjectives frequently occurring as post-Deictic

Type	Subtype		Examples
Expansion	elaborating	identity	identical, same; different ('non-identical'), other [note a + other, another]; respective
		exemplification	certain, particular, given; various, different ('various'), odd; famous, well-known, infamous, notorious; special
	extending		complete, entire, whole
	enhancing	space-time	above, aforementioned, earlier, preceding; subsequent, future
		comparison	similar, different ('non-similar'), comparable
Projection	modality: modalization	probability	certain, possible, probable
		usuality	customary, habitual, normal, ordinary, typical, usual, regular
	modality: modulation	obligation	necessary, required
		readiness	intended, desired
	evidentiality (report)	locution	alleged, so-called, self-styled
		idea	hypothetical, purported, expected, evident, obvious
	attitude	positive	lovely, splendid, magnificent
		negative	miserable, wretched, lousy

In an incongruent nominal group, the post-Deictic may correspond to an interpersonal Adjunct in the related congruent clause (cf. further Chapter 10, Section 10.5). For example, in

> Immediately, the religious groups of the city were embroiled in an angry dispute over the **alleged** invasion of a man's right to freedom of religious belief and conscience. [BROWN1_F]

the incongruent nominal group *the alleged invasion of a man's right to freedom of religious belief and conscience* corresponds to the more congruent clause *allegedly a man's right ... was invaded*, where *allegedly* serves as a comment Adjunct.

Post-Deictic items referring to space-time may alternatively be interpreted as a type of Numerative expressing place in order (see next section).

6.2.1.2 Numerative

The Numerative element indicates some numerical feature of the particular subset of the Thing: either quantity or order, either exact or inexact. Items serving as Numerative are exemplified in Table 6-9.

Table 6-9 Items (numerals, or [embedded] nominal groups) functioning as Numerative

	Definite	**Indefinite**
quantitative	one two three, etc. [a couple of], etc. [a quarter of], etc.	few little [a bit of], etc. several [a number of],etc. many much [a lot of], etc. fewer less more [the same amount of], etc.
ordinative	first second third, etc. next last	preceding subsequent, etc.

(a) The quantifying Numeratives (or 'quantitatives') specify either an exact number (cardinal numerals, e.g. *two trains*) or an inexact number (e.g. *many trains, lots of trains*); for example:

the Senate confirmed **seven** Cabinet secretaries [Text 113]

they have identified **several** proteins that help Ephs and ephrins control the cytoskeleton [Text 398]

many visitors prefer the fine beaches of Redondo Beach State Beach, Torrance County Beach, and Malaga Cove, south of the city [Text 140]

I see **fewer** experimental stories than I did in the decades previous to the eighties. [Text 21]

An unknown number of passengers are still missing [Text 5]

(b) The ordering Numeratives (or 'ordinatives') specify either an exact place in order (ordinal numerals, e.g. *the second train*) or an inexact place (e.g. *a subsequent train*); for example:

For the **third** time in a decade, the telephone company is changing people's phone numbers. [Text 15]

On this short London holiday, he began writing a sea novel, which, after surviving **subsequent** jungle travel, shipwreck on the Congo, and a railway cloakroom in Berlin, came into the hands of Edward Garnett and through him to a London publisher. [Text 153]

An inexact Numerative expression may be exact in the context; for example, *just as many trains* ('as mentioned before'), *the next train* ('from now on'). On the other hand, an exact Numerative expression may be made inexact by **submodification**, as in *about ten trains, almost the last train*. For discussion of the related category of 'measure nominals', see Section 6.2.6.

In an incongruent nominal group that stands as a metaphoric variant of a clause, the Numerative may correspond to a conjunction; for example, *subsequent jungle travel* can be reworded as a congruent clause: *subsequently it travelled through the jungle*.

375

6.2.1.3 Epithet

The **Epithet** indicates some quality of the subset, e.g. *old, long, blue, fast*; since qualities are denoted by adjectives, Epithets are often realized by adjectives (but see Section 6.2.1.5 below for other possibilities). Tucker (1998) provides a detailed, lexicogrammatical and semantic description of adjectives in English, with system networks showing the potential for construing qualities. (i) The quality of the subset may be an objective property of the thing itself, construed as a depiction of the experience of the entity that it represents; or (ii) it may be an expression of the speaker's subjective attitude towards it, e.g. *splendid, silly, fantastic* (see Poynton, 1996). We refer to these as (i) **experiential Epithets** and (ii) interpersonal, or **attitudinal**, **Epithets**, respectively. Examples:

(i) experiential Epithet

Naval authorities believe the boat may have capsized because it was carrying a **heavy** load of construction materials in **choppy** waters. [Text 5]

Then he saw it – a **large red** feather barely sticking out of the straw mat. [Text 65]

New numbers also will be inserted between the **new** area code and the **old** phone number. [Text 15]

It is spring, moonless night in the small town, starless and bible-black, the cobblestreets silent and the hunched, courters'-and-rabbits' wood limping invisible down to the **sloeblack, slow, black, crowblack, fishingboat-bobbing** sea. [Text 194]

(ii) interpersonal Epithet

Oh God Maitland was a **really cute little** town. [UTS/Macquarie Corpus]

I knocked on the door and an **awfully sweet** lady came. [LLC]

He lives in what Alec Guinness has called 'a stately pleasure dome', a 17th century 'pavilion' with **splendid** gardens in the depths of Buckinghamshire. [Text 25]

So I've seen more of prisons and children's institutions than most people – And they really are **horrendous**; I mean they're **ugly scary** places, which you wouldn't put anybody; I mean they really are just **such awful** places you know. [Text 85]

There is no hard and fast line between these two; but the former are experiential in function, whereas the latter, expressing the speaker's attitude, represent an interpersonal element in the meaning of the nominal group (thus contributing to appraisal, in the sense of Martin & White, 2005). This distinction is reflected in the grammar in various ways.

The principal difference is that experiential Epithets are potentially defining, whereas interpersonal ones are not. Take the example of *long* in *long train*. If I say *a long train*, you cannot tell which particular train I am talking about, because the Deictic *a* is non-specific; but if I say *the long train*, the specific Deictic *the* indicates that you can tell, and that the necessary information is contained in the experiential Epithet *long*. This particular train, in other words, is defined by its length, relative to some norm – perhaps some other train or trains that are present in the context. If I use an attitudinal Epithet, on the other hand, such as *mighty* in *along there came a mighty train*, this is not defining and it does not become defining even following the specific Deictic *the*. In *the mighty train came thundering down the track*, the word *mighty* does not identify this particular train by contrast with some unmighty ones.

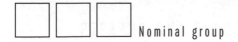

Even in the superlative, which, with experiential Epithets, is almost always used to define (e.g. *ours was the longest train*), an attitudinal Epithet is still not defining. For example, *he said the silliest things* is normally equivalent to *he said some very silly things*. A word like *silliest* can be used to define, as in *the silliest things of all were said by the chairman*; but in that case it has an experiential function. Note that, in general, the same word may act as either experiential or interpersonal Epithet; many of the latter are adjectives of size, quality or age, e.g. *lovely, little, old*:

> I've been writing this **old** novel so long I can't wait. [Text 21]

> I saw it in this **dinky little** magazine. [Text 119]

Since expressions of attitude tend to be strung prosodically throughout the clause, rather than being associated with one particular place, there are very few words that serve only an attitudinal function.

Interpersonal Epithets tend to precede the experiential ones. As we have seen, many of them may also occur as post-Deictic; in that case their deictic function consists rather in referring to, or even in constructing, an occasion of shared experience as in *a miserable few dishes of peanuts*. But whereas with adjectives of experiential quality the difference between Epithet and post-Deictic is rather clear (e.g. *the three famous musketeers, the famous three musketeers*), with the interpersonal ones the difference is much less, and there is no sense of ambiguity in the meaning (contrast *those lovely two evenings in Bali* and *those two lovely evenings in Bali*). Interpersonal Epithets also tend to be reinforced by other words, or other features, all contributing to the same meaning: synonyms (e.g. *a horrible ugly great lump*), intensifiers, swear-words, particular intonation contours, voice quality features, and the like.

6.2.1.4 Classifier

The Classifier indicates a particular subclass of the thing in question, e.g. *electric trains, passenger trains, toy trains*. Sometimes the same word may function either as Epithet or as Classifier, with a difference in meaning: e.g. *fast trains* may mean either 'trains that go fast' (*fast* = Epithet) or 'trains classified as expresses' (*fast* = Classifier). The line between Epithet and Classifier is not a very sharp one, but there are significant differences. Classifiers do not accept degrees of comparison or intensity – we cannot have *a more electric train* or *a very electric train*; and they tend to be organized in mutually exclusive and exhaustive sets – *a train* is either *electric, steam* or *diesel*. The range of semantic relations that may be embodied in a set of items functioning as Classifier is very broad; it includes material, scale and scope, purpose and function, status and rank, origin, mode of operation – more or less any feature that may serve to classify a set of things into a system of smaller sets; for example:

> **Prison** guards restrain the inmates with **electric shock stun** guns, **leg** irons, **pepper** spray and **restraint** chairs. [Text 1]

> Macquarie laid the **foundation** stone of the Cathedral the following year. [Text 22]

> Even the **jointed wooden** lion put on airs. [Text 28]

> Famous organists go into raptures over the **tonal** excellence of the Centennial Hall's organ, one of the two largest original **19th century** organs in the world, with 8,500 pipes. [Text 22]

With a wave and a shy smile, Elian Gonzalez said goodbye to America Wednesday, ending a **seven-month** saga that swept the 6-year-old **Cuban** castaway into a controversy over **parental** rights and U.S. relations with his **communist** homeland. [Text 85]

Classifiers are used in texts of all kinds of registers; but they are of course put to hard work in registers where space is at a premium (headlines, in particular, e.g. *oil windfall profit tax bill*) and in registers where classification is an important aspect of the field of discourse, as in scientific and technological registers (Text 6-2 below illustrates the use of Classifiers in a taxonomic report dealing social classes during a period of Korean history). Texts dealing with complex technology or scientific models often rely on extended classification sequences (see e.g. Rose, 1998), including labels used in technical and scientific drawings (e.g. *oil cooler bypass valve*, *radio noise burst monitor*, *hydrogen internal combustion engine vehicle*; *ventral spino-thalamic tract*, *inferior cervical sympathetic ganglion*). Since the relations between the nouns in such classification sequences are implicit, expert field knowledge is often required to process them.

Text 6-2: Expounding – categorizing: beginning of a taxonomic report

The **yangban** aristocracy literally meant the members of the 'two orders' of officialdom who served in the bureaucracy as **civil and military** officials. This **elite** class, which began to be formed toward the end of the **Koryō** Kingdom (918–1392), directed the government, economy and culture of the subsequent **Chosŏn** Kingdom (1392–1910).

Members of the yangban owned vast land and slaves, and alone enjoyed a variety of **social** privileges including the opportunity for education and **public** service and exemption from **service** obligations like **military** duty or **corvee** labor.

A sequence of Classifier + Thing may be so closely bonded that it is very like a single compound noun, especially where the Thing is a noun of a fairly general class, e.g. *train set* (cf. *chemistry set*, *building set*). In such sequences the Classifier often carries the tonic prominence (see Chapter 8, Section 8.4), which makes it sound like the first element in a compound noun. Noun compounding is outside the scope of the present book; but the line between a compound noun and a nominal group consisting of Classifier + Thing is very fuzzy and shifting, which is why people are often uncertain how to write such sequences, whether as one word, as two words, or joined by a hyphen (e.g. *walkingstick, walking stick, walking-stick*).

In an incongruent nominal group corresponding to a congruent clause, the Classifier may correspond to either a participant or circumstance in the transitivity structure of the clause (cf. further Chapter 10, Section 10.5); for example:

I would have thought the entry of the Americans into the war, the **British and French** efforts, and the losses sustained in Ludendorf's final offensive had something to do with it, [ACE_G]

Unlike nominal groups embedded as possessive Deictics, nouns serving as Classifier have no determination system, so they do not refer to particular participants only to generalized ones: contrast *the Minister's decision* with *ministerial decision*.

378

6.2.1.5 Experiential functions and word classes

We have now identified the nominal group functions of Deictic, post-Deictic (or Deictic$_2$), Numerative, Epithet, Classifier and Thing. The classes of word that most typically realize these functions are as follows (cf. Chapter 2, Figure 2-10):

Deictic	Deictic$_2$	Numerative	Epithet	Classifier	Thing
determiner	adjective	numeral	adjective	noun or adjective	noun

But there are other possibilities: for example, numeral occurring as Classifier, as in *first prize*, or embedded nominal group as possessive Deictic, e.g. *the day before yesterday's paper*.

These word classes – noun (= common noun), adjective, numeral and determiner – are all different kinds of **noun**; they are sub-classes of this one primary class. This larger class can be referred to as 'nominals', to avoid confusion with 'noun' in its narrower, more specific sense. Other words also enter into the nominal group, namely words of the class **verb**, which may function as Epithet or Classifier. Verbs function in the nominal group in one of two forms:

(i)   present (active) participle, V-*ing*, e.g. *losing*, as in *a losing battle*;

(ii) past (passive, or intransitive) participle, V-*en*, e.g. *lost*, as in *a lost cause*.

When functioning as Epithet, these forms usually have the sense of the finite tense to which they are most closely related: the present participle means 'which is (was/will be) ... ing', the past participle means 'which has (had/will have) been ... ed'. When functioning as Classifier, they typically have the sense of a simple present, active or passive: present (= active) 'which ... s', past (= passive) 'which is ... ed'.
Examples:

Verb as Epithet
(i)   a galloping horse ('a horse which is galloping')

a bleeding nose ('a nose which is bleeding')

If however the verb is one which does not normally take the 'present in present' tense *be ... ing* (i.e. a verb expressing a mental or relational process), the distinction between 'which ... s' and 'which is ... ing' is neutralized; the next pair of examples are also Epithets:

the resulting confusion ('the confusion which results')

a knowing smile ('a smile which [suggests that the smiler] knows')

(ii) a wrecked car ('a car which has been wrecked')

a fallen idol ('an idol which has fallen')

379

Verb as Classifier

(i)   a stopping train ('a train which stops')

    a travelling salesman ('a salesman who travels')

(ii) a tied note ('a note which is tied')

    spoken language ('language which is spoken')

It is natural that the more lasting attribute should tend to have a classifying function. But the present participle as Classifier does not exclude the sense of 'which is ... ing', as in *the rising/setting sun*; and conversely, the past participle as Epithet does not always carry the meaning of 'which has been ...', since many such forms are in fact adjectives, as in *a haunted house, a crowded train*. The same word may be now one, now the other: in *Would you like a boiled egg? boiled* is Classifier, 'which gets boiled', contrasting with *fried, poached* or *scrambled*; while in *You must drink only boiled water here, boiled* is Epithet 'which has been boiled'. In *He got stuck in a revolving door*, either interpretation is possible: Classifier 'of the kind which revolves', Epithet 'which was revolving' (cf. *fast trains* above). Note finally that the fact that a particular expression is a cliché does not imply that the modifying element is necessarily a Classifier – the 'permanence' is merely a feature of the wording! Thus in *a considered opinion, a heated argument, the promised land, a going concern*, the verbs are all Epithets: 'which has been considered', 'which has become heated', 'which has been promised', 'which is going [well]'.

Often the participle is itself further modified, as in *a fast-moving train, a hard-boiled egg*. The resulting compound may embody any one of a number of different experiential relations, e.g. *well-meaning, habit-forming, fund-raising, right-angled, fruit-flavoured, pear-shaped, architect-designed, simple-minded, bottled-nosed, iron-fisted, two-edged*. What is happening here is that some part of the experiential structure of a clause is being downgraded to function as Epithet or Classifier; it is a reduced form of a non-finite clause and hence agnate to a (finite or non-finite) Qualifier (see next Section). We have already glossed *boiled water* as 'water which has been boiled'; but the latter is itself another possible form of wording, systematically related to the first: *boiled water/water which has been boiled*. Compare *a train which was moving fast, eggs which are* (Classifier)/*have been* (Epithet) *boiled hard, a house designed by an architect, activities which (are intended to) raise funds*, and so on.

6.2.2 Experiential structure of the nominal group: interpretation of ordering; the Qualifier

6.2.2.1 Ordering

We can now follow the experiential pattern that is embodied in nominal group structure. Proceeding from left to right, we begin with the immediate context, the identification of the item in terms of the here-&-now, e.g. *those trains* 'the trains you can see over there'. Of course, this identification is often in terms of the surrounding text rather than the situation, e.g. *those trains* 'the trains you've just been talking about'; but the point of reference is still the speech event. From there we go on to quantitative features: place in order, and number. These are less naturally definitive than this or that, mine or yours, but more so than a merely qualitative attribute; and the ordinals, being the more definitive of the two, come first. An

ordinal is a kind of superlative cardinal: *third* = 'three-est', i.e. identified by being at number three. Next come the qualitative features, again with superlatives preceding others: *the oldest trains* 'trains for which oldness is the identifying feature'. Often there is an intensifier, such as *very*, or an attitudinal element like *nice, terrible* as a marker of the quality. Finally, comes class membership; this reduces the size of the total set referred to in the noun by specifying a sub-set, e.g. *passenger train* 'kind of train that is for carrying passengers'. We are talking here, it should be made clear, of the identifying **potential** of these elements. In any actual instance, the item in question may or may not be identifying; and this is the function of the word *the* at the beginning of the group – to signal that something that is capable of identifying is actually functioning in this way.

So there is a progression in the nominal group from the kind of element that has the greatest specifying potential to that which has the least; and this is the principle of ordering that we have already recognized in the clause. In the clause, the Theme comes first. We begin by establishing relevance: stating what it is that we are using to introduce this clause into the discourse, as 'this is where I'm starting from' – typically, though by no means necessarily, something that is already 'given' in the context. In the nominal group, we begin with the Deictic: 'first I'll tell you which I mean', *your, these, any, a*, etc. So the principle that puts the Theme first in the clause is the same as that which puts the Deictic first in the nominal group: start by locating the Thing in relation to the here-&-now – in the space-time context of the ongoing speech event. From there we proceed to elements that have successively less identifying potential – which, by the same token, are increasingly permanent as attributes. By and large, the more permanent the attribute of a Thing, the less likely it is to identify it in a particular context. So we proceed with the very impermanent, quantitative characterization that is nearest to a Deictic, e.g. *three* in *three balls*; through various qualitative features such as *new* in *new ball*; and end up with the most permanent, the assignment to a class, e.g. *tennis ball*. Within the qualitative characteristics, if more than one is specified there is, again, a tendency to more from the less permanent to the more permanent; e.g. *a new red ball* rather than *a red new ball*.

6.2.2.2 Qualifier

What of the element which **follows** the Thing? The original example, *Look at those two splendid old electric trains with pantographs*, ended with the phrase *with pantographs*; this also is part of the nominal group, having a function we shall refer to as Qualifier.

Unlike the elements that precede the Thing, which are words (or sometimes word complexes, like *two hundred, very big*; see Section 6.3.2), what follows the Thing is either a phrase or a clause. For example:

Guinness, who was knighted in 1959, had a long film partnership [**with director David Lean**]. [Text 90]

The course [**of science**] and the course [**of military endeavors**] is very close. After all, Archimedes was designing devices [**for military purposes**]. [Text 234]

The smoking [**of tobacco**] altered daily custom, as did the drinking [**of coffee or tea or cocoa**]. [Text 122]

Do you read any English novelists [[**who seem to you Kafkaesque**]]? [Text 125]

First, I divided the presidents between bibliophiles and those [[**to whom books were more or less alien territory**]] . [Text 110]

381

With only rare exceptions[6], all Qualifiers are **rankshifted**. What this means is that position following the Thing is reserved for those items that, in their own structure, are of a rank higher than or at least equivalent to that of the nominal group; on these grounds, therefore, they would not be expected to be constituents of a nominal group. Such items are said to be 'rankshifted' – by contrast with **ranking** ones, which function prototypically as constituents of the higher unit. We may also use the term 'embedded', taken from formal grammars; but with the proviso that this term is often used to cover both rankshift (where the item is downgraded as a constituent) and hypotaxis (where the item is dependent on another one but is not a constituent of it; see Chapter 7, Section 7.4 and 7.5). Here we shall use embedded only as an alternative term synonymous with rankshifted. Examples are:

that has been entered	*in*	the plea 〚that has been entered〛
being handed down	*in*	the judgement 〚being handed down〛
before the court	*in*	the matter [before the court]

Note that 〚 〛 signifies an embedded clause, finite or non-finite; [ ] an embedded phrase (or group).

Like the other, 'ranking' (i.e. non-embedded) elements of the nominal group, the Qualifier also has the function of characterizing the Thing; and again the Deictic *the* serves to signal that the characteristic in question is defining. But the characterization here is in terms of some process within which the Thing is, directly or indirectly, a participant. It may be a major process – that is, a clause, finite or non-finite; or a minor process – a prepositional phrase (see Section 6.5). Figure 6-3 exemplifies these three variants.

The non-finite clause may appear in this environment with no verb present, e.g. *the poles with flags on* (cf. *the poles which have flags on, the poles on which there are flags*); compare the discussion on hypotactic non-finite clauses in Section 7.4.4. Cf. *a clause with no verb present* (*a clause in which no verb is present*).

It is also possible for a nominal group to function as Qualifier inside the structure of another nominal group, for example *my brother the lawyer*, where *the lawyer* defines which brother is being referred to. Such instances typically have a possessive determiner as the Deictic element.

---

[6]   Adjectives and nouns can occur after the Thing in wordings borrowed from languages where Epithets and Classifiers follow the Thing, e.g. *professor emeritus*, *salade Niçoise*; and this may be used to give a person a foreign flavour, as with Agatha Christie's linguistic portrayal of Hercule Poirot: *a crime most horrible*. However, certain types of adjective also appear after the Thing as part of the pattern of the nominal group in English; they often include a sense of potentiality. There are reasons for interpreting these as Qualifier rather than as Epithet or Classifier. Bolinger (1967) drew attention to contrasts such as *a navigable river* and *a river navigable*, and his suggestions have been followed up in the literature (see e.g. McCawley, 1988: Ch. 12; Blöhdorn, 2009). The sequence with Thing: noun ∧ Qualifier: adjective is much less common than the sequence with the adjective before the Thing, but it does occur, e.g. (from COCA): *Throughout the U.S., there are more than 30,000 miles of waterways **navigable** by small boats.*; *So did the idea of making the Danube a river **fully navigable** by large vessels.*; *It was the best solution **possible**.* The sense is that of a Qualifier rather than that of an Epithet or Classifier, and it would be possible to interpret such adjectives as Attributes in reduced intensive attributive relative clauses, as in *a river that is fully navigable by large vessels*, and, by a further step ('unpacking' the potential form of the adjective), *a river that can be fully navigated by large vessels*.

(a)

the	children	[in [blue hats]]
Deictic	Thing	Qualifier
determiner	noun	prepositional phrase

(b)

the	children	[[wearing blue hats]]
Deictic	Thing	Qualifier
determiner	noun	clause, non-finite

(c)

the	children	[[who are wearing blue hats]]
Deictic	Thing	Qualifier
determiner	noun	clause, finite

Fig.6-3 Nominal group with (a) prepositional phrase, (b) non-finite clause, and (c) finite clause as Qualifier

A clause functioning as Qualifier in the nominal group is referred to as a **relative clause**; more specifically, as a **defining relative clause** (in contrast to a non-defining relative clause, which is not embedded but hypotactically dependent: see Sections 7.4.1 and 7.4.5).

In an incongruent nominal group corresponding to a congruent clause, Qualifiers correspond to participants or circumstances in the transitivity structure of the clause; or when the Head/Thing of the nominal group is a nominalization of a verb of sensing or saying, they may correspond to projected clauses in a clause nexus.

Carnation has been available in the UK since 1946, but the main marketing effort dates only from 1954 with the removal [**of restrictions [on sales]**]. [LOB_E]

THE decision [**by the Arbitration Commission**] [[**to award the 2.3 percent pay increase**]] is unfortunate, but it was to be expected. [ACE_B]

This is the real meaning of the US Senate's decision [**last week**] [[**to override any possibility of a presidential veto for real, hard-hitting sanctions against the separate, increasingly desperate tribes** [[**that make up the political entity of South Africa**]]]]. [ACE_B]

As the examples illustrate, participants reconstrued as Qualifiers are realized by prepositional phrases with either *of* or *by*; circumstances are realized in the same way that they would be realized in clauses, by either prepositional phrases or adverbial groups.

6.2.3 Experiential structure of the nominal group: the Thing

The element we are calling **Thing** is the semantic core of the nominal group. It may be realized by a common noun, proper noun or (personal) pronoun.

The personal pronoun represents the world according to the speaker, in the context of a speech exchange. The basic distinction is into speech roles (*I, you*) and other roles (*he, she, it, they*); there is also the generalized pronoun (*one*). These categories are set out in Figure 6-4.

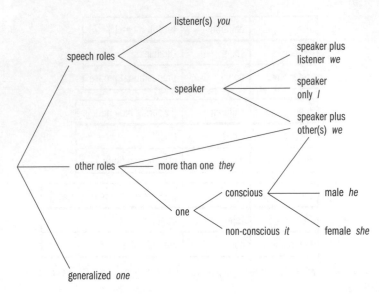

Fig. 6-4 The English person categories

Proper names are names of particular persons, individually or as a group; institutions of all kinds; and places. They may consist of one word or many; those consisting of two or more words, such as *Polly Perkins*, *Ayers Rock* or *Cathay Pacific Airlines*, obviously have their own internal structure; but we shall treat all such instances simply as Thing, since it is beyond our scope here to go into the functional analysis of noun compounds.

Personal pronouns and proper names are alike in that, for both, the reference is typically unique. With pronouns, the referent is defined interpersonally, by the speech situation. With proper names it is defined experientially: there exists only one, at least in the relevant body of experience. In both cases, this means that typically there is no further specification; pronouns and proper names usually occur without any other elements of the nominal group. Sometimes they need further defining, like *you in the back row*, *Henry the Eighth* (this was how surnames started, as Qualifiers of personal names); and they may carry attitudinal Epithets, like *poor Tom* – cf. *pretty little Polly Perkins of Paddington Green*, which has both.

Common nouns, on the other hand, as their name implies, are nouns that are common (that is, generalized) to a class of referents. These name all the classes of phenomena that the language admits as things, and hence as participants in processes of any kind. There is a long tradition of characterizing such phenomena, in grammar books, as a list of very general categories, for example 'persons, other living beings, objects (concrete or abstract), collectives, institutions'. These are relevant grammatically because they relate to a cline of potential agency – that is, the likelihood of functioning as Actor/Agent in the clause; the most likely being persons (human nouns), and the least likely being concrete objects. More delicate categorizations have been suggested along these lines.

But there are obviously many ways in which things can be grouped into categories. The thesaurus, as first devised by Peter Mark Roget, sets up a semantic taxonomy which includes all word classes, so verbs, adjectives and adverbs as well as nouns; this also has implications

for the grammar, in terms of the likelihood of nouns to appear as participants in different process types, but its conceptual framework is lexical rather than grammatical. We cannot attempt a detailed categorization here. But we can identify a small number of vectors along which words capable of functioning as Thing are ordered in terms of the grammar, so that the functional potential of any one noun or pronoun will be suggested by its location on each of these vectors (cf. also Halliday & Matthiessen, 1999). These are:

(1)   countability: count/mass

(2)   animacy: conscious/non-conscious

(3)   generality: general/particular

(1) Countability. Things are represented in English as either (a) discrete, and therefore countable, or (b) continuous, and therefore uncountable; the grammar thus makes a categorical distinction into **count nouns** and **mass nouns**, such that count nouns select for NUMBER: singular/plural, while mass nouns do not. As pointed out above (Section 6.1), mass nouns are treated as singular where the deixis is specific, e.g. *do you like this poetry/ this poem?*, and as plural where the deixis is non-specific, e.g. *I've written some poetry/some poems*.

The distinction is not quite as clear-cut as this suggests. Mass nouns are often itemized, and hence also pluralized; the meaning is either 'a kind of', as in *I've found a new polish*, or 'an amount of', as in *three coffees please*. There will then be an agnate expression having a **measure/type** word as Head (see Section 6.2.6): *a new type of polish, three cups of coffee*.

Mass nouns representing abstract things, and also things that are concrete but general, often move into the count category: *experiences, researches, informations, fruits, furnitures* are all relatively recent plural forms. We could think in terms of a **cline of countability**, ranging from those nouns (and pronouns) which construe things as fully itemized, at one end, to those which treat them as totally unbounded at the other. Typically, living beings and concrete objects are itemized, abstract entities (and nominalized processes and qualities) are unbounded, with institutions and collectives falling in between. But the distinction is made by the grammar, so the same entity may be construed in more than one way; e.g. *hat(s) ~ headgear, fish(es) ~ fish, novel(s) ~ fiction*.

(2) Animacy. Here again the grammar makes a categorical distinction: (a) **conscious** things, which are those referred to as *he/she*, (b) **non-conscious** things, those referred to as *it*. This was brought up in Chapter 5, Section 5.3.1, where we showed that, while there is a clear foundation in the world of experience, with people at one end and inanimate or abstract objects at the other, many things (like non-human animals) lie in between; and, as always, the grammar is free to construe the world as it pleases.

The conscious/non-conscious distinction can also therefore be looked at as a cline; and it is one that has received a lot of attention in typological linguistics, under the name of **animacy**. This, as already remarked, refers to the likelihood of any thing to occur as Actor in a transitive material process, the 'most animate' in this sense being, obviously, post-infancy humans. We noted in Chapter 5 that it is in mental processes that the category of conscious things is clearly delineated, so that any thing functioning as Senser is thereby construed as a conscious being. The grammar has to work harder to turn inanimate objects into agents (cf. Halliday, 1990); but this is a notable feature of the discourse of ecology, which attempts to construe an eco-social reality in which the potential for effective action is not limited to the class of human beings, e.g. see Text 6-3

Text 6-3: Exploring – arguing (spoken, dialogic)
[7-year-old son:] If there weren't trees on the earth, we would all be dead, 'cause there wouldn't be oxygen; trees make oxygen, so we can breathe, so if we had heaps of trees around us, it produces heaps of oxygen, so we can breathe; so trees, big trees are really good because heaps of oxygen comes out of them. – [Father:] So that is the argument for having trees around us. [UTS/Macquarie Corpus]

And from scientific discourse:

These enhanced levels can catalytically destroy ozone in the lower stratosphere. [Text 33]

Contrast more traditional discourse: *The very next morning Noah and his sons went to the cypress forest to cut down the tallest trees for timber* (cf. Chapter 5, Section 5.7).

(3) Generality. Many classes of things are organized in the form of taxonomies: a wild strawberry is a kind of strawberry, a strawberry is a kind of berry, a berry is a kind of fruit. One could take this further and say that fruit is a kind of food. But at the most general level, a strawberry is a kind of thing; and this is construed in the grammar, such as when, being given a dessert decorated by a tough and tasteless specimen, the customer says hopefully to her husband *Would you like that strawberry? I've no use for the thing.*

This is the nearest thing to a categorical distinction made in the grammar along the cline from particular to general: there is a category of **general noun** that functions cohesively to refer to a more specific one that has preceded – and is always unstressed (i.e. cannot carry tonic prominence). These are described in Chapter 9, Section 9.6.1.3; they include a number of very general items like *thing, stuff, place, idea,* plus many words that are interpersonally loaded, usually for disapproval, like *bastard, brute, nonsense.* But, again, the membership is not exactly defined, and other items can be transferred into this category by being used without stress to function cohesively – provided they embody a move up in the scale of generality.

On this scale, the most general type of noun is in fact a **pronoun**, which is the limiting case of anaphoric generalization; this subclass of thing is very clearly marked off in the grammar. There is no clear grammaticalizing towards the particular end of the cline, though it is perhaps worth remarking that the function of Classifier in the nominal group provides the resource for expanding any class of thing into more particular subclasses.

We can use these scales – countability, animacy, generality – as a way of locating the thing in lexicogrammatical space (cf. also Halliday & Matthiessen, 1999: 189–196). A fourth factor, that of the metaphoric propensity of nouns (their potential for construing qualities and processes as things), will be discussed in Chapter 10. Certain special classes of noun can be identified by reference to the grammar of process types: for example, nouns construing different types of projection (see Chapter 7, Section 7.5.6). But a more detailed categorization of things, in terms of their association with roles in the various process types, should emerge after more systematic investigation of the large-scale corpus data that are now available.

6.2.4 A note on interpersonal and textual contributions

We noted at the beginning of the chapter that in analysing group structure it is not necessary to set up three distinct 'lines' corresponding to the experiential, interpersonal and textual metafunctions. A single structural representation will suffice.

We have been able to express this in experiential terms, because it is a general principle of linguistic structure that it is the experiential meaning that most clearly defines constituents (cf. Chapter 2, Table 2-7; see also Halliday, 1979). Interpersonal meanings tend to be scattered prosodically throughout the unit; while textual meanings tend to be realized by the order in which things occur, and especially by placing of boundaries. These are very general tendencies, worked out differently in every language but probably discernible in all. In Part I we saw this pattern in the clause, and it will become clearer by the end of Part II. The textual meaning of the clause is expressed by what is put first (the Theme); by what is phonologically prominent (and tends to be put last – the New, signalled by information focus); and by conjunctions and relatives which if present must occur in initial position. Thus it forms a wave-like pattern of periodicity that is set up by peaks of prominence and boundary markers. The interpersonal meanings are expressed by the intonation contour; by the 'Mood' element, which may be repeated as a tag at the end; and by expressions of modality that may recur throughout the clause (cf. Halliday, 1970). The pattern here is prosodic, 'field'-like rather than wave-like. To complete the triad, first proposed by Pike (1959), of 'language as particle, wave and field', the kind of meaning that is expressed in a particle-like manner is the experiential; it is this that gives us our sense of the building blocks of language. Since we are using particle theory (constituency) as the foundation of the present analysis – it tends to be conceptually and operationally simpler than models of wave or field – it is natural to represent the structure of the nominal group, in which the functional components are (in English) rather clearly defined, in straightforwardly experiential terms.

We shall say little more about the other components, beyond recognizing their presence in what has already been discussed. (1) Interpersonal meanings are embodied (a) in the person system, both as pronouns (person as Thing, e.g. *she*, *you*) and as possessive determiners (person as Deictic, e.g. *her*, *your*); in forms of assessment serving as post-Deictic (e.g. probability *possible* and evidentiality *alleged*); (c) in the attitudinal type of Epithet, e.g. *splendid* in our earlier example; (d) in connotative meanings of lexical items functioning in the group, and (e) in prosodic features such as swear-words and voice quality (cf. Poynton, 1996).

(2) Textual meaning is embodied throughout the entire structure, since it determines the order in which the elements are arranged, as well as patterns of information structure just as in the clause (note, for example, that the unmarked focus of information in a nominal group is on the word that comes last, not the word that functions as Thing: on *pantographs*, not on *trains*). This means that there is a certain potential for assigning experientially similar meanings different textual statuses within the structure of the nominal group. In particular, they may be presented either as Classifier or as Qualifier (e.g. *wooden table* ~ *table of wood*) and as either Deictic or as Qualifier (e.g. *my brother's house* ~ *house of my brother*)[7], with

---

[7]   And there are further possibilities; for example, Keats wrote *A thing of beauty is a joy for ever* with *of beauty* as Qualifier rather than *A beautiful thing is a joy for ever* with *beautiful* as Epithet.

the Qualifier having the greater potential as news. Thus in the following example, the study has already been introduced, and it is presented as Deictic (*the study's* ...) rather than as Qualifier (... *of the study*):

> A research team member, Professor John Hattie of the University of Western Australia, said this was one of **the study's** most surprising results. [ACE_A]

Similarly, compare *Mr Palme's ... death* and *the death of Mr Palme*:

> The circumstances of **Mr Palme's** untimely death draw properly from the Prime Minister and the House universal condemnation of such mindless and unjustified acts of terrorism [ACE_H]

> On behalf of the members of the National Party of Australia, I too would like to endorse the motion of condolence submitted to this House by the Prime Minister (Mr Hawke) on the death **of Mr Olof Palme, the Prime Minister of Sweden**. [ACE_H]

If a property or class relating to a thing has been introduced in the discourse preceding a nominal group, it is likely to be presented as an Epithet or Classifier of the Thing rather than as (part of) a Qualifier; for example:

> If excess carbohydrate is taken in, this can be converted into <u>fat</u> and ***stored***. The **stored** <u>fat</u> is utilized when the liver is empty of glycogen. [Text 150]

Figure 6-5 shows the structure of the example we introduced at the beginning of this section, *those two splendid old electric trains with pantographs* (cf. Figure 6-1), as interpreted so far.

those	two	splendid	old	electric	trains	with		pantographs
Deictic	Numerative	Epithet		Classifier	Thing	Qualifier		
		Attitude	Quality					
determiner	numeral	adjective	adjective	adjective	noun	prepositional phrase		
						'Process'		'Range'
						preposition group		nominal group
						Head		Thing

Fig. 6-5   Nominal group, showing multivariate experiential structure

6.2.5 Logical structure of the nominal group

We now need to consider the structure of the nominal group from a different, and complementary, point of view; seeing it as a logical structure. This does not mean interpreting it in terms of formal logic; it means seeing how it represents the generalized logical-semantic relations that are encoded in natural language. These will be discussed in greater detail in Chapter 7; for the purposes of the nominal group we need to take account

of just one such relationship, that of **subcategorization**: '*a* is a subset of *x*'. This has usually been referred to in the grammar of the nominal group as **modification**, so we will retain this more familiar term here.

Let us first consider the same example, but this time starting with the most general term, *trains*. Moving to the left, we get: (which trains? –) *electric trains*; (which electric trains? –) *old electric trains*; (which old electric trains? –) *splendid old electric trains*; and so on. Calling *trains* the Head, we can represent this as in Figure 6-6, using the letters of the Greek alphabet.

those	two	splendid	old	electric	trains
				Modifier	Head
ζ	ε	δ	γ	β	α

Fig. 6-6   Head and Modifier

The basis of the subcategorization, of course, shifts as we move to the left: 'what type of ...?', 'what quality of ...?', 'how many ...?' and so on – this is the principle underlying the experiential structure. Here, however, we are not concerned with the differences but with the similarities: with the general relationship that runs throughout the pre-Head modification of the nominal group, whatever the experiential function of the individual elements. Figure 6-7 gives another example.

a	magnificent	ornamental	eighteenth-century	carved	mahogany	mantelpiece
					Modifier	Head
η	ζ	ε	δ	γ	β	α

Fig. 6-7   Modification: a further example

Within this logical structure there may be **submodification**: that is, internal bracketing, as in Figure 6-8; for example:

> The discussion of the optimal policy when the outcome of one stage is not known before passing to the next is a **very much** more difficult matter. [BROWN1_J]

> I only wish, too, naturally, they could be sitting here, my father, who spent 40 years helping to administer the public school systems in San Francisco, and my mother, who taught us by example that the education of her children meant **so very much** more than material comforts. [COCA]

> It's **way** more expensive than your average ultrabook, but it's got **way** more horsepower, too.

Submodification may have the effect of disturbing the natural order of elements in the group; this accounts for additional items occurring before the Deictic, as in *almost the last buttercup* (rather than *the almost last buttercup*), *such a bright moon* (rather than *a such bright moon*), and also for displaced elements, as in *not so very difficult a task* (instead of *a not so very difficult task*).

389

a	rather	more	impressive	figure
			Modifier	Head
γ		β		α
	Sub-Modifier		Sub-Head	
	βγ	ββ	βα	

Fig. 6-8 Submodification

The same phenomenon of internal bracketing is also found in examples such as *apple-green pyjamas, second-hand car salesman, full-time appointment,* all of which are ββ ^ βα ^ α. Formally this is identical with submodification, although it is usually not referred to as such, the term being kept for grammatical rather than lexical expansion. As usual there are borderline cases, e.g. *dark/deep* or *light/pale* with colour words (is *deep red* more like *very red* or more like *blood-red*?). But as long as the structural representation is clear it is really unnecessary to introduce a distinct term.

The element following the Head is also a modifying element; we can distinguish the two positions by using the terms Premodifier and Postmodifier. The distinction is not a functional one, but depends, as noted above, on the rank of the modifying term; compare *a weatherboard shack by the roadside* with *a roadside shack made out of weather board*. These two are not synonymous, but the difference lies in the information structure: the item located at Postmodifier has the greater potential as news. But the Postmodifier does not itself enter into the logical structure, because it is not construed as a word complex. What the logical analysis does is to bring out the hypotactic basis of premodification in the nominal group, which then also explains its penchant for generating long strings of nouns such as are found in the names of institutions and parts of machinery, and also in newspaper headlines (cf. above on classification), e.g. *investment trust cash management account, weigh shaft lever balance weight, live steam injector feed water valve, jobs plan grant bid*. We refer to this kind of structure as a **univariate** structure, one which is generated as an iteration of the same functional relationship (cf. Halliday, 1965, 1979): α is modified by β, which is modified by γ, which is ... . By contrast, the type of structure exemplified by Deictic + Numerative + Epithet + Classifier + Thing we call a **multivariate** structure: a configuration of elements each having a distinct function with respect to the whole. Most cases of grammatical structure fall into one type or the other; the nominal group is unusual in that, in order to understand how it functions as a resource for construing complex things by taking off from a simple noun, we do best to interpret its structure in both these ways at once.

6.2.6 Head and Thing

We have assumed so far that the Head of the univariate structure is also always the Thing, in the multivariate structure. But this is not so. There is always a Head in the nominal group (unless it is 'branched', like *one brown* in *one blue eye and one brown* [∅]); but there may be no Thing. It is quite normal to have Numerative or Deictic as Head, as in Figure 6-9:

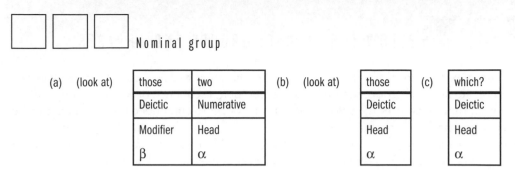

Fig. 6-9   Nominal group with (a) Numerative as Head, (b) and (c) Deictic as Head

There is one functional environment in which we regularly find Epithet as Head, namely when the nominal group occurs as Attribute, typically in an attributive relational clause (see Chapter 5, Section 5.4.3). Here, beside forms with noun (Thing) as Head, typically with non-specific Deictic as in *you're a very lucky boy*, there is the equally common type with adjective (Epithet) as Head, e.g. *you're very lucky*. This type of nominal group (sometimes referred to distinctively as 'adjectival group'[8]) is unique in that it is normally unable to function as Subject in the clause. As noted in Chapter 5, these represent classes defined by reference to a property (*lucky* = 'a member, or instance, of the class of lucky ones'); they readily become Subject by the addition of a noun or noun substitute as Head, e.g. *lucky people*, *a lucky one like you*. A few adjectives occur simply following *the*, like *the rich*; but this is not a productive configuration[9].

Other than this type, Epithets and Classifiers do not normally function as Head. The exception is the superlative, which in other ways also (e.g. place in sequence) resembles a Numerative of the ordering kind rather than an Epithet: for example *(he wants) the smallest*. With other Epithets, and with Classifiers, if the Thing is not made explicit it is realized as a substitute *one/ones*; for example, *(he wants) a small one/a wooden one*. The substitute is then both Head and Thing, as in Figure 6-10:

(we want)	some	very	small	wooden	ones
	Deictic	Epithet		Classifier	Thing
				Modifier	Head
	δ	γ		β	α
		Sub-Mod.	Sub-Head		
		γβ	γα		
	determiner	adverb	adjective	adjective	noun: substitute

Fig. 6-10   Nominal group with substitute one

---

8   Or 'quality group', in the Cardiff grammar: see e.g. Fawcett (2000: 164, 206–207).

9   In Modern English, this is restricted to certain abstractions (*And then the inevitable happened* [KOHL_P]) and general classes of beings (e.g. *Instead he goes down and lives among and with the poor and oppressed* [ACE_D]); but in German and other Germanic languages, such wordings can be used to refer not only to general classes of people but also to particular members of a class.

The complex functional entity formed by the conflation of Head and Thing acts as the fulcrum of the nominal group: before it, as Premodifier, a sequence of words having distinct experiential functions; after it, as Postmodifier, one or more embedded items which may be prepositional phrase or non-finite or finite clause. The Premodifier can then be interpreted in logical terms as a hypotactic word complex.[10] The Premodifier may accommodate both hypotactic word complexes like *a very much better argument*, and wordrank embeddings like *a four-post bed, a left-handed batsman*; including compressed phrases and clauses like *your in-flight magazine, a never-to-be-forgotten experience*. The word complexes derive from the potential for logical expansion built into the noun as Head; the embeddings from the functional scope of the experiential configuration into which the noun enters as Thing.

But there is a further resource in the nominal group that combines these two potentialities, whereby Head and Thing are both present but are dissociated one from the other, not conflated. What happens here is that one of the premodifying functions is taken on by something that is itself a nominal group, in such a way that the Thing gets embedded in a prepositional phrase with *of*, which then functions as post-Head Qualifier, as in *a cup of tea* (see Figure 6-11). Of course, the two dimensions of structure are both present throughout; what we are showing here is the way the total meaning is construed by mapping the headhood of cup onto the thinghood of tea.

a	cup	of	tea
Numerative			Thing
Premodifier	Head	Postmodifier	
β	α		

Fig. 6-11 **Internal structure of the measure expression (or other embedded Numerative)**

Where the Head is dissociated from the Thing in this way, it can be conflated with any of the premodifying functions (see Table 6-10).

(i) Head as Deictic. All non-specific Deictics (see Table 6-3) can function as Head in this construction; note that *a(n)*, *no*, *every* become *one*, *none*, *every one*, and weak *some* [sm] becomes *some*. For example:

I think we're seeing **another one** of those periodic eruptions [COCA]

Well, I get rather fed up of **some** of these youngsters and the claptrap they talk sometimes. [LLC_01]

I can't offer you **any** of Malcolm's sherry because he hasn't got much. [LLC_01]

(ii) Head as Numerative. This may be cardinative or ordinative, definite or indefinite (see Table 6-9 above):

---

[10] In the first two editions of IFG, the Postmodifier also was brought into the scope of the logical representation. But this appears to complicate the description without adding further to its explanatory power.

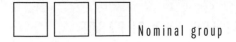

these two women have always got **loads** of washing out, **loads** of tablecloths [LLC_04]

and I think you've **all four** of you given your own subjective reactions to **three** of these four phenomena [LLC_05]

And it may not be the **last** of the storms for Washington and the rest of the country. [COCA]

(For expressions of extended Numeratives, see below.)

(iii) Head as Epithet. This is a more restricted type in which the Head is almost always an attitudinal noun (rather than adjective) embodying some positive or more usually negative appraisal. This appraisal may be extended prosodically by adjectives modifying the attitudinal noun. For example:

I met this feisty, wonderful, paradoxical **genius** of a woman that I'm nuts about [COCA]

In the row ahead of ours, a blond-haired, blue-eyed Christmas-tree **angel** of a teenager turned out to be awaiting trial for shooting a nun pointblank in the head. [COCA]

He's a **hell** of a pitcher, probably the best in the game right now, and as long as he knows he can go to another level, the sky's the limit for that kid. [COCA]

The Chronicle called it 'a beached **whale** of a building'. [COCA]

he has apparently been an absolute **nightmare** of a client [Text 82]

that some thieving **bastard** of a cop had walked off with his cigarettes [BROWN1_L]

I had been dragging and pulling and tugging my stupid **fool** of a brother all the while [KOHL_K]

... ordinary people, many of whom have never been involved politically before, who are feeling extraordinarily concerned about this gigantic **monster** of a bill that seems to be, you know, being rammed down everybody's throats [COCA]

A number of these have become well-worn clichés like *having a whale of a time*.

(iv) Head as Classifier. This occurs in examples such as

The **concept** of an intercolonial exhibition was a new one [ACE_J]

The RBC model includes **concepts** of Leadership, Teamwork, Professional Practice, Care Delivery, Resources, and Outcomes. [COCA]

Mixer fell into the **category** of mutt, an English shepherd and something or the other. [COCA]

Over the next fortnight, the Brisbane Olympic Games delegation will filter into the small Swiss **city** of Lausanne, on the shores of Lake Geneva. [ACE_B]

He's likely to point to the capture over the weekend of the **cities** of Brega and Ras Lanuf by anti-Qaddafi forces. [COCA]

where the Head word specifies the class to which the Thing is being said to belong. This construction is close in meaning to a variant without *of*, as in *the word 'freedom'*; cf. above, Section 6.2.2.2, on Qualifiers realized by nominal groups, as the example given there, *my brother the lawyer*. When the Head is Classifier, both Head and Thing can be either singular or plural, as illustrated above. However, when the Head is Epithet, the construction is, as already noted, more restricted, and plurals seem much less likely; compare *my stupid fool of a brother* with the less likely *my stupid fools of siblings*.

The relationship the Head and the Thing is either (1) an extending one or (2) an enhancing one: see Table 6-10. (1) When the Head is conflated with the Deictic or the Numerative, the relationship between the Head and the Thing is an extending one: 'Head is a subset of Thing'. (2) When the Head is conflated with the Epithet or the Classifier, the relationship between the Head and the Thing is an elaborating one (which is why this type of construction has been called appositive): 'Head is Thing'.

Table 6-10 Nominal groups with Head dissociated from Thing and conflated with one of the Premodifiers

	Deictic	Numerative	Epithet	Classifier
	[determiner: non-specific]	[numeral]	[noun]	[noun]
Head /	one/some/all/none of my **friends**	two/many/of my **friends**; the second/last of my **friends**	my hero/monster of a **friend**	the concept of **friendship**; the city of **Rome**
relationship between Head and Thing	(1) extending		(2) elaborating	

There is one other significant variety of nominal group that is construed in the same way, with the Head dissociated from the Thing and the two linked by *of*, as in *a cup of coffee*. We noted above (Section 6.2.3) that such expressions often figure as agnate to a 'counted' mass noun: *a new polish/type of polish, three coffees/cups of coffee*. These could be regarded as **extended Numeratives**, the Head being a word of measure or type[11]. They can be represented as a matrix of two variables (see Table 6-11): (i) measure (quantity)/type (quality), (ii) the set relationship of Head to Thing (collective (Head > Thing), partitive (Head < Thing), quantitative (Head = Thing)).

What all these have in common is that, while the Thing (e.g. *coffee*) is the entity that is functioning as participant in the transitivity structure of the clause, the logical Head of the construction is something that constrains the entity in terms of the two variables mentioned above. It is the Head that determines the value of the entity in the mood system, and therefore as a potential Subject.

The word *of* is the generalized marker of a structural relationship between nominals. All these instances can be related to the different senses of *of* occurring in a Qualifier; e.g. (aggregate) *the House of Lords*, (portion) *both Houses of Parliament*, (quantum) *a house full of treasure*, (variety) *a house of respite*, (facet) *the House of Windsor*, (make-up) *a house of three storeys*. In all such examples, *house* is both Head and Thing. In measure/type expressions, on the other hand, the Head word has become partially grammaticalized; hence it is often phonologically weak (non-salient), and there is often indeterminacy about the location of other elements in the nominal group, such as plural markers and Epithets.

A **measure** item may be followed by a fully elaborated nominal group, as in *a cup of that good strong Indian tea*. It often happens that the Epithet is transferred to the Head, as in *a*

---

[11] Compare the 'selector' in the account of the nominal group in the Cardiff Grammar (e.g. Fawcett, 2000: 304, 306).

Table 6-11 Extended Numeratives

	Measure (quantity)	**Type (quality)**
Head > Thing collective	**aggregate** a pack of cards such a crowd of people	**variety** a kind of owl my dialect of English
Head < Thing partitive	**portion** a slice of cake the fragment of a novel	**facet** the front of the house three sides of a square
Head = Thing quantitative	**quantum** a cup of coffee some area of land	**make-up** a drink of water their sense of insecurity

strong cup of tea, although clearly it is the tea that is strong, not the cup. Similarly: *a bloody good cup of coffee* [COCA]. It is partly the rather ambivalent nature of this structure, in which Head and Thing are separated, that causes this to happen; but it also arises because in many instances the Epithet could apply equally well to either, as in *a cloud of thick smoke*, *a thick cloud of smoke*, which provides the model for *a strong cup of tea*. (Classifiers, on the other hand, do not get transferred; we do not say *a brown slice of bread*.) Sometimes the Epithet belongs more naturally with the Numerative, as in *a large cup of tea*; but even here one can never have an Epithet that characterizes the item in question in any way other than its function as a Numerative – one cannot say *a blue cup of tea* to mean 'a cup of tea in a blue cup'. Finally, it is not unusual to have an Epithet in both positions, as in *a thick layer of powdery snow, a plastic cup of red, watery punch* [COCA].

While measure items delimit the Thing in terms of quantity, those of **type** delimit it in terms of generality: some species of it, some aspect of it, or its composition. Those of variety include a few very general terms such as *kind, sort, type*; these are the expressions that have led to the use of *kind of, sort of* as little more than markers of hesitation in casual speech. The words *example, instance, specimen* sometimes function in a similar way, especially in exemplifying identifying clauses, e.g. *a toad is an example of an amphibian*, whereas with a word like *kind* the meaning of classification is embodied in the clause structure and is construed by the clause structure even where the classifying word is omitted (*a toad is an amphibian*).

In expressions of facet such as *the front of the house, the entire length of the narrative*, the Head noun *front, length* is related in function to the preposition in a prepositional phrase: *before/in front of the house, throughout the narrative*. There is, in fact, a cline from one to the other: for example *at the summit of the hill* (where *summit* is both Head and Thing) – *at/on the top of the hill* – *on top of the hill* – (*atop the hill —*) *on the hill* (where *hill* is both Head and Thing). In *on top of the hill*, *on top of* is a preposition group (see Section 6.4.3 below); here *top* has no Deictic, cannot be pluralized, and can be used with abstract Things (*I think we've got on top of the problem*). But *at/on the top of the hill* forms a prepositional phrase (see Section 6.5): the preposition is *at* or *on*; *the top of the hill* is the Complement, where *top* can be pluralized ((*on*) *the tops of the hills*), but not made abstract – we will not find *on the top(s) of the problem(s)*. Here *top* is a facet term, and the analysis will be as in Figure 6-12.

[there was snow on]	the	tops	of	the	hills
experiential	Facet			Deictic	Thing
	Deictic	Thing			
logical	(Modifier)	Head	Qualifier		
	β	α		(Modifier)	Head
				β	α

Fig. 6-12   Nominal group with facet expression

In all such nominal expressions where Head and Thing are not conflated although both are clearly present, what is being construed is a phenomenon that from one point of view appears as a single entity and from another point of view as two. Such expressions have their basis in the concrete realms of our experience, such as cups and coffee; they then become an extremely rich resource for construing the virtual entities that make up so much of the environment of our adult existence.

> We need to take more initiative in showing how the halting progress we are making across **the broad front of understanding** really is improving our ability to deal with specific problems. [Text 32]

> The evils of poverty and unemployment are recording a steep rise, raising **the quantum of discontent** among the masses, which might soon reach a peak of no return, ending perhaps in a serious revolution. [KOHL_G]

> Is there still **some area of our soul**, we wonder, which has not yet been appropriated by religion, nor colonized by business, **a forlorn area of deep experience** to which only art has access? [KOHL_G]

6.3 Verbal group

The verbal group is the constituent that functions as Finite plus Predicator (or as Predicator alone if there is no Finite element) in the mood structure of the clause (clause as exchange; see Chapter 4); and as Process in the transitivity structure of the clause (clause as representation; see Chapter 5). In the clause

> someone's been eating my porridge

the verbal group is *has been eating*.

A verbal group is the expansion of a verb, in the same way that a nominal group is the expansion of a noun; and it consists of a sequence of words of the primary class of verb. If we consider *has been eating* just as a word sequence, it contains a **lexical verb** *eat*, which comes last; a **finite verb** *has*, which comes first; and an **auxiliary verb** *been*, which comes in between. No other ordering of these three components is possible.

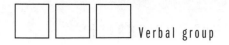

As with the nominal group, we can express this both as an experiential and as a logical structure. Because there is very much less lexical material in the verbal group – only one lexical item, in fact – the experiential structure is extremely simple; and most of the semantic load is carried by the logical structure, including the tense system.

6.3.1 Experiential structure of the verbal group

The experiential structure of the finite verbal group is **Finite** (standing for 'Finite operator') plus **Event**, with optional elements **Auxiliary** (one or more) and Polarity. Finite verbal groups range from short, one-word items such as *ate*, where the Finite is fused with the Event and there is no Auxiliary, to long strings like *couldn't have been going to be being eaten* (Figure 6-13).

(a)

ate
Finite/Event

(b)

couldn't	have	been	going to	be	being	eaten
Finite	Auxiliary1	Auxiliary2	Auxiliary3	Auxiliary4	Auxiliary5	Event

Fig. 6-13   Experiential structure of the verbal group

A striking feature of this structure is its parallelism with the nominal group. The verbal group begins with the Finite, which is the verbal equivalent of the Deictic, relating the process to the 'speaker-now'; the Finite does so by tense or modality (cf. Chapter 4, Section 4.2.2.1) whereas the Deictic does so by person or proximity, but each of these provides the orientation of the group. The verbal group ends with the Event, which is the verbal equivalent of the Thing; the former expresses a process, which may be event, act of consciousness or relation, whereas the latter expresses an entity of some kind, but both represent the core of the lexical meaning.

This is not, of course, a coincidence. Both verbal and nominal group begin with the element that 'fixes' the group in relation to the speech exchange; and both end with the element that specifies the representational content – the difference being that, since things are more highly organized than events, there are additional lexical elements in the nominal but none in the verbal group. And it is not difficult to explain why the structures should be this way round. Initial position is thematic; and the natural theme of a process or participant is its relation to the here-and-now. Final position is informative; and the newsworthy component of a process or participant is some aspect of its lexical content. So the structure of groups recapitulates, in the *fixed* ordering of their elements, the meaning that is incorporated as *choice* in the message structure of the clause.

Just as with the nominal group, therefore, there is no call to give a separate analysis corresponding to each of the three semantic components experiential, interpersonal, textual. The textual meaning is embodied in the ordering of the elements. The interpersonal meaning resides in the deictic features associated with finiteness – primary tense or modality – and polarity together with any attitudinal colouring that may be present in the lexical verb (e.g. *praise* vs. *criticize*; cf. Chapter 2, Figure 2-7). And further systematic distinctions of both kinds may be realized by intonation and rhythm: contrast the neutral *he hasn't been working*

// ^ he /hasn't been /**working** //

with a variant such as *he has not BEEN working*

// ^ he has /not /**been** /working //

which has 'marked negative (polarity)' and 'contrastive past (tense)', as in Figure 6-14. However, the structural labelling of the words that make up the verbal group is of limited value, not only because the meaning can be fully represented in terms of grammatical features (of tense, voice, polarity and modality), but also because it is the logical structure that embodies the single most important semantic feature of the English verb, its recursive tense system, and the elements of the logical structure are not the individual words but certain rather more complex elements. These are described in the next sub-section.

has	not	**been**	working
Finite:	Polarity:	Auxiliary:	Event
present	negative: marked	past: contrastive	

Fig. 6-14   Verbal group with marked polarity and contrastive tense

6.3.2 Logical structure of the verbal group

The verbal group is also structured logically, but in a way that is quite different from, and has no parallel in, the nominal group. The logical structure of the verbal group realizes the system of tense.

Consider the verbal group *has been eating*. This actually makes three separate tense choices: (1) present, expressed by the *-s* in *has* (i.e. by the fact that the first verb is in the present form); (2) past, expressed by the verb *have* plus the *-en* in *been* (i.e. plus the fact that the next verb is in the past/passive participle form v-*en*); (3) present, expressed by the verb *be* plus the *-ing* in *eating* (i.e. plus the fact that the next verb is in the present/active participle form v-*ing*). The complete tense can be built up as in Figure 6-15.

eats		has	eaten		has	been	eating
-s ('does')		-s	have ... -en		-s	have ... -en	be ... -ing
		α	β		α	β	γ

Fig. 6-15   Building up the 'present in past in present' tense

Thus tense in English is a ***recursive*** system. The primary tense is that functioning as Head, shown as α. This is the Deictic tense: past, present or future relative to the speech

event. The modifying elements, at β and beyond, are secondary tenses; they express past, present or future relative to the time selected in the previous tense. Realizations are shown in Table 6-12. Examples:

So when is this thing scheduled to produce results, Frank? – Oh, it's **been producing** results for a long time. [LLC]

When I'd **been teaching** apprentices at Vauxhall, I **could have gone** straight there, but I just couldn't get there [LLC]

They never know in the long vac or in the summer what they **are going to be doing** the next year. [LLC]

We live in Arizona, so they'**ll be going to be traveling** back and forth during the course of the season. [COCA]

But long term, the tax cut will 'generally drain funds that **should have been going to be saved** for Medicare and Social Security'. [COCA]

I think that there'**s going to be** some of that, but for some people they'**re going to have been pulled back** into a process in which they had not participated at all. [COCA]

Table 6-12 Realization of primary and secondary tenses

	Primary	**Secondary**
past	V-ed (simple past tense) as in *was/were, took, walked*	*have* + V-*en* as in *have been, have taken, have walked*
present	V-s (simple present tense) as in *is/are, takes, walks*	*be* + V-*ing* as in *be being, be taking, be walking*
future	*will* + V (infinitive) as in *will be, will take, will walk*	*be going to* + V (infinitive) as in *be going to be, be going to take, be going to walk*

In naming the tenses, it is best to work backwards, beginning with the deepest and using the preposition *in* to express the serial modification. Thus the tense in Figure 6-16 is 'present in past in future in past'.

It is useful to have a notation also for the tenses themselves; we use - for 'past', + for 'future' and ∅ (zero) for 'present'.

Clearly it is possible to represent every instance of a verbal group by a structural analysis showing the Auxiliaries, in a way that is parallel to what is done for the nominal group. However, the elements of the verbal group are purely grammatical (that is, the options they represent are closed – past/present/future, positive/negative, active/passive – not open-ended); so it is simpler just to use logical notation. The tense of the verbal group in Figure 6-16 could be shown as α- ^ β+ ^ γ– ^ δ∅, or simply as – + – ∅. There are no general symbols for polarity and voice, but these can be shown by abbreviations: pos./neg., act./pass./; with perhaps only neg. and pass. needing to be marked.

was	going to		have		been		working	
(past)	be going to ...	(inf.)	have ...	(-en)	be ...	-ing	(work)	
past:	future:		past:		present:			
'present	in past	in future	in past'					

Fig. 6-16   Naming of tenses

The expression of polarity is tied to that of finiteness, as has already been explained (Chapter 4, Section 4.2.2). The expression of voice is an extension of that of tense. The active has no explicit marker; the passive is expressed by *be* ['neutral'] or *get* ['mutative'] plus V-*en* (past/passive participle), appearing as an additional modifying element at the end (for a study of the 'mutative' voice, see Downing, 1996). The passive thus functions like an extra secondary tense; and it displays a distinctive combination of presentness (*be*) and pastness (V-*en*) suggesting 'to be in a present condition resulting from a past event', e.g. *are joined* as in *the two halves of the city are joined by a bridge*. For this reason there is no very clear line between passives and attributes having passive form. Examples of the passive are given in Figure 6-17.

is		eaten	
(present)	be ...	-en	(eat)
αØ		β	
present	passive		

has		been		eaten	
(present)	have ...	-en	be ...	-ing	(eat)
αØ	β–			γ	
present	past		passive		

has		been		being		eaten	
(present)	have ...	-en	be ...	-en	be ...	-en	(eat)
αØ	β–				γØ		δ
present	past		present		passive		

Fig. 6-17   Passive verbal groups

For most of the known history of English the number of passive tenses has, as far as we can tell, lagged behind the number of the active ones. But since the system opened up in the way it has done the passives have caught up, and now every active tense has its passive

counterpart, formed in this manner as an extension of the logical structure (on the systemic expansion of the secondary present, cf. Mair & Leech, 2006: 322–325; Smith & Raylson, 2007). The longest tense forms I have recorded in use (five serial tense choices) include an instance of the passive:

it'll've	been	going	to've been	being	tested
α+	β–	γ+	δ–	εØ	ζ

This is 'passive: present in past in future in past in future'.

Since the tense system is recursive, there should be no longest possible tense. However, in practice there are certain restrictions that limit the total set of those that occur. These restrictions, or 'stop rules', are as follows:

(i) Apart from α, future occurs only once.

(ii) Apart from α, present occurs only once, and always at the deepest level.

(iii) Apart from α, the same tense does not occur twice consecutively.

That is: following (i), we do not hear *she is going to have been about to do it*; following (ii), we do not hear *he has been having done it*; following (iii), we do not hear *they will have had done it*. These restrictions limit the total number of finite tenses to 36. These 36 finite tenses are shown in Table 6-13.

Table 6-13 The finite and non-finite/modalized tense systems

ε	δ	γ	Non-finite, and finite modal, tenses (12): read as far as β		Finite non-modal tenses (36): read as far as α		Finite non-modal tense		Non-finite, and finite modal tense (perfective, imperfective; modal)
			β		α				
			(none)	I	past	1	take/did take	I	to take, taking; can take
					present	2	take(s)/do(es) take		
					future	3	will take		
			past	II	past	4	had taken	II	to have, having; can have + taken
					present	5	has taken		
					future	6	will have taken		
			present	III	past	7	was taking	III	to have, having; can have + taking
					present	8	is taking		
					future	9	will be taking		

401

Table 6-13 The finite and non-finite/modalized tense systems (*contd*)

ε	δ	γ	β		α		Finite non-modal tense		Non-finite, and finite modal tense (perfective, imperfective; modal)
			Non-finite, and finite modal, tenses (12): read as far as β		Finite non-modal tenses (36): read as far as α		Finite non-modal tense		Non-finite, and finite modal tense (perfective, imperfective; modal)
			future	IV	past	10	was going to take		to have, having; can have + going/about to take
					present	11	is going to take	IV	
					future	12	will be going to take		
					past	13	was going to have taken		to have, having; can have + going to have taken
	past		in future	V	present	14	is going to have taken	V	
					future	15	will be going to have taken		
					past	16	had been taking		to have, having; can have + been taking
		present	in past	VI	present	17	has been taking	VI	
					future	18	will have been taking		
					past	19	was going to be taking		to have, having; can have + going to be taking
		present	in future	VII	present	20	is going to be taking	VII	
					future	21	will be going to be taking		
					past	22	had been going to take		to have, having; can have + been going to take
		future	in past	VIII	present	23	has been going to take	VIII	
					future	24	will have been going to take		

Table 6-13 The finite and non-finite/modalized tense systems (*contd*)

ε	δ	γ	β		α		Finite non-modal tense		Non-finite, and finite modal tense (perfective, imperfective; modal)
			Non-finite, and finite modal, tenses (12): read as far as β		Finite non-modal tenses (36): read as far as α		Finite non-modal tense		Non-finite, and finite modal tense (perfective, imperfective; modal)
	past	in future	in past	IX	past	25	had been going to have taken	IX	to have, having; can have + been going to have taken
					present	26	has been going to have taken		
					future	27	will have been going to have taken		
	present	in past	in future	X	past	28	was going to have been taking	X	to have, having; can have + going to have been taking
					present	29	is going to have been taking		
					future	30	will be going to have been taking		
	present	in future	in past	XI	past	31	had been going to be taking	XI	to have, having; can have + been going to be taking
					present	32	has been going to be taking		
					future	33	will have been going to be taking		
present	in past	in future	in past	XII	past	34	had been going to have been taking	XII	to have, having; can have + been going to have been taking
					present	35	has been going to have been taking		
					future	36	will have been going to have been taking		

6.3.3 Finite, sequent and non-finite tense systems

There are, in fact, three distinct systems of tense in English:

System I:	finite	36 tenses
System II:	sequent	24 tenses
System III:	non-finite/modalized	12 tenses

The finite system, System I, is the one displayed in the centre columns of Table 6-13. The way it works can be illustrated by building up clauses with associated time expressions. Figure 6-18 shows a four-degree tense, *she's been going to have known*, built up from one end and then demolished from the other; each form is accompanied by an appropriate time Adjunct. It will be noted that the order of time Adjuncts is the reverse of that of the tenses; there is what is known as 'mirror concord' between them, invariable except that the one corresponding to the primary tense can be picked out and made thematic, e.g. *by now she's known for some time, for a while she was going to have known already by tonight*. The clause chosen is one of mental process, so as to be able to be built up naturally from the simple present.

Fig. 6-18 Building up a complex tense form from the left and from the right, with associated temporal Adjuncts showing mirror concord

System II is that which is available following a past projection (see Chapter 7, Section 7.5) such as *they said*. Note the following equivalences:

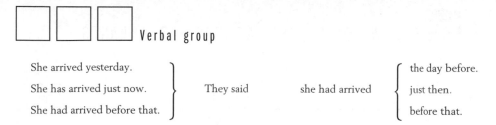

She arrived yesterday.	⎫			⎧ the day before.
She has arrived just now.	⎬ They said	she had arrived		⎨ just then.
She had arrived before that.	⎭			⎩ before that.

What happens here is that in the environment of a 'past' feature, the past element in three of the System II tenses is neutralized; past, past in present and past in past all represented as past in past. Since there are six such triads, System II has $2 \times 6 = 12$ fewer tenses than System I.

System III is the tense system available in non-finite and in modalized forms of the verbal group. Here a further neutralization takes place, i.e. **both** that in System II (affecting the past) **and** a parallel one affecting the future. Derivation of System III by the neutralization of certain contrasts in System I shows the combined effect of both these steps. By step (1), *arrived*, *has arrived* and *had arrived* are all represented by the one form *have arrived*. (This appears as *have arrived* following a modal Finite, and as *to have arrived* [perfective] or *having arrived* [imperfective] when non-finite.) This is the same neutralization as that which produced System II, the only difference being that the System II form is a finite one, *had arrived*. By step (2), *will arrive*, *is going to arrive* and *will be going to arrive* are all represented by the one form *be going to arrive*, or *be about to arrive* (the two are synonymous as far as tense is concerned), these again having modalized, perfective and imperfective variants.

What happens here is that (i) past, past in present and past in past are all represented by past; (ii) future, future in present and future in future are all represented by future. There are twelve such triads; the total number of tenses in System III is therefore $36 - (2 \times 12) = 12$.

The difference between this and System II is that in System III the effect is simply to eliminate the entire choice of primary tense. System I minus the 'α' tense gives System III. The non-finite or modalized verbal group has no deictic tense element: non-finites because they have no deictic at all (that is what non-finite implies: not anchored in the here-&-now); modalized because, while they have a deictic element (being finite), their deixis takes the form of modality and not tense. Strictly speaking, the first secondary tense of the non-finite should be labelled α, since that becomes the Head element; but it seems simpler and clearer to retain the association of α with finiteness and show non-finites as beginning with β.

Here is an example of a clause complex consisting of two clauses each of whose verbs has selected a System III tense:

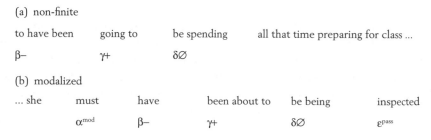

(a) non-finite

to have been	going to	be spending	all that time preparing for class ...
β–	γ+	δØ	

(b) modalized

... she	must	have	been about to	be being	inspected
	α^{mod}	β–	γ+	δØ	ε^{pass}

The tenses of System III are shown in the right-hand column of Table 6-13. Note that, to save duplication, the **labelling** of tenses for both systems is shown on the left. The class I form of System III is tenseless: that is *taking*, *to take*, *must* (or other modal) + *take* (Table 6-14).

Table 6-14 Derivation of System III by the neutralization of certain contrasts in System I

	System I		System III	
(1)			**(a) non-finite**	
	She arrived	yesterday	Having arrived	yesterday, she …
	She has arrived	just now		just now, she …
	She had arrived	before that		before that, she …
			(b) modalized	
			She must have arrived	yesterday
				just now
				before that
(2)			**(a) non-finite**	
	She will arrive	tomorrow	Being about to arrive	tomorrow
	She is going to arrive	just now		just now
	She will be going to arrive	after that		after that
			(b) modalized	
			She must be going to arrive	tomorrow
				just now
				after that

6.3.4 Features of serial tense

It would be possible, obviously, to think of all the tenses in any one of these systems – finite, sequent or non-finite – as making up a simple set. But this would leave unaccounted for both the relations among the three systems and the serial character of the tense system as a whole.

What is remarkable about serial tense is its regularity: the way in which each choice of tense, whether past, present or future, defines a location in time which is then used as the point of departure for a further choice among the same three tenses. This regularity is obscured, and distorted, by the categories of the structuralist analysis, and especially the 'aspect' nomenclature of perfect and progressive (or continuous). The serial nature of past and future tense is not difficult to illustrate with short dialogic sequences:

Did it snow? – It was snowing, when I first arrived.

α–   α– β+   α–

That is, I transport myself to that moment in past time, and now the snowing is in the present. Likewise:

Will it melt? – It will have melted, by the time you have arrived.

α+   α + β–   α ⌀ β–

That is, transport yourself to that moment in future time and now the melting is in the past. The initial move in time may, of course, be repeated:

Did it snow? – It had snowed, before I arrived.

α–   α– β–   α–

At that (past) moment, the snowing was already in the past. Likewise:

Will it melt? – It will just be going to melt, by the time you arrive.

α+   α+ β+   α⌀

At that (future) moment, the melting will just be in the future.

Perhaps the most misleading term is 'continuous', when used for present-in-present. Again, we can illustrate dialogically:

Does it snow? – It is snowing now, though it doesn't usually.

Notice how the secondary tense narrows down and sharpens the focus of the primary one: at this (present) moment, the snowing is in the present. The complication here is that, as we saw in Chapter 5, the exact force of this narrowing depends on the type of process. With a mental or relational process, the unmarked choice is that of simple present, and the present-in-present is rather sharply focused (cf. Section 5.3.3.4):

I don't really like Grand Opera. But I**'m liking** this performance quite a lot.

Oh, she is playing with you. She sees the power she has. And she **is liking** it. [COCA]

Liz Brous, of New York City, mom of 18 month-old Alex, says, 'Charlie and I made one lifetime rule: He gets up in the middle of the night; I get up in the morning, which begins at 6:00 A.M. If Alex starts crying at 5:30, Charlie gets up. If he's still going at 6:00, Charlie wakes me up to take over.' Alex hasn't woken up for six nights in a row, so Liz **is hating** the rule right now. 'But Charlie **was hating** it a few months ago when Alex was up all night teething,' she says. [COCA]

With a material process, on the other hand, the present-in-present has become the norm, and the simple present has a noticeably 'habitual' sense, as in the snowing example given above.

Treating the tenses as a simple list also suggests that there is a clear-cut distinction between those tenses that exist and others that don't, whereas the system varies for different speakers; moreover it is tending to expand all the time, although it has probably just about reached its limits. What has happened is that relative time – before, at or after a defined time reference – has come to be interpreted, in the semantics of English, as a kind of logical relation (cf. Matthiessen, 1983; 1984; 1996); a way of subcategorizing events similar to the subcategorizing of things, except that the latter is multidimensional (and hence lexicalized) whereas the former is based on a single semantic dimension and can therefore be expressed entirely by grammatical means.

Table 6-15 gives an alternative arrangement of the tenses of System I, ordered from the 'Finite' end. This is the opposite to that used in Table 6-13. Column 1 shows past, present and future in $time_2$ – that is, time *relative to* the time chosen as $time_1$. Column 2 shows past, present and future in $time_3$ – again, time relative to the time chosen at $time_2$; and so on. This corresponds with the way the more complex tenses tend to get built up in the course of dialogue (cf. Halliday, 1992b/2003: 369); for example,

Does the machine work?				present
– It's not working now.			present in	present
But it'll be working when you next need it.			present in	future
– Is it going to be working by tomorrow?		present in	future in	present
– It was going to've been working already before you came in; but ...	present in	past in	future in	past
	t_4	t_3	t_2	t_1

It is interesting to compare those in Column 3, where out of 27 theoretically possible tenses only 12 are typically found to occur (cf. the 'stop rules' referred to earlier), with the remaining 15 that could be constructed:

(regularly occurring)		(not normally found)	
$++\varnothing$	will be going to be working	$+++$	will be going to be about to work
$++-$	will be going to have worked	$+\varnothing+$	will be being about to work
		$+\varnothing\varnothing$	will be being working
$+-+$	will have been going to work	$+\varnothing-$	will be having worked
$+-\varnothing$	will have been working	$+--$	will have had worked
$\varnothing+\varnothing$	is going to be working	$\varnothing++$	is going to be about to work
$\varnothing+-$	is going to have worked	$\varnothing\varnothing+$	is being about to work
		$\varnothing\varnothing\varnothing$	is being working
$\varnothing-+$	has been going to work	$\varnothing\varnothing-$	is having worked
$\varnothing-\varnothing$	has been working	$\varnothing--$	has had worked
$-+\varnothing$	was going to be working	$-++$	was going to be about to work
$-+-$	was going to have worked	$-\varnothing+$	was being about to work
		$-\varnothing\varnothing$	was being working
$--+$	had been going to work	$-\varnothing-$	was having worked
$--\varnothing$	had been working	$---$	had had worked

Table 6-15 System I tenses, showing construction of serial time

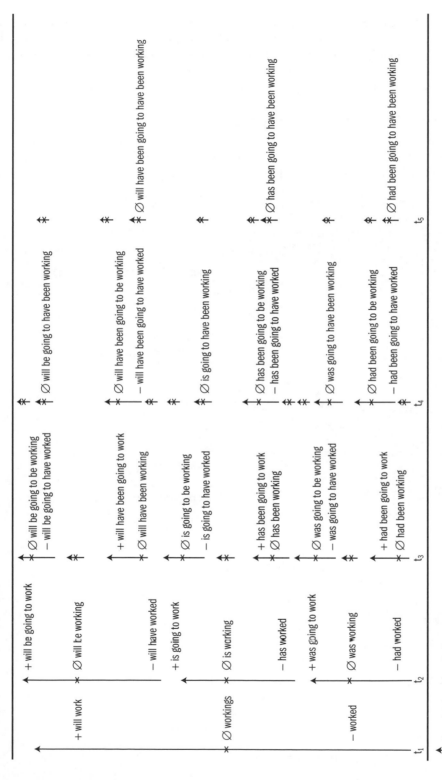

It is not impossible to construct contexts in which there would be strong pressure for one or other of the latter set to appear. Unfortunately this cannot be tested experimentally, because these complex forms are almost always spontaneous; people cannot produce them under experimental conditions. But the system itself has the potential for being further expanded in this way; there is no clear boundary between what is in and what is out.

6.3.5 The system network of the verbal group

As we have seen, the verbal group is highly grammaticalized: all elements of its structure except for the Event are realized by grammatical items, the Event being the only one that is realized by a lexical item. It follows that the system network of the verbal group

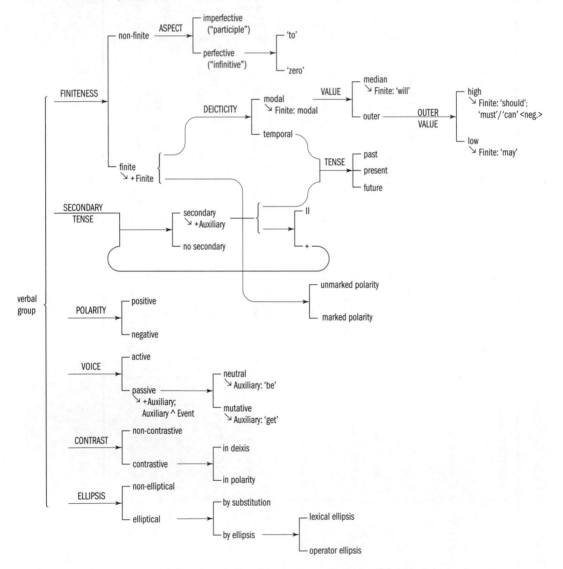

Fig. 6-19 The verbal group system network

410

is a network of systems representing contrasts that are purely grammatical in nature: see Figure 6-19. The only system that extends in delicacy towards distinctions that are realized lexically is the system of EVENT TYPE – the verbal group analogue of the THING TYPE system of the nominal group. This system is concerned with distinctions among verbs relating to their temporal properties (thus complementing the clausal system of PROCESS TYPE, which is concerned with distinctions among processes relating to configurations of process plus participants). However, we have not included this system in the verbal group network presented here.

The systems of the verbal group derive from different metafunctions:

(i)   Textual: VOICE, CONTRAST, and ELLIPSIS;

(ii)   Interpersonal: POLARITY, FINITENESS, and MODALITY;

(iii) Experiential: ASPECT and EVENT TYPE;

(iv) Logical: SECONDARY TENSE.

The logical system of SECONDARY TENSE provides the key to the organization of the verbal group: this is the system that defines the logical structure discussed above. The system of VOICE also contributes an auxiliary to this structure (*be ... -en*), which functions like a final secondary tense right before the Event.

Realization are set out in Table 6-16. (Note that each selection of 'secondary tense' is realized by the insertion of a new Auxiliary element.)

Notes to the system network. (1) There is no system of MOOD in the verbal group. If a clause is 'free: indicative' or 'bound: finite', the verbal group is 'finite'. If a clause is either 'free: imperative' or 'bound: non-finite', the verbal group is 'non-finite'. The verbal group of an imperative clause is 'perfective' in aspect and 'no secondary' or 'present' in (secondary) tense; negative variants have the special realization *don't*. (In various languages, clausal contrasts in MOOD correlate with verbal contrasts in MODE; cf. Chapter 4, Footnote 7.)

(2) The distinction between 'contrastive in tense' and 'contrastive in polarity' is realized only if at least one secondary tense is chosen; it is, however, regarded as systemic in **all** instances, with ambiguity arising where there is no secondary tense.

6.3.6 Phrasal verbs

The class of word functioning as Event in the verbal group structure is the verb. We can refer to this more specifically as the 'lexical verb' to distinguish it from grammatical verbs, the finites and auxiliaries.[12]

---

[12] A major point of difference between the verbal group and the nominal group is that the Event (unlike the Thing) is not the point of departure for the recursive modifying relationship. Hence it does not figure as an element in the notation. It could be argued that a phrasal verb represents an expansion of the Event, giving something like

come	along	up	out	from	under (that table)
α	β	γ	δ	ε	ζ

(or, more seriously, the adverbial part of it, as far as the word *out*). But we have not explored this line of approach here.

Table 6-16 Realizations of terms in verbal group system network

System	Term	Realization
	verbal group	+Event; Event: lexical verb
FINITENESS	finite	+Finite; # ^ Finite
	non-finite	—
ASPECT	imperfective	Auxiliary if present, otherwise Event: v-*ing* /v-*en*
	perfective	Auxiliary if present, otherwise Event: v
PERFECTIVE MARKING	'zero'	—
	'to'	Event: to ^ v
DEICTICITY	modal	Finite: modal
	temporal	—
MODAL VALUE	median	Finite: 'will'
	outer	—
OUTER VALUE	high	Finite: 'should'; 'must' /'can' <negative>
	low	Finite: 'can', 'may'
TENSE [primary]	past	Finite: v-*d*
	present	Finite: v-*(s)*
	future	Finite: 'will'
TENSE [secondary]	past	Auxiliary: 'have ... v-*en*'
	present	Auxiliary: 'be ... v-*ing*'
	future	Auxiliary: 'be going ... to ^ v'
POLARITY	positive	—
	negative	+Polarity; Polarity: 'not'; [temporal: past /present] Finite: 'do' ^ Polarity; [non-finite] # ^ Polarity
POLARITY MARKING	unmarked polarity	[positive] —; [negative] Finite/Polarity
	marked polarity	[positive] Finite: salient; [negative] Polarity: salient; [positive & temporal: past /present] Finite: 'do'
VOICE	active	—
	passive	+Auxiliary; Event: v-*en*
PASSIVE TYPE	neutral	Auxiliary: 'be'
	mutative	Auxiliary: 'get'

Table 6-16 Realizations of terms in verbal group system network (*contd*)

System	Term	Realization
CONTRAST	non-contrastive	–
	contrastive: in tense	
	contrastive: in polarity	
ELLIPSIS	non-elliptical	–
	elliptical: by substitution	Event: 'do'
	lexical ellipsis	
	operator ellipsis	

Phrasal verbs are lexical verbs that consist of more than just the verb word itself (also discussed under a number of other headings, including 'verb particle construction', or 'VPC', and 'multi-word verb', or 'MWV'). They are of two kinds, plus a third, which is a combination of the other two:

(i)   verb + adverb, e.g. *look out* 'unearth, retrieve'

(ii) verb + preposition, e.g. *look for* 'seek'

(iii) verb + adverb + preposition, e.g. *look out for* 'watch for the presence of'

Examples:

(i)   Could you look out for a good recipe for me?

    – Yes I'll look one out in a moment.

(ii) I'm looking for a needle; could you help me find one?

    – Yes I'll look for one in a moment.

(iii) Look out for snakes; there are lots around here.

    – Yes I'll look out for them.

Expressions of this kind are lexical items; *look out, look for* and *look out for* belong as separate entries in a thesaurus or dictionary. They are thus tending more and more to function as grammatical constituents; but this tendency is far from complete, and grammatically they are rather unstable.

Experientially, a phrasal verb is a single Process, rather than Process plus circumstantial element. This can be seen from their assignment to process types[13]. For example, the verb

---

[13] With many phrasal verbs, the meaning of the phrasal verb cannot be predicted from its component parts. For example, the meaning of the phrasal verb *carry off*, 'perform successfully', cannot be 'computed' from *carry* plus *off*. Thus an example such as *they carried it out* is ambiguous. If *carry out* means 'perform successfully', then *it* is likely to refer to something like a plan (as in *as a result of this continued problem, much experimenting was carried out*); but if it means 'carry to an outside location', then *it* is likely to refer to a physical entity (as in *carefully I carried the tray out to him*).

see represents a mental process, and so has simple present as its unmarked present tense, as in *do you see that sign?* (not *are you seeing that sign?*). But *see off* is material, and so has present in present: *are you seeing your brother off?* (not *do you see you brother off?*, which can only be habitual). The transitivity analysis is therefore as in Figure 6-20.

In the case of *see off* and many other phrasal verbs, the phrasal verb is thus not agnate with a non-phrasal counterpart. For example, there is no systemic proportionality such that *see* is related to *see off* as *sound* is to *sound off*. However, with many verbs, the simple verb is agnate with the combination of verb + adverb, e.g. *break ~ break off* ('separate'), *kill ~ kill off* ('kill in large numbers, rendering extinct'), *take ~ take off* ('remove (clothing)'), *beat ~ beat up* ('beat severely, inflicting injury'), *drink ~ drink up* ('drink to the last drop'), *go ~ go up* ('ascend'), *go ~ go on* ('continue going'), although specialized senses may also evolve, as with *break off* in the sense of 'abruptly stop talking', *beat up* in the sense of 'drum up support', and *go on* in the sense of 'talk at great length'. Where there are agnate pairs of verb ~ verb + adverb, the 'phrasal' variant involves a specification of **phase** (cf. Chapter 8, Section 8.5.1), similar to the phasal specifications in Chinese by post-verbs (see Halliday & McDonald, 2004: Section 6.5.2.2) although the English range of options is much more restricted since it involves adverbs rather than verbs. There are three types of phase, **temporal**, **spatial** (directional) and **resultative**: see Table 6-17.[14] These occur with various semantic fields; among these, motion is an important one, as illustrated by the following examples from J.R.R. Tolkien's *The Lord of the Rings*:

> In terror they <u>stumbled **on**</u>; as they <u>flitted **across**</u>; they <u>scrambled **on**</u> to the low parapet of the bridge; slowly and painfully they <u>clambered **down**</u>; Frodo and Sam <u>plodded **on**</u>; [they] <u>went **forward**</u> cautiously; they came upon dark pools fed by threads of water <u>trickling **down**</u> from some source higher up the valley; he <u>crawled **back**</u> into the brambles; but the hobbits <u>crept **by**</u> cautiously

As the examples illustrate, verbs of motion are phased temporally to indicate durative motion ('continue to go') and spatially to indicate directed motion ('go' + direction). With the second type, the verb often denotes some specific manner of motion such as *flit* and *clamber* in the examples above; the phrasal verb thus makes it possible to combine manner and direction: verb [manner] + adverb [direction]. Similar patterns are found in languages with 'serial verb constructions' and 'verb compounding'. Direction occurs naturally with motion, of course; but it may also be used as a phasal extension verbs of other kinds, as with direction of perception:

> Frodo and Sam <u>gazed **out**</u> in mingled loathing and wonder on this hateful land.

The phrasal verbs in Table 6-17 are paired with non-phrasal counterparts. However, even where the phrasal verb has evolved a sense that is unrelated to the simple verb in the verb + adverb combination, this sense often involves a feature of phase, as with *see off* ('take leave

---

[14] Note that a number of the items functioning as spatial adverbs can also serve as prepositions; cf. *they clambered down* and *the clambered down the hill*. These combinations of verb of motion + adverb of place are less like prototypical phrasal verbs in that the adverb can be treated textually (see below) in the same way as a circumstance of Place: *down they clambered*, *it was down that they clambered*.

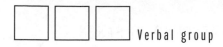

Table 6-17 Examples of phasal types of phrasal verb

Type	Subtype	Adverb	Non-phrasal	Phrasal	Gloss
temporal	durative	on	walk	walk on	'continue to walk'
		away	talk	talk away	'talk continuously, persistently'
spatial (directional)	vertical	up	go	go up	'ascend'
		down	go	down	'descend'
	interior/exterior	in	go	go in	'enter'
		out	go	go out	'exit'
	horizontal	forward	go	forward	'proceed'
		back	go	back	'return'
	path	across	go	go across	'cross'
		along	go	go along	'follow'
		around	go	go around	'circle'
		past	go	past	'pass'
resultative	separative	off	break	break off	'break, separating'
			cut	cut off	'cut, separating'
			fence	fence off	'separate, with a fence'
	completive	up	drink	drink up	'drink to the last drop'
			grow	grow up	'grow, reaching maturity'
			use	use up	'use completely'
			cover	cover up	'cover completely, conceal'
		out	burn	burn out	'burn, being completely consumed'
			fill	fill out	'fill to completion
			try	try out	'try to determine effect'
		through	think	think through	'think about, arriving at conclusion'

of'), *take off* ('leave the ground, rising into the air'), *kick off* ('get started'), where there is a sense of separation, and with *see out* ('work on until completion'), *run out* ('be used up'), *turn out* ('evict').

The experiential configuration is reflected in the thematic variation. If the prepositional phrase *for a needle* was a circumstantial element it should be able to be thematized; but

415

we do not say *for that I'll look*; the more likely form is *that I'll look for*. Similarly with the adverbial ones: *see off* is a single process, so whereas we would say *there I'll see John* (= *I'll see John there* but with *there* instead of *I* as Theme), there is no form *off I'll see John* thematically related to *I'll see John off*.

I	'm seeing	my brother	off
		Goal	
Actor	Process		

I	'm looking for	a needle
Actor	Process	Goal

Fig. 6-20   Transitivity analysis of phrasal verb

The grammar enables us to explain why phrasal verbs have evolved to the extent that they have done in modern English. The leading edge is formed by those of type (i), the adverbial ones, which are particularly widely spread. Typically these have non-phrasal, one-word synonyms, or near-synonyms; yet the phrasal form tends to be preferred, and is strongly favoured in the spoken language. Why is this?

Suppose we have a two-participant clause, active in voice, in which the main item of news is the Goal. The Goal comes at the end, and this is where the prominence – the information focus – typically falls. We can express the process either phrasally or non-phrasally – there is nothing very much to choose between the two:

they cancelled **the meeting**   they called off **the meeting**

Suppose however that I want the focus of information to be the Process rather than the Goal. At this point a significant difference arises. If I say

they **cancelled** the meeting

the result is that the information focus is now non-final; this is a marked, strongly foregrounded option, and therefore carries additional overtones of contrast, contradiction or unexpectedness. I may not want these overtones; but the only way I can avoid them is to leave the focus unmarked – i.e. at the end. This means that the Process, not the Goal, must come last. In Chinese, which has a similar word order and information structure, there is a special construction, the *ba* [ă] construction, for achieving this (see Halliday & McDonald, 2004); but in English it is impossible – I cannot say *they the meeting cancelled* – unless the Process is split into two parts. This, therefore, is what happens, with a phrasal verb: it splits the Process into two parts, one functioning as Predicator and the other as Adjunct[15], with the Adjunct coming in its normal place at the end:

they called the meeting **off**

---

[15]   Note that this means that in an unmarked imperative clause of the jussive type, the Predicator part of a phrasal verb is Theme, while the Adjunct part appears within the Rheme, as illustrated in Chapter 3, Figure 3-10.

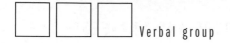

This also explains something that is often presented as an arbitrary rule of English, but is in fact anything but arbitrary: that if the Goal is a pronoun it almost always occurs **within** the phrasal verb (*they called it off* rather than *they called off it*). This is part of the same story; a pronoun is hardly ever newsworthy, since it refers to something that has gone before, so if the Goal is a pronoun it is virtually certain that the Process will be under focus. (But not quite; the pronoun may be contrastive, and if so it **can** come finally, e.g. *they rang up me, but apparently nobody else.*)

Figure 6-21 gives the analysis of a clause with a phrasal verb of the adverbial type (i) in it, in terms of (a) transitivity and (b) mood. Similarly with the prepositional type (ii): in *I'm looking for a needle*, the mood constituents are *looking* Predicator, *for a needle* Adjunct, and this accounts for the ordering relative to other Adjuncts, e.g. *I've looked everywhere for a needle*. The third type includes some where both adverb and preposition are (or may be) part of the Process, e.g. *look out for, put up with, put in for;* and others where only the adverb is within the Process, e.g. *let in for, put up to*, as in *he let me in for it, he put me up to it*. Analysis is shown in Figure 6-21. There will often be doubt about whether these complex lexical items can be interpreted grammatically as a single Process or not. In such cases it is important to consider the transitivity of the clause as a whole, to see whether it appears to be structured as process plus participant or process plus circumstance. Thematic variation often shows a preference one way or the other (cf. Chapter 5, Section 5.7).

(a)

they	called		the meeting	off
			Goal/Medium	
Actor/Agent	Process: material			

(b)

Subject	'past'	'call'	Complement	Adjunct
	Finite	Predicator		
Mood		Residue		

Fig. 6-21   Phrasal verb in transitivity and mood structure

Further examples of phrasal verbs are given in Figure 6-22.

As we have shown above, there are three types of phrasal verb: verb plus preposition, verb plus adverb or verb plus both. We can also note combinations verbs with nouns such as

<u>Taking</u> account of the fact that such a move on our part would be unpopular in world opinion, he argued that the responsibility of the United States is 'to do, confidently and firmly, not what is popular, but what is right'. [BROWN1_B]

And the commission promises **to pay** more attention to the economic consequences of future wage decisions. [ACE_B]

In the Stalag, Helion came to know and love his comrades, most of them plain folk, who, in their extremity, showed true courage and <u>ran great risks</u> to help each other. [BROWN1_G]

(a)

he	put		in	for	the job
Actor	Process				Goal
Subject	'past' Finite	'put' Predicator	Adjunct	Adjunct	

(b)

he	put		him	up	to the job
			Goal		
Actor	Process				Location
Subject	'past' Finite	'put' Predicator	Complement	Adjunct	Adjunct

Fig. 6-22 Further examples of phrasal verbs

Job reservation **must give** <u>way to</u> more equitable systems [LOB_D]

Anyone **setting out** <u>in search of</u> adventure should have the sense to ensure that he or she **is not about to put** someone else's life <u>at risk</u>. [ACE_B]

An era **came** <u>to an end</u> on 31 December when the RAAF Academy transferred from the University to the new Defence Forces Academy in Canberra. [ACE_H]

Wagait was discussed and finally all the full-bloods were asked to go and sit down together and <u>**come** to a decision</u>. [ACE_B]

I thought since we employ and are expert in the medium of radio, what I should do is bring in something which has no words in it so that we're completely **made** <u>fools of</u>. [COCA]

Such combinations are investigated by Allerton (2002) under the heading of 'stretched verb constructions' (cf. our reference in Chapter 1 to research on 'phraseology', in the region midway between grammar and lexis). However, while it can be argued that these are also lexicalized verbs, just as phrasal verbs, 'stretched verbs' can still be accommodated in terms the transitivity patterns of the clause. They involve combinations of Process + Range (see Chapter 5, Section 5.7.3.2), e.g. *take + account of, pay + attention (to), run + risk, reach + conclusion*, or Process + abstract circumstance of Place, e.g. *put + at risk, come + to an end, arrive + at conclusion*. The lexical verb serving as the Event of the verbal group functioning as Process tends to be fairly general, and the lexical content is represented by the noun serving as Thing in the nominal group functioning as Range in the clause, or in the prepositional phrase serving as Place. There tend to be collocational combinations of verb and noun, as illustrated by the examples above; compare also *wreak + havoc, tender + resignation, lend + support*. This noun is often a nominalization of a verb, as with *attention, conclusion*, which reflects the fact that 'stretched verb constructions' embody grammatical metaphor (see Chapter 10). Like other instances of grammatical metaphor, clauses with 'stretched verb constructions' can thus be given more than one analysis, as illustrated in Figure 6-23.

An era	came	to an end
Actor	Process	Place

An era	ended
Actor	Process

Fig. 6-23   Clause with 'stretched verb construction'

6.4 Adverbial group, conjunction group, preposition group

6.4.1 Adverbial group

The adverbial group serves as Adjunct in the modal structure of the clause – either circumstantial Adjunct or modal Adjunct (mood or comment). Examples:

(1)   circumstantial Adjunct

But you mustn't take it **personally**. [UTS/Macquarie Corpus]

Yeah but it didn't **aggressively** market them. [UTS/Macquarie Corpus]

You've coped **beautifully** tonight; you've coped **so well** compared to how I would have coped. [UTS/Macquarie Corpus]

(2a)   interpersonal Adjunct, mood

I **actually** didn't have a lot of chicken; I had **probably** more vegetables. [UTS/Macquarie Corpus]

(2b)   interpersonal Adjunct, comment

Apparently he's got a wife and a couple of kids. [UTS/Macquarie Corpus]

And I nearly I nearly smashed him in the face **frankly**. [UTS/Macquarie Corpus]

Otie, stop licking plates. There's one person in this room who just loves that lasagne. **Unfortunately**, he isn't human. [UTS/Macquarie Corpus]

Specifically what have you been working on this evening Bruno? [UTS/Macquarie Corpus]

The adverbial group has an adverb as Head, which may or may not be accompanied by modifying elements. Adverbial groups serving as circumstantial Adjunct have an adverb denoting a circumstance as Head – for example, a circumstance of time (e.g. *yesterday*, *today*, *tomorrow*) or of quality (e.g. *well*, *badly*; *fast*, *quickly*, *slowly*). Adverbial groups serving as modal Adjunct have an adverb denoting an assessment as Head – for example, an assessment of time (e.g. *still*, *yet*, *already*) or of intensity (e.g. *really*, *just*, *only*, *actually*). Examples are given in Table 6-18. As the table shows, some classes of adverb have interrogative and demonstrative forms.

Premodifiers are grammatical items like *not* and *rather* and *so*; there is no lexical premodification in the adverbial group. What there is is therefore more like what we have called 'submodification' in the nominal group, with SubModifiers relating to an adjective as their SubHead.

We can represent the adverbial group as a logical structure as shown in Figure 6-24.

419

Table 6-18 Classes of adverb serving as Head in adverbial groups

Type of Adjunct	Head	Type		Interrogative	Demonstrative
circumstantial	circumstance	time	*yesterday, today, tomorrow*	*when*	*now/then*
		place	*abroad, overseas, home, upstairs, downstairs, inside, outside; out, up, down, behind; left, right, straight*	*where*	*here/there*
		manner: quality	*well, badly; fast, quickly, slowly; together, jointly, separately, all, both* [(other) adverbs in *-ly, -wise*] *skillfully, gracefully, clumsily; reproachfully, hopefully*	*how*	*thus*
		manner: degree	*much, little, a little* [adverbs in *-ly*] *greatly, considerably, deeply, totally*	*how much*	
		manner: comparison	*differently*		
		manner: means	[adverbs in *-ly*] *microscopically, telescopically*	*how*	*thus*
modal	assessment	comment	*please, kindly; frankly; admittedly, supposedly* – Table 3-5, set II		
		mood	*probably, certainly, perhaps, maybe; still, yet* – Table 3-5, set I		

easily
Head

more	easily
Modifier	Head
β	α

not	so	very	much	more	easily
				Modifier	Head
ζ	ε	δ	γ	β	α

Fig. 6-24 Premodification in the adverbial group

The items serving as Premodifiers are adverbs belonging to one of three types – polarity (*not*), comparison (*more, less; as, so*) and intensification. The classes of adverbs that can serve as Premodifier are thus considerably more restricted than the classes that can serve as Head; they correspond largely to adverbs from the degree class in Table 6-18 above. Those of intensification indicate higher or lower intensity; they are either general intensifiers that

are interpersonally neutral (*very, much, quite, really, completely, totally, utterly; rather, fairly, pretty; almost, nearly*), including the interrogative adverb *how*, or specific ones that derive from some interpersonally significant scale (*amazingly, astonishingly, awfully, desperately, eminently, extraordinarily, horribly, incredibly, perfectly, terribly, terrifically, unbelievably, wonderfully*). Examples:

(1) polarity

Apparently **not** surprisingly Leggos are spitting chips about it all. [UTS/Macquarie Corpus]

Not surprisingly all of these abstract concepts turned out to be mostly metaphorical. [Text 237]

Not infrequently, the supply of communication services in fact precedes the growth in incomes. [Kolhapur]

(2) comparison

And I can see that they've, you know they've changed and I think the one I did **more** recently is more better in terms of the writing. [UTS/Macquarie Corpus]

they reckon that the food industry over there is growing **so** phenomenally that um the there are a lot people are starting to join the food industry and study food science [UTS/Macquarie Corpus]

(3) intensification

old men who dance **terrifically** well were dancing with 18-year-olds and there's just a whole mixture of people dancing with each other and it was very, very, it was a nice scene really. [UTS/Macquarie Corpus]

They signed an agreement a week or so ago and it fell apart **pretty** quickly after that. [KING_Interviews]

She danced well, but **very, very** slowly, and an expression came into her eyes as though her thoughts were far, far away. [Of Human Bondage]

I was in there **fairly** recently. [UTS/Macquarie Corpus]

She took me **quite** seriously. [UTS/Macquarie Corpus]

She writes **totally** differently. [UTS/Macquarie Corpus]

How badly were you hurt by the stories? [KING_Interviews]

Note that in the case of polarity, the negative adverb *not* has the adverbial group as its domain, not the clause in which the adverbial group serves; this can be checked by adding a Moodtag: with the clause *not infrequently the supply of communication services in fact precedes the growth of incomes* the unmarked tag would be negative (*doesn't it*), following the general principle of reversed polarity and thus showing that the clause itself is positive.

The different types may, of course, combine, as with polarity + intensification and intensification + comparison; for example:

Not altogether surprisingly, my wife had fainted. [LOB]

Another thing I think in terms of this committee of scores is the stuff I was talking to Olga about earlier, in that I found it has been extraordinarily useful in my teaching, in working with students who are also struggling with writing and encouraging, often, often just taking what we've done here into the next class, you know, using the same sort of exercises and ... being able to, I think, resource students **much more** productively than I was before about their writing tasks ... and that's been very important I think. [UTS/Macquarie Corpus]

Postmodification is of one type only, namely comparison. As in the nominal group, Postmodifiers are rankshifted, or embedded; they may be (a) embedded clauses, or (b) embedded prepositional phrases. Examples:

(a) much more easily [[than you would have expected]]

as grimly [[as if his life depended on it]]

too quickly [[for us to see [[what was happening]]]]

not long enough [[to find my way around]]

(b) as early [as two o'clock]

faster [than fifteen knots]

There are also the type favoured in grammar tests, such as *John runs faster than Jim*, where the embedded element is said to be a clause with the Finite and Residue presupposed by ellipsis: 'than Jim runs'. It appears however that these are now embedded prepositional phrases, since the normal form of a personal pronoun following *than* or *as* is oblique/absolute rather than nominative: *John runs faster than me* (not *than I*). The same applies in the nominal group when the Head is an adjective: *John isn't as tall as me*.

This is the only instance of embedding other than in a nominal group. All other embedding in English is a form of nominalization, where a group, phrase or clause comes to function as part of, or in place of (i.e. as the whole of), a nominal group. See further Chapter 7, Sections 7.4 and 7.5.

Strictly speaking the domain of these comparative Postmodifiers is not the Head of the group but an item within the Premodifier: *as, more, less, too* (the exception is -*er* comparatives like *faster*). This could be shown as in Figure 6-25 (a); cf. the nominal group, where given *a*

(a)	much	more	quickly	than I could count
	Modifier		Head	Postmodifier
	γ	β	α	
		SubHead		SubModifier
		βα		ββ

(b)	much	more	quickly	than I could count
		much	faster	
		too	quickly	for me to count
	Modifier		Head	Postmodifier
	γ	β	α	

Fig. 6-25   Adverbial groups with embedded Postmodifiers

better man than I am we could show *than I am* as dependent on *better* rather than on *man*.[16] But this is not really necessary: structure is not the appropriate concept for interpreting semantic domain, and the locus of comparison may in any case be part of the Head (the *-er* in *faster, readilier*) or even part of the Postmodifier (the exceptional form *enough*, which follows the Head). It seems unnecessary to represent pairs such as *too fast (for me) to follow, slowly enough (for me) to follow*, or *as fast as I could count, faster than I could count*, as having different structures. They can be analysed as in Figure 6-25 (b).

6.4.2 Conjunction group

Within the 'primary' word class of adverbials, there is another class besides adverbs, namely conjunctions. Their roles in the grammar are described in Chapter 7; they form three sub-classes, namely linker, binder and continuative.

Conjunctions also form word groups by modification, for example *even if, just as, not until, if only*. These can be represented in the same way, as β ^ α structures (or α ^ β in the case of *if only*). Note however that many conjunctive expressions have evolved from more complex structures, e.g. *as soon as, in case, by the time, nevertheless, in so far as*. These can be treated as single elements without further analysis. They are themselves, of course, subject to modification, e.g. *just in case, almost as soon as*.

6.4.3 Preposition group

Prepositions are not a sub-class of adverbials; functionally they are related to verbs. But they form groups by modification, in the same way as conjunctions; e.g. *right behind, not without, way off* as in *right behind the door, not without some misgivings, all along the beach, way off the mark*.

Again, there are more complex forms, such as *in front of, for the sake of*, which can be left unanalysed. These are also subject to modification, as in *just for the sake of, immediately in front of*. It is important to make a distinction between a **preposition group**, such as *right behind* or *immediately in front of*, which is a Modifier-Head structure expanded from and functionally equivalent to a preposition, and a **prepositional phrase,** which is not an expansion of anything but a clause-like structure in which the Process/Predicator function is performed by a preposition and not by a verb. Prepositional phrases are discussed in the final subsection of this chapter (6.5).

Complex prepositions such as *in front (of), for the sake (of)*, have evolved from prepositional phrases, with *front, sake* as 'Complement'. Many expressions are indeterminate between the two, for example *by the side of, as an alternative to, on the grounds of*; expressions like these are on the way to becoming prepositions but have not quite got there. In general, however, there is a difference; those that have become prepositions typically occur without a Deictic preceding the noun (*in front of*, not *in the front of*), and the noun occurs in the singular only (*in front of*, not *in fronts of*). In some instances duplex forms occur: *beside* has become a full preposition, but because it is often used in an abstract or metaphorical sense a modern version of the original complex form *by the side of* has reappeared along with it, and this, in its turn, is now starting to follow the same route towards prepositional status.

---

[16] Cf. *the brightest star in the sky*, where *in the sky* would modify *brightest*.

6.5 Prepositional phrase

The prepositional phrase serves as Adjunct in the modal structure of the clause. Like the adverbial group, it can serve as circumstantial Adjunct or, less commonly, as interpersonal Adjunct; and like the conjunction group, it can serve as conjunctive Adjunct. In addition, it can be rankshifted to serve as Postmodifier in a nominal group or an adverbial group. Examples:

(1a) Ranking, circumstantial Adjunct

Stop **for lunch and a swim at Kuta**. [Text 142]

Yeah, we were doing that **in Adelaide** too. [Text 371]

(1b) Ranking, interpersonal Adjunct

Because literature is **in some cases** the product of the imagination, isn't it? [Text 125]

Anarcho-capitalism, **in my opinion**, is a doctrinal system which, if ever implemented, would lead to forms of tyranny and oppression that have few counterparts in human history. [Text 212]

(1c) Ranking, conjunctive Adjunct

S02: Do they tend to pay; how do they – S04: Per issue. – S02: Per issue. Well **in that case** do they pay after the issues come out? – S04: I think so. [UTS/Macquarie Corpus]

(2a) Rankshifted, Postmodifier in nominal group (Qualifier)

Across the Atlantic, Benjamin Franklin engaged in well-known experiments [**with that curious phenomenon, electricity**]. [Text 122]

(2b) Rankshifted, Postmodifier in adverbial group

But I can run faster [**than a crocodile**]. [UTS/Macquarie Corpus]

The ER-2 aircraft could not climb higher [**than 18.5 km**] because of the very cold, dense atmosphere and the need to carry a lot of fuel for safety reasons. [Text 33]

(2c) Rankshifted, SubPostmodifier

as soon as they wanted better output [**than the average VHS tape**], matters became complicated. [Text 120]

Gore received 539,947 more votes [**than Bush**] on Nov. 7 [Text 113]

A prepositional phrase consists of a preposition plus a nominal group, for example, *on the burning deck*. We have explained a preposition as a minor verb. On the interpersonal dimension it functions as a minor Predicator having a nominal group as its Complement; and, as we saw in Sections 4.3 and 5.7, this is felt to be essentially no different from the Complement of a 'full' Predicator – prepositional Complements increasingly tend to have the same potential for becoming Subject, as in *this floor shouldn't be walked on for a few days*. No doubt one reason for this tendency has been the lexical unity of phrasal verbs, referred to in Section 6.3; because *look up to* is a single lexical item, with a one-word near-synonym *admire*, it is natural to parallel *people have always looked up to her* with *she's always been looked up to*.

Thus the internal structure of *across the lake* is like that of *crossing the lake*, with a non-finite verb as Predicator. In some instances there is a non-finite verb that is more or less

interchangeable with the preposition, e.g. *near/adjoining* (*the house*), *without/not wearing* (*a hat*), *about/concerning* (*the trial*). There is, in fact, an area of overlap between prepositional phrases and non-finite clauses; some instances can be interpreted as either, and some non-finite verb forms can be classified as prepositions, e.g. *regarding, considering, including*. In principle, a non-finite clause implies a potential Subject, whereas a prepositional phrase does not; but the prevalence of so-called 'hanging participles' shows that this is not always taken very seriously (e.g. *it's cold not wearing a hat*). More significant is the fact that **non-finite clauses are clauses**; that is, they can be expanded to include other elements of clause structure, whereas prepositional phrases cannot. One can say either *he left the city in his wife's car* or *he left the city taking his wife's car*; but only the latter can be expanded to *he left the city taking his wife's car quietly out of the driveway*.

Likewise on the experiential dimension the preposition function as a minor Process. The nominal group corresponds in function to a Range. But the constituency is the same whether we represent the prepositional phrase experientially, as in Figure 6-26 (a), or interpersonally, as in Figure 6-26 (b).

(a)

the boy	stood		on	the burning deck
Subject	(past) Finite	'stand' Predicator	Adjunct	
Mood		Residue		
			'Predicator'	'Complement'

(b)

the boy	stood	on	the burning deck
Actor	Process	Location	
		'Process'	'Range'

Fig. 6-26   Representation of prepositional phrase

But note that prepositional phrases are phrases, not groups; they have no logical structure as Head and Modifier, and cannot be reduced to a single element. In this respect, they are clause-like rather than group-like; hence when we interpret the preposition as 'minor Predicator' and 'minor Process' we are interpreting the prepositional phrase as a kind of 'minor clause' – which is what it is.

We noted above that prepositional phrases serve either as Adjunct or as Postmodifier. The exception is prepositional phrases with *of*, which normally occur only as Postmodifier; the reason is that they are not typical prepositional phrases, because in most of its contexts of use *of* is functioning not as minor Process/Predicator but rather as a structure marker in the nominal group (cf. *to* as a structure marker in the verbal group). Hence *of* phrases occur as clause elements only in two cases: (1) as circumstance of Matter, e.g. *Of George Washington it is said that he never told a lie*, (2) as one of a cluster of circumstances expressing a sense of 'source', all ultimately deriving from abstract locative 'from': *died/was cured of cancer, accused/convicted/acquitted of murder*, and so on.

425

If prepositional phrases are interpreted as 'compressed' or 'shrunken' clauses with the structure of Predicator/Process + Complement/Range, then it makes sense to ask whether alongside these 'ranged' phrases, there are 'non-ranged' ones: this is a question that arises automatically from our clause-like analysis of prepositional phrases. Consider an agnate pair of clauses such as *he crossed* and *he crossed the street*. Here the agnation has to do with the absence or presence of the Range; the two clauses are 'non-ranged' and 'ranged', respectively. Are these two clauses analogous to a pair of phrases such as *across* and *across the street*? In other words, is there a proportion:

> he crossed : he crossed the street ::
>
> (he walked) across : (he walked) across the street

If there is, this would mean that in traditional terms prepositions can be either intransitive (*across*) or transitive (*across the street*). Jespersen (1924: 87) noted that 'in nearly all grammars adverbs, prepositions, conjunctions and interjections are treated as four distinct "pars of speech", the difference between them being thus put on a par with that between substantives, adjectives, pronouns, and verbs'. But he felt that this classification meant that 'the dissimilarities between these words are grossly exaggerated, and their evident similarities correspondingly obscured', so he opted for 'the old terminology' according to which they are all 'particles'. Interjections are certainly quite different from adverbs, prepositions and conjunctions; they tend to be protolinguistic remnants in adult languages. However, prepositions may be similar to **certain** adverbs and conjunctions (conjunctive prepositions; cf. Chapter 7). In discussing prepositions and adverbs, Jespersen (1924: 88) suggests that there is an 'exact parallel' between examples such as *put your cap on* and *put your cap on your head*, on the one hand, and *he was in* and *he was in the house*, on the other. More recently, in their reference grammar of English, Huddleston & Pullum (2002: 612 ff.) argue that certain 'adverbs' should be analysed as prepositions without 'NP complements'; for example, they show that *in* belongs to the same category in *the owner is not in* and in *the owner is not in the house*. In our terms, this would mean that prepositional phrases can be 'non-ranged' (*in*) as well as 'ranged' (*in the house*).

6.6 Word classes and group functions

At the beginning of this chapter, we presented a table showing the relationship between group and phrase classes and clause functions (Table 6-1). As the table shows, the mapping between classes at group/phrase rank and functions at clause rank is fairly complex: a group/phrase of a given class can typically serve a number of different clause functions (the exception being the verbal group). When we move down one step along the rank scale to consider the relationship between word classes (see Figure 2-8 in Chapter 2) and group/phrase functions, we find that there is a stronger tendency towards a one-to-one relationship: a word of a particular class tends to serve only one group/phrase function: see Table 6-19. The major exception is the class of adverb; but this is partly a matter of delicacy: certain adverbs function only as Head, whereas others function only as Modifier or Sub-Modifier.

Table 6-19 Word classes and their typical functions in groups

Primary class	Secondary class	Tertiary class	Nominal group	Verbal group	Adverbial group	Conjunction group	Preposition group
nominal	noun	common	Thing, Classifier				
		proper	Thing				
		pronoun	Thing				
	adjective		post-Deictic	Event[17]			
			Epithet, Classifier				
	numeral		Numerative				
	determiner		Deictic				
verbal	verb	lexical	Epithet, Classifier [V-ing, V-en]	Event			
		auxiliary		Auxiliary			
		operator		Finite			
	preposition						Head
adverbial	adverb		(Sub-Modifier)		Head, Modifier	(Sub-Modifier)	Modifier
	conjunction	linker				Head	
		binder				Head	
		continuative				Head	

---

[17] Certain adjectives can serve as Event in a verbal group in a hypotactic verbal group complex (see Chapter 8), e.g. (conation: potentiality:) *be able/apt/prone/likely* → *to do*; (modulation: time: frequency:) *be wont* → *to do*; (modulation: manner: quality:) *be wise/right/wrong* → *to do*; (projection:) *be willing/keen/eager* → *to do*; *be afraid/scared* → *to do*.

CHAPTER
SEVEN

ABOVE THE CLAUSE: THE CLAUSE COMPLEX

7.1 The notion of 'clause complex'

7.1.1 Introductory examples

In Chapters 3 through 5, we explored the internal organization of the clause as a multifunctional construct; and in Chapter 6 we discussed the make-up of the units functioning as elements in this construct – groups and phrases. We shall now investigate how clauses are linked to one another by means of some kind of logico-semantic relation to form **clause complexes** representing sequences of figures (or moves) that are presented as textually related messages. In Chapter 1, we introduced symbols for representing boundaries between clauses in a clause complex and between clause complexes (Table 1-1), and we noted the relationship between clause complexes in the grammar and (orthographic) sentences in the graphology (and tone sequences in the phonology):

> ||| The people just stick together || **because** they have to || **because** it's socially unacceptable [[to be divorced]]. ||| [LLC_5]

> ||| Okay it comes to a total of $18.95 okay || **so if** you can have as close as possible to the correct change || the driver should be with you in approximately thirty minutes. ||| [UTS-Macquarie Corpus]

> ||| The disappearance rate of hGH from plasma is multiexponential (Cameron *et al.* 1969) || **and therefore** the significance of half life estimates of 20 to 30 minutes is difficult to state. ||| [ACE_J]

> ||| I think || he <u>thought</u> || he'd withdraw from business || **but** Fan <u>says</u> || he's now doing something else. ||| [LLC-1]

Let's begin by exploring this phenomenon 'from above' – that is, from the point of view of how the flow of events is construed in the development of text at the level of semantics.

For example, in narrative text, the flow of events is construed as a series of episodes. Each episode is typically developed step by step as sequences of

figures (see Chapter 5) that are linked by means of temporal relators. Thus Text 7-1 is a climactic episode in a narrative; the basic relator linking the figures is '(and) then', although other relators also occur:

– [**figure**: Kukul walked on through the forest] – [**relator**: then] → [figure: he came to a thicket] – [**relator**: meanwhile] → [**figure**: he heard the faint rustling of leaves] – [**relator**: then] → [**figure**: he pointed his arrow] – [**relator**: yet] → [**figure**: he saw nothing] – [**relator**: then] → [**figure**: he crouched low to the ground] ... –

This sequence of figures **_realizes_** a generic element from the 'middle' part within the overall structure of narratives (see e.g. Hasan, 1984/1996: 54); this element is the Sequent Event, which follows the Initiating Event. The dominant strategy for realizing the Sequent Event is the relation of temporal sequence; so if readers are familiar with the structure of narratives, they will expect to find passages developed through this kind of relation – thus even if this relation is not marked explicitly by the lexicogrammar, it can be inferred by the listener or reader based on the properties of the figures that make up the episode. For example, there is no conjunctive item marking the relationship between _he pointed his arrow, but saw nothing_ and _Kukul crouched low to the ground and moved slowly_; but we can infer that the relationship is one of temporal sequence – or possibly one of cause.

Text 7-1: Recreating – narrating (written, monologic): extract from a folk tale [Text 65]

||| Kukul walked on through the forest. ||| **As** he came to a thicket, || he heard the faint rustling of leaves. ||| He pointed his arrow, || **but** saw nothing. ||| Kukul crouched low to the ground || **and** moved slowly. ||| He had not gone far || **when** ... sss ... it came. ||| An arrow pierced his chest. |||

In pain, Kukul pulled out the arrow || **and** headed for the river || **to** wash his wound. ||| 'Surely, it is not deep,' || he <u>tried to convince</u> himself, || **but** his strength began to fade || **as** his chest turned scarlet with blood. |||

A few more steps || **and** Kukul had to lean against a tree. ||| 'It is so dark,' || he <u>moaned</u>. ||| He fell onto a sea of emerald grass || **and there** he died. Alone. Betrayed. |||

At the same time, the semantic sequence of figures **_is realized by_** a series of clause complexes; the grammar is in fact doing a good deal of work in construing the episode. It realizes the figures that make up the episode as clauses; and it combines these clauses into complexes of clauses – _as he came to a thicket, he heard the faint rustling of leaves; he pointed his arrow, but saw nothing_; and so on. These complexes serve to construe semantic **sequences of figures** – not the whole episode, but **_local_** sequences in the flow of events that together make up the episode. For example, while _Kukul walked on through the forest_ is a single clause that is not related grammatically to other clauses, the clause _in pain, Kukul pulled out the arrow_ is related to the clause _[he] headed for the river_, which is in turn related to the clause _[for him] to wash his wound_; together these three clauses form the clause complex _In pain, Kukul pulled out the arrow_ [→] _and headed for the river_ [→] _to wash his wound_, as shown in Figure 7-1 (the different representations of the first and second link will be explained later). Here the clauses are related structurally by the grammar; the first structural link is marked by the structural conjunction _and_ and the second by a certain non-finite form of the verb, the perfective _to wash_. It is reflected in patterns of ellipsis that are possible only within a clause complex; thus the Subject is ellipsed in both _headed for the river_ and _to wash his wound_.

429

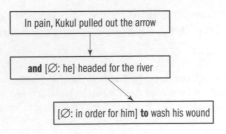

Fig. 7-1   Clause complex representing a sequence in a narrative episode

Semantically, the effect of combining clauses into a clause complex is one of ***tighter integration in meaning***: the sequences that are realized grammatically in a clause complex are construed as being subsequences within the total sequence of events that make up a whole episode in a narrative. For example, *he pointed his arrow, but saw nothing* is construed by the grammar of clause complexing as a subsequence; but the clauses *he heard the faint rustling of leaves* and *he pointed his arrow* are not brought together within a complex, so they are not construed grammatically as a subsequence. This does not mean that these two clauses are semantically unrelated. They are linked by a relation of temporal sequence, or possibly even causal sequence: 'he heard the faint rustling of leaves – [then/so] → he pointed his arrow'. But *he pointed his arrow* is more tightly integrated, both grammatically and semantically, with *but saw nothing*. There is clearly a choice here; the narrator could have said *As he came to a thicket, he heard the faint rustling of leaves, so he pointed his arrow. However, he saw nothing.* But this version is a slightly different narrative. The whole passage in Text 7-1 is set out in Table 7-1. The table shows how clauses are grouped together into clause complexes (also indicating the structural analysis, which will be explained later). The general principle is that the episode is realized by a series of clause complexes. There are in fact only two 'clause simplexes', numbers (1) and (6); and they stand out precisely by virtue of the fact that they do not conform to the pattern of complexing. (1) marks the beginning of the episode, following the end of the previous episode:

‖‖ 'Be careful, Kukul,' ‖ said the bird. ‖‖ Then it flew away. ‖‖

The status of (6) as a simplex serves to foreground its pivotal role in the narrative – *An arrow pierced his chest.*

This integrating of a series of events into a subsequence is a feature of narratives in general, including not only fictional stories but also narrative passages in biographical recounts, news reports and other kinds of text where past experience is construed in terms of a time-line. The extract in Text 7-2 illustrates how clause complexing is used in a narrative of personal experience in a gossip text. The extract is organized grammatically as a single clause complex, developed by temporal sequence ('and then I/she said ...') and quoting ('I/she said ...'). This clause complex is very intricate, consisting of over 20 clauses. Such intricate clause complexes are characteristic of unselfconscious, casual conversation rather than of written discourse (cf. Halliday, 1985a, 1987a; Matthiessen, 2002a). They illustrate how the resources of clause complexing are used to 'choreograph' the rhetorical development of text in real time.

430

Table 7-1 Clause complexes in an episode within a narrative

Number	Type of relation	Structure	Clause
(1)			|||**Kukul walked on through the forest.** |||
(2)	temporal	×β	**As** he came to a thicket, ||
		α	he heard the faint rustling of leaves. |||
(3)		1	He pointed his arrow, ||
	concessive	×2	**but** saw nothing. |||
(4)		1	Kukul crouched low to the ground ||
	temporal	×2	**and** moved slowly. |||
(5)		1	He had not gone far ||
	temporal	×2	**when** ... sss ... it came. |||
(6)			An arrow pierced his chest. |||
(7)		1	In pain, Kukul pulled out the arrow ||
	temporal	×2α	**and** headed for the river ||
	purposive	×2×β	**to** wash his wound. |||
(8)	quoting	1"1	Surely, it is not deep, ||
		12	he <u>tried to convince</u> himself, ||
	adversative	+2α	**but** his strength began to fade ||
	temporal	+2×β	**as** his chest turned scarlet with blood. |||
(9)		1	A few more steps ||
	temporal	×2	**and** Kukul had to lean against a tree. |||
(10)	quoting	"1	It is so dark, ||
		2	he <u>moaned</u>. |||
(11)		1	He fell onto a sea of emerald grass ||
	spatial	×2	**and there** he died. Alone. Betrayed. |||

Text 7-2: Sharing – sharing values (spoken, dialogic): gossiping, using personal experience to substantiate unacceptable behaviour [Text 73]

\|\|\| And Joanne came up \|\| **and** she <u>said</u>, \|\| 'Oh, can you do this?' \|\| **and** I <u>said</u>, \|\| 'Look you're at the end of a very long line; \|\| be prepared to wait!' \|\| **and** she <u>said</u>, \|\| 'Well, she's at the Oncology clinic right now.' \|\| **and** I <u>said</u>, \|\| 'But these have to be done as well, \|\| I can't help.' \|\| **and** sort of smiled all the way through it \|\| **and** she <u>went</u>,... \|\| I <u>said</u>, \|\| 'Look, it's three minutes to three; \|\| these should be done in a minute \|\| **if** you want to wait till then.' \|\| **and** she <u>went</u> ... \|\| '(sigh) ahhh.' \|\| **then** she went away \|\| and I <u>thought</u> \|\| 'Oh yeah!'.

431

But the integrating and choreographing effect achieved by clause complexes is not, of course, restricted to narrative passages in stories, recounts and procedures; it is a feature of texts of all kinds. The extract in Text 7-3 illustrates the typical pattern in enabling texts of the instructional type (including centrally procedures and demonstrations). This particular text is a 'topographic procedure' – a walking tour taken from a guidebook. As in narratives, temporal sequence is a favourite complexing relation. Here the sense is 'do this, then do this' rather than 'this happened, then that happened'; but the temporal principle of development is the same.

> **Text 7-3: Enabling – instructing (written, monologic): topographic procedure [Text 22]**
> The Chinese Gardens
>
> ||| Make your way back towards the Pump House || **and** walk under Pier Street to the southern end of Darling Harbour. ||| Continue walking || **and** after a short distance you can see on your right the Chinese Gardens. ||| The 'Garden of Friendship' was designed according to southern Chinese tradition by Sydney's sister city, Guangzhou in China. ||| A doublestorey pavilion, 'the Gurr', stands above a surrounding system of interconnected lakes and waterfalls. ||| Follow the pathways around the landscaped gardens and over bridges || **before** resting at the Tea House || **where** the scent of lotus flowers mingles with that of freshly brewed tea and traditional cakes. ||| The Garden is open Monday to Friday 10.00 am to sunset || **and** weekends 9.30 am to sunset. |||

Finally, let us illustrate the use of the resources of clause complexing in everyday reasoning: see Text 7-4. Here the son construes 'the argument for having trees around us' by means of a single clause complex. He develops the argument out of the logico-semantic relations of condition (marked by *if*), reason (marked by *because*, *'cause*, *so*) and restatement (marked simply by juxtaposition without an explicit conjunctive marker).

> **Text 7-4: Exploring – arguing (spoken, dialogic): exposition [Text 84]**
> Son: ||| If there weren't trees on the earth, um earth, || we would all be dead, || **'cause** there wouldn't be oxygen; || trees make oxygen, || **so** we can breathe, || **so if** we had heaps of trees around us, || it produces heaps of oxygen, || **so** we can breathe; || **so** trees, big trees, are really good || **because** heaps of oxygen comes out of them. |||
>
> Father: ||| **So** that is the argument for having trees around us. |||

The various examples of clause complexes at work in the creation of text are all based on the same general principle: clause complexes are formed out of logico-semantic relations that link clauses, typically one pair at a time, as interdependent on one another.

7.1.2 Clause complexing and (circumstantial) transitivity in clauses

We have seen examples of a few different types of relation used in linking clauses to form clause complexes. Interestingly, these relations turn out to be manifestations of the same general semantic types that we have already met in another area of the grammar – that of circumstances in the transitivity system of the clause (Chapter 5, Section 5.6). Circumstances **augment** the configuration of process + participants in the clause in terms of either projection or expansion: see Table 5-28. These two types of relation correspond, in turn, to different process types: projection corresponds to verbal and mental clauses, and expansion corresponds to relational clauses. Projection and expansion are also manifested as the logico-semantic relations that link clauses together to form clause complexes. The manifestations of projection and expansion in the clause and the clause complex are set out in Table 7-2.

432

Table 7-2 Projection and expansion manifested in clause and clause complex

	Clause		Clause complex
	process type	**circumstance type**	**logico-semantic type**
projection	[verbal:] he says	[angle:] according to him (that's enough)	[quoting locution:] he says 'that's enough'
	[mental:] he thinks	[angle:] to him (it's too hot)	[reporting idea:] he thinks that it's too hot
expansion	[relational: intensive] she was the leader	[role:] as the leader	[elaborating:] being the leader
	[relational: possessive] he has a dog; he has a nice smile	[accompaniment:] with a dog; with a nice smile	[extending:] he walked to the market and the dog did too; he addressed her, smiling nicely
	[relational: circumstantial] dinner followed the celebration	[location, extent, cause, manner, etc.:] after the celebration	[enhancing:] they dined after celebrating

The table shows patterns of agnation that hold between circumstance types in the clause and the logico-semantic types of relation between clauses in the clause complex. (The patterns of agnation involving process type typically involve grammatical metaphor; this will be discussed in Chapter 10, Section 10.5.4). For example, the circumstance of Means *with all her heart* in the clause

||| Each day, she prayed **with all her heart**. ||| [Text 65]

is agnate with a (non-finite) clause linked to *each day she prayed* in a clause complex:

||| Each day, she prayed || using all her heart. |||

The phrase *with all her heart* augments the clause circumstantially within the domain of the clause; in contrast, the clause *using all her heart* **expands** the clause, relating it to a full-fledged clause (rather than to a prepositional phrase or adverbial group) and thereby opening up a clause complex. Here are some additional examples of circumstances serving within the domain of the clause with suggested agnate clauses within the domain of the clause complex:

[enhancement: time] **Under his rule**, there was peace throughout the land. ~ **when** he ruled [Text 65]

[enhancement: reason] **because of this child**, he would never become hala uinic. ~ **because** this child lived [Text 65]

[extension: alternation] **In place of the usual expensive, elaborate costumes**, the Motleys created simple but beautiful sets and costumes, made from inexpensive materials often picked up at sales. ~ **instead of** creating the usual expensive, elaborate costumes [Gielgud, 168]

[projection: angle] Torture and sexual violence against prisoners is widespread in jails across the United States, **according to a report published yesterday** ~ **says** a report published yesterday [Text 2]

The pattern of agnation works the other way around too, of course; we can often find circumstances that are agnate to clauses:

[elaboration: role] but after a time, Chirumá was chosen ‖ **to be the new chief**. ~ **as** the new chief [Text 65]

As these examples illustrate, a circumstantial element in a clause contains only a ***minor*** process, not a major one; so unlike a clause it cannot construe a full figure, it cannot enact a proposition/proposal and it cannot present a message. In contrast, clause complexing always involves assigning clause-hood to a unit related to clause through expansion or projection: this unit has the full potential of a clause, in terms of experiential, interpersonal and textual systems. So while the circumstantial prepositional phrase *with all her heart* and the (non-finite) clause *using all her heart* are fairly close to one another (prepositional phrases being a miniature clause, as suggested in Chapter 6, Section 6.5), only the latter has the grammatical potential of a clause: for example, it can itself be augmented circumstantially and assessed modally, as in *happily using all her heart for her family's sake*. And being a clause in a clause complex, it can form part of a chain: *each day she prayed, using all her heart as her godmother had taught her all those years ago and focusing her energy on her little brother's recovery*. That is, while circumstantial elements are part of the 'configurational' structure of the clause, clauses in clause complexes are part of a chain-like or serial structure. In the creation of text, we choose between augmenting a clause 'internally' by means of a circumstantial element and augmenting it 'externally' by means of another clause in a complex. The decision depends on many factors; but the basic consideration has to do with how much textual, interpersonal and experiential semiotic 'weight' is to be assigned to the unit: the more weight it has, the more likely it is to be constructed as an interdependent clause in a clause complex rather than as a circumstantial phrase (or adverbial group) augmenting a clause.

We can now bring together the strands of our discussion in order to locate the resources of clause complexing within the overall grammatical resources for realizing a semantic sequence of projection or expansion. A sequence of projection or expansion may be realized by two clauses that are combined structurally to form a clause complex, as in *a happened and then b happened* or *after a happened, b happened*. But there are two alternative forms of realization. On the one hand, the sequence may be realized by two clauses that are not combined structurally but are linked cohesively instead: *A happened. Then b happened.* Here the grammar provides a 'clue' as to the nature of the semantic link; but it does not integrate the two clauses into a grammatical construction. On the other hand, the sequence may be realized by a single clause with a prepositional phrase (or adverbial group) serving as a circumstantial element within it: *after the time of a, b happened*.

These grammatical opportunities for realizing a sequence of projection or expansion form a scale defined by two poles: one pole is the simple clause with a circumstantial element and the other is the cohesive sequence within a text of two independent clauses. The clause complex thus covers the region intermediate between these two poles. But the clause complex is in fact not a single point on this scale; it covers two regions of the scale: closer to the pole of circumstantial augmentation, there are clause combinations where one clause is dependent on a dominant clause, the two thus being of unequal status (as in *when a happened, b happened*); closer to the pole of cohesive sequences, there are

clause combinations where the two clauses are interdependent on one another, the two having equal status (as in *a happened, then b happened*). This scale of degree of grammatical integration and interdependence in the realization of projection and expansion is represented diagrammatically in Figure 7-2.

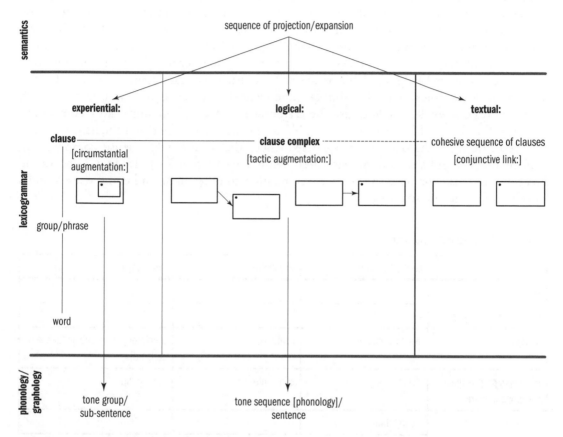

Fig. 7-2   The location of the clause complex in terms of stratification, metafunction and rank

This figure also shows other facets of the location of the clause complex in the overall system of English. (1) In terms of metafunction, it is organized by the logical mode of the ideational metafunction, contrasting with circumstantial augmentations of the clause (experiential) and cohesive sequences (textual). This means that the organization of the clause complex is based on a univariate model rather than a multivariate one, just like complexes at other ranks and like groups (see Chapter 6, Sections 6.1 and 6.2.5; see also Halliday, 1979). (2) In terms of rank, it is located at the highest rank of the grammar – clause rank; and it is thus related to the clause in terms of logical complexing rather than in terms of experiential constituency. (3) In terms of stratification, a clause complex realizes a semantic sequence of projection or expansion; and it is, in turn, realized by a sequence of tones in speech and by a sentence in writing (cf. Chapter 1, Figure 1-4). Before beginning our systematic survey of the clause complex, we shall comment on a few of these points.

7.1.3 Clause complexing, formation of groups and the sentence

As the examples given above illustrate, the clause complex is realized graphologically as a 'sentence', in the way that this has evolved, over the centuries, as a unit in the written language (Chapter 1, Section 1.1.2). The sentence is the highest unit of punctuation on the graphological rank scale and has evolved in the writing system to represent the clause complex as the most extensive domain of grammatical structure.[1] We will use the term **sentence** to refer only to this highest-ranking graphological unit of punctuation. (In various other descriptions, the term sentence has also been used to refer to a grammatical unit (as in 'sentence grammar').) Hence in the analysis of a written text each sentence can be treated as one clause complex, with the 'simple' (one clause) sentence as the limiting case. With a spoken text, we will be able to use the grammar to define and delimit clause complexes, in a way that keeps them as close as possible to the sentences of written English. We have referred briefly to the patterns of tone sequences that characterize clause complexes in spoken English and shall summarize these below (see Section 7.6). Table 7-3 shows the location of clause complex and sentence in relation to other units and complexes of units in the total linguistic system.

Table 7-3 Ranking units across strata

Semantics	Lexicogrammar	Graphology	Phonology
text	–		
(rhetorical) paragraph	–		
sequence	clause *complex*	sentence	tone groups [in tone sequence or concord]
message/proposition (proposal)/figure	clause	sub-sentence	tone group
element	group/phrase	–	–
	word	orthographic word	–
	morpheme	–	–

In some tagmemic and systemic descriptions (e.g. Longacre, 1970, 1996; Gregory, 1983), the sentence is posited as a grammatical unit above the rank of the clause: here sentences are said to consist of clauses just as clauses consist of groups/phrases and groups consist

---

[1]   As always, once a pattern of realization has been established, new options can emerge making it possible to depart from the basic pattern. For example, sentence punctuation can be used to indicate that a clause is chunked into more than one information unit: ||| *He fell onto a sea of emerald grass* || *and there he died. Alone. Betrayed.* ||| This is a common strategy in advertisements (see Fries, 1992).

436

of words[2]. This analysis is analogous to our analysis of groups. Although groups are word complexes, they cannot be fully accounted for as complexes. Groups have developed their own multivariate constituent structures with functional configurations such as the Deictic + Numerative + Epithet + Classifier + Thing of the nominal group in English. Here the elements are (i) distinct in function, (ii) realized by distinct classes, and (iii) more or less fixed in sequence. A configuration of such a kind ***has*** to be represented as a multivariate structure. Treating the group simply as a 'word complex' does not account for all these various aspects of its meaning. It is for this reason that we recognize the group as a distinct rank in the grammar.

But does the clause complex need to be interpreted as a ranked unit (a 'sentence') analogous to the group? We believe the answer is no; the essential nature of a clause complex is brought out by treating it as a univariately structured complex rather than as a multivariately structured unit. In a clause complex, the tendency is much more for any clause to have the potential for functioning with any value in a multi-clausal complex. In other words, the relations among the clauses in a clause complex are generally more like that of a string of nouns such as *railway ticket office staff*, which could be explained as a (univariate) word complex, than that of *these two old railway engines*, which could not. We shall assume, therefore, that the notion of 'clause complex' enables us to account in full for the grammatical combination of clauses.

There are syntagms that may look as if they need to be interpreted in terms of a multivariate sentence structure, involving textual or modal Adjuncts or Vocative elements as Theme:

||| **However** << after the results of many studies were published, >> there was a shift towards the theory being quite unacceptable. ||| [Text 123]

||| **Interestingly**, <<< as I left my small town || and explored the world via the military >>> I realized || I really like to learn, || and I was good at it. ||| [COCA]

||| **Larry, Larry, Larry,** << when you're in the public eye >> you don't do anything. ||| [KING_Interviews]

||| **Well, Larry, unfortunately,** <<< as you know – || we discussed it the other night – >>> the reason [[our commission came to the conclusion [[[that terrorism was the No. 1 threat – || we talked about chemical, biological and nuclear]]] – and the reason [[we came to that conclusion]] is [[we had information, intelligence and other, over the last 3 1/2 years [[[that indicated to us || that efforts were under way [[to manufacture a number of instrumentalities [[[that could be delivered to this country || to cause mass destruction, << which is [[what this is doing]], >> as opposed to mass destruction, || which is [[what would happen with certain types of chemical and certainly nuclear weapons]]]]]]]]. ||| [KING_Interviews]

However, these can all be analysed as hypotactic clause combinations, where the dependent clause is included within the main clause after the textual and/or interpersonal Theme and before the topical Theme: main clause << dependent clause >> – more specifically, main clause [textual + interpersonal Theme] << dependent clause >> main clause [topical

---

[2]   It is important to maintain the terminological distinction between **group** and **phrase**, which is lost if a nominal group is referred to as a 'noun phrase'. Although group and phrase are both of intermediate rank as constituents, they have arrived there from different ends: a group is a bloated word, whereas a phrase is a shrunken clause. In Bloomfield's (1933: 194–195) terms, groups are **endocentric** constructions whereas phrases are **exocentric** ones.

Theme ^ Rheme]. The motivation behind such sequences with included dependent clauses is thus textual: the main clause is powerfully contextualized first by its own textual and/or interpersonal Theme, and then, within the domain of the clause complex, by the dependent clause that qualifies it, and finally by its own topical Theme[3].

7.2 Types of relationship between clauses

In the previous section we introduced the basic patterns of clause complexing. Let us now map out the resources of clause complexing systemically. Two basic systems determine how one clause is related to another; they are set out in Figure 7-3, together with some more delicate subsystems that will be discussed below: (i) TAXIS (degree of interdependency); (ii) the LOGICO-SEMANTIC RELATION. We shall summarize these in the present section, and then go on to examine each in greater detail.

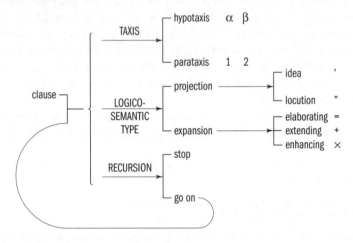

Fig. 7-3   The systems of clause complexing

7.2.1 Taxis (degree of interdependency): hypotaxis/parataxis

All clauses linked by a logico-semantic relation are interdependent: that is the meaning of relational structure – one unit is interdependent on another unit. Two clauses related as interdependent in a complex may be treated as being of **equal status**, as in

||| Kukul crouched low to the ground || **and** moved slowly. ||| [Text 65]

Here there are two clauses that are potentially independent of one another. For example, each constitutes a proposition in its own right and could thus be tagged – *Kukul crouched*

---

[3] Such included clauses, or combinations of clauses, thus 'interrupt' the structure of the main clause they are dependent on; and they may, in fact, even interrupt elements within it, if such interruptions are textually motivated. For example, the clause complex *Any person (even if baptised a Catholic, as Justice Murphy had been) who had publicly repudiated a faith, could not 'in conscience' be given a Christian burial.* ([ACE_A]) is a textual variant of *Even if baptised a Catholic, as Justice Murphy had been, any person who had … .*

low to the ground, didn't he? and *he moved slowly, didn't he?* They could in fact select for different moods; e.g. *Kukul crouched low to the ground but did he move slowly?* For example:

declarative + interrogative

||| I know || it is a copy || **but** is it a real copy? ||| [ACE_G]

||| All these are laudable objects, || **but** is any one of them new? ||| [LOB_E]

declarative + imperative

||| However, firelighting equipment, maps and compasses are useless || unless you know how to use them, || **so** don't blithely wander off into the back-country without some practice first. ||| [ACE_E]

||| I don't plan to marry || **so** don't talk about husbands. [KOLH_K]

Certain mood combinations evolved particular meanings; for example:

interrogative: yes/ no or interrogative: yes/ no – alternative question

||| Does the Church possess divine truth and the unique means to salvation || **or** is it just another benevolent group in a pluralist society? ||| [ACE_G]

||| Do they pull the rope || **or** is there a different arrangement? ||| [KOLH_L]

imperative or declarative – conditioned command

||| Move from the line || **or** I will settle the whip on you. ||| [BROWN1_P]

imperative and declarative – motivated command (warning, advice) / conditioned statement

||| 'Say something against them || **and** you will cop a writ, || even though [[what you say]] may well be harmless or totally true,' || he said. ||| [ACE_A]

||| Listen to voices || **and** you will learn how to improve your own. ||| [LOB_F]

||| Fly with us || **and** you'll experience the dedication to excellence [[that could only be Korean]]. ||| [Korean Air advertisement]

||| Laugh, || **and** the world laughs with you: || Weep, || **and** you weep alone; ||| ['Solitude' by Ella Wheeler Wilcox]

Such sequences of clauses may in fact involve interpersonal metaphor, giving them more than one layer of interpretation. The additional layer of interpretation makes it possible to bring out multiple readings, and the connection between imperatives and conditions based on the sense of irrealis; see the analysis of *don't move or I will shoot* 'if you move, I'll shoot' in Figure 10-10 (b), Chapter 10.

When clauses are combined with the status of equal, there is a closely agnate version where the two clauses are not brought together structurally in a clause complex but rather form a **cohesive sequence**: *Kukul crouched low to the ground. He moved slowly.* In this version the elliptical Subject of the second clause has to be reinstated, since such Subject ellipsis is not possible outside the domain of a clause complex. The two versions are treated differently in the graphology: in the cohesive sequence, the two clauses are separated by a full stop; but in the clause complex, there is no full stop separating the clauses (though there could have been a comma or even semi-colon). This reflects the typical realization in the phonology: in the cohesive sequence, the first clause would be spoken on tone 1 (falling), and then followed by the second clause also on tone 1; but in the clause complex, the first clause would be spoken on tone 3 (level), and then followed by the second clause on tone 1. Here tone 3 indicates that there is more to come – by the expansion of the clause to form a clause complex (see Section 7.6).

Alternatively, two clauses related as interdependent may be treated as being of **unequal status**, as in

||| **As** he came to a thicket, || he heard the faint rustling of leaves. ||| [Text 65]

Here there is only one clause that could stand on its own – *he heard the faint rustling of leaves*. This is treated as the 'main' clause, and the other clause is related to it as a (temporal) qualification, as in the case of the Head + Modifier structure of the nominal group. While the main clause constitutes a proposition in its own right and can thus be tagged (*he heard the faint rustling of leaves, didn't he?*) or queried (*did he hear the faint rustling of leaves?*), the qualifying clause does not and cannot be tagged or queried (we would not expect to find *as he came to a thicket, didn't he, he heard the faint rustling of leaves*; *as did he come to a thicket, he heard the faint rustling of leaves*). This combination of clauses would typically be spoken as a sequence of tone 4 (falling-rising) and tone 1, with the qualifying clause thus marked off in the same way as a marked Theme. There is no closely agnate non-structural, cohesive version; or rather, such a version is agnate only via an intermediate version where the two clauses are related as having equal status within a clause complex: (clause complex, equal status:) *He came to a thicket and at that time he heard the faint rustling of leaves* – (cohesive sequence:) *He came to a thicket. At that time he heard the faint rustling of leaves*. Interestingly, the qualifying clause can be placed either before or after the 'head' clause: *as he came to a thicket he heard the faint rustling of leaves*: *he heard the faint rustling of leaves as he came to a thicket*. The choice is determined by textual considerations. The version that appears in the original text presents the temporal qualifying clause as thematic within the clause complex. This is highly motivated in the context of the narrative flow of events: the clause introduces a new stage in the narrative, and this is foregrounded thematically (see further at the end of Section 7.3). As already noted, this sequence of modifying clause + main clause would typically be spoken on tone 4 followed by tone 1. In contrast, the sequence where the modifying clause is not thematic would be likely to be spoken on a single tone contour – tone 1 (see further Section 7.6 below).

Degree of interdependency is known technically as **taxis**; and the two different degrees of interdependency as **parataxis** (equal status) and **hypotaxis** (unequal status). **Hypotaxis** is the relation between a dependent element and its dominant, the element on which it is dependent.[4] Contrasting with this is **parataxis**, which is the relation between two like elements of equal status, one initiating and the other continuing.

---

4 An earlier name for the higher term in the dependency relation, that on which something is dependent, was **terminant**. The problem with this turns out to be that it is too readily misinterpreted as 'coming last in sequence'. The dependency relation, however, is neutral as regards the sequence in which the elements occur. Another possible set of terms would be 'main clause' for the dominant clause and 'subordinate clause' for the dependent clause. However, this could lead to confusion since 'subordination' has usually been used to refer to both hypotaxis and embedding without the critical distinction between the two (cf. Matthiessen & Thompson, 1988). Further, the term 'parataxis' does not correspond to 'coordination' (in contrast with 'subordination'); it covers not only 'coordination' but also 'apposition': see Section 7.2.3 below. For an early characterization of taxis in SFL, see Halliday (1965).

Hypotactic structures will be represented by the Greek letter notation already used for modification in the structure of the group (see Chapter 6, Section 6.2.5). For paratactic structures we shall use a numerical notation 1 2 3 ..., with nesting indicated in the usual way: 11 12 2 31 32 means the same as 1(1 2) 2 3(1 2). This notation was used in the analysis shown in Table 7-1.

The distinction between parataxis and hypotaxis has evolved in languages as a powerful grammatical strategy for guiding the rhetorical development of text, making it possible for the grammar to assign different statuses to figures within a sequence. The choice between parataxis and hypotaxis characterizes each relation between two clauses (each **nexus** of clauses; see below) within a clause complex; and clause complexes are often formed out of a mixture of parataxis and hypotaxis, as in the clause complex diagrammed in Figure 7-1: *In pain, Kukul pulled out the arrow and headed for the river to wash his wound.* Here the main sequence is represented paratactically as two clauses of equal status and the second clause is qualified hypotactically by a purpose clause. This purpose clause has a 'lower' status; it is brought in to support its main clause. This can also be seen very clearly in procedural texts, as in the following example in Text 7-5 from a walking tour in Sydney:

Text 7-5: Enabling – instructing (written, monologic): extracts from a topographic procedure

||| **If** you are feeling a little more energetic, || walk up Kirribilli Road, || turn right into Waruda Avenue, then right again into Waruda Street || **where** you will find Mary Booth Reserve. ||| [Text 103]

||| Follow the map through the back streets of Sydney's Lower North Shore suburbs, || pass the Zoo into the virgin bushland of Ashton Park, || then pay off the cab driver || **when** the road reaches the old fortifications at Bradley's Head. ||| [Text 103]

||| **When** the path reaches the road, || follow the road downhill for about 200 metres to the cable car, || **which** takes you on a two-and-a-half minute ride over the hippos and alligators to the top entrance to Taronga Zoo. ||| [Text 103]

In the first example, the procedure is represented by the paratactic sequence *walk up Kirribilli Road + turn right into Waruda Avenue, then right again into Waruda Street.* This is supported by two hypotactically related clauses. The first is a conditional one and introduces the sequence as a choice in the walking tour. The second is an elaboration, presenting information about a point of interest. In the second example, the procedure is represented by a paratactic sequence of three clauses. The third clause is hypotactically qualified by a temporal clause (*when the road reaches the old fortifications at Bradley's Head*), which represents the termination of the procedure. This contrasts with the third example, where the clause complex starts with a hypotactically related temporal clause (*when the path reaches the road*) representing the condition under which the new procedure represented by the clause complex is to be started.

As we illustrated in Section 7.1, a clause complex is formed by means of tactic relations; and it is developed or built up as a chain, one pair of clauses at a time. We will refer to any one pair of clauses related by interdependency, or 'taxis', as a **clause nexus**. Thus in the following clause complex

||| I went to school in New York City || **and then** we lived up on the Hudson for a while, || **then** moved to Connecticut. ||| [Text 7]

441

there are two clause nexuses: *I went to school in New York City → and then we lived up on the Hudson for a while*, and *and then we lived up on the Hudson for a while → then moved to Connecticut*. The clauses making up such a nexus are **primary** and **secondary**. The primary is the initiating clause in a paratactic nexus, and the dominant clause in a hypotactic; the secondary is the continuing clause in a paratactic nexus and the dependent clause in a hypotactic. This is set out in Table 7-4. For most purposes we shall be able to refer to 'primary' and 'secondary' clauses and avoid using the more specific terms.

Table 7-4 Primary and secondary clauses in a clause nexus

	Primary	**Secondary**
parataxis	1 (initiating)	2 (continuing)
hypotaxis	α (dominant)	β (dependent)

The clause complex just quoted above is formed out of a linear sequence of clause nexuses; each nexus consists of a pair of related clauses. Many clause complexes are linear sequences of this kind. But we also often find internal bracketing, or **nesting**. This is where what is being linked by a logico-semantic relation is not a single clause but rather a 'subcomplex' – a clause nexus in its own right. Thus in the clause complex diagrammed in Figure 7-1, the initiating clause is a simple clause but the continuing clause is in fact a subcomplex – a hypotactic nexus (see Figure 7-4).

1		In pain, Kukul pulled out the arrow
2	α	**and** headed for the river
	β	**to** wash his wound.

Fig. 7-4 Clause complex with nesting

The concept of nesting is a general property of logical structure and was introduced in our discussion of submodification groups in Chapter 6, Section 6.2.5. We can show nesting in either of two ways. (i) The nesting can be represented explicitly as internal bracketing – e.g. 1 ^ 2(α ^ β); (ii) or it can be represented as a simple string – e.g. 1 ^ 2α ^ 2β.

All 'logical' structures in language are either (a) paratactic or (b) hypotactic. The clause complex involves relationships of both kinds. A typical clause complex is a mixture of paratactic and hypotactic sequences, either of which may be nested inside the other; for example

I would	if I could,	but I can't
1 α	1 β	2

There is a paratactic relationship between *I would if I could* and *but I can't*, shown as 1 2; and a hypotactic relationship between *I would* and *if I could*, shown as α β.

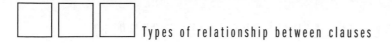
7.2.2 Logico-semantic relation: expansion/projection

There is a wide range of different logico-semantic relations, any of which may hold between a primary and a secondary member of a clause nexus. But it is possible to group these into a small number of general types, based on the two fundamental relationships of (1) **expansion** and (2) **projection**.

(1) **Expansion:**   the secondary clause expands the primary clause, by (a) elaborating it, (b) extending it or (c) enhancing it.

(2) **Projection:**   the secondary clause is projected through the primary clause, which instates it as (a) a locution or (b) an idea.

For example:

expansion:

||| **If** we get enough time, || nobody in the audience will be able to see through the disguises. ||| [KOHL_G]

||| Well that's the idea, you see; || **but** so far it only recognizes people [[whose accents are fairly Queen's English type]], you see, || **because** they're the accents [[it's been trained to recognize]]. ||| [LLC_1]

projection:

||| Gandhi next <u>asked</u> her || **if** she knew what a spinning wheel was. ||| [KOHL_G]

||| 'Good work,' || he <u>acknowledged</u>. ||| [ACE_M]

expansion & projection:

||| And then we <u>knew</u> || we were going up to Cairns at Christmas || **and** we'd be away, || **so** we, we deadlocked everything || **and** we told people || we were going away; || we told the neighbours, || we got mum to go and check the place || **while** we were away || **and** on Christmas night they came back || **and** they took all our music equipment which [inaudible]. ||| [Text 371]

Expansion relates phenomena as being of the same order of experience, while projection relates phenomena of one order of experience (the processes of saying and thinking) to phenomena of a higher order (semiotic phenomena – what people say and think). This basic logico-semantic relation made by the grammar has come to be reflected in the conventions of comic strips, as illustrated schematically in Figure 7-5. Expansion develops the text by linking the frames that make up the strip (and also events within frames); this constitutes

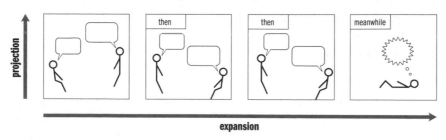

Fig. 7-5   Projection and expansion represented by the conventions of comic strips

the 'horizontal' development of the text. Projection transcends this sequence of events linked by expansion by linking events of saying and thinking to the content of saying and the content of thinking. The content of saying is typically represented in 'balloons', and the content of thinking in 'clouds' – both being a higher order of experience than that represented pictorially in the comic strip.

Within the general categories of expansion and projection, we recognize first of all a small number of subtypes: three of expansion, and two of projection (cf. the classification of circumstances in Chapter 5, Section 5.6). The names of these, with suggested notation, are as follows:

(1) Expansion:

    (a) elaborating = ('equals')

    (b) extending + ('is added to')

    (c) enhancing × ('is multiplied by')

(2) Projection:

    (a) locution " (double quotes)

    (b) idea ' (single quotes)

Below is a brief definition of each of these categories, with examples:

(1a)	Elaborating: 'i.e., e.g., viz.'	one clause expands another by elaborating on it (or some portion of it): restating in other words, specifying in greater detail, commenting, or exemplifying.
(1b)	Extending: 'and, or'	one clause expands another by extending beyond it: adding some new element, giving an exception to it, or offering an alternative.
(1c)	Enhancing: 'so, yet, then'	one clause expands another by embellishing around it: qualifying it with some circumstantial feature of time, place, cause or condition.
(2a)	Locution: 'says'	one clause is projected through another, which presents it as a locution, a construction of wording.
(2b)	Idea: 'thinks'	one clause is projected through another, which presents it as an idea, a construction of meaning.

Examples of expanding complexes (of the enhancing subtype) are analysed in Figure 7-6.
Example (a) involves hypotaxis, while (b) through (e) involve parataxis. Examples of projecting complexes (of the idea subtype) are:

||| Maybe they do not know || that he's got a son. ||| – ||| People don't, you know; || you assume || that newspapers know these things || and you know || that they don't you know. ||| – ||| There's a terrible lack of knowledge. ||| [UTS/Macquarie Corpus]

||| Calypso knew || that her aunt knew || she knew || how unwelcome Richard would be in Enderby Street. ||| [Mary Wesley]

The analysis of this is given in Figure 7-7.

444

(a)	**When** all had been done	**as** God had ordered,	Noah closed the door.	
	×β	×γ	α	
(b)	I went to school in New York City	and then we lived up on the Hudson for a while,	then moved to Connecticut.	
(c)	He ran out on his wife and children,	became a merchant seaman,	was washed off a deck of a cargo ship	and miraculously picked up, not his own ship but another one, way out in the middle of nowhere.
(d)	New designs were drawn up by architect William Wardell,	construction was started in 1868,	the Cathedral was in use by 1882	and was finished September 2, 1928.
(e)	Go under the Santa Monica Freeway,	turn left, west,	and follow the signs to the west-bound onramp;	proceed west to the San Diego Freeway.
	1	×2	×3	×4

Fig. 7-6   Clause complexes of the 'expansion' type

Maybe they do not know	that he's got a son.		
you assume	that newspapers know these things		
you know	that they don't you know		
Calypso knew	that her aunt knew	she knew	how unwelcome Richard would be in Enderby Street
Head	Modifier		
α	'β	'γ	'δ

Fig. 7-7   Clause complex of the 'projection' type

7.2.3 Intersection of taxis and logico-semantic relation; basic set of clause nexuses

The systems of TAXIS and LOGICO-SEMANTIC RELATION intersect to define the basic set of clause nexuses, as exemplified in Table 7-5, where traditional terms are given in quotes for those categories that were recognized in traditional accounts. The examples illustrate how the symbols for parataxis and hypotaxis combine with those for logico-semantic relation types (for a text illustration, see Table 7-1). The logico-semantic relation type symbol is placed before the number or letter representing the continuing clause in a clause nexus (with the exception of certain cases of paratactic projection; see below), e.g. 1 ×2 and α +β. In hypotaxis, the secondary clause is the dependent one, which can either precede the dominant clause (+β ^ α) or follow it (α ^ +β). Examples of the β ^ α sequence are:

While Fred stayed behind,	John ran away	$+\beta \wedge \alpha$
Because he was scared,	John ran away	$\times\beta \wedge \alpha$
That John had run away	no one believed	$`\beta \wedge \alpha$
β	α	

In parataxis, only the order 1 ^ 2 is possible – because the question of which is the primary clause in a paratactic relation is simply a matter of which comes first. In a paratactic expansion, therefore, it is always the secondary clause that elaborates, extends or enhances; if we say

John ran away;	he didn't wait	1 ^ =2
1	2	

the structure is still 1 ^ =2.

With a paratactic projection, on the other hand, it is possible for the primary clause to be the projected one, as in

"I'm running away,"	said John	"1 ^ 2
1	2	

This is because projection is inherently a directional (asymmetrical) relation.

The systems of TAXIS and LOGICO-SEMANTIC TYPE are simultaneous and independently variable: as we can see from Table 7-5, all intersections of terms in these two systems are systemically possible. However, they are not equally likely to be selected in text, as shown by the counts we have given in the table. In a sample of 6,832 clause nexuses in spoken and written texts from a fairly wide range of registers, there are clear quantitative patterns, shown graphically in Figure 7-8[5]. While 'parataxis' and 'hypotaxis' are roughly equally frequent (around 52% and 48%, respectively), 'expansion' is considerably more frequent than 'projection' (around 80% and 20%, respectively) – the two thus coming close to the contrast between systems with equiprobable terms and systems with skew terms discussed in Halliday (1991).

Taking one step further in delicacy, we can see that within projection 'locution' is the more common type than 'idea', but the relationship is not a skew one (around 57% and 43%, respectively); and within expansion, 'enhancing' relations account for almost half of all instances (around 49%), while 'elaborating' and 'extending' ones have almost equal shares of the other half (24% and 27%, respectively).

---

[5] See also Matthiessen (2002a); since that publication we have been able to extend the number of clauses nexuses analysed considerably, but the relative frequencies are very similar. The first study to reveal quantitative patterns in clause complex was Nesbitt & Plum (1988).

Table 7-5 Basic types of clause complex

		(i) Paratactic	(ii) Hypotactic
(1) expansion	(a) elaboration	1 John didn't wait; =2 he ran away. "apposition"	α John ran away, =β which surprised everyone. 'non-defining relative'
		(701 occurrences [52.5%])	(633 occurrences [47.5%])
	(b) extension	1 John ran away, +2 and Fred stayed behind. "coordination"	α John ran away, +β whereas Fred stayed behind.
		(1,368 occurrences [94.2%])	(84 occurrences [5.8%])
	(c) enhancement	1 John was scared, ×2 so he ran away.	α John ran away, ×β he was scared. "adverbial clause"
		(855 occurrences [32.3%])	(1,799 occurrences [67.8%])
(2) projection	(a) locution	1 John said: "2 "I'm running away" "direct speech"	α John said "β he was running away. "indirect speech"
		(368 occurrences [46.2%])	(429 occurrences [53.8%])
	(b) idea	1 John thought to himself: '2 'I'll run away'	α John thought 'β he would run away.
		(15 occurrences [2.5%])	(580 occurrences [97.5%])

Returning now to the intersections of terms from the two systems of TAXIS and LOGICO-SEMANTIC TYPE, we can see that there are three clearly favoured combinations – 'idea' and 'hypotaxis', 'extending' and 'parataxis', and 'enhancing' and 'hypotaxis', and two clearly disfavoured ones, with 15 instances of 'idea' and 'parataxis' (2.5%) and 84 instances of 'extending' and 'hypotaxis' (5.8%). The remaining two combinations are closer to a balance; with 'locution', 'hypotaxis' is favoured slightly over 'parataxis' (46.2% and 53.8%, respectively); and with 'elaborating', there is no very significant difference. These quantitative patterns can be related to qualitative properties of the system; we shall return to these as we discuss first expansion and then projection.

The examples of expansion in Figure 7-6 and of projection in Figure 7-7 all involve only a single type of logico-semantic relation combining with either hypotaxis or parataxis. However, clause complexes are frequently built up through clause nexuses involving different types of taxis, different kinds of logico-semantic relation, or both. Examples:

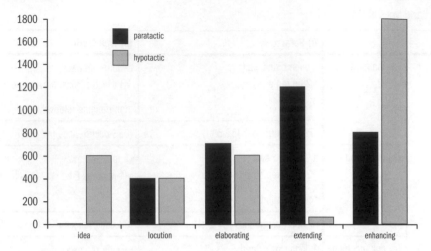

Fig. 7-8 Quantitative profile of intersection of taxis and logico-semantic type in a sample of texts from spoken and written registers (n = 6,832 clause nexuses)

(1) **parataxis + hypotaxis (expansion: enhancing)**

||| Go off the San Diego Freeway at the Wilshire Boulevard-West offramp, || circle right down the offramp, || and turn right onto Wilshire, westbound, || going about one-half mile to San Vicente Boulevard. ||| [Text 140]

||| Some ruined bridges, one of the canals, and the camouflaged oil pumps can be seen || by continuing south on Pacific Avenue to the entrance channel of the Marina del Rey, || turning left at Via Marina, || following Via Marina to its junction with Admiralty Way, || and rejoining the route || by turning right into Admiralty Way. ||| [Text 140]

||| Turn right, west, onto Fiji Way; || go to its ending, || turn around || and return to Admiralty Way; || cross Admiralty || and go 1 short block || to turn right, southeast, on Lincoln Boulevard, Route 1. ||| [Text 140]

(2) **projection + expansion**

||| Yet somebody told me || that I mustn't repudiate my non-fiction, || because it's saying very much || what the fiction is saying. ||| [Text 7]

||| I came back to Mr. Shawn || and said, || 'Listen, I can do the article, || but I'm going to hold back the best material.' ||| [Text 7]

||| He just shakes his head || and shoves it at her again || and says || 'Give Massin,' || as if he knew || there'd be no problem at all. ||| [Text 7]

(3) **projection (hypotaxis + parataxis) + expansion (hypotaxis + parataxis)**

||| Before he was despatched, || folklore has it || that upon being asked || if he had anything further to say, || Morgan calmly surveyed the scenery from the top of Rock Island || and said, || 'Well it certainly is a fine harbour you have here.' ||| [Text 22]

Some of these examples are analysed in Figure 7-9 below.

(1a)

Go off the San Diego Freeway at the Wilshire Boulevard-West offramp,	circle right down the offramp,	and turn right onto Wilshire, westbound,	going about one-half mile to San Vicente Boulevard.

(i)

1	×2	×3α	×3×β

(ii)

1	×2	×3	
		α	×β

(1b)

Some ruined bridges, ... can be seen	by continuing south ...,	turning left at Via Marina,	following Via Marina ...,	and rejoining the route,	by turning right into Admiralty Way.

(i)

α	×β1	×β×2	×β×3	×β×4α	×β×4×β

(ii)

α	×β				
	1	×2	×3	×4	
				α	×β

(2a)

Yet somebody told me	that I mustn't repudiate my non-fiction,	because it's saying very much	what the fiction is saying.

(i)

α	"βα	"β×βα	"β×β"β

(ii)

α	"β		
	α	×β	
		α	"β

(2b)

He just shakes his head	and shoves it at her again	and says	"Give Massin,"	as if he knew	there'd be no problem at all.

(i)

1	×2	×3α1	×3α"2	×3×βα	×3×β'β

(ii)

1	×2	×3			
		α		×β	
		1	"2	α	'β

Fig. 7-9   Examples involving more than one type of taxis and/or logico-semantic relation (*continued overleaf*)

(3)	Before he was despatched	folklore has it	that upon being asked	if he had anything further to say,	Morgan calmly surveyed the scenery ...	and said,	"Well it certainly is a fine harbour you have here."
(i)	×β	αα	α"β×βα	α"β×β"β	α"βα1	α"βα×21	α"βα×2"2

(ii)							
	×β	α					
		α	"β				
		×β	α				
			α	"β	1	×2	
					1	"2	

Fig. 7-9 Examples involving more than one type of taxis and/or logico-semantic relation

The examples in Figure 7-9 all involve the phenomenon of internal bracketing or **nesting**, which we noted above (e.g. Figure 7-4). These examples illustrate the principle that internal nesting always occurs when there is a change in taxis. That is, any logical sequence of clauses is always either paratactic (1 2 3 ...) or hypotactic (α β γ ...). It is never a mixture of the two; for example, a sequence such as 1 ^ β ^ 3 ^ γ is not possible. If there is a switch in taxis, this automatically leads to nesting, as with 1 ^ 2 (α ^ β) in the examples above. By the same token, any logical sequence of clauses is also always constant in logico-semantic type – projection of ideas, projection of locutions, elaboration, extension or enhancement. It is never a mixture of types; for example, a sequence such as 1 ^ ×2 ^ +3 is not possible. If there is a switch in logico-semantic type, then nesting automatically occurs, as with 1 ^ ×2 (1 ^ +2).

In Figure 7-9, the analysis of the univariate structure of each clause complex is given in two forms. In (i), the analysis is given as a single line with the internal nesting factored in for each clause, as with

1 ^ ×2 ^ ×3α ^ ×3×β

in example (1a). But in (ii), the analysis given as a hierarchic structure with the internal nesting factored out so that each new descending row represents a new layer of internal nesting. This corresponds to the use of brackets to show the internal nesting, as with:

1 ^ ×2 ^ ×3 (α ^ ×β)

These two forms of representation are simply notational variants (as in algebra, e.g. x + ya + yb ~ x + y(a + b)). The single line with the internal nesting factored in is convenient

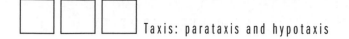

and compact, but the bracketed notation (and the corresponding hierarchic box diagram) can be helpful in sorting out intricate cases of internal nesting. We shall discuss forms of representation further below.

Parataxis and hypotaxis are discussed in more detail in the next section (Section 7.3). Following that we take up the more specific categories of expansion (Section 7.4) and then of projection (Section 7.5).

7.3 Taxis: parataxis and hypotaxis

The tactic structures of complexes are relational in nature; they are the kind of structure that we have called **univariate**, to distinguish it from the **multivariate** structures (see Chapter 6, Section 6.2.5; see further Halliday, 1965/1981: 31–33; 1978: 131): see Table 7-6. This table represents an expansion of the principle we articulated towards the end of Chapter 2, Section 2.6. This principle is that the different metafunctional modes of meaning tend to be realized by different structural modes (Table 2-8; see also Halliday, 1979; Matthiessen, 1988, 2004b; Martin, 1996).

(i) A **univariate** structure is an iteration of the same functional relationship: for example 'and' as in *Bill Brewer, Jan Stewer, Peter Gurney, Peter Davy, Dan'l Whiddon, Harry Hawk, Old Uncle Tom Cobbley and all*; 'equals' as in *Tom, Tom, the piper's son* (Tom = Tom = the piper's son); 'is a subset of' as in *newfashioned three-cornered cambric country-cut handkerchief* (what kind of handkerchief? – country-cut; what kind of country-cut handkerchief? – cambric, ...); and so on. Such **iterative structures** are unique to the logical mode of meaning; they are, as noted, formed out of logico-semantic relations.

(ii) A **multivariate** structure is a configuration of different functional relationships, like Theme + Rheme, Mood + Residue + Moodtag, or Actor + Process + Recipient + Goal. Note that, although it is the functions that are labelled, the structure actually consists of the relationships among them. While we have modelled all multivariate structures in terms of constituency, this structural mode is in fact most appropriate for the experiential mode of meaning. That is, the relationships among the elements in a multivariate structure can be characterized as segmental from an experiential point of view but as prosodic from an interpersonal point of view and as culminative from a textual one. A prototypical example of a segmental structure is the transitivity structure of a clause, a prototypical example of a prosodic structure is the tone contour that typically extends over a clause, and a prototypical example of a culminative structure is thematic prominence at the beginning of the clause (followed by rhematic non-prominence).

The concepts of 'univariate' and 'multivariate' thus allow us to bring out the way in which the structural make-up of the logical mode of meaning differs from the structural make-up characteristic of the other metafunctional modes of meaning. Here we are thus concerned with univariate structures. These are, as we have seen, formed out of a small number of logico-semantic relations such as exemplification, addition and temporal sequence. In all univariate structures the units related in this way are interdependent; but two degrees of interdependency have evolved – parataxis and hypotaxis. This is the distinction in the system of **taxis** introduced above. Parataxis and hypotaxis are general relationships that are the same throughout the grammar: they define complexes at any rank (clause complex, group or phrase complex (see Chapter 8), word complex; in addition hypotaxis defines the logical organization of groups (see Chapter 6). (In contrast, multivariate structures

Table 7-6 Univariate and multivariate structure

Type of structure	Mode of meaning	Mode of structure	Example of structure
(i) univariate	logical	iterative	paratactic: $1 \rightarrow 2 \rightarrow 3 \rightarrow 4 \dots$
			hypotactic: $\alpha \rightarrow \beta \rightarrow \gamma \rightarrow \delta \dots$
(ii) multivariate	experiential	segmental	e.g. [clause:] Medium + Process + Agent + Place + Time [nominal group:] Numerative + Epithet + Classifier + Thing + Qualifier
	interpersonal	prosodic	e.g. [clause:] Mood + Residue + Moodtag [tone group:] // tone 2 //
	textual	culminative	e.g. [clause:] Theme + Rheme [information unit:] Given + New [nominal group] Deictic + ... [verbal group] Finite + ...

differ from one grammatical unit to another.) The distinctive properties and patterns of realization of parataxis and hypotaxis are summarized in Table 7-7.

Parataxis is the linking of elements of equal status, as in Figure 7-4 (b) through (e) above. Both the initiating and the continuing elements are free, in the sense that each could stand as a functioning whole. In principle, the paratactic relation is logically (i) symmetrical and (ii) transitive. This can be exemplified with the 'and' relation. (i) 'salt and pepper' implies 'pepper and salt', so the relationship is symmetrical; (ii) 'salt and pepper', 'pepper and mustard' together imply 'salt and mustard', so the relationship is transitive.

Hypotaxis is the binding of elements of unequal status, as in Figure 7-4 (a) and Figure 7-6 above. The dominant element is free, but the dependent element is not. The hypotactic relation is logically (i) non-symmetrical and (ii) non-transitive. For example, 'when': (i) 'I breathe when I sleep' does not imply 'I sleep when I breathe'; (ii) 'I fret when I have to drive slowly' and 'I have to drive slowly when it's been raining' together do not imply 'I fret when it's been raining'.

This basic pattern may be modified by the nature of the logico-semantic relationship; for example, 'quote' as a paratactic relation is obviously not symmetrical: 'John says, quote: it's raining' cannot be reworded as 'it's raining, quote: John says'. But whenever it is logically possible, a given semantic relationship will be symmetrical and transitive in combination with parataxis but not in combination with hypotaxis. For example, the 'and' relation with hypotaxis is expressed by structures such as *besides* plus non-finite clause; and it is clear that *besides undergoing the operation he also had to pay for it* does not imply *besides having to pay for the operation he also underwent it*. Conversely, if 'when' is expressed paratactically, it will be by such expressions as *at the same time*; and *I sleep, and at the same time I breathe* does imply *I breathe, and at the same time I sleep*. Even with projection the difference appears;

Table 7-7 Properties of parataxis and hypotaxis

		Parataxis	Hypotaxis
'projection' & 'expansion'	status	equal status: initiating + continuing	unequal status: dominant + dependent
	(i) symmetry	symmetrical [except for projection]	non-symmetrical
	(ii) transitivity	transitive	non-transitive
	sequence	1 ∧ 2	$\alpha \wedge \beta,\ \beta \wedge \alpha.,\ \alpha \ll\beta\gg,\ \beta \ll\alpha\gg$
'projection'		quoting: two free-standing clauses	reporting: report dependent on verbal/ mental clause
	primary	projecting [if 1 ∧ "2] / projected [if "1 ∧ 2]	projecting dominant
	secondary	projected [if 1 ∧ "2] / projecting [if "1 ∧ 2]	projected dependent – determined by dominant
	conjunction	–	secondary: binder [*that*; *whether, if*]
	characteristic tone	[see Table 7-30]	[see Table 7-30]
'expansion'	primary	expanded	expanded
	secondary	expanding	expanding
	conjunction	secondary: linker [but some extending correlatives: *either ... or, neither ... nor, both ... and*][6]	secondary: binder, conjunctive preposition (with some non-finite clauses) [but some enhancing correlatives – binder + (cohesive) conjunction: *if ... then, although ... yet, because ... therefore*; binder + binder: *as ... so*; the *the + the* construction]
	characteristic tone	tone 3: 1 [tone 3] ∧ 2	tone 4: β [tone 4] ∧ α

for example, hypotactic *John said that Mary said that it was Tuesday* does not imply *John said that it was Tuesday*, because the projected clause is being treated as what John meant; whereas *John said: 'Mary said: "It's Tuesday".'* does imply *John said: 'It's Tuesday'*, because here the projection refers to what John said and in reporting Mary John did in fact speak those words. (This is not casuistry; it is related to the distinct semantic properties of the two kinds of projection. See Section 7.5 below.)

---

6   In addition, there are patterns with negative polarity *not* and *but*: *not ... but, not only ... but also*.

Conjunctions may be used to mark the secondary clause in both parataxis and hypotaxis; but different classes of conjunction are used (cf. Chapter 6, Section 6.4.2). With parataxis, **linkers** are used, but only when logico-semantic relation is one of expansion (e.g. *and, or, but*). Linkers may also serve a cohesive function (cf. Chapter 9). With hypotaxis, **binders** are used, in the environment of both projection (*that; whether, if*) and expansion (e.g. *when, while; because, since, if, although*) and also, in the case of certain non-finite clauses, conjunctive prepositions (e.g. *after, before; because of, despite*). Both parataxis and hypotaxis may involve correlative conjunctions, where a second conjunction marks the primary clause. Examples of conjunctive markers:

[parataxis: linkers]

Make your way back towards the Pump House **and** walk under Pier Street to the southern end of Darling Harbour.

[hypotaxis: binders, conjunctive prepositions]

Follow the pathways around the landscaped gardens and over bridges **before** resting at the Tea House.

[parataxis: correlatives]

He's **either** holidaying **or** he's on another job. [UTS/Macquarie Corpus]

I would **not only** not finance it, **but** I wouldn't take a big sponsor for any cigarette or any liquor or any other drug that was bad. [KING_Interviews]

Not only was I from the western suburbs **but** my father was a Labor politician. [UTS/Macquarie Corpus]

[hypotaxis: correlatives]

If the majority say well we go **then** we're prepared to go with it. [UTS/Macquarie Corpus]

… **because** we're completely mobile **so** we have to take completely mobile communication. [UTS/Macquarie Corpus]

In a hypotactic clause nexus, dependent clauses may be finite or non-finite:

As he came to a thicket,	he heard the faint rustling of leaves.
† On coming to a thicket,	
×β	α

he headed for the river	† so that he could wash his wound.
	to wash his wound.
α	×β

I told him	to send it off.
	† that he should send it off.
α	"β

In a non-finite dependent clause, the Subject is typically ellipsed. It is generally co-referential with the Subject of the dominant clause – and the prescriptive rule is that it has to be; but

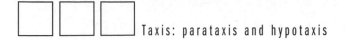

it is not difficult to find examples where it is not co-referential with the Subject of the dominant clause:

||| ×β By [∅:] placing Goffman's work in the context of the writings of other thinkers, || α a beneficial link between the micro- and macro-structures of society becomes visible. ||| [Text 188]

Here the Subject of the dominant clause is *a beneficial link between the micro- and macro-structures of society*, but it is clearly not the Subject of the dependent clause. The dependent Subject is presumably a generalized 'one', 'we'.

Other clauses in the clause complex are finite. Paratactically related clauses that are nested within a dependency are, of course, dependent for this purpose; for example,

α	She set to work very carefully,
=β 1	nibbling first at one and then at the other,
=β +2 α	and growing sometimes taller and sometimes shorter,
=β +2 ×β	until she had brought herself down to her usual height.

In parataxis there is no dependence of either element on the other; so there is no ordering other than that which is represented by the sequence. This is why we use the numerical notation:

pepper	and salt	
1	2	

salt	pepper	and mustard
1	2	3

The only modification is that which arises through internal bracketing or **nesting**, as in

soup	or salad;	meat,	chicken	or fish;	and cheese	or dessert
11	12	21	22	23	31	32

These are word complexes, but the same principles apply to paratactic clause complexes, as in

John came into the room and sat down, Lucy stood in the doorway, and Fred waited outside

where the structure is 11 12 2 3.

In a hypotactic structure the elements are ordered in dependence, and this ordering is largely independent of the sequence. Hence we can have various sequences: dependent clause (i) following dominant, (ii) preceding dominant, (iii) enclosed in or (iv) enclosing dominant:

(i)   α ^ β: ||| You never can tell || till you try. |||

(ii) β ^ α: ||| If wishes were horses, || beggars would ride. |||

(iii) α<<β>>: ||| Picture, << if you can, >> a winkle. |||

(iv) β<<α>>: ||| He might, << he said, >> finish it himself. |||

See further below on textual considerations.

Hypotactic structures may also involve nesting, as illustrated in (2a) and (3) in Figure 7-9 above. Sometimes there are two possible interpretations, as with *she took her umbrella in case it rained when she was leaving*:

	She took her umbrella	in case it rained	when she was leaving
(a)	α	β	γ
(b)	αα	αβ	β

In (a) it rained when she was leaving, or at least that was what she was anticipating; in (b), she took her umbrella when she was leaving. So in (b) there is internal bracketing of the first two clauses.

Typically, hypotactic and paratactic structures combine in the same clause complex, as illustrated above in e.g. Figure 7-4 and Figure 7-9. Here is a more complicated example taken from spontaneous discourse; it was spoken by a girl aged nine:

> Our teacher says that if your neighbour has a new baby and you don't know whether it's a he or a she, if you call it 'it' well then the neighbour will be very offended.

Using this example, let us explore a few different ways of representing the logical structure. We can begin with the kind of box diagram we have already used in Figure 7-9 above, giving two forms of presentation of the analysis: see Figure 7-10 below. Version (i) can be represented as:

α ^ ββ1 ^ ββ2α ^ ββ2β1 ^ ββ2β2 ^ βαβ ^ βαα

and version (ii), using brackets (and showing type of interdependency), as:

α ^ "β (×β (1 ^ +2 (α ^ "β)1 ^ +2))) ^ α (×β ^ α))

This version can also be shown by means of a tree diagram, as in Figure 7-11. The box diagram and the tree diagram both show how the clause complex is made up of clauses; but they have the disadvantage that they make the structure of the clause complex look like a constituency structure even though it is in fact a dependency structure. We experiment with other types of diagram to bring out the dependency nature of the structure: see Figure 7-12. Diagram (c) is based on the graphic conventions of Rhetorical Structure Theory (e.g. Mann, Matthiessen & Thompson, 1992) for representing the rhetorical-relational organization of a text as a semantic unit.

456

Our teacher says	that if your neighbour has a new baby	and you don't know	whether it's a he	or a she,	if you call it 'it'	well then the neighbour will be very offended.
(i) α	"β×β1	"β×β+2α	"β×β'β1	"β×β'β+2	"βα×β	"βαα

(ii) α	"β					
	×β				α	
	1	+2			×β	α
		α	'β			
			1	+2		

Fig. 7-10   Hypotaxis and parataxis combined: box diagram

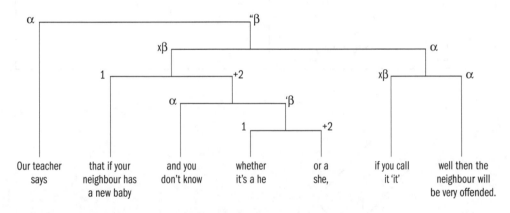

Fig. 7-11   Hypotaxis and parataxis combined: tree diagram

Finally, we present a diagrammatic form of representation that brings out both constituency and dependency relations, as in Figure 7-13.

There is a reason for exploring these different types of notation and diagram. The clause complex is of particular interest in spoken language, because it represents the dynamic potential of the system – the ability to 'choreograph' very long and intricate patterns of semantic movement while maintaining a continuous flow of discourse that is coherent without being constructional. This kind of flow is very uncharacteristic of written language. Since grammatical theory evolved as the study of written language, it is good at synoptic-type 'product' representations, with constituency as the organizing concept, but bad at dynamic-type 'process' representations, which is what are needed for the interpretation of speech. A ball-and-chain picture of this kind is a small experiment in choreographic notation – something which unfortunately cannot be pursued further here (on the dynamic nature of clause complexing, cf. Bateman, 1989).

457

(a)

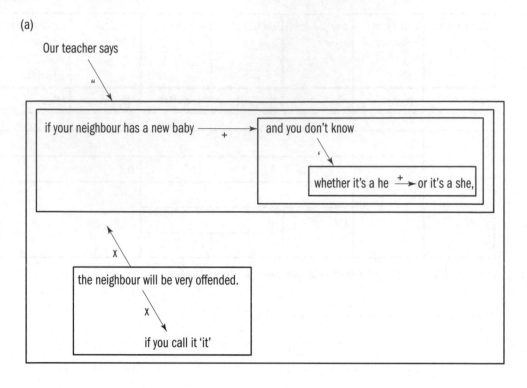

(b)

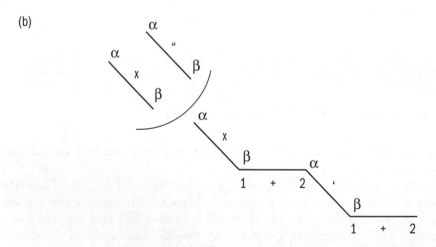

Fig. 7-12(a–b) Hypotaxis and parataxis combined: dependency diagram

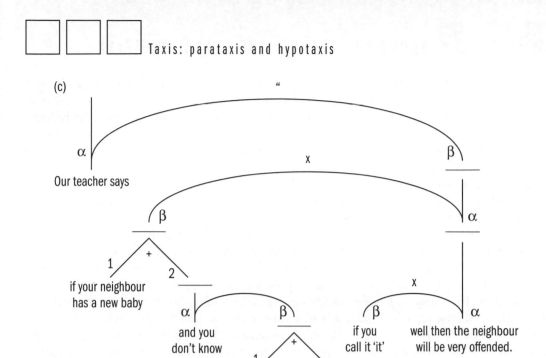

Fig. 7-12(c)   Hypotaxis and parataxis combined: dependency diagram

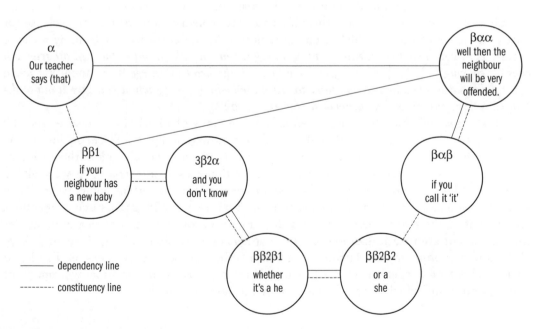

Fig. 7-13   Alternative diagram for a clause complex

The relations of projection and expansion, which (when combined with parataxis and hypotaxis) constitute the 'logical' component of a natural language, are not reducible to elementary logical relations of a non-linguistic kind. As an example, consider the relation of 'and' in its paratactic environment. It was remarked above that 'pepper and salt' implies 'salt and pepper'; but this is not to say that the wordings *pepper and salt* and *salt and pepper* are synonymous – they are clearly not. There is a clear priority accorded to the one that comes first, as is shown by the fact that we do not say *butter and bread*; or rather we do say *butter and bread* – as a way of censuring someone who we consider has spread the butter too thickly: *that's not bread and butter, it's butter and bread!* Thus, although each implies the other, they are not identical in meaning, because while parataxis is a symmetrical relationship, expansion is not. In a hypotactic environment even the implication does not hold, because hypotaxis itself is not symmetrical; thus there is a considerable semantic distance between the examples cited earlier (*besides undergoing the operation he also had to pay for it/besides having to pay for the operation he also underwent it*), despite the fact that one of the semantic features which this structure realizes is still that of 'and'.

It is important to interpret these 'logical' relationships in their own terms as part of the semantics of a language, and not to expect them to fit exactly into formal logical categories – although since the latter were derived from natural language in the first place there will obviously be a close relationship between the two (cf. Halliday & Matthiessen, 1999: 104–106).

7.4 Elaborating, extending, enhancing: three kinds of expansion

In Section 7.2 we introduced the notion of expansion: given a clause (or part of a clause complex, if there is nesting) then this may enter into construction with another clause (or part of a clause complex) which is an expansion of it, the two together forming a clause nexus, as in *you have to crack the head of an egg **when** you take it out of the pan **otherwise** it goes on cooking* [LLC_1], where *you have to crack the head of an egg* is expanded by **when** *you take it out of the pan* and *you have to crack the head of an egg **when** you take it out of the pan* is in turn expanded by **otherwise** *it goes on cooking*.

It was suggested that there are essentially three ways of expanding a clause (see the system network in Figure 7-3 above): elaborating it, extending it and enhancing it.[7] As with all other systems such as the system of process type, we have to think of the system of TYPE OF EXPANSION as defining regions within a continuous semantic space. As we shall see later, the different types of expansion shade into one another at certain points (cf. p. 241); and expansion itself can come very close to projection (cf. pp. 238, 250). Such connections are evident in the current language, and they are also brought out very clearly in studies that document grammaticalization paths of markers of expansion (see e.g. Traugott, 1985, 1997; and cf. comments in Matthiessen, 2002a). When the secondary clause is abandoned (perhaps because of speaker overlap), as may happen in casual conversation, we cannot, of course, determine which kind of expansion might have emerged:

---

[7]   For those who like similes (others should ignore the comparison), these could be compared with three ways of enriching a building: (i) elaborating its existing structure; (ii) extending it by addition or replacement; (iii) enhancing its environment.

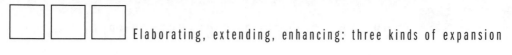

||| No I wouldn't; || my brother ... ||| [Text 10]

7.4.1 Elaboration

In **elaboration**, one clause elaborates on the meaning of another by further specifying or describing it; for example:

||| [α:] Is there any way of disputing || [×β1:] when a priest, any priest, says, || [×β"21:] "This is my conviction, || [×β"2=2:] this is [[what the god [[I serve]] thinks about this]]." ||| [Text 16]

||| [α:] Moo, however, and the novel [[I'm writing now]], << [=β:] **which** is a racehorse novel,>> are comic. ||| [1α:] They are set in a more stable time, || [1=β:] **where** things aren't crushed and lost, || [=2:] they simply go on. ||| [Text 17]

The secondary clause does not introduce a new element into the picture but rather provides a further characterization of one that is already there, restating it, clarifying it, refining it, or adding a descriptive attribute or comment. Thus in the first example above, *This is my conviction* is elaborated through restatement by *this is what the gods I serve think about this*. The thing that is elaborated may be the primary clause as a whole, or it may be just some part of it – one or more of its constituents. Thus *which is a racehorse novel* elaborates part of the clause *Moo, however, and the novel I'm writing now are comic*; it elaborates *the novel I'm writing now* and, being a hypotactic elaboration, it follows its domain of elaboration directly and is as a result included with in the dominant clause (the traditional category of 'non-defining relative clause').

As the examples above illustrate, elaboration may be either paratactic or hypotactic, which are almost equally common in text, as shown in Figure 7-8; the two are contrasted in terms of meaning and realization in Table 7-8. In terms of realization, the two tactic forms of elaboration have one property in common – tone concord (cf. Section 7.7). That is, each clause in an elaborating clause nexus is realized by a tone group, and each tone group selects the same tone (see further under hypotaxis below), as in:

// 13 there's a **bolt** at this **side**, // 13 just sticking out **ahead**, which is what's **holding** us //

The elaborating relationship in meaning is thus symbolized by the identity of tones. However, hypotactic elaborating clauses differ from paratactic ones in that they have a special grammar – the grammar of relative clauses: they are introduced by a relative item (*who, whose ..., which; where, when;* see Chapter 3, Section 3.4 and Table 3-6), which serves as both structural textual Theme and topical Theme[8]. Paratactic elaborating clauses are, in contrast, often without a marker of the elaborating relationship, especially in speech where the relationship is indicated by tone concord.

---

[8]   That is, relative pronouns in English and in many other languages fuse the features of 'pronominal reference' and 'relative marker'; but in a number of other languages, these features are realized separately, as in Arabic (cf. examples in casual spoken English with resumptive pronouns such as *that's because I prefer small boats, **which** other people don't necessarily like **them**,* from Halliday, 2002a/2005: 168); ... *workshop, **which** I videotaped most of **it** until the camera broke down.*

Table 7-8 Paratactic and hypotactic elaboration

	Parataxis	Hypotaxis
meaning	exposition, exemplification, clarification	description
realization	primary + secondary: tone concord	primary + secondary: tone concord
	secondary: often unmarked; may be introduced by *i.e.*, *e.g.*, *viz.* or other conjunctive marker	secondary: non-defining relative clause, either (i) finite introduced by *wh-* element, or (ii) non-finite

In terms of meaning, paratactic elaboration and hypotactic elaboration are largely complementary, covering different aspects of elaboration. Paratactic elaboration involves exposition, exemplification and clarification, while hypotactic elaboration involves description. Certain elaborations have fairly close paratactic and hypotactic agnates; for example:

[α:] Moo, however, and the novel ⟦I'm writing now⟧, << [=β:] which is a racehorse novel,>> are comic. [Text 17]

[1:] Moo, however, and the novel ⟦I'm writing now⟧, are comic; ‖ [=2:] the latter is a racehorse novel.

This is often the case when the elaborating clause is a 'relational' one. In the hypotactic variant, there is always a relative element that refers back to the domain of elaboration; in the agnate paratactic variant this corresponds to a non-relative anaphoric reference (see Chapter 9, Section 9.4) such as a personal or demonstrative pronoun or *the latter*, as in the example above. However, while such close agnation does exist, paratactic elaboration does not have to involve reference to the domain of elaboration; the link is often a lexical one, as with *my conviction = what the god I serve thinks about this*, where *conviction* is glossed in the elaborating clause, with 1: *I just hate it*; =2: *I just loathe it*, where *loathe* is a near synonym of *hate*, or with 1: *this is the image of a poet*, =2: *you're not supposed to see an ordinary African here*, where there is a lexico-semantic relationship between *poet* and *ordinary African*. The lexical link may thus involve lexical cohesion (see Chapter 9, Section 9.6), as in [repetition: *novel ~ novel*] *In the Spirit of Crazy Horse would make a marvelous novel – I could turn that into a novel in a few months*; [hyponymy: *LSD ~ drugs*] *We were both interested in LSD, we were doing a lot of drugs*; [synonymy: *starving ~ hungry*] *I'm starving; I'm so hungry I can't eat*. In this sense, paratactic elaboration covers a wider semantic range of relations. This makes good sense. Hypotactic elaboration has evolved a special clausal construction – that of the non-defining relative clause, with an obligatory anaphoric reference item, the relative, in finite clauses; but paratactic elaboration simply involves an ordinary clause without any special grammatical constraints.

7.4.1.1 Paratactic elaboration

Paratactic (notation 1 =2). The combination of elaboration with parataxis yields three types, the first two of which could be regarded as **apposition** between clauses:

(i)   exposition 'in other words' P i.e. Q

(ii) exemplification 'for example' P e.g. Q

(iii) clarification 'to be precise' P viz. Q

462

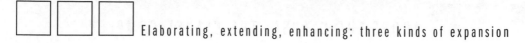

(i) Exposition. Here the secondary clause restates the thesis of the primary clause in different words, to present it from another point of view, or perhaps just to reinforce the message; for example:

||| She wasn't a show dog; || I didn't buy her as a show dog. |||

||| I probably needed that; || it was very healthy. ||| [Text 7]

||| I really enjoyed it, || I thought || it was good. ||| [Text 17]

||| Yeah, I just hate it; || I just loathe it. ||| [Text 76]

||| That British stiff upper lip is trembling in the face of a crisis of sorts: || for the third time in a decade, the telephone company is changing people's phone numbers. ||| [Text 15]

The relationship may be made explicit by conjunctive expressions such as *or* (*rather*), *in other words*, *that is to say* or *I mean*; or, in writing, *i.e.* There is often also a lexico-semantic link accompanying the elaboration (cf. Chapter 9, Section 9.6), as in *need – healthy, enjoy – good, hate – loathe, crisis – changing phone numbers*. In the limiting case, the second clause more or less repeats the first through lexical repetition or synonymy, reinforcing the message, as in *Where's our cake? – It's coming, it's coming.* In casual conversation, the kind of reformulation that is characteristic of real-time editing shades into exposition:

||| Well, what do you ... – why do want to read? ||| [Text 10]

(ii) Exemplification. Here the secondary clause develops the thesis of the primary clause by becoming more specific about it, often citing an actual example; for example

||| We used to have races || – we used to have relays. |||

||| Your face is the same [[as everybody else has]] || – the two eyes so, nose in the middle, mouth under. |||

||| You're too old for that game; || you couldn't bend over. ||| [Text 10]

||| Someone comes along with a great idea for an expedition || – for example, I did a book [[called Sand Rivers]], just before the Indian books, || and it was a safari into a very remote part of Africa. ||| [Text 7]

||| Have you read pre-Shakespearian drama? || have you read any Marlowe say? ||| [Text 135]

Here the explicit conjunctives are *for example, for instance, in particular*; or, in writing, *e.g.* The relationship of exemplification is often accompanied by a lexical-cohesive relationship (cf. Chapter 9, Section 9.6); this is typically one of hyponymy or meronymy, as in *races – relays, expedition – safari, face – eyes, nose, mouth*; but it may involve other relations as well: *too old – couldn't bend over*.

(iii) Clarification. In this case the secondary clause clarifies the thesis of the primary clause, backing it up with some form of explanation or explanatory comment.

||| Tove Jansson was an artist || long before she began to write in the 1940s; || in that respect she was on the receiving end of both nature and nurture from her parents, || both of whom were well-known artists in Finland. ||| [Text 100]

||| They used to work over here; || that's [[how they met]]. ||| [Text 69]

463

The clarification often involves a shift in polarity, from positive to negative or the other way around:

> ||| They weren't show animals; || we just had them as pets. |||

> ||| He never said anything to her; || in fact his last remark was evidently addressed to a tree. |||

> ||| I wasn't surprised || – it was [[what I had expected]]. |||

> ||| 'Now the world can see || that [[what the government says]] is a lie. ||| Brazil wasn't discovered; || our land was invaded,' || said Hugo Xavante. ||| [Text 12]

The clarification may be an evaluative comment:

> ||| You pulled the unqualified statement, Keith; || I expected better from you. ||| [Text 10]

Expressions such as *in fact*, *actually*, *indeed*, *at least* are common in this type; the nearest written abbreviation is again *i.e.*, or sometimes *viz*.

The conjunctives are cohesive rather structural markers of the paratactic relationship (see Chapter 9, Section 9.3). Very often the two clauses are simply juxtaposed. This often makes it difficult to decide, in spoken language, whether they form a clause complex or not; but if the intonation pattern is repeated so that there is tone concord (see Section 7.6), and the semantic relationship of elaboration is clearly present, this can be taken as a criterion for treating them as forming a nexus. In written language the apposition may be signalled by a special punctuation mark, the colon; but this is a fairly recent innovation, never very consistently used, and the lack of any clear structure signal is no doubt the reason why the abbreviations *i.e.*, *e.g.* and *viz*. were first introduced and why they continue to be used today.

7.4.1.2 Hypotactic elaboration

Hypotactic (notation α = β). The combination of elaboration with hypotaxis gives the category of **non-defining relative clause** (also called 'non-restrictive', 'descriptive'). This functions as a kind of descriptive gloss to the primary clause, as in

> ||| Yu, << **who** has been visiting Taiwan this week, >> did not elaborate. ||| [Text 13]

> ||| 'Here' || said Nana, || **who** ruled the nursery. ||| [Text 28]

> ||| So we picked Iowa || because that was closer to Wyoming, || **where** he was from. ||| [Text 17]

> ||| You followed them with The Greenlanders, || **which** seems to me more ambitious. ||| [Text 17]

> ||| The abundance of shale is somewhat less [[than is predicted from the abundance of clay-forming silicate minerals]], || suggesting [[that some clay is deposited in the deep sea basins]]. ||| [Text 68]

> ||| Pyramids, palaces, and temples of stone stand silent and abandoned, || hidden by dense rain forests. ||| [Text 65]

As the examples illustrate, hypotactic elaboration is a strategy for introducing into the discourse background information (in narrative, often, though not necessarily, with a secondary past tense), a characterization, an interpretation of some aspect of the dominant clause, some form of evaluation (as can also happen with paratactic clarification). There

may be a sense of explanatory comment, just as with paratactic elaboration of the type 'clarification':

||| Limestone is presently being formed by chemical precipitation on the shallow Bahama Banks || **where** the factors discussed are favourable. ||| [Text 68]

||| Barak, << trailing badly in the polls in his bid for re-election Feb. 6, >> wants to limit the control over parts of East Jerusalem [[that he already has offered the Palestinians]]. ||| [Text 108]

One special case is where the dominant clause in an elaborating nexus is elaborated more than once:

||| The two big books you've done since then, << if I've got the chronology right, >> are *In the Spirit of Crazy Horse*, << **which** deals with American Indian issues, >> and *Men's Lives*, || **which** deals with your friends, the commercial fisher men, at home. ||| [Text 7]

Here the structure can be represented as $\alpha <<=\beta_1>> \wedge =\beta_2$. Both elaborating clauses are marked by tone concord – first 3 - 3, and then 1 - 1.

As the examples above illustrate, elaborating dependent clauses may be either finite or non-finite. We will consider these two in turn.

(i) Finite. If the secondary clause is finite, it has the same form as a defining relative clause of the WH- type, which is embedded as Qualifier in a nominal group (see Chapter 6, Section 6.2.2). It differs from a defining relative clause, however, in two ways: there is a distinction in the meaning, and there is a corresponding distinction in the expression, both in speech and in writing.

As far as the meaning is concerned, these clauses do not define subsets, in the way that a defining relative clause does. In *the only plan which might have succeeded* the defining clause *which might have succeeded* specifies a particular subset of the general class of plans. A non-defining relative clause, on the other hand, adds a further characterization of something that is taken to be already fully specific. This 'something', therefore, is not necessarily just a noun; the domain of a non-defining relative may be a whole clause, as in the example above, or any of its constituents. It is helpful to treat them under three headings according to the domain within the primary clause, although these are not sub-types, simply convenient groupings:

(a) Clauses with *which* whose domain is either the whole of the primary clause or some part of it that is more than a nominal group (the paratactic and cohesive agnates being extended text references with *it* or *this*); e.g.

||| He talks down to people, || **which** automatically puts people's backs up. ||| [Text 71]

||| I've always thought || that my real writing was the fiction, || **which** seems odd, || since I've done over twice as many non-fiction books as fiction books. ||| [Text 7]

||| In this individual, India has lost an intellectual or an expert; || but it must not be forgotten || that the expert has lost India too, || **which** is a more serious loss in the final reckoning. ||| [Text 254]

meaning 'talking down to people automatically puts people's backs up', and so on. Here the sequence is always $\alpha \wedge =\beta$. The elaborating β-clause is often an 'attributive relational'

465

one, with an Attribute such as *no good*, *a serious loss*, *odd* that provides an evaluation of the primary clause (this thus being one grammatical strategy for 'appraising' a proposition).

(b) Clauses with *which* (occasionally *that*), *who* or *whose* whose domain is a nominal group (the paratactic and cohesive agnates being personal references with *he*, *she*, *it*, *they* and their possessive equivalents); e.g.

> ||| People had trouble || working with Doc Humes, || so I got hold of George Plimpton, || **who** was at Cambridge then. ||| [Text 7]

> ||| This meant [[allowing the Commission to raise charges on these lines to the point [[where they would pay for themselves]]]] || – **which** charges would probably be more [[than the traffic could bear anyway]]. |||

> ||| This was the first English Department class at the University of Ibadan, || **which** had just been founded. ||| [Text 16]

When the nominal group is non-final in the primary clause, the secondary clause is often enclosed, so as to follow immediately after it, as in

> ||| Yu, << **who** has been visiting Taiwan this week, >> did not elaborate. ||| [Text 13]

> ||| Inflation, << **which** was necessary for the system ,>> became also lethal. |||

> ||| Parliament, << **whose** historic role was to make laws, vote taxes and redress grievances, >> allowed the redress of industrial grievances to be mooted and contested elsewhere. |||

Here the structure is α << =β >>; the angle brackets denote enclosure, doubled as always where the delimited element is a clause. (The paratactic agnate of an enclosed hypotactic elaborating clause would follow the primary clause, as in *Yu did not elaborate*; *he has been visiting Taiwan this week*.)

(c) Clauses with *when* or *where*, having as domain some expression of time or place, e.g.

> ||| The first few days are a time for adjustment, || **when** the kitten needs all the love and attention [[you can give it]]. |||

> ||| Go up three flights of escalators to the Podium Level, || **where** lifts leave for the Sydney Tower Observation Deck ($5.00 adults, $3.00 children). ||| [Text 22]

The meaning is 'which is when . . .,' 'which is where . . .'. Those with *where* often refer to abstract space, as in

> ||| Now consider the opposite situation, || **where** the velocity decreases. |||

In this group also the secondary clause may be enclosed, as in

> ||| One evening, << **when** the boy was going to bed, >> he couldn't find the china dog [[that always slept with him]]. ||| [Text 28]

> ||| On October 6, << **when** the edge of the strongly depleted region was poleward of the Palmer station, >> the ozone showed a fairly normal vertical profile. ||| [Text 33]

> ||| In Moominpappa At Sea, << **where** the family go on a long journey to an uninhabited island,>> they have difficulty finding the same wavelength, || until their natural sympathy shows them the way. ||| [Text 100]

As in the examples above, such clauses often elaborate marked Themes of time or place. In addition to *when* and *where* we also find elaborations of temporal expressions introduced by *as*, *when*; for example:

||| That night, << **as** Kukul slept on his straw mat, >> Chirumá came upon him. ||| [Text 65]

As the examples illustrate, this strategy of a nominal group denoting a time plus a hypotactically elaborating clause is common in narratives when the time is being set or reset in the episodic sequence of events.

As far as their expression is concerned, non-defining relative clauses are clearly signalled both in speech and in writing. In written English, a non-defining relative clause is marked off by punctuation – usually commas, but sometimes by being introduced with a dash; whereas a defining relative clause is not separated by punctuation from its antecedent. This, in turn, reflects the fact that in spoken English, whereas a defining relative clause enters into a single tone group together with its antecedent, a non-defining relative forms a separate tone group. Furthermore, the primary and secondary clauses are linked by **tone concord**: that is to say, they are spoken on the same tone (see Section 7.6). For example, in *if I ever did fall off – which there's no chance of*, the tone would probably be tone 4, falling-rising:

//4 if I / ever / did fall / off //4 ^ which there's / no / chance of //

while in *have you been to Wensleydale, where the cheese comes from?*

//2 have you / been to / Wensley/dale where the //2 cheese / comes from //

both clauses would have tone 2, rising.[9] More specifically, the secondary clause is in tone concord with that part of the primary clause that constitutes its domain. Thus where the secondary clause is enclosed, a typical sequence would be 4 - 4 - 1, as in

//4 ^ in/flation //4 ^ which was / necessary for the system // 1 ^ became / also / lethal //

Here the concord is between the secondary clause and its antecedent inflation, both of which have tone 4; this tone suggests that they are non-final, and the sequence is then completed with a tone 1. Whichever tone is used, however, it will be the same in both parts; the tone selected for the (relevant portion of the) primary clause is repeated in the secondary clause. This tone concord is the principal signal of the apposition relationship in English, and applies also to paratactic clause complexes of exposition and exemplification referred to above (though not to clarification, where there is greater semantic distance between the primary and secondary clause). We should also note that this pattern is very frequently accompanied by a rhythmic feature, by which the secondary clause is introduced by a silent beat.

---

9 In British English this would be likely to be the 'sharp fall-rise' variant, tone 2, signalling *Wensleydale* as New (see Chapter 3, Sections 3.5–3.6).

467

There is one group of non-defining relative clauses that strictly speaking would belong with extension rather than elaboration; for example,

||| She told it to the baker's wife, || who told it to the cook. |||

Here the *who* stands for 'and she' and the clause is semantically an additive: the agnate paratactic variant would be *... and she told it to the cook*[10]. Compare also (where the sense is 'and in that case'):

||| It might be hungry, || in which case it would be very likely to eat her up. |||

Note that such instances are not characterized by tone concord. Also extending rather than elaborating are possessives with *whose* or its variants (*of whom/which*), which do not further characterize the noun that constitutes their domain but add a new one related to it by possession; contrast elaborating *come and meet Mary, whose birthday we're celebrating* ('the girl whose ... ') with extending *the shop was taken over by an Indian, whose family came out to join him*. But for most purposes these and all other non-defining relatives can be treated as elaborating clauses.

(ii) Non-finite. Here the same semantic relationship obtains as with the finites, and again the domain may be one nominal group or some larger segment of the primary clause, up to the whole clause. For example:

||| It's my own invention || – to keep clothes and sandwiches in. |||

||| The hairy coat holds a layer of air close to the skin, || insulating the body against changes in the outside temperature. |||

||| [He was an] absolute loner of a man, || pursuing some dream of exploration in the jungles. ||| [Text 7]

||| The document also calls for greater respect for traditional Indian medicine and better protection of intellectual property rights, || threatened by the incursion of foreign drug companies seeking patents on traditional cures. ||| [Text 12]

||| Meanwhile, a list of top Cabinet members in Taiwan's new government was announced, || featuring prominent numbers of women, technocrats and academics who will be key in the push to improve relations with China and clean up corruption. ||| [Text 13]

||| In Nashville, Tennessee, I met Tom Burrell, || now running for the U.S. Senate on the Green Party line. ||| [Text 174]

These also contrast with defining clauses, as in *I needed something to keep sandwiches in, she met some people just leaving the building*, where *to keep sandwiches in, just leaving the building* are embedded as Postmodifier, and do not form a separate tone group – there is no tonic

---

[10] There may also be an explicit marker of an enhancing relationship, a cohesive conjunction such as *then, later, therefore*, e.g. *The daughter is the property of her father* || *who **then** hands it over to his son-in-law* [KOHL_F]; *This differs from Brown's collision theory (1939)* || *in explaining segregation* || *where it is postulated that smaller particles are brought to rest on collision much more readily than large ones* || *which **therefore** can travel further* [ACE_J].

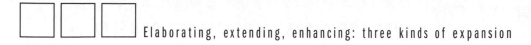

on *something, people*. Again the non-defining clause does form a separate tone group, usually with tone concord; and again there is the corresponding distinction in the punctuation.

When the non-defining clause is an 'intensive relational' one, the Process may be left implicit; for example:

> ||| DPP lawmaker Chen Ting-nan will be the justice minister, || responsible for helping Chen keep his promise to clean up graft. ||| [Text 13]

where *responsible for* ... is Attribute; compare the non-finite version with the Process: [Process:] *being* [Attribute:] *responsible for* ...

As is usual with non-finite clauses, the meaning is less specific; both the domain of the dependent clause and its semantic relationship to its domain are left relatively inexplicit. There is no WH- form, as there is with the finites[11]; nor is there usually any preposition acting conjunctively, as there typically is with non-finite clauses of extension and enhancement such as *besides* or *on* in *besides selling office equipment, on leaving the building*.

The non-finite dependent clauses exemplified above have finite agnates with a wh- element: *he was an absolute loner of a man, pursuing* ... : *he was an absolute loner of a man, who pursued* .... However, there are also non-finites without agnate wh- finites. Here the elaborating relationship is one of clarification, as with parataxis (iii) above; for example:

> ||| I worked for a local firm at that time, || selling office equipment. |||

> ||| 'We really have to have mandatory child safety trigger locks, and photo license IDs for the purchase of new handguns,' || Gore told the crowd, || sounding a frequent Clinton administration theme. ||| [Text 20]

> ||| Goffman, as a product of the Chicago School, writes from a symbolic interactionist perspective, || emphasizing a qualitative analysis of the component parts of the interactive process. ||| [Text 188]

In such cases, there may be an explicit Subject in the dependent clause, as in

> ||| The entire plant was organised around the through movement of ships [[bringing new materials]], || railways bringing some manufactured parts || then the assembly, then dispersing of the single product. ||| [ACE_J]

> ||| I noticed this tow-truck on the other side of the road, next to the ti-tree, || the driver having a fag behind the wheel. ||| [ACE_K]

> ||| It's a much bigger house, || for the children to have their own rooms. |||

But in most instances of non-finite elaboration, the Subject is left implicit, to be presupposed from the primary clause; and it is often difficult to identify it exactly – e.g. in *the hairy coat holds a layer of air close to the skin, insulating the body against changes in the outside temperature*, is it the hairy coat which insulates the body, or is it the holding of a layer of air close to the skin? The question is really irrelevant; it is precisely the function of the non-finite to make it unnecessary to decide: the decreases the arguability of the clause.

With non-finite elaborating hypotactic nexuses, there is a special construction where the dependent precedes the dominant; for example:

---

[11] In this respect, non-finite non-defining relative clauses differ from defining ones.

||| [=β:] A science and transport museum, || [α:] the Powerhouse has over 11,000 objects on display, including the heaviest item, a ten ton steam locomotive [[that ran on Sydney's first rail line between Sydney and Parramatta]]; the tallest, a 10 metre high Boulton and Watt steam engine; and the widest, a Catalina flying boat with a wingspan of 32 metres. ||| [Text 22]

||| [=β:] A New York Times bestseller and a sell-out at megastores, || [α:] this is a lively yet responsible rendering by the Nobel laureate of one of English literature's oldest heirloom. [Text 186]

||| [=β:] Widely considered to be his most inventive work of fiction, || [α:] it is experimental in form, || consisting mainly of dialogue with varied typographic formats. ||| [Text 18]

These elaborating clauses are always 'intensive attributive relational' ones (see Section 5.4.3, Chapter 5) where the Process is implicit and the Attribute is typically the only explicit element of the clause. In fact, such nexuses look like nominal group complexes when they only involve two juxtaposed nominal groups – as with *a science and transport museum* plus *the Powerhouse*. But when we probe further, we find that the nearest agnates are non-finite and finite non-defining relative clauses: *being a science and transport museum, the Powerhouse has over ... / the Powerhouse, which is a science and transport museum, has over ...*; and this explains among other things why clausal elements may be present together with the Attribute (thus showing that the nominal group is an element in a separate clause rather than an element in the clause that follows): [Adjunct: comment] *reportedly* [Complement/Attribute:] *a science and transport museum* [Adjunct/Time] *since 1973, the Powerhouse has over ....* The effect of the construction is to give thematic status within the elaborating clause nexus to the Attribute of the elaboration; and this is a strategy that is often used in biographical texts (e.g. *One of the most famous Indian writers in English Language, R.K Narayan was born in 1906 in Madras*)[12].

Finally, before we leave elaboration, we should note examples that include **asides**:

||| For me, by the time I come to the end of a particular form || —The Greenlanders is an epic || and A Thousand Acres is a tragedy – || I am not all that pleased anymore with [[what I got from it]] || and I'm fed up with [[what I had to give up]]. ||| [Text 17]

||| You watch [[him create Apple]], || then in one of the worst human-resources mistakes in the history of Silicon Valley << – the only thing worse was [[when the French fired Napoleon]] – >> they fire Steve Jobs || and Apple almost completely disintegrates. ||| [Text 260]

Such asides may be analysed as clauses or clause complexes that are enclosed within a clause complex but which are not part of the structure of that clause complex, having only a non-structural, cohesive link to the complex they are enclosed within. However, if there is felt to be a strong pressure to read or speak the enclosed clause or clause complex with tone concord, this suggests a relationship of elaboration, since tone concord is often the

---

[12] As with other cases of hypotactically dependent clauses that are non-finite and lack an explicit conjunctive marker, the logico-semantic relationship may be somewhat indeterminate; in the case of the intensive relational clause consisting of Attribute only, without an explicit Process, there may be a causal feature of enhancement, e.g. *A Shi'a Muslim, Mr Sahhaf is an outsider in the Sunni-dominated government that has been in power since 1968* ('since he is a Shi'a Muslim, Mr Sahhaf is an outsider ...'). Compare thematic circumstances of Role with a temporal connotation: *As a child she lived at Herne Bay* [LOB_A] ('when she was a child, she lived ...').

only marker of elaboration. Interpreted in this way, the tactic structure of the first example would be $\times\beta1 \wedge \times\beta=21 \wedge \times\beta=2+2 \wedge \alpha$, where the aside is analysed as an elaboration of the hypotactically enhancing temporal clause *by the time I come to the end of a particular form.*

7.4.2 Extension

In **extension**, one clause extends the meaning of another by adding something new to it. What is added may be just an addition, or else a replacement, or an alternative. There is a closer parallel with extension between parataxis and hypotaxis than we find with elaboration; we can operate with a single system of categories for both kinds of taxis, although there are certain gaps in the paradigm (e.g. negative additive relations are only paratactic, not hypotactic). The principal categories are set out in Table 7-9, together with a summary of the principal markers of extending clause nexuses. As can be seen from the table, the gaps in the paradigm are found particularly with 'hypotaxis', and we can relate this fact to the skew in frequency between 'parataxis' (around 94%) and 'hypotaxis' (around 6%) in text, as shown in Figure 7-8. The markers of paratactic extension are prototypically markers of extension; that is their core use – *and, or, but, nor*; in contrast, the markers of hypotactic extension are of mixed origin: most of them seem to have been pressed into service from other areas of the grammar – enhancing binders (*while, if* in *if … not (… then)*), linkers followed by *that* (*except that, but [for the fact] that*) and conjunctive prepositions and preposition groups (e.g. *besides, without, apart from, instead of, other than*), and the two additive markers of finite clauses (*while, whereas*) are used both in the sense of 'and' (additive: positive) and in the sense of 'but' (adversative).

Table 7-9 Categories of extension and principal markers

	Category	Meaning	Paratactic	Hypotactic	
				finite	**non-finite**
(i) addition	'and', additive: positive	X and Y	(both …) and; not only … but also	while, whereas	besides, apart from, as well as
	'nor', additive: negative	not X and not Y	(neither …) nor	–	–
	'but', adversative	X and conversely Y	but, (and) yet	while, whereas	Without
(ii) variation	'instead', replacive	not X but Y	but not; not … but	–	instead of, rather than
	'except', subtractive	X but not all X	only, but, except	except that, but (for the fact) that	except for, other than
(iii) alternation	'or'	X or Y	(either …) or (else)	if … not (… then)	–

7.4.2.1 Paratactic extension

Paratactic (notation 1 + 2). The combination of extension with parataxis yields what is known as **co-ordination** between clauses. It is typically expressed by *and, nor, or, but*. We can recognize three major subtypes of paratactic extension, (i) addition, (ii) variation and (iii) alternation.

(i) Addition. Here one process is simply adjoined to another; there is no implication of any causal or temporal relationship between them. Addition falls into three subtypes – (a) 'additive: positive' ('and'), (b) 'additive: negative' ('nor'), and (c) 'adversative' ('but' – 'and conversely'). Paratactic additions are often accompanied by cohesive expressions serving as conjunctive Adjuncts such as *too, in addition, also, moreover, on the other hand*.

(a) Examples of clauses linked by an **'additive: positive'** relation:

||| DPP Secretary-general Yu Shyi-kun was named vice premier || **and** lawmaker Yeh Chu-lan will be transportation minister. ||| [Text 13]

||| Moominpappa himself was a foundling, || **and** we know nothing about his parents. ||| [Text 100]

||| And she had her face painted green with turquoise upside her long nose and around and up and down, || **and** it had all glitter around here. ||| [Text 70]

||| He'd been a medieval history student in college || **and** I was interested in medieval literature, *too*. ||| [Text 17]

||| There was much sickness in the corps, || **and** the men were, ***in addition***, without the clothing, shoes, and blankets needed for the winter weather. ||| [BROWN1_G]

The referents of the two processes may be related in the world of experience; if they share the same semiotic plane then they must be, at the very least by simultaneity or succession, but this is not represented explicitly by the conjunctions in the examples above.

Paratactically related clauses that are introduced by *and* are often additive extensions; but other possibilities exist (just as with *but* and *or*). When the sense is 'and then', 'and so' and the hypotactic version is an enhancing dependent clause, we can interpret the paratactic nexus as one of enhancement instead of one of extension (cf. Section 7.4.3). When the clause starts with *and that* or *and this*, with the *that/this* referring back to (some part of) the previous clause, the sense may be one of elaboration, particularly if the continuing clause is a 'relational' one:

||| [1] But we've got to find those || [=2] and that is the hard part. ||| [Text 77]

The nearest hypotactic equivalent would be a non-restrictive relative clause, *which is the hard part*. Note that many such examples lie on the borderline between elaboration and extension. We have already noted examples of this indeterminacy between elaboration and extension from the other side, with non-defining relative clauses with *who* where the sense is 'and + personal pronoun': see Section 7.4.1.2.

(b) Examples of clauses linked by an **'additive: negative'** relation:

||| Untouchability was observed in matters of food even by Muslims; || they would never dine at the same table with Christians || **nor** touch what was cooked by them. ||| [KOHL_P]

||| He could **neither** explain the whole situation to the editor || **nor** could he accept his rebuke. ||| [KOHL_P]

(c) Examples of clauses linked by an '**adversative**' relation:

||| We liked that breed of dog, || **but** we felt || we weren't in a position [[to own one at the time]]. |||

||| The solar elevation angle is comparatively low by October, || when the hole was at its deepest, || **but** is much higher in November, || when the ultraviolet (UV) effect might be stronger at the surface. ||| [Text 33]

Note that since the linker *nor* embodies negative (clausal) polarity, it attracts the Finite, so the sequence is *nor* ^ Finite ^ Subject (unless the Subject is ellipsed). The linker *but* contains the semantic feature 'and', so we do not say *and but*. For the same reason we do not say *although ... but*, because that would be a mixture of hypotaxis and parataxis; whereas *although ... yet* is quite normal – there is no paratactic 'and' in *yet*.

(ii) **Variation.** Here one clause is presented as being in total or partial replacement of another. Variation falls into two subtypes – 'replacive' ('instead') and 'subtractive' ('except').

(a) Examples of clauses linked by the '**replacive**' relation:

||| The vortex is not a uniform cylinder || **but** has a shape [[that varies with altitude || and is strongest and most isolated above the 400-K isentropic surface, around 15 km and above]]. ||| [Text 33]

||| Witnesses said || the sand dredger seemed to go past the Marchioness || **but** suddenly smashed into the side || and went right over it. ||| [Text 30]

||| They should not be broad statements [[saying || where we hope to be]], || **but *instead*** plans [[specifying || what we want to do next || and exactly how we are going to do it]]. ||| [Text 32]

The clauses related in this way often differ in polarity value, one being 'positive' and the other 'negative'. Note that the *but* here is not adversative, and so is not replaceable by *yet*; nor is it concessive – it does not correspond to hypotactic *although* (see Section 7.4.3.2). Cohesive expressions used with total replacement include *instead, on the contrary*.

(b) Examples of clauses linked by the '**subtractive**' relation:

||| He should have had them before, || **only** he hurt his shoulder at football or some such || and there was a long time spent in treatment, || so it was all deferred, || but finally he went. ||| [LOB_L]

||| Nelly looked rather put out || and replied || that he was quite all right, || **only** the poor little chap was highly strung. ||| [LOB_P]

Here the secondary clause presents an exception to what has been said in the primary clause.

(iii) **Alternation.** Here one clause is presented as an alternative to another. Examples of clauses linked by the **alternative** relation:

||| **Either** you go ahead || and take the plunge || **or** you wait || till you think || you can afford it, || which you never will. |||

||| ["11:] "The death penalty is often enacted in vengeance, || ["1+2:] applied in an arbitrary manner, || ["1+3:] subject to bias because of the defendant's race or economic status, || ["1+4:] **or** driven by the political ambitions of those [[who impose it]]," || [2:] the report said. ||| [Text 1]

||| Can I go on the computer, || **or** have something to eat. ||| [Text 76]

|| Guided tours of the Cathedral take place the first Sunday of every month, || **or** a self-guide booklet about the Cathedral can be picked up inside. ||| [Text 22]

||| Did you have to educate yourself about traditional culture and mythology || **or** did you grow up with that? || [Text 16]

||| The melt is then cooled at a few degrees per hour || until crystals start to form, || **or** *alternatively* the flux is evaporated at a constant rate. ||| [LOB_J]

Here one clause is offered as alternative to another. The correlative pairing is *either – or*, and the associated cohesive conjunctions include *conversely, alternatively, on the other hand*.

7.4.2.2 Hypotactic extension

Hypotactic (notation α +β). The combination of extension with hypotaxis also embraces (a) addition, (b) variation and (c) alternation, but with the extending clause dependent. The dependent clause may be finite or non-finite. Compared with paratactic extension, the hypotactic type appears to be fairly rare; it is, in fact, the least common of the combinations of types of expansion with types of taxis (cf. Nesbitt & Plum, 1988; Matthiessen, 2002a).

(i) Finite. (a) **Addition.** Hypotactic clauses of addition are introduced by the conjunctions *whereas, while*. There is no clear line between the (positive) additive and the adversative; these clauses sometimes have an adversative component, sometimes not. (There is no negative additive type of hypotactic extension.) For example:

||| **Whereas** most children's fathers worked at an office, || my father worked at the studio, || so I went on the set. ||| [Text 134]

||| They have no patience with our official style or tempo, || **whereas** an Indian at home would accept the hurdles as inevitable Karma. ||| [Text 254]

||| And yet Frank grows up, || **while** Huck never grew up. ||| [Text 17]

||| He will be an institutional dealer in New York, || **while** Mr Hayward will be an equity salesman. ||| [ACE_A]

||| **While** 'Joe Gould's Secret' and 'The Sweet Hereafter' played to small audiences in limited release, || Holm has a couple of potential blockbusters [[coming up]]. ||| [Text 73]

(b) **Variation.** There is no finite form for replacement. For **subtraction** the finite clause is introduced by *except that, but (for the fact) that*; e.g.

||| Camera pulls back to show Kane and Susan in much the same positions as before, || **except that** they are older. ||| [Citizen Kane]

||| Language began || when interjections ended || **but that** man still utters cries and uses interjections || and that their significance is merely affective, i.e., expressing fear, surprise, etc. ||| [KOHL_J]

Finite clauses with *whereas, while, except that*, if they follow the primary clause, have a strongly paratactic flavour (cf. on *because, though* in Section 7.4.3.2). The line between parataxis and hypotaxis is not very sharp; as a working rule, if the extending clause could precede (thereby becoming thematic in the clause complex), the relationship is hypotactic (since +β ^ α is a possible sequence, but +2 ^ 1 is not). An example where the extending clause could not precede is

||| He pretended to know all about it || – whereas in fact he had no idea of what was happening. |||

474

This would be interpreted as paratactic. In such instances the conjunction is always unaccented.

(c) **Alternation.** The hypotactic form of the alternative relation is *if ... not* (i.e. 'if not a, then b', with the dependent clause typically coming first). For example,

||| If they're **not** in their usual place || they could have fallen through onto the – ||| [Text 76]

||| If it doesn't come from [[what's outside us]], from our experience, || it's got to come from our inner nature. ||| [Text 173]

||| If you haven't lost it, || then it's in that cupboard. |||

'either you've lost it, or else it's in that cupboard'. Either clause can be construed as the negative condition; we could just as well say *if it's not in that cupboard then you've lost it*, the only difference being which one is chosen as Theme.

(ii) Non-finite. Non-finite hypotactic extending clauses cover both (a) addition and (b) variation. Two subtypes are absent from the non-finite system: 'negative additive' addition and 'alternative' variation. The non-finite form of hypotactic extending is an imperfective clause; for example (structure α +β):

||| We used to go away at the weekend, || taking all our gear with us. |||

The non-finite clause is often introduced by a preposition or preposition group functioning conjunctively, e.g. *besides*, *apart from*, *instead of*, *other than*, *without*; for example

(a) **addition**

additive
||| **Apart from** being amusing || what else does The Nun's Priest's Tale do? ||| [Text 125]

||| **Besides** being gifted with literary talent, || Amir Khusrau was a musician, too. ||| [KOHL_C]

||| Most families are dependent on two salaries coming into the home, || **with** women now constituting almost half the country's workforce. ||| [Text 388]

adversative
||| Until we do that, || the opportunities may come and go || **without** our having a compelling rationale [[for pushing commitment and action]]. ||| [Text 32]

||| The arrow changed its course || and fell to the ground || **without** harming anyone. ||| [Text 65]

(b) **variation**

replacive
||| **Instead of** finding the perpetrators, || they criminally charged the Earth First! activist, || who was left crippled for life. ||| [Text 214]

subtractive
||| We call him a murderer, || but for him there is no way out || **other than** doing the deed. ||| [KOHL_K]

With the additive and adversative, however, there may be no conjunctive expression; such clauses are therefore identical with non-finite elaborating clauses, except that in speech they are not marked by tone concord. Examples:

(additive)

||| So she wandered on, || talking to herself as she went. ||| ('and talked')

(adversative)

||| Hardly knowing || what she did, || she picked up a little bit of stick || and held it out to the puppy. ||| ('she hardly knew ... , but she picked up ... ')

But where the sequence is β ^ α, such a nexus is likely to be neither elaborating nor extending but enhancing; see Section 7.4.3.

With the additive, the Process of a relational dependent clause may be implicit; the marker is the conjunctive preposition *with* (positive) or *without* (negative):

||| I told the whole story of the six-minute Louvre at The Kennedy Center || **with** President Carter there, || and I said, || 'Mr. President, we have the man [[who brought the six-minute Louvre back to America]]!' ||| [Text 119]

||| **Without** chlorine in the antarctic stratosphere, || there would be no ozone hole. ||| [Text 33]

The sense here is 'and several thousand more are still expected to be found', and so on.

7.4.3 Enhancement

In **enhancement** one clause (or subcomplex) enhances the meaning of another by qualifying it in one of a number of possible ways: by reference to time, place, manner, cause or condition. As with extension, the parallel between parataxis and hypotaxis is very close, although there are certain gaps in the paradigm; the principal categories are set out in Table 7-10 together with the principal markers of enhancement[13].

As with extension, long sequences are more likely to be construed paratactically than hypotactically; paratactic temporal sequences play a significant role in the construction of event lines in stories, recounts, procedures and other (passages of) text where chronology is an important organizing principle: see e.g. clause complexes (b), (c) and (d) in Figure 7-6 and clause complex (2b) in Figure 7-9 above. With parataxis, the enhancing subtype is often the same throughout the whole paratactic series, as in (b), (c) and (d) in Figure 7-6, where the subtype is 'different time: later' throughout. Extended hypotactic chains also occur and may maintain the same logico-semantic subtype throughout, as in the following example with causal-conditional: purpose throughout:

||| [α:] Everyone at VES is working hard || [×β:] to change the law || [×γ:] **so that** we will have voluntary euthanasia legalized in England within the next five years. ||| [Text 24]

But they typically involve a shift in the subtype of enhancement, as in complex (a) in the same figure, where β (*when all had been done*) enhances by time and γ (*as God had ordered*) by manner. Similarly:

---

[13] Note that the cohesive conjunctives such as *afterwards*, *nevertheless*, *in that way* are simply examples of a large class of expressions that can co-occur with and in this context (see Chapter 9, Section 9.3).

476

Table 7-10 Categories of enhancement and principal markers

	Category	Meaning	Paratactic	Hypotactic		
				finite	**non-finite: conjunction**	**non-finite: preposition**
(i) temporal	same time	A meanwhile B	(and) meanwhile; (when)	[extent] as, while	while	in (the course/ process of)
				[point] when, as soon as, the moment	when	on
				[spread] whenever, every time	–	–
	different time: later	A subsequently B	(and) then; and + afterwards	after, since	since	after
	different time: earlier	A previously B	and/ but + before that/ first	before, until/ till	until	before
(ii) spatial	same place	C there D	and there	[extent] as far as	–	–
				[point] where	–	–
				[spread] wherever, everywhere	–	–
(iii) manner	means	N is via/ by means of M	and + in that way; (and) thus	–	–	by (means of)
	comparison	N is like M	and + similarly; (and) so, thus	as, as if, like, the way	like	
(iv) causal-conditional	cause: reason	because P so result Q	[cause ^ effect] (and) so; and + therefore			
			[effect ^ cause] for; (because)	because, as, since, in case, seeing that, considering		with, through, by at, as a result, because of, in case of
	cause: purpose	because intention Q so action P	–	in order that, so that	–	(in order/ so as) to; for (the sake of), with the aim of, for fear of
	cause: result			so that	–	to
	condition: positive	if P then Q	(and) then; and + in that case	if, provided that, as long as	if	in the event of
	condition: negative	if not P then Q	or else; (or) otherwise	unless	unless	but for, without

477

Table 7-10 Categories of enhancement and principal markers (*contd*)

	Category	Meaning	Paratactic	Hypotactic		
				finite	non-finite: conjunction	non-finite: preposition
	condition: concessive	if P then contrary to expectation Q	[concession ∧ consequence] but; (and) yet, still; but + nevertheless [consequence ∧ concession] (though)	even if, even though, although, while	even if, even though, although, while	despite, in spite of, without

||| [1α:] Two men were killed by lethal injection in Texas this year, || [1×β:] **even though** they were 17 || [1×γ:] **when** they committed their offences, || [+2:] and another 65 juveniles are on death row across the country. ||| [Text 2]

||| [α:] At least 20 people – including two Australian women and a pregnant Thai woman – died || [×β:] **when** the boat capsized in early morning darkness on Wednesday || [×γ:] **while** travelling to Koh Tao, an island popular with young travellers. ||| [Text 5]

||| [α:] Entry to the Art Gallery is free, || [×β:] **although** << [×γ:] **if** a travelling world exhibition is on display there may be a charge for that section. ||| [Text 22]

In the first example, there is a switch from concession to time; in the second from time: point to time: spread; in the third from causal-conditional: concession to causal-conditional: condition.

7.4.3.1 Paratactic enhancement

Paratactic (notation 1 ×2). The combination of enhancement with parataxis yields what is also a kind of coordination but with a circumstantial feature incorporated into it; the most frequently occurring subtypes are those of time and cause. The circumstantial feature is typically expressed (a) by the conjunctions *then, so, for, but, yet, still*; (b) by a conjunction group with *and*: *and then, and there, and thus, and so, and yet*; or (c) by *and* in combination with a conjunctive (that is, a conjunctive expression that is not structural but cohesive; cf. Chapter 9, Section 9.3) such as *at that time, soon afterwards, till then, in that case, in that way*. Note also that some conjunctives, such as *meanwhile, otherwise, therefore, however, nevertheless*, are extending their use in modern spoken English so as to become paratactic structural conjunctions; in this function they are unaccented (spoken without salience). Some examples are given below.

(i) temporal

same time

||| It's the Cheshire Cat: || **now** I shall have somebody to talk to. |||

||| Three days later, the edge of the chemically disturbed and depleted region moved northward past the station, || and the profile **then** [= 'at that time'] showed a decrease of around 95 percent between 15 and 20 km. ||| [Text 33]

later time

||| The three soldiers wandered about for a minute of two, || **and then** quietly marched off after the others. |||

||| I served in World War II || **and then** [= 'subsequently'] I went to Yale. ||| [Text 7]

As noted earlier, paratactic temporal complexes of the type 'later time' play an important role in construing an event line; a whole narrative episode may be construed by a single clause complex, particularly in spoken discourse, as illustrated in clause complexes (b), (c) and (d) in Figure 7-6. It is common for the Subject/Theme to remain constant throughout the complex, the continuity often being marked by ellipsis. The tense selections are typically a succession of (simple) 'past' tenses (as in *ran – became – was –* [*was*]). Circumstances of Time may help construe the chronology. Instructional sequences in procedural discourse are similar, except that the clauses are 'imperative' instead of 'past declarative': see e.g. (e) in Figure 7-6.

(ii) spatial

same place

||| I ran downstairs || **and there** he was nearly fully dressed, all back to front. ||| [Text 24]

||| He fell onto a sea of emerald grass || **and there** he died. ||| [Text 65]

(iii) manner

means

||| Keep on subtracting the difference, || **and in that way** you will arrive at the correct figure. |||

||| England and France became busy suppliers to the Spanish aristocrats || **and thus** developed an important trade || as they accumulated capital. ||| [Text 122]

comparison

||| Your body goes on changing every instant || **and so** does your mind. ||| [KOHL_J]

||| Factory women wear sandals more frequently than do farmers' wives; || **and similarly** male industrial workers use trousers and shoes or foot-gear more often than their farm counterpart. ||| [KOHL_H]

(iv) causal-conditional

cause: reason

(a) cause ^ effect

||| In her books, Tove Jansson spoke initially to children, || **so** the hero is himself quite young. ||| [Text 100]

||| Literacy is spreading, || it's not contracting, in Africa, || **and so** reading is obviously something [[[which has come in || and is going to grow]]]. ||| [Text 16]

(b) effect ^ cause

||| It is amazing [[how effective this system is]], || **for** the tower stays as stiff as a ram-rod even in the most blustery conditions. ||| [Text 22]

condition: positive

||| That would save a fortune || **and then** we'd have the cash [[that we need to, you know, go on to the next step]]. ||| [UTS/Macquarie Corpus]

||| I have stress at work, || **and then** I sail and fly. ||| [Text 230]

condition: negative

||| This is very much essential, || **otherwise** a lot of time is usually wasted for sighting the staff. ||| [KOHL_J]

||| He must have had a fall the night before, || **otherwise** why should there be bruises and clotted blood on his body? ||| [KOHL_L]

condition: concessive

(a) concession ^ consequence

||| Through mounting irritation I kept telling him that I needed a cure for my son and nothing for myself; || **still** I answered his questions with all the politeness I could muster. ||| [KOHL_L]

(b) consequence ^ concession

||| Well, because I've done a lot of television, || I'm sort of a generalist. ||| I'm not a pastry cook, || **but** I've had to learn a certain amount about it. ||| I'm not a baker, || **though** I've had to learn how to do it. ||| I'm sort of a general cook. ||| [KING_Interviews]

||| I was an English major, || **but** I took courses in biology and ornithology. ||| [Text 7]

||| He carefully searched Kukul's sleeping body, || **but** found nothing. ||| [Text 65]

A typical sequence of paratactic clauses of this kind, each marked with a specific 'enhancing' conjunction, is the following:

||| I had to write this play for Mrs Grundie || **but** I got it wrong || **so** I had to re-write it all again || **and then** she got really interested in it. |||

Here the structure is clearly $1 \times 2 \times 3 \times 4$.

Frequently, however, a sequence of paratactic clauses which have to be interpreted as being in some circumstantial relation to each other, especially a temporal sequence, is marked simply by *and*, without any further conjunctive expression; e.g. *I got the interest and started showing and I got another dog and started breeding* ... It could be argued that these are 'enhancement' by time, since the events described take place in a temporal sequence: they are agnate with enhancing hypotaxis, as in † *after I got the interest, I started showing*. However, the speaker could have used *then* (and had done, in fact, in the immediately preceding discourse: *so I bought one as a pet, and then it progressed from there*). This is a situation where the 'trinocular' perspective gives us different analyses: (1) while the view 'from below' suggests 'extension', since *and* is prototypically a marker of extension and there is no other overt indication of enhancement, (2) the view 'from around' suggests 'enhancement' since agnate hypotactic nexuses are enhancing and (3) the view 'from above' also suggests 'enhancement' since the rhetorical development of the text involves a circumstantial relation[14]. If we allow

---

[14] In temporally organized discourse such as stories, recounts and procedures, clause complexes where the continuing clauses are only marked by *and* typically represent semantic sequences of temporal succession, as was illustrated under (i) above.

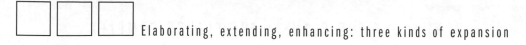

for the enhancing interpretation of a single *and*, then it would be analogous to *but* (extension: adversative, enhancement: concessive); and examples with *and* such as the following would be ambiguous:

> ⫴ I had done well in creative writing classes before that, ⫽ **so** I signed up for the senior creative writing class ⫽ **and** I started writing a novel. ⫴ [Text 17]

The example would be interpreted either as 'and then', in which case the structure would be 1 ^ ×2 ^ ×3, or as 'and also', in which case it would be 1 ^ ×21 ^ ×2+2.

Certain conjunctions that are normally hypotactic ('subordinating conjunctions'), especially *when, till, because* and *though*, often occur in what seems closer to a paratactic function when the enhancing clause follows the primary one; e.g.

> ⫴ Survivor Bethany Rice, from Alaska, said ⫽ passengers were asleep ⫽ '**when** the boat began rocking ⫽ and suddenly pitched. ⫴ Shortly afterward, (the ship) started filling with water. ⫴ We tried to open windows ⫽ to escape'. ⫴ [Text 5]

> ⫴ Did you read that column eight article the other day about this woman ⟦who was driving along somewhere on the this country road ⫽ **when** hail just suddenly started pouring down⟧. ⫴ So she got really scared ⫽ and she stopped ⫽ and she pulled over to the side of the road. ⫴ [UTS/Macquarie Corpus]

Here, the process in the clause introduced by *when* represents the new direction taken by the narrative; it does not serve merely as circumstantial support (cf. Matthiessen & Thompson, 1988: 308, 310). However, when the enhancing clause precedes the enhanced one, the relation is clearly one of hypotaxis:

> ⫴ **Though** Amnesty has long criticised the widespread US use of the death penalty, ⫽ it found ⫽ there has now been another worrying development in this process. ⫴ [Text 2]

We return to these conjunctions following the discussion of hypotaxis below.

7.4.3.2 Hypotactic enhancement

Hypotactic (notation α ×β). The combination of enhancement with hypotaxis gives what are known in traditional formal grammar as 'adverbial clauses'. As with parataxis, these are clauses of time, place, manner, cause, and condition: see above in Table 7-10. Typically, hypotactically enhancing chains are limited to two clauses, with one clause (or subcomplex) qualifying another clause (or subcomplex); for example:

> ⫴ [1α:] I'd parted with the Zen master ⟦⟦I was working with originally⟧⟧, ⫽ [1×β:] as had most of his senior students, ⫽ [×2:] so I was without a teacher. ⫴ [Text 7]

> ⫴ But [×β1:] if you are constantly drinking ⫽ [×β+2:] and borrowing money ⫽ [×β+3:] and never paying back, ⫽ your children are going to be in difficulty. ⫴ [Text 16]

> ⫴ And [×β:] when the priest says this, ⫽ [α1:] how much is his own wish and will and ⫽ [α+2:] how much of it is the will of the gods, ⫽ [α+3:] or is it the will of the community? ⫴ [Text 16]

However, hypotactic chains of more than two clauses are not uncommon – although, as illustrated at the beginning of our discussion of enhancement, the subtype of enhancing

481

relation typically changes as the chain is developed. Their contribution to the development of discourse is, naturally, very different from that of paratactic chains: in a hypotactic chain, each new link in the chain moves further away from the place in the discourse where the dominant clause is located. In contrast, paratactic chains of enhancement move the discourse forward, as happens in narratives and procedures. However, hypotactic enhancement makes another kind of contribution because of the existence of textually distinct sequences – $\alpha \wedge \beta$, $\beta \wedge \alpha$, and $\alpha <<\beta>>$; see Section 7.3 and Section 7.6.

Hypotactically enhancing clauses may be finite or non-finite. The finite ones are introduced by a **binder** ('subordinating conjunction'). The non-finite are introduced either (a) by a preposition such as *on*, *with*, *by* functioning conjunctively – note that sometimes the same word is both conjunction and conjunctive preposition, e.g. *before*, *after*; or (b) by one of a subset of the binders – there are a few of these, such as *when*, which can function also with a non-finite clause. The most usual of these conjunctions and conjunctive prepositions are listed together in a single table, Table 7-10.

(i) Finite

The following are some examples of hypotactic enhancing clauses which are finite:

(a) **time**

||| Moomintroll, that chubby, cheerful being, came into existence as a family joke || **when** Tove Jansson was a young girl |||. [Text 100]

||| **By the time** I was to page sixty, || I felt a certain click. ||| [Text 17]

||| The first draft was that way, || but **as soon as** I finished it, || I felt it was not quite right. ||| [Text 16]

||| **Whenever** they are cruelly attacked for their self-sacrifice || we must find our voices. ||| [Text 328]

||| **Ever since** 'Wildlife in America' appeared in 1959, || and **especially since** 'The Snow Leopard' won a 1978 National Book Award, || Peter Matthiessen has been building up, book by book, a formidable reputation as one of the 20th century's most important wilderness writers. ||| [Text 117]

||| **Once** he had the sense of the guy's nose, || then bit by bit other things about the character would come to it || and magnetize around it. ||| [Text 17]

(b) **place**

concrete place

||| The Ibo never accept anything [[which is rigid and final and absolute]]: || 'wherever one thing stands, || another thing will stand beside it.' ||| [Text 16]

||| Arrows never fall || **where** he places himself. ||| [Text 65]

abstract place

||| As a result, disagreement is carried out in the absence of an audience, || **where** ideological and performance changes may be made without the threat of damage to the goals of the team, as well as the character of the individual. ||| [Text 188]

abstract place shading into matter

||| **As far as** it can, || the Zoo tries to be self-supporting, || and you will notice the names of companies and individuals on many of the cages [[who sponsor the animals]]. ||| [Text 103]

(c) manner

quality

||| **As** it happens, || Margo was an extremely rich woman. ||| [Text 24] 'by chance'

||| Limestone can form in many ways || **as** shown in Table 4-4. ||| [Text 68] 'in the way'

comparison

||| He just shakes his head || and shoves it at her again || and says || 'Give Massin,' || **as if** he knew | there'd be no problem at all. ||| [Text 7]

means

||| These theories include the solar theory, || **whereby** periodically the amount of nitrogen compounds is enhanced. ||| [Text 33]

(d) cause-condition

cause: reason

||| Gradually, they outgrow their baby shoes || – if the expression is pardoned, || **as** Snufkin is in fact the only one of them [[who uses footwear at all]]. ||| [Text 100]

||| The problem isn't simply going to go away || **because** people are laughing. ||| [Text 16]

||| There was no point || **since** you got the same rate from him [[you did at the bank]]. ||| [Text 119]

cause: purpose

||| Everyone at VES is working hard || to change the law || **so that** we will have voluntary euthanasia legalized in England within the next five years. ||| [Text 24]

||| in the Royal Mews, they've been up since four a.m., polishing, cleaning, grooming, feeding, and exercising the horses || **so that** they're not too frisky along the processional route ||| [LLC_10]

cause: result

||| After that, the ozone hole developed rapidly, especially after September 5, || **so that** by October 5, the ozone over the middle of Antarctica had dropped from 320 Dobson units (DU) to 120 DU. ||| [Text 33]

concession

||| **Even though** it was a somewhat silly book about the grand passions of college students, || it really was a novel. ||| [Text 17]

||| They stripped her clean of every bit of jewellery she ever had, || **though** that's neither here nor there. ||| [Text 24] internal concession: 'I'm telling you although ...'

||| Tempting **as** it may be, || we shouldn't embrace every popular issue [[that comes along]]. ||| [Text 6]

||| Africans in Southern Rhodesia do not want to lose [[what they have gained in the past]], || little **though** it may be. ||| [LOB_B]

||| She lived mechanically, || and **while** physically rested, || even as the days became a week and then two, || she found it impossible to overcome the desolation building up around her. [LOB_P]

condition: positive

||| **If** I had a different view, || **then** perhaps I would write more novels. ||| [Text 16]

||| But **if** I can get into the House of Commons || and talk to somebody || and make a fuss somewhere; || **if** I can talk to the young doctors and the nursing people || and impress upon them the reality of human suffering, || **then** perhaps I will have an effect. ||| [Text 24]

||| Now we're only worried about smallpox || because we dared to hold on to some of these viruses || **in case** we wanted to need to use them some day. ||| [KING_Interviews]

||| Many of the restaurants offer a Chinese breakfast || **if** you've missed your breakfast. ||| [Text 22] (internal condition: 'I'm telling you in case ...')

||| **If** it is not too personal an inquiry, || what limits do you set as an acceptable 'quality of life' for yourself? ||| [Text 24] (internal condition: 'I'm asking you in case ...')

condition: negative
||| You will cherish them on your bookshelves for a long time – || **unless**, of course, someone borrows them || and somehow 'forgets' to return them. ||| [Text 100]

As illustrated above, the enhancing relation may be internal rather than external (cf. Halliday & Hasan, 1976: Ch. 5; Martin, 1992: Ch. 4; Mann & Matthiessen, 1991); that is, the β-clause may relate to the enactment of the proposition or proposal realized by the α-clause rather than to the figure that it represents. For example, *if it is not too personal an inquiry, what limits do you set* ... means 'if it is not ..., I ask you ...'; that is, the condition is on the act of questioning, not on the content of the question.

With concession, there is a special hypotactic construction that may be used when the β-clause is an attributive relational one: the Attribute is given the status of marked Theme and the Rheme begins with *as* or *though* – the item that would be the structural Theme in the unmarked case (as in *tempting as it may be*; *little though it may be*).

With a finite clause, the conjunction serves to express both the dependency (the hypotactic status) and the enhancing relationship. As well as simple conjunctions such as *because*, *when*, *if*, and conjunction groups like *as if*, *even if*, *soon after*, *so that*, there are three kinds of complex conjunction, one derived from verbs, one from nouns and the third from adverbs.

(a) Verbal conjunctions are derived from the imperative or from the present/active or past/passive participle + (optionally) that: *provided* (*that*), *seeing* (*that/how*), *suppose/ supposing* (*that*), *granted* (*that*), *say* (*that*). In origin these are projections; their function as expanding conjunction reflects the semantic overlap between expansion and projection in the realm of 'irrealis': 'let us say/think that ... ' = 'if ... ', as in *say they can't mend it, shall I just throw it away?* (Compare the brief reference to grammaticalization paths at the beginning of Section 7.4.)

(b) Nominal conjunctions include *in case*, *in the event that*, *to the extent that*, and *the* + various nouns of time or manner, e.g. *the day*, *the moment*, *the way*. These last have evolved from prepositional phrases with the enhancing clause embedded in them, e.g. *on the day when we arrived*; but they now function to introduce hypotactic clauses just like other conjunctions, e.g. *their daughter was born the day we arrived*, *the way they're working now the job'll be finished in a week*. One clear indication that such constructions have been reanalyzed from nominal groups with embedded clauses to nominal conjunctions introducing hypotactically dependent clauses is that the former 'nominal groups' no longer have the potential for modification; thus while we can say *on the beautiful day when we arrived*, it would be odd (or impossible) to say *their daughter was born the beautiful day we arrived*.

(c) Adverbial conjunctions are *as/so long as*, *as/so far as*, (*as*) *much as*, e.g. *as long as you're here* ... , *as far as I know* ... , *much as I'd like to* ... (compare non-finite *as well as*, which is extending not enhancing). In origin these express limitation, a particular point up to which a certain circumstance is valid.

(ii) Non-finite

Some examples of non-finite enhancing clauses:

(a) Enhancing relationship explicitly marked by a structural conjunction (e.g. *when, while; if; although, though*) or conjunctive preposition (e.g. *before, after, since; because of; without; by*):

time

||| Follow the pathways around the landscaped gardens and over bridges || **before** resting at the Tea House || where the scent of lotus flowers mingles with that of freshly brewed tea and traditional cakes. ||| [Text 22]

||| The issue was raised by elderly presidential adviser Sun Yun-suan, || whom Chen visited || **while** making traditional courtesy calls to influential figures in the current government. ||| [Text 13]

concession

||| Similarly Mr. G. S Sawhney, largely due to the recommendation of Mr. K. K. Shah, then Governor of Tamil Nadu, was transferred from Collector of Customs, Bombay, || to become Director of Revenue Intelligence, || **despite** having himself been under investigation by the CBI || and having been listed as a suspect in the Directorate of Revenue Intelligence. ||| [KOHL_A]

condition

||| I've found || that I can't go more than three days || **without** doing something physically invigorating, || because it makes me uptight and tense. ||| [Text 206]

manner: means

||| Bacteria can also aid chemical precipitation of calcite || **by** making the water more alkaline. ||| [Text 68]

(b) Enhancing relationship left implicit:

time

||| Catch a ride on the monorail to the ritzy shopping centre of Sydney, || taking in the Queen Victoria Building and Centrepoint on the way. ||| [Text 22]

||| Leaving the Gardens, || walk through Tumbalong Park with its fountains and groves of native eucalypts. ||| [Text 22]

cause: reason

||| This view was not empirically based, || having arisen from an a priori philosophy. ||| [Text 237]

||| You must have thought || this would be a fun profession to get involved in, || being so immersed in it as a child. ||| [Text 134]

cause: purpose

||| He grew up in an orphanage || and ran away from it || to seek Freedom and Adventure. ||| [Text 100]

||| To jazz up the title, || use the mouse || to click on the text || and type something new. ||| [Text 121]

cause: result

||| He was taken away from the city, ||| never to be seen again. ||| [Text 65]

||| In practice, these are blended || to produce a practical classification as follows. ||| [Text 68]

||| Thus much chert is recrystallized, || making the origin difficult to discern. ||| [Text 68]

Note that perfective non-finite clauses (e.g. *to jazz up the title*) typically express purpose, but they sometimes express result instead, just as finite clauses introduced by *so that* may express either result or purpose; in other words, purpose ('irrealis') may shade into result ('realis').

As with extending clauses, the non-finite dependent clause without a Subject is interpreted by reference to the Subject of the dominant clause. However, we also find examples where the Subject of the dependent clause is not co-referential with the Subject of the dominant clause; in such cases the dependent Subject typically refers to the speaker –

||| But, of course, << [Ø] having said that, >> the hope is that at least now we know. ||| [Text 16]

– but it may alternatively refer to the Agent in a 'receptive' clause (whether it is structurally present or not),

||| If this occurs in limestone, || beautifully preserved fossils with delicate features intact can be recovered || **by** [Ø] dissolving the limestone with acid. ||| [Text 68]

or to some non-specific entity whose identity is treated as unimportant:

||| If the amount of carbon dioxide is reduced || **by** [Ø] warming the water, || as would occur in shallow tropical water, || calcite may be precipitated. ||| [Text 68]

The dependent clause often has an explicit Subject of its own; when this can show a contrast in case, it appears either in oblique (e.g. *him*) or in possessive (e.g. *his*) form:

||| In order for **there** to be curvature in space time, || the time axis must be extended || – it cannot be just one point, the present. ||| [Text 237]

||| (In order) for **him** to take time off || everyone has to work harder. |||

||| With **him/his** taking time off || everyone has to work harder. |||

Where both are possible (i.e. in the imperfective type) etiquette prescribes the possessive, which reflects the earlier status of these non-finite clauses as rankshifted; but the preferred form in current usage is the 'oblique' case (distinct from the 'nominative' only in the pronouns *him, her, me, us, them*), showing that in the modern language these clauses are not rankshifted but dependent.

If the dependent clause is non-finite, the circumstantial relationship is made explicit by the structural conjunction or conjunctive preposition. The conjunctions are a subset of those occurring in finite clauses, and their meaning is essentially the same. The prepositions tend to be somewhat less specific, e.g. *in turning the corner, on thinking it over, with you being away, without John knowing*; and the meaning of the clause introduced by a preposition may vary according to the sense of the primary clause:

||| Without having been there || I can't say what happened. |||

    (cause: reason 'because I wasn't there')

||| Without having been there || I know all that happened. |||

    (condition: concessive 'although I wasn't there')

||| Without having been there || I rather like the place. |||

    (indeterminate)

Nevertheless, it is usually possible to assign these clauses to the categories of time, manner and cause, and to match the prepositions up in a general way with the conjunctions, as in Table 7-10.

7.4.4 Expansion clauses that are not explicitly marked for any logical-semantic relation

Certain markers of expansion are multivalent; they can mark either elaboration and extension or extension and enhancement. For example, there are three distinct meanings of *but*: (i) adversative, as in *they're pretty, but I can't grow them* ('on the other hand'); (ii) replacive, as in *don't drown them, but give them just enough* ('instead'); (iii) concessive, as in *I don't look after them, but they still grow* ('nevertheless'). Only the last embodies a logical opposition between the two terms; there will therefore be an agnate hypotactic nexus *although I don't look after them they still grow* (not found with the other meanings). Examples of such conjunctive markers with two (or more) senses are listed in Table 7-11.

Clauses introduced by conjunctive markers with two or more senses can, of course, be difficult to analyse. The best strategy is to explore close agnates and to see if these are elaborating, extending or enhancing expansions. Clauses without conjunctive markers naturally pose an even greater challenge. Two kinds of problem arise in analysis, one with finite, the other with non-finite clauses.

(i) A **finite** clause is in principle independent; it becomes dependent only if introduced by a binding (hypotactic) conjunction. If it is joined in a clause complex, its natural status is paratactic. In this case its logical-semantic relationship to its neighbour is typically shown by a linking (paratactic) conjunction.

Table 7-11 Conjunctive markers used for more than one type of expansion

	Elaboration	Extension	Enhancement
and		additive: 'and also'	temporal: 'and then' causal: 'and so'
but		adversative: 'on the other hand' replacive: 'instead'	concessive: 'nevertheless'
yet		adversative: 'on the other hand'	concessive: 'nevertheless'
or	exposition: 'or rather'	alternative: 'or instead'	
while		additive: 'and also' adversative: 'and yet'	temporal: same time: spread: 'and meanwhile' concessive: 'nevertheless'
as			temporal: same time: spread: 'when' causal: reason: 'because'
since			temporal: different time: later: 'after' causal: reason: 'because'
if		alternative (*if ... not [then]*) 'or'	conditional: positive: 'in case'

Frequently, however, two or more finite clauses with no conjunction in them are nonetheless related by expansion; and this is recognized in writing by their being punctuated as one sentence. Typically in such instances the relation is one of elaboration as described above. But in both spoken and written English we find unconjoined sequences which seem to be functioning as clause complexes, yet which do not seem to be restricted to the elaborating type. Here is an example from spontaneous speech, with the clauses related by expansion marked off by commas:

> At the last meeting somebody almost got drowned, he was practising rescuing somebody, no one had really shown how to do it, he had to be dragged out by some of the older lads, nobody really thought it was that bad, they just thought he'd got cramp or something.

Ignoring the projections, there are six clauses, of which only the first and the last pairs seem to be linked by elaboration. There are two ways of approaching this situation. One is to say 'wherever I could recognize a relation of extension or enhancement, as shown by the possibility of inserting a conjunction without changing the logical-semantic relation, I will do so'; this would suggest re-wording along the lines of:

1	At the last meeting somebody almost got drowned;
=21	he was practising rescuing somebody
=2+21α	'but' no one had really shown
=2+21'β	how to do it,
=2+2×2	'so' he had to be dragged out by some of the older lads.
1α	Nobody really thought
1'β	it was that bad;
=2α	they just thought
=2'β	he'd got cramp or something.

The alternative is to say 'if the speaker had wanted to relate these by extension or enhancement he could have done so; he didn't, so I will treat them as semantically unrelated, whatever the sequence of the events to which they refer'. This would give:

1	At the last meeting somebody almost got drowned;
=2	he was practising rescuing somebody.
α	No one had really shown
'β	how to do it,
	He had to be dragged out by some of the older lads.
1α	Nobody really thought
1'β	it was that bad;
=2α	they just thought
=2'β	he'd got cramp or something.

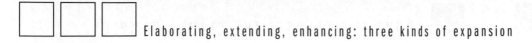

This latter principle is the same as that discussed with reference to the interpretation of 'and' in Section 7.4.3.1.

(ii) A **non-finite** clause, on the other hand, is by its nature dependent, simply by virtue of being non-finite. It typically occurs, therefore, without any other explicit marker of its dependent status. Hence when a non-finite clause occurs without a conjunction, there is no doubt about its hypotactic relation in a clause complex; but there may be no indication of its logical-semantic function. Here, therefore, the same question arises, with examples such as

||| In 1983 he and Mary Hesse delivered the Gifford Lectures in Natural Theology at the University of Edinburgh, || since published as The Construction of Reality, || **extending** schema theory || to provide a coherent epistemology for both individual and social knowledge. ||| [Text 86]

||| Until the 1960s, with very rare exceptions, academic scholarship was grossly falsifying the history, || **suppressing** the reality of [[what happened]]. ||| [Text 234]

||| You try to be a physicist after Newton, || **spinning** off ideological fanaticism, || and you're just out of the game. ||| [Text 234]

||| To meet these new conditions, || certain modifications were introduced from time to time, || **giving** the theory a flexibility [[that would allow it to cover all cases]]. ||| [Text 259]

Unlike the finites, however, these cannot be assigned unmarkedly to just one category; they may be elaborating or extending, and even enhancing, given the appropriate context. The best solution here is to find the nearest finite agnate clause. If this is a non-defining relative clause, the non-finite is elaborating. If it is a coordinate clause, the non-finite is extending. If it is an enhancing clause, the non-finite is enhancing and could probably be introduced by a conjunctive preposition. For example:

He left the house, closing the door behind him.

          and closed the door ... [extending]

I worked for a local firm, selling office equipment

          ; I sold ... ('I was doing some work, which was ... ') [elaborating]

Not wanting to offend, Mary kept quiet.

Because she did not want ... [enhancing]

Having said goodbye, John went home.

After he had said ... [enhancing]

Some precipitation is expected, falling as snow over high ground.

          which will fall ... [elaborating]

The Sonora road was opened by Mexican explorers, supplanting the Anza trail.

          and supplanted ... [extending]

Instances such as *Alice walked on in silence, puzzling over the idea*, illustrate an area of overlap between extension and enhancement; they can be interpreted as 'while'-type temporals (same time extent), but unless the simultaneous time factor is foregrounded, as it is perhaps in *he scrambled back into the saddle*, 'while' *keeping hold of Alice's hair with one hand*, they are probably best treated as straightforward 'and'-type additives.

There is one type of non-finite dependent clause which is often not recognized because it has no verb in it; for example *with no one in charge, with everyone so short of money*. These are in fact 'attributive relational' clauses, with zero alternation of the non-finite verb *being* (less commonly they may be identifying, e.g. *with that the only solution*). The verb *be* will always be present in the agnate finite clause (e.g. *since no one is in charge*); and in the non-finite it is always possible to insert *being*, with very little difference in meaning.

We could summarize the issue raised in this Section as follows. There is a gradual loss of information, in the way a process is construed in the grammar, as one moves from the finite free clause to the prepositional phrase; for example 'soon you will reach the monument; then continue straight ahead':

clause complex	(1)	free (finite) clause	You will reach the monument; ...
	(2)	bound finite clause	When you reach the monument, ...
	(3)	bound non-finite clause	(On) reaching the monument, ...
clause	(4)	prepositional phrase	At the monument ...

(1) shows transitivity, with Process and Medium; bound mood, with Subject, and primary tense (system I). (2) shows transitivity, with Process and Medium; free mood, with Subject, and reduced primary tense (system II). (3) shows transitivity with Process but no Medium; no mood, and no explicit Subject; no primary tense (system III). (4) shows no transitivity (minor process only), no mood, and no tense. (We shall see in Chapter 10 that this loss of information is carried still further through the use of grammatical metaphor.) With no. (3), however, we have a system of ASPECT: imperfective/perfective. The imperfective represents the real, or actual, mode of non-finiteness ('realis'), while the perfective represents the potential, or virtual ('irrealis'). So for example:

||| Reaching the monument, || continue straight ahead. |||

||| To reach the monument, || continue straight ahead. |||

Historically the imperfective combined with the preposition 'at, in' (cf. *a-doing* in the folksy *what are you a-doing of?*); the perfective combined – and still does, in the infinitive form – with the preposition 'to'. The meaning of the two aspects is very fluid and indeterminate; in the most general terms, the imperfective means act in progress, actual, present, ongoing, steady state or (dependent) proposition, while the perfective means goal to be attained, potential, future, starting and stopping, change of state or (dependent) proposal. Sometimes the distinction is quite clear, as in the example above; sometimes it is very tenuous, as between *the first person leaving* and *the first person to leave*. Numerous examples of this given in Chapter 8.

7.4.5 Embedded expansions

7.4.5.1 Embedding vs. hypotaxis; environments of embedding

It is important to distinguish between the 'tactic' relations of parataxis and hypotaxis, on the one hand, and embedding (cf. Chapter 1, Section 1.1.3; Chapter 6), on the other. Whereas

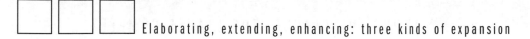

parataxis and hypotaxis are relations *between* clauses (or other ranking elements; see Section 7.6 below), embedding is not. Embedding is a semogenic mechanism whereby a clause or phrase comes to function as a constituent within the structure of a group[15], which itself is a constituent of a clause, e.g. *who came to dinner* in *the man who came to dinner*. Hence there is no direct relationship between an embedded clause and the clause within which it is embedded; the relationship of an embedded clause to the 'outer' clause is an indirect one, with a group as intermediary. The embedded clause functions in the structure of the group, and the group functions in the structure of the clause.[16] Embedding (rankshift) and hypotaxis are contrasted diagrammatically in Figure 7-14. We represent embedded clauses as ⟦ ⟧ and embedded phrases as [ ]:

the man ⟦ who came to dinner ⟧ / ⟦ coming to dinner ⟧

the man [at the next table]

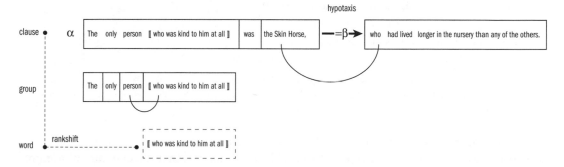

Fig. 7-14   Elaborating clauses – rankshifted within nominal group vs. hypotactically related within clause nexus

Embedding is thus the 'rank shift' by which a clause or phrase comes to function within the structure of a group. The characteristic function of an embedded element is as Postmodifier

---

[15] We can say that it's a mechanism whereby a clause or word comes to function as a word, and there may be agnation between words as Premodifiers and phrases or clauses as Postmodifiers, e.g. *an new car ~ a car ⟦that is new⟧*; *a passenger car ~ a car for passengers*; *an electric car ~ a car ⟦ [that is] powered by electricity⟧*. This is reflected in the use of terms such as 'adjective clause' (for relative clauses serving as Postmodifier) and 'noun clause' (for clauses serving as Head). However, often downranked phrases and clauses construe meanings that are more complex than those lexicalized by words that can serve as Premodifiers. For example, relative clauses typically construe meanings that are in some sense more complex than those construed by adjectives, and the qualities they construe are often instantial ones rather than permanent ones inherent in the Thing (cf. Chapter 6, Footnote 6); cf. *his new car* with *his car ⟦that gave off macho growls at the traffic lights⟧* [ACE_P] and *the only kind person* with *the only person ⟦who was kind to him at all ⟧*.

[16] Where the embedded element functions as Head, we may leave out the intermediate (nominal group) step in the analysis and represent the embedded clause or phrase as functioning directly in the structure of the outer clause, as Subject or whatever. This is a notational simplification; it does not affect the status of the embedded element as a nominalization. Note that this still does not make it resemble hypotaxis; in hypotaxis one clause is dependent on another, but in no sense is it a constituent part of it.

in a nominal group, as in the above examples. Other functions are: as Head of a nominal group (i.e. as a nominalization); and as a Postmodifier in an adverbial group. Examples:

[Postmodifier/Qualifier in a nominal group:]

||| The only person [[who was kind to him at all]] was the Skin Horse, || who had lived longer in the nursery than any of the others. ||| [Text 28]

||| If the planned global change programs are as successful [[as they promise to be]], || they are going to create many more problems for the policy and management community [[than they solve]], at least in the short run. ||| [Text 32]

[Head/Thing in a nominal group:]

||| It's not nice [[what's happening to him]] || but he is creating the situation just as much as [[what they are]], || because he's been caught || drinking on the job, || (whisper) which is no good you know. ||| [Text 71]

||| She comes back from two months away, || organises an extra month the following year || and [[how she accumulates so many holidays]] is beyond me. ||| [Text 70]

[Postmodifier in an adverbial group:]

||| He left Weeks as quickly [[as he could]]. ||| [Of Human Bondage]

||| We need to get that message across at least as much [[as we need to be concerned [[[with getting the FY 1989 budget secured || or getting a congressional hearing on immediate solutions to immediate problems]]]]]. ||| [Text 32]

These are summarized in Table 7-12. All embedding falls into one or other of these major categories; there are no further types. It should be remembered that the category of nominal group includes those having adjective (Epithet) as Head, e.g.

||| His face grew very flushed || and his little body was so hot [[[that it burned the Rabbit || when he held him close]]]. ||| [Text 28]

||| The abundance of shale is somewhat less [[than is predicted from the abundance of clay-forming silicate minerals]], ||| [Text 68]

Here the embedded clause serves to represent a standard of comparison (cf. Fries, 1977).

Table 7-12 Types of embedding (rankshift)

Function	Class	In nominal group	In adverbial group
Postmodifier	clause: finite	the house [[that Jack built]]	sooner [[than we had expected]]
	clause: non-finite	the house [[being built by Jack]]	sooner [[than expected]]
	phrase	the house [by the bridge]	sooner [than the rest of us]
Head	clause: finite	[[what Jack built]]	–
	clause: non-finite	[[for Jack to build a house]]	–
	phrase	[by the bridge]	–

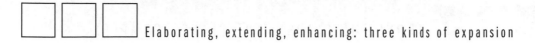

As always, the fact that the two categories of tactic relations and embedding are clearly distinct in principle does not mean that every instance can be definitively assigned to one or the other on some fixed and easily identifiable criterion. The vast majority of instances are clear; but there are anomalous and borderline cases which are bound to cause difficulty. We shall attempt to describe and illustrate the categories as explicitly as possible in what follows.

Like clauses in a paratactic or hypotactic relation, an embedded element may also be either an expansion or a projection. Embedded projections are discussed in Section 7.5.6 below. Here we are concerned with expansions. All the examples cited above were examples of expansion.

The meaning of an embedded clause, or phrase, that is functioning as an expansion is essentially to define, delimit or specify. Thus the characteristic embedded expansion is the 'defining relative clause' (also called 'restrictive'), like *that Jack built* in *the house that Jack built*. Its function is to specify which member or members of the class designated by the Head noun, in this instance *house*, is or are being referred to. Similarly in the following examples *that ever were invented* defines *poems*, and (*who is*) *taking the pictures* defines *girl*.

(this is) the house ⟦that Jack built⟧

(I can explain) all the poems ⟦that ever were invented⟧

(do you know) the girl ⟦ (who is) taking the pictures ⟧

Figure 7-15 shows the analysis of a clause containing a nominal group containing an embedded clause. (The analysis is given in terms of Mood; the embedding could, of course, equally well be incorporated into an analysis in terms of transitivity.)

Within embedded clauses, the distinction among the three categories of elaborating, extending and enhancing, as found in parataxis and hypotaxis, is less foregrounded. However, since the range of semantic relations is roughly equivalent, and since there are subcategories that need to be distinguished, it may be helpful if we continue to refer to the same framework.

do	you	know	the	girl	who	is	taking	the pictures
Mood		Residue						
Finite	Subject	Predicator	Complement					
			nominal group					
			Modifier β	Head α	Postmodifier			
					⟦clause: defining relative⟧			
					Mood		Residue	
					Subject	Finite	Predicator	Complement

Fig. 7-15 Analysis of a clause containing a nominal group with embedded clause as Postmodifier

493

7.4.5.2 Embedding: elaborating

The typical defining relative clause, introduced by *who, which, that*, or in its so-called 'contact clause' form without any relative marker (e.g. *he told* in *the tales he told*), is elaborating in sense. The following example illustrates the contrast between an embedded, defining relative clause and a hypotactically dependent, non-defining one.

> ||| The only person [[who was kind to him at all]] was the Skin Horse, || who had lived longer in the nursery than any of the others. ||| [Text 28]

The relative element in an embedded clause restates the nominal antecedent; thus in

> the man [[who came to dinner]] stayed for a month

the man who came to dinner and the man who stayed for a month are the same man. This is the same principle by which non-defining relatives are also elaborating in function; cf. Section 7.4.1.2. The defining ones, however, do not form a separate tone group, because there is only one piece of information here, not two – *who came to dinner* is not news, but simply part of the characterization of that particular participant.

The elaborating clause is either (a) finite, where the relative is *who(m)*, *which*, *that*[17] or implicit (a 'contact' relative), or (b) non-finite, where the relative is typically implicit; for example:

(a) **finite**

> ||| she said || 'Do you know of anyone else [[**who**'s taken any photos of me at the fancy dress]]?' ||| [Text 70]

> ||| Hafez Assad, Syria's autocratic president [[[**who** dreamed of Arab unity || but watched his neighbors sign peace deals with Israel]]], died Saturday || before he was able to win back the treasured Golan Heights [[he lost to the Jewish state 33 years ago]]. ||| [Text 66]

> ||| She wore this suit with a no top, a pair of Lurex tights without feet in them, you know || and then, and ... she had this old green olive green jumper [[**that** her mother must have had]] ||| [Text 71]

(b) **non-finite**

[imperfective:]

> ||| There was an affair [[going on between the cook and this other girl]], you know. ||| [Text 69]

> ||| Computers [[reading DNA]] are sending more than 10,000 sequences an hour into a public data bank. ||| [Text 77]

[perfective:]

> ||| Still, since cost cuts totaled only $300 million in the first quarter, || there would seem to be plenty of pain [[to come this year]]. ||| [Text 26]

> ||| Examples of advances in atmospheric sciences include acid deposition programs, the stratospheric ozone programs [[to be discussed in this symposium]], and climate change programs. ||| [Text 32]

---

[17] Note that *relative that* must be distinguished from the binder *that*. The latter is used in 'fact' clauses, as in *Leaders of both a publically funded project and a competing private company issued statements Friday [[that they jointly would announce the status of their work on Monday]]*; these are discussed in Section 7.5.7.

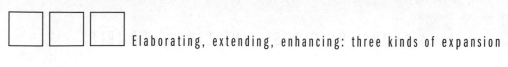

[neutral:]

||| He thought || it would be a long time before this magic [[called Real]] happened to him. ||| [Text 28]

||| Chalk is soft, white limestone [[formed by the accumulation of the shells of microscopic animals]]. ||| [Text 68]

With the non-finite clauses, note again the difference between imperfective and perfective, as in the following set:

[imperfective:]
(a) operative   the person taking pictures ('who is/was taking')

(b) receptive   the pictures taken by Mary ('which were/are taken') (according to the tense of the outer clause)

[perfective:]
(a) operative   (1) the (best) person to take pictures ('who ought to take') [relative = Subject]

                     (2) the (best) pictures to take ('which someone ought to take') [relative = Complement]

(b) receptive   the pictures to be taken ('which are/were to be taken')

Glosses in parenthesis suggest the nearest equivalent finite form. In non-finite elaborating clauses, the implicit relative is normally the Subject, but in perfective operative clauses it may be either the Subject (as in *the person to take pictures*) or the Complement (as in *the pictures to be taken*). Here we thus see two principles in operation, viz. (1) the Subject may be presupposed in a non-finite clause; (2) the Complement may be presupposed in a defining relative clause. The second principle also extends to Adjuncts, as in *the best time to take pictures* ('the best time at which to take pictures'); these are treated as enhancing – see under (iii) below.

Note that in examples such as *the first person who came in*, *the best person to do the job*, the embedded clause strictly has as its domain not the Head noun person but a premodifying element; the meaning is 'the first-who-came-in person', 'the best-to-do-the-job person'. Compare *a hard act to follow*, *the longest bridge ever built*. We can express this relationship structurally as in Figure 7-16. But as already pointed out (Chapter 6, Section 6.4.1) constituency is not a very appropriate concept for representing semantic domain, and for most purposes it suffices to show the clause simply as embedded in the nominal group: *a hard act [[to follow]]*. More such examples will be found under 'enhancing' below.[18]

Although a non-finite embedded clause with a preposition is generally circumstantial in meaning, and hence enhancing, there is one other type (in addition to the perfectives with *to*, already noted) that is elaborating; namely those with *of* where the relation is appositive, e.g. *the job of cleaning the barracks* where the job consists in cleaning the barracks. Some of these are uncertain, e.g. *the advantage of shopping early*, *the problem with asking directions* where *shopping early*, *asking directions* could be either elaborating (appositive) 'which consists in' or enhancing (circumstantial) 'which results from'.

---

[18] Note the distinction between *a better person to do that would be Mary*, where [[*to do that*]] is embedded on the Premodifier *better*, and *you'd have to be a better person to do that* where *to do that* is a hypotactic ×β clause of purpose 'in order to (be able to) do that' (i.e. 'only if you were a better person could you do that').

the	first		person	who came in
a	hard		act	to follow
Premodifier			Head	Postmodifier
	β		α	
	Sub-Head			Sub-Modifier
	βα			ββ

Fig. 7-16   Embedding on a Premodifier

In all the examples that have been discussed so far, the embedded clause functions as Postmodifier. It was pointed out in Chapter 6 that there are structures in which the Head is fused with the relative element in the embedded clause: this happens with *what*, meaning 'that which', and with *whoever, whatever, whichever* meaning 'anyone who, anything that/which', as in *what we want* 'the thing + that we want', *whoever gets there first* 'anyone/the one + who gets there first'.

> We have to recognize that the opportunity for doing such harm is monumental if the exercise is not conducted with very close attention to [[[**what** works already || and therefore does not need fixing or extra coordinating]]]. [Text 32]

> You find some humorous proverbs, for instance, and the humor is that [[**whoever** made these proverbs]] was not going around the world with his eyes closed. [Text 16]

> I have kind of an eclectic mind so I get interested in lots of different things, and I generally get very focused on [[**whatever** it is I'm interested in]]. [Text 17]

The effect of this fusion is that the embedded clause comes to function as Head, although it may be helpful to represent it separately in the analysis (Figure 7-17).

whoever		gets	there	first	wins	a prize
Actor					Process	Scope
'he	who'					
Head	= Postmodifier					
	Actor	Process	Place	Attribute		

Fig. 7-17   Elaborating embedded clause (finite) as Head

This analysis brings out the fact that such embedded clauses function as nominals rather than as clauses; so they take on the range of roles we find with nominals *that* (cf. *what = that which*), *s/he* (cf. *whoever = s/he who*), *the way* (cf. *how = the way in which*), and so on. This is reflected in forms like *the one who* (cf. Section 3.2 on thematic equatives, Chapter 3). For a further type of embedded clause functioning as Head see Section 7.4.6.

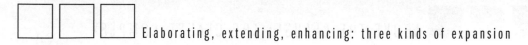

7.4.5.3 Embedding: extending

There are no embedded clauses corresponding to the paratactic and hypotactic categories of addition, replacement and alternation (*and, instead, except, or*).

The only sense of extension which produces embedded clauses is that of possession, introduced by *whose, of which/which ... of* or a 'contact' relative ending with *of*:

> 'Did I tell you the John Hurt story?' he asks, referring to the fellow British actor ⟦ + **whose** character was host to the embryonic alien ⟦that ravaged the crew of the spaceship Nostromo⟧ ⟧. [Text 73]

> In the case of other writers ⟦⟦ = who fail, ‖ + **whose** late work is a falling-off rather than a gathering-in,⟧⟧ it's a failure of connection. [Text 17]

> I recently read an incredibly well-written story about a couple ⟦ + **whose** thirty-something-year-old son dies of an illness⟧. [Text 21]

> In one of those cities – one ⟦ + **whose** name has long been forgotten⟧ – there lived an old halac uinic, or chief. [Text 65]

The category of possessive in the non-defining relative clause was referred to in Section 7.4.1.2; these are the equivalent in the 'defining' type. Note that here, as elsewhere in the grammar, possession is generalized possession; it includes not only concrete ownership but various kinds of concrete and abstract association.

7.4.5.4 Embedding: enhancing

Here the relation between the embedded clause and the Head noun is a circumstantial one of time, place, manner, cause or condition. There are two types, according to where this relationship is construed: (i) those where the circumstantial sense is located in the embedded clause itself; (ii) those where it is located in the noun functioning as Head. With both these types, the embedded clause may be either (a) a relative clause or (b) an enhancing clause. The different combinations are set out in Table 7.13 below, for both (1) finite and (2) non-finite clauses.

(i) Circumstantial feature in embedded clause

In this type it is the clause that expresses the temporal, causal or other enhancing relation (in the same way as in a dependent clause):

> the house ⟦ × (**which/that**) she lived **in** _ / **where** she lived ⟧

> I was invited to one ⟦ × **which** I spent the entire time **in** _ ⟧ [Text 82]

Such clauses are defining relative clauses, like the elaborating ones except that here the definition is circumstantial. Enhancing embedded clauses are either (1) finite or (2) non-finite.

There are two types, (a) embedded enhancing relative clauses and (b) embedded enhancing clauses.

(i.a) Embedded enhancing relative clauses. Here the embedded clause contains a relative that serves as a circumstance in the clause. The clause may be either (1) finite or (2) non-finite.

Table 7-13 Embedding involving circumstantial relations

	(i) Circumstantial feature in embedded clause serving as Postmodifier			(ii) Circumstantial feature in noun serving as Head	
	(a) relative clause		(b) enhancing clause	(a) relative clause	(b) enhancing clause
(1) finite	[i.a] the house [[(which) she lived **in**/**where** she lived]]		[i.b] the scar [[**where** the bullet entered]]	[ii.a] the **reason** [[(that) I like her]]; the **time** [[(that) we plant]]	[ii.b] the **reason** [[**why/for which** I like her]]; the **time** [[**when/at which** we plant]]
(2) non-finite	[i.a] the house [[being lived **in**]]	[i.a] a house [[**for** living **in**]];	[i.b] death [[**by** drowning]]	[ii.a] the **time** [[of planting]]	[ii.b] the **reason** [[**for** (me) liking her]]
		[i.a] a house [[**(for** you) to live **in**]]		[ii.a] the **reason** [[(for me) to like her]]; [ii.a] the **time** [[(for us) to plant]]	[ii.b] the **reason** [[**why/for which** to like her]]; the **time** [[**when/at which** to plant]]

(1) Finite. If the embedded clause is finite, the relative is a WH- prepositional phrase: that is, a prepositional phrase with WH- Complement (e.g. *in which*) or one of its variants *which ... in, that ... in, ... in*:

> (the Council were expected to make available) the funds [[× **without which** no new hospital services could be provided]]

> (you're) the one [[× I've always done the most **for**]]

> (she couldn't find) anyone [[× she could give the message **to**]]

> The Rabbit grew to like it, for the Boy made nice tunnels for him under the bedclothes that he said were like the burrows [[× the real rabbits lived **in**]]. [Text 28]

Sometimes *where* or *when* can be used in this 'defining relative' function, for example:[19]

> Some may precipitate directly from sea water in areas [[× **where** volcanism releases abundant silica]]. [Text 68]

> I mean, it was the laughing stock of the whole hospital and we got to the stage [[× **where** we'd really play on it]] because if we needed anything from the other side we'd sort of ring up ... [Text 69]

---

[19] Alternatively these could be interpreted as type (a) with *area, stage, history* as, by extension, nouns of place and time. But if they were it should be possible to use a *that* or a contact relative clause and say *in areas that volcanism releases abundant silica, the stage that we'd really play on it, in history that the options are finished*. The fact that these are not possible suggests that nouns like these are not (yet) nouns of the place, time class (contrast *the first occasion that professionals took part*).

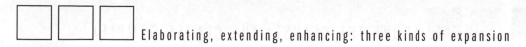

> We are at a juncture in history ⟦ × **when** the options are finished⟧. [Text 16]

Here *where* and *when* are relative adverbs serving as the Head of an adverbial group.

(2) Non-finite. The non-finite clause corresponds to the finite, having some variant of a WH- prepositional phrase as the relative; these may be ordinary imperfectives in *-ing*, e.g.

> the solution ⟦now being experimented with⟧

but perhaps the most typical are 'destiny' clauses with *to* or *for*, e.g.

> a cause ⟦× for which to fight/to fight for ⟧, a glass ⟦× for drinking out of ⟧, someone ⟦× to give the message to ⟧, nothing ⟦× to write home about ⟧
>
> New progressivism is a cause ⟦× to fight for ⟧
>
> When you have nothing ⟦× to write about ⟧, write about it. [Web column]
>
> He has never, himself, done anything ⟦× for which to be hated ⟧ [BROWN1_F]

Only the 'destiny' type allow an explicit Subject, with *for*:[20]

> Together they would create an artwork ⟦× **for** the community to celebrate⟧. [Text 16]
>
> Dr. M—— gave him antibiotic capsules ⟦ × **for** him to take⟧ ... [Text 34]

(i.b) Embedded enhancing clauses. Here the embedded clause is not a relative clause with a relative of enhancement; rather it is the same type of enhancing clause that occurs non-rankshifted in hypotactic nexuses. In general, the noun functioning as Head is the name of a process or property. There is (1) a finite variant and (2) a non-finite one.

(1) Finite. The finite variant is illustrated by examples such as *the applause* ⟦ × *when she finished singing*⟧, *the scar* ⟦ × *where the bullet entered*⟧, *the difference* ⟦ × *since I started taking Brandex*⟧. These are condensed variants of an embedded nexus consisting of an elaborating clause with an enhancing clause dependent on it:

> the applause ⟦ = which erupted ‖ × β when she finished singing ⟧
>
> the scar ⟦ = which has formed ‖ × β where the bullet entered ⟧

The items *when* and *where* are structural conjunctions rather than relative adverbs; they do not have the sense of preposition + *which*: we cannot say e.g. *the scar at which the bullet entered*. Contrast *Some may precipitate directly from sea water in areas* ⟦*where volcanism releases abundant silica*⟧. Here *where* is a relative adverb; and it is related to the prepositional phrase *in which*: ... *in areas in which volcanism releases abundant silica*.

---

[20] If the relative functions as means (instrument), where the usual preposition is *with*, there may in fact be no preposition, the sense of instrument being derived from the 'destiny' sense of the clause as a whole: e.g. *Alice had no more breath* ⟦× *for talking*⟧, i.e. 'for talking with', 'with which to talk'. Contrast the elaborating type *no more water* ⟦ = *for drinking*⟧, where there is no circumstantial sense (and therefore no preposition could occur).

(2) Non-finite. The non-finite variant corresponds to the dependent enhancing clauses with conjunctive preposition; e.g.

death ⟦ × by drowning⟧

a pain ⟦ × like having a red-hot needle stuck into you⟧

Blu-ray: death ⟦× **by** streaming⟧

The trouble ⟦× **with** predicting climate change⟧

Children need help ⟦× **in** learning to control their emotions⟧. [BROWN1_J]

In Seoul, there seems to be anger ⟦× **at** being taken for granted as an American satellite⟧: [KOHL_B]

Since the noun functioning as Head is generally the name of a process or property, these often have close hypotactic parallels, e.g. *he was angry* ‖ × β *at being accused; if you help me* ‖ × β *in cooking the dinner; it's difficult* ‖ × β *with everyone having a part.*

The non-finites could in fact be reworded in the same way as the finites; e.g. *the trouble with everyone having a part* as *the trouble* ⟦⟦ = *which arises* ‖ × β *with everyone having a part*⟧⟧. But there is no need to treat either kind as other than embedded enhancing clauses.

Like elaborating clauses, enhancing clauses of this type may have some premodifying element as their strict semantic domain, typically either Numerative or Epithet in a nominal group or an intensifying Premodifier in an adverbial group; these are clauses of comparison and result used in comparative constructions, e.g.

[comparison:]
I'm <u>as</u> certain of it ⟦ × **as if** his name were written all over his face ⟧

The actual formation of shale is <u>somewhat more</u> complex ⟦ × **than** indicated in Table 4-3⟧. [Text 68]

[result:]
Another survivor, soaked, wide-eyed with shock and <u>too</u> distressed ⟦ × to give his name⟧, said 'We were having a wonderful time when it turned into a nightmare.' [Text 30]

Within the vortex, temperatures become cold <u>enough</u> ⟦ × to form stratospheric ice crystals⟧. [Text 33]

Then he told us anecdotes of how he had gone across the Channel when it was <u>so</u> rough ⟦ × **that** the passengers had to be tied into their berths, and he and the captain were the only two living souls on board who were not ill⟧. [Text: Three Men in a Boat]

The embedded clauses relate respectively to *more, as; too much, such, not ... enough, so.* Again, however, there is no need to represent this relationship in terms of a different structure.

(ii) Circumstantial feature in noun serving as Head
There is a second type of embedded enhancing clause in which the circumstantial relation is construed not in the clause itself but in the Head noun to which the clause stands as Postmodifier. These nouns form a distinct class, with two subclasses: those that can take either finite or non-finite postmodifying clauses and those which can take only non-finite – see Table 7-14.

Table 7-14 Nouns of expansion

Type of expansion		Finite [[why, etc. for, etc. which / (that)]]	Non-finite [[of doing]]
time		*time, day, occasion*	
place		*place*	
manner		*way*	
cause	reason	*reason*	
	purpose		*purpose, point, aim*
	result		*result*

(1) Finite. The special characteristic of the finite clauses is that, since these nouns are inherently 'enhancing' in sense, the circumstantial relation may, or may not, be restated within the clause: we may have either *the day when/on which you came*, with *when, on* signalling time, or simply *the day (that) you came*, with no indication of the temporal relation other than the Head noun *day*. In other words, the finite clauses are either like those of type (i) above or like elaborating clauses – that is, typical 'defining relative' clauses, except that they cannot take *which* without a preposition (you cannot say *the day which you came*). Examples:

I don't see any particular <u>reason</u> [[× **why** I should]] [Text 8]

This was the first <u>occasion</u> [[× **that** I had to help in doing an experiment on a living man]]. [KOHL_M]

Fortunately I had that natural, built-in structure of the dates themselves; the book is faithful to the <u>time</u> [[× **in which** it took place]]. [Text 7]

That stands like a pillar in the course of their history, a <u>place</u> [[× **from which** they can take bearing]]. [Text 16]

The only other <u>place</u> [[× I would want to live]] (is New Zealand)

The people downstairs – there's no <u>way</u> [[× they could have got out]]. [Text 30]

That's the only <u>reason</u> [[× I quit with Far Tortuga]]. [Text 7]

We shared a place in Italy the <u>summer</u> [[× I was working on it]]. [Text 7]

All of these have four variants, two explicitly enhancing (e.g. *the reason why/for which I like her*) and two like elaborating (e.g. *the reason (that) I like her*).

An expression beginning *the time* ... may thus have three distinct functional values: (1) as hypotactic enhancing clause '(on the occasion) when ... ', e.g.

||| [×β:] the time we first met || [α:] he hardly spoke to me at all |||

(2) as nominal group with elaborating embedded clause 'the time which ... ', e.g.

||| the time [[= (which) I like best]] is the hour before dawn |||

(3) as nominal group with enhancing embedded clause 'the time when ... ', e.g.

||| the time ⟦ × (when/that) you should leave ⟧ is when the lights go out |||

A hypotactic enhancing clause introduced by *the time* is agnate with other hypotactic temporal clauses and, by a further step, with paratactic temporal clauses: *when we first met, he hardly ... ; we first met in June; then he hardly ...* . The expression *the time* has come to serve as a structural conjunction; and the item *time* can thus no longer be modified in the way the Head noun of a nominal group can be (an example such as *the early time we first met, he hardly spoke to me at all* is impossible).[21] In contrast, the nominal groups in (2) and (3) can be expanded, since they have the full potential of nominal groups: *the early time (which) I like best is the hour before dawn; the latest time (when/that) you should leave is when the lights go out*. As illustrated by the examples, such enhanced nominal groups typically serve as participants in 'relational' clauses.

(2) Non-finite. The non-finite clauses may occur with or without explicit Subject, e.g.

When the First Fleet arrived in Sydney, 'Rock Island', as it was then known, was a convenient <u>place</u> ⟦ × to punish recalcitrant convicts⟧, who were left in chains on the island for a week on bread and water. [Text 22]

There is no easy <u>way</u> ⟦⟦ × to assess ‖ how much books matter either to presidential performance or to public esteem⟧⟧, but to start the ball rolling, I experimented with a homemade litmus test. [Text 110]

They are sometimes astonishingly like people in their <u>way</u> ⟦⟦ × of thinking, ‖ talking ‖ and relating to each other⟧⟧. [Text 100]

I just don't see the <u>point</u> ⟦ ×of having three or four different lists of people⟧. [UTS/Macquarie Corpus]

That's the <u>reason</u> ⟦ × for keeping the sheets⟧. [UTS/Macquarie Corpus]

There is <u>reason</u> ⟦⟦ × to think ‖ that our embodied conceptual resources may not be adequate to all the tasks of science⟧⟧. [Text 237]

Since then I haven't missed an <u>occasion</u> ⟦⟦×to mix in a crowd ‖ or stand next to a policeman⟧⟧. [KOHL_K]

Soon the <u>time</u> came ⟦⟦ × for Kukul to take his place among the men of his nation⟧⟧. [Text 65]

Sometimes the enhancing relation is marked by an explicit binder, e.g. *why, where, when*; here the Subject has to be implicit:

Chinchilli day is a <u>reason</u> ⟦ **why** to go to Las Vegas⟧. [Blog entry]

Carrasco, a <u>place</u> ⟦⟦ × **where** to return from work ‖ and feel on holidays⟧⟧

There is the same difference between imperfective and perfective as with dependent clauses: other things being equal (that is, if occurring simply with their respective structure markers *of* and *to*), the imperfective is associated with the actual (e.g. *the time of planting*), the perfective with the potential, or virtual (e.g. *the time to plant*); sometimes the difference is minimal, as with *the best way of finding out/the best way to find out* – although even here it

---

[21] However, certain conjunctive features may be included in the nominal expression: *the first time we met/the last time we met/the only time we met, he hardly spoke to me at all.*

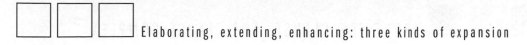
can still be recognized. But the specific semantic force of the Head noun, or the conjunction or conjunctive preposition, will always dominate; e.g. *the purpose of raising funds*, *the best occasion for trying out new methods*.

A typical context for a nominal group with embedded enhancing clause is as Value in an identifying clause; cf. Figure 7-18. In this example the Token is also an embedded enhancing clause, this time functioning as Head. Such clauses often display a similar variation; for example:

> Another reason is [[that the quantity of the literature is not overwhelming yet]]. [Text 16]

> Now the reason [[they hired me]] is [[[because they knew || I didn't know anything about food]]]. [Text 119]

Identifying clauses of this kind, with nouns of expansion as the Head of the nominal group realizing the Value, make an important contribution to the creation of discourse, making it possible to distribute information. Thus the textual impact of *the time to leave is when people start to yawn* is very different from that of *you leave when people yawn*: the former sets up the relationship as an exclusive identity, with the Value/Identified as Theme and the Identifier/Token as New (cf. the discussion of thematic equatives in Chapter 3, Section 3.2).

the	time	[[to leave]]	is	[[when	people	start to yawn]]
Identified/Value			Process	Identifier/Token		
nominal group				nominal group		
Premodifier	Head	Postmodifier		Head		
β	α			α		
		clause		clause		
		Process		Time	Behaver	Process

Fig. 7-18 Circumstantial identifying clause with embedded enhancing clauses

7.4.6 Acts

There is one further function of embedded clauses which is related to expansion in that, although there is no Head noun (so the embedded clause itself functions as 'Head'), the embedded clause is the nominalization of a process. For example, [[threatening people]] *will get you nowhere*.

Such a clause is the name of an action, event or other phenomenon involving a process as the nucleus. It represents a 'macro-phenomenon', as we put it in our discussion of what kinds of phenomenon can enter into a mental clause (Chapter 5, Section 5.3); let us call it an **act**. An 'act' clause may also occur as Postmodifier to a Head noun of the appropriate class, e.g. *the act* [[= of threatening people]]. Hence it is reasonable to treat these as elaborations. Other examples:

503

[relational: attributive]

||| 1 [[= Having a wrong view]] is of course deplorable || + 2 but [[[= α attacking other people || × β for having views]]] is more deplorable. |||

It was careless of him [[= to put another man's helmet on]]

It would be very easy [[[= for the artist to say, || 'I withdraw, you see, to my contemplation.']]] [Text 16]

It's easy [[[= to see how || the Ibo culture, << being a pantheistic culture, >> could incorporate Christianity]]]. But it's harder [[[= to understand || the Christians being able to live side by side with the traditional culture]]]. [Text 16]

Of what use was it [[[= to be loved || and become Real]]] if it all ended like this? [Text 28]

As with igneous rocks, it is more important [[= to interpret the formation of these rocks]] than merely to name them. [Text 68]

[relational: identifying]

[[= Restoring an attractive retirement program for all active duty members]] is therefore my top legislative priority in the FY 2000 Budget. [Text 115]

[[[= Knowing the origin of the materials that compose a sedimentary rock || and understanding the origin of its sedimentary features]]] will permit such interpretation. [Text 68]

[[Not being much of a reader]] hardly affected the ascent of George W. Bush or his father. [Text 110]

These examples show typical contexts for such nominalizations (see Table 7-15): relational clauses, especially attributive ones where the attribute is an evaluative term and identifying ones where they are related to a nominalization. There is one other common environment, namely that of clauses of perception, either mental (inert perception) or behavioural (active perception). Examples:

[behavioural + mental: perceptive]
We were watching [[= the catch being brought in]] and you could see [[[= the boats turn || × as they rounded the headland]]]

[behavioural: perceptive]
We went and watched [[= these kids try to produce 'Hair']]. [KING_Interviews]

But we watched [[= the town struggle with morality]] and we watched [[[= a man try to introduce the teaching of creation, || or sometimes they now call it creation science, alongside evolution]]]. [KING_Interviews]

[mental: perceptive]
Here you can see [[= beer being brewed 'on sight']], [Text 22]

Nakisha Johnson, 17, said she saw [[[= one young man open fire || after a feud between youths became violent]]]. [Text 20]

He had heard [[[= the captain on the radio being warned by a crew member from another boat || that there were big waves ahead || and he should turn back]]]. [Text 4]

I've heard [[[= you mention || that editors often see stories [[that are technically proficient and stylistically sophisticated, || yet lack a quality [[that makes them memorable]]]]]]]. [Text 21]

Here what is being perceived is again some action or event; the clause is typically imperfective, but sometimes perfective (without *to*) to highlight the end state as distinct from the process (cf. Kirsner & Thompson, 1976):

[imperfective:]

I saw the boats turning/(passive) being turned

[perfective:]

I saw the boats turn/(passive) turned

If the embedded clause is used as Postmodifier the Head noun is usually one of sight or sound: *I heard the noise of ...* , *I had a view of ...* , etc. (cf. *the smell of something burning*); e.g.

Just as he was withdrawing into the room to keep the mirror aside he heard the noise ⟦ = of a motorcycle approaching from the other side of the crossing ⟧. [KOHL_K]

In this case the clause is always imperfective.

We have now reached a point where we can relate these clauses to their close relatives that lie just beyond the bounds of expansion, on different frontiers.

(1) Process nominal groups: *we saw the turning of the boats*. Here the process has been nominalized at the word rank, with *turning* as noun; cf. *the departing/departure of the boats* (cf. Chapter 10, Section 10.3, on ideational metaphor). The structure is that of a nominal group having a prepositional phrase with *of* as Postmodifier; the Complement of the *of* phrase corresponds to what would be the Complement if the process was realized as a clause. Examples:

| The building [of [the bridge]] | presented a problem.

Devaluation is taken to be | a humiliation [akin to [the defacing [of [statues [of [national heroes]]]]]] |

Where there would be an explicit Subject, if the process was realized as a clause, what corresponds to this is the 'possessor' of the process serving as Deictic in the structure of the nominal group, as in *his handling of the situation, nobody's peeling of potatoes is as careful as mine,* or as Qualifier, marked by either *by* or *of,* as in *Letters to the press indicate a ground-swell of rejection of this display, by catholic and non-catholic members of church communities* [ACE_B] and *Yet another contributory factor is the disappearance of the horse from our farms* [LOB_F].[22]

(2) Projections: *we saw that the boats had been turned*. If I say *I can see the boats turning,* this is an event. A process 'the boats are turning' is being treated as a single complex phenomenon – a 'macrophenomenon' as we put it in Chapter 5, Section 5.3. If I say *I can see that the boats are turning,* this is a projection. The process 'the boats are turning' is being treated as the projection or idea of a phenomenon – a 'metaphenomenon', something not just bigger but of a different order of reality. So we can say *I can see that the boats have been*

---

[22] Since a possessor can also be realized as an *of* phrase, this leads to the well-known ambiguity of expressions such as *the visiting of relatives*: going to visit relatives, or having relatives come to visit? Cf. the note on non-finite enhancements in Section 7.4.3.2.

Table 7-15 Process type environments of 'act' clauses

PROCESS TYPE		Lexical items	Examples
material		Process: *change, destroy, affect*	Actor: [[worrying over what happened]] won't change anything
behavioural	perceptive	Process: *watch, listen to, feel, taste, smell*	she watched [Phenomenon:] [[the plane take/taking off]]
mental	perceptive	Process: *see, notice, glimpse, hear, overhear, feel, taste, smell*	she could see [Phenomenon:] [[the plane take/taking off]]
	cognitive	–	–
	desiderative	–	–
	emotive	–	–
verbal		–	–
relational	intensive & attributive	Attribute: [manner] *easy, hard, difficult, challenging*; *a piece of cake, a cinch*; [comment] *important*; *(of) what/no/little use* [[*(for x) to do*]]	[manner] it's easy [[(for him) to revise the manuscript]] ~ he can revise ... easily/ with difficulty [comment] it's important [[(for him) to revise the manuscript]] ~ [[that he should revise the manuscript]] is important
		Attribute: [comment] *thoughtful, considerate, kind, helpful, clever, wise, smart*; *careless, negligent, thoughtless, stupid, silly, foolish, deplorable (of x)* [[*to do*]]	it's thoughtless (of him) [[to neglect his family]] ~ thoughtlessly, he neglected his family
	intensive & identifying	Value: [manner] *challenge, difficulty, task*; nouns of expansion (Nouns of expansion)	[Value:] the challenge is [Token:] [[(for him) to revise the manuscript]]
	possessive	–	–
	circumstantial	–	–

turned but not *I can see the boats having been turned* – because you cannot see a past event. You can see the state of affairs resulting from that past event; but the past event itself can only be treated as a projection. In the present, both are possible; but the meaning is slightly different. If the 'seeing' is understanding, or what is seen is a report in writing, then again the relationship must be one of projection.

Metaphenomena – projections – can be associated only with certain types of process, essentially saying and sensing, plus in certain circumstances being; the details are given in Section 7.5 below. Macrophenomena – expansions – can enter into material processes. Thus you can say [[= *crushing him like that*]] broke his bones. But you cannot say *it broke his bones that you crushed him like that*, because finite *that* ('indirect') clauses can only be

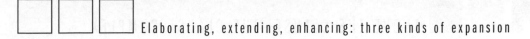

projections, not expansions. (You can on the other hand say *it broke his heart that you crushed him like that,* because heart-breaking, unlike bone-breaking, is a mental process.) Complication arises because the **names** of metaphenomena, nouns such as *belief* and *fact,* can sometimes enter into material processes where the metaphenomena by themselves cannot. For example, although we cannot say *it destroyed his life that the experiment had failed,* we can say *the knowledge that the experiment had failed destroyed his life* – not the idea as such, but his knowledge of it, was the destroyer. We may also note abstract material processes used metaphorically to construe mental phenomena:

> The passage of time, romantic travellers' tales – of which Marco Polo's supply the classic example – and wishful thinking, all combined **to build up** the late medieval belief ⟦ that Prester John was a mighty, if probably schismatical Christian priest-king ⟧. [LOB_J]

We might also say *the fact that the experiment had failed destroyed his life;* here fact stands for a state of affairs, rather than for a projected metaphenomenon as in its prototypical sense (cf. Section 7.5.7). In other words, although projections cannot participate in processes other than those of consciousness, the names of projections can, because they can be used to label events or states of affairs. Here we have reached the borderline between expansion and projection; the two come together under conditions of nominalization, where there is metaphor in the grammar and many of the semantic distinctions expressed in the clause tend to be neutralized (cf. Chapter 10 below).

The different environments in which expansion is manifested are summarized in Table 7-16.

Table 7-16 Paratactic, hypotactic and embedded expansions

	Taxis		Embedding	
	parataxis	**hypotaxis**		**Acts**
elaborating	John ran away; this surprised everyone. John didn't run wait; he ran away.	John ran away, which surprised everyone. John, who came to dinner last night, ran away.	the man ⟦ who came to dinner ⟧ (stayed for a month)	–
	–	John ran away, surprising everyone	the man ⟦ coming to dinner ⟧	I heard ⟦ the water lapping on the crag ⟧
extending	John ran away, and Fred stayed behind.	John ran away, whereas Fred stayed behind.	–	–
	–	John ran away, with Fred staying behind.	–	–
	–	–	the people ⟦ whose house we rent ⟧ (are returning)	–
	–	–	–	–

Table 7-16 Paratactic, hypotactic and embedded expansions (*contd*)

	Taxis		Embedding	
	parataxis	**hypotaxis**		**Acts**
enhancing	John was scared, so he ran away.	John ran away, because he was scared.	**(i) enhancing clause:** [1] the applause ⟦ when she finished singing ⟧	–
	–	John ran away, because of being scared.	death ⟦ by drowning ⟧	–
	–	–	[2] the house ⟦ where she lived ⟧	–
	–	–	nothing ⟦ to write home about ⟧	–
	–	–	**(ii) enhancing noun:** the reason ⟦ why I like her ⟧	–
	–	–	the purpose ⟦ of raising funds ⟧	

7.5 Reports, ideas and facts: three kinds of projection

In Section 7.2 we introduced the notion of projection, the logical-semantic relationship whereby a clause comes to function not as a direct representation of (non-linguistic) experience but as a representation of a (linguistic) representation. Here are some text examples:

||| When did you know || you were a writer? ||| – ||| I always knew. ||| I can't remember even considering doing anything else || after I was about fifteen or sixteen. ||| [Text 7]

||| Mum, do you know || where the scissors are? ||| I desperately, desperately need them. ||| – ||| What? ||| – ||| The scissors. ||| – ||| Yes, I hung the scissors up, in their usual spot. ||| [Text 76]

||| Yet somebody told me || that I mustn't repudiate my non-fiction, || because it's saying very much || what the fiction is saying. ||| [Text 7]

||| You've done it again, || I told you || not to bloody do it, you bloody wog. ||| [Text 10]

||| If policymakers believe || that we should protect ozone over Antarctica, || then it is quite clear that the Montreal Protocol will have to be revised || and the measures made much more stringent. ||| [Text 33]

||| Nakisha Johnson, 17, said || she saw ⟦one young man open fire || after a feud between youths became violent⟧. ||| [Text 20]

||| 'We really have to have mandatory child safety trigger locks, and photo license IDs for the purchase of new handguns,' || Gore told the crowd. ||| [Text 20]

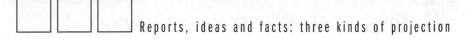
These examples illustrate some of the common discourse uses of projection – to attribute to sources in news reporting, to represent views in scientific discourse, to construct dialogue in narrative (as in 7-2), to frame questions in conversation.

The examples also illustrate that there are different kinds of projection. There are in fact three systems involved in the differentiation of different kinds of projection: (i) the level of projection (idea vs. locution), (ii) the mode of projection (hypotactic reporting vs. paratactic quoting), and (iii) the speech function (projected proposition vs. projected proposal).

(i) Level of projection. Through projection, one clause is set up as the representation of the linguistic 'content' of another – either the content of a 'verbal' clause of saying or the content of a 'mental' clause of sensing. For example, *that we should protect ozone over Antarctica* is the content of the 'mental' clause *policymakers believe*; and *she saw one young man open fire after a feud between youths became violent* is the content of the 'verbal' clause *Nakisha Johnson, 17, said*. There are thus two kinds of projection. On the one hand, the projection may be a representation of the content of a 'mental' clause – what is thought; we call such projections **ideas**. On the other hand, the projection may be a representation of the content of a 'verbal' clause – what is said; we call such projections **locutions**. Projection may thus involve either of the two levels of the content plane of language – projection of meaning (ideas) or projection of wording (locutions). This distinction made by the grammar is reflected in the conventions of cartoons: ideas are represented in 'clouds', whereas locutions are represented in 'balloons' (cf. Figure 7-5).

(ii) Mode of projection. It was pointed out in Section 7.2 that projection combines with the same set of interdependencies that have been shown to occur with expansion – (1) the two tactic interdependency relations of parataxis and hypotaxis and (2) the constituency relation of embedding. For instance, *'We really have to have mandatory child safety trigger locks, and photo license IDs for the purchase of new handguns,'* is projected paratactically by *Gore told the crowd*. This means that the projection is represented as a **quote.** In contrast, *she saw one young man open fire after a feud between youths became violent* is projected hypotactically by *Nakisha Johnson, 17, said*. This means that the projection is represented as a **report** – as something that is dependent on the projecting clause and thus cannot serve on its own. We can see the contrast clearly if we consider the paratactic variant of the hypotactic projection: *'I saw one young man open fire ...'*. The distinction between these two modes of projection was recognized in traditional accounts as the contrast between direct and indirect speech; but as we have already noted, we need to take account of direct and indirect thought as well. In addition to the two tactic modes of projection – paratactic projection of quotes and hypotactic projection of reports, there is one further environment in which projected clauses occur – that of embedding: *the witness's claim that she saw one young man open fire seems plausible*.

Level of projection and mode of projection intersect to define four kinds of projection nexus (we set aside embedding until we return to it in Section 7.5.6): see Table 7-17 (the counts of occurrences in a sample of texts will be discussed below).

509

Table 7-17 Four kinds of projection nexus

	Paratactic ("direct, quoted") 1 2	Hypotactic ("indirect, reported") α β
idea ' mental	1 '2 Brutus thought, 'Caesar is ambitious' [Section 7.5.3]	α 'β Brutus thought that Caesar was ambitious [Section 7.5.2]
	(15 occurrences [2.5%])	(580 occurrences [97.5%])
locution " verbal	1 "2 Brutus said, "Caesar is ambitious" [Section 7.5.1]	α "β Brutus said that Caesar was ambitious [Section 7.5.3]
	(368 occurrences [46.2%])	(429 occurrences [53.8%])

As already shown in the graph in Figure 7-8 above, all combinations of taxis and mode of projection are not equally probable; while some are very frequent in text, others are relatively rare. As the numbers in Table 7-17 indicate, out of 1,392 instances of projection nexuses in a sample of texts from a range of spoken and written registers, there were only 15 instances of paratactically projected ideas; in other words, 97.5% of all 595 projected ideas in the sample were reported rather than quoted (for an explanation of this skew, see the end of Section 7.5.2). In contrast, projected locutions were more evenly balanced between quoting and reporting in the total sample – around 46% and 54%, respectively. The sample contains more projection nexuses from spoken texts (845) and from written texts (557); but it is still interesting to note that in spoken discourse paratactic locution (quoting: 53%) is favoured over hypotactic locution (reporting: 47%)[23], whereas in written discourse it is the other way around: paratactic locution (quoting: 39%) is significantly less common than hypotactic locution (reporting: 61%). We can now turn to the third system mentioned above.

(iii) The speech function of the projection. The projections in Table 7-17 are all propositions; more specifically, they are all statements. But speech functions other than statements can also be projected. For example, *where the scissors are* in *Mum, do you know where the scissors are?* is a projected proposition of the question type; and *not to bloody do it* in *I told you not to bloody do it* is a projected proposal. Both these examples are instances of hypotactic nexuses. But we find the same speech functional range in the paratactic mode of projection. In fact, paratactic projection allows for a greater range: we can quote not only propositions and proposals but also minor speech functions such as greetings and exclamations (e.g. *they said 'Goodbye, Mr Chips'*). This is part of the general principle whereby reporting reduces the potential for projecting dialogic features. For example, while Vocative elements can be quoted, as in *Gable said 'Frankly, my dear, I don't give a damn'*, they cannot be reported (cf. *Gable said that frankly he didn't give a damn* without the Vocative element; we cannot say *Gable said that frankly, my/his dear, he didn't give a damn*).

---

[23] In spoken casual conversation, this difference is even more marked: quoting accounts for two thirds (65%) and reporting for one third (35%). In written news reports, the ratio is almost the reverse.

Adding this third systemic variable to our account, we can now expand Table 7-17: see Table 7-18. This is represented systemically in Figure 7-19 below. The fact that minor clauses cannot be reported is represented by means of a conditioning relationship: 'if minor, then quoting'. The interaction between taxis and type of projection will be explored in Section 7.5.5. We shall now discuss the different kinds of projection nexus in more detail, as indicated by the section references in the tables. We start with paratactic projection of locutions.

Table 7-18 Projection of propositions and proposals

Type of projecting process	projected speech function	Quote paratactic 1 2	Report hypotactic α β
idea ' mental	major: proposition	1 '2 She thought, 'I can' [Section 7.5.3]	α 'β She thought she could [Section 7.5.2]
	major: proposal	He willed her 'Do' [Section 7.5.4]	He wanted her to do [Section 7.5.4]
locution " verbal	major: proposition	1 "2 She said, "I can" [Section 7.5.1]	α "β She said she could [Section 7.5.3]
	major: proposal	He told her "Do" [Section 7.5.4]	He told her to do [Section 7.5.4]
	minor	1 "2 She said, "Wow!"	–

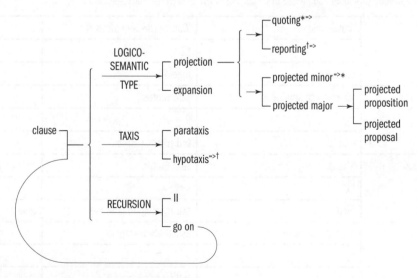

Fig. 7-19　System network of projection

7.5.1 Quoting ('direct speech'): verbal process, parataxis

The simplest form of projection is 'direct' (quoted) speech, as in

||| I <u>said</u> || 'I'm getting old; || I'm going to have to sit down in the shade,' || and she <u>said</u>, || 'Thank God, at least we can do it.'. ||| [Text 24]

||| 'What is REAL?' || the Rabbit asked the Skin Horse one day. ||| [Text 28]

The projecting clause is a verbal process clause, one of saying, and the projected clause represents that which is said. There are innumerable uses of this quoting kind of nexus – eyewitness material in the news, dialogic passages in narrative, scenes in biography, quotes in scientific writing.

In a quoting nexus the 'tactic' relationship, the type of dependency, is parataxis; the two parts have equal status. The projected clause retains all the interactive features of the clause as exchange, including the full mood potential (with the option of mood tagging in 'declarative' and 'interrogative' clauses), vocatives and expletives, tone selections, and (textual) continuatives. In written English, the projection is signalled by quotation marks ('inverted commas'; for the significance of double and single quotation marks see below). In spoken English, the projecting clause is phonologically less prominent than the projected: if it comes first, it is often proclitic (non-salient and prerhythmic: see Chapter 1, Section 1.2), while if it follows all or part of the projected, instead of occupying a separate tone group, it appears as a 'tail', a post-tonic appendage that continues the pitch movement of the preceding projected material; examples are given in Table 7-19. Typically, in (a) *Brutus said* will be proclitic; in (b), *said Brutus* will fall, continuing the falling tone (tone 1) on *ambitious*; in (c) it will rise, continuing the falling-rising tone (tone 4) on *Caesar*; in (d) *asked Mark Anthony* will rise, continuing the rise (tone 2) or fall-rise (tone 2) on *ambitious*.

Table 7-19 Paratactic projection: sequence of clauses in nexus and typical tone selections

(a)	1 ^ "2	Brutus said:	'Caesar was ambitious'	
		1	"2	
		proclitic	tone 1	
(b)	"1 ^ 2	'Caesar was ambitious'	said Brutus	
		"1	2	
		tone 1	**tail** (continued fall)	
(c)	"1 <<2>>	'Caesar'	said Brutus	'was ambitious'
		"1	<<2>>	
		tone 4	**tail** (continued fall-rise)	tone 1
(d)	"1 ^ 2	'Was Caesar ambitious?'	asked Mark Anthony	
		"1	2	
		tone 2 (2)	**tail** (continued rise)	

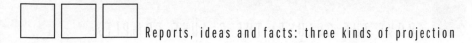

The reason for this is that the main function of the projecting clause is simply to show that the other one is projected: someone said it. There is nothing in the wording of a paratactic projected clause to show that it is projected; it could occur alone, as a direct observation. In written English it is signalled prosodically, by punctuation; and if the quoted matter extends to a new paragraph the quotation marks are usually repeated, as a reminder:

> 'Across the USA, thousands are victims of human rights violations,' said Mr Pierre Sane, Amnesty's international secretary-general. 'Too often, human rights in the US are a tale of two nations – rich and poor, white and black, male and female.' [Text 2]

The parallel to this, in spoken English, is the repetition of the projecting clause, as in the following example:

> My brother, he used to show dogs, and he said to me, he said, 'Look,' he said, 'I really think you've got something here,' he said. 'Why don't you take it to a show?' And I said 'Oh, yea. Right-oh.'

Without this kind of repetition, the fact that a passage of discourse is projected may easily be lost sight of.[24] In written English typically only the first clause complex will be explicitly accompanied by a projecting clause. Note that the analysis accurately reflects the paratactic pattern, showing projection where it occurs in the structure but not where it is simply presumed by cohesion; cf. the following example:

Text 7-6: Recreating – narrating (written, dialogic): extract from a story for children with dramatic dialogue

||| Thomas could just see out of the hole, ||		but he couldn't move. |||
1		×2

||| "Oh dear," ||	<< he said, >>	"I'm a silly engine."
"1	<< 2 >>	

||| "And a very naughty one too,"	|| said a voice behind him.	||| "I saw you." |||
"1	2	1

||| "Please get me out; ||		I won't be naughty again." |||
1		+2

||| "I'm not so sure," ||	replied the Fat Controller. |||	"We can't lift you out with a crane, ||	the ground's not firm enough." |||
"1	2	1	×2

Since the amount and type of explicit projection is a significant discourse variable it is important to show exactly where and in what form it occurs.

---

24 Some speakers introduce a special voice quality into their quoted speech, which could in principle serve as an ongoing prosodic marker and obviate the need for repeating the 'saying' clause – although the acoustic effect probably depends mainly on the initial change of tambre, and if so it will tend to diminish as the quoted speech continues.

What is the nature of the projected clause? The projected clause here stands for a 'wording': that is, the phenomenon it represents is a lexicogrammatical one. Take for example *'I'm not so sure,' replied the Fat Controller*. While the projecting clause *replied the Fat Controller* represents an ordinary phenomenon of experience, the projected clause *I'm not so sure* represents a second-order phenomenon, something that is itself a representation. We will refer to this as a 'metaphenomenon'. If we want to argue, the issue is not 'is he, or is he not, so sure?' – that is a separate question;[25] it is 'did he, or did he not, say these words?' The total structure, therefore, is that of a paratactic clause complex in which the logical-semantic relationship is one of projection; the projecting clause is a verbal process, and the projected clause has the status of a wording.

Verbs used in quoting 'verbal' clauses include those listed in the 'proposition' column in Table 7-20.

Table 7-20 Verbs serving as Process in 'verbal' clauses used to quote

	Proposition	Proposal
(1) general member	*say*[26]	*say*
(2) verbs specific to speech function: (a) giving	(a) statements: *tell* (+ Receiver), *remark, observe, point out, report, announce*	(a) offers: *suggest, offer; threaten* ('offer: undesirable'), *vow* ('offer: sacred'), *promise* ('offer: desirable'), *agree* ('offer: in response')
(b) demanding	(b) questions: *ask, demand, inquire, query*	(b) commands: *call, order, request, tell, propose, decide; urge* ('command: persuasive'), *plead* ('command: desperate'), *warn* ('command: undesirable consequences')
(3) verbs with additional circumstantial feature: (a)	*reply* ('say in response'), *explain* ('say in explanation'), *protest* ('say with reservation'), *continue* ('go on saying'), *add* ('say in addition'), *interrupt* ('say out of turn'), *warn* ('say: undesirable consequences')	[see (2) above]
(b) manner specifying connotation	*insist* ('say emphatically'), *complain* ('say irritably'), *cry, shout* ('say loudly'), *boast* ('say proudly'), *murmur* ('say sotto voce'), *stammer* ('say with embarrassment'), *enthuse* ('say with approval'), *gush* ('say effusiveness'), *rave* ('say with enthusiasm')	[largely the same as for propositions] *blare, thunder* ('order imperiously'), *moan* ('plead whiningly'), *yell* ('order vociferously'), *fuss* ('order officiously')

---

[25] In order to argue this we should have to turn it into a first-order phenomenon: *and is he?*

[26] In addition, we find the verb *go* used in quoting clauses. This verb is also used to project representations of non-linguistic semiosis, as in *the tires went* [sound of screeching]. A more recent addition to quoting verbs in casual speech is *be like*; for example: *I was like 'Are you in the right show?'; 'My friends were like, "Eddie, you're drinking too much, you're out too much, you've got to, like, slow down." And that was true,' he said...*

A very wide range of different verbs can be pressed into service under this last heading, verbs which are not verbs of saying at all but serve in 'behavioural' clauses (see Chapter 5, Section 5.5.1), especially in fictional narrative, to suggest attitudes, emotions or expressive gestures that accompanied the act of speaking, for example *sob, snort, twinkle, beam, venture, breathe*; e.g.

> 'It is a great thing, discretion,' mused Poirot.

Here the implication is that Poirot is trying to give the impression of thinking aloud, while making sure the listener 'overhears'.

Verbs used in clauses quoting proposals – offers and commands – are also listed above and will be discussed in Section 7.5.4.1.

7.5.2 Reporting ('indirect speech'): mental process, hypotaxis

Talking is not the only way of using language; we also use language to think. Hence a process of thinking in a 'mental' clause also serves to project; the process is typically of the 'like' type, but the 'please' type is also possible (see Section 5.3.2, for this distinction):

(a) 'like' type

   ||| So you **believe** || that the short story is better at dealing with real-life, human emotions. ||| [Text 21]

   ||| Mum, **do** you **know** || where the scissors are? ||| I desperately, desperately need them. ||| – What? ||| – The scissors. ||| – Yes, I hung the scissors up, in their usual spot. ||| [Text 76]

   ||| Naval authorities **believe** || the boat may have capsized || because it was carrying a heavy load of construction materials in choppy waters. ||| [Text 5]

   ||| Therefore, I **believe** || that the protocol will do absolutely nothing [[to protect the antarctic region]]. ||| [Text 33]

(b) 'please' type

   ||| It **strikes** me || that Eve's disloyalty and ingratitude must be contagious! ||| [Blade Runner]

   ||| When I attended at Bombay's C.J. Hall the Kal Ke Kalakar festival, || it **struck** me || that, although we did not have the resources, || this particular festival had the potential of an Avignam Nervi or Spoletto. ||| [KOHL_G]

   ||| It **did not occur** to him || that I might want to stay on and watch the cricket. ||| [LOB_P]

   ||| Then it **dawned on** me || that I was talking to a cricketer [[who had so recently been crucified at the altar of expediency]]. ||| [KOHL_G]

The uses of this kind of projecting nexus include (i) the representation of the speaker's thinking in dialogue (often as a way of assessing what is projected, where the projecting clause comes to stand for a modality of probability; see Section 10.3); (ii) the representation of the addressee's thinking in dialogue, often as a way of probing for information; (iii) the representation of a character's consciousness in narrative; (iv) the representation of institutional or expert opinions and beliefs in news reporting and scientific discourse; (v) the representation of the speaker's angle in scientific discourse, often as the result of a chain of reasoning.

As with nexuses projecting locutions, nexuses projecting ideas consist of a phenomenon – the projecting clause – and a metaphenomenon – the 'content' of the projecting clause; for example, in *some experts believe that people someday will have their unique genetic code on smart cards* ... , the phenomenon is *some experts believe* and the metaphenomenon is *that people someday will have their unique genetic code on smart cards* ... . The difference between this and the examples given in Section 7.5.1 above is that here (i) the projecting clause is a 'mental' process clause, more specifically one of cognition, rather than a 'verbal' one; and (ii) the projected clause represents a meaning rather than a wording – that is, an idea rather than a locution.

(i) Examples of verbs serving as Process in 'mental' clauses projecting ideas are set out in Table 7-21. The verbs are largely restricted to two of the four types of sensing identified in Chapter 5, Section 5.3 – cognition and desideration (but usually not perception and never emotion). So far we have concentrated on clauses of the 'cognitive' type; these always project propositions. Here a proposition is, as it were, created cognitively; it is brought into existence by a process of thinking. (We shall turn to the projection of proposals by 'desiderative' clauses in Section 7.5.4 below and we shall explain the place of 'emotive' clauses within the full paradigm of projection in Section 7.5.7. 'Perceptive' clauses were discussed in Section 7.4.6.)

The projected idea clause is either an indirect statement or an indirect question; as the table indicates, different sets of verbs are associated with these two types. In the environment of 'mental' projection, the contrast between statement and question is not concerned with the speech functional orientation of giving vs. demanding information but rather with the status of the validity of the information. In a statement, it is fixed with respect to the polarity and the elements of transitivity (realized by an indirect declarative clause optionally introduced by *that*), but in a question, it is open with respect to the polarity (realized by an indirect yes/no interrogative clause introduced by *whether* or *if*) or one (or more) of the elements of transitivity (realized by an indirect wh- interrogative clause introduced by *who, which, when, where, etc.*). Consequently, mental clauses representing an 'undecided' state of mind are used to project indirect questions. These include clauses of wondering and doubting, finding out and checking, and contemplating, which tend to be characterized by special lexical verbs such as *wonder, ascertain*; for example:

||| Israeli Prime Minister Ehud Barak said Tuesday || he **doubted** || President Clinton could broker an Israeli-Palestinian peace deal before the end his presidential term on Jan. 20. ||| [Reuters, 02/01/01]

||| I'll ask Jenny about laptops || and **find out** || whether we have got any. ||| [UTS/Macquarie Corpus]

||| She had not been in || when he had phoned || **to check** || whether they were going out for dinner that night. ||| [KOHL_L]

||| It should be noted || that the first step taken by the underwriter or agent is [[to examine the policy || **to ascertain** || whether the loss is recoverable thereunder]]. ||| [KOHL_E]

||| He **investigated** || whether his feeling [[that the veena produced the most exquisite musical sound]] was a subjective reaction || or has a sound physical basis. ||| [KOHL_G]

||| Let us now **consider** || whether the arrangement of the stanzas in the particular order bears out any such meaning [[as we have got from it]]. ||| [KOHL_G]

But they also include clauses where the uncertainty is represented grammatically in the projecting clause by a feature of negative polarity or interrogative mood, or by projection or expansion within the verbal group serving as Process, or by perfective aspect in a purpose clause; for example:

||| I **do not know** || whether you have seen it. ||| [KOHL_R]

||| It **is not known** || whether the mystics could give objective certainty to their experiences. ||| [KOHL_J]

||| Who **knows** || whether his debt was true or false? ||| [KOHL_K]

||| So I **want to know** || whether this devious and hypocritical me could have been whole and innocent at least as a boy. ||| [KOHL-K]

Table 7-21 Verbs serving as Process in 'mental' clauses reporting ideas

		Proposition		Proposal
		statement [indirect declarative clause: *(that)* ...]	question [indirect interrogative clause: *whether/if; who, which, when ...*	[perfective non-finite clause, or modulated indirect declarative clause]
perceptive				–
cognitive	'like' type	*believe, guess, think, know, imagine, doubt., remember, forget, dream, predict*	*wonder, doubt; consider; find out, ascertain, check; determine, judge; predict* [interrogative/negative clause:] *know, remember* [= the answer to the question] *know*	–
		e.g. *she knew* || *that he'd left*	e.g. *she wondered (didn't know)* || *whether he'd left*	
	'please' type	*strike, occur to, dawn on*		
		e.g. *it struck her that he'd left*		
desiderative	'like' type	–	–	*want, would like, wish, intend, plan for, hope for*
				e.g. *she wanted* || *him to leave (that he should leave)*
emotive		–	–	–

(ii) Something that is projected as a meaning is still a phenomenon of language – it is what was referred to above as a 'metaphenomenon'; but it is presented at a different level – semantic, not lexicogrammatical. When something is projected as a meaning it has already

517

been 'processed' by the linguistic system – it is a phenomenon of experience that has been construed as a meaning; but processed only once, not twice as in the case of a wording, where a phenomenon of experience is construed first as a meaning and then in turn as a wording. So, for example, the phenomenon of water falling out of the sky may be construed as a meaning, by a mental process of cognition, in *(she thought) it was raining*; but when the same phenomenon is represented by a verbal process, as in *(she said:) 'it's raining'*, it is the **meaning** 'it is raining' that has been reconstrued to become a wording. A wording is, as it were, twice cooked. This is symbolized in an interesting way by the punctuation system of English, which uses both single and double quotation marks; in principle, single quotation marks stand for a meaning and double quotation marks stand for a wording.[27] We are unconsciously aware that when something has the status of a wording it lies not at one but at two removes from experience; it has undergone two steps in the realization process. This symbolism has been adopted in our present notation, in which ' stands for a projected meaning and " for a projected wording:

Some experts believe	that people someday will have their unique genetic code on smart cards ...
α	'β

We have described the process 'from above', from the point of view of how experience is first construed as meaning ('semanticized') and then as wording ('grammaticalized'). But looked at 'from below', a wording is closer to expression than a meaning is; and this seems to be reflected in the conventions of cartoons: ideas are represented as 'clouds', but locutions more concretely as balloons (cf. Figure 7-5).

When something is projected as a meaning, we are not representing 'the very words', because there are no words. If we want to argue about whether or not the experts held this opinion, we have no observed event as a point of reference. Hence, in combination with the tactic system, the basic pattern for projecting meanings is not parataxis, which treats the projection as a free-standing event, but hypotaxis, which makes it dependent on the mental process clause. In other words, the typical pattern for representing a 'thinking' is the hypotactic one: we noted above that in a sample of texts containing 592 nexuses of projected ideas, 97.5% were hypotactic but only 2.5% paratactic (see Table 7-17 and Figure 7-8 above).

As pointed out earlier, the hypotactic relationship implies a different perspective. If we contrast the following pair of examples:

(a) Mary said: 'I will come back here to-morrow'.

(b) Mary thought she would go back there the next day.

then in (a) the standpoint in the projected clause is that of the Sayer, Mary; she is the point of reference for the deixis, which thus preserves the form of the lexicogrammatical event, using *I*, *here*, *come*, *tomorrow*. In (b) on the other hand the standpoint in the projected clause is simply that of the speaker of the projecting one; so Mary is 'she', Mary's present location is 'there', a move towards that location is 'going', and the day referred to as that

---

[27] Regrettably, publishers often do not allow authors to follow this principle in their works.

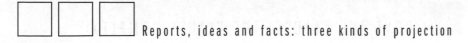

immediately following the saying is not the speaker's tomorrow but simply 'the next day'. Furthermore, since the saying clause has past time the projected clause carries over the feature of temporal remoteness: hence *would* (future in past – the past defined by *thought*), not *will* (simple future). Hypotactic projection preserves the deictic orientation of the projecting clause, which is that of the speaker; whereas in paratactic projection the deixis shifts and takes on the orientation of the Sayer. And while paratactic projection can represent any dialogic features of what was said, hypotactic projection cannot; for example, vocative elements and minor speech functions can be quoted but not reported (cf. the discussion of Table 7-18).

7.5.3 Reporting speech, quoting thought

Returning now to Table 7-17, we can see that we have discussed two of the four basic kinds of projection nexus. These two represent the basic pattern of projection – quoting speech and reporting thought; they are represented diagrammatically in Figure 7-21. But, by the familiar semogenic process of recombination of associated variables (more simply known as filling up the holes; see Halliday, 1992d), other forms have come to exist alongside – reporting speech and quoting thought. We discuss these in turn.

7.5.3.1 Reporting speech

It is possible to 'report' a saying by representing it as a meaning. This is the 'reported speech', or 'indirect speech', of traditional Western grammars; for example, *the noble Brutus hath told you Caesar was ambitious* (Figure 7-20).

In this instance, Brutus had, indeed, said those very words:

> **Text 7-7: Recreating – dramatizing (written, dialogic): extract from Shakespeare's Julius Caesar**
>
> Brutus: As Caesar loved me, I weep for him; as he was fortunate, I rejoice at it; as he was valiant, I honour him: but, as he was ambitious, I slew him.
>
> Mark Antony: The noble Brutus Hath told you Caesar was ambitious. If it were so, it was a grievous fault.

But the principle behind this hypotactic representation of a verbal event is that it is not, in fact, being presented as true to the wording; the speaker is reporting the gist of what was said, and the wording may be quite different from the original, as in the following (where A is a shopkeeper, B an elderly, hard-of-hearing customer and C is her grandson):

Brutus	hath	told	you	Caesar	was	ambitious
α				"β		
Mood		Residue		Mood		Residue
Subject	Finite	Predicator	Complement	Subject	Finite	Complement
Sayer	Process: verbal		Receiver	Carrier	Process	Attribute

Fig. 7-20 Reported speech

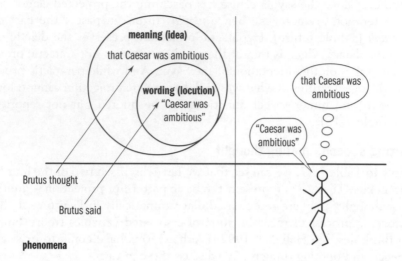

Fig. 7-21 The two basic patterns of projection – quoting speech and reporting thought

Text 7-8: Doing – collaborating: transacting (spoken, dialogic): service encounter

A. It doesn't work; it's broken. You'll have to get it repaired.

B. What does he say?

C. He says it needs mending.

This is not to suggest, of course, that when a speaker uses the paratactic, 'direct' form he is always repeating the exact words; far from it. But the idealized function of the paratactic structure is to represent the wording; whereas with hypotaxis the idealized function is to represent the sense, or gist. Here are some text examples of reported speech, distinguished according to the reported mood:

[indirect declarative:]

||| Coming back to Clinton and Blair || – I **would** certainly **say** || that I regard them as criminals. ||| [Text 381]

||| Now, in an article in the September 13th issue of the journal Nature, the researchers **report** || that they have identified several proteins [[that help Ephs and ephrins control the cytoskeleton]]. ||| [Text 398]

||| From this he **argued** || that all combustible substances must contain a common principle, || and this principle he named phlogiston. ||| [Text 259]

||| This theory **states** || that these intellectual differences are innate among the different races. ||| [Text 123]

||| Then, in August, it **was rumoured** || that the couple were on the rocks || because Ben hadn't been to visit Julia on the set of The Mexican, || which she was filming in Mexico with Brad Pitt. ||| [Text 206]

[indirect interrogative, yes/no:]

||| In India, for quite some time, we **debated** || whether the Court should have the power to review a constitutional amendment. ||| [KOHL_J]

520

||| But **will** you first **tell** me || whether you remember Meera or not? ||| [KOHL_P]

||| Of course, as Patel, who had already left Wardha, was **not** my informant, I am **not** in a position **to say** || whether the editor of the Hindu or my informant had received the correct report. ||| [KOHL_F]

||| It **is** often **asked** || whether acute pulmonary embolism can be prevented and, furthermore, whether it is worth preventing since the mortality due to this complication is extremely low and all prophylactic measures require supervision, extra work, organization, and vigilance. ||| [KOHL_J]

[indirect interrogative, wh-:]

||| I**'ve** always **been asked** || what the highlights of my fourteen years in Paris were. ||| [Text 119]

||| Well, which **would** you **say** || was his majorest? ||| [Text 125]

||| You **can't explain** || why you become a writer, actually, in one word. || But you can certainly show strands of the story, || and that certainly was one. ||| [Text 16]

||| These indicators **show** us || where we've been || and will help us project future readiness trends [[based on current funding and OPTEMPO]] . ||| [Text 115]

||| I **was** just **telling** her || how I was coming up this way this weekend. ||| [Text 82]

While minor clauses can be quoted, they cannot be reported; that is, the quoting clause nexus *He said 'Ah!'* has no reporting agnate. Similarly, while non-linguistic sounds can be quoted (often with *go* as the Process, as in *she went* (sound of a sigh)), they cannot be reported.

Verbs used in reporting statements and questions are often the same as those used in quoting (see Table 7-23; projection of proposals will be discussed below); but there is one significant difference. In quoting, the independent status of the proposition, including its mood, is preserved; hence the speech function is as explicit as in the 'original'. In reporting, on the other hand, the speech function is, or may be, obscured, and is therefore made explicit in the reporting verb. Three things follow. (1) In quoting, the word *say* can project sayings of every mood, whereas in reporting we find *say*, *ask* and *tell*: see examples in Table 7-22.

Table 7-22 Quoting and reporting across mood types

MOOD	Quoting	Reporting
declarative	Henry said, 'Mary's here'.	Henry said that Mary was there.
interrogative: yes/no	Henry said, 'Is Mary here?'	Henry asked whether Mary was there.
interrogative: wh-	Henry said, 'Who's here?'	Henry asked who was there.
imperative	Henry said, 'Stay here!'	Henry told [Fred] to stay there.
minor	Henry said, 'Ouch!'	–

Note also the reporting form *Henry told Janet who was there* 'answered Janet's question "who's here?" ', to which there is no quoting equivalent. (2) Many semantically complex verbs for elaborated speech functions are used only in reporting, e.g. *insinuate, imply, remind, hypothesize, deny, make out, claim, maintain*. These verbs are seldom used to quote; there is too much experiential distance between them and the actual speech event. (3) On the other hand, many verbs that assign interpersonal and/or behavioural features to the speech event, and are used to quote especially in narrative contexts, are never used to report because they do not contain the feature 'say'. Thus we are unlikely to find, corresponding to the example at the end of the previous subsection, *Poirot mused that discretion was a great thing*, and even more unlikely to find examples involving behavioural processes that are closer to the physiological end of the behavioural end of the spectrum.[28]

In addition to the verbs listed in Table 7-23, we also find a pattern with verb: *express* + a noun of sensing such as *belief, confidence, suspicion; hope, desire; apprehension, concern, disappointment, frustration, fear(s), anger, outrage, regret* (+ *to* nominal group) + *that*-clause. This pattern could be analysed as a ranged 'verbal' clause: Process: *express* + Verbiage: [nominal group: Head: *fear, etc.* + Qualifier: *that*-clause] (cf. Section 7.5.6 below on embedded projections); we also find such nouns of sensing (often nominalizations of verbs of sensing) serving as Head and configured with phrases as Qualifier, as in *express + fear of attack / childbirth / for safety / about labour unrest*. However, looked at 'from above', this pattern can be interpreted as a strategy for construing processes of saying externalizing processes of consciousness. They may be configured with an element that can be interpreted as Receiver, and they often occur in the environment of hypotactically projecting verbal clauses; for example:

> Assange **expressed fears that** cyberspace had its limits.

> The coach of the Peruvian Football, Sergio Markarian, **expressed confidence that** their pupils achieve a victory over Colombia and ***said*** it is in the semi-finals of the Copa America.

> Many viewers have **expressed frustration that** the supposedly feminist Joss Whedon would create a story about a glorified, high-tech form of prostitution. However, I ***argue*** here that in his feminist repertoire, Dollhouse gives us just as much fodder for thinking about gender, feminism, and power as Buffy the Vampire Slayer, which drew its appeal by resisting the very forms of systemic oppression, both male and female disempowerment, that Dollhouse sought to make explicit.

> After Warren died from HIV in 1995, I **expressed regret to Kirk that** I hadn't seen more of Warren in his last years, and Kirk ***suggested*** that one way I could respond would be by seeing more of *him* – which I did, and was glad to do.

7.5.3.2 Quoting thought

This combination of a verbal process with 'reporting', although we are treating it as logically subsequent to quoting, being arrived at by analogy with the reporting of a mental process, is the normal way of representing what people say, in most registers of English today. The

---

[28] But they do occur when they embody assessment, as is illustrated by the following selection from the web: (a) *Drinking in the view across the Potomac River, Kennedy reportedly **mused that** he could stay in that spot forever*; (b) *When we invented the wheel, people **moaned that** we'd forget how to walk*; (c) *Citizens have long **grimaced** that their votes are the only input they gave into government*; (d) *I muttered, embarrassed, something about having never been to see him all this time and she **frowned that** I had never gone to see him*; (e) *The careful telephonic questions of Dictator Mussolini were followed by abrupt commands. Consul Riccardi **gulped that** he understood, hung up, donned resplendent attire, and fairly strutted to the residence of Provincial Governor Stumpf*. However, there do not (at the time of writing!) appear to be examples of reporting with *hiccupped (hiccoughed) that, coughed that, spat that*.

Table 7-23 Verbs serving as Process in 'verbal' clauses reporting propositions and proposals

		Proposition	Proposal
(1) general:	(a) giving	[statement] *say, tell*	[offer] *offer*
	(b) demanding	[question] *ask*	[command] *tell, ask*
(2) elaborated speech function:	(a) giving	[statement] *insinuate, imply, remind, hypothesize, deny, make out, claim, maintain*	[offer] *promise, threaten, undertake*
	(b) demanding	[question] *enquire, ascertain*	[command] *command, demand, persuade, forbid, encourage, recommend, implore, plead (with sb), cajole (sb into v-ing), suggest discourage (from v-ing)*

opposite combination, that of a mental process with 'quoting', is also found, although considerably more restricted (see 7-8). Here a thought is represented as if it was a wording, for example

I saw an ad in the paper for dachshunds, and I thought 'I'll just inquire' – not intending to buy one, of course.

||| I thought ||	'I'll just inquire' |||
1	'2

||| 'The gods must watch out for Kukul,' || he thought to himself. ||| [Text 28]

||| So I figured ||'Well, then obviously it's going to be a nineteenth-century American novel'. ||| [Text 17]

||| 'When all's said and done,' << he reflected, >> 'she hasn't had much chance.' ||| [Of Human Bondage]

The implication is 'I said to myself ... '; and this expression is often used, recognizing the fact that one can think in words. Only certain mental process verbs are regularly used to quote in this way, such as *think, wonder, reflect, surmise*.

7.5.4 Projecting offers and commands

So far we have considered just the projection of propositions (see above, Table 7-18): that is, statements and questions. We must now turn to the projection of clauses of the 'goods-&-services' kind, offers and commands, to which we gave the general name 'proposals'.

7.5.4.1 Quoting offers and commands

Offers and commands, and also suggestions which are simply the combination of the two (offer 'I'll do it', command 'you do it', suggestion 'let's do it'), can be projected paratactically (quoted) in the same way as propositions, by means of a verbal process clause having a quoting function. For example (using an exclamation mark as an optional notational variant),

||| If we're talking || when she's writing up on the board, || all of a sudden she'll turn round || and go || 'will you be quiet!' |||

||| she'll go ||	will you be quiet |||
1	"2!

Here the verb *go* is the quoting verb. Further examples:

||| I said to Peter, || 'Don't say anything.' ||| [Text 119]

||| 'The ark must be 450 feet long, 75 feet wide, and 45 feet high,' || he said, || 'big enough for you and your wife, your three sons, and their wives'. ||| [Text 14]

||| He said, || 'I could fix that hot-water heater!' ||| [Text 119]

||| 'Let's celebrate today, || because beginning tomorrow || there's a lot of work [[to do]],' || he said. ||| [Text 87]

As with propositions, there is an extensive set of verbs used in 'verbal' clauses for quoting proposals, especially in narrative fiction: see the 'proposal' column in Table 7-20. As with verbs used to quote propositions, many class (3b) verbs such as *moan* serve in 'behavioural' clauses pressed into quoting service; for example:

||| 'Say something nice to me,' || she murmured. ||| [Of Human Bondage]

||| 'Oh, don't go yet,' || he cried. ||| 'I must,' || she muttered. ||| [Of Human Bondage]

||| 'Oh, don't take him away yet,' || she moaned. ||| [Of Human Bondage]

These are the 'direct commands' of traditional grammar, to which we would need to add 'direct offers (and suggestions)'; in other words, all proposals projected as 'direct speech'. Just like non-projected proposals, quoted proposals may be realized by 'imperative' clauses; but they may also be realized by modulated 'indicative' ones (cf. Chapter 10, Section 10.4.2):

Text 7-9: Recreating – narrating (written, monologic): extract from a Mills & Boon novel, with dramatic dialogue

||| 'Then please tell him', || Liz begged like a child. |||

||| 'Don't be ridiculous', || Julia snapped. |||

||| 'Perhaps you and your wife would like to look around together', || Richard suggested with frosty politeness. |||

||| 'You could still apply for it, you know – the managership', || Andrew was suggesting helpfully. |||

||| 'I shouldn't keep him waiting, || if I were you', || Eleanor tossed over her shoulder || as she left. ||| [Edwina Shore, 1991, *Not His Property*, Mills & Boon]

7.5.4.2 Reporting offers and commands

Like propositions, proposals can also be reported: projected hypotactically (1) by 'verbal' clauses as 'indirect speech' or (2) by 'mental' clauses as 'indirect thought'. The former involves indirect commands, offers and suggestions; the latter desired (ideas of) states of

affair. One central feature they share is the mode of the projected proposal: it is 'irrealis', or non-actualized, and the projecting clause represents the verbal or mental force of actualization. The mode is reflected in the realization of the reported clause. (Both mental and verbal reporting of proposals can be used to realize direct proposals: see Chapter 10, Section 10.4.)

With propositions, the reported clause is finite.[29] With proposals, it may be (a) finite or (b) non-finite. (a) The finites are declarative, usually modulated with a modal auxiliary of obligation (*should, ought to, must, has to, is to, might, could, would*) serving as Finite, e.g.

[verbal]

||| The doctor **ordered** || that all the books and toys [[that the Boy had played with in bed]] ***must*** be burned. ||| [Text 28]

||| Yet somebody **told** me || that I ***mustn't*** repudiate my non-fiction, || because it's saying very much || what the fiction is saying. ||| [Text 7]

||| He **told** Philip || that he ***should*** demand higher wages, || for notwithstanding the difficult work [[he was now engaged in]], he received no more than the six shillings a week [[with which he started]]. ||| [Of Human Bondage]

[mental]

||| I **wish** || you'***d*** do something about that wall, Jane. ||| [UTS/Macquarie Corpus]

||| But until you've got kids || and are bringing them up ||| ... I **wish** || mine ***would*** hurry up || and grow up || and leave home. ||| [UTS/Macquarie Corpus]

In American English in particular, reported proposals are often in the 'subjunctive' (where the third person singular is the base form of the verb); for example:

||| The negotiations were suspended in January || when Syria **insisted** || Israel ***commit*** to returning to prewar 1967 borders. ||| [Text 66]

||| **Did** they **suggest** || the attorney general ***investigate***? ||| [KING_Interviews]

||| When Evans returned to Sydney with glowing reports of this fertile land [[he'd found]], || the Governor **ordered** || that a road ***be*** built. ||| [Text 126]

||| Perhaps it was history that **ordained** || that it ***be*** here, at the Cape of Good Hope [[that we should lay the foundation stone of our new nation]]. ||| [Text 181]

(b) The non-finites are typically perfective, e.g.

[verbal]

||| I **tell** people || ***to say*** thank you. ||| [UTS/Macquarie Corpus]

||| As a first step to correcting this disparity, I **urge** the Congress || ***to eliminate*** the 40 percent Redux retirement formula || and to restore the '50% of base pay' formula for 20 years of active-duty service, || as proposed in the President's FY2000 budget. ||| [Text 115]

---

[29] Except for certain projected ideas, which may take a non-finite form on the model of the Latin 'accusative + infinitive', e.g. ||| *I understood* || *them to have accepted* ||| *he doesn't consider* || *you to be serious* |||. These shade into attributed intensive relational clauses, e.g. [Attributor:] *he* [Process:] *doesn't consider* [Carrier:] *you* [Attribute:] *serious*.

||| And then, finally, I **was invited** || *to create* the interior of the United States Pavilion at the New York World's Fair in 1964. ||| [Text 101]

[mental]
||| Of course I **want** || Labour *to win* || but I don't think || they will. ||| [UTS/Macquarie Corpus]

||| **Do** you **want** || me *to explain* that? ||| [UTS/Macquarie Corpus]

||| She **wanted** || a glass of sherry *to be delivered* to her room, || so she said over the phone to the bar or whatever: || 'Je voudrais un cheri, s'il vous plait.' ||| [Text 119]

However, a few verbs take imperfective projections, e.g. *she suggested talking it over*. Unlike reported propositions, reported proposals take the same form regardless of whether they are giving or demanding in orientation:[30] (giving) *he promised me to wash the car*; (demanding) *he told me to wash the car*. This applies to both locutions and ideas. However, these typically differ with respect to the status of the Subject of the reported proposal. With reported locutions, the Subject is implicit; it is presumed from the Receiver of the reporting 'verbal' clause: *he told/promised me* || *to wash the car*. This is shown by the agnate finite variant (*he told me* || *that I should wash the car*; *he promised me* || *that he would wash the car*) and by the fact that the 'verbal' clause has a passive variant with the Receiver as Subject – *I was told* || *to wash the car*. In contrast, with reported ideas, the Subject is explicit as part of the projected proposal: *he wanted* || *me to wash the car*; *he intended/planned/hoped* || *for me to wash the car*. Here there is no passive variant of the reporting clause – we cannot say *I was wanted* || *to wash the car*, *I was hoped* || *(for) to wash the car*; but there is a passive variant of the reported idea clause – we can say *he wanted* || *the car to be washed (by me)*. Not surprisingly, there are intermediate cases; more specifically, certain nexuses of reported locutions have properties usually associated with nexuses of reported ideas. Thus with *order* we can say *I was ordered* || *to wash the car* (cf. *I was told* || *to wash the car*); but we can also say *he ordered* || *the car to be washed (by me)* (cf. *he wanted* || *the car to be washed (by me)*).

Let us add a few notes first on verbal projection and then on mental.

(1) 'Verbal' reporting of proposals

The parallel between quoting and reporting is not so close with proposals as with propositions, because reported proposals merge gradually into causatives (cf. Chapter 8, Section 8.7) without any very clear line in between. Thus not only are there many verbs used in quoting which are not used in reporting – again the complex ones: we would not write *his driver soothed him to be steady* or *soothed that he should keep steady* – but also there are many verbs used to report that are not used to quote, verbs expressing a wide variety of rhetorical processes such as *persuade, forbid, undertake, encourage, recommend*, as illustrated above; see Table 7-23.

---

[30] This is true of the form of non-finites; but they differ with respect to the source of the presumed Subject of the non-finite clause, as is shown by the agnate finite variant of the reported clause: when the orientation is demanding, the source is the Receiver of the verbal clause (*he told **me** || to wash the car – that I should ...*); when it is given, the source is the Sayer (***he** promised me || to wash the car – that he would ...*). Finites differ between giving and demanding in the choice of modal: (giving: inclination) *he promised that he would wash the car*; (demanding: obligation) *he demanded that we should wash the car*.

How do we decide where to draw the line between these and causatives such as *she got him to talk it over?* (1) As a first step, if there is a quoted equivalent with the same verb, the structure is clearly a projection; e.g. the form

||| he threatened ||	to blow up the city |||
α	"β!

could be paralleled by *'I'll blow up the city!' he threatened.* (2) Typically if a proposal is projected it may not actually eventuate; hence we can say without contradiction *he threatened to blow up the city, but didn't,* or *the Queen ordered the executioner to cut off Alice's head, but he didn't* – whereas it is self-contradictory to say *the Queen got the executioner to cut off Alice's head but he didn't.*

(3) More generally, we can assume that any verb denoting a speech act can in principle be used to project. Hence a verbal process with a non-finite dependent clause can normally be interpreted as a projection; and if the non-finite dependent clause could be replaced by a finite one with modulation this makes it more certain, since it rules out purpose clauses:

||| he promised ||	to make her happy |||
||| he promised ||	he would make her happy |||
α	"β!

as distinct from *he promised, (in order) to make her happy,* which is an expansion with structure α ^ ×β. Causatives are excluded because they are not verbal processes; they also usually do not have finite equivalents – we do not say *I'll make that you should regret this!* cf. Chapter 8, Section 8.7.

(2) 'Mental' reporting of proposals

With the 'mental' reporting of ideas, there is an important distinction between propositions and proposals, deriving from their fundamental nature as different forms of semiotic exchange. Whereas propositions, which are exchanges of information, are projected mentally by processes of cognition – thinking, knowing, understanding, wondering, etc. – proposals, which are exchanges of goods-&-services, are projected mentally by processes of desire, as illustrated by the examples given above under 'mental' (for examples of verbs of desire, see above Table 7-21). Thus, while propositions are thought, proposals are hoped. As with those that are projected verbally, so with those that are projected mentally the exact limits are fuzzy; they merge with causatives and with various aspectual categories. The relevant criteria are similar to those set up for propositions, except that we cannot realistically test for quoting, since mental proposals are rarely quoted.[31] For reporting, however, if the process in the dominant clause is one of desire, and the dependent clause

---

[31] Note that *'I wish he'd go away,' thought Mary* is a quoted proposition incorporating a reported proposal, not a quoted proposal, which would be *'Let him go away!' wished Mary.* As with mental propositions, so also with mental proposals: the notion behind quoting is generally that of 'saying to oneself', or saying silently to a deity as in prayer.

is a future declarative, or could be replaced by a future declarative, then the structure can be interpreted as a projection; for example *we hope you will not forget*. In Chapter 8, Section 8.8, we shall suggest an alternative interpretation for those where the dependent clause is non-finite and its Subject is presupposed from the dominant clause, e.g. *he wanted to go home* (where it is difficult to find a closely equivalent finite form); but there will always be a certain amount of arbitrariness about where the line is drawn.

Notice therefore that there is a proportion such that

	she wanted	him to go	(mental)	proposal
is to	she told him	to go	(verbal)	
	as			
	she knew	he was going	(mental)	proposition
is to	she said	he was going	(verbal)	

We have now covered all the cells in Table 7-18 representing the intersection of (1) level of projection, (2) mode of projection, and (3) speech function of projected clause. Having sketched the overall space of projection, we can now explore some further possibilities.

7.5.5 Quoting vs. reporting; free indirect speech

7.5.5.1 Quoting and reporting as modes of projection

Quoting and reporting are not simply formal variants; they differ in meaning. The difference between them derives from the general semantic distinction between parataxis and hypotaxis, as it applies in the particular context of projecting. In quoting, the projected element has independent status; it is thus more immediate and lifelike, and this effect is enhanced by the orientation of the deixis, which is that of drama not that of narrative. Quoting is particularly associated with certain narrative registers, fictional and personal; it is used not only for sayings but also for thoughts, including not only first-person thoughts, as in

> ... and watching that trial wondering whether in fact he was innocent or not and I couldn't make up my mind, after a while I thought 'No, I'm sure he's guilty'. [UTS/Macquarie Corpus]

but also third-person thoughts projected by an omniscient narrator, as in

> 'And that's the jury-box,' thought Alice.

> So after about two hours he thought 'Well they're not coming back' and he started hitchhiking. [UTS/ Macquarie Corpus]

Reporting, on the other hand, presents the projected element as dependent. It still gives some indication of mood, but in a form which precludes it from functioning as a move in an exchange; the mood is projected, not straight. And the speaker makes no claim to be abiding by the wording.

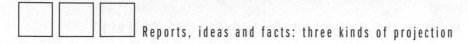

In many registers, quoting and reporting are used together to achieve projection; and this sheds light on how they complement one another. For example, in news reports, reporting often precedes quoting, as in:

Text 7-10: Reporting – chronicling (written, monologic): news report [Reuters, 01/01/01]

A car bomb exploded during the evening rush hour Monday in the busy center of the Israeli city of Netanya, wounding more than 40 people, hospital officials **said**.

'There was a boom, boom and another boom,' **said** a witness who gave his name only as David as he wept. 'All the windows were blown out. It was terrifying.'

Here reporting is associated with a general Sayer (*city officials*) whereas quoting is associated with a particular one (*a witness* ...); and this is often the case: after the general situation has been reported, details and opinions uttered by important people, spokespeople or eye witnesses are quoted (for an example extending over a whole news article, see Matthiessen, 1995a: 849–852). There is thus a cline from the reporter's own voice via reported voices to quoted ones. The quoted material is closest to the reporter's news source whereas the reported material is already, at least potentially, at some distance from what was actually said.

As we have seen, a reported proposition typically takes on a set of related features collectively known as 'indirect speech'. What happens is that all deictic elements are shifted away from reference to the speech situation: personals away from first and second person (speaker and listener) to third, and demonstratives away from near (here-&-now) to remote. A part of this effect is the 'sequence of tenses': if the verb in the reporting clause has 'past' as its primary tense (see Chapter 6, Section 6.3), then typically each verb in the reported clause has its finite element in the corresponding System II ('sequent') form: see Table 7-24.

Table 7-24 Non-sequent and sequent systems

Primary tense		Modality	
Non-sequent	**Sequent**	**Non-sequent**	**Sequent**
am/is/are	was/were	can/could	could
have/has	had	may/might	might
do/does (etc.)	did (etc.)	will/would	would
shall/will	should/would	should	should
was/were	had been	ought to	ought to
did (etc.)	had done (etc.)	must/has to	had to

In other words, an additional 'past' feature is introduced at the Finite element in the mood structure of the projected clause. The use of the sequent form is not obligatory; it is less likely in a clause stating a general proposition, for example *they said they close at weekends*. But overall it is the unmarked choice in the environment in question.

If the reported clause is interrogative it typically shifts into the declarative; the declarative is the unmarked mood, and is used in all clauses that do not select for mood independently, including all dependent clauses. A yes/no interrogative becomes declarative, introduced by *if* or *whether* (*he asked 'is she coming at noon?'* : *he asked whether she was coming at noon*); a WH- interrogative becomes declarative with the WH- element remaining at the front (*he asked 'when is she coming?'* : *he asked when she was coming*).

With the imperative the relationship is less clear. We noted in Chapter 4 that the imperative is a somewhat indeterminate category, having some features of a finite and some features of a non-finite clause. Similarly the category of reported imperative ('indirect command') is not very clearly defined. But non-finite clauses with *to*, following a verb such as *tell* or *order*, can be interpreted as reported proposals. They likewise display the properties of 'indirect speech', although without sequence of tenses, since the verb does not select for tense. For example,

'I know this trick of yours.'	She said ‖ she knew that trick of his.
'Can you come tomorrow?'	He asked ‖ if she could come the next day.
'Why isn't John here?'	She wondered ‖ why John wasn't there.
'Help yourselves.'	He told them ‖ to help themselves.
'We must leave to-night.'	She said ‖ they had to leave that night.

Traditional school exercises of the kind 'turn into direct/indirect speech' suggest that the two always fully match. This is true lexicogrammatically, in that it is always possible to find an equivalent – although not always a unique one: given *Mary said she had seen it*, the quoted equivalent might be *I have seen it, I had seen it* or *I saw it*, or *she* (someone else) *has seen it*, etc. (cf. Chapter 6, Section 6.3). But it is not true as a general statement about usage. Semantically the two do not exactly match, and there are many instances where it does not make sense to replace one by the other. Note, for example, *Alice thought that that was the jury-box*, where we should have to change *Alice thought* to something like *Alice said to herself* in order to avoid the sense of 'held the opinion', which is the natural interpretation of a verb of thinking when it is projecting by hypotaxis.

There are different ways of referring back to what is quoted and what is reported. Typically a reference item, usually *that*, is used to pick up a quoted passage, while a substitute, *so/not*, is used with a report. For example,

She said, 'I can't do it.'– Did she really say that?

She said she couldn't do it.– Did she really say so?

(For the difference between reference and substitution, see Chapter 9; see also Halliday & Hasan, 1976: 88–90.) This is because the act of quoting implies a prior referent, some actual occasion that can then be referred back to, whereas in reporting there is nothing but the reported text. This explains the difference in meaning between *I don't believe that* 'I do not accept that assertion as valid' and *I don't believe so* 'in my opinion such is not the case'. Compare:

The sky is about to fall. (i) – Who said that? (ii) – Who said so?

It is clear that both *that* and *so* stand for something that is projected, as shown by the verb *said*. In (i) this projected element is being treated as a quote: 'who produced that verbal act?' – hence we can ask *who said that?* if we want to identify a speaker from among a crowd, like a teacher finding out who was talking in class. In (ii), on the other hand, the expression *the sky is about to fall* is being treated not as anybody's verbal act but as a text; the meaning is 'who affirmed that that was the case?', with the implication that the contrary is conceivable.

In 'verbal' process clauses, therefore, *he said that* simply attests his production of the wording, whereas *he said so* raises the issue of whether what he said is in fact the case. With 'mental' process clauses the picture is more complex, since the reference form *that* tends to be associated with certainty and the substitute *so* with uncertainty; the principle is actually the same, but it is operating in a different environment (cf. the different senses of thought in quoting and reporting, referred to above). The principle is that a substitute does not refer; it simply harks back. It thus has the general semantic property of implying, and so excluding, possible alternatives; cf. the nominal substitute *one* as in *a big one*, meaning 'there are also small ones, and I don't mean those'. This is why *so*, which is a clause substitute, has the general sense of 'non-real', by contrast with what is 'real'; besides (i) projection, where it signifies what is asserted or postulated, it is used in two other contexts: (ii) hypothetical, as opposed to actual, and (iii) possible, as opposed to certain. Hence:

(i)	I think so	*but*	I know [that]	*not*	I know so
(ii)	if so	*but*	because of that	*not*	because so
(iii)	perhaps so	*but*	certainly	*not*	certainly so

See Chapter 9 for further discussion.

7.5.5.2 A third mode of projection: free indirect speech

Quoting and reporting are thus two distinct modes of projection, representing two degrees of remove from the original source. In certain kinds of discourse, we find a mode of projection that combines features of quoting and reporting; the projected clause is set up as a reported clause introduced by the binder *that* but quoting is then introduced at some point in the development of the clause:

||| Narayan is today a Hindu || and says || that he 'can't write a novel without Krishna, Ganesa, Hanuman, astrologers, pundits, temples and devadasis, or temple prostitutes.' ||| [Text 163]

||| It was reported on BBC Radio 4's Today programme || that 'Sir John Gielgud celebrates his 90th birthday || and causes controversy || by admitting to Hello! magazine || that he doesn't understand Shakespeare properly'. ||| [Text 25]

||| Addressing the people of Israel before a largely Jewish audience, || Clinton said || 'you have hardly had one day of peace and quiet || since your state was created.' ||| He said || 'your dream of a homeland has come true,' || but when the Jewish people returned home || beginning a century ago, || they found || 'it was not vacant. ||| You discovered || that your land was also their land, the homeland of two peoples.' ||| [Text 108]

Here the mixture of quoting and reporting is not very extensive; but there is another mode of projection which is sometimes described as 'intermediate between direct and indirect speech', namely **free indirect speech**:[32]

Quoted ('direct')	'Am I dreaming?' Jill wondered
'Free indirect'	Was she dreaming, Jill wondered
Reported ('indirect')	Jill wondered if she was dreaming

Strictly speaking it is not so much intermediate as a blend: it has some of the features of each of the other two types. The structure is paratactic, so the projected clause has the form of an independent clause retaining the mood of the quoted form; but it is a report and not a quote, so time and person reference are shifted – *was she* not *am I*. This is another example of the semogenic principle whereby the system fills up a slot it has created for itself (see Halliday, 1992d). Here are some natural text instances:

||| He said || he was starting a new magazine, The Paris News-Post, || and would I become its fiction editor. ||| [Text 119]

||| He was asked || to leave after one term. ||| 'They said || I had no talent || and was wasting my money and their time || and would I please just go away.' ||| [ACE_A]

||| Someone once asked Adrian || what was the name of his first wife. ||| [Text 82]

To accommodate free indirect speech in our account, we thus need to expand Table 7-18 by dissociating the quote vs. report variable from the parataxis vs. hypotaxis one: see Table 7-25. As the table shows, free indirect speech can be projected both verbally and mentally, and includes both propositions and proposals – everything, in fact, that can be both quoted and reported (thus excluding minor speech functions since they can only be quoted).

The intonation pattern of free indirect speech is still further anomalous, since it follows that of quoting and not that of reporting: the projected clause takes the intonation that it would have had if quoted (that is, identical with its straight, unprojected form), and the projecting clause follows it as a 'tail'. This is because the projected clause still has the status of an independent speech act.

With our discussion of free indirect speech, we have completed our overview of the ways in which projection may be manifested tactically – that is, as a relationship between interdependent clauses. We shall now turn to another grammatical environment, that of embedding. Here the projected clause does not stand in a tactic relationship to a projecting clause in a clause nexus but it is instead downranked to serve within a nominal group.

---

[32] 'Free indirect speech' encompasses a range of different feature combinations; it is a projection 'space' rather than a single invariant pattern. The account given here represents it in its prototypical form.

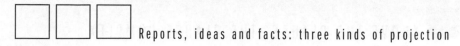
Table 7-25 Direct, free indirect and indirect speech

Type of projecting process	Projected speech function	Quoting [orientation] paratactic [taxis] 1 2	Reporting [orientation]	hypotactic [taxis] α β
verbal:		wording 1 "2	wording represented as meaning (except intonation)	wording represented as meaning α "β
	major: proposition: statement	"I can," he said.	He could, he said.	He said he could.
"locution	major: proposition: question	"Are you súre?" asked Fred.	Was he súre, Fred asked.	Fred asked if he was sùre.
	major: proposal	"Wait here." she told him.	Wait there, she told him.	She told him to wait there.
	minor	1 "2 She said, "Wow!"	–	–
mental:		meaning represented as wording 1 '2	meaning (intonation represented as wording)	meaning α 'β
	major: proposition: statement	'I can,' he thought.	He could, he thought.	He thought she could.
'idea	major: proposition: question	'Am I dreáming?' wondered Jill.	Was she dreáming, Jill wondered.	She wondered if she was dreàming.
	major: proposal	'Wait here,' she willed him.	Wait there, she willed him.	She wanted her to wait there.
		'direct'	'free indirect'	'indirect'

7.5.6 Embedded locutions and ideas

Like the three types of expansion, both locutions and ideas can be embedded. Besides entering into paratactic and hypotactic clause nexuses, they can be 'rankshifted' to function as Qualifiers within a nominal group (cf. Chapter 6, Section 6.2.2.2), as in:

Leaders of both a publically-funded project and a competing private company issued **statements** Friday [[that they jointly would announce the status of their work on Monday]]. [Text 77]

I was very intrigued by your take on Huck Finn in that piece, and your **argument** [[that the great American novel of that century was Uncle Tom's Cabin]]. [Text 17]

To what extent do you buy into the **belief** [[[that if the individual becomes enlightened, || that adds to the betterment of the universe in and of itself]]]? [Text 7]

AT&T's stock slid 14 percent Tuesday as the company issued its first profit warning under chief executive C. Michael Armstrong, fueling **worries** about [[whether his radical remake of the nation's largest long-distance company will succeed]]. [Text 26]

The man was impressive in some ways, Oxford educated, very twenties British bohemian, a great dancer and seducer of women, who suppressed his wife's **desire** [[to be a 'real' archaeologist]] and whose own career really was a joke up until his early death from a sudden illness. [Text 21]

The structure of a nominal group with an embedded projection is shown in Figure 7-22, part [i].

	the/their	assertion		that	Caesar	was	ambitious
[i] nominal group	Deictic	Thing		Qualifier			
	determiner	noun: verbal nominalization		"[[clause: projection			]]
					Carrier	Process: relational	Attribute
					nom. gp.	verbal gp.	nom. gp.
[ii] clause:	α			"β			
projecting nexus	clause: verbal			clause: projection			
	Sayer	Process					
	they	asserted		that	Caesar	was	ambitious

Fig. 7-22   Nominal group with embedded projection

Such instances are still projections; but here the projecting element is the noun that is functioning as Thing, in this case *assertion*. As we shall see later in Chapter 10, Section 10.5, such instances of projection are all metaphorical: a projecting sequence is realized congruently as a clause nexus of projection – part [ii] of Figure 7-22, but it may alternatively be realized metaphorically as a nominal group – part [i] of Figure 7-22. When we align them as in Figure 7-22, we see how the nominal group construction with an embedded projection clause is agnate with a clause nexus of projection: the nominal group is a metaphorical, nominalized version of the clause nexus; and the noun *assertion* serving as Head/Thing is in fact a nominalized variant of the verb *assert* serving as Process in the agnate clause. The congruent Sayer may be left out in the nominal group; or it may be represented either as the Deictic (*their assertion that ...*) or as a Qualifier (*the assertion by the government that ...*). Part of the rhetorical power of the metaphorical group is the potential for leaving the Sayer unspecified.

The fact that the projected clause is embedded as the Qualifier in a nominal group means that it can occur in a range of grammatical environments not open to non-embedded, tactically related projected clauses (see further Section 7.5.7). This is important in the creation of discourse; one of the central uses of nominal groups with embedded projections is in the representation of arguments, as in newspaper reports and scientific discourse:

There is bitter opposition to his **proposal** [[that Palestinians renounce their **demand** [[for more than three million refugees to return to areas inside Israel that were abandoned in the 1948 war]]]].

Israelis have rejected Mr Clinton's **proposal** [[that they give up control of the Temple Mount in Jerusalem's walled Old City, the holiest place in Judaism and the third most sacred in Islam]]. [SMH 03/0i/01]

Boyle's tentative **suggestion** [[that heat was simply motion]] was apparently not accepted by Stahl, || or perhaps it was unknown to him. [Text 259]

Here proposals and demands are opposed, renounced and rejected. The contribution to the creation of discourse is further enhanced by the fact that such nouns of projection can be used anaphorically to refer back to propositions and proposals already established in the discourse (cf. Chapter 9, Section 9.4):

The Labour Party opposed Thor missiles, because, he said, they were out of date and vulnerable and would attract enemy action. That **argument** did not apply to the Polaris submarine. [LOB_A]

The cohesive effect is similar to that created by text references achieved by means of *this*, *that*, *it*:

The talks lasted for three hours. **This** was a surprise, for they had only been scheduled to last two hours. [LOB_A]

(cf. *it was a surprise that the talks lasted for three hours* with a fact clause: see Section 7.5.7 below); but nouns of projection make it possible to construe the class of projection explicitly.

Nouns that project belong to clearly defined classes, verbal process nouns (locutions) and mental process nouns (ideas); they correspond rather closely to, and in many instances are derived from, the verbs used in the projecting clause, especially the reporting ones. Some of the principal nouns of projection are set out in Table 7-26. (The table also includes nouns of fact; these will be discussed in the next subsection.) The nature of the realization of the embedded clause depends on the speech functional subcategory:

(I)   Propositions

    (a)   stating: projected clause either (i) finite, *that* + indirect indicative, or (ii) non-finite, *of* + imperfective

    (b)   questioning: projected clause either (i) finite, *if/whether* or WH- + indirect indicative, or (ii) non-finite, *whether* or WH- + *to* + perfective

(II)   Proposals

    (a)   offering (incl. suggesting): projected clause either (1) non-finite, *to* + perfective or *of* + imperfective, or (ii) finite, future indirect indicative

    (b)   commanding: projected clause either (i) non-finite, *to* + perfective, or (ii) finite, modulated or future indirect indicative

As illustrated by the examples given earlier, the noun is the name of a locution or an idea, and the clause that it projects serves to define it in exactly the same way that a 'restrictive' relative clause defines the noun that is expanded by it. Hence any noun that belongs to a projecting class may be defined (restricted) in either of these two ways, either by projection (e.g. *the thought* [[*that she might one day be a queen*]]) or by expansion (e.g. *the thought* [[*that came into her mind*]]). This leads to ambiguities such as *the report* [[*that he was submitting*]], referred to in Section 7.5.8 below.

535

Table 7-26 Nouns of projection and nouns of fact

			Projection nouns	Fact nouns
propositions	stating	locutions	statement; report, news, rumour, claim, assertion, argument, insistence, proposition, assurance, intimation	(1) 'cases' (nouns of simple fact [non-modalized]): fact, case, point, rule, principle, accident, lesson, grounds
		ideas	thought, belief, knowledge, feeling, notion, suspicion, sense, idea, expectation, view, opinion, prediction, assumption, conviction, discovery	(2) 'chances' (nouns of modalization): chance, possibility, likelihood, probability, certainty, offchance, impossibility (3) 'proofs' (nouns of indication – caused modalization): proof, indication, implication, confirmation, demonstration, evidence, disproof
	questioning	locutions	question; query, inquiry; argument, dispute	(1') 'cases': issue, problem, conundrum
		ideas	doubt, question	(2') 'chances': uncertainty
proposals	offering	locutions	offer, suggestion, proposal, threat, promise	
		ideas	intention, desire, hope, inclination, decision, resolve	
	commanding	locutions	order, command, instruction, demand, request, plea	(4) 'needs' (nouns of modulation): requirement, need, rule, obligation, necessity, onus, expectation, duty
		ideas	wish, desire, hope, fear	

Where the projected clause is non-finite the Subject can be presupposed from the primary clause provided it is the participant that is actually doing the projecting – Senser or (more rarely) Sayer. So *the thought of being a queen* (*encouraged her*), *her desire to be a queen* ... , *her assertion of being a queen* ... , where 'she' is doing the thinking, etc.; but *the news of her being a queen* (*proclaimed by someone else*), *the thought of her being a queen* (*in someone else's mind*), and so on. These correspond to the non-finite forms with hypotaxis referred to in Section 7.5.4: *she wanted to be a queen, they wanted her to be a queen*. In the finite forms, of course, the Subject is always made explicit.

7.5.7 Facts

Thus verbal processes, and mental: cognitive processes, project in the indicative mode (propositions), while verbal processes, and mental: desiderative processes, project in the imperative mode (proposals). The projecting environment may be a verbal or mental process clause, or a (metaphorical) nominal group with a verbal or mental process noun (locution or idea) as its Head.

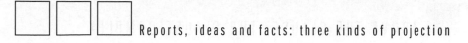

There is one other type of projection, where the projected clause is not being projected by a verbal or mental process with Sayer or Senser, or by a verbal or mental process noun in a metaphorical nominal group, but comes, as it were, ready packaged in projected form. We refer to this type as a **fact**. For example:

> The irony is even further compounded by the **fact** [[that while every people must have those [[[who say, || 'Here I stand,']]] the *fact* is [[[Okonkwo loses a child to the forces of Christianity, || and Ezeulu loses his community to Christianity]]]]]. [Text 16]

> The **fact** [[that fourteen of the original eighteen Julian Ashton nudes still decorate the Marble Bar's walls]], perchance contributed to the bar winning Australian Playboy's survey for Best Bar in Australia in 1986. [Text 22]

> The **fact** [[that Lear never even alluded to that at the end]] is a **sign** [[that he didn't learn very much through the course of the play]]. [Text 17]

> He's trapped by the **fact** [[that the river flows south]]. [Text 17]

Here a 'fact' noun serves as the Head/Thing of a nominal group with a projected clause as Postmodifier/Qualifier.

Consider *That Caesar was dead was obvious to all*. Here *that Caesar was dead* is certainly a projection; but there is no process of saying or thinking which projects it. Its status is simply that of a fact; and it can indeed function as Qualifier to the noun *fact*, e.g. *the fact that Caesar was dead was obvious to all*. There are four sub-classes of fact noun: (1) **cases**, (2) **chances**, (3) **proofs** and (4) **needs**. The first three go with embedded projections whereas the last goes with embedded proposals; see Table 7-26 for examples of nouns. The first three differ in terms of modality of the subtype modalization:

(1) **cases** (nouns of simple fact) relate to ordinary non-modalized propositions 'it is (the case) that ... '

(2) **chances** (nouns of modality) relate to modalized propositions 'it may be (the case) that ... '

(3) **proofs** (nouns of indication) relate to propositions with indications, which are equivalent to caused modalities, 'this proves/implies (i.e. makes it certain/probable) that ... '

(Nouns of 'need' are discussed lower down.) Cases were exemplified above, but we can add examples of chances and proofs:

(2) chances

   I think really if you just keep a good eye on him and keep him quiet, and just keep him mostly to fluids and light things over the next few days, there's a good **chance** [[that it will settle down enough [[[for you to go away || and come back next week]]]]]. [Text 34]

(3) proofs

   There is a huge antarctic ozone hole today with chlorine at 3 ppbv, and there is evidence [[that the ozone hole is enlarging and spreading]]. [Text 33]

The 'fact' noun serving as Head/Thing of the nominal group may thus embody a form of assessment of the projected clauses serving as Postmodifier/Qualifier – assessment involving modalization. Premodifiers may provide further assessments of the projected clause, either

537

as attitudinal Epithet (e.g. *painful, interesting, obvious*; cf. *good* in *good chance* above) or as post-Deictic (e.g. *alleged*), e.g.

'The U.S. government has to come to terms with the **painful fact** ⟦⟦that the good old days ⟦⟦when it could just borrow its way out of messes of its own making⟧⟧ are finally gone⟧⟧,' Xinhua wrote. [News report]

It's an **interesting fact** ⟦⟦⟦that, <<compared with other countries, >> Australians are not very heavy drinkers⟧⟧⟧. [Australia fact website]

The **alledged** (*sic*) **fact** ⟦⟦that a motor breakes (*sic*) more easily under moderated modifications⟧⟧ isn't a symptom of anything going wrong with it –# just that the stock setup/tune is closer to its limits than it used to be. [Web forum; spelling as in original]

No one would like to contend the **blatantly obvious fact** ⟦⟦that thought and consciousness (*sic*) do not fall into the category of material objects according to the current definitions of matter⟧⟧. [KOHL_F]

These often correspond to comment Adjuncts in 'declarative' clauses (e.g. *interestingly, Australians are not* ...); but unlike statements realized by 'declarative' clauses, facts are not open to direct challenge in dialogic interaction (cf. Hoey, 2000; cf. also Chapter 10, Section 10.5.3).

Like nouns of projection, fact nouns can be used anaphorically (or cataphorically) to create cohesion in discourse (cf. Francis, 1985, on her category of 'anaphoric nouns', and cf. the discussion of general nouns in Chapter 9, Section 9.6); for example:

Warwick Town Council originally decided to build its own crematorium, but in April last year it abandoned **the idea** and entered into a joint scheme with Leamington Town Council and Warwick Rural District Council. [LOB_A]

The Bill is short and modest in scope, and it is doubtful whether the other Private Members' Bills in the offing will fill all the gaps. **This fact** may give the Government an extra excuse for counselling patience until the next report from the Molony committee. [LOB_B]

In the first place our business is foreign policy, and it is the business of the Presidential leadership and his appointees in the Department to consider the domestic political aspects of a problem. Mr Truman emphasized **this point** by saying, 'You fellows in the Department of State don't know much about domestic politics'. [BROWN1_H]

Here a passage of text is picked up by anaphoric reference, as in the case of text reference by means of *this* and *that* on their own (see Chapter 9, Section 9.4.3); but fact nouns add a classification and often an assessment (which may be supported by post-Deictics or Epithets) of the discursive antecedent:

There is a subdued aspect of the current political voices: with all the tension generated by the electoral process, it is only a means to an end. The end actually is the transformation in the quality of lives of the people. We must never lose focus of **this** as an issue. **This obvious point** can certainly not be over-emphasised. [Web blog]

A fact clause serving as Head in a nominal group without a fact noun can be related to the first class of fact noun – that of 'cases', since such a fact clause is always agnate with an expanded nominal group with *fact* as Head. Whether the nominal group has a fact noun as Head or not, the fact clause is embedded. Because there is no projecting process involved, to which it could be paratactically or hypotactically related, a fact can appear only in embedded form: either as Qualifier to a 'fact' noun, or as a nominalization on its own (Figure 7-23); for example:

Historically, the **fact** is [[[that Uncle Tom's Cabin was the most popular novel of the nineteenth || century and had a huge effect on American history]]]. [Text 17]

[[that	Caesar	was	dead]]	was	obvious	to all
Carrier				Process: relational	Attribute	Angle
nominal group				verbal group	nominal group	prepositional phrase
Head/Qualifier						
clause: fact						
	Carrier	Process	Attribute			

Fig. 7-23 Attributive clause with projected fact

While there is no participant doing the projecting – no Sayer or Senser – a fact may be projected impersonally, either by a relational process ('it is the case that ...') or by an impersonal mental or verbal process, as in

[i] relational

it is/may be/is not (the case) that ...

it happens (to be the case) that ...

it has been shown/can be proved (to be the case) that ...

it happened/came about that ...

[ii] mental: impersonal

it seems/appears/is thought (to be the case) that ...

[iii] verbal: impersonal

it is said/rumoured (to be the case) that ...

Here the *it* is not a participant in the projecting process but is simply a Subject placeholder (see Chapter 4, Section 4.7 (especially Figure 4-29) and Section 4.8, on the modal structure, and Chapter 3, the end of Section 3.7, on the thematic structure with substitute *it* and a postposed fact clause; cf. with *the fact* instead of *it* as Subject: *the fact is that* ...); hence the fact clause can occupy its position at the front: *that Caesar was ambitious is certainly the case/is widely held/is generally believed*, etc. By contrast we do not normally say *that Caesar was ambitious was thought/said by Brutus* – at least not in a reporting context, only in the special sense of 'these lines were spoken by ...'; and this is because, as we have seen, where there is a personal projecting process, mental or verbal, the clause that is projected by it is not embedded but hypotactic.

Other than with impersonals such as *it is said*, *it is rumoured*, *it seems*, the typical environment for a fact is a 'relational' process clause of the 'intensive' type, either 'attributive' or 'identifying', e.g.

[attributive]

Earl Russell says it is **inevitable, though profoundly regrettable,** [[that the agitation against the Polaris base has generated some antagonism to the policy of the United States]]. [LOB_A]

In that article, it's no **coincidence** [[that I have a big fight with Twain and Eliot]], || because I disagree with them on issues [[that concern all of us]]. [Text 17]

Until 1940 it was an **observable fact** [[that there were composers whose music was highly prized in some countries and entirely neglected by their neighbours]], and this was explained by the difference in national characters. [LOB_A]

It is **clear** [[that the Princess and her husband are settling down in London]] and for this purpose, Kensington Palace is well suited. [LOB_A]

[attributed variant]

The Federal Government has made it **clear** [[that it would have no part in any project for the development of long-range missiles – which in any case would contravene the provisions of the Brussels treaty]]. [LOB_A]

[identifying]

The third **reason** is [[that the supreme interest for the whole world – East and West and uncommitted nations – is the prevention of nuclear war]]. [LOB_A]

The **lesson** [[that's learned]] is [[that they aren't Kangan]]; Kangan is everybody, as represented by the people gathered in Beatrice's apartment at the end of the novel. [Text 16]

Perhaps the most important **point** of all is the **fact** [[that capital was available for expansion as required]]. [LOB_E]

The plain **fact** is [[[that it is extremely difficult [[for MPs to accept invitations from foreign Governments, or from public relations organisations [[working for them]]]], || without being compromised]]]. [LOB_B]

[identifying clause of proving]

But the **fact** [[that they are caught]] proves [[that they do not lift above the headline]]. [LOB_E]

Here the fact is an embedded clause standing as a nominalization on its own, functioning as the realization of an element in the relational process clause (Carrier or Identifier/Token, in these examples).[33] Since it is embedded, there is always an agnate version where the fact clause serves as a Qualifier of a noun of the 'fact' class, e.g. *the fact that Caesar was ambitious*.

In an 'attributive' clause, the Attribute ascribed to the fact clause serving as Carrier is realized by a nominal group with an adjective or noun as Head belonging to one of a small number of classes. These are illustrated in Table 7-27. Several of the types are similar to classes of interpersonal Adjunct (Chapter 4, Section 4.3.2) and two of them can also be

---

[33] Strictly speaking the embedded 'fact' clause functions as Head of a nominal group which, in turn, functions as an element in the ranking clause. This analysis shows how clauses serving as Head are agnate with clauses serving as Postmodifier in nominal groups with a fact noun as Head: *that Caesar was ambitious is obvious*: *the fact that Caesar was ambitious is obvious*. But since a fact clause functioning as Head takes up the whole of that nominal group we can just as well leave out that stage in the structural analysis and show it as directly embedded into the clause, as in Figure 7-15 above. Cf. Footnote 16 earlier in this chapter.

related to types of sensing in 'mental' clauses.[34] We shall return to this area in Chapter 10, Section 10.3.1, showing that certain 'attributive' clauses with fact clauses as Carrier and Attributes of assessment form part of the realization of a semantic system of assessment. The nouns in *it is* include fact nouns such as *fact, idea*, but they also include nouns of evaluation such as *pity, shame, nuisance* that are less likely to function as Head/Thing in nominal groups with a fact clause as Postmodifier/Qualifier.

In an 'identifying' clause, the fact clause serving as Token is identified with a Value realized by a nominal group with a noun as Head that typically belongs to the class of fact nouns (exemplified above in Table 7-26; see below); this fact noun may itself be qualified by an embedded fact clause. The Value is an interpretation of the fact clause, identifying it as a particular fact of some class of fact such as reason, problem, lesson, difficulty. As the examples above illustrate, the Value nominal group may include an Epithet (*thorniest, most important, plain* in the examples above; cf. *obvious, indisputable, appalling, significant, simple, mere*) assessing the fact represented by the Token (in the same way as Epithets within Attributes do) or a Numerative (*third* in the examples above; cf. *first, next, last*). This latter is important in the development of discourse, being agnate with an internal temporal conjunction (cf. *thirdly, the supreme interest for the whole world* ...): the enumerated Value is

Table 7-27 *it is* Attribute: adjective/ noun *that ...*

			Adjective	Noun
proposition	(1)	cognition	doubtful, sure, plausible, (un)believable, (un)imaginable	
		probability	certain, likely, probable, possible	possibility, likelihood, certainty, coincidence (~ it happens that ...)
		usuality	(un)common, (un)usual [*that ... ; for ... to ...*]	tendency, trend [*that ... ; for ... to ...*]
		obviousness	clear, evident, obvious	(clear, obvious) fact
	(2)	attitude	happy, sad, delightful, pleasing, amusing, surprising, (un)fortunate	pity, shame, relief, tragedy, surprise, regret
		judgement	inconvenient, immoral, good, excellent	nuisance, bad/mistaken idea good/ excellent idea
		importance	important, significant, critical	priority
proposal	desire		desirable, acceptable	requirement
	obligation		necessary, required	necessity, rule, principle, law

---

[34] The 'attributive' clause may have an agnate 'mental' clause of the "please" type: *it is surprising (to me) that ... ~ it surprises me that ...*; the equivalent of the Senser in the 'mental' clause is a circumstance of Angle, as illustrated in Figure 7-23 above.

the thematic point of departure of the clause and this Theme locates the clause as a message in the unfolding text.

The 'attributive' clauses illustrated and discussed above are all 'impersonal': the Carrier is realized by a nominal group with a fact clause and the Attribute by one that includes the kind of noun or adjective listed in Table 7-27. However, we also need to take note of 'attributive' clauses where the Carrier is realized by a nominal group denoting a person and the Attribute is a nominal group with an embedded fact clause, either 'possessive' with a noun as Head (e.g. *idea, notion, inkling* [[*that ...*]]) or 'intensive' with an adjective as Head of the nominal group (e.g. *sure, certain, aware, cognizant, oblivious (of the fact)* [[*that ...*]]); for example:

> They would have no **idea** [[[that the current British theatrical renaissance is having an effect far beyond the West End of London, || so that Broadway is heavily influenced by the highly successful plays of today [[that it has imported from Britain]]]]. [LOB_A]

> However, I am not **sure** [[that [[what probabilists and what physicists mean here by 'fields']] are quite synonymous]], [LOB_J]

These 'personal' 'attributive' clauses are closely agnate with projecting 'mental' clauses: *they have no idea ~ they don't know, I'm not sure ~ I don't know*.

Another, minor but significant, environment in which fact clauses occur is that of 'existential' clauses (an environment favoured by *evidence*):

> There is **evidence** [[that the Russians were just as surprised as anyone else at the suddenness and violence of them]], but it is, of course, a situation ideal for exploitation. [LOB_B]

> If the serum of a D negative individual agglutinates the D positive but not the D negative control cells, there is **a high probability** [[that the serum contains anti-D]], but the specificity should be confirmed by testing against several more examples of D-positive and D-negative red cells. [LOB_J]

There is no mental process corresponding to fact or chance, no implication of a conscious participant that is doing the projecting. Unlike nominal groups with nouns of projection, nominal groups with fact nouns are not nominalizations of projection nexuses (cf. Figure 7-22). A fact, as already pointed out, is an impersonal projection. However, it is possible for a fact to enter into a 'mental' process clause without being projected by it. In this case it functions as a Phenomenon within the mental process clause. For example:

> The fact [[that he rides in such exalted company]] **will not deter** Scott. [LOB_A]

> With the heavy expenditure on new rating, plus a new street costing 1,000,000, the cost of the Pump Room, new Municipal Offices, and so on, the eventual rates are likely to deter people from coming to live in the town, as they **would** probably **be influenced** more by excessively high rates than by the fact [[that there was a luxury swimming bath for use in winter]]. [LOB_B]

> He **overlooked** the fact [[that Ceylon had to be governed not only in the first few years after independence but for all time]]; and this raises several questions.[LOB_G]

> Sternberg himself photographed the film, reveling in such pure artificiality, **regretting** only [[that he had to use real water]]. [David Thomson, *A biographical dictionary of film*, p. 780]

> You know I smoke and I hate it. I **hate** [[that I do it]]. And I'm at that point where I have to make the decision. I can't go on any longer with it. [Text 83]

I just **love** [[that he is my dad]]. [TV interview]

I **like** the idea [[[of Tom Robbins waiting for me, || Tim Robbins waiting for me on a beach somewhere]]]. [Text 82]

Note the following pair (Figure 7-24):

(a)

||| Mark Anthony |	thought ||	that Caesar was ambitious |||
α		'β
Senser	Process	

(b)

||| Mark Anthony |	regretted	' [[(the fact) that Caesar was dead]] |||
Senser	Process	Phenomenon: fact

Fig. 7-24   Mental process with (a) idea, (b) fact

In (a) the clause *that Caesar was dead* is projected as an 'idea' by *Mark Antony thought*. It is therefore a separate, hypotactic clause; and hence (i) it cannot be preceded by *the fact*; (ii) it cannot be replaced by Caesar's death; (iii) it can be quoted: '*Caesar is dead*,' *thought Mark Antony*; (iv) it can be replaced by the substitute *so*: *Mark Antony thought so* (cf. Section 7.5.5.1 above). In (b), however, the clause *that Caesar was dead*, although it is a projection, is not projected by *Mark Antony regretted*, which is a clause of emotion not of cognition. It is not an idea but a fact; hence it is embedded, and hence (i) it can be preceded by a 'fact' noun; (ii) it can be replaced by a nominal group *Caesar's death*; (iii) it cannot readily be quoted: *Mark Antony regretted*, '*Caesar is dead*' is very forced; and (iv) it can be replaced by the reference item *it*, but not by the substitute *so*: *Mark Antony regretted it* (not *so*). The form *Mark Antony dreaded that Caesar was dead* is an example of a type that allows both interpretations, and hence is ambiguous: as idea (hypotactic), 'he thought (and wished otherwise)', or as fact (embedded), 'he was afraid because'.

The meaning of (a) in the preceding paragraph is that Mark Antony's thinking brought the idea that Caesar was dead into existence (as with *Mark Anthony believed/imagined that Caesar was dead*); but the meaning of (b) is that the already existing fact that Caesar was dead impinges on Mark Antony's consciousness (as with *that Caesar was dead scared Mark Anthony*). In fact, the 'emotive' type with a fact clause as Phenomenon is more common in the 'effective' variant of agency (the 'please' type) than the 'middle' one (the 'like' type): the Phenomenon is explicitly construed as an Agent bringing about the Medium/Senser's involvement in the process of emotion.

It **did not surprise** him very much [[to find [[that the door opened on the latch]]]], for it was so old and worn that it offered little security. [LOB_L]

She had never reconciled herself to things which hurt her, and sometimes he **was frightened** [[[that when bad things began to happen || she would have so little habit of optimism to support her]]]. [LOB_K]

The evidence against him was by no means decisive, but both judge and jury **seem to have been influenced** by the fact [[that the doctor himself was a morphine addict]]. [LOB_K]

Like 'middle mental' clauses, 'effective' ones either project ideas within a clause nexus or include fact clauses as Phenomenon, e.g.

(a)	||| it strikes me ||	that there's no one here |||
	α	'β
(b)	||| it worries me	'[[that there's no one here]] |||

The first means 'in my opinion there's no one here', with *there's no one here* as an idea. The second means 'there's no one here, and that worries me', with *there's no one here* as a fact. The fact exists prior to the occurrence of the mental process; but the idea does not – it is brought into existence in the course of the mental process. Thus the second is agnate with *there's no one here, which worries me*; but we cannot say *there's no one here, which strikes me*. The two are very distinct in speech, thanks to the intonation pattern (see below); the different analyses are given in Figure 7-25.

(a)

it	strikes	me	that there's no one here
α		→	'β
clause			clause
	Process: mental: cognition	Senser	

(b)

it	worries	me	[[that there's no one here]]
	Process: mental: emotion	Senser	
Pheno-			-menon
nominal ...			... group
Head			Postmodifier
			[[clause: fact]]

Fig. 7-25 Hypotactic projection (a), contrasted with fact as postposed subject (b)

The difference in structure is clear from the intonation pattern. That of (a) corresponds to *I rather think there's no one here*, with falling tonic (tone 1) on *here* and perhaps a separate falling-rising tonic (tone 4) on *strikes/think*; that of (b) corresponds to *it worries me, the emptiness of the place*, a compound tone group with tone 1 on *worries* and tone 3 on *here/emptiness*, showing clearly that that *there's no one here* is functioning as a postposed Subject. Again, *it strikes me* is a cognitive process clause, and so can project an idea, whereas *it worries me* is and emotive one and cannot.

But even with some cognitive and verbal processes, a projected element may occur which is **not projected by that process**; for example:

544

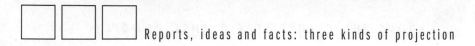

[cognitive]

Just before dress rehearsal, under pressure from the company, he reluctantly **accepted** [[that such ideas were outmoded]], and dropped them. [Gielgud, 166]

The second category of temple land was particularly important and it **was accepted** [[that the holders of this land could sub-lease it]]. [World History, 85]

[verbal]

'That was pretty obvious,' smiled Sir Cedric, 'and I **admit** [[I once had doubts about you]]'. [LOB_L]

With sly winks and discreet sniggering he **conveyed** [[[that he knew very well || that there was a great deal more than Philip confessed]]]. [Of Human Bondage]

And there will always be 'borderline cases', instances where the line is hard to draw. Table 7-28 summarizes the distribution of hypotactic projection of idea and locution clauses in clauses nexuses vs. embedded fact clauses across process types. The table includes both propositions and proposals; we now turn to proposals as embedded fact clauses.

Table 7-28 Hypotactic projection vs. fact clauses across process types

		Report (idea, locution) α β	Fact
mental	perceptive	we saw that the boats had been turned - see § 7.4.6	
	cognitive	✓ Process: believe, consider, guess know, reckon, think/strike; fear, dread (= 'think with fear that ... ')	Process: accept, overlook, recognize + Phenomenon/Range
	desiderative	✓ Process: want, wish, would like, hope, intend, plan	–
	emotive	–	✓ Process: fear, dread (= 'be afraid because of the fact that ...')/frighten, scare; rejoice, grieve, mourn/sadden; worry/worry; resent + Phenomenon/(Range or Agent)
verbal	indicating: declarative	✓ Process: say, tell, explain, notify	Process: admit, acknowledge, convey + Verbiage
	indicating: interrogative	✓ Process: ask, enquire, query	–
	imperating	✓ Process: tell, command, order; promise, undertake, threaten	–
relational	intensive & attributive	–	✓ Process: be (become, seem, etc.) + Attribute: obvious, clear, evident; certain, likely, possible, etc. [see Table 7-27]
	intensive & identifying	–	✓ Process: be (become, seem)/show, prove, ensure etc. + Value: fact noun [see Table 7-26]

545

Finally, as may be expected an embedded projection may belong to the class of proposals rather than propositions, as in

> The thorniest **problem** for next week's conference is [[to settle the relationships between them and the rest of the country]]. [LOB_A]

> The **surprise** was [[to meet Russians (not intellectuals, but common folk) [[who took a contrary view]]]]. [LOB_A]

> You mentioned the **need** of the artist and the right of the artist [[to withdraw]] and yet you have lived consistently a public life. [Text 16]

> if I had not been asked to terminate a life, I would not be so vehement about the **need** [[to help people who are begging for death]] [Text 24]

> The two-year study by Amnesty International, its first comprehensive analysis of North America, accuses Washington of failing in its **duty** [[to provide a moral lead to the rest of the free world]]. [Text 2]

This defines the fourth category of 'fact' nouns referred to earlier (see above, Table 7.26):

> (4) **needs** (nouns of modulation) relate to proposals, which are inherently modulated – e.g. 'it is necessary for ... to ...'.

These, again, have no corresponding mental process verbs; they differ from nouns like *order* (the name of a verbal process) and *insistence* (the name of a mental process) in the same way that *fact* differs from *thought* and *statement* – they do not imply a Sayer or a Senser. Like a proposition, a proposal may either be embedded as Qualifier to one of these nouns, as in the examples above, or may function on its own as a nominalization e.g.

> You've said that one of your editorial **rules** is [[not to publish your buddies]]. [Text 21]

> Again, a first **requirement** is [[to do no harm to organizational frameworks [[that, through years of evolution, are finally at the stage [[where they are supporting programs [[that are actually helping us to get on with the business [[of increasing understanding]]]]]]]]. [Text 32]

> The title for king fell out of use because its final **requirement** was [[that the man [[who aspires to be king]] would first pay all the debt [[owed by every single man and every single woman in the community]]]]! [Text 16]

and we can construct similar pairs, for example

> (a) ||| he insisted || that they had to wait in line |||

>   α   'β!

> (b) ||| he resented (the rule) [['! that they had to wait in line]]

where in (a) it is the 'mental' clause *he insisted* that does the projecting, while in (b) the projected clause is embedded. The 'mental' clause with the embedded fact clause is of the 'emotive' subtype, just as with propositions. But the 'mental' clause projecting the idea clause in (a) is not a 'cognitive' one but rather a 'desiderative' one. With 'mental' clauses, the general principle is that embedded fact clauses serve as Phenomenon in 'emotive' clauses,

whether the facts are propositions or proposals; and that propositions are projected by 'cognitive' clauses whereas proposals are projected by 'desiderative' ones: see Table 7-28.

As with propositions, there is an impersonal form of expression, *it is required/expected that you wait in line*; these are the imperative (proposal) equivalents of *it is said/thought that* ... with propositions. They have an important function as explicitly 'objective modulations' whereby the speaker disclaims responsibility for making the rules (see Chapter 10 below).

What kind of projection is a fact? It is still a meaning, a semantic abstraction, not some third type differing both from meanings and from wordings (indeed, there is no third level to which it could belong). But it is not a meaning created in anybody's consciousness, nor is it emitted by any signal source; it is simply got up so as to function as a participant in some other process – typically a relational process, but sometimes also a mental or a verbal one. Not, however, in a material process; facts cannot do things, or have things done to them (for apparent exceptions to this principle see Section 7.4.6 above).

A fact is thus analogous, as a form of projection, to what we called an 'act' as a form of expansion. Each represents the least prototypical form of its own general category; and hence the least differentiated. Whereas there is a clear distinction between expansion and projection in their finite clausal forms – between, say, (projection) *he never asked if/whether it was snowing* and (expansion) *he never came if/when it was snowing* – there is only a minimal distinction, and perhaps even blending, between (projection: fact) *she liked the snow falling* (*that the snow was falling*) and (expansion: act) *she watched the snow falling* (*as the snow was falling*). Seeing that facts and acts come so close together in this way, we can understand how it is that the same scale of interdependency types (parataxis/hypotaxis/rank shift) is associated with both these logical-semantic relations.

Let us now expand our projection table once more, to take account of quotes, reports and facts, both as meanings and as wordings (Table 7-29).

7.5.8 Summary of projection

Jill says something; this is a verbal event. To represent it, I use a 'verbal' clause *Jill said*, plus a quote of her verbal act *'It's raining'*. The two have equal status (paratactic), because both are wordings. That is to say, both my locution *Jill said* and Jill's locution *it's raining* are lexicogrammatical phenomena.

Fred thinks something; this is a mental event. To represent it, I use a 'mental' clause *Fred thought*, plus a report of his mental act (*that*) *it had stopped*. The two have unequal status (hypotactic), because one is a wording while the other is a meaning. That is to say, my locution *Fred thought* is a lexicogrammatical phenomenon, but Fred's idea 'that it had stopped' is a semantic one.

Thus parataxis is naturally associated with verbal projections and hypotaxis with mental ones. But, as we have seen, the pattern can be inverted. I can choose to report a verbal act, presenting a locution as a meaning; and I can choose to quote a mental act, presenting an idea as a wording. If we report speech, we do not commit ourselves to 'the very words': if I say *Henry said he liked your baking*, you would not quarrel with this even if you had overheard Henry expressing his views and knew that what he had actually said was *That was a beautiful cake*.

Table 7-29 Projection of propositions and proposals

Type of projecting process	projected speech function	Clause complex			Nominal group		
		Quote	Report		Fact		
		paratactic **1 2**		hypotactic $\alpha\ \beta$	embedded **[[ ]]**	as Postmodifier	as Head
idea ' mental	proposition	1 '2 She thought, 'I can' [Section 7.5.3]		α 'β She thought she could [Section 7.5.2]			
	proposal	He will her 'Do' [Section 7.5.4]		She wanted her to do [Section 7.5.4]			
locution " verbal	proposition	1 "2 She said, "I can" [Section 7.5.1]		α "β She said she could [Section 7.5.3]			
	proposal	He told her "Do" [Section 7.5.4]		He told her to do [Section 7.5.4]			
		'direct'	'free indirect'	'indirect'	'indirect qualifying'	impersonal qualifying	impersonal

Both verbal and mental acts have names, such as *statement, query, belief, doubt*; and these also serve to project, with the projected clause embedded as Postmodifier: *the belief that the sky might fall on their heads*. There is a point of overlap between these and embedded expansions of the elaborating type (relative clauses): both may be introduced by *that*, and this produces ambiguities such as *the report that he had submitted disturbed everyone*:

(a)   the report [[= that he had submitted]]

    'the document which he had drafted'

(b)   the report [[" I that he had submitted]]

    'to hear that he had yielded'

Parallel to projected information (propositions) is the projection of goods-&-services (proposals), which likewise may be paratactic, hypotactic, or embedded as Qualifier to a noun; and again the phenomenon may be verbal (locution, projected by the processes *offer, command, suggest/suggestion*, etc.) or mental (idea, projected by *intend/intention, wish, hope*, etc.). The difference in the mental processes is that propositions are projected by cognitive processes whereas proposals are projected by desiderative ones (see Table 7-28).

However, it is possible for an idea to be associated with a mental process while not being projected by it, as in *they rejoiced that their team had won.* When one clause projects another, the two always form a clause nexus; but here, where *that their team had won* comes ready-made as a projection, rather than being turned into one by the process of rejoicing, the idea is embedded as Phenomenon and the whole forms a single clause. This happens particularly when a proposition is an object of emotion: when the fact that ... is a source of pleasure, displeasure, fear, surprise, amusement, interest or some other emotion (see Table 7-28).

Such projections may be embedded as they stand, as nominalizations – equivalent to functioning as Head. But frequently they occur as Postmodifier to a noun of the 'fact' class (see Table 7-26), e.g. *the fact that their team had won.* Fact nouns include 'cases', 'chances' and 'proofs', related to propositions; and 'needs', related to proposals. We refer to these projections, therefore, as facts. Whereas any clause that is projected by another clause, verbal or mental, is either a quote (paratactic) or a report (hypotactic, or embedded if the process is a noun), any clause that has the status 'projected' but without any projecting process is a fact and is embedded, either as a nominalization serving as Head or as Postmodifier to a 'fact' noun serving as Head. This includes some of those functioning in mental clauses, as mentioned above, and all projections functioning in relational clauses (since a relational process cannot project). It also includes 'impersonal' projections such as *it is said ... , it is believed ... , it seems ... ,* where the 'process' is not really a process at all, but simply a way of turning a fact into a clause.

7.6 The clause complex as textual domain

The clause complex is, as we have emphasized, the most extensive domain of grammatical patterning – of patterns of wording, patterns organized in terms of logical, recursive systems and structures. It makes a major contribution to the organization of text, serving to realize (rhetorical) sequences within (rhetorical) paragraphs. In other words, it contributes to the rhetorical-relational development of text by providing grammatical resources for 'choreographing' local rhetorical complexes (cf. Figure 7-2, Table 7-3 above, and see Matthiessen, 2002a; cf. also Cloran, Stuart-Smith & Young, 2001, 2007). The grammar also provides resources for guiding the development of text beyond the domain of the clause complex, but these resources are concerned with cohesion rather than with structure: see Chapter 9.

At the same time as it contributes to the rhetorical-relational organization of text, the clause complex also serves as a domain of organization within the textual metafunction. We have seen that from a textual point of view clauses serve as messages – as quanta of information in the flow of discourse (Chapter 3); based on this insight into the textual nature of the clause, we can characterize the clause complex as a **message complex**.

(i) The sequence of clauses within a clause complex is textually significant from a thematic point of view. This sequence is fixed in the case of parataxis (with the exception of parataxis in the environment of projection), as in 1 *He pointed his arrow*, 2 *but saw nothing* in Figure 7-26; here the primary clause is in a sense thematic in relation to the secondary one even though the sequence is fixed: the primary clause may serve as a point of departure or orientation for the secondary clause. However, in the case of hypotaxis, the sequence is not fixed; it can be progressive ($\alpha \wedge \beta$) or regressive ($\beta \wedge \alpha$) – or the hypotactically dependent clause may be included within the dominant clause ($\alpha << \beta >>$). For example, in the narrative passage in Figure 7-26, the hypotactic nexus β *as he came to a thicket,* α

549

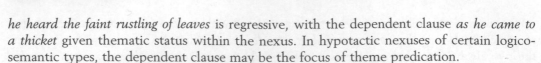

he heard the faint rustling of leaves is regressive, with the dependent clause *as he came to a thicket* given thematic status within the nexus. In hypotactic nexuses of certain logico-semantic types, the dependent clause may be the focus of theme predication.

(ii) In spoken English, the sequence of clauses within a clause complex may be mapped onto one or more information units; that is, there are textually different ways in which a clause complex can be mapped onto an **information unit complex** (see Halliday & Greaves, 2008: Section 5.3). The unmarked mapping is one (ranking) clause = one information unit. Thus the paratactic sequence 1 ^ 2 and the hypotactic sequence β ^ α would each be chunked into two information units (realized by different tone sequences, tone 3 followed by tone 1, and tone 4 followed by tone 1, respectively: see Section 7.7 below). However, there are regular departures from this unmarked pattern. (1) When the dependent clause in a hypotactic nexus is included within the dominant clause, the nexus may be chunked into three information units, with three points of New information (as in //4 **John** //4 who arrived **late** //1 missed the **speeches** // (Halliday, 1967a: 35)). (2) When the dependent clause follows its dominant clause in a hypotactic nexus (progressive sequence), it may be included in the same information unit as the dominant clause, with the focus of New information within the dependent clause (as in //1 I came because he **told** me // (Halliday, 1967a: 33)). (3) When the logico-semantic relation of the nexus is one of projection, the projecting clause may be part of the same information unit as the projected clause, being tonally cliticized to it. See further below, Section 7.7, on clause complexing and tone.

(iii) The sequence of clauses within a clause complex is also textually significant as a **cohesive domain** (see Chapter 9 on COHESION); in particular, the clause complex licenses certain pattern of 'ellipsis' that may involve co-reference. Thus in the paratactic sequence 1 *He pointed his arrow*, 2 *but saw nothing* in Figure 7-26, the Subject of the secondary clause is 'elliptical' (*but* [Subject:] ∅ [Finite/Predicator:] *saw* [Complement:] *nothing*), and is interpreted as co-referential with the Subject of the primary clause (*he*). Similarly, 'elliptical' Subjects of non-finite dependent clauses, tend to be interpreted as co-referential with the Subjects of their dominant clauses (as in α *I went on to birds* β *starting with my mother's feeder*)[35]. Thus in a clause complex, paratactic and hypotactic co-referential ellipsis may work together to signal the continuity of thematic Subjects, e.g.:

||| 1 <u>The scientific community</u> is beginning to recognize the opportunity || 2α but [Subject:] ∅ has done little so far || 2β [Subject:] ∅ to provide useful conceptual tools and means of [[communicating these linkages]] [[[that can be used || to build the social and political consensus necessary for action]]]. [Text 32]

Let us return briefly to thematic considerations within a hypotactic clause nexus. Compare the following two hypotactic nexuses from a procedural text:

α ^ β   fry the onions **until** slightly brown [Text 218]

β ^ α   **if** you want a more substantial stuffing add a little mashed potato [Text 218]

---

[35] And this tendency has been turned into a 'rule' in prescriptive style-guides. However, it is easy to find exceptions, even in formal writing, e.g.: ||| *In doing that,* || *the first requirement is one [[that is analogous to a principle [[accepted by the medical community]]]]:* || *Do no harm to existing programs [[that are under way]].* ||| Here the understood Subject of *in doing that* is not the Subject of the dominant clause (*the first requirement*).

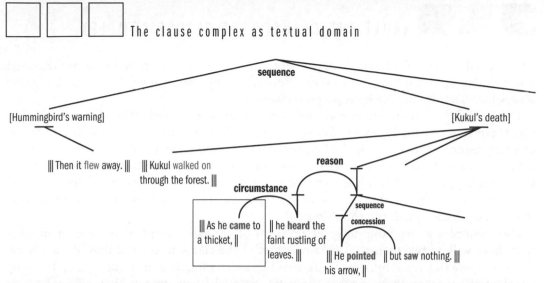

Fig. 7-26   Clause complex with thematic hypotactic clause in the development of a narrative episode

In the first nexus, the sequence is α ^ β (**progressive** sequence). Here the dependent clause is given rhematic status. In the procedure, the process of frying the onions is started before the change of colour takes place: the sequence of clauses is iconic with the sequence of events. In the second nexus, the sequence is β ^ α (**regressive** sequence). Here the dependent clause is given thematic status: see the first structural layer (Theme$_1$ ^ Rheme$_1$) in Figure 7-27. This thematic clause signals a break in the procedure and introduces a variation on the basic method. This re-orientation in the development of the text is achieved by giving the conditional dependent clause thematic status.

The contrast between progressive and regressive sequence illustrated above is quite typical of procedural texts: temporal clauses delimiting the performance of actions tend to be rhematic, but conditional clauses and purpose clauses re-orienting the development of the text are thematic. In general, thematic β-clauses serve to set up a local context in the discourse for the α-clause: they re-orient the development (as in the staging of a narrative), often distilling some aspect of what has gone before to provide the point of departure for the dominant clause, thus creating a link to the previous discourse (cf. Longacre, 1985; Thompson, 1984; Ford & Thompson, 1986). For example:

‖‖ I remember an example ⟦⟦that happened ‖ when I was probably no more than four years old⟧⟧. ‖‖ My brother and I were playing in a neighbourhood friend's garage, ‖ and he disappeared for a minute. ‖‖ When our friend came back ‖ he said ‖ that we had to go home, ‖ 'because my father doesn't want any niggers in his house.' ‖‖ We didn't even know ‖ what the word was. ‖‖ [Text 206]

‖‖ The DMK is already annoyed with the BJP government at the Centre ‖ for not favorably considering its demand ⟦to recall TN Governor Fathima Bheevi for her swearing in Jayalalitha as CM⟧. ‖‖ If the Centre accepts the AIADMK government's objection ‖ and drops the earlier list, ‖ facilitating the AIADMK government to appoint its choice of judges to the Madras High Court, ‖ then the DMK may voice its opposition to such a move. ‖‖ [Text 261]

‖‖ If ifs and ans were pots and pans, ‖ there'd be no need for tinkers. ‖‖ [Proverb]

551

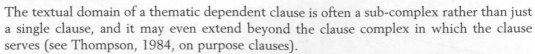

The textual domain of a thematic dependent clause is often a sub-complex rather than just a single clause, and it may even extend beyond the clause complex in which the clause serves (see Thompson, 1984, on purpose clauses).

The last of the examples above comes from a time when people still talked in proverbs and there was a saying for every occasion, as happened in our great-grandmothers' day. It was the response given to a child who prevaricated, who claimed that all would have been well if ... (*an* is an older synonym of *if*, now lost). For granny, the theme of her discourse was 'let's suppose', and this had two strands to it, one verbal 'if talk could achieve', and the other non-verbal 'if things were as we fantasize them'; both neatly encapsulated by thematizing back to him the child's own *if*.

The examples above pose no great problem of analysis; the point to bear in mind is that there will be two thematic domains – that of the clause nexus and that of the clause. We can show this layered thematic pattern by representing it as in Figure 7-27. The only problem arises when there is other thematic material (thematic vocative, conjunctive or continuative elements or thematic interpersonal Adjuncts), as in:

> ||| Lord, if it be thy will, || let this cup pass from me. ||| [Text 17]

> ||| Alternatively, if you've had enough of colonial relics, || a Captain Cook Cruise can be booked on the same number. ||| [Text 22]

> ||| But, of course, if you pursue the responsibility, || you're likely to be denied the privileges [[of exercising the intellectual effort]]. ||| [Text 234]

> ||| Well, if they say it in the parliament, || it's true [[that everyone can hear them]]. ||| [Text 184]

> ||| Ironically, if Ofsted asked its inspectors || to identify 'schools in need of special support', rather than 'failing schools', || the list would be five times as long. ||| [Text 97]

Here there are three possibilities: the first is to treat the thematic material before the dependent clause (*Lord*; *alternatively*; *but, of course*; *well*; *ironically* in the examples above) as part of the Theme of the first clause in the nexus (corresponding to Theme$_2$ in Figure 7-27); the second is to treat is as part of the dominant clause following the thematic dependent clause, analysing this dependent clause as an 'interruption' included within the dominant clause (cf. Footnote 3 earlier in this chapter); and the third is to treat it as part of the Theme of the clause nexus (corresponding to Theme$_1$ in the figure). Strictly speaking this depends on the intonation: if it is spoken as a separate tone group it is part of the Theme of the clause nexus (Theme$_1$) or of the Theme of the dominant clause (Theme$_3$); if not, it is part of the Theme of the dependent clause in the nexus (Theme$_2$). But it does not matter very much, so long as it is shown to be thematic.

if	you	want a more substantial stuffing	add	a little mashed potato
Theme$_1$			Rheme$_1$	
structural	topical		topical	
Theme$_2$		Rheme$_2$	Theme$_3$	Rheme$_3$

Fig. 7-27   Theme in clause nexus and tactically related clauses

552

Hypotactically dependent clauses may thus serve as Theme within the domain of a clause nexus. In addition, certain hypotactically dependent clauses of the 'enhancing' type may be predicated within the system of THEME PREDICATION. For example, a temporal enhancing clause may be predicated to foreground a timeframe defined by an event:

> In fact, despite some ominous undertones even in Britain and France, not to mention Mussolini's increasing grip of Italy, it might be assumed that democratic prospects were on the mend between 1925 and the great 'economic blizzard' which began towards the end of 1929. It was [[when German unemployment began rising again catastrophically in 1930]] [[[that Hitler, whose denunciation of Jews, Versailles, and traitors, sold to Moscow or the *Entente*, had become part of the German political scene, scented his first chances of establishing an altogether more formidable dictatorship than Mussolini's]]]. [LOB_J]

Here the thematic effect is the same as with theme-predicated elements of the clause: the Theme is given the sense of contrastive selection among a set of alternative candidates. Similarly, an enhancing clause of reason may be predicated:

> The International War Crimes Tribunal has been subject to abuse from people [[who have much to hide]]. It has been said that the conclusions of this Tribunal were known in advance. The conclusions of our Tribunal are built out of the evidence. The evidence is abundant. It is [[precisely because the knowledge of crime is a cause for inquiry]] [[that we are holding this session]]. [Text 328]

This is possible with certain clauses of time, place, reason and manner, but seldom with clauses of condition or concession and never with 'elaborating' or 'extending' hypotactically dependent clauses (cf. Matthiessen, 1995a: 157–158).

7.7 Clause complex and tone

Table 7-30 summarizes the intonation patterns that have been discussed in this chapter as realizing systemic selections within the clause complex. These include (i) tone concord: sequences of two or more instances of the same tone; (ii) tone sequences: sequences of two tones, 1 1, 3 1, 4 1; (iii) tonality: post-tonic prolongation of tone group.

The tone sequences 1-1, 3-1, and 4-1 are the unmarked realizations of these three grammatical relationships, respectively (for more detail, see Halliday & Greaves, 2008: Section 5.3.1). However, as is typical of such associations of grammatical and phonological variants, the tonal patterns construe meaning of their own, so that the tonal and structural features may be combined in any of the possible ways. Here, as we have represented things, there are nine possibilities; and each has its own particular nuance. If, for example, the speaker says

// 4 ^ she / packed her / **bags** // 1 then she / left / **home** //

a tension is set up between the lexicogrammatical pattern, which treats the two parts as cohesive but not structurally related, and the prosodic pattern, which treats the first clause as not only incomplete but dependent on the second for its interpretation. We get the opposite effect in

// 1 ^ as / soon as she'd / packed her / **bags** she // 1 left / **home** //

Table 7-30 Tone concord and tone sequence in clause complexes

	Meaning	Tone pattern	Environment	Examples
(i) tone concord	elaboration (paratactic/hypotactic)	repeated tone (1 1, 2 2, 4 4)	hypotactic clause complex	// 1 where's my / green **hàt** // 1 ^ which I / had on / **yèsterday** //
			group complex (Ch. 8)	// 2 have you / seen my / green / **hát** the // 2 one with / two little / **feáthers** //
(ii) tone sequence	degrees of interdependence	1 – 1	cohesive	// 1 ^ she / packed her / **bàgs** // 1 then she / left / **hòme** //
		3 – 1	paratactic	// 3 ^ as / soon as she'd / packed her / **bāgs** and // 1 left / **hòme** //
		4 – 1	hypotactic	// 4 ^ she / packed her / **bǎgs** she // 1 left / **hòme** //
(iii) tonality	projection marking	tonal cliticization: enclitic	"1 ^ 2	// 2 ^ does it / **mátter** / said / Henry //
		tonal cliticization: proclitic	1 ^ "2	// 1 ^ Henry said / what's the / **màtter** //

In writing, the unmarked sequences typically come out as follows:

> She packed her bags. Then she left home.   (1-1)
>
> She packed her bags, and left home.   (3-1)
>
> As soon as she'd packed her bags she left home.   (4-1)

The effect of the marked combination can be represented like this:

> She packed her bags then she left home.   (4-1)
>
> As soon as she'd packed her bags. She left home.   (1-1)

The problem is, of course, that because these are marked forms the writing system has no clear way of indicating them. At best, it can signal that something unusual is afoot, and leave it to the reader to discern what that something is.

7.8 Texts

Text 1 [child, age 7, and parent]

Structure	Speaker	Clause	Tone
α	Son:	‖‖ How do you see ‖	1
'βα		‖ what happened long **ago** ‖	
'β×β		‖ before you were **born**? ‖‖	1
	Parent:	‖‖ You read about it in **books**? ‖‖	2
	Son:	‖‖ **No** ‖‖	2
α		‖‖ Use a **microscope** ‖	1
×β		‖ to look **back** ‖‖	1
	Parent:	How do you do **that**?	1
	Son:	‖‖ **Well** ‖	1
1×β1		‖ if you're in a **car** ‖	4
1×β+2		‖ or you're in an **observation** coach ‖	4
1α1		‖ you look **back** ‖	3
1α×2α		‖ and then you see ‖	1
1α×2'β		‖ what happened **before** ‖	
+2αα		‖ but you need a **microscope** ‖	1
+2α×βα		‖ to see ‖	4
+2α×β'β		‖ what happened long **ago** ‖	
+2×β		‖ because it's very far **away** ‖‖	1

Text 2 [monologue]

×β1	||| But while you're being kept waiting ||
×β=21	|| while there's this long delay ||
×β=2+2α	|| and people [[wearing uniforms]] stride up and down ||
×β=2+2=βα	|| looking ||
×β=2+2=β×β	|| as if they have some serious business [[to attend to]] ||
αα	|| you don't realize ||
α'βα	|| that you're being kept waiting deliberately ||
α'β×β	|| so that the people [[you're going to be employed by]] can observe you ||
α'β×γα	|| so as to see ||
α'β×γ'βα	|| how you behave ||
α'β×γ'β×β1	|| when you feel under stress ||
α'β×γ'β×β+2	|| or start to lose confidence in yourself |||

CHAPTER EIGHT

GROUP AND PHRASE COMPLEXES

8.1 Overview of complexing at group/phrase rank

Now that we have described 'complexes' of the clause, we can return briefly to a consideration of complex structures involving groups and phrases. We started the previous chapter with the following example of a 'paratactic' clause complex:

> ||| I went to school in New York City || **and then** we lived up on the Hudson for a while, || **then** [∅: we] moved to Connecticut. ||| [Text 7]

Here whole clauses are related by enhancement to form a temporal sequence: '1 then 2 then 3'. As the example illustrates, a clause entering into a clause complex in this way may be elliptical, the typical case being ellipsis of the Subject (as in *and moved to Connecticut*, where the Subject *we* has been ellipsed); but it is still the whole clause as a configuration of elements that enters into a combination with another clause. However, instead of combining whole clauses we may combine parts of clauses – groups/phrases realizing single elements within a simple clause – to form complexes in the same way; for example:

> ||| We had a wonderful piece of property in Connecticut, back up in the hills, || and <u>my brother and I</u> were both very interested in snakes and birds. ||| [Text 7]

Here the nominal groups *my brother* and *I* form a 'paratactic' nominal group complex, where *my brother* is extended by *I*; and this complex serves as the Subject of a simple clause. The complexing is thus focused on a single element within that clause; it does not affect the clause as a whole. There are in fact two more instances of complexing below clause rank in this example: *a wonderful piece of property in Connecticut* is elaborated by *back up in the hills*; and *snakes* is extended by *birds*. These instances of complexing are all local to one particular element of the clause. The complex *snakes* and *birds* can in fact be treated as a word complex rather than a group complex. If the speaker had said *poisonous snakes and migratory birds*, we would clearly have a nominal group complex because the structure here is Classifier: *poisonous* ^ Thing: *snakes* 'and' Classifier: *migratory* ^ Thing: *birds*. But while *snakes and birds* can be interpreted as Thing: *snakes* 'and' Thing: *birds*, it can equally be interpreted as Thing: *snakes and birds*. By the same token, in *all the snakes and birds living on the property*, the combination of *snakes and birds* has to be interpreted as a noun complex serving as Thing within a single nominal group, since it is configured with Premodifiers (*all the*) and a Postmodifier (*living on the property*).

Group and phrase complexes thus serve to develop single elements within a clause (or, if these complexes are embedded, a single element within a group or phrase), serving the same function as a simple group or phrase would. Textually, this means there is a single message; interpersonally, it means there is a single proposition or proposal; and experientially, it means that there is a single figure. Here are some further examples:

> ⦀ He had <u>a little kit – maps, a spare shirt, spare underpants</u>. ⦀ [Text 7]

> ⦀ I took a freighter <u>from New York, all the way up the Amazon into Peru</u>; ‖ I went all the way down to Tierra del Fuego. ⦀ [Text 7]

> ⦀ The moths fly off into the moon, ‖ and <u>finally, in that last scene</u>, he builds the bonfire. ⦀ [Text 7]

In any one of these examples, the complexing could be 'upgraded' to clause rank; but this would create two messages, two propositions (proposals), and two figures. Thus there is a clear semantic difference between the following two variants:

> ⦀ It just felt right, ‖ it felt exactly right. ⦀ [Text 7]

> † ⦀ It just felt right, exactly right. ⦀

Note that we have to differentiate group and phrase complexes from clause complexes involving ellipsis. In clause complexes where the Subject or the Subject and the Finite have been ellipsed in a continuing clause, it is easy to see that a whole clause is involved:

> ⦀ Then he went in the Navy ‖ and [Ø: he] helped design various gunnery training devices ⟦used during World War II⟧. ⦀ [Text 7]

But the whole clause is still involved in cases where other elements have been ellipsed:

> The Land-Rover was to take him to Santander, **then** the train [Ø: was to take him] to Bilbao for the late afternoon flight. [Beneath the Mountains]

Here *the train to Bilbao for the late afternoon flight* is an elliptical clause consisting of three explicit elements – Subject: *the train* + Adjunct: *to Bilbao* + Adjunct: *for the late afternoon flight*, with Finite/Predicator and Complement left out by ellipsis. The general principle is that as long as only one element is involved, we can analyse the complexing at group/phrase rank, but as soon as more than one element is involved, we have to analyse the complexing at clause rank and posit ellipsis in one of the clauses.

Group and phrase complexes are formed out of series of nexuses just as clause complexes are formed out of series of clause nexuses. Groups and phrases form nexuses in the same way that clauses do, by a combination of parataxis or hypotaxis with some type of logico-semantic relation; the different possibilities are set out in Table 8-1. Only elements having the same function can be linked in this way. Typically this will mean members of the same class: verbal group with verbal group, nominal group with nominal group, and so on. But it also includes other combinations, especially: adverbial group with prepositional phrase, since these share many of the same circumstantial functions in the clause; and nominal group with prepositional phrase, as Attribute (e.g. *plain or with cream*).

Table 8-1 taxis and logico-semantic type at group rank

		Parataxis	Hypotaxis
expansion	elaboration	nominal group: *his latest book, 'The Jaws of Life'* [APPOSITION]	nominal group: *my new hat, with the green feather* [description]
		adverbial group/prep. phr.: *alone, without help*	adverbial group/prep. phr.: *from now until Thursday* [path]
		verbal group: *got killed, got run over*	verbal group: *begin to do; seem to do* [PHASE]
	extension	nominal group: *either you or your head*	nominal group: *his teacup instead of the bread and butter*
		adverbial group/prep. phr.: *swiftly and without a moment's hesitation*	adverbial group/prep. phr.: *on time instead of two hours late*
		verbal group: *neither like nor dislike*	verbal group: *try to do; learn to do* [CONATION]
	enhancement	nominal group: *all those on board, and hence all the crew*	nominal group: –
		adverbial group/prep. phr.: *calmly enough, although not without some persuasion*	adverbial group/prep. phr.: *tomorrow before lunch* [narrowing]
		verbal group: *tried, but failed*	verbal group: *hasten to do* [MODULATION]
projection		nominal group: *the examiner's assessment, 'a brilliant work', seems hard to justify*	nominal group: –
		adverbial group/prep. phr.: –	adverbial group/prep. phr.: –
		verbal group: –	verbal group: *want to do; claim to do*

The kinds of paratactic nexus formed with groups or phrases are fairly general and easy to state. The hypotactic patterns that may be construed at this rank are, however, much more complex; they tend to be specific to one or other primary class of group or phrase, and also to cover a range of different logical-semantic relations – especially hypotaxis in the verbal group. We will begin with a short discussion of parataxis, and then consider hypotaxis in each of these contexts in turn. Most of the discussion (Sections 8.4–8.6) will be on types of nexus in the hypotactic verbal group.

8.2 Parataxis: groups and phrases

When groups and phrases are linked paratactically, they are given equal status; any of the members of the complex could, in principle, serve the same function as the whole complex. Thus alongside *In the mid-'80s, Apple introduced the LaserWriter – the first PostScript laser printer*, we could also have ... *introduced the LaserWriter* or ... *introduced the first PostScript laser printer*. Groups and phrases can be linked paratactically by apposition and by coordination. As with paratactic clauses the former are elaborating in function, the latter extending. Instances of the enhancing type are less common, since the meanings are too specific to be readily expressed as a relationship between units smaller than clauses; but they do occur. There are no paratactic group/phrase complexes linked by projection, except for nominal group complexes such as *the examiner's assessment, 'a brilliant work', seems hard to justify*, which lie on the borderline of elaborating parataxis.

8.2.1 Elaborating

This is the traditional category of 'apposition'. As with clauses, appositional group or phrase complexes are characterized by tone concord, signalling the semantic relationship of elaboration (cf. Chapter 7, Section 7.6). The elaborating group/phrase may restate or particularize; restatements include naming, explanatory glossing and shifts in perspective: a number of the themes of elaborating clause complexes are replayed on a smaller scale. Examples:

[verbal group:]
(Unfortunately she) got killed, got run over, (by one of those heavy lorries).

Yes, yes you can; ‖ but then I think ‖ emotion has to be – should be, anyhow – shaped by thought. [Text 135]

To build that library, ‖ Apple recommends ‖ copying, or "ripping," individual songs from CDs ⟦you already own⟧ ‖ and converting them into compressed MP3 files. [Text 121]

[nominal group:]
"Too often, human rights in the US are a tale of two nations – rich and poor, white and black, male and female." [Text 2]

... it's because we, the elites, are so great ⟦⟦that we carried through the changes⟧⟧. [Text 234]

Have you done any serious literary criticism ‖ since you left school; ‖ written anything ‖ or thought about it – literature, critically? [Text 125]

... and had long been guided by a world view, a cosmology, ⟦⟦that denied mutability – change through time – of both biological and social life⟧⟧. [Text 122]

In the mid-'80s, Apple introduced the LaserWriter – the first PostScript laser printer – ‖ and near-typeset output came into range for desktop users. [Text 120]

Freedom and steam – a political ideal and a source of energy – these were the forces ⟦⟦that drove the new age on⟧⟧. [Text 122]

While attending the Christian Missionary School there, ‖ he acquired his interest in the Hindu gods – a deliberate defiance of the school chaplain, ‖ who had ridiculed Indian religion. [Text 163]

... the Old Regime remained agrarian and rural, ‖ with most of the population engaged in the cultivation of grain crops, in particular – wheat, barley, and oats – ⟦⟦that were distributed regionally⟧⟧. [Text 122]

How does it differ from other ideologies ⟦⟦that are often associated with socialism⟧⟧, such as Leninism? [Text 212]

Have you read any poetry in the eighteenth century recently – any Pope? [Text 135]

[adverbial group/prepositional phrase:]
(I couldn't have done it) alone, without help.

This has just been when? – over the last few days? [Text 34]

Aesthetically, in terms of the vision in your head, what is the relationship between the fiction and the non-fiction? [Text 7]

In an elaborating nominal group complex, the secondary nominal group may be used to include an embedded clause as Qualifier:

‖‖ Near the San Diego Freeway interchange is the huge Shell Chemical Company plant, part of an industrial district ⟦⟦⟦that was established ‖ before the plain became almost covered with tract housing⟧⟧⟧. ‖‖ [Text 140]

Note also that the secondary nominal group may be delayed for textual reasons, giving rise to a discontinuous complex:

While each of these elements is absolutely essential, ‖ one must come first – peòple. [Text 115]

As with elaborating complexes in general, this is spoken on two tone groups, with tone concord.

It is important to distinguish between an elaborating group and an embedded group occurring as Qualifier: e.g. (taxis, elaborating) *his latest book, 'The Jaws of Life',* (embedded) *his book 'The Jaws of Life'.* The former is related to a non-defining relative; it means 'his latest book – which is "The Jaws of Life"', and is marked by tone concord:

//4 ^ his /latest /book the //4 jaws of /life was a //1 ghastly suc/cess //

The latter is related to a defining relative clause; it means 'this particular book of his (he has written others)' and has no tonic prominence on book.

Note that *or* in the sense of an alternative name for something is elaborating not extending; e.g.:

In one of those cities – one ⟦⟦whose name has long been forgotten⟧⟧ – there lived an old halac uinic, **or** chief. [Text 65]

I understand ‖ that later, you come to an age of hope, **or** at least resignation. [Text 17]

561

8.2.2 Extending

This is the traditional category of 'coordination'. Here the semantic relationship is one of 'and, or, nor, but, but not', as in the following examples:

[verbal group:]

(I) **neither** like **nor** dislike (it).

America can – **and** should – be proud of its soldiers, sailors, airmen, and marines. [Text 115]

There are, **and** can be, no general answers. [Text 212]

[nominal group:]

All the King's horses **and** all the King's men (couldn't put Humpty Dumpty together again).

Bruce **and** Philip were friends, ‖ Jane **and** I were friends ‖ and then you **and** – [Text 82]

Either you **or** your head (must be off, and that in about half no time).

Do you prefer say the Four Quartets to The Waste Land – **or** poems in The Waste Land period? [Text 125]

To import an iMovie (**or** any other QuickTime video file), ‖ just drag and drop the icon onto the iDVD template. [Text 121]

… they see the consequences of the doctrines [[they espouse]], **or** their profound moral failings. [Text 212]

[adverbial group/prepositional phrase:]

Swiftly **and** without a moment's hesitation (he leapt into the fray).

And the French author Voltaire gained, among his many honors, the reputation [[for being the first writer of note [[to earn his keep by his own words – **and** by some speculation on the market]]]]. [Text 122]

But many do it very self-consciously, very honestly, **and** even very constructively. [Text 234]

The idea of "free contract" between the potentate and his starving subject is a sick joke, perhaps worth some moments in an academic seminar [[exploring the consequences of (in my view, absurd) ideas]], **but** nowhere else. [Text 212]

Yes, insofar as they are driven to work by the need for survival; **or** by material reward, … [Text 212]

So there's a kind of an honest intelligentsia ‖ if you like, ‖ meaning not serving power, **either** as Red bureaucracy **or** as state capitalist, commissar equivalents. [Text 234]

Every list of persons or objects formulated by the grammar in the typical way (like a shopping list) is an instance of a paratactic nominal group complex:

Other 'Malgudi' novels are The Dark Room (1938), The English Teacher (1945), Mr. Sampathy (1949), The Financial Expert (1952), The Painter of Signs (1977), A Tiger for Malgudi (1983), The Talkative Man (1986). [Text 152]

An extending nominal group complex may be reinforced by a circumstantial Adjunct of Manner such as *both, jointly, separately, individually, respectively*:

||| We had a wonderful piece of property in Connecticut, back up in the hills, ‖ and my brother **and** I were **both** very interested in snakes and birds. ||| [Text 7]

||| Ross, << expected to go to the Middle East on Tuesday, >> intends to meet **separately** with Israeli Prime Minister Ehud Barak **and** Palestinian leader Yasser Arafat. ||| [Text 108]

562

||| For FY99, our requests for regular and supplemental appropriations |||[to fund these operations, || totaling $1.9 billion **and** $850 million **respectively,**|||[were also approved. ||| [Text 115]

These indicate how the element realized by the nominal group complex takes part in the process of the clause – either jointly or separately.

A number of common expressions like *slowly but surely, last but not least, by hook or by crook* belong to this general pattern. Extension can be used iconically to indicate degree; for example:

Television is very dangerous || because it <u>repeats **and** repeats **and** repeats</u> our disasters instead of our triumphs. [Text 101]

8.2.3 Enhancing

Here the semantic relationship involves a circumstantial relationship; this was not recognized as a distinct type in traditional accounts. As noted above, enhancing relationships are essentially between figures as a whole, and only rarely can they be interpreted as holding between particular elements of a figure. Examples are typically instances of time or cause:

[verbal group:]
(He) tried, **but** failed, (to extract the poison). 'although he tried, he failed' – concession

[nominal group:]
All those on board, **and hence** all the crew, (must have known that something was amiss).

Film hadn't been important until the Italians with realism and Rossellini and De Sica, **then** the French nouvelle vague. [Text 119]

Optimistu's true nature dawned slowly. It became slightly nasty, **then** really rather awful, **then** unremittingly horrendous **and then** lethal only by degrees. [Beneath the Mountains]

[adverbial group/prepositional phrase:]
(She took it) calmly enough, **although** not without some persuasion.

I imagined my framed survey of Xitu hanging above the fire for a few years, then being moved to the spare room, **then** into the bathroom, then finally being confined to the attic. [Beneath the Mountains]

From this crossroads town follow the main road south through increasingly arid landscapes towards Rembitan, a pretty little village claiming a 17th-century mosque, **then** Sade, where tall, thatched lumbung (rice-barns) climb the slopes. [Text 142]

Again, there are some cliché-like instances, e.g. (*he's been here*) *thirty-five years if a day*.

As with paratactic clauses, a paratactic group or phrase complex is not limited to two members. For example: (elaborating) *that old theatre, the Empire, the one they demolished last year*; (extending) (*you've been listening*) *at doors – and behind trees – and down chimneys*. This includes the possibility of nesting (see Section 7.2 above).

We are not in general going below the rank of the group. But note that paratactic relationships are also found within group structures, as relationships between words, as in *three or four* (*days*), *bigger and better* (*bananas*), (*he*) *either will or won't* (*object*), (*a*) *firm but gentle* (*voice*). Figure 8-1 gives an example of a nominal group incorporating both a paratactic and a hypotactic word complex; the structure is:

Deictic / γ ^ Epithet / β 1 ^ β 2 δ ^ β 2 γ ^ β 2 β ^ β 2 α ^ Thing / α

The	immediate	and	not	too	far	distant	future
γ	β						α
Deictic	Epithet						Thing
	1	+2					
		δ	γ	β	α		

Fig. 8-1   Nominal group with word complexes

8.3 Hypotaxis: nominal group

When groups and phrases are linked hypotactically, they are given unequal status, one serving as the dominant element (α) and the remainder as dependent ones (β γ δ ...). Hypotactic verbal group complexes involve either expansion or projection (see below), but hypotactic nominal group complexes and hypotactic adverbial group/prepositional phrase complexes are based only on expansion.

In a hypotactic nominal group complex, the dominant element can, in principle, serve the same function as the whole complex, but dependent elements cannot. Thus instead of *have you seen* (α) *my new hat,* (β) *with the feather in*, we can also say *have you seen my new hat*, but not *have you seen with the feather in*. While the dominant element has to be a nominal group, dependent elements can be adverbial groups or prepositional phrases. In nominal group complexing, hypotactic relations are either (i) elaborating, or (ii) extending; but we do not find enhancing ones.

(i) Elaborating. We saw in Chapter 6 that a nominal group can have as Postmodifier not only an embedded clause ('defining relative' clause) but also an embedded prepositional phrase, as in *the man* = [*in the moon*].

There is the same contrast between embedding and hypotaxis with a phrase as there is with a clause. Parallel to

(a)   ‖ (this is) my new house, = ‖ β which Jack built ‖

(b)   ‖ (this is) the house = ⟦ that Jack built ⟧ ‖

we have

(c)   (have you seen) | my new hat, = | β with the feather in

(d)   (have you seen) | my hat = [with the feather in] |

The secondary element in (c) is a descriptive phrase, 'note that it has a feather in it', not a defining one as in (d). Examples:

It began with worship at <u>St. John's Episcopal Church, across Lafayette Park from the White House</u> [Text 113]

Before the Opera House was completed ‖ <u>the Town Hall's Centennial Hall, with seating for 2,000,</u> was Sydney's main concert venue. [Text 22]

564

Note that *with a little of me thrown in* in the following example

> Those two guys, << with a little of me thrown in, >> came together as Lewis Moon. [Text 7]

is a clause, not a phrase; there are two elements of transitivity (*a little of me + thrown in*): see Chapter 7, Section 7.4.2.2 on clauses without an explicit Process introduced by *with(out)*.

   (ii) Extending. In exactly the same way as with elaboration, a nominal group may be extended hypotactically by a prepositional phrase, the preposition having the same sense as when used to introduce a non-finite extending clause (see Chapter 7, Table 7-9) – (1) addition (positive): *as well as, in addition to*; (2) variation, replacement: *instead of, rather than, unlike*; (3) variation, subtraction: *except for*. Examples:

> Its four levels include a sculpture garden, contemporary collections of Australian and European prints and drawings, 20th century British and European art, an impressionist exhibition **as well as** a new coffee shop and theatre space. [Text 22]

> We have pursued a number of initiatives in recent years ‖ to enhance the capabilities of **both** our forces forward-deployed on the peninsula and our reinforcing elements, **as well as** the forces of our South Korean Allies. [Text 115]

> Our intent is ⟦to develop the most advanced, reliable, and effective equipment ‖ and to field it ‖ when and where it's needed, ‖ using the Chairman's Combating Terrorism Readiness Initiative Fund **in addition to** resources ⟦allocated by the formal budget process⟧ ⟧. [Text 115]

> Venice was developed in 1904 ‖ and was intended to be a western American cultural center like its Italian namesake, with canals **instead of** streets, and opera houses **rather than** amusement piers. [Text 140]

> The nitrogen compounds (**except for** nitrous oxide) dropped from 8 to 10 parts per billion by volume (ppbv) to only 1.5 to 2 ppbv. [Text 33]

> Proteins, **unlike** carbohydrates and fats, cannot be stored for future use. [Text 150]

8.4 Hypotaxis: adverbial group/prepositional phrase

As with parataxis, adverbial groups and prepositional phrases can be linked hypotactically: the tactic relationship is based on identity in function rather than difference in internal structure. Hypotaxis is used to construe spatial and temporal paths and to construe gradual narrowing of the specification of a location. It combines with (i) elaborating, (ii) extending and (iii) enhancing relations.

   (i) Elaborating. This is the relationship that is found in sequences such as:

> She remained in Lincoln **from** 1911 **until** 1919 when she moved owing to the illness of her father, one time Archdeacon of Leicester, and later Canon of Peterborough, and settled in Kettering. [LOB_B]

> I took a freighter **from** New York, **all the way up** the Amazon **into** Peru ... [Text 7]

> This twists around a shady, lush river gorge ⟦thick with bamboo⟧ to Bagudesa, ‖ then continues **through** extensive rice-fields **to** Kumbung. [Text 142]

> In 1990, London prefixes had changed **from** 01 **to** 071 or 081. [Text 15]

> In the present period, the issues arise across the board, <<as they commonly do>>: **from** personal relations in the family and elsewhere, **to** the international political/economic order [Text 212]

Here the hypotactic complex construes a **path** through time or space, including abstract space. Note the difference between these, which have two prepositional phrases in hypotactic relation, and phrases with *between*, which consist of one prepositional phrase with two paratactic nominal groups as Complement:

(he stood) between [the door + | 2 and the window]

It may be helpful to diagram these, as shown in Figure 8-2.

(a)	the rope	stretched	from	one end	to		the other
	Carrier	Process	Attribute/Circumstance				
			prepositional phrase (complex)				
			α		=β		
			'Process'	'Range'	'Process'		'Range'
(b)	she	stood	between	the door	and		the window
	Carrier	Process	Attribute/Circumstance				
			prepositional phrase (simplex)				
			'Process'	'Range'			
				nominal group (complex)			
				1	+2		

Fig. 8-2 (a) Two hypotactic (elaborating) prepositional phrases, (b) one prepositional phrase with paratactic nominal group complex as Complement

(ii) **Extending.** The hypotactic extension of adverbial groups/prepositional phrases is essentially the same as that for nominal groups, with *as well as, instead of, rather than,* etc.:

In government **as well as** in commerce, obviously, power was being defined as wealth, the accumulation of economic resources ⦀by which to live more comfortably ‖ and to command more authority⦀. [Text 122]

It was far better for a weapon used for retaliatory purposes to be under the sea **rather than** on land. [LOB_A]

A very important development is the building of research stations on the farms **instead of** in neighbouring towns. [LOB_G]

By the time the Great Central was built ‖ the trains could manage the gradients much more easily ‖ and the Great Central line usually went across the valleys ... **instead of** round them like the earlier railways ‖ so the distances were shorter ‖ and you got better views. [Text 19]

(iii) **Enhancing.** With prepositional phrases and adverbial groups of place and time there is also a hypotactic relation of enhancement, with the special semantic feature of 'narrowing', as in *tomorrow before lunch*. Examples, starting with a constructed sequence:

(it's) I α upstairs I ×β to the left of the landing I ×γ in the main bedroom I ×δ against the far wall I ×ε in the small cupboard I ×ζ in the top drawer I ×η at the back right hand corner I

Starting from Narmada, ‖ take the main turn-off <u>south towards Praya</u>. [Text 142]

From Beleka the road continues north, ‖ rejoining the main east-west axis <u>near Kopang, about 30km east of Mataram</u>. [Text 142]

You know ‖ what's happening <u>tomorrow at five o'clock</u>, don't you? [Text 82]

Perversely, however, English tends to go the other way, and this employs embedding not hypotaxis (hence many of the prepositions could be replaced by *of*):

(it's) [at [the back right-hand corner [in/of [the top drawer [in/of [the small cupboard [against [the far wall [in/of [the main bedroom [to the left of [the landing [upstairs]]]]]]]]]]]]]

The address on the outside of an envelope forms a similar sequence.

This 'narrowing' relationship is in fact the same as that found in the nominal group, where the 'logical' structure of the Premodifier is a hypotactic sequence of words. This also goes 'in reverse', hence the ordering … γβα; but it is hypotactic, not embedded:

ζ those ε two δ splendid γ old β electric α trains

This brings us round by another route to the analysis given in Chapter 6.

8.5 Hypotaxis: verbal group, expansion (1): general

Like a paratactic verbal group complex and a simple verbal group, a hypotactic verbal group complex, e.g. *tried to do*, serves only one set of functions in the clause (and only in the clause, since it cannot be embedded on its own): it is the Process in the experiential transitivity structure, and the Finite (…) Predicator in the interpersonal modal structure.[1] For example:

---

[1] The traditional analysis was to treat the primary group as Predicator in its own right and the secondary group together with elements following it in the clause as an embedded non-finite clause serving as Complement, and this type of analysis was taken over in modern formal approaches, at least initially. Comparing the two types of analysis in a meaningful way is not possible within the space available here. However, we can note that while the traditional analysis is forced on us if our only model of structural organization is that of constituency, the analysis we present here becomes possible once we recognize tactic interdependency structures. It allows us to show the analogy, and agnation, between sequences of verbs, and sequences of clauses, with areas of indeterminacy between the two (see Section 8.8). It enables us to throw light on so-called 'serial verb constructions' in a range of languages (cf. e.g. Matthiessen, 2004b: especially 572–580), interpreting the findings that have emerged, particularly in the past 15 years or so. Further, it enables us to show how categories of the simple verbal group have evolved from verbal group complexes (cf. references below to tense, modality and voice). And it also makes it possible to avoid one of the major drawbacks of the traditional analysis: the secondary verbal group plus the elements following it do not in fact behave as Complements. For example, if they were Complements, the wh- interrogative should be *what is she trying?*; but it is not: it is *what is she trying to do?*. Verbal group complexes have also been discussed under the heading of 'catenatives', reflecting the fact that the verbs in such a series are concatenated (see e.g. Palmer, 1974: Ch. 7; Huddleston & Pullum, 2002: 64–65, 1194 ff.).

||| We <u>tried to open</u> windows || to escape. ||| [Text 5]

||| In 1960 he <u>began to travel</u>. ||| [Text 162]

The center <u>is helping field</u> the 150,000 inquiries [[flooding in nationally each day]]. [Text 15]

... these doctrines, || which are highly serviceable to power and authority, || but <u>seem to have</u> no other merits. [Text 212]

||| I always <u>tried to avoid tearing</u> her web || and save her repair work, || but she was a quick and efficient spinner. ||| [Text 187]

||| I've been reading a lot of Lawrence; || I'<u>ve been trying to read</u> most of the works of Lawrence. ||| [Text 125]

The hypotactic sequence is always progressive – α ^ β (as in *tried to do*), α ^ β ^ γ (as in *began to try to do*), α ^ β ^ γ ^ δ (as in *wanted to begin to try to do*) .... While the groups making up the complex are typically contiguous, as in the examples above, the complex may be discontinuous:

||| DPP lawmaker Chen Ting-nan will be the justice minister, || responsible [[for <u>helping</u> Chen <u>keep</u> his promise [[to clean up graft]]]]. ||| [Text 13]

||| Again, a first requirement is [[to do no harm to organizational frameworks [[that, through years of evolution, are finally at the stage [[where they are supporting programs [[that <u>are</u> actually <u>helping</u> us <u>to get</u> on with the business [[of increasing understanding]]]]]]]]]]. ||| [Text 32]

(The analysis of such discontinuous verbal group complexes will be illustrated below, as in Figure 8-11.) The primary group (α) may be finite or non-finite; it is the primary group that carries the mood of the clause, e.g. *she tried to do it, what was she trying to do, was she trying to do it, try to do it, having tried to do it* etc. The secondary group (β γ δ ...) is always non-finite, this being the realization of its dependent status. It is the secondary group, or last secondary group if there is more than one, that realizes the process type of the clause, e.g. [material:] *she seemed to mend it*, [behavioural:] *she seemed to laugh*, [mental:] *she seemed to like him*, [verbal:] *she seemed to tell us*, [relational:] *she seemed to be nice*.[2]

The secondary group may be perfective, with or without *to*, e.g. (*to*) *do*; or imperfective, e.g. *doing*, in aspect. The other non-finite form, the 'past/passive participle', e.g. *done*, usually stands for the perfective, as in *I want it* (*to be*) *done, consider it* (*to have been*) *done*; but in itself it is neutral, and in other contexts it neutralizes the distinction, e.g. *I saw it* (*be/being*) *done*.

The difference in meaning between perfective and imperfective was referred to above (see Section 7.4.4). The general principle is that the perfective is 'unreal' and the imperfective is 'real'; they may be opposed in any one of a number of contrasts, as future to present,

---

[2] Non-final verbal groups may realize features that relate to the transitivity of the clause (and this is always the case with causative constructions: see Section 8.7). For example, while phase does not constrain the interpretation of the Subject as a particular type of participant, connation does; it implies that the Subject is like a Behaver in addition to whatever other participant roles it serves (cf. the beginning of Section 8.6.2). Contrast [phase:] *she seemed to like him* with [conation:] *she tried to like him*. This is why phased existential clauses present no problem, but conative ones are odd: *there seemed to be a person on top of the hill* vs. *there tried to be a person on top of the hill*. As we have seen in Chapter 5, *there* in existential clauses serves as Subject, but it does not play a participant role; so when a participant role interpretation is 'imposed' by a conative verbal group complex, there is a clash in the grammar.

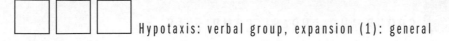

appearance to reality, starting off to going on, goal to means, intention to action, or proposal to proposition; and sometimes the difference between them is minimal. The pairs of examples in Table 8-2 will give some feeling for the distinction.

Table 8-2 Perfective and imperfective in the secondary verbal group

	Perfective	Imperfective	
	'irrealis' (*to-*) *do*	'realis' (*a-*, i.e. 'at, in') *doing*	
Appearance	seems to know	[no special form]	Reality
Appearance leading to realization	turns out to know	turns out knowing	Realization following appearance
Initial state	starts to win	ends up winning	Final state
Activating	begins to work	keeps working	Maintaining
Goal	try to relax	try relaxing	Means
Intention	decides to write	gets down to writing	Action
Proposal	would like to paint	likes painting	Proposition
Attempt leading to success	managed to open	succeeded in opening	Success following attempt

There are numerous types of hypotactic relation, which could be approached in various different ways. It turns out, however, that they correspond fairly systematically to the different patterns in the clause complex: expansion (elaboration, extension, enhancement) and projection (locution, idea); so we will interpret them along these lines (for the system network, see Figure 8-15). The present section deals with those related by expansion.

8.5.1 Elaborating a process: PHASE

Here the verb in the primary group is a very general one of the 'intensive: ascriptive' class (Chapter 5, Section 5.4.3), and it is elaborated by the verb in the secondary verbal group. The semantic relation between the two is one of PHASE (see Table 8-3; cf. Chapter 6, Section 6.3.6, on phase in phrasal verbs, and the reference to phase in Chinese). The basic notion is 'be (intensive) + do', using 'do' to stand for any process.

The two dimensions of phase are time-phase and reality-phase. (i) The **reality-phase**, or realization, system is based on the contrast between 'apparent' (seems to be) and 'realized' (turns out to be); both are perfective, the first being unreal, the second unreal emerging into real.

Witnesses said ‖ the sand dredger <u>seemed to go</u> past the Marchioness ‖ but suddenly smashed into the side ‖ and went right over it. [Text 30]

This offensive <u>appears to be</u> a sign of their strength, ‖ but their position is highly contradictory. [Text 97]

Both in terms of quantity and quality, FY 1998 <u>proved to be</u> a very challenging recruiting year. [Text 115]

The 22 bibliophiles <u>turned out to trail</u> clouds of glory. [Text 110]

Table 8-3 PHASE

Category: Meaning	System	Term	Aspect of β-verb	Examples
[be	time-phase => tense	present in	imperfective	is doing]
[be	time-phase => tense (=> modality)	future in required to)	perfective	is to do]
keep	time-phase	durative	imperfective	keeps (on)/goes on doing
start	time-phase	inceptive	imperfective/perfective	starts/begins doing /to do; gets doing; stops doing, ceases doing /to do
start + keep	time-phase	inceptive-durative	imperfective	takes to doing
[be	reality-phase => voice	passive	neutral	is done]
seem	reality-phase	apparent	perfective	seems/appears to do
prove	reality-phase	realized	perfective	prove/turns out to do

There is a variant of the 'realized' which is imperfective, e.g. *she turns out knowing all about it*; this is looking at it from the 'real' end, as reality emerging from appearance. We can also relate the passive voice to this general meaning, with its original sense of 'is (in a state of) having been realized'.

(ii) The **time-phase** system has split into two. The original opposition is *doing/is to do* (meaning, in modern terms, 'keeps doing' and 'will do') has disappeared, since both have turned into grammatical categories of the verbal group (see Chapter 6, Section 6.3). The former has evolved into tense, defined along the dimension of future/present/past. Thus the *be ... ing* form, as in *he is doing*, which was originally two verbal groups like modern *keeps doing*, is now the secondary present tense form within the one group, meaning 'present in ...'; e.g. *is doing* 'present in present', *was doing* 'present in past', *will have been doing* 'present in past in future', *was going to be doing* 'present in future in past', etc. The latter, the *be to ... * form, as in *he is to do*, similarly turned into a secondary future; but here there has been a further change: *is to* has now turned into a modal form, and its function as secondary tense has been taken over by *is going to*.

The other part of the time-phase system that has remained as a category of phase is that of 'duration/inception': 'durative' going on, contrasting with 'inceptive/conclusive', starting and stopping.[3] For example:

---

[3] When the verbs serving in the primary, elaborated verbal group occur in simple, non-elaborated verbal groups that serve as Process in their own right, they tend to combine with metaphorical nominal groups, as in *Tove Janson's experimentation with slightly different themes began in 1957*: see Chapter 10, Section 10.5.4.

||| In Comet in Moominland and Moomin-summer Madness they are all still having funny, exciting and at times somewhat childish adventures, || but in 1957, << about ten years after the first Moomin book was published, >> Tove Jansson <u>began to experiment</u> with slightly different themes. ||| [Text 100]

||| I <u>keep telling</u> them || I give them the money || so long as they'll leave. ||| [UTS/Macquarie Corpus]

||| The line <u>needs to keep being shut down</u> || to have mechanical work done on there. ||| [UTS/Macquarie Corpus]

||| Meanwhile, the women back in the mangroves <u>had started to hear</u> the cries of the children || because they were all terrified, || and so was I, || and they came racing towards us out of the mangroves, || and then they saw the crocodile || and they got big rocks and branches || and <u>started throwing</u> things at it too || and it <u>started to drift</u> out to sea. ||| [UTS/Macquarie Corpus]

||| If they <u>stop performing</u> their task, || they're likely to be deprived of the opportunities [[to dedicate themselves to intellectual work]]. ||| [Text 234]

Of these, the 'go on' term takes the imperfective; starting and stopping take either, with little difference in meaning – except that *stop* requires imperfective; *stop* + perfective is now interpreted as a hypotactic clause complex of purpose, as in

||| α she stopped || ×β to think ||| 'she stopped, in order to think'

There is also an inceptive-durative 'start to go on', as in *they've taken to coming in at the back door instead of the front.*

At the deepest level time-phase and reality-phase are the same thing: both are concerned with the stages of becoming. A process is something that emerges out of imagination into reality, like the rising of the sun. Before dawn, the sun shines only in the future, or only in the imagination – as future turns into present, imagination turns into reality. The two categories of phase are related to modality and tense; but whereas modality and tense are interpreted as subcategorizations of one process (they are grammatical variants within one verbal group), phase is interpreted as a hypotactic relation between two processes: a general one of becoming, that is then elaborated by the specific action, event, mental process or relation that is being phased in or out. The analysis of one of the examples above is given in Figure 8-3. (Note that just like finite simple verbal groups, the primary verbal group splits into Finite and Predicator: Finite 'did' + Predicator 'seem'. The Predicator then extends to include the secondary verbal group: 'seem' + 'to go'. This is brought out by versions of the clause where Finite and Predicator are discontinuous, as with *did ... seem to go* in *did the sand dredger seem to go past the Marchioness?*)

the sand dredger	seemed		to go	past the Marchioness
Subject	Finite 'past'	Predicator		Adjunct
Actor./Medium	Process: material			Location: Place
	verbal group (complex)			
	α	⟶ =β		

Fig. 8-3 Hypotactic verbal group complex: phase

571

8.5.2 Extending a process: CONATION

Here the basic notion is that of 'have (possession) + do'; in other words, success. The semantic relation between the primary and the secondary verbal group is one of CONATION: trying, and succeeding (for illumination of conation through comparison with Chinese, see Halliday & Matthiessen, 1999: Ch. 7). (The verb of the primary verbal group is usually one that can serve in a 'behavioural' clause: see Section 8.6.2.) This too has provided the resources for another tense form and another modality (see Table 8-4). Examples:

||| Aware of his child's ignorance of Indian life, the Indian parent tries to cram into the child's little head all possible information during an 'Excursion Fare' trip to the mother country. ||| [Text 254]

||| You try and do something responsible for your children || and you get forgotten. ||| [Text 82]

||| I'm just going to try and attach my first semantics chapter for you || 'cause it's not too big || and then you can start reading || when you have time. |||

||| If I tried to swan around, || I wouldn't know how to behave. ||| [Text 90]

||| I always tried to avoid tearing her web || and save her repair work, || but she was a quick and efficient spinner. ||| [Text 187]

||| And, while our military strength remains unmatched, || state or non-state actors may attempt to circumvent our strengths || and exploit our weaknesses || using methods [[that differ significantly from our own]]. ||| [Text 115]

||| The wide range of potential contributions by the RC has proven to be a bright spot || as we strive to match available resources to a demanding mission load, || and demonstrates clearly the enduring value and relevance of the citizen-soldier. ||| [Text 115]

||| We succeeded to take our last steps to freedom in conditions of relative peace. ||| [Text 104]

||| He feels || that he rarely succeeded in reaching the fiber of the characters [[that he desperately wanted to attain]]. ||| [Text 205]

||| He learned to walk in a certain way ||| [Text 17]

Table 8-4 CONATION

Category: Meaning	System	Term	Aspect of β-verb	Examples
[have	=> tense	past in	neutral	has done]
[have	=> modality	required to	perfective	has to do]
try	conation	conative	perfective	try to/and do, attempt to do, strive to do, contrive to do; avoid doing/(can't) help doing
succeed	conation	reussive	imperfective/perfective	succeed in doing; manage/get to do; fail (in) doing/to do
[can	=> modality	be able to	perfective	can do]
can	potentiality	be able to	perfective	be (un)able/(not) know how to do
learn	potentiality	become able to	perfective/imperfective	learn to do; practise doing

Again, there are two dimensions: there is the potential, and the actual. The potential means having, or alternatively not having, the ability to succeed. The actual means trying, or not trying; and succeeding, or not succeeding. The form with *have* has evolved like the forms with *be* above. Originally two verbal groups, it is now either (i) + *done*, a secondary tense form 'past in', e.g. *has done* 'past in present', *will have done* 'past in future', *was going to have done* 'past in future in past' and so on; or (ii) + *to do*, a modal form (of the 'modulation' type; see Chapter 10, Section 10.3), e.g. *has to do* 'must do'. In other words, 'possessing' a process, if combined with past/passive, means past (success); if combined with 'unreal', it means (future) obligation.

The other form that has turned into a finite element within the verbal group is the potential form *can*, in the sense of 'have the ability to'; it is cognate with *know*, so 'know how to'. This is now also a modal form, again of the modulation type – in this case not obligation but readiness (inclination/ability).

Of the remainder of this type, most take the perfective form of the secondary verbal group, as in *try to do*. The imperfective occurs only (i) with the negative terms *avoid*, and (with *in*) *fail*: *avoid doing, fail in doing*; and (ii) with *succeed* (again with *in*). (Cf. footnote in Section 8.6.2 on the non-conative use of *fail*.) The difference between *manage to do* and *succeed in doing* is slight; the former implies attempt leading to success, the latter success following attempt. For *try* + imperfective ('do as a means to an end'), e.g. *try counting sheep*, see the next subsection.

Once again these forms are related to tense and modality, the hypotactic verbal group complex being intermediate between the simple verbal group, as in *has done, has to do*, and the clause complex, as in, say, *by trying hard Alice reached the key*. One of the examples given above is analysed below in Figure 8-4:

state or non-state actors	may	attempt	to circumvent	our strengths
Subject	Finite: modal	Predicator		Complement
Agent/Actor	Process			Medium/Goal
	verbal group (complex)			
	α	⟶	+β	

Fig. 8-4   Hypotactic verbal group complex: conation

8.5.3 Enhancing a process: MODULATION

Here the basic notion is that of 'be (circumstantial) + do', e.g. *help to do* 'do being-with (someone)'. As with all instances of enhancement, there are a number of different kinds; the principal ones are set out in Table 8-5. Examples:

||| Yeah, I think || a good many writers <u>tend to open</u> their books || and groan. ||| [Text 21]

||| Well that would be my contention || but let me <u>hasten to add</u> || that since the first Speaker was also the first Member for Wakefield || I'm not that anxious to emulate the first Speaker. ||| [Text 184]

||| They don't really own them, you see, || they just <u>happened to be lying</u> around in the same place as these things. ||| Text 16]

||| You will cherish them on your bookshelves for a long time – || unless, of course, someone borrows them || and somehow 'forgets' to return them. ||| [Text 100]

||| Perhaps we could start by talking about that. ||| [Text 234]

||| I came to love it || from drinking it in the war years, || but the fact must be faced, || it is an acquired taste. ||| [LOB_E]

Here the primary verbal group is again not a separate process; but this time it is a circumstantial element in the process expressed by the secondary verbal group. If we say *Alice ventured to ask something*, this means she did ask it; but she did so tentatively. (The doubtful one here is *hesitate*, which perhaps belongs with the 'projection' type (discussed in Section 8.8) as a mental process.) Probably all of these would turn out to be metaphorical in the terms described in Chapter 10 (Sections 10.4–10.5). One of the examples above is analysed in Figure 8-5.

a good many writers	tend		to open	their books
Subject	Finite 'present'	Predicator		Complement
Agent/Actor	Process: material			Medium/Goal
	verbal group (complex)			
	α	⟶ ×β		

Fig. 8-5   Hypotactic verbal group complex: modulation

Table 8-5 Modulation

Category	Aspect of β-verb	Example
Time	imperfective	begin by, end up (by) doing 'do first, last'
	perfective	tend to do; be wont to do 'do typically'
Manner: quality	imperfective	insist on doing 'do perversely'
	perfective	hasten to do 'do quickly'
	perfective/imperfective	venture to do/risk doing 'do tentatively'
	perfective	hesitate to do 'do reluctantly'
	perfective	regret to do 'do sadly'
Cause: reason	perfective	happen to do 'do by chance'
	perfective	remember/forget to do 'do /not do according to intention'
Cause: purpose	imperfective	try doing 'do as means to end'
Contingency: concession	perfective	come to do, get to do 'do contrary to expectation'
Accompaniment	perfective/imperfective	help (to) do/(in, with) doing 'do together with someone'

8.6 Hypotaxis: verbal group, expansion (2): passives

A clause containing a verbal group complex is still a single clause, and represents a single process. It has only one transitivity and voice structure (cf. Chapter 5, Section 5.7; Chapter 6, Section 6.3.2).[4]

If it is a paratactic complex, this process consists of two happenings – two actions, events or whatever. If the verbal group complex is hypotactic, on the other hand, there is only one happening. Thus in a paratactic complex each verbal group has a definite voice, although the voice must be the same in each case; but in a hypotactic complex only the group that expresses the happening, the secondary group, actually embodies a feature of voice. The primary group is active in form, but there is no choice involved. (The exception to this is when the clause is causative; see Section 8.7 below.)

The different types of hypotactic complex have different potentialities as regards the passive. If the secondary verbal group is passive, the meaning of the categories of phase is unaffected; but there is an effect on the interpretation of conative forms. We will discuss the three types in turn, starting with phase.

8.6.1 Elaborating: PHASE

Here the transitivity functions remain the same whether the clause is passive or active; there is an exact proportion *ants are biting me*: *I'm getting bitten by ants* :: *ants keep biting me*: *I keep getting bitten by ants*:

(ants) | keep | = β biting | (me)

(I) | keep | = β getting bitten | (by ants)

Compare:

no one <u>seems to have mended</u> the lights yet

the lights <u>don't seem to have been mended</u> yet

when <u>will</u> they <u>start printing</u> the book?

when <u>will</u> the book <u>start being printed</u>?

Further examples:

It <u>began to be realized</u> that it was a great waste of labour and effort to have to turn the whole mill whenever the wind changed and by the end of the 17th century, tower mills were being built. [LOB_E]

At first the prerogative of the *lit de justice* was restricted to royal personages, but the idea was obviously so attractive, allowing as it did a combination of ease and authority, that it <u>began to be</u> more widely <u>adopted</u>. [LOB_F]

Presumably, domestic ritual objects <u>began to be made</u> at much the same time. [LOB_J]

See Figure 8-6 for the analysis in mood and transitivity.

---

[4]   Where there is a shift in transitivity, as in *you'll either kill someone else or get killed yourself*, the structure is that of a clause nexus, not a verbal group nexus.

(a)

ants	keep		biting	me
Mood		Residue		
Subject	Finite 'present'	Predicator		Complement
Actor/Agent	Process: material			Goal /Medium
	verbal group (complex)			
	α	→ =β		

(b)

I	keep		getting bitten	by ants
Mood		Residue		
Subject	Finite 'present'	Predicator		Adjunct
Goal/Medium	Process: material			Actor/Agent
	verbal group (complex)			
	α	→ =β		

Fig. 8-6   Active/passive phased hypotactic verbal group complex

8.6.2 Extending: CONATION

Here the relation of passive to active is different, because a conative verb, although not constituting a separate happening, does in fact represent a behavioural process, and it retains its behavioural sense when the clause is passive. Thus an elaborating active/passive pair such as *people started to accept her/she started to be accepted* is not paralleled by the corresponding extending pair

(people) | tried | + β to accept | (her)

(she) | tried | + β to be accepted |

(see analysis in Figure 8-7). Examples:

He tried to be pleased at the idea. [LOB_N]

Francesca and Grazie were habitual committee chairmen and they usually managed to be elected co-chairmen, equal bosses, of whatever PTA or civic project was being launched. [BROWN1_R]

The extending complex is a two-part process, in which the Subject fills a dual participant role: Behaver (in the conative component) plus Actor, or some other role, in the happening itself.[5]

---

[5] Note the incongruence of the form *people failed to accept her*, meaning 'people did not accept her despite her efforts'. Here *failed to* is functioning as a simple negative, such that there is a proportion

she was not accepted : people did not accept her ::

she failed to be accepted : people failed to accept her

Compare examples such as *I sent them a letter but it failed to arrive, the banks failed to support them*. These should perhaps be interpreted as a form of enhancement, meaning 'do negatively'!

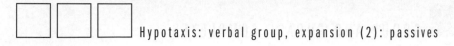

For the same reason, Adjuncts in the clause may relate semantically to the conative component like *hard, quickly* in *she tried hard to write well, she quickly learnt to tell them apart.*

> The Filipino <u>tried</u> *hard* <u>to put in</u> a storming finish, but his attacks were nearly all neatly countered by the clever champion. [LOB_E]

There is no need in the analysis to tie these structurally to the primary verbal group; but it is useful to specify their function, by labelling them as 'conative Adjunct'.

(a)

people	tried		to accept	her
Mood		Residue		
Subject	Finite 'past'	Predicator		Complement
Behaver Actor/Agent	Process: material			Goal/Medium
	verbal group (complex)			
	α ⟶ +β			

(b)

she	tried		to be accepted	by people
Mood		Residue		
Subject	Finite 'past'	Predicator		Adjunct
Behaver Initiator/Medium	Process: material			Actor/Agent
	verbal group (complex)			
	α ⟶ +β			

Fig. 8-7 Active/passive conative hypotactic verbal group complex

8.6.3 Enhancing: MODULATION

Many of the 'enhancing' verbal group complexes are simply inappropriate in the passive; they characterize an approach or attitude to the process, and this is likely to apply to an Actor but not to a Goal – it does not make much sense to say *she hastened to be reassured,* or *your word ventures to be doubted*. Others, such as *happen* and *tend*, are impersonal and so are indifferent to the selection of voice; e.g.

> The house <u>happened to have been built</u> facing the wrong way.

> If the student is of the right calibre to pursue a course, which the Ministry enacts is a worthwhile full-time course, he shall receive the same justice from Britain whatever authority he <u>happens to have been born</u> under. [LOB_H]

How I <u>happened to be marooned</u> at Balicou doesn't interest you in the faintest degree. [LOB_N]

One other aspect of oral work – the memorization and speaking of prose and verse – <u>tends to be considered</u> by many teachers as quite extraneous to the normal class work. [LOB_H]

If conduct in prison were a deciding consideration selection <u>would tend to be left</u> to a time near the date of release. [LOB_H]

Since they are all metaphorical, in the sense that the verbal group is representing a circumstance and not some aspect of a process, the functional analysis provides only a partial interpretation; to get the full picture we would need to take account of the congruent form (see Chapter 10), e.g. *by chance the house had been built facing the wrong way*. There would be no change of role in the passive (see Figure 8-8).

(a)

two guards	hastened happened		to assist	her
Mood		Residue		
Subject	Finite 'past'	Predicator		Complement
Actor/Agent	Process: material			Goal/Medium
	verbal group (complex)			
	α	⟶ ×β		

(b)

she	happened		to be assisted	by two guards
Mood		Residue		
Subject	Finite 'past'	Predicator		Adjunct
Goal/Medium	Process: material			Actor/Agent
	verbal group (complex)			
	α	⟶ ×β		

Fig. 8-8   Active/passive modulated hypotactic verbal group complex

8.7 Hypotaxis: verbal group, expansion (3): causative

The hypotactic verbal group complexes we have looked at so far are, in principle, confined to features of the Process itself – features of phase, conation and modulation. But we have noted that conative hypotactic verbal group complexes with verbs of behaviour in the primary verbal group tend to add the role of Behaver to the experiential interpretation of the Subject, as is brought out by the contrast in voice (see Figure 8-7). We shall now turn to hypotactic verbal group complexes of expansion that also include a feature of causation. Such complexes are involved in the realization of the transitivity system of AGENCY. We saw in Chapter 5 that there is a causative element in the structure of the English clause

(Section 5.7). For example, *John rolled the ball* can be interpreted either as 'John (Actor) did something to the ball (Goal)' or as 'John (Agent) caused the ball (Medium) to do something'.

We can always express this agency analytically, by saying *John made the ball roll*, where *made ... roll* is a hypotactic verbal group complex. Here the causative verbal group complex is thus an alternative realization of the feature of 'effective' agency: an additional participant is introduced into the clause through the expansion of the verbal group realizing the Process. In the ergative analysis this looks the same as *John rolled the ball*; but in the transitive it does not, and this enables us to interpret the difference between them: in *John rolled the ball*, he acted directly on it, whereas in *John made the ball roll* he may have done so by leverage, psychokinesis or some other indirect force (Figure 8-9).

	John	rolled	the ball		John	made	the ball	roll
transitive:	Actor		Goal		Initiator		Actor	
ergative:	Agent		Medium		Agent		Medium	

Fig. 8-9   Interpretation of causative forms

As always, it is the combination of the two analyses, the transitive and the ergative, that gives the essential insight.

In the transitive analysis we introduced the notion of an Initiator, a participant who brings about the action performed by the Actor. This function appears in the explicit causative structure with the verb *make*. We can then, of course, extend the agency further: *Mary made John roll the ball*, as in Figure 8-10:

	Mary	made	John	roll	the ball
transitive:	Initiator		Actor		Goal
ergative:	Agent		Agent		Medium

Fig. 8-10   A three-participant causative

Note that in the ergative analysis the function of Agent recurs, allowing for indefinite expansion along the lines of *Fred made Mary make John ...*

But there is still only one process, that of rolling; so we can still represent it as two verbal groups in hypotactic relationship. In this instance, however, they are discontinuous, as shown in Figure 8-11). Further examples, with *make, compel, get, have* and *let* as causative verbs are as follows:

||| Stanley has a love affair with Oliver Platt, too, || who <u>makes</u> him <u>laugh</u>. ||| I <u>didn't make</u> him <u>laugh</u>, || I <u>made</u> him <u>cry</u>. ||| [Text 73]

||| You'<u>re made to think</u> || the only thing [[that's going to save you]] is that specialness. ||| [Text 17]

||| When the evidence on aggression and the systematic bombardment of the entire population of Vietnam becomes known to the public, || we are in no doubt || that all men of integrity [[who examine this evidence]] <u>will be compelled to reach</u> the same conclusions. ||| [Text 328]

579

||| However, the occurrence of the hole at about that time served as a major driving force [[to get the Europeans to view ozone as a serious issue || and to get them to the table]]. ||| [Text 33]

||| The promise of DVD-quality output from your DV camcorder should get most creative minds spinning; ... ||| [Text 120]

||| In addition to movies, iDVD lets you store pictures [[that can be viewed as a slide show]]. ||| [Text 121]

||| If he would come to know || that the officer had recorded on file the message [[he had received from him]], || he would have him transferred to an unimportant post. ||| [KOHL_G]

John	made	the ball	roll
	Pro-		-cess
	α		×β

Mary	made	John	roll	the ball
	Pro-		-cess	
	α		×β	

Fig. 8-11   Hypotactic verbal group complex: causative

Causatives with *make, get/have* and *let* are of the enhancing type. But there are causative forms in all three types of expansion: see Table 8-6. We will consider each of them in turn.

Table 8-6 CAUSATIVES

Expansion type	Category		Aspect of β-verb	Example
elaborating	reality-phase		perfective	consider ... to do => mental; prove ... to do => verbal
	time-phase		imperfective	keep ... doing; start ... doing, stop ... doing
extending	conation	conative	perfective	encourage ... to do
		reussive	perfective	help ... (to) do, enable ... to do
	potentiality	potential	perfective	enable ... to do
		achieval	perfective	teach ... to do
enhancing	cause	reason	perfective	remind ... to do
	agency	high	perfective	make ... do; force ... to do; require ... to do
		median	perfective	have ... do; get ... to do; oblige ... to do
		low	perfective	let ... do; allow ... to do; permit ... to do

8.7.1 Elaborating: PHASE

(a) **Reality-phase.** It would be possible to recognize causative forms of reality-phase, as follows:

(1) apparent: John seems to be responsible

(caus.)   Mary considers John to be responsible

580

(2) realized: John turns out to be responsible

    (caus.)   that proves John to be responsible

But *consider* and *prove* are better treated as, respectively, mental and verbal processes, with the proposition/process being projected; note the closely agnate finite clauses with *that*, and cf. *it seems/turns out that John is responsible*.

(b) **Time-phase.** Here the same verbs *keep, start/stop*, also function causatively:

(1) durative: the ball kept rolling

    (caus.)   John kept the ball rolling

(2) inceptive: the ball started/stopped rolling

    (caus.)   John started/stopped the ball rolling

Examples:

... || but I suppose || we have to keep ... have to try and do something || to keep the ball rolling. ||| [UTS/Macquarie Corpus]

I keep them going all day || and then write up the stuff at night. [Text 96]

||| But there is still a very strong sense that I want to maintain that until, because it will be the thing that will push me back into writing the Ed D and it certainly kept me going the, and the partnership with E, ah Elizabeth too, that, that too, has ah... assisted in the process of keeping me writing. ||| [UTS/Macquarie Corpus]

||| I had to sit down || and stop her talking about it. ||| [Text 82]

Note that these then have passives: *the ball was kept/started/stopped (from) rolling (by John)*.

8.7.2 Extending: CONATION

(a) **Conation.** There is no causative form of the conative – that is, no word meaning 'make ... try'; this can, of course, be expressed analytically, for example

(she) | α made | (him) | ×β try | +γ to eat | (it)

The causative of the reussive has *help*, and perhaps *enable*:

reussive: John managed to open the lock

(caus.) Mary helped John to open the lock

||| DPP lawmaker Chen Ting-nan will be the justice minister, || responsible [[for helping Chen keep his promise [[to clean up graft]]]]. ||| [Text 13]

||| But he never knew || that it really was his own Bunny, || come back || to look at the child [[who had first helped him to be Real]]. [Text 28]

||| We have, << I am certain, >> an obligation [[to study these questions || and to pronounce on them, after thorough investigation,]] || for in doing so || we can assist mankind in understanding || why a small agrarian people have endured for more than twelve years the assault of the largest industrial power on earth, || possessing the most developed and cruel military capacity. ||| [Text 327]

(b) Potentiality. Here there are causative forms as follows:

(1) potential: the patient can see clearly

    (caus.)   this enables the patient to see clearly

(2) achieval: John learnt to fly

    (caus.)   Mary taught John to fly

Again, these causatives have passives: *the patient is enabled to see clearly, John was taught to fly by Mary*. Further examples:

||| I – and his night nurse Anna – <u>learned to understand</u> him || by lying with our heads on his chest; || we got a vibration [[which <u>enabled</u> us <u>to understand</u> more or less what he was saying]]. ||| [Text 24]

||| The first generation of cognitive scientists <u>was trained to think</u> that way, || and many textbooks still portray cognitive science in that way. ||| [Text 237]

||| This strong support <u>has enabled</u> us <u>to execute</u> these missions || without taxing our already-stressed readiness and modernization accounts. ||| [Text 115]

8.7.3 Enhancing: MODULATION

Only one or two modulations have causative equivalents; e.g.

       John remembered to do it

(caus.) Mary reminded John to do it

with the sense of 'John did it according to attention' and 'Mary caused John to do it according to attention' (cf. Chapter 5, Footnote 24 on the different senses of *remind*). However, there is a special set that exist only as causatives, where the meaning is simply that of agency: *make, cause, force, require, let, allow, permit*, etc. These admit of three degrees of modulation:

(high:)   this made (forced, required) them (to) accept our terms

(median:)   this had (got, obliged) them (to) accept our terms[6]

(low:)   this let (allowed, permitted) them (to) accept our terms

The concept of agency is inherently a circumstantial one. We have already seen in Chapter 5 that the Agent, which from one point of view is a participant in the clause (*John did it*), is from another point of view a kind of Manner (*it was done by John*). It is thus not surprising that the causative Agent enters into this kind of hypotactic structure, with the agency expressed as a process through verbs like *force* and *allow*.

Furthermore, causatives have passives; so we can have

---

[6]   Also imperfective: *got them working, had him begging for mercy.*

(high)	they were made/forced/required to accept
(median:)	they were got/obliged to accept
(low:)	they were allowed/permitted to accept

and this enables us to interpret modulation as it occurs within the verbal group:

(high)	they are required to accept	they must accept
(median:)	they are obliged to accept	they should accept
(low:)	they are allowed to accept	they may accept

Verbal modulation with *must*, etc., is now a kind of modality (see Chapter 4, Table 4-5, and Chapter 10, Section 10.3.2); it is semantically related to those passive causative modulations which have the circumstantial senses of 'do under compulsion/from obligation/with permission'. What links this semantically to modality in the other sense, that of probability, is that both represent a judgement on the part of the speaker: just as in *that may be John* the *may* expresses the speaker's judgement of likelihood ('I consider it possible'), so in *John may go* the *may* expresses the speaker's judgement of obligation ('I give permission'). Analyses are shown in Figure 8-12. Further examples:

||| The Air Force met its quantity goal, || but <u>was forced to dig</u> deep into its reserve of delayed entry applicants. ||| [Text 115]

||| The hydraulic equipment for the control and operation of the two pairs of lock gates <u>was required to be capable of being operated</u> either under power by the lock keeper from local control pedestals located near

(a)

circumstances	forced	him	to resign
Initiator Agent	Pro-	Actor Medium	-cess
	α		×β

(b)

he	was	required	to resign
Actor Medium	Process		
	α		×β

(c)

he	had	to resign
Actor Medium	Process	

Fig. 8-12 Modulation (a) as causative verbal group complex with Agent (b) as verbal group complex (c) as modality (finite element of verbal group)

583

each pair of gates or manually from the same pedestals by members of the general public, after the lock keeper's working hours. ||| [LOB_E]

||| The Comptroller returned || without discovering anything suitable, || and de Soto <u>was obliged to make</u> his landfall somewhere in the capacious, many-armed Bahia del Espiritu Santo, || now known as Tampa Bay, || which had been the starting point for the ill-fated Narvaez expedition eleven years before. ||| [LOB_F]

||| So most of these villains applied to the serious offenders review board || to have their sentences reviewed, || and [2 syllable name] for example <u>was allowed to go</u> after nineteen years ... ||| [Text 82]

||| That kind of left intelligentsia <u>is allowed to have</u> publicity and prominence. ||| [Text 234]

8.8 Hypotaxis: verbal group, projection

We pointed out in the previous subsection that a hypotactic verbal group complex of the 'expansion' type represented a single happening. Thus, there is only one time reference; if the reference is to tomorrow, then the tense of the primary group will be future:

(i)   phase: he'll start to do it tomorrow (not: he starts)

(ii) conation: he'll try to do it tomorrow (not: he tries)

(iii) modulation: he'll help to do it tomorrow (not: he helps)

An expression such as *want to do* looks at first sight very similar to these; but whereas we can say *he'll want to do it tomorrow*, it is also quite normal to say *he wants to do it tomorrow*. The wanting and the doing have distinct time references. We can even say *yesterday I wanted to do it tomorrow* – but not *yesterday I started to do it tomorrow*.

The relation between *want* and *to do* is one of projection. A projection of *do it*, as in *wants to do it*, is a meaning, and thus does not imply 'does it' – whereas an expansion, such as *tries to do it* or *starts to do it*, does imply 'does it', even though the doing may be partial or unsuccessful.

We saw in Chapter 7, Section 7.5.4.2 that a mental process of desideration projects an exchange of the goods-&-services type, i.e. a proposal. If the Subject of the projection is the same as that of the mental process clause, the proposal is an offer, as in *she wants to do it*; if the two are different, then the proposal is a command, as in *she wants you to do it*. In the first type, the Subject is not repeated, but is carried over from the desiderative clause. (It can then be made explicit by a reflexive, as in *she wants to do it herself*.)

All such projections could be treated as clause nexuses, as in Figure 8-13.

||| she	wants	'|| β !	to do it |||
||| she	wants	'|| β !	him to do it |||
α			'β
Senser	Process: mental		

Fig. 8-13   **Projecting clause nexus with want**

However, there are some respects in which they resemble nexuses of the verbal group. (1) The projected element, a (typically perfective) non-finite, has – like the expansion types – given birth to what are now tenses of the verb, namely the two future forms *will* and *be going to*. (2) The WH- probe is *what does she want to do?*, rather than simply *what does she want?*; compare *what is she trying to do?* not *what is she trying?*. (3) The command forms – those with change of Subject – resemble some of the causative expansions; compare the following pairs, including the passives:

she wants him to do it	she causes him/gets him to do it
he is wanted to do it	he is caused/got to do it
she wants it (to be) done	she causes it to be done/gets it done

It is in this area that expansion and projection come to meet and overlap. Causing something to be done means that it is done, with 'external agency' as a circumstantial feature. Wanting something to be done means that it is envisaged, or projected, but may or may not happen: its status is that of a metaphenomenon, not a phenomenon. But the line between the two is fuzzy. In general, if the relationship can be expressed by a finite *that* clause, as in *she wished that he would come*, then in principle it is a projection; but in this respect too there is a 'grey' area: *she wanted that he should come* is possible, but uncommon, whereas *she allowed that he should come* is uncommon, but possible.[7]

Despite the borderline cases, projection is, as we have pointed out, a different kind of relationship from expansion. It is always, in fact, a relationship between processes – between a mental or verbal process on the one hand, and another process (of any kind) that is mentalized or verbalized (projected) by it. Nevertheless it is not inappropriate on grammatical grounds to treat some projections as verbal group nexuses, on the analogy of the types of expansion to which they are somewhat similar in meaning. Figure 8-14 gives some analyses for purposes of comparison. Examples under (a) and (b) are analysed (i) as verbal group nexus, (ii) as clause nexus. Those under (c), with *that* clause, are analysed only as clause nexus, since here the alternative does not arise.

To go into all the types of projection that cluster around this area would be beyond our present scope. Table 8-7 lists some of the more common types. All of them **could** be analysed as clause complexes; but there is a case for treating some of them as complexes of the verbal group – perhaps just those that are proposals, are perfective in aspect, and have the same Subject in both halves. This would **exclude** (1) propositions, like *pretend* and *claim* (*she claims to be infallible = she claims that she is infallible*); (2) imperfectives, e.g. *she doesn't like/mind John leaving so early*; and (3) 'causatives', e.g. *I didn't mean/expect you to notice*, and all 'indirect commands' such as *who asked you to comment?*. It would also exclude those where the projecting process is itself causative, like *tempt* ('make want'), *decide* in *she tempted John to stay, what decided them to change their plans?*. All these would thus be interpreted as projecting clause nexuses along the lines discussed in Section 7.5.

---

[7]   Note also that *want to*, which is particularly frequent in dialogue with first- and second-person Subject, *I* or *you*, is then often phonologically reduced, with *wanna*, like *gonna*, *gotta*, etc.

(a)   **(i)**

Mary	wanted		to go
Mood		Residue	
Subject	Finite: 'past'	Predicator	
		α	'β
Actor	Process: material		

(b)   **(i)**

Mary	wanted		John	to go
Mood		Residue		
Subject	Finite: 'past'	Predi-	Comp.	-cator
			α	'β
Initiator	Process: material		Actor	

(ii)

Mary	wanted		to go
α			'β
Mood		Residue	Residue
Subject	Finite: 'past'	Predicator	Predicator
Senser	Process: mental		Process: material

(ii)

Mary	wanted	John	to go
α		'β	
Mood	Residue	Mood	Residue
Subject	Finite: 'past'	Predicator	Subject	Predicator
Senser	Process: mental	Actor	Process: material

(c)

Mary	wished		that	she	could		go
			that	John	would		go
α			'β				
Mood		Residue		Mood		Residue	
Subject	Finite: 'past'	Predicator		Subject	Finite: 'modul'	Predicator	
Senser	Process: mental			Actor	Process: material		

Fig. 8-14   **Projecting verbal group/clause nexuses: (a) Mary wanted to go (i) as verbal group complex [preferred], (ii) as clause complex; (b) Mary wanted John to go (i) as verbal group complex, (ii) [preferred] as clause nexus; (c) Mary wished that she could/John would go as clause nexus**

Table 8-7 includes some verbal group nexuses with adjectival forms serving as the Event of the projecting verbal group: (i) desideration: *be willing/keen/eager/anxious to do*; (ii) fear: *be afraid/scared to do*. The forms *afraid* and *scared* are verbal in origin, but they function as adjectives now, as can be seen by the form taken by intensification (*very* rather than *much*): *be very afraid/scared to do*. Since these forms are adjectival, they are obviously anomalous as verbal groups. But they fit in **systemically**: they are agnate with verbal forms, and all the forms of the desiderative set are agnate expressions of modulation. We could try to push the analysis even further to include patterns with nominal forms such as (i) desideration:

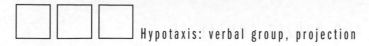

Table 8-7 Some types of projection in the hypotactic verbal group complex

	Category: meaning	System	Term	Aspect of β-verb	Examples
Proposal: idea	[will	desideration => tense	future	perfective	will do]
	[going to	intention => tense	future in (secondary)	perfective	is going to do]
	want	desideration	desiderative	perfective	want/wish/desire/long to do be willing/keen/eager/anxious//reluctant to do
			(negative)		would like/prefer to do would rather do would hate to do
			(negative)	imperfective	like/enjoy doing mind/hate/can't stand doing
	intend	intention	resolving	perfective	mean/plan/intend to do decide/resolve/make up mind to do
			considering	imperfective	intend/consider/anticipate doing
	expect	expectation	expectative	perfective	hope/expect/aspire to do
	need	need	needing	perfective	need/require to do
	fear	fear	fearing	perfective	fear/be afraid/be scared to do
Proposal: locution	ask	demand	demanding	perfective	ask/demand/request to do
	consent	consent	consenting (negative)	perfective	agree/consent to do refuse/decline to do
	promise	promise	promising	perfective	promise/vow/undertake to do threaten to do
Proposition: idea	pretend	pretence	pretending	perfective	pretend to do
Proposition: locution	claim	claim	claiming	perfective	claim/profess to do
		hearsay		perfective	be said/rumoured to do

have a mind to do, and (ii) intention: *make up one's mind to do.* But here we are really going beyond what can be accommodated within the verbal group since these constructions involve grammatical metaphor of the ideational kind (cf. Chapter 10, Section 10.5).

We conclude with some text examples of projecting hypotactic verbal group complexes:

[proposal: idea]

||| Because I like English very much; || I admire literature || and I <u>want to study</u> literature || – this is my field; || it always has been. ||| [Text 125]

||| Well look in that case, I'<u>d like to do</u> it; || I mean I really <u>want to do</u> it. ||| [Text 135]

||| He feels || that he rarely succeeded in reaching the fiber of the characters [[that he desperately <u>wanted to attain</u>]]. ||| [Text 205]

||| I <u>don't want to tell</u> you || that I'm giving you everything [[I saw]], || because I'm not. ||| [Text 7]

||| Following the recent ban on the Students' Islamic Movement of India, || the government has <u>decided to come down</u> heavily on these Islamic religious schools. ||| [Text 320]

||| I <u>can't remember even considering doing</u> anything else || after I was about fifteen or sixteen. ||| [Text 7]

||| I <u>remember going</u> to a little film center || to see [[what we were told || was an interesting avant-garde film]]. ||| [Text 119]

||| ... it's helped me certainly to feel as though I have a worth while voice and I <u>shouldn't be afraid to use</u> it in text, um which is something I've always been very nervous about. ||| [UTS/Macquarie Corpus]

[proposal: locution]

||| Now, come on, || that was Margo saying || "For Christ's sake, let me go! || I'm [[where I <u>promised never to be</u>]]!" ||| [Text 24]

||| Bush <u>promised to make</u> America "more just and generous" || and set a handful of specific goals: ... ||| [Text 113]

||| He <u>vowed to use</u> his remaining days in the White House || to narrow differences between Israel and the Palestinians, || but with less than two weeks left he made no prediction of success. ||| [Text 108]

[proposition: idea]

||| There, he meets up with an attractive nurse (Linda Fiorentino) [[[who eventually figures out || that he <u>is</u> merely <u>pretending to be</u> sick]]]. ||| [Text 205]

[proposition: locution]

||| His one line was [["here is the number of the slaughter'd French"]] || and <u>claims to have delivered</u> it rather badly. ||| [Text 25]

||| Although it <u>can be said to be</u> a reaction to the structuralist views of sociology in the 1960s, and the dangers of totalitarianism, || in taking a relativist stance || ethnomethodology cannot make moral judgements about meanings. ||| [Text 189]

The various options open to non-causative hypotactic verbal group complexes are represented as a system network in Figure 8-15.

8.9 Logical organization: complexes at clause and group/phrase structure, and groups

A verbal group nexus is intermediate between a clause nexus and a verbal group: a verbal group construes a single event, and a clause nexus construes two distinct processes; but a verbal group nexus construes a single process consisting of two events. These different options are available to speakers and writers when they construe their experience of the flow of events. They choose whether they construe a given experience as a process consisting of a single event, as a process consisting of a chain of two (or more) events, or as a chain of two (or more) processes.

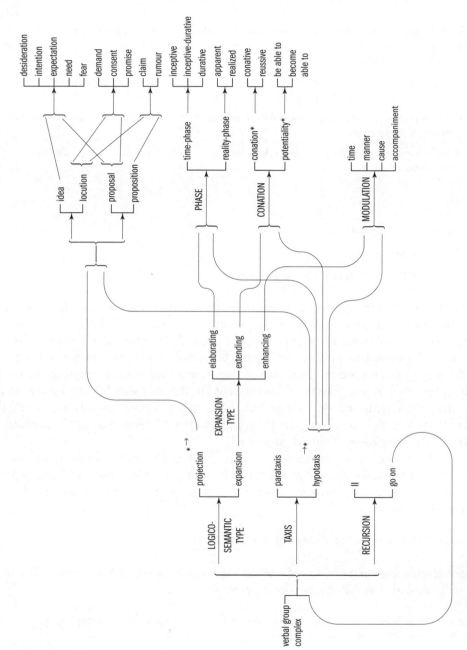

Fig. 8-15 The systems of the verbal group complex

589

The different options may appear as alternatives within and the same text, as often happens in news reporting. Thus in a report of a 'London disco boat disaster' on the Thames, the disaster is construed several times by means of clause nexuses:

Text 8-1: Reporting – chronicling (written, monologic): news report [Text 30]

[4] ||| Thirty people were feared drowned last night after a floating night club [[carrying as many as 150 on a late-night party cruise]] **collided** with a huge dredging barge || and **sank** in London's River Thames. |||

[9] ||| The Marchioness, <<which had been hired for a birthday party,>> **was hit** by the dredger, the Browbelle, near Blackfriars Bridge || and **sank** within two minutes in strong tides. |||

[27] ||| Witnesses said || the sand dredger **seemed to go past** the Marchioness || but suddenly **smashed** into the side || and **went** right over it. |||

[31] "I thought || it **would go** past us, it **was travelling** too fast. [32] ||| It **hit** us in the side, || **smashed** into us || and **went** straight over us." |||

The pattern is

[clause:] approach <barge> ⟶

[clause:] impact <barge, disco boat> ⟶

[clause:] sinking <disco boat>/[clause:] passing over <barge>.

This pattern is created by the serial structure of the clause complex, one clause nexus at a time. The clause complex thus makes it possible to construe the flow of events as an unfolding series of processes. These processes are all single events realized by simple verbal groups – with the exception of one: the hypotactic verbal group complex *seemed to go past* in [27]. This is a phased process, consisting of two events together representing the barge's apparent, rather than actual, passage. This is related to the only simple verbal group that is 'modal' rather than 'temporal' – *would go*; but this verbal group occurs within a clause that is projected. We can thus recognize the three options here: *it **went** past us – it **seemed** ⟶ to go past us ~ I **thought** ⟶ it **would go** past us*.

The 'disco boat disaster' might have been construed in compacted form by means of a single clause as *barge sinks disco boat*. Here the flow of events is compressed into a single quantum of experience, as in *Sydney Morning Herald*'s report of another maritime disaster, the sinking of a Thai ferry:

||| Two Australians missing || as storm **sinks** Thai ferry ||| [Text 4]

This might alternatively have been represented as *storm causes Thai ferry to sink*. This same disaster was construed as follows by *The Australian*:

||| Naval authorities believe || the boat **may have capsized** || because it was carrying a heavy load of construction materials in choppy waters. ||| [Text 5]

This might have been represented as *heavy load causes boat to capsize in choppy waters*, or *heavy load capsizes boat in choppy waters*. We see here that the clausal system of AGENCY is also involved: *storm sinks Thai ferry* is an 'effective' clause in which the cause is represented

as the Agent, while *Thai ferry sinks* is a 'middle' clause in which the cause is not represented as a participant involved in the process. The cause may be represented circumstantially, or as an enhancing clause in a clause nexus, as in *the boat may have capsized* ⟶ *because* ... .

Let us take one further example, this time starting with a clause where the Process is realized by a causative hypotactic verbal group complex:

> When overloading **has caused** the fuse **to blow** it will immediately blow again if the same appliances remain connected. [KOHL_E]

Here we have an analytical causative: *overloading has caused the fuse to blow*. A more 'compressed' version of this would be the synthetic variant with a simple verbal group *overloading has blown the fuse*. Both these clauses are 'effective'. A more 'expanded' version would be *because the fuse was overloaded, it blew* or *the fuse was overloaded, so it blew*. Here the causal relation is construed by means of a clause nexus, with the outcome being represented by the 'middle' clause *the fuse blew*. We can thus identify a scale of strategies for construing the causal relation:

(i)   clause nexus, paratactic – middle clause: the fuse **was overloaded**, so it **blew**

(ii) clause nexus, hypotactic – middle clause: because the fuse **was overloaded**, it **blew**

(iii) verbal group nexus – effective clause: overloading **caused** the fuse **to blow**

(iv) verbal group – effective clause: overloading **blew** the fuse

Some of them involve grammatical metaphor, which will be discussed in Chapter 10.

The point of these examples is to show how the grammar gives us considerable flexibility in construing the flow of events by providing a range of strategies. These strategies are all ideational, but they range from purely logical [(i) and (ii) above] via logical and experiential [(iii)] to purely experiential [(iv)].

The logical structures are all the same: they are tactic patterns of elements – clauses (the clause nexus), groups (the verbal group nexus) or words (the verbal group). As the grammatical system evolves over time, new options emerge – typically by a downwards move along the scale. Thus hypotactic verbal group nexuses are often the source of verbal groups: nexuses of groups are 'compressed' over time to become simple groups, and as part of this process, lexical verbs that started as the Event of a verbal group are reconstrued as grammatical verbs that serve as Auxiliary in a simple verbal group. We have given a number of examples in tables given above, indicating verbal group sources of tense, modality and voice.

Verbal group nexuses thus shade into verbal groups. In text analysis, it can therefore be hard to draw the line between the two, just as it can be hard to draw the line between clause nexuses and verbal group nexuses (see Section 8.8). For example, why is *be going to do* analysed as a simple verbal group but *be required to do* as a nexus of two verbal groups? As always, we have to adopt the trinocular perspective (Chapter 1, Section 1.4.1), balancing considerations 'from above', 'from around' and 'from below':

(i)   'From above': does *be going to do/be required to do* represent a single event or two – is *be going* an event in its own right?

(ii) 'From around': does *be going to do/be required to do* have access to one set of verbal group systems or two – for example, is there one contrast in polarity or two, is there one choice of tense or two?

(iii) 'From below': can *going* in *be going to do* or *required* in *be required to do* be non-salient, and if so, can it be phonologically reduced?

(i) 'From above': *be going to do* represents a single event, whereas *be required to do* represents two. Thus it is possible to vary *be required* lexically, since *require* is a lexical verb representing an event in its own right: *be obliged to do*, and also *be permitted/allowed to do* and *be forced to do*; but it is not possible to vary *be going* lexically – there is no *be walking to do*, *be running to do*, *be sauntering to do*, because *going* is no longer a form of the lexical verb of motion *go*. Instead, there is a grammatical variant of *be going to do* (rather than a lexical one): *be about to do*.

(ii) 'From around': *be going to do* operates as a single verbal group, whereas *be required* and *to do* operate as two separate verbal groups. Thus *be going to do* is the domain of a single series of tense selections, whereas *be required to do* is of two. For example, while we cannot say *is going to be going to do* since two secondary future tenses cannot be selected in succession, we can say *is going to be required to be going to do* since *is going to be required* and *to be going to do* are two distinct verbal groups.

(iii) 'From below': *going* in *be going to do* can be phonologically non-salient and *going to* may be reduced to *gonna*. In contrast, *required*, *obliged* in *be required/obliged to do* are salient. (But *be supposed to do* has its own phonology – /s(ə)poustə/; and (as noted above) *want to* is often reduced to *wanna* with interactant Subject.)

CHAPTER
NINE

AROUND THE CLAUSE: COHESION AND DISCOURSE

9.1 The concept of text; logogenetic patterns

Text is something that happens, in the form of talking or writing, listening or reading (cf. Chapter 1, Section 1.1). When we analyse it, we analyse the **product** of this **process**; and the term 'text' is usually taken as referring to the product – especially the product in its written form, since this is most clearly perceptible as an object (though now that we have recording devices – tape recorders and now various digital recorders – it has become easier for people to conceive of spoken language also as text). In the last resort, of course, a clause (or any other linguistic unit) is also a happening (cf. Halliday, 1961, on linguistic units as patterned activity); but since a clause has a tight formal structure we do not seriously misrepresent it when we look at it synoptically as a configuration. The organization of text is semantic rather than lexicogrammatical, and (at least as far as cohesion is concerned; we are not going into questions of register/contextual structure in this book; see Halliday & Hasan, 1985; Hasan, 1984; Martin, 1992: Ch. 7, Martin & Rose, 2003, 2008) much looser than that of grammatical units. The organization of text has typically been represented in terms of some form of structural notation. But it is important to be able to think of text dynamically, as an ongoing process of meaning.

How can we model text as an ongoing process of meaning? To do this, we return to the concept of the **cline of instantiation**: we introduced it as one of the semiotic dimensions of the organization of language in context in Chapter 1, Section 1.3.4. The system of a language is instantiated as text, the two representing the poles at either end of the cline of instantiation. System and text are not different phenomena; they are simply complementary phases of one and the same phenomenon. When seen up close, this phenomenon appears to us as text; but when we adopt a more distant observer perspective, we can build up a picture of it as system. System and text form a cline rather than a dichotomy, because between these two poles there is a semiotic region of intermediate patterns (conceived of as instance types – as **text types**, or as subsystems – as **registers**).

Text is thus the **process of instantiation**; and we can characterize it by reference to the **system** as the selection of systemic options unfolding through time. Throughout this book, we have given many examples of how selections are made locally in the creation of text – clause by clause, or group/phrase by group/phrase, and of how the structures that realize these selections build up patterns as the text unfolds. We have included many examples of short texts or extracts from longer texts interpreted and classified in terms of the contexts that they operate in (cf. Chapter 1, Section 1.4.1).

Let us introduce a somewhat longer extract from a text as the initial basis for discussion in this chapter: see Text 9-1 This text is the beginning of a long conversation around the dinner table among the members of a family (Mother, Father, Jane and Kate) and their friend and host (Craig). They are all at Craig's vacation home north of Sydney. This is the physical setting – the 'material situational setting' in Hasan's (e.g. Halliday & Hasan, 1985) terms. In material terms, the setting is unified; but in social and semiotic terms it is more varied: within one and the same material setting around the dinner table, the interactants are engaged in different socio-semiotic processes (see Chapter 1, Figure 1-1). The predominant one is that of 'sharing' – they have come together to share experiences and values, as friends and family members do (cf. Eggins, 1990; Eggins & Slade, 2005); but they also engage in other types of activity, e.g. managing food and implements ('doing') and instructing one another in the use of equipment ('enabling'), as shown in 9-1. This extract starts almost right at the beginning of the dinner. Kate has just served a fish dish that she's prepared and Craig turns this into a topic of conversation by making an appreciative comment.

Text 9-1: Sharing – casual conversation: extract from beginning of dinner table conversation among friends (spoken & dialogic), on occasion suspended by 'doing' contexts (text in italics) and 'enabling' contexts [Text 82]

	'Sharing' context	'Doing' context	'Enabling' context
Craig:	Kate I must say this fish is cooked beautifully.		
Mother:	It's lovely darling.		
Kate:	Thanks. Thank you Craig so much for saying so. Jane's not happy.		
Jane:	Mine's cold and ...		
All:	[general laughter]		
Mother:	You're having me on.		
?:	[inaudible overlap]		
Kate:	Well Jane think of smoked salmon.		
Craig:		*Grab the pan.*	
Jane:		*Oh no I'll grab the pan I think.*	
Kate:		*Oh.*	
Jane:		*Oh no no. It's ... I'm sorry.*	

	'Sharing' context	'Doing' context	'Enabling' context
Craig:	Mmm. Mine is sensational. Sensational.		
Jane:	It's alright Kate.	*Oh the pan's been washed, has it?*	
Craig:		*It hasn't, has it?*	
	God, mine's terrific.		
			Do you know how to turn the stove on? Look everybody watch this is the stove turning on demo. Stand back so you can see. Turn it to the right. Turn it on like that; press the button. Very easy.
Father:			Oh automatic.
Craig:			You don't even need a match.
Kate:			Mmm.
Craig:			You don't even need a match.
Father:			Is that electricity, is it?
Craig:			It's gas.
Mother:	The salsa's –		
		Oh can you get some napkins? They're in the back. Unfortunately –	
Craig:		*They're in the top drawer now, Kate, Kate.*	
Mother:		*We only have paper.*	
Craig:		*Over there, that drawer. I know it's like pick a box in this kitchen. Should label the cupboards, shouldn't I? Top drawer second drawer keep going until you find the right.*	

Interactants:

Kate, 41 year-old woman – Jane's sister

Craig, 47 year-old man

Jane, 47 year-old woman – Kate's sister

Mother, 74 year-old woman – Jane & Kate's mother

Father, 77 year-old man – Jane & Kate's father; Mother's husband

We can see how the text unfolds when we examine the systemic selections that have been made, together with their structural realizations clause by clause: see Table 9-1. The

table includes three columns of analysis, one for each metafunction. Each clause is analysed both systemically and structurally. The structural analysis is confined to the key structural pattern within the total structure, as can be seen by comparison with the full analysis given for *well Jane think of smoked salmon* in Figure 9-1.

Table 9-1 Clause analysis of initial 'sharing' phase of Text 9-1, with interleaved 'doing' phase

Speaker		THEME	MOOD	TRANSITIVITY
Craig	Kate I must say	unmarked <subject-theme>, +interpersonal theme	declarative & modal: modulated & +vocative & positive	middle: non-ranged & verbal: locution
		Theme = *Kate I*	Mood = *I must*	Process = *must say*; Medium = *I*
	this fish is cooked beautifully	unmarked <subject-theme>	declarative [bound] & temporal: present & non-interactant & positive	middle: ranged & relational: attributive & intensive
		Theme = *this fish*	Mood = *this fish is*	Process = *is*; Medium = *this fish*
Mother	It's lovely darling.	unmarked <subject-theme>	declarative & temporal: present & non-interactant & positive & +vocative	middle: ranged & relational: attributive & intensive
		Theme = *it*	Mood = *it's*	Process = *'s*; Medium = *it* [fish]; Range = *lovely*
Kate	Thanks. Thank you Craig so much	minor	minor	minor
	for saying so.	unmarked <subject-theme> [implicit]	bound: non-finite & interactant: addressee & positive	middle: non-ranged & verbal: locution [substitute]
		Theme = *for*	[Mood = ∅]	Process = *saying*
	Jane's not happy.	unmarked <subject-theme>	declarative & temporal: present & non-interactant & negative	middle: ranged & relational: attributive & intensive
		Theme = *Jane*	Mood = *Jane's not*	Process = *'s not*; Medium = *Jane*; Range = *happy*
Jane	Mine's cold and ...	unmarked <subject-theme>	declarative & temporal: present & non-interactant & positive	middle: ranged & relational: attributive & intensive
		Theme = *mine*	Mood = *mine's*	Process = *'s*; Medium = *mine* [fish]; Range = *cold*

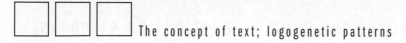

Table 9-1 Clause analysis of initial 'sharing' phase of Text 9-1, with interleaved 'doing' phase (*contd*)

Speaker		THEME	MOOD	TRANSITIVITY
	[general laughter]			
Mother	You're having me on.	unmarked <subject-theme>	declarative & temporal: present & interactant: addressee & positive	
		Theme = *you*	Mood = *you're*	Process = *'re having … on*
	[inaudible overlap]			
Kate	Well Jane think of smoked salmon.	unmarked <predicator-theme>, +textual, +interpersonal	imperative & interactant: addressee & positive	middle: non-ranged & mental: cognitive & matter
		Theme = *well Jane think*	[Mood = ∅]	Process = *think*; Medium = 'you'
Craig	Grab the pan.	unmarked <predicator-theme>	imperative & interactant: addressee & positive	effective: operative & **material**: transformative: elaborating
		Theme = *grab*	[Mood = ∅]	Process = *grab*; Medium = *the pan*; Agent = 'you'
Jane	Oh no I'll grab the pan I think.	unmarked <subject-theme>, +textual	declarative & temporal: present & interactant: speaker & positive	effective: operative & **material**: transformative: elaborating
		Theme = *oh no I*	Mood = *I'll*	Process = *'ll grab*; Medium = *the pan*; Agent = *I*
Kate	Oh.	minor	minor	minor
Jane	Oh no no. It's …			
	I'm sorry.	unmarked <subject-theme>	declarative & temporal: present & interactant: speaker & positive	middle: ranged & relational: attributive & intensive
		Theme = *I*	Mood = *I'm*	Process = *'m*; Medium = *I*; Range = *sorry*
Craig	Mmm.	minor	minor	minor
	Mine is sensational. Sensational.	unmarked <subject-theme>	declarative & temporal: present & non-interactant & positive	middle: ranged & relational: attributive & intensive
		Theme = *mine*	Mood = *mine's*	Process = *'s*; Medium = *mine* [fish]; Range = *sensational, sensational*

Table 9-1 Clause analysis of initial 'sharing' phase of Text 9-1, with interleaved 'doing' phase (*contd*)

Speaker		THEME	MOOD	TRANSITIVITY
Jane	It's alright Kate.	unmarked <subject-theme>	declarative & temporal: present & non-interactant & positive & vocative	middle: ranged & relational: attributive & intensive
		Theme = *it*	Mood = *it's*	Process = *'s*; Medium = *it* [fish]; Range = *alright*
	Oh the pan's been washed, has it?	unmarked <subject-theme>, +textual	declarative & temporal: present & non-interactant & positive & tagged: constant	effective: receptive: non-agentive & **material**: transformative: elaborating
		Theme = *oh the pan*	Mood = *the pan's*	Process = *'s been washed*; Medium = *the pan*
Craig	It hasn't, has it?	unmarked <subject-theme>	declarative & temporal: present & non-interactant & negative & tagged: reversed	effective: receptive: non-agentive & **material**: transformative: elaborating
		Theme = *it*	Mood = *it hasn't ...* Moodtag = *has it*	Process = *hasn't* [∅: been washed]; Medium: *it* [pan]
	God mine's terrific.	unmarked <subject-theme>, +interpersonal	declarative & temporal: present & non-interactant & positive	middle: ranged & relational: attributive & intensive
		Theme = *God mine*	Mood = *mine's*	Process = *'s*; Medium = *mine* [fish]; Range = *terrific*

	Well	Jane	think	of smoked salmon.
unmarked <predicator-theme> & + textual & + interpersonal	textual	interpersonal	topical	
	Theme			Rheme
free: imperative & interactant: addressee & positive & +vocative			Predicator	Adjunct
	Adjunct	Vocative	Residue	
middle: non-ranged & mental: (cognitive & non-phenomenalized) & matter			Process	Matter
	conj. gp.	nom. gp.	verbal gp.	prep. phrase

Fig. 9-1 Systemic and structural analysis of one clause in Table 9-2

(i) Within the **textual** metafunction, unmarked theme selections emerge as the dominant textual motif. The first few selections give 'fish' prominence as topical Theme, with positive assessment of it as the focus of New information (*cooked beautifully*; *lovely*). Then 'Jane' is introduced as another topical Theme, alternating first with 'fish' and then with two successive Themes in imperative clauses (*well Jane think*; *grab*) before being sustained in a series of three clauses. Craig then returns to the topic of 'fish', which is repeated once, then suspended for two clauses where 'the pan' is given thematic status, and finally reinforced by Craig again. The notion of 'fish' thus emerges as the dominant topical theme in this phase of the conversation, with Jane, the pan and actions as minor thematic motifs. There are thus a few different chains of thematic progression, with progression from Theme to Theme as the major strategy (although the thematic *pan* is picked up from the Rheme of *grab the pan*). At the same time, there is a consistency in the nature of new information – expressions of appreciation and of emotion.

(ii) Within the **interpersonal** metafunction, declarative mood is selected again and again. Craig initiates by contributing a proposition revolving around the fish dish – grammatically, the Subject. This move is realized by a clause that is both grammatically and lexically positive: *is* (rather than *isn't*) + *cooked beautifully* (rather than *badly* or the like). (The very first clause, *I must say*, is in fact a modal assessment rather than a proposition in its own right; it is an example of interpersonal metaphor: see Chapter 10, Sections 10.3 and 10.4.) Craig's move is successful in the sense that it sets the tone of the beginning of the dinner table conversation: variants of this proposition occur throughout, with 'the fish is' as the Mood element and positive lexical selections within the Residue. The main exceptions are a couple of proposals realized by imperative clauses – one relating to the fish (*well Jane think of smoked salmon*) and one relating indirectly to the meal (*grab the pan*). The latter is then picked up in a couple of propositions revolving around the pan. The interpersonal selections create patterns of dialogic exchange. For example, Craig's expression of his appreciation of the fish elicits an expression of gratitude in response. Similarly: *grab the pan – I'll grab the pan; the pan's been washed, has it? – it hasn't, has it?*

(iii) Within the **experiential** metafunction, middle relational clauses of the subtype of intensive attribution emerge as the favourite type: all but two have the fish as Medium/Carrier and a quality assigned to it as Range/Attribute; the remaining two intensive attributive variants of mental clauses of emotion with a person as Medium/Carrier and a mental quality as Range/Attribute (*Jane's not happy*; *I'm sorry*). In addition to this dominant relational motif, a minor material motif is introduced about half-way through the passage. These material clauses are effective; the Process is one of manipulation – *grab*, *wash*, the Medium/Goal is a nominal group denoting the pan, and the Agent/Actor (whether explicit or implicit) is one of the interactants. There are thus two dominant domains of experience, both of which are concrete and relate to the shared experience around the dinner table: the qualitative classification of the fish and the manipulation of the pan. (In addition, there is one congruent mental clause – *think of salmon*, one metaphorical mental clause – *I think*, and one metaphorical verbal one – *I must say*.)

These three metafunctional contributions are all essential to the creation of to the patterns of meaning created in Text 9-1. However, like other texts operating in sharing contexts, this text is centrally concerned with the tenor of relations among the interactants, and thus draws heavily on the resources of the interpersonal metafunction (see Chapter 1,

Section 1.4.1 for field vs. tenor orientation, Halliday, 2001, for interpersonal vs. ideational orientation in text, and Eggins & Slade, 2005, for the deployment of interpersonal resources in casual conversation). In the passage quoted above, the interactants' evaluation of the food is an important motif, and it also serves to allow them to calibrate and negotiation their relationships.

The textual, interpersonal and experiential selections create patterns of meaning as the text unfold. These selections are represented as a **text score** (see Matthiessen, 1995a, 2002b) in Table 9-2. Here it is easy to see how favourite motifs emerge and how less common selections stand out against these favourite motifs. Such patterns of favoured and disfavoured selections typically form **phases** in the development of a text (cf. Gregory, 1983, 2002; Cloran, Stuart-Smith & Young, 2007). For example, about half-way through

Table 9-2 Text score for the beginning of a dinner table conversation

Minor	Major												
	THEME		MOOD			POLARITY		AGENCY		PROCESS TYPE			
	un-marked theme	marked theme	free: decl.	free: imp.	bound	pos.	neg.	middle	eff.	mater.	mental	verbal	rel.
3	16	0	13	2	1	14	2	11	5	4	1	2	8

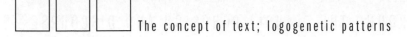

the extract we can see that there is phasal change involving both interpersonal mood selections and experiential transitivity selections. This begins when declarative gives way to imperative, and when relational gives way to mental.

The example in Table 9-2 illustrates how meaning is created in the course of the unfolding of a text. It is helpful to have a term for this general phenomenon – i.e. the creation of meaning in the course of the unfolding of text. We shall call it **logogenesis**, with 'logos' in its original sense of 'discourse' (see Halliday & Matthiessen, 1999: 18; Matthiessen, 2002b). Since logogenesis is the creation of meaning in the course of the unfolding of a text, it is concerned with patterns that appear gradually in the course of this unfolding; and the gradual appearance of patterns is, of course, not limited to single texts but is rather a property of texts in general instantiating the system of language. Such patterns have been called **emergent patterns** and when we focus on grammar we are concerned with patterns of **emergent grammar** (as formulated by Hopper, e.g. 1987, 1998). We shall refer to the version of the system created in the course of the unfolding of a text as an **instantial system** since it represents a distillation of patterns at the instance pole of the cline of instantiation.

Logogenesis pertains to the entire meaning potential of a language – all the strata and all the metafunctions. For example, alliteration in a poem is an example of logogenesis at work at the stratum of phonology. All systems that we identified within the function-rank matrix in Chapter 2, Table 2-8, create such logogenetic patterns. Logogenesis is thus at work throughout the entire system of language. In this book, we are largely limiting ourselves to the lexicogrammatical subsystem, and within this subsystem we have had to focus on the grammatical part of the lexicogrammatical continuum. But since our focus is on grammar rather than on semantics, the concept of logogenesis is all the more important: it allows us to explore how *local* grammatical selections accumulate to create logogenetic patterns that become part of the **systemic history** of an unfolding text (cf. Halliday, 1992b). As we have noted, we can identify phases of selections within such logogenetic patterns; and we can then match them up with contextual and semantic structures of a more global nature (or, alternatively, let these emerge as interpretations of the lexicogrammatical logogenetic patterns). For instance, in our example, Craig's first contribution – *I must say this fish is cooked beautifully* – can be interpreted as the beginning of a contextual stage in dinner parties where somebody other than the cook expresses appreciation of the food. This is why – generically speaking – Mother chimes in with *it's lovely darling*. Since Kate and Jane are sisters, Kate can suggest that Jane does not appreciate the dish, and Jane can, in turn, express negative appreciation – jocularly, as the Mother's *you're having me on* makes explicit. Craig's *God mine's terrific* brings this stage of the conversation to a close; but this interpersonal concern with the appreciation of the food re-appears almost 250 clause complexes later when Kate reactivates it: see Text 9-2. Like so many other interpersonal issues, evaluation has to be explored prosodically.

Text 9-2: Sharing – casual conversation (spoken, dialogic): later extract from beginning of dinner table conversation among friends (spoken & dialogic) in Text 9-1 [Text 82]

Kate:	Mum, you're not enjoying your dinner, are you?
Mother:	I am.
Craig:	She is. Her fish. Look at these chefs; they're so sensitive, aren't they?

Mother:	But you know that I have a very small appetite.
Kate:	Si.
Mother:	Si. I'm not even having any vegetables that I cooked, because I know —

The logogenetic patterns involving selections in the major systems of the clause are summarized and exemplified in Table 9-3. Such patterns emerge from successive selections in lexicogrammatical systems. As we noted in Chapter 1, Section 1.3.3, language is stratified into semantics, lexicogrammar, and some medium of expression – phonology/graphology (or sign). The kind of logogenetic patterns we have illustrated very briefly here within the stratal domain of lexicogrammar operate at the other strata as well. In any text, logogenetic patterns of meaning, wording and sounding (writing) will emerge. Since phonological and graphological patterns are largely 'arbitrary' in relation to lexicogrammar (and, by a further stratal step, in relation to semantics), logogenetic patterns here are largely confined to their own stratum. For example, the frequency of 'open' vs. 'closed' syllables in any given text may be phonologically significant; but it does not, in the general case, affect lexicogrammar

Table 9-3 Logogenetic patterns for higher-ranking units

Metafunction	Unit	System	Logogenetic pattern
logical	clause (nexus)	TAXIS & LOGICO-SEMANTIC TYPE	phases of dominant logico-semantic type (e.g. 'temporal/causal enhancement' in narrative episodes; elaboration in reports concerned with entities); movement from one type to another (e.g. 'reporting' to 'quoting' in news articles)
textual	clause	THEME	phases of favoured ('unmarked'/'marked') theme selections, giving prominence to organizational path through field ('method of development'; e.g. chronology and protagonist focus in narrative and biographical discourse) and angles of assessment (e.g. hypothesis and conjecture in scientific discourse)
	info unit	INFORMATION	phases of gradual accumulation of 'main points' as elaboration of a field (e.g. [state of] product in procedures]) and/or intensification of affect (e.g. positive features of product in advertisements)
interpersonal	clause	MOOD	local phases of negotiation, with one mood selection complementing another (e.g. 'interrogative' ∧ 'declarative' ∧ 'minor'), building up over a text into mood type motifs (e.g. a recipe as a 'macro-imperative' text) and interactant profiles - patterns of favoured interpersonal selections in the clause (e.g. interviewer and interviewee in admissions interviews, parent and child in the home)
experiential	clause	TRANSITIVITY	phases of favoured process type selections (e.g. 'material' in method part of recipes; 'existential' and 'relational' in setting of narratives), building up over a text into process type motifs (e.g. a recipe as a 'macro-material' text) and profiles of participation (e.g. child as Medium and adults as Agent in a narrative)

or semantics: there is no resonance in patterns of wording or meaning (the major exception being the prosodic features)[1]. However, the situation with lexicogrammar is different. As we emphasized in Chapter 1 and have illustrated throughout this book, lexicogrammar stands in a natural relation to semantics, not an arbitrary or conventional one. This means, among other things, that logogenetic patterns that emerge at the level of lexicogrammar are also at the same time semantically significant. For example, logogenetic patterns emerging from successive selections in the system of mood can be interpreted semantically by reference to the notion of exchange structure (Berry, 1981; Martin, 1992: Ch. 2; Eggins & Slade, 2005; Matthiessen & Slade, 2010).

9.2 The lexicogrammatical resources of COHESION

As already noted, the concept of logogenesis enables us to see how the local, blow by blow selections within clauses and other grammatical units build up to create patterns that extend through whole phases of unfolding text, or, indeed, through the whole of a text. We have arrived at this picture simply by reviewing the accounts given of grammatical resources in the previous chapters. We are now in a position to consider additional resources relevant to the processing of text. On the one hand, there is a set of lexicogrammatical systems that have evolved specifically as a resource for making it possible to transcend the boundaries of the clause – i.e. the domain of the highest-ranking grammatical unit. These lexicogrammatical systems originate in the textual metafunction and are collectively known as the system of COHESION (see Halliday & Hasan, 1976, 1985; Martin, 1992, 2001; Fine, 1994). On the other hand, outside lexicogrammar, there are semantic and contextual resources for creating and interpreting text. In keeping with our focus on lexicogrammar, we shall focus on the system of cohesion here; but towards the end of the chapter we shall discuss cohesion in relation to semantics.

There are four ways by which cohesion is created in English: by (i) conjunction, (ii) reference, (iii) ellipsis, and (iv) lexical organization. We can illustrate all of these from the familiar passage of the dinner table conversation in Text 9-1. It is clearly tied to the here-&-now of the material setting, as indicated by outward pointing or 'exophoric' references such as *this fish, the pan*. Still, we find all four types of cohesive strategies at work in creating text-internal cohesive links, as set out in Table 9-4.

(i) CONJUNCTION: Conjunction includes both conjunction proper and continuity (cf. Chapter 3, Section 3.4, on textual Theme). In the opening of our dinner table conversation, there are markers that indicate that a clause in new turn relates to a previous one; for example: *Mine's cold and ... – Well, Jane, think of smoked salmon; Grab the pan! – Oh no, I'll grab the pan*. Such markers serve in the system of **continuity**; they are a characteristic feature of dialogic text. Conjunction proper is not used cohesively in this opening phase of the conversation, but it does appear later in the same text – see Text 9-3:

---

[1]   There are, of course, special registers – especially those of poetry and performance – where logogenetic patterns at the level of phonology construe patterns at the level of lexicogrammar or semantics.

Table 9-4 Cohesion in a conversational passage

Speaker		CONJ.	REFERENCE		ELLIP.	LEXICAL COH.	
Craig	Kate I must say		I (exoph.)				say
	this fish is cooked beautifully		this fish (exoph.)			fish + beautifully	
Mother	It's lovely darling.		it (anaph.)			(it) + lovely	
Kate	Thanks. Thank you Craig so much						
	for saying so.				so (clausal)		saying
	Jane Jane's not happy.						
Jane	Mine's cold and …		mine (exoph.)		mine [= 'my + one'] (nominal)	(mine) + cold	
	[general laughter]						
Mother	You're having me on.		you (exoph.)				
	[inaudible overlap]						
Kate	Well Jane think of smoked salmon.	[continuity:] well				salmon + –	
Craig	Grab the pan.			the pan (exoph.)			grab + pan
Jane	Oh no I'll grab the pan I think.	[continuity:] oh no	I (exoph.)	the pan (anaph.)			grab + pan
Kate	Oh.						
Jane	Oh no no. It's …						
	I'm sorry.		I (exoph.)				
Craig:	Mmm. Mine is sensational. Sensational.		mine (exoph.)		mine [= 'my + one'] (nominal)	(mine) + sensational, sensational	
Jane:	It's alright Kate.		it (anaph.)			(it) + alright	
	Oh the pan's been washed has it.	[continuity:] oh		the pan (anaph.)			wash + pan
Craig:	It hasn't has it.		it (anaph.)		[∅: been washed] (verbal)		
	God mine's terrific.		mine (exoph.)		mine [= 'my + one'] (nominal)	(mine) + terrific	

Text 9-3: Sharing – casual conversation (spoken, dialogic): later extract from beginning of dinner table conversation among friends in Text 9-1 [Text 82]

Jane: 'Cause that was one of those weird things that we had – that we all had friendships with each of them. Bruce, Bruce and Philip were friends, Jane and I were friends, and then you and –

Mother: – David. *Well* you were in the same – you were in the same class.

Jane: We were all exactly * the same.

Kate: * **But** I don't know that we were friends.

Jane: ***Oh*** I think you were friends: you were friendly enough.

Here the conjunction *but* marks a relationship between *I don't know that we were friends* and the preceding discourse: the exact domain is often hard to determine, but here it is most likely to be Jane's contribution. The conjunction *but* is a structural one (a linker) that can be used cohesively, as in our passage; this is typical of casual conversation, where the more elaborated cohesive conjunctions are relatively rare. In Text 9-3, there are also two markers of continuity, viz. *well* and *oh*. Such markers serve in the system of continuity; they are a characteristic feature of dialogic text.

Conjunctive relations marked by explicit cohesive conjunctions may hold between clauses in a clause complex (cf. Chapter 7, e.g. Section 7.4.2.1), between text segments realized by clause complexes, or between longer text segments such as rhetorical paragraphs. For example *meanwhile* and *so* in Texts 9-4 and 9-5 which are passages from a later stage of the dinner table conversation:

Text 9-4: Sharing – casual conversation (spoken, dialogic): later extract from beginning of dinner table conversation among friends in Text 9-1 [Text 82]

Kate: Well I think that's the thing. But you've tried the patches once before, haven't you?

Craig: Oh, once before it did work. Look: there've been plenty of periods when I don't smoke – big blocks of time. And I don't smoke during the day, and it's usually with a drink and all that sort of thing. But, you know, I smoke and I hate it. I hate that I do it. And I'm at that point where I have to make the decision. I can't go on any longer with it.

Kate: **Meanwhile** go and have a fag. [laughs]

Text 9-5: Sharing – casual conversation (spoken, dialogic): later extract from beginning of dinner table conversation among friends in Text 9-1 [Text 82]

Kate: She's got – she's got Big Pond, which she said – which is   apparently not a terribly good provider.

Mother: No.

Craig: Mmm. No. I thought Yahoo was one of the better ones.

Mother: No no no but –

Craig: Isn't it?

Mother: No but Yahoo is a search engine. Um – ah Big Pond is a is a provider.

Craig: Oh okay.

Mother: **So** there's a difference. Like Ozemail and all those things.

(ii) REFERENCE: While conjunction (including continuity) links whole clauses or combinations of clauses, reference creates cohesion by creating links between elements. It is a relationship between things, or facts (phenomena, or metaphenomena); it may be established at varying distances, and although it usually serves to relate single elements that have a function within the clause (processes, participants, circumstances) as exemplified in

605

Table 9-4, it can give to any passage of text the status of a fact, and so turn it into a clause participant (as exemplified in Section 9.4.3 below). Since our dinner-table conversation has an immediate material setting shared by the interactants, there are various references to elements that are part of the dining situation – in particular, the first mention of the fish (*this fish*), the pan (*the pan*), and the stove (*the stove*), where they are introduced into the discourse by reference to these entities on and around the dinner table. Such reference is **exophoric** – pointing outward from the text. However, once introduced in this way, they are picked up through **anaphoric** reference again and again, forming **referential chains** in the unfolding conversation: *this fish – it ...* ; *the pan – the pan – the pan – it.* It is these references within the text that create cohesion of the referential kind. These references are to non-interactants. In addition, there are references to interactants, for example, Jane: *mine – I.* Such interactant determiners and pronouns refer outside the text to roles defined by the speech events – speaker, speaker plus others, addressee; but they can still form chains within the text, of course.

(iii) SUBSTITUTION & ELLIPSIS: Reference creates cohesion by creating links between referents – elements at the level of meaning; but there is also a resource operating at the level of wording, either a clause or some smaller item. This takes two forms, substitution and ellipsis; but we shall refer to it simply as **ellipsis**, since substitution can be interpreted as a systemic variant. Ellipsis makes it possible to leave out parts of a structure when they can be presumed from what has gone before. Ellipsis indicates continuity, allowing speaker and addressee to focus on what is contrastive, as in the first interaction between Kate and Craig in Text 9-1: *Kate, I must say this fish is cooked beautifully – Thank you, Craig, so much for saying **so***. Here the substitute item *so* stands for the hypotactically projected clause *that this fish is cooked beautifully*. This wording is presumed, giving more prominence to the expression of gratitude. Similarly, the noun *fish* serving as Head/Thing is presumed on three occasions by the nominal group *mine*, which can be interpreted as a fusion of Deictic and Thing – *my* plus 'one', standing for *fish*, i.e. *my fish*. This makes it possible to treat *fish* as continuous and give prominence to the ownership.

Unlike reference, ellipsis is usually confined to closely contiguous passages, and is particularly characteristic of question + answer or similar 'adjacency pairs' in dialogue. For example, in Table 9-4 above: *Oh the pan's been washed, has it? – It hasn't [Ø: been washed], has it?* Similarly: *I'm about to throw Joanne out the window. – [Ø: you're about to throw] Joanne who [Ø: out of the window]? – [Ø: I'm about to throw Joanne] Lattimer [Ø: out of the window].*

(iv) LEXICAL COHESION: While conjunction, reference and substitution & ellipsis are cohesive resources within the grammatical zone of lexicogrammar (cf. Chapter 2, Section 2.2), lexical cohesion operates within the lexical zone and is achieved through the choice of lexical items. Most typically, such cohesive relations hold between single lexical items, either words or larger units, e.g. *locomotive* (word), *steam engine* (group), *in steam* (phrase), *steam up, get up steam* ('phrases' in the dictionary sense); but also involving wordings having more than one lexical item in them, such as *maintaining an express locomotive at full steam*. In Text 9-1, two major motifs are established in the 'sharing' and 'doing' phases of. The first is *fish* (often presumed by *mine*, which means 'my one' – i.e. 'my fish') plus an evaluative term from the set *beautifully, lovely, (cold,) sensational, alright, terrific – cold* being interpretable as a negative evaluation in the local discourse environment. The lexical item *fish* is also related to *salmon*; and these combine,

in turn, with terms for modes of preparation, viz. *cook* and *smoke*. The second motif is not as central to the conversation, but it still plays an important role in the creation of cohesion. It consists of *pan* plus a term for manipulating the pan, first *grab* and then *wash*.

Lexical ties are independent of structure and may span long passages of intervening discourse; for example, *fish* and *salmon* are separated by several turns in the conversation in Cohesion in a conversational passage, and distances may be even greater. Thus in

> [the little] voice was drowned by a shrill scream from the engine

the lexical item *engine* was separated from the latest previous occurrence of a related lexical item *(railway journey)* by thirty-six intervening clauses.

As is clear from the analysis set out in Table 9-4, the cohesive selections in a text form logogenetic patterns. In the case of conjunction, such patterns take the form of favoured selections of logico-semantic relations for developing the text rhetorically. In the case of the other types of cohesive resources, such patterns take the form of **logogenetic chains** – chains of reference, ellipsis and lexical cohesive links (as shown in the columns of the table), and of interactions among such chains within and across different types of cohesion. Sometimes the patterns are very local and transient; but often they are sustained over longer periods and become part of the instantial system that develops as the text unfolds. For example, while the pan enters the discourse is maintained for a while by reference, and the combination of *grab/wash* plus *pan* is established over several moves, the history of these cohesive chains in the text is fairly short. In contrast, the combination of specific determiner 'this' or 'my' + *fish* or ellipsis + evaluative term (*beautifully, lovely, cold, sensational, alright, terrific*) emerges gradually as a major motif in the early phase of the dinner table conversation. It is easy to imagine that it would become part of collective memory and be picked up on a later occasion when the interactants meet again. We shall return to such logogenetic patterns in the creation of cohesion in Section 9.7.

The cohesive resources make it possible to link items of any size, whether below or above the clause; and to link items at any distance, whether structurally related or not. Many instances of cohesion involve two or three ties of different kinds occurring in combination with one another. For example:

> 'You don't know much,' said the Duchess; 'and that's a fact.'

> Alice did not at all like the tone of this remark, and thought it would be as well to introduce some other subject of conversation.

where the nominal group *this remark* consists of a reference item *this* and a lexical item *remark*, both related cohesively to what precedes. Similarly *in some other subject of conversation*, both *other* and *subject* relate cohesively to the preceding discussion, which was about whether or not cats could grin. Typically any clause complex in connected discourse will have from one up to about half a dozen cohesive ties with what has gone before it, as well as perhaps some purely internal ones like the *that* by which the Duchess refers back to the first part of her own remark.

Thus the different types of cohesion make distinct contributions to the creation and interpretation of text, contributions that complement one another. This complementarity

607

can be described in terms of two distinctions, (i) one having to do with the extent of the elements that are linked cohesively and (ii) the other with the location of cohesive resources within lexicogrammar.

(i) We can make a distinction between CONJUNCTION and the three other resources of cohesion. As we have seen, conjunction is concerned with rhetorical **transitions** – transitions between whole 'messages', or even message complexes. Conjunction indicates the relations through which such textual transitions are created. In contrast, the other cohesive resources are concerned with textual **statuses** – statuses having to do with how 'components' of messages are processed as information (cf. Matthiessen, 1992)[2]. We shall have more to say about textual transitions and statuses in Section 9.7 when we relate the systems of cohesion to the structure-forming systems of theme and information (textual) and of clause complexing (logical).

(ii) At the same time, we can also recognize that the systems of cohesion operate within either the grammatical zone or the lexical zone of the lexicogrammatical continuum. CONJUNCTION, REFERENCE and ELLIPSIS are all grammatical systems, and are thus all manifestations of what we might call grammatical cohesion. The point of origin of each of these systems falls within one or more particular grammatical unit; and terms within these systems are realized either by grammatical items that have some particular place within the structure of that unit or (in the case of ellipsis) by the absence of elements of grammatical structure. For example, the systemic environment of conjunction is that of the clause; and conjunctions serve as conjunctive Adjuncts in the structure of the clause (see Chapter 3, Section 3.4 and Chapter 4, Section 4.3.3). In contrast, LEXICAL COHESION operates within the lexical zone of the lexicogrammatical continuum; and it follows the general principle that lexical items are not defined in terms of particular grammatical environments (cf. Chapter 2, Section 2.2; Halliday, 1966b). Table 9-5 shows how (i) and (ii) intersect to define the overall space of cohesive systems in English.

Table 9-5 Types of cohesion

General type		Grammatical zone [(location in) grammatical unit]	Lexical zone [lexical item]
transitions between messages		CONJUNCTION [unit: clause]	
statuses of elements	in meaning	REFERENCE [unit: nominal, adverbial group]	LEXICAL COHESION [synonymy, hyponymy]
	in wording	ELLIPSIS-&-SUBSTITUTION [unit (complex): clause, nominal group, adverbial group]	[repetition, collocation]

---

[2] Compare Hasan's distinction between **organic** and **componential** cohesion in Halliday & Hasan (1985).

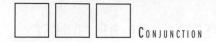

9.3 CONJUNCTION

9.3.1 From clause complexing to conjunction

In Chapter 7, we described the clause complex as the most extensive domain of grammatical structure, representing this structure on the univariate model as being developed out of logico-semantic relations between multivariately organized clauses. These relations link pairs of clauses (or subcomplexes) into nexuses. The relations are either hypotactic or paratactic; and any given complex may be formed out of a combination of hypotactic and paratactic clause nexuses. Then, in Section 9.1, we showed how this strategy for forming clause complexes is used to guide the local development of text, and we also showed that clause complexing has considerable logogenetic power to establish favoured strategies for expanding a text.

The clause complex thus provides the resources for realizing logico-semantic relations grammatically as tactic patterns. This is the most extensive domain of grammatical structure (see Chapter 7, Table 7-3). However, in the semantic organization of text, logico-semantic relations extend beyond the semantic sequences that are realized by clause complexes; they extend to rhetorical paragraphs and even to whole texts (cf. Chapter 1, Section 1.4.2). The semantic organization of text in terms of logico-semantic relations is brought out by different forms of analysis, including the conjunctive reticular analysis developed by Martin (e.g. 1992: Chapter 4) drawing on the work by the Hartford stratificationalists and the rhetorical-relational analysis based on the framework of Rhetorical Structure Theory (RST) developed by Mann, Matthiessen & Thompson (e.g. 1992). The latter form of analysis is illustrated for a persuasive text in Figure 9-7 below: see the discussion in Section 9.7.2.

While the grammar does not provide any grammatical structure beyond the clause complexes, it still provides 'clues' to indicate logico-semantic relations operating on any scale within text. This is the cohesive system of CONJUNCTION, which has evolved as a complementary resource to clause complexing: it provides the resources for marking logico-semantic relationships that obtain between text spans of varying extent, ranging from clauses within clause complexes to long spans of a paragraph or more[3]. A key difference between clause complexing and cohesive conjunction is that while the clause complexing specifies (i) the nature of the logico-semantic relation, (ii) the degree of interdependency, and (iii) the clausal domains being related through the formation of univariate structure, cohesive conjunction only specifies (i) – the nature of the logical-semantic relation. In this sense, cohesive conjunctions are 'clue words' (a term used in natural language processing, e.g. Cohen, 1984), providing listeners and readers with information about (i) that may also allow them to infer (ii) and (iii).

---

[3] Cohesive conjunctions have also been called 'discourse markers', but many other terms have been used as well (e.g. 'discourse particle', 'connective'; and in computational linguistics/natural language processing: 'clue word', 'cue phrase') and the term 'discourse marker' has also been used to include items other than cohesive conjunctions, e.g. textual continuatives but also interpersonal items (see, e.g., Schiffrin, 1987, 2001; Fraser, 2006, and other contributions to Fischer, 2006). Fraser (2006) uses the term 'discourse marker' in the sense of 'conjunction', treating it as a type of 'pragmatic marker'; Schiffrin (1987) uses the term 'discourse marker' in a broader sense. Aijmer & Simon-Vandenbergen (2009) present different senses of the term 'pragmatic marker', and make the point that in systemic functional linguistics such markers are either interpersonal or textual.

Cohesive conjunctions may be used within clause complexes, as in

||| Someone comes along with a great idea for an expedition || – **for example**, I did a book called Sand Rivers, just before the Indian books, || and it was a safari into a very remote part of Africa. ||| [Text 7]

(We exemplified cohesive conjunctions that commonly occur together with structural ones in clause complexes in Chapter 7, Sections 7.4.1.1, 7.4.2.1 and 7.4.3.1.) But their real cohesive contribution is made when they are used to indicate logico-semantic relations that extend beyond the (grammatical) domain of a single clause complex. They may mark relations that obtain between two clause complexes, as in:

||| New numbers also will be inserted between the new area code and the old phone number. ||| **For example:** An old inner London phone number of 0171-555-5555 becomes 020-7555-5555 and an outer London 0181-555-5555 becomes 020-8555-5555. ||| [Text 25]

||| Taiwan's newly elected leader expressed interest Friday in considering a confederation with rival China – a relationship a visiting Chinese policy expert said Beijing would surely reject. ||| **Meanwhile**, a list of top Cabinet members in Taiwan's new government was announced, featuring prominent numbers of women, technocrats and academics who will be key in the push to improve relations with China and clean up corruption. ||| [Text 13]

The relation may, in fact, even link to part of an earlier clause complex, as in:

||| Given the demanding pace of military operations, || <u>service members should be allowed to focus on their mission free from worry about the welfare of their families.</u> ||| **Accordingly**, funding for quality DOD schools, child development activities, and other family assistance programs is important, particularly today || when the stresses of operational deployments are higher than ever before. ||| [Text 115]

But the relation may also link domains that are more extensive than single clause complexes; for example, see Texts 9-6 and 9-7.

Text 9-6: Sharing – casual conversation (spoken, dialogic): gossip [Text 69]
J: She'd sort of make things up in the assembly room.

S: Right.

J: They used to work over here; that's how they met.

S: And is he still here?

D: Yeah.

J: He's on holidays at the moment.

S: Mmm.

D: Is she on holidays? I haven't seen her since I've been back.

J: No, no, she's not.

D: **Actually**, it's really ridiculous

Text 9-7: Exploring – arguing: extract from an open letter (written, monologic) [Text 6]; for the full text, see Table 9-20 below
||| I don't believe || that [[endorsing the Nuclear Freeze initiative]] is the right step for California CC. ||| (7 clause complexes) ||| **Therefore**, I urge you || to vote against a CCC endorsement of the nuclear freeze initiative. |||

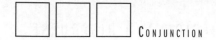

In the last example, the conjunction *therefore* introduces the first clause of the last clause complex, and the domain of the causal relation that it marks is the whole of the preceding text. The text is a persuasive one, where the author first presents arguments and then appeals to readers to vote against the endorsement, presenting this as a rational conclusion (for a rhetorical analysis of the whole text, see Section 9.7). This *therefore* links steps in the internal organization of the discourse (see further below). Such conjunctions often relate fairly extensive passages of discourse (up to entire generic elements: see Martin, 1992: 181, 219).

The logico-semantic relation is marked by a conjunction (see Chapter 6, Section 6.4.2) – either by a non-structural one that is used only in this way, i.e. only cohesively, such as *for example*, *furthermore*, *consequently*; or by a structural one whose prototypical function is to mark the continuing clause in a paratactic clause nexus (see Chapter 7, Section 7.3). The former serve as conjunctive Adjuncts (Chapter 4, Section 4.3.3) and are very commonly thematic; the latter are simply analysed as structure markers and are obligatorily thematic as structural Theme. In fact, since conjunctions are commonly thematic, we listed frequent ones in Chapter 3, Table 3-4.

9.3.2 The system of CONJUNCTION

As already noted, the logico-semantic relations that are manifested in the system of conjunction fall into the same three types of expansion we met in our exploration of clause complexing – that is, conjunctions mark relations where one span of text elaborates, extends or enhances another, earlier span of text. The system is set out in Figure 9-2. It is taken to a certain point in delicacy; we list conjunctions used for each of the most delicate features in Table 9-6, but we will not differentiate the members of these sets further in delicacy.

As we have seen, elaborating, extending and enhancing conjunctions mark relations between semantic domains, i.e. between text segments. These text segments are simultaneously ideational and interpersonal; they construe experience as meaning, e.g. an episode in a narrative or a recount, and they enact roles and relations, e.g. an exchange in a conversation or consultation, or an argument in an exposition. Relations link text segments either in their ideational guise or in their interpersonal guise: they relate either chunks of experience or chunks of interaction. For example, in the following extract from a folk tale, the conjunctions *soon* and *then* mark temporal relations in the episode being narrated:

> Quickly, the hunters grabbed their harpoons and tied the dogs to the sledges. Ka-ha-si rode with the leader as they raced in the direction of the walruses. **Soon** they turned the sledges over and anchored them in the snow. **Then** they pushed their umiak into the water. Ka-ha-si sat silently in the bow.

Relations between representations of segments of experience are called **external relations**, and conjunctions marking such relations are called **external conjunctions**. In contrast, in the argument presented in Text 9-7, a text operating in an exploring context, the conjunction *therefore* marks a causal relation in the argument, not in the experience being represented: 'I tell you ... therefore I urge you ...'. Similarly, *rather* in the same text (see Table 9-20) marks a relation between two steps in the writer's argument. Relations linking text segments in their interpersonal guise are called **internal relations** – internal to the text as a speech event, and conjunctions marking such relations are called **internal conjunctions**. As we noted in

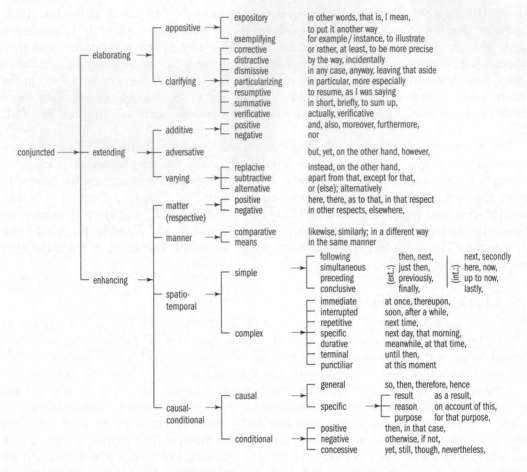

Fig. 9-2 The system of CONJUNCTION

Chapter 1, Section 1.4.1, internal relations are favoured in the global organization of texts that operate in tenor-oriented contexts (as illustrated by the persuasive text in Table 9-20), whereas external relations are favoured in the global organization of texts that operate in field-oriented contexts (e.g. procedural texts and recounts).

The distinction between external and internal relations was introduced by Halliday & Hasan (1976: Chapter 5) and developed by Martin (e.g. 1992: Chapter 4) in his account of conjunction as a semantic system. It also plays a central role in the account of rhetorical relations in RST, as shown by Mann & Matthiessen (1991). For the grammatical system of CONJUNCTION, we can explore the possibility of adding a system of ORIENTATION in parallel with the system of expansion TYPE shown in the system network in Figure 9-2: see Figure 9-3. This interpretation of conjunction as a system embodying two variables brings out the underlying principle. However, the two systemic variables are not entirely independent of one another. The 'elaborating' type tends to be 'internal' rather than 'external', and while 'extending' and 'enhancing' relations can be either 'internal' or 'external', particular conjunctions may be either one or the other. Thus when we extend it in delicacy, we

Table 9-6 Examples of items serving as conjunctive Adjuncts

TYPE OF EXP.	Subtypes			Items
elaboration	apposition	expository		in other words, that is (to say), I mean (to say), to put it another way
		exemplifying		for example, for instance, thus, to illustrate
	clarification	corrective		or rather, at least, to be more precise
		distractive		by the way, incidentally
		dismissive		in any case, anyway, leaving that aside
		particularizing		in particular, more especially
		resumptive		as I was saying, to resume, to get back to the point
		summative		in short, to sum up, in conclusion, briefly
		verifactive		actually, as a matter of fact, in fact, indeed
extension	addition	positive		*and*, also, moreover, in addition
		negative		*nor*
		adversative		*but*, yet, on the other hand, however
	variation	replacive		on the contrary, instead
		subtractive		apart from that, except for that
		alternative		alternatively
enhancement	spatio-temporal: temporal	simple	following	then, next, afterwards [including correlatives first ... then]
			simultaneous	just then, at the same time
			preceding	before that, hitherto, previously
			conclusive	in the end, finally
		complex	immediate	at once, thereupon, straightaway
			interrupted	soon, after a while
			repetitive	next time, on another occasion
			specific	next day, an hour later, that morning
			durative	meanwhile, all that time
			terminal	until then, up to that point
			punctiliar	at this moment

Table 9-6 Examples of items serving as conjunctive Adjuncts (*contd*)

TYPE OF EXP.	Subtypes			Items
		simple internal	following	next, secondly ('my next point is') [incl. correlatives first ... next]
			simultaneous	at this point, here, now
			preceding	hitherto, up to now
			conclusive	lastly, last of all, finally
	manner	comparison	positive	likewise, similarly
			negative	in a different way
		means		thus, thereby, by such means
	causal-conditional	general		*so, then,* therefore, consequently, hence, because of that; *for*
		specific	result	in consequence, as a result
			reason	on account of this, for that reason
			purpose	for that purpose, with this in view
			conditional: positive	then, in that case, in that event, under the circumstances
			conditional: negative	otherwise, if not
			concessive	yet, still, though, despite this, however, even so, all the same, nevertheless
	matter	positive		here, there, as to that, in that respect
		negative		in other respects, elsewhere

would need to take account of the all the possible combinations of type and orientation: (i) a number of conjunctions can be used to mark either external or internal relations, but a number of other conjunctions can be used only to mark either (ii) external or (iii) internal relations. For example:

(i) external/internal: *and, or, but, however, then, next, so, therefore*

(ii) external: *just then, previously, soon, meanwhile, next time*

(iii) internal: *in fact, actually, incidentally, in short, briefly, finally, in conclusion, furthermore, moreover, in this respect, otherwise*

(cf. Halliday & Hasan, 1976: 242–243). Certain items that serve as 'elaborating' conjunctions that are 'internal' only in orientation may also serve as modal adverbs (e.g. *actually, in fact,*

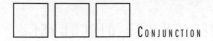
indeed, as a matter of fact), functioning either as mood Adjuncts of intensity (see Chapter 4, Section 4.3.2.1) or as comment Adjuncts of factuality (see Chapter 4, Section 4.3.2.2). In fact, these are related historically through processes of grammaticalization: starting from an experiential source, items such as these tend to develop into textual conjunctions, and by a further step into interpersonal modal adverbs: see e.g. Traugott (1997) and Brinton (2009).

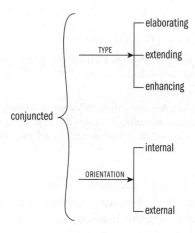

Fig. 9-3 The system of conjunction interpreted as two simultaneous systems, (expansion) type and (metafunctional) orientation

We will now return to the three types of expansion in Figure 9-2, and discuss each type and its immediate subtypes in turn, starting with elaborating conjunctions.

9.3.2.1 Elaboration

There are two categories of elaborating relation, (a) apposition and (b) clarification. The overall range is the same as that of paratactic elaboration; but the category of apposition used here groups exposition and exemplification together. We will consider the appositive type first.

(a) apposition. In this type of elaboration some element is re-presented, or restated, either (i) by exposition, the 'i.e.' relation, or (ii) by example, the 'e.g.' relation.

(i) expository:

I guess the main editorial rule that we work by is to treat all manuscripts equally. **I mean**, it doesn't make any difference who the author is. [Text 21]

(ii) exemplifying:

Our humor is founded on very close observation, very, very close observation of reality. You find some humorous proverbs, **for instance**, and the humor is that whoever made these proverbs was not going around the world with his eyes closed. **For example**, the dog says that those who have buttocks do not know how to sit. [Text 16]

(b) clarification. Here the elaborated element is not simply restated but reinstated, summarized, made more precise or in some other way clarified for purposes of the discourse. There are seven subtypes (corrective, distractive, dismissive, particularizing, resumptive, summative, verifactive), realized by different sets of conjunctions[4]; they are set out in Table 9-6, and illustrated below:

Calculations by Anderson show that ozone depletion at the 410- and 420-K isentropic surfaces between August 23 and September 22 can be almost entirely explained by the amount of ClO present if one assumes that the ClO-ClO mechanism is effective. At the 360-K surface, the calculated ozone loss is somewhat less than the observed loss. **At least** we can say that above about the 400-K level, there does seem to be enough ClO to explain the observed ozone loss. [Text 33] [corrective]

Customer: What's pepperoni? – Operator: Pepperoni? It's a round, it's a pork product. – Customer: Is it? Oh okay. No I don't want that. **Anyway**, um – can I have one of them? I'll pay the two dollar extra: the – what do you call it? the seafood. [11PH12] [dismissive]

Interviewer: You grew up in St. Louis, Missouri, went to Vassar as an undergraduate, and then came back to Iowa for your graduate work. – Smiley: **Actually**, there was a year in there where after I finished Vassar I went to Europe with my then husband and we hitchhiked around, wondering what to do. [Text 17] [verifactive]

9.3.2.2 Extension

Extension involves either addition or variation. Addition is either positive *and*, negative *nor* or adversative *but*; but since the adversative relation plays a particularly important part in discourse it is best taken as a separate heading on its own. Variation includes replacive *instead*, subtractive *except* and alternative *or* types.

(a) addition

(i) positive:

||| The ozone amount was also the lowest on record at all latitudes south of 60°S latitude in 1987. ||| **Furthermore**, the occurrence of strong depletion was a year-long phenomenon south of 60°S || and was not confined to the spring season as in preceding years, || although the greatest depletion occurred during the Southern Hemisphere spring. ||| [Text 33]

(ii) negative:

||| When Kukul awoke, || he saw ⟦that the feature was gone⟧. ||| He searched everywhere, || but he could not find it. ||| **Nor** could he remember the words of the priest on the day ⟦he was born⟧. || [Text 65]

---

4   Some of the items that are used as conjunctions with verifactive senses also have assessment senses and serve as mood or comment Adjuncts (see Chapter 4, Table 4-14): *actually, in fact, indeed* – (i) verifactive ('in reality'), (iia) intensity: counterexpectancy ('even'), and (iib) factual (speech functional comment: 'really'); *as a matter of fact* – (i) verifactive ('in reality'), and (ii) factual (speech functional comment: 'really'). The link between the verifactive and assessment senses is the orientation towards the interpersonal: in their assessment senses, these items are, of course, purely interpersonal; and in their verifactive senses, they are internal in orientation (cf. Halliday & Hasan, 1976: 240ff.): the clarification relates to the speech function rather than to the experiential content of the proposition or proposal being exchanged – 'I'll tell you by way of clarification of what I said before'. Thus in the following example, *in fact* serves as a cohesive conjunctive Adjunct and *actually* as a mood Adjunct: *But that basic training helped me in the part. In fact, when Tom Quayle (Tom Jennings) actually did knock me down in the fight scene, I saw red and had to take a few deep breaths and hold myself back.* [ACE_C] Traugott (1997) shows how both *indeed* and (during a later period in the history of English) *in fact* developed (in our terms) from items serving as circumstantial Adjuncts, to items serving as interpersonal Adjuncts and also to items serving as conjunctive Adjuncts. They follow one of the grammaticalization paths she has identified.

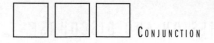
(iii) adversative:

||| After the Bay of Pigs fiasco, he said ruefully, || "It would have been better || if we had left it to James Bond." ||| **On the other hand**, his reputed attempts [[to get Castro to extinguish himself with either an exploding cigar or a poison pen]] may have owed all too much to Bond. ||| [Text 110]

(b) variation

(i) replacive:

||| Assad, a career air force officer [[who took power in a bloodless coup in 1970]], has been grooming Bashar for future leadership, || but the British-educated ophthalmologist has held no major political office. ||| **Instead**, Bashar has been going abroad as his father's special envoy. ||| [Text 66]

(ii) subtractive:

||| Naturally though, it has to be within walking distance of Mayfair, || but, **apart from that**, an attic with only a shower and a gas ring will suffice. ||| [LOB_R]

(iii) alternative:

||| If there's still time, || you may wish to round off the day with a visit to Fort Denison [[conducted by the Maritime Services Board]]. ||| Tours leave from Circular Quay at 10.15am, 12.15am and 2.00pm Tuesday to Sunday, || although you will certainly need to book in advance || by ringing Captain Cook Cruises on 2515007. ||| **Alternatively**, if you've had enough of colonial relics, || a Captain Cook Cruise can be booked on the same number. ||| [Text 22]

9.3.2.3 Enhancement

The various types of enhancement that create cohesion are (a) spatio-temporal, (b) manner, (c) causal-conditional and (d) matter. Each of these will be briefly discussed and exemplified.

(a) spatio-temporal. Place reference may be used conjunctively within a text, with *here* and *there*, spatial adverbs such as *behind* and *nearby*, and expressions containing a place noun or adverb plus reference item, e.g. *in the same place, anywhere else*. Here spatial relations are being used as text-creating cohesive devices.

Note however that most apparently spatial cohesion is in terms of metaphorical space; for example *there* in *there you're wrong*; cf. expressions like *on those grounds, on that point*. These are actually expressions of Matter. Many conjunctive expressions of the expanding kind are also in origin spatial metaphors; e.g. *in the first place, on the other hand* (*hand* involves a double metaphor: 'part of the body' – 'side' [on my right hand] – 'side of an argument').

Temporal conjunction covers a very great variety of different relations; we can distinguish between (i) simple and (ii) complex ones, as set out in Examples of items serving as conjunctive Adjuncts. They are important in registers where sequence in time is a major organizing principle – narratives, biographies, procedures. Examples:

(i) simple

||| "I am   Real!" || said the little Rabbit. ||| "The Boy said || so!" ||| **Just then** there was the sound of footsteps, || and the two strange rabbits disappeared. ||| [Text 28] [simultaneous]

||| The Atlantic took a second story, || and I got an agent. ||| **Then** I started my first novel || and sent off about four chapters || and waited by the post office || for praise to roll in, calls from Hollywood, everything. ||| **Finally** my agent sent me a letter [[that said || "Dear Peter, James Fenimore Cooper wrote this a hundred and fifty years ago, || only he wrote it better. ||| Yours, Bernice."]] ||| [Text 7] [following; conclusive]

617

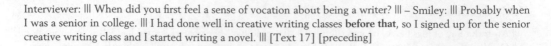

Interviewer: ||| When did you first feel a sense of vocation about being a writer? ||| – Smiley: ||| Probably when I was a senior in college. ||| I had done well in creative writing classes **before that**, so I signed up for the senior creative writing class and I started writing a novel. ||| [Text 17] [preceding]

(ii) complex

||| Kukul fought bravely, || at times at the very front. ||| But wherever he was, || not a single weapon fell on him. ||| Chirumá observed this. ||| "The gods must watch out for Kukul," he thought to himself. ||| **All at once**, Kukul saw an arrow flying straight toward Chirumá, || and Kukul positioned himself like a shield in front of his uncle. ||| [Text 65] [immediate]

||| In another story [[that we recently published]], Robert Olen Butler's "Titanic Victim Speaks through Waterbed," a midlevel colonial official [[who is on the Titanic]] falls in love with a woman || as the ship is about to sink. ||| He has led a dry life **until then**, || and the whole story is told through the eerie perspective of this guy after death, || as he continues to float around in water, at various times in the ocean, in a cup of tea, a pisspot, and finally a waterbed. ||| [Text 21] [terminal]

||| Place the aubergine slices in a colander, || sprinkle with salt || and leave || to drain for 10 minutes. ||| Rinse and dry thoroughly. ||| **Meanwhile**, mix the flour with the cayenne pepper in a bowl. ||| [N.B. Highton & R.B. Highton, 1964, *The home book of vegetarian cookery*. London: Faber & Faber] [durative]

Those that are called 'complex' are the simple ones with some other semantic feature or features present at the same time.

Many temporal conjunctives have an 'internal' as well as an 'external' interpretation (cf. Chapter 7, Section 7.4.3.2; Halliday & Hasan, 1976: Ch. 5; Martin, 1992: Ch. 4; cf. also Mann & Matthiessen, 1991); that is, the time they refer to is the temporal unfolding of the discourse itself, not the temporal sequence of the processes referred to. In terms of the functional components of semantics, it is interpersonal not experiential time. Parallel to the 'simple' categories above we can recognize the simple internal ones set out in Examples of items serving as conjunctive Adjuncts. These play an important role in argumentative passages in discourse. Examples:

(iii) simple internal

||| Organizationally, there are equally strong imperatives and challenges. ||| Again, a ***first*** requirement is [[to do no harm to organizational frameworks [[that, through years of evolution, are finally at the stage [[where they are supporting programs [[that are actually helping us to get on with the business of increasing understanding]]]]]]]]. ||| **Second**, having ensured [[that we do as little harm as possible]], || we must make sure [[that the interdisciplinary linkages [[mentioned earlier]] do not fall between organizational stools]]. ||| **Third**, we must take steps to ensure [[that the organizations [[we do have in place]] do not impede research [[that is crossing over their historical boundaries of self-definition]]]]. ||| **Finally**, the ultimate challenge is [[to identify which, if any, new organizational frameworks would make a positive contribution to our ability [[to get on with the substantive work of [[understanding global change]]]]]]. ||| [Text 32] [following; conclusive]

These shade into temporal metaphors of an expanding kind such as *meanwhile, at the same time* (*meanwhile let us not forget that ...* , *at the same time it must be admitted that ...*)

(b) manner. Manner conjunctives create cohesion (i) by comparison, (ii) by reference to means: see Examples of items serving as conjunctive Adjuncts. Comparison may be (a) positive ('is like'), or (b) negative ('is unlike'). Examples:

618

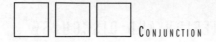

(i) comparison:

||| One area [[that holds considerable promise for RC involvement]] is Information Operations. ||| By exploiting the technical skills [[that many reservists use on a daily basis in their civilian jobs]], || the military can take advantage of industry's latest techniques [[for protecting information systems]]. ||| **Similarly,** [[defending our homeland from terrorism || and responding to chemical attack]] are natural roles for our Guard and Reserve forces. ||| [Text 115] [positive]

(ii) means:

||| Chert originates in several ways. ||| Some may precipitate directly from sea water in areas [[where volcanism releases abundant silica]]. ||| Most comes from the accumulation of silica shells of organisms. ||| These silica remains come from diatoms, radiolaria, and sponge spicules, || and are composed of opal. ||| Opal is easily recrystallized to form chert. ||| **Thus** much chert is recrystallized, || making the origin difficult to discern. ||| [Text 68]

Expressions of means are however not often conjunctive; those that *are* are usually also comparative, e.g. *in the same manner, otherwise.*

(c) causal-conditional. In many types of discourse the relation of cause figures very prominently as a cohesive agent. Some cause expressions are general, others relate more specifically to result, reason or purpose: see Examples of items serving as conjunctive Adjuncts. Examples:

(i) general:

||| We understand it still || that there is no easy road to freedom. ||| We know it well || that none of us [[acting alone]] can achieve success. ||| We must **therefore** act together as a united people, for national reconciliation, for nation building, for the birth of a new world. ||| [Text 104]

(ii) specific
[a] result:

||| Now prices have sunk for secondary schools || and experienced secondary inspectors are shifting into primary and special schools with minimal training. ||| **As a result**, primary schools and teachers are being judged 'failing' by inspectors [[who have never taught younger children, || but only watched a couple of lessons on video during their training]]! ||| [Text 97]

[b] reason:

||| But you wouldn't marry me? || – No. ||| I'm not your type. ||| I'd make you miserable. ||| I mean that. ||| I'd very probably be unfaithful || and that'd kill you. ||| Then I'd be unfaithful too, || to teach you a lesson. ||| It wouldn't work. ||| You'd do it || to spite me. ||| I would never do it **for that reason**. ||| [LOB_K]

[c] purpose:

Laertes: ||| I will do't! ||| And **for that purpose** I'll anoint my sword. ||| [Hamlet]

||| In 2011 the SUN Road Map will be translated into action || with a view to helping countries [[affected by under-nutrition]] to achieve long-term reduction in under-nutrition || and realize the first Millennium Development Goal, || and to start demonstrating this impact within three years. ||| **For that purpose** the SUN Road Map envisages an open system of support to the implementation of SUN efforts by countries. ||| [http://www.unscn.org/en/scaling_up_nutrition_sun/sun_purpose.php]

619

Conditionals subdivide into (i) positive, (ii) negative and (iii) concessive. Examples:
(i)positive:

[S02:] ||| That's the DEET account. ||| Well there must be more money coming from that. ||| Do they tend to pay – || how do they – ||| – [S04:] ||| Per issue. ||| – [S02:] ||| Per issue. ||| Well **in that case** do they pay after the issues come out? ||| [Text 129]

(ii) negative:

||| "I mustn't say anything about it. ||| **Otherwise**, I'll get shot by the lady [[who just shut the door]]," || Holm said, || referring to a publicist [[who had just left the room]]. ||| [Text 73]

(iii) concessive:

||| The outstanding performance of U.S. and other NATO military units has enabled SFOR to fulfill the military tasks [[spelled out in the Dayton Accords]]. ||| **Nevertheless**, success [[in achieving the civil, political, and economic tasks [[identified at Dayton]]]] has been slower in coming. ||| [Text 115]

(d) matter. Here cohesion is established by reference to the 'matter' that has gone before. As noted earlier, many expressions of matter are spatial metaphors, involving words like *point*, *ground*, *field*; and these become conjunctive when coupled with reference items. The relation is either (i) positive or (ii) negative: see Table 9-6. Examples:
(i) positive:

||| Without chlorine in the antarctic stratosphere, || there would be no ozone hole. ||| (**Here** "hole" refers to a substantial reduction below the naturally occurring concentration of ozone over Antarctica.) ||| [Text 33]

(ii) negative: in other respects, elsewhere

||| The serial dilutions of the serum are made in AB serum || and the standard cells are suspended in 30 per cent bovine albumin. ||| **In all other respects** the method is identical with technique No. 17. ||| [LOB_J]

9.3.3 The system of CONJUNCTION instantiated in text

In the previous subsection, we have presented the system of CONJUNCTION, illustrating how conjunctions are used to mark rhetorical relations by which a text is developed. The examples always involved a single relation being marked conjunctively, as in the case of narrative discourse, where conjunctions are often used to mark temporal relations. However, more than one relation may be involved in the development of a text (cf. Martin, 1992):

Text 9-8: Reporting – chronicling (spoken, dialogic): media interview [Text 21]
Morgan: ||| Yeah, I wandered in in blue jeans to her office || and cut my finger on an aluminum Coke can, || so there I was bleeding || when she arrived. ||| She refused to even look at me || until I had sat there bleeding a while. ||| I wandered around looking at letters from famous authors on the walls, || feeling more cowed by the minute. |||

Somerville: ||| What famous authors? |||

Morgan: ||| There were a number of letters from Flannery O'Conner. ||| This lady went back. ||| **Anyway**, she **finally** called me in || and summarily dismissed me. |||

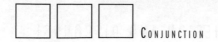

Here Morgan first needs to indicate that he is leaving the proposition that Somerville introduced, thus interrupting his narrative; he does this by means of the 'dismissive corrective' conjunction *anyway*. At the same time, he also picks up the narrative that was temporarily suspended because of Somerville's question; and he does this by means of the 'conclusive temporal' conjunction *finally*.

When we meet a conjunction in text, we often have to decide which relation it marks among different types. For example, is a given instance of *however* 'adversative' or 'concessive' (the same issue arises with structural conjunctions; cf. Chapter 7, Table 7-11)? It is clear that a number of the different types of conjunctive relation set out in Figure 9-2 overlap with one another. The conjunctive relation of 'matter' is very close to some of those of the elaborating kind, and the concessive ('despite X, nevertheless Y') overlaps with the adversative ('X and, conversely, Y'). Such pairs are characterized by differences of emphasis, and some instances can be assigned to one member or the other; but others cannot, and may be interpreted either way. As always, we can try to bring out the most likely interpretation by checking close agnates to examples occurring in the text (cf. Chapter 7, Section 7.4.4). The categories given here are those that have been found most useful in the interpretation of texts, and their schematization is such as to relate to other parts of the system of the language.

One question that arises in the interpretation of a text is what to do about a conjunction that is implicit. It often happens, especially with temporal and causal sequences, that the semantic relationship is clearly felt to be present but is unexpressed; for example

George Stephenson died on 12 August 1848 ... He was buried at Holy Trinity, Chesterfield.

where there is obviously a temporal relationship between the two parts; cf. the following where the relation is one of cause:

Hudson decided next to establish himself in London. He bought what was then considered to be the largest private house in London, Albert House, ...

It is clear that texture is achieved through conjunctive relations of this kind, and there is no reason not to take account of it. On the other hand, the attempt to include it in the analysis leads to a great deal of indeterminacy, both as regards whether a conjunctive relation is present or not and as regards which particular kind of relationship it is. Consider the extract:

Around 1823, certain normally staid and sensible firms in the city of London got themselves very worked up about the possibilities of great fortunes to be made in South America. The idea was admittedly very exciting. Everybody knew the old stories, even if many of them were legendary, about the Inca gold mines, about the Spanish conquistadores and the undreamt of mineral wealth which they had found. These mines had been worked by hand, without machines, and long since left abandoned. Think what can now be done, suggested some bright speculator, using all our new and marvellous steam engines!

This is a highly cohesive passage; but it is difficult to say what implicit conjunctive relationship would hold between pairs of adjacent sentences, or between each sentence and anything that precedes it.

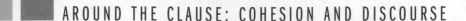

It is perhaps as well, therefore, to be cautious in assigning implicit conjunction in the interpretation of a text. It is likely that there will always be other forms of cohesion present, and that these are the main source of our intuition that there is a pattern of conjunctive relationships as well. (For example, when a lexical relation of hyponymy obtains between lexical items in two successive Themes, a relation of elaboration such as exemplification presence or successive Themes, a relation of elaboration such as exemplification can often be inferred, as would typically be the case in taxonomic reports.) Moreover the absence of explicit conjunction is one of the principal variables in English discourse, both as between registers and as between texts in the same register; this variation is obscured if we assume conjunction where it is not expressed. It is important therefore to note those instances where conjunction is being recognized that is implicit; and to characterize the text also without it, to see how much we still feel is being left unaccounted for.

Table 9-7 gives an example of a text showing conjunctive relations. The headings that may be found useful for most purposes of analysis are the general ones of (i) elaborating: appositive, clarificative; (ii) extending: additive, adversative, variative; (iii) enhancing: temporal, comparative, causal, conditional, concessive, matter.

Table 9-7 Expounding text analysed for conjunction[5]

	Elaborating	Extending	Enhancing
"Heat is only the motion of the atoms I told you about."			
"Then what is *cold*?"			cond
"Cold is only absence of heat."			
"Then if anything is cold it means that its atoms are not moving."			cond
"Only in the most extreme case.			
There are different degrees of cold.			
∅ A piece of ice is cold compared with warm water.	ap		
But the atoms of a piece of ice are moving –			conc
they are moving quite fast, **as a matter of fact**.	ap		
But they are not moving as fast as the atoms of warm water.			conc
So that compared with water, the ice is cold.			caus
But even the water would seem cold, if compared with a red-hot poker.		ad	
Now I'll tell you an experiment you ought to try one day."			temp

[5] ap = appositive; ad = additive, caus = causal, cond = conditional, conc = concessive; temp = temporal;
∅ = implicit conjunction

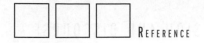

9.4 Reference

In the previous section, we discussed one of the two major cohesive types – the system of CONJUNCTION, a resource for marking **transition** in the unfolding of a text. We will now turn to the other major cohesive type – resources for marking textual **status** (see Table 9-5). By textual statuses, we mean values assigned to elements of discourse that guide speakers and listeners in processing these elements. We have, in fact, already met two kinds of textual status – thematicity and newsworthiness. Theme and New are processed quite differently when interactants manage the flow of text; while Theme is the point of departure for integrating the information being presented in the clause, New is the main point to retain from the information presented. But whereas Theme and New are parts of textual structures – Theme ^ Rheme in the clause and Given + New in the information unit, respectively (see e.g. Figure 3-19, Chapter 3), the textual statuses that come under the heading of cohesion, REFERENCE and ELLIPSIS, are not. That is, while an element is marked cohesively as identifiable by means of a grammatical item such as the personal pronoun *they*, or as continuous by means of a grammatical item such as the nominal substitute *one*, the textual statuses of identifiability and continuity are not structural functions of the clause or of any other grammatical unit. They can occur freely within Theme or Rheme, and within Given or New (although there are certain unmarked associations). We shall start with the system of REFERENCE.[6]

9.4.1 The nature of reference; types of reference

The textual status at issue in the system of reference is that of **identifiability**: does the speaker judge that a given element can be recovered or identified by the listener at the relevant point in the discourse or not? If it is presented as identifiable, then the listener will have to recover the identity from somewhere else (for a systemic description of this as a semantic system, see Martin, 1992). If it is presented as non-identifiable, then the listener will have to establish it as a new element of meaning in the interpretation of the text. For example, in the following introduction to a narrative –

||| There was once <u>a velveteen rabbit</u>. ||| **He** was fat and bunchy, || **his** coat was spotted brown and white, || and **his** ears were lined with pink sateen. ||| [Text 28]

– the protagonist is first introduced as non-identifiable by means of the non-specific nominal group *a velveteen rabbit* (cf. Chapter 6, Section 6.2.1.1), allowing the reader to establish this creature as a node in the network of meanings created in the course of the interpretation of the narrative. After having been introduced in this way, the velveteen rabbit is then presented as identifiable by means of the personal pronoun *he* and possessive determiner *his*. These latter are instances of reference.

---

6   Note that the term 'reference' has been used in different ways. For example, in philosophical and formal semantic works on meaning it indicates ideational denotation, as when expressions are said to refer to phenomena. (In such contexts, reference (or extension) and sense (or intension) are often taken as complementary aspects of meaning, going back to Frege's distinction between Sinn and Bedeutung.) Here we are using the term in the way it has been used in functional work (e.g. Halliday & Hasan, 1976) to indicate the textual cohesive strategy discussed in this section.

In the example above, the reference items *he* and *his* presume the identity of the rabbit by pointing backwards to the preceding text. This is typical of a great many types of discourse: the identity that is presumed can be recovered from the preceding text – or, in effect, from the instantial system of meanings that is built up by speaker and listener as the text unfolds. However, it seems quite likely that reference first evolved as a means of linking 'outwards' to some entity in the environment. So, for example, the concept of 'he' probably originated as 'that man over there' – a reference to a person in the field of perception shared by speaker and listener.

In other words we may postulate an imaginary stage in the evolution of language when the basic referential category of PERSON was deictic in the strict sense, 'to be interpreted by reference to the situation here and now'. Thus *I* was 'the one speaking': *you*, 'the one(s) spoken to'; *he, she, it, they* were the third party, 'the other(s) in the situation'.

The first and second persons *I* and *you* naturally retain this deictic sense; their meaning is defined in the act of speaking. The third person forms *he, she, it, they* can also be used in this way; for example, in the extract in Text 9-9 from a coffee-break conversation at a workplace, the third person forms *he, him* point 'outwards', to a person in the environment:

Text 9-9: Sharing – casual conversation (spoken, dialogic): bantering [Text 10]

J: And don't make such a noise.

C: It wouldn't matter to **him** really; **he**'s half deaf * after all these years ** working at this place.

A: * Yeah.

K: ** Yeah.

J: Yep its true.

E: You're right, very deaf.

But more often than not, in all languages as we know them, such items point not 'outwards' to the environment but 'backwards' to the preceding text, as in our earlier example from the beginning of a narrative. There is, of course, no difference in the forms of the reference items; it is a question of how they are used. Which uses are most favoured will depend on the nature of the text.

It will be helpful to introduce the technical terms for the different kinds of pointing or **phora**: see Table 9-8. The basic distinction is between pointing 'outwards' and pointing 'inwards' – between (i) **exophora** and (ii) **endophora**.

(i) **Exophoric reference** means that the identity presumed by the reference item is recoverable from the environment of the text, as in the example just given above. Here the

Table 9-8 Types of phora

Reference to:		Before	Current	After
environment	exophoric		exophoric ↑	
text	endophoric	anaphoric ←	reference item	→ cataphoric

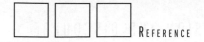
reference links the text to its environment; but it does not contribute to the cohesion of the text, except indirectly when references to one and the same referent are repeated, forming a chain. Such chains are common in dialogue with repetition of references to the interactants by means of forms of *I, you, we*, as in the conversational passage analysed in Table 9-4.

(ii) Endophoric reference means that the identity presumed by the reference item is recoverable from within the text itself – or, to be more precise, from the instantial system of meanings created as the text unfolds. As the text unfolds, speakers and listeners build up a system of meanings – this is part of the process of logogenesis we discussed above. Once a new meaning has been introduced, it becomes part of that system, and if it is the right category of thing, it can be presumed by endophoric reference. There are actually two possibilities here. Endophoric reference may point 'backwards' to the history of the unfolding text, that is, to a referent that has already been introduced and is thus part of the text's system of meanings. This was illustrated above in the conversational passage in Table 9-4 (e.g. *this fish – it; the pan – it*). This type of endophoric reference is called **anaphora**, or anaphoric reference, and the element that is pointed to anaphorically is called the antecedent. Anaphora is very common; it makes a significant contribution to many kinds of text – for example, it is a hallmark of narrative, where we find long chains of anaphoric references. Alternatively, endophoric reference may point 'forwards' to the future of the unfolding text, that is, to a referent that is yet to be introduced. Thus in the following example, *this guy* indicates that more about this referent is to come:

> ||| One day I was sitting in the Dôme, a street café in Montparnasse quite close to [[where we were living]], || and **this guy** walked up || and said, || "I met you in 1948 or 1949. ||| My name is Harold Humes." ||| He said || he was starting a new magazine, The Paris News-Post, || and would I become its fiction editor. ||| [Text 119]

This is strategy for introducing a person into narrative passages in conversation. An even clearer example is the use of *this* on its own to anticipate a passage of text; for example:

> ||| In brief, the soon widely held assumption was **this**: || man could understand the universe || because it was natural || and he was rational. ||| Moreover, he might be able to control, even reorder his environment, || once he had knowledge of it. ||| [Text 122]

This type of endophoric reference is called **cataphora**, or cataphoric reference. Cataphora is quite rare compared with anaphora. The only exception is **structural cataphora** (cf. Halliday & Hasan, 1976: 72), which is common. Here the reference is resolved within the same nominal group where the reference item appears; a Deictic *the* or *that/those* is used to indicate that the Qualifier of a nominal group is to be taken as defining. For example:

> The age was one of transition as much as of transformation, the ongoing process or movement that has led all of us today to use the expression "What's new?" as a common and casual greeting. **Those who were opposed and fearful**, as well as **those who were excited and hopeful**, recognized that the key to an understanding of the age was change. [Europe in Retrospect]

Exophora and endophora are different directions of pointing – either to referents in the environment outside the text, or to referents introduced in the text itself before or after the reference expression. But how does this reference expression achieve the effect of 'pointing'? All such expressions have in common the fact that they presuppose referents; but they

differ with respect to whether what is presupposed is the same referent (**co-reference**) or another referent of the same class (**comparative reference**): see Table 9-9. All the examples we have discussed so far have involved co-reference and before we discuss comparative reference, we shall explore co-reference in some more detail.

Table 9-9 Types of reference expression

		Nominal group: Head or Premodifier	Nominal or adverbial group: SubModifier	Adverbial group: Head
co-reference	personal	personal pronoun as Thing/Head; possessive determiner as Deictic/Premodifier or Head	–	–
	demonstrative	demonstrative pronoun as Thing/Head; demonstrative determiner as Deictic/Premodifier or Head	–	demonstrative adverbs as Head (*here, there*)
comparative reference	general	adjective as post-Deictic (*same, similar, other,* etc.); adjective *such* as Epithet	comparative adverb (*identically, similarly, otherwise,* etc.) as SubModifier in nominal, adverbial group or as Premodifier, Head in adverbial group	
	specific	comparative adverb (*more, fewer,* etc.) as SubModifier of numeral serving as Numerative; comparative adverb (*more, less, etc.*) as SubModifier of adjective serving as Epithet (or simply comparative form of that adjective)	comparative adverb (*more, less, etc.*) as SubModifier in nominal, adverbial group or as Premodifier in adverbial group (or simply comparative form of adverb)	

As the table indicates, there are two types of co-reference: personal reference and demonstrative reference. They differ with respect to the category that is used to indicate the referent – either person or proximity. We shall explore personal co-reference first, then turn to demonstrative co-reference.

9.4.2 Personal reference

In personal reference, the category of person is used to refer: we described the basic principle in the previous subsection, suggesting that non-interactant personal pronouns and possessive determiners have come to be used primarily in anaphoric reference. The personal reference items of English are set out in Table 9-10. They are either 'determinative' or

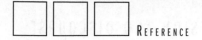

'possessive' (see Chapter 6, Section 6.2.1.1). If 'determinative', they are personal pronouns serving as Thing/Head in the nominal group (as in *a velveteen rabbit ... **he***). If 'possessive', they are determiners serving as Deictic in the nominal group and are conflated with either Head or Premodifier (as in *a velveteen rabbit ... **his** coat*).

We have already seen a simple example of personal reference in operation. The text extract in Cohesion in a conversational passage illustrates the use of *it* to achieve anaphoric reference: *this fish – it, the pan – it*. For a somewhat more extended example, we can refer to a narrative for children about a Velveteen Rabbit. After this Velveteen Rabbit has been introduced, there are anaphoric references to this rabbit, forming a **reference chain** that runs throughout the narrative. The chain running through the extract consists of the following items:

> [*a velveteen rabbit*] – *he* – <u>*his (coat)*</u> – <u>*his (ears)*</u> – <u>*he*</u> – *his (paws)* – *him* – *the Velveteen Rabbit* – *he* – <u>*he*</u> – *him*
> – ... – <u>*the Rabbit*</u> – <u>*he*</u> – *him*

Several of these reference items occur within the Theme (thematic references underlined): while reference items can occur anywhere, there is an unmarked relationship between referential identifiability and status as Given information, and between Given and Theme. There is therefore a strong tendency for reference items to be thematic. Most of the anaphoric references involve simply a personal pronoun or a possessive determiner; there are only two references with demonstrative *the* as Deictic and the lexical noun *rabbit* as Thing. This is the typical pattern in extended reference chains.

That is, there are two primary anaphoric strategies for tracking a referent as a text unfolds. The speaker or writer can use either (i) a personal reference item (personal pronoun or possessive determiner) or (ii) a specified noun. A 'specified noun' is either an inherently specific one – a proper noun – or else a common noun (serving as Thing) modified by a demonstrative determiner as Deictic. For example: *he* vs. *the Rabbit* or *his* vs. *the Rabbit's* (or *of the Rabbit*). The term 'pronoun' suggests that a pronoun stands for a noun; and the term 'pronominalization' suggests that something is turned into a pronoun. But both terms are misleading: the unmarked anaphoric strategy is to use the pronoun, and the lexical variant or a proper name is used only if there is a good reason to vary from the unmarked strategy.

Good reasons include (i) the need to indicate the beginning of a new rhetorical stage in the unfolding text and (ii) the need to further elaborate the reference when there are alternative antecedents around in the discourse. Thus in the following passage from Bertrand Russell's autobiography (p. 216 onwards), Joseph Conrad is introduced into the discourse by means of his proper name, *Joseph Conrad*; but once this introduction has been achieved, the default strategy is that of personal reference, and we find a chain of personal reference items (*he, him, his*) until Russell uses the proper name again as he shifts to a discussion of the nature of the relationship between him and Conrad:

Text 9-10: Reporting – recounting (written, monologic): extract from Russell's autobiography

An event of importance to me in 1913 was the beginning of my friendship with **Joseph Conrad**, which I owed to our common friendship with Ottoline. I had been for many years an admirer of <u>his</u> books, but should not have ventured to seek acquaintance without an introduction. I travelled down to <u>his</u> house near Ashford

627

in Kent in a state of somewhat anxious expectation. My first impression was one of surprise. <u>He</u> spoke English with a very strong foreign accent, and nothing in <u>his</u> demeanour in any way suggested the sea. <u>He</u> was an aristocratic Polish gentleman to <u>his</u> fingertips. <u>His</u> feeling for the sea, and for England, was one of romantic love – love for the sea began at a very early age. When <u>he</u> told <u>his</u> parents that <u>he</u> wished for a career as a sailor, they urged <u>him</u> to go into the Austrian navy, but <u>he</u> wanted adventure and tropical seas and strange rivers surrounded by dark forests; and the Austrian navy offered <u>him</u> no scope for these desires. <u>His</u> family were horrified at <u>his</u> seeking a career in the English merchant marine, but <u>his</u> determination was inflexible.

<u>He</u> was, as anyone may see from <u>his</u> books, a very rigid moralist and by no means politically sympathetic with revolutionaries. <u>He</u> and I were in most of our opinions by no means in agreement, but in something very fundamental we were extraordinarily at one.

My relation to **Joseph Conrad** was unlike any other that I have ever had. I saw <u>him</u> seldom, and not over a long period of years. In the out-works of our lives, *we* were almost strangers, but *we* shared a certain outlook on human life and human destiny, which, from the very first, made a bond of extreme strength. I may perhaps be pardoned for quoting a sentence from a letter that <u>he</u> wrote to me very soon after *we* had become acquainted. ...

Somewhat later in Russell's account of Conrad, we find an illustration of the second reason for departing from the unmarked strategy of pronominal reference:

<u>He</u> was very conscious of the various forms of passionate madness to which men are prone, and it was this that gave <u>him</u> such a profound belief in the importance of discipline. <u>His</u> point of view, one might perhaps say, was the antithesis of Rousseau's: "Man is born in chains, but <u>he</u> can be free". <u>He</u> becomes free, so I believe **Conrad** would have said, not by letting loose <u>his</u> impulses, not by being casual and uncontrolled, but by subduing wayward impulse to a dominant purpose.

Here *Conrad* is used instead of *he* because there are other antecedents in the immediately preceding discourse – *man* (to which the previous *he* refers) and *Rousseau*.

Table 9-10 Personal reference items

		Head		Premodifier
		Thing: pronoun	Deictic: determiner	
		determinative	possessive	
singular	masculine	he/him	his	his
	feminine	she/her	hers	hers
	neuter	it	[its]	its
plural		they/them	theirs	their

9.4.3 Demonstrative reference

Personal reference items create co-reference in terms of the category of person. As we noted above, there is another related, but distinct, co-referential strategy – that of demonstrative reference. Here the reference item is a **demonstrative**, *this/that*, *these/those* (cf. the brief account given in Chapter 6). Demonstratives (see Table 9-11) may also be either exophoric

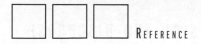

or anaphoric; in origin they were probably the same as third-person forms, but they retain a stronger deictic flavour than the personals, and have evolved certain distinct anaphoric functions of their own.

Table 9-11 Demonstrative reference items

		Nominal group		Adverbial group
		Head/Thing	Premodifier/Deictic	Head
		pronoun	determiner	adverb
specific	near	this/ these	this/ these	here (now)
	remote	that/ those	that/ those	there (then)
non-specific		it	the	

For example:
(i) exophoric

||| Here, I'll help with **this one**. ||| [Text 76]

||| Yes, Dad, but we mustn't even lean on **this** guitar today. ||| [Text 75]

||| We could move **that** table. ||| [Text 75]

||| It wouldn't matter to him really; || he's half deaf after all these years working at **this** place. ||| [Text 10]

||| I've been eating like **this** for the last ten years || and nothing happens. ||| [Text 10]

||| What is **that**? ||| Hmm, Hungarian pastry. ||| [Text 10]

(ii) endophoric: anaphoric

||| Though Amnesty has long criticised the widespread US use of the death penalty, || it found || there has now been another worrying development in **this** process.||| [Text 2]

||| The way that Icelandic expresses the phrase "I dreamed something last night" is "It dreamed me". ||| Though **that**'s also modern Icelandic, || **this** is a medieval idea. ||| [Text 17]

||| During the European scramble for Africa, Nigeria fell to the British. ||| It wasn't one nation at **that** point; || it was a large number of independent political entities. ||| The British brought **this** rather complex association into being as one nation || and ruled it until 1960 || when Nigeria achieved independence. ||| [Text 16]

||| They have to be given instruction of course || and learn to read the signals; || then they'll take a driving test || and there are track circuits as on all electrified lines || so that once a train gets into a section || no other train can move on to **that** section || and run into it || but **that**'s just standard equipment. ||| [Text 19]

(iii) endophoric: cataphoric

||| Rather, I think || we will be stronger and more effective || if we stick to **those** issues of governmental structure and process, broadly defined, that have formed the core of our agenda for years. ||| [Text 6]

The basic sense of 'this' and 'that' is one of proximity; *this* refers to something as being 'near', *that* refers to something as being 'not near'. The 'that' term tends to be more inclusive, though the two are more evenly balanced in English than their equivalents in some other languages. Proximity is typically from the point of view of the speaker, so this means 'near me'. In some languages, as pointed out earlier, there is a close correspondence of demonstratives and personals, such that there are three demonstratives rather than two, and the direction of reference is near me (*this*), near you (*that*) and not near either of us (*yon*). This pattern was once widespread in English and can still be found in some rural varieties of Northern English and Scots. In modern standard English *yon* no longer exists, although we still sometimes find the word *yonder* from the related series *here*, *there* and *yonder*; but another development has taken place in the meantime.

Given just two demonstratives, *this* and *that*, it is usual for *that* to be more inclusive; it tends to become the unmarked member of the pair. This happened in English; and in the process a new demonstrative evolved which took over and extended the 'unmarked' feature of *that* – leaving *this* and *that* once more fairly evenly matched. This is the so-called 'definite article' *the*. The word *the* is still really a demonstrative, although a demonstrative of a rather particular kind.

Consider the following examples:

(a) The sun was shining on the sea.

(b) This is the house that Jack built.

(c) Algy met a bear. The bear was bulgy. The bulge was Algy.

In (a) we know which 'sun' and which 'sea' are being referred to even if we are not standing on the beach with the sun above our heads; there is only one sun, and for practical purposes only one sea. There may be other seas in different parts of the globe, and even other suns in the heavens; but they are irrelevant. In (b) we know which 'house' is being referred to, because we are told – it is the one built by Jack; and notice that the information comes after the occurrence of the *the*. In (c) we know which bear – the one that Algy met; and we know which bulge – the one displayed by the bear; but in this case the information had already been given before the *the* occurred. Only in (c), therefore, is *the* anaphoric.

Like the personals, and the other demonstratives, *the* has a specifying function; it signals 'you know which one(s) I mean'. But there is an important difference. The other items not only signal that the identity is known, or knowable; they state explicitly how the identity is to be established. So

my house = 'you know which: the one belonging to me'

this house = 'you know which: the one near me'

but

the house = 'you know which – the information is there somewhere if you look for it'

In other words, *the* merely announces that the identity is specific; it does not specify it. The information is available elsewhere. It may be in the preceding text (anaphoric), like (c) above; in the following text (**cataphoric**), like (b); or in the air, so to speak, like (a).

630

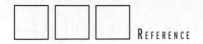

Type (a) are self-specifying; there is only one – or at least only one that makes sense in the context, as in *Have you fed the cat?* (**homophoric**).

Thus *the* is an unmarked demonstrative, while *this* and *that* are both 'marked' terms – neither includes the other. Their basic deictic senses are 'near' and 'remote' from the point of view of the speaker. But they are also used to refer within the text. The 'near' term *this* typically refers either anaphorically, to something that has been mentioned immediately before, or by the speaker, or is in some way or other being treated as 'near', as in (a) below; or else cataphorically, to something that is to come, as in (b):

(a.1) ||| "You may look in front of you, and on both sides, || if you like," || said the Sheep; || "but you can't look all round you || – unless you've got eyes at the back of your head."

But **these**, <<as it happens,>> Alice had not got. |||

(a.2) ||| The animals roared and mooed and trumpeted and crowed and chirped and chattered and squeaked. ||| **These** were the first joyful sounds || since the rain had started. ||| [Text 14]

(b.1) ||| "The great art of riding, <<as I was saying>>, is – [[to keep your balance]]. ||| Like **this**, you know –" ||| He let go the bridle, || and stretched out both his arms || to show Alice [[what he meant]].

(b.2) ||| She said, || "You're not going to believe **this**, || but I was in Nepal with my daughter || and we took a trek to Manang. ||| One night in camp this rude sherpa, << who was a friend of our sherpa, >> came over to me || and said in very, very bad English, || "You America?" ||| ..." [Text 7]

(Example (b.1) is **exophoric** in the immediate context, but cataphoric in the text.) The singular *this* is also used to refer in the same way to extended passages of text, as in (c):

(c.1) ||| "Come back!" || the Caterpillar called after her. ||| "I've something important to say!" ||| **This** sounded promising, certainly: || Alice turned || and came back again. |||

(c.2) ||| Then she went over to Zen – || **this** was in the late '60s – || and she and I weren't getting along very well. ||| [Text 7]

(c.3) ||| You have to be able to feed your family, || and if you don't, || it's a matter of shame. || so Okonkwo's whole life is an attempt to make up for what his father didn't achieve. ||| **This** is a great mistake. ||| [Text 16]

(c.4) ||| But all around him, Noah's neighbors were lying || and fighting || and cheating || and stealing. ||| **This** made God sad. ||| [Text 14]

(c.5) ||| In the worst scenario, if most of a teacher's lessons are 'poor', || he or she will be asked || to sign a sheet explaining any extenuating circumstances. ||| **This** they should refuse || until there is union advice. ||| [Text 97]

The 'remote' term *that* refers anaphorically to something that has been mentioned by the previous speaker, now the listener, as in (d), or is being treated as more remote or from the listener's point of view, as in (e):

(d) ||| "But he's coming very slowly || – and what curious attitudes he goes into!" ||| . . .

"Not at all," || said the King. ||| "He's an Anglo-Saxon Messenger || – and **those** are Anglo-Saxon attitudes." |||

(e.1) ||| "I'll put you through into Looking-glass House. ||| How would you like **that**?" |||

631

(e.2) ⫾⫾⫾ So we picked Iowa ⫾⫾ because **that** was closer to Wyoming, ⫾⫾ where he was from. ⫾⫾⫾ [Text 17]

(e.3) ⫾⫾⫾ I had done well in creative writing classes before that, ⫾⫾ so I signed up for the senior creative writing class ⫾⫾ and I started writing a novel. ⫾⫾⫾ It took me about **that** school year [[to write it]]. ⫾⫾⫾ [Text 17]

Again, the singular *that* often refers back to an extended passage of text, as in (f):

(f.1) ⫾⫾⫾ You cannot do without cream, mate. ⫾⫾⫾ – ⫾⫾⫾ I agree with **that**. ⫾⫾⫾ [Text 10]

(f.2) ⫾⫾⫾ Fortunately, I worked one summer as an intern in a law firm ⫾⫾ and realized ⫾⫾ that I didn't want to do **that**. [Text 21]

(f.3) ⫾⫾⫾ "If **that**'s all [[you know about it]], ⫾⫾ you may stand down," continued the King. ⫾⫾⫾

In (f.3) *that* refers to the whole of the preceding interrogation taking up two pages of the story. Note that the reference item *it* is similarly used for text reference, as in (g)

(g) ⫾⫾⫾ "So here's a question for you. ⫾⫾⫾ How old did you say you were?" ⫾⫾⫾

Alice made a short calculation, ⫾⫾ and said ⫾⫾ "Seven years and six months." ⫾⫾⫾

"Wrong!" ⫾⫾ Humpty Dumpty exclaimed triumphantly. ⫾⫾⫾ "You never said a word like **it**." ⫾⫾⫾

The locative demonstratives *here* and *there* are also used as reference items; *here* may be cataphoric, as in (g) above, or anaphoric and 'near' as in (h); *there* is anaphoric but not 'near', as in (j), where it means 'in what you said':

(h) ⫾⫾⫾ "I think you ought to tell me ⫾⫾ who you are, first." ⫾⫾⫾

"Why?" ⫾⫾ said the Caterpillar. ⫾⫾⫾

Here was another puzzling question; ... ⫾⫾⫾

(j) "Suppose he never commits the crime?" ⫾⫾ said Alice. ⫾⫾⫾

"That would be all the better, wouldn't it?" ⫾⫾ the Queen said, ... ⫾⫾⫾

Alice felt there was no denying that. ⫾⫾⫾ "Of course it would be all the better," ⫾⫾ she said: ⫾⫾ "but it wouldn't be all the better [[his being punished]]." ⫾⫾⫾

"You're wrong **there**, at any rate," ⫾⫾ said the Queen. ⫾⫾⫾

The temporal demonstratives *now* and *then* also function as cohesive items, but conjunctively rather than referentially (see Section 9.3 above).

9.4.4 Comparative reference

Whereas personals and demonstratives, when used anaphorically, set up a relation of co-reference, whereby the same entity is referred to over again, comparatives set up a relation of contrast. In comparative reference, the reference item still signals 'you know which'; not because the same entity is being referred to over again but rather because there is a frame of reference – something by reference to which what I am now talking about is the same or different, like or unlike, equal or unequal, more or less. Comparative reference items function in nominal and adverbial groups; and the comparison is made with reference

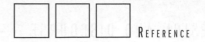

either to general features of identity, similarity and difference or to particular features of quality and quantity: see Table 9-12.

Table 9-12 Comparative reference items

		Nominal group			Adverbial group[7]
		post-Deictic	Numerative	Epithet	Head
		adjective	adverb	adjective; adverb	adverb
general	identity	*same, equal, identical*, etc.			*identically, (just) as*, etc.
	similarity	*similar, additional*, etc.		comparative adjective: *such*	*so, likewise, similarly*, etc.
	difference	*other, different*, etc.			*otherwise, else, differently*, etc.
particular			SubModifier: *more, fewer, less, further* &c.; *so, as*, etc. + Subhead: numeral	comparative adjective: *bigger*, etc. OR SubModifier: *more, less, so, as*, etc. + Subhead: adjective	comparative adverb: *better*, etc. OR SubModifier: *more, less, so, as*, etc. + Subhead: adverb

Any expression such as *the same, another, similar, different, as big, bigger, less big*, and related adverbs such as *likewise, differently, equally*, presumes some standard of reference in the preceding text. For example, *such, other, more* in (a), (b) and (c):

(a) ||| Two men were killed by lethal injection in Texas this year, || even though they were 17 || when they committed their offences, || and another 65 juveniles are on death row across the country. ||| "**Such** executions are rare world-wide," || the report says. ||| [Text 2]

(b) ||| Zoo visitors were shaken by the episode. ||| "I am not bringing them back. || These are my grandkids. || It is not safe," || said Sandra Edwards, || who was visiting the zoo with her grandchildren || when she heard the shots || and saw youths fighting. ||| Nakisha Johnson, 17, said || she saw one young man open fire || after a feud between youths became violent. ||| She said || the children who were wounded were caught in the middle of the two groups of youths. ||| "He was just shooting at the people he was fighting" || but struck the children bystanders, || Johnson said. ||| **Other** witnesses said || the shooting occurred || when a bottle was thrown from one group of youths to another. ||| [Text 20_16]

(c) ||| Survey results, combined with feedback [[gathered by leaders from all the Services during field and fleet visits]], have convinced us || that long-term retention is not well served by the Redux retirement plan. ||| Our men and women deserve a retirement system [[that **more** appropriately rewards their service]]. ||| [Text 115]

---

7 Also as SubModifier in adverbial group or nominal group.

Like personals and demonstratives, comparative reference items can also be used cataphorically, within the nominal group; for example *much more smoothly than a live horse*, where the reference point for the *more* lies in what follows.

As has already been made clear, there is no structural relationship between the reference item and its referent. In order to mark the cohesive relationship in the text, we can devise some form of notation such as that shown in Table 9-13.

Table 9-13 Text analysed for reference[8]

	Personal	Demonstrative	Comparative
Alice looked on with great interest as **the** King took		exo/homo	
an enormous memorandum book out of **his** pocket,	ana		
and began writing.			
A sudden thought struck **her**	ana		
and **she** took hold of	ana		
the end of **the** pencil,		cata; ana	
which came some way over **his** shoulder,	ana		
and began writing for **him**.	ana		
The poor King looked puzzled and unhappy,		ana + exo/homo	
and struggled with **the** pencil for some time		ana	
without saying anything,			
but Alice was too strong for **him**,	ana		
and at last **he** panted out	ana		
"My dear! I really *must* get a **thinner** pencil.			ana
I can't manage **this** one a bit;		ana	
it writes all manner of things that I don't intend —"	ana		
"What manner of things?"			
said **the** Queen,		exo/homo	
looking over **the** book		ana	
(in which Alice had put			
"**The** White Knight is sliding down **the** poker.		exo/homo + ana; exo/homo	
He balances very badly.")	ana		
"**That**'s not a memorandum of *your* feelings!"		ana	

[8] ana = anaphoric (cohesive); cata = cataphoric; exo/homo = exophoric/homophoric

9.5 ELLIPSIS and SUBSTITUTION

9.5.1 Nature of ELLIPSIS and SUBSTITUTION

Reference is a relationship in meaning (cf. Table 9-5). When a reference item is used anaphorically, it sets up a semantic relationship with something mentioned in the preceding text; and this enables the reference item to be interpreted, as either identical with the referent or in some way contrasting with it.

Another form of anaphoric cohesion in the text is achieved by ELLIPSIS, where we presuppose something by means of what is left out. Like all cohesive agencies, ellipsis contributes to the semantic structure of the discourse. But unlike reference, which is itself a semantic relation, ellipsis sets up a relationship that is not semantic but lexicogrammatical – a relationship in the wording rather than directly in the meaning. For example, in

> Attacks on our information systems, use of weapons of mass destruction, domestic and international terrorism, and even man-made environmental disasters are all examples of asymmetric threats [[that could be employed against us]]. Indeed, **some** [Ø: asymmetric threats] already have. [Text 115]

the listener has to supply the words *asymmetric threats*. Ellipsis marks the textual status of **continuous information** within a certain grammatical structure. At the same time, the non-ellipsed elements of that structure are given the status of being **contrastive** in the environment of continuous information. Ellipsis thus assigns differential prominence to the elements of a structure: if they are non-prominent (continuous), they are ellipsed; if they are prominent (contrastive), they are present. The absence of elements through ellipsis is an iconic realization of lack of prominence.

Sometimes an explicit indication may be given that something is omitted, by the use of a substitute form; for instance *one* in the following examples:

> ||| He ran out on his wife and children, || became a merchant seaman, || was washed off a deck of a cargo ship || and miraculously picked up, not his own <u>ship</u> but another **one**, way out in the middle of nowhere. ||| [Text 7]

> ||| ... so my decision was [[that I should do three separate <u>books</u>, one on each generation]]. ||| – ||| What happened to the middle **one**? ||| [Text 16]

> ||| ... if I am totally incapable of doing anything || or go into a <u>stroke</u> again || (the last **one** I had was on my right) || if I got a really whopping **one** || and could neither see || nor speak || –I would ask to be taken away. ||| [Text 34]

The substitute is phonologically non-salient and serves as a place-holding device, showing where something has been omitted and what its grammatical function would be; thus *one* functions as Head in the nominal group and replaces the Thing (with which the Head is typically conflated). Ellipsis and substitution are variants of the same type of cohesive relation. There are some grammatical environments in which only ellipsis is possible, some in which only substitution is possible, and some, such as *I preferred the other* [*one*], which allow for either.

9.5.2 Grammatical domains of ELLIPSIS and SUBSTITUTION

There are three main contexts for ELLIPSIS and SUBSTITUTION in English. These are (1) the clause, (2) the verbal group and (3) the nominal group: see Table 9-14. We shall consider each of these in turn.

635

Table 9-14 Types of ELLIPSIS and SUBSTITUTION

Rank	Type	Extent		Substitution	Ellipsis
clause	yes/no	whole clause	polarity (only)	so, not Is he at home? – I think ‖ so. / Perhaps not.	yes, no + [∅] Is he at home? – Yes [∅: he is at home],
		part of clause	Mood		Mood + [∅: Residue] Is he at home? – Yes, he is [∅: at home].
			Mood + polarity	so, nor/ neither ∧ Mood He is at home. – So is she. Mood + do, do so Has he arrived? – He might do.	
	wh	whole clause	Wh (only)		He is at home. – Who? Who is at home? – John.
		part of clause	Wh + Mood		Will you help us? – I could tomorrow.
			Wh + polarity		We mustn't lean on it. – Why not? Who will help us? – Not me.
group	verbal			do	
	nominal			one	

9.5.2.1 ELLIPSIS and SUBSTITUTION in the clause

Ellipsis in the clause is related to mood, and has been illustrated already in Chapter 4. Specifically, it is related to the question-answer process in dialogue; and this determines that there are two kinds: (a) yes/no ellipsis, and (b) WH- ellipsis. Each of these also allows for substitution, though not in all contexts. We will consider the yes/no type first.

(a) yes/no ellipsis: (i) the whole clause. In a yes/no question-answer sequence the answer may involve ellipsis of the whole clause, e.g.

‖‖ You mean ‖ you were interested in him as a man in private life. ‖ – ‖‖ **Yes, yes**. [∅: I was interested in him as a man in private life.] ‖‖ [Text125]

‖‖ Have you been interviewed by Bedford yet? ‖ – ‖‖ **No**. [∅: I haven't been interviewed by Bedford yet.] ‖‖ [Text 125]

‖‖ ... and the value deal is three large pizzas delivered from $22.95. ‖‖ Would you like to try that? – ‖‖ Ah **no thanks**. [∅: I would not like to try that.] ‖‖ [PH]

The first clause in such a pair is not necessarily a question; it may have any speech function, e.g.

||| I think || it is it must be very tough indeed. ||| – ||| **Yes**. [∅: It is very tough.] ||| [Text125]

||| You feel || it must be English. ||| – ||| **Yes** [∅: I feel it must be English]; || because I am English, || I feel || that I must study English literature || – that's why. ||| [Text125]

||| I mean || that should mean [[that an autobiography is your ideal]]. ||| – ||| **Yes** [∅: an autobiography is my ideal]; || but it also is a very good novel || I think. ||| [Text125]

Here *yes* and *no* serve as mood Adjuncts of polarity (cf. Chapter 4, Section 4.5) and the rest of the clause is elided. Corresponding in meaning to *yes* and *no* are the clause substitutes *so* and *not*. (Etymologically the word *yes* contains the substitute *so*; it is a fusion of (earlier forms of) *aye* and *so*.) In certain contexts these substitute forms are used: (i) following *if* – *if so, if not*; (ii) as a reported clause – *he said so, he said not*; (iii) in the context of modality – *perhaps so, perhaps not*. Examples (and cf. Chapter 7, Section 7.5.3 above):

||| Better than The Rainbow? ||| – ||| I think || **so** [∅: that it is better than The Rainbow], yes, || because I think || it shows Lawrence as a man more Lawrence in his life. ||| [Text125]

||| Well, do I have to do more in the afternoon? ||| – ||| No, [∅: you] probably [∅: do] **not** [∅: have to do more in the afternoon]. ||| Just do half an hour now. ||| [Text 75]

The general principle is that a substitute is required if the clause is projected, as a report (cf. Chapter 7, Section 7.5.5 (i)); with modality (*perhaps*) and hypothesis (*if*) being interpreted as kinds of projection, along the lines of:

he said so–I thought so–I think so–it may be so–perhaps so–let us say so–if so

In addition, the substitute *not* is used when the answer is qualified by a negative in some way:

||| Is that [[what it really is about]], a cock and a fox? ||| – ||| No, not really. ||| [Text 125]

where a positive clause is simply presupposed by ellipsis:

||| Did you feel || that you were taking a risk || in being so open about [[what you were doing]]? ||| – ||| Oh, sure, in some ways. ||| [Text 17]

(a) yes/no ellipsis: (ii) part of the clause. As an alternative to the ellipsis of the whole clause, there may be ellipsis of just one part of it, the Residue. For example:

||| Mum, you're not enjoying your dinner, are you? ||| – ||| I am [∅: enjoying my dinner]. ||| [Text 82]

||| I've had a headache. ||| – ||| Have you [∅: had a headache]? ||| [Text 34]

||| Could you put your issue of Rapale literacy in the numeracy study. ||| – ||| Oh I suppose || I could [0: put my issue of Rapale literacy in the numeracy study]. ||| [UTS/ Macquarie Corpus]

With a declarative response, if there is a change of Subject only, we may have substitute *so, nor, neither* in initial position (= 'and so', 'and not') followed by the Mood element (cf. Chapter 4, Section 4.2).

... but I heard some water in it. – I did too. – **So** did I. [Text 78]

I love them. – **So** did I. – Me, too. [Text 79]

||| This drags down the bibliophiles' score; || and **so** does the disgraced Nixon, || ranked at 23 in Siena. ||| [Text 110]

I didn't want to see it all. – No, **neither** did I. [UTS/Macquarie Corpus]

The order is Finite ^ Subject (to get the Subject under unmarked focus). If the Subject is unchanged, so that the focus is on the Finite, the order is Subject ^ Finite:

S04: At their age you were an orphan. You didn't have to. – S05: Not quite. – S04: You were. – S05: Oh yes. **So I was**. [UTS/Macquarie Corpus]

The negative has various forms:

They've never replied. – So they haven't/Nor they have/Neither they have [∅: replied].

Not infrequently, the Residue is substituted by the verbal substitute *do*, as in:

They say an apple a day keeps the doctor away. – It should do [∅: keep the doctor away], if you aim it straight.

If the focus is on the Residue (and hence falls on *do*), the substitute form *do so* may be used (as an alternative to ellipsis):

||| Tempting as it may be, || we shouldn't embrace every popular issue [[that comes along]]. ||| When **we** <u>do</u> <u>so</u> || we use precious limited resources || where other players with superior resources are already doing an adequate job. ||| [Text 6]

(b) WH- ellipsis: (i) the whole clause. In a WH- sequence the entire clause is usually omitted except for the WH- element itself, or the item that is the response to the WH- element:

I desperately, desperately need them. – What? – **The scissors**. [Text 76]

What have you read? – [∅: I have read] **Lord of the Flies**. [Text 135]

Well I prefer Lord of the Flies. – **Why** [∅: do you prefer Lord of the Flies]? – Because I don't think I understood Pincher Martin. [Text 135]

The substitute *not* may appear in a WH- negative:

The kind of approach to reality and to ideas which the book offers us, is it a realistic book? – No, I don't think so. – **Why** [∅: do you] **not** [∅: think so]? [Text 135]

Substitution is less likely in the positive, except in the expressions *how so?, why so?*.

(b) WH- ellipsis: (ii) part of the clause. Sometimes in a WH- clause, or its response, the Mood element is left in and only the Residue is ellipsed. For example, with WH- Subject:

Has the time come for these local divinities [[to give way to perhaps a bigger concept of deity, a bigger concept of religion]]? – **Who** knows [∅: whether the time has come ...]? [Text 16]

And Hugo told you that, too. – **Who** did [∅: tell me that too]? [Text 79]

Similarly if the WH- element is part of the Residue:

||| I think || that's why my generation is so tediously over-serious. ||| **How** could we not be [∅: so tediously over-serious]? ||| [Text 17]

Yes, I think you'd better look at it. – I don't see any particular reason **why** I should [∅: look at it]. [Text 8]

The Mood element may be represented by negative polarity alone:

Yes, Dad, but we mustn't even lean on this guitar today. – **Why** [∅: must we] not [∅: lean on this guitar today]? [Text 75]

Thus clausal ellipsis/substitution occurs typically in a dialogue sequence where in a response turn everything is omitted except the information-bearing element. Examples of such responses were given in Table 9-14. A clause consisting of Mood only, such as *I will*, could equally occur in either the yes/no or the WH- environment; typically, in a yes/no environment, the focus would be on *will*, which bears the polarity ('Will you ... ?' – *I **will**.*), whereas in a WH- environment, the focus would be on *I*, which carries the information ('Who will ... ?' – *I will.*).

The elliptical or substitute clause requires the listener to 'supply the missing words'; and since they are to be supplied from what has gone before, the effect is cohesive. It is always possible to 'reconstitute' the ellipsed item so that it becomes fully explicit. Since ellipsis is a lexicogrammatical resource, what is taken over is the exact wording, subject only to the reversal of speaker-listener deixis (*I* for *you* and so on), and change of mood where appropriate.

9.5.2.2 Ellipsis and substitution in the verbal group

Since the verbal group consists of Finite plus Predicator, it follows automatically that any clausal ellipsis in which the Mood element is present but the Residue omitted will involve ellipsis within the verbal group: the Predicator will be ellipsed together with the rest of the Residue, as in *Have a shower! – I **can't** [∅: **have a shower**]*. There is no need to repeat the discussion of this phenomenon. The ellipsis may affect only part of the Predicator, as when the Predicator is realized by a verbal group complex (see Chapter 8) and only the first part of the complex is retained together with the infinitive marker *to*:

Have you do you read very much Kafka? I am **trying to** [∅: read very much Kafka], yes, ... [Text 125]

"Can you hop on your hind legs?" asked the furry rabbit. – "I don't **want to** [∅: hop on my hind legs]," said the little Rabbit. [Text 28]

Here the rest of the verbal group serving as Predicator is ellipsed together with the remainder of the Residue.

639

Substitution in the verbal group is by means of the verb *do*, which can substitute for any verb provided it is active not passive, except *be* or, in some contexts, *have*. The verb *do* will appear in the appropriate non-finite form (*do, doing, done*). Examples:

> Does it hurt? –Not any more. It was doing last night.

> Yeah but I'm doing night shift too. If I have to teach people on night shift as I have **done**, I do night shift and then I do day shift and get a couple of hours off and then do night shift and day shift. [UTS/Macquarie Corpus]

As we have seen, this *do* typically substitutes for the whole of the Residue (or, what amounts to the same thing, when the verb is substituted by *do*, the rest of the Residue is ellipsed).

Since there are no demonstrative verbs – we cannot say *he thatted, he whatted?* – this need is met by combining the verb substitute *do* with demonstratives *that, what* (serving as Range in the transitivity structure). For example:

> I did cross-eye in the middle of my art. – I can't **do that**. – I can. [Text 79]

> **What** did your father **do**? – He was an architect. [Text 7]

> **What** are you going to **do** with Blubba? – Oh, I don't know. [Text 10]

> This is one thing I haven't worked out with this phone whether, cause my old phone used to ring you to let you know you had a message. – Yeah. Does this one not **do it**? [UTS/ Macquarie Corpus]

The form *do not* functions as a single reference item. (For the difference between reference and ellipsis-substitution, see the note at the end of the present section.)

9.5.2.3 ELLIPSIS and SUBSTITUTION in the nominal group

Ellipsis within the nominal group was referred to in Chapter 6, where it was shown that an element other than the Thing could function as Head; for example *any* in

> I'll ask Jenny about <u>laptops</u> and find out whether we have got **any** [Ø: laptops]. [UTS/ Macquarie Corpus]

There is a nominal substitute *one*, plural *ones*, which functions as Head; it can substitute for any count noun (that is, any noun that is selecting for number, singular or plural); for example,

> A: But I've got a <u>depression quilt</u> at home. – B: You've got that **one** that Marcia gave you. – A: That Marcia gave me from the American. – B: The Amish **one**, isn't it? [UTS/ Macquarie Corpus]

> She's got she's got Big Pond which she said which is apparently not a terribly good <u>provider</u>. – No. – Mmm. No. I thought Yahoo was one of the better **ones** [providers]. [UTS/ Macquarie Corpus]

> I have always had <u>hot water bottles</u>. I think they're, the last couple disintegrated. I had a nice bright yellow koala shaped **one**. [UTS/ Macquarie Corpus]

> There's <u>reefs</u> around bloody Australia, isn't there? – Yeah; a Great Barrier **one**, I believe. – It's a big **one**, I think. [UTS/ Macquarie Corpus]

With mass nouns, ellipsis is used instead of substitution:

Do you want some more <u>wine</u>? **White or red** [∅: wine]? – **White** [∅:wine]. [UTS/ Macquarie Corpus]

Like *do* in the verbal group, the nominal substitute *one* is derived by extension from an item in the structure of the full, non-elliptical group – in this case the indefinite numeral *one*, via its function as Head in a group which is elliptical as in

Anyone for teas or coffees? – Yeah, I'll have **one**; I'll have a coffee. [UTS/ Macquarie Corpus]

The following passage illustrates the use of both numeral *one* with ellipsis and substitute *one*:

A: Do those fireplaces at your house work? Do you use them? – B: Yes. Yes. – C: Oh yeah. – B: Have you not had **one** [∅: fireplace] ? – A: No I don't think so. There's – what? **one** [∅: fireplace] in the lounge room. – B: **One** [∅: fireplace] in the sitting room and the other <u>one</u> [fireplace] does work. We have had them both working together. – C: You don't use the other <u>one</u> [fireplace] very much. [UTS/ Macquarie Corpus]

The parallel development of the two substitutes, verbal *do* and nominal *one*, is as shown in Table 9-15:

Table 9-15 Parallel development of substitutes *do* and *one*

	Auxiliary as Finite	**Auxiliary as Finite with ellipsis**	**Verb as substitute Event**
verbal *do*	he **does** know	perhaps he **does**	he may **do**
	he **does**n't know	surely he **doesn't**	he never has **done**
	does he know		
nominal *one*	**one** green bottle	there was **one**	a green **one**
	a green bottle	there wasn't **one**	then green **ones**
	determiner as Deictic	**determiner as Deictic with ellipsis**	**noun as substitute Thing**

In some instances the nominal substitute fuses with a Modifier, as in *yours*, *none* in the following:

I haven't finished the crocodile story completely. And then we'll hear **yours** [your story], okay? [UTS/ Macquarie Corpus]

But he won't get any benefit for his early plea of guilty or contrition. – No absolutely **none** [no benefit]. [UTS/ Macquarie Corpus]

These can be analysed as elliptical, the elements *my*, *your*, *no*, etc. having a special form when functioning as Head.

9.5.3 Ellipsis and reference

We remarked earlier that ellipsis is a relationship at the lexicogrammatical level: the meaning is 'go back and retrieve the missing words'. Hence the missing words must be grammatically appropriate; and they can be inserted in place. This is not the case with reference, where, since the relationship is a semantic one, there is no grammatical constraint (the class of the reference item need not match that of what it presumes), and one cannot normally insert the presumed element. Reference, for the same reason, can reach back a long way in the text and extend over a long passage, whereas ellipsis is largely limited to the immediately preceding clause.

But the most important distinction, which again follows from the different nature of the two types of relationship, is that in ellipsis the typical meaning is not one of co-reference. There is always some significant difference between the second instance and the first (between presuming item and presumed). If we want to refer to the same thing, we use reference; if we want to refer to a different thing, we use ellipsis: *Where's your hat?—I can't find it.—Take this (one)*. Each can take on the other meaning, but only by making it explicit: *another hat* (reference, but different), *the same one* (substitution, but not different). Thus reference signals 'the same member' (unless marked as different by the use of comparison); ellipsis signals 'another member of the same class' (unless marked as identical by *same*, etc.). The difference is most clear-cut in the nominal group, since nouns, especially count nouns, tend to have clearly defined referents; it is much less clear-cut in the verbal group or the clause.

Within the nominal group, 'another member' means a new modification of the Thing; Deictic (*this one, another one, mine*), Numerative (*three, the first (one)*), or Epithet (*the biggest (one), a big one*). In the verbal group, it means a new specification of polarity, tense or modality through the Finite element (*did, might (do), hasn't (done)*); and there is a slight tendency for ellipsis to be associated with change of polarity and substitution with change of modality. This tendency is more clearly marked with the clause, where ellipsis adds certainty (yes or no, or a missing identity), whereas substitution adds uncertainty (if, maybe, or someone said so); this is why, in a clause where everything is ellipsed except the modality, it is quite usual to use a substitute (*possibly so, perhaps so*) unless the modality is one of certainty – here we say *certainly* (elliptical), rather than *certainly so*:

> Have you got a nicorette on you? – **Certainly**. [UTS/ Macquarie Corpus]

Table 9-16 presents a short text marked for ellipsis and substitution. For the sake of the exposition, the ellipsed items have been shown at the side, although this is not a necessary part of the analysis.

9.6 LEXICAL COHESION

The types of cohesion we have discussed so far all involve grammatical resources – grammatical items (conjunctions, reference items, substitute items) and grammatical structure (absence or substitution of elements of structure). However, cohesion also operates within the lexical zone of lexicogrammar (cf. Table 9-5). Here a speaker or writer creates cohesion in discourse through the choice of lexical items. This was illustrated above in Table 9-4: we discussed the lexical cohesive patterns involving (i) food: fish plus evaluation, and (ii) cooking utensil: pan plus action. In this way, lexical cohesion comes about through the selection of items that are related in some way to those that have gone before.

Table 9-16 Text analysed for ELLIPSIS (E) and SUBSTITUTION (S)

	Clausal	Verbal	Nominal
"Being so many different sizes in a day is very confusing."			
"It isn't [∅]."	E [very confusing]		
"Well, perhaps you haven't found it **so** yet;	S [to be very confusing]		
but when you have to turn into a chrysalis –			
you will **do** some day, you know –		S [turn into a chrysalis]	
and then after that [∅] into a butterfly,	E [you have to turn]		
I should think you'll feel it a little queer, won't you?"			
"Not a bit [∅]."	E [I shall (not) feel it (a bit) queer]		
"Well, it would feel very queer to *me*."			
"You! Who are *you*?"			
"I hardly know [∅], sir, just at present."	E [who I am]		
"So you think you're changed, do you?"			
"I'm afraid I am [∅], sir."		E [changed]	

Just as ellipsis and substitution take advantage of the patterns inherent in grammatical structure (ellipting and substituting particular elements of structure such as the Head of a nominal group), so lexical cohesion takes advantage of the patterns inherent in the organization of lexis. Lexis is organized into a network of lexical relations such as the 'kind of' relations obtaining between *fish* and *salmon*. In the text analysed in Table 9-4, there is a cohesive link between *fish* and *salmon* precisely because they are related in the lexical system of English.

The primary types of lexical relations are listed in Table 9-17. They derive from either the paradigmatic or the syntagmatic organization of lexis (cf. Chapter 2, Section 2.1). (i) The paradigmatic relations are inherent in the organization of lexis as a resource, as represented in *Roget's Thesaurus*. They can be interpreted in terms of elaboration and extension, two of the subtypes of expansion that are already familiar from the logico-semantic relations used in forming clause complexes (Chapter 7, Section 7.2) and the corresponding conjunctive relations presented earlier in this chapter (Section 9.3). (ii) The syntagmatic relations hold between lexical items in a syntagm that tend to occur together, or **collocate** with one

Table 9-17 Kinds of lexical relations playing a role in lexical cohesion

Nature of relation	Type of expansion		Type of lexical relation	Examples
paradigmatic [lexical set]	elaborating	identity	repetition	bear – bear
			synonymy	sound – noise
				sound – silence [antonymy]
		attribution	hyponymy	tree – oak, pine, elm ...
				oak – pine – elm ... [co-hyponyms]
	extending		meronymy	tree – trunk, branch, leaf ...
				trunk – branch – leaf ... [co-meronyms]
syntagmatic [collocation]	(enhancing)		collocation[9]	fire – smoke ('comes from')

another (Section 9.6.3). Collocates of a lexical item can be found in the entries of certain modern dictionaries based on corpus investigations. Since syntagmatic organization and paradigmatic organization represent two different dimensions of patterning, any pair of lexical items can involve both.

9.6.1 Elaborating relations: repetition, synonymy and hyponymy

9.6.1.1 Repetition

The most direct form of lexical cohesion is the repetition of a lexical item; e.g. *bear* in

Algy met a bear. The **bear** was bulgy

Here the second occurrence of *bear* harks back to the first.

In this instance, there is also the reference item *the*, signalling that the listener knows which bear is intended; and since there is nothing else to satisfy the *the*, we conclude that it is the same bear. But this referential link is not necessary to lexical cohesion; if we had *Algy met a bear. Bears are bulgy*, where *bears* means 'all bears', there would still be lexical cohesion of *bears* with *bear*. In this case, however, there would be only one tie; whereas in the example cited first there are two, one referential (*the*) and one lexical (*bear*).

As the last example shows, in order for a lexical item to be recognized as repeated it need not be in the same morphological shape. For example, *dine, dining, diner, dinner* are all the same item, and an occurrence of any one constitutes a repetition of any of the others. Inflexional variants always belong together as one item; derivational variants usually do, when they are based on a living derivational process, although these are less predictable. (For example, *rational* and *rationalize* are probably still the same lexical item, though the

---

9   Collocation includes, but is not confined to, relationships that can be interpreted as enhancing.

relationship between them has become rather tenuous; but neither now goes with *ration* – *rational* is closer to *reason*, though not close enough to be considered the same item.)

In Landor's line

> I strove with none, for none was worth my strife

there is a strongly felt cohesion between *strife* and *strove*, suggesting that *strive*, *strove* and *strife* are one and the same lexical item.

9.6.1.2 Synonymy

In the second place, lexical cohesion results from the choice of a lexical item that is in some sense synonymous with a preceding one; for example *sound* with *noise*, *cavalry* with *horses* in

> He was just wondering which road to take when he was startled by a noise from behind him. It was the noise of trotting horses. ... He dismounted and led his horse as quickly as he could along the right-hand road. The sound of the cavalry grew rapidly nearer ...

Here again the cohesion need not depend on identity of reference. But once we depart from straightforward repetition, and take account of cohesion between related items, it is useful to distinguish whether the reference is identical or not, because slightly different patterns appear.

(1) with identity of reference. Here the range of potentially cohesive items includes synonyms of the same or some higher level of generality: synonyms in the narrower sense, and **superordinates**. For example, in

> Four-&-twenty blackbirds, baked in a pie.
>
> When the pie was opened, the birds began to sing.

we have one instance of repetition (*pie ... pie*) and one of synonyms (*blackbirds ... birds*). *birds*, however, is at a higher level of generality than *blackbirds*; it is a superordinate term. In fact we might have (disregarding the scansion, of course) any of the following sequences:

four-&-twenty blackbirds ...	the blackbirds began to sing
„	the birds began to sing
„	the creatures began to sing
„	they began to sing

the reference item *they* being simply the most general of all. Compare *ankylosaur ... creature* in the following description of a dinosaur quoted in Table 5-13:

> As an added means of self-defense the **ankylosaur** had a club on its tail. The **creature** may have been able to swing the club with great force and aim a savage blow at an enemy.

Such instances are typically accompanied by the reference item *the*. This interaction between lexical cohesion and reference is the principal means for tracking a participant through the

645

discourse. Instead of *the creature* we might simply have had the personal reference *it*; and earlier in the same text, we find such examples:

> Ankylosaurus – the "fused lizard" – was the largest of the ankylosaurs, but in spite of **its** size and frightening appearance **it** fed only on plants.

Related to these are examples such as the following, where there is still identity of reference, although not to a participant, and the synonym may not be in the same word class (*cheered ... applause*; *cried ... tears*):

> Everyone cheered. The leader acknowledged **the applause**.

> I wish I hadn't cried so much! I shall be punished for it, I suppose, by being drowned in **my own tears**!

(2) without necessary identity of reference. The occurrence of a synonym even where there is no particular referential relation is still cohesive; for example, see Text 9-11

Text 9-11: Recreating – narrating (written, monologic): limerick

There was a man of Thessaly
    And he was wondrous wise.
He jumped into a hawthorn bush
    And scratched out both his eyes.
And when he saw his eyes were out
    With all his might and main
He jumped into a quickset hedge
    And scratched them in again.

where the quickset hedge is not the same entity as the hawthorn bush but there is still cohesion between the synonyms *hedge* and *bush*.

A special case of synonymy is its opposite, antonymy. Lexical items which are opposite in meaning, namely antonyms, also function with cohesive effect in a text. For example, *woke* and *asleep* in

> He fell asleep. What woke him was a loud crash.

9.6.1.3 Hyponymy

Repetition and synonymy are both elaborating relations based on identity; one lexical item restates another. There is a second kind of elaborating relationship – attribution. This is based on classification (specific to general): the first lexical item represents a class of thing and the second either (i) a superclass or a subclass or (ii) another class at the same level of classification. For example:

> Open government, campaign finance reform, and fighting the special interests and big money – these are our kinds of **issues**. [Text 6]

> You take over a main line like the Great Central and a few branch lines that run off from it, you electrify it, and then instead of running **trains** as they're run at present as public **vehicles** you hire out small trains to individual drivers. [Text 19]

And do you know anything about medieval literature; have you ever heard of any other kinds of **literature** in the medieval period besides **Chaucer**? [Text 125]

Most limestone probably originates from **organisms** that remove calcium carbonate from sea water. The remains of these **animals** may accumulate to form the limestone directly, or they may be broken and redeposited. [Text 68]

Noah's wife and his sons' wives went to the fields to gather **fruit** and **grain** and **vegetables**. They would need plenty of **food** for themselves and the animals on the ark. The remains of these animals may accumulate to form the limestone directly, or they may be broken and redeposited. [Text 14]

Thus in the last example, *fruit*, *grain* and *vegetables* are co-hyponyms of *food*. Hyponymy is common where a passage of text is being developed by means of elaboration. For example, see Texts 9-12 and 9-13:

Text 9-12: Expounding – categorizing (written, monologic): The Fuels of the Body
<u>The fuels of the body</u> are **carbohydrates**, **fats** and **proteins**. These are taken in the diet. They are found mainly in cereal grains, vegetable oils, meat, fish and dairy products. **Carbohydrates** are the principal source of energy in most diets. [...] **Fats** make up the second largest source of energy in most diets. [...] **Proteins** are essential for the growth and rebuilding of tissue, but they can also be used as a source of energy. [...]

Text 9-13: Expounding – categorizing (written, monologic): Primates
Fossil and living forms in the order <u>Primates</u> can be divided into two groups: the **archaic primates** (**Plesiadapiformes**) and the **modern primates** (**Euprimates**). **Plesiadapiforms** became extinct in the Euocene. They lacked most of the characteristic primate specialisations of the head, hands and feet, and it has recently been suggested that at least some members of this group were more closely related to culagos or 'flying lemurs' (order Dermoptera) than to modern primates. [*The Cambridge encyclopedia of human evolution*, p. 26.]

We referred in Chapter 6 to the category of general nouns, terms such as *thing, stuff, creature* which refer to a superordinate member of some taxonomic class of entity. These items perform a strongly cohesive function when they occur following one or more hyponymous terms. Here the general word does not carry the information focus, even if (as is typically the case) it occurs in a normally prominent position – as the final lexical item in the unit. For example:

||| Chen said || he did not have the power [[to single-handedly determine the future of Taiwan]] || and that there would have to be public consensus || before Taiwan pressed ahead || in trying to establish a confederation with the mainland. But he said || it was an example of "new thinking [[that could bring a breakthrough]]." Chen added, || "There's a lot of room for discussion of **this matter**." ||| [Text 13]

||| Then somewhere in the middle of the desert – about six hundred miles later << I didn't see a connection with anything >> – he bangs on the side of the car || and I let him out. ||| Now I know Indian people better, || and I know || that **the guy** probably didn't speak English, || or if he did, || he was ashamed of it. ||| [Text 7]

9.6.2 Extending relations: meronymy

The general sense of hyponymy is 'be a kind of', as in 'fruit is a kind of food'. There is a similar relation in the extending domain (Kinds of lexical relations playing a role in lexical cohesion). This is **meronymy** – 'be a part of'. These two lexical relations are contrasted diagrammatically in Figure 9-4: given a lexical set consisting of either hyponyms, where x, y and z are all 'kinds of' a, or meronyms, where p, q and r are all 'parts of' b. The occurrence of any pair of items within the set will be cohesive; for example

> ||| On the left of the park lies the Exhibition **Centre** [[which covers a massive 25,000 square metres of column-free space under the one **roof**]]. ||| Opened in January 1988, || the **Centre** is designed to hold major international exhibitions. ||| The glassed eastern **facade** is stepped back in five separate stages [[that can be partitioned off to form smaller **halls**]]. ||| The fifth **hall** is linked by covered walkway to the Convention Centre. ||| [7 Days in Sydney]

> ||| Elfrida had a beautiful little glass scent-**bottle**. ||| She had used up all the scent long ago; || but she often used to take the little **stopper** out ||| ...

> ||| She knelt down || and looked along the passage into the loveliest **garden** [[you ever saw]]. ||| How she longed to get out of that dark hall, || and wander about among those beds of bright **flowers** and those cool **fountains**, || ...

where *roof, facade, hall* are meronyms of *centre*, *stopper* is a meronym of *bottle*, and *flowers* and *fountains* are co-meronyms of garden. Passages in texts describing entities typically draw heavily on meronymic relations; this is illustrated by the guidebook passage above, and another such example is the encyclopedic entry on ankylosaurus presented in Chapter 5, Table 5-13. Here we find meronymic relations such as *ankylosaurus – skin, body, teeth, jaws, head, plates, beak, tail; head – teeth, jaws, beak*. The general tendency in such descriptions is to introduce the whole first, and then extend this meronymically in terms of the parts.

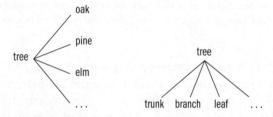

Fig. 9-4 Hyponymy and meronymy

Hyponymy and meronymy often work together in the development of text, as when some entity is being subclassified into subclasses by reference to properties of their parts (cf. Halliday & Matthiessen, 1999: 89–91). This illustrated by the passage on primates quoted above as Text 9-13.

There is no very clear line between meronymy and hyponymy, especially with abstract terms; and a given set of items may be co-hyponyms of one term but co-meronyms of another – for example, *chair, table, bed* are 'kinds' (hyponyms) of *furniture*, but 'parts' (meronyms) of *furnishings; forward, half-back, back* are 'kinds' of *players* but 'parts' of a *team*, and so on. But since either relationship is a source of lexical cohesion it is not necessary to insist on deciding between them.

9.6.3 Collocation

At the same time there are other instances of lexical cohesion that do not depend on any general semantic relationship of the types just discussed, but rather on a particular

association between the items in question – a tendency to co-occur. This 'co-occurrence tendency' is known as **collocation**. For example,

Text 9-14: Recreating – narrating (written, monologic): limerick

A little fat man of Bombay
Was smoking one very hot day.
  But a bird called a snipe
  Flew away with his pipe,
Which vexed the fat man of Bombay.

There is a strong collocational bond between *smoke* and *pipe*, which makes the occurrence of *pipe* in line 4 cohesive.

Clearly there is a semantic basis to a collocation of this kind; a pipe is something you smoke, and the words *pipe* and *smoke* are typically related as Range to Process in a behavioural process clause. Hence *pipe* here will be interpreted as 'the pipe that he was smoking at the time'. In general, the semantic basis of many instances of collocation is the relation of enhancement, as with *dine + restaurant, table; fry + pan; bake + oven*. These are circumstantial relationships (for collocations involving Process + Manner: degree, e.g. *love + deeply, want + badly, understand + completely*, see Matthiessen, 2009b), but as the example with *smoke + pipe* illustrates, participant + process relationships also form the basis of collocation – the most important ones involving either Process + Range (e.g. *play* + musical instrument: *piano, violin*, etc.; *grow + old*) or Process + Medium (e.g. *shell + peas, twinkle + star, polish + shoes*); and there are also combinations involving functions in the nominal group, in particular, Epithet + Thing (e.g. *strong + tea, heavy + traffic, powerful + argument*) and Facet + Thing (e.g. *pod + wales, flock + birds, school + fish, herd + cattle, gaggle + geese*).

While we can typically find a semantic basis to collocation in this way, the relationship is at the same time a direct association between the words; if *pipe* is in the text then *smoke* may well be somewhere around, at least with considerably greater probability than if we just pulled words out of a hat on the basis of their overall frequency in the language. We get ready for it, so to speak; and hence if it does occur it is strongly cohesive (cf. Hoey's, 2005, notion of lexical priming).

As a matter of fact, even where there is a relation of synonymy between lexical items, their cohesive effect tends to depend more on collocation, a simple tendency to co-occur. Of course, if both relationships are present they reinforce each other; but if a pair of synonyms are not regular collocates their cohesive effect is fairly weak, whereas words that are closely associated but without any systematic semantic relationship are nevertheless likely to have a noticeably cohesive effect. This is because collocation is one of the factors on which we build our expectations of what is to come next.

So, for example, there is a strong collocational bond between *cold* and *ice*, but not nearly so strong between *cold* and *snow*, though it would make just as good sense; *snow* is more likely to conjure up *white*. We collocate *friends* and *relations*, and also *friends* and *neighbours*; but not very often *relations* and *neighbours*, although *family* and *neighbourhood* seem to be associated. The extreme cases of such collocational patterns are to be found in fixed phrases and clichés, like *flesh and blood, stretch of the imagination*; but these actually contribute little to cohesion, since they are so closely bound together that they behave almost like single lexical items.

649

Notice, finally, that collocations are often fairly specifically associated with one or another particular register, or functional variety of the language. This is true, of course, of individual lexical items, many of which we regard as 'technical' because they appear exclusively, or almost exclusively, in one kind of text. But it is also noteworthy that perfectly ordinary lexical items often appear in different collocations according to the text variety. For example, *hunting*, in a story of the English aristocracy, will call up *quarry* and *hounds* (or, at another level, *shooting* and *fishing*); in an anthropological text, words like *gathering*, *agricultural* and *pastoral*; as well as, in other contexts, *bargain*, *souvenir*, *fortune* and such-like.

Table 9-18 presents an example of a text marked for lexical cohesion, using the categories set out earlier in Table 9-17.

9.7 The creation of texture

We have identified the following features as those which combine to make up the textual resources of the lexicogrammar of English:

(A) structural

    1   thematic structure: Theme and Rheme (clause: Chapter 3; clause complex: Chapter 7, Section, 7.6)

    2   information structure and focus: Given and New (clause: Chapter 3, Sections 3.5 and 3.6; clause complex: Chapter 7, Section, 7.6)

(B) cohesive (Chapter 9)

    1   conjunction

    2   reference

    3   ellipsis (that is, ellipsis and substitution)

    4   lexical cohesion

Looked at 'from below', these textual resources fall into two categories – those that engender grammatical structure (theme and information) and those that do not (conjunction, reference, ellipsis, lexical cohesion). Looked at 'from above', these textual resources are concerned either with textual transitions between messages or with textual statuses of components (elements) of these messages. These two classificatory perspectives are intersected in Table 9-19. The table indicates that structural and cohesive resources work together in the marking of textual transitions and in the marking of textual statuses. In the latter case, all the resources are indeed textual; but in the former, the structural resources are logical rather than textual – the logical relations of clause complexing (Chapter 7). We shall return to this metafunctional alignment between the textual and the logical in Chapter 10, Section 10.2.1. The table does not include lexical cohesion. This is like reference and ellipsis in that it involves components of messages rather than whole messages; but it often works together with conjunction in the creation of relations in text. We shall thus have occasion to refer to it both in our discussion of textual statuses and in our discussion of textual transitions.

Table 9-18 Text analysed for lexical cohesion[10]

	Rep.	Syn.	Ident.	Hyp.	Mer.	Coll.
Peter rushed straight up to the *monster*						
and aimed a *slash* of his *sword* at its side.						
That **slash** never			[slash]			
reached the **Wolf**.			[monster]			
Quick as **lightning** it turned round,						[quick]
its eyes flaming,						
and its *mouth* wide open in a *howl* of *anger*.						
If it had not been so **angry**	[anger]					
that it simply had to **howl**	[howl]					
it would have got him by the **throat** at once.					[mouth]	[mouth]
As it was –						
though all this happened too **quickly** for Peter to think at all –	[quick]					
he had just **time** to duck down						[quick]
and plunge his **sword**	[sword]					
as hard as he could,						
between the **brute's** forelegs into its heart.			[Wolf]			
Then came a horrible, confused **moment**				[time]		
like something in a **nightmare**.						[monster]
He was *tugging* and **pulling**						[tugging]
and the Wolf seemed neither *alive* nor **dead**,						[alive]
and its bared **teeth** knocked against his forehead,					[mouth]	[mouth]
and everything was blood and heat and hair.						
A **moment** later he found	[moment]					
that the **monster**	[monster]		[Wolf]			
lay **dead**.	[dead]					

---

[10] Bold represents item analysed for cohesion; italics represents cohesively related item.

Table 9-19 Textual resources

	Structural	Cohesive
textual transitions ['organic']	(logical: TAXIS [clause complex])	CONJUNCTION
textual statuses ['componential']	THEME: Theme ∧ Rheme; INFORMATION: Given + New	REFERENCE; ELLIPSIS

9.7.1 Textual statuses: THEME, INFORMATION, REFERENCE & ELLIPSIS

The systems of THEME, INFORMATION, REFERENCE and ELLIPSIS are all concerned with textual statuses. Speakers assign these statuses to components of messages to help themselves produce texts and to help their listeners interpret them. These textual statuses are independently variable. For example, as we have seen (Chapter 3, Section 3.6), thematic status may be combined with either given or new, and the same is true of rhematic status. However, there are certain unmarked combinations: in the unmarked case, Theme is Given and New falls within Rheme. The thematic statuses and the favoured combinations are shown in Figure 9-5.

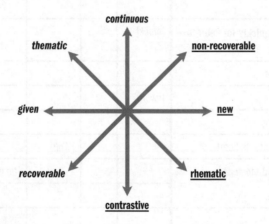

Fig. 9-5   Unmarked combinations of different textual statuses – shown in bold italics (continuous, thematic, given and recoverable) and bold underlining (contrastive, rhematic, new and non-recoverable)

Let us return to our dinner table conversation to investigate how the textual statuses are deployed in this passage. When Craig says *this fish is cooked beautifully*, he gives *this fish* the status of Theme, treating it as Given information that is recoverable (identifiable) to his listeners; and he gives *cooked beautifully* the status of New, treating it as rhematic and (by implication) as non-recoverable. There is no ellipsis or substitution, so the distinction between continuity and contrast is not in operation. With the textual choices in this clause, Craig uses a common pattern of the unmarked combinations set out in Figure 9-5. This pattern is repeated again and again in our dinner table extract, as can be seen from the analysis represented diagrammatically in Figure 9-6.

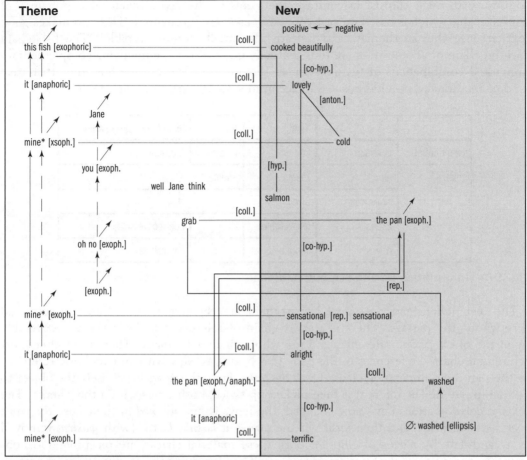

*mine = 'my + one' [personal reference + substitution]

Fig. 9-6   Theme, information and cohesion in Text 9:1

In this figure, the logogenetic chains created by selections within reference, ellipsis and lexical cohesion (cf. Table 9-4) are represented vertically. For example, the figure shows the 'fish' chain involving both reference and ellipsis. The fish is first referred to exophorically (*this fish*) and then picked up anaphorically (*it*). The next node in the chain is *mine*, which means 'my one = fish'. This nominal group involves personal reference to the speaker ('my'), which is thus exophoric, and also ellipsis ('one' = 'fish'): the variant with re-instated ellipsis is *my fish*. The Thing of the nominal group is thus given the textual status of continuous information, so that the Deictic is highlighted as contrastive.

As the diagram in Figure 9-6 shows, the nodes of the logogenetic chains have the textual status of either Theme or New. In fact, it turns out that the nodes within a given chain are consistently given the same status, with only a few exceptions. Thus the nodes of the 'fish' chain are thematic throughout. This makes good textual sense: they are referentially recoverable (being either exophoric or anaphoric) and several of them also involve

653

continuity through ellipsis. In contrast, the items in the lexical chain of expressions of appreciation, which is based on co-hyponymy, are new throughout. This also makes good textual sense: they are rhematic and they are referentially non-recoverable[11]. The 'fish' chain and the chain of appreciation are thus textually quite distinct, embodying complementary unmarked combinations of textual statuses (Figure 9-5). We can see how the attributive kind of relational clause has evolved to accommodate this pattern: Figure 9-7.

		'fish'	'be'	'quality of appreciation'
experiential	TRANSITIVITY	Carrier	Process	Attribute
textual	THEME	Theme	Rheme	
	INFORMATION	Given		New
	REFERENCE	recoverable	–	non-recoverable
	ELLIPSIS	continuous		contrastive

Fig. 9-7   Information flow in attributive clause

The 'fish' chain and the appreciation chain are the major ones; they are sustained throughout the passage. There is a short chain of references to Jane: she is recoverable by virtue of exophoric reference, and the whole chain is thematic. There is another short referential chain – references to the pan. This begins as New with an exophoric reference to the pan in an imperative clause (*grab the pan*). Here the news is precisely the object to be manipulated. The referent is then picked up twice, both times within the Theme. The textual considerations have now changed: the news is first *washed* in the clause *the pan's been washed, has it* and then *hasn't* in the clause *it hasn't, has it* (with *washed* removed as a candidate by means of ellipsis). Both these material clauses are receptive and non-agentive: these voice selections create the conditions for giving the Medium/Goal the status of unmarked Theme.

Unlike REFERENCE and ELLIPSIS, the resource of LEXICAL COHESION is, in general, neutral with respect to textual statuses; that is why we have not included it in Table 9-4. A given lexical item can be assigned any of the textual statuses; it is not predisposed to any particular status. Similarly, a given lexical relation is also neutral with respect to textual statuses. However, a particular lexical chain in a text is very likely to show some systematic pattern in relation to textual status. This is illustrated by the chain of appreciation in our text: there is a good reason why all the items are treated as New (within Rheme) rather than as Theme (within Given). The speakers consistently treat their appraisal of the fish as their main point of news. By the same token, they consistently select the fish as their point of departure. (The only place where 'fish' becomes news is in *well Jane think of salmon*, where a hyponym of *fish* is given the status of New.)

---

[11]   For example, *terrific* in *mine's terrific* is a nominal group with Epithet: adjective as Head. Such nominal groups are always 'non-specific', as is shown by the agnate variant with Thing: noun as Head: *mine's a terrific one*; and non-specificity is an indication of non-recoverability.

Texts vary in how lexical chains relate to textual status, but this variation usually reflects systematic strategies associated with the registers that the texts belong to. For example, Fries (1993) shows how there is a strong tendency in the persuasive register of advertising for chains relating to the product to be thematic and chains embodying positive appraisal to be treated as new, as illustrated by the extract in Text 9-15:

Text 9-15: Recommending – promoting (written, monologic): extract from an advertisement

Are you ready to rock? <u>The Autora Fuse™ PCI digital video capture card</u> gives you **the power to inexpensively view and edit your full motion, full screen video at a phenomenal 9 MB per second. Immediate feedback on all displays, tight A/V synch, QuickTime™ compatible and 3 bundled software options.** <u>The Igniter™</u> boasts **13.3 MB per second performance** and is **upgradeable to component, uncompressed and more!** Made **for PCI PowerMacsTM G3s & G4s** and **very affordable!** For detailed brochure and more information contact: ... [Australian Macworld 02.2003]

Similarly, in factual reports, there is a clear division of lexical labour between chains serving as Theme and New (as can be seen in Text 9-12): see Halliday & Martin (1993: 244). Lexical chains may thus be foregrounded either as Theme or as New.

9.7.2 Textual transitions: CONJUNCTION and TAXIS

While textual statuses are assigned to components of messages, textual transitions hold between whole messages, or groups of whole messages. Such transitions may, of course, be left to the listener or reader to infer, without the help of any explicit markers; but they may also be marked explicitly by means of textual or logical resources. The textual resource for indicating such transitions is the system of CONJUNCTION (see Section 9.3). Here the type of relation is indicated, but there is no distinction between paratactic and hypotactic relations. The logical resource combines type of relation with TAXIS in the univariate structure of clause complexing (Chapter 7). These two resources complement one another in the grammatical realization of transitions in text. The general principle of complementarity is this: clause complexing does relatively more work locally, while conjunction does relatively more work non-locally and even globally. Clause complexing 'choreographs' the local development of text by means of univariate structure, indicating both taxis and type of logico-semantic relation. Conjunction can work together with clause complexing, reinforcing local relations, but it tends to take over from clause complexing as the relations become less local and more global. Looked at from the point of view of lexicogrammar, this means that the local organization tends to be 'tighter' whereas the more global organization tends to be 'looser'. At the same time, looked at from the point of view of context, the more global organization is subject to more contextual guidance in the form of generic structure. In this way, grammar and context complement one another in their contributions to the semantic organization of text.

Let us illustrate these aspects of the relational organization of text in reference to a persuasive text: see Table 9-20. The clause complexes all serve to link clauses locally; the two most intricate complexes consist of three clauses each, but all the others consist only of two. All combinations are hypotactic, either projecting or enhancing – with the exception of one elaborating nexus. There are only three instances of conjunction. One is fairly local in its scope, the enhancing *but* in [12]. The punctuation treats [11] and [12] as separate

655

Table 9-20 Clause complexing and conjunction in a persuasive text

	CONJ.	COMPLEX	
[1]		α:	I don't believe
		'β:	that endorsing the Nuclear Freeze initiative is the right step for California CC.
[2]		×β:	Tempting as it may be,
[3]		α:	we shouldn't embrace every popular issue that comes along.
[4]		×β:	*When* we do so
[5]		αα:	we use precious limited resources
[6]		α×β:	where other players with superior resources are already doing an adequate job.
[7]	extending: variation	α:	***Rather***, I think
		'βα:	we will be stronger and more effective
[8]		'β×β:	*if* we stick to those issues of governmental structure and process, broadly defined, that have formed the core of our agenda for years.
[9]			Open government, campaign finance reform, and fighting the special interests and big money – these are our kinds of issues.
[10]			Let's be clear:
[11]			I personally favour the initiative and ardently support disarmament negotiations to reduce the risk of war.
[12]	enhancing: concession	α:	***But*** I don't think
		'β:	endorsing a specific freeze proposal is appropriate for CCC.
[13]		α:	We should limit our involvement in defense and weaponry to matters of process,
		=β:	*such as* exposing the weapons industry's influence on the political process.
[14]	enhancing: cause	α:	***Therefore***, I urge you
		"β:	to vote against a CCC endorsement of the nuclear freeze initiative.
			(Signed) Michael Asimow, California Common Cause Vice-Chair and UCLA Law Professor

sentences, so under the assumption that the sentence is the graphological realization of a clause complex, we have analysed them as separate clause complexes. If read aloud, [11] would probably be spoken on tone 1 rather than tone 3, thus confirming our analysis.

However, there is a closely agnate variant where [11] and [12] are grouped into one clause complex. In contrast, the other two conjunctions – the extending: replacive *rather* and the enhancing: causal *therefore* – are less local in terms of their scopes. The extending *rather* indicates a relationship of antithesis between 2 through 6 and 7 through 9. The enhancing *therefore* indicates a relationship of motivation between [1] through [13] and [14]. It is thus even more global in its scope. The relationship is an internal one, and such fairly global internal relationships are typical of persuasive texts. This is where the organization of the text follows the general schema of persuasive texts where the key unit is a proposal ('vote against ...!'): Motivation [Claim ^ Evidence] ^ Appeal.

This schematic organization is contextual: it is projected onto the text from the context of persuasion in which it operates. At the same time, the text is organized semantically as a complex of rhetorical relations, and it is these relations that are realized by the combination of conjunction and clause complexing: see Figure 9-8. The figure shows a rhetorical-relational analysis of the text as a semantic unit, with grammatical realization by clause complexes and conjunction superimposed (for the rhetorical analysis of this text, see Mann & Thompson, 1985; for this type of analysis in general, see Mann, Matthiessen & Thompson, 1992, and for the relation to clause complexing, see Matthiessen & Thompson, 1988, and Matthiessen, 2002a).

This example illustrates how conjunction and clause complexing complement one another in the grammatical realization of rhetorical relations. However, this pattern of complementarity varies significantly across registers. In particular, in unselfconscious spoken text, clause complexing does relatively more work and conjunction relatively less. Here clause complexes can extend well beyond local relations, reaching a span of up to 20 to 30 clauses (cf. Halliday, 1985a; Matthiessen, 2002a). Conversely, in planned written text, clause complexing does relatively less work and conjunction relatively more.

657

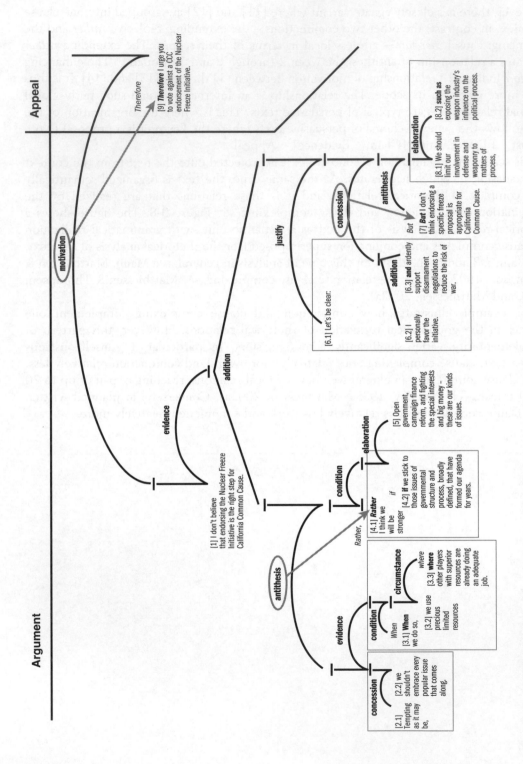

Argument

Appeal

motivation

[9] **Therefore** I urge you to vote against a CCC endorsement of the Nuclear Freeze Initiative.

Therefore

antithesis

justify

concession

antithesis

elaboration

[8.1] We should limit our involvement in defense and weaponry to matters of process,

[8.2] **such as** exposing the weapon industry's influence on the political process.

But [7] **But** I don't think endorsing a specific freeze proposal is appropriate for California Common Cause.

addition

[6.3] **and** ardently support disarmament negotiations to reduce the risk of war.

[6.1] Let's be clear:

[6.2] I personally favor the initiative.

evidence

addition

[1] I don't believe that endorsing the Nuclear Freeze Initiative is the right step for California Common Cause.

condition

elaboration

[5] Open government, campaign finance reform, and fighting the special interests and big money – these are our kinds of issues.

[4.1] *Rather,* I think we will be stronger

Rather,

if [4.2] **if** we stick to those issues of governmental structure and process, broadly defined, that have formed our agenda for years.

antithesis

evidence

concession

condition

circumstance

[2.1] *Tempting as it may be,*

[2.2] we shouldn't embrace every popular issue that comes along.

When [3.1] **When** we do so,

[3.2] we use precious limited resources

where [3.3] **where** other players with superior resources are already doing an adequate job.

Fig. 9-8   Rhetorical analysis of the 'California Common Cause' text (revised from Mann & Thompson, 1985), with lexicogrammatical realizations superimposed

BEYOND THE CLAUSE: METAPHORICAL MODES OF EXPRESSION

10.1 Lexicogrammar and semantics

In the previous chapter, we explored how the resources of lexicogrammar are deployed in the processing – creation and interpretation – of text. We found that although the grammar does not extend its compositional organization beyond the rank of clause (cf. Chapter 1, Section 1.1.3), the resources of lexicogrammar make two fundamental contributions beyond this upper limit of grammatical units: (i) the creation of logogenetic patterns and (ii) the marking of cohesion.

(i) On the one hand, in the course of unfolding of text, lexicogrammatical selections create **logogenetic patterns** at all ranks. This is patterning in the text that has nothing to do with composition or size: instead of composition (the relationship between a whole and its parts), the patterning is based on instantiation (the relationship between an instance and a generalized instance type). The patterning represents a slight move up this cline from the single instance to a pattern of instances, as in a news report where one projecting verbal clause after another is selected until this emerges as a favourite clause type. The logogenetic patterns that emerge as a text unfolds form a transient system that is specific to that text; but from repeated patterns over many such transient systems may, in turn, emerge a generalized system characteristic of a certain type of text or register (see e.g. the discussion of the evolution of scientific English in Halliday, 1988).

(ii) On the other hand, lexicogrammar has evolved textual resources for creating cohesive links that have the ability to indicate semantic relationships in the unfolding text beyond the domain of grammar. These resources are known collectively as the **system of** COHESION (Chapter 9). Cohesion includes (1) the system of CONJUNCTION for marking textual transitions in the unfolding of text and (2) the systems of REFERENCE, ELLIPSIS & SUBSTITUTION, and LEXICAL COHESION for giving elements different textual statuses in the unfolding of text.

Through the accumulation of logogenetic patterns and through the resources of cohesion, lexicogrammar makes a considerable contribution to the development of patterns in a text that extend beyond a single grammatical unit such as the clause, or even a complex of units such as the clause complex; and this is, of course, why lexicogrammatical analysis of a text can tell us so much about how it works, as we showed in Chapter 9. The patterns that are developed in this way are, however, patterns of meaning, not patterns of wording; they are patterns at the level of semantics rather than at the level of lexicogrammar. This is so because text is, as we have emphasized, a semantic phenomenon in the first instance; it is meaning unfolding in some particular context of situation. For example, the grammatical system of conjunction gives speakers and writers the resources to mark transitions in the development of a text – i.e., to mark rhetorical relations used to expand the text step by step; and the rhetorical relations that are marked in this way by conjunctions are semantic relations organizing the text as a flow of meaning.

A text is thus a unit of meaning – more accurately, a unit in the flow of meaning that is always taking place at the instance pole of the cline of instantiation (cf. Chapter 1, Section 1.3.4). How does this semantic unit relate to the units and unit complexes of grammar – the clause (clause complex), the groups (group complexes) and so on? The folk view is that a text *consists of* clauses (or 'sentences'); but this is a misleading simplification of a more indirect – but much more flexible and powerful – relationship. A text does not 'consist of' clauses (clause complexes) – there is no part-whole or 'constituency' relationship between a text and a clause (complex) and there is no single rank scale with text and clause as ranks (cf. Chapter 1, Section 1.1.3). Rather a text is *realized by* clauses (clause complexes), the two being located on different strata – semantics (the stratum of meaning) and lexicogrammar (the stratum of wording) respectively (see Halliday & Hasan, 1976; Halliday, 1982; Martin, 1992; Halliday & Matthiessen, 1999). The notion that language is stratified into an ordered series of levels or strata that are related by realization was first introduced in Chapter 1, Section 1.1.3; and this type of organization of language was represented diagrammatically in Figure 1-10.

While our focus has been on the lexicogrammatical stratum throughout this book, the stratal, realizational relationship between lexicogrammar and the strata above it (semantics) and below it (phonology) has also been a key motif throughout. We have discussed the realizational relationship between lexicogrammar and phonology, noting that in the unmarked case a clause is realized by a tone group and showing how options in the grammar of mood are realized phonologically (by tone within the interpersonal metafunction: Chapter 4, Section 4.4.4) and how options in the grammar of information are realized phonologically (by tonicity within the textual metafunction: Chapter 3, Section 3.5). We have also discussed the realizational relationship between semantics and lexicogrammar, showing, for example, how options in the semantic system of speech function (proposition/ proposal) are realized lexicogrammatically by mood (clause; see Chapter 4, Section 4.1). Let us now briefly review the stratal relationship between semantics and lexicogrammar.

The upper bound of the semantic stratum is, as we have said, the **text**: this is the most extensive unit of meaning. The upper bound of the lexicogrammatical system is the **clause**: this is the most extensive unit of wording (cf. Chapter 7, Table 7-3).[1] In the grammar,

---

[1] By saying that they are the upper bounds, we are not ruling out complexes – text complexes and clause complexes; for example, a cookery book can be analysed as a macro-text consisting of sets of additive sequences of recipes, elaborating background information, and so on (cf. Martin's, e.g. 1995, 1997: 16, notion of macro-genres as complexes of genres). But complexes are, as we have seen in Chapter 7, not higher-ranking units but rather expansions of units of a given rank.

there is a single, generalized compositional scale – the grammatical rank scale introduced in Chapter 1, Section 1.1.3 (clause – group/phrase – word – morpheme); and we can specify not only the upper and lower bounds of this scale – the clause and the morpheme, respectively – but also the intermediate units of patterning: group/phrase and word. But in the semantics, it is far from clear whether there is a single compositional scale: such a scale would have to be generalized across all registerial varieties of a language, but we know that texts vary considerably from one register to another. It is quite possible that different registers operate with different compositional scales; for example, one such scale was identified in the organization of class room discourse by Sinclair & Coulthard (1975) and another in the organization of certain types of conversation by Cloran (1994). This issue can only be settled after a great deal more research into the semantics of text has been carried out (for discussion, see Matthiessen & Halliday, in prep.).

However, even though we have to leave open the question of whether there is a single semantic compositional scale or more than one, we can say something about the lower region of such a scale or such scales. This is the region where semantic units are realized by lexicogrammatical ones. We have already referred to these semantic units throughout the book, and the principle that emerges here is the familiar metafunctional one. The clause is a multifunctional construct in the grammar, one that realizes three different semantic units, one for each metafunction: textual – message (Chapter 3), interpersonal – proposition/ proposal (Chapter 4), and experiential – figure (Chapter 5). These relationships are shown in Figure 10-1: the three semantic units deriving from the three metafunctions are all mapped onto the clause, which thus unifies the three metafunctional strands of meaning.

What is intermediate in the semantics between text on the one hand and message, proposition/proposal and figure on the other hand? Messages, propositions/proposals and figures can combine with units of the same metafunctional type to form more extensive semantic patterns in the creation of text. These patterns are distinct for each metafunction.

(i) Textual. Messages combine to form periodic movements of information in the way illustrated in Chapter 3 and discussed again in Chapter 9 (e.g. in reference to the thematic progression in Text 7-1, Chapter 7). For example, the paragraph dealing with The Chinese Gardens in Text 7-3 in Chapter 7 starts with a phase of messages concerned with (the reader's) motion through space and then moves on to a phase of messages concerned with points of interest. Such phases of messages help construct the flow of information as the text unfolds and we can refer to them simply as **information flow patterns**.

(ii) Interpersonal. Propositions/proposals combine to form **patterns of exchange** involving two or more interactants, as in Text 10-1.

Text 10-1: Reporting – admissions interview [Text 135]
Professor Hart: Will you have any domestic work at all to do?

Mrs Finney: Well I shall have to organize.

Professor Hart: But not washing or cleaning or cooking?

Mrs Finney: Oh good heavens, no no no; I've got a full-time {{Professor Hart: Good.}} charwoman as well as this creature. {{Professor Hart: Yes.}} She's a nice girl.

Professor Hart: Oh have you?

semantics

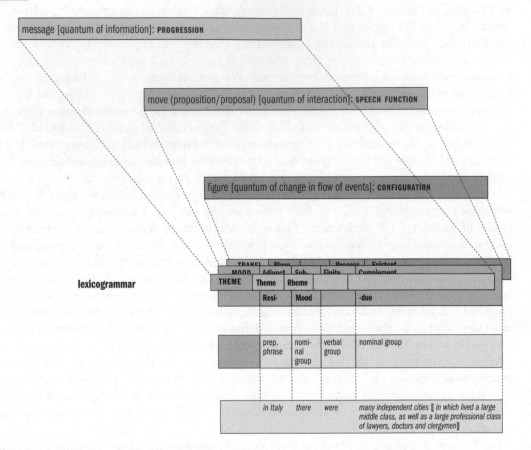

Fig. 10-1   Clause as a tri-functional construct

Mrs Finney: Yes, yes.

Professor Hart: Yes oh well you are very well situated, I must say.

This passage is taken from an admissions interview: Mrs Finney has applied to do English honours at a university and Professor Hart and a colleague interview her to determine whether they find her suitable or not. The interview is essentially a series of information exchanges consisting of propositions: the interviewers demand information by asking questions and Mrs Finney gives on demand by making statements. But the dialogic pattern is more complex than simple Question + Statement sequences. In her second turn, Mrs Finney supplements her answer by giving more information about her domestic arrangements: *I've got a full-time charwoman as well as this creature*. Professor Harts responds by demanding information as a check: *Oh have you?* And Mrs Finney responds in turn by giving information: *Yes, yes*. The phase is concluded by Professor Hart when he gives information evaluating what Mrs Finney has said: *Yes oh well, you are very well situated, I*

must say. The pattern of exchange has thus been Question (Professor Hart) ^ Statement (Mrs Finney) ^ Question [follow-up] (Professor Hart) ^ Statement [supplementary] (Mrs Finney) ^ Question [checking] (Professor Hart) ^ Statement [confirming] (Mrs Finney) ^ Statement [evaluating] (Professor Hart). In this way, speakers combine propositions/proposals to create dialogue.

At least in some registers such as interviews, classroom discourse and quiz shows, the patterns are regular and predictable enough to appear to be compositional in nature: interpersonal units of exchange consisting of certain sequences of propositions/proposals (see Martin, 1992: Section 2.3, on "exchange structure"; Eggins & Slade, 2005). But whatever the status is of such exchange patterning, the critical point is that it is interpersonal rather than textual or ideational, and that it is intermediate between propositions/proposals and the whole text.

(iii) Ideational. Figures combine to form sequences; and these, in turn, may combine to form **episodic patterns**, as in narratives and other chronologically organized texts or chronological passages within other kinds of text. This was illustrated in Chapter 7 by reference to an extract from a narrative, Text 7-1; another example is Pat's anecdote in Text 5-7, Chapter 5. Such episodes typically consist of several sequences, each of which is realized by a clause complex. There is, of course, considerable variation in how a given episode is construed. One good source of illustration of this kind of variation is the modern news report (cf. Nanri, 1994; Iedema, Feez & White, 1994; Martin & Rose, 2008: 75–81), where one and the same episode is usually construed several times, often from different angles, including the vantage points of eyewitnesses, as illustrated in Text 10-2.

Text 10-2: Reporting – chronicling: extract from a news report [Text 30]

THIRTY people were feared drowned last night after a floating night club carrying as many as 150 on a late-night party cruise collided with a huge dredging barge and sank in London's River Thames.

[...]

Witnesses said the sand dredger seemed to go past the Marchioness but suddenly smashed into the side and went right over it. Art student Mike Mosbacher, 22, said he saved himself by diving through an open cabin window on the top deck. He saw the sand dredger heading for the cruiser. "My friend pointed it out to me. I thought it would go past us, it was travelling too fast. It hit us in the side, smashed into us and went straight over us. I dived out of the window. The people downstairs – there's no way they could have got out. There were people swimming in the water and people screaming."

The sinking of a disco boat on the Thames is recounted first in the reporter's voice as a single sequence (realized by a single clause complex: α: people + drowned ^ ×β1: club + collided ^ ×β×2: club + sank), and later in the news report in the voices of eyewitnesses as a series of clauses and clause complexes. The eyewitness account quoted above increases the delicacy of focus, construing the disastrous episode into six sequences. The sequences that make up an episode may be linked through the relations of expansion (elaboration, extension and enhancement), effectively forming a macro-sequence; but they also form a more multivariate configuration with a kind of Beginning ^ Middle ^ End structure (cf. Halliday, 2001). Thus the account given above starts out with anticipation of the disaster (*My friend ... travelling too fast*), then moves on to the actual collision (*It hit us ... straight over us*) plus escape (*I dived out of the window*), and finishes off with the outcome (*The people*

downstairs ... people screaming). The dominant type of expansion here is enhancement; and the dominant type of transitivity is that of 'material' clauses.

The examples referred to above all involve sequence in time; but there are, of course, other, non-temporal patterns extending beyond a single sequence. For example, descriptive passages are sequences in detail, developing a characterization of some phenomenon. Thus in the text in Table 5-13, Chapter 5, the characterization of Ankylosaurus proceeds as follows: placement in taxonomy of Ankylosaurs in general (clause 1) – size (clause complex 2: α ^ +β) – anatomy: build & exterior (clause 3) – anatomy: elaboration of exterior (clause complex 4: 1 ^ ×2) – Ankylosaurus as the largest member of Ankylosaurs and size in relation to feeding habit (clause complex 5: 1 ^ ×2) – food source and anatomy [teeth and jaws] (clause 6) – anatomy: head and beak (clause complex 7: α << =β>>) – predators (clause 8) – self-defence and anatomy: tail (clause 9) – use of tail (clause complex 10: 1 ^ ×2). While the dominant type of expansion in narrative episode is that of enhancement (temporal sequence, possibly with the addition of cause) with some kind of Beginning ^ Middle ^ End structure, passages such as this one are based on elaboration and extension with some kind of General/Whole ^ Specific/Part structure. Similarly, they differ in transitivity. Narrative episodes are dominated by 'material' clauses, while characterizations are dominated by 'relational' ones.

The account that we have outlined is summarized in Table 10-1. (This table extends Table 1-5, Chapter 1.) The table shows the intersection of two content strata (semantics and lexicogrammar) with the three metafunctions. Within each metafunction there are semantic patterns that are intermediate between (1) the local semantic units that are realized by the clause and the clause complex and (2) the global semantic unit, i.e. the text. These intermediate patterns are the ones that are very likely to vary from one register to another: there will be variation both in the nature of the patterns and in the degree to which there is a compositional scale between the text and the message/proposition (proposal)/figure. For example, within the interpersonal metafunction, the patterns intermediate between proposition/proposal and text (in its interpersonal guise) are patterns of (dialogic) exchange; and these patterns vary considerably from, say, casual conversation to interviews

Table 10-1 Some semantic and lexicogrammatical units

	Logical	Experiential	Interpersonal	Textual
semantics	text			
	(episodic patterns)		(exchange patterns)	(information flow patterns)
	sequence ⬊	figure ⬊	proposition/proposal ⬊	message ⬊
lexicogrammar	complex of ...	clause		
	TAXIS & LOGICO-SEMANTIC TYPE	TRANSITIVITY	MOOD	THEME; INFORMATION [info unit]
	complex of ...	group/phrase		

to classroom discourse to courtroom trials or panel debates (see e.g. Martin, 1992: Ch. 2; Eggins & Slade, 2005; Matthiessen & Slade, 2010).[2]

Table 10-1 shows how semantic units are mapped onto grammatical ones. The principle is that of rank-based constituency – semantic unit $a \searrow$ grammatical unit m; the key grammatical unit is the clause, as shown diagrammatically in Figure 10-1. But while this is the foundation on which the relationship between semantics and lexicogrammar is based, there are two other principles affecting this relationship, making it more complicated but also extending the meaning potential of language: (i) transgrammatical semantic domains – domains of meaning extending across different grammatical units, and (ii) metaphor – incongruent realizational relations between semantics and lexicogrammar.

(i) On the one hand, there are semantic domains that range over more than a single grammatical unit. Thus the semantic domain of modality (Chapter 4, Section 4.5.2) is realized in more than one place in the grammar; for example, it is realized by 'mental' clauses such as *I suppose* and by 'relational' clauses such as *it is possible*, by verbal groups with finite modal operators such as *may* and by adverbial groups with modal adverbs such as *perhaps*. These modal patterns within different grammatical units are not interchangeable synonyms; they have distinct values within the overall semantic system of modality. As we shall see below, while the forms above can all realize 'low probability', *I think* is explicitly subjective, *it is possible* is explicitly objective, *may* is implicitly subjective and *perhaps* is implicitly objective. This means that the semantic system of modality is more extensive than the modal features of any one given grammatical unit would suggest; it is realized not by a single grammatical unit but by a range of units: semantic unit $a \searrow$ grammatical units m, n & o. We shall discuss such **transgrammatical semantic domains** in Section 10.2 below.

(ii) On the other hand, there are realignments in the realizational relationship between semantic units and grammatical ones. According to Table 10-1, a sequence is realized by a clause complex; the combination of a figure, a proposition/proposal and a message is realized by a clause; and we could add further realizational correspondences: for example, a participant is realized by a nominal group, a process by a verbal group and a circumstance by an adverbial group or a prepositional phrase. But once these couplings between the two strata of the content plane have been established, 'cross-couplings' become theoretically possible (cf. Chapter 1, Section 1.3.1). For example, while sequences are realized by clause complexes and figures by clauses, it is theoretically possible that, under certain conditions, sequences would be realized by clauses – that is, as if they were figures. This is the possibility of **metaphorical realization**, which has been taken up in English and many other languages, creating a more complex relationship between semantics and lexicogrammar than the one shown in Table 10-1. For example, instead of saying *we and this common homeland are spiritually and physically united, so we were deeply pained as we saw ...*, we can say *that spiritual and physical oneness we all share with this common homeland explains the depth of the pain we all carried in our hearts as we saw ...*. But the two forms of realization are not, of course, synonymous, so the effect is one of expanding the meaning potential of the language. We shall discuss this phenomenon of **grammatical metaphor** in Sections 10.4 and 10.5.

---

[2] In conversational analysis, such differences have been discussed in terms of different kinds of turn allocation system; but while this is part of the picture, there are other, deeper considerations as well.

10.2 Semantic domains

Every lexicogrammatical system realizes some semantic system. For example, we have seen that the grammatical system of MOOD [clause] realizes the semantic system of SPEECH FUNCTION [proposition/proposal] (Chapter 4, Section 4.1). Here one lexicogrammatical domain, the clause, corresponds to one semantic domain, the proposition/proposal. In addition, there are semantic systems that are realized by grammatical systems operating in more than one place in the grammar. These semantic domains range over two or more grammatical domains, spanning two or more grammatical units, as in the case of MODALITY noted above (see Chapter 4, Section 4.5.2).

There are two fundamental semantic domains of this kind – expansion and projection. For example, the expanding relation of 'addition' may be realized (1) cohesively by a conjunction such as *also* or (2) structurally by (a) an additive paratactic clause nexus marked by the structural conjunction *and*, (b) a circumstance of accompaniment marked by the preposition *with* or (c) an additive paratactic group nexus marked by *and*:

(1) She went to the market. Her son **also** went to the market.

(2a) She went to the market **and** so did her son.

(2b) She went to the market **with** her son.

(2c) She **and** her son went to the market.

These realizational variants are dispersed in the grammar, since they constitute different grammatical environments; but they are semantically agnate in that they all have the feature of 'addition'. The fact that they are semantically agnate does not mean that they are synonymous; they share the feature 'addition' but they differ in other respects. For example, (2b) and (2c) construe one event, whereas (2a) and (1) imply two events. One semantic system, the system of EXPANSION, has thus evolved to bring together patterns of wording within grammatically distinct units, thereby extending its overall meaning potential.

The semantic system of EXPANSION may be contrasted in this respect with that of FIGURATION: see Figure 10-2. The grammatical realization of FIGURATION is 'compact', being confined to the TRANSITIVITY system of the clause. In contrast, the grammatical realization of EXPANSION is 'dispersed', ranging over more than one grammatical unit. (We shall see later that compactly realized systems such as configuration may become dispersed in their realization through the process of grammatical metaphor.) We shall now briefly survey dispersed semantic systems, starting with expansion and then moving on to projection.

10.2.1 Expansion

We have met expansion in a number of different grammatical domains. The most detailed account was given in Chapter 7, Section 7.4, where we found that the three subtypes of expansion (elaboration, extension and enhancement) combine with tactic relations to link one clause to another in the formation of clause complexes. The same pattern was found to operate in the formation of group and phrase complexes (Chapter 8). In clause complexes and in group/phrase complexes, expansion is manifested within the logical mode of the ideational metafunction. But we had already met two experiential manifestations of expansion within the system of transitivity (Chapter 5). On the one hand, expansion is manifested in

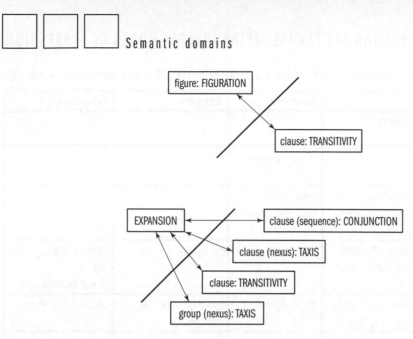

Fig. 10-2   Relationship between semantic systems and lexicogrammatical ones: (a) compact realization, (b) dispersed realization

the augmentation of the clause by circumstances: these circumstantial augmentations cover all three types of expansion, with enhancement being the most highly developed one (see Chapter 5, Table 5-28). On the other hand, expansion is manifested in the process of a 'relational' clause (cf. Chapter 5, Section 5.4.2): 'intensive' clauses embody elaboration, 'possessive' clauses extension, and 'circumstantial' clauses enhancement. In the domain of the nominal group, there are also various manifestations of the three types of expansion. Thus the Qualifier may elaborate, extend or enhance the Thing; this was discussed with reference to embedded clauses serving as Qualifier (see Chapter 7, Section 7.4.5).

The range of different manifestations of expansion mentioned above occurs in texts of all kinds; but different text types (registers) favour different expansion types and also different kinds of grammatical manifestation. This can be illustrated by reference to an extract from a topographic procedure in Table 10-2. The favourite type of expansion here is enhancement. This is hardly surprising. On the one hand, the representation of space is very central to topographic procedures, and the category of space is included within enhancement. On the other hand, the representation of temporal sequence is a key aspect of procedures in general, and time is also included within enhancement. Thus in the enhancement column we find circumstances of Place (e.g. *to the Art Gallery of N.S.W.*) and also spatial Qualifiers (e.g. *at Darling Harbour*); and we find temporal relations combined with tactic relations in clause complexes (e.g. *after seeing the Chinese Gardens ... catch a ride ...*) and with cohesive relations of conjunction (*Then cross Hyde Park ...*).

Elaboration and extension are, by comparison, minor motifs in the extract, although both play distinctive roles. Elaboration is manifested mainly within nominal groups as Epithets and Classifiers; these elaborating elements serve to characterize and evaluate phenomena that will be encountered on the tour (e.g. *enticing aromas, Chinese breakfast*). Extension is also manifested within the nominal group; here the sense is that of generalized possession –

667

Table 10-2 Manifestations of expansion in an extract from an enabling: instructing text, a topographic procedure [Text 22]

	Clause	Elaboration	Extension	Enhancement
1	Start the day <u>at Sydney's Chinatown</u>; ||			clause, trans.: Place
=2α	see ||	clause complex: 1 =2		
=2'β	if you can resist the enticing aromas [[<u>wafting through the doors of the many restaurants</u>]] . |||	group: Epithet (*enticing*); Qualifier =[[		
×β	<u>After</u> seeing the Chinese Gardens, Festival Markets and museums [at Darling Harbour], ||			clause complex: ×β α group: Qualifier ×[
αα	catch a ride on the monorail <u>to the ritzy shopping centre of Sydney</u>, ||	group: Epithet (*ritzy*)	group: Qualifier (*of Sydney*)	clause, trans.: Place
α×β	taking in the Queen Victoria Building and Centrepoint <u>on the way</u>. |||			clause, trans.: Place
1	Then cross <u>Hyde Park and the Domain to the Art Gallery of N.S.W.</u>, ||		group: Qualifier (*of N.S.W.*)	clause, conj.: Conjunctive clause, trans.: Scope clause, trans.: Place
×2	<u>and</u> finish the afternoon <u>with</u> a visit to Fort Denison on Sydney Harbour, <u>or with</u> a Captain Cook Cruise <u>on</u> the Harbour. |||		group complex: 1 +2	clause complex: 1 ×2 clause, trans.: Means group: Qualifier ×[
	Hail a cab <u>to</u> Dixon Street in the centre of Sydney's Chinatown. |||		group: Qualifier (*of Sydney's Chinatown*); Deictic (*Sydney's*)	clause, trans.: Place
α	Many of the restaurants offer a Chinese breakfast ||	group: Classifier (*Chinese*)		
×β	<u>if</u> you've missed your breakfast. |||		group: Deictic (*your*)	clause complex: α ×β
α	<u>Nearby</u>, <u>on</u> the corner of Hay Street and Harbour Street, the Sydney Entertainment Centre, the largest indoor auditorium <u>in</u> Australia, << >> <u>is</u> a venue for concerts, ice skating events, indoor tennis tournaments and so on.	clause, trans: Process: intensive group: Epithet (*largest*)	group: Qualifier (*of Hay Street and Harbour Street*)	clause, trans: Place group: Classifier (*indoor*); Qualifier ×[
=β1	<<opened <u>in</u> 1983 ||			clause, trans.: Time
=β+2	<u>and</u> seating up to 12,50>>		clause complex: 1 +2	

Table 10-2 Manifestations of expansion in an extract from an enabling: instructing text, a topographic procedure [Text 22] (*contd*)

	Clause	Elaboration	Extension	Enhancement
×β1α	To find out ‖			
×β1'β	who's in town ‖			clause, trans.: Process: intensive + Attribute: circ.
×β+2	and to make bookings ‖		clause complex: 1 +2	
α1	go to the booking office in the Entertainment Centre ‖			clause, trans: Place group: Classifier (*booking*)
α+2	or ring Mitchells Bass on 266 4800. ‖‖		clause complex: 1 +2	

either a possessive Deictic (*your, Sydney's*) or a possessive Qualifier (*of Sydney*). In addition, extension is manifested within the domains of clause and group/ phrase complexes (e.g. *go to the booking office ... or ring Mitchells Bass*; *with a visit to Fort Denison on Sydney Harbour, or with a Captain Cook Cruise on the Harbour*). Here the sense is addition or alternation.

The extract from the topographic procedure illustrates how pervasive elaboration, extension and enhancement are as semantic types that are manifested throughout the grammatical system. Our sketchy analysis illustrates how we can develop a picture of these three types of expansion in a given text – or, if we enlarge the sample, in a particular register. Topographic procedures are dominated by enhancement at different ranks, within both simplexes and complexes; but any given register will be characterized by its own distribution of these types of expansion. As we shall see in Section 10.3, registers also vary with respect to where along the rank scale elaboration, extension and enhancement tend to appear.

Let us now present a systematic and comprehensive summary of the different grammatical environments in which elaboration, extension and enhancement are manifested: see Table 10-3. As the table shows, the environments of manifestation can be differentiated in terms of (i) metafunction – textual (CONJUNCTION), logical (INTERDEPENDENCY; MODIFICATION) and experiential (CIRCUMSTANTIATION; PROCESS TYPE: relational), and (ii) rank – clause and group/phrase. (The table could, in fact, be extended downwards along the rank scale to take account of patterns below the rank of group/phrase within the logical metafunction: word and morpheme complexes also embody interdependency relations that combine with expansion.)

From a grammatical point of view, the environments set out in Table 10-3 are, of course, all different. But seen from above, from the vantage point of semantics, they are all agnate ways of construing expansion. Collectively they thus construe expansion as a semantic system. This means that for any given type of expansion we want to express, we have at our disposal a range of resources. For example, if we want to express an enhancing relationship of cause, the opportunities made available by the grammar include the one set out in Table 10-4.

Table 10-3 Synoptic summary of expansion

			Textual clause — CONJUNCTION between clause complexes (non-structural)	Logical clause nexus — INTERDEPENDENCY between clauses in clause nexus — paratactic	hypotactic	[non-finite clause]	Experiential nom. group — embedding: DEFINING RELATIVE CLAUSE	clause — CIRCUM-STANTIATION	Logical verbal group (nexus) — PHASE, CONATION &c. in verbal group nexus (TENSE, VOICE in verbal group)		Experiential Clause — ATTRIBUTION or IDENTIFICATION as relational process
elaboration	apposition	Expository	in other words	that is	which, who	[non-finite clause]	which, who; that [non-finite clause]	as ROLE	PASSIVE VOICE is $[v^n]$	PHASE (a) TIME start, keep (b) REALITY seem, turn out	INTENSIVE 'is' be, mean, etc.;
		Exemplificatory	for example								exemplify, illustrate
	clarification	(various types)	or rather, anyway, actually, etc.	at least							
extension	addition	positive	also	and	while	besides	whose, of which	with, including, ACCOMP.	PAST TENSE has $[v^n]$	CONATION try; succeed; can, learn	POSSESSIVE 'has' complement; include
		negative	neither	nor		without		without			exclude
		adversative	however	but	whereas	—		—	OBLIGATION has to $[v^p]$		
	variation	replacive	on the contrary			besides		instead of			replace
		subtractive	otherwise	only	except that; if not ... then	other than		except (for)			
	alternative	alternative	alternatively	or				—			
enhancement	spatio-temporal: place	extent	—	—	as far as	—	(a) place (where/that); (b) where/at which	DISTANCE for	PRESENT TENSE is (at) $[v^n]$	MODULATION —	CIRCUMSTANTIAL 'is at' (a) take up, cover; (b) —

		Textual: clause — CONJUNCTION between clause complexes (non-structural)	Logical: clause nexus — INTERDEPENDENCY (paratactic)	INTERDEPENDENCY (hypotactic)	Experiential: nom. group — embedding; DEFINING RELATIVE CLAUSE	embedding; DEFINING RELATIVE CLAUSE	clause — CIRCUM-STANTIATION	Logical: verbal group (nexus) — PHASE, CONATION &c. in verbal group nexus (TENSE, VOICE in verbal group)	Experiential: Clause — ATTRIBUTION or IDENTIFICATION as relational process
spatio-temporal: time	point(s)	there	there	where(ver)	—		PLACE at, in, etc.	EXPECTATION is to [v^0]	(a) contain, face, line &c; (b) be at, etc.
	extent	throughout	—	while	while, in	(a) time (when/that); (b) when/on which	DURATION for	begin by, end up (by), tend	(a) last, take up; (b) be throughout
	point(s)	simultaneously	now	when(ever)	when, on		TIME at, on		(a) – (b) be at
	prior	previously	—	before, until	before, until		before		(a) precede; (b) be before
	subsequent	next	then	after, since	after, since		after		(a) follow; (b) be after
	various complex types	finally, at once, meanwhile, etc.	—	as soon as, etc.	—		during, etc.		(a) conclude, coincide with
manner	means	thus	—	—	by	way (how/that)	MANNER by, with	—	(a) enable; (b) be through
	quality	—	—	—	—		[adverb]	venture, hasten, hesitate, regret	
	comparison	likewise	so	as, as if	like, as if		like	—	(a) resemble; (b) be like

Table 10-3 Synoptic summary of expansion (*contd*)

		Textual	Logical			Experiential		Logical	Experiential
		clause	clause nexus			nom. group	clause	verbal group (nexus)	Clause
		CONJUNCTION between clause complexes (non-structural)	INTERDEPENDENCY between clauses in clause nexus			embedding: DEFINING RELATIVE CLAUSE	CIRCUM-STANTIATION	PHASE, CONATION &c. in verbal group nexus (TENSE, VOICE in verbal group)	ATTRIBUTION or IDENTIFICATION as relational process
			paratactic	hypotactic					
causal-conditional: cause	reason	therefore	so, for	because	with, by	reason (why/that)	CAUSE because of	happen, remember	(a) cause; (b) be because of
	result	consequently	thus	so that	as a result of				
	purpose	to that end	–	in order that, so that	(so as/ in order) to, for		for	try	
	insurance	–	–	in case	in case of		in case of		
causal-conditional: condition	positive	in that case	then	if, as long as	if, in the event of		in the event of		(a) depend on; (b) be in the event of
	negative	otherwise	otherwise	unless	without		in default of		
	concessive	nevertheless	though	although	despite		despite		
matter	respective	in this respect	–	–	as for		MATTER about		(a) concern; (b) be about

672

Table 10-4 Manifestations of the enhancing relationship of cause

Domain	System	Metafunction	Example
cohesive sequence:	conjunction	textual	She didn't know the rules. Consequently, she died.
clause, complex:	parataxis	logical	She didn't know the rules; so she died.
	hypotaxis		Because she didn't know the rules, she died.
clause, simplex:	causation	logical + experiential	Her ignorance of the rules caused her to die.
	circumstantiation	experiential	Through ignorance of the rules, she died.
	relational process		Her death was due to ignorance of the rules.
			Her ignorance of the rules caused her death.
			The cause of her death was her ignorance of the rules.
nominal group:	qualification		Her death through ignorance of the rules.

These patterns of wording are agnate, but just like agnate patterns in general they are not synonymous: agnation always embodies both similarity and difference. The similarity is the basis for interpreting the patterns as alike, bringing them together within a paradigm, while the difference is the basis for treating them as variant types rather than as tokens of the same type. The patterns are similar in that they are all manifestations of different kinds of expansion, as illustrated by the examples of the enhancing notion of cause above. But how do the agnate variants differ in meaning? As always with questions of meaning, the answer can be found in its metafunctional organization: differences turn out to be (i) ideational, (ii) textual and (iii) interpersonal.

   (i) Ideational. From an ideational point of view, the difference in meaning relates most directly to the question of what is construed as a quantum of change in the flow of events (cf. Chapter 8, Section 8.9). The examples in Table 10-4 form a scale extended between two poles. At one pole, the experience of the flow of events is construed as two distinct quanta of change, realized by two independent clauses that are related cohesively but not structurally (*She didn't know the rules. Consequently, she died.*). At the other pole, the experience of the flow of events is construed as a component part of a quantum of change – a participant that can itself be an element of some other quantum of change (cf. *the quite incredible ignorance on which it is based must be a cause for grave concern*), realized by a single nominal group (*her death through ignorance of the rules*). Intermediate between these two poles are various manifestations that represent a move from two distinct quanta of change via two interdependent ones to a single one.

   The scale is thus one of **degree of integration of two quanta of change**. This scale of integration is based on the rank scale. At one pole, the sequence of cohesively related clauses transcends the rank scale, and, at the other, the nominal group is located at the rank below that of the clause. These two poles are thus connected by a move down the rank scale. At the same time, this move involves a shift in metafunction: textual – logical – logical + experiential – experiential. Here the meaning of expansion changes with the

673

change of metafunctional manifestation. For example, the manifestation of cause changes from rhetorical relation (textual: *consequently*) via logico-semantic relation (logical: *so*, *because*) to process or minor process and even participant (experiential: *cause*, *through*; *cause*). This means that the category meaning of 'cause' changes; so while, for example, *consequently* and *through* share the meaning of cause, they differ in the category meanings they assign to it. (We shall see below that some of these realizations of cause are, in fact, ideational metaphors within the domain of the grammar.)

(ii) Textual. The different domains of manifestation of expansion, illustrated for cause in Table 10-4, are textually distinct. When the domain of manifestation is a cohesive sequence of clauses or a nexus of tactically related clauses, the conjunction group realizing the causal relation is given a textual status within the clause in which it appears: it is either textual Theme or part of the Rheme. While a conjunction group with a structural conjunction such as *so* or *because* as Head is obligatorily thematic, there is a choice for conjunction groups with a cohesive conjunction such as *consequently* as Head:

Consequently, the fields had to remain dry while the authorities "dwelled on the matter." [KOHL_A]

Encouraged by the favourable Chinese pronouncements, the Indian Maoists **consequently** did not undertake any independent ideological studies and discussions. [KOHL_C]

These two factors **consequently** lead to a prediction, lower than the actual settlement value for the pile group. [KOHL_J]

In a hypotactic nexus, there is a further textual contrast that is not open to cohesive sequences and paratactic nexuses: the dependent β clause representing the cause may be either thematic or rhematic within the clause nexus; for example:

<u>Because the supply of tortoise shell has decreased with the years</u> the work is not produced profusely any more. [KOHL_E]

They do this strenuous and risky work <u>because it would be difficult to make both ends meet</u> if they relied solely on the income of the male members. [KOHL_A]

When the domain of manifestation of expansion is a simple clause, the potential textual status of the manifestation of the cause depends on how it manifested – (1) as minor Process within a prepositional phrase serving as a circumstance of Cause, (2) as Process, or (3) as Thing within a nominal group serving as a participant in a circumstantial relational clause.

(1) When it is manifested within a circumstance of Cause, the cause may be given the status of either Theme or Rheme, and, if it is Theme, it may be given the status of predicated Theme; for example:

<u>**Because of this action**</u> physiological responses have been possible. [KOHL_B]

||| It was **because of the protracted delays** [[**caused by litigation**]] [[that land ceiling laws were put in the Ninth Schedule of the Constitution || to give them immunity [[from being challenged in the courts]]]]. ||| [KOHL_B]

||| <u>The country</u> was incurring a loss of Rs. 4,000 crores in industrial production every year, **because of the acute power crisis**, || Mr. S. K. Birla, President, Indian Chamber of Commerce, said here yesterday. ||| [KOHL_A]

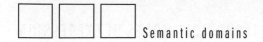

(2) When the causal relation is manifested as Process (either in a hypotactic verbal group complex in a clause of any process type, or as the nuclear process in a circumstantial relational clause), its textual status will most likely be rhematic. More specifically, it is likely to be (part of) the transition between Theme and New. For example:

> Encouraged by the favourable Chinese pronouncements, the Indian Maoists consequently did not undertake any independent ideological studies and discussions. They just mechanically applied Chinese strategy, emulating particularly the ideological activities of the Chinese Red Guards during the Cultural Revolution. This **caused** an ideological stagnation, whose impact was noticed in 1973. [KOHL_C]

(3) When the cause is manifested as the Thing in a nominal group serving as a participant, it will have the thematic status assigned to that nominal group as a whole – either thematic or rhematic. But, in addition, it will be within the domain of operation of another textual system – the system of REFERENCE (see Chapter 9, Section 9.4). This means that it is given a textual status as a discourse referent – either recoverable (identifiable) or non-recoverable (non-identifiable), and that it can be tracked in the development of the discourse. For example:

> India, the World Cup winners of 1975, had been pushed down five places in the 1978 World Cup: the world champions of one time had been wiped out. The opposition had been improving all along. Pakistan, who won the gold at Buenos Aires, Holland who won the silver, Australia who won the bronze, West Germany who were fourth, Spain who were fifth, and New Zealand, who did not play at this World Cup but who won the gold at Montreal in 1976, all these countries had been taking longer, and faster strides in world hockey. India had also been striding, with the strides becoming longer, and faster. But India had been striding backwards. Towards the destruction of its own hockey. **The real cause** had been the power-game which the Indian hockey bosses play. The 1978 Buenos Aires experience was a consequence. It was one massive stride backwards. It was <u>an effect of **the same cause**</u>. The alleged mismanagement of the Indian team at Buenos Aires was merely a symptom, an indication that **this cause** was working. It was not **the cause** itself, as it has been made out to be. And Indian hockey continues to stride backwards. The strides are becoming longer. The pace is increasing. **The cause** still exists. The power-game continues to be played. [KOHL_E]

(iii) Interpersonal. Just as the different domains of manifestation are textually distinct, they are also interpersonally distinct. When the domain of manifestation is a cohesive sequence of clauses, or a paratactic nexus of (free) clauses, the two figures related by expansion are enacted interpersonally as propositions or proposals. This means that each of them can be negotiated in their own right – accepted or denied, complied with or refused, and so on, as in *she didn't know the rules – oh yes, she certainly did*. The same is true of the dominant (α) clause of a hypotactic nexus, since if it is a free clause, it realizes a negotiable proposition or proposal. However, while the dependent (β) clause supports a proposition or proposal, it does not constitute one itself (cf. Matthiessen & Thompson, 1988); and if it is non-finite, it is even further removed from the realm of negotiation. A causal dependent clause (e.g. *because she didn't know the rules*) is thus not presented as directly accessible to negotiation; it has to be accepted without argument.

When the domain of manifestation is a simple clause, there is just a single proposition rather than two. This obviously restricts the scope for negotiation; but when the causal relation is construed within the Process, it has become propositionalized or proposalized, and can be assessed, e.g.

675

(permanent loss of the sense of smell) **may be caused** by a disorder affecting the part of the brain responsible for interpreting smell sensations [ACE]

and negotiated, e.g.

Hi, Mr. Jennings, if the United States goes to war with Iraq, **wouldn't** the unprovoked nature of U.S. military action **lead to** even greater resentment of the U.S. in the Arab world, and thus make the United States even more vulnerable to future terrorist attacks? [King Interviews]

Here it is no longer the cause or the effect that is held up for negotiation but rather the causal relation. Being construed as nominal groups, the cause and the effect are not negotiable at all.

10.2.2 Projection

Let's now turn to the semantic domain of projection. Like expansion, projection is manifested both logically and experientially within the ideational metafunction; but outside the ideational domain, it is manifested interpersonally rather than textually, thus contrasting with the textual manifestation of expansion: see Table 10-5. That is, while there are conjunctions marking rhetorical relations of elaboration, extension and enhancement (as shown in Table 9-6), there are no conjunctions marking relations of quoting or reporting; and while there are interpersonal resources for realizing projection (e.g. *allegedly* 'they allege'; *probably* 'I think'), there are no interpersonal Adjuncts or other interpersonal manifestations of expansion. There is thus a significant difference between expansion and projection. We shall explore this difference further; but let us first consider some text examples illustrating the dispersal of projection in the grammatical system.

Table 10-5 Manifestation of expansion and projection at clause rank

		Expansion	Projection
textual	CONJUNCTION	types of conjunction	–
logical	INTERDEPENDENCY	expansion nexuses	projection nexuses (quoting & reporting)
experiential	PROCESS TYPE	relational: intensive/possessive/circumstantial	mental/verbal
	CIRCUMSTANTIATION	role/accompaniment/ location, extent, cause, etc.	angle/matter
interpersonal	MODAL ASSESSMENT	–	modality, polarity; comment

When the need arises in discourse to attribute information to some source, this can be done logically by means of clause nexus of projection (Chapter 7, Section 7.5); but it can also be done experientially by means of a circumstance of Angle (Chapter 5, Section 5.6.2). Both strategies are uses in news reports, as illustrated in Text 10-3.

Text 10-3: Reporting – chronicling: extract from a news report

Gunfire rang through the National Zoo on Monday evening as a feud between youths turned violent, leaving six children wounded. A 12-year-old boy was in grave condition, **according to witnesses and authorities**.

Capt. Brian Lee, a spokesman for the District of Columbia Fire and Emergency Medical Services, <u>said</u> one boy suffered grave wounds to the head and the others did not appear to have life-threatening injuries. One girl was in serious condition with a gunshot wound to the chest. A seventh victim suffered a seizure, Lee <u>said</u>. [Text 20]

Here the status of *a 12-year-old boy was in grave condition* is represented circumstantially by means of the Angle *according to witnesses and authorities*; the projecting feature has thus been incorporated into the clause as one element of the transitivity configuration. In contrast, the next two manifestations of projection both involve clause nexuses. In such a nexus, the projected part and the projecting part are both given the status of clauses in their own right.

Projection can also be manifested interpersonally in the form of a modal Adjunct (Chapter 4, Section 4.3.2). Thus in Text 10-4, projection is manifested both logically as clause nexus and interpersonally as modal Adjunct. Both strategies are aspects of the journalistic need to indicate the status of the information being imparted.

Text 10-4: Reporting – chronicling: extract from a news report [Text 5]

||| Storm stops search for ferry survivors |||

From AP and AAP correspondents in Bangkok

24oct98

||| THE search for passengers [[[missing || after a ferry capsized in the Gulf of Thailand]]] has been delayed by a storm, || marine police <u>said</u> yesterday. |||

||| At least 20 people – including two Australian women and a pregnant Thai woman – died || when the boat capsized in early morning darkness on Wednesday || while travelling to Koh Tao, an island [[popular with young travellers]] . |||

||| The Australians were Melbourne scuba diving instructor Gabrielle Sandercock, 33, << whose family come from Adelaide >>, and Naomi Leslie, 24, of Perth, || who had been working on the island resorts [[near where the accident occurred]]. |||

||| The heavy storm has delayed the operation for a second straight day, || <u>said</u> an officer. |||

||| An unknown number of passengers are still missing || and police <u>presume</u> || they are dead. |||

||| The ferry was **reportedly** carrying about 40 passengers || when it capsized. ||| German agency DPA <u>said</u> || 24 people were still missing. ||| Survivors <u>told</u> police || they had to kick out glass windows in the section [[where they were sleeping]] || to escape from the sinking boat. ||| ...

Unlike the logical and experiential manifestations, the interpersonal manifestation does not represent the Sayer or Senser; rather it enacts the speaker's opinion – an enactment of his or her degree of commitment to the proposition: the proposition is assessed as being projected by somebody other than the speaker. This type of assessment is known as 'evidentiality': the modal Adjunct is used to indicate the evidential status of the proposition. The nearest logical equivalent would be 'people say/they say that ...', or 'I hear that': evidentiality is related to 'verbal' clauses and 'mental' clauses of perception.

In Chapter 4, we called this kind of modal assessment **presumption** (see Figure 4-26); the comment Adjunct is realized by adverbial groups with adverbs as Head such as

677

evidently, supposedly, reportedly, allegedly; arguably; presumably and they may have cognate verbs such as *report, allege, argue* serving as Process in a 'verbal' clause or *suppose, presume* serving as Process in a 'mental' clause. The following example illustrates the force of 'presumption':

> iTunes deletes foreign files? **Evidently** iTunes will delete a WinAmp playlist file if the user attempts to open it from iTunes. John Willsey **writes**: "My Mac is on a network which has a volume of shared files with MP3 files and several PC-created WinAmp playlists. I was surprised to see the playlist files show up with an iTunes icon and identified as iTunes documents on the Mac. However, when opening the playlist instead of displaying an error that the file count not be read, iTunes promptly deleted the playlist file." [www.maxfixit.com]

The writer first indicates by means of *evidently* that the status of the proposition is presumed and then goes on to provide the basis for this presumption, which is represented by means of a projecting clause nexus (*John Willsey writes: "My Mac is ..."*).

Projection is thus manifested interpersonally as modal assessment of the presumption type; but it extends beyond presumption to cover quite a few other types of modal assessment as well (cf. Matthiessen, 2007c). These are exemplified below. As the examples show, projection includes both hypotactic projection of ideas/reports and pre-projected facts serving in a 'mental' or 'relational' clause (cf. Chapter 4, Table 4-3). A hypotactic projection is always 'subjective'; the speaker is represented explicitly as the Senser (e.g. *I presume*) or Sayer (e.g. *I admit*). A pre-projected fact in a 'mental' clause is like hypotactic projection in representing the assessment as 'subjective' – the speaker is explicitly represented as the Senser (e.g. *I regret*). In contrast, a pre-projected fact in a 'relational' clause represents the assessment as 'objective' (e.g. *it is regrettable*); but it may be 'prefaced' by a 'mental' clause with a 'subjective' orientation:

> **I think** || **it is astounding** [[that hardly any of the original families are left]]. [ACE_G]

The spread in manifestation can be illustrated for two types of modal assessment, prediction and admission:

propositional: prediction
The instructors, **surprisingly**, are human, helpful, good humoured, and have the uncanny knack when partnering you to make you feel like a good dancer. [LOB_E]

Not surprisingly, No. 9, the "playing at horses" number, used most probably for the lovers' meeting, is precisely the same as Bordeaux No. 8, even to the extent of reproducing a bowing indication – a great rarity in the Herold score. [LOB_G]

I'm not surprised [[[he died || thinking the novel was a failure]]] || because its structure and its sentiments collided at that point [[where they pass Cairo]]. [Text 17]

In these circumstances, **it is not surprising** [[[to find || that the philosophes looked for reform from above, not below]]]. [Text 122]

speech-functional: admission
I like surprise in stories || and **quite frankly** I like humor, ... [Text 21]

Indian media, on their part, must, **admittedly**, within financial limitations, stir themselves a little more and discover some more Sayeed Naqvis abroad, who have dash, enterprise, contacts and talent, so that such interviews and coverage for Doordarshan are not sporadic but steady. [KOHL_C]

"That was pretty obvious," smiled Sir Cedric, "and **I admit** I once had doubts about you." [LOB_L]

It is to be admitted, however, that a few drill attachments have been put on the market which are unsound in design and poor in quality, and should be avoided. [LOB_E]

It's true [[that there are times [[when the odd homily might be offered by (*laughs*) me]]]], || but generally speaking I think || the parliament is, by parliamentary standards, well behaved. [Text 184]

Projection is thus dispersed across different grammatical environments. But the different manifestations of projection are not, of course, synonymous. The ideational manifestations make explicit the orientation of the assessment: the logical manifestation is explicitly subjective (e.g. *I regret*) whereas the experiential manifestation is explicitly objective (e.g. *it's regrettable*). In contrast, the interpersonal manifestation leaves the orientation implicit:

ideational, logical – nexus:	explicit orientation: subjective (*I regret*)
ideational, exper. – 2 clauses:	explicit orientation: objective (*it's regrettable*)
interpersonal – 1 clause:	implicit orientation (*regrettably*)

The difference between 'subjective' and 'objective' orientation in the ideational manifestation follows from the general difference between a projecting 'mental' or 'verbal' clause with a Senser or Sayer and a 'relational' clause without such a 'projector' (see Chapter 7, Section 7.5.7). When the assessment is explicitly 'subjective', the Senser or Sayer has to be the speaker *I* if the clause is 'declarative' or the addressee *you* if it is 'interrogative' (as in *Do you regret that it's taken so long for you and your dad to get to work together?*). If it is a person other than the speaker or addressee, the clause will still be a projecting one; but it will not be agnate with an interpersonal assessment. Thus in the following example –

Grudgingly, Manning admitted that the other's guess had not been too bad a one. [LOB_L]

Manning's admission is construed as part of the experiential representation of a figure of saying, and the clause does not enact the speaker's admission. We shall come back to this point below, explaining it by reference to interpersonal metaphor.

The full range of modal assessment is shown in Table 10-6. The table indicates the different realizational domains of modal assessment, and it gives an indication of where categories of modal assessment correspond to categories of appraisal as described by J.R. Martin, Peter White and others (see e.g. Eggins & Slade, 2005; Martin & Rose, 2003). We have also noted assessments that may be realized as the Epithet of a nominal group. Such nominal groups serve as the Attribute of an intensive attributive relational clause with a fact as Carrier – the explicitly objective form of assessment. However, such Epithets of assessment may be assigned to things as well as to metathings: either the nominal group in which the Epithet serves is the Attribute assigned to a Carrier denoting a thing rather than a metathing, or else the Epithet is assigned directly to the Thing of the nominal group in which it serves. For example:

propositional: prediction
It is worth noting that the appearance of the ozone hole was an **unexpected** event in the sense that the models referred to by Albritton did not predict the hole. [Text 33]

Table 10-6 Modal assessment: domains of realization

TYPE OF MODAL ASSESSMENT				Domain of manifestation									nominal group	
				clause						clause				
				clause + clause						Angle	modal Adjunct	Predicator	post-Deictic	Epithet
				verbal clause	mental 'like' clause	mental 'please' clause	relational 'I am' clause	relational 'it is' clause						
				finite				finite	non-finite	prep. phrase	adv. gp.; prep. phrase	verbal group	adjective	adjective
comment: propositional	on Subject	wisdom	wise						it is wise of x [[to …]]	–	wisely, cleverly	x is wise to …		wise, clever
			unwise						it is foolish of x [[to …]]	–	foolishly, stupidly	x is foolish to		foolish, stupid
		morality	moral						it is right of x [[to …]]	–	rightly, justly, correctly	x is right to …		right, just, correct
			immoral						it is wrong of x [[to …]]	–	wrongly, unjustifiably	x is wrong to …		wrong, unjustifiable
		typicality							it is typical of x [[to …]]	–	characteristically, typically	x is wont to …		characteristic, typical
	on whole	asseverative [tone 1]	natural					it is natural [[that …]]		–	naturally, inevitably, of course			natural, inevitable
			obvious					it is obvious [[that …]]		–	obviously, clearly, plainly, of course		obvious, clear, transparent	
			sure		I + not + doubt		I + have + no doubt	it is indubitable [[that …]]		–	doubtless, indubitably, no doubt			indubitable
		qualificative [tone 4]	prediction / predictable		I + expect			it is predictable [[that …]]		–	unsurprisingly, predictably			unsurprising, predictable

Domain of manifestation

Type of modal assessment		clause + clause						clause			nominal group	
		verbal clause	mental 'like' clause	mental 'please' clause	relational 'I am' clause	relational 'it is' clause		Angle	modal Adjunct	Predicator	post-Deictic	Epithet
		finite				finite	non-finite	prep. phrase	adv. gp.; prep. phrase	verbal group	adjective	adjective
	unpredictable		I + not + expect			it is surprising [[that ...]]		–	surprisingly, unexpectedly			surprising, unexpected
presumption	hearsay	they + say; it + be said	I + hear					according to + x	evidently, allegedly, supposedly	be said/ rumoured to	alleged, so-called, self-styled, putative	
	argument	I + argue				it is arguable [[that ...]]		–	arguably		arguable	
	guess		I + presume					–	presumably, supposedly		presumed, supposed	
desirability	desirable: luck		I + rejoice					–	luckily, fortunately			lucky, fortunate, happy, encouraging
	[desirable: reaction]			it fascinates + me [[that ...]]		it is wonderful [[that ...]]		–	wonderfully, fascinatingly			wonderful, fascinating, lovely
	[undesirable: security]				I am confident [[that ...]]			–	–			confident, assured

Table 10-6 Modal assessment: domains of realization (*contd*)

TYPE OF MODAL ASSESSMENT	Domain of manifestation										
	clause						clause			nominal group	
	clause + clause						Angle	modal Adjunct	Predicator	post-Deictic	Epithet
	verbal clause	mental 'like' clause	mental 'please' clause	relational 'I am' clause	relational 'it is' clause		prep. phrase	adv. gp.; prep. phrase	verbal group	adjective	adjective
	finite				finite	non-finite					
[desirability: dissatisfaction]			it interests +me [[that ...]]		it is interesting [[that ...]]		–	interestingly			interested, absorbed
desirable: hope		I + hope					–	hopefully			hopeful
undesirable		I + regret					–	sadly: unfortunately, regrettably, to my distress			sad, unfortunate, regrettable, distressing
[undesirable: reaction]			it disgusts +me [[that ...]]		it is horrible/ [[that ...]]		–	horribly, boringly			horrible, boring, revolting
[undesirable: insecurity]				I + am + anxious [[that ...]]			–	–			worried, anxious, uneasy
[undesirable: dissatisfaction]			it displeases +me [[that ...]]		it is tiring [[that ...]]		–	annoyingly, tiresomely			tired, fed up, exasperate
amusement			it amuses +me [[that ...]]		it is funny [[that ...]]			funnily, amusingly			
significance					it is important [[that ...]]			importantly, significantly			

		Domain of manifestation									nominal group	
		clause + clause						clause		Predicator	post-Deictic	Epithet
		verbal clause	mental 'like' clause	mental 'please' clause	relational 'I am' clause	relational 'it is' clause		Angle	modal Adjunct			
		finite				finite	non-finite	prep. phrase	adv. gp.; prep. phrase	verbal group	adjective	adjective
comment: speech-functional	**unqualified**											
	persuasive 'I grant you'	I + admit						–	admittedly, certainly			
	'I assure you'	I + assure						–	honestly, truly, seriously			
	factual	I + tell + you							actually, really			
	qualified [tone 4]											
	validity (degree of) general	I + tell + you + in general terms						–	generally, broadly, roughly			
	specific	I + tell + you + in terms of the law						–	academically, legally, politically			
	personal engagement (claim for) honesty	I + tell + you + honestly						–	frankly, candidly			
	secrecy	I + tell + you + in confidence						–	confidentially, between you and me			
	individuality							to + x	personally, for my part			
	accuracy	I + tell + you + strictly						–	truly, strictly			

Table 10-6 Modal assessment: domains of realization (*contd*)

TYPE OF MODAL ASSESSMENT			Domain of manifestation										
			clause + clause						clause		Predicator	nominal group	
			verbal clause	mental 'like' clause	mental 'please' clause	relational 'I am' clause	relational 'it is' clause		Angle	modal Adjunct		post-Deictic	Epithet
			finite	finite			finite	non-finite	prep. phrase	adv. gp.; prep. phrase	verbal group	adjective	adjective
mood		hesitancy	I + suggest + to you						–	tentatively, provisional			
	temporality	relative to now								eventually, soon, once, just			
		relative to expectation								still, already, no longer, not yet			
	modality	modalization — probability		I guess/think/know → that ...			it is possible/probable/certain [[that ...]]		–	perhaps, probably, certainly		possible, probable, certain	
		usuality	–					it is usual/common [[for ... to ...]]	–	sometimes, often, always		usual, common	
		modulation — potentiality						it is possible [[for ... to ...]]	–	–	be able to		
		inclination							–	–	be willing/keen/eager to		

TYPE OF MODAL ASSESSMENT

		Domain of manifestation										
		clause									nominal group	
		clause + clause				clause						
		verbal clause	mental 'like' clause	mental 'please' clause	relational 'I am' clause	relational 'it is' clause		Angle	modal Adjunct	Predicator	post-Deictic	Epithet
		finite				finite	non-finite	prep. phrase	adv. gp.; prep. phrase	verbal group	adjective	adjective
	obligation	I want → you to …						–	–	be allowed/ expected/ required to		
intensity	degree — total								totally, utterly			total, utter, complete
	degree — high								almost, quite, nearly			
	degree — low								scarcely, hardly			
	counter-expectancy								even, actually; just, simply			

propositional: presumption

So now in 1945 the Russians were quick to take advantage of the all too **evident** disunity among those from whose efforts they had, since 1941 only, been glad to benefit. [LOB_G]

propositional: desirability

"Killing Mister Watson" is Peter Matthiessen's sixth and **most impressive** novel, a fiction in the tradition of Joseph Conrad, as fiercely incisive as the work of Sinclair Lewis, a virtuoso performance [[that powerfully indicts the heedlessness and hidden criminality [[that are part and parcel of America's devotion to the pursuit of wealth, to its cult of financial success]]]]. [Text 117]

speech-functional: admission

He exercised his discretion in favour of the husband's **admitted** adultery. [LOB_A]

Here the Thing of the nominal group is assessed by means of an interpersonal Epithet (Chapter 6, Section 6.2.1.3); for example, *impressive* in the nominal group *most impressive novel* constitutes the writer's positive evaluation of the entity denoted by the nominal group. Certain assessments serve as post-Deictic rather than as Epithet, as in *these alleged two burglars*. Here the referent's membership in the class denoted by the Thing is assessed; the sense is 'these two are allegedly burglars'. But whether the assessment is Epithet or post-Deictic, it can be related to projection: 'this novel impresses me the most', 'they allege that these two are (the) burglars'.

The range of assessments assigned to propositions within the domain of the clause and the range of assessments assigned to things within the domain of the nominal group are not, of course, the same. They overlap; but there are kinds of assessment specific to the realm of propositions, just as there are other kinds specific to the realm of things. The common foundation is that they are both projections of the speaker's assessment. This explains why clausal assessment can in fact be transformed into nominal assessment, as in *disappointingly they forecast that ... => the disappointing forecast*. Such instances of grammatical metaphor will be discussed below.

One type of clausal assessment we have not yet discussed is modality. We shall now turn to this, using it as the way into grammatical metaphor.

10.3 MODALITY

10.3.1 Metaphorical expansion of MODALITY

In the previous section, we gave an account of modal assessment as a semantic domain extending across more than one grammatical environment. We treated these different grammatical environments as alternative forms of expression, in the same way that we diagrammed the domain of expansion in Figure 10-2. But this is only part of the story, as we see when we turn to the kind of modal assessment known as MODALITY (see Chapter 4, Section 4.5). With modality, it is very clear that certain grammatical environments constitute metaphorical realizations of modality.

An example of metaphor in modality was given in Chapter 3 (see Figure 3-17): *I don't believe that pudding ever will be cooked*, where it was pointed out that *I don't believe* is functioning as an expression of modality, as can be shown by the tag, which would be *will it?*, not *do I?*. The example was brought in at that point in order to explain the thematic structure; let us now represent this same clause in a way that brings out the metaphoric element in its modal structure (see Figure 10-3).

686

'probably'			'that pudding	never	will	be cooked'
Modality: probability			Subject	Modality: usuality	Finite	Predicator
Mood						Residue

I	don't	believe	that pudding	ever	will	be cooked
α			'β			
Subject	Finite	Predicator	Subject	Modality	Finite	Predicator
Mood		Residue	Mood			Residue

Fig. 10-3   An interpersonal metaphor of modality

Here the cognitive mental clause *I don't believe* is a metaphorical realization of probability: the probability is realized by a mental clause **as if** it was a figure of sensing. Being metaphorical, the clause serves not only as the projecting part of a clause nexus of projection, but also as a mood Adjunct, just as *probably* does. The reason for regarding this as a metaphorical variant is that the proposition is not, in fact, 'I think'; the proposition is 'it is so'. This is shown clearly by the tag; if we tag the clause *I think it's going to rain* we get

I think it's going to rain, isn't it?

not *I think it's going to rain, don't I?*. In other words the clause is a variant of *it's probably going to rain* (*isn't it?*) and not a first-person equivalent of *John thinks it's going to rain*, which does represent the proposition 'John thinks' (tag *doesn't he?*). Thus in

You know ‖ what's happening tomorrow at five o'clock, don't you? [Text 82]

the 'mental' clause *you know* was able to be tagged because it does not stand for a modality.

It is the fact that mental clause is a modal clause and serves as mood Adjunct that explains the tag. If it was just an ordinary mental clause in a clause nexus of projection, *I don't believe* should be able to be tagged. But since it has a metaphorical status and serves as mood Adjunct, it cannot be tagged. Instead, the Moodtag picks up the Mood element of the modalized proposition: *that pudding probably never will ... will it?*

What's happened here is that there has been a **realignment** in the realizational relationship between semantics and grammar. The non-metaphorical alignment was set out in Figure 10-1: one message, one proposition and one figure are jointly realized by one clause. But in examples such as the one analysed in Figure 10-3, a modalized proposition is realized as if it was a sequence, by a clause nexus of projection. The effect is that the modality and the modalized proposition are separated, each being realized by a clause in its own right: the modality is realized by the projecting mental clause and the proposition by the projected idea clause.

The example in Figure 10-3 represents a very common type of interpersonal metaphor, based on the semantic relationship of projection. In this type the speaker's opinion regarding the probability that his observation is valid is coded not as a modal element within the clause, which would be its congruent realization, but as a separate, projecting clause in a hypotactic clause nexus. To the congruent form *it probably is so* corresponds the metaphorical variant *I think it is so*, with *I think* as the primary or 'alpha' clause.

687

There is, in fact, a wide range of variants for the expression of modality in the clause, and some of these take the form of a clause nexus. This range is comparable to what we found with other types of modal assessment. If we limit ourselves first to the meaning of 'probability', the principal categories are as shown in Table 10-7; corpus examples are given below:

(1a) Subjective, explicit ↘ as projecting mental clause + idea clause

||| **I guess** || we were a pretty pragmatic lot – including me. ||| [Text 21]

||| Em, **I suppose** || that made your pain worse, did it? ||| [Text 34]

||| No **I don't think** || it was superficial for him; || **I suppose** || he did feel it || but he he didn't think enough for me; || he he felt too much. ||| [Text 135]

||| So I wrote a column back to the paper [[[in which I said, || "**I know** || I'm not going to get invited to the wedding || because the Grimaldis and the Buchwalds have been feuding for five hundred years!"]]] ||| [Text 119]

(1b) Subjective, implicit ↘ clause, Mood – as Finite: modal auxiliary

||| Tsai, << who **could** be on the front line in possible talks with Beijing, >> **may** have been tapped for her experience [[in helping to negotiate Taiwan's bid [[to join the World Trade Organization]]]]. ||| [Text 13]

||| Family background, fellow artists and friends **may** be glimpsed in amiable disguise. ||| [Text 100]

(2a) Objective, implicit ↘ clause, Mood – as mood Adjunct: modal adverb

||| Under the Montreal Protocol, the concentration of chlorine will **certainly** rise to at least 5 ppbv || and **possibly** to as high as 8 or 9 ppbv. ||| [Text 33]

||| Now I know Indian people better, || and I know || that the guy **probably** didn't speak English, || or if he did, || he was ashamed of it. ||| [Text 7]

||| He felt || they **surely** would understand || when he talked like that! ||| [Text 119]

(2b) Objective, explicit ↘ relational clause with factual Carrier: clause and modal Attribute: nominal group

||| **It is certain** [[that he would never yield to the blackmail of the insubordinate generals]]. ||| [LOB_B]

||| **It is probable** [[that the benefit is continuous]], || and so the indefinite use of aspirin is recommended. ||| [COCA]

||| In other words, even in those circumstances [[where **it isn't possible** [[simply to bar the door to an inspection]]]], we have a range of tactics for struggle [[which will subvert the Ofsted process and the very reasons for its existence]]. ||| [Text 97]

What happens is that, in order to state explicitly that the probability is subjective, or alternatively, at the other end, to claim explicitly that the probability is objective, the speaker construes the proposition as a projection and encodes the subjectivity (I think), or the objectivity (it is likely), in a projecting clause. (There are other forms intermediate between the explicit and implicit: subjective *in my opinion*, objective *in all probability*, where the modality is expressed as a prepositional phrase, which is a kind of halfway house between clausal and non-clausal status.)

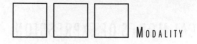
Table 10-7 Expressions of probability

Category		Type of realization	Example
(1) subjective	(a) explicit	I think, I'm certain	I think Mary knows
	(b) implicit	will, must	Mary'll know
(2) objective	(a) implicit	probably, certainly	Mary probably knows
	(b) explicit	it's likely, it's certain	it's likely Mary knows

Suppose now that Mary doesn't know, or at least we don't think she knows. There are now two possibilities in each of the 'explicit' forms:

(1) Subjective

I think Mary doesn't know/I don't think Mary knows

(2) Objective

it's likely Mary doesn't know/it isn't likely Mary knows

Here another metaphorical process has taken place: the transfer of the polarity feature into the primary clause (*I don't think, it isn't likely*). On the face of it, these are nonsensical: it is not the thinking that is being negated, nor can there be any such thing as a negative probability. But non-thought and negative probabilities cause no great problems in the semantics of natural language. Since the modality is being dressed up as a proposition, it is natural for it to take over the burden of yes or no.

Figure 10-4 gives the analysis of two of these examples.

10.3.2 A further account of modality

It is not always possible to say exactly what is and what is not a metaphorical representation of a modality. But speakers have indefinitely many ways of expressing their opinions – or rather, perhaps, of dissimulating the fact that they are expressing their opinions; for example:

It is obvious that this prediction has never yet been fulfilled, and looks on to a future day. [LOB_D]

It stands to reason that if a horse is too backward to race during his first season in training, he is most unlikely to be sufficiently mature to beat the best of his generation in the late May or early June of the following year, and it is a number of years now since a horse that embarked upon its three-year-old career unraced has won the Derby. [LOB_A]

Nobody tries to deny that the problem of immigration into Britain is primarily a problem of colour: the need for control was never raised so long as immigrants were largely European, as, until recently, they were. [LOB_A]

In the case of loans, therefore, **it is particularly difficult to avoid the conclusion that** they count as distributions even if they are made on commercial terms; but I do not regard the decision in the Chappie case as throwing no light on the construction of the rest of this Sub-section. [LOB_H]

There can be no doubt, however, **that** the imperial Byzantine silks have a power and a dignity, a feeling for design and texture, seldom rivalled in the history of textiles. [LOB_J]

'probably'				'Mary'	knows'	
Modality				Subject	Finite 'present'	Predicator know
Mood						Residue

it	seems		likely	that	Mary	knows	
α					'β		
Subject	Finite 'present'	Predicator seem	Complement		Subject	Finite 'present'	Predicator know
Mood		Residue			Mood		Residue

			'Mary'	won't	know'
			Subject	Finite/Modality/ Polarity	Predicator
			Mood		Residue
'in my opinion'			'Mary'	doesn't	know'
Modality			Subject	Finite/Polarity	Predicator
Mood					Residue

I	don't	think	Mary	knows	
α			'β		
Subject	Finite/Polarity	Predicator	Subject	Finite 'present'	Predicator know
Mood		Residue	Mood		Residue

Fig. 10-4 Analysis of probability expressions

Whatever the rights or wrongs of the dispute, **the impartial spectator** – if one can still be found – **will surely agree that** rarely has trade union loyalty faced a more baffling test. [LOB_B]

Any teacher will agree that it is impossible to pursue both lines effectively during a single year. [LOB_B]

Most people would agree that Immanuel Kant was a great thinker and also that he was hard to understand. [LOB_D]

And **everyone knows** that the changes have largely come from young people. [Text 209]

no sane person would pretend that ... not ...

commonsense determines that ...

all authorities on the subject are agreed that ...

you can't seriously doubt that ...

and a thousand and one others, all of which mean 'I believe'.

The reason this area of the semantic system is so highly elaborated metaphorically is to be found in the nature of modality itself. A very brief account of modality was given in Chapter 4, Section 4.5; now that we have introduced the concept of grammatical metaphor we can give a somewhat more systematic description of the principal features of the modality system.

Modality refers to the area of meaning that lies between yes and no – the intermediate ground between positive and negative polarity. What this implies more specifically will depend on the underlying speech function of the clause. (1) If the clause is an 'information' clause (a proposition, congruently realized as indicative), this means either (i) 'either yes or no', i.e. 'maybe'; or (ii) 'both yes and no', i.e. 'sometimes'; in other words, some degree of probability or of usuality. (2) If the clause is a 'goods-&-services' clause (a proposal, which has no real congruent form in the grammar, but by default we can characterize it as imperative), it means either (i) 'is wanted to', related to a command, or (ii) 'wants to', related to an offer; in other words, some degree of obligation or of inclination. We refer to type (1) as MODALIZATION and to type (2) as MODULATION; this gives a system as in Figure 10-5.

The four types are set out in diagrammatic form in Figure 10-6.

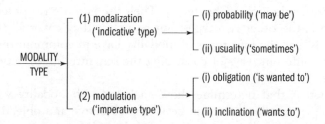

Fig. 10-5 **System of types of modality**

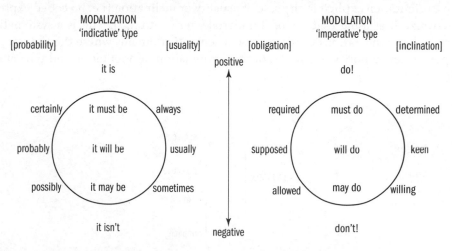

Fig. 10-6 **Diagram showing relation of modality to polarity and mood**

691

Note that modulation refers to the semantic category of proposals; but all modalities are realized as indicative (that is, as if they were propositions). Thus imperative *go home!*, when modulated, becomes indicative *you must go home!* (In philosophical semantics and linguistic accounts influenced by 'modal logic' (see e.g. Lyons, 1977: Ch. 17), probability is referred to as 'epistemic' modality (from Greek *episteme*, for 'knowledge') and obligation as 'deontic' modality (from Greek *deon*, for 'what is binding'). Readiness has been referred to as 'dynamic' modality, and deontic and dynamic modalities have been grouped together as 'root' modality – our modulation type of modality; but usuality tends to be left out of accounts of modality. See, e.g., Depraetere & Reed (2006: Section 4.2, Table 12-2). (For the place of *can* 'be able to' in the system, see below.)

Here is an example of each of the four types:

1.i	[probability]	There can't be many candlestick-makers left.
1.ii	[usuality]	It'll change right there in front of your eyes.
2.i	[obligation]	The roads should pay for themselves, like the railways.
2.ii	[inclination]	Voters won't pay taxes any more.

As these examples show, the modal operators can occur in all four types (for the full list of modal operators see Table 4-5 in Chapter 4). Their use is more restricted in usuality and in inclination than in the other two types; but as a class they cover all these senses. This brings out what it is that the four types of modality have in common: they are all varying degrees of polarity, different ways of construing the semantic space between the positive and negative poles.

The basic distinction that determines how each type of modality will be realized is the ORIENTATION: that is, the distinction between subjective and objective modality, and between the explicit and implicit variants, discussed (with reference to probability) in the preceding section. The system is as in Figure 10-7. These combine with all four types of modality, but with gaps; for example, there are no systematic forms for making the subjective orientation explicit in the case of usuality or inclination (i.e. no coded expressions for 'I recognize it as usual that ... ' or 'I undertake for ... to ... '). This is a systematic gap; these particular combinations would represent semantic domains where the speaker cannot readily pose as an authority. Examples of the combination of orientation and type are given in Table 10-8.

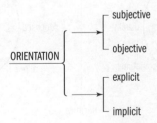

Fig. 10-7 System of types of orientation in modality

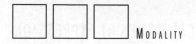

Table 10-8 Modality: examples of 'type' and orientation combined (realization of modality in bold)

	Subjective: explicit ⬂	Subjective: implicit ⬂	Objective: implicit ⬂	Objective: explicit ⬂
	projecting mental clause as mood Adjunct	modal operator as Finite	[1] modalization: modal adverb as mood Adjunct; [2] modulation: modal verb as passive/ adjectival verbal group in verbal group complex as Predicator	relational clause with modal Complement/ Attribute
Modalization: probability	**I think** → Mary knows; [*in my opinion* Mary knows]	Mary**'ll** know	Mary **probably** knows [in all probability] [Mary **is likely** to]	**it's likely** [[that Mary knows]]
Modalization: usuality		Fred**'ll** sit quite quiet	Fred **usually** sits quite quiet	**it's usual** [[for Fred to sit quite quiet]]
Modulation: obligation	**I want** → John to go	John **should** go	John**'s supposed** to go	**it's expected** [[that John goes]]
Modulation: inclination		Jane**'ll** help	Jane**'s keen** to help	

The third variable in modality is the VALUE that is attached to the modal judgment: high, median or low. These values are summarized in Table 10-9, with 'objective implicit' forms as category labels. The median value is clearly set apart from the two 'outer' values by the system of polarity: the median is that in which the negative is freely transferable between the proposition and the modality:

	direct negative	transferred negative
(prob.)	it's likely Mary doesn't know	it isn't likely Mary knows
(usu.)	Fred usually doesn't stay	Fred doesn't usually stay
(obl.)	John's supposed not to go	John's not supposed to go
(incl.)	Jane's keen not to take part	Jane's not keen to take part

With the outer values, on the other hand, if the negative is transferred the value switches (either from high to low, or from low to high):

693

Table 10-9 Three 'values' of modality

	Probability	**Usuality**	**Obligation**	**Inclination**
High	certain	always	required	determined
Median	probable	usually	supposed	keen
Low	possible	sometimes	allowed	willing

direct negative	transferred negative
(p: high) it's certain Mary doesn't know	it isn't possible Mary knows
(p: low) it's possible Mary doesn't know	it isn't certain Mary knows
(u: high) Fred always doesn't stay	Fred doesn't sometimes stay
[Fred never stays	Fred doesn't ever stay]
(u: low) Fred sometimes doesn't stay	Fred doesn't always stay
(o: high) John's required not to go	John isn't allowed to go
(o: low) John's allowed not to go	John isn't required to go
(i: high) Jane's determined not to take part	Jane isn't willing to take part
(i: low) Jane's willing not to take part	Jane isn't determined to take part

These are illustrated here with the 'objective implicit' orientation, except for those of probability which are 'objective/explicit' – the purpose being to choose those where the system is displayed most obviously and clearly. In fact, the possibility of transferring the negative from proposition to modality applies throughout, always with the same switch between high and low; for example (probability/subjective/explicit):

	direct negative	transferred negative
(median)	I think Mary doesn't know	I don't think Mary knows
(high)	I know Mary doesn't know	I can't imagine Mary knows
(low)	I imagine Mary doesn't know	I don't know that Mary knows

The most complex pattern of realization is the 'subjective/implicit', that with the modal operators; for example (probability/subjective/implicit):

	direct negative	transferred negative
(median)	that'll [will] not be John	that won't be John
(high)	that must not be John	that can't be John
(low)	that may not be John	that needn't be John

These are further complicated by a great deal of dialectal and individual variation (cf. Mair & Leech, 2006, on changes in the frequency of modal operators over the past few decades).

694

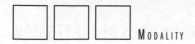

But the underlying pattern can be discerned throughout, and is useful in throwing light on all the variants that are found to occur.

We have arrived at the network of modality systems presented in Chapter 4, Figure 4-23. This generates a set of $4 \times 4 \times 3 \times 3 = 144$ categories of modality. Thirty of these are illustrated in Figure 10-8 (the key for which is provided in Table 10-10).

Table 10-10 Key to examples in Figure 4-23

	TYPE	POLARITY	TRANSF.	DEGREE	ORIENTATION		modal item
1	probability	positive	–	high	implicit	subjective	*must*
2			–			objective	*certainly*
3			–	median		subjective	*will*
4			–			objective	*probably*
5			–	low		subjective	*may*
6			–			objective	*possibly*
7		negative	transferred	high		subjective	*can't*
8			direct			objective	*certainly … n't*
9			transferred		explicit		*n't possible*
10				median	implicit	subjective	*won't*
11			direct			objective	*probably … n't*
12			transferred		explicit		*n't probable*
13				low	implicit	subjective	*needn't*
14			direct			objective	*possibly … n't*
15			transferred		explicit		*n't certain*
16	obligation	positive	–	high	implicit	subjective	*must*
17			–			objective	*required*
18			–	median		subjective	*should*
19			–			objective	*supposed*
20			–	low		subjective	*can*
21			–			objective	*allowed*
22		negative	transferred	high		subjective	*can't*
23			direct			objective	*required not*
24			transferred		explicit		*not allowed*

Table 10-10 Key to examples in Figure 4-23 (*contd*)

	TYPE	POLARITY	TRANSF.	DEGREE	ORIENTATION		modal item
25				median	implicit	subjective	*shouldn't*
26			direct			objective	*supposed not*
27			transferred		explicit		*not supposed*
28				low	implicit	subjective	*needn't*
29			direct			objective	*allowed not*
30			transferred		explicit		*not required*

There is one further category that needs to be taken into account, that of ability/ potentiality, as in *she can keep the whole audience enthralled*. This is on the fringe of the modality system. It has the different orientations of subjective (implicit only) realized by *can/can't*, objective implicit by *be able to*, and objective explicit by *it is possible (for ...) to*. In the last of these, the typical meaning is 'potentiality', as in *it was possible for a layer of ice to form*. In the subjective it is closer to inclination; we could recognize a general category of 'readiness', having 'inclination' and 'ability' as subcategories at one end of the scale (*can/is able to* as 'low'-value variants of *will/is willing to*). In any case *can* in this sense is untypical of the modal operators: it is the only case where the oblique form functions as a simple past, as in *I couldn't read that before; now with my new glasses I can*.

This is as far as we shall take the description of modality here. The actual number of systematic distinctions that are made in this corner of the language runs well into the tens of thousands; among the many variants that are being left out of account are those expressed by the different modal operators within each of the values high, median and low:

> high: must ought to need has to is to

> median: will would shall should

> low: may might can could

But this is the same limitation that is being imposed throughout. If we want to range over the grammar from the clause complex to the word group within a single volume, we cannot expect to give more than a thumbnail sketch, such that no one portion can be explored very far in delicacy.

But we need to return to the categories of orientation, in order to complete the account of metaphor in modality. The general difference in meaning between the subjective and the objective orientation can be seen from the effect of the tag. Compare the following two clauses:

> he couldn't have meant that, could he?

> surely he didn't mean that, did he?

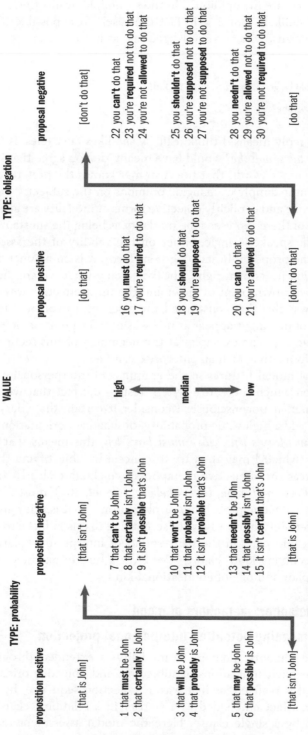

Fig. 10-8 Probability and obligation with positive and negative propositions and proposals (Note: No. 22 is now more commonly _mustn't_, from the direct negative _must not_.)

In the first, the speaker wants the listener to confirm his estimate of the probabilities: 'I think it unlikely; do you share my opinion?'. In the second, he wants the listener to provide the answer: 'I think it unlikely, but is it in fact the case?'. It is possible to switch from a subjectively modalized clause to a non-modalized tag, as in this exchange in a store selling children's books:

What do you reckon would be good for a five-year-old kid?

– She'll like fairy tales, does she?

Here the salesperson's reply means 'I think it likely she likes fairy tales; is that the case?' – whereas *she'll like fairy tales, will she?* would have meant 'do you agree that it is likely?'. The speaker is assuming, in other words, that the customer knows the preferences of the child; there would be no point in simply exchanging opinions on the subject.

The explicitly subjective and explicitly objective forms of modality are all strictly speaking metaphorical, since all of them represent the modality as being the substantive proposition. Modality represents the speaker's angle, either on the validity of the assertion or on the rights and wrongs of the proposal; in its congruent form, it is an adjunct to a proposition rather than a proposition in its own right. Speakers being what we are, however, we like to give prominence to our own point of view; and the most effective way of doing that is to dress it up as if it was this that constituted the assertion ('explicit' *I think* ...) – with the further possibility of making it appear as if it was not our point of view at all ('explicit objective' *it's likely that* ...). The examples at the beginning of this section show some of the highly elaborated forms that such an enterprise can take.

The importance of modal features in the grammar of interpersonal exchanges lies in an apparent paradox on which the entire system rests – the fact that we only say we are certain when we are not. If unconsciously I consider it certain that Mary has left, I say, simply, *Mary's left*. If I add a high value probability, of whatever orientation, such as *Mary's certainly left*, *I'm certain Mary's left*, *Mary must have left*, this means that I am admitting an element of doubt – which I may then try to conceal by objectifying the expression of certainty. Hence whereas the subjective metaphors, which state clearly 'this is how I see it', take on all values (*I'm sure*, *I think*, *I don't believe*, *I doubt*, etc.), most of the objectifying metaphors express a 'high' value probability or obligation – that is, they are different ways of claiming objective certainty or necessity for something that is in fact a matter of opinion. Most of the 'games people play' in the daily round of interpersonal skirmishing involve metaphors of this objectifying kind. Figure 10-9 gives a further example, containing both an interpersonal metaphor and one of an ideational kind.

10.4 Interpersonal metaphor: metaphors of mood

10.4.1 Expansion of meaning potential; interpersonal projection

As we have seen, the semantic domain of modality is extended through grammatical metaphor to include explicit indications of subjective and objective orientation: a modal proposition or proposal is realized, as if it was a projection sequence, by a nexus of two clauses, or as if it was a fact embedded as a Carrier in a relational clause with a modal Attribute, rather than by a single clause. Here the modal assessment itself is given the

'surely'	'it is required that'	'money	shouldn't	go on	being invested'
Modality: prob/o: m/high	Modality: ob/o: ex/high	Subject	Finite	Predicator	
Mood				Residue	
		Goal	α Aspect: imperfective	=β Process: material	

Surely	commonsense	dictates		there	should	be	a	limit	to	the	money	invested
α				"β								
Modality: prob/o: m/high	Subject	'pres' Finite	dictate Pred.	Subject	Finite	Pred.	Complement					
Mood			Residue	Mood		Residue						
	Sayer	Process: verbal				Process: existential	Existent					
								Thing	Qualifier			
									'Process'	'Range'		
											Thing	Qualifier

Fig. 10-9 Example with modal and transitivity metaphors

status of a proposition in its own right; but because the projecting clause of the nexus is metaphorical in nature, standing for an interpersonal assessment of modality, it is also, at the same time, a modal Adjunct in the clause realizing the proposition/proposal. This is the general effect of grammatical metaphor: it construes additional layers of meaning and wording. To capture this layering in our grammatical analysis, we introduce one or more *additional structural layers* in the box diagram, as in Figure 10-4 and Figure 10-9 above.

The representation of grammatical metaphor in such diagrams shows how the metaphor is embodied in the structural organization as an increase in the layers of meaning and wording. But there is, of course, also a systemic effect. Systemically, metaphor leads to an *expansion of the meaning potential*: by creating new patterns of structural realization, it opens up new systemic domains of meaning. And it is the pressure to expand the meaning potential that in fact lies behind the development of metaphorical modes of meaning. Thus in the system of MODALITY shown in Figure 4-16, the system of ORIENTATION is expanded by the addition of a systemic contrast in MANIFESTATION between 'explicit' and 'implicit': the metaphorical modalities described above make it possible to make the orientation explicit in wordings such as *I think* and *it is likely that*, which, in turn, makes it possible to increase the delicacy of differentiations (cf. *I think/imagine/expect/assume/suppose/reckon/*

guess; *I would think/I would have thought*; *I imagine/I can imagine*; and so on). As we have already seen, this same principle extends beyond modality and applies to modal assessment more generally (e.g. *I regret, it is regrettable that*). The metaphoric strategy is to **upgrade** the interpersonal assessment from group rank to clause rank – from an adverbial group or prepositional phrase serving within a simple clause to a clause serving within a clause nexus of projection.

There is thus a fundamental relationship between modal assessment, including modality, and projection. To bring this out, we can interpret modal assessment as **interpersonal projection** (see Matthiessen & Teruya, forthc.). Interpersonal projection always involves the speaker or addressee as 'projector': 'I think', 'I say'; 'do you think', 'do you say'. It is always implicit unless it is made explicit through grammatical metaphor, by 'co-opting' ideational resources to do interpersonal service. But the notion of interpersonal projection is not, in fact, limited to modal assessment. Consider the short persuasive text in Text 10-5 (for the rhetorical-semantic analysis of this text, see Figure 9-7 above, and Mann & Thompson, 1985; cf. also Martin, 1992: 244–246):

> **Text 10-5: Exploring – arguing: open letter appealing to members of an organization [Text 6]**
>
> *I don't believe* that endorsing the Nuclear Freeze initiative is the right step for California Common Cause. Tempting as it *may* be, we **shouldn't** embrace every popular issue that comes along. When we do so we use precious limited resources where other players with superior resources are already doing an adequate job. Rather, *I think* we will be stronger and more effective if we stick to those issues of governmental structure and process, broadly defined, that have formed the core of our agenda for years. Open government, campaign finance reform, and fighting the special interests and big money – these are our kinds of issues.
>
> Let's be clear: I personally favour the initiative and ardently support disarmament negotiations to reduce the risk of war. But *I don't think* endorsing a specific freeze proposal is appropriate for CCC. We **should** limit our involvement in defense and weaponry to matters of process, such as exposing the weapons industry's influence on the political process. Therefore, **I urge you** to vote against a CCC endorsement of the nuclear freeze initiative.

Expressions of modulation are bolded and expressions of modalization are italicized; metaphorical expressions are underlined.[3] Subjective assessment of modality permeates the text, like a prosody. In the case of modalization, it is largely explicit; in the case of modulation, it is implicit until the very last clause. This clause realizes the nucleus of the whole text; it is here that the key proposal is presented with a nuclear punch, as 'macro-New' (cf. Halliday, 1982; Martin, 1993). But what is the key proposal? One variant of *I urge you to vote ...* is *you must vote ...*, the two being relatable as explicit and implicit variants of subjective, high modulations of the type obligation. However, we can take one step further in the analysis. What the author is saying is *Vote against ...*, which is an 'imperative' clause – the congruent realization of a proposal of the subtype 'command'. This indicates

---

3 Like persuasive texts in general, this text is suffused with interpersonal meanings – the modal assessment extends to the lexis. For example, *right* in *the right step for California Common Cause* is a moral judgement that can be related to modulation of the type obligation. A more congruent version would be *California Common Cause shouldn't endorse Nuclear Freeze* (with the negative polarity coming from its transferred placement in *I don't believe*).

the connection between 'imperative' clauses and modulation, which is why modulation was characterized as the 'imperative type' of modality. On the one hand, an 'imperative' clause imposes an obligation; on the other hand, the imperative tag checks the addressee's inclination to comply (*will you?*). But the example also illustrates the connection between mood and projection.

10.4.2 Metaphorical realizations of propositions and proposals

The command 'vote against ...' is realized metaphorically by a hypotactic clause nexus; it is realized as if it was a report of what the speaker says. This is just like the metaphorical realization of modality of the explicitly subjective orientation. Thus the reported command can be tagged: *I urge you to vote against ... will you?* In other words, just like modality, speech function can be represented as a substantive proposition in its own right; and this proposition is a figure of sensing or saying that projects the original [i] proposal or [ii] proposition:

[i] proposal ↘ projected proposal in projection nexus
(1a) declarative, speaker Subject, simple present

> ||| **I want** || you to have a bit more of the rice, Dano. ||| [UTS/ Macquarie Corpus]

> ||| As a first step to correcting this disparity, **I urge the Congress** || to eliminate the 40 percent Redux retirement formula || and to restore the "50% of base pay" formula for 20 years of active-duty service, || as proposed in the President's FY2000 budget. ||| [Text 115]

> ||| While I fully endorse your attitude to the Commonwealth Immigrants Bill, || and am repelled by that section of its supporters [[who detergently echo the racialist slogan, "Keep Britain White,"]] || nevertheless **I urge** || that the particular problem of immigrants from any source crowding into congested areas in London, Birmingham, and elsewhere must not be evaded. ||| [LOB_B] [**generalized appeal**]

(1b) declarative, speaker Subject, modal

> ||| **I would strongly advise you** || to pay a visit to your doctor in the very near future. ||| [LOB_P]

(1c) interrogative: yes/no, speaker Subject, modal: modulation

> ||| If, as a by-product of such research, it is found || that in recent years the habit of discussing certain Rulings with the Chair has increased, || **may I ask you** || not to hesitate to say || so, || so that we may conform to the more orderly methods of our predecessors? ||| [LOB_H]

(2) speaker-plus Subject

> ||| Your essay, if I may just cut across for one moment || **we'd like** || you to re-read this little passage [[beginning the last paragraph]] as an example. ||| [Text 135]

[ii.a] proposition [demanding] ↘ projected proposition in projection nexus
(1) interrogative: yes/no, speaker Subject, modal: modulated

> ||| **Can I ask you** first, as a very prominent Liberal MP || how you think || the row over Shane Stone's memo has affected the party? ||| [Text 184]

(2) interrogative: yes/no, addressee Subject, modal: modulated

||| **Would you say** || that a lot of fiction lacks this compassion or empathy? ||| [Text 21]

||| Well, **which would you say** || was his majorest? ||| [Text 125]

||| **What kind of category of novel would you say** || generally speaking Lord of the Flies belongs to; || is it a realistic novel || or is it a symbolic novel || or – how would you describe it? ||| [Text 135]

(3) declarative, speaker Subject + projected interrogative, addressee Subject

||| You mentioned || that the composition of The Snow Leopard was your Zen practice for several years, || and **I wonder** || if **you'd explain** || what that means? ||| [Text 7] 'what does that mean?'

[ii.b] **proposition [giving]** ⬎ projected proposition in projection nexus

||| And **I tell you** || we had a good laugh out of that; || couldn't stop laughing (*Laughs*). ||| [Text 11]

||| Now, Congressman Kennedy, **I can assure you** || that America thanks you for your retirement. ||| [COCA]

The patterns illustrated by these examples are set out in Table 10-11. The projecting 'verbal' and 'mental' clauses are interpersonally constrained with respect to the nature of the Mood element. On the one hand, the SUBJECT PERSON is 'interactant' rather than 'non-interactant'; typically the Subject is either the speaker (*I*) or the addressee (*you*). On the other hand, the DEICTICITY is either 'temporal: present' (e.g. *want, urge*) or 'modal: modulation' (e.g. *can, may, would*). There are, of course, departures from these constraints. For example, the Subject may be 'non-interactant', as in a 'passive verbal' clause with the Receiver as Subject or in an active one with some source of authority as Subject:

[i] proposal
(1) Source of authority as Subject

||| **Section 15(2) of the Act requires** || leases to be stamped within thirty days of execution, || and if this is not done || the lessee is liable to a fine of ten pounds and a further penalty equivalent to the stamp duty || unless there is a reasonable excuse for the delay in stamping the lease || and the Commissioners of Inland Revenue mitigate or remit the penalty. ||| [LOB_J]

(2) Receiver as Subject, Sayer implicit

||| **Staff who cannot attend on the day scheduled for their College/Office are encouraged** || to attend one of the other sessions. ||| [Macquarie University administrative circular]

[ii] proposition

||| **They say** || that films are like a director's children. ||| [Text 134]

These are departures from the explicitly subjective orientation of the proposal or proposition, in the sense that the speaker or writer shifts the modal responsibility embodied in subjecthood to somebody or something else. But are there explicitly objective variants,

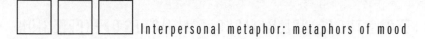

analogous to the explicitly objective metaphorical realizations of modality presented in the previous section? In the realm of proposals, the line between an explicitly objective command and an explicit modulation seems to disappear: as they are 'experientialized', they are neutralized as facts. It is certainly possible, however, to find passages where explicitly objective wordings such as *it is demanded that, it is asked that; it is imperative that, it is important that* serve together with congruently realized commands, as in Text 10-6.

Text 10-6: Enabling – regulatory (written, monologic): administrative circular
<u>Please be</u> aware that the University has a legal obligation to conform with the requirements of the Privacy and Personal Information Protection Act. The University could incur financial penalties or damage to its reputation if it is found to be in breach of the Act. **It is** therefore **important that** all staff understand their obligations under the Act. [Macquarie University administrative circular]

Such explicit objective variants are common in the discourse of bureaucracy, where people's activities are regulated; and they may be backed up by other renderings of obligation in *their obligations under the Act*.

In the realm of propositions, the line between explicitly objective propositions and modal assessment seems to disappear. Forms such as *it is said that, it is rumoured that* serve as assessments of the nature of the evidence for a proposition: it is, as it were, represented as being projected by somebody other than the speaker (thus *it is said* and *they say* are very close in meaning); the projection thus serves as a device enabling speakers to distance themselves from the proposition. For example:

||| **Of Samuel it is said** || that when he asked the people || to bear witness || that he had not taken anything of theirs || the people said || that they were witnesses. ||| [LOB_D]

||| **It is said** || that television keeps people at home. ||| But you, at any rate, have proved that wrong. ||| And **they say**, too, || that television makes its appeal to those of lesser intelligence. ||| [LOB_F]

||| Furthermore, it **is claimed,** || there are no known connections between the languages of the Old World and those of the Americas. ||| [Text 196]

In the type of mood metaphor shown in Table 10-11, the proposition/proposal is realized by a clause nexus of projection rather than by a simple clause. The interpersonal projection embodied in speech function has thus been realized as if it was an ideational projection. This has two consequences for the expansions of the meaning potential of speech function, just as in the case of modality. On the one hand, the option of making the subjective orientation of the speech functional selection explicit is added to the system, as in *vote against ...* (implicit) vs. *I urge you to vote against* (explicit). On the other hand, the speech functional system can be further elaborated in delicacy by drawing on the extensive resources of the lexicogrammar of 'verbal' and 'mental' clauses. Thus in addition to *vote against ...*, we now have, for example, ('verbal') *I tell you/command you/order you/ask you/urge you/implore you/beseech you/plead with you/suggest to you → to vote against ...*; ('mental') *I want/desire/'d like/intend/plan → (for) you to vote against ....* And while these clauses are constrained in terms of SUBJECT PERSON and DEICTICITY, they still allow for additional systemic variation; for example: *I urge you/I would urge you/I should urge you/I must urge you//can I (please) urge you/could I perhaps urge you → to vote against ....*

Table 10-11 Examples of metaphorical realizations of proposals and propositions involving projection nexuses

	Declarative		Interrogative: yes/no		
speaker (speaker+)	I (we) implore you → to I (we) want → you to	I (we) would advise you → to I (we) would want → you to	may I (we) advise you → to		proposal: command
	I (we) assure you → that	I (we) can assure you → that	may I (we) assure you → that		proposition: statement
	I (we) ask you → whether I (we) wonder → whether	I (we) must ask you → whether I (we) must wonder → whether	may I (we) ask you → whether		proposition: question
addressee	you are urged by me (us) → to	you would be advised by me (us) → to	could you possibly be persuaded by me (us) → to		proposal: command
		you must believe → that	would you believe → that		proposition: statement
		you must tell me → whether	would you say → that could you tell me → whether	do you mean → that	proposition: question
	temporal: present	modal: modulation		temporal: present	

As we have noted, metaphors of mood make it possible for the semantic system of SPEECH FUNCTION to be further elaborated in delicacy. Why does the speech functional system need to be expanded in this way; why has it been expanded beyond the basic system sketched in Chapter 4, Section 4.1? The basic principle is this: the expansion of the speech functional system has increased the meaning potential available to interactants for negotiation in dialogue. For instance, in the following examples 'commands' are all realized metaphorically by modulated declarative clauses with addressee Subjects – *can you* ...:

(a) Oh. Stefan, can you turn off the tape? – [Non-verbal response: tape is turned off.] [Text 76]

(b) Can you tell us about the political and cultural makeup of Nigeria? – One quarter of the entire population of Africa is in Nigeria, so we say that every fourth African is a Nigerian. [Text 16]

(c) And Joanne came up and she said, "Oh, can you do this?" and I said, "Look you're at the end of a very long line; be prepared to wait" ... [Text 72]

(d) Interviewee: Well can you give me any further help then? I'm sorry. I'm holding up your *time to see me.* – Interviewer 1: *Well not* just at the moment I'm afraid. – Interviewer 2: No no, because we've got a whole list of interviewees but you see our point. [Text 135]

The preferred response to a command is an offer to comply – as in (a) and (b) above; but the metaphorical realization gives more discretion to the addressee, and in (c) and (d) the response is a refusal to comply. The potential for negotiation in dialogue created by metaphors of mood is directly related to the different contextual variables within **tenor**. Metaphors of mood expand the interpersonal resources for **negotiation**, whether the negotiation involves consensus or conflict (see Matthiessen, Teruya & Wu, 2008, and references therein). The tenor variables are usually discussed in terms of status, formality, face, tact and politeness (and their negative counterparts; see Watts, 2003, for a critical survey of different approaches). What these have in common is a very general sense of the **social distance** between the speaker and the addressee. Here interpersonal metaphor is part of a principle of interpersonal iconicity: metaphorical variants create a greater semiotic distance between meaning and wording, and this enacts a greater social distance between speaker and addressee. The semiotic distance is often manifested directly in the lexicogrammar as a syntagmatic extension of the wording. For example, in the following extract from an interview, the interviewer says

‖‖ You mentioned ‖ that the composition of The Snow Leopard was your Zen practice for several years, ‖ and I wonder ‖ if you'd explain ‖ what that means? ‖‖ [Text 7]

using a three-clause clause complex, *I wonder* → *if you'd explain* → *what that means* instead of just asking *What does that mean?* This extension of the wording also reflects the interpersonal tendency towards prosodic expression (see Chapter 2, Section 2.7).

In addition to metaphors based on ideational projection, there are other kinds of metaphor of mood as well. One prominent type involves a shift in the realizational domain of commands from 'imperative' to 'indicative' clauses. The 'indicative' clause can be either 'declarative' or 'interrogative'; for example:

[iii] proposal ⟍ modulated indicative

(1) declarative

‖‖ Yes, well, if you apply that criterion, ‖ then **surely you must** start to rearrange your estimates of Lawrence's novels, **surely**. ‖‖ [Text 125]

‖‖ **Perhaps you should** tell me about your current project. ‖‖ [Text 21]

‖‖ You just don't think about it; ‖ **you shouldn't**. ‖‖ [Text 101]

‖‖ Well look, honestly, Mrs Finney, my suggestion to you would be [[[that if you want to read English honours ‖ **you should** spend a year in solid preparation for it ‖ and then reapply]]]. ‖‖ [Text 135]

‖‖ **I think** ‖ **you should** talk to David Hawker, ‖ whose committee, <<I think,>> put this in train. ‖‖ [Text 184]

(2) interrogative

‖‖ Oh **can you** get some napkins? ‖‖ [Text 82]

‖‖ **Can you** name a moment, or an image [[[that you can point to ‖ and say ‖ this is [[when you decided ‖ that you were going to write The Greenlanders]]]]]? ‖‖ [Text 17]

‖‖ **Would you** like to take the comfortable chair? ‖‖ [Text 125]

‖‖ **Could you** tell us about a poem [[which lives up to this ideal of yours]] in whatever period? ‖‖ [Text 135]

705

Here the Mood element of the 'indicative' clause is constrained in terms of the systems of SUBJECT PERSON and DEICTICITY. The SUBJECT PERSON selection is 'addressee' – Subject = *you*; and the DEICTICITY is 'modal', more specifically 'modulation'. In other words, the Subject is the same as that of a 'jussive imperative' clause and the modality is of the proposal kind – the 'imperative' type (see Chapter 4, Section 4.5.2 (2)). The fact that the 'indicative' clause realizes a kind of command can be seen in the way the addressee treats it in the exchange, complying with it (or refusing to comply); for example:

Interviewer: **Perhaps you should** tell me about your current project.

Interviewee: It's set during the summer of 1934 in my old stomping grounds, Western Arkansas, Eastern Oklahoma. [Text 21]

The presence of the Mood element expands the potential for negotiation. Alongside the fixed value of the 'imperative' *do!*, we now have e.g. (declarative) *you must/ought to/should/ will/may/can + do* with modulation of the 'obligation' kind, and (interrogative) *must you* ('do you insist on')/*would you/can you* with modulation of the 'readiness' kind. These may combine with modal assessments, including modalization, or negative polarity, as in *perhaps you should* in one of the examples above. These 'indicative' variants provide a range of more delicate ways of commanding. For example, *must you do that* means 'don't do that!', but adds the sense of rebuke and exasperation, which is further intensified in the 'wh-' version with *why*:

"Why must you always be getting at me, Dad? Nothing I ever do is right!" [LOB_N]

In contrast, examples with *you should* as the Mood element are typically milder versions of a command, as in *perhaps you should tell me* ... above, where the low modalization of probability reinforces the sense of a mild command or suggestion (that is, 'it is possible that it is your duty to tell me'). The 'indicative' potential is thus 'co-opted' as a grammatical realization of the semantic category of 'command' so that interactants have a richer semantic potential to negotiate their positions relative to one another in socio-semiotic space.

The 'indicative' realization of proposals has the effect of blurring the line between proposals directed to the addressee and propositions about how the world ought to be. For example, through the extension of *you* from 'addressee' to 'generalized person, including the addressee' (in contrast with generalized *they*), we get general rules, general advice, and the like:

||| If you find [[yourself coming back the next day || and erasing more of the so-called improvements [[than you keep]]]], || **you'd better** get the hell out of that book. ||| [Text 7]

||| If you are writing about something [[that you have not experienced]], || then **you must** supply yourself with experience. ||| [Text 17]

||| **You cannot** drink on the job. ||| [Text 71]

This move away from responsibility directly and explicitly assigned to the addressee includes modulated declarative clauses with non-interactant Subjects, as in regulatory texts, see Text 10-7:

Text 10-7: Enabling – regulating (written, monologic): extract from Road User's Handbook

You and everyone in the vehicle must wear a seat belt whenever there is one available. That means if there is an empty seat with a seat belt, **a passenger must** move to it and not sit in a seat without a belt. If there are no seat belts fitted, it is safer for a passenger to sit in the back. [...] **Drivers should** make sure children travel in restraints suitable for their size and age. **Children under 12 months must** use a suitable, approved child restraint if the vehicle has a child restraint anchorage point to attach it to. [Road User's Handbook (Roads and Traffic Authority, June 1994)]

Here the Subjects are still people being held responsible for complying with the 'commands' – except in the last case, *children under 12 months must*. But this is further attenuated when the Subject is not a potential carrier of obligation; for example:

Any notice of termination must be in writing, give the required period of notice and set out the grounds for termination (if any). [Residential Tenancy Agreement]

Here the ones being held responsible are the parties to the agreement, the people who would produce the notice of termination – not that notice itself.

We have explored certain key strategies involved in the metaphorical expansion of the interpersonal meaning potential, showing that they are not random or *ad hoc* features of the system but rather motivated and principled extensions of the congruent system. There are, of course, other strategies as well. The lexicogrammatical resources of MOOD, and the associated patterns of MODALITY and KEY, carry a very considerable semantic load as the expression of interpersonal rhetoric. Not surprisingly, these categories lend themselves to a rich variety of metaphorical devices; and it is by no means easy to decide what are metaphorical and what are congruent forms. Some common speech-functional formulae are clearly metaphorical in origin, for example (i) *I wouldn't ... if I was you*: command, congruently *don't ... !* functioning as warning; (ii) *I've a good mind to ... :* modalized offer, congruently *maybe I'll ...*, typically functioning as threat; (iii) *she'd better ... :* modulated command, congruently *she should ... ,* typically functioning as advice. Some words, such as *mind*, seem particularly to lend themselves to this kind of transference: cf. *would you mind ... ?, mind you!, I don't mind ...* (including *I don't mind if I do*, positive response to offer of drink in the environment of a pub), and so on.

Metaphors of this kind have been extensively studied in speech act theory, originally under the heading of 'perlocutionary' acts. From a linguistic point of view they are not a separate phenomenon, but one aspect of the general phenomenon of metaphor, just like the ideational metaphors to be discussed in the next section. Both interpersonal and ideational metaphors can be represented in the same way, by postulating some congruent form and then analysing the two in relation to each other. Some examples are given in Figure 10-10.

10.5 Ideational metaphors

Interpersonal metaphors may prove a challenge for children – and a source of interpersonal confusion; but many of them are handled by young children before they start school. In fact, in a case study of one child, Painter (1993, 1999) shows how his path into mental projection was through the type that crosses over into the interpersonal domain of modality – that is, *I think* and the like with speaker as Subject/Senser and the verb in present tense.

(a)

'tentatively			is	the position		still	available?'
Modal Adjunct			Finite	Subject		Adjunct	Complement
Mood							Residue

I	was	wondering	if	the position	is	still	available

logical:	α				'β			
interpersonal:	Subject	Finite	Predicator		Subject	Finite	Adjunct	Complement
	Mood		Residue		Mood			Residue

(b)

'if	you	move			I	'll	shoot'
logical:	×β				α		
interpersonal:	Subject	'do Finite	move' Predicator		Subject	Finite	Predicator
	Mood		Residue		Mood		Residue

	don't	move		or	I	'll	shoot
logical:	1				+2		
interpersonal:	Finite	Predicator			Subject	Finite	Predicator
	Mood	Residue			Mood		Residue

(c)

'you	shouldn't	say	such a thing'
Subject	Finite	Predicator	Complement
Mood		Residue	

how	could	you	say	such a thing
WH-/Adjunct	Subject	Finite	Predicator	Complement
	Mood			
Residue				

(d)

'the evidence	is	(the fact) that	they		cheated	before'
Subject	Finite	Complement: clause	Subject	'did Finite	cheat' Predicator	Adjunct
Mood		Residue	Mood		Residue	

look		at	the way	they	cheated	before
'do Finite	look' Predicator	Adjunct				
		'Predicator'	Complement: clause		as above	
Mood	Residue					

Fig. 10-10 **Further examples of interpersonal metaphors**

The interpersonal metafunction defines the environment in which children first learn the strategy of grammatical metaphor.[4] No doubt this is partly because interpersonal metaphors tend to make selections more explicit, as when probability is realized by a 'mental' clause projecting the modalized proposition ('explicit' orientation in Figure 4-23), and partly because the interpretation of interpersonal metaphors is often both supported and 'tested' immediately in the ongoing dialogic interaction. For example:

Oh. Stefan, can you turn off the tape? – [Non-verbal response: tape is turned off.] [Text 76]

Here the responses show that the 'yes/no interrogative' clauses are interpreted as metaphorically realized commands rather than as congruently realized questions. The expansion of the interpersonal semantic system through grammatical metaphor provides speakers with additional, powerful resources for enacting social roles and relations in the complex network of relations that make up the fabric of a community of any kind (cf. Rose's, 2001, exploration of tenor and interpersonal resources in Western Desert).

10.5.1 Introductory example

Unlike interpersonal metaphor, the other type of grammatical metaphor, ideational metaphor, is learned later by children and is not part of the grammar of ordinary, spontaneous conversation that children meet in the home and neighbourhood; rather, it is associated with the discourses of education and science, bureaucracy and the law. Children are likely to meet the ideational type of metaphor when they reach the upper levels of primary

---

[4] This is a manifestation of a more general principle: see Halliday (1993c).

school (see e.g. Christie & Derewianka, 2008; Derewianka, 1995); but its full force will only appear when they begin to grapple with the specialized discourses of subject-based secondary education. Here are some examples of ideational metaphors they are likely to meet early in their experience with written text:

> Slate is a metamorphic rock. Slate was once shale. But over millions of years, tons and tons of rock *pressed* down on it. The pressure made the shale very *hot*, and the heat and pressure changed it into slate. ... Other metamorphic rocks are made the same way slate it, by heat and pressure. [Gans, 1984, *Rock collecting*. New York: Harper & Row. Ages 4–8. p. 24.]

> With its great size and strength it must have had little resistance from smaller animals. ... It may be that the creature's large size prevented it from moving quickly. [Wilson, 1986, *100 Dinosaurs from A to Z*. New York: Grosset & Dunlap.]

The first example comes from a book for young readers written by an author who produced many books for this kind of audience. It contains two nominalizations, one verbal nominalization (*press > pressure*) and one adjectival nominalization (*hot > heat*). These nominalizations are in fact examples of ideational metaphors where processes and qualities are construed as if they were entities – they are reified; but they are likely to be accessible to young readers because in the text itself they follow congruent forms, so that the readers have enough information to tackle the metaphors: *tons and tons of rocks pressed down on it > the pressure made the shale very hot > the heat and pressure* .... The sequence in text from congruent to metaphorical is in fact quite common: the metaphor can be interpreted against the background of its congruent variant (see e.g. Halliday & Martin, 1993; Halliday & Matthiessen, 1999: Ch. 6). In contrast to the first example, the other two examples are likely to be less accessible to young readers because congruent wordings do not prepare them for the metaphorical variants (cf. Christie & Derewianka, 2008).

Let us now consider in Text 10-8 an extract from a book blurb where projection is a central motif:

Text 10-8: Recommending – promoting: book blurb [Text 196]

This book presents a series of illuminating studies which conclusively demonstrates that the prevailing conception of historical linguistics is deeply flawed. Most linguists today **believe** that there is no good evidence that the Indo-European family of languages is related to any other language family, or even any other language. In like manner, the New World **is deemed to contain** hundreds of language families, among which there are no apparent links. Furthermore, it **is claimed**, there are no known connections between the languages of the Old World and those of the Americas. And finally, the strongest belief of all is that there is no trace of genetic affinity – nor could be – among the world's language families.

The author argues that all of these firmly entrenched – and vigorously defended – beliefs are false, that they are myths propagated by a small group of scholars who have failed to understand the true basis of genetic affinity. ...

As we have seen interpersonal metaphor is a strategy for expanding the potential for negotiation, and we see this at work in the passage above; for example, *it is claimed* extends the domain of modal assessments like *allegedly*: through projection, the writer assigns a certain modal status to the proposition 'there are no known connections'. The passage

also contains examples of ideational metaphor involving projection. Consider the following steps in the text:

(a)   Most linguists today believe → that there is no good evidence ...

(b)   the strongest belief of all is [[that there is no trace ...]]

(b)   these firmly entrenched – and vigorously defended – beliefs

In (a), we find a hypotactic clause nexus of projection of the familiar kind: one clause represents people thinking (*most linguists today believe*), and the other represents the 'content' of their process of thinking (*that there is no good evidence ...*). The process of thinking is represented as a verbal group (*believe*) serving as the Process of a 'mental' clause.

In (b), we find a simple 'relational' clause of the 'identifying' kind. Here the Value and the Token correspond to the two halves of a projection nexus. (1) The Value of this identity is the nominal group *the strongest belief of all*. Here the process of believing is represented (as if it was an entity) by *belief*, a nominalization of the verb *believe* that serves as the Thing of the nominal group; and the degree of believing is represented as an adjectival Epithet (*strongest*) characterizing the Thing. This corresponds to the 'mental' clause (*people*) *believe most strongly*, except that the nominal group does not include an equivalent of the Senser of the clause. While there is no equivalent of the Senser, the nominal group has a feature of determination that is not present in the clause; this is expressed by the Deictic reference item *the* and is a property of 'things' rather than of 'processes'. In this instance, the reference item is structurally cataphoric (see Section 9.4.1). (2) The Token of the identity is the embedded clause *that there is no trace ....* This is a 'fact' clause and it corresponds to the projected 'idea' clause of a projection nexus such as (a); that is, the projected 'idea' is represented as if it was a pre-projected 'fact'. This type of 'identifying' clause with an embedded 'fact' clause as Token was discussed and exemplified in Section 7.5.7.

To sum up: a projection sequence of figures in the semantics is realized congruently by a projection clause nexus in the grammar, and the two figures forming the sequence are realized by clauses. This is what we find in example (a); but in (b), a projection sequence has been realized not by a clause nexus but by a simple clause, and the figure of sensing is realized not by a clause but by a nominal group, while the projected figure has been realized not by a dependent 'idea' clause but by an embedded 'fact' clause. The congruent and metaphorical modes of realization are combined in Figure 10-11. Just like interpersonal metaphor, ideational metaphor introduces additional layers of meaning that are construed by the grammar as additional layers of wording.

In (c), we find a nominal group that is like the nominal group *the strongest belief of all* in (b): *these firmly entrenched – and vigorously defended – beliefs*. That is, this nominal group can again be interpreted as a metaphorical variant of a 'mental' clause: it has a verbal nominalization, *beliefs*, as Thing, corresponding to the Process of the clause. The nominal group serves as Carrier in an 'intensive attributive relational' clause, where it is assigned the Attribute *false*. The Deictic is the reference item *these*, which refers back anaphorically to earlier instances of 'beliefs': *most linguists today believe ..., the New World is deemed to*

711

'congruent'	'(people)	most strongly	believe			that there is no ...'
	α				∅	'β
	clause: mental					clause: projected
	Senser	Manner: degree	Process			
	nom. gp.	adv. gp.	verbal gp.			
'metaphorical'	the	strongest	belief	of all	is	that there is no ...
	clause: relational					
	Value				Process	Token
	nom. gp.				verbal gp.	nom. gp.: clause
	Deictic	Epithet	Thing	Qualifier	Finite/Event	Thing
	determiner	adjective	noun: nominalization	prep. phrase	verb	clause

Fig. 10-11   Congruent and metaphorical wordings combined

contain ..., it is claimed there are no known connections ..., and *the strongest belief of all.*[5] What has happened here is that since the process of believing has been realized metaphorically as an entity serving as the Thing in a nominal group, it can now be treated textually as a discourse referent, in the same way as ordinary, non-metaphorical entities. In fact, this referent is picked up again in the following clause by the pronoun *they* 'the beliefs'. So there is a textual motivation behind the metaphor in (c). But there is also an experiential one: as an entity, the process of believing can be assigned the Epithet *firmly entrenched – and vigorously defended*; these are in the first instance properties of entities (construed in the grammar of the nominal group) rather than of processes (construed in the grammar of the clause). At the same time, the metaphorical entity can serve as Carrier in a 'relational' clause and be assigned the Attribute *false*, which is a property of propositions rather than of entities: while there is no overt projection associated with the nominal group *these ... beliefs*, it is used to refer back to be propositions in the preceding text and can stand as the value of a proposition in an identity (cf. *the belief is that there is no trace ...*).

10.5.2 Re-mapping between semantics and lexicogrammar

As illustrated by the example analysed in Figure 10-11, grammatical metaphor within the ideational metafunction involves a 're-mapping' between sequences, figures and elements

---

[5]   Since, as pointed out in Chapter 9, reference is a semantic relation rather than a lexicogrammatical one, it is the sense of 'belief' that is picked up, not the lexical item *believe/ belief*; the use of the reference in *these ... belief*s shows very clearly that *deemed* and *claimed* are also associated with 'belief' in the semantic system.

in the semantics and clause nexuses, clauses and groups in the grammar. In the congruent mode of realization that we described in Chapters 5 and 7, a sequence is realized by a clause nexus and a figure is realized by a clause. In the metaphorical mode, the whole set of mappings seems to be shifted 'downwards': a sequence is realized by a clause, a figure is realized by a group, and an element is realized by a word. The two modes of realization are contrasted diagrammatically in Figure 10-14 below. Examples:

> It is false to say the <u>absence</u> of a peace treaty with Germany **causes** no real <u>danger</u>. [LOB_A] 'although (Britain) has no peace treaty with Germany, (the situation) is not dangerous'

> Lord de l'Isle's <u>appointment</u> **has caused** a certain protocol <u>confusion</u>, with the Melbourne Herald announcing it first and congratulating Mr. Menzies, the Australian Prime Minister, on his "acceptable choice." [LOB_A] 'because Lord d l'Isle was appointed, (people) were confused about the protocol'

> The ***cause*** of the present <u>clash</u> with the Russians **is** the <u>decision</u> of the West Germans to hold Parliamentary committee meetings in Berlin and a session next week of the Federal Parliament's upper house there. [LOB_A]

> In particular, the shortage of grazing [[**caused** by drought]] **necessitated** heavy <u>purchases</u> of feeding stuffs. [LOB_A] '(farmers) had too little land where (cattle) could graze because it hasn't rained, so they had to buy a great deal of feeding stuffs'

The 're-mapping' is possible because semantic motifs such as cause are manifested repeatedly in the different environments of the grammar so that each environment is a possible domain of realization for such a motif. These motifs are of the two primary types, expansion and projection, that have been discussed at various places above (e.g. Sections 10.2.1 and 10.2.2); cf. summaries in Table 10-3 and Table 10-6. Ideational metaphor is based on patterns that exist already in the congruent mode of realization; but it expands these patterns significantly, as can be seen when we analyse scientific, legal or administrative discourse – or, indeed, other kinds of discourse that the metaphorical mode has spread to in a systematic way. The following example produced by a general in a 'posture statement' to the House Armed Services Committee of the United States' House of Representatives is a typical specimen:

> In our units, the perception of an inadequate retirement program consistently surfaces as a primary cause of our recruiting and recruiting and retention problems. [Text 115]

In the grammar of the home and the neighbourhood, this would be *people think that what we do when they retire is not good enough, so we can't recruit them and we can't keep them*; but this sequence of figures that is realized congruently as a complex of clauses has been re-mapped by the general in the metaphorical mode of realization as a simple clause, where the figures are realized as groups and phrases.

The metaphorical mode has come to be associated with prestige discourses of power and authority. But what is the underlying significance of this kind of 're-mapping' between the semantics and the grammar? As we have seen, the ideational metafunction is a resource for construing our experience of the world that lies around us and inside us. In the congruent mode, the grammar construes sequences (of figures), figures and elements as the basic phenomena of experience, as shown schematically in Figure 10-14. In the metaphorical mode, the model is enriched through combinations of these categories:

713

in addition to the congruent categories, we now also have metaphorical combinations of categories – sequences construed as figures, figures construed as elements, and so on. These combinations open up new meaning potential. For example, in a sequence, there is a temporally invariant logico-semantic relation such as cause, but in a sequence construed as a figure, this relation is typically construed as a process. Unlike a logical relation, a process is construed as unfolding through time, and in the grammar of the verbal group it is marked for tense or modality:

> In the first case, it is the absence of a voluntary euthanasia law [[that **causes** so much suffering]]; ‖ in the second it was the absence of a signed "living will" or advance directive document [[that wrecked havoc with my cousin]]. [Text 24] 'voluntary euthanasia law is absent, so many people suffer'

> Within the hills are several faults; ‖ displacement along these faults **caused** failure of the Baldwin Hills Reservoir in 1963, ‖ when 250 million gallons of water poured through the residential areas at the northern base of the hills, ‖ **caused** heavy damage, ‖ and finally drained into Ballona Creek. [Text 140]

> A central aisle often enhances the impression of spaciousness, and the new ceremonious <u>regard</u> for the Communion Table, brought by the contemporary sacramental revival, **has usually caused** the <u>removal</u> of the pulpit to the side of the church. [LOB_D]

> A magnitude-6 quake **can cause** severe damage ‖ if it is centered under a populated area. [Text 94]

Here the logical relation of 'cause' is construed as a full-fledged process, thus gaining access to the potential for construing time embodied in the tense system of the verbal group (Chapter 6, Section 6.3.3). In a similar way, figures construed as participants are realized by nominal groups, so the potential for construing participants embodied in the nominal group systems of classification and characterization become available. For example, when 'somebody remembering something' is reconstrued as 'memory', it can be classified and characterized just like other entities (cf. Matthiessen, 1993a, 1998b). Thus, in non-technical discourse we find examples such as:

> Martin had not liked to go on questioning him, suspecting that this would be an intrusion on some **private memory** which he wanted to respect. [LOB_K]

> When she didn't, she went on in her brisk, clackety voice, that reminded Lea of nothing so much as a **childhood memory** of the boy next door playing with a morse set. Clack, clack, clackety, clack. It was just the same. [LOB_L]

> This reprieve (which for all I know is a common occurrence) began soon after one of my aunts recommended yeast to me as a cure for **failing memory**. [LOB_R]

> So you have to do research ‖ and you have to ponder it ‖ and sort of work it into your mind ‖ as if it's something [[that you remember]]. You try to give yourself a **historical memory**. [Text 17]

And in the technical discourse of cognitive science we find *working memory*, *long term memory*, *short term memory*, *semantic memory*, *visual memory* and so on:

> **Semantic memory** is concerned with the structure of knowledge, with [[how knowledge is stored, cross-referenced and indexed]]: it is concerned with the organization of everyday world knowledge, and with the representation of meaning. **Semantic memory** is not just an internal dictionary [[in which linguistic terms are listed and defined]]. [Gillian Cohen, 1977. The psychology of cognition. New York: Academic Press.]

As we have just illustrated, the metaphorical mode thus makes available a great deal of further ideational potential that is not accessible in the congruent mode. At the same time, the metaphorical mode also denies access to significant aspects of the potential that is associated with the congruent mode: there is a loss of ideational meaning. For example, the tactic patterns of clause complexing (with the distinction between paratactic interdependency and hypotactic dependency) are not available to sequences that are realized metaphorically as clauses, and the configurational patterns of participant roles are lost or obscured when figures are realized as groups or phrases. Thus in the nominal group *the perception of an inadequate retirement program*, it is likely that *an inadequate retirement program* is what is perceived, but this has to be inferred (contrast *the perception of concerned citizens*, where *concerned citizens* is likely to be the perceiver, not what is perceived); and the perceiver is left implicit. In more congruent versions, such underspecification does not occur: *people see the retirement program as inadequate, people think that the retirement program is inadequate*, and so on. This is because the grammar of the clause construes participants as inherent in the process, and only allows them to be absent through ellipsis if they are recoverable.

10.5.3 Textual and interpersonal considerations

Within the ideational metafunction, the general effect of this realignment in the semantic system is a shift from the logical to the experiential – an experientialization of our construal of experience (see Halliday & Matthiessen, 1999: 264). Thus logical sequences of figures are reconstrued as experiential configurations of elements. But the significance of grammatical metaphor of the ideational kind extends beyond the ideational metafunction to both the textual and interpersonal ones. The textual and interpersonal effects of ideational metaphor are due to the fact the **realignment** of ideational patterns described above also means that there is a realignment of the textual and interpersonal environments in which ideational systems operate.

(i) **Textual effects.** When a sequence is realized metaphorically by a clause, this means not only that it is mapped onto the transitivity patterns of the clause but also that it falls within the domain of the Theme + Rheme organization of the clause and also, by extension, that of the Given + New organization of the information unit (see Chapter 3, Sections 3.5 and 3.6). Thus the following sequence –

Displacement along these faults **caused** failure of the Baldwin Hills Reservoir in 1963 [Text 140]

– is realized metaphorically as a 'relational' clause, and the figures making up the sequence are realized metaphorically as nominal groups serving as elements of the clause. Since they function within the clause, these nominal groups can be assigned textual statuses: the nominal group *displacement along these faults* serves as Theme, and the nominal group *failure of the Baldwin Hills Reservoir in 1963* serves as New: see Figure 10-12. The metaphoric 'relational' clause thus creates a textual pattern of Theme: figure 'displacement' + New: figure 'failure'.

This textual patterns is an effective resource in the rhetorical development of scientific discourse (see Halliday, 1988; Halliday & Martin, 1993). There is thus a gain in textual meaning in the shift from the congruent mode of realization to the metaphoric mode. In

clause	displacement along these faults	**caused**	failure of the Baldwin Hills Reservoir in 1963
	Token/Identified	Process	Value/Identifier
	Theme	Rheme	
	Given		New
clause nexus	x was displaced along these faults	so	the Baldwin Reservoir failed in 1963
	1	×2	

Fig. 10-12   Metaphorically realized sequence: textual organization

this way, the ideational metaphor accommodates the textual metafunction: the experiential configuration of Identified + Process + Identifier structures the sequence into two textual quanta, one figure as Theme followed by another as New. In some cases, this kind of textual accommodation may be the main reason behind the ideational metaphor. Mental clauses of perception may be used in this way:

> The second day of the convention **saw** [[the advantage pushed further]]: each Territory had its representation increased threefold; of contesting delegations those who represented the gold element in their respective States were unseated to make way for silverites; and Stephen M. White, one of the California senators, was made permanent chairman. [The Agrarian Crusade]

> It was a pomp-filled end to a campaign [[which **saw** [[Bush finish second in the popular vote but a narrow winner in the all-important electoral competition]]]]. [Text 113]

Here the pattern is Theme/Senser: time or event + Process + New/Phenomenon: act; that is, the structure of the mental clause is used to redistribute information, creating two textual groupings, with a circumstantial feature as unmarked Theme and an act clause as unmarked New, as in Figure 10-13. Here the Phenomenon serves to group Goal (*the advantage*) + Process (*pushed*) + Distance (*further*) together as one element of information. The act-clause serving as Phenomenon may be reconstrued as a reified process realized by a nominalization:

> Whatever the case may have been, this conquest **saw** an overwhelming replacement or absorption of the existing Celtic linguistic community by the newly arrived Germanic speakers. [Denison & Hogg, 2006, "Overview", *A history of the English language.* Cambridge: Cambridge University Press]

To sum up: when a sequence is realized by a clause rather than by a clause nexus, it will be structured textually into Theme + Rheme and, since a clause is an information unit in the unmarked case, also into Given + New. This means that the figures that make up the sequence can be given thematic or newsworthy status. In addition, such a figure, realized metaphorically by a nominal group rather than congruently by a clause, gains access to the textual systems of the nominal group – most significantly, the system of DETERMINATION. This means that it can be treated textually as a discourse referent (cf. Chapter 9, Section 9.4). It is marked either as 'non-specific' or as 'specific', in which case its identity is presented as recoverable to the addressee. For example:

716

The second day of the convention		saw		the advantage	pushed	further
Given		New				
Theme		Rheme				
Senser		Process		Phenomenon		
nominal group		verbal group		nominal group: clause		
Time				Goal	Process	Distance
'on the second day				the advantage	was pushed	further'

Fig. 10-13   Regrouping of information in metaphorical mental clause

(1) non-specific

Additionally, in a number of cases, <u>transnational movements</u> threaten our interests, our values, and even our physical security here at home. [Text 115]

There has also been <u>a dramatic decline in ozone concentration over Antarctica that was not predicted</u>. [Climate Change]

(2a) specific: cataphoric (structural)

<u>**The** migration of millions of peasant families</u> has radically changed Peruvian culture, || beginning with the slow but steady abandonment of Indian dress and language || and expressed more recently in the arts, particularly in music [[that combines Andean tradition with contemporary Latin and Caribbean motifs]]. [Text 229]

(2b) specific: anaphoric

Formerly one of the city's finest residential areas, Bunker Hill has been cleared of its old buildings, lowered thirty feet, and reshaped to provide sites for high-rise offices, apartments, and shops. Beyond it loom the closely spaced high-rise buildings of the downtown Los Angeles financial and office center (3). Most have been built since removal of the height ceiling in 1957. **This** <u>concentration</u> indicates the westward movement of the downtown core, which to a large degree has been halted by the Harbor Freeway. [Text 140]

In this way, a metaphorically realized figure can be tracked as a discourse referent as the discourse unfolds:

However, worldwide manufacture and use of these compounds <u>have increased</u> dramatically in recent years, leading to <u>a renewed upswing</u> in global CFC production at a rate of several percent a year. **This** <u>renewed increase</u> in CFC emissions was one of the main reasons that interest was rekindled in abatement regulations. [Climate Change]

The new colonial wealth crowded the wharves of bustling ports like Bristol and Bordeaux, || from which it <u>was transshipped</u> not only to other cities in England and France, but to those European metropolitan areas [[not directly involved in maritime commerce with the New World and the Far East]]. **This** <u>localized transshipment</u> was the means [[[by which the new goods were widely distributed throughout Europe || so that – by way of obvious example – the pungent odor of the coffeehouse filled the streets of Berlin and Brussels as well as those of London and Paris]]]. [Text 122]

The models also predict <u>a 10 percent increase in ozone amount below 30 km</u>. **This** would lead to a warming of the lower atmosphere and surface and would constitute a significant fraction of total surface and tropospheric warming that is predicted for all of the combined greenhouse gases. [Climate Change]

(ii) Interpersonal effects. Ideational metaphor thus leads to a realignment in the grammar between the ideational and the textual domains: sequences gain access to textual resources that are congruently associated with figures, and figures gain access to textual resources that are congruently associated with participants. At the same time, ideational metaphor also realigns the ideational in relation to the interpersonal. When a sequence is realized metaphorically by a clause, it is given the interpersonal status of a proposition or proposal, making it arguable. For example:

||| Too many unprogrammed deployments will inevitably disrupt operating budgets, || sap morale, || cause lost training opportunities, || and accelerate wear and tear on equipment. ||| [Text 115]

||| A magnitude-6 quake can cause severe damage || if it is centered under a populated area. ||| [Text 94]

||| This is consistent with the concept [[that the antarctic ozone hole phenomenon causes a dilution effect throughout much of the Southern Hemisphere]]. ||| [Text 33]

As the examples illustrate, a 'propositionalized' sequence can be modalized, doubted, argued and negotiated interpersonally in numerous other ways. By the same token, when a figure is realized metaphorically by a group or phrase, it is deprived of the interpersonal status of a proposition or proposal, making it inarguable. It is thus presented as something already established; and any modifications, including interpersonal evaluative ones, have to be taken for granted (cf. Hoey, 2000):

<u>A **standard** empirical hypothesis</u> is that one component of the mind/brain is a *parser*, which assigns a percept to a signal (abstracting from other circumstances relevant to interpretation). [Chomsky, 1995, *The minimalist program*. Cambridge, Mass.: The MIT Press, p.18.]

<u>Any **serious** approach to complex phenomena</u> involves innumerable idealizations, and the one just sketched is no exception. [Chomsky, *The minimalist program*, p.19.]

But **interesting** (and **conflicting**) arguments have been presented. [Chomsky, *The minimalist program*, p. 22.]

<u>Much of the **fruitful** inquiry into generative grammar in the past years</u> has pursued the working hypothesis that UG is a simple and elegant theory, with fundamental principles that have an intuitive character and broad generality. [Chomsky, *The minimalist program*, p. 29.]

As we have seen, grammatical metaphor of the ideational kind is primarily a strategy enabling us to transform our experience of the world: the model of experience construed in the congruent mode is reconstrued in the metaphorical mode, creating a model that is further removed from our everyday experience – but which has made modern science possible. At the same time, there are also textual and interpersonal consequences of this metaphorical realignment in the grammar: ideational metaphor can be a powerful textual resource for managing the creation of text, creating new mappings between the ideational and textual quanta of information; and it can also be a powerful interpersonal resource for organizing the ongoing negotiation of meaning, creating new mappings between the ideational and interpersonal propositions/proposals.

718

10.5.4 Types of ideational metaphor

In our presentation of interpersonal metaphor, we identified a number of common types. The general tendency is for interpersonal metaphor to 'upgrade' the domain of grammatical realization; for example, while the congruent realization of modality is a group serving in the clause, the metaphorical realization is a clause that projects (*I think* ... , etc.) or embeds (*it is probable* ... , etc.) the clause to which a modal value is assigned. In this way, interpersonal metaphor tends to expand interpersonal systems by adding explicit variants – that is, variants where the subjective or objective orientation is made explicit.

In contrast, the general tendency for ideational metaphor is to 'downgrade' the domain of grammatical realization of a semantic sequence, figure or element – from clause nexus to clause, from clause to group/phrase, and even from group/phase to word: see Figure 10-14. Such downgrading affects both the unit whose domain of realization is downgraded, and the units of which it is composed: the downgrading proceeds down the rank scale by a kind of 'domino effect'. The downgrading may start with (i) a whole sequence of figures, (ii) with a single figure, or (iii) with a single element within a figure.

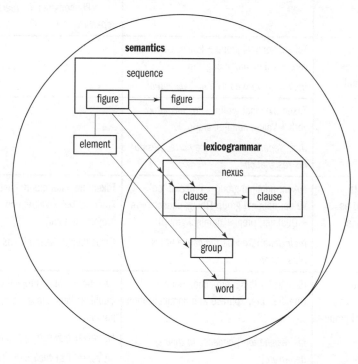

Fig. 10-14 Congruent mode of realization and metaphorical mode involving 'downgrading'

(i) **Sequence.** In the congruent mode, a sequence of two figures is realized by a nexus of two clauses; but in the metaphorical mode, the domain of realization is downgraded from clause nexus to clause. In the metaphorical mode, the domain of realization of either one or both of the figures is, in turn, downranked from clause to group/phrase. These

719

successive steps in downgrading are possible because, as we have seen (in Section 10.2), both projection and expansion are motifs that are manifested throughout the grammatical system: a sequence of projection can thus be realized not only by the manifestation of projection in the clause nexus, but also by its manifestation in the clause or the group/phrase. The same principle applies to expansion. The possibilities of downgrading include the four types set out in Table 10-12.

Table 10-12 Congruent and incongruent realization of sequences – downgrading of one or both clauses

	(1) Expansion	**(2) Projection**
(0) congruent: clause + clause	*he resigned because they had departed*	*he explained that (why) they had departed* *he regretted that they had departed*
(1) incongruent: one clause downgraded as element of the other clause	Cause: prepositional phrase *he resigned because of their departure*	Range: nominal group … /Verbiage *he explained their departure* … /Phenomenon *he regretted their departure*
(2) incongruent: both clauses downgraded as elements of 'relational' clause	Token: nominal group + Process: causal verb + Value: nominal group *their departure caused his resignation* Token: nominal group + Process: proof verb + Value: nominal group *their departure proved the correctness of his resignation*	
(3) incongruent: both clauses downgraded as elements of 'relational' clause	Token: nominal group + Process: 'be' + Value: nominal group [Thing: causal noun + Qualifier: prep. + nominal group] *their departure was the cause of his resignation*	Token: nominal group: 'fact' clause + Process: 'be' + Value: nominal group [Thing: projection noun] [[*that they departed*]] *was his regret*
(4) incongruent: both clauses downgraded as elements of nominal group	(Deictic +) Thing: projection noun + Qualifier: prep. phrase with nominalization *his resignation* [*because of their departure*]	(Deictic +) Thing: projection noun + Qualifier: 'fact' clause/prep. phrase with nominalization *his regret* [[*that they had departed*]] *his regret* [*at their departure*]

(1.1) With expansion, one figure of the sequence may be realized congruently by a clause, while the other is realized incongruently as a prepositional phrase serving as a circumstance of Cause within that clause; here the relator of the sequence is realized as the minor Process of the phrase. The relator and the minor Process are matched in terms of subtype of expansion; for example, 'so' is realized by *because of* or another causal preposition:

||| Many of these lessons may have gone wrong **because of** nervousness due to inspection, ... ||| [Text 97] 'many of these lessons may have gone wrong because teachers were nervous because the school was being inspected'

(1.2) With projection, the projecting figure may be realized congruently as a 'verbal' or 'mental' clause, while the projected figure is realized incongruently as the Range – the Verbiage or the Phenomenon:

|||| I think || I'll have to wait a few years, however, || before I explain to him the reality of their likeness within the order Hymenoptera. ||| [Text 187]

||| He does not regret his decision to discontinue academic studies. ||| [KOHL_G]

(2) With expansion, both figures of the sequence may be realized incongruently as Token and Value in a 'circumstantial relational' clause; here the relator of the sequence is realized, also incongruently, as the Process element in the clause (cf. Chapter 5, Table 5-20). The expansion type of the relator is matched by the nature of the circumstantial Process (but for internal cause, see below):

||| Within the hills are several faults; || displacement along these faults **caused** failure of the Baldwin Hills Reservoir in 1963, || when 250 million gallons of water poured through the residential areas at the northern base of the hills || caused heavy damage, || and finally drained into Ballona Creek. ||| [Text 140]

||| Severe wave erosion of the former Redondo Beach waterfront **led to** construction of the breakwater and creation of the King Harbor Marina (30). ||| [Text 140]

||| Overcrowding, largely the result of long sentences for drug offenses, **has brought** a shift in emphasis from rehabilitation to punishment and incapacitation, || Amnesty said. ||| [Text 21]

Alternatively, the 'circumstantial relational' clause is 'attributive' rather than 'identifying', with the expanding figure as Attribute and the expanded one as Carrier:

||| Hence evidence from numerous studies above clearly shows [[[that the Genetic explanations cannot be true, || that differences in IQ among races and groups **is because of** genetic differences]]]. ||| [Text 123] 'races and groups differ in IQ because they differ genetically'

Relations of internal cause – cause in the sense of 'x so I think/say y' – are construed metaphorically by verbs of proving such as *prove, show, demonstrate, argue, suggest, indicate, imply* in 'intensive identifying relational' clauses (cf. Chapter 5, Table 5-14):

||| The wide range of potential contributions by the RC has proven to be a bright spot || as we strive to match available resources to a demanding mission load, || and **demonstrates** clearly the enduring value and relevance of the citizen-soldier. ||| [Text 115]

||| Further experiments **proved** [[[that the dye lowered fertility in rats, || induced still-births || and even produced malformed and macerated foetuses]]]. ||| [KOHL_E]

||| Large amounts of feldspar in a sandstone **may imply** rapid deposition and burial [[before chemical weathering could decompose the feldspar]], || or it might imply a cold climate [[in which chemical weathering is very slow]]. ||| [Text 68]

721

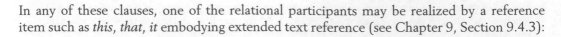

In any of these clauses, one of the relational participants may be realized by a reference item such as *this*, *that*, *it* embodying extended text reference (see Chapter 9, Section 9.4.3):

||| TOMS data from the Northern Hemisphere show a decrease in ozone from 1979 through 1985. ||| **This** is consistent with an increase in trace gases, primarily chlorofluorocarbons (CFCs), and a decline in solar output (solar maximum in 1979-1980, minimum in 1985–1986). ||| [Text 33]

(3.1) With expansion, both figures of the sequence may be realized incongruently as Token and Value in an 'intensive relational' clause; but the relator is nominalized as the Thing of the nominal group serving as Value, and the expanding figure is embedded as a Qualifier. The nominalized relator is a noun of expansion such as *time*, *place*, *cause*, *result*, *reason* (see Chapter 7, Section 7.4.5):

||| Closer to the mark is the metaphysical argument [[offered by the French romantic author Chateaubriand]]: || the French Revolution was the **result** of the "slow conspiracy of the ages." ||| [Text 122]

||| The **reason** for the general formlessness and intellectual vacuity <<< (often disguised in big words, || but that is again in the self-interest of intellectuals) >>> is [[[that we do not understand very much about complex systems, such as human societies; || and have only intuitions of limited validity as to [[[the ways they should be reshaped || and constructed]]]]]] . ||| [Text 122]

(3.2) With projection, the projected figure may be realized metaphorically as an embedded 'fact' clause (see Chapter 7, Section 7.5.7) serving as Token in an 'intensive identifying' relational clause with the projecting figure realized incongruently as a nominal group serving as Value:

||| My original intention **was** [[to write a saga [[covering three generations of the Okonkwo family in one book]]]]. [Text 16]

(4.1) With expansion, the expanded figure is realized incongruently as a nominal group with the process as Head/Thing and the expanded figure is realized incongruently as a prepositional phrase in this nominal group serving as Qualifier:

||| Some ten to twelve children have obvious hypotrophy (emaciation and loss of muscle tone), || and several have cachexia (the final stages of **exhaustion and corporeal depletion** due to malnourishment and starvation, || as may be observed, for example, in the final stages of cancer). |||

(4.2) With projection, the projecting figure in a sequence may be realized incongruently as a noun of projection (cf. Chapter 7, Section 7.5.7) serving as the Head/Thing of a nominal group and the projected figure as a downranked clause serving as Qualifier:

||| It was helpful || but revealed no significant wastage || and supported **my contention** [[that 150,000 litres a year is a most unrealistic level on which to base future water taxes]]]]. ||| [ACE_B]

||| Little research developed along these lines over the next 20 to 30 years || because there were neither data nor instruments nor testable theories [[that would let anyone go beyond the **assertion** [[that the integrated, interdisciplinary perspective might be a useful approach]]]]. ||| [Text 32]

||| Appearing on CNN's "Late Edition," || Secretary of State Madeleine Albright challenged **assertions** [[that Clinton's last-ditch peace efforts were an attempt [[to ensure his legacy]]]]. ||| [Text 108]

||| Despite the **claim** [[that inspection is about 'improving schools']], Ofsted instructs inspectors || to 'make judgements, || and not give advice'. ||| [Text 97]

In all the cases identified above, a sequence of two figures is realized metaphorically as a simple clause. There is always a domino effect: as the realizational domain of the sequence is downgraded, so are the realizational domains of its component parts. At least one of the figures is, in turn, realized metaphorically as a ranking group/phrase, and elements within figures are realized either by downranked groups/phrases or by words. Thus in the example analysed in Figure 10-12, *Displacement along these fault lines caused failure of the Baldwin Hills Reservoir in 1963*, both the figures in the causal sequence 'x displaced y along these fault lines, so the Baldwin Hills Reservoir failed in 1963' are realized by nominal groups. In the nominal group serving as Token, (1) the process is reconstrued as the noun *displacement* serving as Thing and (2) the circumstance of location is reconstrued as the downranked prepositional phrase *along these fault line*s serving as Qualifier. As often happens in such metaphorical nominal groups, the participants in the process have been left implicit: we are not told what displaces what. In the nominal group serving as Value, (1) the process of the figure is also reconstrued as the noun *failure* serving as Thing, (2) the participant in this process, the Medium, is reconstrued as the downranked prepositional phrase *of the Baldwin Hills Reservoir* (i.e. structure marker *of* + nominal group) serving as Qualifier, and (3) the circumstantial element of time is reconstrued as the downranked prepositional phrase *in 1963* serving as Qualifier. Either of these last two elements could in fact have been downgraded even further to be realized as words serving as Classifier in the nominal group – *the 1963 failure*, *the Baldwin Hills Reservoir failure*; compare:

||| The science of "political economy," or early economics, was a <u>seventeenth-century</u> **creation**, and an indication of the close relationship [[now accepted between power and wealth]]. ||| [Text 122]

||| If, as was now asserted, || society was a <u>human</u>, not a <u>divine</u> **creation**, || it could be reordered || so that mankind could more easily engage in "the pursuit of happiness." [Text 122]

||| Severe <u>wave</u> **erosion** of the former Redondo Beach waterfront led to construction of the breakwater and creation of the King Harbor Marina (30). ||| [Text 140]

At this point they lose their status as elements in their own right, becoming sub-elements of the 'failure' element. For example, they can no longer be treated as discourse referents – entities that can be introduced and tracked referentially in discourse (see Chapter 9, Section 9.4). Thus we can say *the failure of the Baldwin Hills Reservoir in 1963 ... its failure in 1973*, referring back to the reservoir by means of *its*, this is not possible if *Baldwin Hills Reservoir* is a word complex serving as Classifier (that is, *the Baldwin Hills Reservoir failure*, rather than an embedded nominal group with a Deictic serving as Qualifier).

(ii) Figure. As we have seen, the downgrading of the realizational domain of a sequence will start a metaphorical chain reaction that moves down the rank scale until it has reached downranked groups/phrases or words. But such metaphorical chains need not start with sequences; they may start with figures instead.

(1) The incongruent realization of the figure may retain the clause as the domain of realization, but downgrade –

(1.1) all of the figure as a metaphorical nominal group (see below, under (iii) element), creating a new Process. This Process may have the sense of 'happen', thus supplying the

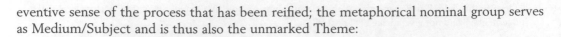

eventive sense of the process that has been reified; the metaphorical nominal group serves as Medium/Subject and is thus also the unmarked Theme:

||| <u>A considerable redevelopment and intensification of land use</u> **is occurring**, particularly construction of apartments, hotels, and motels. ||| [Text 140]

This is close to an 'existential' clause with the nominalized figure as Medium/Existent and *there* as Subject; but such clauses are textually different: they serve as a strategy for introducing the figure as the focus of New information:

||| In spite of a considerable time span, the fact [[that these diverse prehistoric people should have retained a basic similarity in the structure and proportions of their skulls]] strongly supports the idea [[that there was <u>a relatively rapid diffusion of the Modern human stock out of Africa</u>]]. ||| [J. Kingdon, 1993, *Self-made man*, New York: John Wiley, p. 99.]

(1.2) part of the figure as a metaphorical nominal group. This occurs either (a) when the phasal part of a process realized by an elaborating hypotactic verbal group complex (Chapter 8, Section 8.5.1) is reconstrued as if it were a process in its own right, with the incongruent nominal group as Medium –

||| It remains our position [[[that the Duma must ratify START II || before <u>formal negotiations</u> **can begin** on START III]]]. ||| [Text 115]

– or, (b) when the process is reconstrued as a participant of the Range type and is combined with a new process with the general sense of 'perform':

||| Look, Danko, **have** <u>a shower</u> – ||| [Text 76]

||| But he says || he always carries along with him Andean music cassette tapes, || and he readily **belts out** <u>an Andean song</u> on request. ||| [Text 229]

||| He **made** <u>mathematical calculations</u>. ||| [Text 65]

Metaphors of this last type only affect the Process of the clause, creating a contrast between congruent Process and incongruent Process + Range. The Process + Range pattern makes it possible to present the semantic process as the (focus of) unmarked New, and it also makes it possible to classify this process as if it were an entity, as in *Andean song* and *mathematical calculation*. Unlike ideational metaphors in general, this pattern is quite common in casual, everyday English. In most cases, it has, in fact, become the norm so that there is a strong tendency for 'middle' clauses of all process types (not just relational clauses) to be configured as Process + Range (cf. Chapter 5, Section 5.7.3.2; Halliday, 1967/8/2005: 29–30).

(2) The incongruent realization of the figure may downgrade the domain from clause to group/phrase. Grammatically, this is only possible in an environment of rankshift, as when the congruent clause/metaphorical group/phrase serves as the Head or Postmodifier of a nominal group.

Taken together, <u>the deterioration of relations with Laos and Cambodia</u> worried the Thai military regime. [Wyatt, 284] ~ the fact [[that relations ... deteriorated]] worried the Thai military regime

Her eyesight was none too good, || but when moths and flies blundered into her trap, || she could feel the vibration of one of the web's guying threads || and she would rush out onto it. [Text 187] ~ she could feel [[one of the guying threads vibrating]]

As the examples above illustrate, the process element of the figure is usually realized metaphorically as the Thing of a nominal group. However, when the figure is one of qualitative attribution, with the quality as Attribute, it is the Attribute that is construed as Thing; for example:

The importance of impression management is most visible with these individuals, ... [Text 188] ~ the fact [[that impression management is important]] is most visible ...

In addition to the general cases discussed above, there are special cases involving particular elements. For example, a comment that would be realized as a modal Adjunct in a congruent clause may be assigned as a quality to a nominalized process in a nominal group, either as Epithet in that incongruent nominal group or as Attribute in an 'intensive attributive' relational clause where the incongruent nominal group serves as Carrier:

||| Though the four boys and two girls, the youngest nineteen years of age, the oldest twenty-four, came from varying backgrounds || and had different professional and personal interests, || there was **surprising** agreement among them. ||| [Brown1_G] 'surprisingly they agreed with one another'

||| The growing loss of pilots is **troubling**, not only because of its direct impact on combat effectiveness, but also because of the heavy investment [[we make in training them]], the costs of replacing them, and the many years [[required to produce competent combat pilots]]. ||| [Text 115] 'Troublingly, pilots are increasingly being lost ...'

(iii) Element. When the realization of a whole figure is downgraded through metaphor from clause to nominal group, its elements will, of course, also be downgraded: the process is nominalized and serves as Thing (except in the case of a qualitative attributive relational clause, where it is the Attribute that is reconstrued as Thing, as noted above); the other elements of the figure are realized either as downranked groups/phrases serving as Qualifier or Deictic (instead of as ranking ones, serving in a clause) or, by a further step, as words serving as Classifier, Epithet or post-Deictic. For example, *my original intention* in *my original intention was to write a saga covering three generations of the Okonkwo family in one book* is structured as Deictic ^ Post-Deictic ^ Thing, corresponding to the congruent clause Subject ^ Adjunct ^ Predicator: see Figure 10-15. Further examples:

severe wave erosion of the former Redondo Beach waterfront – Epithet/Manner ^ Classifier/Agent ^ Thing/ Process ^ Qualifier/ Medium

the growing loss of pilots – Epithet/Manner ('more and more') ^ Thing/Process ^ Qualifier/Medium

nervousness due to inspection – Thing/Attribute ^ Qualifier/ Cause [from an enhancing figure]

a first important observation – post-Deictic/Conjunctive ^ Epithet/comment Adjunct ^ Thing/ Process

These are examples of elements that are realized metaphorically as a consequence of serving in figures that are realized metaphorically. But elements may also be internally metaphorical in figures that are otherwise congruent.

'I'	'originally'	'intended'
Subject	Adjunct	Finite/ Predicator
Senser		Process
nominal group	adverbial group	verbal group
my	original	intention
Deictic	Post-Deictic	Thing
determiner	adjective	noun

Fig. 10-15   Metaphorical nominal group realizing a figure

The typology of ideational metaphors that we have sketched above is intended to identify general tendencies; but it leaves out both details and distinct types (such as that of metaphorical 'mental' clauses of perception, discussed above in relation to textual considerations). In Halliday & Matthiessen (1999: Ch. 6) we present a much more detailed typology of ideational metaphor, identifying the various features that make up the tendencies we have identified here. For other investigations of ideational metaphor, see the contributions in Vandenbergen, Taverniers & Ravelli (2003); for approaches to metaphor in different traditions, see Taverniers (2002); for the role of ideational metaphor in education, see e.g. Halliday & Martin (1993), Derewianka (1995), Martin & Veel (1998), Painter, Derewianka & Torr (2007), and Christie & Derewianka (2008). Let us round off the discussion of types by showing an analysis that relates the metaphorical and congruent versions of an example through a series of steps: see Figure 10-16.

10.5.5 Spoken and written language

The factor that perhaps tends most to determine the extent of metaphor in the grammar of a text is whether that text is spoken or written; speech and writing are rather different in their patterns of metaphoric usage. This is because they have different ways of constructing complex meanings.

It might be assumed that metaphor, while not inherently value-laden, is nevertheless inherently complex, and that the least metaphorical wording will always be the one that is maximally simple. The often professed ideal of 'plain, simple English' would seem to imply something that is in general what we are calling congruent. But the concept of 'plain and simple' is itself very far from being plain and simple; anything approaching technical language, for example, tends to become noticeably more complex if one tries to 'simplify' it by removing the metaphors. As a test of this, try constructing a congruent variant of the clause *braking distance increases more rapidly at high speeds*.

The explanation is that there is more than one kind of complexity (see e.g. Halliday, 1985a, 1987a). Typically, written language becomes complex by being **lexically dense**: it packs a large number of lexical items into each clause; whereas spoken language becomes complex by being **grammatically intricate**: it builds up elaborate clause complexes out of parataxis and hypotaxis.

Consider the following sentence, from *The Horizon Book of Railways*, pp. 74–75:

advances	in technology	are speeding up		the	writing	of business programs
Actor		Process: material		Goal		
nominal group		verbal group		nominal group		
Thing	Qualifier: Place (abstract)			Deictic	Thing	Qualifier/Medium

advances in technology		are enabling	people	to write	business programs	faster
			Actor			
Initiator		Process: α causative		β material	Goal	Manner: quality

because	technology	is advancing		people	are (becoming) able to write	business programs	faster
		×β			α		
	Actor	Process: material		Actor	Process: material/ modulation	Goal	Manner: quality

because	technology	is getting	better	people	are able to write	business programs	faster
		×β			α		
	Carrier	Process: attributive	Attribute	Actor	Process: material/ modulation	Goal	Manner: quality

Fig. 10-16   Step-by-step analysis of a transitivity metaphor

In bridging river valleys, the early engineers built many notable masonry viaducts of numerous arches.

The clause complex and transitivity analysis is given in Figure 10-17.

To measure lexical density, simply divide the number of lexical items by the number of ranking clauses. This example has eleven lexical items (*bridging, river, valleys, early, engineers, built, notable, masonry, viaducts, numerous, arches*), and two clauses; hence lexical density 5.5. Note that the grammatical structure both of the clause complex as a whole and of each constituent clause is rather simple.

Let us now reword this in a form more typical of the spoken language. If we retain the same lexical items, but reword in a more naturally spoken form, we might arrive at something like the following:

in	bridging	river valleys	the early engineers	built	many notable masonry viaducts of numerous arches
×β			α		
	Process: material	Goal	Actor	Process: material	Goal

Fig. 10-17 An example of high lexical density

In the early days when engineers had to make a bridge across a valley and the valley had a river flowing through it, they often built viaducts, which were constructed of masonry and had numerous arches in them; and many of these viaducts became notable.

Here the structure of the clause complex is

$$1×β1 \wedge 1×β+2 \wedge 1α α \wedge 1α =β1 \wedge 1α=β+2 \wedge +2$$

There are now six grammatically related clauses, rather than just two. The total number of lexical items has gone up to seventeen, mainly because there is some repetition; but since there are six ranking clauses, the lexical density is slightly under 3.

In other words, the written version is more complex in terms of lexical density, while the spoken version is more complex in terms of grammatical intricacy (cf. Matthiessen, 2002a). The lexical items in the written version thus have fewer clauses to accommodate them; but obviously they are still part of the overall grammatical structure – what typically happens is that they are incorporated into nominal groups. The nominal group is the primary resource used by the grammar for packing in lexical items at high density. An example is that in Figure 10-18. Here the relationships which are expressed **clausally** in the spoken version (*the viaducts were constructed of masonry and had numerous arches in them*) are instead expressed **nominally** (*masonry viaducts of numerous arches*). The clause complex is replaced by the nominal group.

many	notable	masonry	viaducts	of	numerous	arches
Numerative	Epithet	Classifier	Thing	Qualifier		
				'Predicator'	'Complement'	
					Numerative	Thing

Fig. 10-18 A dense nominal group

In spoken language, the ideational content is loosely strung out, but in clausal patterns that can become highly intricate in movement: the complexity is dynamic – we might think of it in choreographic terms. In written language, the clausal patterns are typically rather simple; but the ideational content is densely packed in nominal constructions: here the complexity is more static – perhaps crystalline. These are, it should be made clear, general tendencies; not every particular instance will conform. But they do bring out the essential

character of the relationship between the two. And it is the written kind of complexity that involves grammatical metaphor.

10.5.6 Ideational metaphors and nominalization

The example discussed in the last section was concerned with a material process of a concrete kind, namely building viaducts; and it was taken from a book written to be read by children. There was some degree of grammatical metaphor in it, e.g. *early engineers*, *notable viaducts*, but not a great deal. Here for comparison is an example from writing from adults:

> The argument to the contrary is basically an appeal to the lack of synonymy in mental language.

This is a relational process clause, identifying, with structure Id/Vl ^ Ir/Tk. The lexical density is 8 (one clause, eight lexical items). We might reword it as:

> In order to argue that [this] is not so [he] simply points out that there are no synonyms in mental language.

This is four clauses, structure ×βα β'β αα α'β, with six lexical items in them; lexical density 1.5.

The original version has two nominal groups: *the argument to the contrary* and *an appeal to the lack of synonymy in mental language*; and both involve grammatical metaphor. The negative existential clause *there are no synonyms* is nominalized as *the lack of synonymy*; the projecting clause complex [*he*] *points out that there are no synonyms* is nominalized (via [*he*] *appeals to the lack of ...*) as *an appeal to the lack of synonymy*; the clause [*this*] *is not so* is nominalized as *the contrary*, and the projecting clause complex *to argue that ... not* is nominalized (via *to argue to the contrary*) as *the argument to the contrary*. As always, there would be other ways of 'unpacking' these metaphors; but whatever the more congruent wording that is constructed, when it is then reworded back to the original metaphorical form this will mainly involve turning clausal patterns into nominal ones.

Nominalizing is the single most powerful resource for creating grammatical metaphor. By this device, processes (congruently worded as verbs) and properties (congruently worded as adjectives) are reworded metaphorically as nouns; instead of functioning in the clause, as Process or Attribute, they function as Thing in the nominal group. Thus, for example:

is impaired by alcohol	alcohol impairment
they allocate an extra packer	the allocation of an extra packer
some shorter, some longer	of varying length
they were able to reach the computer	their access to the computer
technology is getting better	advances in technology

What then happens to the original 'things'? They get displaced by the metaphoric ones, and so are reduced to modifying these: *alcohol* becomes a Classifier of *impairment*; *the computer*, *one extra packer* and *technology* go into prepositional phrases functioning as Qualifier to, respectively, *access*, *allocation* and *advances*.

This kind of nominalizing metaphor probably evolved first in scientific and technical registers (cf. Halliday, 1967b, 1988), where it played a dual role: it made it possible on the one hand to construct hierarchies of technical terms, and on the other hand to develop an argument step by step, using complex passages 'packaged' in nominal form as Themes. It has gradually worked its way through into most other varieties of adult discourse, in much of which, however, it loses its original *raison d'être* and tends to become merely a mark of prestige and power. Notice that when clausal patterns are replaced by nominal ones, some of the information is lost: for example, the Classifier + Thing construction *alcohol impairment* gives no indication of the semantic relation between the two and could be agnate to *alcohol impairs* (*alcohol* as Actor), *alcohol is impaired* (*alcohol* as Goal), and maybe other transitivity configurations besides. The writer presumably knows exactly what it means; but the reader may not, and so this kind of highly metaphorical discourse tends to mark off the expert from those who are uninitiated.

How far should one pursue the analysis of ideational metaphors? There can be no universally valid answer to this question; it depends on what one is trying to achieve. In an example such as *The second day of the convention saw the advantage pushed further*, there is an obvious tension between *day* as Senser and *saw* as mental Process which needs explaining (cf. Figure 10-13). But in most instances of contemporary discourse it is only when we start to analyse that we become aware of the grammatical metaphors involved. The important point to make is that a piece of wording that is metaphorical has, as it were, an additional dimension of meaning: it 'means' both metaphorically and congruently. Thus, to go back to *alcohol impairment*: here *impairment* is a noun functioning as Thing, and hence takes on the status of an entity participating in some other process, as in:

> Because alcohol impairment effects are well established and documented, alcohol impairment can be used as a benchmark for other forms of driving impairment, such as fatigue, or in comparison to the effects of other drugs.

It does not thereby lose its own semantic character as a process, which it has by virtue of the fact that congruently it is realized as a verb; but it acquires an additional semantic feature by becoming a noun. Compare *failure* in

> Engines of the 36 class only appeared on this train in times of reduced loading, or engine failure.

– where a more congruent version would be *whenever an engine failed*. Thus, however far one may choose to go in unpacking ideational metaphor, it is important also to analyse each instance as it is. A significant feature of our present-day world is that it consists so largely of metaphorically constructed entities, like *access*, *advances*, *allocation*, *impairment* and *appeal*.

The concept of grammatical metaphor enables us to bring together a number of features of discourse which at first sight look rather different from each other. But when we recognize the different kinds of meaning that come together in the lexicogrammar, and especially the basic distinction between ideational and interpersonal meaning, we can see that what look like two different sets of phenomena are really instances of the same phenomenon arising in these two different contexts. In all the instances that we are treating as grammatical metaphor, some aspect of the structural configuration of the clause, whether in its ideational

function or in its interpersonal function or in both[6], is in some way different from that which would be arrived at by the shortest route – it is not, or was not originally, the most straightforward coding of the meanings selected. This feature is not to be interpreted as something negative or deviant; it is partly in order to avoid any such connotations that we have used the term 'metaphorical rather than 'incongruent'. But it is something that needs to be accounted for in an adequate interpretation of a text.

How far we go in pursuing metaphorical forms of discourse in any given instance will depend on what we are trying to achieve. In the most general terms, the purpose of analysing a text is to explain the impact that it makes: why it means what it does, and why it gives the particular impression that it does. But within this general goal we may have various kinds and degrees of interest in exploring this or that specific instance; sometimes a note to the effect that the expression is metaphorical is all that is needed, whereas at other times we may want to trace a whole series of intermediate steps linking the clause to a postulated 'most congruent' form. These are not to be thought of as a 'history' of the clause; as we have seen, in some areas the metaphorical form has become the typical, coded form of expression in the language, and even where it is not, there is no way of tracking the process whereby a speaker or writer has arrived at a particular mode of expression in the discourse. What the metaphorical interpretation does is to suggest how an instance in the text may be referred to the system of the language as a whole. It is therefore an important link in the total chain of explanations whereby we relate the text to the system. A text is meaningful because it is an actualization of the potential that constitutes the linguistic system; it is for this reason that the study of discourse ('text linguistics') cannot properly be separated from the study of the grammar that lies behind it.

---

[6] While some scholars have explored the possibility of grammatical metaphor within the textual metafunction, we do not see any evidence that the textual metafunction engenders metaphor. It is certainly a factor in the metaphorical mode of realization – particularly, in ideational metaphor, as we have illustrated above; but the origins of metaphor lie in the need to re-construe experience (ideational) and to re-enact roles and relations (interpersonal). The role of the textual metafunction is of a different nature (cf. Matthiessen, 1992).

REFERENCES

Aarts, B. & McMahon, A. (eds) 2006. *The handbook of English linguistics*. Oxford: Blackwell.

Abercrombie, D. 1967. *Elements of general phonetics*. Chicago: Aldine Publishing Company & Edinburgh: Edinburgh University Press.

Aijmer, K. & Simon-Vandenbergen, A-M. 2009. Pragmatic markers. In: Östman, J-O. & Verschueren, J. (eds) *Handbook of pragmatics*. 2009 Installment. Amsterdam & Philadelphia: John Benjamins. 223–247.

Allerton, D.J. 2002. *Stretched verb constructions in English*. London & New York: Routledge.

Andersen, T., Petersen, U.H. & Smedegaard, F. 2001. *Sproget some resource: dansk systemisk functionel lingvistik i teori og praksis*. Odense: Odense Universitetsforlag.

Bateman, J.A. 1988. Aspects of clause politeness in Japanese: an inquiry semantic treatment. *The 26th Annual Meeting of the Association for Computational Linguistics*. 147–154.

Bateman, J.A. 1989. Dynamic systemic-functional grammar: a new frontier. *Word* **40** 1–2: 263–287.

Bateman, J.A. 2008. *Multimodality and genre: a foundation for the systematic analysis of multimodal documents*. London & New York: Palgrave Macmillan.

Bateman, J.A., Matthiessen, C.M.I.M. & Zeng, L. 1999. Multilingual language generation for multilingual software: a functional linguistic approach. *Applied Artificial Intelligence: An International Journal* **13** 6: 607–639.

Bateman, J., Matthiessen, C., Nanri, K. & Zeng, L. 1991. The rapid prototyping of natural language generation components: an application of functional typology. *Proceedings of the 12th International Conference on Artificial Intelligence, Sydney, 24–30 August 1991*. San Mateo, CA: Morgan Kaufman. 966–971.

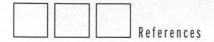

Beavers, J., Levin, B. & Thao, S.W. 2010. The typology of motion expressions revisited. *Journal of Linguistics* **46**: 331–377.

Beckner, C., Blythe, R., Christiansen, M.H., Croft, W., Ellis, N.C., Holland, J., Ke, J., Larsen-Freeman, D. & Shoenemann, T. 2009. Language is a complex adaptive system: position paper. *Language Learning* **59**: Supplement 1, *Language as a complex adaptive system*, edited by Ellis, N.C. & Larsen-Freeman, D. 1–26.

Beekman, J., Callow, J. & Kopesec, M. 1981. *The semantic structure of written communication*. Dallas, TX: Summer Institute of Linguistics.

Benson, J.D. & Greaves, W.S. 1992. Collocation and field of discourse. In: Mann, W.C. & Thompson, S.A. (eds) *Discourse description: diverse analyses of a fund-raising text*. Amsterdam: Benjamins. 397–410.

Benson, J.D., Cummings, M.J. & Greaves, W.S. (ed.) 1988. *Linguistics in a systemic perspective*. Amsterdam: Benjamins.

Berry, M. 1981. Systemic linguistics and discourse analysis: a multi-layered approach to exchange structure. In: Coulthard, M. & Montgomery, J. (eds) *Studies in discourse analysis*. London: Routledge & Kegan Paul.

Biber, D., Johansson, S., Leech, G., Conrad, S. & Finnegan, E. 1999. *The Longman grammar of spoken and written English*. London: Longman.

Blöhdorn, L.M. 2009. *Postmodifying attributive adjectives in English: an integrated corpus-based approach*. Frankfurt am Main: Peter Lang.

Bloomfield, L. 1933. *Language*. London: Allen & Unwin.

Bloor, T. & Bloor, M. 1995. *The functional analysis of English: a Hallidayan approach*. London: Edward Arnold.

Bloor, T. & Bloor, M. 2004. *Functional analysis of English*. Second edition. London: Hodder & Stoughton Educational.

Bod, R., Hay, J. & Jannedy, S. (eds) 2003. *Probabilistic linguistics*. Cambridge, Mass: MIT Press.

Bolinger, D. 1967. Adjectives in English: attribution and predication. *Lingua* **18**: 1–34.

Brinton, L. 2009. Pathways in the evelopment of pragmatic markers in English. In: van Kemenade, A. & Los, B. (eds) *The handbook of the history of English*. Oxford: Wiley-Blackwell. 307–334.

Brown, P. & Levinson, S. 1987. *Politeness: some universals in language usage*. Cambridge: Cambridge University Press.

Brown, R. & Gilman, A. 1960. The pronouns of power and solidarity. In: Sebeok, T.A. (ed.) *Style in language*. Cambridge, Mass.: MIT Press. 253–76. Also in: Giglioli, P.P. (1972) (ed.) *Language and social context: selected readings*. 252–282.

Butler, C.S. 1988. Politeness and the semantics of modalised directives in English. In: Benson, J.D., Cummings, M.J. & Greaves, W.S. (eds) *Linguistics in a systemic perspective*. Amsterdam: Benjamins. 119–154.

Butt, D.G. & Matthiessen, C.M.I.M. forthc. *The meaning potential of language: mapping meaning systemically*. Book in MS.

Butt, D.G. & Wegener, R.K.A. 2007. The work of concepts: context and metafunction in the systemic functional model. In: Hasan, Matthiessen & Webster (eds) (2007). 589–618.

REFERENCES

Butt, D., Fahey, R., Feez, S., Spinks, S. & Yallop, C. 2000. *Using functional grammar: an explorer's guide*. Second edition. Sydney: Macquarie University, NCELTR (National Centre for English Language Teaching and Research).

Butt, M. 2003. The light verb jungle. In: *Harvard Working Papers in Linguistics*, Ay-gen, G., Bowern, C. and Quinn, C. (eds.) 1–49. *Volume 9*, Papers from the GSAS/Dudley House Workshop on Light Verbs.

Byrnes, H. (ed.) 2006. *Advanced instructed language learning: the complementary contribution of Halliday and Vygotsky*. London & New York: Continuum.

Caffarel, A. 2000. Interpreting French theme as a bi-layered structure: discourse implications. In: Ventola, E. (ed.) *Discourse and community: doing functional linguistics*. Tübingen: Gunter Narr Verlag. 247–272.

Caffarel, A. 2004. Metafunctional profile of the grammar of French. In: Caffarel, Martin & Matthiessen (eds). 77–137.

Caffarel, A. 2006. *A systemic functional grammar of French: from grammar to discourse*. London & New York: Continuum.

Caffarel, A., Martin, J.R. & Matthiessen, C.M.I.M. (eds) 2004. *Language typology: a functional perspective*. Amsterdam: Benjamins.

Capra, F. 1996. *The web of life: a new synthesis of mind and matter*. London: Harper Collins.

Catford, J.C. 1977. *Fundamental problems in phonetics*. Indiana: Indiana University Press.

Catford, J.C. 1985. 'Rest' and 'open transition' in a systemic phonology of English. In: Benson, J.D. & Greaves, W.S. (eds) *Systemic perspectives on discourse*. Norwood NJ: Ablex.

Cheng, W. 2011. *Exploring corpus linguistics: language in action*. London: Routledge.

Cheng, W., Greaves, C., Sinclair, J. McH. & Warren, M. 2009. Uncovering the extent of the phraseological tendency: towards a systematic analysis of concgrams. *Applied Linguistics* **30** 2: 236–252.

Christie, F. & Derewianka, B. 2008. *School discourse: learning to write across the years of schooling*. London & New York: Continuum.

Christie, F. & Martin, J.R. (eds) 1997. *Genre and institutions: social processes in the workplace and school*. London & New York: Continuum.

Cloran, C. 1994. *Rhetorical units and decontextualisation: an enquiry into some relations of context, meaning and grammar*. University of Nottingham: Monographs in Systemic Linguistics Number 6.

Cloran, C., Stuart-Smith, V. & Young, L. 2007. Models of discourse. In: Hasan, Matthiessen & Webster (eds) 2007. 645–668.

Coffin, C. 2006. *Historical discourse*. London & New York: Continuum.

Coffin, C., Donohue, J. & North, S. 2009. *Exploring English grammar: from formal to functional*. London: Routledge.

Cohen, R. 1984. A computational theory of the function of clue words in argument understanding. *Proceedings of COLING 84*. 251–258.

Collins, P.J. 1991. *Cleft and pseudo-cleft constructions in English*. London and New York: Routledge.

Coulthard, M. 1993. On beginning the study of forensic texts: corpus, concordance, collocation. In: Hoey, M. (ed.) *Data, description, discourse: papers on the English language in honour of John McH Sinclair on his sixtieth birthday*. London: HarperCollins. 86–97.

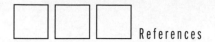

Covington, M.A. 1984. *Syntactic theory in the High Middle Ages: modistic models of sentence structure*. Cambridge: Cambridge University Press.

Davidse, K. 1991. *Categories of experiential grammar*. Catholic University of Leuven: Ph.D. thesis. Published in the Nottingham University series Monographs in Systemic Linguistics, 1999.

Davidse, K. 1992. A semiotic approach to relational clauses. *Occasional Papers in Systemic Linguistics* 6.

Davidse, K. 1992. Existential constructions: a systemic perspective. *Leuven Contributions in Linguistics and Philology* 81: 71–99.

Davidse, K. 1996. Turning grammar on itself: identifying clauses in linguistic discourse. In: Butler, C., Berry, M., Fawcett, R. & Huang, G. (eds) *Meaning and form: systemic functional interpretations*. Norwood, NJ: Ablex. 367–393.

Davies, H. 1980. *George Stevenson: the remarkable life of the founder of the railways*. Feltham, Middx: Hamlyn Paperbacks.

Davies, M. 1986. Literacy and intonation. In: Couture, B. (ed.) *Functional approaches to writing: research perspectives*. Norwood, NJ: Ablex. 199–230.

Depraetere, I. & Reed, R. 2006. Mood and modality in English. In: Aarts & McMahon (eds) 269–290.

Derewianka, B. 1995. *Language development in the transition from childhood to adolescence: the role of grammatical metaphor*. Macquarie University: Ph.D. thesis.

Dik, S. 1978. *Functional grammar*. Amsterdam: North-Holland.

Dixon, R.M.W. 2010. *Basic linguistic theory. Volume 1: methodology*. Oxford: Oxford University Press.

Downing, A. 1990. The discourse function of presentative *there* in existential structures in Middle English and Present-Day English: a systemic functional perspective. *Occasional Papers in Systemic Linguistics* 4.

Downing, A. 1996. The semantics of get-passives. In: Hasan, Cloran & Butt (eds). 179–207.

Eggins, S. 1990. *Conversational structure: a systemic-functional analysis of interpersonal and logical meaning in multiparty sustained talk*. Department of Linguistics, University of Sydney: Ph.D. thesis.

Eggins, S. 2004. *An introduction to systemic functional linguistics*. Second edition. London & New York: Continuum.

Eggins, S. & Slade, D. 1997. *Analysing casual conversation*. London: Cassell.

Eggins, S. & Slade, D. 2005. *Analysing casual conversation*. Second edition. London: Equinox.

Eggins, S., Wignell, P. & Martin, J.R. 1993. The discourse of history: distancing the recoverable past. In: Ghadessy (ed.). 75–109.

Ellegård, A. 1953. *The Auxiliary 'do': the establishment and regulation of its use in English*. Stockholm: Almqvist and Wiksell.

Ellis, J.M. 1993. *Language, thought, and logic*. Evanston, Ill.: Northwestern University Press.

Elmenoufy, A. 1988. Intonation and meaning in spontaneous discourse. In: Benson, Cummings & Greaves (eds). 1–27.

Ervin-Tripp, S. 1972. On sociolinguistic rules: alternation and co-occurrence. In: Gumperz, J. & Hymes, D. (eds) (1972). *Directions in sociolinguistics: The ethnography of communication*. New York: Holt, Rinehart and Winston. 213–250.

 REFERENCES

Fawcett, R.P. 1987. The semantics of clause and verb for relational processes in English. In: Halliday, M.A.K. & Fawcett, R.P. (eds) *New developments in systemic linguistics: theory and description*. London: Pinter. 130–183.

Fawcett, R.P. 1988. What makes a 'good' system network good? Benson, J.D. & Greaves, W.S. (eds) *Systemic functional approaches to discourse*. Norwood, NJ: Ablex. 1–28.

Fawcett, R.P. 1999. On the subject of Subject in English: two positions on its meaning (and how to test for it). *Functions of Language* **6** 2: 243–275.

Fawcett, R.P. 2000. *A theory of syntax for systemic functional linguistics*. Amsterdam: Benjamins.

Fillmore, C.J. 1968. The case for case. In: Bach, E. & Harms, R.T. (eds) 1968. *Universals in linguistic theory*. New York: Holt, Rinehart and Winston. 1–88.

Fillmore, C.J. 2002. Mini-grammars of some time–when expressions in English. In: Bybee, J. & Noonan, M. (eds) *Complex sentences in grammar and discourse: essays in honor of Sandra A. Thompson*. Amsterdam & Philadelphia: Benjamins. 31–59.

Fine, J. 1994. *How language works: cohesion in normal and nonstandard communication*. Norwood, NJ: Ablex.

Firbas, J. 1992. *Functional sentence perspective in written and spoken communication*. Cambridge: Cambridge University Press.

Firth, J.R. 1957. A synopsis of linguistic theory, 1930–1955. In: Firth, J.R. (1957). *Papers in linguistics*. London: Oxford University Press.

Fischer, K. (ed.) 2006. *Approaches to discourse particles*. Amsterdam: Elsevier.

Foley, W.A. & Van Valin, R.D. 1984. *Functional syntax and universal grammar*. Cambridge: Cambridge University Press.

Ford, C.E. & Thompson, S.A. 1986. Conditionals in discourse: a text-based study from English. In: Traugott, E., Ferguson, C., Reilly, J. & ter Meulen, A. (eds) *On conditionals*. Cambridge: Cambridge University Press.

Francis, G. 1985. *Anaphoric nouns*. Discourse Analysis Monographs 11. English Language Research, Department of English, University of Birmingham.

Fraser, B. 2006. Towards a theory of discourse markers. In: Fischer (ed.) 189–205.

Fries, P.H. 1977. English predications of comparison. In: DiPietro, R. & Blansitt, E. (eds) *The Third LACUS Forum 1976*. Columbia, SC: Hornbeam Press. 545–556.

Fries, P.H. 1981. On the status of theme in English: arguments from discourse. *Forum Linguisticum* **6** 1: 1–38. Reprinted in Petöfi, J. & Sözer, E. (eds) *Micro and macro connexity of texts*. (Papers in Linguistics 45.) Hamburg: Helmut Buske Verlag. 116–152.

Fries, P.H. 1985. How does a story mean what it does? A partial answer. In: Benson & Greaves (eds). 295–321.

Fries, P.H. 1992. Information flow in written advertising. In: Alatis, J. (ed.) *Language, communication and social meaning*. Washington, DC: Georgetown University Press. 336–352.

Fujimura, O. & Erickson, D. 1997. Acoustic phonetics. In: Hardcastle, W.J. & Laver, J. (eds) *The handbook of phonetic sciences*. Oxford: Blackwell. 65–115.

Garvin, P. (ed.) 1964. *A Prague School reader on esthetics, literary structure, and style*. Washington, DC: Georgetown University Press.

Ghadessy, M. (ed.) 1993. *Register analysis: theory and practice*. London & New York: Pinter.

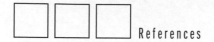 References

Ghadessy, M. (ed.) 1995. *Thematic development in English text*. London: Pinter.

Ghadessy, M. (ed.) 1999. *Text and context in functional linguistics*. Amsterdam: Benjamins.

Gleason, Jr., H.A. 1965. *Linguistics and English grammar*. New York: Holt, Rinehart and Winston, Inc.

Gledhill, C.J. 2000. *Collocations in science writing*. Tübingen: Gunter Narr Verlag.

Grabe, E. & Low, E.L. 2002. Durational variability in speech and the rhythm class hypothesis. In: Gussenhoven, C. & Varner, N. (eds) *Papers in Laboratory Phonology 7*. Berlin: Mouton de Gruyter. 515–546.

Greaves, C. 2009. *ConcGram 1.0: A phraseological search engine*. Amsterdam & Philadelphia: Benjamins.

Gregory, M.J. 1983. Clause and sentence as distinct units in the morphosyntax of English and their relation to semological propositions and predications. In: Morreall, J. (ed.) *The Ninth LACUS Forum*. Columbia: Hornbeam Press.

Gregory, M.J. 2002. Phasal analysis within communication linguistics: two contrastive discourses. In: Cummings, M., Fries, P.H. & Lockwood, D. (eds) *Relations and functions within and around language*. London & New York: Continuum.

Grimes, J.E. 1975. *The thread of discourse*. The Hague: Mouton.

Gruber, J.S. 1976. *Lexical structures in syntax and semantics*. Amsterdam: North-Holland.

Gu, Y. 1999. Towards a model of situated discourse. In: Turner, K. (ed.) *The semantics/pragmatics interface from different points of view*. Oxford: Elsevier. 150–178.

Halliday, M.A.K. 1956. Grammatical categories in Modern Chinese. *Transactions of the Philological Society*. 177–224.

Halliday, M.A.K. 1959. *The language of the Chinese 'Secret history of the Mongols'*. Oxford: Blackwell. (Publications of the Philological Society 17.)

Halliday, M.A.K. 1961. Categories of the theory of grammar. *Word* **17** 3: 242–292. Reprinted as Chapter 2 in Halliday, M.A.K. (2002), *On grammar, Volume 1* of *The collected works of M.A.K. Halliday* edited by Jonathan J. Webster. London & New York: Continuum.

Halliday, M.A.K. 1963a. The tones of English. *Archivum Linguisticum* **15** 1: 1–28.

Halliday, M.A.K. 1963b. Intonation in English grammar. *Transactions of the Philological Society*. 143–169.

Halliday, M.A.K. 1963c. Class in relation to the axes of chain and choice in language. *Linguistics* **2**: 5–15. Reprinted in Halliday, M.A.K. (2002) *On grammar. Volume 1* of *The collected works of M.A.K. Halliday* edited by Jonathan Webster. London & New York: Continuum. Chapter 3: 95–117.

Halliday, M.A.K. 1964. Syntax and the consumer. In: Stuart, C.I.J.M. (ed.) *Report of the Fifteenth Annual (First International) Round Table Meeting on Linguistics and Language*. Washington, DC: Georgetown University Press. 11–24. Reprinted in Halliday & Martin (1981), 21–28, and in Halliday (2003), 36–49.

Halliday, M.A.K. 1965. Types of structure. The OSTI Programme in the Linguistic Properties of Scientific English. In: Halliday & Martin (eds) (1981).

Halliday, M.A.K. 1966a. Some notes on 'deep' grammar. *Journal of Linguistics* **2** 1: 57–67.

Halliday, M.A.K. 1966b. Lexis as a linguistic level. In: Bazell, C.E. *et al.* (eds), *In memory of J.R. Firth*. London: Longman.

Halliday, M.A.K. 1966c. The concept of rank: a reply. *Journal of Linguistics* **2** 1: 110–118.

Halliday, M.A.K. 1967a. *Intonation and grammar in British English*. The Hague: Mouton. (Janua Linguarum Series Practica 48.)

Halliday, M.A.K. 1967b. *Grammar, society and the noun*. London: H.K Lewis for University College London. Reprinted in Halliday, M.A.K. (2003) *On language and linguistics, Volume 3* of *The collected works of M.A.K. Halliday* edited by Jonathan Webster. London & New York: Continuum. Chapter 2: 50–73.

Halliday, M.A.K. 1967/8. *Journal of Linguistics* **3** 1: 37–81, **3** 2: 199–244, **4** 2: 179–215. Reprinted in Halliday, M.A.K. (2005) *Studies in English language, Volume 7* in *The collected works of M.A.K. Halliday* edited by Jonathan Webster. London & New York: Continuum. Chapter 1: 5–54. Chapter 2: 55–109. Chapter 3: 110–153.

Halliday, M.A.K. 1969. Options and functions in the English clause. *Brno Studies in English* **8**: 81–8.

Halliday, M.A.K. 1970. Functional diversity in language, as seen from a consideration of modality and mood in English. *Foundations of language* **6**: 322–361. Reprinted in Halliday, M.A.K. (2005) *Studies in English language, Volume 7* in *The collected works of M.A.K. Halliday* edited by Jonathan Webster. London & New York: Continuum. Chapter 5: 164–204.

Halliday, M.A.K. 1971. Linguistic function and literary style: an enquiry into the language of William Golding's 'The inheritors'. In: Chatman, S. (ed.) *Literary style: a symposium*. New York: Oxford University Press. 330–368. Reprinted in M.A.K. Halliday (2002) *Linguistic studies of text and discourse, Volume 2* in *The collected works of M.A.K. Halliday* edited by Jonathan J. Webster. London and New York: Continuum. Chapter 3: 88–125.

Halliday, M.A.K. 1973. *Explorations in the functions of language*. London: Edward Arnold.

Halliday, M.A.K. 1975. *Learning how to mean*. London: Edward Arnold. Reprinted in M.A.K. Halliday (2003) *The language of early childhood, Volume 4* of *The collected works of M.A.K. Halliday* edited by Jonathan J. Webster. London & New York: Continuum.

Halliday, M.A.K. 1976a. *System and function in language*. Edited by Gunther Kress. London: Oxford University Press.

Halliday, M.A.K. 1976b. The teacher taught the student English: an essay in applied linguistics. In: Reich, P.A. (ed.) The Second LACUS Forum. Hornbeam Press: Columbia. 344–349. Reprinted in Halliday, M.A.K. (2005) *Studies in English language, Volume 7* in *The Collected Works of M.A.K. Halliday* edited by Jonathan Webster. London & New York: Continuum. Chapter 11: 297–305.

Halliday, M.A.K. 1977. Ideas about language. In M.A.K. Halliday, *Aims and perspectives in linguistics*. Applied Linguistics Association of Australia (Occasional Papers 1). 32–49. Reprinted in Halliday, M.A.K. (2003) *On language and linguistics, Volume 3* of *The Collected Works of M.A.K. Halliday* edited by Jonathan Webster. London & New York: Continuum. Chapter 4: 92–115.

Halliday, M.A.K. 1978. *Language as social semiotic: the social interpretation of language and meaning*. London: Edward Arnold.

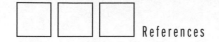

Halliday, M.A.K. 1979. Modes of meaning and modes of expression: types of grammatical structure and their determination by different semantic functions. In: Allerton, D.J. Carney, E. & Holdcroft, D. (eds) *Function and context in linguistic analysis: a Festschrift for William Haas.* Cambridge: Cambridge University Press. 57–79. Reprinted in in Halliday, M.A.K. (2002) *On grammar, Volume 1* of *The collected works of M.A.K. Halliday* edited by Jonathan Webster. London & New York: Continuum. 196–218.

Halliday, M.A.K. 1982. How is a text like a clause? In: Allén, S. (ed.), *Text processing: text analysis and generation, text typology and attrition (Proceedings of Nobel Symposium 51).* Stockholm: Almqvist & Wiksell. 209–247. Reprinted as Text semantics and clause grammar: how is a text like a clause? in Halliday, M.A.K. (2002) *On grammar, Volume 1* of *The collected works of M.A.K. Halliday* edited by Jonathan Webster. London & New York: Continuum. Chapter 9: 219–260.

Halliday, M.A.K. 1984a. 'Language as code and language as behaviour: a systemic-functional interpretation of the nature and ontogenesis of dialogue.' In: Halliday, M.A.K., Fawcett, R.P., Lamb, S. & Makkai, A. (eds) *The semiotics of language and culture.* London: Frances Pinter. *Volume 1:* 3–35.

Halliday, M.A.K. 1984b. On the ineffability of grammatical categories. In: Manning, A., Martin, P. & McCalla, K. (eds) *Tenth LACUS Forum.* Columbia: Hornbeam Press. 3–18. Reprinted in Halliday, M.A.K. (2002) *On grammar, Volume 1* of *The collected works of M.A.K. Halliday* edited by Jonathan J. Webster. London & New York: Continuum. Chapter 11: 291–322.

Halliday, M.A.K. 1985a. *Spoken and written language.* Geelong, Vic.: Deakin University Press.

Halliday, M.A.K. 1985b. Systemic background. In: Benson, J.D. & Greaves, W.S. (eds) *Systemic perspectives on discourse.* Norwood, NJ: Ablex. 1–15. Reprinted in Halliday, M.A.K. (2003) *On language and linguistics, Volume 3* of *The collected works of M.A.K. Halliday* edited by Jonathan Webster. London & New York: Continuum. 185–198.

Halliday, M.A.K. 1985c. Dimensions of discourse analysis: grammar. In: van Dijk, T.A. (ed.) 1985. *The handbook of discourse analysis.* New York: Academic Press. 29–56.

Halliday, M.A.K. 1985d. *An introduction to functional grammar.* London: Edward Arnold.

Halliday, M.A.K. 1987. Spoken and written modes of meaning. In: Horowitz, R. and Samuels, S.J. (eds), *Comprehending oral and written language.* New York: Academic Press. 55–82.

Halliday, M.A.K. 1988. On the language of physical science. In: Ghadessy, M. (ed.) *Registers of written English: situational factors and linguistic features.* London & New York: Pinter Publishers. 162–178. Reprinted in Halliday & Martin (1993).

Halliday, M.A.K. 1990. New ways of meaning: a challenge to applied linguistics. Greek Applied Linguistics Association, *Journal of Applied Linguistics* 6 (Ninth World Congress of Applied Linguistics Special Issue): 7–36. Reprinted in Halliday (2003), Chapter 6: 139–174.

Halliday, M.A.K. 1991. Corpus linguistics and probabilistic grammar. In: Aijmer, K. & Altenberg, B. (eds) *English corpus linguistics: studies in honour of Jan Svartvik.* London: Longman. 30–43.

Halliday, M.A.K. 1992a. The notion of 'context' in language education. In: Le, T. &

REFERENCES

McCausland, M. (eds) *Interaction and development: proceedings of the international conference*, Vietnam, 30 March–1 April 1992. University of Tasmania: Language Education.

Halliday, M.A.K. 1992b. The history of a sentence: an essay in social semiotics. In: Fortunait, V. (ed.) *La cultura italiana e le leterature straniere moderne*. Bologna: Longo Editore [for University of Bologna]. 29–45. Reprinted in Halliday (2003), Chapter 16: 355–374.

Halliday, M.A.K. 1992c. A systemic interpretation of Peking syllable finals. In: Tench, P. (ed.) *Studies in systemic phonology*. London: Pinter. 98–121.

Halliday, M.A.K. 1992d. How do you mean? In: Davies, M. & Ravelli, L. (eds) *Advances in systemic linguistics: recent theory and practice*. London: Pinter. 20–35. Reprinted in Halliday, M.A.K. (2002) *On grammar, Volume 1* of *The collected works of M.A.K. Halliday* edited by Jonathan Webster. London & New York: Continuum. Chapter 13: 352–368.

Halliday, M.A.K. 1992e. Systemic grammar and the concept of a 'science of language'. *Waiguoyu* (Journal of Foreign Languages, Shanghai International Studies University) **2**: 1–9. Reprinted in Halliday, M.A.K. (2003) *On language and linguistics, Volume 3* of *The collected works of M.A.K. Halliday* edited by Jonathan Webster. London & New York: Continuum. Chapter 9: 199–212.

Halliday, M.A.K. 1993a. Quantitative studies and probabilities in grammar. In: Hoey, M. (ed.) *Data, description, discourse: papers on the English language in honour of John McH. Sinclair*. London: Harper Collins. 1–25.

Halliday, M.A.K. 1993b. *Language in a changing world*. Canberra, ACT: Applied Linguistics Association of Australia.

Halliday, M.A.K. 1993c. Towards a language-based theory of learning. *Linguistics and Education* **5** 2: 93–116.

Halliday, M.A.K. 1994. Language and the theory of codes. In: Sadovnik, A. (ed.) *Knowledge and pedagogy: the sociology of Basil Bernstein*. Norwood, NJ: Ablex. 124–142.

Halliday, M.A.K. 1995a. A recent view of 'missteps' in linguistic theory (Review article of John M. Ellis, Language, thought and logic). *Functions of Language* **2**.2: 249–267.

Halliday, M.A.K. 1995b. On language in relation to the evolution of human consciousness. Allén, S. (ed.) *Of thoughts and words: proceedings of Nobel Symposium 92 'The relation between language and mind'*, Stockholm, 8–12 August 1994. Singapore, River Edge, NJ & London: Imperial College Press. 45–84.

Halliday, M.A.K. 1996. On grammar and grammatics. In: Hasan, Cloran & Butt (eds). 1–38.

Halliday, M.A.K. 1998. On the grammar of pain. *Functions of Language* **5** 1: 1–32. Reprinted in Halliday (2005), Chapter 12: 306–337.

Halliday, M.A.K. 2001. On the grammatical foundations of discourse. In: Ren, S., Guthrie, W. & Ronald Fong, I.W.R. (eds) *Grammar and discourse: proceedings of the International Conference on Discourse Analysis*, University of Macau (in conjunction with Tsinghua University, China), 16–18 October 1997. Macau: University of Macau Publication Centre. 47–58.

Halliday, M.A.K. 2002a. The spoken language corpus: a foundation for grammatical theory. In: Aijmer, K. & Altenberg, B. (eds) *Proceedings of ICAME 2002: The theory and use of corpora*, Göteborg 22–26 May 2002. Amsterdam: Editions Rodopi.

Reprinted in Halliday, M.A.K. (2005) *Computational and quantitative studies, Volume 6* in *The collected works of M.A.K. Halliday* edited by Jonathan Webster. London & New York: Continuum. 157–189.

Halliday, M.A.K. 2002b. *On grammar*, Volume 1 of *The collected works of M.A.K. Halliday*, edited by Jonathan J. Webster. London & New York: Continuum.

Halliday, M.A.K. 2002c. *Linguistic studies of text and discourse*. Volume 2 of *The collected works of M.A.K. Halliday*, edited by Jonathan J. Webster. London & New York: Continuum.

Halliday, M.A.K. 2002d. Computing meanings: some reflections on past experience and present prospects. In: Huang, G. & Wang, Z. (eds) *Discourse and language functions*. Shanghai: Foreign Language Teaching and Research Press. 3–25. Reprinted in Halliday, M.A.K. (2005) *Computational and quantitative studies, Volume 6* in *The collected works of M.A.K. Halliday* edited by Jonathan Webster. London & New York: Continuum. 239–267.

Halliday, M.A.K. 2003. *On Language and linguistics, Volume 3* of *The collected works of M.A.K. Halliday* edited by Jonathan J. Webster. London & New York: Continuum.

Halliday, M.A.K. 2003/2006. Written language, standard language, global language. *World Englishes* **22** 4: 405–418. Also in Kachru, Kachru & Nelson (eds). 349–365.

Halliday, M.A.K. 2004. *The language of early childhood, Volume 4* of *The collected works of M.A.K. Halliday* edited by Jonathan Webster. London & New York: Continuum.

Halliday, M.A.K. 2005. *Studies in English language, Volume 7* in the *The collected works of M.A.K. Halliday* edited by Jonathan Webster. London & New York: Continuum.

Halliday, M.A.K. 2008. *Complementarities in language*. (Halliday Centre Series in Appliable Linguistics.) Beijing: The Commercial Press.

Halliday, M.A.K. 2010. Text, discourse and information: a systemic-functional overview. Paper presented at Tongji University, November 2010.

Halliday, M.A.K & Greaves, W.S. 2008. *Intonation in the grammar of English*. London: Equinox.

Halliday, M.A.K & Hasan, R. 1976. *Cohesion in English*. London: Longman.

Halliday, M.A.K & Hasan, R. 1985. *Language, context and text: a social semiotic perspective*. Geelong, Vic.: Deakin University Press.

Halliday, M.A.K & James, Z.L. 1993. A quantitative study of polarity and primary tense in the English finite clause. In: Sinclair, J.M., Hoey, M. & Fox, G. (eds), *Techniques of description: spoken and written discourse (A Festschrift for Malcolm Coulthard)*. London and New York: Routledge. 32–66.

Halliday, M.A.K. & McDonald, E. 2004. Metafunctional profile of the grammar of Chinese. In Caffarel, Martin & Matthiessen (eds). 305–396.

Halliday, M.A.K., McIntosh, A. & Strevens, P. 1964. *The linguistic sciences and language teaching*. London: Longman.

Halliday, M.A.K. & Martin, J.R. (eds) 1981. *Readings in systemic linguistics*. London: Batsford.

Halliday, M.A.K. & Martin, J.R. 1993. *Writing science: literacy and discursive power*. London: Falmer.

Halliday, M.A.K. & Matthiessen, C.M.I.M. 1999. *Construing experience through meaning: a language-based approach to cognition*. London: Cassell.

741

Halliday, M.A.K. & Matthiessen, C.M.I.M. 2006. *Construing experience through meaning: a language-based approach to cognition.* (Study edition.) London & New York: Continuum.

Halliday, M.A.K., Teubert, W., Yallop, C. & Čermáková, A. 2004. *Lexicology and corpus linguistics.* London & New York: Continuum.

Halliday, M.A.K. & Webster, J. (eds) 2009. *Continuum companion to systemic functional linguistics.* London & New York: Continuum.

Harris, A.C. & Campbell, L. 1995. *Historical syntax in cross-linguistic perspective.* Cambridge: Cambridge University Press.

Harvey, A. 1999. Definitions in English technical discourse: a study in metafunctional dominance and interaction. *Functions of Language* **6** 1: 55–96.

Hasan, R. 1973. Code, register and social dialect. In: Bernstein, B. (ed.) *Class, codes and control: applied studies towards a sociology of language. Volume 2.* London: Routledge & Kegan Paul. 253–292.

Hasan, R. 1984. The nursery tale as a genre. *Nottingham Linguistic Circular* **13**. Reprinted in Hasan (1996), 51–72.

Hasan, R. 1985a. Lending and borrowing: from grammar to lexis. *Beiträge zur Phonetik und Linguistik* **48**: 56–67.

Hasan, R. 1985b. *Linguistics, language and verbal art.* Geelong, Vic.: Deakin University Press.

Hasan, R. 1987. The grammarian's dream: lexis as most delicate grammar. In: Halliday, M.A.K. & Fawcett, R.P. (eds) *New developments in systemic linguistics: theory and description.* London: Pinter. 184–211.

Hasan, R. 1996. *Ways of saying: ways of meaning. Selected papers of Ruqaiya Hasan* edited by Cloran, C., Butt, D. & Williams, G. (Open Linguistics Series). London: Cassell.

Hasan, R. 1999. Speaking with reference to context. In: Ghadessy (ed.) 1999. 219–328.

Hasan, R., Cloran, C. & Butt, D (eds). 1996. *Functional descriptions: language form and linguistic theory.* Current Issues in Linguistic Theory, No. 121. Amsterdam & Philadelphia: Benjamins.

Hasan, R., Cloran, C., Williams, G. & Lukin, A. 2007. Semantic networks: the description of linguistic meaning in SFL. In: Hasan, Matthiessen & Webster (eds) 697–738.

Hasan, R. & Fries, P. (eds) 1995. *On subject and theme: a discourse functional perspective.* Amsterdam and Philadelphia: Benjamins.

Hasan, R., Matthiessen, C.M.I.M. & Webster, J. (eds) 2005. *Continuing discourse on language: a functional perspective. Volume 1.* London: Equinox Publishing.

Hasan, R., Matthiessen, C.M.I.M. & Webster, J. (eds) 2007. *Continuing discourse on language: a functional perspective. Volume 2.* London: Equinox Publishing.

Hetzron, R. 1975. The presentative movement, or why the ideal word order is VSOP. In: Li, C. (ed.) *Word order and word order change.* New York: Academic Press. 346–388.

Hockett, C.F. 1958. *A course in modern linguistics.* New York: Macmillan.

Hoey, M. 2000. Persuasive rhetoric in linguistics: a stylistic study of some features of the language of Noam Chomsky. In: Hunston, S. & Thompson, G. (eds) *Evaluation in text: authorial stance and the construction of discourse.* Oxford: Oxford University Press. 28–37.

Hoey, M. 2005. *Lexical priming: a new theory of words and language*. London & New York: Routledge.

Hoffmann, S. 2006. Tag questions in Early and Late Modern English: historical description and theoretical implications. *Anglistik* **17** 2: 35–55.

Holmes, J. 2000. Victoria University's Language in the Workplace Project: An overview. *Language in the Workplace Occasional Papers 1*. (Available at: http://www.victoria. ac.nz/lals/lwp/docs/ops/op1.pdf.)

Hood, S. 2011. Body language in face-to-face teaching: a focus on textual and interpersonal meaning. In: Dreyfus, S., Hood, S. & Stenglin, M. (eds) *Semiotic margins: meaning in multimodalities*. London & New York: Continuum. 31–52.

Hopper, P. 1987. Emergent grammar. *Berkeley Linguistic Society* **13**: 139–157.

Hopper, P. 1998. Emergent grammar. In: Tomasello, M. (ed.) *The new psychology of language*. Mahwah, NJ: Lawrence Erlbaum Associates, Publishers. 155–175.

Hopper, P. & Traugott, E.C. 1993. *Grammaticalization*. Cambridge: Cambridge University Press. (Cambridge Textbooks in Linguistics.)

Hori, M. 2006. Pain expressions in Japanese. In: Thompson & Hunston (eds). 206–225.

Hornby, A.L. 1954. *A guide to patterns and usage in English*. London: Oxford University Press.

Huddleston, R.D. 1965. Rank and Depth. *Language* **41**: 574–586. Reprinted in Halliday, M.A.K. & Martin, J.R. (eds) (1981) *Readings in systemic linguistics*. London: Batsford. 42–53.

Huddleston, R.D. & Pullum, G. 2002. *The Cambridge grammar of the English language*. Cambridge: Cambridge University Press.

Hunston, S. & Francis, G. 2000. *Pattern grammar: a corpus-driven approach to the lexical grammar of English*. Amsterdam: Benjamins.

Hunston, S. & Thompson, G. (eds) 2006. *System and corpus: exploring connections*. London: Equinox.

Iedema, R., Feez, S. & White, W. 1994. *Media literacy*. (Write it right industry research report no. 2.) Sydney: NSW, Department of Education, Disadvantaged Schools Program Metropolitan East.

Jackendoff, R. 1972. *Semantic interpretation in generative grammar*. Cambridge, Mass.: MIT Press.

Jespersen, O. 1924. *The philosophy of grammar*. London: George Allen & Unwin Ltd.

Jespersen, O. 1928. *A modern English grammar on historical principles III*. London: Allen and Unwin.

Jespersen, O. 1937. *Analytic syntax*. London: Allen & Unwin.

Jespersen, O. 1942. *A modern English grammar on historical principles. Part VI*. Copenhagen: Ejnar Munksgaard.

Jones, S. 1999. *Almost like a whale: the Origin of Species updated*. London & New York: Doubleday.

Kachru, B.B., Kachru, Y. & Nelson, C.L. (eds) 2006. *The handbook of World Englishes*. Oxford: Blackwell.

Kay, P. & Fillmore, C.J. 1999. Grammatical constructions and linguistic generalizations: *What's X doing Y?* construction. *Language* **73** 1: 1–33.

Kirsner, R. & Thompson, S.A. 1976. The role of inference in semantics: a study of sensory verb complements in English. *Glossa* **10**: 200–240.

Kortmann, B., Burridge, K., Mesthrie, R., Schneider, E.W. & Upton, C. (eds) (2004) *A handbook of varieties of English. Volume II: Morphology and syntax*. Berlin & New York: Mouton de Gruyter.

Kress, G. & van Leeuwen, T. 1996. *Reading images: the grammar of visual design*. London: Routledge.

Kress, G. & van Leeuwen, T. 2001. *Multimodal discourse*. London: Arnold.

Lamb, S. 1999. *Pathways of the brain: the neurocognitive basis of language*. Amsterdam: Benjamins.

Landau, S.I. 1989. *Dictionaries: The art and craft of lexicography*. Cambridge: Cambridge University Press.

Lascaratou, C. 2007. *The language of pain: expression or description?* Amsterdam: John Benjamins.

Lavid, J., Arús, J. & Zamorano-Mansilla, J.R. 2009. *Systemic functional grammar of Spanish: a contrastive study with English*. London & New York: Continuum.

Law, V. 2003. *The history of linguistics in Europe: from Plato to 1600*. Cambridge: Cambridge University Press.

van Leeuwen, T. 1999. *Speech, music, sound*. London & New York: Palgrave Macmillan.

Leimgruber, J.R.E. 2011. Singapore English. *Language and Linguistics Compass* **5** 1: 47–62.

Lemke, J.L. 1984. *Semiotics and education*. Toronto: Toronto Semiotic Circle.

Levin, B. 1993. *English verb classes and alternations: a preliminary investigation*. Chicago & London: The University of Chicago Press.

Li, C.N. & Thompson, S.A. 1976. Subject and Topic: a new typology of language. In: Li, C.N. (ed.) *Subject and topic*. New York: Academic Press. 458–489.

Linn, A. 2006. English grammar writing. In: Aarts & McMahon (eds). 72–92.

Lock, G. 1995. *Functional English grammar: an introduction for second language teachers*. Cambridge: Cambridge University Press.

Longacre, R.E. 1970. Sentence structure as a statement calculus. *Language* **46**: 783–815.

Longacre, R.E. 1985. Sentences as combinations of clauses. In: Shopen, T. (ed.) *Language typology and syntactic descriptions: III Complex constructions*. Cambridge: Cambridge University Press. 235–287.

Longacre, R.E. 1996. *The grammar of discourse*. Second edition. New York: Plenum.

Longacre, R.E. & Hwang, S.J.J. 2012. *Holistic discourse analysis*. Dallas, TX: SIL International Publications.

Lukin, A., Moore, A., Herke, M., Wegener, R. & Wu, C. 2008. Halliday's model of register revisited and explored. *Linguistics and the Human Sciences* **4**.2: 187–243.

Lyons, J. 1977. *Semantics. Volume 2*. Cambridge: Cambridge University Press.

McArthur, T. 1986. *Worlds of reference: lexicography, learning and language from the clay tablet to the computer*. Cambridge: Cambridge University Press.

McCawley, J. 1988. *The syntactic phenomena of English*. Two volumes. Chicago: Chicago University Press.

McEnery, T. & Gabrielatos, C. 2006. English corpus linguistics. I: Aarts & McMahon (eds) 33–71.

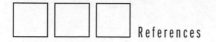 References

McEnery, T. & Hardie, A. 2012. *Corpus linguistics: method, theory and practice*. Cambridge: Cambridge University Press.

McNeill, D. (ed.) 2000. *Language and gesture*. Cambridge: Cambridge University Press.

Macnamara, J. 2010. *The 21st century media: (r)evolution – emergent communication practices*. New York: Peter Lang.

Mair, C. & Leech, G. 2006. Current changes in English syntax. In: Aarts & McMahon (eds). 318–342.

Malinowski, B. 1944. *A scientific theory of culture and other essays*. Chapel Hill: University of North Carolina Press.

Mann, W.C. & Matthiessen, C.M.I.M. 1991. Functions of language in two frameworks. *Word* **42** 3: 231–249.

Mann, W.C., Matthiessen, C.M.I.M. & Thompson, S.A. 1992. Rhetorical Structure Theory and text analysis. In: Mann & Thompson (eds) 39–79.

Mann, W.C. & Thompson, S.A. 1985. Assertions from discourse. *Proceedings of the Eleventh Berkeley Linguistics Society*. Berkeley: Berkeley Linguistics Society.

Mann, W.C. & Thompson, S.A. (eds) 1992. *Discourse description: diverse linguistic analyses of a fund-raising text*. Amsterdam: Benjamins.

Martin, J.R. 1988. Hypotactic recursive systems in English: towards a functional interpretation. In: Benson, J.D. & Greaves, W.S. (eds) *Systemic functional approaches to discourse: Selected papers from the Twelfth International Systemic Workshop*. Norwood, NJ.: Ablex. 240–270.

Martin, J.R. 1990. Interpersonal grammaticalisation: mood and modality in Tagalog. *Philippine Journal of Linguistics* (Special Monograph Issue celebrating the 25th Anniversary of the Language Study centre, Philippine Normal College) 21(1): 2–51.

Martin, J.R. 1991. Intrinsic functionality: implications for contextual theory. *Social Semiotics* **1** 1: 99–162.

Martin, J.R. 1992. *English text: system and structure*. Amsterdam: Benjamins.

Martin, J.R. 1993. Life as a noun. In: Halliday, M.A.K. & Martin, J.R. *Writing science: literacy and discursive power*. London: Falmer. 221–267.

Martin, J.R. 1995. Text and clause: fractal resonance. *Text* **15** 1: 5–42.

Martin, J.R. 1996. Types of structure: deconstructing notions of constituency in clause and text. In: Hovy, E. & Scott, D. (eds) *Burning issues in discourse: a multidisciplinary perspective*. Heidelberg: Springer. 39–66.

Martin, J.R. 1997. Analysing genre: functional parameters. In: Christie & Martin (eds). 3–39.

Martin, J.R. 1999. Grace: the logogenesis of freedom. *Discourse Studies* **1** 1: 31–58.

Martin, J.R. 2001. Cohesion and texture. In: Schiffrin, Tannen & Hamilton (eds). 35–53.

Martin, J.R. 2004. Metafunctional profile of Tagalog. In: Caffarel, Martin & Matthiessen (eds). 255–304.

Martin, J.R. & Matthiessen, C.M.I.M. 1991. Systemic typology and topology. In: Christie, F. (ed.) *Literacy in social processes: papers from the Inaugural Australian Systemic Functional Linguistics Conference, Deakin University, January 1990*. Darwin: Centre for Studies of Language in Education, Northern Territory University. 345–383. Reprinted in Martin, J.R. (2010), *SFL theory, Volume 1* in *The collected works of J.R. Martin*, edited by Wang Zhenhua. Shanghai: Shanghai Jiao Tong University Press. 167–215.

REFERENCES

Martin, J.R., Matthiessen, C.M.I.M. & Painter, C. 1997. *Working with functional grammar*. London: Edward Arnold.

Martin, J.R., Matthiessen, C.M.I.M. & Painter, C. 2010. *Deploying functional grammar*. Extensively revised, new edition of 1997 edition. Shanghai: Commercial Press.

Martin, J.R. & Rose, D. 2003. *Working with discourse: meaning beyond the clause*. London & New York: Continuum.

Martin, J.R. & Rose, D. 2007. *Working with discourse: meaning beyond the clause*. Second edition. London & New York: Continuum.

Martin, J.R. & Rose, D. 2008. *Genre relations: mapping culture*. London & Oakville: Equinox.

Martin, J.R. & Veel, R. (eds) 1998. *Reading science: critical and functional perspectives on discourses of science*. London: Routledge.

Martin, J.R. & White, P.R.R. 2005. *The language of evaluation: appraisal in English*. London & New York: Palgrave Macmillan.

Martinec, R. 2005. Topics in Multimodality. In: Hasan, Matthiessen & Webster (eds). 2005. 157–181.

Matthiessen, C.M.I.M. 1983. Choosing primary tense in English. *Studies in Language* **7** 3: 369–430.

Matthiessen, C.M.I.M. 1984. *Choosing tense in English*. USC/ISI Report: ISI/RR: 84–143.

Matthiessen, C.M.I.M. 1988. Representational issues in systemic functional grammar. In: Benson, J.D. & Greaves, W.S. (eds) *Systemic functional perspectives on discourse*. Norwood, NJ: Ablex. 136–175.

Matthiessen, C.M.I.M. 1990. Two approaches to semantic interfaces in text generation. *Proceedings of COLING-90, Helsinki, August 1990*.

Matthiessen, C.M.I.M. 1991a. Language on language: the grammar of semiosis. *Social Semiotics* **1** 2: 69–111.

Matthiessen, C.M.I.M. 1991b. Lexico(grammatical) choice in text-generation. In: Paris, C., Swartout, W. & Mann, W.C. (eds) *Natural language generation in artificial intelligence and computational linguistics*. Boston: Kluwer. 249–292.

Matthiessen, C.M.I.M. 1992. Interpreting the textual metafunction. In: Davies, M. & Ravelli, L. (eds) *Advances in systemic linguistics: recent theory and practice*. London: Pinter. 37–82.

Matthiessen, C.M.I.M. 1993a. The object of study in cognitive science in relation to its construal and enactment in language. In: *Language as Cultural Dynamic* (Special issue of *Cultural Dynamics* VI.1–2: 187–243, ed. M.A.K. Halliday).

Matthiessen, C.M.I.M. 1993b. Register in the round: diversity in a unified theory of register analysis. In: Ghadessy (ed.). 221–292.

Matthiessen, C.M.I.M. 1995a. *Lexicogrammatical cartography: English systems*. Tokyo: International Language Sciences Publishers.

Matthiessen, C.M.I.M. 1995b. Fuzziness construed in language: a linguistic perspective. Proceedings of FUZZ/IEEE, Yokohama, March 1995. Yokohama. 1871–1878.

Matthiessen, C.M.I.M. 1995c. THEME as an enabling resource in ideational 'knowledge' construction. In: Ghadessy (ed.). 20–55.

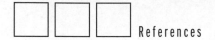

Matthiessen, C.M.I.M. 1996. Tense in English seen through systemic-functional theory. In: Butler, C., Berry, M., Fawcett, R.P. & Huang, G. (eds) *Meaning and form: systemic functional interpretations*. Norwood, NJ: Ablex. 431–498.

Matthiessen, C.M.I.M. 1998a. Lexicogrammar and collocation: a systemic functional exploration. To appear in *Issues in English Grammar. Volume II*. Hyderabad: Central Institute of English and Foreign Languages. Translated into Spanish as Matthiessen (2009b).

Matthiessen, C.M.I.M. 1998b. Construing processes of consciousness: from the commonsense model to the uncommonsense model of cognitive science. In: Martin, J.R. & Veel, R. (eds) *Reading science: critical and functional perspectives on discourses of science*. London: Routledge. 327–357.

Matthiessen, C.M.I.M. 1999. The system of TRANSITIVITY: an exploratory study of text-based profiles. *Functions of Language* **6** 1: 1–51.

Matthiessen, Christian M.I.M. 2001. The environments of translation. In: Steiner, E. & Yallop, C. (eds) *Beyond content: exploring translation and multilingual text*. Berlin: de Gruyter. 41–124.

Matthiessen, C.M.I.M. 2002a. Combining clauses into clause complexes: a multi-faceted view. In: Bybee, J. & Noonan, M. (eds) *Complex sentences in grammar and discourse: essays in honor of Sandra A. Thompson*. Amsterdam: Benjamins. 237–322.

Matthiessen, C.M.I.M. 2002b. Lexicogrammar in discourse development: logogenetic patterns of wording. In: Huang, G. & Wang, Zongyan (eds) *Discourse and language functions*. Shanghai: Foreign Language and Research Press.

Matthiessen, C.M.I.M. 2004a. The evolution of language: a systemic functional exploration of phylogenetic phases. In: Williams, G. & Lukin, A. (eds) *Language development: functional perspectives on evolution and ontogenesis*. London: Continuum. 45–90.

Matthiessen, C.M.I.M. 2004b. Descriptive motifs and generalizations. In: Caffarel, Martin & Matthiessen (eds), 537–673.

Matthiessen, C.M.I.M. 2005. Remembering Bill Mann. *Journal of Computational Linguistics* **31** 2: 161–171.

Matthiessen, C.M.I.M. 2006a. Frequency profiles of some basic grammatical systems: an interim report. In: Hunston, S. & Thompson, G. (eds) 103–142.

Matthiessen, C.M.I.M. 2006b. The multimodal page: a systemic functional exploration. In: Royce, T.D. & Bowcher, W.L. (eds) 2006. *New directions in the analysis of multimodal discourse*. Hillsdale, NJ: Lawrence Erlbaum. 1–62.

Matthiessen, C.M.I.M. 2006c. Educating for advanced foreign language capacities: Exploring the meaning-making resources of languages systemic-functionally. In: Byrnes, H. (ed.) *Advanced instructed language learning: the complementary contribution of Halliday and Vygotsky*. London & New York: Continuum. 31–57.

Matthiessen, C.M.I.M. 2007a. The 'architecture' of language according to systemic functional theory: developments since the 1970s. In: Hasan, Matthiessen & Webster (eds). 505–561.

Matthiessen, C.M.I.M. 2007b. Lexicogrammar in Systemic Functional Linguistics: descriptive and theoretical developments in the 'IFG' tradition since the 1970s. In: Hasan, Matthiessen & Webster (eds). 765–858.

747

REFERENCES

Matthiessen, C.M.I.M. 2007c. The lexicogrammar of emotion and attitude in English. Published in electronic proceedings based on contributions to the Third International Congress on English Grammar (ICEG 3), Sona College, Salem, Tamil Nadu, India, 23–27 January, 2006.

Matthiessen, C.M.I.M. 2009a. Multisemiotic and context-based register typology: registerial variation in the complementarity of semiotic systems. Ventola, E. & Guijarro, A.J.M. (eds). *The world shown and the world told*. Basingstoke: Palgrave Macmillan. 11–38.

Matthiessen, C.M.I.M. 2009b. Léxico-gramática y colocación léxica: Un estudio sistémico-funcional. [Translation of Lexicogrammar and collocation: A systemic functional exploration.] *Revista Signos* **42** 71: 333–383.

Matthiessen, C.M.I.M. 2009c. Ideas and new directions. In: Halliday, M.A.K. & Webster, J. (eds) *A companion to systemic functional linguistics*. London & New York: Continuum. 12–58.

Matthiessen, C.M.I.M. forthc. Extending the description of process type in delicacy: verb classes. Accepted by *Functions of Language*.

Matthiessen, C.M.I.M. & Bateman, J.A. 1991. *Systemic linguistics and text generation: experiences from Japanese and English*. London: Frances Pinter.

Matthiessen, C.M.I.M. & Halliday, M.A.K. 2009. *Systemic functional grammar: a first step into the theory*. Bilingual edition, with introduction by Huang Guowen. Beijing: Higher Education Press.

Matthiessen, C.M.I.M. & Halliday, M.A.K. in prep. *Outline of systemic functional linguistics*. Two volumes.

Matthiessen, C.M.I.M. & Nesbitt, C. 1996. On the idea of theory-neutral descriptions. In Hasan, R., Cloran, C. & Butt, D. (eds) *Functional descriptions: theory in practice*. Amsterdam: Benjamins. 39–85.

Matthiessen, C.M.I.M. & Slade, D. 2010. Analysing conversation. In: Wodak, R., Johnston, B. & Kerswill, P. (eds) *The SAGE Handbook of Sociolinguistics*. Los Angeles, London, New Delhi, Singapore & Washington DC: SAGE. 375–395.

Matthiessen, C.M.I.M. & Teruya, K. forthcoming. Ideational and interpersonal projection: constancy and variation across languages.

Matthiessen, C.M.I.M., Teruya, K. & Canzhong, W. 2008. Multilingual studies as a multi-dimensional space of interconnected language studies. In: Webster, J.J. (ed.) *Meaning in context*. London & New York: Continuum. 146–221.

Matthiessen, C.M.I.M., Teruya, K. & Lam, M. 2010. *Key terms in systemic functional linguistics*. London & New York: Continuum.

Matthiessen, C.M.I.M. & Thompson, S.A. 1988. The structure of discourse and 'subordination'. In: Haiman, J. & Thompson, S.A. (eds) *Clause combining in grammar and discourse*. Amsterdam: Benjamins. 275–329.

Michael, I. 1970. *English grammatical categories and the tradition to 1800*. Cambridge: Cambridge University Press.

Muntigl, P. 2004. Modelling multiple semiotic systems: the case of gesture and speech. In: Ventola, E., Cassily, C. & Kaltenbacher, M. (eds) *Perspectives on multimodality*. Amsterdam: Benjamins: 31–50.

Nanri, K. 1994. *An attempt to synthesize two systemic contextual theories through the*

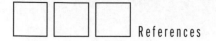

investigation of the process of the evolution of the discourse semantic structure of the newspaper reporting article. University of Sydney: Ph.D. thesis.

Neale, A. 2006. Matching corpus data and system networks: using corpora to modify and extend the system networks for transitivity in English. In: Hunston, S. & Thompson, G. (eds) *System and corpus: exploring connections*. London & Oakville: Equinox. 143–163.

Nesbitt, C.N. & Plum, G. 1988. 'Probabilities in a systemic grammar: the clause complex in English.' In: Fawcett, R.P. & Young, D. (ed.) *New developments in systemic linguistics, Volume 2: theory and application*. London: Frances Pinter. 6–39.

Nooteboom, S. 1997. The prosody of speech: melody and rhythm. In: Hardcastle, W.J. & Laver, J. (eds) *The handbook of phonetic sciences*. Oxford: Blackwell. 640–673.

O'Donnell, M. 1994. *Sentence analysis and generation: a systemic perspective*. Sydney University: Ph.D.

O'Donnell, M. 2011. UAM CorpusTool: Version 2.7 User Manual.[1]

O'Donnell, M. & Bateman, J.A. 2005. SFL in Computational Contexts. In: Hasan, Matthiessen & Webster (eds) 2005. 343–382.

O'Halloran, K.L. 2005. *Mathematical discourse: language, symbolism and visual images*. London & New York: Continuum.

O'Toole, M. 1994. *The language of displayed art*. London: Leicester University Press (Pinter).

Painter, C. 1984. *Into the mother tongue: a case study in early language development*. London: Frances Pinter.

Painter, C. 1993. *Learning through language: a case study in the development of language as a resource for learning from 2 1/2 to 5 years*. University of Sydney: Ph.D. thesis.

Painter, C. 1999. *Learning through language in early childhood*. London: Cassell.

Painter, C., Derewianka, B. & Torr, J. 2007. From microfunctions to metaphor: learning language and learning through language. In Hasan, Matthiessen & Webster (eds) 563–588.

Palmer, F.R. 1974. *The English verb*. London: Longman.

Partington, A. 1998. *Patterns and meanings using corpora for English language research and teaching*. Amsterdam: Benjamins.

Patpong, P. 2005. *A systemic functional interpretation of Thai grammar: an exploration of Thai narrative discourse*. Macquarie University: Ph.D. thesis.

Pike, E.G. 1992. How I understand a text – via the structure of the happenings and the telling of them. In: Mann & Thompson (eds). 227–261.

Pike, K.L. 1959. Language as particle, wave, and field. *The Texas Quarterly* **2** 2: 37–54. Reprinted in Brend, R. (ed.) *Kenneth L. Pike: selected writings*. The Hague: Mouton. 129–144.

Poutsma, H. 1926. *A Grammar of late modern English: Part II*. Groningen: P. Noordhof.

Poynton, C. 1984. Forms and functions: names as vocatives. *Nottingham Linguistic Circular* **13**.

---

[1] Available at: http://www.wagsoft.com/CorpusTool/UAMCorpusToolManualv27.pdf (iv/2011).

■ ■ ■ REFERENCES

Poynton, C. 1996. Amplification as a grammatical prosody: attitudinal modification in the nominal group. In: Butler, C., Berry, M., Fawcett. R. & Huang, G. (eds) *Meaning and form: systemic functional interpretations*. Norwood, NJ: Ablex. 211–229.

Prakasam, V. 2004. Metafunctional profile of Telugu. In: Caffarel, Martin & Matthiessen (eds) 433–478.

Quirk, R., Greenbaum, S., Leech, G. & Svartvik, J. 1972. *A grammar of contemporary English*, London: Longman.

Quirk, R., Greenbaum, S., Leech, G. & Svartvik, J. 1985. *A comprehensive grammar of the English language*. London: Longman.

Robins, R.H. 1966. The development of the word class system of the European grammatical tradition. *Foundations of Language* **2**: 3–19. Reprinted in Robins (1970) *Diversions of Bloomsbury: selected writings on linguistics*. Amsterdam: North-Holland. 185–203.

Rosch, E. 1978. Principles of categorization. In: Rosch, E. & Lloyd, B.B. (eds) *Cognition and categorization*. Hillsdale, NJ: Erlbaum. 27–48.

Rose, D. 1998. Science discourse and industry hierarchy. In: Martin, J.R. & Veel, R. (eds) *Reading science: critical and functional perspectives of discourses of science*. London: Routledge. 236–265.

Rose, D. 2001. *The Western Desert Code: an Australian cryptogrammar*. Canberra: Pacific Linguistics.

Schachter, P. 1976. The subject in Philippine languages: topic, actor, actor-topic, or none of the above. In: Li, C. (ed.) *Subject and topic*. New York: Academic Press. 491–518.

Schachter, P. 1977. Reference-related and role-related properties of subjects. In: Cole, P. & Sadock, J.M. (eds) *Syntax and semantics, Volume 8: grammatical relations*. New York: Academic Press. 279–306.

Schachter, P. 1994. The subject in Tagalog: still none of the above. *UCLA Occasional Papers in Linguistics* **15**: 1–61.

Schiffrin, D. 1987. *Discourse markers*. Cambridge: Cambridge University Press.

Schiffrin, D. 2001. Discourse markers: language, meaning, and context. In: Schiffrin, Tannen & Hamilton (eds) 54–75.

Schiffrin, D., Tannen, D. & Hamilton, H. (eds). 2001. *The handbook of discourse analysis*. Oxford: Blackwell.

Schneider, E.W. 2007. *Postcolonial English: varieties around the world*. Cambridge: Cambridge University Press.

Seuren, P.A.M. 1998. *Western linguistics: an historical introduction*. Oxford: Blackwell.

Sinclair, J. McH. 1987. Collocation: a progress report. In: Steele, R. & Threadgold, T. (eds) *Language topics: essays in honour of Michael Halliday*. Amsterdam: Benjamins. 319–332.

Sinclair, J. McH. 1991. *Corpus Concordance Collocation*. Oxford: Oxford University Press.

Sinclair, J. McH. & Coulthard, M. 1975. *Towards an analysis of discourse: the English used by teachers and pupils*. London: Oxford University Press.

Smith, N. & Raylson, P. 2007. Recent change and variation in the British English use of the progressive passive. *IJAME Journal* **31**: 129–160.

Starosta, S. 1988. *The case for lexicase: an outline of lexicase grammatical theory*. London: Pinter.

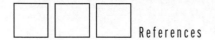

Steiner, E. & Teich, E. 2004. Metafunctional profile of German. In: Caffarel, Martin & Matthiessen (eds). 139–184.

Stenström, A-B. 1994. *An Introduction to spoken interaction.* London: Longman.

Strang, B.M.H. 1970. *A history of English.* London: Methuen.

Stuart-Smith, V. 2001. *Rhetorical structure theory as a model of semantics: a corpus-based analysis from a systemic-functional perspective.* Macquarie University: Ph.D. thesis.

Talmy, L. 1985. Lexicalisation patterns. In: Shopen, T. (ed.) *Language typology and syntactic description. Volume III. Grammatical categories and the lexicon.* Cambridge: Cambridge University Press. 57–149.

Taverniers, M. 2002. *Metaphor and metaphorology. A selective genealogy of philosophical and linguistic conceptions of metaphor from Aristotle to the 1990s.* (Studia Germanica Gandensia: Libri, 1) Ghent: Academia Press.

Teich, E. 2009. Computational linguistics. In: Halliday & Webster (eds). 113–127.

Tench, P. 1990. *The roles of intonation in English discourse.* Frankfurt: Peter Lang.

Tench, P. 1996. *The intonation systems of English.* London: Cassell.

Teruya, K. 2004. Metafunctional profile of Japanese. In: Caffarel, Martin & Matthiessen (eds). 185–254.

Teruya, K. 2007. *A systemic functional grammar of Japanese.* London and New York: Continuum.

Teruya, K., Akerejola, E., Andersen, T.H., Caffarel, A., Lavid, J., Matthiessen, C., Petersen, U-H., Patpong, P. & Smedegaard, F. 2007b. Typology of MOOD: a text-based and system-based functional view. In: Hasan, Matthiessen & Webster (eds). 859–920.

Tesnière, L. 1959. *Éléments de syntaxe structurale.* Paris: Librairie C. Klincksieck.

Thai, M. D. 2004. Metafunctional profile: Vietnamese. In Caffarel, Martin & Matthiessen. (eds).

Thibault, P. J. 2004. *Brain, mind and the signifying body: an ecosocial semiotic theory.* London & New York: Continuum.

Thompson, G. 1996. *Introducing functional grammar.* London: Hodder Education.

Thompson, G. 2004. *Introducing functional grammar.* Second edition. London: Hodder & Stoughton Educational.

Thompson, G. & Hunston, S. (eds) 2006. *System and corpus: exploring connections.* London & Oakville: Equinox.

Thompson, S.A. 1984. Grammar and written discourse: initial vs. final purpose clauses in English. Nottingham Linguistic Circular 13. Also in *Text* 5(1/2): 55–84.

Thomson, D. 1994. *A biographical dictionary of film.* London: André Deutsch.

Tognini-Bonelli, E. 2001. *Corpus linguistics at work.* Amsterdam: Benjamins.

Tottie, G. & Hoffmann, S. 2006. Tag questions in British and American English. *The Journal of English Linguistics* **34**: 283–311.

Trask, R.L. 1993. *A dictionary of grammatical terms in linguistics.* London: Routledge.

Traugott, E.C. 1985. Conditional markers. In: Haiman, J. (ed.) *Iconicity in syntax.* Amsterdam & Philadelphia: Benjamins. 289–307.

Traugott, E.C. 1997. The role of the development of discourse markers in a theory of grammaticalization. Paper presented at ICHL XII, Manchester 1995, Version of 11/97. Published as Le rôle de l'évolution des marqueurs discursifs dans une théorie de la

grammaticalization, in Fernandez-Vest, M.M.J. & Carter-Thomas, S. (eds) *Structure Informationallée et Particules Énonciatives: Essai de Typologie*. Paris: L'Harmattan. 295–333.

Tucker, G.H. 1998. *The lexicogrammar of adjectives: a systemic functional approach to lexis*. London: Cassell.

Tucker, G. 2001. Possibly alternative modality. *Functions of Language* 8 2: 183–215.

Tucker, G. 2007. Between grammar and lexis: towards a systemic functional account of phraseology. In: Hasan, Matthiessen & Webster (eds). 953–977.

Vandenbergen, A-M., Taverniers, M. & Ravelli, L. (eds) 2003. *Grammatical metaphor: views from systemic functional linguistics*. Amsterdam: John Benjamins.

van Dijk, T.A. (ed.). 1985. *Handbook of discourse analysis*. Volume 2. New York: Academic Press.

Van Valin, Jr., R.D. & LaPolla, R.J. 1997. *Syntax: structure, meaning and function*. Cambridge: Cambridge University Press.

Veel, R. 1997. Learning how to mean – scientifically speaking: apprenticeship into scientific discourse in the secondary school. In Christie, F. & Martin, J.R. (eds) *Genre and institutions: social processes in the workplace and school*. London: Cassell. 161–195.

Watts, R.J. 2003. *Politeness*. Cambridge: Cambridge University Press.

Webster, J.J. 1993. Text processing using the Functional Grammar Processor. In: Ghadessy (ed.). 1993. 181–195.

Wells, J.C. 2006. *English intonation: an introduction*. Cambridge: Cambridge University Press.

Whorf, B.L. 1956. *Language, thought, and reality: selected writings*. With an introduction by John B. Carroll. Cambridge, Mass.: The MIT Press.

Williams, G. 2005. Grammatics in schools. In: Hasan, Matthiessen & Webster (eds). 281–310.

Wilson, R. 1986. *100 Dinosaurs from A to Z*. New York: Grosset & Dunlap.

Wu, C. 2000. *Modelling linguistic resources*. Macquarie University: Ph.D. thesis.

Wu, C. 2009. Corpus-based research. In: Halliday & Webster (eds). 128–142.

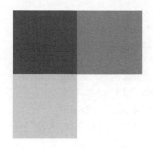

INDEX

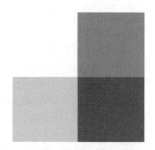

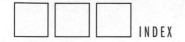

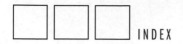 **INDEX**

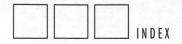

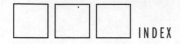

773

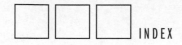

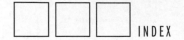

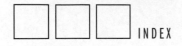